Handbook of Applied Cognition
Second Edition

Edited by

Francis T. Durso
Texas Tech University, USA

Associate Editors

Raymond S. Nickerson
Tufts University, USA

Susan T. Dumais
Microsoft Corporation, USA

Stephan Lewandowsky
University of Western Australia, Australia

Timothy J. Perfect
University of Plymouth, UK

BICENTENNIAL 1807 WILEY 2007 BICENTENNIAL

John Wiley & Sons, Ltd

John Wiley & Sons Ltd, The Atrium, Southern Gate, Chichester,
West Sussex PO19 8SQ, England
Telephone (+44) 1243 779777

Email (for orders and customer service enquiries): cs-books@wiley.co.uk
Visit our Home Page on www.wiley.com

Reprinted July 2007

Other Wiley Editorial Offices

John Wiley & Sons Inc., 111 River Street, Hoboken, NJ 07030, USA

Jossey-Bass, 989 Market Street, San Francisco, CA 94103-1741, USA

Wiley-VCH Verlag GmbH, Boschstr. 12, D-69469 Weinheim, Germany

John Wiley & Sons Australia Ltd, 42 McDougall Street, Milton, Queensland 4064, Australia

John Wiley & Sons (Asia) Pte Ltd, 2 Clementi Loop #02-01, Jin Xing Distripark, Singapore 129809

John Wiley & Sons Canada Ltd, 6045 Freemont Blvd, Mississauga, ONT, L5R 4J3

Wiley also publishes its books in a variety of electronic formats. Some content that appears in print may not be available in electronic books.

Anniversary Logo Design: Richard J. Pacifico

Library of Congress Cataloging-in-Publication Data

Handbook of applied cognition / edited by Francis T. Durso ; associate editors, Raymond S. Nickerson . . . [*et al.*]. – 2nd ed.
p. cm.
Includes index.
ISBN-13: 978-0-470-01534-6
1. Cognitive psychology. I. Durso, Francis Thomas. II. Nickerson, Raymond S.
BF201.H36 2007
153–dc22 2006024838

British Library Cataloguing in Publication Data

A catalogue record for this book is available from the British Library

ISBN-13 978-04-70-01534-6 (H/B)

Typeset in 10/12 pt Times by SNP Best-set Typesetter Ltd., Hong Kong
Printed and bound in Great Britain by Antony Rowe Ltd, Chippenham, Wiltshire
This book is printed on acid-free paper responsibly manufactured from sustainable forestry in which at least two trees are planted for each one used for paper production.

Handbook of Applied Cognition

Second Edition

To our mentors

Contents

About the Editors

Frank Durso received his PhD from SUNY at Stony Brook and his BS from Carnegie-Mellon University. He is Professor of Psychology at Texas Tech University on the faculties of the human factors program and the applied cognition program. He currently is president-elect of APA's Applied Experimental division, is chair of the Aerospace Technical Group of Human Factors and on the executive council of the Society for Applied Research on Memory and Cognition. He was President of the Southwestern Psychological Association and founder of the Oklahoma Psychological Society. A fellow of APA and APS, he serves on the editorial boards of the *Journal of Experimental Psychology: Applied*, *Human Factors*, *Air Traffic Control Quarterly*, and *Cognitive Technology*. He is recipient of the Regents' Award for Research and the Kenneth E. Crook award for instruction from the University of Oklahoma where he served as professor and founding director of OU's Human–Technology Interaction Center. He has been funded by NSF and the FAA, the latter continuously since 1990. His research interests have focused on cognitive factors in dynamic situations, in particular air traffic control. He is coauthor (with Nancy Cooke) of the forthcoming book titled *Stories of Human–Technology Failures and Cognitive Engineering Successes* designed to promote cognitive engineering to students and the public.

Raymond S. Nickerson received a PhD in experimental psychology from Tufts University in 1965. He was a researcher and manager at Bolt Beranek and Newman Inc. for 25 years and retired as a senior vice president; he is now a research professor at Tufts University. He is a fellow of the American Association for the Advancement of Science, the American Psychological Association (Divisions 1, 3, 21), the Association for Psychological Science, the Human Factors and Ergonomics Society, the Society of Experimental Psychologists, and a recipient of the Franklin V. Taylor award from the APA's Division of Applied Experimental and Engineering Psychology (1991). Dr Nickerson was founding editor of the *Journal of Experimental Psychology: Applied* and of *Reviews of Human Factors and Ergonomics,* and is a past chair of the National Research Council's Committee on Human Factors. He is the author of several books, the more recent of which are *Looking Ahead: Human Factors Challenges in a Changing World* (1992), *Psychology and Environmental Change* (2003), and *Cognition and Chance: The Psychology of Probabilistic Reasoning* (2004).

Susan Dumais is a Principal Researcher in the Adaptive Systems and Interaction Group at Microsoft Research. She has been at Microsoft Research since 1997 and has published widely in the areas of human–computer interaction and information retrieval. Her current research focuses on personal information management, user modeling and personalization, novel interfaces for interactive retrieval, and implicit measures of user interest and activity. She has worked closely with several Microsoft product groups on search-related innovations. Prior to joining Microsoft Research, she was at Bellcore and Bell Labs for many years, where she worked on Latent Semantic Indexing (a statistical method for concept-based retrieval), combining search and navigation, individual differences, and organizational impacts of new technology. Susan has published more than 170 articles in the fields of information science, human–computer interaction, and cognitive science, and holds several patents on novel retrieval algorithms and interfaces. She is Past-Chair of ACM's Special Interest Group in Information Retrieval (SIGIR), and was elected to the CHI Academy in 2004. She serves on numerous government panels, editorial boards and conference organizing committees. Susan is an adjunct professor in the Information School at the University of Washington, and has been a visiting faculty member at Stevens Institute of Technology, New York University, and the University of Chicago.

Stephan Lewandowsky obtained his PhD from the University of Toronto in 1985 and has held academic posts at the University of Toronto, University of Oklahoma, and University of Western Australia since then. He has been a Professor of Psychology at the University of Western Australia since 2000. He has held posts as Visiting Professors at the University of Potsdam, Germany, and the University of Bristol, UK. He is currently serving on the editorial board of *Psychological Review* and is Associate Editor of the *Journal of Experimental Psychology: Learning, Memory, and Cognition.* His research seeks to synthesize basic scientific research in the context of potential application to everyday problems. His research has been funded by several agencies, including the US Federal Aviation Administration and the Australian Research Council. He has edited three books and has published 26 refereed articles since 2000 (with a lifetime total of over 90 publications).

Timothy Perfect graduated with his PhD in 1989 from the University of Manchester. From there he worked first at the University of Liverpool and then the University of Bristol. He is currently Professor of Experimental Psychology at the University of Plymouth, where he heads the Memory Research Group. His research interests are broadly in the area of the applied psychology of memory, and he has published on topics of eyewitness confidence, face recognition, retrieval induced forgetting, unconscious plagiarism and cognitive aging. His work has been funded by several UK funding councils and charitable trusts: the Economic and Social Research Council, the Biotechnology and Biology Research Council, the Medical Research Council, The Leverhulme Trust, and The Nuffield Foundation. He is currently on the editorial board of the journals *Applied Cognitive Psychology* and *Memory*, and is a member of the Experimental Psychology Society, the Society for Applied Research in Memory and Cognition, and the Psychonomic Society. He is married (to Tara) and has two sons (Jake and Sam), and he harbours the ambition to score a century at cricket for his local team.

Contributors

Bruce Abernethy, University of Hong Kong, Institute of Human Performance, 111 Pokfulam Road, Pokfulam, Hong Kong and School of Human Movement Studies, University of Queensland, Australia

Lyn Y. Abramson, University of Wisconsin, Department of Psychology, 1202 W. Johnson Street, Madison, WI 53706, USA

Phillip L. Ackerman, Georgia Institute of Technology, Room 227, J. S. Coon Building, 654 Cherry Street, Atlanta, GA 30332-0170, USA

Joseph W. Alba, Department of Marketing, 212 Bryan Hall, PO Box 117155, University of Florida, Gainesville, FL 32611-7155, USA

Lauren B. Alloy, Temple University, Department of Psychology, 1701 N. 13th Street, Philadelphia, PA 19122, USA

Julie M. C. Baker, Department of Psychology, PO Box 5190, Kent State University, Kent, OH 44242-0001, USA

Christopher P. Barlett, Kansas State University, Bluemont Hall 492, 1100 Mid-Campus Drive, Manhattan KS 66506-5302, USA

Margaret E. Beier, Department of Psychology, Rice University, MS-25, 6100 Main Street, Houston, TX 77005, USA

Robert A. Bjork, Department of Psychology, University of California, Los Angeles, Los Angeles, CA 90095-1563, USA

Aysecan Boduroglu, Department of Psychology, Bogazici University, 34342 Bebek, İstanbul, Turkey

Elizabeth T. Cady, Kansas State University, Bluemont Hall 492, 1100 Mid-Campus Drive, Manhattan KS 66506-5302, USA

Curt A. Carlson, Department of Psychology, 455 W. Lindsay, University of Oklahoma, Norman, OK 73019, USA

Peter Chapman, School of Psychology, University of Nottingham, Nottingham NG7 2RD, UK

Nancy J. Cooke, Applied Psychology Program, Arizona State University Polytechnic, 7001 E. Williams Field Rd., Bldg. 140, Mesa, AZ 85212, USA

David Crundall, School of Psychology, University of Nottingham, Nottingham NG7 2RD, UK

Graham M. Davies, School of Psychology, Leicester University, University Road, Leicester LE1 7RH, UK

Frank A. Drews, Department of Psychology, The University of Utah, 380 S. 1530 E. RM 502, Salt Lake City, Utah 84112, USA

John Dunlosky, Department of Psychology, PO Box 5190, Kent State University, Kent, OH 44242-0001, USA

Francis T. Durso, Department of Psychology, Texas Tech University, PO Box 42051, Lubbock, TX 79409-2051, USA

Arthur D. Fisk, School of Psychology, 654 Cherry Street, Georgia Institute of Technology, Atlanta, GA 30332-0170, USA

Sara Girotto, Department of Psychology, Texas Tech University, P.O. Box 42051, Lubbock, TX 79409-2051, USA

Jamie C. Gorman, Cognitive Engineering Research Institute, 5810 S. Sossaman, Ste. 106, Mesa, AZ 85212, USA

Edith Greene, Department of Psychology, University of Colorado, PO Box 7150, Colorado Springs, CO 80933, USA

Scott D. Gronlund, Department of Psychology, 455 W. Lindsay, University of Oklahoma, Norman, OK 73019, USA

Richard Jackson Harris, Kansas State University, Bluemont Hall 492, 1100 Mid-Campus Drive, Manhattan KS 66506-5302, USA

Erik Hollnagel, Industrial Safety Chair, École des Mines de Paris, Pôle Cindyniques, Sophia Antipolis, France

Megan E. Hughes, Temple University, Department of Psychology, 1701 N. 13th Street, Philadelphia, PA 19122, USA

J. Wesley Hutchinson, Department of Marketing, 746 Jon M. Huntsman Hall, The Wharton School, University of Pennsylvania, Philadelphia, PA 19104-6340, USA

Robin C. Jackson, University of Hong Kong, Institute of Human Performance, 111 Pokfulam Road, Pokfulam, Hong Kong

William Jones, University of Washington, The Information School, Box 352840, Seattle, WA 98195-2840, USA

Michael L. Kalish, Institute of Cognitive Science, University of Louisiana at Lafayette, Lafayette, LA 70504

Gary Klein, Klein Associates, 1750 Commerce Center Blvd. North, Fairborn, OH 45324-6362, USA

Stephan Lewandowsky, School of Psychology, University of Western Australia, Crawley, WA 6009, Australia

Marcia C. Linn, Graduate School of Education, Education in Mathematics, Science, and Technology; University of California, Berkley, 4611 Tolman Hall, Berkeley, CA 94720-1670, USA

Daniel Little, School of Psychology, University of Western Australia, Crawley, WA 6009, Australia

Bernd Lorenz, German Aerospace Centre (DLR), Institute of Flight Guidance, 7 Lilienthalplatz, 38108 Braunschweig, Germany

Ruth H. Maki, Department of Psychology, Texas Tech University, PO Box 42051, Lubbock, TX 79409-2051, USA

William S. Maki, Department of Psychology, Texas Tech University, PO Box 42051, Lubbock, TX 79409-2051, USA

Richard S. W. Masters, University of Hong Kong, Institute of Human Performance, 111 Pokfulam Road, Pokfulam, Hong Kong

Jonathan P. Maxwell, University of Hong Kong, Institute of Human Performance, 111 Pokfulam Road, Pokfulam, Hong Kong

Giuliana Mazzoni, School of Psychology, University of Plymouth, Drake Circus, Plymouth PL4 8AA, UK

Meredith Minear, Department of Psychology, Washington University, One Brookings Drive, Campus Box 1125, Saint Louis, MO 63130, USA

Neville Moray, Professor Emeritus University of Surrey, Villa Cantegril, 17 Avenue des Genets, 06520 Magagnosc, France

Raymond S. Nickerson, Department of Psychology, Tufts University, 5 Gleason Rd., Bedford, MA 01730, USA

Gary M. Olson, School of Information, University of Michigan, 1075 Beal Avenue, Ann Arbor, MI 48109-2122, USA

Judith S. Olson, University of Michigan, School of Business Administration, C2416 Bus Admin, Ann Arbor, MI 48109, USA

Richard Pak, Clemson University, Department of Psychology, 418 Brackett Hall, Clemson, SC, 29634, USA

Catherine Panzarella, Child, Adolescent and Family Division; Mental Health Association of Southeastern Pennsylvania; 11th Floor, 1211 Chestnut Street; Philadelphia, PA 19107, USA

Raja Parasuraman, Professor of Psychology, 2056 David King Hall, George Mason University, MS 3F5, 4400 University Drive, Fairfax, VA 22030-4444, USA

Vimla L. Patel, Laboratory of Decision making and Cognition, Department of Biomedical Informatics, Columbia University Medical Center, VC5, 622 West 168th Street, New York, NY 10032, USA

Peter Pirolli, Palo Alto Research Center, 3333 Coyote Hill Road, Palo Alto, CA 94304, USA

Katherine A. Rawson, Kent State University, Department of Psychology, P.O. Box 5190, Kent, OH 44242, USA

Lindsey E. Richland, University of California, Irvine, Education, Irvine, CA 92697-5500, USA

Wendy A. Rogers, School of Psychology, 654 Cherry Street, Georgia Institute of Technology, Atlanta, GA 30332-0170, USA

Brian H. Ross, Beckman Institute and Department of Psychology, University of Illinois , 405 N. Mathews Ave., Urbana, IL 61821, USA

Alan Scoboria, University of Windsor, 173 Chrysler Hall South, 401 Sunset Avenue, Windsor, Ontario N9B 3P4, Canada

Michael J. Serra, Department of Psychology, PO Box 5190, Kent State University, Kent, OH 44242-0001, USA

Priti Shah, Department of Psychology, University of Michigan, 2004 East Hall 530 Church Street, Ann Arbor, MI 48109-1043, USA

Winston R. Sieck, Klein Associates, 1750 Commerce Center Blvd. North, Fairborn, OH 45324-3987, USA

David L. Strayer, Department of Psychology, The University of Utah, 380 S. 1530 E. RM 502, Salt Lake City, Utah 84112, USA

Debra Tower, Department of Psychology, 455 W. Lindsay, University of Oklahoma, Norman, OK 73019, USA

Geoffrey Underwood, School of Psychology, University of Nottingham, Nottingham NG7 2RD, UK

Christopher Wickens, University of Illinois at Urbana-Champaign, Institute of Aviation, Aviation Human Factors Division #1 Airport Rd., Savoy, IL 61874, USA

Barbara A. Wilson, Medical Research Council, Cognition and Brain Sciences Unit, Box 58, Addenbrookes Hospital, Hills Rd., Cambridge CB2 2QQ, UK

Jennifer L. Winner, Applied Psychology Program, Arizona State University Polytechnic, 7001 E. Williams Field Rd., Bldg. 140, Mesa, AZ 85212, USA

Ryan J. Winter, Florida International University, University Park Campus, 11200 S.W. 8th Street, Miami, FL 33199, USA

Daniel B. Wright, Psychology Department, University of Sussex, BN1 9QH, UK

Jiajie Zhang, School of Health Information Sciences, University of Texas at Houston, 7000 Fannin, Suite 600, Houston, TX 77030, USA

Reviewers

Erik Altmann
Paul Atchley
Simon Banbury
Kate Bleckley
Neil Brewer
Andrew Butler
Mike Byrne
Leanne Casey
Nancy Cooke
Jason Dana
Rick DeShon
Dennis Devine
Mike Dougherty
Frank Drews
John Dunlosky
Randy Engle
Anders Ericsson
Jonathan Evans
Susan Fussell
David Gallo
Carmella Gottesman
Rob Gray
Wayne Gray
Irene Greif
Scott Gronlund
Dana Grzybicki
Sowon Hahn
Zach Hambrick
Craig Harvey
Kelly Henry
Doug Herrman
Robert Hoffman
Mark Horswill
Reed Hunt
Chris Johnson
Dave Kaber
Mark Lansdale
Jeff Larsen
Kevin Larsen
Vance Locke
Gloria Mark
Ruth Maki
Richard Mayer
Dave McCabe
David McDonald
Dick McGlynn
Janet Metcalfe
Anne Miller
Dan Morrow
Kathleen Mosier
Chris Moulin
Emily Patterson
Robert Proctor
Richard Reardon
Steven Richards
Doug Rohrer
Ernst Rothkopf
Eduardo Salas
Mark Scerbo
Stephanie Sharman
Baba Shiv
David Strayer
Rick Thomas
Pamela Tsang
Tom Van Vleet
Steve Whittaker
Kevin Williams

Preface

ALL THE DIFFERENCE

It has been over a decade since I received the original proposal from the Society for Applied Research in Memory and Cognition (SARMAC) to put together a handbook that brought together the myriad of work in applied cognition. That first edition appeared in 1999, and we were gratified by the favorable comments we received in the press and personally. Thus, I was happy to take on the second edition when approached by Gillian Leslie of John Wiley & Sons.

The field of applied cognition is different than it was 10 years ago. Some of the changes were anticipated in the first edition. Others are the consequence of the unhappy circumstance in which the world finds itself. For example, there is no doubt that as the initial work matures, topics like security will find their way into a future edition of this handbook. Applied cognitive researchers should also become involved in issues such as the evacuation of cities and the transfer of information between teams and between organizations.

The second edition is substantially different from the first. Some topics that continue to characterize work in applied cognition, such as aviation, eyewitness testimony, and decision making remain, although many of these are written by new authors, who add their perspective to the ones admirably conveyed by contributors to the first edition. Even those chapters from authors reprising their roles are substantially revised and updated. Readers familiar with the first edition will note that some chapters have not reappeared in the second edition making way for areas not covered in the first edition that have made substantial progress. Thus, we were able to add many new chapters covering domains not included in the first volume but which are important arenas of applied cognition, for example, personal information management, sports, media, and false memory to mention a few.

In other respects, the second edition shares much in approach and philosophy with the first. As before, here we leave the lab to understand cognition in the uncontrolled world of interesting people. The focus is on applied work, not applicable work that could, potentially, be applied someday. As before, this edition does not assume that applied cognition necessarily means applied cognitive psychology. In fact, some of the authors are quite clear in eschewing traditional cognitive psychology. For example, cognitive systems engineering will seem quite un-cognitive to a traditional cognitive psychologist. Finally, the current edition attempts to gather a variety of applied work on cognition from a variety of domains and perspectives. Each of these chapters is intended as a broad review of the relevant literature, but perhaps one with more pedagogy than a chapter written exclusively for experts already inculcated in the area. Instead, basic researchers interested in taking a step into an applied domain, and applied researchers interested in undergirding their work with basic research will find value in these pages.

The 30 chapters that make up this handbook could obviously be put together in more than one way. We chose to organize the chapters into three large sections. Section 1 comprises 10 chapters that reflect the processes generally considered when people talk about the cognitive activities that happen in applied settings. When potential contributors were approached, the instructions for authors to the first section differed from those given to the contributors of the remaining chapters. Authors of chapters in the first section were asked to consider the basic science of their construct and then to take a slice through the applied work that showed that construct as it is studied in applied domains. Interestingly, although no one was asked to compare basic and applied research in those chapters, several did. Resolving the relation between basic and applied seems especially important to researchers doing work under the banner, applied cognition.

The remaining chapters draw from on the work discussed in the first 10. Whereas authors of Section 1 took a broad horizontal slice through the literature, the 20 chapters in Sections 2 and 3 sliced the literature vertically, into domains and applied areas of research. These final 20 chapters, although all about application, show differences. They seemed to me to form two collections. One collection, *Applied Cognition in Human–Technical Systems,* tends to focus on domains and issues in which the "system" is primarily the human working with technology. The other collection, *Applied Cognition in Human–Social Systems,* comprise chapters in which domain issues focus on a system of the human operating within a social milieu.

It is interesting that there is another apparent, at least to me, difference in these two collections. I think of the second section of the *Handbook* as research by human factors, or cognitive engineering, types. These authors tend to be known to members of, for example, *The Human Factors and Ergonomics Society, Division 21 of APA,* and *SIGCHI.* On the other hand, the authors of the third section might be regarded as applied cognitive psychologists, known to members of *SARMAC* and the *Psychonomics Society* for instance. Of course there are exceptions; many are known to all applied experimental psychologists and some have intentionally stretched beyond their home turf to address an issue in a different type of system.

Nevertheless, the fact that there is substantial association between the system focus that characterizes a section and the people who conduct that type of research suggests that there are at least two brands of researchers, both of whom are applied cognitive scientists in the sense that they both take advantage of the basic work reviewed in the first section of this handbook.

What does this difference between the subfields of applied cognition, between Sections 2 and 3, tell us about the field? At one level, it tells us that human cognition is an important part of much of what we do and what we ask industrial operators to do. Unlike at the turn of the last century, when most workers earned a living doing physical labor, today's jobs – and today's problems – are heavily cognitive. Our ability to address issues in such complex and dynamic real-world environments is also a testament to the knowledge that has accumulated about human cognition over the past 60 years. On the other hand, the expansiveness of applied cognition captured by two relatively distinct collections of research (together with the explosion of interest in neurocognition) suggest that the pressures on the basic cognitive paradigm are taking their toll. Yet, it remains unclear how the new paradigm will shift. Will applied cognitive psychology and cognitive engineering proceed down separate paths, or will a synthesis of applied cognitive work emerge?

So, should these cognitive engineers and applied cognitive psychologists interact more, or is it unavoidable that scientists in Section 2 interact little with those in Section 3 while both groups borrow tenuously from Section 1? After all, it is difficult enough to keep up with one's own specialization, and maybe another within your "section," but to read so far afield as to read a chapter from another section may simply be unrealistic. Although it is difficult to ignore the pragmatics behind such a position, I believe there will be rewards for those willing to take such a journey. There is the added perspective not only on the field generally but on one's own work as well. There is the realization that the old work on vigilance might inform my new work on prospective memory; that the old work on eyewitness testimony seems relevant to this new work on driving. We hope that the second edition of the *Handbook of Applied Cognition* can serve as a travel guide for such a journey, or, at least, a map that points out that there is indeed a fork in the road. Which road in the wood should you take? That question has been answered by writers wiser and more eloquent than I.

This handbook is a cooperative accomplishment in the truest sense. The associate editors are world authorities in applied cognition and were gracious in assenting to help, some for a second time. Each was an effective steward of several of the chapters you will read. They advised me from the beginning on content and structure. They cajoled colleagues to serve as reviewers. In fact, each chapter was reviewed by two or three experts in the field and at least one of the five editors, often two. Some of our reviewers agreed to help out with impossible deadlines, some helped with more than one chapter, and one reviewer did both. A special thanks. Several of the chapters were subjected to the reviews of my graduate Cognitive Ergonomics class at Texas Tech. Their critiques were often insightful and routinely contributed to my reviews of the chapters. Finally, and most importantly, there are the world-class contributors from throughout applied cognition. We are honored by their participation and appreciative of their cooperation.

The book also benefited from the cooperation and understanding of my colleagues at Texas Tech University. Thanks to Ruth Maki and David Rudd, who chaired my department during the preparation of this volume, for their patience and assistance, and to my graduate students who tolerated this intrusion. Special thanks to Lana Jackson, my sedulous office manager, who is now off to graduate school. Lana helped with every onerous task associated with a production of this size, from nudging late reviewers to organizing the submissions. Throughout, I have enjoyed working with the representatives of Wiley. Gillian Leslie has been an important factor and a pleasant one from the initial invitation until now. An editor could have no better publisher. Gillian's patience as well as the help and patience of Ruth Graham, Nicole Burnett, and Claire Ruston at Wiley and their affiliate Richard Lawrence made production of this volume a great experience. Finally, to my *raisons d'être,* Kate, who has been my partner through this edition and the last, and my son, Andrew, who has grown since the last edition into the finest young man I know.

The contributions of the authors speak for themselves in the pages that follow.

F. T. D.
September 2006
Texas Tech University

Preface to the First Edition

During the past 40 years a large number of bright people have embraced the reemergence of human mental functioning as a viable topic of scientific study. Indeed, the theories, models, and methodologies that have been developed to understand the human mind stand as tributes to the enthusiasm and intelligence of these scholars. Much of this progress has been in gaining an understanding of basic or fundamental cognitive functioning. Psychology has participated in, and often led, this initiative as one of the empirical arms of the cognitive science movement.

This *Handbook* explores another dimension of what it means to be interested in human mental functioning: the attempt to understand cognition in the uncontrolled world of interesting people. When I was first asked to edit this volume, I thought the timing was right for a number of reasons. First, a large amount of applied work was being conducted that was very strong, but not easily accessed – hidden in this specialty journal or tucked away in those proceedings. A *Handbook* devoted to applications of cognitive research could help bring this work to the notice of others. Second, exactly how to characterize basic research to applied researchers seemed a noble although difficult problem. Leaders in the applied community had routinely stated that basic cognitive research was not worth very much. Explicit condemnation of the value of cognitive psychology had been the topic of more than one thought-provoking address, including Don Norman's eloquent address at SARMAC, the organization that initiated this volume. Thus, for applied researchers, this volume offers a collection of chapters of successful and not-so-successful applications of basic principles. These chapters include reviews from the perspective of a basic cognitive process as well as reviews from the perspective of an applied domain. Third, basic research did not always appreciate the value of applied cognition, and even when cognitive research looked applied it was often what Doug Herrmann has called "applicable," not applied. More important than the under-appreciation of applied work, there did not seem to be the realization that good applied work was being conducted by people other than cognitive psychologists – a fact that should interest scientists who believe the empirical study of mind should be the province of cognitive psychology. Such a *Handbook* would supply a compendium of research that would move such debates from the general "useful/useless," "good/bad" debates to more sophisticated considerations of science, engineering, and mental functioning. Finally, and of most interest conceptually, a number of pressures on the current paradigm of cognitive psychology seemed to revolve around the ability to apply cognitive psychology. Debates occurred and are continuing on qualitative methods, hypothesis testing, situated cognition, the AI agenda, and Gibson. At their hearts, these debates confront various issues about the real-world applicability of what applied researchers would call academic cognitive psychology. As one looks over the pressures on cognitive psychology, the paradigm pressures seem to have a ring of familiarity.

Kuhnians amongst us would argue that cognitive psychology replaced neobehaviorism as the dominant paradigm in scientific psychology. In fact, a popular textbook of the early 1980s (Lachman, Lachman & Butterfield, 1979) stood out for its attempt to supply young cognitive psychologists a context from which to understand the demise of one paradigm and the rise of the other. Neobehaviorism had been under a number of paradigm pressures:

1. Models were attacked as becoming overly complex sequences of Ss and Rs.
2. Concepts like reinforcement and stimulus control looked circular outside the laboratory.
3. Applied researchers challenged fundamental assumptions of neobehaviorism by making it clear that humans were not passive recipients of impinging events.
4. Advances in technology (i.e. computer science) provided new opportunities, but neobehaviorists tended to ignore or under-utilize the new technology.
5. Finally, and perhaps most critical, neobehaviorism was not making advances in areas it should have (like language and perception) but, importantly, other disciplines were.

Today, modern cognitive psychology is buffeted by paradigm pressures just as its predecessor was. Several of these points are eloquently discussed elsewhere in the literature. In my view, the pressures seem surprisingly reminiscent:

1. Cognitive psychology's typical method of explanation is the construction of underlying mechanisms (e.g. short-term memory) and not by inducing abstract categories for the experimental variables (e.g. this is a force, this is a mass). The proliferation of cognitive models is apparent. From the perspective of the applied community, large amounts of effort and talent have been spent on relatively small, model-specific problems.
2. Like reinforcement and stimulus control, cognitive constructs are often not well specified in the applied arena. Consider elaborative rehearsal versus maintenance rehearsal. Although they are important additions to our theories of short-term memory and are supported by ingenious laboratory experiments, it is difficult for the applied researcher to employ the concepts. An air-traffic controller remembers one plane, but not another. The first must have undergone elaborative rehearsal because it is remembered better, and so on.
3. It is becoming clear that, not only are humans active processors of events, but that humans impinge on events as well as being impinged by them. The fact that humans control and modify their environment, have choices about what to look at and what to do, is not only abundantly clear in a field setting, but becomes critical in any attempt to apply basic research to an applied problem. Typically, when an expert is doing his or her job, the experimental intervention is the least interesting part of the environment; in the laboratory it is often the most interesting, if not only, part of the environment. This assertion is perhaps made most clearly by the distributed cognition initiatives. An important part of a human's environment is often other humans. We could say that such issues are the responsibility of social cognition, but that is just second millenium think-

ing. Besides, many social psychologists have affirmed their intent to become more like cognitive psychologists, making it difficult for cognitive psychologists to become more like them.

4. New technologies today include virtual reality and high fidelity simulations. Ignoring these technologies makes sense within the current cognitive paradigm where the environment plays a role secondary to internal cognition. However, to cash out the promise of cognitive psychology in the applied marketplace will require complex, dynamic, interactive, yet controllable environments. Use of these technologies can take advantage of new methodologies and statistical procedures for the understanding of sequential data.
5. Despite these paradigm pressures, if neobehaviorism could have made reasonable contributions to language and perception, not only might Chomsky have read *Verbal Behavior* before he reviewed it, but neobehaviorism may have participated in a Hegelian synthesis rather than being the paradigm lost. How well is cognitive psychology doing in the applied arena? The answer is not a simple one. The many chapters of this *Handbook* are attempts to characterize cognitive research in applied settings, but not necessarily applied cognitive psychology. Several of the chapters do not rely much on cognitive psychology and make that point explicitly. Several other chapters have easily imported the findings and views of cognitive psychology into their applied domains. In addition, several authors draw heavily from social psychology. The domains covered in this *Handbook* clearly vary from relatively new areas about which little is understood, to large, well-researched, well-understood domains.

The *Handbook* begins with a chapter on applying cognitive psychology and then continues with six chapters that overview applied research from perspectives familiar to most cognitive psychologists. These overviews are followed by chapters that focus on particular applied domains. These domains fall roughly into four broad arenas: business and industry, computers and technology, information and instruction, and health and law, but it will be clear that issues raised in one section of the *Handbook* will echo in others.

There are a number of people who were critical to the production of this volume. The panel of associate editors served as vital advisers and coordinated helpful reviews for a number of the chapters. Several of the early drafts were reviewed by my graduate-level Applied Cognition class; these discussions often helped me clarify my view of the chapters. Many colleagues agreed to review chapters often within impossibly short timeframes, and the chairs of the Psychology Department, Ken Hoving and Kirby Gilliland, were gracious in allowing me access to departmental resources. I was director of the University of Oklahoma's Human–Technology Interaction Center while this volume was being produced, and appreciate the support of my HTIC colleagues during the past year. My graduate students were tolerant of the demands placed on me by this task. Patience and tolerance were particularly plentiful from the people at Wiley, Comfort Jegede and Melanie Phillips, who held my hand throughout the process. My assistants, Paul Linville and Helen Fung, were absolutely invaluable, with special thanks to Paul who was my right hand through all but the final phase of the project. Finally, thanks to the great loves of my life, Kate Bleckley who found the time to continue her degree at GaTech while giving me editorial assistance, cognitive aid, and emotional support, and to my son,

Andy, who took time from being a teenager to let me know he thinks it's cool I'm editing a book.

The contributions of the authors speak for themselves in the pages that follow.

F. T. D.
June 23, 1998
University of Oklahoma

REFERENCES

Chomsky, N. (1959). A review of Skinner's *Verbal Behavior. Language*, 35, 26–58.
Lachman, R., Lachman, J. L. & Butterfield, E. C. (1979). *Cognitive Psychology and Information Processing: An Introduction*. Hillsdale, NJ: Lawrence Erlbaum.

SECTION 1

Applied Cognition Fundamentals

CHAPTER 1

Applied Cognitive Psychology in the Context of Everyday Living

Wendy A. Rogers
Georgia Institute of Technology, USA
Richard Pak
Clemson University, USA
and
Arthur D. Fisk
Georgia Institute of Technology, USA

Psychological science is the study of behavior. We all learned that definition in our introductory psychology class. What then is the difference between "basic psychological science" and "applied psychological science? Some would argue that there is no difference – understanding behavior is the focus of psychology whether that behavior occurs inside or outside of the laboratory. However, others argue that the difference is the purpose of the research – is it intended to contribute fundamental knowledge (i.e., basic) or is it intended to solve a specific problem (i.e., applied)." (See the enlightening debate between Hoffman & Deffenbacher 1993, 1994; Vicente 1994.)

Another perspective concerning the dichotomization of basic and applied psychology is that theories are developed in basic scientific endeavors and simply put into action in applied science. There is certainly some benefit in attempting to apply psychological theories as Broadbent (1973) elegantly stated: "the test of intellectual excellence of a psychological theory, as well as its moral justification, lies in its application to concrete practical situations" (p. 7). However, as is clear from Broadbent's work, the goal is not to develop theories of behavior and only then attempt to apply those theories. Instead, applied psychological science provides a *problem space* within which principles of behavior can be developed (see also Brunswik 1952, 1956). The behavior in question is often complex, influenced by multiple variables, and susceptible to contextual influences as well as

Handbook of Applied Cognition: Second Edition. Edited by Francis T. Durso.

individual differences. Attempting to understand such behavior is the essence of applied psychological science.

This perspective is not new. In fact, this view was well stated by Thorndike in the context of discussing the importance of psychological science contributions during the First World War:

> Applied psychology is much more than cleverness and common sense using the facts and principles found in standard texts. It is scientific work, research on problems of human nature complicated by the conditions of the shop or school or army, restricted by time and labor cost, and directed by imperative needs . . . The secret of success in applied psychology . . . is to be rigorously scientific. (Thorndike 1919, p. 60)

Applied psychology, done well, has the potential to solve specific problems, to lead to the development of general principles of behavior, and to improve lives. Thorndike concluded his paper with the following statement: "the psychologists of America worked to help win the war" (Thorndike 1919, p. 60).

Too often it seems that the distinction between applied and basic psychology is made with trite or stereotypic definitions. Such thinking can constrain progress in psychological science (Landauer 1989; Fisk & Kirlik 1996). Our perspective is that applied psychology, to be effective, should be thought of as "use-inspired basic research" (Stokes 1997, p. 73). A prominent general science example of such research described by Stokes is Louis Pasteur's quest to understand microbiological processes and to control these processes so as to minimize spoilage and conquer disease. Examples from the field of applied cognitive psychology are the focus of this chapter.

Much of human behavior involves cognitive processes such as perception, attention, memory, language, reasoning, decision-making, and problem-solving. Consequently, applied cognitive psychology may be defined as the science of the cognitive processes involved in activities of daily living. In this chapter we first provide a general discussion of applied cognitive psychology. We then describe the knowledge, skills, and abilities required for applied cognitive psychologists. Next we provide examplars of research conducted within different problem spaces that have successfully contributed to our understanding of human behavior. We conclude with a more in-depth discussion of applied cognitive psychology in the context of advanced technological solutions designed to improve the health and well-being of older adults. This discussion is meant to illustrate the potential for applied cognitive psychology to contribute to an important social issue facing the world today.

OVERVIEW OF APPLIED COGNITIVE PSYCHOLOGY

There is a variety of misconceptions about applied cognitive psychology and clearing up misconceptions about a research field can aid in defining that field. We address just a few of these misconceptions here (adapted from Fisk & Kirlik 1996; see also Landauer 1989).

Misconception #1 – Applied Cognitive Research is, by Definition, Designed to Answer a Practical Question for a Specific Task in a Specific Context

Although some applied research may be conducted to answer a specific question, that is not the hallmark definition of all applied cognitive research; nor should it be. The same criticism can be levied at some basic cognitive research which may be overly specific. Ideally, the goal should be to develop general principles that will have relevance to a range of problems and to specify the boundary conditions under which such principles will be valid. This is really a concern for generality (Petrinovich 1989). Certainly, external validity may be lacking in some applied research. However, the problem with, and limitation of, such research seems to rest on its piecemeal approach and the fact that such research is often driven primarily by technology. Hence, the integration of some bodies of applied research is quite difficult, as is the generality of that research beyond the specific targeted problem or context. Recognizing the importance of advancing both the practice of cognitive psychology and theories within cognitive psychology can do much to overcome this problem.

Misconception #2 – The Critical Basic Cognitive Psychology Research Must be Conducted First and Only then Can the Application be Made

Applied cognitive research is not simply the application of cognitive theories. Basic and applied science should be considered as having a symbiotic relationship whereby attempts at application can bring to light the inadequacy of a theory, but application should also guide the study of fundamental issues in psychology. The idea that application must follow basic research assumes that "basic" and "applied" research represent ends of a linear continuum. We think of "basic" and "applied" cognitive psychology as part of a circular continuum with both giving to and taking from the other (see also Hoffman & Deffenbacher 1993).

Misconception #3 – Applied Cognitive Research Does Not Allow Proper Research Control

Conducting applied research does not imply that research is not done well or is not done with consideration for control (see Cook & Campbell 1979). Well-designed research efforts must consider internal validity as well as external validity. Such designs may ultimately be complex but are not impossible.

Misconception #4 – Tasks That Are Context-rich Weaken Generalization

Some researchers argue that understanding "pure" cognitive processes necessitates studying them in controlled situations that remove potentially influential environmental contexts. An extension of this view might be that the study of complex tasks that are embedded in a representative context will not yield generalizable results because few other situations will have exactly the same context. However, stripping a task of its context does not assure that a context-independent activity is being engaged through performance of that task and the resultant task may not be at all representative of typical behaviors. Moreover, understanding the role of environmental context in performance may provide more generality to the principles of behavior that can be developed on the basis of contextually-rich research studies. This idea is grounded in the ideas of "ecological validity" and "representative design," as suggested by Brunswik (see Hoffman & Deffenbacher 1993; Hammond & Stewart 2001).

Moving beyond the Misconceptions

This discussion of misconceptions is not meant to imply that we do not recognize the important contributions of fundamental cognitive psychology. Indeed, we consider ourselves cognitive psychologists searching for basic, fundamental knowledge. Cognitive psychologists have conducted many elegant, detailed, and controlled studies to understand the fundamentals of cognitive processes. Consider the cognitive process(es) of attention: it is well documented that there are varieties of attention (Parasuraman & Davies 1984), that through extensive consistent practice attentional demands can be reduced (e.g., Schneider & Shiffrin 1977), that attentional capabilities change with age (Rogers & Fisk 2001), and that different attentional functions are localized in different areas of the brain (Posner & Petersen 1990; Parasuraman 1998). Yet without taking an applied cognitive psychology approach we would not know how attention affects driving behavior, flying an airplane, or monitoring gauges in a control center.

KNOWLEDGE, SKILLS, AND CAPABILITIES OF APPLIED COGNITIVE PSYCHOLOGISTS

The knowledge and skill set of an applied cognitive psychologist must be a *superset* of the skills held by a cognitive psychologist. That is, in addition to the training that a cognitive psychologist receives (e.g., cognitive psychology, research design, statistics), applied cognitive psychologists need collateral knowledge and skills.

To illustrate this point, consider the curricula of graduate programs in cognitive psychology and applied cognitive psychology. A review of cognitive psychology graduate programs reveals that the typical coursework involves cognitive psychology (with specialized courses in perception, memory, language, etc.), statistics, research design, and other optional, specialized courses (e.g., neuroscience, aging). On the other hand, applied cognitive psychology programs (sometimes called engineering psychology or applied experimental psychology) include the above curriculum as well as courses in engineering psychology methods, human factors, human performance, biomechanics, computer science, industrial design, and so on. Such declarative knowledge is required to study applied problems that may span many content areas. In addition to coursework, special emphasis is placed on skills and tools used to analyze the person, environment, and machines that make up a system. Applied cognitive psychologists also require the capability to work as a part of a multidisciplinary team and to translate principles and theories from simple to complex task environments.

It is worth noting that similar knowledge, skills, and capabilities are required in the field of cognitive engineering which may be considered the engineering companion to the psychology of applied cognition. Cognitive engineering generally focuses on complex work domains such as nuclear power plants and hospitals, using techniques such as cognitive task analysis, focusing on the human–system interaction, and taking a problem-driven approach (Rasmussen 1986).

Knowledge

If one of the goals of applied cognitive psychologists is to study complex behavior in complex situations, they must possess a certain breadth as well as depth in many areas of psychology. This knowledge includes the core areas of psychology such as perception, cognition, and movement control. This fundamental knowledge illuminates the cognitive, perceptual, and physical capabilities or limitations of individuals. But applied cognitive psychologists may also need to be aware of social and industrial/organization psychology to understand the larger surrounding context in which the behavior of interest is situated. Or to have knowledge of developmental psychology to understand how age-related changes in cognition affect the behavior of interest.

Additionally, depending on the problem domain of study, domain-specific knowledge will be required. For example, if the focus is on behavior that is situated in computer systems, a technical understanding of human–computer interaction issues would generally be necessary. Similarly, understanding general aviation would inform studies of pilots and cockpit design, whereas knowledge of driving would enhance studies of intelligent vehicles and highway signage. The psychologist in this case does not need performance expertise, but solid domain knowledge. If one were investigating how best to train the perceptual decision-making skills required of an NFL quarterback, a thorough knowledge of what a quarterback must do as well as the perceptual cues used to "read defenses," and so on is required (Walker & Fisk 1995), but having the physical prowess to be a football quarterback would not be necessary.

Skills

A powerful aspect of applied cognitive psychological research lies in the production of general principles about behavior in complex situations. This capacity of the field of applied cognition comes from the design of studies that sample a wide range of user characteristics in different situations (i.e., representative design; Hammond 1998). As a beginning, it is critical to understand the user and the system or environment in which that user is interacting (e.g., Rogers *et al.* 2001). There are methods, tools, and techniques that can be used to garner the requisite understanding such as knowledge engineering and task analysis (Nichols *et al.* 2004). There are clear benefits to having multiple methods and techniques available to study a problem domain (Vicente 1994). The scientific method should be used in conjunction with these additional methods to enhance understanding of human behavior in situ (Durso & Manning 2002).

Knowledge Engineering

In addition to understanding the capabilities and limitations of people in the task context, it is critical to understand the knowledge and experience that people bring to various situations. Such an understanding can be obtained through the use of knowledge engineering which is a systematic method to examine the knowledge and cues that people use to make decisions (Sanchez *et al.* in press). This knowledge can be obtained by conducting focus groups, interviews, questionnaires, or observing operators in their environment. Therefore, skills in survey development, interviewing techniques, questionnaire design, and ethnographic methods are required.

Analysis of the data from knowledge engineering studies requires specialized skill. Qualitative data analysis is a process of reducing the massive quantities of text that can come from the transcription of focus groups or structured interviews. The process involves an analysis of the common themes that frequently occur in the raw data (i.e., transcripts). These themes constitute the *coding scheme*. Although qualitative data analysis can be extremely time-consuming, it offers a way for researchers to "study things in their natural settings, attempting to make sense of, or interpret phenomena in terms of the meanings people bring to them" (Denzin & Lincoln 1998, p. 3). It is also important to recognize that qualitative data can be quantified and analyzed statistically (for an example, see Melenhorst *et al.* 2006).

Knowledge engineering is also referred to as "knowledge acquisition" or "knowledge elicitation," and this process has been used extensively in the development of expert systems (see Hoffman *et al.* 1995; Cooke 1999 for reviews). For example, the development of an intelligent system can be based on an understanding of how experienced operators interact with a system. Similarly, knowledge engineering can be used to guide the transition from a manually controlled system into one with a higher degree of automation.

Knowledge engineering can be used to understand information-processing components of a task. For example, Fisk and Eggemeier (1988) used knowledge engineering to identify consistent trainable components in a real-world tactical command and control mission and to develop a part-task training approach based on those components. Another example is the work by Klein (1998), where he used a knowledge engineering approach to investigate the decision-making processes of firefighters operating in stressful situations. These findings have since been applied to aid in the design of military decision support systems.

Task Analysis

To understand the system and environment, a critical skill for applied cognitive psychologists is the capability to conduct a thorough task analysis. A task analysis is a general class of techniques that can provide a detailed analysis of the individual steps of a task and how the steps are arranged (Luczak 1997). The levels of detail can vary depending on the method, but a properly executed task analysis can be a powerful tool to reveal the physical and cognitive demands placed on a user by the system and environment.

For example, a blood glucose meter is a device used by diabetics to monitor the level of glucose in their blood. Rogers *et al.* (2001) found that although a manufacturer of blood glucose meters advertised their system as consisting of three easy steps, a task analysis revealed that proper use of the device required 52 individual, sequential steps. The task analysis was crucial in identifying the complexity of the "simple" task of using a blood glucose meter. Table 1.1 presents a portion of the task analysis to illustrate the level of detail that a task analysis can provide concerning the task the user has to perform at each step, the knowledge required for each task, the feedback (or lack thereof) provided by the system, and the potential problems the user might encounter.

Psychometric Methods

In addition to general statistics (e.g., analysis of variance, regression), measurement and modeling tools are a valuable part of the arsenal of an applied cognitive psychologist. For example, Gillan and Schvaneveldt (1999) described the utility of network models to understand knowledge differences between novices and experts, to make predictions about student learning, and to design computer interfaces.

Developing valid and reliable questionnaires and surveys will also be a critical component of successful applied projects (Babbie 1990; Moroney & Cameron 2004, unpubl. manuscript). It is a challenge to develop outcome measures that capture the complexity of behaviors that may be manifested in various task domains. The measures must provide reliable estimates across testing occasions and across the people being tested (who may vary widely in their level of performance). Moreover, the measures must provide a valid index of the behavior of interest whether it be performance, learning, expertise, retention over time, transfer across tasks, and so on.

Capabilities

Being Part of a Team

Because of the desire to study behavior in complex settings, an applied cognitive psychologist often works on interdisciplinary teams. For example, research in aviation psychology may involve collaboration work with aircraft designers and pilots. Someone interested in older adults' ability to use medical devices may be working with computer scientists, industrial designers, cognitive psychologists, medical doctors, and independent living facility coordinators. Because of the need to ground psychological research in a domain representative of the target behavior's context, working in diversified teams is often a requirement for applied cognitive psychologists.

Translation

Many talented scientists can interpret the psychological literature. However, given the goal of understanding behavior in contextually rich and often complex environments, applied cognitive psychologists must be able to abstract the critical principles of theories of perception or attention or memory and translate those ideas into testable hypotheses for tasks that comprise perception, attention, *and* memory components. Something as seemingly simple as the selection of an input device for a system is complicated by issues such as task demands, the specific controls being manipulated (e.g., radio buttons or scroll bars),

Table 1.1 Partial Task Analysis for a Standard Blood Glucose Meter

Task Number	Task	Task/Knowledge requirements	Feedback	Potential problems
1.0	Set up the meter			
1.1	Select the display language			
1.1.1	Press and hold the C button	Location of C button	Tactile (feel button action)	Cannot locate button
1.1.2	Press and release the On/Off button	Location of On/Off button	Meter beeps when turned on; meter displays last reading	Cannot locate buttonfail to release button
1.1.3	Release the C button	Location of the C button	Tactile (feel button action)	Cannot locate button
1.2	Code the meter			
1.2.1	Turn on the meter	Location of On/Off button	Meter beeps when turned on; meter displays last reading	Cannot locate button
1.2.2	Compare the code numbers on the meter and test strip package	Location of correct code number	None	Cannot find correct code number on package
1.2.3	Press the C button until the codes match	Location of the C button	Tactile (feel button action); code changes on display	Enter incorrect code number
2.0	Check the system			
2.1	Perform a check strip test			
2.1.1	Make sure the test area is clean	Location of test area	None	Test area not cleaned
2.1.2	Turn the meter on	Location of On/Off button	Meter beeps when turned on; meter displays last reading	Cannot locate button
2.1.3	Wait for meter to say "INSERT STRIP"	Location of display	Meter displays instructions	Does not observe instructions on display; inserts strip too early
2.1.4	Slide side 1 of the check strip into the test strip holder	Location of the test strip holder; proper orientation of check strip	Meter displays "APPLY SAMPLE" when it detects something	Insert check strip incorrectly; insert something other than a check strip
2.1.5	Wait for the meter to say "APPLY SAMPLE"	Location of the display; correct procedure	Meter displays instructions	Does not remove check strip from holder; applies blood or control solution; does not wait for instructions
2.1.6	Slide the check strip out of the test strip holder	Correct procedure	Meter displays "INSERT SIDE 2" when strip is removed	Does not remove check strip
2.1.7	Wait for the meter to say "INSERT SIDE 2"	Location of the display; correct procedure	Meter displays instructions	Does not wait for the instructions

Note: The full task analysis of the 52 steps is presented in Rogers *et al.* (2001).

the context of use, and the age of the user (McLaughlin *et al.* 2003; Charness *et al.* 2004; Rogers *et al.* 2005).

THE NEED FOR APPLIED COGNITIVE PSYCHOLOGY

During the First World War, a critical issue was selecting the right person for the right job in the military and ensuring that task-appropriate training was provided. These goals were met through applied psychology (Thorndike 1919). The Second World War brought issues of human–technology collaborations that revealed the limitations of a purely reductionist approach to psychological theories (Schvaneveldt 2005). The wartime needs required psychologists to solve complex problems in complex settings and to develop principles of behavior that would transcend the specific instance to guide design and training more generally (Hoffman & Deffenbacher 1992; Taylor 1994; Parsons 1999).

Today, technology continues to evolve, and quite rapidly; population demographics are changing; and psychologists recognize the importance of trying to understand behavior in the context of complex and varied environments. Applied cognitive psychologists are intrigued by design and training problems they observe; and their curiosity and concern for society lead them to want to understand, and perhaps improve, the world around them.

To illustrate applied cognitive psychological research, we selected six exemplar papers. We chose these examples to illustrate a range of cognitive functions (perception, attention, monitoring, learning, decision-making, memory, and comprehension) in a variety of everyday contexts (driving, security, sports, collaboration with technology, and safety). These examples are illustrative of the philosophy of use-inspired basic research (Stokes 1997), but they are by no means exhaustive. Myriad other examples are presented in other chapters of this book.

For each paper, we first present the impetus for the research, which we learned through a personal query sent to the lead author of each paper. We then describe the specific research question and the key findings. These examples illustrate the range of problems that are studied (i.e., the breadth of applied cognitive psychology), the variety of research methods used, and the contributions of this research to our daily lives, as well as to the science of psychology.

Training New Drivers

> At the time I started thinking about undertaking research on driving simulators, I had two young children. I thought constantly about my daughters' safety . . . Personally I was in a near fatal crash as a teenager . . . And professionally, as a mathematical psychologist, I was used to predicting behaviors that differed by only a few milliseconds. But those behaviors were relatively inconsequential. In the car, however, those few milliseconds can make the difference between life and death. (Don Fisher)

Novice drivers are more likely to suffer fatal accidents than are other drivers (Insurance Institute for Highway Safety 1988). In addition to a lack of experience among novice drivers, another potential reason for their increased fatality could be a lack of the higher-level cognitive skill of risk perception. One reason that novice drivers may suffer more fatal accidents could be that they are less likely to understand the consequences of risky driving. Fisher *et al.* (2002) examined the degree to which the skill of risk perception could be trained using low-cost personal computers (PCs). Determining how to train the complex cognitive skill of risk perception could lead to the widespread adoption of a low-cost way to train young drivers.

The question in the research was how best to train risk perception, a skill requiring perceptual and cognitive components. Could training encourage young drivers to drive more cautiously during demanding driving situations, and if so what are the psychological properties of training that would most facilitate the skill development? Another question Fisher *et al.* (2002) addressed was the extent to which PC-based training would generalize to more complex, riskier situations. They tested three groups: (1) college-aged bus drivers; (2) high school-aged novice drivers enrolled in a driver education course; and (3) high school-aged novice drivers enrolled in a driver education course and given the PC-based risk-awareness training program. The risk-awareness training program was composed of 80 scenarios that contained film of the windshield view and the driver's and rearview mirrors. Depending on the mode of the training program, users were asked to identify all potential risky elements in the scenario (e.g., a child playing on the sidewalk). In another mode, the training program was stopped and users had to report on important elements of the situation (e.g., "was there a vehicle approaching you?").

All three groups were tested in a high-fidelity driving simulator where they experienced various potentially risky driving situations (e.g., needing to pass a parked truck that obscures the view). The results showed that novice young drivers who participated in the risk-awareness training were indeed more cautious (i.e., made superior driving-related decisions) in risk-related driving scenarios compared with novice drivers who did not participate in risk-awareness training. This cautious driving was even apparent in situations with no apparent risk. For example, trained drivers were slower in their approach to an empty pedestrian cross walk. The driving patterns of the trained novice drivers were more similar to the untrained experienced drivers. The importance of the results is that risk-awareness training through a low-cost means (PC-based risk-awareness training) can have a pronounced effect on driving behavior in a highly vulnerable population (novice young drivers). Most importantly, the results generalized to novel situations in a high-fidelity driving simulator, which suggests that they may translate to actual driving.

Driving while Talking on a Cell Phone

> While observing drivers on the roadway, it became clear that the multi-tasking demands of the driver were beginning to increase in ways that were similar to the increases in workload of pilots years ago . . . What began as a simple exploration has become a sustained research project . . . Our latest series of studies came about because the aging and dual-task literature suggests that older adults have more difficulty multi-tasking than younger adults . . . we are now exploring the other side of the age continuum – 16 & 17 year-olds just learning to drive. . . . (Dave Strayer)

With decreasing costs, cell phones have been enthusiastically adopted by an estimated 160 million Americans (CTIA 2004). Previous research has shown that driving while talking on a cell phone is disruptive to driving performance among young adults (e.g.,

Strayer & Johnston 2001) such that when driving and talking on a cell phone, they were more likely to miss critical events such as stop signs and traffic lights.

Driving is a complex activity that involves the coordination of many activities. The literature on dual-task performance and aging has shown consistent effects, with older adults having more difficulty performing multiple tasks than other age groups (see Rogers 2000). Age-related differences in the ability to divide attention to multiple tasks may make driving and talking on a cell phone more difficult for older adults. However, older adults have more driving experience, which may moderate potential dual task decrements of driving and talking on a cell phone.

Strayer and Drews (2004) investigated whether talking on a hand-free phone while driving would disrupt driving performance and whether the effects would differ for younger and older adults. They examined age-related differences in dual-task performance in a research context representative of the target behavior: talking on a cell phone and driving in a simulator. Based on the literature in dual-task performance and aging, they predicted that older adults' performance on the driving task would deteriorate more rapidly than younger adults'.

In the driving-only condition of the study, participants followed a "pace car" in a driving simulator. The task was to avoid collision with the pace car by applying the brakes when the pace car applied the brakes. In the driving and talking condition, participants followed the pace car, but also engaged in a conversation with a research assistant (sitting out of view of the driver). This latter condition was meant to simulate talking on a hand-free cell phone. The dependent measures were how quickly the brakes could be applied in response to the pace car's brakes, the distance between the pace car and the driver, speed, and how quickly participants could recover speed lost during braking. The results showed that drivers who were conversing and driving took longer to brake and longer to recover lost speed, but they also had longer following distance than participants who were not conversing on a cell phone. Interestingly, older adults' driving was not more affected by hand-free conversations than younger adults'. The authors explained that this could be due to the high fidelity of the simulator, which allowed older adults to draw upon their extensive experience in a driving task.

The research conducted by Strayer and Drews (2004) illustrates that theories based on novel tasks used in basic cognitive aging research studies of dual-task performance may overestimate the effect of aging on everyday task performance (see also Walker *et al.* 1997). However, for both younger and older adults, talking on a cell phone, even when it is hand-free, has the potential to disrupt driving performance.

Support for Baggage Screeners

> We began the work largely because the screening task gave us a nice real-world domain in which to do theoretical work/apply theoretical knowledge. Basically, we saw an RFP [Request for Proposals] from the FAA [Federal Aviation Administration], and the topic seemed relevant to our general research interests (vision, attention, eye movements) so we pursued it. (Jason McCarley)

Most travelers are familiar with the process of getting their bags checked at the airport. Looking at the images of x-rayed baggage, one is likely to wonder how anyone can discern potentially threatening objects in the images (e.g., guns, bombs). Searching x-ray images for threatening objects in the presence of noise, clutter, and degraded image quality is a difficult task, which is made more difficult by time pressures and other external stressors. Whereas research has been conducted examining how expert radiologists examine medical x-rays, radiologists have additional information that may help guide their search. For example, anatomical constraints guide their search to very specific areas. Security screening of x-ray images represents a more difficult task because there are fewer constraints that may guide visual search. There seems to be little trial-to-trial regularity, even for training at the category level (Fisk & Schneider 1983). Additionally, the potential shape of targets (i.e., threatening objects) is vast. Consequently training detection of particular target shapes may not transfer to novel shapes that may also represent threats.

McCarley *et al.* (2004) examined the question of whether practice on a simulated baggage screening task improved performance in that task. Specifically, did training enhance search skills, recognition skills, or both? The second goal of their study was to determine how well training of search and recognition skills transferred to novel situations.

The observer's task was to view images of x-rays of bags. In some of the images, a picture of a knife was inserted. The training phase consisted of five sessions of 300 trials per session. Feedback was given after each trial. In the fifth session, the transfer phase, observers were told that they would be again searching for knives, but the shape of the knives was different than that on which they had been trained.

The results may not be surprising but they are important. The data indicated that across the training phase (comparing sessions 1–4), sensitivity improved; that is, observers were better able to recognize targets with practice. To determine whether training benefits would transfer, session 4 was compared to the transfer session, session 5. Results indicated that observers were less able to recognize the new knife shapes, suggesting that the training of target shapes was indeed stimulus-specific and did not transfer.

Did the practice provide any advantage to searching? McCarley *et al.* (2004) compared session 1 performance (first exposure to the task and to the targets) with session 5 (familiar with the task but searching for new targets). This comparison showed that recognition performance as well as target detection time was significantly better for session 5, suggesting some general benefit of task practice.

These results suggest that training efforts for baggage screeners should focus on training them to detect a wide variety of threats instead of modifying visual scanning behavior. McCarley *et al.* (2004) used eye-tracking measurements and found that the effectiveness of scanning did not change with practice; it was learning the targets that improved performance. Because of the heterogeneity of potential targets in this task domain, training programs should provide a wide variety of potentially threatening targets, possibly extending the research to examine superordinate or higher-order categories as suggested by the perceptual decision-making literature (e.g., Kirlik *et al.* 1996, 1998).

Deciding Where to Throw the Ball

> When I was in graduate school I was taught that practice (albeit practice of a particular sort) was *the* royal road to skill acquisition. But if that was the whole story, why could I rapidly learn to use technologies designed in one way, but only slowly and painfully learn to use other sorts of designs? I realized that skill acquisition simply had to have

> an environmental dimension . . . I wrote in 1995 on what I called Ecological Task Analysis, a technique for specifying the environmental support for, and impediments to, fluent behavior. [This article showed] that the presence of perceptual information that did a good job of specifying the environmental constraints on behavior facilitated skill acquisition. (Alex Kirlik) [Kirlik 1995]

Operators engaged in complex, dynamic situations often rely on simple perceptual heuristics to guide behavior. Kirlik *et al.* (1996) wondered whether specifically training simple perceptual and pattern-recognition heuristics would help performance in a complex task. The idea was that decision-making in complex environments is most likely dominated by the use of heuristics ("automatic" processes) rather than cognitively intensive procedures ("controlled" processes).

Although the heuristic aspect of decision-making may be a very important contributor to performance in complex decision-making tasks, very little work had been done to examine how best to train this kind of behavior. The purpose of the Kirlik *et al.* (1996) study was to examine how best to support skilled decision-making through display augmentation (highlighting important aspects of the display) with the goal of allowing an operator to quickly extract critical, task-relevant information.

Playing the role of an American football quarterback, participants had to decide to whom to throw the ball, as well as the exact time to throw the ball. In general, this decision-making behavior is dictated by specific rules based on general patterns of players on the field. If a specific pattern of players was evident, there was always one correct answer. Participants were assigned to one of four training conditions (the factorial combinations of rule training vs. no rule training, and visual enhancement vs. no visual enhancement). After training, participants were given similar tasks with no enhancement (transfer tasks) to measure the effects of training.

Simple rule training was better than no rule training, but the addition of visual enhancement (highlighting important task aspects in the display) improved response speed at transfer. The first study showed the performance benefits of static perceptual augmentation given during training; a second study showed that perceptual augmentation was also beneficial in a dynamic decision-making task.

The results of these studies illustrate how complex decision-making can be enhanced by exposing operators to concrete task situations. Such exposure allows operators to learn the relationships between abstract concepts (rules) and the perceptual information from the environment to which the rules are referring. Understanding these relationships informs theories of dynamic decision-making, provides guidance for training, and informs display design.

Let the Computer Do it: Automation

> The idea for the study did not stem from any one single observation of real world behavior, but from many, which all converged on the issue at hand. That is, when a task that is formerly done manually is given over to a computer, memory for the skill relevant to the task declines and people tend to become over-reliant on the computer, sometimes not bothering to check the computer results manually. I had noticed the same phenomenon in such diverse domains as my kids using an electronic calculator, myself using a spell checker in a word processing program, airline pilots using the autopilot in commercial aircraft, and control room personnel going through an "electronic check list" in a power plant. (Raja Parasuraman)

Automated systems are embedded in many products and systems we use throughout daily life. Some systems are completely automated with nothing required of the user other than to turn it on and push a button to activate it (e.g., disposable cameras). In these systems, the system takes over all functions (exposure, flash control, etc.), and allows the user only rudimentary control (take the picture or not). Other systems are more adaptive, allowing users to maintain control when they desire it. For example, the cruise control function in most cars offloads the driver's need to monitor the speed of the car, but the driver can obtain control when needed (e.g., to brake when the car ahead brakes). It has been suggested that with strict allocation of functions (as in traditional automation), users are left "out of the loop"; that is, they are not aware of what is going on in the system. On the other hand, adaptive systems may be less prone to the "out of the loop" syndrome because the operator is always in the loop, deciding when to turn off automation.

The question of whether adaptive task allocation (sometimes the machine has control, sometimes the human) would result in improved monitoring performance was examined in a study by Parasuraman *et al.* (1996). Two groups of participants monitored three control panels: engine status, fuel status, and tracking task. For one group, detection and correction of engine anomalies was automated throughout the study. This condition represented an instance of automation that is not adaptive. For the other group, the automation for the engine was turned on for the beginning of the study, turned off and under human control in the middle of the study, and turned back on for the rest of the study (adaptive automation). The automation in both conditions was not perfectly reliable and sometimes failed to detect engine problems. The dependent variable was the operator's detection rate of automation failures. The group that had the engine automation turned off for part of the study was better able to detect automation failures when the automation was turned back on. The results suggest that turning over control of certain automated monitoring tasks to the operator, at least for brief periods, has a beneficial effect on the ability detect automation failures. The results are important because operator failure to detect automation errors can, in some cases, lead to disastrous consequences. However, keeping human operator "in the loop" enabled them to better detect failures of automation and initiate corrective actions.

How do People Interpret Warning Symbols?

> The idea originated with thinking about how people who are not primary English speakers might need to accurately interpret a symbol's meaning in one word or a short phrase. When they first see the symbol, they shouldn't have to … think of a meaning that consists of several sentences. In everyday living situations, upon viewing a safety symbol, someone might have to make a snap judgment and only have time for a quick, concise thought, an instinctive impression … Furthermore the thought should be in line with the intended message of the symbol. (Holly Hancock)

Looking around one's home or workplace, one is likely to notice that most products contain a warning label or image. These warnings are provided to inform the user of potential hazards of products. However, are people easily able to decipher the symbols used in many warning labels? The American National Standards Institute (National Electrical Manufacturers Association 1998) recommends that symbols be used only if they are recognizable by 85 per cent of the general population. However, there is evidence that symbols often are not comprehended at this level, especially by older adults (Hancock *et al.* 2001) although other studies failed to find age-related differences in symbol comprehension (e.g., Halpern 1984). The inconsistency was hypothesized to be due to differences in testing methods to assess comprehension (e.g., some studies used multiple-choice responding while other studies used ranking tests).

Hancock *et al.* (2004) further examined age-related differences in symbol comprehension by using a methodology new to the warnings research area (phrase generation procedure) to assess symbol comprehension. In the phrase generation procedure (based on Battig & Montague 1969), the participants were presented with a safety symbol and asked to write down all the phrases that came to mind. The benefit of this type of procedure was that it allowed global comprehension to be evaluated from all of the phrases that participants generated. The procedure also allowed an analysis of the first phrase that came to mind which would represent the concept that was most strongly associated with the particular symbol.

The first phrase that was generated by younger adults more closely matched the actual meaning of the symbol compared to older adults. Younger adults also had better overall symbol comprehension than older adults (the sum of all the generated phrases more closely matched the intended meaning of the presented symbol). Another important finding was that accuracy rates among both younger and older adults was well below the 85 per cent recommended by ANSI. These results show that important safety-related symbols commonly in use may not be comprehensible by people of different ages.

SUCCESSFUL AGING

As we have argued, applied cognitive psychology is rooted in understanding behavior in context, extending psychological theories to more complex tasks and environments, and developing principles and guidelines that might improve lives. In this section we explore one specific area in more depth, namely, the potential of applied cognitive psychology to provide solutions for an important societal dilemma: how to support the desire of older adults to maintain their independence and autonomy.

It is a fact that the average age of members of most developed countries is increasing. For example, in the US, approximately 12 per cent of the population was over age 65 in 2000 with a projection of 20 per cent by the year 2030.This translates to roughly 71.5 million people (US Census Bureau 2000).

Longer life, however, does not mean life without disease, physical frailty, or cognitive decline. There are age-related changes in capabilities that make everyday activities more challenging as individuals grow older. There are perceptual changes (Kline & Scialfa 1997; Schieber 2003), cognitive changes (Craik & Salthouse 2000; Park & Schwarz 2000), movement control changes (Vercruyssen 1996; Ketcham & Stelmach 2004), and changes in functional anthropometry (Kroemer *et al.* 2001; Kroemer 2006). The research discussed in this book (as well as in the first edition; Durso *et al.* 1999) has the potential to support successful aging.

Everyday Activities

What does it mean to age successfully? The specific answer probably varies by individual, but there are likely common themes. One must be able to perform basic activities of daily living (ADLs) such as bathing, toileting, and eating (Katz 1983). Also critical is the ability to maintain one's household, manage a medication schedule, keep track of financial records, and prepare nutritious meals. These are referred to as instrumental activities of daily living (IADLs; Katz 1983; Lawton 1990). Performance of ADLs and IADLs is critical, but successful aging means more than performing these activities. Successful aging also involves being able to perform activities that contribute to the quality of life such as communicating with family and friends, continuing a hobby, or learning a new skill. These are referred to as enhanced activities of daily living (EADLs; Rogers *et al.* 1998).

How can applied cognitive psychology support these everyday activities? We will focus our discussion on IADLs and EADLs, which are more heavily influenced by cognitive capabilities (ADL performance is mostly influenced by physical functioning). Even with that constraint, supporting aging-in-place is a complex, multifaceted problem. What are the activities that need to be supported? What is the optimal way to provide support? Will older adults accept the supports into their daily activities? The tools of applied cognitive psychology can be used to begin to answer these questions. However, there is much work to be done if these efforts are to be successful.

What are the Activities that Need to be Supported?

To answer this question requires a needs analysis. The older adult user population has unique needs, capabilities, and limitations that must be considered throughout the design process. "Needs assessment and requirements analysis are the most important activities for initiating system improvement because, done well, they are the foundation upon which all other activities build" (Beith 2001, p. 14).

If home technologies are to be successful in supporting the independence of older adults, they must be designed with the needs of those older adults in mind. On the surface, this is an easy principle to follow. However, by not considering capabilities and limitations of older adults as well as the perceived benefits of technology, useful and acceptable technologies will not be developed. "Needs arise from the ways in which people perceive their everyday world and how they decide and act upon their own self-determined priorities. The ways in which needs arise thus depend upon the individual, but are also driven by the norms shared with other people within their social group … technological solutions must adequately account for the full complexity of human experience if they are to be useful" (Sixsmith & Sixsmith 2000, p. 192).

How do older adults spend their time? Moss and Lawton (1982) conducted a time-budget analysis of data from two samples (mean age 75 and 79). They found that 82 per cent of all waking behaviors of older adults occurred in the home. In a similar, more recent study, Baltes *et al.* (1999) examined activity patterns for two age groups. For individuals aged 70–84, primary activities were as follows: self-care activities such as getting up, eating, shopping (19 per cent), instrumental activities such as household chores, banking, and medical treatments (17 per cent), leisure activities such as cultural events, reading, gardening, watching television (42 per cent), social activities such as talking to people, visiting, telephoning (7 per cent), work (1 per cent), and resting (12 per cent). The distribution pattern was similar for their sample of adults over age 85, except for a marked increase in resting behavior (25 per cent). Approximately 80 per cent of the behaviors of both groups occurred in the home.

To move toward development of supports to bridge the gap between the demands of the tasks that must be performed and the capabilities of the individuals who must perform them, we need to have more detailed analyses of the sources of the problems, the nature of the problems, and the contexts in which they occur. In particular, more focus needs to be placed on the role of *cognition* in home functioning. Willis *et al.* (1999) suggested that qualitative research focusing on patterns and processes of behavior represents a useful tool for understanding age-related functional changes. They conducted a detailed analysis of the types of errors that older adults made on the Everyday Problems for Cognitive Challenged Elderly test (see Willis *et al.* 1998 for details). The strength of Willis *et al.*'s (1999) error analysis was that it provided specific information about the types of error participants made. Most notably, 90 per cent of their sample (aged 70–94) made "incomplete processing" errors. For example, they were deficient in combining and integrating information, they made procedural memory errors such as leaving steps out of a process, or they made selective attention errors such that they only processed portions of the necessary information. In addition, 22 per cent of the participants made errors indicating an inappropriate reliance on prior experience, which may indicate a tendency for older adults to rely on their intact semantic knowledge even when it may not be appropriately applicable. This study illustrates the role of cognitive processes in everyday home activities.

What is the Optimal Way to Provide Support?

We need to understand within the home context where and when cognitive supports are needed. For example, it is crucial to establish the prevalence of memory problems within the home-based environment. Currently, existing databases do not provide such information. Also important is understanding the knowledge and human information-processing demands placed on the human when interacting with the "system." It is through understanding the vulnerabilities of older adults, and capitalizing where possible on strengths, that a principled approach to effective aware home cognitive augmentation is possible.

Unfortunately, general principles of age-related system design that can be systematically applied to aware home technology design and development have not yet emerged. We believe that such principles can emerge; however, they will be tied to an understanding of age-related interactions with characteristics of the system interface, human information-processing demands, and goals associated with use of the system. Indeed, in domains more fully explored (e.g., "standard" technology such as computer input devices) such principles have emerged (Fisk *et al.* 2004).

One logical focus area for aware home technology is the support of memory-related tasks. There is substantial evidence in the literature that older adults have declines in their memory capabilities (for recent reviews, see Anderson & Craik 2000; Balota *et al.* 2000; Zacks *et al.* 2000), and that perceived memory complaints have an influence on the well-being of older adults (Verhaeghen *et al.* 2000). In addition, cognitive capabilities such as memory contribute to everyday cognitive competence, which is considered essential for independent living (Willis 1996).

To maintain their functional independence, older adults must remember to do certain things: pay the electricity bill before it is overdue; adhere to a specific medication regimen; purchase the appropriate items at the grocery store; go to scheduled physician's appointments on the appropriate day at the appropriate time; eat nutritious meals; exercise regularly; and take the roast out of the oven or the kettle off the stove. If these tasks are not carried out, individuals may not adequately be tending to their nutrition, health, and safety needs; indeed performing such tasks is, arguably "essential for independent living" (Maylor 1996, p. 192).

Future research must identify characteristics of the memory complaints reported by older adults in the context of the home and develop and test empirically-based methods of providing cognitive aids to support recovery from memory failures. To do so, it will be necessary to study the ecology of forgetting in the home – the "everyday content" of memory-intensive activities. Everyday content is loosely defined as the continually shifting set of information that a person uses to perform tasks (Mynatt *et al.* 1999). This flow of information is often incomplete, unnamed, informal, heavily context-dependent, and transient. Examples are notes, to-do lists, drafts, reminders, sketches, and the like that are in sharp contrast to archival material typically filed electronically or physically. Everyday content in the home includes a written or unwritten list of tasks, other reminders, frequently used objects, notes, messages, and other transient pieces of information common to daily living. Intuitively it is clear that memory functioning (in a variety of ways) is critical to the myriad tasks we carry out. However, "relatively little research has been done on the rich and complex strategies and tactics that we use every day to interrogate our memory systems" (Baddeley 1998, p. 217).

Will Older Adults Accept These Supports into Their Daily Activities?

"Older adults prefer to do things the old-fashioned way." "You can't teach an old dog new tricks." "New technologies are for the young." While it is true that older adults are slower to adopt many new technologies, and they typically require more training to learn to use them, these myths about older adults and new technologies are overstated. Rogers *et al.*'s (1998) focus group study illustrated a variety of new technologies that older adults reported encountering. Some technologies they had little choice about using, such as telephone menus, new gas pumps, or medical devices. However, some participants had voluntarily learned to use new devices, and most were eager to learn. These individuals did not wish to insulate themselves from changing technology. However, because of inadequate design and lack of accessible training, many had not been able to use a host of new technologies. An encouraging finding was the older adults' willingness to learn. Although they often acknowledged that they might have difficulty learning and require more time to learn, older individuals were eager to learn how to use various technologies.

Systems must be well designed and proper training must be provided. Does that guarantee that older adults will adopt new technologies to perform daily tasks? Not necessarily – adoption of new technologies is influenced by a variety of factors such as the relative advantage of the technology (in comparison to the previous method of accomplishing the activity) and the degree to which the innovation is compatible with one's values, experiences, and needs (Rogers 2003).

The factors that influenced adoption of new communication technologies were investigated by Melenhorst *et al.* (2006). In a focus group study, older adults were asked about how they would decide what communication method would be best suited for a particular communication goal such as sharing good news or making an appointment. The goal was to investigate perceived context-related benefits of communication technologies by older adults. Internet users and non-users were questioned about their preferences to use the telephone, a face-to-face visit, a letter, or the Internet. Of particular interest was the reasoning the participants used – why they selected a particular method of communication. The results revealed that older adults made their decisions primarily on the basis of the perceived benefits (or lack thereof) of the particular communication method afforded by the technology. These data are important as they indicate that the decision process seemed to rely mostly on whether the method suited their needs (i.e., was fast enough or personal enough or easy enough). Contrary to myths about older adults' use of technology, their decisions were not primarily based on negatives such as whether the method was too difficult or too costly or too time-intensive. These data support the notion that technology will be adopted by older individuals when the benefits of the technology are clear to them and meet their needs. Older adults seem willing to invest the time, resources, and money necessary to learn new technologies, if such benefits are clear. An implication of these results may be that introduction of new technology should involve making conscious the specific benefits, from the user's perspective.

We specifically assessed older adults' attitudes to advanced home technologies in a structured interview study to assess utility, privacy concerns, and the social acceptability of these systems (Melenhorst *et al.* 2004, in press; Mynatt *et al.* 2004). Issues of technology acceptance were examined in detail. The questions addressed both the participants' opinions about specific technological devices and the general concept of a technology-rich environment. The analyses of the qualitative data indicated a conditional acceptance of technology in the home by older adults. The perception of technology benefit or technology need seems to be an important incentive for older adults to overcome barriers such as expenses, lack of skills, and unfamiliarity. This study provides insight into preconditions of acceptance related to features of the technology. Insight into context- and person-related preconditions regarding technology use is necessary for a successful implementation of technology in the home, and for the development of supportive living environments.

Summary

There is no such thing as "the older adult." Older adults are a heterogeneous group with diverse needs, capabilities, and experiences (Lawton 1990). Cognitive aging theories (see Craik & Salthouse 2000 for a review) provide a general overview of typical, age-related changes in sensation, perception, and cognitive functioning. However, it is applied cognitive psychology that will lead to the scientific developments to provide support for older adults. But the problem domain is complex – there are many factors that must be considered when designing studies to test various hypotheses. It is critical that applied cognitive psychologists be prepared to employ numerous qualitative research approaches as well as the experimental and quasi-experimental approaches that are so well taught in the typical cognitive psychology graduate program of study.

When older people are asked about their hopes and aspirations, they often mention remaining independent and being able to take care of themselves. A serious fear among older adults is becoming dependent on others and losing their dignity (Lawton 1990). Current technology has the power to aid in the reduction of such fears by facilitating activities required for successful aging. Such technology can aid performance and leave intact, and indeed even enhance, a person's dignity. Unfortunately, investigation of the science and engineering of such advanced technology has been lacking from the perspective of the *human* in the human–machine system. The development of such technology is currently under-informed by the needs, capabilities, concerns, desires, and goals of older adults. Moreover, the factors that affect acceptance of such technologies are only beginning to be understood.

CONCLUSIONS

Applied cognitive psychology has a great deal of potential to enhance understanding of human behavior and improve lives. In fact, such efforts have already improved system design, education, job training, and health care – examples abound throughout this book (see also Durso *et al.* 1999; Vicente 2004).

Naturally, however, there is more to be learned. The fruits of applied psychological science may only provide a solution space, rather than the specific solution for a given problem. Such research is grounded in a problem space, but it is by no means atheoretical. Applied researchers must understand the relevance of theory and the importance of testing theory. It is important to emphasize that applied cognitive psychology is *not* simply applying the findings of so-called basic research.

Why haven't we solved all the problems yet? Because the problems are difficult! In addition, we probably have not even yet identified all of the problems that need to be solved. We have tried to illustrate the complexity of research problems in the domain of aging-in-place. Even though there have been decades of research on cognitive aging and many books have been written on the topic, it is not clear how to support the cognitive needs of older adults to enable them to maintain their functional independence.

There is nothing as practical as a good theory – this phrase was attributed to Lewin (Marrow 1969) and the concept is frequently debated (e.g., Eysenck 1987; Sandelands 1990). In our view, a theory may be practically relevant, but the theory had better be developed to accommodate the scale of complexity that surrounds many everyday activities. The success of applied cognitive psychology will be in the development of theories and principles that describe behavior, wherever that behavior occurs, be it in the workplace, the cockpit, the driver's seat, or the home.

AUTHOR NOTES

The authors were supported in part by a grant from the National Institutes of Health (National Institute on Aging) Grant P01 AG17211 under the auspices of the Center for Research and Education on Aging and Technology Enhancement (CREATE) and Award 0121661 entitled "The Aware Home: Sustaining the Quality of Life for an Aging Population" from the National Science Foundation.

Special thanks to Don Fisher, Holly Hancock, Alex Kirlik, Jason McCarley, Raja Parasuraman, and Dave Strayer for sharing their experiences about how they became involved in their respective research areas described in this chapter.

REFERENCES

Anderson, N. D. & Craik, F. I. M. (2000). Memory in the aging brain. In E. Tulving & F. I. M. Craik (eds.), *The Oxford Handbook of Memory* (pp. 411–425). Oxford: Oxford University Press.

Babbie, E. (1990). *Survey Research Methods* (2nd edn). Belmont, CA: Wadsworth.

Baddeley, A. (1998). *Human Memory: Theory and Practice* (2nd edn). Boston: Allyn and Bacon.

Balota, D. A., Dolan, P. O. & Duchek, J. M. (2000). Memory changes in healthy older adults. In E. Tulving & F. I. M. Craik (eds.), *The Oxford Handbook of Memory* (pp. 395–409). Oxford: Oxford University Press.

Baltes, M. M., Maas, I., Wilms, H.-U. *et al.* (1999). Everyday competence in old and very old age: theoretical considerations and empirical findings. In P. B. Baltes & K. U. Mayer (eds.), *The Berlin Aging Study: Aging from 70 to 100* (pp. 384–402). Cambridge: Cambridge University Press.

Battig, W. F. & Montague, W. E. (1969). Category norms for verbal items in 56 categories: a replication and extension of the Connecticut category norms. *Journal of Experimental Psychology Monograph, 80*, 1–46.

Beith, B. H. (2001). Needs and requirements in health care for the older adult: Challenges and opportunities for the new millennium. In W. A. Rogers & A. D. Fisk (eds.), *Human Factors Interventions for the Health Care of Older Adults* (pp. 13–30). Mahwah, NJ: Lawrence Erlbaum Associates.

Broadbent, D. E. (1973). *In Defence of Empirical Psychology.* London: Methuen.

Brunswik, E. (1952). *The Conceptual Framework of Psychology.* Chicago: University of Chicago Press.

Brunswik, E. (1956). *Perception and the Representative Design of Psychological Experiments* (2nd edn). Chicago: University of Chicago Press.

Charness, N., Holley, P., Feddon, J. & Jastrzembski, T. (2004). Light pen use and practice minimize age and hand performance differences in pointing tasks. *Human Factors, 46*, 373–384.

Cook, T. D. & Campbell, D. T. (1979). Quasi-experimentation: Design and Analysis for Field Settings. Chicago: Rand-McNally College Publishing.

Cooke, N. J. (1999). Knowledge elicitation. In F. T. Durso, R. S. Nickerson, R. W. Schvaneveldt, S. T. Dumais, D. S. Lindsay & M. T. H. Chi (eds.), *Handbook of Applied Cognition* (pp. 479–509). Chichester: John Wiley & Sons.

Craik, F. I. M. & Salthouse, T. A. (2000). *The Handbook of Aging and Cognition* (2nd edn). Mahwah, NJ: Lawrence Erlbaum Associates.

CTIA (2004). *Semi-annual Wireless Industry Survey* [electronic version]. Retrieved February 24, 2005, Available at: http://www.ctia.org/research_statistics/index.cfm/AID/10030.

Denzin, N. K. & Lincoln, Y. S. (1998). *Strategies of Qualitative Inquiry.* Thousand Oaks, CA: Sage.

Durso, F. T. & Manning, C. A. (2002). Spinning paper into glass: transforming flight progress strips. *Human Factors and Aerospace Safety, 2*, 1–31.

Durso, F. T., Nickerson, R. S., Schvaneveldt, R. W. *et al.* (1999). *Handbook of Applied Cognition.* Chichester: John Wiley & Sons.

Eysenck, H. J. (1987). There is nothing more practical than a good theory. In W. J. Baker & M. E. Hyland (eds.), *Current Issues in Theoretical Psychology* (pp. 49–64). Oxford: North-Holland.

Fisher, D. L., Laurie, N. E., Glaser, R. *et al.* (2002). Use of a fixed-base driving simulator to evaluate the effects of experience and PC-based risk awareness training on drivers' decisions. *Human Factors, 44*, 287–302.

Fisk, A. D. & Eggemeier, F. T. (1988). Application of automatic/controlled processing theory to training tactical and command control skills: 1. Background and task analytic methodology. *Proceedings of the Human Factors Society 32nd Annual Meeting.* Santa Monica, CA: Human Factors Society.

Fisk, A. D. & Kirlik, A. (1996). Practical relevance and age-related research: can theory advance without practice? In W. A. Rogers, A. D. Fisk & N. Walker (eds.) *Aging and Skilled Performance: Advances in Theory and Application* (pp. 1–15). Mahwah, NJ: Lawrence Erlbaum Associates.

Fisk, A. D., Rogers, W. A., Czaja, S. J. *et al.* (2004). *Designing for Older Users: Principles and Creative Human Factors Approaches*. Boca Raton, FL: CRC Press.

Fisk, A. D. & Schneider, W. (1983). Category and word search: generalizing search principles to complex processing. *Journal of Experimental Psychology: Learning, Memory, and Cognition*, *9*, 177–195.

Gillan, D. J. & Schvaneveldt, R. W. (1999). Applying cognitive psychology: bridging the gulf between basic research and cognitive artifacts. In F. T. Durso, R. S. Nickerson, R. W. Schvaneveldt, S. T. Dumais, D. S. Lindsay & M. T. H. Chi (eds.), *Handbook of Applied Cognition* (pp. 3–31). Chichester: John Wiley & Sons.

Halpern, D. F. (1984). Age differences in response time to verbal and symbolic traffic signs. *Experimental Aging Research*, *10*, 201–204.

Hammond, K. R. (1998). Representative design [electronic version]. Retrieved February 27, 2005, Available at: http://www.albany.edu/cpr/brunswik/notes/essay3.html.

Hammond, K. R. & Stewart, T. R. (2001). *The Essential Brunswik: Beginnings, Explications, Applications*. New York: Oxford University Press.

Hancock, H. E., Rogers, W. A. & Fisk, A. D. (2001). An evaluation of warning habits and beliefs across the adult lifespan. *Human Factors*, *43*, 343–354.

Hancock, H. E., Rogers, W. A., Schroeder, D. & Fisk, A. D. (2004). Safety symbol comprehension: Effects of symbol type, familiarity, and age. *Human Factors*, *46*, 183–195.

Hoffman, R. R. & Deffenbacher, K. A. (1992). A brief history of applied cognitive psychology. *Applied Cognitive Psychology, 6*, 1–48.

Hoffman, R. R. & Deffenbacher, K. A. (1993). An analysis of the relations between basic and applied psychology. *Ecological Psychology*, *5*, 315–352.

Hoffman, R. R. & Deffenbacher, K. A. (1994). Alternate schemes for the analysis of basic versus applied science: beauty is still in the eye of the beholder. *Ecological Psychology*, *6*, 125–130.

Hoffman, R. R., Shadbolt, N. R., Burton, A. M. & Klein, G. (1995). Eliciting knowledge from experts: a methodological analysis. *Organizational Behavior and Human Decision Processes*, *62*, 129–158.

Insurance Institute for Highway Safety (1988). Sixteen-year-old drivers' death rates rising at alarming rate. *Status Report*, *33*, 1–2.

Katz, S. (1983). Assessing self-maintenance: activities of daily living, mobility, and instrumental activities of daily living. *Journal of the American Geriatric Society*, *31*, 721–727.

Ketcham, C. J. & Stelmach, G. E. (2004). Movement control in the older adult. In R. W. Pew & S. B. Van Hemel (eds.), *Technology for Adaptive Aging* (pp. 64–92). Washington, DC: The National Academies Press.

Kirlik, A. (1995). Requirements for psychological models to support design: Toward ecological task analysis. In J. M. Flach & P. A. Hancock (eds.), *Global Perspectives on the Ecology of Human–Machine Systems* (pp. 68–120). Hillsdale, NJ: Lawrence Erlbaum Associates.

Kirlik, A., Fisk, A. D., Walker, N. & Rothrock, L. (1998). Feedback augmentation and part-task practice in training dynamic decision making skills. In J. A. Cannon-Bowers & E. Salas (eds.), *Making Decisions under Stress: Implications for Individual and Team Training* (pp. 91–113). Washington, DC: American Psychological Association.

Kirlik, A., Walker, N., Fisk, A.D. & Nagel, K. (1996). Supporting perception in the service of dynamic decision making. *Human Factors*, *38*, 288–299.

Klein, G. A. (1998). *Sources of Power: How People Make Decisions*. Cambridge, MA: MIT Press.

Kline, D. & Scialfa, C. T. (1997). Sensory and perceptual functioning: basic research and human factors implications. In A. D. Fisk & W. A. Rogers (eds.), *Handbook of Human Factors and the Older Adult* (pp. 27–54). San Diego, CA: Academic Press.

Kroemer, K. H. E. (2006) *"Extra-ordinary" Ergonomics: How to Accommodate Small and Big Persons, the Disabled, and Elderly, Expectant Mothers, and Children*. Boca Raton, FL: CRC Press and HFES.

Kroemer, K. H. E., Kroemer, H. B. & Kroemer-Elbert, K. E. (2001). *Ergonomics: How to Design for Ease and Efficiency*. Upper Saddle River, NJ: Prentice-Hall.

Landauer, T. K. (1989). Some bad and some good reasons for studying memory and cognition in the wild. In L. W. Poon, D. C. Rubin & B. A. Wilson (eds.), *Everyday Cognition in Adulthood and Late Life* (pp. 116–125). Cambridge: Cambridge University Press.

Lawton, M. P. (1990). Aging and performance on home tasks. *Human Factors, 32*, 527–536.

Luczak, H. (1997). Task analysis. In G. Salvendy (ed.), *Handbook of Human Factors and Ergonomics* (2nd edn, pp. 340–416). New York: John Wiley & Sons.

McCarley, J. S., Kramer, A. F., Wickens, C. D. *et al.* (2004). Visual skills in airport-security screening. *Psychological Science, 15*, 302–306.

McLaughlin, A. C., Rogers, W. A. & Fisk, A. D. (2003). Effects of attentional demand on input device use in younger and older adults. In *Proceedings of the Human Factors and Ergonomics Society 47th Annual Meeting* (pp. 247–251). Santa Monica, CA: Human Factors and Ergonomics Society.

Marrow, A. J. (1977). *The Practical Theorist: The Life and Work of Kurt Lewin.* New York: Teachers College Press.

Maylor, E. A. (1996). Does prospective memory decline with age? In M. Brandimonte, G. O. Einstein & M. A. McDaniel (eds.), *Prospective Memory: Theory and Applications* (pp. 173–197). Mahwah, NJ: Lawrence Erlbaum Associates.

Melenhorst, A. S., Fisk, A. D., Mynatt, E. D. & Rogers, W. A. (2004). Potential intrusiveness of aware home technology: perceptions of older adults. In *Proceedings of the Human Factors and Ergonomics Society 48th Annual Meeting* (pp. 266–270). Santa Monica, CA: Human Factors and Ergonomics Society.

Melenhorst, A. S., Rogers, W. A. & Bouwhuis, D. G. (2006). Older adults' motivated choice for technological innovation: evidence for benefit-driven selectivity. *Psychology and Aging, 21*, 190–195.

Melenhorst, A. S., Rogers, W. A. & Fisk, A. D. (in press). When will technology in the home improve older adults' quality of life? In H. W. Wahl, C. Tesch-Römer & A. Hoff (eds.), *New Dynamics in Old Age: Individual, Environmental, and Societal Perspectives.* Amityville, NY: Baywood Publishing.

Moroney, W. F. & Cameron, J. A. (2004). The Design of Questionnaires and Surveys. Unpublished manuscript, University of Dayton.

Moss, M. S. & Lawton, M. P. (1982). Time budgets of older people: a window on four lifestyles. *Journal of Gerontology, 37*(1), 115–123.

Mynatt, E. D., Igarashi, T., Edward, W. K. & LaMarca, A. (1999). Flatland: new dimensions in office whiteboards. In *Proceedings of the 1999 ACM Conference on Human Factors in Computing Systems* (pp. 346–353). Pittsburgh, PA: CHI 99.

Mynatt, E. D., Melenhorst, A. S., Fisk, A. D. & Rogers, W. A. (2004). Aware technologies for aging in place: Understanding user needs and attitudes. *IEEE Pervasive Computing, 3*, 36–41.

National Electrical Manufacturers Association (1998). *American National Standard for Criteria for Safety Symbols* (ANSI Z535.5). Washington, DC: National Electrical Manufacturers Association.

Nichols, T. A., Stronge, A. J., Fisk, A. D. *et al.* (2004). Human factors and ergonomics: bridging psychology and technology in telemedicine applications. *International Journal of Healthcare Technology and Management, 6*, 3–19.

Parasuraman, R. (1998). The attentive brain: issues and prospects. In R. Parasuraman (ed.), *The Attentive Brain* (pp. 3–15). Cambridge, MA: MIT Press.

Parasuraman, R. & Davies, D. R. (1984). *Varieties of Attention.* San Diego, CA: Academic Press.

Parasuraman, R., Mouloua, M. & Malloy, R. (1996). Effects of adaptive task allocation on monitoring of automated systems. *Human Factors, 38*, 665–679.

Park, D. C. & Schwarz, N. (2000). *Cognitive Aging: A Primer.* New York: Psychology Press.

Parsons, H. M. (1999). A history of division 21 (applied experimental and engineering psychology). In D. A. Dewsbury (ed.), *Unification through Division: Histories of the Divisions of the American Psychological Association* (Vol. 3, pp. 43–72). Washington, DC: American Psychological Association.

Petrinovich, L. (1989). Representative design and the quality of generalization. In L. W. Poon, D. C. Rubin & B. A. Wilson (eds.), *Everyday Cognition in Adulthood and Late Life* (pp. 11–24). Cambridge: Cambridge University Press.
Posner, M. I. & Petersen, S. E. (1990). The attention system of the human brain. *Annual Review of Neuroscience, 13*, 25–42.
Rasmussen, J. (1986). *Information Processing and Human–Machine Interaction: An Approach to Cognitive Engineering*. New York: North-Holland.
Rogers, E. M. (2003). *Diffusion of Innovations* (5th edn). New York: Free Press.
Rogers, W. A. (2000). Attention and aging. In D. C. Park & N. Schwarz (eds.), *Cognitive Aging: A Primer*. Philadelphia, PA: Psychology Press.
Rogers, W. A., Campbell, R. H. & Pak, R. (2001). A systems approach for training older adults to use technology. In N. Charness, D. C. Park & B. A. Sabel (eds.), *Communication, Technology, and Aging: Opportunities and Challenges for the Future* (pp. 187–208). New York: Springer.
Rogers, W. A. & Fisk, A. D. (2001). Understanding the role of attention in cognitive aging research. In J. E. Birren & K. W. Schaie (eds.), *Handbook of the Psychology of Aging* (5th edn, pp. 267–287). San Diego, CA: Academic Press.
Rogers, W. A., Fisk, A. D., McLaughlin, A.C. & Pak, R. (2005). Touch a screen or turn a knob: choosing the best device for the job. *Human Factors, 47*, 271–288.
Rogers, W. A., Meyer, B., Walker, N. & Fisk, A. D. (1998). Functional limitations to daily living tasks in the aged: a focus group analysis. *Human Factors, 40*, 111–125.
Rogers, W. A., Mykityshyn, A. L., Campbell, R. H. & Fisk, A. D. (2001). Analysis of a "simple" medical device. *Ergonomics in Design, 9*, 6–14.
Sanchez, J., Bowles, C. T., Rogers, W. A. & Fisk, A. D. (in press). Human factors goes to the golf course: knowledge engineering of a "simple" mowing task. *Ergonomics in Design*.
Sandelands, L. E. (1990). What is so practical about theory? Lewin revisited. *Journal for the Theory of Social Behavior, 20*, 235–262.
Schieber, F. (2003). Human factors and aging: identifying and compensating for age-related deficits in sensory and cognitive function. In N. Charness & K. W. Schaie (eds.), *Impact of Technology on Successful Aging* (pp. 42–84). New York: Springer Publishing Company.
Schneider, W. & Shiffrin, R. M. (1977). Controlled and automatic human information processing: I. Detection, search and attention. *Psychological Review, 84*, 1–66.
Schvaneveldt, R. W. (2005). Finding meaning in psychology. In A. F. Healy (ed.), *Experimental Cognitive Psychology and Its Application* (pp. 211–224). Washington, DC: American Psychological Association.
Sixsmith, A. & Sixsmith, J. (2000). Smart care technologies: meeting whose needs? *Journal of Telemedicine and Telecare, 6*, 190–192.
Stokes, D. E. (1997). *Pasteur's Quadrant: Basic Science and Technological Innovation*. Washington, DC: Brookings Institute Press.
Strayer, D. L. & Drews, F. A. (2004). Profiles in driver distraction: effects of cell phone conversations on younger and older drivers. *Human Factors, 46*, 640–649.
Strayer, D. L. & Johnston, W. A. (2001). Driven to distraction: dual-task studies of simulated driving and conversing on a cellular telephone. *Psychological Science, 12*, 462–466.
Taylor, H. L. (1994). *Who Made Distinguished Contributions to Engineering Psychology*? Washington, DC: American Psychological Association.
Thorndike, E. L. (1919). Scientific personnel work in the army. *Science, 49*, 53–61.
US Census Bureau (2000). Retrieved October 30, 2004, Available at: www.census.gov/population/www/projections/natproj.html.
Vercruyssen, M. (1996). Movement control and the speed of behavior. In A. D. Fisk & W. A. Rogers (eds.), *Handbook of Human Factors and the Older Adult* (pp. 55–86). San Diego, CA: Academic Press.
Verhaeghen, P., Geraerts, N. & Marcoen, A. (2000). Memory complaints, coping, and well-being in old age: a systemic approach. *The Gerontologist, 40*, 540–548.
Vicente, K. (1994). A pragmatic conception of basic and applied research: commentary on Hoffman and Deffenbacher (1993). *Ecological Psychology, 6*, 65–81.
Vicente, K. (2004). *The Human Factor: Revolutionizing the Way People Live with Technology*. New York: Routledge.

CHAPTER 2

Attention

David L. Strayer and Frank A. Drews
University of Utah, USA

WHAT IS ATTENTION AND WHY IS IT IMPORTANT?

A fundamental characteristic of human cognition is our *limited capacity* for processing information. We cannot see, attend to, remember, or react to everything that we encounter in our environment. Nowhere does this limited capacity play a more central role than with attention. This attentional bottleneck implies that paying attention to one source of information causes the processing of other things to suffer. For example, when a driver of a motor vehicle begins to chat on a cell phone, the driver's performance degrades as attention is withdrawn from driving and directed toward the phone conversation. Another important characteristic of attention is that it can be *flexibly allocated*, based on the task demands and goals of the operator. In the following paragraphs, we briefly describe the varieties of attention.

Selective attention refers to the ability to selectively process some sources of information while ignoring others (Johnston & Dark 1986). Given that we cannot process all the information that is constantly bombarding our sensory systems, it is important to be able to select the information that is most important to our current set of goals for further processing and exclude irrelevant sources of information from analysis. Researchers speculate that a combination of facilitatory and inhibitory processes work together to aid in the selective processing of the environment (e.g., Houghton & Tipper 1994). Facilitatory processes are assumed to amplify the processing of task-relevant information and inhibitory processes dampen the processing of irrelevant information. For the most part, the mechanisms of selection are quite effective. People are good at selectively processing task-relevant information and excluding irrelevant material, although performance is not always perfect. In the extreme, attention-related patient disorders, such as schizophrenia, provide examples where patients fail to effectively suppress the processing of irrelevant stimuli or thoughts (Beech *et al.* 1989).

Divided attention[1] refers to the ability to perform two or more concurrent tasks or activities. In this context, attention has been conceptualized as a commodity that can be flexibly allocated between different tasks, based on the *processing priority* assigned to each (Kahneman 1973; Navon & Gopher 1979). Because the capacity of attention is

Handbook of Applied Cognition: Second Edition. Edited by Francis T. Durso.

limited, it implies that there is an upper limit to how well people can perform any two tasks in combination. In many instances, when an operator attempts to concurrently perform two tasks, performance on one task prospers at the expense of the other; however, there are important exceptions (e.g., perfect time-sharing) which will be discussed below. The demands of dual-task performance are also closely associated with mental workload; as the cognitive demands increase, there is a corresponding increase in mental workload. In some instances, practice can facilitate the development of efficient automatic processing, resulting in significant improvements in dual-task performance. There are also interesting individual differences in multi-tasking ability. For example, in their review of the literature on aging and dual-task performance, Kramer and Larish (1996) noted that "one of the best exemplars of a mental activity in which large and robust age-related differences have been consistently obtained is dual-task processing" (p. 106).

Sustained attention refers to the ability to maintain the focus of attention for prolonged periods. In one variant of the sustained attention task, observers might be required to monitor a display for some task-relevant target information (e.g., a concealed weapon in airport carry-on luggage) occurring intermittently in a stream of non-target material. Not surprisingly, performance degrades when the focus of attention drifts from the monitoring task or if the observer becomes bored. As with the other variants of attention, there are important individual differences in the ability to sustain the focus of attention. For example, individuals with the predominantly inattentive type of attention deficit hyperactivity disorder (ADHD) exhibit difficulty in sustaining attention and often avoid tasks requiring sustained effort (DSM-IV 1994).

The remainder of this chapter is organized into three sections. The first provides a brief theoretical and historical overview of attention. The second gives examples of the different roles attention plays in applied settings such as aviation, medicine, surface transportation, and human–computer interaction. The final section considers future directions in basic and applied attention research.

THEORETICAL AND HISTORICAL PERSPECTIVES ON ATTENTION

William James' (1890) prescient treatment of attention is one of the earliest in the psychological literature. James observed that there are *varieties of attention* (sensory vs. intellectual, immediate vs. derived, passive vs. active), considered the effects of attention (on perceiving, conceiving, distinguishing, remembering and shortening reaction time), and the span of consciousness (i.e., how many things we can attend to at once, ranging from four to six distinct objects). According to James,

> Every one knows what attention is. It is the taking possession by the mind, in clear and vivid form, of one out of what seem several simultaneously possible objects or trains of thought. Focalization, concentration, of consciousness are of its essence. It implies withdrawal from some things in order to deal effectively with others, and is a condition which has a real opposite in the confused, dazed, scatterbrained state which in French is called distraction and *Zerstreutheit* in German. (pp. 403–404)

James also discussed the limits on performing two tasks at once, and the role of practice in dual-task performance. He commented on the role of attention in forming memories, noted that intense, sudden, or moving stimuli were processed reflexively, and commented on the difficulties of sustaining the focus of attention for prolonged periods of time. In short, James' characterization established the foundation for much of contemporary theorizing about attention.[2]

Attention became a central focus of research in the 1950s and 1960s, following Shannon and Weaver's (1949) work on *information theory* and the notion of a *limited capacity channel*. Broadbent (1957, 1958) applied the concept of a limited capacity channel to attention, proposing that attention acts as a filter allowing only relevant information to pass to higher levels and excluding irrelevant information from the information-processing system. Broadbent's *filter theory* operated as a gatekeeper and selection was based on the physical properties of the input. As evidence mounted that sources of "irrelevant" information, such as the listener's name, were noticed by the listener (e.g. Morray 1959; Treisman 1960), the concept of an all-or-none filter was modified so that irrelevant information was *attenuated*, but not completely blocked from access (Treisman 1960, 1969; Treisman & Geffen 1967). By contrast to these *early selection* theories, Deutsch and Deutsch (1963) proposed a *late selection* model in which all information was processed for meaning, and selection occurred at the level of the response. For several years, researchers debate the location of the filter ("early" vs. "late"). The issue was largely resolved when Johnston and Heinz (1978) demonstrated that the attentional bottleneck was flexible, based on task demands. Accordingly, selection is thought to occur so as to minimize the capacity demands on the individual.

In the 1970s and early 1980s, the predominant metaphor of attention was *resources*, based on principles borrowed from economic theory. Attention was viewed as an energetic, with performance improving as more attention (i.e., energy) was allocated to the task (Norman & Bobrow 1975). Research focused on *divided attention* tasks with performance trading off between tasks as a function of the attention allocated to each (Kahneman 1973). Later resource models considered attention to be made up of multiple pools of resources (Navon & Gopher 1979; Wickens 1980, 1984). Wickens (1984) conceptualized multiple resources as a multidimensional space formed by modalities of input (e.g., auditory vs. visual), mental codes (e.g., verbal vs. spatial), stages of processing (e.g., perceptual/cognitive vs. response), and output modalities (e.g., vocal vs. manual). According to this model, dual-task performance is predicted to be good when the resource demands of two tasks are far apart in the multidimensional resource space. When the two tasks compete for the same multidimensional space, performance will trade off as a function of processing priority. Some researchers have suggested that it may be fruitful to consider multiple resources in terms of neural structures, such as the left and right cerebral hemispheres (Kinsbourn & Hicks 1978; Friedman & Polson 1981). On the other hand, Navon (1984) has questioned the utility of the concept of resources, likening it to a theoretical *soup stone* with little explanatory power. Instead, Navon (1984; Navon & Miller 1987) suggests that dual-task interference may be due to *cross-talk* between concurrent tasks. That is, like the situation in which you can hear the "cross-talk" from another line when you are making a long-distance telephone call, the information-processing operations of the one task can contaminate the information-processing operations of a concurrent task.

Another important theme emerging in the 1970s and 1980s was the role that automatic and controlled processing play in human information-processing (e.g., Laberge & Samuels, 1974; Posner & Snyder 1975; Schneider & Shiffrin 1977; Shiffrin & Schneider 1977; Anderson 1982; Logan 1988). Novice performance is thought to rely on controlled attentional processing, which is often characterized as flexible, slow, effortful, and reliant on limited capacity attention. The transition from novice to expert involves the acquisition of automatic processing routines that have been characterized as fast, efficient, and no longer governed by limited capacity attention. Much of the theoretical work in this area has focused on the mechanisms underlying the development of automatic processing. For example, strength-based theories (e.g., Shiffrin & Schneider 1977) suggest that the associative strength of stimulus–response mappings is strengthened with consistent practice, yielding highly efficient information-processing. By contrast, memory-based theories (e.g., Logan 1988) suggest that automatic processing stems from memory retrieval processes that result in faster performance as more instances are stored in memory.

In the same period, other metaphors were developed to describe the spatial distribution of attention. Wachtel (1967; see also Posner 1980; Posner *et al.* 1980; LaBerge & Brown 1989) characterized attention as a *spotlight* that illuminated information that fell within its beam. The selective properties of spatial attention were represented by what fell within vs. outside the spotlight of attention. Posner and Cohen (1984) demonstrated that spatial attention could be directed with both *exogenous* and *endogenous cues*. In the case of exogenous cuing, a peripheral cue automatically draws (i.e., orients) attention to a spatial location. In the case of endogenous cuing, a central cue directs attention to peripheral locations in a controlled, goal-oriented fashion. Exogenous cuing is characterized as fast and effortless, whereas endogenous cuing is slow and effortful (Jonides 1981). Posner *et al.* (1984) suggest that the endogenously controlled movement of attention involves three separate mechanisms: one to *disengage* from the current focus of attention, one to *move* attention to a new location, and one to *engage* attention on a new object/location. Eriksen and St. James (1986; see also Eriksen & Yeh 1985) developed a *zoom lens* metaphor to describe other attributes of spatial attention. Like a zoom lens, the resolution of attention was hypothesized to be variable, with the magnification inversely proportional to the field of view. At low resolution, attention can be distributed over larger regions of space, with less ability to resolve fine detail. At higher resolution, attention can be distributed over a smaller region of space, but with greater ability to discriminate fine detail.

Attention also plays a critical important role in *binding features* together (Treisman & Gelade 1980; Treisman 1996). Whereas searching for a *feature singleton* (e.g., red items) can be accomplished *pre-attentively* (i.e., without capacity limitations), limited capacity attention is required to conjoin two or more features in a *conjunction search task* (e.g., searching for red squares in a field of red and blue triangles and blue squares). Metaphorically speaking, attention has been referred to as the *glue* that cements visual information together (Briand & Klein 1987), and in some instances attention can incorrectly bind features, resulting in *illusory conjunctions* (Treisman & Schmidt 1982). Treisman & Souther (1985) also observed interesting *search asymmetries.* When a task required searching for the presence of a feature (e.g., searching for a Q in a field of Os), search is easy and efficient. By contrast, when searching for the absence of a feature (searching for an O in a field of Qs), search is slow and effortful.

Meanwhile, another focus of research examined whether attention operated on *space-based* representations or on *object-based* representations. Duncan (1984; see also Kahneman & Henik 1981; Kahneman & Treisman 1984; Treisman 1988, 1992; Kahneman *et al.* 1992; Vecera & Farah 1994) suggested that attending to an object forms an *object file* and that all the attributes of the object are processed in parallel. Accordingly, it is easier to divide attention between two dimensions of a single object than to divide attention between two dimensions of different objects. However, when the task involves ignoring irrelevant or interfering material, it is often easier if the irrelevant information is on a different object than if the irrelevant information is part of the same object. Kramer and Jacobson (1991) found evidence that attention is influenced by both object-based and space-based representations, but that object-based effects often override the effects of spatial proximity.

More recently, research has focused on the role that a central processing bottleneck plays in limiting dual-task performance (e.g., Pashler 1994, 1999; Pashler *et al.* 2001; see also de Jong, 1993, 1995). Much of the evidence for this assertion comes from studies using the *psychological refractory period*, in which subjects are presented with two stimuli presented in rapid succession, each of which requires a separate discrete response. As the asynchrony in stimulus onset between the first stimulus and the second increases, reaction time to the second stimulus systematically decreases until reaching an asymptote. The delay in reaction time is often identical to the interval between the onsets of the two stimuli, indicating that processing of the second stimulus cannot begin until the first has completed. Pashler (1999) suggests that central mental operations are forced to queue while waiting to pass through the bottleneck. There has been considerable debate over whether the bottleneck is part of the cognitive architecture or whether it is strategic (e.g., Ruthruff *et al.* 2000).

Researchers have also focused on the role attention plays in executive functions and cognitive control using a variety of task-switching paradigms (Jerslid 1927; Rogers & Monsell 1995). In the task-switching paradigm, participants alternate between tasks, and the costs of switching is measured by the difference in performance from the beginning and end of a block of trials. When the two tasks use a common stimulus set (e.g., digits) with different mental operations (e.g., subtraction vs. addition), participants respond more slowly when the tasks alternate between blocks. In contrast, when the two tasks have distinct stimulus sets (e.g., digits vs. letters), there is little cost in switching between tasks (e.g., Allport *et al.* 1994). Switch costs are thought to provide an estimate of the time needed to reconfigure the cognitive network to perform a different task. Logan and Gordon (2001) suggest that the switch costs reflect an executive control process controlling subordinate automatic processes by reconfiguring their parameters in accordance with the current task demands.

Current advances in cognitive neuroscience are also beginning to shed some light on the neurobiology of attention (for a review of the neuroscience of attention, see Posner 2004). For example, evidence from fMRI studies of differential processing in the lateral geniculate nucleus (O'Connor *et al.* 2002) and single unit recordings from primary visual cortex (e.g., Reynolds *et al.* 1999) indicate that selective attention can be observed at very early stages in vision.[3] Evidence of top-down modulation of visual attention appears to come from posterior parietal and dorsal lateral prefrontal cortices (Nobre 2004). Anterior cingulated cortex also plays a major role in the selection for action and error processing (Posner *et al.* 1988; Holroyd & Coles 2002). Although our current understanding of the neurobiology of attention is far from complete and the role that this line of research will play in applied cognition is indeterminate, what is clear is that several brain regions work in tandem to regulate the flow of human information processing.

The *metaphors of attention* described in this section have been used by researchers to characterize different properties of human performance. On the one hand are theories that focus on conditions encouraging the operator to selectively process information in the environment. On the other are theories that focus on situations in which the operator engages in some form of multitasking operation. In each case, there are situations in which the mechanisms of attention operate effectively and efficiently, and situations in which capacity limitations affect the performance of the observer.

EXAMPLES FROM THE APPLIED LITERATURE

In this section, we consider selected examples of the varieties of attention and related concepts applied to real-world settings. Topics of consideration include selective attention, divided attention, sustained attention, mental workload, effects of practice, executive control, and individual differences. In each case, we have selected examples that illustrate the diverse ways in which attention influences performance.

Selective Attention

Consider the task of *selective attention*, in which the observer is overloaded with sensory stimulation and must select the most task-relevant information for further processing while excluding irrelevant sources of information. In such circumstances, it is useful to consider how successful the observer is at filtering out the irrelevant information. Simons and Chabris (1999; see also Neisser & Becklen 1975) provide a compelling example of the efficiency of selective attention in excluding irrelevant material from further analysis. Participants were asked to watch a short video clip of two teams passing a basketball back and forth and report the number of times that the team wearing white jerseys passed the ball. Midway through, a person dressed in a gorilla suit walked into the scene, stood in the middle of the basketball players, beat his chest, and then sauntered off the screen. Amazingly, 58 per cent of the people watching the video failed to see the gorilla! This *inattentional blindness* indicates that the mechanisms of selective attention are actually quite effective in filtering out highly salient, but irrelevant, information.

Attention can also be too selective, resulting in *cognitive tunnel vision*. In many cases, stress, workload, and fatigue can increase the likelihood of tunnel vision (Weltman *et al.* 1971; Baddeley 1972). In these situations, information that is critical to the observer may be ignored. For example, on December 29, 1972, Eastern Airlines Flight 401 developed problems with its landing gear on approach to Miami Airport. While the pilots focused on solving the landing gear problem, the plane was put on autopilot. Inadvertently, the autopilot was disabled and the plane began a gradual descent of 200 feet per minute. Transcripts indicate that the pilots, believing the autopilot was still engaged, focused so intently on solving the landing gear problem that they failed to respond to the ground proximity alarm until it was too late. The ensuing crash resulted in the loss of 98 lives.

Selective attention is also not perfect in filtering out irrelevant information. The Stroop color word interference task provides an excellent example of the inability of attention to exclude irrelevant information from being processed (Stroop 1935; MacLeod 1991). In the classic Stroop task, observers are presented with color word names (e.g., RED printed in blue ink). When asked to name the ink color and ignore the color word name, observers suffered considerable interference, indicating that selective attention was not successful in filtering out the irrelevant material. *Stroop-like interference* has also been observed when irrelevant information flanks critical target information (Eriksen & Eriksen 1974). Another example of a failure to suppress irrelevant or incompatible information comes when a speaker's voice is fed back with about a one second delay (as is often the case with two-way satellite communication). Speakers often find hearing the delayed audio feedback of their own voice quite disruptive to speech production (Howell & Powell 1987).

There are a number of factors that contribute to the efficiency of selective attention in searching for information in visual displays. Search is efficient if critical target information can be defined by a single feature such as color or shape (Christ 1975; Treisman & Gelade 1980; Wolfe 1994). For example, Agutter *et al.* (2003) found that anesthesiologists detected and treated myocardial ischemia more rapidly with graphical displays that changed the shape of a heart object during a heart attack. Similarly, Yeh and Wickens (2001) found color coding to be an effective attentional filtering technique for segmenting electronic battlefield maps; Fisher *et al.* (1989) reported that color coding could substantially reduce the time to search for a highlighted target in a computer menu; and Remington *et al.* (2000) found that air traffic controllers could identify traffic conflicts more rapidly when the aircraft altitude was color-coded. In each of these cases, performance was enhanced by the use of simple features making selective attention more efficient (i.e., targets seem to "pop out" of the display).

By contrast, search is slow and effortful when the observer must search for a target defined by a conjunction of features (Treisman & Gelade 1980). An entertaining example of the difficulty of conjunctive search comes from the children's cartoon book *Where's Waldo?* in which observers are given the task of finding Waldo, who is dressed in blue trousers, a red and white striped shirt, a stocking cap, and black-rimmed glasses. The task is surprisingly difficult because many of the other characters in the scene are also wearing some of the clothes from Waldo's wardrobe. Thus, observers must search for the set of features that uniquely identifies Waldo. Of course, in scenes where Waldo's wardrobe is unique, he immediately stands out in the crowd. Search is also more effective when observers are searching for the presence of an object than the absence of an object (Treisman & Souther 1985). For example, if there is a problem with the oil pressure in your automobile, it is more likely that you will notice this problem if a warning indicator comes on (presence of a feature) rather than if a status light turns off (absence of a feature).

Attention can also be captured by sudden onset stimuli (Yantis & Jonides 1990; Yantis 1993) and movement (McLeod *et al.* 1991; Franconeri & Simons 2003). If the critical target information is identified by sudden onsets (e.g., flashing) or movement, then it is more likely to be detected quickly and efficiently. In aviation, the air traffic controller's display uses flash coding to rapidly draw attention to situations requiring immediate attention (Yuditsky *et al.* 2002). Another example of using onset cues to direct attention is the blinking cursor on the computer monitor. Attention is directed to the location of the cursor which tends to pop out of the static display, making it easy for the computer user to know where they are typing. On the other hand, if irrelevant information in the display appears as an onset stimulus or with movement, then this may automatically divert attention from the task of successfully locating and identifying the target material. Sagarin *et al.* (2003, 2005) provide evidence that dynamic Internet pop-up advertisements (which often include both onset and movement stimuli) are a form of intrusive technology that "steals" consumer attention from the processing of desired content on an internet browser. New electronic billboards with bright images, flashing messages, and moving objects that are placed along the roadway can also be a potent source of driver distraction. Indeed, billboard advertisements suggest that "motorists can't miss" the new electronic signs because attention is captured by the moving display.

Expectancy also plays a major important role in selective attention. We often see what we expect to see. For example, on September 7, 2000, the pilots of a Boeing 737 airliner thought they were on final approach to runway 5 at Adelaide Airport, Australia. The pilots had expected to see the runway from the co-pilot's window, but because of strong northerly winds on final approach, the lights that they thought were from runway 5 were, in fact, lights from Anzac Highway. Fortunately, the pilot realized the error in time to abort the errant landing and later successfully landed on runway 23. Another example of expectancy bias is when an owner of a new vehicle suddenly notices many of the same vehicles on the road. Of course, the other vehicles were there prior to the purchase, but they are only noticed by the observer because *top-down processes* bias the processing of information in the environment.

Divided Attention

When attention is divided between two or more concurrent activities, this is referred to as a *divided attention* task.[4] In this context, attention has often been conceptualized as a resource that can be flexibly allocated between tasks based on processing priority (Kahneman 1973; Norman & Bobrow 1975; Navon & Gopher 1979; Wickens 1980, 1984, but see Navon 1984). Norman and Bobrow (1975) differentiated between *data-limited* and *resource-limited* regions of a theoretical function relating attentional resources and performance (i.e., the *performance–resource function*). In the data-limited region of the curve, allocating more attention to a task does not improve performance (in many cases, this is due to ceiling or floor effects in performance). For example, if a novice pilot attempted to fly a high-performance fighter aircraft, it is unlikely that allocating more attention would improve performance. In the resource-limited region of the curve, allocating more attention to a task improves performance. When an operator attempts to concurrently perform two resource-limited tasks in this "zero-sum game," performance on one task prospers at the expense of the other (but see Wickens 1980, 1984).

Dual-task combinations typically fall into one of two categories. The first includes situations in which performance of a task in dual-task conditions is similar to the performance of that task when performed in isolation. This occurs when one or both tasks are in data-limited regions of their respective performance resource functions or when the two tasks tap separate pools of resources (Wickens 1980). For example, some skills may become so automatic that they can be combined with another activity with little or no cost. In one such case, Spelke *et al.* (1976; see also Solomons and Stein 1896) trained subjects for 17 weeks so that they could take dictation while reading unrelated sentences with no decrement in reading speed or comprehension. Conditions such as this are referred to as *perfect time-sharing* (Wickens 1984).

The second category of dual-task combinations includes situations in which performance of a task in dual-task conditions varies as a function of the processing priority allocated to the two tasks. In this case, both tasks are in the resource-limited regions of their respective performance resource functions. As more attention is allocated to one task, performance on that task improves and performance on the concurrent task deteriorates.

Below, we consider examples of dual-task combinations that fall into the latter category and defer discussion of perfect time sharing to the section examining the effects of practice on attention and performance.

One dual-task activity that is commonly engaged in by over 100 million drivers in the US is the use of cell phones while driving. Studies indicate that drivers are more likely to miss critical traffic signals (e.g., traffic lights, a vehicle in front braking, etc.), slower to respond to the signals that they do detect, and are more likely to be involved in rear-end collisions when they were conversing on a cell phone (Brookhuis *et al.* 1991; McKnight & McKnight 1993; Alm & Nilsson 1995; Redelmeier & Tibshirani 1997; Strayer & Johnston 2001; Strayer *et al.* 2003). Not only does the use of a cell phone interfere with driving, but there is evidence that driving interferes with the cell phone conversation (Briem & Hedman 1995). That is, the cell-phone/driving dual-task combination is a good example of dual-task interference in which the driving and cell phone tasks compete for limited capacity attention.

Intuition might lead you to suspect that walking would be a task that is automatic and could be combined with other activities without costs. However, O'Shea *et al.* (2002) found that the stride length of patients with Parkinson's disease and control subjects was reduced when they engaged in either a motoric coin transfer secondary task or a cognitive digit subtraction secondary task. Anecdotal evidence suggests that talking on a cell phone also interferes with walking. Thus, there may be some merit to the saying that some people have difficulty walking and chewing gum at the same time (Kahneman 1973).

Finally, in considering divided attention it is worth examining how finely attention can be divided; that is, how many *independent* things can be attended to at the same time. James (1890) suggested that the range was between four and six. Interestingly, current estimates are within James' proposed 4–6 range. For example, Halford *et al.* (2005) asked participants to interpret graphically displayed statistical interactions. Task complexity increased as a function of the number of independent variables. These authors found that both the accuracy and speed of performance declined significantly between three and four variables, and performance on a five-way interaction was at chance. Similarly, Fisher (1984) suggested that the maximum number of cognitive comparison operations that can be executed simultaneously is restricted to about four, and Julez (1981) suggested that observers can subitize brief presentations of up to four objects without error. Using a different method, Pylyshyn and Storm (1988; Pylyshyn 2004) had participants monitor the location of four randomly moving targets in a field of four randomly moving distractors. The target and distractor objects were identical and were cued just before a trial began by briefly flashing the target objects. Then all eight items in the display moved randomly and independently for 10 seconds. When the motion stopped, the observers were required to locate the target objects. When initially confronted with this task, most observers had the impression that the task was too difficult and could not be done. Yet, location accuracy was about 87 per cent and observers were able to monitor the location the targets without keeping track of their identities. However, performance in the multiple-object tracking task falls rather dramatically as the number of target items increases beyond four (e.g., Oksama & Hyona 2004).

Mental Workload

> The stream of our thought is like a river. On the whole easy simple flowing predominates in it, the drift of things is with the pull of gravity, and effortless attention is the rule. But at intervals an obstruction, a set-back, a log-jam occurs, stops the current, creates an eddy, and makes things temporarily move the other way. If a real river could feel, it would feel these eddies and set-backs as places of effort. (James 1890, pp. 451–452)

Daniel Kahneman's (1973) book, entitled *Attention and Effort*, suggests that there is a relationship between attention and mental effort. Trying harder means allocating more attention to the task, often with corresponding increases in the mental workload experienced by the operator. In general, there is an inverted U-shaped function relating mental workload and performance (Yerkes & Dodson 1908). If workload is too low, then fatigue and boredom can set in and performance will deteriorate. If workload is too high, then the operator will be overloaded and performance will suffer. The "middle ground" of mental workload is a situation where the task demands are high enough to keep the operator alert and functioning at high levels of performance, but not so high as to overtax the individual.

Mental workload describes the interaction between an operator and the task (Gopher & Donchin 1986). Workload is a multifaceted construct, with no single measure completely capturing the experience. Researchers have used a variety of methods to measure workload. One measure is based on *primary task* performance, with the assumption that as performance degrades, workload must have increased. For example, as the mental workload of drivers increases, they may exhibit greater difficulty in keeping the vehicle in the center of the lane. Researchers have also added a *secondary task* while people perform the primary task, with the assumption that performance on the secondary task declines because the mental workload of the primary task increases. For example, Baddeley (1966; see also Logie *et al.* 1989) found that an operator's ability to generate a series of random numbers (as a secondary task) decreased as the primary task difficulty increased. Mental workload has also been assessed using a wide variety of *physiological measures* including electrocardiographic (ECG), electrooculographic (EOG), and electroencephalographic (EEG) recordings. Finally, workload is often assessed using *subjective* assessments of the individual performing the task. With subjective measures, the operator evaluates their phenomenological experience along several dimensions. For example, using the NASA-TLX (Task Load Index), operators are asked to rate their mental demand, physical demand, temporal demand, performance, effort, and frustration level (Hart & Staveland 1988). Primary task measures, secondary task measures, physiological measures, and subjective measures all capture important aspects of mental workload and each is associated with different strengths and weaknesses (O'Donnell & Eggemeier 1986).

Sirevaag *et al.* (1993) provide an interesting example of a comprehensive evaluation of the mental workload of military helicopter pilots in a high-fidelity flight simulation. In this study, the four methods described above for assessing mental workload were used to assess the demands on the pilot. Primary task measures included how well pilots performed each segment of their mission (e.g., to avoid anti-aircraft fire, pilots were instructed to fly 6 feet above the ground and deviations above or below this were taken to indicate higher levels of workload). Secondary task measures included presenting occasional tones over headphones, and pilots were instructed to keep a running tally of the number of tones that they had detected. In more difficult sections of the mission, the accuracy of the count tally decreased, indicating higher levels of mental workload in the primary task (i.e., flying the helicopter). Physiological measures included recording event-related brain potentials (ERPs) elicited by the secondary task tones. As the demands of flying the helicopter increased, the amplitude of the attention-sensitive components of the ERPs diminished. Finally, after each segment of the mission, pilots filled out subjective ratings of their workload. Taken together, these four methods provided converging evidence for determining the pilot's mental workload as they performed different maneuvers in the simulator.

In an example from a different operational environment, Weinger *et al.* (2004) evaluated mental workload of anesthesiologists during teaching and non-teaching anesthesia cases. Mental workload was assessed using a combination of primary task measures (i.e., observer ratings), secondary task measures (i.e., reaction to alarm lights on the patient monitor), physiological measures (i.e., heart rate), and subjective measures. Converging evidence from the four measures indicated that the workload of the clinician systematically increased from non-teaching baseline cases to situations in which when they performed their joint role as a clinician/instructor. As noted by the authors of the study, the increased workload suggests the need for caution when teaching during the delivery of patient care. As with the preceding example, the multiple measurement techniques help to provide valid and reliable estimates of the workload demands faced by the user.

With advances in computer technology and sophisticated psychophysiological techniques, it is now possible to estimate the mental workload of an operator in real time and adjust the demands of the task through computer automation when workload becomes excessive. In the case of *adaptive automation*, computer automation takes over lower priority tasks that the operator cannot perform under high workload and as the task demands and mental workload decrease, the computer automation relinquishes control to the operator (Pope *et al.* 1995). Wilson & Russell (2003) used artificial neural networks to classify in real time psychophysiological measures of mental workload while subjects performed different variations of the NASA multi-attribute task battery.[5] In this study, measures of ECG, EOG, EEG, and respiratory rate were taken while participants performed both low and high difficulty versions of the NASA task. The authors reported that classification accuracy for the artificial neural networks ranged from 82 to 86 per cent correct. Similarly, Prinzel *et al.* (2003) described a *biocybernetic* system that dynamically changed the task demands based on a combination of EEG and ERP measures, and Hillburn *et al.* (1997) used psychophysiological measures to adjust the task demands of an air traffic controller so as to maintain acceptable levels of workload.

Sustained Attention and Vigilance

Situations in which an observer must sustain attention for prolonged period of times are referred to as *vigilance tasks* (Mackworth 1948; Parasuraman, 1979, 1985; Parasuraman *et al.* 1987). In the typical vigilance task, the observer searches for target signals (e.g., enemy planes on a radar display, tumors in a radiograph, hidden weapons in a luggage x-ray, etc.) that are unpredictable and infrequent. Vigilance tasks are often quite taxing, performed under time pressure, associated with high levels of mental workload, and have levels of performance that are less than desirable (Hitchcock *et al.* 1999; Temple *et al.*

2000). The task of airport baggage screening provides an excellent example of a vigilance task in which the screener must monitor x-ray images for prolonged periods of time searching for prohibited items (e.g., guns, knives, bombs, etc.). McCarley *et al.* (2004) used an eye-tracker to measure fixation patterns in x-ray images of luggage and found that airport baggage screeners missed 15 per cent of the hunting knives that were fixated upon and 44 per cent of knives that appeared in locations that were not fixated on by the screener. This performance is clearly less than desirable.

Moreover, in sustained attention tasks there is a characteristic decrement in vigilance performance over a work shift that occurs in conditions where observers must hold information in active memory and use it to make decisions (i.e., the *vigilance decrement*).[6] For example, Parasuraman (1979) found decrements in detection sensitivity when the task required that target templates be held in working memory and observers to make *successive discriminations* (i.e., by comparing the item in question to an internal template in working memory). This vigilance decrement appears to stem in large part from the capacity drain brought about by prolonged effortful attention (Grier *et al.* 2003). By contrast, the decrements in detection sensitivity are less prevalent in *simultaneous discrimination* conditions in which the task does not overload working memory. In the latter case, an external template may be provided for comparison purposes to ease the burden on working memory.

Airport baggage screening provides a good example of successive discrimination. Because the list of prohibited items is quite large and there is considerable variation in the features within each category, the screening task places a considerable load on working memory. Thus, it is not surprising that McCarley *et al.* (2004) found poor detection rates, even when the screeners looked at the prohibited items in the x-ray. However, in cases where a template can be provided (e.g., in a production assembly-line) and the task does not overburden working memory, vigilance decrements should not be as pronounced.

Several methods have been proposed to improve vigilance performance (Davies & Parasuraman 1982). One suggestion is to provide consistent practice to make critical target information automatically capture attention (Shiffrin & Schneider 1977; see below for more details). If the potential set of target items is well defined, then consistent practice is likely to improve performance by increasing the *detection sensitivity* of the observer. However, as in the case of baggage screeners, if the critical target information varies based on viewing angle and from instance to instance, then it will be difficult to develop automatic detection of the targets (McCarley *et al.* 2004). Another option is to provide incentives to increase the motivation of the observer. For example, a baggage screener could get a bonus for detecting prohibited weapons. Incentives that increase the payoff for target detection are likely to decrease the observer's *response criterion*, resulting in an increase in *hits* (i.e., correctly indicating that a target is present) and *false alarms* (i.e., erroneously indicating that a target is present) and a decrease in *misses* (i.e., erroneously indicating that a target is absent), and *correct rejections* (i.e., correctly indicating that a target is absent) (see Green & Swets 1966). A final possibility considered here is the introduction of "false" signals that increase the probability of an event. In the case of airport baggage screening, prohibited items have been introduced into the screening process by transportation security officials. The introduction of false signals is also likely to result in a decrease in the response criterion (and lead to an increase in hits and false alarms and a decrease in misses).

Effects of Training

The old adage *practice makes perfect* implies that performance improves when people perform a task routinely. Indeed, one of the most important characteristics of human cognition is the ability to acquire new skills and expertise (Posner & Snyder 1975; Shiffrin & Schneider 1977; Anderson 1982, 1987, 1992; Logan 1985, 1988). Novice performance is typically characterized as slow, effortful, and reliant on limited capacity attention. At the other end of the continuum, an expert's performance is often characterized as fast, effortless, and automatic. In their classic studies of controlled and automatic human information-processing, Shiffrin and Schneider (1977) demonstrated that performance improves with certain types of practice, whereas other types of practice do not improve performance (even with tens of thousands of trials of practice). When there is a *consistent mapping* of stimulus to response over trials, performance will improve with practice and may eventually be characterized as automatic (e.g., free of capacity limitations, autonomous, ballistic). By contrast, when the mapping of stimulus to response varies across blocks of trials (i.e., *varied mapping*), performance does not improve with practice and remains subject to the capacity limitations of attention. For example, people who drive different vehicles can become frustrated because the process of activating the windshield wipers, headlights, and other devices varies from vehicle to vehicle (i.e., variable mapping). Other aspects of operating a motor vehicle, such as controlling the gas pedal or steering wheel, are consistent from vehicle to vehicle, making transfer from one vehicle to another relatively easy (i.e., consistent mapping). One implication of these findings is that benefits of practice are only to be had with parts of a task where there is consistency in the input–output mappings.[7]

An important characteristic of tasks as they become more automatic is that they place fewer demands on limited capacity attention. Anyone who watches an expert in action cannot help but be amazed at the mastery of his/her skill. Experts can make a seemingly impossible task for a novice look routine and effortless. At high levels of automatization, attention can be withdrawn from the task (Schneider & Fisk 1982) and the skills can be performed autonomously (i.e., without attentional control). In fact, there is evidence to show that paying too much attention to the automatic components of a task can interfere with the performance of an expert. Beilock *et al.* (2002, 2004) found that experienced golfers benefited from dual-task conditions that limited, rather than encouraged, attention to the execution of their swing.

Consequently, tasks that are processed automatically can be combined in dual-task situations with little change in performance from single-task levels (i.e., perfect time-sharing). For example, Schneider and Fisk (1982) found that subjects can sometimes perform two visual search tasks without noticeable deficit when one of the search tasks is automatic. In their dual-task study, subjects searched for a target letter in a series of 12 rapidly presented frames. Subjects searched for a consistently mapped target on one diagonal of a 2×2 character array and searched for a variably mapped target on the other diagonal of the array. When subjects performed the dual-task condition with a strong emphasis on the variably mapped search task, target detection sensitivity on the consistently mapped search task did not differ from single-task baseline levels. These data indicate that subjects were able to perform automatic visual search without allocating attention to the task.[8] Another example of perfect time-sharing comes from the dual-task studies described earlier requiring participants to take dictation and read unrelated passages (Spelke *et al.*

1976; see also Solomons & Stein 1896). After extensive practice, two hearty souls were able to take dictation with no decrement in reading speed or comprehension. Moreover, with additional encouragement, these subjects were able to detect relations among the dictated words and categorize the dictated words for meaning without interference on the reading task. Likewise, Allport *et al.* (1972) reported that a skilled pianist could shadow a series of aurally presented words without decrements in concurrent sight-reading performance. Similar evidence of perfect time-sharing has been reported with experienced ice hockey players (Leavitt 1979) and soccer players (Smith & Chamberlin 1992).

Given that consistent practice improves performance, an effective strategy for training is to provide extensive practice on the parts of the task that are amenable to improvement (Schneider 1985). With *part-task training*, a task analysis is used to identify the consistent components of a task. These sub-tasks are practiced in isolation until performance is proficient, before being integrated into the whole task. Wightman and Lintern (1985) differentiated between two forms of part-task training. *Segmentation* refers to situations in which practice is provided on segments of the whole task. In the case of segmentation, the components of the part and whole task are identical and transfer is expected to be good. A good example of segmentation is when a musician practices a particularly difficult part of a score several times before performing the entire piece. *Fractionation* refers to situations in which practice is provided on the individual components of two or more tasks that must eventually be performed together in the whole task. In the case of fractionation, the time-sharing demands of the part and whole task are likely to differ and part-task training is not likely to be effective. Indeed, researchers have found that part-task training has varying degrees of success. For example, using a space fortress videogame, Fabiani *et al.* (1988) found that participants who received part-task training performed better than participants trained for the same amount of time on the whole task. Likewise, Drews *et al.* (2005) found that part-task training improved resident anesthesiologists' ability to detect and diagnose critical events during simulated surgeries. However, when the demands of integrating task components are high, practicing each task in isolation may not be any more effective than practicing the whole task, and in some instances may result in negative transfer if the integrative dual-task components go unpracticed.

A variation on part-task training designed to avoid the limitations associated with fractionation is *variable priority training* (Gopher *et al.* 1989, 1994). With variable priority training, participants always perform the whole task, but they are systematically instructed to emphasize some components of the whole task while deemphasizing the other parts of the whole task. Note that with variable priority training the integrality of the dual task is maintained while trainees flexibly allocate attention to the different components of the task. Kramer *et al.* (1995) compared the effectiveness of variable priority training with a fixed priority training strategy. Subjects were initially trained to concurrently perform a monitoring task and an alphabet-arithmetic task, and then were transferred to a scheduling and a running memory dual task combination. Not only did variable priority training better facilitate the rate of learning and the level of mastery during the initial training period, but subjects trained under variable priority showed better transfer to the scheduling and running memory tasks. Thus, variable priority training appears to be an effective technique for training the flexible allocation of attention in dual-task conditions.

Executive Control

Working memory capacity, as measured by counting, operation, and reading span tasks, is thought to play a critical role in helping to keep task-relevant information active and accessible during the execution of complex tasks (e.g., Daneman & Carpenter 1983; Kane *et al.* 2001; Conway *et al.* 2005; Cowan *et al.* 2005). From this perspective, Engle *et al.* (1999) have suggested that working memory capacity reflects an executive attentional system[9] reliant upon prefrontal cortical brain regions in which "the memory representations are maintained in a highly active state in the face of interference, and these representations may reflect the action plans, goal states, or task-relevant stimuli in the environment" (Kane & Engle 2002, p. 638). As an illustrative example, consider the operation span task originally developed by Turner and Engle (1989) and recently used by Watson *et al.* (2005, Exp. 1) to study how individuals with low and high operation span differ in the susceptibility for creating false memories. In the first phase of the study, participants were asked to read and solve aloud a math problem followed by a to-be-remembered word (e.g., $2 \times 5 - 3 = 6$? cow). The number of math problem-word items was randomly varied from 2 to 6 and at the end of each list participants were prompted to recall the words from the list in order they were presented. Participants were subsequently classified as having low operation span if they correctly recalled between 0 and 9 words in the correct order, whereas participants were classified as having a high operation span if they correctly recalled more than 20 words in the correct order. In the second phase of the study, Watson *et al.* (2005) compared low- and high-span individuals' susceptibility for false memories by creating lists of words to be memorized where the list items are strong associates of a critical missing word (e.g., the critical missing word might be "sleep" and the presented list items are bed, rest, awake, dream, blanket, etc.). Participants were given explicit task instructions warning them how the lists were designed to induce false memories. Nevertheless, low-span individuals were more susceptible to false memories than were high-span individuals, and this was interpreted as reflecting differences in the ability of low- and high-span individuals to actively maintain the task goal of not falsely recalling items that were not on the list.

There are a number of important individual differences in the executive control of attention that have been reported in the literature (see below for additional discussion of individual differences). For example, working memory span tasks have been found to be predictive of reading comprehension and verbal SAT scores (Friedman & Miyake 2004), differences in the spatial distribution of attention (Bleckley *et al.* 2004), performance on dichotic listening tasks (Conway *et al.* 2001), ability to perform the anti-saccade task (Kane *et al.* 2001), and the degree of interference in a Stroop color naming task (Kane & Engle 2003). Working memory span tasks have also been shown to decline with senescence (Balota *et al.* 1999; Watson *et al.* 2004) and to be reduced for patients with Alzheimer's dementia (Balota *et al.* 1999; Watson *et al.* 2001). Thus, the executive attentional system appears to be a critical component in people's ability to successfully perform a task when confronted with distraction or interruption.

In a similar vein, Altmann and Trafton (2002) developed an activation-based model for memory for goals which has been successfully applied to understand the ability to recover from an interruption in an ongoing activity. Indeed, in the workplace we are often interrupted by ringing phones, beeping emails, queries from colleagues, alarms, etc., and it is often a challenge to resume the interrupted task at the appropriate place in the sequence. These interruptions can have harmful consequences if the task is resumed in such way that an important item is omitted. For example, a National Transportation Safety Board (1988) investigation of the crash of Northwest Airlines Flight 255 determined that the first officer was distracted by several intervening events which diverted his attention from the task of adjusting the flaps and slats. Consequently, the flaps and slats were not fully extended and the airliner crashed immediately after takeoff, killing 148 passengers, six crew, and two people on the ground. In fact, Dismukes *et al.* (1998) concluded that nearly half of the NTSB reported aviation accidents attributed to crew error involved lapses of attention associated with interruptions, distractions, or preoccupation with one task to the exclusion of another. Similarly, interruptions have been shown to negatively interfere with operating a motor vehicle (e.g., Strayer & Johnston 2001; Monk *et al.* 2002; Strayer *et al.* 2003), the delivery of patient care in the emergency room (e.g., Chisholm *et al.* 2000, 2001) and in the intensive care unit (e.g., Drews 2006). Given the potential adverse consequences of interruptions, it may prove fruitful to include working memory span tasks in the battery of selection instruments used during the initial screening of employees in operational environments where task-item omission is of concern.

Individual Differences

As with all aspects of human cognition, there are important individual differences in the diverse varieties of attention and, in the extreme, deficits in attentional processing are important defining characteristics for several psychopathologies (e.g., schizophrenia, attention deficit hyperactivity disorder, etc.; for details, see DSM-IV 1994). Here we consider non-pathological differences in attention and performance.

Ackerman (1987, 1988) demonstrated that *between-subject* variability in performance decreases with consistent practice on a task such that individual differences tend to be greater early in training than they are later in training. To better understand the role skill acquisition plays on individual differences, Ackerman (1988) developed a theoretical framework incorporating differences in general ability, perceptual speed ability, and psychomotor ability. As the consistency of a task increases, the role that these ability differences play in skill acquisition grows. Ackerman's framework builds on the three phases of skill acquisition developed by Anderson (1982, 1987, 1992). The first phase of skill acquisition is the *declarative stage* and is dependent upon the general processing abilities of the individual. The second phase is the *knowledge compilation phase* and is dependent on an individual's perceptual speed ability. The third phase is the *procedural stage* and is dependent on psychomotor ability.

In applied settings, an important goal is to select the right people for the right job. Individuals differ in their abilities and each job has unique requirements. For example, the requirements for an anesthesiologist differ from those of a fighter aircraft pilot and from an NFL lineman. In considering the task of selecting the right person for the right job, it is important to identify the goal of selection. Using Ackerman's (1988) framework, if the goal of selection is to identify those individuals who will do well during the early stages of training, then general abilities are likely to be good predictors of success. By contrast, if the goal of selection is to identify those who will do well in the later stages of training, then at least in some cases psychomotor abilities may be good predictors of success.

Of course, as illustrated in the preceding section, not all ability differences can be practiced away and differences in attention can have important consequences for performance in applied settings. Surprisingly, this area has not been a major focus of research for non-pathological populations. However, several investigators have demonstrated that individual differences in attention are predictive of real-world performance. For example, Gopher (1982) found that individual differences in a selective attention dichotic listening task were correlated with individual differences in performance in flight training. Jones and Martin (2003) suggest that an individual's ability to distribute attention is a predictor of successfully avoiding the accidental loss of computing work. Finally, Schweizer *et al.* (2000) found that performance on a sustained attention task was correlated with measured intelligence and that the correlation grew in strength as the cognitive demands of the sustained attention task increased.

CONCLUSIONS AND FUTURE DIRECTIONS

Looking back over the years since James (1890) published his chapter on attention in *The Principles of Psychology*, it is clear that his original framework is still with us. Attention is Balkanized into subcategories (e.g., selective attention, divided attention, etc.) and we still have no unified theory of attention. Although a number of paradigms have been developed to study attention and many of the details have fallen into place, advancement toward a coherent theoretical picture has been unsatisfactory. This has led some to lament the progress in the field (e.g., Johnston & Dark 1986). Pashler (1999) suggests that "no one knows what attention is, and that there may not even be an 'it' to be known about" (p. 1). Pashler argues for "the inadequacy of the term attention" (p. 317), suggesting that our folk psychological use of the term may be getting in the way of understanding the phenomenon. By contrast, Logan (2004) paints an optimistic picture of cumulative progress in theories of attention.

Our brief survey of the theoretical literature indicates that researchers have used a number of metaphors to describe attention, including: filter, gatekeeper, spotlight, zoom lens, resources, object file, glue, and bottleneck. Each metaphor describes important characteristics of attention, but each falls short of helping to explain the underlying mechanisms. Gentner and Jeziorski (1993; Gentner 1998) suggest that metaphors (and analogies) exploit partial similarities between different systems which can be misleading as well as helpful. From a scientific perspective, a useful metaphor maps the knowledge from one *well-understood* domain onto another, such that a system of relationships that holds for the former also holds for the latter. In some cases, metaphor can lead to new insight into a phenomenon. However, it is important not to be misled by superficial similarity of a metaphorical relation.

From an applied perspective, it is useful to consider whether it is *necessary* to have a general unified theory of attention in order to apply the principles derived from basic research on attention to the real world. Clearly, as outlined in the preceding section, the properties of human performance associated with selective processing of the environment have important consequences in applied settings. Likewise, capacity limitations play a fundamental role in human performance in real-world multitasking situations. Moreover, related concepts, such as workload, practice, executive control, and individual differences, are undeniably important in applied contexts. We suggest that even an inchoate theory of attention can be useful in helping to understanding human performance in the real world.

From our viewpoint, the distinction between basic and applied research is somewhat arbitrary. Good applied research has often provided important insights into the basic mechanisms of human cognition, and basic research can lead to new directions in applied research. What should be the role of applied attention research given the theoretical ambiguity of the term attention? Among other things, we suggest that applying our current understanding of the mechanisms of attention to applied issues provides useful information for how well a theory scales from the laboratory to the real world. The ultimate arbitrator on the utility of a theory of attention is how well it explains human behavior in everyday life.

NOTES

1 We use the terms divided attention and dual task interchangeably throughout this chapter.
2 A notable exception is James' concept of an *effect theory of attention*, which has largely been ignored by contemporary researchers (but see Johnston & Dark 1986). With effect theory, attention is the *effect* of differential processing, rather than the *cause* of differential processing.
3 Note, however, that evidence of the effects of selective attention in lower visual areas may be indicative of feed-forward "early selection" or "late selection" feedback from higher cortical levels.
4 It often proves difficult to determine if dual-task performance is the result of sharing attention between tasks or rapidly switching attention between the two tasks. However, estimates of the time to switch attention between to sources of input range from 80 ms (Peterson & Juola 2000; Logan 2005) to 300 ms (Weichselgartner & Sperling 1987), which would seem to preclude rapid shifts of attention in many dynamic dual-task configurations.
5 The NASA multi-attribute task battery subtasks include light and dial monitoring, manual tracking, resource management, and auditory communication.
6 However, Adams (1987) suggests that typical laboratory paradigms may overestimate the real-world decrements in vigilance performance.
7 It is interesting to note that in commercial aviation, pilots are certified to fly specific types of aircraft so as to avoid the inconsistency (i.e., varied mapping) that would result from switching from one model of aircraft to another. By contrast, in healthcare the configuration of equipment (e.g., in the different operating rooms of a hospital) often varies as a function of equipment manufacture and purchasing policies, thereby requiring physicians to operate in an environment with higher levels of inconsistency that is optimal.
8 Although single-task and dual-task *detection sensitivity* did not differ in Schneider and Fisk's (1982) study, the overall accuracy of detection dropped by 17 per cent from single- to dual-task conditions. This suggests that even in ideal settings, perfect time-sharing may not be truly "perfect."
9 The executive attention system has also been referred to as a central executive (e.g., Baddeley & Hitch 1974; Baddeley 1993), controlled processing (e.g., Posner & Snyder 1975; Shiffrin & Schneider 1977), and the supervisory attentional system (e.g., Norman & Shallice 1986; Shallice 1988).

REFERENCES

Ackerman, P. L. (1987). Individual differences in skill learning: an integration of psychometric and information processing perspectives. *Psychological Bulletin, 102*, 3–27.

Ackerman, P. L. (1988). Determinants of individual differences during skill acquisition: cognitive abilities and information processing. *Journal of Experimental Psychology: General, 117,* 288–318.

Adams, J. A. (1987). Criticisms of vigilance research: a discussion. *Human Factors, 29,* 737–740.

Agutter, J., Drews, F. A., Syroid, N. D. *et al.* (2003). Evaluation of a graphical cardiovascular display in a high fidelity simulator. *Anesthesia & Analgesia, 97,* 1403–1413.

Allport, D. A., Antonis, B. & Reynolds, P. (1972). On the division of attention: a disproof of the single channel hypothesis. *Quarterly Journal of Experimental Psychology, 24,* 225–235.

Allport, A., Styles, E. A. & Hsieh, S. (1994). Shifting intentional set: exploring the dynamic control of tasks. In C. Umilta & M. Moscovitch (eds.). *Attention and Performance XV: Conscious and Nonconscious Information Processing* (pp. 421–452), Cambridge, MA: MIT Press.

Alm, H. & Nilsson, L. (1995). The effects of a mobile telephone task on driver behaviour in a car following situation. *Accident Analysis & Prevention, 27*(5), 707–715.

Altmann, E. M. & Trafton, J. G. (2002). Memory for goals: an activation-based model. *Cognitive Sciences, 26,* 39–83.

Anderson, J. R. (1982). Acquisition of cognitive skill. *Psychological Review, 89,* 369–406.

Anderson, J. R. (1987). Skill acquisition: compilation of weak-method problem solutions. *Psychological Review, 94,* 192–210.

Anderson, J. R. (1992). Automaticity and the ACT* theory. *American Journal of Psychology, 105,* 165–180.

Baddeley, A. D. (1966). The capacity for generating information by randomization. *Quarterly Journal of Experimental Psychology, 18,* 119–130.

Baddeley, A. D. (1972). Selective attention and performance in dangerous environments. *British Journal of Psychology, 63,* 537–546.

Baddeley, A. D. (1993). Working memory or working attention? In A. Baddeley & L. Weiskrantz (eds.), *Attention: Selection, Awareness, and Control* (pp. 152–170). Oxford: Clarendon Press.

Baddeley, A. D. & Hitch, G. J. (1974). Working memory. In G. A. Bower (ed.), *The Psychology of Learning and Motivation* (pp. 47–89). New York: Academic Press.

Balota, D. A., Cortese, M. J., Duchek, J. M. *et al.* (1999). Veridical and false memories in healthy older adults and in dementia of the Alzheimer's type. *Cognitive Neuropsychology, 16,* 361–384.

Beech, A., Baylis, G. C., Smithson, P. & Claridge, G. (1989). Individual differences in schizotypy as reflected in cognitive measures of inhibition. *British Journal of Clinical Psychology, 28,* 117–129.

Beilock, S. L., Bertenthal, B. I., McCoy, A. M. M. & Carr, T. H. (2004). Haste does not always make waste: expertise, direction of attention, and speed versus accuracy in performing sensorimotor skills. *Psychonomic Bulletin & Review, 11,* 373–379.

Beilock, S. L., Carr, T. H., MacMahon, C. & Starks, J. L. (2002). When paying attention becomes counterproductive: impact of divided versus skill-focused attention on novice and experienced performance of sensorimotor skills. *Journal of Experimental Psychology: Applied, 8,* 6–16.

Bleckley, M. K., Durso, F. T., Crutchfield, J. M. *et al.* (2004). Individual differences in working memory capacity predict visual attention allocation. *Psychonomic Bulletin & Review, 10,* 884–889.

Briand, K. A. & Klein, R. M. (1987). Is Posner's "beam" the same as Treisman's "glue"?: on the relation between visual orienting and feature integration theory. *Journal of Experimental Psychology: Human Perception and Performance, 13,* 228–241.

Briem, V. & Hedman, L. R. (1995). Behavioural effects of mobile telephone use during simulated driving. *Ergonomics, 38,* 2536–2562.

Broadbent, D. A. (1957). A mechanical model for human attention and immediate memory. *Psychological Review, 64,* 205–215.

Broadbent, D. A. (1958). *Perception and Communication.* London: Pergamon Press.

Brookhuis, K. A., De Vries, G. & De Waard, D. (1991). The effects of mobile telephoning on driving performance. *Accident Analysis & Prevention, 23,* 309–316.

Chisholm, C. D., Collison, E. K., Nelson, D. R. & Cordell, W. H. (2000). Emergency department workplace interruptions: are emergency physicians "interrupt-driven" and "multitasking"? *Academic Emergency Medicine, 7,* 1239–1243.

Chisholm, C. D., Dornfeld, A. M., Nelson, D. R. & Cordell, W. H. (2001). Work interrupted: a comparison of workplace interruptions in emergency departments and primary care offices. *Annals of Emergency Medicine*, *38*, 146–151.

Christ, R. E. (1975). Review and analysis of color coding research for visual displays. *Human Factors*, *17*, 542–570.

Conway, A. R. A., Cowan, N. & Bunting, M. F. (2001). The cocktail party phenomenon revisited: the importance of working memory capacity. *Psychonomic Bulletin & Review*, *8*, 331–335.

Conway, A. R. A., Kane, M. J., Bunting, M. F. *et al.* (2005). Working memory span tasks: a methodological review and user's guide. *Psychonomic Bulletin & Review*, *12*, 769–786.

Cowan, N., Elliott, E. M., Saults J. S. *et al.* (2005). On the capacity of attention: its estimation and its role in working memory and cognitive attitudes. *Cognitive Psychology*, *51*, 42–100.

Daneman, M. & Carpenter, P. A. (1983). Individual differences in integrating information between and within sentences. *Journal of Experimental Psychology: Learning, Memory, and Cognition*, *9*, 561–584.

Davies, D. R. & Parasuraman, R. (1982). *The Psychology of Vigilance*. London: Academic Press.

de Jong, R. (1993). Multiple bottlenecks in overlapping task performance. *Journal of Experimental Psychology: Human Perception and Performance*, *19*, 965–980.

de Jong, R. (1995). The role of preparation in overlapping-task performance. *Quarterly Journal of Experimental Psychology: Human Experimental Psychology, 48A,* 2–25.

Deutsch, J. A. & Deutsch, D. (1963). Attention: some theoretical considerations. *Psychological Review, 70*, 80–90.

Dismukes, K., Young, G. & Sumwalt, C. R. (1998). Cockpit interruptions and distractions. *ASRA Directline Magazine*, December.

Drews, F. A. (2006). The frequency and impact of task interruptions on patient safety. In *Proceedings of the 16th World Congress of the International Ergonomics Association*. Maastricht.

Drews, F. A., Johnson, K., Syroid, N. & Strayer, D. (2005). Human factors meets anesthesia: advanced training to improve airway management. In *Proceedings of the 49th Annual Meeting of the Human Factors and Ergonomics Society*. Orlando, FL.

DSM-IV (1994). *The Diagnostic and Statistical Manual of Mental Disorders* (4th edn). Washington, DC: American Psychiatric Association.

Duncan, J. (1984). Selective attention and the organization of visual information. *Journal of Experimental Psychology: General*, *113*, 501–517.

Engle, R. W., Thuolski, S., W., Laughlin, J. E. & Conway, A. R. A. (1999). Working memory, short-term memory and general fluid intelligence: a latent variable approach. *Journal of Experimental Psychology: General*, *128*, 309–331.

Eriksen, B. A. & Eriksen, C. W. (1974). Effects of noise letters upon the identification of a target letter in a nonsearch task. *Perception & Psychophysics, 42*, 60–68.

Eriksen, C. W. & St. James, J. D. (1986). Visual attention within and around the field of focal attention: a zoom lens model. *Perception & Psychophysics*, *40*, 225–240.

Eriksen, C. W. & Yeh, Y. Y. (1985). Allocation of attention in the visual field. *Journal of Experimental Psychology: Human Perception and Performance*, *11*, 583–597.

Fabiani, M., Gratton, G., Karis, D. & Donchin, E. (1988) The definition, identification, and reliability of measurement of the P300 component of the event-related brain potential. In P. K. Ackles, J. R. Jennings & M. G. Coles (eds.), *Advances in Psychophysiology: Vol. 2*. Guilford, CT: JAI Press.

Fisher, D. L. (1984). Central capacity limits in consistent mapping visual search tasks: four channels or more? *Cognitive Psychology*, *16*, 449–484.

Fisher, D. L., Coury, B. G., Tengs, T. O. & Duffy, S. A. (1989). Minimizing the time to search visual displays: the role of highlighting. *Human Factors*, *31*, 167–182.

Franconeri, S. L. & Simons, D. J. (2003). Moving and looming stimuli capture attention. *Perception & Psychophysics*, *65*, 999–1010.

Friedman, A. & Polson, M. C. (1981). Hemispheres as independent resource systems: limited-capacity processing and cerebral specialization. *Journal of Experimental Psychology: Human Perception and Performance*, *7*, 1031–1058.

Friedman, N. P. & Miyake, A. (2004). The reading span test and its predictive power for reading comprehension ability. *Journal of Memory & Language*, 51, 136–158.

Gentner, D. (1998). Analogy. In W. Bechtel & G. Grahm (eds.), *A Companion to Cognitive Science* (pp. 107–113). Oxford: Blackwell.
Gentner, D. & Jeziorski, M. (1993). The shift from metaphor to analogy in western science. In A. Ortony (ed.), *Metaphor and Thought* (2nd edn, pp. 447–480). Cambridge: Cambridge University Press.
Gopher, D. (1982). A selection attention test as a predictor of success in flight training. *Human Factors, 24*, 173–183.
Gopher, D. & Donchin, E. (1986). Workload: an examination of the concept. In K. Boff, L. Kaufmann & J. Thomas (eds.), *Handbook of Perception and Performance (Vol. 2): Cognitive Processes and Performance* (pp. 1–49). New York: John Wiley & Sons.
Gopher, D., Weil, M. & Barekt, T. (1994). Transfer of skill from a computer game trainer to flight. *Human Factors, 36*, 387–405.
Gopher, D., Weil, M. & Siegel, D. (1989). Practice under changing priorities: an approach to training in complex skills. *Acta Psychologica, 71*, 147–179.
Green, D. M. & Swets, J. A. (1966). *Signal Detection Theory and Psychophysics*. New York: John Wiley & Sons.
Grier, R. A., Warm, J. S., Dember, W. N. *et al.* (2003). The vigilance decrement reflects limitations in effortful attention, not mindlessness. *Human Factors, 45*, 349–359.
Halford, G. S., Baker, R., McCredden, J. E. & Bain, J. D. (2005). How many variables can humans process? *Psychological Science, 16*, 70–76.
Hart, S. G. & Staveland, L. E. (1988). Development of NASA-TLX (Task Load Index): results of empirical and theoretical research. In P. A. Hancock & N. Meshkati (eds.), *Human Mental Workload*. Amsterdam: North-Holland.
Hillburn, B., Jorna, P. G., Byrne, E. A. & Parasuraman, R. (1997). The effect of adaptive air control (ATC) decision aiding on controller mental workload. In M. Mustapha & J. M. Koonce (eds.), *Human–Automation Interaction: Research and Practice* (pp. 84–91). Mahwah, NJ: Lawrence Erlbaum Associates.
Hitchcock, E. M., Dember, W. N., Warn, J. S. *et al.* (1999). Effects of cuing and knowledge of results on workload and boredom in sustained attention. *Human Factors, 41*, 365–372.
Holroyd, C. B. & Coles, M. G. H. (2002). The neural basis of human error processing: reinforcement learning, dopamine, and the error-related negativity. *Psychological Review, 109*, 679–709.
Houghton, G. & Tipper, S. P. (1994). A model of inhibitory mechanisms in selective attention. In D. Dagenbach & T. Carr (eds.), *Inhibitory Processes in Attention, Memory, and Language* (pp. 53–112). San Diego, CA: Academic Press.
Howell, P. & Powell, D. J. (1987). Delayed auditory feedback with delayed sounds varying in duration. *Perception and Psychophysics, 42*, 166–172.
James, W. (1890). *The Principles of Psychology* (Vol. 1). New York: Holt, Rhinehart & Winston.
Jerslid, A. T. (1927). Mental set and shift. *Archives of Psychology, 89*, whole issue.
Johnston, W. A. & Dark, V. J. (1986). Selective attention. *Annual Review of Psychology, 37*, 43–75.
Johnston, W. A. & Heinz, S. P. (1978). Flexibility and capacity demands of attention. *Journal of Experimental Psychology: General, 107*, 420–435.
Jonides, J. (1981). Voluntary versus automatic control over the mind's eye's movement. In J. B. Long & A. D. Baddeley (eds.), *Attention and Performance IX* (pp. 187–203). Hillsdale, NJ: Lawrence Erlbaum Associates.
Jones, G. F. & Martin, M. (2003).Distribution of attention and failure to save computer work. In M. Rauterberg *et al.* (eds.), *Human–Computer Interaction – Interact '03* (pp. 789–792). Amsterdam: IOS Press IFIP.
Julez, B. (1981). Figure and ground perception in briefly presented isodipole textures. In M. Kubovy & J. R. Pomerantz (eds.). *Perceptual Organization* (pp. 27–54). Hillsdale, NJ: Lawrence Erlbaum Associates.
Kahneman, D. (1973). *Attention and Effort*. Englewood Cliffs, NJ: Prentice-Hall.
Kahneman, D. & Henik, A. (1981). Perceptual organization and attention. In M. Kubovy & J. R. Pomerantz (eds.), *Perceptual Organization* (pp. 181–211). Hillsdale, NJ: Lawrence Erlbaum Associates.

Kahneman, D. & Treisman, A. (1984). Changing views of attention and automaticity. In R. Parasuraman & D. R. Davies (eds.), *Variety of Attention* (pp. 29–61). New York: Academic Press.

Kahneman, D., Treisman, A. & Gibbs, B. (1992). The reviewing of object files: object-specific integration of information. *Cognitive Psychology*, *24*, 175–219.

Kane, M. J., Bleckley, M. K., Conway, A. R. A. & Engle, R. W. (2001). A controlled-attention view of working memory capacity. *Journal of Experimental Psychology: General*, *130*, 169–183.

Kane, M. J. & Engle, R. W. (2002). The role of prefrontal cortex in working memory capacity, executive attention, and general fluid intelligence: an individual-differences perspective. *Psychonomic Bulletin & Review*, *9*, 637–671.

Kane, M. J. & Engle, R. W. (2003). Working memory capacity and the control of attention: the contribution of goal neglect, response competition, and task set to Stroop interference. *Journal of Experimental Psychology: General*, *132*, 47–70.

Kinsbourn, M. & Hicks, R. E. (1978). Functional cerebral space: a model for overflow, transfer, and interference effects in human performance. In J. Requin (ed.), *Attention and Performance VII* (pp. 345–362). Hillsdale, NJ: Lawrence Erlbaum Associates.

Kramer, A. F. & Jacobson, A. (1991). Perceptual organization and focused attention: the role of objects and proximity in visual processing. *Perception & Psychophysics*, *50*, 267–284.

Kramer, A. F. & Larish, J. (1996). Aging and dual-task performance. In W. Rogers, A. D. Fisk & N. Walker (eds.), *Aging and Skilled Performance* (pp. 83–112). Hillsdale, NJ: Lawrence Erlbaum Associates.

Kramer, A. F., Larish, J. & Strayer, D. L. (1995). *Training* for attentional control in dual task settings: a comparison of young and old adults. *Journal of Experimental Psychology: Applied*, *1*, 50–76.

LaBerge, D. & Brown, V. (1989). Theory of attentional operations in shape identification. *Psychological Review*, *96*, 101–124.

LaBerge, D. & Samuels, S. J. (1974). Towards a theory of automatic information processes in reading. *Cognitive Psychology*, *6*, 293–323.

Leavitt, J. (1979). Cognitive demands of skating and stick handling in ice hockey. *Canadian Journal of Applied Sport Sciences*, *4*, 46–55.

Logan, G. (1985). Skill and automaticity: relations, implications, and future directions. *Canadian Journal of Psychology*, *39*, 367–386.

Logan, G. (1988).Towards an instance theory of automatization. *Psychological Review*, *95*, 492–527.

Logan, G. D. (2004). Cumulative progress in formal theories of attention. *Annual Review of Psychology*, *55*, 207–234.

Logan, G. D. (2005). The time it takes to switch attention. *Psychonomic Bulletin & Review*, *12*, 646–653.

Logan.G. D. & Gordon, R. D. (2001). Executive control of visual attention in dual-task situations. *Psychological Review*, *108*, 393–434.

Logie, R., Baddeley, A., Mane, A. *et al.* (1989). Working memory in the acquisition of complex skills. *Acta Psychologica*, *71*, 53–87.

McCarley, J. S., Kramer, A. F., Wickens, C. D. *et al.* (2004). Visual skills in airport-security screening. *Psychological Science*, *15*, 302–306.

McKnight, A. J. & McKnight, A. S. (1993). The effect of cellular phone use upon driver attention. *Accident Analysis & Prevention*, *25*(3), 259–265.

Mackworth, N. H. (1948). The breakdown of vigilance during prolonged visual search. *Quarterly Journal of Experimental Psychology*, *1*, 5–61.

MacLeod, C. M. (1991). Half a century of research on the Stroop effect: an integrative review. *Psychological Bulletin*, *109*, 163–203.

McLeod, P., Driver, J., Dienes, Z. & Crisp, J. (1991). Filtering by movement in visual search. *Journal of Experimental Psychology: Human Perception and Performance*, *17*, 55–64.

Monk,.C. A., Boehm-David, D. A. & Trafton, J. G. (2002). The attentional costs of interruption task performance at various stages. In *Proceedings of the 46th Annual Meeting of the Human Factors and Ergonomics Society* (pp. 1824–1828). Santa Monica, CA: HFES.

Morray, N. (1959). Attention in dichotic listening: affective cues and the influence of instruction. *Quarterly Journal of Experimental Psychology, 11*, 56–60.
Navon, D. (1984). Resources: a theoretical soup stone. *Psychological Review, 91*, 216–334.
Navon, D. & Gopher, D. (1979). On the economy of the human processing system. *Psychological Review, 86*, 214–255.
Navon, D. & Miller, J. (1987). Role of outcome conflict in dual-task interference. *Journal of Experimental Psychology: Human Perception and Performance, 13*, 435–448.
Neisser, U. & Becklen, R. (1975). Selective looking: attending to visually specified events. *Cognitive Psychology, 7*, 480–494.
Nobre, A. C. (2004). Probing the flexibility of attentional orienting in the human brain. In M. I. Posner (ed.). *Cognitive Neruroscience of Attention* (pp. 157–179). New York: Guilford Press.
Norman, D. A. & Bobrow, D. G. (1975). On data-limited and resource-limited processes. *Cognitive Psychology, 7*, 44–64.
Norman, D. A. & Shallice, T. (1986). Attention to action: willed and automatic control of behavior. In R J. Davidson, G. E. Schwartz & D. Shapiro (eds.), *Consciousness and Self-Regulation: Advances in Research and Theory* (Vol. 4, pp. 1–18). New York: Plenum.
NTSB (1988). *Aircraft Accident Report: Northwest Airlines, Inc., McDonnell Dougless DC-9–82, N312RC, Detroit Metropolitan Wayne County Airport, Romulus, Michigan, August 16, 1987* (NTSB/AAR-88–05). Washington, DC: National Transportation Safety Board.
O'Connor, D. H., Fukui, M. M., Pinsk, M. A. & Kastner, S. (2002). Attention modulates responses in the human lateral geniculate nucleus. *Nature Neurosciences, 5*, 1203–1209.
O'Donnell, R. D. & Eggemeier, F. T. (1986). Workload assessment methodology. In K. Boff, L. Kaufman & J. Thomas (eds.), *Handbook of Perception and Performance* (Vol. 2). New York: John Wiley & Sons.
O'Shea, S., Morris, M. E. & Iansek, R. (2002). Dual task interference during gait in people with Parkinson disease: effects of motor versus cognitive secondary tasks. *Physical Therapy, 82*, 888–897.
Oksama, L. & Hyona, J. (2004). Is multiple object tracking carried out automatically by an early vision mechanism independent of higher-order cognition? An individual difference approach. *Visual Cognition, 11*, 631–671.
Parasurman, R. (1979). Memory load and event rate control sensitivity decrements in sustained attention. *Science, 205*, 925–927.
Parasurman, R. (1985). Sustained attention: a multifactorial approach. In M. I. Posner & O. S. M. Marin (eds.), *Attention and Performance XI* (pp. 493–511). Hillsdale, NJ: Lawrence Erlbaum Associates.
Parasurman, R., Warm, J. S. & Dember, W. N. (1987). Vigilance: taxonomy and utility. In L. S. Mark, J. S. Warm & R. L. Huston (eds.), *Ergonomics and Human Factors* (pp. 11–32). New York: Springer-Verlag.
Pashler, H. E. (1994). Dual-task interference in simple tasks: data and theory. *Psychological Bulletin, 16*, 220–244.
Pashler, H. E. (1999). *The Psychology of Attention*. Cambridge, MA: MIT Press.
Pashler, H., Johnston, J. C. & Ruthruff, E. (2001). Attention and performance. *Annual Review of Psychology, 52*, 629–651.
Peterson, M. S. & Juola, J.F. (2000). Evidence for distinct attentional bottlenecks in attention switching and attentional blink tasks. *Journal of General Psychology, 127*, 6–27.
Pope, A. T., Bogart, E. H. & Bartolome, D. (1995). Biocybernetic system evaluates indices of operator engagement. *Biological Psychology, 40*, 187–196.
Posner, M. I. (1980). Orientation of attention. *Quarterly Journal of Experimental Psychology, 32*, 3–25.
Posner, M. I. (2004). *Cognitive Neruroscience of Attention*. New York: Guilford Press.
Posner, M. I. & Cohen, Y. (1984). Components of visual orienting. In H. Bouma & D. Bonwhuis (eds.), *Attention and Performance X: Control of Language Processes* (pp. 551–556). Hillsdale, NJ: Lawrence Erlbaum Associates.
Posner, M. I., Petersen, S. E., Fox, P. T. & Raichle, M. E. (1988). Location of cognitive operations in the human brain. *Science, 240*, 1627–1631.

Posner, M. I. & Snyder, C. R. R. (1975). Attention and cognitive control: In R. Solso (ed.), *Information Processing and Cognition: The Loyola Symposium*. Pontomac, MD: Lawrence Erlbaum Associates.
Posner, M. I., Snyder, C. R. R. & Davidson, B. J. (1980). Attention and the detection of signals. *Journal of Experimental Psychology: General*, *109*, 160–174.
Posner, M. I., Walker, J., Friedrich, F. & Rafal, R. (1984), Effects of parietal injury on covert orienting of attention, *Journal of Neuroscience*, *4*, 1863–1874.
Prinzel, L. J., Freeman, F. G., Scerbo, M. W. & Mikulka, P. J. (2003). Effects of a psychophysiological system for adaptive automation on performance, workload, and the event-related potential P300 component. *Human Factors, 45*, 601–613.
Pylyshyn, Z. W. (2004). Some puzzling findings about multiple object tracking (MOT): I. Tracking without keeping track of object identities. *Visual Cognition*, *11*, 801–822.
Pylyshyn, Z. W. & Storm, R. W. (1988). Tracking multiple independent targets: evidence for parallel tracking mechanisms. *Spatial Vision*, *3*, 1–19.
Redelmeier, D. A. & Tibshirani, R. J. (1997). Association between cellular-telephone calls and motor vehicle collisions. *The New England Journal of Medicine*, *336*, 453–458.
Remington, R. W., Johnston, J. C., Ruthruff, E. *et al.* (2000). Visual search in complex displays: factors affecting conflict detection by air traffic controllers. *Human Factors*, *42*, 349–366.
Reynolds, J. H., Chelazzi, L. & Desimone, R. (1999). Competitive mechanisms subserve attention in macaque areas V2 and V4. *Journal of Neuroscience, 19*, 1736–1753.
Rogers, R. D. & Monsell, S. (1995). Costs of a predictable switch between simple cognitive tasks. *Journal of Experimental Psychology: General*, *124*, 207–231.
Ruthruff, E., Pashler, H. E. & Klassen, A. (2000). Processing bottlenecks in dual-task performance: structural limitations of voluntary postponement? *Psychonomic Buelletin and Review*, *8*, 73–80.
Sagarin, B. J., Britt, A. M., Heider, J. D. *et al.* (2005). Intrusive technology: bartering and stealing consumer attention. In W. R. Walker & D. J. Herrmann (eds.), *Cognitive Technology: Essays on the Transformation of Thoughts and Society* (pp. 69–88). Jefferson, NC: McFarland & Company.
Sagarin, G. J., Britt, M. A., Heider, J. D. *et al.* (2003). Bartering our attention: the distraction and persuasion effects of on-line advertisements. *Cognitive Technology*, *8*, 4–17.
Schneider, W. (1985). Training high-performance skills: fallacies and guidelines. *Human Factors*, *27*, 285–300.
Schneider, W. & Fisk, A. D. (1982). Concurrent automatic and controlled visual search: can processing occur without resource cost? *Journal of Experimental Psychology: Learning, Memory, and Cognition*, *8*, 261–278.
Schneider, W. & Shiffrin, R. M. (1977). Controlled and automatic human information processing: I. Detection, search, and attention. *Psychological Review*, *84*, 1–66.
Schweizer, K., Zimmermann, P. & Koch, W. (2000). Sustained attention, intelligence, and the critical role of perceptual processes. *Learning & Individual Differences*, *12*, 271–287.
Shallice, T. (1988). *From Neuropsychology to Mental Structure*. Cambridge: Cambridge University Press.
Shannon, C. E. & Weaver, W. (1949). *A Mathematical Model of Communication*. Urbana, IL: University of Illinois Press.
Shiffrin, R. M. & Schneider, W. (1977). Controlled and automatic human information processing: II. Perceptual learning, automatic attending, and a general theory. *Psychological Review*, *84*, 127–190.
Simons, D. J. & Chabris, C. F. (1999). Gorillas in our midst: sustained inattentional blindness for dynamic events. *Perception*, *28*, 1059–1074.
Sirevaag, E. J., Kramer, A. F., Wickens, C. D. *et al.* (1993). Assessment of pilot performance and mental workload in rotary wing aircraft. *Ergonomics*, *9*, 1121–1140.
Smith, M. D. & Chamberlin, C. J. (1992). Effect of adding cognitively demanding tasks on soccer skill performance. *Perceptual and Motor Skills*, *75*, 955–961.
Solomons, L. & Stein, G. (1896). Normal motor automatism. *Psychological Review*, *3*, 492–512.
Spelke, E. S., Hirst, W. C. & Neisser, U. (1976). Skills of divided attention. *Cognition*, *4*, 215–250.

Strayer, D. L., Drews, F. A. & Johnston, W. A. (2003). Cell phone induced failures of visual attention during simulated driving. *Journal of Experimental Psychology: Applied*, *9*, 23–52.

Strayer, D. L. & Johnston, W. A. (2001). Driven to distraction: dual-task studies of simulated driving and conversing on a cellular phone. *Psychological Science*, *12*, 462–466.

Stroop, J. R. (1935). Studies of interference in serial verbal reactions. *Journal of Experimental Psychology*, *18*, 643–662.

Temple, J. G., Warm, J. S., Dember, W. N. *et al.* (2000). The effects of signal salience and caffeine on performance, workload, and stress in an abbreviated vigilance task. *Human Factors*, *42*, 183–194.

Treisman, A. (1988). Features and objects: the fourteenth Bartlett memorial lecture. *Quarterly Journal of Experimental Psychology*, *40A*, 201–237.

Treisman, A. (1992). Perceiving and re-perceiving objects. *American Psychologist*, *47*, 862–875.

Treisman, A. (1996). The binding problem. *Current Opinion in Neurobiology*, *6*, 171–178.

Treisman, A. & Gelade, G. (1980). A feature-integration theory of attention. *Cognitive Psychology*, *12*, 97–136.

Treisman, A. & Schmidt, H. (1982). Illusory conjunctions in the perception of objects. *Cognitive Psychology*, *14*, 107–141.

Treisman, A. & Souther, J. (1985). Search asymmetry: a diagnostic for preattentive processing of separable features. *Journal of Experimental Psychology: Human Perception and Performance*, *114*, 285–310.

Treisman, A. M. (1960). Contextual cues in selective listening. *Quarterly Journal of Experimental Psychology*, *12*, 242–248.

Treisman, A. M. (1969). Strategies and models of selective attention. *Psychological Review*, *76*, 282–299.

Treisman, A. M. & Geffen, G. (1967). Selective attention: perception of response? *Quarterly Journal of Experimental Psychology*, *19*, 1–17.

Turner, M. L. & Engle, R. W. (1989). Is working memory capacity task dependent? *Journal of Memory & Language*, *28*, 127–154.

Vecera, S. & Farah, M. J. (1994). Does visual attention select objects or locations. *Journal of Experimental Psychology: General*, *123*, 146–160.

Wachtel, P. L. (1967). Conceptions of broad and narrow attention. *Psychological Bulletin*, *68*, 417–419.

Watson, J. M., Balota, D. A. & Sergent-Marshall, S. D. (2001). Semantic, phonological, and hybrid veridical and false memories in healthy older adults and individuals with dementia of the Alzheimer type. *Neuropsychology*, *2*, 254–267.

Watson, J. M., Bunting, M. F., Poole, B. J. & Conway, A. R. A. (2005). Individual differences in susceptibility to false memory in the Deese/Roediger-McDermott paradigm. *Journal of Experimental Psychology: Learning, Memory, and Cognition*, *31*, 76–85.

Watson, J. M., McDermott, K. B. & Balota, D. A. (2004). Attempting to avoid false memories in the Deese/Roediger-McDermott paradigm: assessing the combined influence of practice and warnings in young and old adults. *Memory and Cognition*, *32*, 135–141.

Weichselgartner, E. & Sperling, G. A. (1987). Dynamics of automatic and controlled visual attention. *Science*, *238*, 778–780.

Weinger, M. B., Reddy, S. B. & Slagle, J. M. (2004). Multiple measures of anesthesia workload during teaching and nonteaching cases. *Anesthesiology and Analgesia*, *98*, 1419–1425.

Weltman, G., Smith, J. E. & Egstrom, G. H. (1971). Perceptual narrowing during simulated pressure-chamber exposure. *Human Factors*, *13*, 99–107.

Wickens, C. D. (1980). The structure of attentional resources. In R. Nickerson (ed.), *Attention and Performance VIII* (pp. 239–257). Hillsdale, NJ: Lawrence Erlbaum Associates.

Wickens, C. D. (1984). Processing resources in attention. In R. Parasuraman & R. Davies (eds.), *Varieties of Attention* (pp. 63–101). New York: Academic Press.

Wightman, D. C. & Lintern, G. (1985). Part-task training for tracking and manual control. *Human Factors*, *27*, 267–283.

Wilson, G. F. & Russell, C. A. (2003). Real-time assessment of mental workload using psychophysiological measures and artificial neural networks. *Human Factors*, *45*, 635–643.

Wolfe, J. M. (1994) Guided Search 2.0: a revised model of visual search. *Psychonomic Bulletin & Review*, *1*, 202–238.
Yantis, S. (1993). Stimulus-driven attentional capture. *Current Directions in Psychological Science*, *2*, 156–161.
Yantis, S. & Jonides, J. (1990). Abrupt visual onsets and selective attention: voluntary versus automatic allocation. *Journal of Experimental Psychology: Human Perception and Performance*, *16*, 121–134.
Yeh, W. & Wickens, C. D. (2001). Attentional filtering in the design of electronic map displays: a comparison of color coding, intensity coding, and decluttering techniques. *Human Factors*, *43*, 543–562.
Yerkes, R. M. & Dodson, J. D. (1908). The relation of strength of stimulus to rapidity of habit formation. *Journal of Comparative Neurological Psychology*, *18*, 459–482.
Yuditsky, T., Sollenberger, R. L., Della Rocco, P. S. *et al.* (2002). *Application of Color to Reduce Complexity in Air Traffic Control*. DOT/FAA/CT-TN03/01.

CHAPTER 3

Working Memory

Aysecan Boduroglu
Bogazici University, Turkey
Meredith Minear
Washington University, USA
and
Priti Shah
University of Michigan, USA

WORKING MEMORY APPLIED

Working memory is the ability to actively maintain task-relevant information in the service of a cognitive task (Baddeley & Hitch 1974; Shah & Miyake 1999). Virtually every complex cognitive task requires working memory. In a prototypical example, performing a mental arithmetic task such as multiplying 64 × 27 requires keeping track of intermediate results (such as 4 × 7 = 28) while performing additional calculations.

Given working memory's central role in cognition, understanding its characteristics, functions, and limitations are important for many areas of applied psychology. Indeed, the literature on working memory and its applications is vast: virtually any keyword consisting of a cognitive skill or task coupled with working memory, such as "air traffic control and working memory," or "piano and working memory," yields a result in databases of psychology literature. Thus our review is necessarily highly selective. We focus on domains in which there has been recent interest and data. Our goal is to highlight major findings and their implications for applied fields. In order to place the applied research in context, we first provide a brief introduction to working memory.

HISTORICAL AND CURRENT CONCEPTIONS OF WORKING MEMORY

The notion of working memory was first proposed by Baddeley and Hitch (1974) as an elaboration of the concept of short-term memory (Atkinson & Shiffrin 1968). The Baddeley and Hitch model of working memory (1974) is a tripartite system with a central

Handbook of Applied Cognition: Second Edition. Edited by Francis T. Durso.

executive, and two content-based slave systems for temporary storage: the phonological loop and the visuospatial sketchpad. While the phonological loop is responsible for maintaining verbal information, the visuospatial sketchpad is responsible for maintaining visuospatial information. Each slave system has a limited capacity store that holds only a few items. The contents of these stores are prone to rapid decay unless they are continuously rehearsed (Baddeley 1986). The central executive is the supervisory system that oversees and regulates the activities of these two slave systems, and shares certain features with the supervisory attentional system (SAS) of Norman and Shallice (1986). So-called "executive" processes thought to reflect the functioning of the central executive include various forms of attentional control, such as focusing, switching, and dividing attention, as well as the ability to inhibit unwanted thoughts or actions and to stay focused on a particular goal (Duncan 1995; Miyake *et al.* 2000; Baddeley 2002).

Although Baddeley's is not the only theoretical model of working memory, there are several characteristics of working memory that are standard conclusions of this and other models. A review of several theoretical approaches to working memory can be found in Miyake and Shah (1999a). In this chapter, we focus on recent findings regarding working memory that have important implications.

CHARACTERISTICS OF WORKING MEMORY

In this section, we describe characteristics of working memory that have implications for applied topics. In particular, we first present evidence supporting domain-specific aspects of working memory. Next, we focus on visual and spatial working memory because of recent progress made on understanding these systems. In the third subsection, we summarize recent findings in executive functions research. Finally, we discuss working memory limitations. Following this selective review, we discuss applications.

Domain-Specific Stores

One feature of the Baddeley model is the separation of systems for the active maintenance of verbal and visuospatial information. The verbal/visuospatial distinction has been validated by converging evidence from behavioral, neuropsychological, and neuroimaging studies. Despite evidence of domain-specificity of working memory at a peripheral level, recent research suggests that the central executive component of working memory is likely to be largely domain-general (see, for example, Kane *et al.* 2004). Because this "central" component of working memory is relevant for many complex cognitive tasks, we discuss its measurement and role in complex cognition in more detail later.

One line of evidence for domain-specific stores involves studies demonstrating selective interference of visuospatial and verbal activities on visuospatial and verbal working memory tasks, respectively (Brooks 1968; Baddeley *et al.* 1975). Additional evidence for this separation comes from research demonstrating that verbal and spatial ability measures correlate selectively with performance on verbal and spatial working memory tasks (Shah & Miyake 1996). Finally, neuropsychological evidence from patients with selective damage to the verbal and visuospatial systems, and neuroimaging data, both provide evidence that verbal and visuospatial information-processing is mediated by different neural mechanisms; verbal working memory tasks activate left frontal and spatial memory tasks activate right parietal regions (Gathercole 1994; Smith & Jonides 1997).

In addition to the verbal/visuospatial dissociation, evidence has accumulated indicating a further dissociation between processing of visual object and spatial and movement-related information (Logie 1995). This evidence includes data from interference tasks (for a review, see Pickering 2001), dissociations in patient populations (Gathercole 1994), and findings indicating that different neural streams, the ventral and dorsal, carry what and where information, respectively (Ungerleider & Mishkin 1982). Furthermore, separate projections from these streams to distinct prefrontal sites for short-term maintenance of visual and spatial information have been reported (Smith & Jonides 1999). The applied cognitive literature incorporates these distinctions. Most prominently, the Wickens' Multiple Resources Theory explicitly distinguishes between resources for auditory and visual modalities and verbal and spatial domains (Wickens & Liu 1988).

Verbal, Visual, and Spatial Working Memory

Even though the dissociation between the verbal, visual, and spatial systems was established early on, most previous work selectively focused on verbal working memory. Since the 1960s research has addressed questions on the nature of representations and rehearsal mechanisms in verbal working memory, resulting in a more detailed understanding of the verbal working memory system (for a review, see Baddeley 2000). In contrast to the vast interest in verbal working memory, most research on visuospatial working memory has been at preliminary stages. This asymmetry in the bulk of past research led Baddeley (2000) to conclude that the visual and the spatial components of the tripartite working memory model are in need of further elaboration. Indeed, in recent years important strides have been made in this direction.

A major question of recent interest has been how objects are represented in visual working memory. Specifically, research has been addressing whether or not visual features of objects are represented in an integrated fashion or stored independently. Evidence has indicated that only a few objects can be maintained in visual working memory, each one represented as an object file, a bound representation of its visual features (Luck & Vogel 1997; Wheeler & Treisman 2002; Xu 2002). When people are asked to recall simple geometric forms, capacity estimates are around three or four objects (Luck & Vogel 1997). However, others have shown that the amount of information that can be maintained in visual working memory is influenced by factors such as perceptual complexity and novelty of visual objects (Alvarez & Cavanagh 2004; Eng *et al.* 2005). Our own research has demonstrated limitations of three or four locations in spatial working memory, similar to those in visual working memory (Boduroglu & Shah 2004). Furthermore, as in verbal and visual working memory, stimulus properties such as complexity influence the accuracy with which spatial locations are recalled (Kemps 1999; Boduroglu & Shah 2005; Parmentier *et al.* 2005).

Findings from verbal, visual, and spatial working memory studies regarding capacity limitations highlight a common characteristic of working memory. First, only a small number of items can be accurately maintained in working memory. Second, factors such as complexity impact on how much information can be kept active in working memory. These findings indicate that working memory limitations cannot be easily accounted for by models assuming that capacity is determined by a fixed number of slots. Rather, it is likely that resources are flexibly allocated based on task demands. The similarities and limitations across different domains may reflect some underlying constraint in the working memory system (for a detailed discussion, see Cowan 2001).

Even though studies have indicated that the capacity of visual and spatial working memory is limited, a clear understanding of the tradeoff between resolution of representations and capacity limitations will provide us with an even better understanding of the theoretical limitations of the working memory system. For instance, Luck and Zhang (2004) investigated how the discriminability of visual features influences the amount of information that can be maintained in visual working memory. Similarly, Boduroglu and Shah (2005) demonstrated that people strategically adapt to the requirement of representing more locations by reducing the resolution with which they represent target locations. Further research is necessary to delineate the tradeoff between the resolution of representations and capacity limitations.

Executive Functions

A second major area of recent progress has been in understanding the central executive. As recently as a decade ago, Monsell (1996) and Baddeley (1996) argued that there was virtually no understanding of executive control. Recent years have produced a great deal of behavioral (e.g., Miyake *et al.* 2000; Kane *et al.* 2001), neuroscientific (e.g., D'Esposito *et al.* 1995; Cohen *et al.* 1997; Fuster 1999; Diwadkar *et al.* 2000), and computational modeling (e.g., Meyer & Kieras 1997; O'Reilly *et al.* 1999) approaches to executive functions. This research suggests that there is a small number of "core" executive functions or mechanisms, with somewhat different neuroanatomical bases (Jonides 2001), which collectively regulate the dynamics of human cognition. Some of the most frequently postulated executive control skills include the ability to: maintain and update the contents of working memory (*maintenance and updating*); inhibit irrelevant information or prepotent responses (*inhibition*); shift attention to a new piece of information or a new task (*task-shifting*); keep track of a set of goals and subgoals (*goal management*); coordinate the performance of multiple tasks simultaneously (*multi-tasking*); plan (*planning*) (e.g., Baddeley 1986; Duncan *et al.* 1996; Miyake *et al.* 2000).

Several lines of evidence support the idea that there may be a small number of distinct executive functions. First, damage to the frontal areas of the brain was reported to result in selective impairments in one set of executive tasks but not others (Shallice 1988). Second, Miyake and his colleagues (2000) conducted a latent-variable analysis based on data from a large number of participants who performed a number of maintenance and updating, task-shifting, and inhibition tasks. They found that a three-component model of executive control provided a better fit to the data than a unitary model. This suggests that these three processes are separable components of executive control. Recent neuroimaging data provide converging evidence to support the claim that these three executive control skills are independent; there are distinct neural substrates for these different executive control skills within the prefrontal cortex (Jonides 2001; Kane & Engle 2002). Finally, computational approaches to executive control incorporate similar distinctions (e.g., Meyer & Kieras 1997).

Executive functions have been linked to the notion of general or fluid intelligence (e.g., Duncan 1995; Duncan *et al.* 1996; Engle *et al.* 1999; Duncan *et al.* 2000). In addition, many cognitive disorders, such as attention-deficit hyperactivity disorder (ADHD) (Barkley 1997) and Alzheimer's disease (Brugger *et al.* 1996) are thought to involve deficits in executive control skills. Furthermore, many researchers argue that age-related changes in cognitive function are caused by the progressive decline of executive control skills (Crawford *et al.* 2000).

Executive functions have also been linked very closely to performance on most complex cognitive tasks; this association between executive functions, intelligence, and complex cognition has led to significant work in understanding the limitations and individual differences in the "executive" or controlled attention aspects of working memory.

Working Memory Limitations and Individual Differences

An analysis of a large body of applied work in the area of working memory suggest that the main feature of working memory that is relevant to applications is that its capacity is highly limited. The best-known historical account of working memory limitations is George Miller's (1956) proposal of capacity limits, in which he argued that people are able to keep track of a "magic number 7 ± 2" chunks of information. More recently, Cowan has argued that working memory capacity is somewhat more limited and that specifically people can typically attend to approximately four items at the same time (Cowan 2001).

Working memory is limited in all individuals. However, individuals and groups differ in their working memory capacity. Despite uniform agreement that working memory is highly limited, less agreement exists about the underlying mechanisms responsible for working memory limitations and individual differences in working memory capacity. In addition, there is disagreement as to why individual differences in working memory capacity are responsible for individual differences in other cognitive tasks. These two issues are separable. Individuals may differ in their performance on any particular working memory task for a variety of reasons, but not all of these factors may be responsible for the relationship between working memory and higher-order cognition. In this section, we focus on factors that affect working memory capacity regardless of their involvement in higher-order cognitive tasks.

Historically, some of the major competing theories have been that there are limits in the amount of activation resources available to the cognitive system (e.g., Just & Carpenter 1992; Anderson *et al.* 1996; Daily *et al.* 2001), limits in the efficiency of inhibition mechanisms (Hasher & Zacks 1988), or limits in speed of processing (Salthouse 1992). More recently, Cowan (2005) has proposed that working memory limitations arise via limits in the amount of information that can be in the focus of attention; while Engle and his colleagues have proposed that working memory limitations arise because of limitations in attentional control. Specifically, they argue that there is a fundamental limitation in the ability to retrieve information in the face of interference when information is *no longer* in the focus of attention (Heitz *et al.* 2005; Unsworth & Engle 2006a, 2006b).

Both the Cowan theory and the Engle theory propose a relationship between working memory and attentional limitations. Although the theoretical relationship between working memory and attention is not clear, there is an empirical association between working memory task performance and performance on attentional tasks, ranging from selective attention (Bleckley *et al.* 2003) to dichotic listening (Conway *et al.* 2001).

Alternatives to capacity-based explanations of working memory limitations are those explanations that emphasize domain-specific knowledge and skills (Ericsson & Kintsch 1995). According to Ericsson and Kintsch's (1995) long-term working memory theory the *effective* capacity of working memory is dependent on an individual's prior knowledge and thus on how information is encoded and chunked in working memory. One implication is that working memory limitations are most severe when to-be-maintained information is novel. Thus, novices may be more overloaded by working memory demands than experts. Indeed, Sohn and Doane (2003) found exactly that: in a meaningful airline cockpit scene-awareness task, high-knowledge individuals with high long-term working memory capacity relied on their long-term working memory, but low-knowledge individuals relied more heavily on their short-term working memory.

In summary, there is a number of possible mechanisms underlying working memory limitations, and there is some consensus that there are multiple limitations in working memory capacity (Miyake & Shah 1999b).

Measuring Individual Differences

As discussed above, there are individual differences in working memory capacity. Furthermore, there are special populations with impairments in working memory. Specifically, older adults and individuals with schizophrenia and Alzheimer's disease have diminished working memory capacity (Brugger *et al.* 1996; Park *et al.* 2002; Barch 2005). Working memory deficits have also been reported in Down's syndrome (Hulme & Mackenzie 1992), children with learning disabilities (Swanson & Sachse-Lee 2001), and in children who have undergone chemotherapy (Schatz *et al.* 2000).

Individual differences in working memory are most commonly assessed by measures that evaluate the ability to simultaneously store and process information. An example of a working memory measure is the reading span in which an individual reads a series of sentences and is asked to recall the sentence final words (Daneman & Carpenter 1980). A similar measure is the operation span, which involves solving equations and remembering words (Turner & Engle 1989; Unsworth *et al.* 2005). There are also spatial variants of such tasks such as one that involves judging whether letters are normal or mirror-imaged and remembering the letters' orientations (Shah & Miyake 1996). These processing and storage tasks are better predictors of higher-order cognition than earlier measures of short-term memory, such as digit span.

An important caveat in measuring working memory capacity is that it is not clear what factors are responsible for the covariation between working memory and cognitive tasks (see Kane *et al.* 2006). One recent approach has been to use different measures of performance on working memory tasks (e.g., intrusions) and identify which of these measures predict complex task performance. Using this type of approach, Unsworth and Engle (2006a, 2006b) argued that the component of tasks that predicts fluid intelligence is the ability to retrieve information from memory when it is no longer active. However, a number of competing possibilities still exist. Although this question is not completely resolved, for practical purposes span tasks are reasonably reliable indicators of working memory.

It should also be noted that performance on any individual task necessarily involves both domain-specific and domain-general factors. For prediction of general cognitive ability (i.e., fluid intelligence), it may be more useful for applied researchers to use multiple measures and statistically separate variance associated with task-specific factors and domain-general working memory skills (Conway *et al.* 2005). Similarly, one might be better able to predict performance on domain-specific tasks, such as reading comprehension or spatial ability, by using domain-specific measures (Shah & Miyake 1996).

In addition to measuring "capacity," there has been a substantial recent interest in the measurement of the executive control aspects of working memory (Miyake *et al.* 2000). One "core" executive function that has attracted a great deal of interest in recent years is task-switching (Rogers & Monsell 1995). The task-switching paradigm involves asking individuals to perform two simple tasks and measuring the time to perform an individual task repeatedly compared to switching between the tasks. The ability to inhibit irrelevant information or prepotent responses is also an executive control skill that is frequently measured. Recent studies have suggested that there may be multiple inhibitory functions measured by different tasks. These include the ability to ignore distracting information (e.g., the Flanker task, which requires speeded perceptual identification in the context of distracting stimuli) and the ability to inhibit a prepotent response (e.g., the Stroop task; Nigg 2000; Friedman & Miyake 2004). Finally, the ability to update information in working memory is another core executive function. The n-back task, which involves actively updating working memory representations and judging whether individual items are the same as or different from those presented n items previously, is frequently used as a measure of updating (Jonides & Smith 1997).

APPLICATIONS OF WORKING MEMORY RESEARCH

The following sections focus on several bodies of applied research that are grounded in working memory theory. The ultimate goal in virtually all applied working memory research is to overcome limitations in working memory. In the first section, we consider how mental workload is measured. In the second, we discuss individual differences in working memory capacity. In the third, we review new research on attempts to overcome working memory limitations via remediation and training. In the fourth, we discuss how working memory demands in various types of displays can be reduced. In the next three sections, we consider somewhat more specific limitations and applications. Specifically, the fifth section deals with the issue of change blindness, a consequence of working memory limitations that has implications for numerous design and HCI contexts. The sixth section considers the special case of older adults who may have severe working memory limitations and have special life demands, such as following medical instructions that tax their working memory. The final section discusses performing under pressure or anxiety.

We note that researchers have used at least three strategies to identify the role of working memory in applied tasks. The most direct approach compares task performance with and without working memory load; if a task is working memory demanding, then performance will be impaired under load. A second strategy is to demonstrate that individual variation in working memory capacity predicts performance on a specific task. The third strategy is a task-analytic approach in which researchers make an assumption that a task that has high comprehension and information-processing demands requires working memory. Whenever possible we refer to empirical evidence regarding working memory involvement in tasks. When working memory involvement is assumed by researchers, we provide a task-analytic explanation.

Mental Workload

It has been argued that an overload of working memory is the main culprit for performance errors (e.g., Card *et al.* 1983). Determining task structure and demands and eliminating extraneous task variables has been proposed as one effective way to improve overall task performance (Moran 1981). Task demands, or "mental workload" as it has become known in the human–computer interaction field, is the combination of all demands placed on an operator engaging with an external system. In order to optimize performance, mental workload must be determined. This involves assessing the demands placed by the equipment as well as the resources available from the operator. Measures of mental workload enable comparison of different systems, identification of the most optimal one, and help determine whether operators need additional training with the chosen system. Given the breadth of this field, here we chose to outline major approaches to the measurement of mental workload and focus on some of the recent developments, and refer the interested reader to O'Donnell and Eggemeier (1986) for a more detailed review of the subject matter.

Mental workload assessment techniques can be categorized into four major groups: primary task measures, secondary task measures, psychophysiological and neurophysiological measures, and subjective measures (O'Donnell & Eggemeier 1986). In general, these different indices are highly correlated, but under certain circumstances dissociations between different indices were observed (e.g., Yeh & Wickens 1988). While primary task measures focus on performance on the main task, secondary task measures measure performance on a secondary task in a dual-task paradigm. Secondary task measures are ideal for differentiating two tasks with similar demands. Dual-task methodologies also help determine the available residual resources an operator can utilize in the event of an emergency. Also, identical secondary tasks can be coupled with diverse primary tasks (with different dependent variables, like reaction time and accuracy that cannot be easily compared) to yield an easy-to-compare workload measure. However, secondary task measures are problematic in that they may underestimate workload if the secondary task taps into a different resource than the primary task and the dual-task technique employed may prove to be intrusive, disrupting the primary task performance.

Psychophysiological, neurophysiological, and subjective measures of mental workload are advantageous over the secondary task technique because they are not obtrusive. In addition, psychophysiological and neurophysiological measures provide a continuous assessment of mental workload. There are three typical psychophysiological measures used to determine workload: pupilometry (Kahneman & Beatty 1966), heart-rate variability (Mulder & Mulder 1981), and visual scanning (Bellenkes *et al.* 1997). Recently, it has been demonstrated that different psychophysiological measures provide unique diagnostic information about the mental workload of particular sub-tasks in aviation (Hankins & Wilson 1998). Therefore, Hankins and Wilson (1998) argue that using multiple psychophysiological measures concurrently may provide a more comprehensive account of the overall task demands placed on an operator.

More recently, researchers have started to rely on neurophysiological indices of mental workload (for a review, see Just *et al.* 2003). Neurophysiological indices utilize relatively newer technologies, such as EEG, ERP, PET, and fMRI. We discuss each of these in greater detail. One neurophysiological index that has been correlated with mental effort involves monitoring spectral components of brainwaves (i.e., EEGs) as individuals engage in complex tasks (e.g., Gevins *et al.* 1998). Specifically, Gevins and colleagues (1998) demonstrated that increased mental workload correlates with increases in frontal theta and decreases in alpha activity. It has been argued that measuring EEG activity as oppose to ERP activity is more suitable for determining task demands because EEGs do not require time-locking the signal to specific events as in ERPs. As a result, EEGs provide a temporally continuous measure of mental workload. However, others demonstrated that ERP components (e.g., P300 and slow wave) may be utilized to determine mental workload in real time, and as participants perform complex tasks (Humphrey & Kramer 1994). These findings extend previous simple laboratory and simulator studies in which the P300 component and the slow wave were shown to be modulated by the allocation of resources between the perceptual and cognitive demands placed on the participant under dual-task paradigms (for a review, see Humphrey & Kramer 1994).

Measures of functional brain activity, either fMRI or PET, are also viable candidates in determining mental workload. While fMRI and PET measure different aspects of functional brain activity, fMRI measuring oxygenated blood level and PET measuring glucose metabolism rate (GMR), as both have been reported to correlate with cognitive load. For instance, in a sentence comprehension task, Just and colleagues (1996) reported an increase in fMRI activity in language regions (Broca's, Wernicke's and their right homologues) with increased sentence complexity. In a related vein, in a training study, Haier *et al.* (1992) demonstrated that after four to eight weeks' practice with the game "Tetris," leading to game-playing being less cognitively demanding, GMR was found to be reduced. While this may reflect a cognitive strategy shift due to learning, it might also reflect a reduction in engagement of non-task-relevant cortical regions. Thus, these studies illustrate how measures of PET and fMRI can measure the cognitive demands of tasks.

The final approach to measuring mental workload involves assessing subjective perceptions of mental workload (Moray 1982). When subjective mental workload is measured researchers ask the operator to provide ratings on either a single scale, or on several scales capturing the multidimensional nature of mental workload. The two commonly used multidimensional techniques are the NASA Task Load Index (TLX) (Hart & Staveland 1988) and the subjective workload assessment (SWAT) technique (Reid & Nygren 1988). Even though these two measures were shown to correlate highly, TLD has been favored over SWAT because the former incorporates ratings from seven as opposed to three scales, providing a more reliable measure of subjective mental workload (Hill *et al.* 1992). Recently, Colle and Reid (1998) demonstrated how contextual factors (e.g., varying task difficulty) can influence perceived workload and bias judgments, and outlined ways to standardize context to ensure subjective mental workload ratings are unbiased.

Working Memory in Complex Cognition

Much research on working memory focuses on the relationship between individual differences in working memory and performance on various complex cognitive tasks. At a theoretical level, the goal of this research has been to identify the role of working memory in cognitive activities. At the same time, the identification of tasks that are particularly working memory demanding can have implications for education, training, and personnel selection. In this section we summarize empirical findings regarding the nature of working memory involvement in cognitive tasks.

In educational settings, evaluating working memory skills may help individuals identify students who may have trouble in school later. These students may be provided with extra, early intervention (for a review of working memory and education, see Pickering 2006). In the context of school, individual differences in working memory measures such as reading span have been shown to predict performance on a wide variety of tasks, including vocabulary acquisition (Gathercole & Baddeley 1993), language comprehension (Daneman & Merikle 1996), mathematics (Bull *et al.* 1999), reasoning (Kyllonen & Christal 1990), and following directions (Engle *et al.* 1991).

Working memory, and in particular the executive control aspects of working memory, have also been implicated in a variety of important work-related tasks such as air traffic control (Ackerman 1990; Reder & Schunn 1999) and aircraft and helicopter flight (Gopher *et al.* 1989; Gopher 1993). One military task on which there has been a great deal of research, funded by the Defense Advance Research Projects Agency (DARPA), is the "Space Fortress" task (Mané & Donchin 1989 introduce a special issue of *Acta Psychologica* on this game). This task requires people to control a spaceship, fire missiles, and judge whether mines are "friends' or "foes," and so on. Performance on this task is correlated with executive functions (e.g., Gopher 1993; Day *et al.* 1997). Given the role of working memory and executive functions on such tasks, limitations in working memory and executive control may have detrimental effects. Indeed, it has been suggested that some serious disasters, such as those involved at Three Mile Island and the naval cruiser *Vincennes* might have occurred because the human operators' capacity for control and regulation of working memory had been overtaxed. Such disasters might have been avoided either by improvement in the design of systems to reduce the load on operators' working memory, or by improvements in the training or selection of personnel to handle such loads (Meyer & Kieras 1999). (In a later section, we discuss factors that influence working memory load.)

Researchers have speculated that working memory plays an important role in all complex cognitive activities because individual differences in working memory and executive functions underlie differences in intelligence. Much new empirical evidence supports this contention (Duncan *et al.* 1996; Kane & Engle 2002). In one influential study conducted by Duncan *et al.* (1996), participants performed a *goal-neglect* task to test this hypothesis. In the goal-neglect task, participants viewed pairs of symbols (numbers and/or letters) appearing two at a time on a computer screen. They had to read the letters that appeared on one side, while ignoring numbers on the other side. They occasionally received a signal that either required them to continue attending to the same side or to switch sides. Therefore, throughout the entire task, participants had to maintain information about the meaning of the symbols. They also frequently had to shift their attention between sides. Thus, this task required maintenance and updating, task-shifting, and inhibition. They found a high correlation (up to 0.65) between a test of general intelligence, the Cattell Culture Fair test (Cattell 1973), and performance on the goal-neglect task. This correlation is much higher than typical correlations reported between general intelligence and individual executive control skills. Furthermore, participants who scored lower than one standard deviation below the mean on the intelligence task failed consistently on the goal-neglect task. Thus, Duncan *et al.* (1996) concluded that general intelligence reflects individual differences in the overall efficacy of executive control.

This conclusion is further bolstered by recent neuroimaging data which suggest that performance on IQ tests such as the Raven's Progressive Matrices test (Raven *et al.* 1977) and the Cattell Culture Fair test (Cattell 1973) involve the same prefrontal regions identified as being important for executive control work (D'Esposito *et al.* 1995; Duncan *et al.* 2000; Kane & Engle 2002). Finally, recent correlational studies using latent variable analyses techniques also pinpoint executive control skills as the decisive factor on tests of general intelligence (Engle *et al.* 1999).

Another current approach to understanding the role of working memory and executive functions in complex cognition is the examination of which aspects of working memory function are related to performance on different cognitive tasks. An example is a study by McLean and Hitch (1999), who go beyond previous studies that demonstrate a relationship between working memory and arithmetic ability. Instead, they demonstrate that children with poor arithmetic abilities had impairments in spatial working memory and executive functions but not in verbal working memory. In another study, Miyake and colleagues (2001) demonstrated that performance on different spatial ability tasks (perceptual speed, speeded rotation, and spatial visualization) could be predicted by different aspects of working memory. Finally, in the case of fluid intelligence, Friedman *et al.* (2006) demonstrated that the updating aspects of executive function, and not the inhibition or task-switching aspects, were most highly correlated with general intelligence.

Remediation of Working Memory

Given the importance of working memory, the question naturally arises: Can working memory capacity or performance be improved? If it can, then a second and crucial question must be addressed: Will such improvements translate into better performance on higher-level cognitive tasks such as reading comprehension or navigating an aircraft?

A logical starting point lies in an examination of how exceptional memory performance can be achieved. Work by Ericsson and colleagues have looked at how experts in various fields frequently seem to circumvent capacity-based working memory limitations (Ericsson & Kintsch 1995). Ericsson and Polson (1988), for example, reported that expert waiters could carry on an irrelevant conversation while simultaneously memorizing orders for 16 diners. These waiters did not have greater working memory capacities than non-waiters, but rather with experience, they acquired knowledge and strategies that allowed them to expand the amount of information they could process and retain on-line. This is an illustration of the concept of long-term working memory in which rapid storage and retrieval of information in long-term memory can supplement the basic capacity of working memory (Ericsson & Kintsch 1995). Ericsson *et al.* (1980) dramatically demonstrated that extensive training within a particular domain can lead to remarkable improvements in memory performance. In this study, a college student practiced memorizing strings of digits for over 200 hours spread over almost two years. By the end of this period, the student had increased his digit span from the magic number 7 to a span of 80 digits. However, this improvement was specific to digits; with letters his performance dropped to normal levels. The same is true for experts. When working memory performance is measured outside their field of expertise, their scores fall back into the normal range (Chase & Simon 1973). However, it is possible that some portion of the individual differences seen in working memory performance may be due in part to differences in strategy utilization. For example, individuals with Down's syndrome have been reported as failing to spontaneously rehearse verbal information and when taught to use rehearsal, their performance can improve (Laws *et al.* 1996).

Two recent studies have examined the extent to which training in the use of particular strategies can affect working memory performance. McNamara and Scott (2001) instructed a group of college students to use an effective short-term memory strategy called chaining in which to-be-remembered words are linked by creating a story. Participants' performance on a reading span-like task was improved compared to an uninstructed group. However, the use of the chaining strategy did not lead to a differential improvement in a measure of comprehension for the material presented in the working memory task.

The second paper to examine the effects of strategy training on working memory compared the effects of three strategies: rehearsal, imagery, and a semantic strategy similar to chaining, on operation span (Turley-Ames & Whitfield 2003). They also looked at whether high or low spans would benefit more from any one strategy and the extent to which controlling for individual differences in strategy use would affect the correlation between working memory span and a measure of reading ability. The training of a rehearsal strategy led to a significant improvement in working memory performance, especially for low-span participants. This may have been due in part to the fact that low spans were less likely than high spans to report using any strategy prior to training. Neither the imagery nor the semantic strategy appeared to yield a consistent benefit for either group. Finally, controlling for individual differences in strategy use by rehearsal strategy training led to an increased correlation between operation span and reading ability. The authors reasoned that if strategy use contributed to the relationship between working memory and complex cognition, then controlling for strategy should lead to a decrease in the correlation between working memory and reading ability rather than an increase. These results support theories that describe individual differences in working memory as arising primarily from underlying capacity differences, with high-capacity individuals performing better than low, even when strategy use is equated. Therefore, a second basic approach to improving performance on working memory tasks is to attempt to increase working memory capacity per se.

A number of researchers have employed a variety of different training programs for working memory based on the concept of process-specific training (Sohlberg & Mateer 1987). Originally developed for the rehabilitation of cognitive deficits in brain-injured adults, in process-specific training, the repeated practice of a particular cognitive process is hypothesized to lead to improved performance. Attention process training (APT) is a process-specific approach in which individuals receive repeated practice on focused, selective, sustained, alternating, and divided attention tasks. A number of studies have reported improvements in attention or executive function in both brain-injured (Sohlberg & Mateer 1987; Park *et al.* 1999; Sohlberg *et al.* 2000) and schizophrenic adults (Lopez-Luengo & Vazquez 2003). Other training programs, consisting of repeated practice on executive tasks such as random number generation, dual-task performance, and n-back (Cicerone 2002) or storage and retrieval processes in verbal working memory (Vallat *et al.* 2005), have shown some limited promise in adult patients. However, many of these studies have been criticized for small sample size and limited generality of improvements (Park & Ingles 2001).

More promising work can be found in Klingberg *et al.* (2002), who incorporated basic principles from process-specific training into a working memory training program for children with ADHD. In their study, children were randomly assigned to either an experimental or a control group. Both groups were measured on three tasks commonly used to index working memory and executive function, a visuospatial working memory task, the Raven's Progressive Matrices, and the Stroop task. The children were then trained on the same visuospatial working memory task they were initially measured on and three new tasks: backward digit span, letter span, and a go/no-go reaction time task. Training occurred 20 minutes a day, 4–6 days a week for 5 weeks and the difficulty of the tasks was constantly adjusted based on performance. Control group children received 10 minutes a day of training and difficulty was not increased. At the end of training, both groups were measured on the visuospatial working memory task, Raven's Progressive Matrices, and the Stroop. There were significant differences between the experimental and the control groups, with the experimental group showing significantly greater improvements than the control group on all three tasks. These results were replicated in a second experiment using young non-ADHD adults and, in a more recent follow-up, using a larger sample of ADHD children (Klingberg *et al.* 2005). The authors concluded that these findings constitute evidence that working memory performance can be improved with training and that improvements can generalize to untrained working memory tasks. A neuroimaging study of brain changes elicited after a similar course of working memory training in normal young adults found increased activation in prefrontal and parietal areas associated with working memory. Although preliminary, these results may constitute evidence of plasticity in the neural systems that underlie working memory and possible loci of training effects (Olesen *et al.* 2003). Similar remediation programs are being attempted in children with traumatic brain injury (Van't Hooft *et al.* 2005) and young survivors of chemotherapy and cranial radiation therapy who frequently experience working memory and executive deficits (Butler & Copeland 2002).

The possibility of increases in capacity with process-specific training may not be limited to populations with impaired working memory. Verhaeghen *et al.* (2004) found that with extensive practice on the n-back task, college students could expand their focus of attention from one item to four. Rueda and colleagues (2205) reported that groups of normal four- and six-year-old children demonstrated significant improvements in executive attention after training compared to a control group.

While the above reports of improved working memory performance after process-specific training programs are encouraging, the extent to which there can be measurable transfer to real-world performance is unclear. Butler and Copeland (2002) reported significant improvements on measures of working memory (digit span and sentence memory) and sustained attention (a continuous performance test in which children were required to continuously monitor a computer screen and press a key every time a letter appeared except for the letter "X," in which case they were to withhold their response) for a group of young cancer survivors after a training program that included attention process training compared to a control group of children who did not receive training. However, a fourth measure, a test of arithmetic achievement, showed no difference between groups. The usefulness of these training interventions will be greatly limited until there is a greater understanding of the conditions necessary or even possible for transfer to higher-level cognition (see Minear & Shah 2006 for more detailed discussions).

Reducing Working Memory Demands

Large amounts of complex information are frequently presented to individuals orally, in text, or in static and dynamic multimedia displays. Interpretation of such complex information requires maintaining and mentally manipulating visual and verbal information and consequently much applied working memory research focuses on how to reduce working memory demands on design of text and multimedia (Shah & Hoeffner 2002). In this section, we outline specifically the role of working memory in multimedia displays. Using such displays typically requires integrating or coordinating auditory or textually presented information with visual information (e.g., van Bruggen *et al.* 2002). In addition, viewers may be required to form a mental model or mentally animate visually presented information (Hegarty & Just 1993).

Much research has demonstrated the conditions under which such limitations might constrain the interpretation of displays and others led to guidelines that reduce the impact of these limitations (e.g., Narayanan & Hegarty 1998; Sweller *et al.* 1998; Mayer 2001; Shah *et al.* 2005). One factor that influences cognitive load is the amount of information presented. Mayer *et al.* (2001) found that students who received a basic presentation about lightning (i.e., lacking additional words, sounds, or video) demonstrated superior problem-solving transfer to students who received an expanded version (i.e., with music, sound effects, and/or video). In a related study, Mayer *et al.* (2001) showed that when students viewed a lightning bolt hitting a person on the ground in a lesson about how lightning works, they understood the scientific principles discussed less than when the text did not contain such "seductive details." These studies suggest that cognitive load may be reduced by not having multiple pieces of information competing for limited resources, especially when some of the information is less relevant for learning. In other words, in some cases "less is more."

A second factor that influences working memory demands is the relative difficulty of integrating multiple pieces of information. People are able to integrate information that is within close physical proximity more easily. Sweller *et al.* (1998), for example, found a benefit for presenting statements of relevant theorems used in a geometry proof physically next to relevant portions of a diagram rather than on a different part of a screen or page. Presenting some information in auditory form while visual information is presented on a screen so that viewers do not have to look in more than one place to integrate is also beneficial (Mayer 2001). Thus, by presenting to-be-integrated information close together or in separate modalities supports comprehension of visualizations. This different modality effect holds true not only for multimedia in education, but also in job training. Mousavi *et al.* (1995) conducted a study in which they found that audiovisual displays were better than purely visual displays for electrical engineering tasks because audiovisual displays support integration and reduce cognitive load (Kalyuga *et al.* 1999).

Following this same principle, when AOL launched its email service, they decided to simultaneously present an auditory cue "You've got mail!" as well as a visual icon change to indicate incoming mail. This was in contrast to earlier providers whose email services was not effectively utilized by users, mostly because the visual cue indicating the arrival of new emails was not sufficient to direct attention to the inbox (Varakin *et al.* 2004).

A third factor that influences the working memory demands of a display is the extent to which information must be mentally transformed for comprehension (Larkin & Simon 1987). For example, when maps are presented in a manner that requires mentally aligning or rotating information in order to understand it or use it for navigation, comprehension is difficult (Taylor 2005; Wickens *et al.* 2005). Based on the same principle, Levine (1982) recommended that to ensure the usability of "you are here" maps, such maps should adhere to the "forward is up" principle, and present locations that the viewers are facing in the upper portions rather than in the bottom portions of the map. Similarly, Shah *et al.* (1999) found that students' comprehension of graphs was facilitated when graphs were designed to reduce cognitively demanding transformations. In general, information should be presented in a manner requiring minimal cognitive computation for comprehension of the most important information in a display (see Wickens & Hollands 2000; Shah *et al.* 2005 for reviews).

One general principle for minimizing computation in displays is the *proximity compatibility principle* (Wickens & Carswell 1995). This suggests that if information requires high integration (e.g., identifying a trend in complex data), then the display should be highly integrated (e.g., in a line graph). By contrast, if a task does not require a high degree of integration (e.g., identifying an individual data point), then information should be presented in a less integrated way (e.g., in a bar graph).

A final principle is to use the degree of realism that is relevant for the viewers' task. In many cases, greater realism comes with cognitive costs in that it may reduce viewers' situational understanding of the environment (Wickens 2005). At the same time, realism can help viewers form mental models of visuospatial information that are not available in schematic diagrams. Schwartz and Black (1996) for example, found that viewing realistic pictures of hinges and gears helped viewers mentally animate the working of these mechanical systems compared to schematic drawings. One solution proposed by Narayanan and Hegarty (1998) is to provide both schematic and realistic diagrams that can be selected by the learner depending on his or her goals.

In the preceding paragraphs we summarized principles for reducing cognitive load. Attempts to reduce cognitive load in multimedia have also revealed the ineffectiveness of some intuitions. One example of this lack of effectiveness is in the context of animation. The implicit assumption is that presenting animated displays may reduce the working memory demands of mental animation. However, a recent review suggests that when studies control for information content, viewers' comprehension is no better for animated displays than for non-animated displays (Tversky *et al.* 2002).

In another attempt to reduce working memory demands in aviation, pilots use head-up displays (HUD) that project navigation information on the windshields of planes to prevent pilots from looking down at the display (e.g., Wickens & Long 1995; for a discussion of driving and HUDs, see Tufano 1997). However, a meta-analysis of aviation research on HUDs revealed that there are costs *and* benefits to HUD use (Fadden *et al.* 1998). Among the benefits, HUDs reduce visual accommodation by eliminating the need to switch between displays inside the cockpit and the external world. Also, the superimposition of navigational and outside information has been shown to reduce scanning time, and enable efficient integration of information. On the other hand, especially during unexpected events, HUDs were noted to impair event detection. Haines (1991) reported that, when tested in a simulator, two out of nine pilots were not able to detect another close-by aircraft taxiing during landing. Furthermore, Wickens and Long (1995) noted that even when pilots detected an unexpected situation on the runway, their reaction times to start emergency maneuvers were disproportionately longer than those pilots not using HUDs. Varakin *et al.* (2004) argued that these "cognitive tunneling" or "cognitive capture" effects are partly due to the same attentional and working memory limitations that lead to change blindness. In the next section we elaborate further on the change blindness phenomenon observed in the context of human–computer interaction.

Change Blindness

One consequence of limitations of visual working memory is the phenomenon of change blindness (Rensink 2002; Simons & Rensink 2005). Change blindness refers to a viewer's inability to detect large changes that occur in visual scenes and displays. This phenomenon has been demonstrated under many different conditions, including controlled laboratory experiments (e.g., Rensink *et al.* 1997; O'Regan & Noë 2001) and more naturalistic experiments involving real-world personal interactions (e.g., Simons & Levin 1997). In both types of study, the paradigms involve individuals sequentially viewing two displays identical to one another except for one major change. Sometimes these two display screens are interleaved with a blank screen, sometimes a number of local masks are randomly superimposed on one image, and at other times changes are introduced during eye movements. The "change blindness" effects are robust across all these conditions and are indicative of an inability to maintain and/or compare information in visual working memory across a brief delay interval in the magnitude of hundreds of seconds (Rensink 2002).

This limitation has been the subject of some recent applied research (see Durlach 2004; Pew 2004; Varakin *et al.* 2004, all in a special issue of *Human-Computer Interaction*). Here we briefly summarize some of the major findings from two domains: monitoring of critical information and advertisement.

Complex and critical monitoring tasks such as those of air traffic control officers, army and navy personnel at Combat Information Centers (CIC) require people to keep track of safety-critical information across different monitors, multiple and sometimes superimposed windows and pop-up alerts. Recent research has suggested that under such set-ups operators are particularly prone to change blindness. Tasks demanding operators to attend across a number of separate information panels necessitate operators to distribute their attention broadly, and switch task and focus frequently. Such shifts may act like the blank gray screens or local masks between two alternating screens manipulated in laboratory studies of visual change blindness. Indeed, officers at CIC (DiVita *et al.* 2004), pilots (Nikolic & Sarter 2001), and individuals interacting with army's command brigade system (Durlach & Chen 2003) were all shown to be prone to change blindness. More importantly, changes that were undetected or detected too late were highly salient events.

In one such experiment, Nikolic and Sarter (2001) had experienced pilots report automated mode transitions on the primary flight display while in a flight simulator. Even though automated mode transitions were indicated as in actual cockpits, the pilots in the experiments did not notice major changes such as "ON" vs. "OFF." Similarly, DiVita *et al.* (2004) had civilians experienced with space and naval warfare systems monitor the action of eight contacts in tactical displays. Even when participants were told that there was a change, on average they needed two or more selections to determine which contact had moved. Modeling of task performance indicated that if correct identification was made after three selections, then performance was best characterized as random guessing. Even more striking is how this study might have underestimated the extent of change blindness in these types of task; in real-world settings involving tactical monitoring each person typically monitors 150 to 100 contacts not eight. In yet another study Durlach and Chen (2003) examined change blindness in the context of army's Force XXI Battle Command Brigade and Below system. They reported that critical icon changes during a concurrent task were detected on only half the occasions; this was the case with even a single target icon.

In order to facilitate change detection during critical monitoring tasks, Durlach (2004) summarized a number of factors affecting the speed at which changes are detected, and then noted how operators of such systems may benefit from carefully designed displays and effective training. It is specifically proposed that limiting the number of distractors in displays, increasing the discriminability of icons,[1] and providing system-relevant and knowledge based expertise as opposed to procedural expertise at operating a system might reduce change blindness.

Another domain where similar change blindness results were obtained is advertising. It has been reported that one of the most common forms of advertisement on the Web is the banner (Millward Brown Interactive 1997). However, Benway and Lane (1998) reported that people do not necessarily notice big, colorful banners on web-pages even when they are task-relevant, a phenomenon known as "banner blindness." Despite their ineffectiveness in capturing attention, banner ads have become even more prevalent and larger (Burke *et al.* 2004). Furthermore, despite the lack of empirical validation of the claim that animations do capture the viewer's attention, animated banners have increased as well. When Burke and colleagues (2004) tested the influence of banners on search and memory tasks, they found that banners actually caused distraction (as revealed by an increase in search times) and were not accurately recalled. Also, animated banners were found to be even more distracting than static banners. Therefore, Burke and colleagues concluded that people are not necessarily "blind" to banners; banners actually result in decrements in performance (see also Briggs & Hollis 1997).

Reducing Demands for Older Adults

A population of special concern with regards to applied psychology and working memory is older adults. Older adults, compared to younger adults, perform poorly on various cognitive tasks. Working memory limitations and reduction in the speed of processing have been shown to explain age-related variances in these tasks (e.g., Park *et al.* 2002). One important applied consequence of reduced working memory capacity of older adults has to do with their comprehension of displays. Given that working memory and language comprehension are closely related (e.g., Daneman & Merikle 1996), older adults' working memory impairments are likely to impact their comprehension of various instructional texts and displays. In the following paragraphs, we discuss empirical findings on how older adults interact with interfaces and how well they comprehend warnings, procedural assembly, and medication instructions, and how working memory demands for these comprehension tasks can be reduced.

Despite the increase of middle-aged and older adults in the population and the pervasiveness of computers in many daily tasks, empirical research on interface design and aging is limited. However, Hawthorn (2000) points to a number of principles that might be beneficial to interface designers. First, Hawthorn advises designers to create a system where reliance on working memory is less and where crucial information is readily available and distractors are at a minimum. To facilitate task completion he suggests eliminating time delays between components of sub-tasks and ridding the system of unnecessary steps required for task completion. Also, designers are advised to replace longer instructional paragraphs with directions in the forms of bullet points or simple lists (Morrow *et al.* 1998b). Hawthorn (2000) also discusses that frequently updating or changing interfaces may put older adults at a greater disadvantage than younger adults. Older users need a lot of practice to get comfortable with a new interface, and until they do, they are more likely to rely on their limited working memory. Even though some research exists on how to most effectively train older adults on new interfaces, there is no commonly accepted procedure (e.g., Charness *et al.* 2001).

Limitations in working memory also influence how safety warnings are processed. Even when simple symbols are used to convey warning information, age-related impairments were reported (Hancock *et al.* 2004). Four key features of product warnings are: (1) they must capture attention and be noticed; (2) the warnings should be legible; (3) the warnings must be easy to comprehend; and (4) compliance with the warning should not require excessive mental or physical effort. Working memory limitations are most likely to impact the comprehension of product warnings. While incoherent product warnings are problematic for both younger and older adults, the latter group may be at a greater disadvantage due to their reduced working memory capacity. For instance, Rousseau and colleagues argued that older adults may have a hard time maintaining all of the information present in a warning active in working memory, requiring them to repeatedly examine the warning. Also, older adults may have difficulty following through with the multiple steps necessary to safely comply with the warning (Rousseau *et al.* 1998).

In order to ensure product warning effectiveness, the following principles must be respected. First, warnings should be placed on the product itself rather than in a separate manual (Rousseau *et al.* 1998). Second, since older adults have reduced attentional breadth (e.g., Sekuler *et al.* 2000), warnings should be placed strategically near a main point of interest, such as the label and brand information, as Kline and Scialfa's (1997) findings demonstrate. Third, when possible, warning information should be presented through symbols that are tested to be easy to comprehend (Hancock *et al.* 2004). Finally, the seriousness of the warning should be calibrated by using labels such as "danger," "warning," and "caution" (Wogalter & Silver 1995), and through the redundant color coding of these labels (with colors red through green, with reddish hues implying greater risk) (Braun & Silver 1995).

Another domain in which older adults may face difficulty because of their working memory limitations is the comprehension of instructions in procedural assembly tasks. Typical assembly tasks require individuals to follow detailed instructions, and to switch back and forth between the instruction pamphlet and the items assembled; thus, by definition, these tasks are working memory demanding. Morrell and Park (1993) tested younger and older adults on an assembly task and reported that performance on a spatial working memory task correlated with assembly performance, and that older adults performed worse than younger adults, especially in complex cases. Also, they demonstrated that when instructions included text along with illustrations, the overall number of errors in assembling was reduced compared to when the text or the illustration was presented alone. This finding suggests that instructions that incorporate text and illustrations are more suitable for both age groups; and more so for older populations. Therefore, these types of instructions should be favored over text-only or illustration-only instructions.

Finally, another domain that is of particular importance to older adults due to possible working memory and comprehension deficits has to do with the design of medication instructions. Since the federal legislation (Food and Drug Administration 1995) mandating pharmacies to provide detailed information about prescriptions was introduced, patients have been provided with expanded communication about medications. However, such communication, especially when poorly organized and when requiring inferences to be drawn, was reported to be ineffective in communicating drug-related information (e.g., Park *et al.* 1994; Morrow *et al.* 1998a). Therefore, it is vital to establish effective means of communicating medicine instructions, especially for older adults. Recent research has identified ways to improve the comprehensibility of medicine instructions. For instance, it is helpful to present information in list format rather than in a paragraph (Morrow *et al.* 1998b). Graphic illustrations of medication dose and time also result in better comprehension and consequently better adherence to the drug regimen (Morrow *et al.* 1998a; see Park *et al.* 1999 for further discussion).

Mood and Emotion and Working Memory Capacity

There has been a great deal of research on the effect of affect on working memory and tasks that rely on working memory (Eysenck 1985). Although providing a full discussion of this research is beyond the scope of this review, we briefly describe some work in this area which has important implications. One major theory guiding this research for which there is substantial evidence is that anxiety and possibly other positive and negative mood states lead to intrusive thoughts which in turn reduce working memory capacity (Eysenck 1985, 1992; Oaksford *et al.* 1996); Oaksford *et al.* (1996), for example, found that individuals in a positive mood performed worse on the Tower of London task (a measure of planning ability that is highly working memory demanding) than individuals in a neutral mood.

A great deal of this research has focused on the relationship between anxiety, intrusions, and working memory tasks (Eysenck 1985, 1992). Some recent studies have applied Eysenck's theory of anxiety to the effect of mathematics anxiety and pressure on mathematics problem-solving performance (Ashcraft 2002). For example, Ashcraft and Kirk (2001) measured mathematics anxiety, working memory capacity, and mathematics problem-solving. Individuals with high mathematics anxiety also had lower working memory capacity and reduced performance on mathematics problem-solving tasks. In a related study, Beilock *et al.* (2004) demonstrated that individuals were most affected by pressure on high working memory demanding mathematics problems rather than low working memory demanding problems.

Recent studies have suggested a relatively complex and interesting pattern of effects of pressure on mathematics problem-solving performance. Individuals with high working memory capacity are more likely to show decrements in performance under pressure (Beilock & Carr 2005). This may be because these individuals are most likely to rely on working memory demanding strategies. The Beilock and Carr study is particularly interesting because of its somewhat counterintuitive finding that high working memory individuals are more impacted by pressure than low working memory individuals and has numerous possible implications for performance in applied settings that have yet to be explored.

CONCLUSION

In this chapter we have provided a summary of the characteristics of working memory and its limitations. Based on this selective review, we have discussed implications of working memory limitations on applied cognition. The reason for our selective focus on working memory limitations was two-fold. First, from a theoretical standpoint, understanding limitations of working memory has been an overarching goal for researchers since the inception of the working memory concept. Second, there has been a number of relatively new areas of research that have recently generated lots of empirical data (e.g., visual and spatial working memory, training research, executive functions, etc.), some of which we have already seen applications of (e.g., change blindness effects in human computer interaction, HUDs), and some of which are likely to influence applied cognition, but at the moment requiring further research (e.g., spatial working memory, training and transfer research, attention capturing and yet not distracting alerts, anxiety and mood effects on working memory). Different approaches to applications of working memory can be found in recent books on applied cognitive psychology (e.g., Esgate & Groome 2004; Healy 2005).

NOTE

1 Durlach (2004) noted that when the icons for the currently used systems were initially designed, discriminability of the icons was not attended to.

REFERENCES

Ackerman, P. L. (1990). A correlational analysis of skill specificity: learning, abilities, and individual differences. *Journal of Experimental Psychology: Learning, Memory, and Cognition*, *16*, 883–901.

Alvarez, G. A. & Cavanagh, P. (2004). The capacity of visual short-term memory is set both by visual information load and by number of objects. *Psychological Science*, *15*, 106–111.

Anderson, J. R., Reder, L. M. & Lebiere, C. (1996). Working memory: activation limitations on retrieval. *Cognitive Psychology*, *30*, 221–256.

Ashcraft, M. H. (2002). Math anxiety: personal, educational, and cognitive consequences, *Current Directions in Psychological Science*, *11*, 181.

Ashcraft, M. H. & Kirk, E. P. (2001).The Relationships among working memory, math anxiety, and performance, *Journal of Experimental Psychology: General*, *130*, 224–237.

Atkinson, R. C. & Shiffrin, R. M. (1968). Human memory: a proposed system and its control processes. In K. W. Spence & J. T. Spence (eds.), *The Psychology of Learning and Motivation: Advances in Research and Theory* (Vol. 2, pp. 89–195). New York: Academic Press.

Baddeley, A. (2002). Fractionating the central executive. In D. T. Stuss (ed.), *Principles of Frontal Lobe Function* (pp. 246–260). London: Oxford University Press.
Baddeley, A. D. (1986). *Working Memory*. Oxford: Clarendon Press.
Baddeley, A.D. (1996). Exploring the central executive. *Quarterly Journal of Experimental Psychology, 49A*, 5–28.
Baddeley, A. D. (2000). The episodic buffer: a new component of working memory. *Trends in Cognitive Sciences, 4*, 417.
Baddeley, A. D., Grant, S., Wright, E. & Thomson, N. (1975). Imagery and visual working memory. In P. M. A. Rabbitt & S. Dornic (eds.), *Attention and Performance V* (pp. 205–217). London: Academic Press.
Baddeley, A. D. & Hitch, G. (1974). Working memory. In G. H. Bower (ed.), *The Psychology of Learning and Motivation* (Vol. 8, pp. 47–90). New York: Academic Press.
Barch, D. M. (2005). The cognitive neuroscience of schizophrenia. *Annual Review of Clinical Psychology, 1*, 321–353.
Barkley, R. A. (1997). Behavioral inhibition, sustained attention, and executive functions: constructing a unifying theory of ADHD. *Psychological Bulletin, 121*, 65–94.
Beilock, S. L. & Carr, T. H. (2005). When high-powered people fail. *Psychological Science, 16*, 101–105.
Beilock, S. L., Kulp, C. A., Holt, L. E. & Carr, T. H. (2004). More on the fragility of performance: chocking under pressure in mathematical problem solving. *Journal of Experimental Psychology: General, 133*, 584–600.
Benway, J. P. & Lane, D. M. (1998). Banner blindness: web searchers often miss "obvious" links. *Internetworking, 2*, 1. Retrieved May 22, 2006, Available at: http://www.InternetTG.org/newsletter/dec98/bannerblindness.html.
Bellenkes, A. H., Wickens, C. D. & Kramer, A. F. (1997). Visual scanning and pilot expertise: their role of attentional flexibility and mental model development. *Aviation, Space and Environmental Medicine, 87*(7), 569–579.
Bleckley, M. K., Durso, F., Crutchfield, J. *et al.* (2003). Individual differences in working memory capacity predict visual attention allocation. *Psychonomic Bulleting & Review, 10*, 884–889.
Boduroglu, A. & Shah, P. (2004). Orientation-specific configuration based representations in spatial working memory [Abstract]. *Journal of Vision, 4*(8), 392a.
Boduroglu, A. & Shah, P. (2005). Effects of complexity on the recall of spatial configurations. Poster presentation at the Annual Meeting of the Psychonomics Society, Toronto, ON.
Braun, C. C. & Silver, N. C. (1995). Interaction of signal word and colour on warning labels: differences in perceived hazard and behavioural compliance, *Ergonomics, 38*, 2207–2220.
Briggs, R. & Hollis, N. (1997). Advertising on the Web: is there response before click-through? *Journal of Advertising Research, 37*(2), 33–45.
Brooks, L. R. (1968). Spatial and verbal components of the act of recall. *Canadian Journal of Psychology*, 22, 349–368.
van Bruggen, J. M., Kirschner, P. A. & Jochems, W. (2002). External representation of argumentation in CSCL and the management of cognitive load. *Learning and Instruction, 12*, 121–138.
Brugger, P., Monsch, A. U., Salmon, D. P. & Butters, N. (1996). Random number generation in dementia of the Alzheimer type: a test of frontal executive functions. *Neuropsychologia, 34*, 97–103.
Bull, R., Johnston, R. S. & Roy, J. A. (1999). Exploring the roles of the visual-spatial sketch pad and central executive in children's arithmetical skills: views from cognition and developmental neuropsychology. *Developmental Neuropsychology, 15*, 421–442.
Burke, M., Gorman, N., Nilsen, E. & Hornof, A. (2004). Banner ads hinder visual search and are forgotten. Extended Abstracts of ACM CHI 2004: conference on Human Factors in Computing Systems. New York: ACM, pp. 1139–1142.
Butler, R. W. & Copeland, D. R. (2002). Attentional processes and their remediation in children treated for cancer: a literature review and the development of a therapeutic approach. *Journal of the International Neuropsychological Society, 8*, 115–124.
Card, S. K., Moran, T. P. & Newell, A. (1983). *The Psychology of Human–Computer Interaction*. Hillsdale, NJ: Lawrence Erlbaum Associates.

Cattell, R. B. (1973). Measuring intelligence with the culture fair tests. Champaign, IL: Institute for Personality and Ability Testing.
Charness, N., Kelley, C. L., Bosman, E. A. & Mottram, M. (2001). Word processing training and retraining: effects of adult age, experience, and interface. *Psychology and Aging*, *16*, 110–127.
Chase, W. G. & Simon, H.A. (1973). Perception in chess. *Cognitive Psychology*, *4*, 55–81.
Cicerone, K. D. (2002). Remediation of "working attention" in mild traumatic brain injury. *Brain Injury*, *16*, 185–195.
Cohen, J. D., Perlstein, W. M., Braver, T. S. *et al.* (1997). Temporal dynamics of brain activation during a working memory task. *Nature*, *386*, 604–608.
Colle, H. A. & Reid, G. B. (1998). Context effects in subjective mental workload ratings. *Human Factors*, *40*, 591–600.
Conway, A. R. A., Kane, M. J., Bunting, M. F. *et al.* (2005). Working memory span tasks: a methodological review and user's guide. *Psychonomic Bulletin and Review*, *12*, 769–786.
Conway, R. A., Cowan, N. & Bunting, M. F. (2001). The cocktail party phenomenon revisited: the importance of working memory capacity. *Psychonomic Bulletin & Review*, *8*, 331–335.
Cowan, N. (2001). The magical number 4 in short-term memory: a reconsideration of mental storage capacity. *Behavioral and Brain Sciences*, *24*, 87–185.
Cowan, N. (2005). *Working Memory Capacity*. Hove: Psychology Press.
Crawford, J. R., Bryan, J., Luszcz, M. A. *et al.* (2000). The executive decline hypothesis of cognitive aging: do executive deficits qualify as differential deficits and do they mediate age-related memory. *Aging, Neuropsychology & Cognition*, *7*, 9–31.
Daily, L. Z., Lovett, M. C. & Reder, L. M. (2001). Modeling individual differences in working memory: a source activation account. *Cognitive Science*, *25*, 315–353.
Daneman, M. & Carpenter, P. A. (1980). Individual differences in working memory and reading. *Journal of Verbal Learning and Verbal Behavior*, *19*, 450–466.
Daneman, M. & Merikle, P. M. (1996). Working memory and language comprehension: a meta-analysis. *Psychonomic Bulletin & Review*, *3*, 422–433.
Day, E. A., Arthur, W. & Shebilske, W. L. (1997). Ability determinants of complex skill acquisition: effects of training protocol. *Acta Psychologica*, *97*, 145–165.
D'Esposito, M., Detre, J. A., Alsop, D. C. *et al.* (1995). The neural basis of the central executive system of working memory. *Nature*, *378*, 279–281.
DiVita, J., Obermeyer, R., Nygren, T. E. & Linville, J. M. (2004). Verification of the change blindness phenomena while managing critical events on a combat information display. *Human Factors*, *46*, 205–218.
Diwadkar, V. A., Carpenter, P. A. & Just, M. A. (2000). Collaborative activity between parietal and dorso-lateral prefrontal cortex in dynamic spatial working memory revealed by fMRI. *NeuroImage*, *12*, 85–99.
Duncan, J. (1995). Attention, intelligence, and the frontal lobes. In M. S. Gazzaniga (ed.), *The Cognitive Neurosciences* (pp. 721–733). Cambridge, MA: MIT Press.
Duncan, J., Emslie, H., Williams, P. *et al.* (1996). Intelligence and the frontal lobe: the organization of goal-directed behavior. *Cognitive Psychology*, *30*, 257–303.
Duncan, J., Seitz, R. J., Kolodny, J. *et al.* (2000). A neural basis for general intelligence. *Science*, *289*, 457–460.
Durlach, P. J. (2004) Change blindness and its implications for complex monitoring and control systems design and operator training. *Human–Computer Interaction, 19*, 423–451.
Durlach, P. J. & Chen, J. Y. C. (2003). Visual change detection in digital military displays. In *Proceedings of the Interservice/Industry Training, Simulation, and Education Conference 2003*. Orlando, FL: IITSEC.
Eng, H. Y., Chen, D. & Jiang, Y. (2005). Visual working memory for complex and simple visual stimuli. *Psychonomic Bulletin & Review*, *12*, 1127–1133.
Engle, R. W., Carullo, J. J. & Collins, K. W. (1991). Individual differences in the role of working memory in comprehension and following directions. *Journal of Educational Research*, *84*, 253–262.
Engle, R. W., Tuholski, S. W., Laughlin, J. E. & Conway, A. R. A. (1999). Working memory, short-term memory, and general fluid intelligence: a latent variable approach. *Journal of Experimental Psychology: General*, *125*, 309–331.

Ericsson, K. A., Chase, W. G. & Faloon, S. (1980). Acquisition of a memory skill. *Science*, *208*, 1181–1182.
Ericsson, K. A. & Kintsch, W. (1995). Long-term working memory. *Psychological Review*, *102*, 211–245.
Ericsson, K. A. & Polson, P. G. (1988). An experimental analysis of a memory skill for dinner-orders. *Journal of Experimental Psychology: Learning, Memory, and Cognition*, *14*, 305–316.
Esgate, A. & Groome, D. (2004). *An Introduction to Applied Cognitive Psychology*. New York: Psychology Press.
Eysenck, M. W. (1985). Anxiety and cognitive-task performance. *Personality and Individual Differences*, *6*, 579–586.
Eysenck, M. W. (1992). *Anxiety: The Cognitive Perspective*. Hillsdale, NJ: Lawrence Erlbaum Associates.
Fadden, S., Ververs, P. & Wickens, C. D. (1998). Costs and benefits of head-up display use: a meta-analytic approach. In *Proceedings of the 42nd Annual Meeting of the Human Factors & Ergonomics Society*. Santa Monica, CA: Human Factors Society.
Food and Drug Administration (1995). Prescription drug labeling; medication guide requirements; proposed rule. *Federal Register*, *60*, No. 164, Health and Human Services, Food and Drug Administration. CFR parts 201, 208, 314, 601.
Friedman, N. P. & Miyake, A. (2004). The relations among inhibition and interference control functions: a latent variable analysis. *Journal of Experimental Psychology: General*, *133*, 101–135.
Friedman, N. P., Miyake, A., Corley, R. P. *et al.* (2006). Not all executive functions are related to intelligence. *Psychological Science*, *17*, 172–179.
Fuster, J. M. (1999). Cognitive functions of the frontal lobes. In B. L. Miller & J. L. Cummings (eds.), *The Human Frontal Lobes: Functions and Disorder* (pp. 187–195). New York: Guilford Press.
Gathercole, S. E. (1994). Neuropsychology and working memory: a review. *Neuropsychology*, *8*(4), 494–505.
Gathercole, S. E. & Baddeley, A. D. (1993). Phonological working memory: a critical building block for reading development and vocabulary acquisition? *European Journal of Psychology of Education*, *8*, 259–272.
Gevins, A., Smith, M. E., Leong, H. *et al.* (1998). Monitoring working memory load during computer-based tasks with EEG pattern recognition methods. *Human Factors*, *40*, 79–91.
Gopher, D. (1993). The skill of attention control: acquisition and execution of attention strategies. In D. E. Meyer & S. Kornblum (eds.), *Attention and Performance XIV: Synergies in Experimental Psychology, Artificial Intelligence, and Cognitive Neuroscience* (pp. 299–322). Cambridge, MA: MIT Press.
Gopher, D., Weil, M. & Siegel, D. (1989). Practice under changing priorities: an approach to training of complex skills. *Acta Psychologica*, *71*, 147–179.
Haier, R. J., Siegel, B. V., MacLachlan, A. *et al.* (1992). Regional glucose metabolic changes after learning a complex visuospatial/motor task: a positron emission topographic study. *Brain Research*, *570*, 134–143.
Haines, R. F (1991). A breakdown in simultaneous information processing. In G. Obrecht & L. Start (eds.), *Prebyopia Research: From Molecular Biology to Visual Adaptation* (pp. 171–175). New York: Plenum.
Hancock, H. E., Rogers, W. A., Schroeder, D. & Fisk, A. D. (2004) Safety symbol comprehension: effects of symbol type, familiarity, and age. *Human Factors*, *46*, 183–195.
Hankins, T. C. & Wilson, G. F. (1998). A comparison of heart rate, eye activity, EEF and subjective measures of pilot mental workload during flight. *Aviation Space and Environmental Medicine*, *69*, 360–367.
Hart, S. G. & Staveland, L. E. (1988). Development of NASA-TLS (Task Load Index): results of empirical and theoretical research. In P. A. Hancock & N. Meshkati (eds.), *Human Mental Workload*. Amsterdam: North-Holland.
Hasher, L. & Zacks, R. T. (1988). Working memory, comprehension, and aging: a review and a new view. In G. H. Bower (ed.), *The Psychology of Learning and Motivation* (Vol. 22, pp. 193–225). New York: Academic Press.

Hawthorn, D. (2000). Possible implications of aging for interface designers. *Interacting with Computers*, *12*, 507–528.
Healy, A. (ed.) (2005). *Experimental Cognitive Psychology and Its Applications.* Washington, DC: American Psychological Association.
Hegarty, M. & Just, M. A. (1993). Constructing mental models of machines from text and diagrams. *Journal of Memory and Language*, *32*, 717–742.
Heitz, R. P., Unsworth, N. & Engle, R. W. (2005). Working memory capacity, attentional control, and fluid intelligence. In O. Wilhelm & R. W. Engle (eds.), *Handbook of Understanding and Measuring Intelligence* (pp. 61–78). London: Sage.
Hill, S. G., Iavecchia, H. P., Byers, H. C. *et al.* (1992). Comparison of four subjective workload rating scales. *Human Factors*, *24*, 429–440.
Hulme, C. & Mackenzie, S. (1992). *Working Memory and Severe Learning Difficulties.* Hove: Lawrence Erlbaum Associates.
Humphrey, D. G. & Kramer, A. F. (1994). Toward a psychophysiological assessment of dynamic changes in mental workload. *Human Factors*, *36*(1), 3–26.
Jonides, J. (2001). Modules of executive control. Paper presented at fMRI Workshop, Ann Arbor, MI.
Jonides, J. & Smith, E. E. (1997). The architecture of working memory. In M. D. Rugg (ed.), *Cognitive Neuroscience* (pp. 243–276). Cambridge, MA: MIT Press.
Just, M. A. & Carpenter, P. A. (1992). A capacity theory of comprehension: individual differences in working memory. *Psychological Review*, *99*, 122–149.
Just, M. A., Carpenter, P. A., Keller, T. A. *et al.* (1996). Brain activation modulated by sentence comprehension. *Science*, *274*, 114–116.
Just, M. A., Carpenter, P. A. & Miyake, A. (2003). Neuroindices of cognitive workload: neuroimaging, pupillometric, and event-related potential studies of brain work. *Theoretical Issues in Ergonomics*, *4*, 56–88
Kahneman, D. & Beatty, J. (1966). Pupil diameter and load on memory. *Science*, *154*, 1583–1585
Kalyuga, S., Changler, P. & Sweller, J. (1999). Managing split-attention and redundancy in multimedia instruction. *Applied Cognitive Psychology*, *13*, 351–357.
Kane, M., Miyake, A., Towse, J. *et al.* (eds.) (2006). *Variation in Working Memory.* New York: Oxford University Press.
Kane, M. J., Bleckley, K. M., Conway, A. R. A. & Engle, R. W. (2001). A controlled-attention view of working-memory capacity. *Journal of Experimental Psychology: General*, *130*, 169–183.
Kane, M. J. & Engle, R. W. (2002). The role of prefrontal cortex in working memory capacity, executive attention, and general fluid intelligence: an individual differences perspective. *Psychonomic Bulletin and Review*, *9*, 637–671.
Kane, M. J., Hambrick, D. Z., Tuholski, S. W. *et al.* (2004). The generality of working memory capacity: a latent variable approach to verbal and visuospatial memory span and reasoning. *Journal of Experimental Psychology: General*, *133*, 189–217.
Kemps, E. (1999). Effects of complexity on visuospatial working memory. *European Journal of Cognitive Psychology*, *11*, 335–356.
Kline, D. W. & Scialfa, C. T. (1997). Sensory and perceptual functioning. Basic research and human factors implications. In A. D. Fisk & W. A. Rogers (eds.), *Handbook of Human Factors and the Older Adults* (pp. 27–54). New York: Academic Press.
Klingberg, T., Fernell, E., Olesen, P. J. *et al.* (2005). Computerized training of working memory in children with ADHD – A randomized, controlled trial. *Journal of the American Academy of Child and Adolescent Psychiatry*, *44*, 177–186.
Klingberg, T., Forssberg H. & Westerberg, H. (2002). Training of working memory in children with ADHD. *Journal of Clinical and Experimental Neuropsychology*, *24*, 781–791.
Kyllonen, P. C. & Christal, R. E. (1990). Reasoning ability is (little more than) working-memory capacity? *Intelligence*, *14*, 389–433.
Larkin, J. H. & Simon, H. A. (1987). Why a diagram is (sometimes) worth ten thousand words. *Cognitive Science*, *11*, 65–99.
Laws, G., MacDonald, J. & Buckley, S. (1996). The effects of a short training in the use of a rehearsal strategy on memory for words and pictures in children with Down syndrome. *Down Syndrome: Research & Practice*, *4*, 70–78.

Levine, M. (1982) You-are-here maps: psychological considerations. *Environment and Behavior, 14*(2), 221–237.
Logie, R. H. (1995). *Visuospatial Working Memory.* Hove: Lawrence Erlbaum Associates.
Lopez-Luengo, B. & Vazquez, C. (2003). Effects of attention process training on cognitive functioning of schizophrenic patients. *Psychiatry Research, 119*, 41–53.
Luck, S. J. & Vogel, E. K. (1997). The capacity of visual working memory for features and conjunctions. *Nature, 390*, 279–281.
Luck, S. J. & Zhang, W. (2004). Fixed resolution, slot-like representations in visual working memory [Abstract]. *Journal of Vision, 4*(8), 149.
McLean J. F. & Hitch G. J. (1999). Working memory impairments in children with specific arithmetic learning difficulties. *Journal of Experimental Child Psychology, 74*, 240–260.
McNamara, D. S. & Scott, J. L. (2001). Working memory capacity and strategy use. *Memory & Cognition, 29*, 10–17.
Mané, A. M. & Donchin, E. (1989). The space fortress game. *Acta psychologica*, 71, 17–22.
Mayer, R. E. (2001). *Multimedia Learning.* New York: Cambridge University Press.
Mayer, R. E., Heiser, J. & Lonn, S. (2001). Cognitive constraints on multimedia learning: when presenting more material results in less understanding. *Journal of Educational Psychology, 93*, 187–198.
Meyer, D. E. & Kieras, D. E. (1997). A computational theory of executive cognitive processes and multiple-task performance: II. Accounts of psychological refractory-period phenomena. *Psychological Review, 104*, 749–791.
Meyer, D. E. & Kieras, D. E. (1999). Précis to a practical unified theory of cognition and action: some lessons from EPIC computational models of human multiple-task performance. In D. Gopher & A. Koriat (eds.), *Attention and Performance XVII: Cognitive Regulation of Performance: Interaction of Theory and Application* (pp. 17–88). Cambridge, MA: MIT Press.
Miller, G. A. (1956). The magical number seven, plus or minus two: some limits on our capacity for processing information. *The Psychological Review, 63*, 81–97.
Millward Brown Interactive & Internet Advertising Bureau (1997). *IAB Online Advertising Effectiveness Study.* Millward Brown Interactive & Internet Advertising Bureau. Draft copy only.
Minear, M. & Shah, P. (2006). Sources of working memory deficits in children and possibilities for remediation. In S. Pickering (ed.), *Working Memory and Education* (pp. 274–307). San Diego, CA: Elsevier Press.
Miyake, A., Friedman, N. P., Emerson, M. J. *et al.* (2000). The unity and diversity of executive functions and their contributions to complex "frontal lobe" tasks: a latent variable analysis, *Cognitive Psychology, 41*, 49–100.
Miyake, A., Friedman, N. P., Rettinger, D. A. *et al.* (2001). Visuospatial working memory, central executive functioning, and psychometric visuospatial abilities: how are they related? *Journal of Experimental Psychology: General, 130*, 621–640.
Miyake, A. & Shah, P. (eds.) (1999a). *Models of Working Memory: Mechanisms of Active Maintenance and Executive Control.* New York: Cambridge University Press.
Miyake, A. & Shah, P. (1999b). Toward unified theories of working memory: emerging general consensus, unresolved theoretical issues, and future research directions. In A. Miyake & P. Shah (eds.), *Models of Working Memory: Mechanisms of Active Maintenance and Executive Control* (pp. 442–481). New York: Cambridge University Press.
Monsell, S. (1996). Control of mental processes. In V. Bruce (ed.), *Unsolved Mysteries of the Mind: Tutorial Essays in Cognition* (pp. 93–148). Hove: Lawrence Erlbaum Associates.
Moran, T. P. (1981). An applied psychology of the user. *Computing Surveys, 13*(1), 1–11.
Moray, N. P. (1982). Subjective mental workload. *Human Factors, 24*, 25–40.
Morrell, R. W. & Park, D. C. (1993). Effects of age, illustrations, and task variables on the performance of procedural assembly tasks. *Psychology and Aging, 8*, 389–399.
Morrow, D., Hier, C., Menard, W. & Leirer, V. (1998a). Icons improve older and younger adult comprehension of medication information. *Journal of Gerontology: Psychological Sciences, 53B*, 240–254.
Morrow, D. G., Leirer, V., Andrassy, J. M. *et al.* (1998b). The influence of list format and category headers on age differences in understanding medication instructions. *Experimental Aging Research, 24*, 231–256.

Mousavi, S., Low, R. & Sweller, J. (1995). Reducing cognitive load by mixing auditory and visual presentation modes. *Journal of Educational Psychology, 87,* 319–334.

Mulder, G. & Mulder, L. J. (1981). Information processing and cardiovascular control. *Psychophysiology, 18,* 392–401.

Narayanan, N. H. & Hegarty, M. (1998). On designing comprehensible interactive hypermedia manuals. *International Journal of Human–Computer Studies, 48,* 267–301.

Nigg, J. T. (2000). On inhibition/disinhibition in developmental psychopathology: views from cognitive and personality psychology and a working inhibition taxonomy. *Psychological Bulletin, 126,* 220–246.

Nikolic, M. I. & Sarter, N. B. (2001). Peripheral visual feedback: a powerful means of supporting attention allocation and human-automation coordination in highly dynamic data-rich environments. *Human Factors, 43*(1), 30–38.

Norman, D. A. & Shallice, T. (1986). Attention to action: willed and automatic control of behaviour. Reprinted in revised form in R. J. Davidson, G. E. Schwartz & D. Shapiro (eds.) (1986) *Consciousness and Self-Regulation* (Vol. 4, pp. 1–18). New York: Plenum.

Oaksford, M., Morris, F., Grainger, B. & Williams, J. M. G. (1996). Mood, reasoning, and central executive processes, *Journal of Experimental Psychology: Learning, Memory & Cognition, 22,* 476–492.

O'Donnell, R. D. & Eggemeier, F. T. (1986). Workload assessment methodology. In K. Boff, L. Kaufman & J. Thomas (eds.), *Handbook of Perception and Performance* (Vol. 2). New York: John Wiley & Sons.

Olesen, P. J., Westerberg, H. & Klingberg, T. (2003). Increased prefrontal and parietal activity after training of working memory. *Nature Neuroscience, 7,* 75–79.

O'Regan, J. K. & Noe, A. (2001). A sensorimotor account of vision and visual consciousness. *Behavioral and Brain Sciences, 24*(5), 939–1011.

O'Reilly, R. C., Braver, T. S. & Cohen, J. D. (1999). A biologically based computational model of working memory. In A. Miyake & P. Shah (eds.), *Models of Working Memory: Mechanisms of Active Maintenance and Executive Control* (pp. 375–411), New York: Cambridge University Press.

Park, D. C., Lautenschlager, G., Hedden, T. *et al.* (2002). Models of visuospatial and verbal memory across the adult life span. *Psychology and Aging, 17,* 299–320.

Park, D. C., Morrell, R. W. & Shifren, K. (eds.) (1999). *Processing of Medical Information in Aging Patients: Cognitive and Human Factors Perspectives.* Mahwah, NJ: Lawrence Erlbaum Associates.

Park, D. C., Willis, S. L., Morrow, D. *et al.* (1994). Cognitive function and medication usage in older adults. *Journal of Applied Gerontology, 13,* 39–57.

Park, N. W., Proulx, G. B. & Towers, W. M. (1999). Evaluation of the attention process training programme. *Neuropsychological Rehabilitation, 9,* 135–154.

Park, W. P. & Ingles, J. L. (2001). Effectiveness of attention rehabilitation after an acquired brain injury: a meta-analysis. *Neuropsychology, 15,* 199–210.

Parmentier, F. B. R., Elford, G. & Maybery, M. T. (2005). Transitional information in spatial serial memory: path characteristics affect recall performance. *Journal of Experimental Psychology: Learning, Memory & Cognition, 31,* 412–427.

Pew, R. W. (2004). Introduction to this special section on change blindness. *Human–Computer Interaction, 19,* 387–388.

Pickering, S. J. (2001). Cognitive approaches to the fractionation of visuospatial working memory. *Cortex, 37,* 457–473.

Pickering, S. J. (ed.) (2006). *Working Memory and Education.* San Diego, CA: Elsevier.

Raven, J. C., Court, J. H. & Raven, J. (1977). *Standard Progressive Matrices.* London: H. K. Lewis & Co.

Reder, L. M. & Schunn, C. D. (1999). Bringing together the psychometric and strategy worlds: predicting adaptivity in a dynamic task. In D. Gopher & A. Koriat (eds.), *Attention and Performance XVII: Cognitive Regulation of Performance: Interaction of Theory and Application* (pp. 315–342). Cambridge, MA: MIT Press.

Reid, G. B. & Nygren, T. E. (1988). The subjective workload assessment technique: a scaling procedure for measuring mental workload. In P. A. Hancock & N. Meshkati (eds.), *Human Mental Workload* (pp. 185–213). Amsterdam: North-Holland.

Rensink, R. A. (2002). Change detection. *Annual Review of Psychology, 53*, 245–277.
Rensink, R. A., O'Regan, J. K. & Clark, J. J. (1997). To see or not to see: the need for attention to perceive changes in scenes. *Psychological Science, 8*, 368–373.
Rogers, R. D. & Monsell, S. (1995). Costs of a predictable switch between simple cognitive tasks. *Journal of Experimental Psychology: General, 124*, 207–231.
Rousseau, G. K. Lamson, N. & Rogers, W. A. (1998). Designing warning to compensate for age-related changes in perceptual and cognitive abilities. *Psychology and Marketing, 15*, 643–662.
Rueda, M. R., Rothbart, M. K., McCandliss, B. D. *et al.* (2005). Training, maturation, and genetic influences on the development of executive attention. *Proceedings of the National Academy of Sciences, 102*, 14931–14936.
Salthouse, T. A. (1992). Influence of processing speed on adult age differences in working memory. *Acta Psychologica, 79*, 155–170.
Schatz, J., Kramer, J. H., Albin, A. & Matthay, K. K. (2000). Processing speed, working memory and IQ: a developmental model of cognitive deficits following cranial radiation therapy. *Neuropsychology, 14*, 189–200.
Schwartz, D. L. & Black, J. B. (1996). Analog imagery in mental model reasoning: depictive models, *Cognitive Psychology, 30*, 154–219.
Sekuler, A. B., Bennett, P. J. & Mamelak, M. (2000) Effects of aging on the useful field of view. *Experimental Aging Research*, 26, 103–120.
Shah, P., Freedman, E. & Vekiri, I. (2005). The comprehension of quantitative information in graphical displays. In P. Shah & A. Miyake (eds.), *The Cambridge Handbook of Visuospatial Thinking* (pp. 426–476). New York: Cambridge University Press.
Shah, P. & Hoeffner, J. (2002). Review of graph comprehension research: implications for instruction. *Educational Psychology Review, 14*, 47–69.
Shah, P. & Miyake, A. (1996). The separability of working memory resources for spatial thinking and language processing: an individual differences approach. *Journal of Experimental Psychology: General, 125*, 4–27.
Shah, P. & Miyake, A. (1999). Models of Working Memory: an Introduction. In A. Miyake & P. Shah (eds.), *Models of Working Memory: Mechanisms of Active Maintenance and Executive Control*. New York: Cambridge University Press.
Shah, P., Mayer, R. E. & Hegarty, M. (1999). Graphs as aids to knowledge construction: signaling techniques for guiding the process of graph comprehension. *Journal of Educational Psychology, 91*, 690–702.
Shallice, T. (1988). *From Neuropsychology to Mental Structure*. New York: Cambridge University Press.
Simons, D. J. & Levin, D. T. (1997). Change blindness. *Trends in Cognitive Sciences, 1*, 261–267.
Simons, D. J. & Rensink, R. A. (2005). Change blindness: past, present, and future. *Trends in Cognitive Sciences, 9*, 16–20.
Smith, E. E. & Jonides, J. (1997). Working memory: a view from neuroimaging. *Cognitive Psychology, 33*, 5–42.
Smith, E. E. & Jonides, J. (1999). Storage and executive processes in the frontal lobes. *Science, 283*, 1657–1661.
Sohlberg, M. M ., McLaughlin, K. A., Pavese, A. *et al.* (2000). Evaluation of attention process training and brain injury education in person with acquired brain injury. *Journal of Clinical and Experimental Neuropsychology, 22*, 656–676.
Sohlberg, M. M. & Mateer, C. A. (1987). Effectiveness of an attention training program. *Journal of Clinical Experimental Neuropsychology, 19*, 117–130.
Sohn, Y. & Doane, S. (2003). Roles of working memory capacity and long-term working memory skill in complex task performance. *Memory & Cognition, 31*, 458–466.
Swanson, H. L. & Sachse-Lee, C. (2001). Mathematical problem solving and working memory in children with learning disabilities: both executive and phonological processes are important. *Journal of Experimental Child Psychology, 79*, 294–321.
Sweller, J., van Merrienboer, J. J. G. & Paas, F. G. W. C. (1998). Cognitive architecture and instructional design. *Educational Psychology Review, 10*, 251–296.
Taylor, H. (2005). Mapping the understanding of maps. In P. Shah & A. Miyake (eds.), *The Cambridge Handbook of Visuospatial Thinking* (pp. 295–333). New York: Cambridge University Press.

Tufano, D. R. (1997). Automotive HUDs: the overlooked safety issues. *Human Factors*, *39*(2), 303–311.
Turley-Ames, K. J. & Whitfield, M. M. (2003). Strategy training and working memory task performance. *Journal of Memory & Language*, *49*, 446–468.
Turner, M. L. & Engle, R. W. (1989). Is working memory capacity task dependent? *Journal of Memory and Language*, *28*, 127–154.
Tversky, B., Morrison, J. B. & Betrancourt, M. (2002). Animation: can it facilitate? *International Journal of Human–Computer Studies*, *57*, 247–262.
Ungerleider, L. G. & Mishkin, M. (1982) The two cortical visual systems. In D. J. Ingle, M. A. Goodale & R. J. W. Mansfield (eds.), *Analysis of Visual Behavior* (pp. 549–586). Cambridge, MA: MIT Press.
Unsworth, N. & Engle, R. W. (2006a). A temporal-contextual retrieval account of complex span: an analysis of errors. *Journal of Memory and Language*, *54*, 346–362.
Unsworth, N. & Engle, R. W. (2006b). Simple and complex memory spans: evidence from list-length effects. *Journal of Memory and Language*, *54*, 68–80.
Unsworth, N., Heitz, R. P., Schrock, J. C. & Engle, R. W. (2005). An automated version of the operation span task. *Behavior Research Methods*, *37*, 498–505.
Vallat, C., Azouvi, P., Hardisson, H. *et al.* (2005). Rehabilitation of verbal working memory after left hemisphere stroke. *Brain Injury*, *19*, 1157–1164.
Van't Hooft, I., Andersson, K., Bergman, B. *et al.* (2005). Beneficial effect from a cognitive training programme on children with acquired brain injuries demonstrated in a controlled study. *Brain Injury*, *19*, 511–518.
Varakin, A. D., Levin, T. D. & Fidler, R. (2004). Unseen and unaware: implications of research research on failures of visual awareness for human-computer interface design. *Human-Computer Interaction*, *19*, 389–422.
Verhaeghen, P., Cerella, J. & Basak, C. (2004). A working memory workout: how to expand the focus of serial attention from one to four items in 10 hours or less. *Journal of Experimental Psychology: Learning, Memory and Cognition*, *30*, 1322–1337.
Wheeler, M. E. & Treisman, A. M. (2002). Binding in short-term visual memory. *Journal of Experimental Psychology: General*, *131*(1), 48–64.
Wickens, C. D. (2005). Attentional tunneling and task management. In R. Jensen (ed.), *Proceedings International Symposium on Aviation Psychology*. Dayton, OH: Wright State University.
Wickens, C. D. & Carswell, C. M. (1995). The proximity compatibility principle. *Human Factors*, *37*(3), 473–494.
Wickens, C. D. & Hollands, J. (2000). *Engineering Psychology and Human Performance* (3rd edn). Upper Saddle River, NJ: Prentice-Hall.
Wickens, C. D. & Liu, Y. (1988). Codes and modalities in multiple resources: a success and a qualification. *Human Factors*, *30*(5), 599–616.
Wickens, C. D. & Long, J. (1995). Object versus space-based models of visual attention: implications for the design of head-up displays. *Journal of Experimental Psychology: Applied*, *1*(3), 179–193.
Wickens, C. D., Vincow, M. & Yeh, M. (2005). Design applications of visual spatial thinking: the importance of frame of reference. In P. Shah & A. Miyake (eds.), *The Cambridge Handbook of Visuospatial Thinking* (pp. 383–425). New York: Cambridge University Press.
Wogalter, M. S. & Silver, N. C. (1995). Warning signal words: connoted strength and understandability by children, elders, and non-native English speakers. *Ergonomics*, *38*, 2188–2206.
Xu, Y. (2002). Limitations of object-based feature encoding in visual short-term memory. *Journal of Experimental Psychology: Human Perception and Performance*, *28*(2), 458–468.
Yeh, Y-Y. & Wickens, C. D. (1988). The dissociation of subjective measures of mental workload and performance. *Human Factors*, *30*, 111–120.

CHAPTER 4

Knowledge and Expertise

Stephan Lewandowsky and Daniel Little
University of Western Australia, Australia

and

Michael L. Kalish
University of Louisiana, USA

KNOWLEDGE IN APPLIED SETTINGS

What is knowledge? In fact, it may be simpler to ask, what is *not* knowledge? There is perhaps no single, more all-encompassing concept in cognitive psychology than knowledge. Knowledge contributes to simple perceptual tasks such as object recognition, when people identify an ambiguous stimulus on the basis of prior knowledge (e.g., Bar & Ullman 1996). Knowledge contributes to memory performance in myriad ways, for example when people reconstruct events according to a schema or script (e.g., Roediger *et al.* 2001; Tuckey & Brewer 2003). Finally, knowledge is the fundamental ingredient of human cognition at its best, namely expert performance. Accordingly, the literature on knowledge is vast, and its sheer size prevents a summary by a few simple assertions. To keep our task manageable we have therefore imposed some strong constraints on this chapter.

Charness and Schultetus (1999) defined knowledge as "acquired information that can be activated in a timely fashion in order to generate an appropriate response" (p. 61). We accept this as our working definition, but restrict consideration to manifestations of knowledge that have been variously called declarative or explicit (Reber & Squire 1994; Shanks & Johnstone 1998). These forms of knowledge are characterized by being accessible to awareness and verbal report, for example in response to a query such as "What is the capital of France?" We do not give much consideration to issues of training and knowledge acquisition, which are the domain of Chapter 21. Finally, we use the applied focus of this handbook to guide which topics to foreground and which to downplay. Accordingly, we omit discussion of computational models of knowledge and its acquisition and transfer (e.g., ACT; Anderson 1990) as extensive treatments of those models can be found elsewhere (e.g., Singley & Anderson 1989). Instead, we foreground research on expertise and expert performance; we focus on the fractionation and encapsulation of knowledge; and we examine the success or failure of the transfer of that knowledge.

Handbook of Applied Cognition: Second Edition. Edited by Francis T. Durso.

We proceed as follows. In the first major section we discuss the nature of expert behavior. In particular, we suggest that expertise is the result of specific learned adaptations to cognitive processing constraints. In consequence, expertise turns out to be very specific and "brittle"; that is, experts may encounter difficulties when tasks are altered or when transfer to new problems is expected. We conclude the section on expertise by examining three shortcomings and sources of error that experts frequently encounter. In the second major section, we consider more conventional, non-expert manifestations of knowledge. We begin by considering the widespread view that knowledge is integrated and coherent, exemplified by knowledge space theories as well as the mental model approach. We then consider the alternative position; namely, that knowledge is often fragmented or partitioned, and that multiple alternative pieces of knowledge are often held simultaneously. In the final major section, we consider the mechanisms underlying the transfer of learned knowledge to novel situations. We suggest that transfer succeeds only if people perceive the similarity between their existing knowledge and a novel problem, and we then review the factors that affect the perception of similarity. We conclude the section by examining additional factors that may lead to the failure of transfer. Throughout the chapter, we place particular emphasis on the problems and shortcomings associated with those processes, because they are of major relevance to the practitioner.

EXPERTISE AND ITS LIMITATIONS

We begin by considering the performance of the most skilled of individuals – the experts. Analysis of expertise can illustrate the essential characteristics of human knowledge; indeed, some have gone as far as to argue that expertise is an indicator of consciousness (Rossano 2003). Our intention in this section is to provide a fairly atheoretical summary of the performance characteristics and shortcomings of experts. The subsequent sections provide a more theoretical discussion of the properties of knowledge in general, and in so doing also provide another, more theoretical perspective on expertise.

Although the many definitions of an expert include anecdotal descriptions such as "anyone who is holding a briefcase and is more than 50 miles from home" (Salthouse 1991, p. 286) or "someone who continually learns more and more about less and less" (Salthouse 1991, p. 286), there is common agreement that an expert is characterized by reproducible superior performance in a particular domain. Any coherent set of tasks and problems that is amenable to objective performance measurement (Ericsson 1996) can constitute a domain of expertise. Accordingly, researchers have examined domains as diverse as the linking of car crime series by expert investigators (Santtila *et al.* 2004), the ability to predict the spread of bush fires by expert firefighters (Lewandowsky & Kirsner 2000), medical diagnosis (e.g., Patel *et al.* 1996), seemingly mundane but highly sophisticated activities such as driving a car (see Chapter 15 for more details), or the performance of chess masters (e.g., Charness *et al.* 1996). In all cases, expert performance has been consistently and reliably found to be outstanding and superior to that of novices.[1]

In chess, for example, expertise is associated with an extraordinary ability to remember the location of pieces on a board after a few seconds of viewing, and the ability to play several games at the same time (e.g., de Groot 1965). In medical diagnosis, experienced radiologists reliably outperform residents when inspecting x-rays (Norman *et al.* 1992). A contemporary mnemonist, Rajan, has memorized the digits of π to over 30,000 places and can reproduce sequences of up to 75 random digits with great ease (e.g., Thompson *et al.* 1993). Even relatively mundane tasks such as waiting tables (Ericsson & Polson 1988) and transcription typing (Salthouse 1991) can involve astonishing levels of knowledge and cognitive performance. (Chapter 3, this volume, provides more information about some of those feats.) Notwithstanding the generally high level of performance, expertise is characterized by several attributes which, in addition to supporting exceptional performance, engender intriguing limitations and create the potential for serious error.

Characteristics of Expertise

Circumventing Known Processing Limitations

Expert performance often seems to defy known human processing limitations. For example, it is known that people cannot tap a finger repetitively more than about six times a second, even if they do not have to respond to specific stimuli (Freund 1983). In conjunction with the known lower limit on response latency to successive stimuli (around 550 ms; Salthouse 1984), these constraints seem to dictate a maximum transcription typing speed of somewhere between 20 and 75 words per minute. Yet, expert typists can enter text at a rate exceeding 75 words per minute. Salthouse (1984) showed that typists achieve this high level of performance by developing specific strategies to circumvent these processing constraints. Specifically, the maximum typing speed a typist can achieve is correlated with the number of characters that must be simultaneously visible for the typist to maintain their maximum speed. This correlation indicates that growing expertise is associated with increased parallelism of processing, such as that used to pre-plan keystrokes involving opposite hands. One index of this planning is the strong negative correlation between expertise and the delay between keystrokes involving alternate hands, as when "w" is followed by "o." That is, coordination between the two hands increases with the expertise of a typist. The further fact that the correlation between expertise and inter-key intervals is substantially smaller for repetitions of the same letter – which necessarily involves repeated tapping of the same finger – indicates that expertise often involves the acquisition of skills to circumvent "hard" constraints, rather than a relaxation of those biological or cognitive constraints.

Similarly, outstanding memorial abilities appear to be based on acquired strategies and techniques. To illustrate, consider individuals who gradually raised their digit span by deliberate acquisition of mnemonic techniques. In some particularly dramatic instances, a person's span increased from the standard 7 ± 2 to 80 or even higher (e.g., Ericsson *et al.* 1980; Staszewski 1993). These remarkable abilities relied on the acquisition of increasingly larger, richly integrated hierarchical retrieval structures (e.g., Staszewski 1993), an observation supported by computer simulation (Richman *et al.* 1995). Ericsson *et al.* (2004) recently confirmed that a similar account can capture the immediate memory abilities of the mnemonist Rajan mentioned above, notwithstanding earlier opinions to the contrary (Thompson *et al.* 1993).

The view that expertise represents a learned adaptation to task constraints – as opposed to being the result of innate "talent" – has found a theoretical focus in the work by Anders Ericsson and colleagues (e.g., Ericsson 2003, 2005). The principal tenet of Ericsson's view is that expertise arises not from mere prolonged exposure to a task, but from extensive

Table 4.1 Commonalities between experts in different domains identified by Holyoak (1991)

1	Experts perform complex tasks in their domains much more accurately than do novices
2	Experts solve problems in their domains with greater ease than do novices
3	Expertise develops from knowledge initially acquired by weak methods
4	Expertise is based on the automatic evocations of actions by conditions
5	**Experts have superior memory for information related to their domains**
6	Experts are better at perceiving patterns among task-related cues
7	Expert problem-solvers search forward from given information rather than backward from goals
8	One's degree of expertise increases steadily with practice
9	Learning requires specific goals and clear feedback
10	**Expertise is highly domain-specific**
11	Teaching expert rules results in expertise
12	Performances of experts can be predicted accurately from knowledge of the rules they claim to use

"deliberate practice." Deliberate practice differs from mere exposure and repetition in several important ways. First, deliberate practice involves a well-defined specific task that the learner seeks to master. Second, task performance is followed by immediate feedback. Third, there is opportunity for repetition. Ericsson *et al.* (1993) provided a very extensive characterization of deliberate practice, and Ericsson (2005) surveys specific instances in which the role of deliberate practice has been established in a variety of expert domains.

There is now considerable consensus that, irrespective of the domain of expertise, ten years of deliberate practice are required to attain outstanding levels of performance (e.g., Ericsson 1996). Moreover, experts exhibit some notable commonalities across domains. Table 4.1 lists some of the commonalities that were identified by Holyoak (1991). The bold-faced entries correspond to issues that we take up in this chapter because we consider them to be particularly critical; the reader is referred to Holyoak (1991) for a discussion of the remainder.

The fact that expertise is the result of very specific adaptations to task demands and processing constraints entails two related consequences: First, experience is typically very specific and limited to the trained domain. Second, expertise is often quite brittle, and seemingly small deviations from a routine task can be associated with surprisingly large performance decrements.

Specificity of Expertise

It should come as no surprise that expert archaeologists are not necessarily also outstanding oceanographers, and that expert psychologists are unlikely also to be world-class ornithologists. However, the extent of that specificity may exceed the expectations and intuitions of most practitioners. For example, individuals who acquire a phenomenally large digit span after extended training (e.g., Ericsson *et al.* 1980), somewhat soberingly retain the standard limited capacity for other information – approximately seven symbols (e.g., Chase & Ericsson 1981). That is, the same person may struggle to recall "C F G K L P Z" in the correct order while being able to reproduce the sequence "2 9 0 3 4 1 8 9 2 3 0 5 7 1 4 5 2 2 8 1 0" (or an even longer series of digits) flawlessly. Similarly, expert pianists' acquired ability to tap fingers particularly rapidly (Ericsson *et al.* 1993) does not generalize to an ability to tap feet at a particularly rapid rate (Keele & Ivry 1987). Perhaps the most astounding demonstration of specificity is the finding that one year after learning to read text in an unfamiliar transformation (e.g., letters flipped upside down and mirror reversed), people can re-read pages from a year ago reliably more quickly than new text that is presented in the same transformed script (Kolers 1976).

Brittleness of Expertise

A corollary of the specificity of expertise is its "brittleness"; that is, the deterioration in performance that is observed when a domain-relevant task is altered slightly and thus becomes atypical. A classic example involves memory for chess configurations. Chase and Simon (1973) found that an expert chess player could recall the identity and location of pieces on a chessboard after fairly brief (5 seconds) exposure with remarkable accuracy. However, this striking ability was limited to plausible configurations that might arise during an actual game. When pieces were randomly arranged, and hence no longer formed a meaningful pattern, the performance of the expert deteriorated dramatically. The deterioration of expert memory when domain-relevant stimuli are rendered meaningless by randomization or some other disruption is a fundamental attribute of expertise that has been observed in many domains. A review by Ericsson and Lehmann (1996) cites areas as diverse as the games of bridge, GO, Othello, snooker, basketball, field hockey, volleyball, and football, and professional disciplines such as medicine, computer programming, and dance.

Another intriguing aspect of these results, in particular those involving chess, arises from detailed comparisons between experts and novices. For meaningful game positions, the reproduction skills of chess masters are indubitably far superior to those of novices. For random positions, it used to be a matter of consensus that the expert advantage was completely eliminated. The belief that experts and novices did not differ in their memorial abilities for random board configurations was sufficiently entrenched to be echoed in recent textbooks (e.g., Medin *et al.* 2001). However, when the evidence from numerous studies is considered jointly in a meta-analysis, increasing expertise is found to be associated with a small but clear memory advantage even for random board positions (Gobet & Simon 1996). This small advantage is most likely due to the experts' ability to discover even small regularities in otherwise random positions by matching board positions against a repertoire of an estimated 50,000 or so chess patterns stored in long-term memory (Simon & Gilmartin 1973).

Accordingly, when the degree of randomness (defined by the extent to which basic game constraints are violated) is manipulated, players with greater expertise are better able to exploit any remaining regularities than players with lesser expertise (Gobet & Waters 2003). The specificity of expertise thus extends to highly subtle regularities indeed.

Expert Transfer

The characteristics of expertise reviewed in the foregoing should readily generate expectations about how expertise transfers from one task to another. It would seem safe to assume a fair degree of within-domain transfer, albeit perhaps bounded by the observed brittleness of expertise, combined with the likely absence of transfer to tasks outside the expert's domain.

Indeed, there is considerable support for within-domain transfer. For example, Novick and colleagues (Novick 1988; Novick & Holyoak 1991) showed that mathematical expertise predicts the degree to which solution strategies are transferred from one algebra word problem to another that appears different at the surface but shares the same deep structure. In fact, transfer is observed even when the two problems are presented under two separate experimental cover stories. In one study, the amount of transfer among experts was found to be up to nine times greater than among novices (Novick 1988, Experiment 1).

Similarly, in the domain of accounting, Marchant *et al.* (1991) showed that experts in general exhibit significantly more transfer than novices between problems involving the application of taxation laws. An accompanying finding was that when the problems were "anomalous," that is, constituted exceptions to a general taxation principle, the experts' subsequent transfer was often reduced to the level shown by novices. Marchant *et al.* argued that processing of the first exceptional case "increased the salience of a highly proceduralized strategy that overrides transfer from the analogy in the more experienced group" (p. 283). Thus, while expertise generally facilitates within-domain transfer, it may not do so in cases involving exceptional problems, because experts cannot help but activate their general knowledge even when exceptions to that knowledge must be processed. In consequence, the strongly activated general knowledge may prevent the renewed recognition of an exception to the general knowledge. We revisit the theme of the inevitable activation of expert knowledge below.

Turning to the issue of transfer outside a problem domain, it is unsurprising that such transfer is often absent. What is perhaps more surprising is how little deviation from a routine task it takes in order to eliminate transfer. Sims and Mayer (2002) examined the spatial skills of expert "Tetris" players. "Tetris" is a computer game that requires the player mentally to rotate shapes presented on the screen in a limited amount of time. People who were experienced "Tetris" players (either pre-experimental experts or trained in the experiment) did not differ from novices on a whole battery of spatial tests, with the highly selective exception of mental rotation tests involving shapes used in "Tetris" or very similar ones. That is, even though "Tetris" relies almost entirely on mental rotation skills, and even though people improved those skills during training, this improvement was narrowly limited to a certain type of stimuli and did not transfer to other shapes.

The characteristics of expertise just reviewed can engender specific performance errors and shortcomings that are worthy of the practitioner's attention. We next review those errors and shortcomings before examining the knowledge structures that underlie skilled performance in general and expertise in particular.

Expert Errors and Shortcomings

There is growing recognition that the analysis of performance errors and limitations contributes in fundamental ways to our understanding of the nature of expert knowledge (e.g.,

Table 4.2 Expert Shortcomings (items 1–8 were identified by Holyoak 1991)

1	Inflexibility
2	Expediency
3	Mediocrity
4	Inefficiency
5	Poorer memory for cases outside domain
6	Poorer perception of patterns unrelated to expert performance
7	Aysmptotic performance
8	Domain specificity
9	Subjectivity
10	Lack of knowledge integration
12	Knowledge Inaccessibility

Johnson *et al.* 1992). Holyoak (1991) provided a list of expert limitations that are reproduced in Table 4.2, together with others identified by ourselves. Three of those limitations and shortcomings – inflexibility, expediency, and mediocrity – are particularly relevant here.

Inflexibility

Inflexibility is revealed when experts are confronted with novel task demands that are inconsistent with their existing knowledge base. In those situations, the need for adaptation may prove to be more challenging to experts than to novices (Frensch & Sternberg 1989; Sternberg & Frensch 1992). Using the game of bridge as their domain of expertise, Sternberg and Frensch (1992) examined the effects of various arbitrary rule changes on the performance of expert and novice bridge players. In general, experts were found to suffer more than novices from any rule change, although the extent of their impairment differed with the type of change. When the rule change involved surface modifications, such as introducing new nonsense names for suits and honor cards, experts suffered less of a performance decrement than when the deep structure of the game was changed, for example, by altering the rule determining the opening of each play. The fact that expert disruption was maximal after a change to the deep structure suggests that experts, unlike novices, routinely processed the task at that deep level; a finding that is consonant with much prior research (e.g., Chi *et al.* 1981; Dunbar 1995). Highly skilled performance may thus entail the general cost of reduced flexibility in the face of novel task demands.

In a related vein, Wiley (1998) showed that experts cannot suppress the retrieval of domain-relevant knowledge, even when participants are warned that their knowledge may be inappropriate or misleading in the current task setting. Wiley used a remote association task, in which people have to generate a word that can form a familiar phrase with each one of three presented items. For example, given the stimuli *plate*, *broken*, and *rest*, the word *home* can be used to form the meaningful phrases *home plate*, *broken home*, and *rest home*. Readers with expertise in baseball may have found this example particularly easy because the target phrase *home plate* represents a crucial concept in baseball. But what if the stimuli had instead been *plate*, *broken*, and *shot*? The intended word here is *glass*, although the first two words are compatible with the baseball-consistent completion *home*. Wiley found that baseball experts, unlike novices, had great difficulty with items that implied – but did not permit – a domain-consistent completion.

The experts' difficulty persisted even when they were warned beforehand that their domain knowledge would be misleading, suggesting that activation of expert knowledge is automatic and cannot be suppressed.

Expediency

Expediency, by contrast, concerns the acquisition phase of expertise, and refers to the fact that experts emphasize efficiency when acquiring a skill. They may, for example, trade knowledge for extended search where many cues could be considered (Johnson 1988; Charness 1991). Thus, accumulation of a large knowledge-base allows experts to select the key features of the problem, thereby reducing the number of variables chosen for consideration. An illustrative case of expert expediency was reported by Lewandowsky and Kirsner (2000), who asked experienced wildfire commanders to predict the spread of simulated wildfires. The spread of wildfires is primarily determined by two physical variables: fires tend to spread with the wind and uphill. It follows that with light downhill winds, the outcome depends on the relative strengths of the competing predictors. If the wind is sufficiently strong, the fire spreads downhill with the wind, whereas if the wind is too light, the fire spreads uphill against the wind. Lewandowsky and Kirsner found that (with an intriguing exception that we discuss in a later section) experts completely ignored the slope and based their predictions entirely on the wind. While this gave rise to correct predictions in most circumstances, any fire in which light winds were overridden by a strong slope was systematically mis-predicted.

Mediocrity

Finally, imperfect expert performance has also been associated with situations in which probabilistic cues must be used to predict uncertain outcomes. For example, when predicting the likely success of applicants to medical school from their prior record (e.g., grades, letters of recommendation), expert accuracy is often inferior to that achieved by simple linear regression models, and only slightly superior to that of novices (Johnson 1988; Camerer & Johnson 1991). Most reports of this expert "mediocrity" have relied on domains in which there are no unequivocally correct rules but only sets of more or less accurate heuristics (Johnson 1988), which human experts have difficulty applying and combining in the correct statistical manner. In consequence, performance in those domains can be optimized by forming weighted linear combinations of probabilistic cues, a process embodied in linear regression but apparently difficult to achieve by humans (Camerer & Johnson 1991). To circumvent those difficulties, human experts use a variety of alternative combinatorial strategies. One of them, known as configural reasoning, consists of considering predictor variables in a categorical manner rather than by weighted addition. For example, a configural rule in medical diagnosis might be: "If the patient experiences headaches that have a gradual onset, with no periods of remission, and has high levels of spinal fluid protein, then diagnose a brain tumor" (Schwartz & Griffin 1986, p. 94). Configural reasoning is often observed in experts, but unlike weighted linear regression its all-or-none character renders it vulnerable to small variability in measurements (Camerer & Johnson 1991).

Adaptive Expertise

Thus far, we have limited our discussion to what some have described as "routine expertise," in contrast to what is termed "adaptive expertise" (e.g., Gott *et al.* 1993; Kimball & Holyoak 2000). Adaptive expertise has been defined as "an advanced level of problem-solving performance . . . characterized by principled representations of knowledge . . . as opposed to representations dominated by surface features" (Gott *et al.* 1993, p. 259).

Although routine and adaptive expertise are often seen as two contrasting concepts (e.g., Kimball & Holyoak 2000), we are reluctant to accept this contrast for a variety of reasons. First, we are not aware of an independent criterion that identifies a particular expert, or a particular domain of expertise, as adaptive. Instead, expertise appears to be considered adaptive whenever it transfers well and it is considered routine whenever it does not. Second, empirical examinations of adaptive expertise converge on identification of the same, or similar, cognitive principles that are also involved in non-adaptive settings. For example, Barnett and Koslowski (2002) presented experienced restaurant managers and business consultants without any experience in the hospitality industry with problems relating to the management of hypothetical restaurants. Because the specific problems were novel to both groups of participants, Barnett and Koslowski considered them to represent "transfer" problems. Notwithstanding the lack of domain-specific expertise, the business consultants were found to outperform the restaurant managers, suggesting that the consultants were "adaptive" experts whereas the managers' expertise was more "routine." Further analysis identified the amount of prior consulting history (i.e., strategic business advisory experience) as the crucial variable underlying the performance difference. A crucial characteristic of business consulting, in turn, is the extreme breadth and variability of the problems that consultants tend to encounter. Barnett and Koslowski therefore conclude that "a possible explanation for the observed differences is . . . the wide variety of business problem-solving experience to which the consultants, but not the restaurant managers, have been exposed" (p. 260).

As we review below, variability among training instances is a known strong predictor of transfer in general. We therefore propose that adaptive expertise does not differ qualitatively from routine expertise, and that the observed differences in transfer ability are best explained within known principles of knowledge and expertise.

We now turn to an examination of those broader principles of knowledge in contexts other than expertise. This examination, in turn, provides another, more theoretical perspective on the nature of expertise.

STRUCTURE OF KNOWLEDGE

Overview

By discussing the structure of knowledge, we implicitly assume that knowledge can have a structure – that we can reasonably discuss constructs such as individual parcels of

Siegler 1998; Lovett & Schunn 1999). Reder and Ritter (1992) and Schunn *et al.* (1997) presented participants repeatedly with two-digit × two-digit multiplication problems (e.g., 43 × 19). Before responding, participants had to rapidly indicate whether they could retrieve the correct answer from memory (which they then had to report immediately) or whether they would need to compute the answer (in which case extra time was allotted). Most relevant for present purposes is the finding that across repeated presentations of a given problem, people were found to switch strategies not just once but between two and three times, and switches were separated by up to 50 per cent of all learning trials (reported in Delaney *et al.* 1998). This suggests that both forms of knowledge – retrieval and computation – continued to coexist throughout the experiment.

Prolonged coexistence of alternative knowledge has also been observed at a much larger time-scale, namely across grades in primary school (e.g., Siegler 1987; Shrager & Siegler 1998). This research showed that children approach single-digit mental arithmetic with immense cognitive variability, and that some techniques – such as counting fingers vs. retrieving the answer from memory – may coexist for several years and compete for selection whenever a problem is presented. Correspondingly, even adult performance can be characterized by an interaction between memory retrieval and alternative strategies (Griffiths & Kalish 2002). Griffiths and Kalish showed that many, but not all, systematic aspects of the pattern of errors observed in simple multiplication problems (Campbell 1994) could be explained by the similarity (and thus confusability) of the problems as predicted by a retrieval-based response strategy.

The persistence of competing knowledge structures is consonant with the suggestion that people ordinarily maintain multiple parcels of knowledge that could apply to any given situation (diSessa 1988). This suggestion has two non-trivial implications. First, it presupposes that there is a selection process that can choose among plausible alternative parcels. This selection process is presumably based on the structural and perceptual similarities of the current situation with those stored in memory (Gentner 1989). Second, if the ordinary state of knowledge includes multiple overlapping parcels, then at least some of those parcels might contain mutually inconsistent and contradictory information. This, indeed, appears to be the case.

Knowledge Partitioning

Consider, first, an instance of contradictory knowledge that, though consolidated by experience, is at the lower end of the expertise spectrum. Tirosh and Tsamir (1996) reported inconsistencies in high school students' understanding of the concept of mathematical infinity. Depending on the surface structure of the problem presentation, the distribution of responses differed greatly: Whereas with one surface structure, 80 per cent of participants correctly identified two infinite sets as containing the same number of elements, the vast majority of the same respondents (70 per cent) gave the opposing, inconsistent answer with the other surface structure. In a related study, also involving mathematical knowledge, Even (1998) showed that few prospective secondary mathematics teachers spontaneously linked an expression to its isomorphic graphical representation, even though this linkage would have facilitated solution of the problem.

The reverse was also true: people had difficulty deriving an expression from a graphical representation of the same function. Given that subjects were highly conversant with both representations of all functions used in the study, Even's findings point to heterogeneity even in consolidated knowledge.

Contradictory elements of knowledge have also been revealed in another naturalistic domain known as "street mathematics." This research focused on people who lack formal schooling but are able to solve mathematical problems in everyday contexts, for example street vendors, fishermen, construction foremen, and cooks in Brazil (e.g., Carraher *et al.* 1985; Nunes *et al.* 1993). Notwithstanding their minimal formal schooling, the participants were highly competent at solving mathematical problems associated with their domain of expertise.

Of greatest interest here is a context manipulation involving expert cooks (Schliemann & Carraher 1993). Participants were presented with identical proportionality problems either in a pricing context ("If 2 kg of rice cost 5 cruzeiros, how much do you have to pay for 3 kg?"), or in a recipe context ("To make a cake with two cups of flour you need five spoonfuls of water; how many spoonfuls do you need for three cups of flour?"). Importantly, both problem contexts were familiar to participants and relevant to their domain of expertise. Schliemann and Carraher reasoned that social convention dictated accuracy in the pricing context, whereas estimation might be acceptable for recipes. Those expectations were confirmed. In the pricing context, subjects used a variety of identifiable mathematical strategies in preference to estimation, with the result that accuracy was in excess of 90 per cent. In the recipe context, by contrast, accuracy was dramatically lower (20 per cent) and half of the responses given were based on estimation.

In the preceding cases, contradictory performance arose between variants of problems that differed not only according to the context in which they were presented (e.g., their cover story), but also their surface structure. An even purer instance of contradiction, involving reasoning about materially identical problems that differed only in an irrelevant context, was observed in the study by Lewandowsky and Kirsner (2000) mentioned earlier. Lewandowsky and Kirsner asked experienced wildfire commanders to predict the spread of simulated wildfires. The experts' predictions were found to depend on an additional variable, the physically irrelevant problem context. When a fire was presented as one that had to be brought under control, experts nearly always expected it to spread with the wind. When an identical fire was presented as a "back burn," experts predicted the reverse, namely that the fire would spread uphill and into the wind. Back burns are fires that are lit by firefighters in the path of an advancing to-be-controlled fire to starve it of fuel; back burns obey the same laws of physics as any other fire, in the same way that apples and oranges both obey the laws of gravity.

Before presenting an explanatory framework for these results, it is essential to differentiate them from conventional context effects, such as those reviewed earlier which underscored the specificity of expertise. Four attributes of the Lewandowsky and Kirsner study are relevant in this regard: (1) The nature of the problem and its surface structure arguably did not differ between contexts. That is, unlike the conventional context effects in expertise, the problem was no more typical of the domain in one context than the other. (2) By implication, unlike the related study by Schliemann and Carraher (1993), the change in context was a minimal alteration of a verbal label that accompanied presentation of a problem. (3) Both domain-relevant contexts were part of the training regime of the experts and both regularly occurred in the field. (4) The context shift resulted not only in a reduction of performance – as, for example, observed with chess masters' memory of random board configurations – but in a qualitative reversal of the response. That is, the same problem yielded two mutually exclusive and contradictory predictions, each of which was consistent with application of a domain-relevant predictor variable.

These attributes are sufficiently unique to warrant the assertion that knowledge, even within a well-learned domain, may exhibit little homogeneity. Indeed, it appears that experts may sometimes, perhaps often, have knowledge that is overlapping and contradictory. As we observed earlier, overlapping knowledge parcels are indicative of fragmented knowledge structures, and fragmentation has been assumed to be the norm for naïve theories (diSessa *et al.* 2004). Lewandowsky and Kirsner (2000) suggested that the fragmentation observed in experts be considered an example of knowledge partitioning, caused by associative learning and thus a natural consequence of acquiring expertise.

Lewandowsky *et al.* (2002) proposed that associative learning produces knowledge partitioning in essentially the following way. Early in learning, when few cases are known, the learner acquires information rapidly about the few available cases. As learning continues, the most effective strategy to deal with new problems that are similar to the learned cases is to use the initially learned information. Thus, it is effective for learners to protect their old knowledge and use it whenever it is applicable. People achieve this protection through rapid shifts in attention (Kalish *et al.* 2004). This process of learning new cases when necessary and deflecting change from old cases creates knowledge parcels that may contain contradictory information. So long as the stored cases do not overlap, this is not a problem for the learner, and so the associative theory predicts that partitioning is only sustainable when such conflict does not routinely occur. In the firefighting example, this may indeed have been the case as wildfires tended (in the experts' experience) to occur during high-wind periods and back burns tended to be encountered (or set) primarily when winds were light.

Our discussion of knowledge "parcels" is not to give the impression that knowledge representations are necessarily static. On the contrary, there is evidence that knowledge, specifically conceptual knowledge, is not static and may be created or altered "on the fly." For example, knowledge assembly theory (Hayes-Roth 1977) posits that repeated activation of the same components leads to the unitization of these components into a configuration which is then activated as a single, integrated entity. As another example, Barsalou's (1983) work with ad hoc categories has demonstrated that highlighting or making salient a particular goal can alter one's judgment about an item's category membership, its typicality, and the activation of other related items (Barsalou 1982, 1983, 1985). More recently, Barsalou (1999) has taken the notion of "on the fly" recruitment of knowledge even further, by suggesting that knowledge is fundamentally linked to physical experience. According to his perceptual symbols theory, knowledge of a concept is represented as a modality-specific "simulation" of one's physical experience with that concept. For example, the sweetness of a strawberry is represented by "simulating" (or imagining) its taste. Knowledge is thus fragmented according to modalities, of which Barsalou identifies six: vision, audition, taste, smell, touch, and action (Pecher *et al.* 2004). Which of these is activated for simulation depends on the context in which the concept is encountered (Pecher *et al.* 2004), thus further underscoring the dynamic – and fractionated – nature of knowledge representations within this framework.

Given the ready occurrence of partitioning and fragmentation, the apparent integration of knowledge in the expert may now appear all the more remarkable. However, close examination of the way experts apply their knowledge suggests that this appearance is at least partially an illusion. We have suggested that knowledge is frequently accessible only from an associated context, or, equivalently, that knowledge is often represented at a grain size that is smaller than the domain the knowledge ought to (in a normative sense) cover. One measure of this grain size is the ease of transfer; problems within a knowledge parcel's domain should see transfer, whereas knowledge should be used with more difficulty on problems outside the parcel's boundaries. In the next section, we take up this issue and evaluate the integration of knowledge with respect to transfer.

TRANSFER OF KNOWLEDGE

The use of existing knowledge in new situations, known as transfer, is perhaps the most important test of one's current knowledge structures. Transfer necessarily involves linking or mapping from what is known to a new or novel situation (Holland *et al.* 1986). This mapping entails a tradeoff between expediency, which requires the rapid application of knowledge, and efficiency, which requires the selective application of only those cognitive resources that are necessary for the task (Besnard & Cacitti 2005). Inherent in this tradeoff is the potential for transfer to fail.

Failure of transfer can have drastic consequences in an applied setting. Besnard and Cacitti (2005) described an industrial accident at a French steel factory, where the installation and use of new machinery among several older machines resulted in the death of a factory worker. The worker was operating a thread-drawing machine, a device used to reduce the diameter of a metal thread by gradually increasing its tension. The output of this machine is wound tightly onto a drum and held in place by a set of pressing wheels controlled by the operator. On the new machine, the two key buttons controlling the opening and closing of the pressing wheels were swapped with respect to the older machines. The experienced operator mistakenly opened the pressing wheels on the new machine at a time when the metal thread was tightly wound, causing the thread to uncoil violently and resulting in the death of the worker. Prior experience with the old machines led the worker to transfer an existing skill to a situation that required similar skills, but applied in different manner, with deadly results.

This is not to conclude that successful transfer is impossible or rare; we have already seen that experts are extremely adept at transferring their knowledge within their domain of expertise. There is also evidence for successful within-domain transfer (also called "near" transfer) among novices. For example, having learned a specific rule to categorize stimuli, people are able quickly to learn to categorize novel stimuli that share the same rule but are instantiated by different dimensions (Shepard *et al.* 1961).

However, as we show later, the extent of transfer between tasks often falls short of what intuition might lead one to expect. For example, in the domain of artificial grammar learning, transfer is much better if the surface structure of the training set remains the same during the test phase (Brooks & Vokey 1991; Gomez *et al.* 2000). Slight contextual changes (e.g., replacing colors with color names; Dienes & Altmann 1998) can reduce or eliminate transfer altogether.

We now examine the conditions that determine whether or not transfer is successful. We focus on cognitive factors and do not consider variables that are beyond the scope of this chapter, such as organizational factors (e.g., perceived support; Flint 2003), characteristics of the individual (e.g., IQ; Ceci & Ruiz 1993; Ceci *et al.* 1999); motivation

(Bereby-Meyer & Kaplan 2005), or social factors like mentoring or supervisor support (e.g., Cromwell & Kolb 2004).

Similarity and Transfer

For transfer to occur, people must necessarily *perceive* two tasks as being similar. The emphasis on perception is crucial, because transfer depends primarily on the perceiver's psychological processing rather than objective measurements of the tasks involved. We consider four factors that are known to affect the perception of similarity.

Perceived Similarity: Structure vs. Surface

Perhaps the most important differentiation between forms of similarity involves the distinction between "deep" structural similarity and "surface" similarity, which comprise two potentially independent means of describing the relations between two situations or objects. For example, two fables that involve completely different sets of characters (and hence share little surface similarity) may nonetheless make the same moral point (thus having identical deep structure). Conversely, two fairy tales may involve the same set of characters but provide completely different messages. The latter situation can be particularly harmful because when surface similarity lures people into attempting transfer between tasks that are structurally dissimilar, negative transfer may result (Hershey & Walsh 2000). For example, a novice attempting to understand the game of cricket might mistakenly apply his or her knowledge of American baseball because a bat and a ball are used in both games. This attempt at transfer is fatal because the deep structure of cricket – which is sufficiently grave and complex to be summarized not by mere rules but by "laws" – deviates considerably from the comparatively simple deep structure of baseball.

Conversely, a change in cover story or surface presentation can reduce transfer, notwithstanding deep structural identity between the two tasks. For example, in a now classic study, Gick and Holyoak (1980, 1983) taught participants to solve a problem involving the storming of a fortress surrounded by a minefield, in which the key to successful conquest was to send numerous platoons from all directions simultaneously which then converged onto the target. After learning this solution, people were unable to apply that knowledge to an isomorphic radiation convergence problem, in which removal of a tumor without damaging the surrounding tissue could be achieved only by applying weak intersecting radiation from all directions (Gick & Holyoak 1980, 1983). Hence, while transfer to similar problems is possible, a surprisingly small change in context or cover story can eliminate that transfer quite readily.

Similarity and Expertise

The distinction between surface and structural similarity is particularly relevant when comparing the transfer abilities of novices and experts. One of the primary differences between expert and novice problem-solving is that experts focus on the deep structure of the task (e.g., Chi *et al.* 1981; Dunbar 1995). Accordingly, experts will attempt transfer if two tasks share structural similarities even if their surface similarity is low. As we have seen, mathematical expertise predicts the ease with which people transfer between superficially different word problems with the same structure (Novick 1988). Novices, by contrast, will attempt transfer only if there are salient surface similarities between the source and the target, despite the fact that the same solution process is needed (Cormier 1987). For example, in the earlier convergence problems, novices, after being trained in the radiation context, are more likely to attempt transfer to a problem that is similar at the surface, because it involves x-rays, rather than to a structurally similar problem that is less similar at the surface because it involve ultrasound (Holyoak & Koh 1987).

Conceptual vs. Structural Similarity

Dixon and colleagues (Dixon & Gabrys 1991; Dixon *et al.* 1997) differentiate between conceptual similarity, which is based on information about why a procedure works or how a device operates and allows the application of conceptually similar problem-solving steps, and structural similarity, which is similarity based on the steps that must be performed to solve a problem and allows for the application of identical procedural steps. In their studies, participants were initially trained to operate a complex device through a series of sub-goals comprised of a number of different steps (e.g., for an airplane device, the sub-goal "Engine Start Up" might consist of the steps "engine 1," "engine 2," followed by "ignition"). Consequently, conceptual similarity (which, in this example, is isomorphic to superficial similarity) could be manipulated independently of structural similarity by changing the order of the sub-goals but maintaining the same order of steps within each sub-goal.

Following initial training with one device, transfer to a second, superficially unrelated device (e.g., an alarm system) was impaired compared to transfer to a superficially related device (e.g., an airplane with differently labeled controls) when the order of sub-goals was changed. Transfer was poorer still when the order of steps within the sub-goals was changed, compared to when the steps were unchanged, regardless of whether the sub-goal order was also altered. Hence, the order of the steps comprising the deep structure was not as important to maintaining acceptable transfer as the order of the routines within these steps (Dixon *et al.* 1997).

Similarity and Context

The context in which a judgment is made can greatly alter perceived similarity. For example, changing the context during problem-solving can affect encoding of the problem, which in turn can either facilitate or deter successful transfer. In a "pass-along" task, in which blocks of various sizes are shifted within a frame from an initial configuration to a known goal-state, completion of a difficult problem becomes easier if an analogy can be identified between the difficult problem and an easier one (Zamani & Richard 2000). For instance, in the difficult problem, two rectangular blocks are encoded as either two halves of a square or as two separate rectangles depending on whether an easier problem with an identical solution, but with a square block instead of two rectangular blocks, is shown first or not at all (Zamani & Richard 2000). Furthermore, for the difficult problem to be used as an analogue for an even harder problem, the problems must share the same goal-state. Recognition of similar goal-states allows for the application of the same solution strategies for both problems (Zamani & Richard 2000). If the two difficult problems have different goal-states, and hence different solution procedures, knowledge is not transferred from one to the other (Zamani & Richard 2000).

The context of training can also affect the judgment of similarity between problems. For example, in category learning, if people are trained to associate a context cue with a particular region of category space, then despite the fact that the context cue does not predict category membership, people will use context to gate their responses and will treat an *identical* stimulus differently in two different contexts (Yang & Lewandowsky 2003, 2004; see also the earlier discussion of Lewandowsky and Kirsner 2000).

Failures of Transfer

When people fail to perceive the similarity between what they know and a novel task, transfer does not occur. People may fail to note relevant isomorphisms for a variety of reasons.

Context Specificity

Transfer fails more readily if the first task is more context-specific than the second one. For example, if people are initially trained to answer physics problems and are then tested with more general algebra problems, which nonetheless involve the same concepts, transfer is poor (Bassok & Holyoak 1989). Conversely, if people are initially trained with algebra problems, transfer to physics problems remains intact (Bassok & Holyoak 1989).

Extent of Learning

Failures of transfer can stem from failures of learning, for example when training involves only a limited number of problems (see, e.g., Catrambone & Holyoak 1990; Loewenstein *et al.* 1999). Likewise, if training involves only prototypical examples, then transfer will only be possible for target problems that are suitably similar to the prototypes (Elio & Anderson 1984; see also Gick & Holyoak 1987). The inverse of this statement, that transfer is greater if training involves a broader range of problems, is also true and we have already noted that it may underlie apparent instances of "adaptive" expertise.

Accordingly, techniques that improve learning have also been shown to improve subsequent transfer (Aleven & Koedinger 2002). For instance, compared to rote learning, transfer is better after learning that required participants to generate solutions to problems (Flint 2003) or test hypotheses (Burns & Vollmeyer 2002). Similarly, training which emphasizes different objectives can facilitate the transfer of different skills (Bitan & Karni 2003). For example, when trained to recognize nonsense words (e.g., PON, LOP) composed of a Morse code-like script (e.g., PON = |^**|^|^, LOP = *^|*||^*), people were able to transfer knowledge of the specific "letters" (i.e., they could recognize novel "words" composed of the letters used at training) only when initially instructed on how to decode the script. When people were trained on non-alphabetical words (i.e., the Morse code-like script did not consistently map to specific letters), they were unable to transfer any of the learning to novel words (Bitan & Karni 2003). Importantly, people who learned how to decode the script performed much worse on old words comprised of new symbols than people trained on non-alphabetical words. The demonstration of both positive and negative transfer within the same condition illustrates the differential effects of training with different objectives.

Negative Transfer

Negative transfer is said to occur when performance on a novel task following training is poorer than it would have been without any prior training. Although typically not accompanied by the fatal consequences that struck the unfortunate French steel worker, negative transfer can occur whenever surface similarities mask structural differences. For example, Woltz *et al.* (2000) trained subjects in a complex number reduction task in which the rule for reduction of a larger number to a smaller number was determined by the relationship between the first two digits of the larger number (e.g., if the two digits differ by a value of two, replace those two digits with the midpoint between the two digits, or if two digits are equal remove the first digit). Participants were initially trained solely on stimuli that required the application of one sequence of rules. For example, the numbers 3565 and 9767 both require application of the "midpoint" rule for the first and second reduction and the "equal" rule for the final reduction (e.g., 3565 becomes 465, 465 becomes 55, and 55 becomes 5). Subjects produced errors when new sequences were presented at transfer that initially resembled training sequences but that required the application of a different rule for the last reduction (e.g., 3567 requires application of the midpoint rule twice to reduce the number to 57, but the final reduction is different from the training stimuli). Hence, for these "garden path" stimuli, the initial similarity in rule application masked the necessity of a different final rule and thus resulted in negative transfer compared to stimuli which were either completely dissimilarity or highly similar to the training stimuli.

Moreover, when task complexity was increased (e.g., by increasing the number of possible rules), increased training led not only to increased positive transfer for novel sequences (i.e., faster response latencies), but also to an increase in undetected errors for new "garden path" sequences (Woltz *et al.* 2000, Experiment 2). In this case, as in the case of the French factory worker, increased training and expertise led to enhanced negative transfer.

These instances of negative transfer, which usually occur spontaneously, have often been referred to as "strong-but-wrong" errors (Norman 1981). Reason (1990) linked strong-but-wrong errors to a process of frequency gambling and similarity matching. That is, if a process has been successful in the past, people are more likely to continue applying that same process if it appears similar to the target task (see also Lovett & Anderson 1996). Negative transfer is distinct from other forms of error, such as simply computing an incorrect response from a correct algorithm, because the performance decrement involves the application of prior knowledge or training in a situation that does not require it. In Woltz *et al.*'s (2000) number-reduction task, we can distinguish between negative transfer and calculation error because errors on "garden path" problems were committed with the same speed as correct responses to training problems. By contrast, latencies for novel regular transfer sequences were longer than for training sequences. One implication of negative transfer is that the resultant "strong-but-wrong" errors go unnoticed and thus escape the possibility of discovery and correction (Woltz *et al.* 2000).

Increasing Positive Transfer

On the basis of the preceding discussion, one might be tempted to assume that simply informing people about the similarity between two tasks might enhance transfer. Contrary to that intuition, it turns out that transfer is facilitated if the process of discovering and extracting similarities between tasks, particularly similarities between relational information, is self-initiated (Dixon & Dohn 2003). In their study, people were given problems consisting of different numbers of alternating, connected beams, each supported by a fulcrum, which acted in a seesaw fashion with the action of the first beam affecting the action of the second, and so forth. People were told in which direction the first beam was moving and were asked to predict the direction of movement of the final beam. Participants were either told to classify each beam as an *up* beam or a *down* beam in alternation or were given no instructions. Half of the people who did not receive instructions quickly discovered the up/down strategy, while all of the people given the up/down instructions used that strategy exclusively. When shown new problems involving gear systems, those people who received no instructions and nonetheless discovered the up/down strategy also quickly discovered an analogue of the up/down strategy and applied it to the gear problems. The people who received instructions, however, fell back to a less efficient tracing strategy. Hence, people demonstrated better transfer when allowed to discover more efficient strategies for themselves, a process labeled "redescription" by Dixon and Dohn (2003). It follows that training regimes which allow for self-discovery should lead to more effective transfer, although this notion has yet to be tested.

CONCLUSIONS

We have touched on a variety of issues in research on knowledge and expertise. At the risk of glib oversimplification, we propose to condense our review to the claim that knowledge is best understood by rejecting its existence as a coherent concept: Instead of talking about "knowledge," we prefer to talk about a *set of highly context-specific learned responses*. Adopting this perspective appears to be particularly useful for the practitioner because it automatically accommodates the following major limitations and shortcomings of knowledge and expertise:

1. Expertise is highly domain-specific and brittle. Accordingly, expert performance can suffer dramatically if the deep structure of a task is altered, even if only slightly. In an applied setting, any alteration of an expert's domain is likely to result in decreased performance. This decrease is likely to be more severe if the deep structure of the task,

such as the number and sequence of steps involved in performing a task or a task rule, is altered. It follows that practitioners should ensure that the steps and rules in the current task closely match the steps and rules in the expert's domain of expertise.

2. While expertise transfers well within a domain, little or no transfer can be expected outside a domain. In general, transfer often falls short of what intuition might lead one to expect because it occurs only if people correctly *perceive* two tasks to be similar. In practice, it is crucial that practitioners wanting to ensure positive transfer maximize the likelihood of two tasks being perceived similarly. A pertinent example of this is the release of software updates. If the updated software changes the settings so that different labels are given to identical function, the user's performance will suffer, until he or she is well practiced with the new version.
3. Negative transfer can result, with potentially grievous consequences, if people are misled by the surface similarity between two tasks with very different deep structures. The resulting "strong-but-wrong" errors often escape detection and correction. In practice, this means that tasks which require different operations should be given different surface features to minimize negative transfer. This is particularly true when two tasks with different operations are required in close temporal or spatial proximity.
4. Knowledge frequently reveals itself to be fragmented and partitioned, with people exhibiting quite contradictory behavior on an otherwise identical problem in different contexts. Even experts, who are typically assumed to have a highly integrated knowledge base, may exhibit surprisingly contradictory behavior. In response, practitioners should ensure that training occurs in a variety of contexts, and should make trainees aware of the potential hazards of partitioned knowledge.
5. Experts also often exhibit expediency; that is, the tendency to master a task by focusing on a few key variables at the expense of ignoring other, and sometimes crucial, information. One way to tackle this issue is to highlight the importance of considering all information during training. If training highlights the pitfalls of ignoring relevant information, perhaps by designing a task where ignoring relevant information leads to failure, then the learner will hopefully be more aware of this shortcoming of expertise. It has also been suggested that providing the opportunity for learning by self-discovery can result in more flexible knowledge that is readily transferred.

Although the list of limitations and shortcomings is perhaps sobering, it need not detract from the stunning achievements that people are capable of. Whether considered "knowledge" or a "set of context-specific responses," abilities such as the retention of 30000 digits of π or 50000 chess patterns, or the ability safely to operate a machine as complex as an Airbus A380, are remarkable by any criterion.

NOTE

1 By the same token, research has identified domains in which exceptional performance cannot be detected. For example, people who claim to be speed readers have been found to exhibit remarkable dexterity at turning pages without displaying any comprehension of the text (Homa 1983). Those "domains" are commonly excluded from consideration in research on expertise.

REFERENCES

Aleven, V. A. W. M. M. & Koedinger, K. R. (2002). An effective metacognitive strategy: learning by doing and explaining with a computer-based Cognitive Tutor. *Cognitive Science, 26*, 147–179.

Anderson, J. R. (1990). *The Adaptive Character of Thought.* Hillsdale, NJ: Lawrence Erlbaum Associates.

Bar, M. & Ullman, S. (1996). Spatial context in recognition. *Perception, 25*, 343–352.

Barnett, S. M. & Koslowski, B. (2002). Adaptive expertise: effects of type of experience and the level of theoretical understanding it generates. *Thinking and Reasoning, 8*, 237–267.

Barsalou, L. W. (1982). Context-independent and context-dependent information in concepts. *Memory & Cognition, 10*, 82–93.

Barsalou, L. W. (1983). Ad hoc categories. *Memory & Cognition, 11*, 211–227.

Barsalou, L. W. (1985). Ideals, central tendency, and frequency of instantiation as determinants of graded structure in categories. *Journal of Experimental Psychology: Learning, Memory, and Cognition, 11*, 629–654.

Barsalou, L. W. (1999). Perceptua. Symbol systems. *Behavioral and Brain Sciences, 22*, 577–660.

Barsalou, L. W. & Hale, C. R. (1993). Components of conceptual representation: from feature lists to recursive frames. In I. Van Mechelen, J. Hampton, R. S. Michalski & P. Theuns (eds.), *Categories and Concepts: Theoretical Views and Inductive Data Analysis* (pp. 97–144). San Diego, CA: Academic Press.

Bassok, M. & Holyoak, K. J. (1989). Interdomain transfer between isomorphic topics in algebra and physics. *Journal of Experimental Psychology: Learning, Memory & Cognition, 15*, 153–166.

Bassok, M. & Holyoak, K. J. (1993). Pragmatic knowledge and conceptual structure: determinants of transfer between quantitative domains. In D. K. Detterman & R. J. Sternberg (eds.), *Transfer on Trial: Intelligence, Cognition, and Instruction.* Norwood, NJ: Ablex Publishing Corporation.

Bédard, J. & Chi, M. T. H. (1992). Expertise. *Current Directions in Psychological Science, 1*, 135–139.

Bellenkes, A. H., Wickens, C. D. & Kramer, A. F. (1997). Visual scanning and pilot expertise: the role of attentional flexibility and mental model development. *Aviation, Space & Environmental Medicine, 68*, 569–579.

Bereby-Meyer, Y. & Kaplan, A. (2005). Motivational influences on transfer of problem-solving strategies. *Contemporary Educational Psychology, 30*, 1–22.

Berg, G. (1992). Representational adequacy and the case for a hybrid connectionist/marker-parsing model. In R. G. Reilly & N. E. Sharkey (eds.), *Connectionist Approaches to Natural Language Processing* (pp. 253–272). Hillsdale, NJ: Lawrence Erlbaum Associates.

Besnard, D. & Cacitti, L. (2005). Interface changes causing accidents: an empirical study of negative transfer. *International Journal of Human–Computer Studies, 62*, 105–125.

Bitan, T. & Karni, A. (2003). Alphabetical knowledge from whole words training: effects of explicit instruction and implicit experience on learning script segmentation. *Cognitive Brain Research, 16*, 323–337.

Brooks, L. R. & Vokey, J. R. (1991). Abstract analogies and abstracted grammars: comments on Reber (1989) and Mathews *et al.* (1989). *Journal of Experimental Psychology: General, 120*, 316–323.

Burns, B. D. & Vollmeyer, R. (2002). Goal specificity effects on hypothesis testing in problem solving. *The Quarterly Journal of Experimental Psychology, 55*, 241–261.

Camerer, C. F. & Johnson, E. J. (1991). The process-performance paradox in expert judgment: how can experts know so much and predict so badly? In K. A. Ericsson & J. Smith (eds.), *Towards a General Theory of Expertise: Prospects and Limits* (pp. 195–217). New York: Cambridge University Press.

Campbell, J. I. D. (1994). Architectures for numerical cognition. *Cognition, 53*, 1–44.

Carraher, T. N., Carraher, D. W. & Schliemann, A. D. (1985). Mathematics in the streets and in schools. *British Journal of Developmental Psychology, 3*, 21–29.

Catrambone, R. & Holyoak, K. J. (1990). Learning subgoals and methods for solving probability problems. *Memory & Cognition*, *18*, 593–603.
Ceci, S. J., Rosenblum, T. B. & DeBruyn, E. (1999). Laboratory versus field approaches to cognition. In R. J. Sternberg (ed.), *The Nature of Cognition* (pp. 385–408). Cambridge, MA: MIT Press.
Ceci, S. J. & Ruiz, A. (1993). Transfer, abstractness, and intelligence. In D. K. Detterman & R. J. Sternberg (eds.), *Transfer on Trial: Intelligence, Cognition, and Instruction* (pp. 168–191). Norwood, NJ: Ablex.
Charness, N. (1991). Expertise in chess: the balance between knowledge and search. In K. A. Ericsson & J. Smith (eds.), *Toward a General Theory of Expertise: Prospects and Limits* (pp. 39–63). New York: Cambridge University Press.
Charness, N., Krampe, R. T. & Mayr, U. (1996). The role of practice and coaching in entrepreneurial skill domains: an international comparison of life-span chess skill acquisition. In K. A. Ericsson (ed.), *The Road to Excellence: The Acquisition of Expert Performance in the Arts, Sciences, Sports, and Games* (pp. 51–80). Mahwah, NJ: Lawrence Erlbaum Associates.
Charness, N. & Schultetus, R. S. (1999). Knowledge and expertise. In F. T. Durso, R. S. Nickerson, R. W. Schvaneveldt *et al.* (eds.), *Handbook of Applied Cognition* (pp. 57–81). Chichester: John Wiley & Sons.
Chase, W. G. & Ericsson, K. A. (1981). Skilled memory. In J. R. Anderson (ed.), *Cognitive Skills and Their Acquisition* (pp. 141–189). Hillsdale, NJ: Lawrence Erlbaum Associates.
Chase, W. G. & Simon, H. A. (1973). Perception in chess. *Cognitive Psychology*, *4*, 55–81.
Chi, M. T. H., Feltovich, P. J. & Glaser, R. (1981). Categorization and representation of physics problems by experts and novices. *Cognitive Science*, *5*, 121–152.
Cormier, S. M. (1987). The structural process underlying transfer of training. In S. M. Cormier & J. D. Hagman (eds.), *Transfer of Learning: Contemporary Research and Applications* (pp. 151–181). San Diego, CA: Academic Press, Inc.
Cromwell, S. E. & Kolb, J. A. (2004). An examination of work-environment support factors affecting transfer of supervisory skills training to the workplace. *Human Resource Development Quarterly*, *15*, 449–471.
Delaney, P. F., Reder, L. M., Staszewski, J. J. & Ritter, F. E. (1998). The strategy specific nature of improvement: the power law applies by strategy within task. *Psychological Science*, *9*(1), 1–8.
Delisle, S., Moulin, B. & Copeck, T. (2003). Surface-marker-based dialog modeling: a progress report on the MAREDI project. *Natural Language Engineering*, *9*, 325–363.
Dienes, Z. & Altmann, G. (1998). Transfer of implicit knowledge across domains: how implicit and how abstract? In D. Berry (ed.), *How Implicit is Implicit Learning?* (pp. 107–123). London: Oxford University Press.
diSessa, A. A. (1988). Knowledge in pieces. In G. Forman & P. B. Pufall (eds.), *Constructivism in the Computer Age. The Jean Piaget Symposium Series* (pp. 49–70). Hillsdale, NJ: Lawrence Erlbaum Associates.
diSessa, A. A., Gillespie, N. M. & Esterly, J. B. (2004). Coherence versus fragmentation in the development of the concept of force. *Cognitive Science*, *28*, 843–900.
Dixon, J. A. & Dohn, M. C. (2003). Redescription disembeds relations: evidence from relational transfer and use in problem solving. *Memory & Cognition*, *31*, 1082–1093.
Dixon, P. & Gabrys, G. (1991). Learning to operate complex devices: effects of conceptual and operational similarity. *Human Factors*, *33*, 103–120.
Dixon, P., Zimmerman, C. & Nearey, S. (1997). Prior experience and complex procedures. *Memory & Cognition*, *25*, 381–394.
Dunbar, K. (1995). How scientists really reason: scientific reasoning in real-world laboratories. In R. J. Sternberg & J. E. Davidson (eds.), *The Nature of Insight* (pp. 365–395). Cambridge, MA: MIT Press.
Elio, R. & Anderson, J. R. (1984). The effects of information order and learning mode on schema abstraction. *Memory & Cognition*, *12*, 20–30.
Ericsson, K. A. (1996). The acquisition of expert performance: an introduction to some of the issues. In K. A. Ericsson (ed.), *The Road to Excellence: The Acquisition of Expert Performance in the Arts and Sciences, Sports, and Games* (pp. 1–50). Mahwah, NJ: Lawrence Erlbaum Associates.

Ericsson, K. A. (2003). Memorizers are made, not born. *Trends in Cognitive Science, 7,* 233–235.
Ericsson, K. A. (2005). Recent advances in expertise research: a commentary on the contributions to the special issue. *Applied Cognitive Psychology, 19,* 233–241.
Ericsson, K. A., Chase, W. G. & Faloon, S. (1980). Acquisition of a memory skill. *Science, 208,* 1181–1182.
Ericsson, K. A., Delaney, P. F., Weaver, G. A. & Mahadevan, S. (2004). Uncovering the structure of a memorist's superior "basic" memory capacity. *Cognitive Psychology, 49,* 191–237.
Ericsson, K. A., Krampe, R. T. & Tesch-Römer, C. (1993). The role of deliberate practice in the acquisition of expert performance. *Psychological Review, 100,* 363–406.
Ericsson, K. A. & Lehmann, A. C. (1996). Expert and exceptional performance: evidence of maximal adaptation to task. *Annual Review of Psychology, 47,* 273–305.
Ericsson, K. A. & Polson, P. G. (1988). An experimental analysis of the mechanisms of a memory skill. *Journal of Experimental Psychology: Learning, Memory and Cognition, 14,* 305–316.
Even, R. (1998). Factors involved in linking representations of functions. *Journal of Mathematical Behavior, 17,* 105–121.
Flint, W. (2003). Transfer of learning: evaluating workplace transfer of training techniques. In J. A. Chambers (ed.), *Selected Papers from the 14th International Conference on College Teaching and Learning* (pp. 93–101). Jacksonville, FL: Florida Community College.
Frensch, P. A. & Sternberg, R. J. (1989). Expertise and intelligent thinking: when is it worse to know better? In R. J. Sternberg (ed.), *Advances in the Psychology of Human Intelligence* (Vol. 5, pp. 157–188). Hillsdale, NJ: Lawrence Erlbaum Associates.
Freund, H. J. (1983). Motor unit and muscle activity in voluntary motor control. *Physiological Review, 63,* 387–436.
Gentner, D. (1989). The mechanisms of analogical learning. In S. Vosniadou & A. Ortony (eds.), *Similarity and Analogical Reasoning* (pp. 199–241). London: Cambridge University Press.
Gick, M. L. & Holyoak, K. J. (1980). Analogical problem solving. *Cognitive Psychology, 12,* 306–355.
Gick, M. L. & Holyoak, K. J. (1983). Schema induction and analogical transfer. *Cognitive Psychology, 15,* 1–38.
Gick, M. L. & Holyoak, K. J. (1987). The cognitive basis of knowledge transfer. In S. M. Cormier & J. D. Hagman (eds.), *Transfer of Learning: Contemporary Research and Applications* (pp. 9–46). San Diego, CA: Academic Press.
Glaser, R. (1996). Changing the agency for learning: acquiring expert performance. In K. A. Ericsson (ed.), *The Road to Excellence: The Acquisition of Expert Performance in the Arts and Sciences, Sports, and Games* (pp. 303–311). Mahwah, NJ: Lawrence Erlbaum Associates.
Gobet, F. & Simon, H. A. (1996). The roles of recognition processes and look-ahead search in time-constrained expert problem solving: evidence from grandmaster level chess. *Psychological Science, 7,* 52–55.
Gobet, F. & Waters, A. J. (2003). The role of constraints in xpert memory. *Journal of Experimental Psychology: Learning, Memory & Cognition,* 29, 1082–1094.
Gomez, R. L., Gerken, L. & Schevaneveldt, R. W. (2000). The basis of transfer in artificial grammar learning. *Memory & Cognition, 28,* 253–263.
Gott, S. P., Hall, E. P., Pokorny, R. A. *et al.* (1993). A naturalistic study of transfer: adaptive expertise in technical domains. In D. K. Detterman & R. J. Sternberg (eds.), *Transfer on Trial: Intelligence, Cognition and Instruction* (pp. 258–288). Norwood, NJ: Ablex.
Griffiths, T. L. & Kalish, M. (2002). A multidimensional scaling approach to mental multiplication. *Memory and Cognition, 30,* 97–106.
Griffiths, T. L. & Steyvers, M. (2002). A probabilistic approach to semantic representation. In *Proceedings of the Twenty-Fourth Annual Conference of Cognitive Science Society.* George Mason University, Fairfax, VA.
de Groot, A. D. (1965). *Thought and Choice in Chess.* The Hague: Mouton.
Hayes-Roth, B. (1977). Evolution of cognitive structures and processes. *Psychological Review, 84,* 260–278.
Hershey, D. A. & Walsh, D. A. (2000). Knowledge versus experience in financial problem solving. *Current Psychology: Developmental, Learning & Personality, 19,* 261–291.

Hoffman, T. (1999). Probabilistic latent semantic analysis. In K. B. Laskey & H. Prade (eds.), *UAI '99: Proceedings of the Fifteenth Conference on Uncertainty in Artificial Intelligence*, Stockholm, Sweden, July 30–August 1, 1999. Morgan Kaufmann.
Holland, J. H., Holyoak, K. J., Nisbett, R. E. & Thagard, P. R. (1986). *Induction: Processes of Inference, Learning, and Discovery*. Cambridge, MA: MIT Press.
Holyoak, K. J. (1991). Symbolic connectionism: toward third-generation theories of expertise. In A. Ericsson & J. Smith (eds.), *Toward a General Theory of Expertise: Prospects and Limits* (pp. 301–355). Cambridge: Cambridge University Press.
Holyoak, K. J. & Koh, K. (1987). Surface and structural similarity in analogical transfer. *Memory & Cognition, 15*, 332–340.
Homa, D. (1983). An assessment of two "extraordinary" speed-readers. *Bulletin of the Psychonomic Society, 21*, 123–126.
Johnson, E. J. (1988). Expertise and decisions under uncertainty: performance and process. In M. L. H. Chi, R. Glaser & M. J. Farr (eds.), *The Nature of Expertise* (pp. 209–228). Hillsdale, NJ: Lawrence Erlbaum Associates.
Johnson, P. E., Grazioli, S., Jamal, K. & Zualkernan, I. A. (1992). Success and failure in expert reasoning. *Journal of Organizational Behavior and Human Decision Processes, 53*, 173–203.
Kalish, M. L., Lewandowsky, S. & Kruschke, J. K. (2004). Population of linear experts: knoweldge partitioning and function learning. *Psychological Review, 111*, 1072–1099.
Keele, S. W. & Ivry, R. I. (1987). Modular analysis of timing in motor skill. In G. H. Bower (ed.), *The Psychology of Learning and Motivation* (Vol. 21, pp. 183–228). San Diego, CA: Academic Press.
Kimball, D. R. & Holyoak, K. J. (2000). Transfer and expertise. In E. Tulving & F. I. M. Craik (eds.), *The Oxford Handbook of Memory* (pp. 109–122). London: Oxford University Press.
Kintsch, W. (2000). The control of knowledge activation in discourse comprehension. In W. J. Perrig & A. Grob (eds.), *Control of Human Behavior, Mental Processes, and Consciousness: Essays in Honor of the 60th Birthday of August Flammer* (pp. 137–146). Mahwah, NJ: Lawrence Erlbaum Associates.
Kolers, P. A. (1976). Pattern analyzing memory. *Science, 191*, 1280–1281.
Landauer, T. K. & Dumais, S. T. (1997). A solution to Plato's problem: the Latent Semantic Analysis theory of acquisition, induction and representation of knowledge. *Psychological Review, 104*, 211–240.
Lange, T. E. (1992). Hybrid connectionist models: temporary bridges over the gap between the symbolic and the subsymbolic. In J. Dinsmore (ed.), *The Symbolic and Connectionist Paradigms: Closing the Gap* (pp. 237–289). Hillsdale, NJ: Lawrence Erlbaum Associates.
Lewandowsky, S., Kalish, M. & Ngang, S. K. (2002). Simplified learning in complex situations: knowledge partitioning in function learning. *Journal of Experimental Psychology: General, 131*, 163–193.
Lewandowsky, S. & Kirsner, K. (2000). Knowledge partitioning: context-dependent use of expertise. *Memory & Cognition, 28*, 295–305.
Loewenstein, J., Thompson, L. & Gentner, D. (1999). Analogical encoding facilitates knowledge transfer in negotiation. *Psychonomic Bulletin & Review, 6*, 586–597.
Lovett, M. C. & Anderson, J. R. (1996). History of success and current context in problem solving: combined influences on operator selection. *Cognitive Psychology, 31*, 168–217.
Lovett, M. C. & Schunn, C. D. (1999). Task representations, strategy variability, and base-rate neglect. *Journal of Experimental Psychology: General, 128*, 107–130.
Marchant, G., Robinson, J., Anderson, U. & Schadewald, M. (1991). Analogical transfer and expertise in legal reasoning. *Organizational Behavior & Human Decision Processes, 48*, 272–290.
Marshall, S. P. (1995). *Schemas in Problem Solving*. New York: Cambridge University Press.
Medin, D., Ross, B. H. & Markman, A. B. (2001). *Cognitive Psychology* (3rd edn). Chichester: John Wiley & Sons.
Moray, N. (1999). Mental models in theory and practice. In D. Gopher & A. Koriat (eds.), *Attention and Performance XVII: Cognitive Regulation of Performance: Interaction of Theory and Application. Attention and Performance* (pp. 223–258). Cambridge, MA: MIT Press.
Norman, D. A. (1981). Categorization of action slips. *Psychology Review, 88*, 1–15.

Norman, G. R., Brooks, L. R., Coblentz, C. K. & Babcook, C. J. (1992). The interdependence of feature and category identification in diagnostic radiology. *Memory & Cognition, 20,* 344–355.
Novick, L. R. (1988). Analogical transfer, problem similarity and expertise. *Journal of Experimental Psychology: Learning, Memory and Cognition, 14,* 510–520.
Novick, L. R. & Holyoak, K. J. (1991). Mathematical problem solving by analogy. *Journal of Experimental Psychology: Learning, Memory, and Cognition, 17,* 398–415.
Nunes, T., Schliemann, A. D. & Carraher, D. W. (1993). *Street Mathematics and School Mathematics* (pp. 77–126). New York: Cambridge University Press.
Patel, V. L., Kaufman, D. R. & Magder, S. (1996). The acquisition of medical expertise in complex dynamic decision-making environments. In A. Ericsson (ed.), *The Road to Excellence: The Acquisition of Expert Performance in the Arts and Sciences, Sports and Games* (pp. 127–165). Hillsdale, NJ: Lawrence Erlbaum Associates.
Pecher, D., Zeelenberg, R. & Barsalou, L. W. (2004). Sensorimotor simulations underlie conceptual representations: modality-specific effects of prior activation. *Psychonomic Bulletin & Review, 11,* 164–167.
Reason, J. T. (1990). *Human Error.* New York: Cambridge University Press.
Reber, P. J. & Squire, L. R. (1994). Parallel brain systems for learning with and without awareness. *Learning and Memory, 1,* 217–229.
Reder, L. M. & Ritter, F. E. (1992). What determines initial feeling of knowing? Familiarity with question terms, not with the answer. *Journal of Experimental Psychology: Learning, Memory, and Cognition, 18,* 435–451.
Richman, H. B., Staszewski, J. J. & Simon, H. A. (1995). Simulation of expert memory using EPAM IV. *Psychological Review, 102,* 305–330.
Roediger, H. L. III, Meade, M. L. & Bergman, E. T. (2001). Social contagion of memory. *Psychonomic Bulletin & Review, 8,* 365–371.
Rossano, M. J. (2003). *Evolutionary Psychology: The Science of Human Behaviour and Evolution.* Chichester: John Wiley & Sons.
Salthouse, T. A. (1984). Effects of age and skill in typing. *Journal of Experimental Psychology: General, 13,* 345–371.
Salthouse, T. A. (1991). Expertise as the circumvention of human processing limitations. In K. A. Ericsson & J. Smith (eds.), *Toward a General Theory of Expertise: Prospects and Limits* (pp. 286–300). New York: Cambridge University Press.
Santtila, P., Korpela, S. & Häkkänen, H. (2004). Expertise and decision-making in linking car crime series. *Psychology, Crime & Law, 10,* 97–112.
Schliemann, A. D. & Carraher, D. W. (1993). Proportional reasoning in and out of school. In P. Light & G. Butterworth (eds.), *Context and Cognition: Ways of Learning and Knowing* (pp. 47–73). Hillsdale, NJ: Lawrence Erlbaum Associates.
Schunn, C. D., Reder, L. M., Nhouyvanisvong, A., Richards, D. R. & Stroffolino, P. J. (1997). To calculate or not calculate: a source activation confusion (SAC) model of problem-familiarity's role in strategy selection. *Journal of Experimental Psychology: Learning, Memory & Cognition, 23,* 3–29.
Schwartz, S. & Griffin, T. (1986). Evaluating medical information. In: *Medical Thinking. The Psychology of Medical Judgment and Decision Making* (pp. 56–96). New York: Springer-Verlag.
Shanks, D. R. & Johnstone, T. (1998). Implicit knowledge in sequential learning tasks. In M. A. Stadler & P. A. Frensch (eds.), *Handbook of Implicit Learning* (pp. 533–572). Thousand Oaks, CA: Sage.
Shepard, R. N. (1987). Towards a universal law of generalization for psychological science. *Science, 237,* 1317–1323.
Shepard, R. N., Hovland, C. L. & Jenkins, H. M. (1961). Learning and memorization of classifications. *Psychological Monographs, 75,* 1–43.
Shrager, J. & Siegler, R. S. (1998). SCADS: a model of children's strategy choices and strategy discoveries. *Psychological Science, 9,* 405–410.
Siegler, R. S. (1987). Some general conclusions about children's strategy choice procedures. *International Journal of Psychology, 22,* 729–749.

Simon, H. A. & Gilmartin, K. J. (1973). A simulation of memory for chess positions. *Cognitive Psychology, 5*, 29–46.

Sims, V. K. & Mayer, R. E. (2002). Domain specificity of spatial expertise: the case of video game players. *Applied Cognitive Psychology, 16*, 97–115.

Singley, M. K. & Anderson, J. R. (1989). *Transfer of Cognitive Skill*. Cambridge, MA: Harvard University Press.

Staszewski, J. J. (1993). A theory of skilled memory. In *Proceedings of the 15th Annual Conference of the Cognitive Science Society* (pp. 971–975). Hillsdale, NJ: Lawrence Erlbaum Associates.

Sternberg, R. J. & Frensch, P. A. (1992). On being an expert: a cost–benefit analysis. In R. Hoffman (ed.), *The Cognition of Experts: Psychological Research and Empirical AI* (pp. 191–203). New York: Springer-Verlag.

Thompson, C. P., Cowan, T. M. & Frieman, J. (1993). *Memory Search by a Memorist*. Hillsdale, NJ: Lawrence Erlbaum Associates.

Tirosh, D. & Tsamir, P. (1996). The role of representations in students' intuitive thinking about infinity. *Journal of Mathematical Education in Science and Technology, 27*, 33–40.

Tuckey, M. R. & Brewer, N. (2003). How schemas affect eyewitness memory over repeated retrieval attempts. *Applied Cognitive Psychology, 17*, 785–800.

Vigliocco, G., Vinson, D. P., Lewis, W. & Garrett, M. F. (2004). Representing the meanings of object and action words: the Featural and Unitary Semantic System (FUSS) hypothesis. *Cognitive Psychology, 48*, 422–488.

Wiley, J. (1998). Expertise as mental set: the effects of domain knowledge in creative problem solving. *Memory & Cognition, 26*, 716–730.

Woltz, D. J., Gardner, M. K. & Bell, B. G. (2000). Negative transfer errors in sequential cognitive skills: strong-but-wrong sequence application. *Journal of Experimental Psychology: Learning, Memory & Cognition, 26*, 601–625.

Yang, L-X. & Lewandowsky, S. (2003). Context-gated knowledge partitioning in categorization. *Journal of Experimental Psychology: Learning, Memory, and Cognition, 29*, 563–679.

Yang, L-X. & Lewandowsky, S. (2004). Knowledge partitioning in categorization: constraints on exemplar models. *Journal of Experimental Psychology: Learning, Memory, and Cognition, 30*, 1045–1064.

Zamani, M. & Richard, J-F. (2000). Object encoding, goal similarity, and analogical transfer. *Memory & Cognition, 28*, 873–886.

CHAPTER 5

Episodic Memory

Scott D. Gronlund, Curt A. Carlson, and Debra Tower
University of Oklahoma, USA

On the morning of September 11, 2001, two planes hit the towers of the World Trade Center. Although people will never forget this event, they also report that they will never forget who first told them and where they were when they heard of the attack. Memory for the personal circumstances surrounding events of great consequence is termed flashbulb memory (Brown & Kulik 1977). On September 12, 2001, Talarico and Rubin (2003) had students report memories for a recent everyday event and for the particulars of learning about 9/11. Accuracy decreased similarly for both types of memory, despite participants reporting their flashbulb memories with great confidence. Inaccurate flashbulb memories are the norm (e.g., Schmolck *et al.* 2000; but see Berntsen & Thomsen 2005), no matter how noteworthy your connection to the event. On December 4, 2001 and January 5, 2002, President George W. Bush reported that he watched on television as the first plane flew into one of the towers (though this would have been impossible), while on December 20, 2001 he told the *Washington Post* that Karl Rove told him about the first plane (Greenberg 2004). What kind of memory do we have that at once makes some memories indelible, others quickly forgotten, and still others reconstructions that we mistake for real?

An understanding of memory is central to an understanding of all aspects of cognition. Memory supports object recognition and perceptual categorization (Palmeri & Gauthier 2004), decision-making (Dougherty *et al.* 2003), influences attention (Clark *et al.* 1996), is modified by expertise (Chase & Simon 1973), and affects how you read (Zwaan 1994), speak (Goldinger & Azuma 2004), and plan (Gronlund *et al.* 2005). With that broad scope, it is not surprising that memory plays an important role in many real-world settings: Novice medical students recall more verbatim details about a case whereas expert physicians make more inferences and recall more of the relevant information (Patel *et al.* 1999); air traffic controllers exhibit superior memory for aircraft in conflict (Gronlund *et al.* 1998); and older adults can be confused about whether they have already taken that day's medication (Einstein *et al.* 1998). Furthermore, memory lies at the crux of many important applied problems, such as eyewitness identification (Wells & Olson 2003).

The topic of this chapter is not the entire realm of memory: Tulving and Craik (2000) edited such a volume, which ran to 700 pages. One classification scheme that helps to

Handbook of Applied Cognition: Second Edition. Edited by Francis T. Durso.

delimit our discussion divides long-term memory into implicit and explicit components (e.g., Squire 1992). We utilize explicit memory when we consciously remember an event from the past; implicit memory for a prior event is demonstrated without conscious awareness (Schacter 1987). This chapter focuses on a review of explicit memory and its applications, but there are many examples of applied work in implicit memory (e.g., Bargh *et al.* 1996; Coates *et al.* 2004; Andrade 2005; Holland *et al.* 2005).

Another classification scheme divides memory into episodic and semantic components. Episodic memory, first popularized by Tulving (1972), is the ability to re-experience happenings from one's past. Episodic memory involves the ability to mentally represent a specific event and localize it in time and space. Episodic memory is context-bound; for example, I remember that yesterday I learned that my neighbor's bulldog is named Daisy. In contrast, semantic memory consists of context-free facts. Bulldogs were bred to fight bulls. Controversy remains regarding the relationship between episodic and semantic memory. Some have argued that the two are distinct and supported by different underlying mechanisms (Cabeza & Nyberg 2000; Tulving 2002). Others have suggested that episodic and semantic memory are supported by the same underlying system; semantic memory "represents the residue of many episodes" (Baddeley 2001, p. 1346). Irrespective of the views regarding one vs. two underlying systems, there is an unambiguous heuristic distinction between episodic and semantic memory that is useful for researchers. This is true despite the fact that memory tasks are multiply-determined (Tulving 1991) and none is purely episodic. Although the focus of this chapter is on episodic memory, the role of semantic memory or knowledge will play a prominent role at various points.

We do not take an applied or basic approach to our overview of explicit, episodic memory; neither camp has a monopoly on the desire to explain important phenomena or to solve significant problems. Some have written that basic research has little to offer applied research or everyday memory phenomena (e.g., Neisser 1978), and many basic researchers argue the converse position (Banaji & Crowder 1989). Koriat *et al.* (2000) recast this debate as between two metaphors that guide research: a quantity-oriented storehouse metaphor and an accuracy-oriented correspondence metaphor. The former, which grew out of traditional laboratory research and characteristically involves memory for words from a list, focuses on the number of items remembered. The latter grew out of the everyday memory tradition and considers the degree of correspondence between the original event and what is reported.

Some of the topics we discuss are more easily conceptualized according to the storehouse metaphor and other topics according to the correspondence metaphor. But the best chance of understanding something as complex and pervasive as episodic memory comes from capitalizing on good ideas wherever they are found, be they sophisticated techniques developed in the laboratory (Batchelder & Riefer 1999; see Riefer *et al.* 2002, for the use of multinomial models to analyze the storage and retrieval deficits of Korsakoff's patients and schizophrenics), to questions that arise from real-world experiences (faulty eyewitness identification, Loftus 1979) or spur new areas of investigation (e.g., metacognition, Koriat & Goldsmith 1996). Our understanding is enhanced when we examine questions about memory using both metaphors. For example, a recent finding (Barkin *et al.* 2005) reported that as the number of topics discussed by pediatricians with parents increased, the ability of parents to remember the topics decreased (the well-known list-length effect from the storehouse metaphor; Strong 1912). However, it is equally important to consider the accuracy of the information that was remembered, whether the most important information was remembered, and what was important to the parents (e.g., reminders to parents to apply sunscreen to their children is unnecessary in Duluth in December). Both metaphors have something to offer.

This overview of episodic memory is organized in two sections. The first focuses on the factors that influence what is retained in episodic memory. We consider factors that relate to how much is retained (consistent with the storehouse metaphor) and what is retained (consistent with the correspondence metaphor). These factors are depicted through research and examples. The second section focuses on the underlying processes that support episodic memory, notably a dual-process heuristic consisting of familiarity and recollection. Various methodologies also are highlighted.

FACTORS THAT INFLUENCE EPISODIC MEMORY

Episodic memory is a system that captures prior experiences and utilizes those prior experiences to influence current behavior and plan future behavior. For example, episodic memory is responsible for a fear of tiny, cantankerous dogs because I remember being bitten by one as a child. A useful way to conceptualize episodic memory is to posit that each experience creates a representation of the experience. This so-called exemplar approach has been influential in many fields (e.g., attention, Logan 2002; categorization, Nosofsky 1988; decision-making, Dougherty *et al.* 1999).

Semon (1921) coined the term engram to refer to the physical trace he believed to be recorded in the nervous system as the result of a previous experience. He proposed that events and stimuli left a trace in the brain, which could be replayed and experienced again. Although neuroscientists continue to examine the trace in terms of neural activity and plasticity, cognitive psychologists use it as a metaphor for the mental representation of stored information, despite the fact that some researchers (e.g., Watkins 1990; Clancey 1997) argue that the construct obstructs theoretical progress. Utilizing the trace metaphor, the next section describes factors that *enhance* the retention of a trace, including its strength, the role of repetition and spacing, and the type of information represented by the trace. Then we describe factors that can *decrease* the retention of a trace: forgetting and the overlap between the trace and the retrieval cue used to access it. These factors map onto the storehouse metaphor. Finally, we consider factors that can modify the trace or add information to it, resulting in a reconstructive memory. These factors fit with the correspondence metaphor.

Factors that *Enhance* How Much is Retained

Not all memories are created equal. There are some events we remember easily and in great detail, others that are hazy and seem to fade quickly, and memories at every gradation between. While it is easy to propose that traces differ in strength, it is much more complicated to explain why this is so. One part of the explanation is that not all traces are created equally; that is, certain stimuli or circumstances leave a stronger, more memorable trace than others.

An individual is more likely to remember a trace that encapsulates a performed action rather than one that is spoken (Koriat *et al.* 1998), listened to (Englekamp & Zimmer

2001), imagined (Senkfor *et al.* 2002), or watched (Golly-Häring & Englekamp 2003). For example, for participants assigned either to read aloud or perform tasks such as "lick your lips" and "touch the flower," free recall of the tasks was better for those who had enacted the task (Koriat *et al.* 1998). Additional processes are needed to perform an action and these enrich the memory trace (Zimmer 2001). Sign language seems to tap into this advantage. Deaf individuals who signed an action had better memory than the deaf participants who simply read the action. In addition, people will remember better when the material is self-generated rather than provided (Slamecka & Graf 1978; Foos *et al.* 1994). An important component in the effectiveness of note-taking is that the individual is generating not only material, but an event in which they are involved. Non-linear strategies in note-taking are particularly effective; that is, those who create outlines and graphs to organize the material are more likely to remember than those who simply write down what has been said (Piolat *et al.* 2005).

Better memory for self-performed actions has implications for training and work in today's computer-enhanced world. Automation may deprive learners of crucial experience needed to handle unusual circumstances or create a situation in which the operator lacks full knowledge, awareness, and control of the situation (see Durso & Gronlund 1999 for a review). Baxter and Besnard (2004) believed that, due to the complexity of the flight management system in the cockpit, pilots might not fully comprehend the situation, or if they do, are often required to spend much of their time trying to explain it to the system by typing in data (Sarter & Woods 1995).

Paivio (1971) hypothesized that the ease of imaging a word enhances the ability to learn and remember it. While Paivio (1973) found that participants had much better recall for pictures than for words, this disparity decreased when participants imaged, rather than spoke, the word. A word that evokes an image may create a verbal and a visual trace for that word which can enhance its recall. The use of images can facilitate the learning of a second language. Spanish learners can enhance their memory of vocabulary by using the keyword method (Beaton *et al.* 2005). The learner is presented with a Spanish word that is phonologically similar to an English word and told to create an image of the two items. For example, *vaca* (cow) is similar to vacuum. By imaging a cow using a vacuum cleaner, participants learn this vocabulary word. People are adept at remembering visual information (Shepard 1967), and a picture superiority effect has been found across many studies (e.g., Nelson *et al.* 1976). However, like many of the phenomena in this chapter, the reasons why this benefits memory are still under debate (Glaser & Glaser 1989; Arieh & Algom 2002), but this need not stop the practitioner from capitalizing on the superior memory for a trace containing visual information.

Another characteristic that enhances retention of the trace is the meaningfulness of the stimuli. For example, FBI will be easier to recall than YHP. Craik and Lockhart (1972) discussed the role of the depth of processing of a stimulus and how that affected memorability: The deeper or more meaningfully some information was encoded, the more memorable it became. The first such evidence was reported by University of Oklahoma researcher James Moore (1936; G. Logan, pers. comm., May 4, 2005), who showed that participants told to remember the facts of a story recalled more facts than those told to count the words in the story. A focus on meaning led to better memory than an emphasis on perceptual details. Advertisers are well aware of the relationship between meaningfulness and memory (see MacInnis *et al.* 1991 for a review). One technique in creating an effective commercial is to include rhetorical questions (*Where's the beef?*) instead of just presenting declarative statements. This obliges the viewer to focus on the ad, thereby increasing the likelihood of remembering (and buying?) the brand (Petty *et al.* 1981). Advertisers also know that consumers pay more attention and process ads more deeply if the material is self-relevant (Kendzierski 1980).

It seems trite to suggest that strengthening a trace through rehearsal enhances memory; but, in fact, this is not always the case. (In the next section we illustrate why trace strength, like depth of processing, does not translate into enhanced retention.) Rohrer *et al.* (2005) had participants continue to study geography facts or word definitions beyond perfect performance. Although their recall was better at one week than those who had not over-learned, the information was not retained better over the long term. By nine weeks, most of the high learners' advantage was lost. Although over-learning (strengthening a trace) can be effective for preparing for this morning's exam, if long-term retention is your goal, time is better spent practicing old concepts while learning new ones rather than merely over-learning the new concepts. Such findings emphasize the importance of spaced study.

Ross and Landauer (1978, p. 669) found that "two successive presentations . . . are hardly more effective than a single presentation, while two well-spaced presentations are about twice effective as one." An explanation was offered by Raaijmakers (2003), who implemented Glenberg's (1979) conceptual model using the SAM (Search of Associative Memory) theoretical framework (Raaijmakers & Shiffrin 1981). The key idea is that a new trace is added to memory if the existing trace is not retrieved when it is repeated (resulting in two retrieval routes to the information). However, if the existing trace is retrieved, information is added to it and the existing trace is strengthened.

The spacing effect is an example of what Bjork (1994, 1999) called desirable difficulties: manipulations that often harm short-term retention but result in superior long-term retention. Desirable difficulties also include the aforementioned generation effect and interleaving (better long-term retention if two concepts A and B are experienced as ABAB rather than as AABB). An application of these ideas is taking place as part of the IDDEAS (Introducing Desirable Difficulties for Educational Applications in Science) Project. Richland *et al.* (2005) examined how interleaving and generation affected college students' learning of astronomy facts related to a planet's habitability. Interleaving resulted in better integration of concepts on a posttest, and successful generation enhanced memory for single facts. These results also are an important demonstration of what many basic researchers believe. Findings from the laboratory can scale up to the complexities of the real world.

Distinctiveness is another factor that can enhance how much is retained. In fact, many of the aforementioned factors are effective because they involve the creation of a more distinctive trace (e.g., generation effect, picture superiority). Imagine that you are driving home from work and a song comes on the radio. Not only do you recognize the song, but you know it played during a scene in a movie you saw last month. But you cannot remember which movie if that song has been used in many soundtracks. However, you would remember the movie if the song you heard (the cue) was unique to a particular movie (e.g., the *Jaws* theme). A distinctive cue also improves prospective memory accuracy (McDaniel & Einstein 1993). Prospective memory involves the use of episodic memory to remember future actions (e.g., a dentist's appointment) (Winograd 1988; see also McDaniel & Einstein 2000).

A distinctive cue (Hunt & McDaniel 1993; Hunt 1995) elicits a particular memory because such a cue is not overloaded (Watkins & Watkins 1975). For example, let the degree of match between a cue and a trace equal ten units. If that cue also is weakly matched to ten other cues (one unit each), the likelihood of sampling that trace is 10/20 (using a ratio sampling rule like that implemented in SAM, Raaijmakers and Shiffrin 1981). But if that same cue is an equally good match for two other traces and a weak match to the remaining eight traces, the likelihood of sampling that particular trace falls to 10/38. Note that the matching strength (or overlap) between the cue and the trace did not change, yet the likelihood of retrieving that trace decreased because the cue also was strongly connected to other traces (Nairne 2002). However, a change of the cue used to access the trace can overcome the cue overload and increase the likelihood of successful remembering. For example, an attorney, unable to remember a precedent-setting case during an exchange with the judge might remember it on her way back to the office. The courtroom context is a poor cue for the desired information because it is related to many different aspects of the case. However, on her way to the office, a new cue – spotting an SUV like the one involved in the hit-and-run accident – provides a better cue for the precedent-setting case.

Hunt (2003) distinguished between two types of distinctiveness: item- and event-based. The picture superiority effect is a good example of item-based distinctiveness. Not only are certain stimuli (such as pictures) inherently more distinctive, but non-distinctive stimuli can be made more distinctive via encoding manipulations (event-based distinctiveness). For example, Jacoby *et al.* (1979) found that increasing the difficulty of encoding improved the probability that an item subsequently would be recognized. Participants had to decide which of two words was most related to a third word. The choice between "lake" and "chair" vs. "water" is an example of an easy comparison; the choice between "lake" and "thirst" vs. "water" is a difficult comparison. Participants had better memory for the words that were part of the difficult choices. Thus, the words associated with more difficult choices became more distinctive compared to those words associated with easy choices. For the same reason solving a word problem for the correct answer will lead to higher retention than rote memorization of the correct answer.

Factors that *Decrease* How Much is Retained

To this point the focus has been on how the properties of the trace enhance how much is remembered. However, a common outcome of memory is forgetting. Is forgetting simply the loss or decay of a trace? Explanations that assume that forgetting is due to the decay of a trace have not fared well (Medin *et al.* 2001). An alternative explanation is that forgetting is caused by interference with a trace caused by new learning. Two explanations have been proposed for how new learning can interfere with a trace.

Wixted (2004) proposed a consolidation hypothesis whereby forgetting results when newly formed traces fail to consolidate due to the interfering effect of other mental activities. In an experiment that supports this hypothesis, Sisson (1939) had participants study a ten-item list. A subsequent list was presented either immediately after the initial list, in the middle of the retention interval, or just prior to test. Performance on the initial list was affected by when the subsequent list was learned. Worse performance resulted when the subsequent list was learned immediately after the initial list, thereby interfering with the consolidation process. Dudai (2004) proposed that consolidation of a trace may not happen only once. Reactivation of a trace might make it labile and subject to renewed consolidation. Renewed consolidation opens up possibilities for training the reacquisition of a skill or for the treatment of pathologies that involve obsessive recollection (e.g., post-traumatic stress disorder). For example, the drug propranolol restricts post-traumatic stress disorder by blocking the over-consolidation of a distressing memory (Pitman & Delahanty 2005). Perhaps future treatments will allow therapeutic forgetting; it works in the movies (*Eternal Sunshine of the Spotless Mind*: Williamson *et al.* 2004).

The most commonly accepted explanation for forgetting is retrieval failure. In this case a trace is lost *in* memory rather than *from* memory, much like a library book that has been placed on the wrong shelf. A trace that people initially fail to report often can be "found" with the proper cue (Tulving & Pearlstone 1966). This is why episodic memory is referred to as cue-dependent. Any college student can attest to that after failing to remember *Wernicke's aphasia* on an exam but having it spring to mind when Nikki the roommate asks how the test went.

A key factor governing retrieval failure is the overlap between the information stored at encoding and the retrieval cue used to access it (termed encoding specificity by Tulving & Thomson 1971, 1973). Retrieval failure becomes more likely as the overlap between encoding and retrieval decreases. A typical experiment (Tulving & Thomson 1971) involves learning a series of word pairs (e.g., tiger–lion). In a subsequent recognition test, participants must determine which words were from the initial list. Encoding specificity is responsible for worse performance for recognizing words that are re-paired with a different studied word (e.g., horse–LION), compared to words paired with the original associate (e.g., tiger–LION).

The method of loci mnemonic (Bower 1970) capitalizes on encoding specificity by linking to-be-learned items to sequentially organized locations (e.g., landmarks on your route to work). At retrieval, by mentally retracing your route to work, you regenerate the best possible cue for each item: the cue used when learning that item. An important application of encoding specificity in forensic settings is the cognitive interview (Fisher & Geiselman 1992). One aspect of the cognitive interview involves reinstating the context of the crime. Kohnken *et al.* (1999) found that the cognitive interview elicited between 35 and 75 per cent more information than typical police interviews and did not increase the proportion of incorrect responses. Malpass (1996) suggested other procedures based on context reinstatement that might improve lineup identification accuracy. For example, his guided memory interview involves reminding the witness of key elements from the event while encouraging visualization of the details.

Transfer-appropriate processing is an extension of the encoding specificity principle. Memory retention suffers to the extent that the operations required at retrieval do not overlap or fail to recapture the operations used during encoding (Morris *et al.* 1977; Roediger & Blaxton 1987). Brain imaging experiments illustrate a neural basis for transfer-appropriate processing. Wheeler *et al.* (2000) presented participants with words like "dog," accompanied either by a picture of a dog or a barking sound. At test, they were provided with the same label seen previously and were asked to mentally recall the corresponding referent (i.e., the sound of barking or the picture, only one of which they had experienced at encoding). Event-related functional magnetic resonance imaging (fMRI) showed that successful picture recall activated the same part of the visual cortex as was activated during encoding of the picture, and successful sound recall activated the same auditory cortical regions activated during encoding of the sound. They concluded that the cortical areas involved in the initial perception of an event become part of the trace for that experience. Thus, when the same (or similar) context is reinstated, the same cortical areas become active, paving the way for retrieval of that trace.

Like encoding specificity, transfer-appropriate processing has many applications. Stacy *et al.* (2004) applied transfer-appropriate processing to consumer behavior and public health. To assess adolescents' memory of alcohol advertisements, still-frames from each of several beer commercials from a recent Super Bowl were presented as cues. Could participants remember which were the alcohol ads, and, if so, could they remember the particular brand? Results indicated that commercials were more likely to be recognized as advertising beer in the Super-Bowl cue condition compared to a control group, and two Budweiser commercials (both featuring the Budweiser frogs) were remembered better than any other (which probably has something to do with distinctiveness).

Although Wixted (2005) suggested that forgetting by retrieval failure does not play a substantial role outside of the laboratory, we believe that both consolidation and retrieval failure provide important insights into applied problems. For example, if a patient forgets what the physician told her to do after completing her course of antibiotics, is it because at the initial examination the physician also told her to limit salt intake and begin taking a multivitamin (thereby hampering consolidation of the instructions regarding the antibiotic), or because the patient learned what to do in the context of personal health-related issues and is having trouble remembering it later while walking the dog? In the former case, the correct course of action is no longer in memory and the physician should have provided an external memory aid (a list) to ensure that the directives were followed. In the latter case, thinking back to the situation in the examination room might result in remembering what to do.

Thus far, we have learned about properties of a memory trace that enhance retention of a trace. We also have examined the impact of new learning and how that can decrease access to a trace. Before moving on, we will assimilate these ideas by exploring tactics an instructor could use to enhance retention.

An instructor can shift course content from verbal to visual. Rather than describing the corporate hierarchy, a figure that depicts the information would be better remembered. Retention also will be improved if students complete tasks themselves rather than simply writing down what they are told. Students will perform better on both multiple-choice (based on recognition) and short-answer or essay questions (based on recall) if the material they learn is encoded with some difficulty. These factors serve to make the information more distinctive. There are improvements an instructor can achieve through the appropriate sequencing of course content; creating desirable difficulties by spacing out the learning is beneficial. Providing meaning and structure to the course content supplies the proper context for interpretation. It also helps organize a set of cues to aid subsequent retrieval (much like what the method of loci does). Retention is improved if elements of the test match those used to encode the material. Roediger and Karpicke (2006) found the effect of testing to be more effective than an equivalent amount of additional study. According to transfer-appropriate processing, testing improves performances because it practices retrieval skills that are the same as those needed for the final test. Also, testing results in a more distinctive memory trace and thereby overcomes cue overload. Whenever critical new information is conveyed, an instructor should be mindful to minimize interference from new learning in order to maximize consolidation (i.e., do not attempt to teach a large amount of new information in one class period; rather, teach some new material, followed by examples or practice of that material). In sum, an instructor can use various techniques to increase how much is remembered, but he or she must remain aware of the crucial moderating roles played by the encoding–retrieval overlap and the distinctiveness of the cues used to access the information.

Factors that Affect *What* is Retained

In the two prior sections, the trace was treated as an accurate depiction of what was experienced, and the likelihood of retrieving a trace was shown to be a joint function of the encoding–retrieval overlap (which determines memory strength) and the distinctiveness of the cue. However, we often remember things differently from the way in which they actually happened, or even remember something that never occurred. In the 1930s, Bartlett wrote: "Remembering is not the re-excitation of innumerable fixed, lifeless and fragmentary traces" (1932, p. 213). But for the next 50 years, the study of memory largely focused on exactly that. When the focus is on the number of events remembered, events that are not remembered correctly are considered forgotten. However, when the focus shifts to accuracy, the correspondence between what actually happened and what is reported becomes paramount. We next examine "the consequences of the idea that information is not simply deposited into a memory store, but is assimilated and integrated into cognitive structures (e.g., schemas) and later recreated from those structures" (Koriat *et al.* 2000, p. 487). Although schemata and related retrieval structures benefit memory by aiding in the selection and interpretation of the to-be-learned information (Alba & Hasher 1983), in this section we focus on the factors that decrease the accuracy of what is remembered.

Several taxonomies have been proposed for categorizing factors that decrease the accuracy of what is remembered (e.g., Schacter 1999). We follow the taxonomy of Koriat *et al.* (2000) because it previews the dual-process discussion below: (1) remembering at an incorrect level of abstraction; (2) suggested information changes the original memory; (3) recombining features that belong to different events; (4) false recognition or false recall of events that never happened; and (5) meta-memory monitoring.

(1) Information can be remembered at an incorrect level of abstraction. According to fuzzy-trace theory (Brainerd & Reyna 2002), verbatim information and the gist of the experience are encoded independently and in parallel. However, verbatim information (the man who robbed me was 6′6″) is lost quickly, leaving primarily the gist available at test (he was tall). Workload also may affect the level of abstraction that is retained. Moray (1987) argued that the operators of a complex system create mental models at varying levels within a network defined by different levels of abstraction. Problems arise when an operator works at too low a level of generality; for example, when a pilot needs to know the exact location of the severe weather but only remembers that it is near Tulsa. At a low workload, an air traffic controller might remember the speed of each aircraft, but at a higher workload, might remember only the important aircraft or only the relative speeds (Gronlund *et al.* 1998). Finally, we have meta-cognitive control over the level of abstraction. Goldsmith *et al.* (2005) showed that participants regulated the grain size of reported quantitative information. For example, the height of an individual involved in a bar-room fight could be reported at a detailed grain size (height in feet and inches) or an imprecise grain size (taller than me). As the retention interval increased, Goldsmith *et al.* found that report accuracy declined more slowly for those allowed to regulate their grain size. This

finding has obvious implications for the criminal justice system; testimony is more likely to be accurate if a witness is allowed to report information in the manner (at the grain size) they prefer.

(2) Suggestions can change the original memory. Schooler and Tanaka (1991) called these compromise recollections; Azuma *et al.* (2004) called them blend errors. Azuma *et al.* had participants read homophones (e.g., PAWS) during a study phase while maintaining a memory load that included words (e.g., cause) related to the alternate homophone spelling (pause). A recognition test that included both versions of the homophone (PAUSE and PAWS) found an increased false alarm rate to PAUSE. They argued that a blend memory for PAUSE was created due to the close temporal activation of two related lexical entities (PAWS and cause). Something similar contributed to problems in therapy settings directed at recovering memories of purported abuse (Loftus & Ketcham 1994). A therapist might instruct a client to use journaling, whereby a client free-associates to images she has had. In cases involving false accusations of sexual abuse (e.g., Nadean Cool; see Loftus 1997), the veracity of these images was of little relevance, no matter how bizarre (Clark & Loftus 1996). The problem is that activating two memories (e.g., a memory of your dad and a memory of a bloody knife) at approximately the same time may result in the creation of a new memory (your dad holding a bloody knife). Imagining this new event would further enhance its plausibility (Mazzoni & Memon 2003).

(3) Recombining features that belong to different events or different sources can decrease memory accuracy. Misinformation effects in eyewitness identification provide one example (Loftus 1979). Witnesses are exposed to an event, are subsequently misinformed about a detail in the event (e.g., they originally saw a stop sign but are told it was a yield sign), and later are given a forced-choice recognition test between the original and the suggested detail. Witnesses were less likely to choose the original detail when an alternative was suggested compared to the situation where no alternative was suggested. McCloskey and Zaragoza (1985) argued that both the original detail and the suggested detail were represented in memory, and that the misinformation effect was the result of competition between them. If two memories for the event of interest coexist, techniques can be used to help distinguish between them (e.g., instructions to focus on the perceptual characteristics; Johnson *et al.* 1988). Clearly, this effort is misplaced if a compromise recollection was created and the memory of the original event has been replaced. What if a student's memory for the material from the textbook contradicts what they learn in an ill-prepared study group? This could negatively affect exam performance if the new memory (from the study group) destructively updates the old (from the textbook). If McCloskey and Zaragoza are correct, there will be competition between the two traces and a chance that the incorrect answer prevails.

(4) Some events that never happened can be falsely recognized or recalled due to importing information from a knowledge structure (Bower *et al.* 1979) or due to confabulating information. Zaragoza *et al.* (2001) forced participants to confabulate details about events they saw in a short film. Participants subsequently reported that some of these fake events actually happened. For example, an air traffic controller is importing information from a knowledge structure when he or she "remembers" that AAL123 is landing in Phoenix because that is what it does every day (except today).

Memory typically benefits from a reliance on knowledge structures (Alba & Hasher 1983; Schacter 1999), but the relationship is a complex one. Wiley (2005) found that low-knowledge individuals tended to recall more arguments consistent with their position on a controversial issue, but high-knowledge individuals could remember arguments on both sides of a controversial issue (prior knowledge immunizes against "spin"). Interestingly, when a text was structured such that supporting and opposing arguments were interleaved, differences due to prior knowledge were eliminated. This finding is germane to journalists, web designers, honest politicians, or anyone who presents information for a living.

The self is a uniquely important knowledge structure that influences episodic memory. Although some claim that the influence is better conceptualized as occurring in a related system called autobiographical memory (e.g., Conway 1996; Rubin 2005), others use episodic and autobiographical interchangeably. Tulving (1972) considered using the latter when he first proposed the distinction between the characteristics of memories for personally experienced events (episodic) and memory for general facts (semantic). Some evidence supports the idea that episodic and autobiographical are not the same, including studies of the amnesic patient K. C., who demonstrated some autobiographical but no episodic memory (Tulving *et al.* 1988). However, the autobiographic memory demonstrated by K. C. consisted of general factual information and it would be hard to argue that his autobiographical memory was unaffected. Studies that examine neural activity in an attempt to dissociate episodic from autobiographical memory have been conducted, but Gillihan and Farah (2005) argued that most suffer from confounds and found little support for the idea that memory for the self is qualitatively, or functionally, different from other episodic memories.

We will not resolve this issue here, but note that much of what we have discussed is relevant to autobiographical memory, no matter its relationship to episodic memory. For example, life experiences may be forgotten, changed, emphasized, or even confabulated, in order to maintain a stable self. Furthermore, Conway (2005) emphasized that because many autobiographical memories are interpretations of events, not literal records, we must consider accuracy for the event as well as accuracy for the self-image.

(5) Inferential and decisional processes also play an important role in mediating memory accuracy. The role of decisional processes has long been recognized through applications of signal detection theory (e.g., Banks 1970). However, given the reconstructive nature of memory, the challenge clearly involves more than assessing memory strength and determining whether or not it exceeds a decision criterion. "The rememberer is conceived as facing the challenge of interpreting an ambiguous mental record, applying heuristics that are of limited validity, and engaging in a variety of fallible inferential processes" (Koriat *et al.* 2000, p. 513). For example, as described above, greater inaccuracy results if we fail to regulate the grain size of what we report. An innocent bystander is selected from a lineup if we fail to ascertain why that individual appears familiar. A client might not believe the images revealed while under hypnosis or dreaming unless informed by their therapist that they must be true or they would not have revealed themselves. What is retrieved from memory is only the starting point regarding what we report remembering. In the next section, we turn our attention to the processes that underlie episodic memory and describe a distinction that helps us to understand the memorial, inferential, and decisional contributions to episodic memory.

DUAL PROCESSES IN EPISODIC MEMORY

Familiarity is the feeling we have on seeing our butcher on the bus (Mandler 1980) or a business acquaintance at the gym, without the experience of remembering from where we know him. Recollection is the process responsible for the recall of details surrounding the prior occurrence of an event. Recollection informs us how we know the person at the gym (e.g., he wore aqua bell bottoms on casual Friday). Familiarity is automatic, effortless, and quick; recollection is conscious, effortful, and relatively slow.

Single-process explanations of recognition in episodic memory rely on familiarity and are cast in signal detection terms (for applications of signal detection to memory, see Banks 1970). Familiarity arises from matching a test probe against everything in memory (for an overview of global matching models, see Clark and Gronlund 1996). The resultant global match is compared to a decision criterion that converts continuous match strength into a (typically) binary decision. If the global match exceeds the criterion value, a positive response is made and the event is reported as having been experienced previously. A witness to a crime might rely on familiarity to decide whether the individual presented to her in a show-up stole her purse. If the suspect's familiarity exceeds criterion, the witness exclaims, "That's him!"

Dual-process explanations assume that a recollection process also can contribute to recognition decisions (see review by Yonelinas 2002). In the aforementioned show-up, recollection is thought to play a role if the witness not only reports, "That's him!", but also reports that this is the guy because she remembers the skull tattoo on his forearm. However, in contrast to a continuous familiarity process, recollection typically is assumed to be an all-or-nothing threshold process (recollect the item or not). Although many dual-process models have been proposed (e.g., Jacoby 1991; Wheeler *et al.* 1997; Aggleton & Brown 1999; Yonelinas 1999; Norman & O'Reilly 2003), we will not commit to a particular model, but instead use the familiarity/recollection distinction as a heuristic. In what follows, we equate recollection and recall although the exact relationship between them remains unclear (e.g., Dobbins *et al.* 1998; Kahana *et al.* 2005).

Dual-Process Distinctions

The heuristic distinction between familiarity and recollection subsumes at least three related distinctions. One such distinction involves item and associative (or relational) information (Humphreys 1978). Retrieval of item information, whether an item occurred previously or not, is driven by a familiarity process; retrieval of associative information, whether two previously occurring items occurred together or as part of two separate events, requires a recollection process. A second distinction recasts associative information as memory for the source (Johnson *et al.* 1993) and introduces the important role of recollection as it relates to monitoring. Source confusions contribute to faulty eyewitness identifications when a witness chooses an innocent suspect from a mug-shot and subsequently picks that same person from a lineup. A final distinction involves automatic versus intentional processing (Jacoby 1991). An automatic process is unaffected by dividing attention at test, but an intentional process (based on recollection) is hampered.

All three distinctions are consistent with the idea that familiarity is quick and automatic, while recollection is effortful and under a degree of strategic control. Gronlund and Ratcliff (1989) used the response signal paradigm (Reed 1973) to show that item information was retrieved before associative information. In the response signal paradigm, the time course of information is mapped by requiring that a participant responds upon receiving a signal (e.g., a "beep"), the timing of which varies across trials. Results from their study were consistent with other work that showed that automatic influences occur early in processing while strategic influences occur later (e.g., Yonelinas & Jacoby 1994).

The response signal paradigm is useful for tracing how accuracy and speed trade off in a recognition situation. For example, the pilot of an attack helicopter chooses when and how often to emerge from the trees to assess the battlefield situation. During that brief interval, the pilot must collect information about potential targets and discriminate friend from foe in a complex, dynamic, and hostile environment. To increase the accuracy of these assessments the pilot must spend more time in the open. However, to survive the pilot must decrease the time of these assessments, thereby reducing their accuracy. One way to validate the usefulness of automated target recognition (ATR) systems is to map recognition accuracy across time using the response signal paradigm. This can reveal a series of "snapshots of processing" (Cohen & Tolcott 1992, p. 48) that disclose when particular features are extracted and how the availability of these features is affected by the introduction of the ATR system. For example, if color is important for recognizing targets, and if the availability of color is speeded by the introduction of the ATR system, the system will benefit performance. However, if allies and enemies have tanks of a similar color, reliance on quick familiarity for identification is problematic and slower recollection may need to play a role.

Faulty source monitoring plays an important role in the reconstructive nature of episodic memory. A lack of correspondence between an original event (viewing a stop sign) and memory for that event ("remembering" a yield sign) results from confusion between the original event and the suggestion. Faulty monitoring also results in the misattributed fluency of processing (Jacoby *et al.* 1989; Whittlesea 2002). This is why the apocryphal Sebastian Weisdorf is deemed famous by many participants in memory experiments (Jacoby *et al.* 1989). Mr. Weisdorf's name and other *non-famous* names were studied under divided or full attention. At test, those participants in the divided attention condition were more likely to classify Sebastian Weisdorf as famous. Because recollection is effortful, dividing attention renders source monitoring ineffectual and the relative ease of processing Sebastian Weisdorf's name is attributed to his purported fame rather than to its presence on the prior list. Aging also harms monitoring, which results in greater degrees of false memory in older adults (e.g., Schacter *et al.* 1997).

Measuring Familiarity and Recollection

There is great interest in measuring the respective contributions of the fast, automatic, familiarity process and the slower, strategic, recollection process. We could avoid much embarrassment if we could determine which process was responsible for making a face at the mall seem familiar before we run over and say hello to a total stranger who resembles a golfing buddy. In the courtroom, the jury needs to know if a positive identification is based on familiarity (he looks most like the guy who robbed me) or recollection (he is the robber because he has the same crooked teeth and tattoo). Arthur Carmona was selected from a show-up only after the police placed a Lakers cap on him known to be worn by the assailant. This made Arthur more familiar to the witnesses. He served two years of a 12-year jail sentence before he was released (see http://www.stopwrongfulconvictions.org/learnexonerees.htm).

The difficulty with measuring familiarity and recollection is that memory tasks are not process-pure (Jacoby 1991). Not only are tasks not purely episodic (as mentioned previously with regard to semantic contributions), they also are not based solely on familiarity (F) or recollection (R). To extract estimates of familiarity and recollection we need to make assumptions about how these processes are combined (Wainwright & Reingold 1996). The simplest assumption is to assume that the processes are independent (an assumption that has garnered some controversy; see, e.g., Curran & Hintzman 1995).

Jacoby (1991) introduced a methodology called process dissociation for separating automatic (familiarity) from strategic (recollection) contributions. In the process dissociation procedure, two lists of items are studied. The study phase is followed by a test phase which includes three types of tests: items from list 1 (L1), items from list 2 (L2), and items not viewed previously (New). The tests are conducted in two ways. In an inclusion condition, positive responses are made to L1 and L2 items. In other words, in the inclusion condition a positive response occurs if an item is recollected (R) or if an item is not recollected (1 – R) but is familiar (F) [Eqn 5.1: R + (1 – R) F]. In an exclusion condition, positive responses are reserved for items from only one of the lists (e.g., L1 items). In the exclusion condition, recollection must be used to oppose the familiarity of L2 items and prevent them from receiving a positive response: L2 items will be responded to positively if they are not recollected (1 – R) but are familiar (F) [Eqn 5.2: (1 – R) F]. Subtracting Equation 5.2 from Equation 5.1 gives an estimate of the contributions of R alone. Once obtained, an estimate of F alone also can be achieved. This is depicted graphically in Figure 5.1.

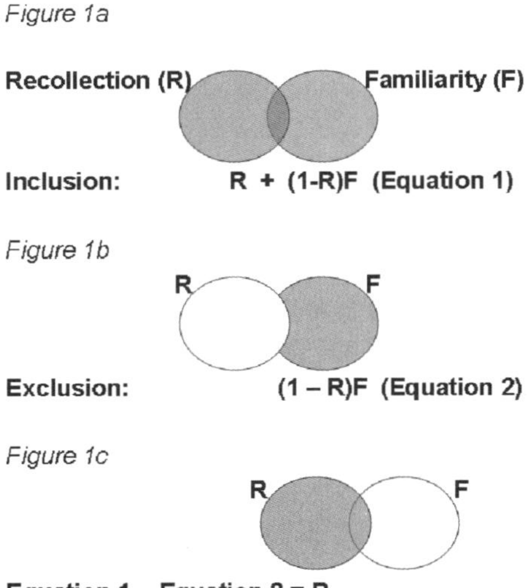

Figure 5.1 An illustration of the independent processes of familiarity and recollection. (a) depicts the inclusion test of the process dissociation procedure (Jacoby 1991), which shows that either familiarity (right circle) or recollection (left circle) can lead to a positive response (Eqn 5.1). (b) depicts Jacoby's exclusion test, which illustrates an incorrect positive response due to familiarity alone (Eqn 5.2). (c) shows that subtracting Equation 5.2 from Equation 5.1 gives an estimate of recollection alone

Separating these two processes by using the process dissociation procedure (or other techniques like receiver operating characteristic curves, see Yonelinas 1999) helped researchers determine that recollection, not familiarity, is harmed by aging (Hay & Jacoby 1999). Once it is known where the problem is, treatment and training options can be targeted to maximum benefit. For example, Jennings and Jacoby (2003) enhanced the memory of older adults by training recollection. A continuous memory task required participants to respond "no" to repeated or novel items, and to respond "yes" to once-presented items. The key was that the growing familiarity of the repeated items, which arises from having experienced them before, must be opposed by recollection. Recollection is used to determine if the item is familiar because it was studied once before (respond "yes") or repeatedly (respond "no"). For one group, the spacing between repetitions increased as training progressed, putting a gradually increasing demand on recollection. For the other group, spacing varied randomly. Performance was enhanced for the former group and the benefit was maintained four months later.

Another popular method for measuring familiarity and recollection is the remember/know procedure (Tulving 1985; Gardiner & Java 1993). As originally conceptualized, familiarity and recollection represented phenomenologically distinct memorial states, and therefore, a participant could specify whether or not a particular memory decision was accompanied by the recollection of a contextual association. Before saying hello to that man in the mall, can I remember a detail about him that places him in the proper context (resulting in a *remember* response)? If no such detail is forthcoming, I make a *know* response (I *know* he is familiar, but cannot specify why).

Despite its popularity, the remember/know procedure is problematic. It makes the strong assumption that familiarity and recollection are mutually exclusive. In other words, a memory decision is based either on familiarity or on recollection, whereas independence allows responses to be based on familiarity, recollection, or both processes. Furthermore, Bodner and Lindsay (2003) showed that *remember* and *know* responses were influenced by the strength of competing memories (operationalized by a word's depth of processing or DOP). Words studied at a medium DOP (is the word commonly used?) were judged *remembered* when pitted against low DOP words (does the word contain the letter A?) but were judged *known* when pitted against high DOP words (does the word reflect something needed if stranded on a desert island?). The classification of medium DOP words should not be affected by this manipulation if memory decisions reflect the processes that give rise to them. Bodner and Lindsay argued that these judgments are better viewed as attributions than as reflections of the underlying memory processes. Wixted and Stretch (2004) highlighted another problem when they argued that a recognition decision was based on the aggregated strength of a combined familiarity and recollection signal, both of which they assumed were continuous variables. They build a strong case for these ideas by showing how remember/know judgments reflect memory strength or confidence rather than distinct underlying memory processes.

There is much that still needs to be learned about when and how familiarity and recollection operate in recognition. In fact, even the debate about the need for dual processes continues (e.g., Dennis & Humphreys 2001; Leboe & Whittlesea 2002; Malmberg *et al.* 2004; Slotnick & Dodson 2005). Despite there being no universally accepted methodology for measuring the contributions of familiarity and recollection, most researchers now agree that two processes are useful for explaining a wide range of phenomena (Yonelinas

2002). Furthermore, it is our opinion that the dual-process heuristic can be profitably applied to many situations of interest to the practitioner.

Applications of the Dual-Process Heuristic

To solidify our understanding of the dual-process heuristic, we next review four topics of significance to the practitioner interested in episodic memory. We show how an understanding of each is enhanced by consideration of a quick, automatic contribution from familiarity and a slower, effortful contribution from recollection. We begin with eyewitness identification.

Eyewitness Identification

Faulty eyewitness identification often results from faulty monitoring (i.e., the failure of recollection, source monitoring, or misattributed familiarity). The witness to a crime may select an innocent bystander from a lineup simply because he looks familiar. The witness fails to remember the context of previously having seen the bystander and thus assumes that he must seem familiar because he is the guilty party (Buckhout 1974). Imagine the situation in which a witness views a photo lineup and makes a selection. During a subsequent live lineup, the witness usually chooses the same familiar individual. The problem is that this familiarity can arise from this being the man that committed the robbery or from having previously selected this individual from the photo lineup. In the misinformation effect (Loftus & Palmer 1974), a witness might choose the lineup member with the crooked nose if another witness previously made such a suggestion about the criminal's appearance and the first witness misattributes it to his own memory. The success of the elimination lineup (Pozzulo & Lindsay 1999) probably is based on enhancing the contribution of recollection. Once a witness makes a choice from the lineup (based on who looks most familiar), they are asked to verify that the person looks familiar because he committed the crime (recollect why he looks familiar).

Procedural recommendations have been proposed to enhance eyewitness identification (Wells *et al.* 1998). One involves presenting lineup members in a sequential manner. Sequential lineups typically result in a reduced false alarm rate compared to simultaneous lineups (where all lineup members are viewed at once; see meta-analysis by Steblay *et al.* 2001). Lindsay and Wells (1985) argued that a sequential lineup leads a witness to adopt an absolute judgment process (comparing the current lineup member to your memory for the perpetrator) while a simultaneous lineup leads a witness to adopt a relative judgment process (comparing among the lineup members to choose the closest match to the perpetrator). Carlson (2004; Gronlund 2005) proposed that an absolute judgment process involves the greater use of recollection in sequential lineups. The enhanced use of recollection could aid performance by helping to accept a familiar-looking lineup member; alternatively, recollection could operate in a recall-to-reject manner (Rotello & Heit 2000) if the witness realizes that a familiar-looking lineup member is not the man who robbed her because this individual lacks the scar the robber had.

Consumer Memory

Advertisers capitalize on mistaken attributions of familiarity and failures of recollection, including an advertising misinformation effect (Braun & Loftus 1998). Shapiro (2005) presented a model of advertising in which he assumed that advertising creates memories of positive experiences with a product, which consumers have difficulty keeping separate from their actual experiences with the product. Holden and Vanhuele (1999) presented fake pharmaceutical brand names during session one. The next day, participants sometimes believed the fake brands to be real, misattributing the familiarity to the actual existence of the brands as opposed to having seen them the day before. Skurnik *et al.* (2005) presented statements about health warnings labeled as true or false (e.g., aspirin is bad for tooth enamel). They presented these statements once or three times to college students and older adults. Three days later, the college students began to mistake some of the once-presented false statements as true. The older adults had even more trouble. At the short delay, the older adults were good at correctly assigning truth to statements that had been presented three times. However, after three days, they believed that about 40 per cent of these false statements were true. They had difficulty opposing the increased familiarity of the statements presented three times. Familiarity has the illusion of truth (Begg *et al.* 1992).

Education

The dual-process heuristic is not useful just for understanding what happens when memory goes awry. It also provides insight into situations where accuracy is highly desirable. There are many instances of the utility of the dual-process heuristic in educational settings. Conway *et al.* (1997) examined learning in the classroom and found that students initially *remember* new information, but as learning progresses they increasingly *know* it. Herbert and Burt (2001) suggested that this *remember*-to-*know* shift is what educators strive for as the information becomes de-contextualized. Clariana (2003) found that a constructed-response study task (fill-in-the-blank) was more effective for long-term learning than a multiple-choice study task. He suggested that the constructed-response task relies on recollection while the multiple-choice task tends to rely on familiarity.

Collaborative Recall/Recognition

An individual's memory for an event is changed (for better or worse) after collaborating with others who witnessed the same event. In a collaborative recall experiment (Gabbert *et al.* 2003), participants witnessed different viewpoints of the same event and then discussed what they saw before giving their individual reports. As a result of faulty source monitoring, participants' accounts incorporated elements from the event that could only be seen from another witness's viewpoint. Clark *et al.* (in press) had dyads of participants study a list of word-pairs (denoted AB, CD, EF). The subsequent test lists consisted of word-pairs from the original list (targets, AB) or rearrangements (distractors, CF). Each participant first individually made a judgment about whether they thought the test pair was a target or not, and then collaborated with the other member of the dyad to determine a group decision. Hinsz (1990) found beneficial effects of such collaboration on the eventual group decision, primarily based on one member of the dyad dissuading the other member from making an incorrect decision. Casting this effect in a dual-process light, Clark *et al.* (in press) argued that familiarity and recollection worked together for targets, but worked in opposition for distractors. Apparently, recollection by one member of the dyad of the word actually paired with the rearrangement was enough to give that person the confidence to discourage his partner from making an incorrect response.

CONCLUSIONS

An understanding of episodic memory is central to an understanding of all aspects of cognition. In this chapter, we have reviewed many aspects of episodic memory, keeping a focus on its applications. We began by describing how characteristics of the memory trace that results from an experience affect what is remembered. Next, we introduced the vital role played by the overlap between what is encoded and what is used to retrieve the information. We next reviewed the reconstructive nature of memory and the resulting errors. Finally, a dual-process perspective was presented as a framework for understanding these disparate phenomena.

The understanding and the usefulness of episodic memory will be enhanced by continued interplay between the factors we have discussed and the challenges arising from applying these findings to real-world problems (work exemplified by this and the first edition of this handbook; Durso 1999). A factor that we believe will prove beneficial to achieving this goal is the increased use of formal models to understand data and dissect real-world challenges. For example, Clark (2003) developed the WITNESS model to begin to systematize eyewitness research. Clark examined three experiments directed at the same issue (whether lineup foils should match a perpetrator's description or his face), which had quite variable results. Through application of the WITNESS model, Clark showed that these differences could be understood as due to the variation across experiments in the foil–suspect similarities. Work like this can help an investigator develop better methodology, design a critical experiment, and extend our understanding of the issues at hand. As knowledge of episodic memory expands, and the phenomena of interest become increasingly multifaceted, formal models will continue to enhance our thinking by providing a test bed for ideas and a means to evaluate their consequences. The work ahead may seem intimidating, and attempting to pull together the myriad lines of research into a single construct called episodic memory often seems an impossible task, but the satisfactions of this pursuit greatly outweigh its frustrations.

AUTHOR NOTE

This work was supported by the National Science Foundation under grant SES-0240182. Any opinions, findings, and conclusions or recommendations expressed in this material are those of the authors and do not reflect the views of the NSF. The authors are indebted to Tim Perfect, David Gallo, Reed Hunt, Mike Dougherty, and Frank Durso for their valuable comments. Several members of Durso's graduate class and Dougherty's DAM lab also provided us with helpful feedback.

REFERENCES

Aggleton, J. P. & Brown, M. W. (1999). Episodic memory, amnesia, and the hippocampal–anterior thalamic axis. *Behavioral & Brain Sciences*, *22*, 425–489.

Alba, J. W. & Hasher, L. (1983). Is memory schematic? *Psychological Bulletin*, *93*, 203–231.

Andrade, J. (2005). Does memory priming during anesthesia matter? *Anesthesiology*, *103*, 919–920.

Arieh, Y. & Algom, D. (2002). Processing picture–word stimuli: the contingent nature of picture and of word superiority. *Journal of Experimental Psychology: Learning, Memory, and Cognition*, *28*, 221–232.

Azuma, T., Williams, E. J. & Davie, J. E. (2004). Paws + cause = pause? Memory load and memory blends in homophone recognition. *Psychonomic Bulletin & Review*, *11*, 723–728.

Baddeley, A. (2001). The concept of episodic memory. *Philosophical Transactions of the Royal Society of London: Biological Sciences*, *356*, 1345–1350.

Banaji, M. R. & Crowder, R. G. (1989). The bankruptcy of everyday memory. *American Psychologist*, *44*, 1185–1193.

Banks, W. P. (1970). Signal detection theory and human memory. *Psychological Bulletin*, *74*, 81–99.

Bargh, J. A., Chen, M. & Burrows, L. (1996). Automaticity of social behavior: direct effects of trait construct and stereotype priming on action. *Journal of Personality and Social Psychology*, *71*, 230–244.

Barkin, S. L., Scheindlin, B., Brown, C. *et al.* (2005). Anticipatory guidance topics: are more better? *Ambulatory Pediatrics*, *5*, 372–376.

Bartlett, F. C. (1932). *Remembering: A Study in Experimental and Social Psychology*. New York: Cambridge University Press.

Batchelder, W. H. & Riefer, D. M. (1999). Theoretical and empirical review of multinomial processing tree modeling. *Psychonomic Bulletin & Review*, *6*, 57–86.

Baxter, G. & Besnard, D. (2004). Cognitive mismatches in the cockpit: Will they ever be a thing of the past? Paper presented at the flight deck of the future: human factors in data links and free flight conference, University of Nottingham.

Beaton, A. A., Gruneberg, M. M., Hyde, C. *et al.* (2005). Facilitation of receptive and productive foreign vocabulary acquisition using the keyword method: the role of image quality. *Memory*, *13*, 458–471.

Begg, I. M., Anas, A. & Farinacci, S. (1992). Dissociation of processes in belief: source recollection, statement familiarity, and the illusion of truth. *Journal of Experimental Psychology: General*, *121*, 446–458.

Berntsen, D. & Thomsen, D. K. (2005). Personal memories for remote historical events: accuracy and clarity of flashbulb memories related to World War II. *Journal of Experimental Psychology: General*, *134*, 242–257.

Bjork, R. A. (1994). Memory and metamemory considerations in the training of human beings. In J. Metcalfe & A. Shimamura (eds.), *Metacognition: Knowing about Knowing* (pp. 185–205). Cambridge, MA: MIT Press.

Bjork, R. A. (1999). Assessing our own competence: heuristics and illusions. In D. Gopher & A. Koriat (eds.), *Attention and Performance XVII. Cognitive Regulation of Performance: Interaction of Theory and Application* (pp. 435–459). Cambridge, MA: MIT Press.

Bodner, G. E. & Lindsay, D. S. (2003). Remembering and knowing in context. *Journal of Memory and Language*, *48*, 563–580.

Bower, G. H. (1970). Analysis of a mnemonic device. *American Scientist*, *58*, 496–510.

Bower, G. H., Black, J. B. & Turner, T. J. (1979). Scripts in memory for text. *Cognitive Psychology*, *11*, 177–220.

Brainerd, C. J. & Reyna, V. F. (2002). Fuzzy-trace theory and false memory. *Current Directions in Psychological Science*, *11*, 164–169.

Braun, K. A. & Loftus, E. F. (1998). Advertising's misinformation effect. *Applied Cognitive Psychology*, *12*, 569–591.

Brown, R. & Kulik, J. (1977). Flashbulb memories. *Cognition*, *5*, 73–99.

Buckhout, R. (1974). Eyewitness testimony. *Scientific American*, *231*, 23–31.

Cabeza, R. & Nyberg, L. (2000). Imaging cognition II: an empirical review of 275 PET and fMRI studies. *Journal of Cognitive Neuroscience*, *12*, 1–47.

Carlson, C. A. (2004). Distinctiveness in sequential and simultaneous lineups: an evaluation of SUSPECTS. Unpublished master's thesis, University of Oklahoma, Norman, OK.

Chase, W. G. & Simon, H. A. (1973). The mind's eye in chess. In W. G. Chase (ed.), *Visual Information Processing* (pp. 215–281). New York: Academic Press.

Clancey, W. J. (1997). Remembering controversies. In *Situated Cognition: On Human Knowledge and Computer Representations* (pp. 46–69). Cambridge: Cambridge University Press.

Clariana, R. B. (2003). The effectiveness of constructed-response and multiple-choice study tasks in computer aided learning. *Journal of Educational Computing Research*, *28*, 395–406.

Clark, S. E. (2003). A memory and decision model for eyewitness identification. *Applied Cognitive Psychology*, *17*, 629–654.

Clark, S. E., Abbe, A. & Larson, R. (in press). Collaboration in associative recognition memory: using recalled information to defend "new" judgments. *Journal of Experimental Psychology: Learning, Memory, and Cognition.*

Clark, S. E. & Gronlund, S. D. (1996). Global matching models of recognition memory: how the models match the data. *Psychonomic Bulletin & Review*, *3*, 37–60.

Clark, S. E. & Loftus, E. F. (1996). The construction of space alien abduction memories. *Psychological Inquiry*, *7*, 140–143.

Coates, S. L., Butler, L. T. & Berry, D. C. (2004). Implicit memory: a prime example for brand consideration and choice. *Applied Cognitive Psychology*, *18*, 1195–1211.

Cohen, M. S. & Tolcott, M. A. (1992). *A Cognitive Basis for Automated Target Recognition Interface Design*. Arlington, VA: Cognitive Technologies, Inc.

Conway, M. A. (1996). Autobiographical memories. In E. L. Bjork & R. A. Bjork (eds.), *Memory* (pp. 165–194). San Diego, CA: Academic Press.

Conway, M. A. (2005). Memory and the self. *Journal of Memory and Language*, *53*, 594–628.

Conway, M. A., Gardiner, J. M., Perfect, T. J. *et al.* (1997). Changes in memory awareness during learning: the acquisition of knowledge by psychology undergraduates. *Journal of Experimental Psychology: General*, *126*, 393–413.

Craik, F. I. M., Govoni, R., Naveh-Benjamin, M. & Anderson, N. D. (1996). The effects of divided attention on encoding and retrieval processes in human memory. *Journal of Experimental Psychology: General*, *125*, 159–180.

Craik, F. I. M. & Lockhart, R. S. (1972). Levels of processing: a framework for memory research. *Journal of Verbal Learning and Verbal Behavior*, *11*, 671–684.

Curran, T. & Hintzman, D. L. (1995). Violations of the independence assumption in process dissociation. *Journal of Experimental Psychology: Learning, Memory, and Cognition*, *21*, 531–547.

Dennis, S. & Humphreys, M. S. (2001). A context noise model of episodic word recognition. *Psychological Review*, *108*, 452–477.

Dobbins, I. G., Kroll, N. E. A., Yonelinas, A. P. & Liu, Q. (1998). Distinctiveness in recognition and free recall: the role of recollection in the rejection of the familiar. *Journal of Memory and Language*, *38*, 381–400.

Dougherty, M. R. P., Gettys, C. F. & Ogden, E. E. (1999). MINERVA-DM: a memory processes model for judgments of likelihood. *Psychological Review*, *106*, 180–209.

Dougherty, M. R. P., Gronlund, S. D. & Gettys, C. F. (2003). Memory as a fundamental heuristic for decision making. In S. L. Schneider & J. Shanteau (eds.), *Emerging Perspectives on Judgment and Decision Research* (pp. 125–164). New York: Cambridge University Press.

Dudai, Y. (2004). The neurobiology of consolidations, or, how stable is the engram. *Annual Review of Psychology*, *55*, 51–86.

Durso, F. T. (ed.) (1999). *Handbook of Applied Cognition*. Chichester: John Wiley & Sons.
Durso, F. T. & Gronlund, S. D. (1999). Situation awareness. In F. T. Durso (ed.), *Handbook of Applied Cognition* (pp. 283–314). Chichester: John Wiley & Sons.
Einstein, G. O., McDaniel, M. A., Smith, R. E. & Shaw, P. (1998). Habitual prospective memory and aging: remembering intentions and forgetting actions. *Psychological Science, 9*, 284–288.
Engelkamp, J. & Zimmer, H. (2001). Categorical and order information in free recall of action phrases. *Psicológica, 22*, 71–96.
Fisher, R. P. & Geiselman, R. E. (1992). *Memory-Enhancing Techniques for Investigative Interviewing: The Cognitive Interview*. Springfield, IL: Charles C. Thomas.
Foos, P. W., Mora, J. J. & Tkacz, S. (1994). Student study techniques and the generation effect. *Journal of Educational Psychology, 86*, 567–576.
Gabbert, F., Memon, A. & Allan, K. (2003). Memory conformity: can eyewitnesses influence each other's memories for an event? *Applied Cognitive Psychology, 17*, 533–543.
Gardiner, J. M. & Java, R. I. (1993). Recognizing and remembering. In A. F. Collins, S. E. Gathercole, M. A. Conway & P. E. Morris (eds.), *Theories of Memory* (pp. 163–188). Hove: Lawrence Erlbaum Associates.
Glaser, W. R. & Glaser, M. O. (1989). Context effects in Stroop-like word and picture processing. *Journal of Experimental Psychology: General, 118*, 13–42.
Glenberg, A. M. (1979). Component-levels theory of the effects of spacing of repetitions on recall and recognition. *Memory & Cognition, 7*, 95–112.
Gillihan, S. & Farah, M. J. (2005). Is self-related processing special? A critical review. *Psychological Bulletin, 131*, 76–97.
Goldinger, S. D. & Azuma, T. (2004). Episodic memory reflected in printed word naming. *Psychonomic Bulletin & Review, 11*, 716–722.
Goldsmith, M., Koriat, A. & Pansky, A. (2005). Strategic regulation of grain size in memory reporting over time. *Journal of Memory and Language, 52*, 505–525.
Golly-Häring, C. & Englekamp, J. (2003). Categorical-relational and order-relational information in memory for subject-performed and experimenter-performed actions. *Journal of Experimental Psychology: Learning, Memory, and Cognition, 29*, 965–975.
Greenberg, D. L. (2004). President Bush's false "flashbulb" memory of 9/11/01. *Applied Cognitive Psychology, 18*, 363–370.
Gronlund, S. D. (2005). Sequential lineup advantage: contributions of distinctiveness and recollection. *Applied Cognitive Psychology, 19*, 23–37.
Gronlund, S. D., Dougherty, M. R. P., Durso *et al.* (2005). Planning in air traffic control: impact of problem type. *International Journal of Aviation Psychology, 15*, 269–293.
Gronlund, S. D., Ohrt, D. D., Dougherty, M. R. P. *et al.* (1998). Role of memory in air traffic control. *Journal of Experimental Psychology: Applied, 4*, 263–280.
Gronlund, S. D. & Ratcliff, R. (1989). Time course of item and associative information: implications for global memory models. *Journal of Experimental Psychology: Learning, Memory & Cognition, 15*, 846–858.
Hay, J. F. & Jacoby, L. L. (1999). Separating habit and recollection in young and elderly adults. Effects of elaborative processing and distinctiveness. *Psychology and Aging, 14*, 122–134.
Herbert, D. M. B. & Burt, J. S. (2001). Memory awareness and schematization: learning in the university context. *Applied Cognitive Psychology, 15*, 617–637.
Hinsz, V. B. (1990). Cognitive and consensus processes in group recognition memory performance. *Journal of Personality & Social Psychology, 59*, 705–718.
Holden, S. J. S. & Vanhuele, M. (1999). Know the name, forget the exposure: brand familiarity versus memory of exposure context. *Psychology & Marketing, 16*, 479–496.
Holland, R. W., Hendriks, M. & Aarts, H. (2005). Smells like clean spirit: nonconscious effects of scent on cognition and behavior. *Psychological Science, 16*, 689–693.
Humphreys, M. S. (1978). Item and relational information: a case for context independent retrieval. *Journal of Verbal Learning and Verbal Behavior, 17*, 175–187.
Hunt, R. R. (1995). The subtlety of distinctiveness: what von Restorff really did. *Psychonomic Bulletin & Review, 2*, 105–112.

Hunt, R. R. (2003). Two contributions of distinctive processing to accurate memory. *Journal of Memory and Language*, *48*, 811–825.
Hunt, R. R. & McDaniel, M. A. (1993). The enigma of organization and distinctiveness. *Journal of Memory and Language*, *32*, 421–445.
Jacoby, L. L. (1991). A process dissociation framework: separating automatic and intentional uses of memory. *Journal of Memory and Language*, *30*, 513–541.
Jacoby, L. L., Craik, F. I. M. & Begg, I. (1979). Effects of decision difficulty on recognition and recall. *Journal of Verbal Learning and Verbal Behavior*, *18*, 585–600.
Jacoby, L. L., Kelley, C. M., Brown, J. & Jasechko, J. (1989). Becoming famous overnight: limits on the ability to avoid unconscious influences of the past. *Journal of Personality and Social Psychology*, *56*, 326–338.
Jacoby, L. L., Kelley, C. M. & Dywan, J. (1989). Memory attributions. In H. L. Roediger III & F. I. M. Craik (eds.), *Varieties of Memory and Consciousness: Essays in Honour of Endel Tulving* (pp. 391–422). Hillsdale, NJ: Lawrence Erlbaum Associates.
Jennings, J. M. & Jacoby, L. L. (2003). Improving memory in older adults: training recollection. *Neuropsychological Rehabilitation*, *13*, 417–440.
Johnson, M. K., Foley, M. A., Suengas, A. G. & Raye, C. L. (1988). Phenomenal characteristics of memories for perceived and imagined autobiographical events. *Journal of Experimental Psychology: General*, *117*, 371–376.
Johnson, M. K., Hashtroudi, S. & Lindsay, D. S. (1993). Source monitoring. *Psychological Bulletin*, *114*, 3–28.
Kahana, M. J., Rizzuto, D. S. & Schneider, A. R. (2005). Theoretical correlations and measured correlations: relating recognition and recall in four distributed memory models. *Journal of Experimental Psychology: Learning, Memory, and Cognition*, *31*, 933–953.
Kendzierski, D. (1980). Self-schemata and scripts: the recall of self-referent and scriptal information. *Personality & Social Psychology Bulletin*, *6*, 23–29.
Kohnken, G., Milne, R., Memon, A. & Bull, R. (1999). The cognitive interview: a meta-analysis. *Psychology, Crime & Law*, *5*, 3–27.
Koriat, A. & Goldsmith, M. (1996). Monitoring and control processes in the strategic regulation of memory accuracy. *Psychological Review*, *103*, 409–517.
Koriat, A., Goldsmith, M. & Pansky, A. (2000). Toward a psychology of memory accuracy. *Annual Review of Psychology*, *51*, 481–537.
Koriat, A., Pearlman-Avnion, S. & Ben-Zur, H. (1998). The subjective organization of input and output events in memory. *Psychological Research*, *61*, 295–307.
Leboe, J. P. & Whittlesea, B. W. A. (2002). The inferential basis of familiarity and recall: evidence for a common underlying process. *Journal of Memory and Language*, *46*, 804–829.
Lindsay, R. C. & Wells, G. L. (1985). Improving eyewitness identifications from lineups: simultaneous versus sequential lineup presentation. *Journal of Applied Psychology*, *70*, 556–564.
Loftus, E. F. (1979). *Eyewitness Testimony*. Cambridge, MA: Harvard University Press.
Loftus, E. F. (1997). Creating false memories. *Scientific American*, *277*, 70–75.
Loftus, E. F. & Ketcham, K. (1994). *The Myth of Repressed Memory: False Memories and Allegations of Sexual Abuse*. New York: St. Martin's Griffin.
Loftus, E. F. & Palmer, J. C. (1974). Reconstruction of automobile destruction. *Journal of Verbal Learning and Verbal Behavior*, *13*, 585–589.
Logan, G. D. (2002). An instance theory of attention and memory. *Psychological Review*, *109*, 376–400.
McCloskey, M. & Zaragoza, M. (1985). Misleading postevent information and memory for events: arguments and evidence against memory impairment hypotheses. *Journal of Experimental Psychology: General*, *114*, 1–16.
McDaniel, M. A. & Einstein, G. O. (1993). The importance of cue familiarity and cue distinctiveness in prospective memory. *Memory*, *1*, 23–41.
McDaniel, M. A. & Einstein, G. O. (2000). Strategic and automatic processes in prospective memory retrieval: a multiprocess framework. *Applied Cognitive Psychology*, *14*, 127–144.
MacInnis, D. J., Moorman, C. & Jaworski, B. J. (1991). Enhancing and measuring consumers' motivation, opportunity, and ability to process brand information from ads. *Journal of Marketing*, *55*, 32–53.

Malmberg, K. J., Zeelenberg, R. & Shiffrin, R. M. (2004). Turning up the noise or turning down the volume? On the nature of the impairment of episodic recognition memory by Midazolam. *Journal of Experimental Psychology: Learning, Memory, and Cognition*, *30*, 537–546.

Malpass, R. S. (1996). Enhancing eyewitness memory. In S. Sporer, R. S. Malpass & G. Koehnken (eds.), *Psychological Issues in Eyewitness Identification* (pp. 177–204). Hillsdale, NJ: Lawrence Erlbaum Associates.

Mandler, G. (1980). Recognizing: the judgment of previous occurrence. *Psychological Review*, *87*, 252–271.

Mazzoni, G. & Memon, A. (2003). Imagination can create false autobiographical memories. *Psychological Science*, *14*, 186–188.

Medin, D. L., Ross, B. H. & Markman, A. B. (2001). *Cognitive Psychology* (3rd edn), Fort Worth, TX: Harcourt College Publishers.

Moore, J. H. (1936). The role of determining tendencies in learning. *American Journal of Psychology*, *48*, 559–571.

Moray, N. (1987). Intelligent aids, mental models, and the theory of machines. *International Journal of Man–Machine Studies*, *27*, 619–629.

Morris, C. D., Bransford, J. D. & Franks, J. J. (1977). Levels of processing versus transfer-appropriate processing. *Journal of Verbal Learning and Verbal Behavior*, *16*, 519–533.

Nairne, J. S. (2002). The myth of the encoding-retrieval match. *Memory*, *10*, 389–395.

Neisser, U. (1978). Memory: what are the important questions? In M. M. Gruneberg, P. E. Morris & R. N. Sykes (eds.), *Practical Aspects of Memory* (pp. 3–24). London: Academic Press.

Nelson, D. L., Reed, U. S. & Walling, J. R. (1976). Picture superiority effect. *Journal of Experimental Psychology: Human Learning & Memory*, *2*, 523–528.

Norman, K. A. & O'Reilly, R. C. (2003). Modeling hippocampal and neocortical contributions to recognition memory: a complementary learning systems approach. *Psychological Review*, *110*, 611–646.

Nosofsky, R. M. (1988). Exemplar-based accounts of relations between classification, recognition, and typicality. *Journal of Experimental Psychology: Learning, Memory, and Cognition*, *14*, 700–708.

Paivio, A. (1971). *Imagery and Verbal Processes*. Oxford: Holt, Rinehart & Winston.

Paivio, A. (1973). Picture superiority in free recall: imagery or dual coding? *Cognitive Psychology*, *5*, 176–206.

Palmeri, T. J. & Gauthier, I. (2004). Visual object understanding. *Nature Reviews Neuroscience*, *5*, 291–303.

Patel, V. L., Arocha, J. F. & Kaufman, D. R. (1999). Medical cognition. In F. T. Durso (ed.), *Handbook of Applied Cognition* (pp. 663–693). Chichester: John Wiley & Sons.

Petty, R., Cacioppo, J. & Heesacker, M. (1981). Effects of rhetorical questions on persuasion: a cognitive response analysis. *Journal of Personality and Social Psychology*, *40*, 432–440.

Piolat, A., Olive, T. & Kellogg, R. T. (2005). Cognitive effort during note taking. *Applied Cognitive Psychology*, *19*, 291–312.

Pitman, R. & Delahanty, D. (2005). Conceptually driven pharmacologic approaches to acute trauma. *CNS Spectrums*, *10*, 99–106.

Pozzulo, J. D. & Lindsay, R. C. L. (1999). Elimination lineups: an improved identification procedure for child eyewitnesses. *Journal of Applied Psychology*, *84*, 167–176.

Raaijmakers, J. G. W. (2003). Spacing and repetition effects in human memory: application of the SAM model. *Cognitive Science*, *27*, 431–452.

Raaijmakers, J. G. W. & Shiffrin, R. M. (1981). Search of associative memory. *Psychological Review*, *88*, 93–134.

Reed, A. V. (1973). Speed-accuracy trade-off in recognition memory. *Science*, *181*, 574–576.

Richland, L. E., Bjork, R. A., Finley, J. R. & Linn, M. C. (2005). Linking cognitive science to education: generation and interleaving effects. In B. G. Bara, L. Barsalou & M. Bucciarelli (eds.), *Proceedings of the Twenty-Seventh Annual Conference of the Cognitive Science Society*. Mahwah, NJ: Lawrence Erlbaum Associates.

Riefer, D. M., Knapp, B. R., Batchelder, W. H. *et al.* (2002). Cognitive psychometrics: assessing storage and retrieval deficits in special populations with multinomial processing tree models. *Psychological Assessment*, *14*, 184–201.

Roediger, H. L. III & Blaxton, T. A. (1987). Retrieval modes produce dissociations in memory for surface information. In D. S. Gorfein (ed.), *Memory and Learning: The Ebbinghaus Centennial Conference* (pp. 349–379). Hillsdale, NJ: Lawrence Erlbaum Associates.

Roediger, H. L. III & Karpicke, J. D. (2006). Test-enhanced learning: taking memory tests improves long-term retention. *Psychological Science*, *17*, 249–255.

Rohrer, D., Taylor, K., Pashler, H. *et al.* (2005). The effect of overlearning on long-term retention. *Applied Cognitive Psychology*, *19*, 361–374.

Ross, B. H. & Landauer, T. K. (1978). Memory for at least one of two items: test and failure of several theories of spacing effects. *Journal of Verbal Learning and Verbal Behavior*, *17*, 669–680.

Rotello, C. M. & Heit, E. (2000). Associative recognition: a case of recall-to-reject processing. *Memory & Cognition*, *28*, 907–922.

Rubin, D. (2005). A basic-systems approach to autobiographical memory. *Current Direction in Psychological Science*, *14*, 79–83.

Sarter, N. B. & Woods, D. D. (1995). How in the world did we ever get into that mode? Mode error and awareness in supervisory control. *Human Factors*, *37*, 5–19.

Schacter, D. L. (1987). Implicit memory: history and current status. *Journal of Experimental Psychology: Learning, Memory, and Cognition*, *13*, 501–518.

Schacter, D. L. (1999). The seven sins of memory: insights from psychology and cognitive neuroscience. *American Psychologist*, *54*, 182–203.

Schacter, D. L., Koutstaal, W. & Norman, K. A. (1997). False memories and aging. *Trends in Cognitive Science*, *1*, 229–236.

Schmolck, H., Buffalo, E. A. & Squire, L. R. (2000). Memory distortions develop over time: recollections of the O.J. Simpson trial verdict after 15 and 32 months. *Psychological Science*, *11*, 39–45.

Schooler, J. W. & Tanaka, J. W. (1991). Composites, compromises, and CHARM: what is the evidence for blend memory representations? *Journal of Experimental Psychology: General*, *120*, 96–100.

Semon, R. (1921). *The Mneme*. London: George Allen & Unwin.

Senkfor, A. J., Van Petten, C. & Kutas, M. (2002). Episodic action for real objects: an ERP investigation with perform, watch, and imagine action encoding tasks versus a non-action encoding task. *Journal of Cognitive Neuroscience*, *14*, 402–419.

Shapiro, J. M. (2005). A "memory-jamming" theory of advertising. Retrieved May 7, 2006, Available at: http://home.uchicago.edu/~jmshapir/advert101805.pdf.

Shepard, R. N. (1967). Recognition memory for words, sentences, and pictures. *Journal of Verbal Learning and Verbal Behavior*, *6*, 156–163.

Sisson, E. D. (1939). Retroactive inhibition: the temporal position of interpolated activity. *Journal of Experimental Psychology*, *25*, 228–233.

Skurnik, I., Yoon, C., Park, D. C. & Schwarz, N. (2005). How warnings about false claims become recommendations. *Journal of Consumer Research*, *31*, 713–724.

Slamecka, N. J. & Graf, P. (1978). The generation effect: delineation of a phenomenon. *Journal of Experimental Psychology: Human Learning and Memory*, *4*, 592–604.

Slotnick, S. D. & Dodson, C. S. (2005). Support for a continuous (single-process) model of recognition memory and source memory. *Memory & Cognition*, *33*, 151–170.

Squire, L. R. (1992). Declarative and nondeclarative memory: multiple brain systems supporting learning and memory. *Journal of Cognitive Neuroscience*, *4*, 232–243.

Stacy, A. W., Pearce, S. G., Zogg, J. B. *et al.* (2004). A nonverbal test of naturalistic memory for alcohol commercials. *Psychology & Marketing*, *21*, 295–322.

Steblay, N., Dysart, J., Fulero, S. & Lindsay, R. C. L. (2001). Eyewitness accuracy rates in sequential and simultaneous lineup presentations: a meta-analytic comparison. *Law & Human Behavior*, *25*, 459–473.

Strong, E. K. Jr (1912). The effect of length of series upon recognition memory. *Psychological Review*, *19*, 447–462.

Talarico, J. M. & Rubin, D. C. (2003). Confidence, not consistency, characterizes flashbulb memories. *Psychological Science*, *14*, 455–461.

Tulving, E. (1972). Episodic and semantic memory. In E. Tulving & W. Donaldson (eds.), *Organization of Memory* (pp. 381–403). New York: Academic Press.

Tulving E. (1985). Memory and consciousness. *Canadian Psychology*, *26*, 1–12.

Tulving, E. (1991). Concepts of human memory. In L. Squire, G. Lynch, N. M. Weinberger & J. L. McGaugh (eds.), *Memory: Organization and Locus of Change* (pp. 3–32). New York: Oxford University Press.

Tulving, E. (2002). Episodic memory: from mind to brain. *Annual Review of Psychology*, *53*, 1–25.

Tulving, E. & Craik, F. I. M. (eds.) (2000). *The Oxford Handbook of Memory*. London: Oxford University Press.

Tulving, E. & Pearlstone, Z. (1966). Availability versus accessibility of information in memory for words. *Journal of Verbal Learning and Verbal Behavior*, *5*, 381–391.

Tulving, E., Schacter, D. L., McLachlan, D. R. & Moscovitch, M. (1988). Priming of semantic autobiographical knowledge: a case study of retrograde amnesia. *Brain & Cognition*, *8*, 3–20.

Tulving, E. & Thomson, D. M. (1971). Retrieval processes in recognition memory: effects of associative context. *Journal of Experimental Psychology*, *87*, 116–124.

Tulving, E. & Thomson, D. M. (1973). Encoding specificity and retrieval processes in episodic memory. *Psychological Review*, *80*, 359–380.

Wainwright, M. J. & Reingold, E. M. (1996). Response bias correction in the process dissociation procedure: approaches, assumptions, and evaluation. *Consciousness and Cognition*, *5*, 232–254.

Watkins, M. J. (1990). Mediationism and the obfuscation of memory. *American Psychologist*, *45*, 328–335.

Watkins, O. C. & Watkins, M. J. (1975). Buildup of proactive inhibition as a cue-overload effect. *Journal of Experimental Psychology: Human Learning and Memory*, *1*, 442–452.

Wells, G. L. & Olson, E. A. (2003). Eyewitness testimony. *Annual Review of Psychology*, *54*, 277–295.

Wells, G. L., Small, M., Penrod, S. *et al.* (1998). Eyewitness identification procedures: recommendations for lineups and photospreads. *Law and Human Behavior*, *22*, 603–647.

Wheeler, M. A., Stuss, D. T. & Tulving, E. (1997). Toward a theory of episodic memory: the frontal lobes and autonoetic consciousness. *Psychological Bulletin*, *121*, 331–354.

Wheeler M. E., Petersen, S. E. & Buckner, R. L. (2000). Memory's echo: vivid remembering reactivates sensory-specific cortex. *Proceedings of the National Academy of Sciences*, *97*, 11125–11129.

Whittlesea, B. W. A. (2002). False memory and the discrepancy-attribution-hypothesis: the prototype-familiarity illusion. *Journal of Experimental Psychology: General*, *131*, 96–115.

Wiley, J. (2005). A fair and balanced look at the news: what affects memory for controversial arguments? *Journal of Memory and Language*, *53*, 95–109.

Williamson, G., Kaufman, C., Bermann, G., Bushell, D. L. [Producers], Gondry, M. [Director] & Kaufman, C. [Writer]. (2004). *Eternal sunshine of the spotless mind* [Motion picture]. United States: Focus Features.

Winograd, E. (1988). Some observations on prospective remembering. In M. M. Gruneburg, P. I. Morris & R. N. Sykes (eds.), *Memory in Everyday Life* (Vol. 1). Chichester: John Wiley & Sons.

Wixted, J. T. (2004). The psychology and neuroscience of forgetting. *Annual Review of Psychology*, *55*, 235–269.

Wixted, J. T. (2005). A theory about why we forget what we once knew. *Current Directions in Psychological Science*, *14*, 6–9.

Wixted, J. T. & Stretch, V. (2004). In defense of the signal detection interpretation of remember/know judgments. *Psychonomic Bulletin & Review*, *11*, 616–641.

Yonelinas, A. P. (1999). The contribution of recollection and familiarity to recognition and source-memory judgments: a formal dual-process model and an analysis of receiver operating characteristics. *Journal of Experimental Psychology: Learning, Memory, and Cognition*, *25*, 1415–1434.

Yonelinas, A. P. (2002). The nature of recollection and familiarity: a review of 30 years of research. *Journal of Memory and Language*, *46*, 441–517.

Yonelinas, A. P. & Jacoby, L. L. (1994). Dissociations of processes in recognition memory: effects of interference and of response speed. *Canadian Journal of Experimental Psychology*, *48*, 516–534.

Zaragoza, M. S., Payment, K. E., Ackil, J. K. *et al.* (2001). Interviewing witnesses: forced confabulation and confirmatory feedback increases false memories. *Psychological Science*, *12*, 473–477.

Zimmer, H. D. (2001). Why do actions speak louder than words? Action memory as a variant of encoding manipulations or the result of a specific memory system? In H. D. Zimmer, R. L. Cohen, M. Guynn *et al.* (eds.), *Memory for Action: A Distinct form of Episodic Memory?* (pp. 151–197). New York: Oxford University Press.

Zwaan, R. A. (1994). Effect of genre expectations on text comprehension. *Journal of Experimental Psychology: Learning, Memory, and Cognition*, *20*, 920–933.

CHAPTER 6

Metamemory

John Dunlosky, Michael J. Serra, and Julie M. C. Baker
Kent State University, USA

METAMEMORY APPLIED

Imagine Beth, a sixth-year graduate student, as she prepares to give an important conference talk about her dissertation research. Her PowerPoint slides are all in order, so she proceeds by practicing her talk as she steps from slide to slide. As Beth practices, she realizes that her introduction – where she provides a broader perspective on her field – is quite weak; she notices herself stumbling and searching for words. Because of these problems, she decides to develop more detailed ideas on what to say, so that the beginning of the talk will be polished. Also, Beth is adamant about not using notes or reading from the slides, and she realizes that it is best to straight-out memorize the short list of caveats about her conclusions. To do so, she repeats each caveat over and over. Beth has already given multiple talks, and it is obvious to her that her anxiety can undermine what should otherwise be a smooth presentation. So to help conquer some anxiety, she decides to practice the talk a bit extra this time, and to do so multiple times with a mock audience.

DEFINING METACOGNITION: CONSTRUCTS AND QUESTIONS

Although many of the activities that Beth engaged in – from preparing her slides to practicing her talk – clearly involve cognitive processes, some of the activities recruit metacognitive processes as well. Taken literally, the term *metacognition* means cognition about cognition. Any component of cognition can bear the *meta*-prefix, such as metalinguistics, metaperception, and metamemory. *Metamemory* refers to a person's cognitions about his or her own memory and is the focus of the present chapter. After we define the core constructs and questions that are fundamental to metacognition, we move to a detailed analysis of metamemory and how advances in this area have led to insights into improving human learning and memory. The same definitions, methods, and theory described in these sections can be applied to exploring other real-world problems that involve people's metacognitive abilities. At the end of the chapter, we touch on two of

Handbook of Applied Cognition: Second Edition. Edited by Francis T. Durso.

these problems – improving juror deliberation and people's comprehension of text – to illustrate the breadth and power of the metacognitive framework. Thus, we do not provide a laundry list of all current and possible applications of metamemory. Instead, this chapter is a guide for researchers who may want to explore how metacognitive abilities may contribute to human performance in their applied domain of interest. To best serve this purpose, we first discuss definitions and theory of metacognition relevant to application – which includes real-world examples to illustrate key points – before we consider applied metamemory in detail.

Concerning a more refined conceptualization of metacognition, ever since Flavell (1979) emphasized the importance of metacognition to cognitive development, *metacognition* has been defined by the numerous kinds of activity that are either about one's cognitive processes or work upon them. Although early debates in the area centered on which activities should be included under the rubric of metacognition (Cavanaugh & Perlmutter 1982), current conceptualizations include these three constructs: knowledge about one's cognition, the monitoring of ongoing cognition, and controlling cognition. We consider each construct in turn, as well as how each one arises as Beth prepares for her conference talk. Beth's preparation for her talk, though, is just one example of how metacognition can influence behavior in everyday situations. The three constructs described above – knowledge, monitoring, and control – can be isolated and studied in many situations in which people perform everyday tasks that involve thinking about and controlling their actions.

Metacognitive knowledge, or knowledge about cognition, is declarative knowledge composed of a person's beliefs about any aspect of cognition. In the introductory scenario, Beth believed that anxiety would undermine her performance (which is likely correct; see Matthews *et al.* 2000, chapter 15), and she obviously knew about some rehearsal strategies. Nevertheless, her belief that rote repetition would ensure excellent memory for her conclusions may not be entirely accurate (e.g., Hertzog *et al.* 1998). Initial research on metacognition concerned people's beliefs and knowledge about cognition (and in particular, children's knowledge, e.g., Kreutzer *et al.* 1975), and a great deal of research has been devoted to understanding the development of people's beliefs about cognition and how these beliefs are related to one's wellbeing and cognitive performance.

Almost everyone will accrue extensive knowledge and beliefs about how cognition operates in general. Beginning in early development, children develop a sophisticated theory of mind, which includes an understanding of mental states such as one's desires, intentions, and emotions (for a recent review, see Flavell 2004). Later in life, many people develop a belief that forgetting becomes more of a problem as we age (McDonald-Miszczak *et al.* 1995), and adults of all ages have knowledge and beliefs about how the mind operates in general (Hertzog & Hultsch 2000). The knowledge obtained is not always accurate, and recent research in the domain of psychopathology has explored the degree to which incorrect beliefs about cognition can contribute to mental disorder (e.g., Cartwright-Hatton & Wells 1997). For instance, Emmelkamp and Aardema (1999) report that obsessive-compulsive behavior is related to thought–action fusion, which is the belief that one's intrusive thoughts are "morally equivalent to carrying out a prohibited action" (p. 139, e.g., having a violent thought is almost as inappropriate as violence itself). Likewise, a doctor may hold the belief that patients understand and will remember the instructions they are given, which may often reflect inaccurate knowledge about others' minds that could undermine patients' wellbeing. In these cases, researchers will need to discover the specific knowledge and beliefs people have about cognition and how such metacognitive knowledge influences thought and action.

In the present chapter, we focus on the more process-oriented constructs of metacognition: monitoring and control.[1] *Monitoring* involves assessing the current state or ongoing progress of any aspect of cognition, and *control* involves the regulation of ongoing cognitive processes. Examples of each abound. Beth monitored her ongoing progress toward developing a competent talk by attending to how often she stumbled during practice. She then exerted control by deciding to continue practicing those parts of the talk on which she stumbled the most. In this case, Beth's monitoring (i.e., checking for stumbling) served in the control of how she practiced (e.g., by devising detailed ideas about how to present parts of the talk where she stumbled).

These definitions and examples provide an excellent beginning (and end for many) concerning monitoring and control. Nevertheless, even though the nature of these two constructs in some ways is quite intuitive, their actual conceptualization in the literature is sometimes vague or overextended to include other processes. For instance, consider the following rationale, which is arguably plausible. If monitoring involves assessing an ongoing cognitive state and self-assessments involve conscious activity, it seems reasonable that an activity must be conscious to count as metacognitive. Whether conscious awareness is necessary for metacognitive activities has stimulated research and debates (Reder 1996), but the definitions of monitoring and control should remain agnostic toward the issue of consciousness. This goal was met by Nelson and Narens (1990, 1994), who defined monitoring and control in terms of the flow of information within a dominance relationship between a metalevel and object-level of cognition. As shown in Figure 6.1 (Panel A), Nelson and Narens (1990) defined monitoring and control in terms of the flow of information between these two levels. In particular, monitoring occurs when the metalevel is informed by information from an object-level cognition, and control occurs whenever information from the metalevel modifies the object-level. Nelson and Narens (1994)

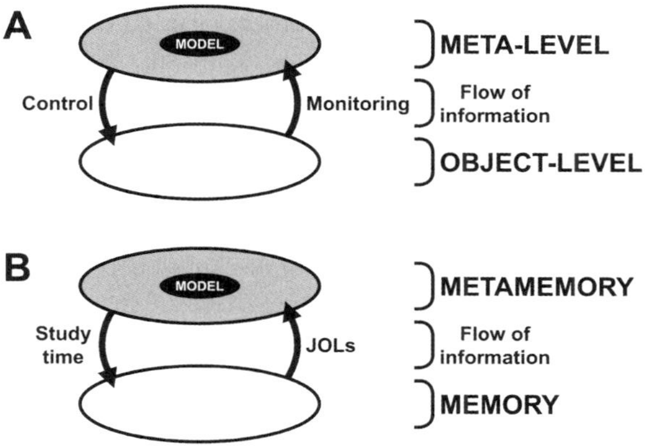

Figure 6.1 Monitoring and control defined as the flow of information between two levels of cognition (Panel A) and a specific instantiation relevant to the allocation of study time (Panel B). Adapted from Nelson and Narens (1994)

described this system in detail and generalized it to more than two levels. Importantly, this model is agnostic as to whether people are conscious of the flow of information or as to whether the two levels of representation are psychologically or physiologically distinct. Both issues will need to be resolved through empirical analyses (for evidence that they are distinct, see Mazzoni & Nelson 1998; Pannu & Kaszniak 2005).

Important advances in our understanding of monitoring and control processes have been achieved over the past three decades. Advances in measurement, methods, and theories have led to a honing of questions relevant to metacognition and to a greater specificity of answers for them. As important, these advances have implications for enhancing human performance in many domains, and some have been validated empirically in the laboratory and in the field.

In the remainder of this chapter, we will discuss monitoring and control mainly as they have been addressed in regards to *metamemory*, which is the facet of metacognition that concerns people's monitoring and control of learning and retrieval processes. We targeted metamemory because progressive – and extensive – research is available concerning both monitoring and control within this domain. We move next to a discussion of standard measures of memory monitoring and control and introduce core questions within this field. This discussion largely comprises a tutorial that may be skipped by more knowledgeable readers. We then review recent research that has sought to answer some of these core questions in one area of metamemory that pertains to how people monitor and control their learning. This review is also meant to showcase how metacognitive methods and theory have been used to investigate metamemory. As important, we describe this research in some detail in hopes that the method and theory can be extended to investigate any real-world task that involves metacognitive processes. After this review, we end with a discussion of how such a metamemory framework has been extended to investigate two applied domains (jury deliberation and text comprehension), so as to showcase the versatility and power of the framework.

MONITORING AND CONTROL: MEASURES AND QUESTIONS

In the domain of metamemory, any memory process can be the object of the metalevel, so that monitoring can potentially be directed toward any one of these processes. A student can monitor his or her ongoing learning of simple materials and can later monitor progress toward retrieving these same materials. To measure monitoring in either case, research participants are often asked to make overt judgments about the particular process under investigation. For instance, to investigate people's monitoring of ongoing learning, participants may judge how well they have learned a particular item by predicting the likelihood of recalling it on a subsequent test. It is important to note that these judgments – or any other kind of metamemory judgment for that matter – are not taken at face value, as if they were a direct and valid measure of on-going monitoring of memory (Nelson 1996a). Instead, researchers obtain objective measures of performance that can be compared to the judgments, so that judgment biases can be described and understood. For instance, to evaluate Beth's metacognitive ability, we might ask her to explicitly judge how well she performed each portion of her talk and then compare those judgments to some objective assessment of her performance, such as ratings obtained from a group of experienced speakers.

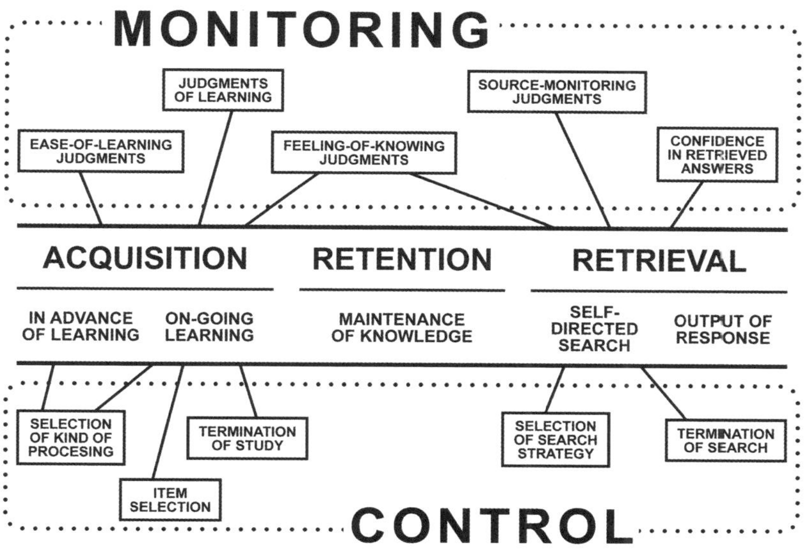

Figure 6.2 Overview of the metacognitive framework first proposed by Nelson and Narens (1990), which now includes judgments that were absent from the original framework

Through the 1970s and 1980s, interest in metamemory grew steadily and investigators explored a variety of monitoring and control processes relevant to learning. Although exceptions exist, research on any one monitoring or control process was largely conducted in isolation from others. Isolationism was curtailed, however, when Nelson and Narens (1990) published a framework that subsequently unified areas of metamemory research. In particular, they organized the different measures of monitoring and control across three stages of learning: acquisition, retention, and retrieval. The measures are illustrated in Figure 6.2 (adapted from Nelson & Narens 1990), and their definitions are presented in Table 6.1.

To make any judgment, a person is asked to evaluate some aspect of learning or test processes. For instance, participants may study paired associates (e.g., dog–spoon), take a test of recall on those items (e.g., recall the correct response to "dog– ?"), and then take a recognition test for all items in which they did not recall the correct response. During these study-test trials, participants may judge several aspects of their progress and performance, and the various metamemory judgments differ with respect to which specific process is being evaluated. For instance, participants may make ease-of-learning judgments prior to learning by judging how easy each item will be to learn during subsequent study trials. For judgments of learning, participants would first study the items and then predict how likely they will be to recall each one on the upcoming criterion test. For feeling-of-knowing judgments, participants first take a recall test over all the items and then judge responses that were not correctly recalled. For these non-recalled items, participants predict the likelihood of recognizing the non-recalled response on a recognition test with multiple alternatives. And for retrospective confidence judgments, participants judge the likelihood that their responses on a test are correct. Each judgment may be

Table 6.1 Names and common definitions of metacognitive judgments and control processes

Name	Definition
	Metacognitive judgments
Ease-of-learning (EOL) judgments	Judgments of how easy to-be-studied items will be to learn.
Judgments of Learning (JOL)	Judgments of the likelihood of remembering recently studied items on an upcoming test.
Feeling of knowing (FOK) judgments	Judgments of the likelihood of recognizing currently unrecallable answers on an upcoming test.
Source-monitoring judgments	Judgments made during a criterion test pertaining to the source of a particular memory.
Confidence in Retrieved Answers	Judgments of the likelihood that a response on a test is correct. Often referred to as retrospective confidence (RC) judgments.
	Control processes
Selection of Kind of Processing	Selection of strategies to employ when attempting to commit to an item to memory.
Item Selection	Decision about whether to study an item on an upcoming trial.
Termination of Study	Decision to stop studying an item currently being studied.
Selection of Search Strategy	Selecting a particular strategy in order to produce a correct response during a test.
Termination of Search	Decisions to terminate searching for a response.

applied to investigate metamemory in real-world tasks. For instance, when students are preparing for an exam, a teacher may ask them to judge how well they have learned the study materials to identify students who are overconfident about how much they have learned. And during the actual exam, students may be asked to judge the correctness of each response in an attempt to determine how often they guess.

In Figure 6.2, the judgments also differ with respect to which control processes that they may inform. For instance, judgments of learning (JOLs) presumably inform the termination of study during ongoing learning, and confidence in retrieved answers informs the control of search during self-regulated retrieval. Such monitoring-and-control dynamics are addressed more specifically in Figure 6.1 (Panel B), which illustrates the relationship between constructs and measures for the termination of study. Termination of study time is hypothesized to rely on an evaluation (as measured by JOLs) of ongoing learning, which then feeds into a decision about terminating study. For instance, students who are overconfident about how much they have learned may stop studying well before achieving their learning goals. Of course, even the model in Figure 6.1 (Panel B) is not highly refined, because although it predicts that JOLs and study time will be related, it does not specify how (or to what degree) these measures should be related. More refined models of the control functions listed in Figure 6.2 have been proposed and evaluated – some of which will be introduced later in this chapter.

Individual literatures have arisen around almost every one of the monitoring and control processes depicted in Figure 6.2. But even with this diversity and breadth of investigations, the questions that have consistently motivated research have been relatively few in number. Four of these questions are listed in Table 6.2; though not exhaustive, they do represent major foci across the areas. The questions pertain to the constructs of monitoring and

Table 6.2 Core questions about monitoring and control from research about adult human cognition

How do people monitor memory?
How accurate is memory monitoring?
Can monitoring accuracy be improved?
How is monitoring used to control?

Table 6.3 Index to references of research relevant to the dominant questions (Table 6.2) and core metacognitive judgments (Figure 6.2)

Questions	Metacognitive judgments				
	EOL	JOLs	FOK	RC	SM
How do individuals monitor memory?	1	2	3	4	5
How accurate is memory monitoring?	6	7	8	9	10
Can monitoring accuracy be improved?	11	12	13	14	15
How is monitoring used to control?	16	17	18	19	20

Note: EOL, ease of learning judgment; JOL, judgment of learning; FOK, feeling of knowing judgment; RC, retrospective confidence judgment; SM, source monitoring judgment. The number in each cell above corresponds to one or more articles that can be used as an entry point to the literature. The numeral within a cell is used to label the corresponding article in the Appendix.

control, and hence within each literature, they have been pursued by investigating the corresponding measures presented in Figure 6.2. Researchers interested in how people monitor memory investigate how they make the various judgments of memory monitoring, such as JOLs and FOK judgments. Researchers interested in the accuracy (or validity) of people's memory monitoring often compare a person's judgments of monitoring (e.g., JOLs) with the objective target of the particular judgment (e.g., eventual test performance). Similarly, those interested in how monitoring influences control processes often examine the empirical relations between a judgment of monitoring (e.g., JOLs) and a corresponding measure of control (e.g., time devoted to study).

Obviously, to review answers to each question in Table 6.2 for all the literatures, we would need much more room than is provided by a single chapter. Thus, we have limited our review to questions most relevant to JOLs and self-regulated study because this particular area of metamemory is relevant to improving human performance (Bjork 1994). In general, the conclusions offered by research on JOLs and self-regulated study will generalize to other monitoring control functions, but we realize some readers' most avid interests will align with these other functions. For instance, you may be concerned with why some grade school students are better at taking exams than are other students who are presumably as knowledgeable. If your intuition is that the poor test-takers are less skilled at evaluating the quality of their answers, then you may want to begin exploring the literature on retrospective confidence judgments that pertains to the question, "How accurate is memory monitoring?" With this possibility in mind, we have constructed Table 6.3, which can be used to locate a key reference from literatures about each question and function. To use this table, locate the numeral within the cell of interest, and then refer to the Appendix to identify the relevant article that can be used as an entry point to the larger literature pertaining to your question and function of interest. In the example above, the relevant entry of Table 6.3 is "9," which would lead you to Gigerenzer *et al.* (1991).

MONITORING DURING ACQUISITION: JUDGMENTS OF LEARNING

In this section, we consider how people judge their learning of newly studied material, the accuracy of these judgments, and how accuracy can be improved. A motivating principle that has stimulated interest in these issues is quite intuitive: obtaining high levels of judgment accuracy can support efficient learning. In the introductory scenario, Beth judged that the beginning of her talk was not quite coherent. If her judgment was accurate, she could efficiently use her time by practicing this portion of her talk instead of others that she already performed well. If instead she had inaccurately judged that her introduction was incoherent when in fact it was fine, she may inadvertently waste time in practicing this portion of the talk. Beyond this anecdote, this principle also appears to hold for judgments of learning and the effectiveness of study. Namely, people who more accurately judge what they have versus have not learned demonstrate faster learning across multiple trials because they are able to isolate and restudy those items that require it most (for a review, see Dunlosky *et al.* 2005).

How People Judge Memories for Newly Learned Materials

Discovering the sources of judgment (in)accuracy can be informed by understanding how people judge memories for newly learned materials. Put differently, explanations of how people make metamemory judgments often have direct implications about why the judgments are (in)accurate. We explore one of the more thoroughly investigated explanations here and pursue their implications for accuracy in the following section.

To investigate how people make judgments of learning, researchers have adopted a relatively standard method. Namely, participants are instructed to study a list of items, such as paired associates (dog–spoon), which are presented individually for study. Sometime after studying each item, a JOL is made in which a participant rates the likelihood of correctly remembering each item. This rating typically is made on a scale from 0 to 100, where 0 means no chance that the item will be remembered and 100 means that it will absolutely be remembered. After items are studied, a test of memory is administered for all items. In some cases, participants are then asked to select which items that they would like to restudy, and/or asked to pace their restudy of each item. These latter control processes – item selection and self-paced study – are considered in a later section, and we focus here on the issues of how people make JOLs and on JOL accuracy. Hypothetical data relevant to these issues are presented in Table 6.4, which we will return to throughout this discussion.

One relatively successful hypothesis has been proposed that attempts to explain how people make almost every one of the judgments presented in Figure 6.2 (for competing hypotheses that have not faired as well, see Hart 1965; Koriat 1993; Metcalfe 2000). This

Table 6.4 Hypothetical data from a single participant

Item	JOL	Recall	Item selection	Study time (s)
King–Crown	80	1	0	1.2
Paint–Artist	90	0	0	1.0
Leaf–Branch	60	0	1	3.4
Weed–Garden	75	1	1	4.0
Suit–Jacket	90	1	0	0
Paper–Pencil	70	1	0	1.3
Dog–Spoon	35	0	1	4.0
Cotton–Lamp	40	1	1	4.7
Lunch–Motor	55	0	1	3.9
Baby–Forest	50	1	0	1.9
Milk–Clerk	35	0	1	5.2
Snake–Brain	45	0	1	6.0

Dependent measure	Across all items	Related items	Unrelated items
Mean judgment	60.4	77.5	43.3
Relative accuracy	+0.43	+0.14	+0.25
JOL/selection correlation	−0.77	−0.75	−0.60
JOL/study time correlation	−0.68	−0.71	−0.29

Note: Hypothetical data from a single participant along with common descriptive analyses. JOL, judgment of learning. Recall: 1, correct; 0, incorrect. Item selection: 1, selected for restudy; 0, not selected. Gamma correlations were used to derive the measures of relative accuracy and the correlational measures of the allocation of stucy time (for rationale, see Nelson 1984).

inference-based hypothesis is that people's metamemory judgments are inferential in nature and are based on any number of available cues that can be used to infer the memorability of an item (for a review, see Schwartz *et al.* 1997). For example, consider a list of paired-associate items composed of both related pairs (king–crown) and unrelated pairs (dog–spoon). A participant studies this list and makes JOLs as described earlier. This participant may attend to the cue of relatedness and then infer its meaning with respect to memory. In particular, she may infer that "being related" means that memory will be quite good for that item. In our opening example, Beth presumably inferred how well she was performing her talk by attending to how often she stumbled. In this case, stumbling (the cue) may be fairly diagnostic of the quality of her talk, although she may also use other cues (e.g., dryness of her mouth) that may not be that diagnostic.

Given that inferential accounts have received substantial support (e.g., Koriat 1993, 1997; Schwartz *et al.* 1997; Benjamin *et al.* 1998), one research goal involves identifying cues that people use to make inferences about memory. To discover these cues, investigators have adapted the standard method either by inserting a possible cue within the task (e.g., item relatedness) or measuring cues as they occur naturally. Several outcomes are noteworthy. JOLs are substantially related to the following cues: (1) the semantic association of words within a paired associate, with JOLs being greater for related word pairs (e.g., king–crown) than for unrelated word pairs (e.g., dog–spoon; Koriat & Bjork 2005); (2) the fluency of processing items during study, with JOLs being greater for items in which mediators (e.g., interactive images) are more quickly generated than are more slowly generated (Hertzog *et al.* 2003); (3) whether the expected criterion test is recognition or recall, with JOLs being greater in anticipation of recognition tests regardless of the relative difficulty of the two kinds of test (Thiede 1996); and (4) the fluency of retrieval, with JOLs being greater for items in which responses are retrieved quickly than for those retrieved less quickly (Benjamin *et al.* 1998). By contrast, various encoding strategies that influence performance (e.g., imagery vs. rote repetition) often have a relatively small influence on JOLs (e.g., Shaughnessy 1981; Dunlosky & Nelson 1994). Although a variety of accounts have been offered for these effects (most notably, see Koriat 1997), a general process-oriented explanation is not yet available, which offers one of the most important challenges for theory development in this area. Moreover, much translational research is needed to discover which cues influence people's judgments of their learning in real-world settings, such as when a clinical graduate studies for a licensing exam or a young physician is learning about new procedures for diagnoses.

In summary, much is now known about how people judge their learning of individual items for an upcoming test. JOLs are largely inferential in nature, being constructed from available cues that learners perceive as relevant to memory. As we discuss next, an inferential account of judgments has much heuristic value both for understanding and improving judgment accuracy.

Accuracy of Judgments of Learning

For any metamemory judgment, accuracy is operationalized as the relationship between the judgment and performance on the corresponding criterion test. In the judgmental literature, accuracy has been conceptualized in two ways (Murphy 1973; Lichtenstein *et al.* 1977; Nelson 1996b). First, *relative accuracy* refers to the degree to which judgments discriminate between the test performance of one item relative to another. In our opening example, Beth may have judged that the opening of her talk was great and that her conclusions need work; if that were truly the case, then her judgments demonstrated excellent relative accuracy at discriminating between what she performed well vs. what she had performed less well. Relative accuracy (also known as *resolution*) has been measured in multiple ways in the literature, but the most widely used measures involve computing an intra-individual correlation between each participant's judgments and his or her own test performance. Correlations that are reliably greater than 0 indicate above-chance relative accuracy, and higher correlations (approaching +1.0) indicate higher levels of relative accuracy. Several correlations have been used to estimate relative accuracy, including Pearson r and the Goodman-Kruskal γ correlation (for other measures, see Nelson 1984; Gonzalez & Nelson 1996).

Which correlation provides the best estimate of relative accuracy? Nelson (1984) described six properties that would be desirable for any measure of relative accuracy, including (a) that if two people have equal levels of overall test performance, then the person with better judgment ability should be higher on the measure of relative accuracy; and (b) that the measure of relative accuracy should be independent of overall test performance. Based on his evaluation of prevalent measures, Nelson (1984) argued that these properties were best met by the γ correlation, which is now the most widely used correlation for estimating relative accuracy. Gamma can be computed using common statistical packages (e.g., SPSS and Systat). For the hypothetical data in Table 6.4, relative accuracy of JOLs across all items as computed by γ is +0.43.

Second, *absolute accuracy* refers to the degree to which the absolute values of ratings reflect the actual level of performance obtained. For instance, a person that predicts he will recall 70 per cent of the items correct on a test and then recalls 70 per cent has excellent absolute accuracy, whereas another person who predicts 70 per cent but only recalls 40 per cent shows overconfidence. To estimate absolute accuracy, researchers must have participants make judgments on a scale – e.g., judging the *per cent* likelihood of correct recall – that is comparable to the measure of test performance – e.g., *per cent* correct recall. Absolute accuracy is measured by computing calibration indices between mean ratings and mean performance (Keren 1991). One common technique involves constructing a calibration curve, where per cent correct on the criterion test is plotted (on the ordinate) as a function of increasing levels of judgment rating (on the abscissa). Values from the calibration curve can be used to estimate the degree to which judgments show under-confidence or overconfidence by computing a weighted mean of the differences between the mean judgment and the corresponding level of text performance for each level of judgment (Lichtenstein & Fischhoff 1977). Positive values indicate overconfidence and negative values indicate under-confidence. (For detailed discussion of how to measure absolute accuracy and some difficulties in interpreting these measures, see Keren 1991; Wallsten 1996.)

In the present review, we highlight results pertaining to relative accuracy, which has been consistently reported in the JOL literature. The earliest investigations typically had participants make *immediate* JOLs in which a JOL was made for an item immediately after it had been studied (e.g., Arbuckle & Cuddy 1969; Zechmeister & Shaughnessy 1980). For instance, a nurse may describe a schedule for taking a new medication to a patient and then immediately ask, "Will you remember this schedule?" In this case, the patient would be making an immediate judgment of his or her learning. Although some exceptions exist, the relative accuracy of immediate JOLs tends to be quite low, but above zero (for a review, Sikström & Jönsson 2005) – which is reflected in mean correlations that are reliably greater than zero but below +0.50. Why do these judgments show above-chance accuracy and how might their accuracy be improved? According to inferential-based accounts, judgments will accurately predict performance as long as the cues that are used to make judgments are empirically correlated with test performance. In the case of immediate JOLs, the available cues apparently are somewhat (but not highly) predictive of subsequent performance, so low levels of accuracy should be expected.

Inferential-based accounts provide insight into improving people's judgment accuracy. Namely, to improve accuracy, techniques are needed that produce cues that are highly diagnostic of test performance. One possibility would be to insert diagnostic cues into the learning environment. For instance, mixing related pairs (king–crown) with unrelated word pairs (dog–spoon) on a list improves accuracy because this cue (relatedness) influences JOLs and is also highly diagnostic of test performance. As illustrated in Table 6.4, relative accuracy computed across related and unrelated pairs yields higher levels of accuracy than is found for either subset of item (as in Dunlosky & Matvey 2001). Unfortunately, this solution for improving accuracy is not highly practical, because learners rarely construct the set of materials that they need to learn. Instead, for practical applications, techniques are needed that enhance judgment accuracy regardless of the set of to-be-learned materials.

In the late 1980s, T. O. Nelson devised a technique that would achieve this goal for associative learning of word pairs (e.g., foreign-language translation equivalents). In particular, instead of having participants make a judgment immediately after each stimulus-response pair (e.g., dog–spoon, where "dog" is the stimulus and "spoon" is the response) had been studied, a short delay (about two minutes) filled with the study of other items occurred between the study and judgment of each item. Delayed judgments were collected using only the stimulus of each pair (e.g., if "dog–spoon" had been studied, the JOL prompt would be "dog– ?"). Most important, relative accuracy was substantially greater for delayed JOLs (M = 0.90) than for immediate JOLs (M = 0.38). This delayed JOL effect (Nelson & Dunlosky 1991) has been replicated numerous times and occurs for a variety of subject populations and conditions. Fortunately, delayed judgments can be easily incorporated into real-world settings; for example, after a nurse describes a medication schedule, he may then turn the conversation briefly to another topic before asking the patient if she will remember the schedule.

A general explanation of the delayed JOL effect fits well with inferential accounts of JOLs. Namely, when the stimulus alone (i.e., "dog– ?") is presented for a delayed JOL, a participant may attempt to retrieve the corresponding response and to use the outcome of this retrieval attempt as a cue for the JOL. Because this retrieval outcome would be highly predictive of subsequent test performance, delayed JOLs achieve high levels of accuracy. Put differently, the technique of delaying JOLs using only the stimulus of each pair provides diagnostic cues that can drive highly accurate inferences about memory for paired-associate learning (Nelson *et al.* 2004). Although most agree with this idea in general, there has been ongoing discussion concerning the specific cause of the delayed JOL effect, which includes debates about why retrieval outcomes at the time of delayed JOLs are diagnostic (Nelson & Dunlosky 1992; Spellman & Bjork 1992; Kimball & Metcalfe 2003; Sikström & Jönsson 2005) and whether participants engage in a full-blown retrieval attempt prior to making delayed JOLs (Nelson *et al.* 2004; Son & Metcalfe 2005). Most important, the accuracy of JOLs for predicting associative recall can be dramatically improved, and the technique to do so was in part discovered by considering how to manipulate task constraints in a way that would provide diagnostic cues for learners.

CONTROL DURING ACQUISITION: ALLOCATION OF STUDY TIME

An important reason for understanding how people monitor learning pertains to its function in the control of learning. As illustrated in Figure 6.1, monitoring may serve to control many aspects of learning and retrieval. For instance, students may decide to restudy essential classroom materials they had judged as not well learned. In this way, accurate monitoring can support efficient control, because learners can study again just those items that they (accurately) judged would benefit most from it. This intuitive conjecture was supported by Thiede (1999), who had participants study paired associates during multiple study-test trials. During the first trial, participants made JOLs and selected which items to restudy. The relative accuracy of each participant's JOLs was computed and compared to subsequent learning. As expected, participants who had more accurate JOLs on the first trial performed better on subsequent trials, presumably because accurate monitoring supported more efficient control of learning.

Given the importance of monitoring to efficient control, how monitoring serves to control memory has been scrutinized for each of the various control functions shown in Figure 6.2. Consider the work by Reder and her colleagues (e.g., Reder 1988; Reder & Ritter 1992), who investigated how people select search strategies during retrieval. More specifically, this work has demonstrated how monitoring informs people's decisions about whether to retrieve an answer to a problem (e.g., $12 \times 12 = ?$ or $13 \times 23 = ?$) or to compute the answer to it. Using a variety of clever procedures, Reder has provided compelling evidence that when a person first reads a problem, the decision to retrieve or to compute an answer is controlled by a quick feeling-of-knowing judgment based on familiarity with the problem itself. If the problem immediately evokes a feeling of familiarity (e.g., $12 \times 12 = ?$), a person will select the strategy of retrieving the answer. If the problem triggers much less familiarity (e.g., $12 \times 23 = ?$), then the person would select the strategy of computing the answer. Their research represents one of many programs aimed at understanding metacognitively controlled systems; examples involving other control processes illustrated in Figure 6.2 can be identified using Table 6.3.

We now examine in some detail how monitoring is used to control study. To describe monitoring–control relationships, researchers have used variations on the following procedure. Participants first briefly study each to-be-learned item of a list and then make a JOL for each one. After this preliminary trial, each item is presented again and participants either select which items they would like to restudy (item selection) or spend as much time as they want studying each item (self-paced study time). Although several dependent measures may be computed to explore how people allocate study time, an often reported measure has been the correlation between JOLs and these measures of allocation. In Table 6.4, values are presented for item selection and termination of study, both of which correlated negatively with JOLs made on the initial study trial. A negative relationship has been found in numerous investigations (for a review, see Son & Metcalfe 2000) and indicates that people often spend more time studying (or more often select for restudy) items that are judged as less well learned.

What mechanisms are responsible for this relationship? One of the earliest explanations was inspired by system models of self-regulation that are based on negative feedback (Powers 1973). At the core of this explanation is a discrepancy-reduction mechanism in which a person continues studying an item until the learning goal set for the item has been met. That is, a person studies until the discrepancy has been reduced between the current state of learning and the desired amount of learning. Because relatively difficult items (vs. less difficult ones) will require more study time to meet a given learning goal, this discrepancy-reduction model predicts that JOLs will be negatively related to study time. This model has yielded numerous predictions that have guided research, and in doing so, some of its weaknesses have been discovered and have led to new discoveries about the flexibility and adaptivity of self-regulated study.

Concerning a weakness, the discrepancy-reduction model cannot explain why JOLs and measures of study-time allocation are sometimes positively correlated (Thiede & Dunlosky 1999; Son & Metcalfe 2000). For instance, Son and Metcalfe (2000) reported that participants chose to study items judged as difficult to learn when they had adequate time to study all to-be-learned items. However, when their participants had a limited time for study, they chose to study first those items judged as easier to learn. Similarly, Thiede and Dunlosky (1999) instructed participants that they only needed to obtain a low performance goal (i.e., to learn six items from a 30-item list), and in this case, participants also chose to restudy those items judged as easier to learn and neglected the more difficult ones. Dunlosky and Thiede (2004) dubbed such outcomes as shift-to-easier-materials (STEM) effects, because people apparently shifted from allocating more time to the difficult-to-learn items to allocating more time to the easier items.

One explanation for the STEM effect is that participants attempt to obtain task goals – in this case, a performance goal for recall – in an efficient manner. For Son and Metcalfe (2000), participants under time pressure to learn items presumably interpreted the explicit goal of "total mastery of all items" as "memorize as many items as you can in the brief time allowed." Efficiently obtaining this goal would arguably involve studying the easier items first. Metcalfe and Kornell (2005) have recently proposed that the particular kind of adaptive control reflected by STEM effects results from students' attempts to allocate the most time to those items within a region of proximal learning, which are unlearned items that a learner believes would benefit from study. Focusing one's time on a region of proximal learning may arise in many real-world contexts. For instance, a student may spend little time studying in a physics class (or even drop it) because he feels that the material is too difficult to learn and instead decide to use the time studying for another class in which he feels he could meet his learning goals in a timely fashion. The current support for a region of proximal learning mechanism is extensive (Metcalfe 2002), although it is clear that other processes are also involved in the allocation of study time (Metcalfe & Kornell 2005).

Admittedly, theories of self-regulated study are in their infancy, and it would be premature to rule out any mechanism without further investigation. Nevertheless, some conclusions are being consistently supported. First, one function of monitoring is in the control of study processes. People attempt to use monitoring to control these processes in an efficient manner, but it is also evident that they can have difficulty in efficiently controlling these processes (e.g., Reder & Ritter 1992; Dunlosky & Thiede 2004). Second, because monitoring serves to control study and retrieval, improving the accuracy of monitoring can improve the efficiency of control. Indeed, it seems almost self-evident that accurate monitoring would be critical for efficiently controlling any cognitive process, not just those involved in memory and learning. If so, the research question shifts from "Does improving accuracy support more efficient control?" to "What is the specific relationship between accuracy and efficient control?" Answering the latter question will involve discovering the level of accuracy required to achieve the most efficient control within a given domain. Perhaps only moderate levels of accuracy will be required for maximizing control in some domains, whereas the highest levels of accuracy will be required in others.

Many of the issues and questions raised about self-regulated study speak directly to improving human performance in other domains, and importantly, can be raised for almost any cognitive process. In the next section, we explore this possibility by describing some examples of how metamemory methods and theory have been applied to domains that have relevance to solving real-world problems.

APPLICATIONS OF A METAMEMORY FRAMEWORK

Our discussion of the JOL literature illustrates how a metamemory framework has been used to investigate monitoring and control processes relevant to learning. As alluded to above, such investigations have direct implications for solving real-world problems relevant to learning and memory that are only now being explored systematically. For instance, Kennedy and her colleagues (Kennedy *et al.* 2003; Kennedy & Yorkston 2004) have applied this framework to understand the monitoring and control abilities of people with acquired brain injury (ABI), with one aim being to help them overcome their learning deficits. Although ABI patients show deficits in learning, Kennedy *et al.* (2003) demonstrated that these patients can achieve relatively high levels of monitoring accuracy by using delayed JOLs. Importantly, learning is faster for ABI participants who use their highly accurate delayed JOLs to regulate study as compared to those who use their (less accurate) immediate JOLs. Thus, training ABI patients to make and use delayed JOLs in acquiring new information provides a promising route in helping them to compensate for learning deficits.

The same metamemory framework – focused on memory, learning, and retrieval – has also been used to examine the capabilities of other subject populations who demonstrate learning deficits and who may benefit from accurate monitoring and appropriate self control. These populations include children and older adults, adults with Alzheimer's disease and Korsakoff's disease, adults who are acutely intoxicated, and adults with frontal lobe damage, to name only a few. Not only is the literature too large to review here (for some excellent reviews, see Hertzog & Hultsch 2000; Perfect & Schwartz 2002; Pannu & Kaszniak 2005) but this list of populations is not close to exhaustive. Just think of any population you may be interested in that is not listed (e.g., children with attentional deficits), and this framework can be readily applied to describe (and potentially improve) their metamemory and learning abilities (e.g., Knouse *et al.* in press). Our key point here is simply that the framework outlined above can be readily applied to assessing people's metamemory capabilities and whether they can use them to enhance their learning and memory. Perhaps most encouraging, over a decade of research has demonstrated that many people who have impaired memories have intact metamemory abilities and hence may be able to use them to compensate for their impairments.

Beyond the realm of learning and memory, a metacognitive framework aimed at improving human performance can be applied to any real-world task that relies in part on cognitive processing. To foster such applications, we offer the following suggestions. First, conduct a componential analysis of the task in as much detail as possible. In this task analysis, the idea is to map out the possible components of the task that could contribute to performance. Second, for each *cognitive* component, two empirical questions inspired by the present framework can be posed to drive research that has applied relevance: (1) Can people accurately monitor how well the given component is operating? (2) Can people use monitoring to control the effectiveness of each component process? These two questions pertain readily to applications aimed at improving human performance, because they concern whether people *can* monitor and control a component process. Pursuing these two empirical questions alone within any particular domain will likely comprise a progressive and productive research program with applied merit, because doing so will naturally lead to other, more detailed questions about how metacognitive abilities may enhance performance.

In the next two sections, we explore how the present metacognitive framework can be applied to two real-world domains – jury deliberation and comprehension. Again, our exploration scratches only the surface of all domains that this framework may inform. A longer, albeit still not exhaustive, list of domains would include mathematical and insight problem-solving (e.g., Metcalfe 1998; Desoete *et al.* 2003), psychopathology (e.g., Teasdale 1999), eyewitness memory (Perfect 2002), writing expository texts (Sitko 1998), unconscious plagiarism (Carroll & Perfect 2002), and even artificial intelligence (Cox 2005). In fact, we do not even include exhaustive reviews of the extensive literature on jury deliberation (see Nietzel *et al.* 1999) or on comprehension (see Maki 1998). Instead, we wanted to illustrate how the framework has been applied to two topics with applied relevance. We decided to focus on these topics for the following reason. For jury deliberation, we describe a recent study that incorporates a kind of metacognitive judgment – called an *aggregate or global* judgment – that has been used extensively in the literature to explore people's judgment abilities, but which we did not discuss earlier. For comprehension, we highlight how the use of a metacognitive framework – methods and theory – have supported recent advances that promise to improve people's retention and comprehension of text materials. We hope these additional sections will stimulate researchers to creatively apply some of the same principles to understand more fully the role of metacognition within their domains of interest.

Juror Duties

Certainly, many different cognitive processes are recruited as a person plays his or her civic duty as a juror. Jury selection, ongoing trial activities, closing arguments, and jury deliberation will all challenge cognition as the jury works toward a verdict. Because componential analyses of these juror duties goes well beyond the scope of this chapter, we discuss only a recent example of how a metacognitive approach has been used to investigate a particularly important component of juror duty, namely, jury deliberation.

When jurors are deliberating the innocence or guilt of a defendant, they often must rely on their memories for the trial proceedings. Jurors who are most confident in their memories also tend to have the largest influence during deliberation (Kassin & Wrightsman 1988). Of course, if a juror's confidence reflects his or her actual memory for the trial, then perhaps his or her particular memory for a trial should be heavily weighted during the deliberation process. This possibility leads to the question: How accurate are jurors at judging their memories for trial proceedings?

To answer this question, Pritchard and Keenan (1999) creatively adapted standard metacognitive methods to investigate the judgment accuracy of mock jurors. The mock jurors watched a video tape of an actual murder trial, and after viewing the tape, each made a global judgment of how well he or she would do overall on a test of memory for the trial. These *global* judgments differ somewhat from item-by-item JOLs (Table 6.1) in that they refer to performance across all items. Although item-by-item JOLs could have been made about people's memories for specific aspects of the trial, global judgments not only tap monitoring of individual memories but also each person's overall efficacy for remembering (Hertzog *et al.* 1990; for a general framework that includes both item-by-item judgments and global judgments, see Dunlosky and Hertzog 2000). That is, global judgments tap people's overall self-efficacy at remembering, which may (or may not) be related to actual performance. As pointed out by the authors, "it is reasonable to think that global JOLs may be a primary factor in determining an individual juror's overall level of participation in the deliberative process. For example, a juror who thinks his or her memory is poor is likely to take a backseat in the deliberations" (p. 154). After making the global judgments, the participants then answered 30 questions about the trial.

How accurate were jurors' predictions? To answer this question, Pritchard and Keenan (1999) correlated (across participants) global judgments with mean test performance. Note that this between-person correlation is interpreted differently than the within-participant correlations introduced earlier in this chapter. The latter measure of relative accuracy indicates how accurately a specific person distinguishes between his or her own memory successes and failures. By contrast, the between-person correlation indicates the degree to which people with more confidence also perform better. Across two experiments, this correlation was not reliably different from zero, which indicates that the most confident jurors did not have the best memories for the trial. A somewhat unfortunate implication is that jurors who will likely "have the largest impact on the verdict may not [have] the most accurate [memories]" (Pritchard & Keenan 1999, p. 161).

Pritchard and Keenan's (1999) research demonstrates how metamemory methods can be applied to investigate aspects of juror decision-making: (a) identify a component of cognition that may influence task performance, in this case, memory for the trial may influence the quality of juror deliberations; (b) adopt or develop a metamemory measure that taps people's ability to evaluate that component, in this case, a global judgment about one's memory for the trial; and (c) compare the metamemory judgment to a corresponding objective measure that pertains to what is being judged, in this case, correlating people's global judgments with their actual trial memory. In any given application, researchers may need to develop new kinds of judgment specifically relevant to the particular cognitive component under investigation. For each judgment, it is critical to obtain an objective measure of performance, so that participants' biases can be described, understood, and potentially mended.

Finally, Pritchard and Keenan's (1999) research provided an answer to the first empirical question introduced at the beginning of this section, namely, "How accurately do jurors monitor their memories of a trial?" Given their poor accuracy, the next steps for this line of research may involve identifying cues that could support higher levels of accuracy to evaluate whether jurors can use them when evaluating their memories for a trial. Other empirical questions concern control processes in this area, such as: How strongly does a juror's confidence in his or her own memory influence whether the memory is offered during deliberation? And is one juror's confidence in his or her memory influential in whether other jurors are persuaded? We suspect that answering these questions will lead to prescriptions on how to improve the performance of individual jurors and jury decision making. Importantly, methods to answer these questions (and many other related ones) can be devised from those already developed in the field.

Text Comprehension

Improving people's comprehension while reading has become one of the most sought-after goals of the American educational system, and literacy is being promoted worldwide. A complete task analysis of comprehension would by no means be straightforward because of the numerous components that contribute individually and interact while a person reads. Many of these components are triggered by promiscuous associative processes that serve to construct and integrate representations of the text as a person reads (Kintsch 1998). It seems unlikely that these associative processes are privy to metacognitive monitoring, and even if they are, it is possible that attempting to monitor them would disrupt text processing. Even so, metacognitive monitoring and control processes could play a significant role in other aspects of reading, such as in evaluating one's understanding after reading and in deciding whether to reread sections of a text.

For present purposes, consider the case of monitoring one's understanding of text, which has received substantial interest in the field. In fact, Ellen Markman's (1977) work on error detection during reading was groundbreaking research for the area of metacognition (see also Glenberg *et al.* 1982). Since her seminal research, monitoring of reading and comprehension has been measured in various ways, such as by eye-tracking, think-aloud protocols collected while reading, detection of errors embedded in text, and explicit judgments of text comprehension. Reviews of these areas are available (e.g., Pressley & Afflerbach 1995; Otero 1998), so we consider here only a few outcomes from the literature on explicit judgments of learning and comprehension for text, which in method are most closely aligned with the monitoring judgments presented in Figure 6.2.

Maki and Berry (1984) were the first to investigate how accurately people could judge their learning and comprehension of text. The methods they developed have been adapted over the past two decades, but in general the procedure is as follows. A person reads a series of short texts (typically 200–400 words in length), and sometime after reading each one, a participant predicts how well he or she will perform on a criterion test. Finally, a criterion test over the text materials is administered. Relative accuracy is measured by computing within-participant correlations between judgments and test performance.

For the first two decades of research in this area, the most resounding conclusion about judgment accuracy was fraught with pessimism. Maki (1998) explains that in her own research, the mean across people's correlations for almost 30 different experiments was on average about +0.30, suggesting the possibility that "students cannot predict performance well, and that prediction is not a teachable skill" (p. 142). And although a good deal has been learned about how people *make* these judgments, a defensible claim even now is that no one has discovered a panacea for consistently obtaining high levels of metacomprehension accuracy.

As we argued in our review of JOLs, discovering techniques to boost metacomprehension accuracy may lead to improved learning. To this end, the inferential account of how people judge memory suggests that accuracy could be improved as long as cues were available that accurately predicted eventual test performance. When people judge their learning and comprehension of texts, the cues that are often available are not highly predictive of test performance. For instance, people's judgments of text comprehension and learning may be influenced by how difficult a passage is to read (Rawson & Dunlosky 2002), or by how quickly they can recall any information from the text in the moments prior to judging it (Morris 1990). Unfortunately, both these cues are not necessarily predictive of test performance and may even be misleading in some circumstances. By contrast, perhaps having participants attempt to retrieve the entire text before judging it would produce valid cues that would be predictive of how well each text was learned and comprehended. Consistent with this possibility, Thiede and Anderson (2003) found that having participants summarize a text after it was read (but prior to judging their comprehension) enhanced metacomprehension accuracy, as long as summarization was delayed after reading (cf. the delayed JOL effect, described earlier).

Moreover, Thiede *et al.* (2003) have been working with a new technique – delayed keyword generation – that promises to boost accuracy under many conditions. Keyword generation is based on the same principle as summarization (i.e., more fully retrieve information about each text at a delay prior to making judgments), except that generating keywords takes much less time and may be more practical to boost accuracy in time-sensitive situations. For keyword generation, participants first read a text and then are asked to generate five keywords. They were instructed to generate keywords that captured the essence of the to-be-judged text, No other constraints were placed on the generation of keywords, so they could either come directly from the text or just be implied by it. Thiede *et al.* (2003) contrasted two groups: participants in one group generated keywords immediately after reading each text, and those in the other first read all the texts and then generated keywords for each one. Whereas predictive accuracy for the immediate generation group was relatively low, the mean accuracy for participants who predicted performance after delayed keyword generation exceeded +0.70. A take-home message here is that achieving high levels of judgment accuracy is possible even for a task as complex as text learning and comprehension.

This particular technique could be extended to other contexts in which people may need to evaluate their understanding. For instance, a patient who just received instructions from a doctor about how to administer his or her medication may take a moment to generate key ideas from the instructions. Failures to generate them may indicate incomplete understanding, which could be remedied through further discussion. After listening to a lecture, students may be encouraged to generate key ideas from each topic covered in the lecture near the end of the class period. Students may identify topics they do not fully understand, which the instructor could begin to clarify in review. Of course, we do not advocate applying this technique widely without further investigating whether it benefits performance in these or other situations. What we do advocate, however, is using the methods, analyses, and theory that have grown from a metamemory tradition to investigate the possible benefits of using these new techniques. By doing so, their limits will be uncovered as we move toward discovering newer and more potent techniques for enhancing human metacognition and performance.

SUMMARY AND CONCLUSIONS

Our main goals of the present chapter included introducing definitions, methods, and theories that have arisen from research on metamemory. The specific discussion of research on JOLs was intended to highlight how these methods have been used to understand students' self-regulated study, which has straightforward implications for enhancing student scholarship. Other approaches have been brought to bear on this problem, and we certainly are not promoting the current approach as the panacea for understanding and improving self-regulated study. Instead, the metamemory framework presented here should be viewed as one more tool that can complement other approaches for enhancing student scholarship.

Beyond reviewing the literature on JOLs and the allocation of study time, we also described how the present framework has been applied to the domains of juror decision-making and text comprehension. These represent only two of many domains where a metacognitive framework has successfully guided empirical enquiry. After a quick spin through the contents of this book, it is evident that a metacognitive framework could be applied judiciously to many other domains. Such an approach is likely to uncover people's potential at monitoring and controlling real-world tasks in various target domains, and it offers a promissory note for discovering techniques to foster this potential as a means to enhance human performance.

ACKNOWLEDGMENTS

This chapter is dedicated to Thomas O. Nelson and Louis Narens, whose scholarship on metacognition has inspired and guided our research program over the past decade and a half. Much thanks to Susan McDonald for informative discussion about juror duties and behavior.

NOTE

1 It is important to emphasize that the particular perspective on metacognition that we present is based largely on information-processing models of metacognition. And even more specifically, we highlight only monitoring and control. Although we believe the perspective presented here holds much promise for improving human performance, other perspectives and research traditions of metacognition do as well, such as those focused on self-efficacy theory or in training general metacognitive abilities. The various traditions are not mutually exclusive and likely represent different pieces of a larger whole. Given that a theoretical analysis of this larger whole is not currently available and goes beyond the scope of this humble chapter, we ask for the reader's forgiveness in biasing this review toward a single perspective.

REFERENCES

Arbuckle, T. Y. & Cuddy, L. L. (1969). Discrimination of item strength at time of presentation. *Journal of Experimental Psychology*, *81*, 126–131.

Benjamin, A. S., Bjork, R. A. & Schwartz, B. L. (1998). The mismeasure of memory: when retrieval fluency is misleading as a metamnemonic index. *Journal of Experimental Psychology: General*, *127*, 55–68.

Bjork, R. A. (1994). Memory and metamemory: considerations in the training of human beings. In J. Metcalfe & A. P. Shimamura (eds.), *Metacognition: Knowing about Knowing* (pp. 185–205). Cambridge, MA: MIT Press.

Carroll, M. & Perfect, T. J. (2002). Students' experiences of unconscious plagiarism: did I beget or forget? In T. J. Perfect & B. Schwartz (eds.), *Applied Metacognition*. (pp. 145–166). New York: Cambridge University Press.

Cartwright-Hatton, S. & Wells, A. (1997). Beliefs about worry and intrusions: the metacognitions questionnaire and its correlates. *Journal of Anxiety Disorders*, *11*, 279–296.

Cavanaugh, J. C. & Perlmutter, M. (1982). Metamemory: a critical examination. *Child Development*, *53*, 11–28.

Cox, M. (2005). Metacognition in computation: a selective research review. *Artificial Intelligence*, *169*, 104–141.

Desoete, A., Roeyers, H. & De Clercq, A. (2003). Can offline metacognition enhance mathematical problem solving? *Journal of Educational Psychology*, *95*, 188–200.

Dunlosky, J. & Hertzog, C. (2000). Updating knowledge about encoding strategies: a componential analysis of learning about strategy effectiveness from task experience. *Psychology & Aging*, *15*, 462–474.

Dunlosky, J., Hertzog, C., Kennedy, M. R. F. & Thiede, K. W. (2005). The self-monitoring approach for effective learning. *International Journal of Cognitive Technology*, *10*, 4–11.

Dunlosky, J. & Matvey, G. (2001). Empirical analysis of the intrinsic-extrinsic distinction of judgments of learning (JOLs): effects of relatedness and serial position on JOLs. *Journal of Experimental Psychology: Learning, Memory & Cognition*, *27*, 1180–1191.

Dunlosky, J. & Nelson, T. O. (1994). Does the sensitivity of judgments of learning (JOLs) to the effects of various study activities depend on when the JOLs occur? *Journal of Memory & Language*, *33*, 545–565.

Dunlosky, J. & Thiede, K. W. (2004). Causes and constraints of the shift-to-easier-materials effect in the control of study. *Memory & Cognition*, *32*, 779–788.

Emmelkamp, P. M. G. & Aardema, A. (1999). Metacognition, specific obsessive-compulsive beliefs and obsessive-compulsive behaviour. *Clinical Psychology & Psychotherapy*, *6*, 139–145.

Flavell, J. H. (1979). Metacognition and cognitive monitoring: a new area of cognitive-developmental inquiry. *American Psychologist*, *34*, 906–911.

Flavell, J. H. (2004). Theory-of-mind development: retrospect and prospect. *Merrill-Palmer Quarterly*, *50*, 274–290.

Gigerenzer, G., Hoffrage, U. & Kleinbolting, H. (1991). Probabilistic mental models: a Brunswikian theory of confidence. *Psychological Review*, *98*, 506–528.

Glenberg, A. M., Wilkinson, A. C. & Epstein, W. (1982). The illusion of knowing: failure in the self-assessment of comprehension. *Memory and Cognition*, *10*, 597–602.

Gonzalez, R. & Nelson, T. O. (1996). Measuring ordinal association in situations that contain tied scores. *Psychological Bulletin*, *119*, 159–165.

Hart, J. T. (1965). Memory and the feeling-of-knowing experience. *Journal of Educational Psychology*, *56*, 208–216.

Hertzog, C., Dixon, R.A. & Hultsch, D. F. (1990). Relationships between metamemory, memory predictions, and memory task performance in adults. *Psychology and Aging*, *5*, 215–227.

Hertzog, C., Dunlosky, J., Robinson, A. E. & Kidder, D. P. (2003). Encoding fluency is a cue used for judgments about learning. *Journal of Experimental Psychology: Learning, Memory, and Cognition*, *29*, 22–34.

Hertzog, C. & Hultsch, D. F. (2000). Metacognition in adulthood and old age. In F. I. M. Craik & T. A. Salthouse (eds.), *The Handbook of Aging and Cognition* (2nd edn, pp. 417–466). Mahwah, NJ: Lawrence Erlbaum Associates.

Hertzog, C., McGuire, C. L. & Lineweaver, T. T. (1998). Aging, attributions, perceived control and strategy use in a free recall task. *Aging, Neuropsychology, and Cognition*, *5*, 85–106.

Kassin, S. M. & Wrightsman, L. S. (1988). *The American Jury on Trial: Psychological Perspectives*. New York: Hemisphere Publishing/Harper and Row.

Kennedy, M. R. T., Carney, E. & Peters, S. M. (2003). Predictions of recall and study strategy decisions after diffuse brain injury. *Brain Injury*, *17*, 1043–1064.

Kennedy, M. R. T. & Yorkston, K. M. (2004). The effects of frontal injury on "on-line" self-monitoring during verbal learning by adults with diffuse brain injury. *Neuropsychological Rehabilitation*, *14*, 449–465.

Keren, G. (1991). Calibration and probability judgments: conceptual and methodological issues. *Acta Psychologica*, *77*, 217–273.

Kimball, D. R. & Metcalfe, J. (2003). Delaying judgments of learning affects memory, not metamemory. *Memory & Cognition*, *31*, 918–929.

Kintsch, W. (1998). *Comprehension: A Paradigm for Cognition*. New York: Cambridge University Press.

Knouse, L., Paradise, M. & Dunlosky, J. (in press). Does ADHD in adults affect the relative accuracy of metamemory judgments? *Journal of Attention Disorders*.

Koriat, A. (1993). How do we know that we know? The accessibility model of the feeling of knowing. *Psychological Review*, *100*, 609–639.

Koriat, A. (1997). Monitoring one's own knowledge during study: a cue-utilization approach to judgments of learning. *Journal of Experimental Psychology: General*, *126*, 349–370.

Koriat, A. & Bjork, R. A. (2005). Illusions of competence in monitoring one's knowledge during study. *Journal of Experimental Psychology: Learning, Memory & Cognition*, *31*, 187–194.

Kreutzer, M. A., Leonard, C. & Flavell, J. H. (1975). An interview study of children's knowledge about memory. *Monographs of the Society for Research in Child Development*, *40*, 1–60.

Lichtenstein, S. & Fischhoff, B. (1977). Do those who know more also know more about how much they know? *Organizational Behavior and Human Performance*, *20*, 159–183.

Lichtenstein, S., Fischhoff, B. & Phillips, L. D. (1977). Calibration of probabilities: the state of the art. In H. Jungermann & G. deZeeuw (eds.), *Decision Making and Change in Human Affairs*. Amsterdam: D. Reidel.

McDonald-Miszczak, L., Hertzog, C. & Hultsch, D. F. (1995). Stability and accuracy of metamemory in adulthood and aging: a longitudinal analysis. *Psychology and Aging*, *10*, 553–564.

Maki, R. H. (1998). Test predictions over text material. In D.J. Hacker, J. Dunlosky & A. C. Graesser (eds.), *Metacognition in Educational Theory and Practice* (pp. 117–144). Mahwah, NJ: Lawrence Erlbaum Associates.

Maki, R. H. & Berry, S. L. (1984). Metacomprehension of text material. *Journal of Experimental Psychology: Learning, Memory, and Cognition*, *10*, 663–679.

Markman, E. M. (1977). Realizing that you don't understand: a preliminary investigation. *Child Development*, *48*, 986–992.

Matthews, G., Davies, D. R., Westerman, S. J. & Stammers, R. B. (2000). *Human Performance: Cognition, Stress, and Individual Differences*. Philadelphia, PA: Psychology Press/Taylor & Francis.

Mazzoni, G. & Nelson, T. O. (eds.) (1998). *Metacognition and Cognitive Neuropsychology: Monitoring and Control Processes*. Mahwah, NJ: Lawrence Erlbaum Associates.

Metcalfe, J. (1998). Insight and metacognition. In G. Mazzoni & T. O. Nelson (eds.), *Metacognition and Cognitive Neuropsychology: Monitoring and Control Processes* (pp. 181–197). Mahwah, NJ: Lawrence Erlbaum Associates.

Metcalfe, J. (2000). Metamemory: theory and data. In E. Tulving & F. I. M. Craik (eds.), *The Oxford Handbook of Memory* (pp. 197–211). New York: Oxford University Press.

Metcalfe, J. (2002). Is study time allocated selectively to a region of proximal learning? *Journal of Experimental Psychology: General*, *131*, 349–363.

Metcalfe, J. & Kornell, N. (2005). A region of proximal learning model of study time allocation. *Journal of Memory and Language*, *52*, 463–477.

Morris, C. C. (1990). Retrieval processes underlying confidence in comprehension judgments. *Journal of Experimental Psychology: Learning, Memory & Cognition*, *16*, 223–232.

Murphy, A. H. (1973). A new vector partition of the probability score. *Journal of Applied Meteorology*, *12*, 595–600.

Nelson, T. O. (1984). A comparison of current measures of the accuracy of feeling-of-knowing predictions. *Psychological Bulletin*, *95*, 109–133.

Nelson, T. O. (1996a). Consciousness and metacognition. *American Psychologist*, *51*, 102–116.

Nelson, T. O. (1996b). Gamma is a measure of the accuracy of predicting performance on one item relative to another item, not of the absolute performance on an individual item. *Applied Cognitive Psychology*, *10*, 257–260.

Nelson, T. O. & Dunlosky, J. (1991). When people's judgments of learning (JOLs) are extremely accurate at predicting subsequent recall: the "delayed-JOL effect". *Psychological Science*, *2*, 267–270.

Nelson, T. O. & Dunlosky, J. (1992). How shall we explain the delayed-judgment-of-learning effect? *Psychological Science*, *3*, 317–318.

Nelson, T. O. & Narens, L. (1990). Metamemory: a theoretical framework and new findings. In G. H. Bower (ed.), *The Psychology of Learning and Motivation* (Vol. 26, pp. 125–173). San Diego, CA: Academic Press.

Nelson, T. O. & Narens, L. (1994). Why investigate metacognition? In J. Metcalfe & A. P. Shimamura (eds.), *Metacognition: Knowing About Knowing* (pp. 1–25). Cambridge, MA: MIT Press.

Nelson, T. O., Narens, L. & Dunlosky, J. (2004). A revised methodology for research on metamemory: pre-judgment recall and monitoring (PRAM). *Psychological Method*, *9*, 53–69.

Nietzel, M. T., McCarthy, D. M. & Kern, M. J. (1999). Juries: the current state of the empirical literature. In R. Roesch, S. D. Hart & J. R. P. Ogloff (eds.), *Psychology and Law: The State of the Discipline* (pp. 23–52). Dordrecht: Kluwer.

Otero, J. (1998). Influence of knowledge activation and context on comprehension monitoring of science texts. In D. J. Hacker, J. Dunlosky & A. C. Graesser (eds.), *Metacognition in Educational Theory and Practice* (pp. 145–164). Mahwah, NJ: Lawrence Erlbaum Associates.

Pannu, J. K. & Kaszniak, A. W. (2005). Metamemory experiments in neurological populations: a review. *Neuropsychology Review*, *3*, 105–130.

Perfect, T. J. (2002). When does eyewitness confidence predict performance? In T. J. Perfect & B. Schwartz (eds.), *Applied Metacognition* (pp. 95–120). New York: Cambridge University Press.

Perfect, T. J. & Schwartz, B. (eds.) (2002). *Applied Metacognition*. New York: Cambridge University Press.

Powers, W. T. (1973). *Behavior: The Control of Perception*. Oxford: Aldine.

Pressley, M. & Afflerbach, P. (1995). *Verbal Protocols of Reading: The Nature of Constructively Responsive Reading*. Hillsdale, NJ: Lawrence Erlbaum Associates.

Pritchard, M. F. & Keenan, J. M. (1999). Memory monitoring in mock jurors. *Journal of Experimental Psychology: Applied*, *5*, 152–168.

Rawson, K. A. & Dunlosky, J. (2002). Are performance predictions for text based on ease of processing? *Journal of Experimental Psychology: Learning, Memory & Cognition*, *28*, 69–80.

Reder, L. M. (1988). Strategic control of retrieval strategies. *The Psychology of Learning and Motivation: Advances in Research & Theory*, *22*, 227–259.

Reder, L. M. (ed.) (1996). Implicit memory and metacognition. Mahwah, NJ: Lawrence Erlbaum Associates.

Reder, L. M. & Ritter, F. E. (1992). What determines initial feeling of knowing? Familiarity with question terms, not with the answer. *Journal of Experimental Psychology: Learning, Memory, and Cognition*, *18*, 435–451.

Schwartz, B. L., Benjamin, A. S. & Bjork, R. A. (1997). The inferential and experiential bases of metamemory. *Current Directions in Psychological Science*, *6*, 132–137.

Shaughnessy, J. J. (1981). Memory monitoring accuracy and modification of rehearsal strategies. *Journal of Verbal Learning & Verbal Behavior*, *20*, 216–230.

Sikström, S. & Jönsson, F. (2005). A model for stochastic drift in memory strength to account for judgments of learning. *Psychological Review*, *112*, 932–950.

Sitko, B. M. (1998). Knowing how to write: metacognition and writing instruction. In D. J. Hacker, J. Dunlosky & A. C. Graesser (eds.), *Metacognition in Educational Theory and Practice* (pp. 93–116). Mahwah, NJ: Lawrence Erlbaum Associates.

Son, L. K. & Metcalfe, J. (2000). Metacognitive and control strategies in study-time allocation. *Journal of Experimental Psychology: Learning, Memory, and Cognition*, *26*, 204–221.

Son, L. & Metcalfe, J. (2005). Judgments of learning: evidence for a two-stage process. *Memory & Cognition*, *33*, 1116–1129.

Spellman, B. A. & Bjork, R. A. (1992). When predictions create reality: judgments of learning may alter what they are intended to assess. *Psychological Science*, *3*, 315–316.

Teasdale, J. D. (1999). Metacognition, mindfulness and the modification of mood disorders. *Clinical Psychology and Psychotherapy*, *6*, 146–155.

Thiede, K. W. (1996). The relative importance of anticipated test format and anticipated test difficulty on performance. *Quarterly Journal of Experimental Psychology: Human Experimental Psychology*, *49A*, 901–918.

Thiede, K. W. (1999). The importance of monitoring and self-regulation during multi-trial learning. *Psychonomic Bulletin & Review*, *6*, 662–667.

Thiede, K. W. & Anderson, M. C. M. (2003). Summarizing can improve metacomprehension accuracy. *Contemporary Educational Psychology*, *28*, 129–160.

Thiede, K. W., Anderson, M. C. M. & Therriault, D. (2003). Accuracy of metacognitive monitoring affects learning of text. *Journal of Educational Psychology*, *95*, 66–73.

Thiede, K. W. & Dunlosky, J. (1999). Toward a general model of self-regulated study: an analysis of selection of items for study and self-paced study time. *Journal of Experimental Psychology: Learning, Memory, and Cognition*, *25*, 1024–1037.

Wallsten, T. S. (1996). An analysis of judgment research analyses. *Organizational Behavior & Human Decision Processes*, *65*, 220–226.

Zechmeister, E. B. & Shaughnessy, J. J. (1980). When you know that you and when you think that you know but you don't. *Bulletin of the Psychonomic Society*, *15*, 41–44.

APPENDIX

See Table 6.3 for instructions on using this Appendix for finding entry points into various areas of enquiry for metacognitive research.

How do Individuals Monitor Memory?

1. Leonesio, R. J. & Nelson, T. O. (1990). Do different metamemory judgments tap the same underlying aspects of memory? *Journal of Experimental Psychology: Learning, Memory, and Cognition*, *16*, 464–470.
2. Koriat (1997). See References.
3. Schwartz, B. L. (1994). Sources of information in metamemory: judgments of learning and feelings of knowing. *Psychonomic Bulletin & Review*, *1*, 357–375.
4. Kelley, C. M. & Lindsay, D. S. (1993). Remembering mistaken for knowing: ease of retrieval as a basis for confidence in answers to general knowledge questions. *Journal of Memory & Language*, *32*, 1–24.
5. Johnson, M. K. & Reeder, J. A. (1997). Consciousness as metaprocessing. In J. D. Cohen & J. W. Schooler (eds.), *Scientific Approaches to Consciousness* (pp. 261–293). Mahwah, NJ: Lawrence Erlbaum Associates.

How Accurate is Memory Monitoring?

6. Underwood, B. J. (1966). Individual and group predictions of item difficulty for free learning. *Journal of Experimental Psychology*, *71*, 673–679.
7. Nelson and Dunlosky (1991). See References.
8. Koriat (1993). See References.
9. Gigerenzer, G., Hoffrage, U. & Kleinbolting, H. (1991). Probabilistic mental models: a Brunswikian theory of confidence. *Psychological Review*, *98*, 506–528.
10. Mitchell, K. J. & Johnson, M. K. (2000). Source monitoring: attributing mental experiences. In E. Tulving & F. I. M. Craik (eds.), *The Oxford Handbook of Memory* (pp. 179–195). New York: Oxford University Press.

Can Monitoring Accuracy be Improved?

11. We are unaware of programmatic research in this area.
12. Weaver, C. A. & Kelemen, W. L. (1997). Judgments of learning at delays: shifts in response patterns or increased metamemory accuracy? *Psychological Science*, *8*, 318–321.
13. Koriat (1993). See References.
14. Arkes, H. R. (1991). Costs and benefits of judgment errors: implications for debiasing. *Psychological Bulletin*, *110*, 486–498.
15. Multhaup, K. S. (1995). Aging, source, and decision criteria: when false fame errors do and do not occur. *Psychology & Aging*, *10*, 492–497.

How is Monitoring Used to Control?

16. Son and Metcalfe (2000). See References.
17. Metcalfe and Kornell (2005). See References.
18. Reder and Ritter (1992). See References.
19. Goldsmith, M., Koriat, A. & Weinberg-Eliezer, A. (2002). Strategic regulation of grain size memory reporting. *Journal of Experimental Psychology: General*, *131*, 73–95.
20. See Johnson and Reeder (1997). 5 above.

CHAPTER 7

Comprehension and Situation Awareness

Francis T. Durso
Texas Tech University, USA

Katherine A. Rawson
Kent State University, USA

and

Sara Girotto
Texas Tech University, USA

The central role of comprehension in human cognition has been recognized by both basic and applied researchers. Basic research in comprehension, conducted under the rubrics of text comprehension, language processing, and reading research, is a large part of the field of psycholinguistics in particular and cognitive science in general. Applied research in comprehension, conducted under the rubric of situation awareness (SA), is a large part of the field of cognitive ergonomics in particular and human factors in general.

Although SA has (many) very specific definitions in the literature (e.g., Endsley 1990; see Rousseau *et al.* 2004), in this chapter we think of SA as comprehension, or understanding, of a dynamic environment. In fact, the origin of the term SA in aviation highlights comprehension: the component of tactical flight operations which involves the pilot's understanding. There are some advantages to this way of thinking. The term *comprehension* carries less baggage than does the term *awareness*. For example, comprehension allows for implicit (e.g., Croft *et al.* 2004) as well as explicit (Gugerty 1997) information. It may also help applied researchers sidestep semantic entanglements, like SA as product and SA as process. Finally, the term *comprehension* acknowledges the connections to the large basic research database on reading comprehension from which SA work has benefited, and invites continued comparisons between comprehension of dynamic situations and comprehension of text.

Lack of understanding when performing complex cognitive tasks can have dramatic consequences (see Casey 1993; Chiles 2002). The incident at Three Mile Island was a result of operators draining coolant because they misunderstood the coolant level to be too high. As another example, nearly 5000 people died between 1978 and 1992 in flights

Handbook of Applied Cognition: Second Edition. Edited by Francis T. Durso.

that were under control but flown into terrain (CFIT: controlled flight into terrain). According to Woodhouse and Woodhouse (1995), 74 per cent of these CFIT accidents were due to a lack of awareness on the part of the flight crew, as opposed to non-adherence or proficiency/skill failure. Similarly, Durso *et al.* (1998b) reported that 62 per cent of the operational errors while controlling flights between airports (en route) were made by air traffic controllers unaware that a loss of separation was developing. In many domains, superior performance is linked to superior SA, and not to other, less cognitive skills. For example, Horswill and McKenna (2004) argue that of all the components of driving the *only* one that correlates with safety is SA, and not for example vehicle control skills.

Currently, there is no clear consensus on how operators understand the dynamic environment in which they work. There are efforts to understand SA from a variety of perspectives. Although it is possible to look at SA from perspectives other than cognitive information-processing (cf. Adams *et al.* 1995), there is certainly reason to treat SA as a cognitive construct (Endsley & Bolstad 1994; Endsley 1995; Durso & Gronlund 1999). As examples, Carretta *et al.* (1996) asked which abilities and personality traits predicted SA in F-15 pilots. They used cognitive measures of working memory, spatial ability, time estimation, and perceptual speed. Psychomotor skills and the Big Five personality traits were also assessed. SA was determined by judgments of peers and supervisors using a Likert scale ranging from 1 (acceptable) to 6 (outstanding). When flying experience was controlled, general cognitive ability was found to predict SA, but not psychomotor skills or personality traits. Similarly, O'Hare (1997), using an SA measure requiring pilots to "scan multiple information sources, evaluate alternatives, establish priorities, and select and work on the task that has the highest priority at the moment" (WOMBAT; Roscoe 1997), was able to discriminate elite pilots from ordinary pilots. Chaparro *et al.* (1999) showed that drivers' ability to recognize hazards was dependent on their divided and selective attention ability.

Endsley and colleagues have championed a general cognitive approach in the literature. In 1995, Endsley sketched a framework of the cognitive processes likely to underlie SA. In this chapter, we add to that work by borrowing from the reading comprehension literature to specify more precisely at least one possible sequence of processes that gives rise to understanding of dynamic situations. As in the reading comprehension literature, in this chapter *comprehension* is not viewed as one stage in a serial sequence of stages. To us comprehension is the phenomenon that emerges from an orchestra of cognitive processes. Perception is involved in all comprehension, but, perhaps less obviously, so are top-down, predictive processes, and bottom-up event integrating processes. Thus, although we break down the comprehension process into constituents for the sake of exposition, all component processes operate in a highly integrated fashion.

Thinking of SA as something like reading comprehension, but in a dynamic environment, is the analogy that drives this chapter. Thus, unlike the previous coverage of SA in the first edition of this book (Durso & Gronlund 1999), which let the extant literature direct the shape of the review, this chapter takes a somewhat more top-down approach. Our intent here is to review the literature on SA, but to do so in the context of a model of situation comprehension. By so doing, we explore the appropriateness of an analogy with reading comprehension for furthering understanding of SA, and review the literature that has accumulated since the Durso and Gronlund review of SA. Like all analogies, there are limits, but comparing something poorly understood (e.g., SA) to something well understood (e.g., reading comprehension), has been useful in every scientific domain (e.g., Oppenheimer 1956).

MEASURING COMPREHENSION

We begin our analogy with methodology. Because basic and applied investigators have differed in their epistemic goals, their methods have also differed. Basic cognitive research explains comprehension by characterizing the underlying cognitive mechanisms involved. In order to do this, researchers have developed particular methodologies that are used in relatively simple, controlled experiments. Because those experiments are about language, the domain is almost universally static text. The empirical facts that have emerged from this work have allowed researchers to reach a surprising level of consensus on the theoretical underpinnings of comprehension. Of course, particular models differ in their specifics, but researchers interested in comprehension in reading agree on much.

Measuring Text Comprehension

A wide variety of measures has been developed to measure text comprehension. The kinds of measures used in text comprehension research may be roughly grouped into three categories, as shown in Table 7.1.

Self-report Measures

Self-report measures include those in which individuals are asked to report their subjective beliefs about their comprehension (metacomprehension judgments) or report on their own thinking during comprehension (verbal protocols). Understanding individuals' beliefs about and conscious experiences of their own comprehension may be important for understanding their subsequent judgments and behaviors. However, metacomprehension judgments and verbal protocols are limited in the extent to which they can be used as measures of comprehension and in the extent to which they reveal the nature of underlying cognitive processes.

Accuracy Measures

The second category includes objective measures of comprehension in which accuracy is the primary dependent variable of interest. These objective measures can be further divided into those that primarily measure memory for text content and those that primarily measure deeper comprehension (Kintsch 1994), although no measure provides a "pure" assessment of either memory or comprehension. Note this important distinction between memory and comprehension – an individual could memorize this paragraph well enough to recite it without really understanding the concepts or ideas in it. Conversely, most of our readers will understand this paragraph quite well while reading, although they may not be able to remember many of the specific details afterwards.

Table 7.1 Kinds of measures used in text comprehension research

Task	Descriptions and examples	Sample references
Self-report measures		
Metacomprehension judgments	Judging how well a text has been understood	Rawson *et al.* (2002)
		Thiede and Anderson (2003)
	Predicting how well one will do on a test	Maki (1998)
		Rawson and Dunlosky (2002)
	Estimating how well one has done on a test	Maki *et al.* (1990)
		Maki *et al.* (1994)
Verbal protocols	Unconstrained "thinking out loud" while reading	Kendeou and van den Broek (2005)
	Answering open-ended questions while reading (e.g., after each sentence of a narrative, explaining why the event described therein happened)	Suh and Trabasso (1993)
		Magliano *et al.* (1999)
Performance accuracy measures		
Memory measures		
Recall	Free recall (e.g., "Write down everything you can remember from the text you just read")	Kintsch (1998)
		Rawson and Kintsch (2004)
	Cued recall (e.g., "What is the definition of ________ ?")	Myers *et al.* (1987)
Recognition	e.g., "Which of the following sentences appeared in the text you just read?"	Zwaan (1994)
		Kintsch *et al.* (1990)
	e.g., "Which item below is the definition of ________ ?"	
Comprehension measures		
Inference questions	Forming a connection between two ideas that was not explicitly stated in the text, forming a connection between an idea and relevant prior knowledge, or drawing valid conclusions from ideas stated in the text	Mayer *et al.* (1996)
		Mayer and Jackson (2005)
Transfer problems	Applying principles from one domain to new problems in another domain	Rawson and Kintsch (2005)
Concept organization	Drawing concept maps or diagrams, concept sorting, similarity judgments	McNamara and Kintsch (1996)

Table 7.1 *Continued*

Task	Descriptions and examples	Sample references
Performance time measures		
Self-paced reading times	Computer presents units of material (words, phrases, sentences, or paragraphs) one at a time and individual advances through units at own pace; amount of time spent reading each unit is recorded. Reading times in different experimental conditions re often compared. Correlations between reading times and variables of theoretical interest are often computed	Graesser *et al.* (1980) Millis *et al.* (1998)
Eye movements	Intact text material is presented and eye tracking equipment records (a) amount of time spent looking at each region and (b) the pattern of eye movement between regions	Just and Carpenter (1980) Rayner (1998) Wiley and Rayner (2000)
Implicit query	Reading is interrupted at target locations by a probe presented for speeded response. These measures are typically used to estimate the activation level of a target concept, based on the extent to which response times to the target are faster than to a control.	Long *et al.* (1992) Klin *et al.* (1999) Wiley *et al.* (2001) McKoon *et al.* (1996) Singer *et al.* (1992) O'Brien and Albrecht (1991)
Lexical decision	Decide whether a string of letters forms a word	
Naming	Pronounce a word as fast as possible	
Recognition	Indicate whether a word appeared in the text just read	
Explicit query	Reading is interrupted at target locations by a question requiring a speeded response (e.g., the sentence "Bob believed Bill because he was gullible" is followed by the query, "Who was gullible?")	

In most studies using accuracy measures, individuals read an entire text and later answer questions based on the text material. These measures are useful for understanding the product readers acquire from a text and the extent to which this information can be retained and used subsequently. However, these measures are limited for investigating the nature of the processes involved during reading. For example, if an individual cannot answer an inference question after reading a text, it does not mean that inferential processing was not taking place during reading (the inference may have been computed but then forgotten). Likewise, the ability to answer the question does not necessarily mean that the inference was made during reading (the inference may have been made at time of test).

Latency Measures

The third category includes measures in which latency is the primary dependent variable of interest. In contrast to the first two kinds of measure, these tasks are accepted as more useful for studying the nature of the underlying cognitive processes and the mental representations involved during reading because the measures are taken at the time of processing (vs. measuring the product after process has been completed, i.e., the representation that is still available after the reading task). For example, to explore whether individuals make predictive inferences while reading, Klin *et al.* (1999) presented readers with short stories in one of two versions, one that was consistent with a target predictive inference and one that was not. To illustrate, one story described the protagonist either as having lost his job or as having been given a healthy raise. The story then goes on to say that the protagonist really wanted to give his wife something special for her birthday, and he noticed a beautiful ruby ring sitting unattended on a department store counter. The story ended with "He quietly made his way closer to the counter." Immediately after the last sentence, the word STEAL appeared on the screen and participants simply had to say the word aloud as quickly as possible. People were faster to say the word when the man had been described as losing his job than when he had been described as getting a raise. Presumably, readers had already activated the concept steal in the former case because they predicted that he was going to steal the ring from the counter (vs. buy it in the latter case).

One measure of time that has been particularly informative in reading research is fixation duration or dwell time. Key assumptions have allowed eye movement research in reading to have powerful implications for underlying cognition (Just & Carpenter 1980). According to the *immediacy assumption*, interpretation of a stimulus (e.g., a word) begins as soon as the stimulus is fixated. According to the *eye–mind assumption*, "the eye remains fixated on a word as long as the word is being processed . . . there is no appreciable lag between what is being fixated and what is being processed" (Just & Carpenter 1980, pp. 330–331).

In summary, performance time measures such as these can support fine-grained analysis of the mental representations and processes involved during comprehension. In the text-comprehension literature, the adoption of one performance time measure over another often depends upon weighing tradeoffs between task intrusiveness that may disrupt or alter normal comprehension processing versus the ease of interpreting the data that are acquired. When possible, the use of converging methods is routinely recommended (e.g., Klin *et al.* 1999).

Measuring Comprehension of Dynamic Environments

A variety of different measures has been developed to measure SA. One scheme (Durso & Gronlund 1999) classifies measures into three general types: subjective measures, query methods, and implicit performance measures. Such a classification can be productively compared with a classification that comes from our analogy to reading comprehension: self-reports, accuracy, and time (see Table 7.2).

Subjective Measures

Subjective measures, as in reading research, typically require the operator to make self-judgments about understanding. One of the most well-known subjective measures is the Situation Awareness Rating Technique (SART) developed by Taylor (1990), which requires operators to make judgments along a number of dimensions, some of which capture impressions of workload, whereas others capture more cognitive dimensions.

As with reading comprehension, subjective measures of SA are metacomprehension, not comprehension, measures. However, this does not mean that subjective measures are not useful. In most industrial situations, it is very important that objective SA and subjective judgments of SA coincide. In a future where the operator must decide whether to turn on an intelligent aid, or in the present where the operator must admit he needs help, research on *meta-SA* is needed. Nevertheless, these measures reveal nothing about the underlying processes of comprehension.

Unlike in reading research, we also find a few subjective measures based on *observer* reports. Unlike reading, in dynamic environments controlled by operators, it is at least possible that behaviors signal the level of situation comprehension. Efforts to formalize such experiences have asked subject matter experts (SMEs) to observe the operator's performance and then to rate the participant's level of SA; the Carretta *et al.* (1996) study with F-15 pilots discussed earlier is one example. See also SA/BARS (Neal *et al.* 1998).

Accuracy Measures

By analogy to the reading comprehension literature, SA measures using accuracy as a dependent variable tend to measure the product of situation awareness, that is, the final product of the situation comprehension processes; for example, location of own ship, awareness of the mode of the aircraft, and navigational awareness are SA products in aviation. SA accuracy measures include query methods and implicit performance measures. Query methods explicitly ask the operator to report a piece of task-relevant information (see Jeannot *et al.* 2003 for a review). Implicit performance measures examine how an operator responds to an SA-revealing event embedded, either naturally or by clever experimenters, into the scenario. It is of fundamental importance that the tasks used as implicit performance measures of SA can be performed successfully by an operator with good SA but unsuccessfully by one with poor SA. Similarly, event detection (Gugerty & Falzetta 2005) requires the operator to detect particular embedded events, like swerves or decelerations.

Table 7.2 Measures of SA comparing a classification scheme from the literature with a classification drawn from the analogy to reading comprehension. One classification scheme reported in the SA literature

		Subjective	Query	Implicit performance
Classification scheme of text comprehension methodologies	Self-reports	SART (Taylor 1990); SAPS (Deighton 1997; Jensen 1999); C-SAS (Dennehy 1997); SASHA_Q (Jeannot *et al.* 2003); SA-SWORD (Vidulich & Hughes 1991); SARS (Waag & Houck 1994); Verbal protocols (Metalis 1993)		
	Accuracy		SAGAT (Endsley 1990); SALSA (Hauβ *et al.* 2000, 2001); SAPS (Deighton 1997; Jensen 1999); Explicit probes (Vidulich *et al.* 1994)	Andre *et al.* (1991) Measures of Effectiveness (Vidulich *et al.* 1994); Implicit probes (Vidulich *et al.* 1994) Gugerty and Falzetta (2005)
	Time		SPAM (Durso *et al.* 1995; 1998); SASHA_L (Jeannot *et al.* 2003)	Busquets *et al.* (1994)

As Table 7.2 suggests, most objective measures of SA, whether query methods or implicit performance methods, rely on accuracy. Examining accuracy is valuable for understanding which types of information about a certain situation the operator retains. The most widely used query method, the Situation Awareness Global Assessment Technique (SAGAT), developed by Endsley (1990), relies on accuracy. In order to administer this measure (see Jones & Kaber 2004), the experimenter prepares a series of questions relevant to the task the operator will have to perform. The simulation is stopped at points, and all the information relevant to the task is physically removed from the operator who, at that point, is asked to answer the questions previously prepared. In addition to the possible effects that the intrusiveness of the method might cause, SAGAT has been criticized for relying too heavily on conscious memory (e.g., Sarter & Woods 1991; Durso *et al.* 1998a). The criticisms raised by reading comprehension researchers apply here as well: If the operator does not have a good picture of the situation when queried, that does not mean that she did not have the picture while performing the task. A common example is highway amnesia. Although the driver may wonder if she stopped at the traffic light for which she has no memory, failure to answer correctly does not mean she had an SA failure at the traffic light. Underwood *et al.* (2002) showed that experienced drivers can be inaccurate in judgments about what they looked at just moments ago. The contrary can hold as well: An operator may form a mental image at the point of query that may differ from the one actually present during task performance.

Latency Measures

Methods that use time as a dependent variable are a step toward investigating the cognitive processes that underlie situation comprehension. Accuracy tells us about SA only when it fails; response time has the potential to help us in investigating what happens when SA succeeds. This logic led to the use of response time to understand human memory and opened research into semantic memory and knowledge structures (Lachman *et al.* 1979).

Thus far, only a few measures have been developed to measure SA using response time, although many can certainly be adapted. Some are implicit performance measures. For example, Busquets *et al.* (1994) had participants land on one runway while another aircraft was to land on another runway. Occasionally, the second aircraft would deviate and try to land on the first runway. The time to take action to avoid the second aircraft was the implicit performance measure of SA.

Query methods collecting response time have also been developed. In the Situation-Present Assessment Method (SPAM; Durso *et al.* 1998a; Durso & Dattel 2004), the operator is given unsolicited requests for information (hence the unusual acronym) while he or she is performing the task. For example, the operator can be asked which one of two airplanes has the lower altitude or, given the current speed, which one will reach a waypoint first. The logic of SPAM is that if the information is immediately available to the operator, response time to the query should be short. If the information is not available, but the operator knows where to find the information, then response time will be longer, but not as long as the case in which the operator does not know where to find the information. Thus, SPAM leaves the operator in context and assumes that knowing where to find a piece of information could be indicative of good SA, even if the information was not available in memory. In fact, if a piece of information was immediately available in the environment, it might be a poor idea to use limited resources to remember it. Other details including how to eliminate workload effects and how to construct the queries can be found in Durso and Dattel (2004). SPAM has recently spawned other measures (Jeannot *et al.* 2003).

SPAM has been shown to improve prediction over a large battery of psychological tests (Durso *et al.* in press). Performance on an ATC simulator was predictable from various cognitive and occasionally noncognitive variables. Of importance here was the finding that SPAM improved predictability of handoff delay times and air traffic errors above and beyond the battery of standard tests, but off-line queries using accuracy did not. Thus, an SA measure like SPAM was able to capture additional variance in performance.

Finally, for fixation duration or dwell time, it is not clear how, or even if, the eye-movement assumptions from text comprehension, hold in a dynamic environment. Rather than process a stimulus and then move on to the next without revisiting the stimulus as does a skilled reader, the skilled industrial operator makes many small fixations (about 2.5/s), revisiting displays for very brief periods (Moray 1990). In the literature there are cases in which experts have longer fixations (Williams & Davids 1998), cases in which their fixations are shorter (Crundall & Underwood 1998), and cases in which no differences in fixation durations are found (Helsen & Pauwels 1993; Williams *et al.* 2002) between experts and novices. Perhaps the best way to understand the difficulty in equating real-world dwell times and cognitive processing is to imagine where you look when driving in the country vs. in the city. Chapman and Underwood (1998) showed that drivers fixate longer on a rural road than an urban one. It seems unlikely that more cognitive processing is occurring on the rural road, and thus researchers must be careful in interpreting eye fixations in real-world dynamic environments, where the operator has choices and where the task is uncontrolled.

Nevertheless, from more controlled, yet dynamic, situations there comes hope that fixation duration may reveal insights into SA. For example, when encountering a dangerous situation, both experts and novice drivers increase fixation durations (Chapman & Underwood 1998). There have even been findings in accord with some of the more subtle discoveries in reading research. For example, when soccer players did not anticipate correctly, they tended to fixate on the player with the ball longer than during correct trials (Helsen & Starkes 1999). This result mirrors nicely those found in reading research when expectations are violated and the offending information receives a longer fixation.

In summary, meta-SA (i.e., self-report) measures are valuable in revealing metacognitive assumptions the operator is making when controlling a dynamic environment, but they tell us little about either the product of comprehension or the processes. SA accuracy measures can tell us about the product of comprehension. Adding latency measures allow insights into the processes as well. Although SA and reading comprehension measures need not agree, they did show a number of similarities. Researchers in both fields must keep several important dimensions in mind when selecting measures, including temporal proximity, availability of external information, invasiveness, and congruence between the SA measure and the performance measure. For example, measures will be more informative about the process of comprehension to the extent that they are temporally proximal to task performance, whereas measures that are taken after task completion are more likely to reflect the products of comprehension. Finally, and perhaps most exciting, additional SA measures can be developed by adapting other reading comprehension measures (Table 7.1) to dynamic environments.

TOWARD A MODEL OF COMPREHENSION OF DYNAMIC SITUATIONS

In this chapter, we use key assumptions from theories of text comprehension to motivate the development of a model of situation comprehension. To foreshadow, an important starting assumption is that text comprehension is not one process. Rather, comprehension is best thought of as a system of cognitive processes. These processes operate together in a coordinated fashion to encode and integrate various kinds of information. In fact, the most widely accepted theoretical claim in text comprehension research is that comprehension processes operate at three basic levels, with different kinds of information encoded at each level (Kintsch 1998). The *surface level* representation includes the exact words and grammatical structures used to form the sentences. In contrast to the linguistic information encoded at the surface level, the *textbase* contains semantic information. That is, the textbase is the representation of the meaning that is extracted from the linguistic input. Finally, like the textbase, the *situation model* also contains meaningful information. However, whereas the textbase primarily includes information that is explicitly stated in the text, the situation model integrates the textbase with prior world knowledge to form a fuller representation of the situation being described in the text. A great deal of research has been dedicated to exploring the processes involved in encoding and integration at each of these levels.

Using these theoretical assumptions of text comprehension models as a foundation, we propose a model of the comprehension of dynamic environments. A schematic of the model appears in Figure 7.1. Each component of the model is described below. To overview, according to our model, situation comprehension involves several different cognitive processes that encode and integrate various kinds of information. By analogy to text comprehension, situation comprehension involves a *surface level* representation that includes the objects in the environment and the structural relationships between them (i.e., scenes). The *eventbase* includes the semantic information that is extracted from the perceptual input. Finally, the *situation model* integrates the semantic information that can be derived from the external input with prior knowledge to form a fuller representation of the situation.

An Illustration

For illustrative purposes, consider an individual who is talking on a cell phone while driving. If she is particularly engaged in the phone conversation, she may fail to check her rearview mirror, an attentional failure at the surface level that results in inadequate sampling of information from the scene behind her. She may encode coarse-grained information about the presence of several cars in the lanes ahead, she may fail to encode the cascade of brake lights on the cars in front of her as they near an intersection.

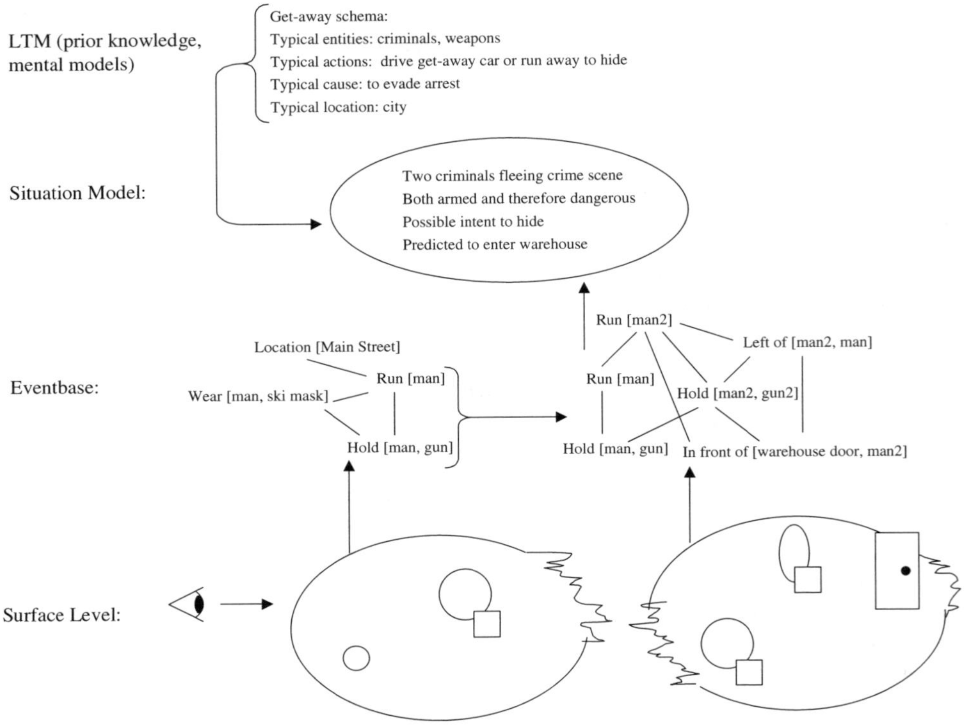

Figure 7.1 A schematic of the model. At the surface level, the operator processes perceptual information: objects and scenes. Information from this level is added to the eventbase, which operates on the basis of promiscuous activation and pruning. A skilled operator will have a mental model containing relevant information, like causation, relevant to the prototypical situation. The mental model, together with the actual situation, instantiates a situation model. Details of the model are contained in the text

Even if adequate surface-level information is processed, the extraction of semantic information may be inadequate, and thus our distracted driver may also have deficient eventbase processing. While sitting at the intersection, she may encode the perceptual features of the red light going off and a green arrow coming on, but fail to process the meaning of the green light (until the annoyed driver behind her sounds his horn). Similarly, as she approaches the four-way stop at the next intersection, she may encode the scene to her left in which a red sedan has just come to a stop. She may also encode the scene to her right in which a blue minivan rolls to a stop about the same time she does. However, what she may fail to do is to integrate the spatial and temporal information from the two scenes and to extract the relevant semantic information – namely, the information that determines who has right of way and should enter the intersection first.

Finally, our driver may have adequate surface and eventbase processing but may still have inadequate situation comprehension if the situation model fails. For example, our driver may process that the driver of an oncoming SUV appears to be oriented toward a child in the backseat. She may also integrate the spatial and temporal information from this scene with information from the other scenes she has sampled, such as that the other three vehicles (hers included) are reaching the intersection before the SUV. She may even successfully extract semantic information, such as encoding from the driver's facial features that he is yelling angrily at the child in the backseat. But if her situation model processing is incomplete, she may fail to grasp the unfolding situation – i.e., although the man in the SUV does not have right of way, he is not attending to the intersection and is not slowing down, and thus our driver should infer the likely outcome that the SUV will run the stop sign. If she fails fully to represent the situation in this way, she may act based only on her eventbase representation (i.e., she has the right of way) thus initiating what will turn out to be a disastrous left turn.

The Surface Level: Encoding Objects and Scenes

The surface level of a text representation includes the particular words and grammatical structures included in each sentence. At first glance, the analogy between text comprehension and situation comprehension may not seem useful, because dynamic environments obviously have different kinds of information than static linguistic information. However, at a broader level, the analogy invites us to ask what the words and sentences of a dynamic environment are. Dynamic environments contain objects and structural relationships between them that must be encoded (much like words and the grammatical relations between them). Thus, as a sentence comprises words and their syntactic relationships, we can think of a scene as a group of characteristic objects (De Graef *et al.* 1990; Bar & Ullman 1996).

According to Endsley's (1995) definition of SA, perceptual processing of individual units is the first step in situation assessment. Many studies have demonstrated that loss of SA is often caused by faulty perception. Jones and Endsley (1996) analyzed 262 pilot SA errors derived from 143 accidents. They found that 72 per cent of SA errors were due to perceptual and attentional processing errors. Durso *et al.* (1998b) reported that 50 per cent of the operational errors caused by air traffic controllers who were unaware that the error was occurring had perceptual or attentional errors underlying them. About 44 per cent of knives carried in baggage are not detected when the airport baggage screener fails to fixate directly on the knife's image, an attentional failure. Even when fixated, 15 per cent of the knives went undetected (McCarley *et al.* 2004). Thus, both attention to and perception of units in the environment are critical to SA.

Of course, the surface level involves not just the encoding of individual objects, but also the encoding of scenes. Scene identification is very quick, sometimes as fast as the identification of a single constituent object (Potter 1976; Friedman 1979; Biederman *et al.* 1982). In many cases, a single fixation can be sufficient to get the "gist" of a scene (Renninger & Malik 2004). For example, Schyns and Oliva (1994; Oliva & Schyns 1997) found that scenes could be identified when pictures were presented for only 45–135 ms.

Operators extract various cues from the environment in order to perform their task, whether it is predicting where the tennis serve will land or whether the approaching aircraft is hostile. These cues can be scenes, objects, or parts of objects. For example, Schyns and Oliva (1994) found that scenes could be identified from holistic cues like low-spatial frequency that preserves the spatial relations between large-scale structures existing in the scene without presenting the visual details needed to identify the individual objects.

Renninger and Malik (2004) found that humans confuse scenes with similar textures and that texture alone was able to account for correct categorization on eight of the ten scene categories presented. Thus, scene level information, independent from information relative to individual objects, can support scene identification (Biederman 1981, 1988; Schyns & Oliva 1994; Oliva & Schyns 2000).

Surface level processing has been shown to be of fundamental importance in hazard perception, or "situation awareness for dangerous situations in the traffic environment" (Horswill & McKenna 2004, p. 155). In typical research, participants watch a monitor and press a button when the situation presents a danger. Reaction time and accuracy both correlate with on-road evaluations of driving instructors (Mills *et al.* 1998). Experts detect hazards faster than novices (McKenna & Crick 1991; Avila & Moreno 2003), in part because experienced drivers know potential hazard locations (see Underwood *et al.*, Chapter 15, this volume). There is some evidence that conceptual categorization of cues (i.e., that is a category member) can be as rapid as perception of the simple presence of the cue (Secrist & Hartman 1993).

Superior SA can result not only if an operator detects a cue more quickly, but also if the cue is more diagnostic (Salas *et al.* 2001). Expert squash players seem to rely at least partially on perceptual extraction of better cues. For example, looking at response latency, Howarth *et al.* (1984) found that experts used information extracted prior to ball contact, whereas less skilled players relied on early ball-flight information. Some of this prior-to-contact information seems to be opponent movement (Abernethy *et al.* 2001) and some seem to be proximal cues (Abernethy & Russell 1987). These results have been replicated in a variety of sports (see Abernethy *et al.*, Chapter 13, this volume).

Clearly, failures to perceive the cues that indicate a danger can travel down the cognitive stream and lead to poor decisions and poor performance. Consider the fact that pilots sometimes decide to fly into storms, often with fatal consequences. Ineffective decision-making related to weather has led researchers to try to identify the psychological reasons why pilots decide to continue a flight when weather conditions are deteriorating (Wiggins & O'Hare 2003). Faulty perceptual classification seems at least partially to blame.

Wiggins and O'Hare (2003) developed a training program for novice pilots to facilitate identification of cues helpful in recognizing dangerous, weather-related situations. One strategy that is promising in teaching operators how to recognize relevant cues in the environment is cognitive apprenticeship (Druckman & Bjork 1991): Trainees work closely with experts on a series of activities that take place in the real environment.

Studies investigating the effectiveness of sport-specific perceptual training found that players improve their performance after they learn to use visual cues (James & Patrick 2004). Experiments (Williams *et al.* 2002; Farrow & Abernethy 2003) in which tennis players were trained with either implicit or explicit cue recognition revealed better performance of the two groups with respect to a control and a placebo group.

In summary, the literature has clear support that perception is an important component of situation comprehension. Perception in a dynamic environment can proceed by sampling and identifying objects and scenes, with the latter often occurring as quickly as the former. Activation of a scene can proceed from a characteristic constituent object or from holistic cues. Once a scene is identified, top-down influences on identification of constituent objects become possible. The perceptual components of SA, such as speed of scene identification and the relationship between scenes and objects, have important consequences for application. Training programs that focus on surface level processing have had success.

The Eventbase: Integrating Sequences of Meaningful Events

The Textbase in Text Comprehension

Whereas the surface level representation in text comprehension includes linguistic information (i.e., the exact words and grammatical structures in a sentence), the textbase represents the semantic information that is derived from the linguistic input, including the concepts denoted by words and the ideas denoted by the structural relationships between them. For example, "The man was bitten by the dog" and "The dog bit the man" have different grammatical structures but express the same idea or *proposition*.

Importantly, in addition to the concepts and propositions themselves, the textbase represents the semantic relationships between them. Such connections can be based on several different dimensions, including reference, causality, time, and space. For example, two propositions could be connected if they express events that occur in the same timeframe or spatial location. Likewise, a connection between two propositions may be represented when they refer to the same entity. The important point is that the representation of concepts and propositions alone is not enough. These elements must also be connected to one another, or integrated, to form a coherent representation. Furthermore, not only must connections between elements within a sentence be represented, but also connections between the elements in different sentences must be represented for a coherent representation of the text. Quite simply, not to represent relations between elements that are explicitly stated or strongly implied is to incompletely understand a text, and thus incoherent representations may lead to comprehension failures. Accordingly, an important issue concerns how connections between elements are formed. According to the construction-integration (CI) theory of comprehension (Kintsch 1988, 1998), only a limited amount of text material can be processed at one time due to limited cognitive capacity. Text comprehension thus proceeds in cycles, with the input in a given cycle roughly equivalent to a sentence. Each cycle involves two phases of processing. In the construction phase, representational "nodes" are created that correspond to the concepts and propositions extracted from the linguistic input. Each node can then activate associated concepts, propositions, and higher-order knowledge structures (e.g., schemata) from long-term memory, which are also included as nodes in the developing network. The other key process involved during the construction phase involves the formation of connections between nodes, based on various factors (e.g., time, space, reference, and causality).

The *integration* phase involves the spreading of activation throughout the network. Highly interconnected nodes will accumulate activation, whereas less well-connected nodes will lose activation and may drop from the network altogether. As a result of the spreading activation process, network nodes will vary in their activation level at the end of integration. Given the limited capacity of the processing system, the entire network cannot be carried over to the next processing cycle because some capacity must be available for the processing of the next input. According to the CI model, the network that remains after integration is stored in long-term memory but only the subset of nodes with the highest ending activation remain in working memory to participate in the next processing cycle. It is this "carrying over" of nodes from one cycle to the next that allows the integration of information across segments of text. Thus, an important part of processing is determining what to carry over from one processing cycle to the next – the success of integrating information across cycles will depend upon which nodes are carried over. The highly activated nodes in one cycle will usually, but not always, represent the information that is most related to the next input. If not, the representation will be incoherent (i.e., one form of comprehension failure) in the absence of additional processing.

Empirical Evidence from Text Comprehension Research

Previous research has provided support for each of these theoretical claims. Several studies have reported evidence for the representation of concepts and propositions (e.g., Kintsch *et al.* 1975; Murphy 1984; O'Brien *et al.* 1997). For example, Murphy (1984) showed that processing a word that introduces a new concept is more time-consuming than processing the same word when it refers to an existing concept. Studies involving multiple regression analyses have shown monotonic increases in sentence reading times, with each additional word introducing a new concept and with each additional proposition in a sentence, after controlling for other related variables (e.g., Graesser *et al.* 1980; Haberlandt *et al.* 1980; Graesser & Bertus 1998; Millis *et al.* 1998).

Research has also provided support for assumptions about the nature of the processes involved in constructing the textbase. For example, concerning the claim that input is processed in cycles, studies using reading time and eye movement measures have reported robust *wrap-up effects*. The wrap-up effect refers to the finding that reading times are substantially longer for the final word of a major clause or sentence than for non-boundary words (e.g., Just & Carpenter 1980; Haberlandt *et al.* 1986; Rayner *et al.* 2000; but see Magliano *et al.* 1993). These effects are attributed to the integration process, which presumably takes place at these boundaries. Some research has focused on investigating how the elements to be carried over from one processing cycle to the next are selected (e.g., Fletcher 1981; Malt 1985; Glanzer & Nolan 1986; Fletcher *et al.* 1990; McKoon *et al.* 1993). Computational models that simulate text processing based on the principles of the CI theory have also been successful at predicting the probability with which humans recall particular propositions from a text (e.g., Goldman & Varma 1995; Kintsch 1998; Rawson & Kintsch 2004), which provides converging evidence for the plausibility of the hypothesized processes.

The Eventbase in Situation Comprehension

By analogy to this work on textbase representations and processes in text comprehension, we posit that a complete representation of a dynamic environment involves the construction of an *eventbase*. Whereas the surface level representation in situation comprehension includes perceptual information (e.g., the objects and the spatial relationships between them in a scene), the eventbase represents the semantic information that is derived from the perceptual input.

Sometimes this information is quite distinct from the perceptual input. For example, an air traffic controller in the tower cab may observe the physical American 767 ascending from Runway 31 to 3 000 feet underneath a nearby Delta 757 that is descending to 3 000 feet, whereas an air traffic controller in the approach control (TRACON) may receive the corresponding information from a radar screen. Although the perceptual input is quite different in the two cases, the two air traffic controllers will likely develop a similar eventbase representation (e.g., each including a "concept" node for Plane A and a "concept" node for Plane B, a "proposition" expressing that Plane A is ascending, a "proposition" expressing that Plane B is descending, and the connections between these elements based on space, time, and reference). Previous applied research has acknowledged that a visual form can differ from a representational form (e.g., Woods 1991). On other occasions, the information in the eventbase is more dependent on the perceptual input. For example, Garsoffky *et al.* (2002) provide data that suggest that viewpoint is retained in the eventbase. Participants watched short (less than 30-second) clips of soccer goals and after each clip made yes/no recognition judgments on video stills. Regardless of level of expertise or from where in the clip the still was taken, recognition hits showed viewpoint dependency. Thus, when witnessing an event, the relationship between perception and semantics is less arbitrary than what would be expected from a strict analogy to reading comprehension. However, even when witnessing an event, the eventbase cannot be equivalent to the raw surface level type of information, nor can it be composed entirely of perceptual information.

According to the analogy, only a limited amount of the situation can be processed at one time due to limited cognitive capacity. Moray (1990) discusses how limited the processing is and how features of the environment allow experienced operators to deal with these limits. Industrial operators sample their environment about 2.5 times a second. If the environment is well structured, then these brief samples can take advantage of redundancies in the world. If it is unstructured, or the operator does not have the experience to take advantage of the structure, then situation awareness will be impaired. A favorite example is that when free-flying moths detect the ultrasonic pulse of a predatory bat, they fly a random flight path (Roeder 1962); such evasive actions make the predictability of the system low, thus limiting the bat's SA. Further, if the bandwidth of the environment is too high, that is if the environment is changing too rapidly, then processing will be beyond the operators' brief samples and again SA will suffer. In most tasks the bandwidth is acceptable (e.g., transportation) or divided up into teams (e.g., Unoccupied Aerial Vehicles) or otherwise reduced, although there are cases like low-altitude combat flying (Haber & Haber 2003) in which the operator is given explicit training on managing the bandwidth by explicitly learning times required to perform tasks as function of altitude.

Importantly, the eventbase also integrates semantic information across scenes. Consider a fighter pilot who encodes perceptual information from the instrument panel including a radar screen indicating two aircraft to the right, one at 45° and one at 120°. The pilot then looks through the right window and physically observes one aircraft flying slightly ahead. Each scene is encoded in one cycle of processing, much as each cycle of processing during text comprehension involves roughly one sentence. However, the information encoded from the first scene (the instrument panel) has yet to be integrated with the information encoded from the second scene (the view through the window). Perceptual information per se will not allow the pilot to make the referential connection between the physical object on the radar screen and the physical object observed through the window, because the two are quite dissimilar perceptually. However, the connection can be established at the semantic level. From the first scene, the pilot may represent a "concept" for Plane A, a "concept" for Plane B, a "proposition" expressing that Plane A is ahead of own ship, and a "proposition" expressing that Plane B is behind own ship. If these elements are carried over to the next cycle of processing, a referential link may be established with the "proposition" from the second scene expressing that a plane is ahead of our pilot's plane.

The analogy leads to the hypothesis that the processes involved in construction of an eventbase are similar to those involved in the construction of a textbase. Processing proceeds in cycles, with one scene processed in each cycle (e.g., a driver looking ahead to a stoplight, checking the rearview mirror, and then looking out the side window). Nodes will be created that correspond to the meaning of the objects in the scene as well as nodes expressing the semantic relationships between them. Each node may activate associated information from long-term memory. Connections will be formed between nodes based on various dimensions (e.g., time, space, reference), and then activation will be spread through the network resulting in the pruning of some nodes. Only those elements that are most highly active at the end of integration will be carried over to participate in the processing of the next scene.

To discriminate cleanly between the eventbase, which is not influenced by domain specific knowledge, and the situation model, which is, it is important to consider the ability to track changes outside of an area of expertise. Exactly this kind of work was begun in the 1960s by Yntema and colleagues (Yntema & Mueser 1960, 1962; Yntema 1963). For example, in the study by Yntema and Mueser (1960), participants saw an 8×8 grid of "doors," with a row representing an object (e.g., object "K") and a column representing an attribute (e.g., shape) that could take on four states (e.g., circle, square, triangle, heart). Messages read to the participant indicated the value that an attribute had and would continue to have until further notice. Occasionally, the procedure was interrupted to interrogate the participant about the present state of one of the variables (e.g., "What is the current shape of object K?"). Yntema and Mueser varied the number of objects with the same single attribute to be monitored and the number of attributes for the same, single object. Accuracy decreased as the number of attributes whose states were to be remembered increased. Monitoring one attribute across different objects was more difficult than monitoring multiple attributes for one object. For example, keeping track of the shape of eight objects was more difficult than keeping track of eight attributes of one object. Propositionally, this might be represented as SHAPE (K, circle), SHAPE (D, square), SHAPE (N, triangle) and so on, versus SHAPE (K, circle), FOOD (K, toast), WEATHER (K, stormy), and so on. These two eventbases could be represented as in Figure 7.2.

The eventbase representations in Figure 7.2 suggest why the Yntema results obtain. Consider how the processing cycles for these two sets of descriptions might proceed. For the left-hand set, the first processing cycle would involve construction of a concept node for "K," a proposition denoting that K was a circle, and the integration of these two nodes. These two nodes would be carried over for inclusion in the next cycle. However, because no connection can be established between these nodes and the subsequent input, they will likely be dropped during the spreading activation process of the next cycle. At a minimum, the more recent input will be more strongly activated and will thus be selected for carryover to the next processing cycle. Either way, the K nodes will not participate in any additional processing cycles. By comparison, consider the processing cycles for the right-hand set. The initial processing cycle would be the same, with construction of the two K nodes

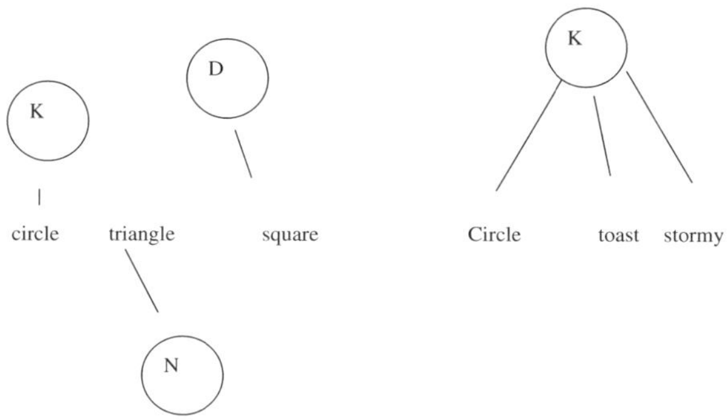

Figure 7.2 Eventbase representation of the monitoring task described in Yntema & Mueser (1960)

and then carryover of those nodes to the next cycle. However, in this case, both nodes can be connected to the nodes constructed for the subsequent input based on argument overlap (i.e., all propositions contain the argument "K"). Thus, the two original nodes are less likely to be dropped from the network during spreading activation. Additionally, even though not all four nodes will be carried over to the next cycle, those nodes that are carried over will probabilistically reactivate the other K nodes with which they are now connected during the construction phase, providing those K nodes with yet another opportunity to become linked to other K nodes and to accrue more activation. Importantly, the CI theory states that the retrievability of any given node is partly a function of the activation it accrues during processing (which increases with the number of processing cycles in which it participates) and the connection strength between that node and the retrieval cue. Both of these factors favor the latter set of descriptions, which provides an explanation for why recall is greater in this condition.

Integrating across scenes and eye fixations to create an eventbase is, in some ways, easier to appreciate in dynamic environments than in reading static text. Scan paths have been studied for years. It is well known that during the early phases of learning to scan, the scan paths are likely to be more variable (Wikman *et al.* 1998) but less flexible (Crundall & Underwood 1998). Recent analyses in some domains are becoming quite intricate. Consider driving. Underwood *et al.* (2003) identified scanpaths of differing number of fixations. Given that experienced drivers have better SA than less experienced ones, it is unlikely that the advantage is due to simple fixations since Underwood *et al.*'s drivers were comparable in that regard. Fixations were heavily dependent on the immediate past for experienced drivers, but regardless of where the novice driver was looking at fixation N, he or she looked at the road far ahead on fixation N + 1. Even though the two groups experienced the same input (comparable single fixations) the information carried from one processing cycle to another (different scan paths) created different eventbases, setting the stage for an ultimate difference in understanding. The difference in scanpaths can be dangerously different: When novice drivers time share with another in-car task, 40 per cent of the males looked away from the road for over three seconds, an amount of time never seen in the data of experienced drivers (Wikman *et al.* 1998).

The information that gets carried from one processing cycle to another in a dynamic environment is likely to be complexly determined and a function of both the operator's intention and the environment's ability to capture attention. Consider the study by Moray and Rotenberg (1989). Their participants were monitoring a simulated thermal hydraulic system. Of interest here is what happened when a second fault occurred shortly after a first. Normally, operators begin to address a fault within seconds, but because they were processing the first fault, the second fault was not addressed for a considerable time. In fact, the first fault resulted in a drop in attention to all the other subsystems except the one with the initial fault. Moray (1990) notes that the operators occasionally looked at the subsystem containing the second fault, but failed to do anything about it. Integrating the second fault into the eventbase would be difficult if all information beyond the first fault subsystem were pruned. Operator intention (to fix the first fault) weights first fault information heavily, increasing the likelihood that it will be carried over, and thus continue to have a heavy influence on spreading activation. Other nodes would drop out, or, at a minimum, would not be selected for carryover.

Consider results from command, control, and communication settings (C3; Wellens & Ergener 1988; Wellens 1993) when multiple threats manifest. Wellens showed that SA was harmed as communication broke down due to time stress. Under high time stress (events distributed over 10 minutes) compared with low stress (events distributed over 40 minutes), the dispatchers were more reactive, attended more to their own monitor, showed deficits in performance and resource allocation, and showed poorer recall. According to the model discussed in the current chapter, the operator would carry over only part of the information – either detail about one emergency at the expense of another, or limited information about multiple emergencies. If the former occurs, the operator understands one of the emergencies but cognitively dismisses the others. If the latter occurs, the operator may carry over some nodes from each emergency, but then not have the information needed to integrate the emergencies and thus would not deeply understand any of the emergencies. Empirically, the dispatcher often allocated nominal resources to all emergencies; thus some node from each emergency makes it to the next cycle, but with little coherence. Thus, understanding and communication suffer.

The Knowledge Level: Going beyond Explicit Information

The Situation Model in Text Comprehension

The textbase contains the semantic information that is denoted by the linguistic content of the text. However, text comprehension involves much more than just a representation of the meaning of the explicit text content itself. In almost all texts, much of the information necessary for comprehension is only implied or is altogether absent from the text. Thus, to understand fully the situations or ideas described in texts, readers must bring a great deal of prior knowledge to bear. Integrating relevant prior knowledge with the semantic information contained in the textbase gives rise to a representation referred to as the *situation model* (e.g., Kintsch 1998; Zwaan & Radvansky 1998).

The nature of the situation model that is constructed for any given text will depend in part on the kinds of prior knowledge that are integrated with the textbase. Many different kinds of knowledge can be involved in text comprehension, from very general world knowledge to very domain-specific knowledge. For example, the nature of the situation model represented for an expository text often depends on the extent to which the reader has prior knowledge about the particular topic discussed in the text. Several studies have demonstrated that readers with high knowledge within a domain construct more complete, coherent situation models than do readers with low domain knowledge (e.g., Bransford & Johnson 1973; Spilich *et al.* 1979; McNamara *et al.* 1996). Importantly, high and low knowledge readers usually differ not only in the amount of domain-relevant knowledge they have, but also in the organization of that information. For example, experts within a domain are more likely to have well-structured and elaborated *mental models,* which here refers to a representation of the causal (and other) relationships between entities and events that are typical across instances of a situation. Mental models can then be integrated with explicit text content to guide the construction of a situation model for the particular situation being described in a text. Mental models and situation models can be thought of as standing in a type–token relationship. In principle, experts and novices may construct the same textbase but still arrive at different situation models due to differences in the prior knowledge they bring to bear, including differences in the completeness, correctness, and coherence of their knowledge.

Orthogonal to the influence of the amount and structure of prior knowledge, the nature of a situation model will also depend on qualitative differences in the kinds of knowledge incorporated into the text representation. As mentioned above, mental models involve knowledge about typical causal relationships between entities and events as well as knowledge about typical spatial relationships between entities, typical temporal relationships between events, typical goals, emotions, and motivations of protagonists, and so on. Thus, situation models are often multidimensional, and the nature of a particular situation model will depend on the extent to which information along one or more of these dimensions is represented. This may depend in part on the kind of situation being described. The spatial dimension may be particularly important when reading a descriptive text (e.g., driving directions) but may be less central when reading other texts (e.g., a romance novel). Although some texts describe static environments, many expository texts and most narratives describe dynamic environments in which the relationships between entities and events change along several dimensions. Thus, different texts will require different kinds of knowledge and will afford different kinds of situation models.

The situation model is the level of representation that is commonly thought to support performance on tasks that require "deep" comprehension, including problem-solving and application. Additionally, the situation model is thought to support predictive inferences during reading (for discussion of the extent to which readers make predictions while reading, see Millis *et al.* 1990; Fincher-Kiefer 1993; Klin *et al.* 1999; Cook *et al.* 2001).

Empirical Evidence from Text Comprehension Research

Several lines of evidence support the claim that situation models are multidimensional (e.g., Bloom *et al.* 1990; Millis *et al.* 1990; Zwaan *et al.* 1995; Zwaan & Radvansky 1998). For example, Zwaan *et al.* (1998) evaluated the processing-load hypothesis, according to which "the fewer indexes that are shared between the current event being processed and other events in the situation model, the more difficult it should be to incorporate that event into the situation model" (p. 201). Zwaan *et al.* coded each clause in their texts with respect to whether that information could be related to the current situation model along several dimensions, including time (if an event occurred in the same time period as the current situation), space (if an event occurred in the same time period as the current situation), causation (if the situation model contained a causal antecedent for the event), reference (if the information referred to an entity in the current situation), and motivation (if an action is consistent with a protagonist's goal). For all dimensions except for space, reading times increased with increases in the number of dimensions along which a connection between the current clause, and the current situation model could not be formed (a follow-up study showed that coherence on the spatial dimension also predicted reading times when readers memorized a map of the location being described in the text before reading).

Other latency measures have also been used to investigate the situational dimensions that individuals monitor while reading (e.g., Glenberg *et al.* 1987; Zwaan 1996; Scott Rich & Taylor 2000). For example, Glenberg *et al.* (1987) developed texts that introduced a character and an object, and the object was then either described as spatially associated with or dissociated from the character (e.g., John put on/took off his sweatshirt and went jogging). After filler sentences (a sentence mentioning the character but not the object), a probe word naming the object (e.g., sweatshirt) was presented for speeded recognition. Reaction times were longer in the dissociated condition than in the associated condition.

The Situation Model in Situation Awareness

Applied researchers have assumed the existence of situation models with properties like time and causation and recognize their applied value. There is evidence of expert knowledge helping organize situations. Stokes *et al.* (1997) had pilots listen to ATC radio communications. Expert pilots recalled twice the number of concept words, but recalled fewer "filler" words than did apprentices. Experts were also asked to "build a mental picture" of the situation and then select from a set of diagrams that best represented the situation. Experts outperformed apprentices in matching the correct diagram with the dialogue. To Stokes *et al.* "[experts] are better able to make practical use of situational schemata to impose form on sensory data in real time" (p. 191).

It is also thought that the temporal and causal properties of a situation model allow users to anticipate the future and to direct subsequent encodings and pattern recognition. In support, Paull and Glencross (1997) conducted a study on baseball players in which they compared batters' ability to anticipate the direction of a pitch. Experts, who presumably had a good situation model, were quicker and more accurate in making predictions about the pitch. Paull and Glenncross point out that the superior knowledge of experts allowed them to have better anticipation and to identify in the visual display cues that were really useful for the task. In Doane and Sohn (2004) novices were especially poor at predicting the result of multiple, meaningfully related control activities, presumably because the novices did not have the internal model needed to generate predictions from the related control activities.

Sometimes having a model of the situation allows anticipation of the future to be immediate and not a matter of choosing among alternatives. In fact, naturalistic decision-making (see Sieck & Klein, Chapter 8, this volume; Zsambok & Klein 1997) has a central tenet that perception can lead directly to appropriate action. Perceiving the present tells the expert operator about the future.

Having a model of the situation can also help overcome cognitive limits. For example, working memory (WM) limits are well documented, but they do not always manifest. Durso and Gronlund (1999) argued that retrieval structures (i.e., long-term working memory; LTWM), selection of only important perceptual information, "gistification" of verbatim information, and chunking are all knowledge-dependent avenues that can allow the skilled operator to bypass cognitive limitations. Consider Sohn and Doane's (2004) work with apprentice and expert pilots. They obtained measures of domain-independent spatial WM and knowledge-dependent LTWM. WM was measured using a rotation span task, and knowledge was based on delayed recall of meaningfully vs. non-meaningfully related pairs of cockpit displays. SA was measured by asking participants if a goal would be reached in the next five seconds given a presented cockpit configuration. Of interest here was the fact that, in some analyses, experts and apprentices seemed to rely differentially on general domain-specific WM: as reliance on domain-specific knowledge increased, reliance on general WM decreased.

Designing for Situation Awareness

We end our consideration of SA by considering recent research on design. Advances in understanding the process of comprehension can greatly contribute to the design of more efficient artifacts. Distribution of attention across a display depends on both the display and the operator. Changes in the environment by chance or design certainly affect such attention allocation. Indeed, cognitive ergonomists have a good understanding of how to employ factors like color (Remington *et al.* 2000) and position (Barfield *et al.* 1995; Wickens & Carswell 1995) in the design of effective alarms and displays (Williams 2002). The reader is directed to the excellent introduction to display–design principles presented in Wickens *et al.* (2004).

Because the importance of maintaining SA and meta-SA has been widely recognized, numerous studies have looked at the design of tools that aid in building and maintaining them. In particular, Endsley *et al.* (2003) argue that addressing SA in the design phase is the key to achieve user-centered design.

In order to establish some guidelines on how to design for SA, Endsley *et al.* (2003) first identified eight possible factors (e.g., errant mental models) that might prevent one from having good SA. Based on these eight factors, Endsley *et al.* (2003) formulated a series of design principles that should be followed when designing for SA. In particular, she suggested: organizing the information around goals; supporting the different phases that result in SA (perception, comprehension, projection); making the important cues salient; helping reduce operator's uncertainty; being as simple as possible; keeping the operator in the loop; and supporting the building of shared SA when teams are involved. It is important to keep in mind that these guidelines are not effective if not based on the SA requirements of the specific domain.

Results of different studies support the fact that designing systems with the specific aim of facilitating and enhancing SA is effective. For example, Tlauka *et al.* (2000) researched the effects of a dual map aircraft display – presenting both ego-centered (ERF) and world-centered reference (WRF) frames – on situation awareness. The purpose of a dual display of this type is to support the operator in maintaining both the current navigational path, by means of the ERF, and support a more global SA, through the WRF. Results of the study showed that, after a moderate amount of training, both ERF tasks and WRF tasks improved when relying on dual displays. As another example, Van Breda and Veltman (1998) compared the use of perspective displays with the use of conventional plan-like displays in a target acquisition task. The use of perspective radar displays allowed pilots a faster target acquisition, apparently an SA-dependent behavior.

Studies investigating the effect of Highway-In-The-Sky (HITS) suggest that flight path awareness is better maintained when using the HITS than when using conventional instruments (Haskell & Wickens 1993; Wickens & Prevett 1995). Farley *et al.* (2000) designed an air–ground data-link system with the specific aim of enabling pilots and air traffic controllers to share information expected to enhance SA and the resulting decision-making. The results showed that SA of traffic and weather, as measured by performance-based testable responses, improved. Also, more information shared led to a more collaborative interaction among operators and improved safety.

CONCLUSIONS

In this chapter, we have attempted to draw an analogy between understanding dynamic environments and the comprehension literature that has evolved to explain how readers understand text. From this analogy, we compared methodologies and suggested that methodologies useful in illuminating reading comprehension could be adapted to reveal details about the processes required to understand dynamic situations. We also sketched a model of situation comprehension that can be applied to research conducted under the rubric of situation awareness. Central to the situation comprehension model were processes allowing encoding objects and scenes, an eventbase that allowed integration of events, and a situation model that allowed the operator to employ knowledge of the situation, including causal knowledge, to anticipate the future. Finally, it seems to us that modern research on comprehension of dynamic environments is ready to benefit from more detailed models of situation comprehension. Experiments designed to test the proposed analogy between text comprehension and situation comprehension would contribute to the development of such detailed models.

AUTHOR NOTE

The authors are grateful for the thorough reviews from Steve Lewandowsky, who managed the review process, and from his two anonymous reviewers. Thanks also to the graduate students in Texas Tech's *Cognitive Ergonomics* class for their comments and criticisms.

REFERENCES

Abernethy, B., Gill, D. P., Parks, S. L. & Packer, S. T. (2001). Expertise and the perception of kinematic and situational probability information. *Perception*, *30*, 233–252.

Abernethy, B., Maxwell, J. P., Jackson, R. C. & Masters, R. S. W. (2007). Cognition and skill in sport. In F. T. Durso, R. Nickerson, S. Dumais, S. Lewandowsky & T. Perfect (eds.), *The Handbook of Applied Cognition* (2nd edn). Chicester: John Wiley & Sons.
Abernethy, B. & Russell, D. G. (1987). Expert–novice differences in an applied selective attention task. *Journal of Sport Psychology*, *9*, 326–345.
Adams, M. J., Tenney, Y. J. & Pew, R. W. (1995). Situation awareness and the cognitive management of complex systems. *Human Factors*, *37*, 85–104.
Andre, A. D., Wickens, C. D., Boorman, L. & Boschelli, M. M. (1991). Display formatting techniques for improving situation awareness in the aircraft cockpit. *International Journal of Aviation Psychology*, *1*, 205–218.
Avila, F. & Moreno, F. J. (2003). Visual search strategies elaborated by tennis coaches during execution error detection processes. *Journal of Human Movement Studies*, *44*, 209–224.
Bar, M. & Ullman, S. (1996). Spatial context in recognition. *Perception*, *25*, 343–352.
Barfield, W., Rosenberg, C. & Furness, T. A. (1995). Situation awareness as a function of frame of reference, computer-graphics eyepoint elevation, and geometric field of view. *International Journal of Aviation Psychology*, *5*, 233–256.
Biederman, I. (1981). On the semantics of a glance at a scene. In M. Kubovy & J. R. Pomerantz (eds.), *Perceptual Organization* (pp. 213–253). Hillsdale, NJ: Lawrence Erlbaum Associates.
Biederman, I. (1988). Aspects and extensions of a theory of human image understanding. In Z. W. Pylyshyn (ed.), *Computational Processes in Human Vision: An Interdisciplinary Perspective* (pp. 370–428). Norwood, NJ: Ablex.
Biederman, I., Mezzanotte, R. J. & Rabinowitz, J. C. (1982). Scene perception: detecting and judging objects undergoing relational violations. *Cognitive Psychology*, *14*, 143–177.
Bloom, C. P., Fletcher, C. R., van der Broek, P. *et al.* (1990). An online assessment of causal reasoning during comprehension. *Memory and Cognition*, *18*, 65–71.
Bransford, J. D. & Johnson, M. K. (1973). Consideration of some problems of comprehension. In W. G. Chase (ed.), *Visual Information Processing*. New York: Academic Press.
Busquets, A. M., Parrish, R. V., Williams, S. P. & Nold, D. E. (1994). Comparison of pilots' acceptance and spatial awareness when using EFIS vs. pictorial display formats for complex, curved landing approaches. In R. D. Gilson, D. J. Garland & J. M. Koonce (eds.), *Situational Awareness in Complex Systems: Proceedings of a CAHFA Conference* (pp. 139–167). Daytona Beach, FL: Embry-Riddle Aeronautical University Press.
Carretta, T. R., Perry, D. C. & Ree, M. J. (1996). Prediction of situational awareness in F-15 pilots. *International Journal of Aviation Psychology*, *6*, 21–41.
Casey, S. (1993). *Set Phasers on Stun and other True Tales of Design, Technology, and Human Error.* Santa Barbara, CA: Aegean Publishing.
Chaparro, A., Groff, L., Tabor, K. *et al.* (1999). Maintaining situational awareness: the role of visual attention. In *Proceedings of the Human Factors and Ergonomics Society* (pp. 1343–1347), Santa Monica, CA: Human Factors and Ergonomics Society.
Chapman, P. & Underwood, G. (1998). Visual search of driving situations: danger and experience. *Perception*, *27*, 951–964.
Chiles, J. R. (2002). *Inviting Disaster: Lessons from the Edge of Technology.* New York: HarperCollins.
Cook, A. E., Limber, J. E. & O'Brien, E. J. (2001). Situation-based context and the availability of predictive inferences. *Journal of Memory and Language*, *44*, 220–234.
Croft, D. G., Banbury, S. P., Butler, L. T. & Berry, D. C. (2004). The role of awareness in situation awareness. In S. Banbury & S. Tremblay (eds.), *A Cognitive Approach to Situation Awareness: Theory and Application* (pp. 82–103). Aldershot: Ashgate.
Crundall, D. E. & Underwood, G. (1998). Effects of experience and processing demands on visual information acquisition in drivers. *Ergonomics*, *41*, 448–458.
De Graef, P., Christiansen, D. & d'Ydewalle, G. (1990). Perceptual effects of scene context on object identification. *Psychological Research*, *52*, 317–329.
Deighton, C. D. B. (1997). Towards the development of an integrated human factors and engineering evaluation methodology for rotorcraft D/NAW systems. *QinetiQ Report No. DERA/AS/FMC/CR97629/1.0*, Dec. Farnborough: QinetiQ Ltd.

Dennehy, K. (1997). *Cranfield – Situation Awareness Scale, User Manual.* Applied Psychology Unit, College of Aeronautics, Cranfield University, COA report No. 9702, Bedford.
Doane, S. M. & Sohn, Y. W. (2004). Pilot ability to anticipate the consequences of flight actions as a function of expertise. *Human Factors, 46*, 92–103.
Druckman, D. & Bjork, R. A. (1991). *In the Mind's Eye: Enhancing Human Performance.* Washington, DC: National Academy Press.
Durso, F. T., Bleckley, M. K. & Dattel, A. R. (in press). Does SA add to the validity of cognitive tests? *Human Factors.*
Durso, F. T. & Dattel, A. R. (2004). SPAM: the real-time assessment of SA. In S. Banbury & S. Tremblay (eds.), *A Cognitive Approach to Situation Awareness: Theory and Application* (pp. 137–154). Aldershot: Ashgate.
Durso, F. T. & Gronlund, S. D. (1999). Situation awareness. In F. T. Durso, R. S. Nickerson, R. W. Schvaneveldt *et al.* (eds.), *Handbook of Applied Cognition* (pp. 283–314). New York: John Wiley & Sons.
Durso, F. T., Hackworth, C., Truitt, T. R. *et al.* (1998a). Situation awareness as a predictor of performance in en route air traffic controllers. *Air Traffic Control Quarterly, 6*, 1–20.
Durso, F. T., Truitt, T. R., Hackworth, C. A. *et al.* (1998b). En route operational errors and situation awareness. *International Journal of Aviation Psychology, 8*, 177–194.
Durso, F. T., Truitt, T. R., Hackworth, C. A. *et al.* (1995). Expertise and chess: comparing situation awareness methodologies. In *International Conference on Situation Awareness*, Daytona, FL.
Endsley, M. R. (1990). Predictive utility of an objective measure of situation awareness. *Proceedings of the Human Factors Society, 34*, 41–45.
Endsley, M. R. (1995). Toward a theory of situation awareness in dynamic systems. *Human Factors, 37*, 32–64.
Endsley, M. R. & Bolstad, C. A. (1994). Individual differences in pilot situation awareness. *International Journal of Aviation Psychology, 4*, 241–264.
Endsley, M. R., Bolté, B. & Jones, D. G. (2003). *Designing for Situation Awareness: An Approach to User-Centered Design.* New York: Taylor and Francis.
Farley, T. C., Hansman, R. J. & Amonlirdviman, K. (2000). Shared information between pilots and controllers in tactical air traffic control. *Journal of Guidance, Control and Dynamics, 23*(5), 826–836.
Farrow, D. & Abernethy, B. (2003). Do expertise and the degree of perception-action coupling affect natural anticipatory performance? *Perception, 32*, 1127–1139.
Fincher-Kiefer, R. (1993). The role of predictive inferences in situation model construction. *Discourse Processes, 16*, 99–124.
Fletcher, C. R. (1981). Short-term memory processes in text comprehension. *Journal of Verbal Learning and Verbal Behavior, 20*, 564–574.
Fletcher, C. R., Hummel, J. E. & Marsolek, C. J. (1990). Causality and the allocation of attention during comprehension. *Journal of Experimental Psychology: Learning, Memory, and Cognition, 16*, 233–240.
Friedman, A. (1979). Framing pictures: the role of knowledge in automatized encoding and memory for gist. *Journal of Experimental Psychology: General, 108*, 316–355.
Garsoffky, B., Schwan, S. & Hesse, F. W. (2002). Viewpoint dependency in the recognition of dynamic scenes. *Journal of Experimental Psychology: Learning, Memory and Cognition, 28*, 1035–1050.
Glanzer, M. & Nolan, S. D. (1986). Memory mechanisms in text comprehension. In *The Psychology of Learning and Motivation* (Vol. 20, pp. 275–317). San Diego, CA: Academic Press.
Glenberg, A. M., Meyer, M. & Lindem, K. (1987). Mental models contribute to foregrounding during text comprehension. *Journal of Memory and Language, 26*, 69–83.
Goldman, S. R. & Varma, S. (1995). CAPping the construction-integration model of discourse comprehension. In C. A. Weaver III, S. Mannes & C. R. Fletcher (eds.), *Discourse Comprehension: Essays in Honor of Walter Kintsch* (pp. 337–358). Hillsdale, NJ: Lawrence Erlbaum Associates.
Graesser, A. C. & Bertus, E. L. (1998). The construction of causal inferences while reading expository texts on science and technology. *Scientific Studies of Reading, 2*, 247–269.

Graesser, A. C., Hoffman, N. L. & Clark, L. F. (1980). Structural components of reading time. *Journal of Verbal Learning and Verbal Behavior, 19*, 135–151.

Gugerty, L. J. (1997). Situation awareness during driving: explicit and implicit knowledge in dynamic spatial memory. *Journal of Experimental Psychology: Applied, 3*, 42–66.

Gugerty, L. J. & Falzetta, M. (2005). Using an event-detection measure to assess drivers' attention and situation awareness. In *Proceeding of the 49th Annual Meeting of the Human Factors and Ergonomics Society*. Santa Monica, CA: Human Factors and Ergonomics Society.

Haber, R. N. & Haber, L. (2003). Perception and attention during low-altitude high-speed flight. In P. S. Tsang & M. A. Vidulich (eds.), *Principles and Practice of Aviation Psychology* (pp. 21–68). Mahwah, NJ: Lawrence Erlbaum Associates.

Haberlandt, K., Berian, C. & Sandson, J. (1980). The episode schema in story processing. *Journal of Verbal Learning and Verbal Behavior, 19*, 635–650.

Haberlandt, K. F., Graesser, A. C., Schneider, N. J. & Kiely, J. (1986). Effects of task and new arguments on word reading times. *Journal of Memory and Language, 25*, 314–322.

Haskell, I. D. & Wickens, C. D. (1993). Two- and three-dimensional displays for aviation: a theoretical and empirical comparison. *International Journal of Aviation Psychology, 3*, 87–109.

Hauβ, Y., Gauss, B. & Eyferth, K. (2000). The evaluation of a future air traffic management: towards a new approach to measure situation awareness in air traffic control. In L. M. Camarinha-Matos, H. Afsarmanesh & H. Herbe (eds.), *Advances in Networked Enterprises: Virtual Organization, Balanced Automation and System Integration* (CD Suppl.). Boston, MA: Kluwer.

Hauβ, Y., Gauss, B. & Eyferth, K. (2001). The influence of multi-sector planning on the controllers' mental models. In D. Harris (ed.), *Engineering Psychology and Cognitive Ergonomics* (pp. 203–209). Aldershot: Ashgate.

Helsen, W. F. & Pauwels, J. M. (1993). The relationship between expertise and visual information processing in sport. *Applied Cognitive Psychology, 13*, 109–134.

Helsen, W. F. & Starkes, J. L. (1999). A multidimensional approach to skilled perception and performance in sport. *Applied Cognitive Psychology, 13*, 1–27.

Horswill, M. S. & McKenna, F. P. (2004). Drivers' hazard perception ability: situation awareness on the road. In S. Banbury & S. Tremblay (eds.), *A Cognitive Approach to Situation Awareness: Theory and Application*. Aldershot: Ashgate.

Howarth, C., Walsh, W. D. & Abernethy, B. (1984). A field examination of anticipation in squash: some preliminary data. *The Australian Journal of Science and Medicine in Sport, 16*, 7–11.

James, N. & Patrick, J. (2004). The role of situation awareness in sport. In S. Banbury & S. Tremblay (eds.), *A Cognitive Approach to Situation Awareness: Theory and Application* (pp. 137–154). Aldershot: Ashgate.

Jeannot, E., Kelly, C. & Thompson, D. (2003). *The Development of Situation Awareness Measures in ATM Systems*. HRS/HSP-005-REP-01. Brussels: EUROCONTROL.

Jensen, S. (1999). Perceived versus real situation awareness: towards more objective assessment of SA. In L. Straker & C. Pollack (eds.), *CD-ROM Proceedings of CybErg 1999: The Second International Cyberspace Conference on Ergonomics* (pp. 327–334). Perth: International Ergonomics Association Press.

Jones, D. G. & Endsley, M. R. (1996). Sources of situation awareness errors in aviation. *Aviation, Space, and Environmental Medicine, 67*, 507–512.

Jones, D. G. & Kaber, D. B. (2004). Situation awareness measurement and the situation awareness global assessment technique. In N. Stanton, A. Hedge, K. Brookhuis, E. Salas & H. Hendrick (eds.), *Handbook of Human Factors and Ergonomics Methods* (pp. 42-1–42-8). Boca Raton, FL: CRC Press.

Just, M. A. & Carpenter, P. A. (1980). A theory of reading: from eye fixations to comprehension. *Psychological Review, 87*, 329–354.

Kendeou, P. & van den Broek, P. (2005). The effects of readers' misconceptions on comprehension of scientific text. *Journal of Educational Psychology, 97*, 235–245.

Kintsch, W. (1988). The use of knowledge in discourse processing: a construction-integration model. *Psychological Review, 95*, 163–182.

Kintsch, W. (1994). Learning from text. *American Psychologist, 49*, 294–303.

Kintsch, W. (1998). *Comprehension: A Paradigm for Cognition*. Cambridge: Cambridge University Press.

Kintsch, W., Kozminsky, E., Streby, W. J. *et al.* (1975). Comprehension and recall of text as a function of content variables. *Journal of Verbal Learning and Verbal Behavior, 14*, 196–214.

Kintsch, W., Welsch, D. M., Schmalhofer, F. & Zimny, S. (1990). Sentence memory: a theoretical analysis. *Journal of Memory and Language, 29*, 133–159.

Klin, C. M., Murray, J. D., Levine, W. H. & Guzmán, A. E. (1999). Forward inferences: from activation to long-term memory. *Discourse Processes, 27*, 241–260.

Lachman, R., Lachman, J. L. & Butterfield, E. C. (1979). *Cognitive Psychology and Information Processing*. Hillsdale, NJ: Lawrence Erlbaum Associates.

Long, D. L., Golding, J. M. & Graesser, A. C. (1992). A test of the on-line status of goal-related inferences. *Journal of Memory and Language, 31*, 634–647.

McCarley, J. S., Kramer, A. F., Wickens, C. D. *et al.* (2004). Visual skills in airport security screening. *Psychological Science, 15*, 302–306.

McKenna, F. P. & Crick, J. L. (1991). *Hazard Perception in Drivers: A Methodology for Testing and Training*. Final Report. Behavioral Studies Unit, Transport and Road Research Laboratory, Crowthorne, UK.

McKoon, G., Gerrig, R. J. & Greene, S. B. (1996). Pronoun resolution without pronouns: some consequences of memory-based text processing. *Journal of Experimental Psychology: Learning, Memory, and Cognition, 22*, 919–932.

McKoon, G., Ratcliff, R., Ward, G. & Sproat, R. (1993). Syntactic prominence effects on discourse processes. *Journal of Memory and Language, 32*, 593–607.

McNamara, D. S., Kintsch, E., Songer, N. B. & Kintsch, W. (1996). Are good texts always better? Interactions of text coherence, background knowledge, and levels of understanding in learning from text. *Cognition and Instruction, 14*, 1–43.

McNamara, D. S. & Kintsch, W. (1996). Learning from texts: effects of prior knowledge and text coherence. *Discourse Processes, 22*, 247–288.

Magliano, J. P., Graesser, A. C., Eymard, L. A. *et al.* (1993). Locus of interpretive and inference processes during text comprehension: a comparison of gaze durations and word reading times. *Journal of Experimental Psychology: Learning, Memory, and Cognition, 19*, 704–709.

Magliano, J. P., Trabasso, T. & Graesser, A. C. (1999). Strategic processing during comprehension. *Journal of Educational Psychology, 91*, 615–629.

Maki, R. H. (1998). Test predictions over text material. In D. J. Hacker, J. Dunlosky & A. C. Graesser (eds.), *Metacognition in Educational Theory and Practice* (pp. 117–144). Hillsdale, NJ: Lawrence Erlbaum Associates.

Maki, R. H., Foley, J. M., Kajer, W. K. *et al.* (1990). Increased processing enhances calibration of comprehension. *Journal of Experimental Psychology: Learning, Memory & Cognition, 16*, 609–616.

Maki, R. H., Jonas, D. & Kallod, M. (1994). The relationship between comprehension and metacomprehension ability. *Psychonomic Bulletin & Review, 1*, 126–129.

Malt, B. C. (1985). The role of discourse structure in understanding anaphora. *Journal of Memory and Language, 24*, 271–289.

Mayer, R. E. & Jackson, J. (2005). The case for coherence in scientific explanations: qualitative details can hurt qualitative understanding. *Journal of Experimental Psychology: Applied, 11*, 13–18.

Mayer, R. E., Bove, W., Bryman, A. *et al.* (1996). When less is more: meaningful learning from visual and verbal summaries of science textbook lessons. *Journal of Educational Psychology, 88*, 64–73.

Metalis, S. A. (1993). Assessment of pilot situational awareness: measurement via simulation. In *Proceedings of the Human Factors Society 37th Annual Meeting* (pp. 113–117). Santa Monica, CA: The Human Factors and Ergonomics Society.

Millis, K. K., Morgan, D. & Graesser, A. C. (1990). The influence of knowledge-based inferences on reading time for expository text. In A. C. Graesser & G. H. Bowers (eds.), *The Psychology of Learning and Motivation: Inferences and Text Comprehension*. New York: Academic Press.

Millis, K. K., Simon, S. & tenBroek, N. S. (1998). Resource allocation during the rereading of scientific texts. *Memory & Cognition*, *26*, 232–246.

Mills, K. L., Hall, R. D., McDonald, M. & Rolls, G. W. P. (1998). *The Effects of Hazard Perception Training on the Development of Novice Driver Skills*. Research Report. London: Department for Transport.

Moray, N. (1990). Designing for transportation safety in the light of perception, attention, and mental models. *Ergonomics*, *33*, 1201–1213.

Moray, N. & Rotenberg, I. (1989). Fault management in process control: eye movements and action. *Ergonomics*, *32*, 1319–1342.

Murphy, G. L. (1984). Establishing and accessing referents in discourse. *Memory & Cognition*, *12*, 489–497.

Myers, J. L., Shinjo, M. & Duffy, S. A. (1987). Degree of causal relatedness and memory. *Journal of Memory and Language*, *26*, 453–465.

Neal, A., Griffin, M., Paterson, J. & Bordia, P. (1998). *Human Factors Issues: Performance Management Transition to a CNS/ATM Environment*. Final Report: Air Services Australia. Brisbane: University of Queensland.

O'Brien, E. J. & Albrecht, J. E. (1991). The role of context in accessing antecedents in text. *Journal of Experimental Psychology: Learning, Memory, and Cognition*, *17*, 94–102.

O'Brien, E. J., Raney, G. E., Albrecht, J. E. & Rayner, K. (1997). Processes involved in the resolution of explicit anaphors. *Discourse Processes*, *23*, 1–24.

O'Hare, D. (1997). Cognitive ability determinants of elite pilot performance. *Human Factors*, *39*, 540–552.

Oliva, A. & Schyns, P. G. (1997). Coarse blobs or fine edges? Evidence that information diagnosticity changes the perception of complex visual stimuli. *Cognitive Psychology, 34*, 72–107.

Oliva, A. & Schyns, P. G. (2000). Diagnostic colors mediate scene recognition. *Cognitive Psychology*, *41*, 176–210.

Oppenheimer, R. (1956). Analogy in science. *American Psychologist*, *11*, 127–135.

Paull, G. & Glencross, D. (1997). Expert perception and decision making in baseball. *International Journal of Sport Psychology*, *28*, 35–56.

Potter, M. C. (1976). Short-term conceptual memory for pictures. *Journal of Experimental Psychology: Human Learning & Memory*, *2*, 509–522.

Rawson, K. A. & Dunlosky, J. (2002). Are performance predictions for text based on ease of processing? *Journal of Experimental Psychology: Learning, Memory, and Cognition*, *28*, 69–80.

Rawson, K. A., Dunlosky, J. & McDonald, S. L. (2002). Influences of metamemory on performance predictions for text. *Quarterly Journal of Experimental Psychology, 55A*, 505–524.

Rawson, K. A. & Kintsch, W. (2004). Exploring encoding and retrieval effects of background information on text memory. *Discourse Processes*, *38*, 323–344.

Rawson, K. A. & Kintsch, W. (2005). Rereading effects depend upon time of test. *Journal of Educational Psychology*, *97*, 70–80.

Rayner, K. (1998). Eye movements in reading and information processing: 20 years of research. *Psychological Bulletin*, *124*, 372–422.

Rayner, K., Kambe, G. & Duffy, S. A. (2000). The effect of clause wrap-up on eye movements during reading. *Quarterly Journal of Experimental Psychology*, *53A*, 1061–1080.

Remington, R. W., Johnston, J. C., Ruthruff, E. *et al.* (2000). Visual search in complex displays: factors affecting conflict detection by air traffic controllers. *Human Factors*, *42*, 349–366.

Renninger, L. W. & Malik, J. (2004). When is scene identification just texture recognition? *Vision Research*, *44*, 2301–2311.

Roeder, K. D. (1962). The behaviour of free flying moths in the presence of artificial ultrasonic pulses. *Animal Behaviour*, *10*, 300–304.

Roscoe, S. N. (1997). *Predicting Human Performance*. Quebec: Helio Press.

Rousseau, R., Tremblay, S. & Breton, R. (2004). Defining and modeling situation awareness: a critical review. In S. Banbury & S. Tremblay (eds.), *A Cognitive Approach to Situation Awareness: Theory and Application* (pp. 3–21). Aldershot: Ashgate.

Salas, E., Cannon-Bowers, J. A., Fiore, S. M. & Stout, R. J. (2001). Cue-recognition training to enhance team situation awareness. In M. McNeese & E. Salas (eds.), *New Trends in Cooperative*

Activities: Understanding System Dynamics in Complex Environments. Santa Monica, CA: Human Factors and Ergonomics Society.

Sarter, N. B. & Woods, D. D. (1991). Situation awareness: a critical but ill-defined phenomenon. *International Journal of Aviation Psychology, 1*, 45–57.

Scott Rich, S. & Taylor, H. A. (2000). Not all narrative shifts function equally. *Memory & Cognition, 28*, 1257–1266.

Schyns, P. G. & Oliva, A. (1994). From blobs to boundary edges: evidence for time and spatial scale dependent scene recognition. *Psychological Science, 5*, 195–200.

Secrist, G. E. & Hartman, B. O. (1993). Situational awareness: the trainability of the near-threshold information acquisition dimension. *Aviation, Space, and Environmental Medicine, 64*, 885–892.

Sieck, W. R. & Klein, G. (2007). A comparison of rationalist and naturalistic decision methods for applied decision research. In F. T. Durso, R. Nickerson, S. Dumais *et al.* (eds.), *The Handbook of Applied Cognition* (2nd edn). Chichester: John Wiley & Sons.

Singer, M., Halldorson, M., Lear, J. C. & Andrusiak, P. (1992). Validation of causal bridging inference in discourse understanding. *Journal of Memory and Language, 31*, 507–524.

Spilich, G. J., Vesonder, G. T., Chiesi, H. L. & Voss, J. F. (1979). Text processing of domain-related information for individuals with high and low domain knowledge. *Journal of Verbal Learning and Verbal Behavior, 18*, 275–290.

Sohn, Y. W. & Doane, S. M. (2004). Memory processes of flight situation awareness: interactive Roles of working memory capacity, long-term working memory, and expertise. *Human Factors, 46*, 461–475.

Stokes, A., Kemper, K. & Kite, K. (1997). Aeronautical decision-making, cue recognition, and expertise under time pressure. In C. E. Zsambok & G. Klein (eds.), *Naturalistic Decision Making* (pp. 183–197). Mahwah, NJ: Lawrence Erlbaum Associates.

Suh, S. & Trabasso, T. (1993). Inferences during reading: converging evidence from discourse analysis, talk-aloud protocols, and recognition priming. *Journal of Memory and Language, 32*, 279–300.

Taylor, R. M. (1990). Situational awareness rating technique (SART): the development of a tool for aircrew systems design. In *Situational Awareness in Aerospace Operations* (AGARD-CP-478; pp. 3/1–3/17). Neuilly-sur-Seine: NATO-AGARD.

Thiede, K. W. & Anderson, M. C. M. (2003). Summarizing can improve metacomprehension accuracy. *Contemporary Educational Psychology, 28*, 129–160.

Tlauka, M., Stanton, D. & McKenna, F. P. (2000). Dual displays. *Ergonomics, 43*(6), 764–770.

Underwood, G., Chapman, P., Bowden, K. & Crundall, D. (2002). Visual search while driving: skill and awareness during inspection of the scene. *Transportation Research Part F, 5*, 87–97.

Underwood, G., Chapman, P., Brocklehurst, N. *et al.* (2003). Visual attention while driving: sequences of eye fixations made by experienced and novice drivers. *Ergonomics, 46*, 629–646.

Underwood, G., Crundall, D. & Chapman, P. (2007). Cognition and driving. In F. T. Durso, R. Nickerson, S. Dumais, S. Lewandowsky & T. Perfect (eds.), *The Handbook of Applied Cognition* (2nd edn). Chicester: John Wiley & Sons.

Van Breda, L. & Veltman, H. A. (1998). Perspective information in the cockpit as target acquisition aid. *Journal of experimental psychology: Applied, 4*, 55–68.

Vidulich, M. A. & Hughes, E. R. (1991). Testing a subjective metric of situation awareness. In *Proceedings of the Human Factors Society 35th Annual Meeting* (pp. 1307–1311). Santa Monica, CA: The Human Factors and Ergonomics Society.

Vidulich, M. A., Stratton, M., Crabtree, M. & Wilson, G. (1994). Performance-based and physiological measures of situational awareness. *Aviation, Space, and Environmental Medicine, 65*, A7–A12.

Waag, W. L. & Houck, M. R. (1994). Tools for assessing situational awareness in an operational fighter environment. *Aviation, Space, and Environmental Medicine, 65*, A13–A19.

Wellens, A. R. (1993). Group situation awareness and distributed decision making: from military to civilian applications. In N. J. Castellan (ed.), *Individual Group and Decision Making: Current Issues* (pp. 267–291). Hillsdale, NJ: Lawrence Erlbaum Associates.

Wellens, A. R. & Ergener, D. (1988). The C.I.T.I.E.S. game: A computer-based situation assessment task for studying distributed decision-making. *Simulation & Games,* 19, 304–327.
Wickens, C. D. & Carswell, C. M. (1995). The proximity compatibility principle: its psychological foundation and relevance to display design. *Human Factors*, *37*, 473–494.
Wickens, C. D., Lee, J., Liu, Y. D. & Becker, S. (eds.) (2004). *An Introduction to Human Factors Engineering.* Upper Saddle River, NJ: Pearson Education.
Wickens, C. D. & Prevett, T. T. (1995). Exploring the dimension of egocentricity in aircraft navigation displays. *Journal of Experimental Psychology: Applied*, *1*, 110–135.
Wiggins, M. & O'Hare, D. (2003). Weatherwise: evaluation of a cue-based training approach for the recognition of deteriorating weather conditions during flight. *Human Factors*, *45*, 337–345.
Wikman, A. S., Nieminen, T. & Summala, H. (1998). Driving experience and time-sharing during in-car tasks on roads of different width. *Ergonomics*, *41*, 358–372.
Wiley, J., Mason, R. A. & Myers, J. L. (2001). Accessibility of potential referents following categorical anaphors. *Journal of Experimental Psychology: Learning, Memory, and Cognition*, *27*, 1238–1249.
Wiley, J. & Rayner, K. (2000). Effects of titles on the processing of text and lexically ambiguous words: evidence from eye movements. *Memory & Cognition*, *28*, 1011–1021.
Williams, A. M. & Davids, K. (1998). Visual search strategy, selective attention and expertise in soccer. *Research Quarterly for Exercise and Sport*, *69*, 111–128.
Williams, A. M., Ward, P., Knowles, J. M. & Smeeton, N. J. (2002). Anticipation skill in a real-world task: measurement, training and transfer in tennis. *Journal of Experimental Psychology: Applied*, *8*, 259–270.
Williams, K. W. (2002). Impact of highway-in-the-sky displays on pilot situation awareness. *Human Factors*, *44*, 18–27.
Woodhouse, R. & Woodhouse, R. A. (1995). Navigation errors in relation to controlled flight into terrain (CFIT) accidents. In *8th International Symposium on Aviation Psychology*. Columbus, OH, April.
Woods, D. (1991). The cognitive engineering of problem representations. In J. Alty & G. Weir (eds.), *Human–Computer Interaction and Complex Systems* (pp. 169–188). London: Academic Press.
Yntema, D. B. (1963). Keeping track of several things at once. Human Factors, *5*, 7–17.
Yntema, D. B. & Mueser, G. E. (1960). Remembering the present states of a number of variables. *Journal of Experimental Psychology, 60*, 18–22.
Yntema, D. B. & Mueser, G. E. (1962). Keeping track of variables that have few or many states. *Journal of Experimental Psychology*, *63*, 391–395.
Zsambok, C. E. & Klein, G. (eds.) (1997). *Naturalistic Decision Making. Expertise: Research and Applications*. Mahwah, NJ: Lawrence Erlbaum Associates.
Zwaan, R. A. (1994). Effect of genre expectations on text comprehension. *Journal of Experimental Psychology: Learning, Memory, and Cognition*, *20*, 920–933.
Zwaan, R. A. (1996). Processing narrative time shifts. *Journal of Experimental Psychology: Learning, Memory, and Cognition*, *22*, 1196–1207.
Zwaan, R. A., Magliano, J. P. & Graesser, A. C. (1995). Dimensions of situation model construction in narrative comprehension. *Journal of Experimental Psychology: Learning, Memory, and Cognition*, *21*, 386–397.
Zwaan, R. A. & Radvansky, G. A. (1998). Situation models in language comprehension and memory. *Psychological Bulletin*, *123*, 162–185.
Zwaan, R. A., Radvansky, G. A., Hilliard, A. E. & Curiel, J. M. (1998). Constructing multidimensional situation models during reading. *Scientific Studies of Reading*, *2*, 199–220.

CHAPTER 8

Decision-Making

Winston R. Sieck and Gary Klein
Klein Associates, a division of Applied Research Associates, Inc., USA

Decision-making is a pervasive, consequential human activity, from laypeople dealing with their own daily life events, to "tactical" professionals such as physicians, lawyers, firefighters, and military commanders whose responsibilities extend beyond themselves, to presidents and other world leaders who are charged with the fate of us all for generations to come. How do such people make their respective decisions? How should they be making them? And how can we close the gap between what is and what should be? These are the questions that decision researchers have been doggedly pursuing from a variety of perspectives.

The purpose of this chapter is to describe in broad terms two of the fields of decision research that have been devoted to tackling applied problems. Our emphasis is on psychological aspects of applied decision-making, although we recognize that decision research is highly interdisciplinary and we hope that researchers from any number of backgrounds will be able to gain some insights from our review. The chapter describes two perspectives on decision research that rarely intersect: the rational choice perspective, and the naturalistic decision-making perspective. These two perspectives are often contrasted at the ideological level, resulting in discussion that quickly degenerates into polemics. In the current chapter, we attempt to re-engage discussion at the methodological level. Specifically, we compare kernel Decision Analysis (DA) and Cognitive Task Analysis (CTA) methodologies employed in the service of each perspective, respectively. The surprising conclusion is that these methods are intended to achieve distinct goals that are more complementary than competing. In particular, our examination resolves the following misperceptions of these methods:

- CTA sanctifies intuition; DA promotes analysis.
- CTA holds up the expert as having reached the apex of decision-making competence; DA strives for a higher ideal.
- Studies demonstrating weakness in expert judgment imply that DA should be used rather than CTA.

Even more surprising is the conclusion that DA and CTA methods have much to offer toward tackling the big problems of their counterpart. Finally, these potential benefits exist, despite important ideological differences that remain to be resolved.

Handbook of Applied Cognition: Second Edition. Edited by Francis T. Durso.

Before delving into that discussion, however, we first note that there are three distinct communities of practice involved in decision research, each with its own set of aims and perspectives: Decision Analysis, Naturalistic Decision-Making, and Behavioral Decision-Making. The Decision Analysis and Naturalistic Decision-Making communities are most directly focused on applied decision research and have coherent, deeply rooted approaches for tackling applications. These communities are the primary focus of the current chapter, and thus will be described in more detail below. However, we want to briefly note the community of psychological researchers studying "behavioral decision-making" or "judgment and decision-making." As a whole, this community of researchers embraces perhaps the widest perspective on decision research issues, and hence is less coherent in promulgating a particular approach for applied work. Such researchers are most typically employing experimental psychological methods to investigate basic research issues, and affiliate primarily with cognitive or social psychology departments. Many are increasingly found in other academic schools, such as marketing, medicine, and law, and with slightly more applied foci. The primary forum for behavioral decision researchers is the Society for Judgment and Decision-making (www.sjdm.org). The two primary journals for judgment and decision-making research are *Behavioral Decision-Making* and *Organizational Behavior and Human Decision Processes*. There is also a very recent online, open-access journal, *Judgment and Decision-Making.*

A second preliminary issue is to define what we mean by applied research in decision-making, given that it is the focus of the current chapter. One approach is to say that applied research is prescriptive in nature. That is, decision researchers have traditionally distinguished descriptive and prescriptive questions to ask about decision-making. The descriptive question concerns how people actually go about making decisions. The prescriptive question, in contrast, asks how people should go about making decisions. Hence, at first blush, basic research could be identified with description, whereas applied research involves prescription. However, this neat distinction is too simplistic. First, many basic psychological decision researchers have prescriptive interests. They sometimes pursue these interests by conducting laboratory studies on college students using rather sparse and simplified decision problems.

As an example, Lichtenstein and Fischhoff (1980) conducted a now classic study to determine whether and to what extent probability judgments could be improved with specialized feedback on their judgment performance. Lichtenstein and Fischhoff were addressing a prescriptive question, namely, the efficacy of a specific approach to improving probability judgment performance. Yet, the study materials and elicited judgments do not particularly reflect those of professionals who are faced with probability judgment tasks, and their participants had no prior experience or current real need to perform in these kinds of situations. As another, recent example, Sieck and Arkes (2005) examined ways of decreasing overconfidence in order to increase undergraduate acceptability and usage of a statistical decision aid in a multiple-cue prediction task. Studies such as these might thus be considered as "basic-prescriptive," and illustrate how basic research on prescriptions can illuminate fundamental decision processes.

Another possibility for identifying research as applied has to do with whether the research is conducted with professionals in their job settings. For example, Dawson *et al.* (1993) had physicians provide estimates on three measures of hemodynamic status, as well as their confidence in those estimates. The physician estimates were compared with values obtained from a catheter to determine accuracy (discrimination and calibration), and neither kind of accuracy was particularly good. In this study, the researchers describe the judgment accuracy of professionals, but without a clear and direct purpose of determining how those professional judgments might be improved. Hence, this research should also not be considered as "applied" by our account.

If neither the prescriptive/descriptive distinction nor the participant population determines whether the research is applied or basic, what is the distinction? In our view, decision research is applied if the project is intended to directly benefit decision-makers who have a genuine need to perform in their respective domain. This emphasis on immediate benefit has a further implication. In basic research, the primary criterion of success is scientific validity. There is no consideration given to how feasible it might be to carry out any recommendations emerging from the findings. Scientific validity is also critical in applied research, but it is insufficient. Applied research has an additional constraint – to consider how the results could be put into practice. In the applied world, usability and acceptability are additional criteria by which success of the project must be measured.

The remainder of this chapter proceeds as follows. First, we provide a brief, general overview of Decision Analysis (DA) methods as employed within a rational choice perspective, and Cognitive Task Analysis (CTA) methods used within the Naturalistic Decision-Making perspective. From this overview, we introduce four themes that form the basis for comparison of the alternative research methodologies. Next, we describe the DA and CTA methods in some detail, including how each theme is addressed from within the perspective. Basic research needs to support each method are also described in the context of the final theme on the role of the psychologist. Finally, we compare and contrast the methods in terms of the themes, and describe some of the ways that they can inform each other.

OVERVIEW OF METHODOLOGIES

The DA and CTA methodological processes are illustrated for ready comparison in Figure 8.1. As can be seen, both methods are analytical processes. However, the topics and products of the analyses differ. The topic of DA is the decision problem, whereas the topic of

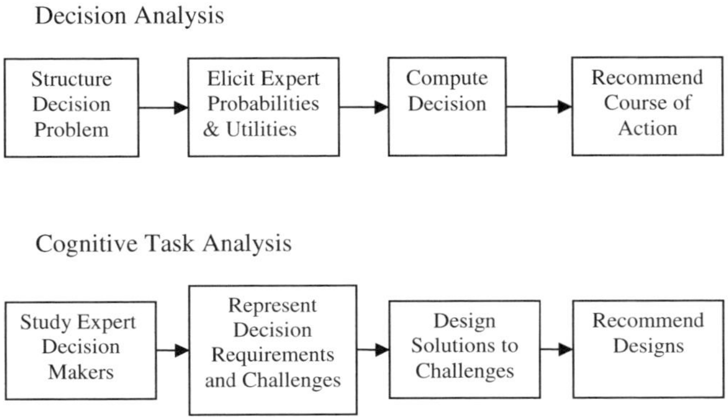

Figure 8.1 Process overviews for decision analysis and cognitive task analysis

CTA is the decision-maker's cognition, including both intuitive and analytical aspects. Also, the product of DA is a recommendation that the decision-maker take a specific course of action. In contrast, CTA produces a set of decision requirements (e.g., the specific difficult decisions for that job), along with designs for interventions such as decision aids or training that support those requirements. As also suggested by Figure 8.1, both DA and CTA researchers are interested in improvement over current practice; neither recommends the status quo or maintains that experts are already achieving their best possible decision performance. At issue are the concepts of quality and improvement themselves. DA relies on formal axioms to define quality and on methods that ensure decisions are consistent with those axioms. For CTA, quality is about how well solutions meet the specifically identified needs of decision-makers, and seeks improvement by bootstrapping expertise. Figure 8.1 also illustrates that experts are incorporated into both kinds of analysis, though the specific roles of the experts differ. Hence, the quality of expert judgment is important for both methods. In CTA, the focus is on judgments actually made by experts on the job, whereas DA elicits quantity judgments that do not necessarily fit the decision-maker's expertise. Given that both methods involve human judgments and other inputs, it is reasonable to ask what roles there are for psychologists. As will be seen, both methods allow for multiple ways in which psychologists could add value to the process, though the psychologist would typically have the lead in CTA. The points of comparison suggested by Figure 8.1 can be summarized in the following themes:

- Topic and product of analysis.
- Quality and achievement.
- Role of the expert decision-maker.
- Role of the psychologist.

Next, we describe DA and CTA in more detail, with an emphasis on these themes.

DECISION ANALYSIS

Decision analysis refers to systematic quantitative approaches for making decisions that are based on a set of formal axioms that guarantee consistent choices (e.g., Clemen 1996). Adherence to the axioms is central to the rational-choice perspective. Decision analysts are most typically associated with operations research engineering, although computer scientists and other computationally oriented researchers are joining the fray. The primary forum for decision analysis research is the Decision Analysis Society of the Institute for Operations Research (OR) and the Management Sciences (www.informs.org/Society/DA). Another group made up primarily of industry practitioners with little interest in academic publishing is the Decision Analysis Affinity Group (DAAG; www.daag.net). The two primary outlets for decision analysis research have been the journals *Interfaces* and *Operations Research.* A new journal, *Decision Analysis*, was launched in 2003. In its preview issue, Keefer *et al.* (2003) provide a thorough review of the field for 1990–2001, including a number of decision analysis trends. A relatively non-technical introduction to decision analysis procedures is provided by Hammond *et al.* (1999). Clemen (1996) and Goodwin and Wright (1998) are two other core texts for the field.

Basic Approach

Decision analyses can become extremely elaborate masses of equations, yet they boil down to three, relatively simple, mathematical rules for normative choice. The first is expected utility maximization, the second is multi-attribute utility, and the third is Bayes' theorem. To describe the rules, suppose that you are faced with a choice between playing a gamble or not. The game is straightforward (at first blush). A six-sided die is rolled. If a 1 or 2 appears, you win \$15. If it lands with a 3, 4, or 5, you win \$2. If a 6 is rolled, you lose \$12. Of course, if you do not play the game, then no money is won or lost; you go home with whatever you had in your pocket. Should you play the game or not?

Before you decide, consider the representation of this decision shown in Figure 8.2. Figure 8.2 is an example of a *decision tree*, and it highlights the various components of your decision problem using typical symbols. The square on the left-hand side denotes a *decision node*, and the two lines running from it represent the available *options*, i.e. to play or not play. The circle lying on the path from the "play" option represents a *chance node*. The lines that stem from the chance node are the *possibilities*. Whereas the lines branching from decision nodes (options) are under your control, those branching from chance nodes (possibilities) are determined by nature. Each possibility has some chance or probability of occurrence. In Figure 8.2, we have listed probabilities for each, assuming that the die is fair. That is, since the chances of obtaining each side of a fair die are 1/6, the chances of a 1 or 2 are 1/3, the chances of a 3, 4, or 5, are 1/2 and the chance of a 6 is 1/6. Finally, the dollar values listed at the ends of each pathway are *outcomes*, and each pathway from decision through to outcome is a *scenario*. That is, each path tells a story about how the situation might play out.

These are the core elements of a decision problem from a decision analysis point of view, and the decision tree is a common means of representing these elements and their interconnections. Now, how would a decision analyst say you should choose? We will start with a simple answer and then add in complications in order to introduce the three rules, and elucidate the basic approach.

The first rule is *expected utility maximization*, in which you should compute the expected utility for each option and then choose the one that is biggest. A simple way to

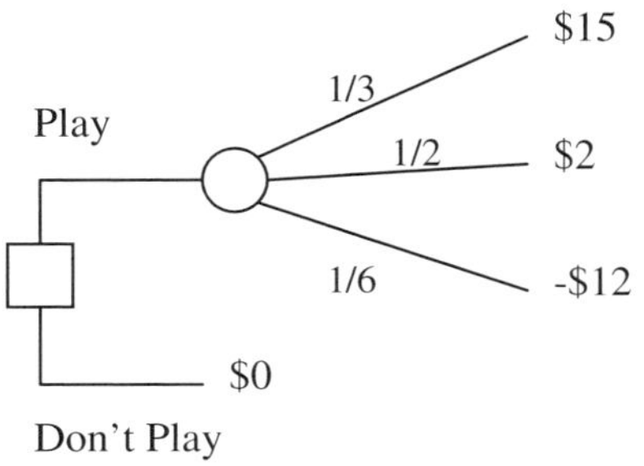

Figure 8.2 Decision tree representation of a gambling problem

do this is to take the dollar value of the gamble as your utility, and compute the expected value (EV) as follows:

$$EV_{play} = 1/3(\$15) + 1/2(\$2) + 1/6(-\$12) = \$5 + \$1 - \$2 = \$4$$

Since the EV of not playing is \$0, and \$4 > \$0, you should play the game, according to this analysis. However, this analysis ignores all the interesting psychological details. First, we simplified your utility or subjective value of each of the outcomes by simply plugging in the objective dollar value. There are at least two ways that these might not line up. First, suppose that you are a teenager, or worse off, a graduate student, and your current total wealth is approximately \$14. If, like many people, you are fairly risk-averse, then the possibility of reducing your total wealth to \$2 will weigh heavily, whereas the possibilities of ending up with \$16 or even \$29 might not feel like much improvement over leaving with \$14. Hence, your subjective values do not correspond with the objective dollar amounts due to your attitude to risk.

The second complication brings into play the second rule, multi-attribute utility, predicated on the idea that utilities often depend on more than one dimension or attribute. For example, suppose you have a slight moral opposition to gambling. Then your total utility for winning the \$15 is determined by:

$$u(\$15, \text{moral failure}) = a \cdot u(\$15) + b \cdot u(\text{moral failure})$$

In this expression, the a and b are weights indicating the importance of each attribute, and the u() indicates that you have to get the money and the feeling of a moral failure onto comparable quantitative scales. That basic mathematical format follows from Multi-Attribute Utility Theory (MAUT).

The final complication involves the probabilities associated with each dollar outcome. We assigned those probabilities based on several assumptions, including that the die was fair. That may have felt reasonable, given the abstract description of the problem. To add some context, suppose that you have encountered this gambling opportunity on a street corner in Brooklyn. The game is being hosted by an unkempt man with an eye patch. It is his die, and he rolls it. He has been on the street corner for a good part of the last three days, though he has not run out of money. As you walked by each day, you saw one play of the game. For the game you saw on the first and third days, he rolled a 6. On the second day, he rolled a 5. It is the fourth day, and you are reflecting on whether or not to stop by the table and play the game. What do you think are the chance of his rolling a 6 (or other number) today? Bayes' rule provides guidance on how you should update your prior beliefs in light of recent evidence to determine a final set of probabilities to include in the expected utility computation. In this case, your priors would be determined in part by your beliefs about chance and probability itself, as well as the situational context. Suppose for simplicity that your subjective probability of a 6, prior to witnessing the three games, is 1/6, but that the context convinces you not to put much stock in that. For the Bayesian analysis, you decide that your prior probability is worth about one real observation. The three rolls that you have witnessed imply that the probability of a 6 is 2/3. Your posterior probability will fall between these two values, specifically it will be: $[1(1/6) + 3(2/3)]/4 \approx \frac{1}{2}$ (Lee 2004). The gamble doesn't look nearly as good at this point.

This example illustrates the basic procedure for conducting a decision analysis, including the components of a decision, the use of a decision tree to graphically represent the problem, and the three fundamental rules for (1) updating beliefs (Bayes' rule); (2) combining outcome attributes into overall utilities (MAUT); and (3) combining beliefs and utilities to determine the overall expected utility of each available option, and then selecting the option with the highest expected utility (EU maximization). However, the simple example does not give much feel for a realistic application of decision analysis. A realistic application is the use for choosing a development strategy for a new drug, Leapogen, at Amgen (Beccue 2001).

In Beccue's study, members of an Amgen leadership team had differing views on the best way to proceed in developing and marketing the drug. They had to resolve their differences and report for a senior management review in two months. The leadership team requested that Amgen's decision sciences group conduct a formal decision analysis to help structure their thinking around the various development options, and to provide a basis for their recommendation to upper management. In response, Beccue formed a cross-sectional team of scientists and managers. They defined eight plausible strategies, and determined the information they would need to complete the analysis. They spent six weeks collecting the data, and built a decision tree with approximately 500,000 scenarios for each strategy. In this case, the optimum marketing focus turned out to be different than any the leadership team had anticipated. Furthermore, the analysis led the team members to unanimous agreement for that under-considered strategy. The team presented the results of the analysis for three of the strategies to senior management, and secured agreement on their recommended strategy from that group.

Topic and Product of Analysis

The topic of decision analysis research is a specific decision problem that requires some resolution. At the end of the process, the decision analysis method delivers the resolution of a decision, or interrelated set of decisions for a particular decision problem of a customer.

Quality and Achievement

The Amgen example illustrates a realistic decision analysis application, as well as providing some insight into how decision analysts think about decision quality. Technically, from the rational choice perspective a good decision is one that satisfies the axioms of consistent choice. This emphasis is seen as an improvement over the idea that a good decision is one that leads to a good outcome. The issue is that the acknowledged element of irreducible chance can produce discrepancies between good decisions and good outcomes. As exemplified in the Amgen example, decision analysts view good decisions as requiring more than satisfaction of the axioms (Edwards *et al.* 1984). Good decisions are typically viewed as those made after comprehensive, analytical deliberation of all options and possibilities. For example, Edwards and Fasolo (2001) described a 19-step process for making a good decision. Their steps include the three normative rules described above, plus supporting processes, such as identifying options and possible outcomes of each option. With eight core strategies and 500000 scenarios per strategy, Beccue's (2001) analysis certainly exemplifies the state of the art in comprehensive analysis. It also makes clear that extensive time and resources are needed to be thorough in deciding. However, even given that the resource constraints are met, what guarantee is there that such extensive analysis actually leads to better decisions, and in what ways are decisions improved? As with any of the approaches, it is difficult to estimate the value of decision analysis. However, decision analysis would appear to provide at least three concrete benefits: (1) identification of valuable options that were not initially considered; (2) means for teams to negotiate conflicting opinions; and (3) justification and documentation in support of the decision that was made.

As an example, Johnson (2003) and his consulting team used decision analysis to help their clients reach consensus on the next steps to take for a cancer drug. The drug was in use, but there was disagreement over what the subsequent development strategy should be. The decision analysis team identified five key stakeholders in senior management who would approve or veto their recommendation. They interviewed those stakeholders to determine their objectives. In a brainstorming session with a cross-sectional team, they produced five distinct strategies to analyze, but also explored variant, hybrid strategies in the analysis. The decision analysis team discovered that a hybrid strategy was best, with a $50 million NPV improvement over the best of the five original strategies, and $100 million improvement over the status quo (Johnson 2003).

In another example of these benefits, Hammond and Adelman (1976) conducted a decision analysis to resolve a dispute between the Denver Police Department and the ACLU and other concerned citizen groups. The police wanted to change from conventional round-nosed bullets to hollow-point bullets in order to increase the stopping effectiveness, or ability to incapacitate and prevent return-fire. The citizen groups were against the hollow-point bullets because they believed that they caused far more injury. The usual legalistic dialogue was not working well in this case, with each side providing experts to justify their favored bullet and no resolution to the debate in sight. Also, the ballistics experts and politicians did not have clarity on their distinct roles. Hammond and his team were called in at this point to attempt a decision analytic solution. The team assessed subjective values from the mayor, city council, and other elected officials along several dimensions, including stopping effectiveness and injury. They also had the ballistics experts judge many possible bullets in terms of degree of expected stopping effectiveness, injury, etc., based on physical characteristics such as weight and velocity. They then combined the judgments into overall acceptability, using MAUT. Interestingly, the politicians had very diverse subjective values, and ended up settling on use of equal weights for each dimension. From their analysis, Hammond's team found a bullet with better stopping effectiveness and injury properties than those considered by either party initially. The previously unconsidered bullet was accepted by all parties, and implemented by the police (Hammond & Adelman 1976).

These examples illustrate the concrete benefits of decision analysis applications. An example of an application in which conflicting opinions were not resolved involved a study on ecological restoration (Cipollini *et al.* 2005). Ecological restoration is concerned with the management of ecosystems in order to restore them to target levels of ecological integrity. In the current case, members of the management organizations for an Appalachian prairie preserve expressed ongoing disagreement about how to manage all the prairies. The science director incorporated decision analysis, and elicited expert objectives and preferences to develop a prioritization scheme for the prairie management. Cipollini *et al.* (2005) found that, although they had diverse backgrounds, most of the experts bought into the prioritization scheme. However, there was one important individual who did not buy into the scheme (K. A. Cipollini, pers. comm.). This person was the burn crew leader, and so had considerable influence over which management actions would actually be implemented. In the past, this individual had primarily made the decisions based on his own opinion, and was not interested in relinquishing that control to a group process. Further, he believed that decisions about restoration management could not be quantified and modeled. Hence, he put up roadblocks throughout the process, and eventually derailed the implementation.

Pollock and Chen (1986) had similar difficulties implementing decision analysis in China. Specifically, they met with resistance against the analytical approaches, and the participants had considerable difficulty in assessing probabilities and subjective values. These cases highlight that, although decision analysis may aid in resolving conflict, it does not constitute a panacea for negotiating differences, since, for example, parties may well disagree on whether the general approach is acceptable. From an applied research standpoint, it is extremely risky to dismiss such findings or attribute them to the imprudence of the decision-maker. In the applied world, usability and acceptability of the analysis and recommendations are critical, in addition to scientific validity.

Role of the Expert Decision-Maker

The subject matter expert's role in the group decision process is to provide particular judgments to support the decision tree (or related) representation, when called upon. In some cases the expert may aid in the initial problem structuring, but this is not a hard requirement. The primary information needed from expert judgment to support decision analysis is a set of probability judgment inputs. For example, the subject matter expert used to populate Hailfinder made 3700 probability judgments (Edwards 1998).

In addition to supplying judgment inputs, the expert typically has some role in reviewing the output of the analysis, and might have some or complete say in whether the recommended option will be accepted.

Role of the Psychologist

There are roles for psychologists to participate directly in the applied decision analysis research, as well as in conducting more basic studies that support decision analysis. In the application studies per se the formal representations and analyses dominate, so that psychologists tend to be placed in supporting roles for the OR engineers. For example, Edwards described the need for skilled quantity judgment elicitors, and elicitation facilitation and training as a primary way for psychologists to contribute (Edwards 1998). Probably a more important role for psychologists is to facilitate the initial framing of the problem, in part to ensure that important aspects from the key players' mental representations are not lost in the rush to formalization. Finally, there is a role for psychologists with knowledge of social/organizational decision-making who can flag and cope with the myriad interpersonal issues that surface throughout the process (Peterson *et al.* 2003).

These requirements for psychologists "in the moment" during conduct of the decision analysis study naturally correspond to the needs for psychologists to carry out supporting basic research. The three points of input for basic research psychologists are described in turn.

Elicitation: Assessing Subjective Probabilities and Values

An obvious role for psychologists conducting basic research to support decision analysis is to research and develop elicitation methods for subjective values and probabilities. Indeed, much basic research in judgment and decision-making has been devoted to discovering new ways to conceptualize and model subjective value and subjective probability. For example, Mellers and her colleagues have developed new models of subjective value that better account for emotional responses (Mellers *et al.* 1999; Mellers 2000). Birnbaum (2004, in press) has conducted a number of tests of several advanced theories of utility. The basic paradigm for this research is to construct mathematical models that accurately predict people's decisions in very transparent situations, and then test their goodness-of-fit as compared with other models. For a decision analysis application, the point would be to use the most psychologically realistic models of subjective value in their analyses of large, "real" decision problems. This approach is predicated on two tacit assumptions: (1) people decide according to their "true" preferences for small, transparent decisions, but not for large decisions that are more opaque; and (2) a highly detailed, accurate model for the transparent decisions is what should be incorporated for use in decision analysis on the opaque decisions. The large decisions are beyond unaided human capacity to jointly consider all of the elements, so the person is "represented" in the equation by a highly realistic mathematical proxy.

The decision analysis examples described above suggest a very different paradigm from the one just described for subjective value elicitation and model development. First, note that the value models were attempting to capture a group's values, not those of any one individual. Also, the people appeared to be more concerned with ensuring that their "position" was represented in the model, and that the various positions are represented in a simple, understandable, and fair way. Hence, a basic line of psychological research on value assessment that would seem to better serve decision analysis would put a group of people in a scenario where they have distinct preferences, and then investigate the group process by which they come to agree on a model of their collective preferences. Note that the criterion here is acceptability, or willingness to use the value model, rather than goodness-of-fit of the model to simple gambles. Most current psychological research appears to be moving in the opposite direction (but see Edwards & Hutton 1994).

Subjective probability is another area that has received considerable attention by psychologists, but in a way that seems disconnected from decision analysis. Edwards and others have noted that probability research in the lab is quite different from the way elicitation is done in the field (Edwards 1998). Rather than studying probability judgment using general knowledge questions, for example, researchers ought to focus on future events (Wright & Wisudha 1982). It should also be useful to study judgments of conditional probabilities clustered within an overall scenario to match those required in decision analyses, rather than investigating judgments of independent items as typified in the lab.

Understanding the Situation

A bigger and more interesting contribution that is needed from basic psychological researchers is in coming to grips with a step that precedes application of the three rules in the decision analysis process, "understanding the situation" (Edwards & Fasolo 2001). Research into understanding falls squarely within the domain of the cognitive psychologists, and presents an ideal phase in which they can make a difference (Weick 1995; Klein *et al.* in press). Understanding the situation, or initial problem structuring, has been held as a crucial and poorly understood component of the process (von Winterfeldt & Edwards 1986). Graphical representations, such as knowledge maps, have been developed and incorporated by decision analysts as an approach to improve problem structuring (Howard 1989). However, situational understanding remains severely underdeveloped in decision analysis, though psychologists have conducted some interesting initial studies (Benson *et al.* 1995; Browne *et al.* 1997).

Organizational Issues

In practice, DA tends to be done with multiple stakeholders. It follows that there is a need to coordinate between analysts, managers, and executives. Decision analysts have developed some of their own processes for managing interactions between stakeholders and decision analysts, and for dealing with multiple decision-makers (Kusnic & Owen 1992; Bodily & Allen 1999). However, as in the case of situational understanding, there is a clear role for psychologists in the development, vetting, validation, and implementation of such processes.

COGNITIVE TASK ANALYSIS

The Naturalistic Decision-Making (NDM) perspective focuses on improving decision-making by first investigating how highly experienced individuals and groups make decisions in field settings. NDM researchers investigate decision-making in settings that are marked by ill-defined goals, shifting conditions, high levels of uncertainty, high stakes, non-defined or ill-defined cues, contextual complexity, and organizational constraints. We need to examine decision-making under these kinds of conditions in order to improve the track record of applications. Therefore, NDM researchers have needed to develop methods for cognitive field research, particularly observations and methods for conducting interviews.

Cognitive Task Analysis (CTA) refers to a set of systematic, qualitative methods for uncovering information about the knowledge, thought processes, and goal structures underlying observable performance (Cooke 1994; Militello & Hutton 1998; Schraagen *et al.* 2000; Crandall *et al.* 2006). NDM researchers and CTA practitioners tend to be associated with applied cognitive and human factors psychology. The primary forum for NDM research is the Cognitive Engineering and Decision-Making technical group of the Human Factors and Ergonomics Society (cedm.hfes.org), and the bi-annual Naturalistic Decision-Making conferences (e.g., www.ndm7.com). The primary outlet for NDM research has been the series of edited volumes resulting from the NDM conferences (e.g. Zsambok & Klein 1997). However, the new *Journal of Cognitive Engineering & Decision-Making* should provide a good, peer-reviewed forum for NDM and other cognitive field research studies. A non-technical introduction to NDM is provided by Klein (1998). Hutchins (1995) gives another good introduction to the same general concept.

Basic Approach

Cognitive Task Analysis provides a set of knowledge elicitation, analysis, and representation tools for identifying and analyzing general domain knowledge, expert knowledge, and task-specific skill sets for critical decisions made in a subject-matter expert's (SMEs) complex, naturalistic environment. These analyses lead to a breakdown of the tasks and functions into critical decision requirements: the critical, challenging, and frequent decisions that are made, and the information, knowledge, and strategies that go into making those decisions. Those decision requirements are then used to develop decision-skills training, inform the design of decision-support systems, or restructure teams and organizations. Next, we lay out the basic approach, and provide a couple of illustrating examples from actual projects.

There are several specific CTA interview methods, perhaps the most central of which is the Critical Decision Method (CDM) (Klein *et al.* 1989; Hoffman *et al.* 1998; Schraagen *et al.* 2000). CDM was originally developed based on an earlier technique for uncovering critical incidents (Flanagan 1954). A CDM session is organized around an initial account of a specific incident that comes from the participant's direct experience. The specific episode carries context with it and reveals how particular aspects and events in the environment impel the decision-maker to action.

The CDM interview requires an initial step, that of guiding the participant to recall and recount a relevant incident, depending on the focus of the study. The interviewer then conducts three additional information-gathering sweeps through the incident. These are: Timeline Verification and Decision Point Identification; Progressive Deepening; and What if Queries.

First Sweep: Incident Identification and Selection

In accord with the goals of the project, interviewers will have decided on an opening query, such as "Can you think of a time when you were fighting a fire and your skills were really challenged?" The idea is to help the SME identify cases that are non-routine, especially challenging, or difficult.

Once the participant identifies a relevant incident, he or she is asked to recount the episode in its entirety. The interviewer acts as an active listener, asking few questions, and allowing the participant to structure the incident account him or herself. By requesting personal accounts of a specific event and organizing the interview around that account, potential memory biases are minimized (Berntsen & Thomsen 2005).

Once the expert has completed his or her initial recounting of the incident, the interviewer retells the story. The participant is asked to attend to the details and sequence and to correct any errors or gaps in the interviewer's record of the incident. This critical step allows interviewers and participants to arrive at a shared view of the incident.

Second Sweep: Timeline Verification and Decision Point Identification

In this phase of the interview, the expert goes back over the incident account, seeking to structure and organize the account into ordered segments. The expert is asked for the approximate time of key events and turning points within the incident. The elicitor's goal is to capture the salient events within the incident, ordered by time and expressed in terms of the points where important input information was received or acquired, points where decisions were made, and points where actions were taken. These decision points represent critical junctures within the event. At the conclusion of the second sweep through the incident account, the elicitor has produced a verified, refined documentation of events.

Third Sweep: Progressive Deepening and the Story Behind the Story

During the third sweep, the CDM interviewer leads the participant back over each segment of the incident account identified in the second sweep employing probes designed to focus attention on particular aspects of the incident, and soliciting information about them. The data collected in the third sweep may include presence or absence of salient cues and the nature of those cues, assessment of the situation and the basis of that assessment, expectations about how the situation might evolve, goals considered, and options evaluated and chosen.

Fourth Sweep: "What if?" Expert Novice Differences, Decision Errors, and More

The final sweep through the incident provides an opportunity for interviewers to shift perspective, moving away from the participant's actual, lived experience of the event to a more external view. During this phase, interviewers often use a "What if?" strategy. They pose various changes to the incident account and ask the participant to speculate on how things would have played out differently. An example query might be: "What if you had taken action Y, instead of action X?" Answers to such questions can provide important insights into domain-specific expertise. Or one might go back over each decision point and ask the expert to identify potential errors and explain how and why those errors might occur in order to better understand the vulnerabilities and critical junctures within the incident.

After a number of such incidents have been collected (*n* is typically between 8 and 40, depending on the size of the project), qualitative analyses on the transcripts are conducted. Analysis of these data reduces and combines the individual incident accounts into the form of essential "decision requirements." The decision requirements encompass the "whats" and "hows" of decision-making. What are the critical decisions? What pieces of information are critical to making those decisions? Decision requirements summarize the key difficult, challenging, and critical decisions within a specific task domain. These descriptions are supported by a host of relevant information about why the decision or cognitive activity is challenging or difficult, what strategies are used to make the decision, what information or patterns of information support the decision-making, what critical background knowledge is required to support the decision, what common errors or difficulties are incoming to a decision, and so forth. The requirements then provide the basis for organization or technology design concepts, process improvements, and the development of training exercises for decision-making (Klein *et al.* 1997; Hollnagel 2002).

One example of a CDM interview is a project conducted by Klein *et al.* (1989) to study how fire ground commanders make life-and-death decisions under extreme time pressure. This was one of the first studies using critical incidents as a basis for interviews, and much of the formal structure of the CDM was developed to facilitate the research. The research team conducted CDM interviews. Each interview yielded one or two critical incidents, and these incidents contained approximately five decision points. The final tally in this study was 156 decision points which were probed. The researchers categorized the way that the fire ground commanders handled each decision point. In 127 instances, the commanders recognized a promising option and adopted it without systematically comparing it to alternatives. In 11 instances, the commanders had to devise a novel course of action because none of the usual methods would work. In 18 instances, the commander recognized two or more promising options and compared them to find the best by imagining what would happen if the course of action was carried out.

Another CDM study was conducted with weather forecasters (Pliske *et al.* 2004). A total of 22 Air Force weather forecasters were interviewed to understand how they generate their predictions. Pliske *et al.* found a large variation in strategies, and hypothesized that the experience level and engagement of the forecaster determined the strategy used. Some forecasters applied formulaic methods to compute their predictions. Others used complex rules. Note that extensive quantitative analysis is among the strategies in the repertoire of these experts, as it fits naturally within the demands and constraints of their jobs. Even so, the expertise of the most skillful forecasters went beyond rendering their predictions. For example, they could identify the "problem of the day" that needed to be closely monitored. As important as this problem detection process is, it has been virtually unstudied. They could also sense when the standard computer projections were not trustworthy. Specifically, they could use scatter in the data as an important indicator, and had a sense of what the necessary level of data-smoothing was in particular situations. They would not use programs that over-smoothed the data, and did not permit the user to adjust the level of smoothing. Without understanding in depth the competence and situations of these experts, the applied decision researcher is at risk of attributing the expert's rejection of such an analysis tool to some inherent character flaw on the expert's part.

Hutton and Miller (2003) described research employing CDM and related CTA methods to understand the cognitive challenges faced by experienced air campaign planners. These challenges included being faced with large amounts of dispersed data, managing conflicting goals, and dealing with unclear criteria for the development and evaluation of plans. Taking the details of these challenges into account, the research team designed and developed a prototype decision support tool, the Bed-Down Critic, for use by the planners in the development and evaluation of their plans. The planner could drag and drop assets onto potential sites (e.g., aircraft onto airfields) and receive immediate feedback on the appropriateness of the allocation, thus alleviating the need to attend to myriad lower-level details and remain focused on the higher-level objectives.

These examples illustrated how a CTA method such as the CDM can be useful for obtaining insights about judgment and decision strategies in complex field conditions, and how those insights can be translated into support systems that are tailored to meet the needs of decision-makers.

Topic and Product of Analysis

The topic of a CTA project is the decision-making process of a set of experts in the context of their work. At the end of the process, CTA delivers insights into the nature of the decision problems from the experts' point of view. More concretely, these insights are captured in the form of decision requirements that guide the design of solutions (e.g., decision aids, training, organizational processes) that fit with the realities of the end-users' situations. There are few a priori constraints on the nature of the recommended solutions; they are truly tailored to fit the decision-makers' requirements.

Quality and Achievement

NDM researchers typically study experts to describe good decision-making processes and define quality decision-making (Klein 1989; Hutton & Klein 1999). Hence, the primary criterion for good decision-making is to act like the experts: to notice the cues and patterns, to make the adaptations, to engage in anticipatory thinking, and so forth. A good decision involves doing these sorts of things in ways that novices would not. If we use expertise as a gold standard, a good decision means complying with the application of expertise. This idea of describing expertise in order to set a gold standard for a domain clearly requires further discussion. For one thing, it brings us back to the description (how do people make decisions) vs. prescription (how should people make decisions) distinction. With that distinction in mind, an immediate question that surfaces is how can we possibly move directly from describing decision-making to prescribing it?

To address this question, consider the analogy to bootstrapping in judgments with specified criterion and cues (Dawes & Corigan 1974). In bootstrapping, the decision researcher builds a descriptive model of judges by capturing their policies in equation form, and then replaces the judge with the equation. The bootstrapped equation is often found to perform better than the original judge. CTA moves from description to prescription in a similar manner, though the endpoint is an aid for the judge, rather than replacement.

In general, CTA studies extract and model the expertise of a group of performers, not individual experts. That pooled information from the group of experts is then used to determine the critical judgments and decisions that the experts actually make on the job, what the challenges are in making those judgments and decisions, and what cues, factors, and strategies they use to make those judgments. Strategies range from intuitive rules of thumb to extensive analytical processes, depending on the constraints of the job. Also, NDM researchers are not drawing random samples in order to describe the characteristics of a general population of performers in a domain. They are attempting to draw samples from the top performers, and to construct descriptive models of the decision-making of that expert group. The resulting descriptive model that culls lessons learned from the set of experts is then used as the gold standard, or current best available practice.

Establishing the cognitive performance of the experts as a gold standard provides several advantages. First, since the description of skilled performance combines cues, strategies, etc. of a group, there are elements of the description that any individual expert might pick up. By clarifying the kinds of cues and relationships that experts are attending to, we can see how to formulate a program for skill development in journeymen and novices. Second, because the model is stable it suggests reliable achievement of the strategies. Hence, individual experts can themselves pursue more reliable application of the described process. This latter point suggests that we might be better off considering the judgment and decision strategy of experts as a baseline reference point than a gold standard. We do not want to place a ceiling or end state on their processes. Rather, we want to take their strategies into account when considering ways to improve processes, in part to ensure that our recommendations are usable and acceptable.

What kinds of impact can a CTA study have? Staszewski (2004) conducted a study of expert minesweepers. He used CTA methods to identify the cognitive strategies they use in detecting small mines with low metal content. For example, he found that experts altered how they swept detectors over the ground, slowing the rate of their sweeps and using the detectors to find the edges and centers of the mines. Their judgment process is more complicated than mapping a set of static cues onto a criterion. Even the newest technology only resulted in a 10–20 per cent success rate in detecting mines. Staszewski used his findings to design a training program to help Army engineers use the strategies of the experts. The results were dramatic. Detection rates rose from 10–20 per cent to 90 per cent and higher. Even an abbreviated training program administered for only an hour resulted in success rates higher than 80 per cent.

Role of the Expert Decision-Maker

The subject matter expert (SME) and decision-maker is the focal point of analysis. The point of the research is to foster a collaboration between researcher and SME, as an active participant in the design process. Taking the experts seriously means realizing that they develop their own tools themselves, and recognize what new solutions will help them. In a CTA study, experts also have the roles of sharing what they have learned, articulating what they notice, admitting mistakes where they think they have made them, and speculating about other approaches or reactions.

Role of the Psychologist

As in Decision Analysis, there are direct roles for psychologists in research using CTA to improve decision-making, as well as in basic research that supports the approach. In direct applied CTA research, the psychologist is the driver of the CTA process and design/development of supporting training or technologies. Technology experts, such as OR experts, play a supporting role, rather than a lead role. Several applied and basic research roles for psychologists are described next.

Knowledge Elicitation

Psychologists working within the NDM framework perform cognitive task analyses to identify the environmental factors and pressures that affect decision strategies and quality. The knowledge elicitation that CTA researchers conduct facilitates the initial framing of the problem and ensures that important aspects from the key players' mental representations are not lost in the rush to develop technological or training solutions. Indeed, CTA methods deliver the kind of broader problem structuring insights that decision analysts have described a need for.

There are also basic supporting research roles. Although CTA methods have been carefully thought out and used in the field for decades, rigorous development of the approach is lacking. Hence, considerable further research is needed to study, develop, and validate CTA and novel methods, especially knowledge elicitation methods, to improve their quality and rigor. For example, Nisbett and Wilson (1977) have criticized the use of verbal reports in decision research by arguing that experts are conscious of the products on their mental processes, but not of the decision processes themselves. CTA researchers are well aware of the limitations of incident recall. Klein (1998) cites two cases where decision-makers believed that they made decisions because of ESP. Not believing that answer, the CTA interviewers emphasized probes about what the participants recalled noticing, rather than asking them to explain their decision strategy. And that procedure uncovered a much more plausible basis for the decisions. Hence, while the Nisbett and Wilson (1977) study cannot be taken as a definitive condemnation of CTA because the specific probes differ, further basic research is clearly needed to determine the real validity constraints on incident-based interview approaches, as well as positive suggestions for methodological improvement. Research into methods for interviewing eyewitnesses is likely to prove a reasonable starting point for such investigations (Geiselman & Fisher 1997).

Expertise

Another clear role for psychologists is to discover the basis for expertise. In basic, supporting research, psychologists are needed to help resolve the process–performance paradox. A first step might be to ensure that the precise judgment selected and task details actually match the critical judgments and details of how they are made on the job. A CTA combined with a modified experimental judgment paradigm might be useful to perform this kind of study. The CTA would be used to identify critical judgments actually made by experts, along with their processing strategies for deriving relevant cues from the environment (e.g., as in Staszewski's minesweeping study). An ecologically valid judgment paradigm that stresses those processes could then be constructed and used for investigation into expert performance. Another related area of importance is the development of assessment approaches for clearly identifying/vetting experts (Shanteau *et al.* 2003).

Solutions Design and Development

Psychologists also have a key role in applying the discoveries made in CTA studies in order to improve performance, whether through training, or information technologies, or incentives, or organizational redesign, or personnel selection. In order to accomplish this application, psychologists have to collaborate with developers of information technology, working to get them to think about the point of view of the expert decision-maker (Hollnagel 2002).

DISCUSSION

Psychologists interested in performing applied decision research might do well to consider how they want to contribute to the broad community interested in improving decision-making. Psychologists conducting basic research might reflect on how they arrived at studying the particular set of issues and paradigms that they are pursuing. What are the originating and extant implications for their work to applied decision research?

To assist psychologists in defining their desired role, in this chapter we have compared and contrasted Decision Analysis (rooted in a rational-choice perspective) with Cognitive Task Analysis (stemming from the Naturalistic Decision-Making perspective). Furthermore, we have attempted to identify needs for psychologist input into each methodology, as understood by scholars in the respective field. The disconnects and gaps uncovered from this analysis suggest opportunities for basic researchers to pursue lines of inquiry that will make a difference for applied decision research.

Table 8.1 summarizes central themes for ready comparison. With respect to the first, note that the topic and product of these two kinds of applied research are distinct. So, at the methodological level, they really are non-competing. Furthermore, CTA comprises a front-end analysis that can provide useful supporting information pertaining to the suitability of DA to the problem at hand, as well as the problem-structuring step of a DA. Combining CTA and DA in this way may seem odd to those who think of CTA as sanctifying intuition, but it is important to keep in mind that some form of analysis is often found among the expert decision-makers' strategies.

A related point of confusion is the idea that CTA is best used for short-term tactical types of problems, whereas DA is best suited for long-range strategic issues. The sponsors for CTA and DA research may cluster toward the tactical or the strategic, creating this impression, but the methods themselves are suited to both tactical and strategic problems. The one possible exception is the use of extensive DA in the midst of tactical decision-making. The time constraints do render application of DA unsuitable for the immediate situation in such cases. However, it is possible to use DA to evaluate policies in research studies outside of those situations, and then employ the results (e.g., via training) in the situations themselves.

Table 8.1 Decision analysis and cognitive task analysis compared

Theme	DA	CTA
Analysis		
Topic	Specific decision	Decision-maker cognition
Product	Recommended course of action	Decision requirements, recommended design
Quality and achievement	Consistency with axioms, extensive analysis	Bootstrapping expertise
Role of the decision-maker	Render probabilities and utilities, judge usability and acceptability of solution	Research participant, collaborator in design, judge usability and acceptability of solution
Role of the psychologist	Elicit probabilities and utilities	Lead research project

The conceptions of decision quality of the two approaches do appear to conflict rather directly. Furthermore, neither conception seems entirely satisfactory. The classic arguments used to support the need for consistency with the axioms, such as avoidance of becoming a money pump, are fairly weak and ad hoc from an applied standpoint. That is, it is far from clear that becoming a money pump is a genuine risk that plagues decision-makers in the real world. As important as the axioms themselves are for the theoretical development of analytical methods (e.g., statistical methods), consistency with them is an insufficient standard of decision performance (cf. Yates 1982). In addition, use of extensive quantitative analysis is a process, not a performance metric. And the link to performance is far from clear (Klein *et al.* 1995; Gigerenzer *et al.* 1999; Gigerenzer 2005).

From the CTA standpoint, significant research and thought are required to determine how the concept of expert performance can be widely appreciated as a gold standard, given the process–performance paradox. The preliminary clarifications made here regarding the concept of "bootstrapping expertise" and examination of the degree to which solutions meet the specific needs of decision-makers allow for some potential points of departure of such research. Also, at this point, the expert model is better thought of as providing a baseline reference to be accounted for in improvement efforts, rather than an ideal standard. NDM does not claim that the expert has reached the pinnacle of good decision-making. This, of course, implies that both approaches are lacking in generally acceptable ideal standards.

A related question is whether experts are, in fact, any good at what they do (Smith *et al.* 2004). A number of studies have compared experts with novices and decision aids on experimentally well-defined tasks that permit convenient quantitative comparisons, finding the experts to be wanting. From our standpoint, "what they do" is a critical issue. This issue has been discussed extensively (Rohrbaugh & Shanteau 1999; Phillips *et al.* 2004). For example, the value is unclear of comparisons between individual expert performance and novices (or decision aids) on experimental tasks generated by relatively uninformed experimenters. That is, the task constraints often appear such that the experiments are not capturing the judgments and processes that make up expertise. For example, Westen and Weinberger (2005) argued that the research showing the limitations of experts does not provide a reasonable assessment. If clinicians are asked a question such as whether a specific client will commit a violent act, the clinician is not likely to give an accurate appraisal simply because clinicians have very few patients who engage in violence. Thus, the clinicians have little expertise at making this type of judgment. If skilled clinicians are asked about client features that they frequently encounter, their accuracy rates are much better. Sieck (2003) made a similar observation regarding differences in calibration between experts who render probability judgments as part of their jobs and those who do not. It is worth pointing out that the mismatch between actual expertise and elicited judgments is of particular concern for the application of DA, where quantity judgments are required in a form that is often incompatible with the decision-maker's expertise.

In sum, a broader perspective is required to get at the nature of decision quality. The discussions provided here, as well as recent research by Yates and his colleagues, may provide serious beginnings for addressing these issues (Yates 2003; Yates *et al.* 2003; Hoffman & Yates 2005).

Our third theme, concerning the role of the expert decision-maker, has non-trivial implications for the acceptability and implementation of the final recommendations. From the NDM perspective, it is essential to include the decision-makers at the front end, and understand the issues from their perspective. Even if some of the extreme critics of expertise are correct (which we seriously doubt), the results of getting decision support tools designed according to DA principles successfully integrated and implemented into practice have been less than satisfactory (Corey & Merenstein 1987; Ashton 1991). Although it is common to berate the decision-makers and trivialize their experience in such cases, such a position does not serve the common goal of improving decision-making. Decision support solutions based on designs that take the challenges of the decision-makers into account are likely to be much more useable and acceptable to those experts. And applied research has to take usability and acceptability of the recommendations into account, in addition to scientific validity of the process.

Our intent here is to get beyond confrontations between DA and CTA for the two methodologies are not necessarily opposed. They are each attempting to meet different objectives. In that frame, we believe that psychologists who can appreciate aspects of both approaches can work on ways to use CTA field research methods to improve DA. Likewise, DA can be used to bolster CTA.

Thus far, decision analysts have concentrated on finding stronger techniques and better ways to do the math. However, the big issues with DA have to do with the people, not the math. The practice of DA can be improved by understanding the broader challenges of knowledge elicitation and problem structuring. DA will improve by devising better methods for gaining acceptance within organizations, and by becoming more sensitive to the work context and organizational issues that have been barriers to adoption. Methods of CTA may be helpful in taking these steps. On the other hand, CTA researchers have focused their efforts on developing methods to investigate expert decision-making in natural settings, with the aim of uncovering a wide range of solutions that meet the specific needs of decision-makers. Little work has been done, however, to generate more external evaluations of recommendations. To achieve broader acceptance of the approach, DA principles could be used to validate and quantify the benefits of CTA. Furthermore, the graphical and formal representations used in DA may provide useful constructs for representing expert decision processes in the data analysis phase of CTA. At this juncture, the investigation of combined CTA–DA approaches for improving decision-making is surely warranted.

AUTHOR NOTE

The authors thank Frank Durso and three reviewers for their patience and comments on an earlier version of this chapter.

REFERENCES

Ashton, R. (1991). Pressure and performance in accounting decision settings: paradoxical effects of incentives, feedback, and justification. *Journal of Accounting Research*, *28*, 148–186.

Beccue, P. (2001). Choosing a development strategy for a new product at Amgen. *Interfaces*, *31*(5), 62–64.

Benson, P. G., Curley, S. P. & Smith, G. F. (1995). Belief assessment: an underdeveloped phase of probability elicitation. *Management Science*, *41*(10), 1639–1653.

Berntsen, D. & Thomsen, D. K. (2005). Personal memories for remote historical events: accuracy and clarity of flashbulb memories related to World War II. *Journal of Experimental Psychology: General*, *134*(2), 242–257.

Birnbaum, M. H. (2004). Tests of rank-dependent utility and cumulative prospect theory in gambles represented by natural frequencies: effects of format, event framing, and branch splitting. *Organizational Behavior and Human Decision Processes*, *95*, 40–65.

Birnbaum, M. H. (2005). Three new tests of independence that differentiate models of risky decision making. *Management Science*, *51*, 1346–1358.

Bodily, S. E. & Allen, M. S. (1999). A dialogue process for choosing value-creating strategies. *Interfaces*, *29*(6), 16–28.

Browne, G. J., Curley, S. P. & Benson, P. G. (1997). Evoking information in probability assessment: knowledge maps and reasoning-based directed questions. *Management Science*, *43*(1), 1–14.

Cipollini, K .A., Maruyama, A. L. & Zimmerman, C. L. (2005). Planning for restoration: a decision analysis approach to prioritization. *Restoration Ecology*, *13*(3), 460–470.

Clemen, R. T. (1996). *Making hard decisions: an introduction to decision analysis*, 2nd Edition. Belmont, CA: Duxbury Press.

Cooke, N. J. (1994). Varieties of knowledge elicitation techniques. *International Journal of Human-Computer Studies*, *41*, 801–849.

Corey, G. A. & Merenstein, J. H. (1987). Applying the acute ischemic heart disease predictive instrument. *The Journal of Family Practice*, *25*, 127–133.

Crandall, B., Klein, G. & Hoffman, R. R. (2006). *Working Minds: A Practitioner's Guide to Cognitive Task Analysis*. Boston, MA: MIT Press.

Dawes, R. M. & Corigan, B. (1974). Linear models in decision making. *Psychological Bulletin*, *81*, 95–106.

Dawson, N. V., Connors, A. F. Jr., Speroff, T. *et al.* (1993). Hemodynamic assessment in managing the critically ill: is physician confidence warranted? *Medical Decision Making*, *13*, 258–266.

Edwards, W. (1998). Hailfinder: tools for and experiences with Bayesian normative modeling. *American Psychologist*, *53*(4), 416–428.

Edwards, W. & Fasolo, B. (2001). Decision technology. *Annual Review of Psychology*, *52*, 581–606.

Edwards, W. & Hutton, B. F. (1994). SMARTS and SMARTER: improved simple methods for multiattribute utility measurement. *Organizational Behavior and Human Decision Processes*, *60*(3), 306–325.

Edwards, W., Kiss, I., Majone, G. & Toda, M. (1984). What constitutes "a good decision?" *Acta Psychologica*, *56*, 5–27.

Flanagan, J. C. (1954). The critical incident technique. *Psychological Bulletin*, *51*, 327–358.

Geiselman, R. E. & Fisher, R. P. (1997). Ten years of cognitive interviewing. In D. G. P. F. G. Conrad (ed.), *Intersections in Basic and Applied Memory Research*. Hillsdale, NJ: Lawrence Erlbaum Associates.

Gigerenzer, G. (2005). Is the mind irrational or ecologically rational? In F. Parisi & V. L. Smith (eds.), *The Law and Economics of Irrational Behavior* (pp. 37–67). Stanford, CA: Stanford University Press.

Gigerenzer, G., Todd, P. M. & Group, T. A. R. (1999). *Simple Heuristics that Make Us Smart*. New York: Oxford University Press.

Goodwin, P. & Wright, G. (1998). *Decision analysis for management judgment,* 2nd Edition. Chichester: Wiley.

Hammond, J. S., Keeney, R. L. & Raiffa, H. (1999). *Smart Choices: A Practical Guide to Making Better Decisions*. Boston, MA: Harvard Business School Press.

Hammond, K. R. & Adelman, L. (1976). Science, values, and human judgment. *Science*, *194*, 389–396.

Hoffman, R. R., Crandall, B. W. & Shadbolt, N. R. (1998). Use of the critical decision method to elicit expert knowledge: a case study in cognitive task analysis methodology. *Human Factors*, *40*(2), 254–276.

Hoffman, R. R. & Yates, J. F. (2005). Decision (?) Making (?). *IEEE Intelligent Systems*, *20*(4), 76–83.
Hollnagel, E. (ed.) (2002). *Handbook of Cognitive Task Design*. Mahwah, NJ: Lawrence Erlbaum Associates.
Howard, R. A. (1989). Knowledge maps. *Management Science*, *35*, 903–922.
Hutchins, E. (1995). *Cognition in the Wild*. Cambridge, MA: MIT Press.
Hutton, R. J. B. & Klein, G. (1999). Expert decision making. *Systems Engineering*, *2*(1), 32–45.
Hutton, R. J. B. & Miller, T. E. (2003). Decision-Centered Design: leveraging cognitive task analysis in design. In E. Hollnagel (ed.), *Handbook of Cognitive Task Design*. Mahwah, NJ: Lawrence Erlbaum Associates.
Johnson, E. (2003). Analyzing the development strategy for apimoxin. *Interfaces*, *33*(3), 57–59.
Klein, G. (1998). *Sources of Power: How People Make Decisions*. Cambridge, MA: MIT Press.
Klein, G., McCloskey, M. J., Pliske, R. M. & Schmitt, J. (1997). Decision skills training. In *Proceedings of the Human Factors and Ergonomics Society 41st Annual Meeting* (pp. 182–185). Santa Monica, CA: HFES.
Klein, G., Phillips, J. K., Rall, E. L. & Peluso, D. A. (in press). A data/frame theory of sensemaking. In R. R. Hoffman (ed.), *Expertise Out of Context: Proceedings of the 6th International Conference on Naturalistic Decision Making*. Mahwah, NJ: Lawrence Erlbaum Associates.
Klein, G., Wolf, S., Militello, L. G. & Zsambok, C. E. (1995). Characteristics of skilled option generation in chess. *Organizational Behavior and Human Decision Processes*, *62*(1), 63–69.
Klein, G. A. (1989). Recognition-primed decisions. In W. B. Rouse (ed.), *Advances in Man-Machine Systems Research*. Greenwich, CT: JAI Press.
Klein, G. A., Calderwood, R. & MacGregor, D. (1989). Critical decision method for eliciting knowledge. *IEEE Transactions on Systems, Man, and Cybernetics*, *19*(3), 462–472.
Kusnic, M. W. & Owen, D. (1992). The unifying vision process: value beyond traditional decision analysis in multiple-decision-maker-environments. *Interfaces*, *22*(6), 150–166.
Lee, P. M. (2004). *Bayesian Statistics: An Introduction* (3rd edn). London: Oxford University Press.
Lichtenstein, S. & Fischhoff, B. (1980). Training for calibration. *Organizational Behavior and Human Performance*, *26*, 149–171.
Mellers, B. A. (2000). Choice and the relative pleasure of consequences. *Psychological Bulletin*, *126*, 910–924.
Mellers, B. A., Schwartz, A. & Ritov, I. (1999). Emotion-based choice. *Journal of Experimental Psychology: General*, *128*, 1–14.
Militello, L. G. & Hutton, R. J. B. (1998). Applied Cognitive Task Analysis (ACTA): a practitioner's toolkit for understanding cognitive task demands. *Ergonomics*, *41*(11), 1618–1641.
Nisbett, R. E. & Wilson, T. (1977). Telling more than we can know: verbal reports on mental processes. *Psychological Review*, *84*, 231–259.
Peterson, M. F., Miranda, S. M., Smith, P. B. & Haskell, V. M. (2003). The sociocultural contexts of decision making in organizations. In S. L. Schneider & J. Shanteau (eds.), *Emerging Perspectives on Judgment and Decision Research* (pp. 512–555). Cambridge: Cambridge University Press.
Phillips, J. K., Klein, G. & Sieck, W. R. (2004). Expertise in judgment and decision making: a case for training intuitive decision skills. In D. J. Koehler & N. Harvey (eds.), *Blackwell Handbook of Judgment & Decision Making* (pp. 297–315). Malden, MA: Blackwell.
Pliske, R. M., Crandall, B. & Klein, G. (2004). Competence in weather forecasting. In K. Smith, J. Shanteau & P. Johnson (eds.), *Psychological Investigations of Competence in Decision Making* (pp. 40–70). Cambridge: Cambridge University Press.
Pollock, S. M. & Chen, K. (1986). Strive to conquer the black stink: decision analysis in the People's Republic of China. *Interfaces*, *16*(2), 31–37.
Rohrbaugh, C. C. & Shanteau, J. (1999). Context, process, and experience: research on applied judgment and decision making. In F. T. Durso, R. S. Nickerson, R. W. Schvaneveldt, S. T. Dumais, D. S. Lindsay & M. T. H. Chi (eds.), *Handbook of Applied Cognition* (pp. 115–139). Chichester: John Wiley & Sons.
Schraagen, J. M., Chipman, S. F. & Shalin, V. L. (eds.) (2000). *Cognitive Task Analysis*. Mahwah, NJ: Lawrence Erlbaum Associates.

Schraagen, J. M., Chipman, S. F. & Shute, V. J. (2000). State-of-the-art review of cognitive task analysis techniques. In J. M. Schraagen, S. F. Chipman & V. L. Shalin (eds.), *Cognitive Task Analysis* (pp. 467–487). Mahwah, NJ: Lawrence Erlbaum Associates.

Shanteau, J., Weiss, D. J., Thomas, R. P. & Pounds, J. (2003). How can you tell if someone is an expert? Performance-based assessment of expertise. In S. L. Schneider & J. Shanteau (eds.), *Emerging Perspectives on Judgment and Decision Research* (pp. 620–639). Cambridge: Cambridge University Press.

Sieck, W. R. (2003). Effects of choice and relative frequency elicitation on overconfidence: further tests of an exemplar-retrieval model. *Journal of Behavioral Decision Making, 16*, 127–145.

Sieck, W. R. & Arkes, H. R. (2005). The recalcitrance of overconfidence and its contribution to decision aid neglect. *Journal of Behavioral Decision Making, 18*, 29–53.

Smith, K., Shanteau, J. & Johnson, P. (2004). *Psychological Investigations of Competence in Decision-making*. Cambridge: Cambridge University Press.

Staszewski, J. (2004). Models of human expertise as blueprints for cognitive engineering: applications to landmine detection. Paper presented at the Human Factors and Ergonomics Society.

Weick, K. E. (1995). *Sensemaking in Organizations*. Newbury Park, CA: Sage.

Westen, D. & Weinberger, J. (2005). In praise of clinical judgment: Meehl's forgotten legacy. *Journal of Clinical Psychology, 61*(10), 1257–1276.

von Winterfeldt, D. & Edwards, W. (1986). *Decision Analysis and Behavioral Research*. Cambridge: Cambridge University Press.

Wright, G. & Wisudha, A. (1982). Distribution of probability assessments for alamanc and future event questions. *Scandinavian Journal of Psychology, 23*(3), 219–224.

Yates, J. F. (1982). External correspondence: decompositions of the mean probability score. *Organizational Behavior and Human Decision Processes, 30*, 132–156.

Yates, J. F. (2003). *Decision Management: How to Assure Better Decisions in Your Company*. San Francisco, CA: Jossey-Bass.

Yates, J. F., Veinott, E. S. & Patalano, A. L. (2003). Hard decisions, bad decisions: on decision quality and decision aiding. In S. L. Schneider & J. Shanteau (eds.), *Emerging Perspectives on Judgment and Decision Research* (pp. 13–63). New York: Cambridge University Press.

Zsambok, C. E. & Klein, G. (eds.) (1997). *Naturalistic Decision Making*. Mahwah, NJ: Lawrence Erlbaum Associates.

CHAPTER 9

Human Error: Trick or Treat?

Erik Hollnagel
École des Mines de Paris, France

In this chapter the status of the concept of "human error" is discussed from an ontological and pragmatic perspective. It is argued that it owes it existence to the assumption about flawless mental (information) processes, in line with the engineering design tradition. A closer examination of the terminological confusion created by researchers and practitioners alike leads to the conclusion that "human error" is best understood as a judgment made in hindsight. By further acknowledging that, philosophically speaking, it is a category mistake, the need for a separate category evaporates. This does not, however, deny that the utility of the term "human error" will lead to its continued use for the foreseeable future. We do need a way to account for the variability of human performance, not least in how this may affect the safety of socio-technical complexes. But we also need models and theories that can express human behavior such that the concept of "human error" becomes superfluous.

THE PEDIGREE OF "HUMAN ERROR"

"Human error" enjoys the rather unique characteristic of being a phenomenon that in an academic sense belongs to one discipline yet is used more by people from other disciplines. Because "human error" refers to an aspect of human behavior the relevant scientific discipline is clearly psychology, defined as the scientific study of human behavior and of the human mind. Yet within psychology "human error" has only recently become a central concept of the kind that warrants a separate chapter in textbooks, and even this is mostly due to external interests. The need to describe and understand actions that go wrong has arisen in other, more practically oriented disciplines, such as human factors engineering, accident analysis, probabilistic risk assessment, and industrial safety management. This need has elevated "human error" to its current cardinal position, which is, perhaps, not altogether justified. From the point of view of these practically oriented disciplines it may seem strange that psychology has neglected a phenomenon as important as "human error." This chapter will, however, argue that this is actually not the case, and that perhaps the practically oriented disciplines have put too much emphasis on it.

Handbook of Applied Cognition: Second Edition. Edited by Francis T. Durso.

Any discussion of "human error" should be based on a definition of what the term means. Yet despite its widespread use, as if the term was unambiguous and referred to a well-defined phenomenon, it is far from simple to define. The problems in providing a definition will be analyzed more thoroughly in the following sections. For the time being "human error" is taken to mean an incorrectly performed human action, particularly in cases where the term is used to denote the cause of an unwanted outcome.

"Human Error" as a Psychological Concept

As a psychological concept, "human error" can be described either using an idiographic or a nomothetic perspective. In the first case "human error" is an individual characteristic or personality trait, while in the second it is something that is common to many or all. The idiographic perspective may lead to hypotheses about error-proneness as an individual trait or a view of risk-taking in terms of subjective preferences. For instance, one of the early candidates for a theory to explain industrial accidents was a single-factor model of accident-proneness (Greenwood & Woods 1919). A more recent example is the zero-risk hypothesis of driving (Summala 1985, 1988), which proposes that drivers aim to keep their subjectively perceived risk at zero level. It is, however, more common to adopt a nomothetic view, where "human error" is described as a general trait and therefore as something that can be treated statistically and described by a general theory. This places "human error" on the same level as a host of other important psychological phenomena such as learning, remembering, problem-solving, decision-making, etc. (The reader may already detect here a bias, as these examples belong to the field of cognition rather than emotion. This is not meant to present a false juxtaposition between cognition and emotion, but simply reflects the traditional position in these types of study.)

A closer look at this list reveals that there is an important difference between "human error" and the other phenomena mentioned. Learning and remembering, for instance, are generic functions or abilities without which we would not have survived as a species. Indeed, they can both be found in organisms that are low on the phylogenetic scale, such as inchworms and slugs. Problem-solving and decision-making are more complex phenomena which to some extent reflect a specific theoretical stance, yet they are also essential for a person's ability to cope with the complexity of the environment – at least in what we call the modern societies.

"Human error" is, however, of a different character. Although it can be argued that error – or doing something wrong – is essential for learning, from a psychological or a control theoretic perspective, these theories refer to the utility of failing rather than to error, or "human error," as a phenomenon per se. For instance, Campbell (1956, 1960) has cogently argued for the importance of error, in the guise of trial-and-error, for both learning and creativity. Similarly, control theory points out the usefulness of failures by noting that they provide an opportunity to learn. Thus if everything always happens as expected and if nothing ever fails, it is impossible to improve. This is known as the *Fundamental Regulator Paradox*, which is defined as follows:

> The task of a regulator is to eliminate variation, but this variation is the ultimate source of information about the quality of its work. Therefore, the better the job a regulator does the less information it gets about how to improve. (Weinberg & Weinberg 1979, p. 250)

Although it is beyond dispute that failure is necessary for the survival of the individual as well as of the species, this does not mean that "human error" as such is necessary. The argument can, however, not really be settled before the status of "human error" has been clarified, both ontologically and pragmatically. Since this is the purpose of this chapter, I will proceed to do so and return to the question of the necessity of "human error" at the end.

The Roots of "Human Error"

In trying to clarify the conceptual status of "human error" it is necessary, however briefly, to look to philosophy. Since many, if not most, philosophers at one time or another have tried to understand the workings of the human mind, they have necessarily also considered "human error". In these cases the meaning of "human error" is often quite different from contemporary interpretations. Whereas we now seem to be preoccupied with error as it manifests itself in action, philosophy has traditionally been concerned with error as the false conclusions that may be reached when thinking or reasoning. In that sense the concern is more with understanding thinking than with explaining or accounting for failure *qua* failure.

A good example is found in the following passage from David Hume's text *A Treatise of Human Nature*.

> There are therefore three proportions, which the mind distinguishes in the general appearance of its objects, and calls by the names of greater, less and equal. But though its decisions concerning these proportions be sometimes infallible, they are not always so; nor are our judgments of this kind more exempt from doubt and error than those on any other subject. We frequently correct our first opinion by a review and reflection; and pronounce those objects to be equal, which at first we esteemed unequal; and regard an object as less, though before it appeared greater than another. Nor is this the only correction, which these judgments of our senses undergo; but we often discover our error by a juxtaposition of the objects; or where that is impracticable, by the use of some common and invariable measure, which being successively applied to each, informs us of their different proportions. And even this correction is susceptible of a new correction, and of different degrees of exactness, according to the nature of the instrument, by which we measure the bodies, and the care which we employ in the comparison. (Hume 1985 [first published. 1739], p. 95) Book I, Part II, Section IV)

What Hume was writing about is what we now would call an error of judgment, in the concrete sense of judging whether one line or surface is equal to, or greater or less than, another. His discussion addressed the fact that this judgment could be incorrect and considered the ways in which an incorrect opinion could be corrected. Hume was therefore less concerned with "human error" in the meaning of an action gone wrong than with the means by which we can learn to make correct judgments – and in general learn to perceive the world correctly in order to act appropriately.

The Duality of "Human Error"

One of the reasons why "human error" is difficult to define is that it can be understood as either a process or product. In the former case, "human error" is the reason why something leads to the wrong outcome; in the latter "human error" is the wrong outcome itself. This duality has been present from the early days of scientific psychology, as the following sections show.

Errors of Memory

One of the most famous psychological experiments is seemingly about error, namely about errors in remembering. We all know that the ability to remember something is imperfect, and that retention of learned material degrades over time in both the short and the long run. While academic psychology traditionally has referred to this as the study of memory, the advent of the information-processing metaphor changed that. Rather than being an ability – the ability to remember – memory became a structure or an entity. Careless use of language therefore led people to talk about storing – or retrieving – something from memory, instead of remembering or recalling, itself an example of a product–process duality.

Hermann Ebbinghaus (1850–1909) achieved fame by inventing a way for experimental psychology to study the "higher mental processes" (Boring 1950, p. 388). His experiments showed retention as a function of number of repetitions, as a function of time, as a function of repeated learning, and as a function of the order of succession of the items to be remembered. Most famously, the studies introduced the *forgetting curve*, which showed retention as a function of time. But unlike contemporary cognitive psychology and cognitive science, which are preoccupied with finding the causes of memory errors, Ebbinghaus did not consider incomplete retention as an error. He was, of course, interested in the difference between complete and partial reproduction of the learned material, the former called a reproduction "without error" and the latter a reproduction with "a probable error," and in explaining how this difference depended on the experimental conditions. Yet the incomplete recall was not an error in the sense that something had gone wrong. Instead, the incomplete recall was accepted as a normal (and therefore unavoidable) phenomenon. In contemporary terms we may say that the focus of Ebbinghaus's studies was on the natural variability of remembering (as performance), rather than on the juxtaposition between correct and incorrect memory functions.

This view is in stark contrast to the modern study of memory, where the concern is for finding ways of explaining the errors of memory, i.e., the error becomes significant *eo ipso*. This change of focus is possibly a side-effect of psychopathology, which puts the spotlight on understanding what is wrong or abnormal, rather than on normal performance. In the case of psychoanalysis and psychopathology, errors, such as slips of the tongue, have a diagnostic significance. In the case of information-processing psychology in general, errors are seen as phenomena in their own right which require an explanation, rather than as symptoms.

While a distinction between something that is correct or normal and something that is incorrect or abnormal is warranted for technological systems such as car engines or computers, it is not justified in describing humans. In the technological world, it makes sense to assume that if something does not work, then something must have gone wrong and therefore to begin a search for what may have failed. But it is not sound to make the same assumption in the case of humans, if for no other reason than because it is difficult to define what is meant by correct performance.

Errors in Learning

Another prominent use of the term error in psychology was in relation to learning, more specifically in the form of the trial-and-error phenomenon. The notable experiments of Edward Lee Thorndike (1874–1949) showed how cats locked in a cage could learn to get out through a series of trial and error. Or rather, how the positive effect of a movement "stamped in" the movements that were the cause of it. The experiments served to demonstrate how an animal's behavior would change from being haphazard and random to become purposive, in the sense that after a number of learning trials it could almost immediately open its cage and get out.

Although Thorndike normally is thought of as espousing trial-and-error learning, he was in fact more interested in the value of success. The more direct and comprehensive theoretical treatment of failure and success in learning theories came later in the writings of Donald Campbell who, in a comprehensive survey and analysis of learning theories, described the role of trial and error as follows:

> In terms of the rudiments of the general selective survival model, habit formation would be based upon (a) random variation of emitted behavior, (b) selective survival of certain variations, and (c) retention and duplication of surviving variations. In terms of conceptual traditions in psychology, this translates into a random trial-and-error learning model. Accepting the general correctness of the model may be made more palatable by noting that most contemporary learning theories contain a random trial-and-error component. While this is most obvious in theories of the Thorndike tradition, as in Hull, Skinner, and especially Guthrie, it is also true of the more Gestaltish theories of Tolman and Meier, as has been pointed out elsewhere. The major unsolved problems lie in the mechanisms of selection and retention, and these problems are formidable. But for the purposes of the present paper it is the randomness that needs emphasis. (Campbell 1956)

Random behavior, or trial-and-error learning, does not, however, represent the kind of error that is implied by the term "human error." The error in learning is, first of all, a necessary step toward success (cf. the *Fundamental Regulator Paradox* mentioned above). Indeed, without making errors, i.e., without failing to achieve the desired outcome, nothing can be learned. Second, random behavior is in a very real sense normal in conditions where the acting organism – be it a cat in a cage or a human faced with an unknown situation – is unable to make sense of what is going on, and hence unable to make an informed choice about the right behavior. Just as the imperfect recall in Ebbinghaus's memory experiments was the norm rather than the exception, so is trial and error the norm in an unknown situation.

As an aside, the utility of trial and error did not become extinct when the classical learning experiments, such as Thorndike's, went out of fashion. In the industrialized world everyone will periodically face a situation where it is uncertain how a certain "gadget" works. This may be as simple as resetting a digital watch when daylight saving time ends, or more complex such as employing a rarely used function in a piece of software. The usual resort in such cases is to rely on a more or less systematic trial and error. Thanks to the unrestrained creativeness of designers, the effects of usability engineering notwithstanding, the opportunities to practice trial and error are in no obvious danger of disappearing.

Error as Process or as Product

The use of the concept of error in memory experiments differs from its use in learning theories. In the former case, error refers to the *process* of remembering, i.e., recall is imperfect and the result is therefore incorrect. In the latter case, error refers to the *product* or outcome, i.e., the inability to achieve the desired outcome, such as Thorndike's cat being unable to get out of the cage. Yet the *activity* leading to the outcome, either as the single activity of trying to open the latch or as the compound activity of trying to get out of the cage, cannot be said to be wrong as such since it is the only way of achieving the desired result.

The difference between process and product is important in trying to define precisely what "human error" is. We can all easily think of situations where the outcome or product is incorrect, and in that sense – following Hume's principle – go on to determine whether it is too large or too small. In other words, we can know that something is wrong – as a product – and try to determine how wrong it is. Yet we cannot use the same binary distinction of a process as being either right or wrong. A process may be of the wrong kind, of course, and in that sense completely inappropriate for the purpose. But apart from such extreme cases, whether a process is right or wrong is normally a matter of degree rather than of absolutes. Learning may be imperfect if the right outcome or product is not achieved, but that learning as such has taken place is beyond dispute. So the cat's failure to escape was not because learning as a process failed but because learning was incomplete or insufficient. A little more practice and the cat would have succeeded.

THE MEANING OF ERROR

The facility by which the terms error and "human error" are used in practice belies the problems of providing a precise definition. This can be illustrated by looking at how leading researchers in the field have approached the problem.

> It is interesting to note that one of the early definitions of human error described it as a failure to perform a prescribed act (or perform a prohibited act) which could result in unwanted consequences. (Hagen 1976)
>
> An active human error is an unintended action or an intended action based on a mistaken diagnosis, interpretation, or other failure, which is not recovered and which has significant negative consequences for the system. (Embrey 1994, p. 43)
>
> Any member of a set of human actions or activities that exceeds some limit of acceptability, i.e., an out of tolerance action [or failure to act] where the limits of performance are defined by the system. (Kirwan 1994, p. 1; quoting a definition provided by Swain 1989)
>
> An error occurs when a planned action fails to achieve its desired outcome, and when this failure cannot be attributed to the intervention of some chance occurrence. (Reason & Mycielska 1982, p. 14)
>
> Error will be taken as a generic term to encompass all those occasions in which a planned sequence of mental or physical activities fail to achieve its intended outcome, and when these failures cannot be attributed to the intervention of some chance agency. (Reason 1990, p. 9)
>
> Error means that something has been done which was (1) not intended by the actor, (2) not desired by a set of rules or an external observer, (3) that led the task or system outside its acceptable limits. (Senders & Moray 1991, p. 25)

> The label "human error" is a judgment made in hindsight. After the outcome is clear, any attribution of error is a social and psychological judgment process, not a narrow, purely technical, or objective analysis. (Woods *et al.* 1994, p. 200)

With the exception of the Woods *et al.* (1994), the definitions focus either on the process aspect or on the product aspect, or on both. There is no strong disagreement among them, but neither is there much analytical accuracy. The general feature seems to be that the human in one way or another has done something that was wrong, in the sense that their action led to an unwanted outcome or failed to achieve the desired outcome. (The two conditions are obviously not identical.) Some definitions include the psychological reasons for why this happens, while others are vaguer. One reason for this difference is that the definitions are based on different premises or made from different perspectives. In human factors engineering, for instance, the human operator is viewed as a system component for which successes and failures can be described in much the same way as for equipments. (This stance also includes information-processing psychology.) In behavioral science, on the other hand, the starting assumption is that human behavior is essentially purposive and that it therefore can be fully understood only by reference to subjective goals and intentions. Finally, in social science, the origins of failure are usually ascribed to features of the prevailing socio-technical system so that management style and organizational structure are seen as the mediating variables influencing error rates.

The problems in providing a concise definition of "human error" may raise the suspicion that it is not a meaningful term at all – or rather that it is ambiguous because it has several meanings. Despite the agreed general usage of the word, "human error" is in practice often used in three quite different ways. The first is that a "human error" denotes the *cause* of something; the second that it denotes the *event* or *action* itself; and the third that it denotes the *outcome* of an action.

- *The failure was due to human error.* Here the focus is on "human error" as the cause of the unwanted outcome. This usage is very common, as illustrated by the following quoted from an EU White Paper on traffic safety, according to which, 95 per cent of all accidents are caused by "human error" in one way or another, and in 76 per cent of cases the human is seen as the only cause of the accident.
- *I forgot to check the water level.* Here the focus is on the action or process itself, whereas the outcome or the consequence is not considered.

  > I intended to pick up a knife to cut the potatoes, but actually picked up the tea towel. I wanted to cut the potatoes I had just peeled for boiling. Normally when I prepare french fries, I dry the potatoes with a tea towel before cutting them. On this occasion I was doing boiled mashed potatoes. (Reason & Mycielska 1982, p. 70)

  It is even possible that the outcome has not yet occurred, yet the person still feels that an error has been made, for instance that some action or operation has been forgotten.
- *I left the key in the lock.* Here the focus is solely on the outcome, although the linguistic description is of the action. In this example, forgetting the key in the lock (in the car or at home) is a condition or result that clearly is unintended and therefore in a very real sense wrong.

The differences in usage are illustrated in Figure 9.1. This illustrates that the term "human error" commonly is used in several different ways. This ambiguity makes the

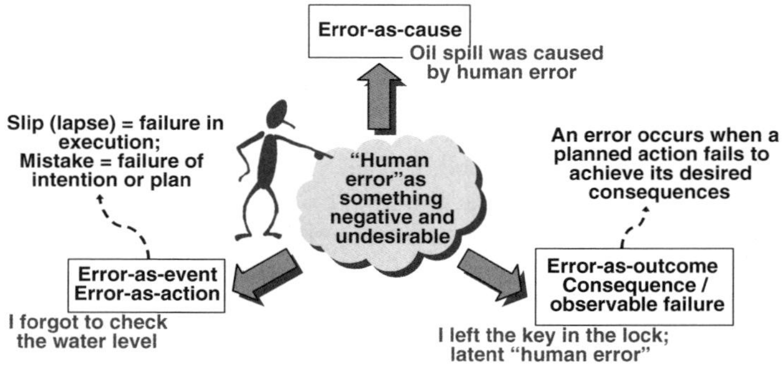

Figure 9.1 Three meanings of the term "human error"

term unsuitable for more systematic analyses, and therefore creates the need for a less ambiguous terminology.

Woods *et al.* (1994, p. xvii) note that "the diversity of approaches to the topic of error is symptomatic that 'human error' is not a well defined category of human performance." This is illustrated by the seven definitions listed above, of which some clearly represent the "error-as-action," others the "error-as-cause," and yet others the "error-as-outcome" interpretation. The definition by Woods *et al.* (1994) alone offers a completely different perspective which will be discussed below.

The Practical Need

The growing interest in "human error" as a phenomenon in its own right did not come from psychology but from practitioners facing the problems of humans working in complex industrial systems. When such socio-technical systems are used in practice, there is always a possibility that something may go wrong, resulting in serious negative consequences. Quite apart from a natural tendency to dislike incidents and accidents because they represent uncertainty – something that the human psyche abhors – accidents also lead to undesirable outcomes such as the loss of property or life.

Indeed, when designing and building such systems it is essential to ensure that they can be relied upon, that nothing will go wrong, and that we can entrust our safety and well-being to them. When a house is built, we want to be sure that neither the roof, floors, nor walls will collapse – certainly not under normal circumstances and preferably not during extreme conditions such as storms, heavy snowfall, or earthquakes. When we develop an electricity distribution system or a water supply system or a communication system or a healthcare system, we want to feel confident that it is reliable, and that it is there when and where we need it. The same goes for systems such as nuclear power plants, emergency admission centers, airplanes and airports, etc.

The need to address these matters led to the development of human factors engineering, risk analysis, and probabilistic risk assessment, i.e., systematic ways of ascertaining and ensuring that there are no obvious or significant ways in which something can go wrong. Risk analysis is a relatively young discipline, most of the common methods being from the later 1950s or early 1960s (Leveson 1995). This is no coincidence, but a consequence of the development of the meta-technical sciences, such as information theory and cybernetics, in the middle of the twentieth century in combination with the invention of digital computers, the transistor, and the integrated circuit.

The scientific interest in risk, of course, is much older than that and goes back at least to the Renaissance (Bernstein 1996). The classical studies of risk, however, aimed at finding ways of expressing, harnessing, or managing the risks that were part of commercial and private life, and were neither concerned with looking into the origin of risk as such nor with "human error." It was only when the industrialized world expanded dramatically that risk at work became an issue, and with that the concern for "human error."

Consequences and Causes

In accident analysis the law of causality, or rather the law of reverse causality, reigns supreme. Where the law of causality states that every cause has an effect, the reverse law states that every effect has a cause. Although this is philosophically reasonable in the sense that it is unacceptable that events happen by themselves, it is not a defensible position in practice. Yet assuming that a cause must exist does not necessarily mean that it can also be found. The belief that this is possible rests on two assumptions: the law of reverse causality and the assumption that it is logically possible to reason backwards in time from the effect to the cause (the rationality assumption). Quite apart from the fact that humans are notoriously prone to reason in ways that conflict with the rules of logic, the rationality assumption also requires a deterministic world that does not really exist.

The role of determinism in accidents has probably never been expressed more clearly than in the axioms of industrial safety, of which the first reads:

> The occurrence of an injury invariably results from a completed sequence of factors – the last one of these being the accident itself. The accident in turn is invariably caused or permitted directly by the unsafe act of a person and/or a mechanical or physical hazard. (Heinrich *et al.* 1980, p. 21)

Yet the belief in the existence of a cause and in our ability to find the cause does not automatically bring "human error" to the fore. Before the mid-1950s, people were quite satisfied if and when a technical cause was found, i.e., that something had broken or did not work. Indeed, much of technology was previously unreliable, at least relative to our present standards, and it was therefore reasonable to look for the cause there. This changed drastically around the 1950s when the availability of affordable digital technology made it possible for many processes to be controlled without relying on humans. As a result, the speed with which things could be done increased significantly – and continues to increase to this day. The effects of computerization, added to those of mechanization, centralization, and automation (Hollnagel & Woods 2005), however, meant that humans were faced with a new world of work for which they were ill suited. In a paradoxical way, technology again became limited by human performance, not on the levels of tracking and regulation of processes, but on the levels of monitoring and planning.

Human factors engineering evolved as a way of solving these problems, and with that the widely accepted view that the human operator was a weak link in the control of processes and in socio-technical systems in general. Accident investigations often seemed to assume that the process as such was infallible, or would have been had the operators not done something wrong. It was therefore natural to stop the analyses once a "human error" had been identified. This was elegantly expressed by Perrow (1984):

> Formal accident investigations usually start with an assumption that the operator must have failed, and if this attribution can be made, that is the end of serious inquiry. Finding that faulty designs were responsible would entail enormous shutdown and retrofitting costs; finding that management was responsible would threaten those in charge, but finding that operators were responsible preserves the system, with some soporific injunctions about better training. (p. 146)

The first axiom of industrial safety, which obviously is no more than an expression of the accepted wisdom among practitioners, expresses both the assumption about reverse causation and the assumption that "human errors" are the root causes of accidents. As Perrow demonstrates, this view is singularly non-constructive for accident analysis.

The Representation of Risk

The practical need is also created by the way in which risk assessments are done. The conventional representation of a scenario used in risk analysis is a forward-branching binary tree, such as the one shown in Figure 9.2. The top row shows the sequence of events that is being considered, and the tree shows how the success or failure of an event may lead the scenario in one direction or another.

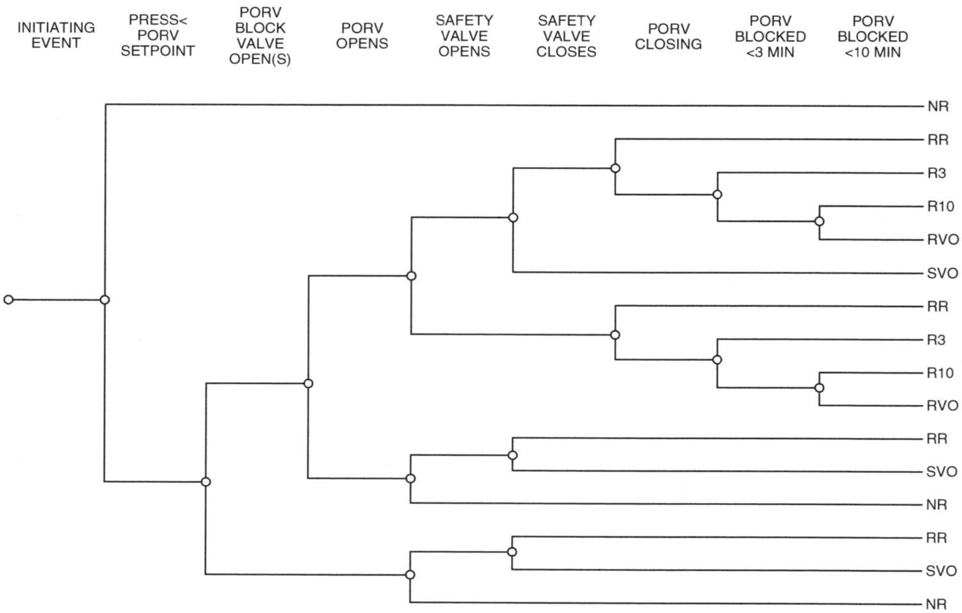

Figure 9.2 Example of an event tree

The event tree was developed to describe combinations of component failures. Each node thus represents the two possible outcomes of an event, either success (traditionally the upward branch) or failure (traditionally the downward branch). In the case that an event represents a human action, the downward branch corresponds to "human error," i.e., the failure somehow to carry out the action as required. In Human Reliability Assessment this led to the notion of "human error" probability, espoused by safety analysts and detested by psychologists (see Dougherty 1990; Hollnagel 1993a; Kirwan 1994 for various views on this).

The Flawless Process

If processes or functions are flawless, i.e., if they always function correctly in an algorithmic fashion, then there is clearly need of an explanation when something goes wrong. Flawless processes unfortunately belong to the ideal world and are conspicuously absent from the real. For instance, an algorithm may mathematically or logically be flawless (cf. the notion of the Turing machine; Turing 1963), but the implementation of the algorithm is rarely so. Despite that, computers, and information-processing systems, are often expected to be the actual embodiment of ideal processes. Indeed, it is only because of human fallibility that programs do not work as they should.

When the information-processing metaphor was adopted, first by psychology and later by cognitive science, it naturally led to the notion that human cognition, seen as human information processes, always should be correct. When that was not the case, and the evidence was quite overwhelming, it was "logical" to look for sources of possible failures in what should have been a flawless process. These sources were at one time proposed as outright error mechanisms (e.g., Rasmussen *et al.* 1981), which is an ironical misuse of the concept of a flawless process (to wit, the error mechanism itself) to explain why information processes were imperfect.

Yet error and "human error" are only necessary if processes are flawless, i.e., if it is assumed that everything always goes right. If instead we assume that processes or functions always are variable, then that variability may by itself be sufficient to account for the occurrence of unwanted outcomes. For example, if a theory of memory (or rather, of remembering) assumes that recall is reproductive, then incorrect recall requires a separate explanation, i.e., a process over and above that of memory itself. If, on the other hand, the theory assumes that recall is reconstructive, then "errors" are inevitable as a logical consequence of reconstruction, thereby eliminating the need of separate mechanisms. From this point of view, the need of "human error" as an explanatory concept is an artifact of the underlying assumption of a flawless process. On the other hand, if we accept that cognition always is approximate, then there is no need for "error" in cognition as such.

THE PRAGMATICS OF ERROR

From a pragmatic point of view it cannot be denied that humans quite often, and sometimes regularly, do things that they did not intend to do, leading to undesired consequences – or the failure to achieve the desired consequences. Irrespective of the above differences it is worthwhile to look more closely at what is required to conclude that an error (in either sense) occurred. When viewed from the perspective of the acting individual there seem to be at least three intuitive parts to any definition of "human error":

- There needs to be a clearly specified *performance standard* or *criterion* against which a deviant response can be measured.
- There must be an *event* or an *action* that results in a measurable *performance shortfall* such that the expected level of performance is not met by the acting agent.
- There must be a degree of *volition* such that the person had the opportunity to act in a way that would not be considered erroneous.

Each of these characteristics of "human errors" has proved controversial and the basic areas of disagreement are considered in more detail below. From the perspective of the acting person all of them are necessary conditions for a "human error" to occur, although this may not be true from other points of view. Together, they may also constitute a sufficient set of conditions.

The Criterion Problem

A "human error" can only be said to exist if a clear performance standard can define the criteria for an acceptable response. In an ideal world, performance criteria are specified prior to the action since otherwise the status of the action becomes nothing more than a value judgment (Woods *et al.* 1994). In general, two broad classes of response criteria have been used by investigators: externalized verifiable models in which "human errors" are defined relative to criteria of objective correctness, and internalized verifiable frameworks in which "human errors" are defined relative to criteria such as transient intentions, purposes, and goal structures of the acting individual.

The use of an external criterion can be illustrated by Miller and Swain's (1987) proposition that "human error" should be defined as: "any member of a set of responses that exceeds some limit of acceptability. It is an out-of-tolerance action where the limits of performance are defined by the system." In this definition "human error" refers to an observable and verifiable action, rather than to the person's own experience of having made an error. This definition thus corresponds to the categories of "error-as-cause" and "error-as-consequence," but not to the category of "error-as-action."

In contrast to that cognitive psychology and human factors have tended to prefer definitions of "human error" that refer to internalized criteria such as the temporary intentions, purposes, and goal structures of the acting individual. From this basis it is possible to define two basic ways that an action can go wrong. A "human error" can occur in the case where the intention to act is adequate but the actions fail to achieve the goal, or in the case where actions proceed according to plan but the plan are inadequate (Reason & Mycielska 1982). In the former case the "human error" is conventionally called a *slip*; in the latter it is usually classed as a *mistake* (Norman 1981). It thus refers to the "error as action" category, rather than to any of the two others.

While the use of an internalized or subjective criterion is necessary for the psychological study of "human errors," it is not essential for human factors. The reason for that is simply that the focus of human factors is on actions that result in undesirable consequences, rather than actions that are considered as erroneous by the perpetrator. It is also impossible for a risk analysis to assume anything about what the state of mind of the operators may be and the internalized criterion is therefore only of academic interest. Human factors nevertheless do need models of human cognition and human performance. It is, indeed, necessary that predictions of human performance can refer to appropriate models. Yet the models should represent the essential (requisite) variety of human performance and of the joint cognitive system, rather than elegant but ephemeral theoretical constructions.

Performance Shortfall

Irrespective of whether "human errors" are defined relative to externalized or internalized criteria, most definitions agree that the actions fail to meet some predefined performance standard. There is, however, little consensus on how best to account for the psychological functions that can be used to explain the "human errors." One school of thought adopts a pessimistic interpretation of human performance capabilities, whilst another attempts to account for "human error" on the basis of competent human performance.

It is in good agreement with the tenets of information-processing psychology to have a pessimistic view of human capabilities and conclude that "human errors" provide strong evidence of "design defects" inherent in the information-processing system. The classical expression of the notion of a limited capacity human information processor is epitomized by the so-called Fitts' List, which was originally used to allocate functions as part of the development of an air traffic control system (Fitts 1951).

Workers in these traditions have been at the forefront of a research strand aimed at identifying the "design defects" of human cognition. Once identified, it is assumed that guidelines can be developed to say where the human operator can, and cannot, be trusted with the care of complex plant and equipment (see, e.g., Human Factors Reliability Group 1985). Although the strict information-processing view has been questioned since the late 1980s, the basic attitude has not changed in any significant way and it is still common to find research and models from this school in the first decade of the twenty-first century.

A more optimistic viewpoint emphasizes that most "human errors" have their origins in processes that perform a useful and adaptive function. Such approaches take a much more beneficial view of tendencies for human cognition to go wrong and relate "error mechanisms" to processes that underpin intelligent cognitive functioning and especially the human ability to deal with complex ambiguous data forms that are characterized by a high degree of uncertainty. This view has an equally long history and several classical descriptions of decision-making have challenged the orthodoxy of the rational decision-maker, the *homo economicus*. The best-known examples are the concepts of *satisficing* (Simon 1957) and "muddling through" (Lindblom 1959). This is also the basis for Resilience Engineering (Hollnagel *et al.* 2006).

It is not difficult to argue that, of the two descriptions, one is more realistic than the other, simply because it corresponds better to what people actually do. In the optimistic view, the shortcomings are not due to specific information-processing limitations but rather to the characteristics of the overall process. The muddling-through types of decision-making, or *satisficing*, have evolved to be effective in real-life situations. Although they do not meet the normative demands of performance, they work well enough in a sufficiently large number of cases to guarantee the survival of the decision-maker. A more recent example of the same principle is the description of performance as entailing efficiency–thoroughness tradeoffs (Hollnagel 2004) and the concept of sacrificing decisions (Dekker 2006).

Volition

The final definitive characteristic of "human errors" concerns the requirement that the acting agent has the opportunity to perform in a way that would be considered appropriate. Thus, as Zapf *et al.* (1990) have observed, it is unreasonable to speak of "human errors" unless the person had some way of avoiding the action. If something is unavoidable, then the cause should rather be attributed to features of the socio-technical system such as technological failures, management oversights, etc. These may, of course, turn out to be due to a "human error" or an incorrect judgment by a person, but that person will most certainly not be the one who is caught up in the situation.

It is now widely recognized that the working and organizational conditions are a common factor in a large number of accidents. As the view on "human errors" gradually became more refined, it was acknowledged that incidents usually evolved through a conjunction of several failures and factors, and that many of these were conditioned by the context. This has been developed into the notion of people at the "sharp end" of a system (Reason 1990; Woods *et al.* 1994) as contrasted with people at the "blunt end." The people at the "sharp end" are those who interact with the processes in their roles as operators, pilots, doctors, physicians, dealers, etc. They are also the people who are exposed to all the problems in the control of the system, and who often have to compensate for them during both normal and abnormal operating conditions. The people at the "blunt end" are those who are somehow responsible for the conditions met by people at the sharp end, but who are isolated from the actual operation – and hence are deprived of effective feedback. They may be managers, designers, regulators, analysts, system architects, instrument providers, etc.

The basic idea in the socio-technical approach is that human performance is a compromise between the demands from the monitored process and the resources and constraints that are part of the working environment. Demands and resources meet at the sharp end, i.e., in the actions that people make. The demands come from the process, but by implication also from the organizational environment in which the process exists. The resources and the constraints are more explicitly given by the organizational context, e.g., in terms of procedures, rules, limits, tools, etc. The cognitive aspects of the actions are characterized using the notions of knowledge, attention dynamics, and strategic factors (Woods *et al.* 1994).

The socio-technical approach is in many ways the inverse of the classic information-processing approach which concentrates on the internal human information-processing mechanisms. The socio-technical approach therefore runs the same danger of focusing on one aspect of the situation, the context, and neglecting the other. Even so, the socio-technical approach is a valuable reminder that we need to consider both cognition and context. Rather than proposing an explanation for "human error," the socio-technical approaches tend to reduce the relative contribution of the operator's cognition to the benefit of the context. In the extreme case, the socio-technical approaches even play down the role of volition. When an undesirable event occurs it is because the cards have been stacked against the person at the "sharp end," who is then subjected to so-called "error-forcing conditions" (Cooper *et al.* 1996). In that case volition plays no role at all, which makes "human error" a meaningless concept, although for a different reason than the usual one.

THE CONSEQUENCES OF A REALISTIC APPRAISAL OF "HUMAN ERROR"

The question was put above of whether "human error" is necessary. The discussion so far has looked at this question from an ontological perspective to determine the need of "human error" as a theoretical concept, and from a pragmatic perspective to determine the need of "human error" as a part of methods for, e.g., accident analysis and risk assessment. The conclusion so far is that the answer is a negative one. In other words, there is no need of "human error," either for theories or methods. It is, as Woods *et al.* (1994) cogently remarked, a judgment in hindsight.

This conclusion echoes the outcome of a similar analysis by Hollnagel and Amalberti (2001), who investigated four arguments against the use of the term "human error." The semantic argument pointed out the fundamental ambiguity in the use of the term "human error," specifically the failure to distinguish between "error-as-action" and "error-as-cause." The philosophical argument referred to the metaphysical status of causation and to the problems in backward causation. The logical argument discussed the arbitrariness of the stop rule in searching for causes, as well as the fact that accident analysis is a matter of expediency as much as of logic. The empirical argument finally illustrated the problems in making observations of "human error," due to the fact that it is necessary to know the context in order to make a reasonably correct classification.

The discussions in this chapter have shown that "human error" is an artifact from both an ontological and a pragmatic perspective. In the ontological sense, "human error" owes it existence to the assumption about flawless cognition or flawless information-processing, which in turn reflects the long tradition of engineering design. If the occurrence of an error means that something has failed, then there clearly is a need to account for how that happened. But if an error is seen as the outcome of a normal variability, then the need for a specific explanation disappears. It is worthwhile pointing out that the concerns about a flawless process came along with human factors engineering and were conspicuously absent in experimental and theoretical psychology prior to that. In the pragmatic sense, "human error" is the result of transferring the methods developed for technological risk analysis to cover also failures of human actions. The clearest example is the representation imposed by the event tree, which implies a binary distinction between correctly and incorrectly executed functions, regardless of whether they are performed by a human or by a machine. This view is exacerbated by the dominance of sequential accident models that predispose analysts to rely on decomposition to understand both accidents and risks, to look for failures of components, and to search for root causes.

Despite the conclusion that the concept of "human error" is not really nor ought to be necessary, it is a manifest fact that it is widely used by researchers and practitioners alike, and that arguments alone are insufficient to change that (cf. Hollnagel 1983). Although there is no pragmatic necessity of "human error," there is an undeniable utility in using the term, if not the concept. Neither should it be neglected that human actions in many cases play a significant role in how accidents happen. It is therefore necessary to consider two consequences of the conclusion reached here. One concerns the utility of the term "human error," which will lead to its continued use for the foreseeable future. The other concerns how theories and models of human behavior should be expressed in order to make the concept of "human error" superfluous. Each of these consequences will be considered briefly below.

The Utility of "Human Error"

One of the practical problems in the use of the term "human error" is that it can mean different things. As Figure 9.1 shows, at least three interpretations are possible. Even though the common underlying sense is that a "human error" refers to an incorrectly performed human action as the cause of an unwanted outcome, it is clearly not very practical if this has several different meanings. It is first of all an obstacle to effective and precise communication, particularly since people take for granted that their own interpretation is automatically shared by others. Second, it is a problem for measurements and statistics, since it leaves uncertain what is actually being counted (e.g., Dekker 2001). And third, it is a hindrance for learning, since the preoccupation with finding "human error" means that the search for alternative – and potentially more effective – explanations is abandoned (e.g., Perrow 1984; Woods & Cook 2002).

The practical basis for the utility of "human error" is that people regularly do things that in one way or another are wrong and which may lead to unwanted consequences. The "wrongness" may be subjective and therefore only noticed by the acting person, or intersubjective and noticed by others as well. Each of us will several times a day experience that we have done something we did not intend to do or not done something we did intend to do (e.g., Reason & Mycielska 1982). Most of these cases concern trivial matters, such as making a typing error or forgetting to buy something at the supermarket, but in some cases there may be a serious effect on what we are doing and perhaps even consequences for others. The "slips and lapses" of everyday actions are easily explained in a number of ways, such as lack of experience, confusing work layout, conflicting demands, insufficient information, etc. In most cases, people fortunately realize what has happened in time to recover from the failure and therefore avoid any significant consequences (Dorieau *et al.* 1997).

As the utility of "human error" lies in the description of the ways in which something can be done wrongly, the issue is how best to describe the manifestations of "human error" or "error-as-action." There is an indisputable need for a practical vocabulary in order to be able to describe such failures in a consistent manner. The term "human error" is, however, of little use both because it is a catchall category and because it confuses actions and causes. What is needed is actually not a theory of "human error" as such, but rather a consistent classification of manifestations. Fortunately, such a classification is not hard to come by. The best-known example is the traditional Hazard and Operability (HAZOP) technique, which in the early 1960s came into use in the engineering disciplines as a way of analyzing all the possible outcomes of equipment failure analysis. The basis of a HAZOP is a set of guidewords that help the analyst to identify all the possible ways in which a function can fail. The guidewords are juxtaposed to all significant functions in order to make the analyst to consider whether such a combination could occur. The guidewords that are used to look for problems are "no," "less," "more," "as well as," "other than," "reverse," and "part of." If, for instance, the function is the opening of a valve, the HAZOP procedure demands that the analyst considers whether "not opening," "opening less," "opening more," etc., may possibly happen (Harms-Ringdahl 2001).

The HAZOP guidewords can obviously be used more or less directly to describe human performance, and several suggestions have been presented for a "human" HAZOP. Once this stance has been adopted, it soon becomes obvious that most classifications of "human error" fail to separate in a consistent manner descriptions of manifestations ("error-as-action") from descriptions of potential explanations ("error-as-cause"). A suggestion to improve this situation is to make a clear distinction between error phenotypes and error genotypes (Hollnagel 1993b), borrowing two terms from biology. Here the phenotype is the manifestation of "human errors," i.e., how they appear in overt action, how they can be observed, hence the empirical basis for their classification. Similarly, the genotype is functional characteristics of human cognition (or of the human mind) that are assumed to be a contributing cause of the "human error." In practice, it turns out that there is only a limited number of ways in which something can be done wrongly, referring to descriptive dimensions such as timing, duration, force, direction, magnitude, etc. For an exhaustive description of how this can be used in practice see, e.g., Hollnagel (1998) and Ljung *et al.* (2004).

The importance of maintaining a clear distinction between phenotype and genotype is easily illustrated by considering a simple failure, such as switching on the wrong light in a lecture hall. In many cases the light switches are placed together at the entrance without any clear indication of which switch corresponds to which light. It therefore easily happens that the wrong light is switched on (or off, as the case may be). In the commonly used terminology, the failure to switch on the right light may be classified as either a slip or a mistake, according to the following definition: "(a) *slips and lapses*, in which actions deviate from current intention due to execution failures and/or storage failures . . . and (b) *mistakes*, in which actions may run according to plan, but where the plan is inadequate to achieve its desired outcome . . ." (Reason 1990, p. 53). Yet following these definitions an action can only be classified as a slip or a mistake if the person's intentions are known, i.e., if it is known which plan(s) s/he was trying to carry out. The phenotype or the observable manifestation of the failure is "wrong object" or possibly "wrong direction," referring to the movement of the switch. The slip/mistake classification therefore describes the genotype or cause, rather than the phenotype or failure, and using this to describe the incorrect action is therefore not justifiable.

Making "Human Error" Obsolete

Since "human error" is an artifact of a specific perspective on human action, namely the assumption about flawless performance or flawless processes, it follows that the concept will disappear if a different perspective is adopted. This observation is not new and can be found in several places. Hollnagel (1983) argued that there is no need of a theory of "human error" because the observed discrepancies in performance should be explained by a theory of normal performance rather than specific "error mechanisms." In a similar vein Rasmussen (1986, p. 150) viewed "human error" as "unsuccessful experiments with unwanted consequences," while Reason (1990, p. 1) noted that "far from being rooted in irrational or maladaptive tendencies . . . recurrent error forms have their origin in fundamentally useful psychological processes." Although both Rasmussen and Reason emphasized the utility of making "errors," they still maintained a distinction between "normal" performance and "errors." From a contemporary perspective this distinction is not necessary.

As soon as it is acknowledged that performance always varies and is never flawless, the need of a separate category for "human error" evaporates. It is, indeed, a category mistake as defined by Ryle (1949) since it ascribes to the mind a property that is only meaningful for technological systems, namely, the property of an incorrect process. What is still needed, of course, is some way to account for the variability of human performance. Since we know that the variability is not random, we can look for the regularities (and irregularities) of performance and try to understand the conditions under which they occur. The psychological literature is full of examples of that, for specific mental processes such as concept formation (Bruner *et al.* 1956), problem-solving (Maier 1968), remembering (Reason & Mycielska 1982), decision-making (Tversky & Kahneman 1975), and for human performance in general. A powerful example of the latter is the concept of satisficing (March & Simon 1993), which describes how people usually settle for that which is satisfactory rather than search for that which is optimal. This is related to both the speed–accuracy tradeoff that characterizes perceptual-motor tasks (e.g., MacKay 1982) and to the sacrificing decisions found at the level of organizational behavior (e.g., Woods 2006).

The view that "human errors" are due to the influence of the working conditions on normal performance rather than "error mechanisms," and hence are exogenic rather than endogenic, is also found in the so-called second-generation human reliability assessment (HRA) methods. The phenomenon has been given different names by different methods, such as "error-forcing conditions" (ATHEANA; Cooper *et al.* 1996), performance variability, and common performance conditions (CREAM; Hollnagel 1998), or "Caractéristique Importante de la Conduite Accidentelle" (MERMOS, Bieder *et al.* 1998). This does not deny, of course, that people every now and then make stupid mistakes or do things wrongly for very trivial reasons, such as being inattentive or relying too much on routine. But it does mean that such cases, as well as situations with serious unwanted outcomes, can be accounted for by a theory of the context-dependent variability of normal performance without invoking a special theory of "human error." This also supports the very reasonable position that psychology – and human factors – should study normal performance rather than the exceptions. We need to understand better the variability of everyday performance and the consequences this may have vis-à-vis the activity to be performed (the task). As a second step, but far beyond this level, we also need to consider the ways in which the variability may aggregate over individuals, to account for the nature of social interaction. This does not imply that social interaction and organizational performance can be explained in a reductionist manner, but it does mean that the understanding of individual performance is a necessary contribution for the still distant understanding of organizational performance.

REFERENCES

Bernstein, P. L. (1996). *Against the Gods: The Remarkable History of Risk.* New York: John Wiley & Sons.

Bieder, C., Le-Bot, P., Desmares, P. & Bonnet, J.-L. (1998). *MERMOS: EDF's New Advanced HRA Method.* Proceedings of PSAM-4. London: Springer-Verlag.

Boring, E. G. (1950). *A History of Experimental Psychology* (2nd edn). Englewood Cliffs, NJ: Prentice-Hall.
Bruner, J. S., Goodnow, J. J. & Austin, G. A. (1956). *A Study of Thinking*. New York: John Wiley & Sons.
Campbell, D. T. (1956). Perception as substitute trial and error. *Psychological Review, 63*(5), 330–342.
Campbell, D. T. (1960). Blind variation and selective retention in creative thought as in other knowledge processes. *Psychological Review, 67*(6), 380–400.
Cooper, S. E., Ramey-Smith, A. M., Wreathall, J. *et al.* (1996). *A Technique for Human Error Analysis (ATHEANA)* (NUREG/CR-6350). Washington, DC: US Nuclear Regulatory Commission.
Dekker, S. W. A. (2001). *The Field Guide to Human Error Investigations*. Aldershot: Ashgate.
Dekker, S. W. A. (2006). Resilience engineering: chronicling the emergence of confused consensus. In E. Hollnagel, D. D. Woods & N. G. Leveson (eds.), *Resilience Engineering: Concepts and Precepts*. Aldershot: Ashgate.
Dorieau, P., Wioland, L. & Amalberti, R. (1997). La détection des erreurs humaines par des opérateurs extérieurs à l'action: Le cas du pilotage d'avion. *Le Travail humain, 60*(2), 131–153.
Dougherty, E. M. Jr (1990). Human reliability analysis – where shouldst thou turn? *Reliability Engineering and System Safety, 29*(3), 283–299.
Embrey, D. E. (1994). *Guidelines for Reducing Human Error in Process Safety*. New York: Center for Chemical Process Safety, American Institute of Chemical Engineers.
Fitts, P. M. (ed.) (1951). *Human Engineering for an Effective Air Navigation and Traffic-control System*. Columbus, OH: Ohio State University Research Foundation.
Greenwood, M. & Woods, H. M. (1919). *The Incidence of Industrial Accidents upon Individuals with Special Reference to Multiple Accidents* (British Industrial Fatigue Research Board, Report No. 4). London: HMS.
Hagen, E. (ed.) (1976). Human reliability analysis. *Nuclear Safety, 17*(3), 315–326.
Harms-Ringdahl, L. (2001). *Safety Analysis. Principles and Practice in Occupational Safety* (2nd edn). London: Taylor and Francis.
Heinrich, H. W., Petersen, D. & Roos, N. (1980). *Industrial Accident Prevention* (5th edn). New York: McGraw-Hill.
Hollnagel, E. (1983). *Position Paper on Human Error*. NATO Conference on Human Error, August 1983, Bellagio, Italy. Available: http://www.ida.liu.se/~eriho/. Accessed December 15, 2005.
Hollnagel, E. (1993a). *Human Reliability Analysis: Context and Control*. London: Academic Press.
Hollnagel, E. (1993b). The phenotype of erroneous actions. *International Journal of Man–Machine Studies, 39*, 1–32.
Hollnagel, E. (1998). *Cognitive Reliability and Error Analysis Method (CREAM)*. New York: Elsevier Science.
Hollnagel, E. (2004). *Barriers and Accident Prevention*. Aldershot: Ashgate.
Hollnagel, E. & Amalberti, R. (2001). The emperor's new clothes or whatever happened to "human error?" In *4th International Workshop on Human Error, Safety, and System Development*. Linköping, Sweden.
Hollnagel, E. & Woods, D. D. (2005). *Joint Cognitive Systems: Foundations of Cognitive Systems Engineering*. Boca Raton, FL: Taylor and Francis.
Hollnagel, E., Woods, D. D. & Leveson, N. G. (2006). *Resilience Engineering: Concepts and precepts*. Aldershot: Ashgate.
Human Factors Reliability Group (1985) *Guide to Reducing Human Error in Process Control*. Warrington: Safety and Reliability Directorate.
Hume, D. (1985). *A Treatise of Human Nature*. Harmondsworth: Penguin Books.
Kirwan, B. (1994). *A Guide to Practical Human Reliability Assessment*. London: Taylor and Francis.
Leveson, N. G. (1995). *Safeware: System Safety and Computers*. Boston, MA: Addison-Wesley.
Lindblom, C. E. (1959). The science of "muddling through." *Public Administration Quaterly, 19*, 79–88.

Ljung, M., Huang, Y., Karlsson, N. & Johannson E. (2004). Close call on the road: a study of driver's near-misses. In *3rd International Conference on Traffic & Transport Psychology*, Nottingham, September 5–9.
MacKay, D. G. (1982). The problems of flexibility, fluency, and speed-accuracy trade-off in skilled behavior. *Psychological Review, 89*(5), 483–506.
Maier, N. R. F. (1968). Reasoning in humans. II. The solution of a problem and its appearance in consciousness. In P. C. Wason & P. N. Johnson-Laird (eds.), *Thinking and Reasoning* (pp. 17–27). Harmondsworth: Penguin Books.
March, J. G. & Simon, H. A. (1993). *Organizations* (2nd edn). Malden, MA: Blackwell.
Miller, D. P. & Swain, A. D. (1987). *Human Error and Human Reliability.* In G. Salvendy (ed.), *Handbook of Human Factors.* New York: John Wiley & Sons.
Norman, D. A. (1981). Categorization of action slips. *Psychological Review, 88*, 1–15.
Perrow, C. (1984). *Normal Accidents: Living with High Risk Technologies.* New York: Basic Books.
Rasmussen, J. (1986). *Information Processing and Human–Machine Interaction.* New York: North-Holland.
Rasmussen, J., Pedersen, O. M., Mancini, G. *et al.* (1981). *Classification System for Reporting Events Involving Human Malfunctions* (Risø-M-2240, SINDOC(81)14). Roskilde: Risø National Laboratory.
Reason, J. T. (1990). *Human Error.* Cambridge: Cambridge University Press.
Reason, J. T. & Mycielska, K. (1982). *Absent-minded? The Psychology of Mental Lapses and Everyday Errors.* Englewood Cliffs, NJ: Prentice-Hall.
Ryle, G. (1949). *The Concept of Mind.* Chicago: University of Chicago Press.
Senders, J. W. & Moray, N. P. (1991). *Human Error: Cause, Prediction, and Reduction.* Hillsdale, NJ: Lawrence Erlbaum Associates.
Simon, H. A. (1957). *Models of Man: Social and Rational.* New York: John Wiley & Sons.
Summala, H. (1985). Modeling driver behavior: a pessimistic prediction? In L.E.A.R.C. Schwing (ed.), *Human Behavior and Traffic Safety* (pp. 43–65). New York: Plenum.
Summala, H. (1988) Risk control is not risk adjustment: the zero-risk theory of driver behavior and its implications. *Ergonomics, 31*(4), 491–506.
Swain, A. D. (1989). *Comparative Evaluation of Methods for Human Reliability Analysis* (GRS-71). Garching, FRG: Gesellschaft für Reaktorsicherheit.
Turing, A. (1963). Computing machinery and intelligence. In E. A. Feigenbaum & J. Feldman (eds.), *Computers and Thought.* New York: McGraw-Hill.
Tversky, A. & Kahneman, D. (1975). Judgment under uncertainty: heuristics and biases. In D. Wendt & C. Vlek (eds.), *Utility, Probability, and Human Decision Making.* Dordrecht: D. Reidel.
Weinberg, G. M. & Weinberg, D. (1979). *On the Design of Stable Systems.* New York: John Wiley & Sons.
Woods, D. D. (2006). Essential characteristics of resilience. In E. Hollnagel, D.D. Woods & N. G. Leveson (eds.), *Resilience Engineering: Concepts and Precepts.* Aldershot: Ashgate.
Woods, D. D. & Cook, R. I. (2002). Nine steps to move forward from error. *Cognition, Technology & Work, 4*(2), 137–144.
Woods, D. D., Johannesen, L. J., Cook, R. I. & Sarter, N. B. (1994). *Behind Human Error: Cognitive Systems, Computers and Hindsight.* Columbus, OH: CSERIAC.
Zapf, D., Brodbeck, F. C., Frese, M. *et al.* (1990). Error working with office computers. In J. Ziegler (ed.), *Ergonomie und Informatik* (Vol. 9, pp. 3–25). Mitteilungen des Fachausschusses 2.3 heft.

CHAPTER 10

Team Cognition

Nancy J. Cooke
Arizona State University, USA
Cognitive Engineering Research Institute, USA

Jamie C. Gorman
New Mexico State University, USA
Cognitive Engineering Research Institute, USA

and

Jennifer L. Winner
Arizona State University, USA
Cognitive Engineering Research Institute, USA

Research and theory on cognitive structure and process occurring inside an individual's head have dominated the last 50 years of scientific psychology. In this regard, cognition has primarily been localized and studied in individuals, and not teams or groups. For the most part, applications of cognitive theories and findings have, as a result, tended to be individual-centric (e.g., cognitive processes involved in using a computer; individual decision-making; situation awareness of one pilot). However, the growing complexity of technological systems and the associated cognitive burden of operating, maintaining, diagnosing, and overseeing such systems has necessitated teams or groups. Problems posed to cognitive engineers in settings ranging from military systems to aviation to nuclear power plant systems depend increasingly on multiple operators interacting with each other and interfacing with complex technology.

There are many examples of errors in *team* cognition, ranging from the relatively mundane failures of business teams to the catastrophic failures seen in the USS *Vincennes* incident (Collyer & Malecki 1998) and in emergency response to Hurricane Katrina (CNN 2005). Because it is clear that assembling a team of experts is not sufficient to produce an expert team (the 2004 US Olympics men's basketball team being a case in point), we need to understand team-level cognition so that we can improve team-level thinking and intervene to prevent team-oriented errors.

Do individually oriented cognitive theories and methods apply to teams? Are teams somehow different from a collection of individuals? How can we measure, assess, and design for *team* cognition? How can team cognition be applied to increase team effectiveness? These are some of the questions to be explored in this chapter.

Handbook of Applied Cognition: Second Edition. Edited by Francis T. Durso.

First, we will define team cognition in order to position this topic within the area of applied cognition and to provide focus for the remainder of the chapter. Team researchers distinguish teams from groups, and in turn, team research and applications from group research and applications. In this chapter we follow convention and define a team as a special type of group. Specifically, Salas *et al.* (1992) define a team as "a distinguishable set of two or more people who interact dynamically, interdependently, and adaptively toward a common and valued goal/object/mission, who have each been assigned specific roles or functions to perform, and who have a limited life span of membership" (p. 4). Thus teams are a type of group that is interdependent and has different, interdependent roles for different team members. A surgical unit is a team, whereas a jury is a group, as is a typing pool. A pilot, co-pilot, and flight attendant constitute a team by this definition, but the faculty of a psychology department functions more as a group, as do religious and political groups. Command-and-control tasks and military planning tasks involve teams. Though these examples seem to clearly distinguish teams from groups, the difference has also been expressed as a continuum (George 1977).

One dimension that tends to distinguish groups from teams is degree of homogeneity in regard to cognitive requirements of individuals. Teams tend to be more heterogeneous than groups by virtue of a division of labor or information (Wittenbaum *et al.* 1996). Related to the notion of a division of labor, heterogeneous team members complement each other, even though they may not be very similar (like vinegar and oil). Nonetheless, they can work well together in the service of some higher-level functionality, such as a common or valued goal.

Much research has been done in the organizational management, computer-supported cooperative work (Olson & Olson, Chapter 19, this volume), and social psychology arenas on small group behavior and decision-making (e.g., Kerr & Tindale 2004). The research in this area tends to be on groups, not teams, and so some theories and findings may not apply. On the other hand, there are probably as many theories and findings that *do* apply to both groups and teams. Thus, in this chapter, we will consider the work on groups that may inform the theories, measures, and applications of team cognition.

Given the Salas *et al.* (1992) definition of a team, what is *team cognition*? In this chapter we define team cognition as cognitive activity that occurs at a team level. This definition deviates from many common views of team cognition in two regards. First, it emphasizes cognitive activity over cognitive structure (i.e., mental models) and second it emphasizes team-level cognition as opposed to aggregated individual level cognition. For instance, planning is a cognitive activity, but independent planning by a team member would not, by definition, involve team cognition. Rather, interdependent planning by two or more team members with a common goal is an example of team cognition. Thus, the team-level stipulation necessitates interaction among the individuals. For example, by definition, team situation awareness is not the respective situation awareness of each individual team member (Endsley & Jones 1997), but is necessarily something based on interaction and probably something emergent.

The difference between an aggregate of individuals and interacting individuals is a very important, and yet often overlooked, distinction in team cognitive research (Cooke & Gorman 2006). These are questions addressed in the remainder of this chapter. How do we measure team cognition? How do we design technology to support this team-level cognition? How do we train teams to support team-level cognition? Answers to these questions are increasingly important as teams continue to supplant individuals in highly complex technological systems (e.g., socio-technical systems; Eason 1988).

The sections in this chapter are organized in a nontraditional sequence that characterizes the historical roots of this new field. Though several precursors to the study of team cognition such as team performance in the industrial/organizational tradition, management in the business tradition, and small-group decision-making in the social psychology tradition are not at all new, the study of team cognition as defined in the preceding paragraphs is no more than 15 years old. Unlike other applied research topics for which application of well-developed theory is the end goal, for team cognition, application has been the main driver. The field was sparked by a need to improve the cognitive activity of teams. Measurement, empirical work, and theoretical development followed. Although existing theory from the precursor disciplines was also influential, the push stemming from application is noteworthy. Therefore, we have decided to structure this chapter accordingly. We start with the applied need, working our way through developments in measurement and empirical work, and finally culminating in the continually evolving theory of team cognition.

THE NEED FOR A SCIENCE OF TEAM COGNITION

We often think of applications in cognitive psychology as the natural product of good cognitive theories. As the story goes, a theory is born, grows, is tested, developed, and eventually matures in the pristine control of a laboratory. When ready, the theory is (sometimes) pushed out into the world of application, often looking for a job and sometimes finding that it is poorly qualified to fit the existing need. This story does not characterize team cognition. While there were theories of team and group decision-making, they did not completely address the problem of team cognition. And there *was* a problem to be addressed.

Indeed, much of the research on team cognition was fueled by a handful of disasters that occurred in a ten-year period and that pointed out problems with team performance in cognitively demanding arenas. The Three Mile Island and Chernobyl nuclear power plant accidents of 1979 and 1986, respectively, both involved problems with the coordinated response of the operating crews in the control rooms (Gaddy & Wachtel 1992). On January 28, 1986 faulty decision-making at the organizational level (i.e., teams of teams) resulted in the mistaken and tragic launch of the space shuttle *Challenger* (Vaughan 1996). Then in July 1988 the USS *Vincennes*, a naval warship, mistakenly shot down an Iranian airbus full of passengers (Collyer & Malecki 1998). This incident, like the others, was tied to a complex web of causes and preexisting system weaknesses (Reason 1997), but also like the others, was partially attributed to coordination problems in command-and-control decision-making.

These events of the 1980s highlighted the complexity of our human–technological systems, not only in terms of the physical system, but also in terms of the socio-cognitive system. It became clear that human decision-making and other cognitive activities were occurring in the context of a complex socio-technical system and that this type of cognition, so foreign from the lab studies that dominate mainstream cognitive psychology, demanded attention. The naturalistic decision-making movement fully appeared on the scene in the 1990s to address cognitive processing in complex dynamic environments (Zsambok & Klein 1997). The cognitive engineering and decision-making technical group of the Human Factors and Ergonomics Society also had its start in the 1990s. The TADMUS (Tactical Decision Making Under Stress) research program of the Navy was initiated in 1990 as a direct result of the *Vincennes* incident with specific naval applications as the target of this research (Cannon-Bowers & Salas 1998). This was the case of a problem in need of a theory. The TADMUS program, for example, fueled some of the first research on team cognition. It is significant that these research efforts were tied heavily to application – to enhancing team decision-making effectiveness in complex cognitive environments. Because an understanding of team cognition is a prerequisite to improving team effectiveness, the theoretical growth has occurred in parallel, but the research has been driven primarily by applied needs. Thus, applications are seen here not as the end result of various research programs, but as drivers of those programs.

Fifteen years have passed since the disasters and ensuing programs that sparked work on team cognition. Theoretical perspectives, methodologies, and research findings have progressed significantly and in parallel with specific applied solutions. With disasters such as the *Vincennes* looming in the recent past, there was no time to wait for a psychology of team cognition. Applications to improve team decision-making, for instance, were needed "yesterday." Thus, the need spawned some initial applied solutions that were based on preliminary conceptions of team cognition primarily drawn from precursor and related disciplines (i.e., social psychology, management, information-processing) and applied by those in industrial/organizational psychology, military psychology, and human factors. Efforts toward these early applications incited many research questions regarding measurement and theories of team cognition. At the same time, the applications evolved with the psychology of team cognition. Thus, in the following sections we highlight some of the early applications of team cognition, saving the more recently applied products of this evolution for the end of the chapter.

Team Training

In applied psychology and specifically industrial/organizational psychology, there has been a long history of applying psychology to training and applying the study of teamwork to improving team training effectiveness (Ford *et al.* 1997). To address the need for training teams in more *cognitively*-laden activities, team training programs began to focus more heavily on the cognitive training of teams.

For instance, Crew Resource Management (CRM) training programs (Helmreich *et al.* 1999; Salas *et al.* 2001) incorporate important interrelated and team-level cognitive skills such as team coordination, communication, and resource allocation. CRM training has been predominant in the aviation community and arose in response to crew-related errors impacting aviation safety. CRM is really a family of instructional strategies, and programs have differed over the years and across organizations in how the training has been implemented (Helmreich *et al.* 1999). CRM training programs have been recently implemented in other team domains such as transportation and medicine (Salas *et al.* 2006). Evaluations of CRM training programs have generally been positive (Salas *et al.* 2006).

Cross-training involves the training of individuals in the job skills associated with other team member positions. Cross-training is generally effective, but the concept of team cognition and, in particular, shared mental models and interpositional knowledge, were drawn upon as explanations for the success of this approach (Volpe *et al.* 1996; Cannon-Bowers *et al.* 1998; Cooke *et al.* 2003). Other training strategies were readily adapted to cognitive tasks and include team leadership training and team self-correction which teaches team members to identify and correct problems in the team without help from an outside instructor (Salas & Cannon-Bowers 2001).

Simulation

In order to study team cognition in a laboratory, it became clear that rich synthetic environments were required to provide empirical test-beds for teams. Althought team test-beds were in place, there was still a need for cognitive simulators for teams. Some initial test-beds grew out of the TADMUS program and were based on tactical decision-making by crews on ships (e.g., TANDEM, Johnston *et al.* 1998).

In the mid- to late 1990s there was a flurry of work devoted to the development of synthetic task environments for teams (Schiflett *et al.* 2004). The Dynamic Distributed Decision-Making Task (DDD, Kleinman *et al.* 1996) was developed as a synthetic version of an Airborne Warning and Control System (AWACS) platform. This synthetic environment has since evolved to simulate a wide range of team tasks (e.g., a snowmobile-based search and rescue mission). Cooke and Shope (2002, 2004) developed a synthetic task environment to simulate Uninhabited Aerial Vehicle (UAV) ground control by a team. This test-bed was unique in its experimenter-friendly design (i.e., affording measurement and manipulation) and its applicability to heterogeneous team tasks in which team members all have very different jobs to do (i.e., navigator, pilot, photographer).

The act of developing these simulations required and generated extensive knowledge about cognitive team tasks in the field. Questions were also raised about the concept of simulator fidelity (Salas *et al.* 1998; Cooke & Shope 2004). As military doctrine changed and concepts such as network-centric warfare became commonplace, the applicability of these test-beds as potential training and interface testing environments also became clear.

Software Tools

Much of the work on decision aids and collaborative tools for teams and groupware had its start in business management and human–computer interaction. This work has been labeled CSCW (Computer Supported Cooperative Work), GDSS (Group Decision Support Systems), and groupware (Olson *et al.* 2001; Olson & Olson, Chapter 19, this volume). These applications were designed to facilitate business meetings, collaborative writing, and organizational decision-making. More specific applications of groupware focused on facilitating the integration of multiple perspectives across a broad decision-making domain (e.g., product development teams, Monplaisir 2002) by improving the ability for collaboration from a distance.

Groupware researchers have experimented with various communication modes for distributed groups such as video, audio, and text (Daft & Lengel 1986) and have examined the impact of groupware technology on decision quality (e.g., McLeod 1992). Indeed the advantages of CSCW applications are dependent on the type of team and task (DeSanctis & Poole 1991).

Some Unanswered Questions

These initial applications for improving team cognition were valuable in identifying research questions and guiding future research and development efforts in team cognition. Team cognition is thus a good example of the problem-driven approach of cognitive engineering.

Interests in team cognition, combined with successful tests of cross-training, gave rise to the concept of the shared mental model and the idea of interpositional knowledge. But there were also questions about scalability of cross-training to large, heterogeneous teams in highly complex settings such as shipboard command-and-control. First, there was the issue of the practicality of cross-training across all positions of a large team (Cooke *et al.* 2003). Second, the practicality of a common mental model to be shared among team members with different roles was also questioned.

Groupware applications provided valuable insight into how distributed decision-making may be facilitated by technology, but it also spawned questions about the costs and benefits of co-located vs. distributed environments. With groupware technology also came an interest in ways to facilitate team situation assessment and group interaction processes associated with group decision-making. Indeed, these were some of the same issues important to those interested in team cognition. However, other questions were raised about differences between small groups and teams and between the "business meeting" and more heterogeneous, interdependent tasks like military command-and-control or hospital emergency room triage.

One very important question kept surfacing: the question of the measurement of team cognition. The answer to this question was central for designing and evaluating the success of training programs, supportive tools and technologies, and even for understanding individual and team differences that may lead to applications in team composition and staffing (Morgan & Lassiter 1992). Further, the measurement problem is not merely about eliciting team cognition from experts to build systems, but also about assessment and diagnosis. In order to target specific team-level cognitive skills for training or design intervention, measures are needed that reveal the deficiencies and strengths of a team and, if possible, the specific sources of these strengths and weaknesses. Accordingly, one of the biggest measurement challenges is to consider how assessment and diagnosis could occur in an embedded, automated, and real-time fashion in an operational setting. We could then monitor team cognition, assess it on the fly, and provide diagnostically appropriate interventions, all in real time. Measurement issues will be discussed in the next section.

MEASURING TEAM COGNITION

Leveraging cognitive work at the individual level, researchers have applied and adapted various individual measurement methodologies to teams. Knowledge elicitation methods have been used to circumscribe the task or domain in terms of the knowledge, skills, and abilities required. Information gleaned from these knowledge elicitation activities is used to construct tests to assess a team with respect to a desired cognitive state. Finally, with a deeper understanding of team cognition in a domain, the researcher can begin to identify diagnostic information for targeted interventions.

Elicitation and Analysis

Knowledge elicitation techniques include observations, interviews, process tracing, and conceptual methods with countless variations within each category (Cooke 1994, 1999). Although knowledge elicitation focuses primarily on knowledge, there are other methods for analyzing the cognition underlying a task more generally. These include cognitive task analysis (Seamster *et al.* 1997) and cognitive work analysis (Vicente 1999). For team cognition, these kinds of measurement activities have been adapted for a variety of purposes, including design of a synthetic task that captures some of the cognitive fidelity of the real task (Gugerty *et al.* 1999; Cooke & Shope 2004), identification of training requirements (Mitchell *et al.* 1993), improvement of team coordination (Klinger & Klein 1999), modeling interactions (Stout *et al.* 1994), and development of assessment metrics (Cooke *et al.* 2001).

For instance, a popular team knowledge elicitation method involves what Cooke (1999) referred to as a "conceptual method," in which judgments of the proximity of domain-relevant concepts to one another are elicited from team members. The set of pairwise judgments can be submitted to multivariate statistical routines, like Pathfinder (Schvaneveldt *et al.* 1989; Schvaneveldt 1990) in order to better visualize "knowledge structure." This approach has been used extensively to examine individual expert-novice differences and specific cognitive constructs such as insight (Durso *et al.* 1994) and has been applied to team cognition in the elicitation of team knowledge and team member mental models (Mohammad *et al.* 2000; Cooke *et al.* 2003) as well as the identification of interaction patterns in teams (Shope *et al.* 2004). In the latter case, the proximities judgments were based on the degree to which two individuals interact.

Assessment and Diagnosis

Although the elicitation and analyses methods provide critical information and are prerequisites for assessment methodologies, they do not alone afford more than qualitative information about team cognition. Thus, questions about how teams compare cognitively, how team cognition develops over time, or the success of interventions to improve team cognition are restricted to qualitative analyses using these methods.

One way to move from description to assessment is to compare the description to a referent or gold standard. For example, a description of team cognition for a high-performing team might be held up as the standard. Alternatively, a standard may be developed directly by subject matter experts (e.g., drawing the "ideal" Pathfinder network). Although the comparison of two descriptions could be done in a qualitative way, there are also quantitative approaches that involve similarity metrics such as correlation coefficients (e.g., Goldsmith *et al.* 1991).

Team process behaviors, which are sometimes associated with team-level cognitive process behaviors, have been assessed in this manner (e.g., Fowlkes *et al.* 1998). That is, expert judges observe and rate team behaviors (e.g., communication, leadership, conflict management) and judges' ratings are assumed to involve implicit comparisons of the team behavior with idealized behavior in the eyes of a judge. However, inter-rater reliability is an issue with generalized ratings of this type. Event-based checklists (e.g., TARGETS; Fowlkes *et al.* 1998) improve observations by grounding them in contextually-relevant events and behaviors (e.g., instead of rating team communication, check whether or not a specific piece of information was passed between team members at a given event). A checklist approach like this is a useful method for assessing the sequencing and timing of the team process behaviors thought to underlie team cognition (Proctor *et al.* 2004).

Team or shared mental models have been assessed primarily through the comparisons of conceptual representations such as those elicited using proximity judgments and represented using Pathfinder (e.g., Stout *et al.* 1999). At the most basic level, the degree to which a mental model is shared by two team members can be estimated through a comparison of the representations of those two team members. For example, Pathfinder similarity can be quantified in terms of proportion of shared links. Accuracy of a conceptual representation can similarly be estimated through comparison with a referent representation.

Situation awareness has been measured using a mixture of subjective, performance-based, and query methods, while team situation awareness has primarily been assessed using aggregate query-based techniques (e.g., SAGAT: Situation Awareness Global Assessment Technique; Endsley 1995) in which queries concerning task- or team-related items are presented to each team member during a break in task performance (Bolstad & Endsley 2003). Team situation awareness is then measured by aggregating (e.g., summing) the accuracy scores of all team members (Endsley & Jones 1997). (However this procedure is contrary to the definition of team cognition offered earlier that is interaction-oriented.) The Situation Present Assessment Method (SPAM; Durso *et al.* 1998) is another query method that has been applied to teams which does not involve separating the team from the visual cues in the situation.

Some Measurement Limitations and Proposed Solutions

The application of measures developed to elicit, analyze, and assess individual cognition to measure team cognition was an important first step, but the jump from individuals to teams brought with it some new measurement challenges (see Table 10.1).

Table 10.1 Some challenges to measuring team cognition and some solutions (Cooke *et al.* 2000, 2004; Gorman *et al.* 2005)

Challenges	Solutions
Measures applicable to heterogeneous teams	Heterogeneous knowledge metrics (e.g., role-specific referents)
Measures that capture emergent cognition	Holistic measures taken at the team level (e.g., consensus ratings)
Holistic, embedded, real-time metrics	Communication pattern analysis
Measures of emergent team situation awareness	CAST: coordinated perception and action of team members in the face of change

The first challenge pertains to the definition of teams offered by Salas *et al.* (1992) especially the part that states that team members have "each been assigned specific roles or functions to perform." Early applications of measurement treated teams as homogeneous and assumed that shared knowledge (or situation awareness, mental models, understanding) is similar knowledge. These metrics have been used to elicit knowledge at the individual level and to examine similarity (and sometimes accuracy) across team members (e.g., Langan-Fox *et al.* 2000). Although this approach seems suited for homogeneous groups like juries, it is less clear how it applies to heterogeneous teams. For example, the concept of "shared mental model" is not straightforward for the anesthesiologist, surgeon, and nurse, or for emergency response team members handling different emergency functions.

Cooke *et al.* (2004) describe knowledge metrics for heterogeneous teams. Their approach derives knowledge referents for each position on the team (e.g., the ideal nurse's knowledge) and assesses positional accuracy for individual team members by comparison of some knowledge output to a role-specific referent. They refer to this as "positional knowledge." "Interpositional knowledge" can similarly be assessed by comparison of each team member's knowledge output with that of each of the other team member's role referents. By examining the team knowledge defined by each of these metrics in high-performing teams, Cooke *et al.* (2003) identified a team task as requiring high degrees of knowledge specialization, partially explaining why cross-training was unsuccessful.

Another characteristic of the metrics that were adapted for measuring team cognition is that they focused on (and for the most part continue to focus on) eliciting and assessing individual knowledge and aggregating (e.g., averaging) results across team members. Not only is the aggregation process questionable for a heterogeneous group (i.e., equating "apples and oranges"), but this approach seems to lose sight of the essence of team cognition. If we view team cognition as an emergent phenomenon, that is, a result that emerges through ongoing interactions among team members, then aggregation-based metrics are unsatisfying. These metrics miss the mark in terms of adaptive interaction on the part of team members that underlies team cognition. But what is the alternative?

One option is to empirically derive the aggregation method, an option realized in social decision scheme literature (Hinsz 1995, 1999). This approach constitutes a more principled aggregation. If there were a leader who dictated the team response, then this would be reflected in the best fitting social decision scheme. Another solution in keeping with the definition of team cognition offered earlier is to focus more on process. Cooke *et al.* (2004) developed "holistic" metrics that do just this. Knowledge is elicited at the team level through a consensus process. For instance, a team, not an individual, will be asked to provide relatedness ratings for pairs of task-related concepts. Results from this holistic approach are different from the aggregate approach as seen in Figure 10.1, in which three-person teams were ranked in terms of aggregate or collective knowledge accuracy or holistic knowledge accuracy (Cooke *et al.* 2004). Though the rank orders are different, the results concerning the validity of one metric over the other are mixed. Indeed, this solution is not completely satisfactory because it assumes that the process used in the consensus task mirrors that of operational team-level cognitive processing, but the consensus process itself may confound the processing. However, this approach does allow for dynamic distribution of team member resources in formulating a team-level response.

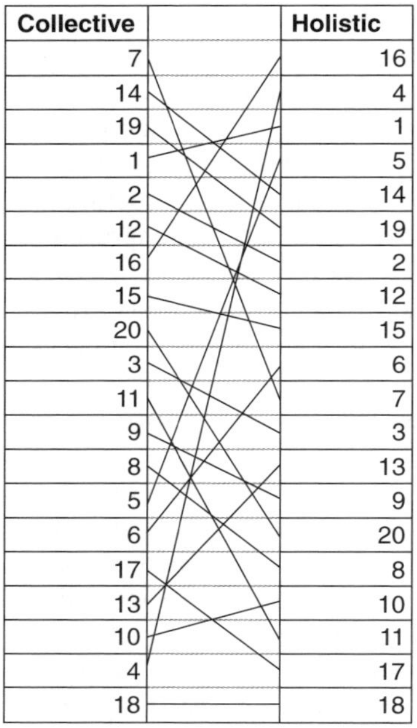

Collective
7
14
19
1
2
12
16
15
20
3
11
9
8
5
6
17
13
10
4
18
Holistic
16
4
1
5
14
19
2
12
15
6
7
3
13
9
20
8
10
11
17
18

Figure 10.1 Teams' rank order according to their collective or holistic task work knowledge (experiment 2, Cooke *et al.* 2004)

Another potential alternative is to measure team cognition through team communication analysis (Kiekel *et al.* 2002). Communications occur naturally in most team tasks, and can thus be thought of as a sort of naturally occurring "think-aloud" and thus a holistic metric of team cognition. Rather than providing merely a "window" to team cognition, communication provides direct access. Team communication is thus an instrument for team cognition, not a representation of it, as is the case for individual think aloud. Many researchers have relied on communication analysis for understanding the cognitive demands and constraints in various task domains in order to generate team-oriented theories of task acquisition or performance (e.g., Kanki & Foushee 1989; Achille *et al.* 1995; Kiekel *et al.* 2004).

As mentioned, most attempts to measure team situation awareness have used aggregate measures that tend to assume homogeneity and do not seem to get at the emergent, dynamically coordinated aspects of teams encountering a quickly changing task environment. An interaction-based method called CAST (Coordinated Awareness of Situation by Teams; Gorman *et al.* 2005) which assesses the patterns of coordinated perception and action that emerge from team member interactions (beyond the static knowledge of team members) when faced with unusual situation constraints or "road blocks" begins to address this limitation.

In summary, measures used to elicit and assess individual knowledge have been applied to team cognition. Whereas this is a useful start, there are limits in extending these metrics to team cognition. In particular, the emergent quality of team cognition that accompanies interactions of heterogeneous team members is not captured by individually-oriented and aggregation approaches. Team-level properties, including team cognition, are not necessarily reducible to the summed properties of heterogeneous team members who do not interact. In this regard, metrics relying on consensus judgments, communication, and coordination have potential for the measurement of team cognition.

EMPIRICAL WORK ON TEAM COGNITION

Early empirical efforts to address the problem of team cognition were conducted in social psychology (e.g., small-group decision-making) and business management with applications to groups that were relatively homogeneous such as juries or business teams (Steiner 1972; Davis 1973). Some concepts relevant to team cognition such as social loafing, social decision schemes, and transactive memory have been studied in this context. Much of the empirical work examined team process and performance, but there was always a strong emphasis on team cognition. In particular, the concepts of shared mental models and team situation awareness received the most attention (e.g., Stout *et al.* 1996). In the typical study variables are manipulated (e.g., distributed vs. co-located environments, workload, team structure, communication mode) and their impact on team performance and cognition are noted.

Empirical Work on Small-Group Decision-Making

Social loafing is a phenomenon in which group size has deleterious effects on group output (Karau & Williams 2001). Specifically, the efforts (or motivations) exhibited by individual team members are inversely related to group size (Latan *et al.* 1979), leading to reduced collective output by the team as a whole. In an additive task, e.g., rope pulling, adding more and more pullers actually decreases the collective amount of exertion in proportion to the summed pulling strengths of individual rope pullers (Schoggen 1989). According to the social loafing effect, the proportion of agents expending maximal effort can be expected to drop as group size increases. Interestingly, this effect cannot be explained in terms of overall process or coordination costs (cf. Steiner 1972). For instance, researchers have replicated the social loafing effect while controlling for process loss (e.g., Ingham *et al.* 1974; Latan *et al.* 1979) by simulating a coordinated task when in reality only one individual was participating. One possible explanation for the social loafing effect is that the level of social pressure for a given task remains constant regardless of group size, and that social loafing manifests itself as this constant level of social pressure is distributed over larger groups of agents.

A number of factors have been studied as possible mediators of the social loafing effect on group output (Karau & Williams 2001). For example, the requirement of individual accountability in a group setting may actually reduce the social loafing effect (Tata 2002) with direct consequences for group performance (cf. Harcum & Badura 1990). Group or team cohesion may also be related to social loafing in that the more cohesive the group, the less inclined individuals would be to loaf. In fact, Everett *et al.* (1992) found a negative relationship between group cohesion and social loafing for female, but not male, swim teams. Social exchange relationships (e.g., leadership, dominance) may also be a useful factor for mediating the effects of social loafing (Murphy *et al.* 2003). Perhaps most germane to the study of team cognition, increased task interdependence (i.e., heterogeneity) in highly critical (meaningful) task domains have been related to decreased social loafing (Wageman 1999), such that agents involved in these types of groups may expend more, rather than less effort proportional to group size. The increased interdependency among individuals in teams may counteract the diffusion of responsibility, however social loafing by any one team member can lead to a loss of integrity for the team.

Overall, social loafing results contradict the intuition that bigger teams are better or more effective teams. These results also suggest that social loafing may affect team cognition of homogeneous teams more than heterogeneous teams. They also support the importance of team member interdependence.

Decision-making in small groups has also been a topic of study for some time originating with the early work of Lewin (1947, 1951). Many others followed, including Festinger (1954) who studied social comparison, and Janis (1972) who investigated groupthink. Festinger (1954) found that members of a group will likely distribute themselves in terms of decision input based upon the decision-making prowess of their counterparts. Through social comparisons to individuals of higher ability (an upward comparison), a group decision can in some sense be of a higher quality than the aggregate of individual decision-making abilities. On the contrary, Steiner's (1972) model promotes the notion that this maximum is rarely, if ever, attained due to process loss that occurs during the group interaction process. Social decision scheme theory (Davis 1973) uses these sorts of views to establish a priori group decision models and then examines the deviation of an observed group decision from a decision based on combining individual inputs via these decision models (e.g., Hinsz 1995, 1999) and it has been established that groups do use explicit or implicit decision rules when making choices, such as majority rules (see Hastie & Kameda 2005). Researchers have recently used signal detection theory to illustrate that the decision rule employed by a group can influence the quality of their choice (Sorkin *et al.* 1998, 2001).

There are a number of factors that influence decision-making by groups. Stasser and Titus (1985) made a distinction between shared or common information, which is available to all team members, and unshared information, which is initially available to individual team members. They found that groups discussed common information more so than information initially held by only one team member. Stasser and Titus (1987) reported a follow-up study in which they manipulated the amount of information that groups had to consider and the percentage of shared information. Although groups with a low load and a low percentage of shared information recalled a larger portion of the unshared items, overall, none of the groups was successful in distributing the unshared information. Larson *et al.* (1994) manipulated the perceived importance of the decision and found that not only did groups fail to discuss the majority of the unshared information, but neither task importance nor training lessened the emphasis on shared information. Still, other factors have been found to increase group discussion of unshared information including being face-to-face (rather than distributed) with low reliance on memory (Hollingshead 1996), as well as having assigned roles or areas of expertise (Stewart & Stasser 1993; Stasser *et al.* 2000).

Group decisions can also be influenced by the manner by which information is presented to the group. In studies assessing the decision-making of mock juries, the order of criminal charges has been found to influence group choices (Nagao & Davis 1980; Davis *et al.* 1984). Additionally, jury verdicts may be influenced by the number of changes (Greene & Loftus 1981; Tanford & Penrod 1982, 1984) and the sequence and the timing of polling techniques (Davis *et al.* 1993). There is also evidence to suggest that the number of hung juries is related to anonymity in polling and jury size (Kerr & MacCoun 1985). To summarize, groups are inclined to discuss shared rather than unshared information and group outcomes may be influenced by the manner by which information is presented to the group.

The concept of individual memory has also been extended to small groups. In fact, decision scheme theory described in the previous paragraph has been applied to group memory (Hinsz 1990). A *transactive memory* system is group memory considered in terms of group members' knowledge about themselves and their knowledge about the capabilities of other group members (Wegner 1986). Numerous researchers have found a positive relationship between transactive memory systems and group performance (Liang *et al.* 1995; Hollingshead 1998; Moreland 1999; Moreland & Myaskovsky 2000). For example, Liang *et al.* (1995) found that participants who trained as a group in a radio assembly task had significantly lower assembly errors and better recall of the procedure (an index of transactive memory) than participants who trained individually.

Efforts have been made to identify the source of the transactive memory benefit to groups. Hollingshead (1998) investigated the effect of communication on learning and recall of words in transactive memory systems. In a study comparing recall in dyads of dating couples or strangers, the effect of communication on word recall was moderated by the nature of the dyad's relationship. Moreland and Myaskovsky (2000) conducted a study to clarify the role of communication in the radio assembly task and concluded that the increase in performance found for groups was not the result of communication during training. Groups trained without the chance to communicate performed as well as those who could communicate once they were able to receive information regarding others' skills. This finding is counter to the suggested centrality of team interaction. Similarly, Rulke and Rau (2000) found that groups with high transactive memory declared domains of expertise early in group interaction, and evaluations of others' expertise and ability increased in frequency over time.

In support of interaction, shared (overlapping) resource knowledge in transactive memory systems has been proposed to elevate the memory capacity of a group to a level greater than the sum of individual agents (Wegner 1986; Liang *et al.* 1995; but see also Pavitt 2003). This result suggests that transactive memory systems are more efficient than systems in which agents do not interact, instead aggregating their memory capacity based on static, individual-level knowledge. In accordance with Steiner's (1972) model of process loss, however, this efficiency may break down as group size increases (e.g., Pavitt 2003; Wittenbaum 2003) due to exponential increases in establishing resource knowledge. Although transactive memory systems may indeed be advantageous constructs for studying smaller groups, the adaptability of transactive memory systems to larger organizations raises some scalability issues. Other factors that may also affect the viability of transactive memory systems include differential information distribution (Fraidin 2004), gender stereotyping in resource knowledge (Hollingshead & Fraidin 2003), and mismatched distribution of expertise across agents (Hollingshead 2000, 2001).

Shared Mental Models

Numerous researchers have reported that team mental model similarity influences team processes and performance (Hinsz *et al.* 1997; Stout *et al.* 1999; Mathieu *et al.* 2000).

Specifically, the shared mental model literature indicates that high similarity within a team should lead to preemptive process behaviors in which one team member anticipates the needs of another (Duncan *et al.* 1996; Wittenbaum *et al.* 1996; Entin & Serfaty 1999) and thus effective team performance (Converse *et al.* 1991; Rouse *et al.* 1992; Stout 1995; Blickensderfer *et al.* 1997; Mathieu *et al.* 2000). Additionally, team member mental models are assumed to converge over time because of increased intra-team interaction (Clark & Brennan 1991; Rentsch & Hall 1994; Liang *et al.* 1995; Moreland 1999; Levesque *et al.* 2001). However, the results have been mixed.

Mathieu *et al.* (2000) reported a study assessing the influence of shared mental models on team process and performance. In the context of a personal computer-based flight combat simulation, both task- and team-based mental models were assessed. Though it was determined that both task- and team-based mental models were positively related to team process and performance, neither type of mental model converged within a team over time. Along these lines, Levesque *et al.* (2001) found that the similarity of mental models decreased over time, which may be functional for teams with highly specialized roles (Cooke *et al.* 2003).

Smith-Jentsch *et al.* (2001) examined convergence over a longer timeframe. They assessed mental model similarity and accuracy for teamwork knowledge through card-sorting techniques and comparison to an empirically-derived referent. They found that similarity with an expert model was higher for Navy personnel with higher rank. Rentsch and Klimoski (2001) found that in a naturalistic setting, factors associated with team homogeneity increased intra-team similarity for teamwork knowledge and in some cases indirectly affected team effectiveness (measured subjectively by the team members).

Mental models have also been "manipulated" through cross-training (e.g., Cooke *et al.* 2003) or information available to participants through displays or instructions. In some of these cases, however, though the manipulation impacted the knowledge or mental model, it did not impact team performance (Cooke *et al.* 2003; Cooke *et al.* 2004).

Thus there are generally mixed results concerning the relationship between shared mental models and team performance. As Cooke *et al.* (2000) point out, there is probably some confusion stemming from the ambiguity of terminology. What is the scope of the team *mental model*? A mental model (Rouse & Morris 1986) may be held at the individual level that is relevant to the task or aspects of the task, the team, or team member beliefs (Mohammad *et al.* 2000). Even the term *sharing* can imply either knowledge similarity among team members in which everyone knows the same thing or knowledge distribution (see Figure 10.2). The measurement issues described earlier follow in the footsteps of the ambiguous conceptualizations with the role of similarity, accuracy, and applicability to heterogeneous teams (Cooke *et al.* 2000; Smith-Jentsch *et al.* 2001). As a result of this early research, the concept of a *shared mental model*, whereby team members are thinking the same thing, has been tempered by use of the concept of *team mental model*, in which team member knowledge is not overlapping, but rather complementary to a degree such that all domain knowledge is represented by the summed knowledge of team members (Klimoski & Mohammed 1994; Cooke *et al.* 2000).

Mixed results may also reflect the variability inherent in tasks and teams. For example, extremely heterogeneous teams may become increasingly dissimilar in regard to their knowledge over time as team members become more specialized. Also, the overlap of individual mental models is likely to be greater for highly structured tasks (Kraiger & Wenzel 1997). Finally, even if all of these measurement, task, and team factors are taken

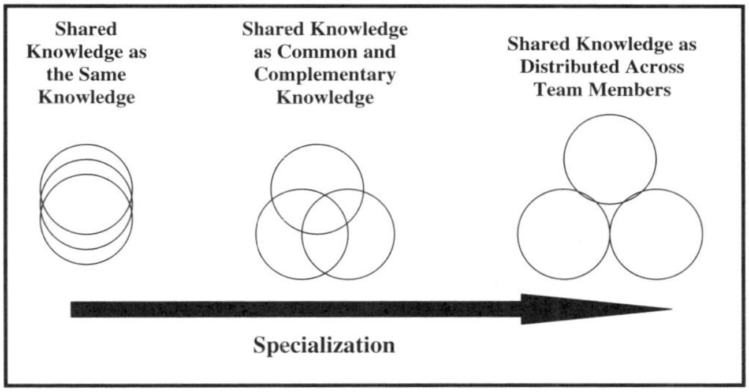

Figure 10.2 Varieties of shared knowledge

into account, it is not clear that the "knowledge construct" is strongly tied to team performance. For example, the fact that highly experienced individuals within the same domain are more cognitively similar than novices has been illustrated in multiple domains such as combat flight maneuvers (Schvaneveldt *et al.* 1985) and computer programming (Cooke & Schvaneveldt 1988); however, this does not mean that the similarity or accuracy of a mental model causes performance. Alternatively, it may be that processes leading to shared cognition are more significant than an outcome reflecting a shared idea (Kameda *et al.* 1997; Ensley & Pearce 2001; Gorman *et al.* 2004; Cooke & Gorman 2006), a point we shall revisit in our later theoretical discussion.

Team Situation Awareness

Situation awareness (SA) at the individual level has been a topic of much recent interest, stemming from the world of aviation and phenomena recognized as important by pilots (Fracker 1989; Wellens 1993; Endsley 1995; Orasanu 1995; Robertson & Endsley 1995; Durso & Gronlund 1999; Durso *et al.*, Chapter 7, this volume). Endsley (1988) provided a commonly cited definition of SA as "the perception of the elements in the environment within a volume of time and space, the comprehension of their meaning, and the projection of their status in the near future" (p. 97). However, the concept of SA originates from the pilots who used it to label critical cognition in the highly dynamic aviation environment. Results in this area have shown that early collection and exchange of information, along with planning, are linked with high levels of SA (Orasanu 1995) and that high levels of SA are linked with high levels of performance.

What, then, is *team* SA? In order to address the issue of heterogeneous teams with different SA requirements, some have distinguished between shared (i.e., common to team members) SA requirements and individual SA requirements, each of which is important to team SA (Endsley & Jones 1997). So, team SA has been primarily defined in terms of the collection of the SA (shared or unique) of individual team members.

Team SA has been challenging to measure because the situation often changes more rapidly than individuals can be questioned. Bolstad and Endsley (2003) reported results for a study involving US Army officers participating in a simulation exercise. SAGAT, administered using the freeze technique, was used to measure each individual's SA. Composite scores were created by averaging the individual query score for each SAGAT stop. Results indicated that accuracy on SA queries varied *across* cells in the Objective Force structure and was not shared to the degree expected *within* cells; however, there was no information on performance provided and it is not clear whether these teams required a common understanding of the information to do their jobs. Cooke *et al.* (2004) measured team SA in a UAV ground control task using individual queries, as well as a consensus procedure. Though they found that collective team SA correlated positively with team performance, they were concerned that the results were an artifact of the participants' experience with the experimental procedure. That is, the measure was not as pertinent to the team's awareness of the situation, as much as the awareness of the experimental procedure (i.e., memorizing queries).

The two constructs of shared mental models and team SA are theoretically linked in that shared mental models or a long-term shared understanding of the task, team, or equipment are thought to be important factors in team SA, and specifically the construction of a team situation model (Cooke *et al.* 2001). Therefore, some empirical work has examined manipulations that would foster both shared mental models (e.g., via shared information) and team SA (e.g., via shared displays) in order to improve team performance (Bolstad & Endsley 1999).

Empirical work on team SA is challenging given the difficulty pinning down a precise and agreed definition and a satisfactory method of measurement. Some ideas and measures emerging from newer theoretical perspectives (e.g., CAST; Gorman *et al.* 2005) may provide reasonable alternatives to measurement.

Summary of Empirical Work

Our understanding of team cognition has benefited greatly from research on small-group decision-making. Findings in this literature tend to be process-focused. For instance, groups tend to discuss shared information more than unshared information; however, manipulations that increase or highlight group heterogeneity tend to lessen this effect. Studies in the areas of shared mental models and team situation awareness have generated findings suggesting that common or shared knowledge is better, although the connection between common knowledge and performance is not altogether straightforward. Transactive memory results also implicate communication processes and interaction more so than the shared mental model literature. However, there are also many differences between these small-group studies and team studies ranging from type of task and team (heterogeneous vs. homogeneous) to type of manipulations or interventions favored. There are also some fundamental differences in the way the two camps have conceptualized team cognition, a topic to which we now turn.

THEORETICAL PERSPECTIVES ON TEAM COGNITION

As we have described, research efforts in team cognition were initiated by need and quickly followed with application, measures, and empirical work. These early developments were inspired by theory, measures, research, and applications in the closely related fields of social, industrial-organizational, and cognitive psychology with close ties to specific areas of small-group behavior, organizational management, groupware, and information-processing. Theoretical developments were no different, with early perspectives borrowing heavily from related disciplines whereby there was some convergence on a theory of team cognition. We refer to this generic perspective as the I-P-O (Input-Process-Output) perspective. This has been the dominant perspective on team cognition. However, recent inquiries have led to some new ways of thinking about team cognition.

The I-P-O Perspective

The earliest models of team cognition were heavily influenced by process-oriented theories coming from the social psychology of small groups and industrial-organizational psychology. For example, Tushman (1979) found that high-performing work teams will match their coordination structure to the changing demands of their work. For instance, under high levels of uncertainty and workload, decentralized coordination structure emerged in order to adaptively distribute resources. Katz (1982) reported that although a stable or fixed coordination structure may be preferable in the short-to-medium term, that same stability can have deleterious effects on team information-processing over the long term if it is not flexible enough to handle the influx of new information. In this tradition Hackman (1987) suggested that interaction processes could be studied as mediators of the effects of individual, group, and environmental factors on team output and cohesiveness. This approach to understanding team performance was called the I-P-O (input-process-output) framework for work team productivity and also became the standard model for early conceptualizations of team cognition.

Applying the I-P-O framework to team cognition, cognition at the team level is analogous to cognition at the individual level, insofar as knowledge structure is distributed over team members, instead of over long-term memory, and is operated on by team process behaviors, instead of memory processes. A generic I-P-O framework is presented in Figure 10.3.

As shown in Figure 10.3, factors at the individual level (e.g., team member demographics, Rentsch & Klimoski 2001; cognitive model similarity, Adelman *et al.* 1986), at the group level (e.g., inter-team member perceptions, Dirks 1999; Fiore *et al.* 2001), and at

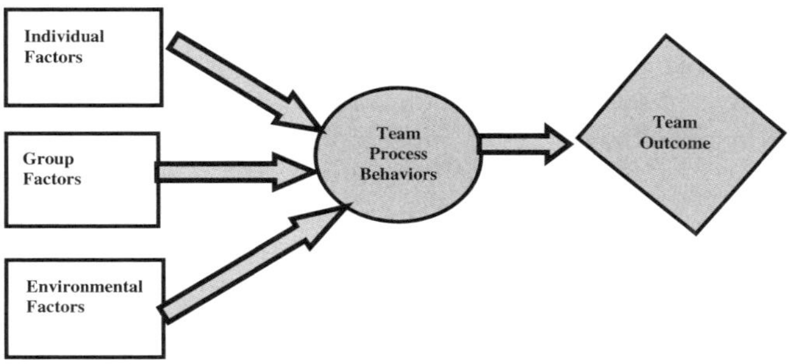

Figure 10.3 A Generic Input-Process-Output (I-P-O) framework

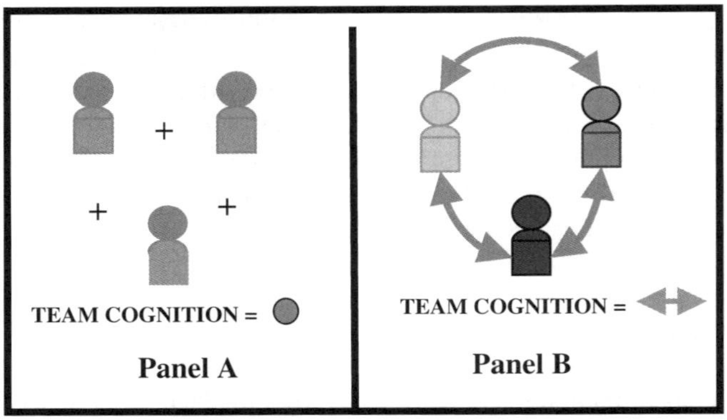

Figure 10.4 Team cognition as viewed from the I-P-O (Panel A) and THEDA (Panel B) perspectives

the environmental level (e.g., data quality, Mallubhatla *et al.* 1991) serve as input to team process behaviors. Processing in the I-P-O framework is analogous to individual-level cognitive processing such as storage and retrieval (Hinsz *et al.* 1997). In terms of team cognition, process behaviors mediate between individual and group knowledge and team outcomes. Various team processes include behaviors such as assertiveness, adaptability, leadership, and communications (Brannick *et al.* 1995).

Team cognition has been implicated across this framework as an input (e.g., Mohammed & Dumville 2001), process (e.g., Brannick *et al.* 1995), and outcome (e.g., Mathieu *et al.* 2000). However, there has been increasing focus on the "I" part in which team cognition is thought of as the collection of inputs (e.g., individual knowledge involving the task and team; Figure 10.4, Panel A). Views of shared mental models and team situation awareness in terms of common understanding have turned the spotlight on the input side of the I-P-O framework. The focus is on the knowledge or mental models more than the sharing processes or interactions. Thus, the I-P-O perspective, the dominant view of team cognition, has become input- or knowledge-centric, rather than process or behavior-centric (e.g., Mohammed & Dumville 2001).

THEDA: Team Holistic Ecology and Dynamic Activity

The THEDA perspective represents an alternative to the I-P-O perspective on team cognition, partially motivated by some limitations of the I-P-O perspective (i.e., applicability to heterogeneous teams, knowledge vs. process focus) and partially motivated by some alternative views of scientific psychology (i.e., distributed cognition, Hutchins 1991; ecological psychology, Reed 1996; dynamical systems theory, Alligood *et al.* 1996; and Soviet era activity theory, Leontev 1990). The THEDA view (Figure 10.4, Panel B) is that team cognition is not equivalent to the aggregate of independent team member cognition, but instead emerges from the dynamic interplay between collective cognition and team member interactions. It is, accordingly, a perspective on team cognition that supports holistic rather than aggregate measurement.

The THEDA perspective advocates holistic thinking about team cognition and holistic measurement (i.e., measurement at the team level) rather than collective measurement (measurement of individuals and aggregation) and is inspired by Gestalt psychology (Cooke *et al.* 2000; see also "collective cognition," Gibson 2001). Simple aggregation rules (e.g., summing of individual data) are inappropriate for heterogeneous teams for which there is a heterogeneous distribution of knowledge and abilities across team members (Gorman *et al.* 2004; Cooke & Gorman 2006). In aggregate, the parts are independent of their relations to each other, whereas in a whole relations help determine the nature of the parts. For holistic team cognition the relations among the parts are of inherent interest, in addition to the static distribution of knowledge among the parts themselves. THEDA is concerned with the team processing mechanisms by which the *whole* team is structured, beyond the sum of the parts. Team communication or discourse data are congruent with this holistic approach. THEDA's emphasis on team member interactions beyond a collection of team knowledge stores is also shared with much of the small-group work on decision-making (Festinger 1954; Steiner 1972), social decision schemes (Davis 1973; Hinsz 1995, 1999), and even transactive memory with its emphasis on transaction or communication (Hollingshead & Brandon 2003). In fact, THEDA's emphasis on interactions or process returns full circle to the origins of the I-P-O perspective with an emphasis on "P."

Borrowing concepts from ecological psychology, teams can be viewed as a set of distributed perception-action systems that can become coordinated to the relatively global stimulus information specifying a team-level event. By analogy, when we encounter fire we see flames, we smell smoke, we feel the heat, we hear the crackle, etc.; our perceptual systems are coordinated to the same stimulus information specific to fire. Similarly, when an event occurs in the team environment, each team member is heterogeneously attuned to different aspects of the event. These "perception-action" systems are all attuned to the same event, they just extract information about it in different ways, in such a manner that these systems need to be coordinated. The THEDA perspective thus emphasizes team coordination (i.e., a team process) in response to events in the team environment. In this manner, team cognition is characterized as a single organism, ebbing and flowing and adapting itself to novel environmental constraints much as a community or institution evolves with respect to a history of changing circumstances. This process of adaptation is also consistent with Soviet activity theory (Leontev 1990) or how a team internalizes new information in terms of information distribution across team members (cf. Artman 2000). Thus, the fundamental units of team cognition could be team members yoked to a knowledge structure or the evolution of relationships among team members. A THEDA perspective invokes the latter.

This perspective is not aligned with Behaviorism, but rather Functionalism. Cognition and team cognition are acknowledged as important activities that can be studied scientifically. But unlike traditional "Cognitivist" views, cognition is an activity possibly involving an organ (i.e., the brain), but this is wholly different from postulating an internal world of reckoning based on a priori "mental structure." Actually observing team processes or interactions over time is a more direct (in the functional sense) measure of team cognition than either measuring what team members collectively think they can do (Cognitivism) or Input–Output "habits" that describe team performance (Behaviorism).

In further contrast to I-P-O-oriented theories of team cognition in which regression is used to predict team outcome at a single point in time, the THEDA perspective considers the dynamic evolution of the "team as a system" using dynamical systems theory (Alligood *et al.* 1996; Latané & Bourgeois 2001; Losada & Heaphy 2004). This is consistent with the view that coordination has to continually evolve in order to handle the flux of information in highly complex team environments. The concepts of circular causality, self-organization, bifurcation theory, and entrainment from dynamic systems theory are particularly helpful in conceptualizing the dynamics (Gorman *et al.* 2005; Cooke & Gorman 2006). For example, whereas I-P-O perspectives consider teams using relatively static, machine-like frameworks we have found evidence of team cognition exhibiting plasticity, at least with respect to learning, over multiple timescales (Gorman 2005).

EMERGING APPLICATIONS

As the study of team cognition has progressed, so have applications designed to facilitate or improve team cognition. Some of these changes evolved with the new measures and theories, whereas others came about as technology itself changed.

Training team cognition has relied more and more on advance training technologies such as simulation of tasks, virtual reality, and models of teammates. Especially for distributed command-and-control environments like those that gave rise to team cognition research, there is a growing tendency to blur the distinction between training and operations. The mantra in the military is "train as we fight." With these new training technologies there is a great need for assessment of cognitive training requirements and examination of issues of learning and transfer and retention in this train-as-we-fight environment. Does learning happen faster and last longer in this setting, or are we better off isolating the essence of what we want to train from the complexities of the environment?

Computer modeling of team cognition has also progressed by leaps and bounds (Carley & Prietula 1998). Modeling team cognition allows us to question a model in order to ascertain answers that would perhaps be very difficult to ascertain in any other way. Individual cognitive modeling approaches have been extended to team modeling (e.g., Team-Soar, Kang *et al.* 1998). The approach starts with the individual cognitive model and populates teams with multiple interacting models (Chapman *et al.* 2004). Computerized or synthetic agents are becoming synthetic teammates and provide a richer training and research context for this work. Synthetic enemy forces are also being used for similar purposes and indeed create the realism in training and simulation that seems critical to battlefield applications. However, this realism is limited by the fact that the enemy forces are programmed and therefore lack the flexibility and rationality of human enemy forces.

Artificial agents are also touted as decision aids, gathering information and disseminating it to the appropriate team members as a way to improve team cognition. However, agent assistants can only perform tasks that are delegated to them (e.g., route planning, information-gathering; Miller *et al.* 2004; Sycara & Lewis 2004). Indeed, groupware has progressed to facilitate much of the information push-and-pull required of command-and-control teams through electronic repositories for ongoing information sharing (e.g., Freeman *et al.* 2003). In general, groupware applications have also been extended from the business domain to the military and have increasingly focused on issues of team rather than group cognition (Hinsz 2001; Klein 2001; Gutwin & Greenberg 2004).

Finally, there have also been movements toward embedded and automated assessment of teams for rapid intervention and improvement – a team version of augmented cognition efforts. The idea is to embed measures of team cognition within an operational environment in order to assess, diagnose, and ultimately intervene to improve team cognition. This is a challenge for a number of reasons discussed in this chapter but due to a concerted effort on team cognition measurement, progress has been made (Cooke 2005).

With new ways of thinking about team cognition, as represented in the THEDA perspective discussed in this chapter, also come new applications. Indeed, though different theoretical perspectives can be used to explain complex team behavior, the real distinction in focus is often revealed in the applications stemming from each perspective. For instance, the THEDA perspective would approach improving team situation awareness quite differently than someone with an I-P-O perspective. The I-P-O solution to this problem has been to design shared displays for teammates to enhance building of a common picture or shared mental model (Langan-Fox *et al.* 2000; Rentsch & Klimoski 2001; Bolstad & Endsley 1999). In contrast to the I-P-O solution for enhanced team SA, the THEDA solution might advocate improving the push-and-pull of information in the face of novel events through an understanding of the long-range correlations among information elements, perhaps employing an artificial agent as an on-line monitoring device. Similarly, whereas the information-processing approach focuses on training teamwork skills and knowledge at the individual level, the THEDA approach suggests more holistic training such as the kind a team might get playing an internet video game.

THEDA would also advocate modeling team cognition at a higher, more abstract level (e.g., dynamic flows or maps) than the agent level modeling that is most common. Multi-agent-based modeling is inspired by information-processing (e.g., Kang *et al.* 1998) and the question is whether groups of agents will be able to replicate phenomena of team cognition. And if they do, the computational needs will be tremendous. The THEDA approach would be to use higher-level modeling approaches such as nonlinear dynamics to model teams and organizations at the level of qualitative coordination states (Gorman *et al.* 2005). Recent approaches to model teams at a higher level as inspired by social network theory (Friedkin 1998) are also consistent with this approach (Sanil *et al.* 1995).

Finally, team cognition conceived as an emergent coordinated state has a very intriguing application in regard to individual cognition. Specifically, cognitive psychologists have struggled with the fact that individual cognition defies direct observation. Alternatively, team cognition, conceived as an emergent team property, is observable in the coordination and communication behavior of teams, as an open system that self-organizes its own constraints, and thus cognitive states. One potential application, then, of team cognition is to use theories, methods, and data to generate hypotheses about individual cognition.

CONCLUSION

Failures of cognitive systems such as the *Vincennes* incident have been pivotal to the field of team cognition. After 15 years' work in the area of team cognition dedicated to problems such as this one, have we improved the situation? Though precise measures of success are few and far between, it certainly seems that the trajectory is a positive one. There is much more work to be done. Questions remain unanswered regarding the measurement of team cognition and the possibilities for empirical research are endless. Applications that directly address the need do not wait for multi-year research programs and so there is also a need to streamline research efforts on teams and organizations. Research in this area is resource-intense in terms of participants, equipment, experimenters, and time. Interestingly, the same technology that is being developed to address the problem (e.g., team-level modeling, embedded team assessment) can also be applied to research programs to streamline these efforts. So, yes, we have learned much about team cognition in the last 15 years and we have developed tools and technologies to improve decision-making under stress and to facilitate team coordination. But as always, there is much more to do.

Specifically, as we have outlined in this chapter, it remains to be decided whether individual-based cognitive theories can be applied to problems stemming from the psychology of teams, or if, rather, the opposite tack might not more fruitful in the long run. The answer to this question will undoubtedly be empirical in nature, yet in the meantime we can achieve better theoretical and applied balance by focusing not only on understanding the knowledge requirements of individual team members, but also on understanding how relationships among team members evolve.

ACKNOWLEDGMENTS

The authors would like to thank Mike Letsky (Office of Naval Research, N00014-03-1-0580), Bob Sorkin and John Tangney (Air Force Office of Scientific Research, FA9550-04-1-0234), and Dee Andrews (Air Force Research Laboratory, FA8650-04-6442) for ongoing support of the CERTT Lab's program in team cognition. We are also grateful to Jasmine Duran and Tamica Smith for their editorial comments on the chapter.

REFERENCES

Achille, L. B., Schultz, K. G. & Schmidt-Nielson, A. (1995). An analysis of communication and the use of military terms in Navy team training. *Military Psychology, 7*, 95–107.

Adelman, L., Zirk, D. A., Lehner, P. E. *et al.* (1986). Distributed tactical decision making: conceptual framework and empirical results. *IEEE Transactions on Systems, Man, and Cybernetics, 16*, 794–805.

Alligood, K. T., Sauer, T. D. & Yorke, J. A. (1996). *Chaos: An Introduction to Dynamical Systems.* New York: Springer-Verlag.

Artman, H. (2000). Team situation assessment and information distribution. *Ergonomics, 43*, 1111–1128.

Blickensderfer, E., Cannon-Bowers, J. A. & Salas, E. (1997). Training teams to self-correct: an empirical evaluation. Paper presented at the Meeting of the Society for Industrial and Organizational Psychology, St. Louis, MO (April 10–13).

Bolstad, C. A. & Endsley, M. R. (1999). Shared mental models and shared displays: an empirical evaluation of team performance. In *Proceedings of The Human Factors and Ergonomics Society 43rd Annual Meeting* (pp. 213–217). Santa Monica, CA: Human Factors and Ergonomics Society.

Bolstad, C. A. & Endsley, M. R. (2003). Measuring shared and team situational awareness in the Army's future objective force. In *Proceedings of the Human Factors and Ergonomics Society 47th Annual Meeting* (pp. 369–373). Santa Monica, CA: Human Factors and Ergonomics Society.

Brannick, M. T., Prince, A., Prince, C. & Salas, E. (1995). The measurement of team process. *Human Factors*, *37*, 641–651.
Cannon-Bowers, J. A. & Salas, E. (eds.) (1998). *Making Decisions under Stress: Implications for Individual and Team Training*. Washington, DC: American Psychological Association.
Cannon-Bowers, J. A., Salas, E., Blickensderfer, E. & Bowers, C. A. (1998). The impact of cross-training and workload on team functioning: a replication and extension of initial findings. *Human Factors*, *40*, 92–101.
Carley, K. M. & Prietula, M. J. (1998). Webbots, trust, and organizational science. In M. J. Prietula, K. M. Carley & L. Gasser (eds.), *Simulating Organizations: Computational Models of Institutions and Groups* (pp. 3–22). Menlo Park, CA: American Association for Artificial Intelligence.
Chapman, R. J., Ryder, J. & Bell, B. (2004). STRATA (Synthetic Teammates for Real-time Anywhere Training and Assessment): an integration of cognitive models and virtual environments for scenario based training. In *Proceedings of the Human Factors and Ergonomics Society 48th Annual Meeting*, New Orleans, LA.
Clark, H. & Brennan, S. E. (1991). Grounding in communication. In L. B. Resnick, J. Levine & S. Teasley (eds.), *Socially Shared Cognition*. Washington, DC: American Psychology Association.
CNN (2005). *Katrina: State of Emergency*. Kansas City, KS: Andrew McMeel Publishing.
Collyer, S. C. & Malecki, G. S. (1998). Tactical decision making under stress: history and overview. In J. A. Cannon-Bowers & E. Salas (eds.), *Decision Making under Stress: Implications for Individual and Team Training* (pp. 3–15), Washington, DC: American Psychological Association.
Converse, S., Cannon-Bowers, J. A. & Salas, E. (1991). Team member shared mental models. In *Proceedings of the 35th Human Factors Society Annual Meeting* (pp. 1417–1421). Santa Monica, CA: Human Factors and Ergonomics Society.
Cooke, N. C. & Gorman, J. C. (2006). Assessment of team cognition. In P. Karwowski (ed.) *International Encyclopedia of Ergonomics and Human Factors* (2nd edn). pp. 270–275. UK: Taylor & Francis Ltd.
Cooke, N. J. (1994). Varieties of knowledge elicitation techniques. *International Journal of Human–Computer Studies*, *41*, 801–849.
Cooke, N. J. (1999). Knowledge elicitation. In F. T. Durso (ed.), *Handbook of Applied Cognition* (pp. 479–509). Chichester: John Wiley & Sons.
Cooke, N. J. (2005). Augmented Team Cognition. Paper presented and session chaired at Augmented Cognition, Human Computer Interaction International, July 22–27, Las Vegas, NV.
Cooke, N. J., DeJoode, J. A., Pedersen, H. K. *et al.* (2004). *The Role of Individual and Team Cognition in Uninhabited Air Vehicle Command-and-Control*. Technical Report for AFOSR Grant Nos. F49620-01-1-0261 and F49620-03-1-0024.
Cooke, N. J., Kiekel, P. A., Salas, E. *et al.* (2003). Measuring team knowledge: a window to the cognitive underpinnings of team performance. *Group Dynamics: Theory, Research and Practice*, *7*, 179–199.
Cooke, N. J., Salas, E., Cannon-Bowers, J. A. & Stout, R. (2000). Measuring team knowledge. *Human Factors*, *42*, 151–173.
Cooke, N. J., Salas, E., Kiekel, P. A. & Bell, B. (2004). Advances in measuring team cognition. In E. Salas & S. M. Fiore (eds.), *Team Cognition: Understanding the Factors that Drive Process and Performance* (pp. 83–106). Washington, DC: American Psychological Association.
Cooke, N. J. & Schvaneveldt, R. W. (1988). Effects of computer programming experience on network representations of abstract programming concepts. *International Journal of Man–Machine Studies*, *29*, 407–427.
Cooke, N. J. & Shope, S. M. (2002). The CERTT-UAV Task: a synthetic task environment to facilitate team research. In *Proceedings of the Advanced Simulation Technologies Conference: Military, Government, and Aerospace Simulation Symposium* (pp. 25–30). San Diego, CA: The Society for Modeling and Simulation International.
Cooke, N. J. & Shope, S. M. (2004). Designing a synthetic task environment. In S. G. Schiflett, L. R. Elliott, E. Salas & M. D. Coovert (eds.), *Scaled Worlds: Development, Validation, and Application* (pp. 263–278). Aldershot: Ashgate.

Cooke, N. J., Stout, R. & Salas, E. (2001). A knowledge elicitation approach to the measurement of team situation awareness. In M. McNeese, E. Salas & M. R. Endsley (eds.), *New Trends in Cooperative Activities: Understanding System Dynamics in Complex Environments* (pp. 114–139). Santa Monica, CA: Human Factors and Ergonomics Society.

Daft, R. & Lengel, R. (1986). Organizational information requirements, media richness, and structural design. *Management Science, 32*, 1268–1287.

Davis, J. H. (1973). Group decision and social interaction: a theory of social decision schemes. *Psychological Review, 80*, 97–125.

Davis, J. H., Stasson, M. F., Parks, C. D. *et al.* (1993). Quantitative decisions by groups and individuals: voting procedures and monetary awards by mock civil juries. *Journal of Experimental Social Psychology, 29*, 326–346.

Davis, J. H., Tindale, R. S., Nagao, D. H. *et al.* (1984). Order effects in multiple decisions by groups: a demonstration with mock juries and trials procedures. *Journal of Personality and Social Psychology, 47*, 1003–1012.

DeSanctis, G. & Poole, M. S. (1991). Understanding the difference in collaborative system use through appropriation analysis. In *Proceedings of the 24th Hawaii International Conference on System Sciences* (pp. 750–757). Piscataway, NJ: IEEE.

Dirks, K. T. (1999). The effects of interpersonal trust on work group performance. *Journal of Applied Psychology, 84*, 445–455.

Duncan, P. C., Rouse, W. B., Johnston, J. H. *et al.* (1996). Training teams working in complex systems: a mental model-based approach. *Human/Technology Interaction in Complex Systems, 8*, 173–231.

Durso, F. D. & Gronlund, S. D. (1999). Situation awareness. In F. T. Durso, R. Nickerson, R. Schvaneveldt, S. Dumais, M. Chi & S. Lindsay (eds.), *The Handbook of Applied Cognition* (pp. 283–314). Chichester: John Wiley & Sons.

Durso, F. T., Hackworth, C. A., Truitt, T. R. *et al.* (1998). Situation awareness as a predictor of performance in en route air traffic controllers. *Air Traffic Control Quarterly, 5*, 1–20.

Durso, F. T., Rea, C. B. & Dayton, T. (1994). Graph-theoretic confirmation of restructuring during insight. *Psychological Science, 5*, 94–98.

Durso, F. T., Rawson, K. A. & Girotto, S. (2007). Comprehension and situation awareness, Chapter 7, this volume.

Eason, K. (1988). *Information technology and organizational change*. London: Taylor & Francis.

Endsley, M. R. (1988). Design and evaluation for situation awareness. In *Proceedings of the Human Factors Society 37th Annual Meeting* (pp. 97–101). Santa Monica, CA: The Human Factors and Ergonomics Society.

Endsley, M. R. (1995). Measurement of situation awareness in dynamic systems. *Human Factors, 37*, 65–84.

Endsley, M. R. & Jones, W. M. (1997). *Situation Awareness, Information Dominance, and Information Warfare* (United States Air Force Armstrong Laboratory Technical Report 97-01). USAF.

Ensley, M. D. & Pearce, C. L. (2001). Shared cognition in top management teams: implications for new venture performance. *Journal of Organizational Behavior, 22*, 145–160.

Entin, E. E. & Serfaty, D. (1999). Adaptive team coordination. *Human Factors, 41*, 312–325.

Everett, J. J., Smith, R. E. & Williams, K. D. (1992). Effects of team cohesion and identifiability on social loafing in relay swimming performance. *International Journal of Sport Psychology, 23*, 311–324.

Festinger, L. (1954). A theory of social comparison processes. *Human Relations, 7*, 117–140.

Fiore, S. M., Salas, E. & Cannon-Bowers, J. A. (2001). Group dynamics and shared mental model development. In M. London (ed.), *How People Evaluate Others in Organizations* (pp. 309–336). Mahwah, NJ: Lawrence Erlbaum Associates.

Ford, J. K., Kozlowski, S. W. J., Kraiger, K. *et al.* (eds.) (1997). *Improving Training Effectiveness in Work Organizations*. Mahwah, NJ: Lawrence Erlbaum Associates.

Fowlkes, J. E., Dwyer, D., Oser, R. L. & Salas, E. (1998). Event based approach to training (EBAT). *The International Journal of Aviation Psychology, 8*, 209–221.

Fracker, M. L. (1989). Attention allocation in situation awareness. In *Proceedings of the Human Factors Society 33rd Annual Meeting* (pp. 1396–1400). Santa Monica, CA: The Human Factors and Ergonomics Society.

Fraidin, S. N. (2004). When is one head better than two? Interdependent information in group decision making. *Organizational Behavior & Human Decision Processes, 93*, 102–113.

Freeman, J., Hess, K. P., Spitz, G. *et al.* (2003). Collaborative critical thinking. In *Proceedings of the 8th International Command and Control Research and Technology Symposium.* Washington, DC.

Friedkin, N. E. 1998. *A Structural Theory of Social Influence.* New York: Cambridge University Press.

Gaddy, C. D. & Wachtel, J. A. (1992). Team skills training in nuclear power plant operations. In R. W. Swezey & E. Salas (eds.), *Teams: Their Training and Performance* (pp. 379–396). Norwood, NJ: Ablex.

George, C. E. (1977). Testing for coordination in small units. *Proceedings of the Military Testing Conference, 19*, 487–497.

Gibson, C. (2001). From knowledge accumulation to accommodation: cycles of collective cognition in work groups. *Journal of Organizational Behavior, 22*, 121–134.

Goldsmith, T. E., Johnson, P. J. & Acton, W. H. (1991). Assessing structural knowledge. *Journal of Educational Psychology, 83*, 88–96.

Gorman, J. C. (2005). The concept of long memory for assessing the global effects of augmented team cognition. In *Proceedings of the 1st International Conference on Augmented Cognition*, Las Vegas, NV, 22–27, July 2005.

Gorman, J. C., Cooke, N. J. & Kiekel, P. A. (2004). Dynamical perspectives on team cognition. In *Proceedings of the Human Factors and Ergonomics Society 48th Annual Meeting.* Santa Monica, CA: Human Factors and Ergonomics Society.

Gorman, J. C., Cooke, N. J., Pedersen, H. K. *et al.* (2005). Coordinated awareness of situation by teams (CAST): measuring team situation awareness of a communication glitch. In *Proceedings of the Human Factors and Ergonomics Society 49th Annual Meeting.* Orlando, FL.

Greene, E. & Loftus, E. S. (1981). When crimes are joined at trial: institutionalized prejudice? Paper presented at the Biennial Convention of the Psychology-Law Society, Cambridge, MA.

Gugerty, L., DeBoom, D., Walker, R. & Burns, J. (1999). Developing a simulated uninhabited aerial vehicle (UAV) task based on cognitive task analysis: task analysis results and preliminary simulator data. In *Proceedings of the Human Factors and Ergonomics Society 43rd Annual Meeting* (pp. 86–90). Santa Monica, CA: Human Factors and Ergonomics Society.

Gutwin, C. & Greenberg, S. (2004). The importance of awareness for team cognition in distributed collaboration. In E. Salas & S. M. Fiore (eds.), *Team Cognition: Understanding the Factors that Drive Process and Performance* (pp. 177–202), Washington, DC: American Psychological Association.

Hackman, J. R. (1987). The design of work teams. In J. W. Lorsch (ed.), *Handbook of Organizational Behavior* (pp. 315–342). Englewood Cliffs, NJ: Prentice-Hall.

Harcum, E. R. & Badura, L. L. (1990). Social loafing as response to an appraisal of appropriate effort. *Journal of Psychology: Interdisciplinary & Applied, 124*, 629–637.

Hastie, R. & Kameda, T. (2005). The robust beauty of majority rules in group decisions. *Psychological Review, 112*, 494–508.

Helmreich, R. L., Merritt, A. C. & Wilhelm, J. A. (1999). The evolution of crew resource management training in commercial aviation. *The International Journal of Aviation Psychology, 9*(1), 19–32.

Hinsz, V., Tindale, R. S. & Vollrath, D. A. (1997). The emerging conceptualization of groups as information processors. *Psychological Bulletin, 121*, 43–64.

Hinsz, V. B. (1990). Cognitive and consensus processes in group recognition memory performance. *Journal of Personality and Social Psychology, 59*, 705–718.

Hinsz, V. B. (1995). Group and individual decision making for task performance goals: processes in the establishment of goals in groups. *Journal of Applied Social Psychology, 25*, 353–370.

Hinsz, V. B. (1999). Group decision making with responses of a quantitative nature: the theory of social decision schemes for quantities. *Organizational Behavior and Human Decision Processes, 80*, 28–49.

Hinsz, V. B. (2001). A groups-as-information-processors perspective for technological support of intellectual teamwork. In M. McNeese, E. Salas & M. Endsley (eds.), *New Trends in Cooperative Activities* (pp. 218–229). Santa Monica, CA: Human Factors and Ergonomics Society.

Hollingshead, A. B. (1996). The rank-order effect in group decision making. *Organizational Behavior and Human Decision Processes, 68*, 181–193.
Hollingshead, A. B. (1998). Communication, learning, and retrieval in transactive memory systems. *Journal of Experimental Social Psychology, 34*, 423–442.
Hollingshead, A. B. (2000). Perceptions of expertise and transactive memory in work relationships. *Group Processes & Intergroup Relations, 3*, 257–267.
Hollingshead, A. B. (2001). Cognitive interdependence and convergent expectations in transactive memory. *Journal of Personality & Social Psychology, 81*, 1080–1089.
Hollingshead, A. B. & Brandon, D. P. (2003). Potential benefits of communication in transactive memory systems. *Human Communication Research, 29*, 607–615.
Hollingshead, A. B. & Fraidin, S. N. (2003). Gender stereotypes and assumptions about expertise in transactive memory. *Journal of Experimental Social Psychology, 39*, 355–363.
Hutchins, E. (1991). The social organization of distributed cognition. In L. B. Resnick, J. M. Levine & S. D. Teasley (eds.), *Perspectives on Socially Shared Cognition* (pp. 283–307). Washington, DC: American Psychological Association.
Ingham, A. G., Levinger, G., Graves, J. & Peckham, V. (1974). The Ringelmann effect: studies of group size and group performance. *Journal of Experimental Social Psychology, 10*, 371–384.
Janis, I. L. (1972). *Victims of Groupthink: A psychological Study of Foreign-policy Decisions and Fiascoes*. Boston, MA: Houghton Mifflin.
Johnston, J. H., Poirier, J. & Smith-Jentsch, K. A. (1998). Decision making under stress: creating a research methodology. In J. A. Cannon-Bowers & E. Salas (eds.), *Making Decisions under Stress: implications for Individual and Team Training* (pp. 39–59). Washington, DC. American Psychological Association.
Kameda, T., Ohtsubho, Y. & Takezawa, M. (1997). Centrality in sociocognitive networks and social influence: an illustration in a group decision-making context. *Journal of Personality and Social Psychology, 73*, 296–309.
Kang, M., Waisel, L. B. & Wallace, W. A. (1998). Team-Soar: a model for team decision making. In M. J. Prietula, K. M. Carley & L. Gasser (eds.), *Simulating Organizations: Computational Models of Institutions and Groups* (pp. 23–45). Menlo Park, CA: American Association for Artificial Intelligence.
Kanki, B. G. & Foushee, C. H. (1989). Communication as group process mediator of aircrew performance. *Aviation, Space, and Environmental Medicine, 60*, 402–410.
Karau, S. J. & Williams, K. D. (2001). Understanding individual motivation in groups: the collective effort model. In M. E. Turner (ed.), *Groups at Work: Theory and Research* (pp. 113–141). Mahwah, NJ: Lawrence Erlbaum Associates.
Katz, R. (1982). The effects of group longevity on project communication and performance. *Administrative Science Quarterly, 27*, 81–104.
Kerr, N. L. & MacCoun, R. J. (1985). The effect of jury size and polling method on the process and product of jury deliberations. *Journal of Personality and Social Psychology, 48*, 349–363.
Kerr, N. L. & Tindale, R. S. (2004). Group performance and decision making. *Annual Review of Psychology, 55*, 623–655.
Kiekel, P. A., Cooke, N. J., Foltz, P. W. *et al.* (2002). Some promising results of communication-based automatic measures of team cognition. In *Proceedings of the Human Factors and Ergonomics Society 46th Annual Meeting* (pp. 298–302). Santa Monica, CA.
Kiekel, P. A., Gorman, J. C. & Cooke, N. J. (2004). Measuring speech flow of co-located and distributed command and control teams during a communication channel glitch. In *Proceedings of the Human Factors and Ergonomics Society 48th Annual Meeting*. Santa Monica, CA.
Klein, G. (2001). Features of team coordination. In M. McNeese, E. Salas & M. Endsley (eds.), *New Trends in Cooperative Activities* (pp. 68–95). Santa Monica, CA: Human Factors and Ergonomics Society.
Kleinman, D. L., Young, P. W. & Higgins, G. (1996). The DDD-III: a tool for empirical research in adaptive organizations. In *Proceedings of the 1996 Command and Control Research and Technology Symposium*. Monterey, CA: NPS.
Klimoski, R. & Mohammed, S. (1994). Team mental model: construct or metaphor? *Journal of Management, 20*, 403–437.

Klinger, D. & Klein, G. (1999). An accident waiting to happen. *Ergonomics in Design, July*, 20–25.
Kraiger, K. & Wenzel, L. H. (1997). Conceptual development and empirical evaluation of measures of shared mental models as indicators of team effectiveness. In M. T. Brannick, E. Salas & C. Prince (eds.), *Performance Assessment and Measurement: Theory, Methods & Applications* (pp. 63–84). Mahwah, NJ: Lawrence Erlbaum Associates.
Langan-Fox, J., Code, S. & Langfield-Smith, K. (2000). Team mental models: techniques, Methods, and Analytic Approaches. *Human Factors*, *42*, 242–271.
Larson, J. R. Jr, Foster-Fishman, P. G. & Keys, C. B. (1994). Discussion of shared and unshared information in decision-making groups. *Journal of Personality and Social Psychology*, *67*, 446–461.
Latané, B. & Bourgeois, M. (2001). Dynamic social impact and the consolidation, clustering, correlation, and continuing diversity of culture. In M. A. Hogg & R. S. Tindale (eds.), *Blackwell Handbook of Social Psychology: Group Processes* (pp. 235–258). Malden, MA: Blackwell.
Latané, B., Williams, K. & Harkins, S. (1979). Many hands make light the work: the causes and consequences of social loafing. *Journal of Personality & Social Psychology*, *37*, 822–832.
Leontev, D. A. (1990). Deyatelnost i potrefnost (Activity and need). In D. B. Davydov & D. A. Leontev (eds.), *Deyatelnostnyi Podhod v Psihologii: Problemy i Perspektivy (The Activity Approach in Psychology: Problems and Perspectives)* (pp. 96–108). Moscow: APN.
Levesque, L. L., Wilson, J. M. & Wholey, D. R. (2001). Cognitive divergence and shared mental models in software development project teams. *Journal of Organization Behavior*, *22*, 135–144.
Lewin, K. (1947). Frontiers in group dynamics. *Human Relations*, *1*, 143–153.
Lewin, K. (1951). *Field Theory in Social Science*. New York: Harper.
Liang, D. W., Moreland, R. L. & Argote, L. (1995). Group versus individual training and group performance: the mediating role of transactive memory. *Personality and Social Psychology Bulletin*, *21*, 384–393.
Losada, M. & Heaphy, E. (2004). The role of positivity and connectivity in the performance of business teams: a nonlinear dynamics model. *American Behavioral Scientist*, *47*, 740–765.
McLeod, P. L. (1992). An assessment of the experimental literature on electronic support of group work: results of a meta-analysis. *Human–Computer Interaction*, *7*, 257–280.
Mallubhatla, R., Pattipati, K. R., Kleinman, D. L. & Tang, Z. B. (1991). A model of distributed team information processing under ambiguity. *IEEE Transactions on Systems, Man & Cybernetics*, *21*, 713–725.
Mathieu, J. E., Goodwin, G. F., Heffner, T. S. *et al.* (2000). The influence of shared mental models on team process and performance. *Journal of Applied Psychology*, *85*, 273–283.
Miller, C., Funk, H., Goldman, R. & Wu, P. (2004). A "playbook" for variable autonomy control of multiple, heterogeneous unmanned air vehicles. In *Proceedings of the 4th Conference on Human Performance*, Situation Awareness and Automation, Daytona Beach, FL; March 22–25.
Mitchell, J. L., Yadrick, R. M. & Bennett, W. Jr (1993). Estimating training requirements from job and training pattern simulations. *Military Psychology*, *5*, 1–20.
Mohammed, S. & Dumville, B. C. (2001). Team mental models in a team knowledge framework: expanding theory and measurement across discipline boundaries. *Journal of Organizational Behavior*, *22*, 89–106.
Mohammad, S., Klimoski, R. & Rentsch, J. R. (2000). The measurement of team mental models: we have no shared schema. *Organizational Research Methods*, *3*, 123–165.
Monplaisir, L. (2002). Enhancing CSCW with advanced decision making tools for an agile manufacturing system design application. *Group Decision & Negotiation*, *11*, 45–63.
Moreland, R. L. (1999). Transactive memory: learning who knows what in work groups and organizations. In L. Thompson, J. Levine & D. Messick (eds.), *Shared Cognition in Organizations: The Management of Knowledge* (pp. 3–31). Mahwah, NJ: Lawrence Erlbaum Associates.
Moreland, R. L. & Myaskovsky, L. (2000). Explaining the performance benefits of group training: transactive memory or improved communication? *Organizational Behavior and Human Decision Processes*, *82*, 117–133.

Morgan, B. B. & Lassiter, D. L. (1992). Team composition and staffing. In R. W. Swezey & E. Salas (eds.), *Teams: Their Training and Performance* (pp. 75–100). Norwood, NJ: Ablex.
Murphy, S. M., Wayne, S. J., Liden, R. C. & Erdogan, B. (2003). Understanding social loafing: the role of justice perceptions and exchange relationships. *Human Relations*, *56*, 61–84.
Nagao, D. H. & Davis, J. H. (1980). The effects of prior experience on mock juror case judgments. *Social Psychology Quarterly*, *43*, 190–199.
Olson, G. M., Malone, T. W. & Smith, J. B. (eds.) (2001). *Coordination Theory and Collaboration Technology*. Mahwah, NJ: Lawrence Erlbaum Associates.
Olson, G. M. & Olson, J. S. (2007). Computer-supported cooperative work, Chapter 19, this volume.
Orasanu, J. M. (1995). Evaluating team situation awareness through communication. In D. J. Garland & M. R. Endsley (eds.), *Proceedings of an International Conference on Experiment Analysis and Measurement of Situation Awareness* (pp. 283–288). Daytona Beach, FL: Embry–Riddle Aeronautical University Press.
Pavitt, C. (2003). Colloquy: do interacting groups perform better than aggregates of individuals? Why we have to be reductionists about group memory. *Human Communication Research*, *29*, 592–599.
Proctor, M. D., Panko, M. & Donovan, S. J. (2004). Considerations for training team situation awareness and task performance through PC-gamer simulated multiship helicopter operations. *The International Journal of Aviation Psychology*, *14*, 191–205.
Reason, J. (1997). *Managing the Risks of Organizational Accidents*. Brookfield, VT: Ashgate.
Reed, E. S. (1996). *Encountering the World: Toward an Ecological Psychology*. New York: Oxford University Press.
Rentsch, J. R. & Hall, R. J. (1994). Members of great teams think alike: a model of team effectiveness and schema similarity among team members. In M. M. Beyerlein & D. A. Johnson (eds.), *Advances in Interdisciplinary Studies of Work Teams: Theories of Self-managing Work Teams* (Vol. 1, pp. 223–262). Greenwich, CT: JAI Press.
Rentsch, J. R. & Klimoski, R. J. (2001). Why do "great minds" think alike? Antecedents of team member schema agreement. *Journal of Organizational Behavior*, *22*, 107–120.
Robertson, M. M. & Endsley, M. R. (1995). A methodology for analyzing team situation awareness in aviation maintenance. In *Proceedings of the International Conference on Analysis and Measurement of Situation Awareness*. Daytona Beach, FL: Embry-Riddle University.
Rouse, W. B., Cannon-Bowers, J. A. & Salas, E. (1992). The role of mental models in team performance in complex systems. *IEEE Transactions on Systems, Man, and Cybernetics*, *22*, 1296–1308.
Rouse, W. B. & Morris, N. M. (1986). On looking into the black box: prospects and limits in the search for mental models, *Psychological Bulletin*, *100*, 349–363.
Rulke, D. L. & Rau, D. (2000). Investigating the encoding process of transactive memory development in group training. *Group and Organization Management*, *25*, 373–396.
Salas, E., Bowers, C. A. & Rhodenizer, L. (1998). It is not how much you have but how you use it: toward a rational use of simulation to support aviation training. *The International Journal of Aviation Psychology*, *8*, 197–208.
Salas, E., Burke, C. S., Bowers, C. A. & Wilson, K. A. (2001). Team training in the skies: does crew resource management (CRM) training work? *Human Factors*, *43*(4), 641–674.
Salas, E. & Cannon-Bowers, J. A. (2001). The science of training: a decade of progress. *Annual Review of Psychology*, *52*, 471–499.
Salas, E., Dickinson, T. L., Converse, S. A. & Tannenbaum, S. I. (1992). Toward an understanding of team performance and training. In R. W. Swezey & E. Salas (eds.), *Teams: Their Training and Performance* (pp. 3–29). Norwood, NJ: Ablex.
Salas, E., Wilson, K. A., Burke, C. S. & Wightman, D. C. (2006). Does CRM training work? An update, extension, and some critical needs. *Human Factors*, *48*, 392–412.
Sanil, A., Banks, D. & Carley, K. (1995). Models for evolving fixed node networks: model fitting and model testing, *Social Networks*, *17*, 65–81.
Schiflett, S. G., Elliott, L. R., Salas, E. & Coovert, M. D. (eds.) (2004). *Scaled Worlds: Development, Validation, and Applications*. Aldershot: Ashgate.
Schoggen, P. (1989). *Behavior Settings*. Stanford, CA: Stanford University Press.

Schvaneveldt, R. W. (1990). *Pathfinder Associative Networks: Studies in Knowledge Organization*. Norwood, NJ: Ablex.

Schvaneveldt, R. W., Durso, F. T. & Dearholt, D. W. (1989). Network structures in proximity data. In G. H. Bower (ed.), *The Psychology of Learning and Motivation: Advances in Research and Theory* (Vol. 24, pp. 249–284). New York: Academic Press.

Schvaneveldt, R. W., Durso, F. T., Goldsmith, T. E. *et al.* (1985). Measuring the structure of expertise. *International Journal of Man–Machine Studies*, *23*, 699–728.

Seamster, T. L., Redding, R. E. & Kaempf, G. L. (1997). *Applied Cognitive Task Analysis in Aviation*. London: Ashgate.

Shope, S. M., DeJoode, J. A., Cooke, N. J. & Pedersen, H. (2004). Using Pathfinder to generate communication networks in a cognitive task analysis. In *Proceedings of the Human Factors and Ergonomics Society 48th Annual Meeting*. Santa Monica, CA: Human Factors and Ergonomics Society.

Smith-Jentsch, K. A., Campbell, G. E., Milanovich, D. M. & Reynolds, A. M. (2001). Measuring teamwork mental models to support training needs assessment, development, and evaluation: two empirical studies. *Journal of Organizational Behavior*, *22*, 179–194.

Sorkin, R. D., Hays, C. J. & West, R. (2001). Signal-detection analysis of group decision making. *Psychological Review*, *108*, 183–203.

Sorkin, R. D., West, R. & Robinson, D. E. (1998). Group performance depends on the majority rule. *Psychological Science*, *9*, 456–463.

Stasser, G. & Titus, W. (1985). Pooling of unshared information in group decision making: biased information sampling during discussion. *Journal of Personality and Social Psychology*, *48*, 1467–1478.

Stasser, G. & Titus, W. (1987). Effects of information load and percentage of shared information on the dissemination of unshared information during group discussion. *Journal of Personality and Social Psychology*, *53*, 81–93.

Stasser, G., Vaughan, S. I. & Stewart, D. D. (2000). Pooling unshared information: the benefits of knowing how access to information is distributed among group members. *Organizational Behavior and Human Decision Processes*, *82*, 102–116.

Steiner, I. D. (1972). *Group Process and Productivity*. New York: Academic Press.

Stewart, D. D. & Stasser, G. (1993, May). Information sampling in collective recall groups versus decision making groups. Poster presented at the 65th Annual Meeting of the Midwestern Psychological Association, Chicago, IL.

Stout, R., Cannon-Bowers, J. A. & Salas, E. (1996). The role of shared mental models in developing team situation awareness: implications for training. *Training Research Journal*, *2*, 85–116.

Stout, R. J. (1995). Planning effects on communication strategies: a shared mental models perspective. In *Proceedings of the Human Factors and Ergonomics Society 39th Annual Meeting* (pp. 1278–1282). Santa Monica, CA: Human Factors and Ergonomics Society.

Stout, R. J., Cannon-Bowers, J. A., Salas, E. & Milanovich, D. M. (1999). Planning, shared mental models, and coordinated performance: an empirical link is established. *Human Factors*, *41*, 61–71.

Stout, R. J., Salas, E. & Carson, R. (1994). Individual task proficiency and team process behavior: what's important for team functioning? *Military Psychology*, *6*, 177–192.

Sycara, K. & Lewis, M. (2004). Integrating intelligent agents into human teams. In E. Salas & S. M. Fiore (eds.), *Team Cognition: Understanding the Factors that Drive Process and Performance* (pp. 203–231). Washington, DC: American Psychological Association.

Tanford, S. & Penrod, S. (1982). Biases in trials involving defendants charged with multiple offenses. *Journal of Applied Social Psychology*, *12*, 453–480.

Tanford, S. & Penrod, S. (1984). Social inference processes in juror judgments of multiple-offense trials. *Journal of Personality and Social Psychology*, *47*, 749–765.

Tata, J. (2002). The influence of accounts of perceived social loafing in work teams. *International Journal of Conflict Management*, *13*, 292–308.

Tushman, M. L. (1979). Work characteristics and subunit communication structure: a contingency analysis. *Administrative Science Quarterly*, *24*, 82–97.

Vaughan, D. (1996). *The Challenger Launch Decision: Risky Technology, Culture, and Deviance at NASA*. Chicago, IL: The University of Chicago Press.

Vicente, K. J. (1999). *Cognitive Work Analysis: Toward Safe, Productive, and Healthy Computer-based Work*. Mahwah, NJ: Lawrence Erlbaum Associates.

Volpe, C. E., Cannon-Bowers, J. A., Salas, E. & Spector, P. E. (1996). The impact of cross-training on team functioning: an empirical investigation. *Human Factors*, *38*, 87–100.

Wageman, R. (1999). Task design, outcome interdependence, and individual differences: their joint effects on effort in task-performing teams (commentary on Huguet *et al.*, 1999). *Group Dynamics*, *32*, 132–137.

Wegner, D. M. (1986). Transactive memory: a contemporary analysis of the group mind. In G. Mullen & G. Geothals (eds.), *Theories of Group Behavior* (pp. 185–208). New York: Springer-Verlag.

Wellens, A. R. (1993). Group situation awareness and distributed decision making: from military to civilian applications. In N. J. Castellan Jr (ed.), *Individual and Group Decision Making* (pp. 267–291). Hillsdale, NJ: Lawrence Erlbaum Associates.

Wittenbaum, G., Stasser, G. & Merry, C. J. (1996). Tacit *coordination* in anticipation of small group task completion. *Journal of Experimental Social Psychology*, *32*, 129–152.

Wittenbaum, G. W. (2003). Putting communication into the study of group memory. *Human Communication Research*, *29*, 616–623.

Zsambok, C. E. & Klein, G. (eds.) (1997). *Naturalistic Decision Making*. Mahwah, NJ: Lawrence Erlbaum Associates.

SECTION 2

Applied Cognition in Human–Technical Systems

CHAPTER 11

Industrial Systems

Neville Moray
Magagnosc, France

INTRODUCTION

This chapter describes the cognitive psychology involved in the operation of *continuous process control systems* (CPCS), such as chemical plants, refineries, and electrical generation, and in *discrete manufacturing systems* (DMS) making products such as automobiles, electronic components, and consumer goods. The characteristics of the work domains and of relevant cognitive activities are described. The chapter draws on extensive early work on cognitive activity in industrial human–machine systems, and concentrates on the individual operator. For the important topic of cognition in groups and teams, see Cooke *et al.* (Chapter 10, this volume).

Humans in CPCS were studied extensively even prior to the 1960s. Lees (1974) cites several hundred references, and Edwards and Lees (1974b) provide over 100 pages of references. Much of that work has not been superseded. For one entering the field, the following early references are essential reading: Edwards and Lees (1974a); Singleton (1978); Rasmussen (1986). More recent books include Rasmussen *et al.* (1995); Salvendy (1997); Vicente (1999); Hollnagel and Woods (2005). The major change that has occurred since the early studies is a great increase in automation; but it is widely accepted that humans should be retained both as collaborative operators with automation, and for sociopolitical reasons (Kuo & Hsu 1990; Vierling 1990). Humans are particularly important as agents of fault management when plants enter states that were not foreseen by their designers. For the important topic of allocation of function between human and machine in automation, see Parasuraman & Lorenz (Chapter 16, this volume).

As we shall see, it is difficult to apply research from laboratory studies of cognition to industrial settings. Field studies are fundamental to such extrapolation, but some laboratory studies have succeeded in achieving sufficient realism to study "real" behavior. In particular, the use of simulators and micro-worlds is of great value. For an excellent discussion of the relation among classical experiments, simulation, and field studies, see Rasmussen *et al.* (1995, pp. 219–224).

Consider Figure 11.1. Cognition at work is located in the world as much as in the head, and is an example of *cultural cognition* and *distributed cognition* (Hutchins 1995;

Handbook of Applied Cognition: Second Edition. Edited by Francis T. Durso.

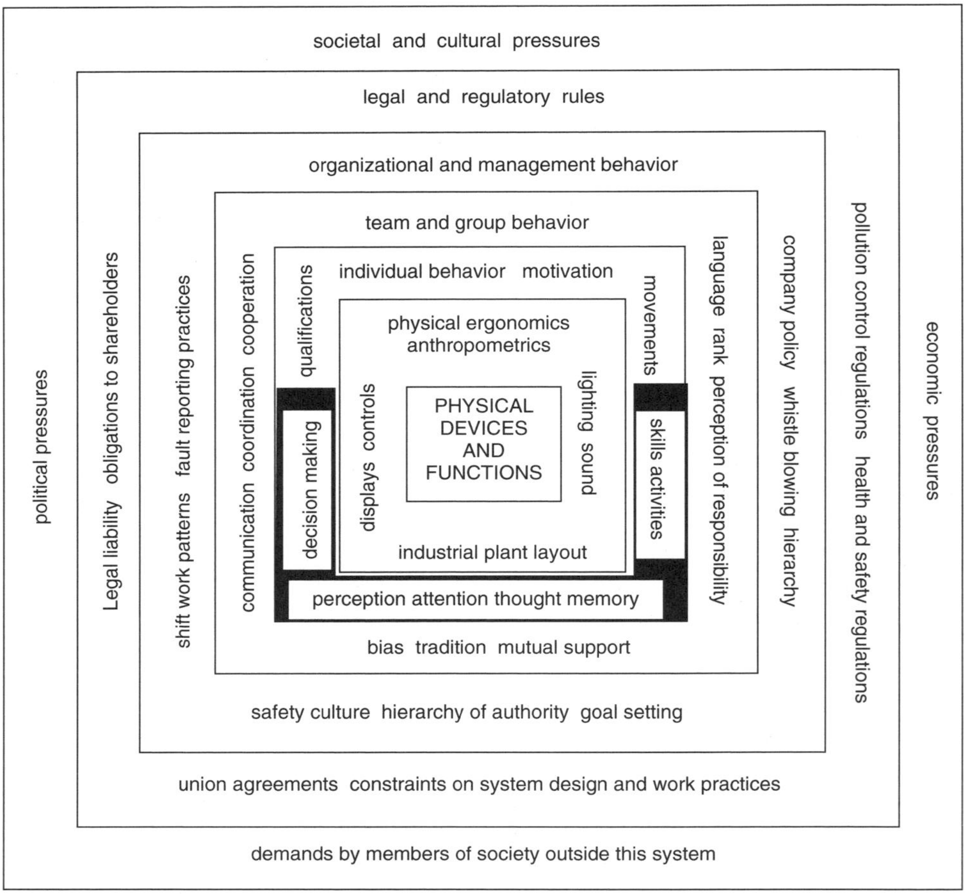

Figure 11.1 Constraints on cognition

Hollnagel & Woods 2005). Laboratory research concentrates typically on the shaded region of Figure 11.1, but the dynamics of organizations, the constraints imposed by the outer levels of Figure 11.1, and team support are as important as individual cognitive abilities in determining performance in real tasks. At the center, the physical ergonomics of control rooms and the factory floor constrain the information available and the possibilities for action.

CHARACTERISTICS OF INDUSTRIAL SYSTEMS

Cognition in industrial settings can only be understood in terms of the constraints on behavior imposed by the task environment (Simon 1981; Hutchins 1995; Rasmussen *et al.* 1995; Moray 1997a; Vicente 1999; Hollnagel & Woods 2005). Cognition is not context-free. *Domain knowledge* is essential for understanding cognition in real-world systems. Four particularly important properties are system size, complexity, temporal characteristics, and mode of control.

Size

Size is significant in two senses. First is *physical size*: a worker cannot know what is happening in all parts of a plant, since the latter may extend over many hectares, and only a subset of information about plant state is displayed in the control room. Even a lone control room operator cooperates with maintenance and field personnel, management, etc., above all during abnormal or fault conditions. It may take many minutes to retrieve information and may involve cooperation by telephone or other means of communication, as well as access to the information displayed in the control room. Second, the *functional size* of a system is measured by its degrees of freedom, which greatly affect the cognitive load on workers. All systems can be analyzed to find a minimal set of variables sufficient to describe and control the plant, and the number of entries in such a list is its degrees of freedom. In a nuclear power plant (NPP) control room there may be 1000–2000 displays and controls, or several hundred pages of computerized displays. An NPP may be several hectares in extent and many meters high, and may contain hundreds of thousands of parts. Such a plant typically has 40–50 degrees of freedom (T. B. Sheridan, pers. comm.). Any successful controller, human or otherwise, must measure and act upon a suitably chosen set of variables at least equal in number to the degrees of freedom of the system, in accordance with the Principle of Requisite Variety (Ashby 1956).

Complexity

There is no formal definition of complexity, but it includes the idea of many interconnected subsystems, parts, and components. A major cognitive consequence of complexity is that it is often difficult to know what will happen elsewhere when one part of a system is changed. Changes may propagate throughout many parts of the system, often with long delays, so that the correlations and causal relations are difficult to perceive, understand, and predict. A central theme in studies of industrial cognition is *coping with complexity* (Woods 1988; Hollnagel & Woods 2005).

Coupling is the causal origin of correlation among variables. If two parts of a system are coupled, change in one part affects the other. Expert personnel with long experience of a system tend to intervene as little as possible in its operation because coupling means that any intervention, even if locally successful in reducing the impact of a disturbance, may have widespread effects and therefore produce undesirable effects distant in time and space. Human and machine intelligence, rather than physical force, are coupled through the human–machine interface. Perrow (1984) maintains that it is tight coupling that causes modern complex industrial systems to be so hazardous in the face of human error and physical faults. Surprisingly little research has been done on the detection, perception, and understanding of coupling in complex systems (Lee & Moray 1989).

Temporal Characteristics

Industrial systems operate in *real time*. Modern DMS seldom hold large inventories of stock, so any order must be completed rapidly in response to the client's demand. The timescale may be a matter of months, days, hours, or minutes, depending on the product. In CPCS there are both explicit and implicit deadlines. Although CPCS may run continuously for many months, rates of heating and cooling may change; casting and annealing metal have characteristic tempi; and in highly dynamic processes such as nuclear fission it may be necessary to shut down a reactor within seconds.

The *time constant* of a system can be thought of informally as the shortest time over which a variable changes significantly, or as the inverse of the highest frequency present in the bandwidth of the system. The time constants of annealing metal are long – of the order of hours or days – while events in the fuel rods of a nuclear power reactor are of the order of microseconds. Scheduling dynamics have time constants of many hours, although individual machines used in DMS may have short time constants. The time constants of complex systems may not be immediately obvious. Fast transient impulses may perturb what is generally a slow process (Crossman 1974; Crossman & Cooke 1974). If there are processes with very short time constants, the system may nonetheless be buffered by others acting as integrators, providing the equivalent of inertia, and hence a longer effective time constant.

The emphasis on "real time" reflects an important difference between laboratory environments and the industrial world. A failure to manage the dynamics of energy in a system with a short time constant can cause anything from minor economic loss to catastrophic failure and death. Action must be taken by deadlines even without complete information, in the face of risk and hazard, and whether or not operators are confident that what they are doing is correct. By contrast, the start-up of an NPP or a petrochemical refinery takes several days, during which dozens or even hundreds of people are involved in more or less continuous decision-making, day and night, with people changing shift, sharing information, and supporting one another's cognitive activity over many hours at a time. European ergonomists have paid particular attention to temporal factors in cognition in industry (Volta 1986; De Cortis 1988; Hoc 1995, 1996; Cellier *et al.* 1996). The idea of "reaction time" in the classical sense is of little value. More important is the timescale for completing series of actions (Wohl 1982; Moray 1986).

To describe the dynamics of cognitive tasks one must know the rate at which the plant processes evolve, the timing of the arrival of information, the distribution in time and space of personnel, and the properties of the communication channels involved. The rate at which people can make decisions is constrained by the rate at which physical events unfold and the way in which information is displayed, often more than by the psychological characteristics of the operators.

Modes of Control

In modern plants many tasks are performed by fully automatic closed-loop controllers, but distributed control is also common, with tactical and strategic decisions being left to humans. Hollnagel and Woods (2005) describe the typical plant as being made of *joint cognitive systems*. Both open-loop and closed-loop control may be present, and a characteristic of increasing expertise and skill is a change from closed-loop reactive control to open-loop predictive control (Kelly 1964; Crossman & Cooke 1974; Moray *et al.* 1986; Hollnagel & Woods 2005). Automation means that operators are no longer a component of the closed loop, and become for long periods observers of the system rather than actors in it. This can produce an "out of the loop syndrome," such that if operators must suddenly take control they are out of touch with the state of the plant and with its dynamics (Endsley & Kiris 1995). It is difficult for operators to retain the necessary expertise for skill-based behavior (see below) if they are not in the loop (Edwards & Lees 1974a; Bainbridge 1978; Singleton 1978; Wickens 1991).

Automation

There is no unique definition of automation, but generally it refers to systems that perform tasks that used to be, or could be, performed by human operators (Parasuraman & Riley 1997; Sheridan 2002; Hollnagel & Woods 2005). Important systems characteristics include the type and degree of automation and the quality of function allocation (i.e., the partition of control between human and machine intelligence). Poor allocation of function ("clumsy automation") means that automation makes the work of operators harder, not easier (Wiener & Curry 1980). Bainbridge (1983), in a classic paper, noted that what is automated is what is well understood by engineers, which ironically leaves the less understandable, more difficult tasks for human operators (Wiener & Curry 1980; Woods 1988; Norman 1990; Rasmussen *et al.* 1995). The pilot of a heavily automated civilian aircraft once told the writer that it was a wonderful aircraft to fly, but that only the most experienced pilots should fly it because the automation was so difficult to use. Given that the purpose of designing so much automation into the aircraft was to compensate less experienced pilots for their lack of skill, this is surely the ultimate "irony of automation," to use Bainbridge's term.

Differences among Industrial Systems

Differences between CPCS and DMS have important consequences for cognition. In CPCS coupling is tight. If a valve is opened, pressure is transmitted through the system at the speed of sound, and since liquids are incompressible, flows are changed instantaneously except in viscous fluids. Temperature differences cause continuous energy fluxes across boundaries according to the laws of thermodynamics. Some parts of such systems show lags or delays, so that a change in one component may take many minutes or even hours to appear in another part of the system (Moray 1997b). A typical example is the effect on temperature of changing energy input. In DMS, coupling is looser. A change in the activity of one numerically controlled machine has no direct effect on others. If an automated guided vehicle (AGV) drops off a pallet on one conveyor, it has no effect on others. If an AGV halts, it may not indicate a fault: the scheduling algorithm may imply that such a pause will support optimal performance over a time horizon of several hours. Often the state of the plant is not readily observable. Temporal delays do not provide an error signal in the same way as do pressure or temperature differences in a chemical process. Above all, causality in scheduling is final causality, that is goal-directed causality,

Table 11.1 Differences between continuous process control and discrete manufacturing systems

Continuous process control	Discrete manufacturing
Newtonian physical causality	Goal-directed causality
Tight and continuous coupling	Distributed and loose coupling
Error signal continuously displayed as feedback, synchronous in real time	Error signal ambiguous intermittent and asynchronous
Intervention tends to produce global propagation of effects	Intervention can be local and with little or no propagation
Time, physical processes, and couplings continuous and synchronous	Time, physical processes, causal and causal couplings discrete and asynchronous
Strong control theory models available available	No accepted strong models
Fundamental problem is the control of physical processes, mass/energy	Fundamental problem is the control of planning and scheduling
Usually serially continuous	Usually partly parallel due to multiple machines, partly sequential due to scheduling constraints
Often require control long after the process has been stopped due to thermal inertia, residual heat and reactivity, secondary reactions	Often can be stopped quickly, and individual subsystems closed down without affecting others

rather than material causality (to use Aristotelian terms). A pallet moves from one machine to another not because a pressure pushes it, but because it is required at the next station in order that something may be done to it. Scheduling pulls events through a DMS, whereas Newtonian physics pushes events through a CPCS.

The differences between continuous and discrete production technology, summarized in Table 11.1, require different operator mental models and different kinds of reasoning supported in turn by different kinds of displays and aids.

To summarize, the characteristics of industrial systems most relevant to cognitive engineering include:

- System size
- System complexity
- System dynamics (time constraints, bandwidth)
- System decomposability into subsystems and components
- System observability
- System mode lability
- Intra-system physical coupling
- Closed-loop and open-loop control characteristics
- Degree and style of automation
- Bases for function allocation
- Modes of human–machine coupling
- Quality of human–machine interface
- Less than complete display of information

CONCEPTUAL FRAMEWORKS

Rasmussen (1986; Rasmussen *et al.* 1995) proposes five conceptual frameworks:

- An abstraction hierarchy
- A means–ends hierarchy
- Part–whole decomposition
- A decision ladder
- A work domain framework (sociotechnical factors).

The first three describe engineering properties of human–machine systems, the fourth is a heuristic (or perhaps a model) of cognitive activities in human–machine systems, and the fifth provides a socio-technical view of work.

Abstraction Hierarchy (AH)

The Abstraction Hierarchy is a description of the properties of the system to be controlled by the human. It is not a description of cognitive activities, or of a mental model, but a system description that must be known and understood by an efficient human operator.

Any complex system can be described at different levels of abstraction (Rasmussen 1986). (See Table 11.2 for the hierarchy and applications to CPCS and DMS.) The most concrete description, *physical form*, lists physical components. In a control room it lists nuts and bolts, switches, sliders, knobs, meters, pen recorders, computer screens, etc. Such a description lists a system's anatomy or topography, the simplest components of the system, but does not define the system's purpose or function.

The next level is *physical function*, where one identifies physical subsystems – a certain set of switches, displays, motors, platforms, etc. comprise a pump or an AGV. Some function is evident – conveyors are to move things; valves control flows. But we still do not know the overall purpose of the system.

At the level of *general function*, we no longer think of the physical characteristics of components, but of local purpose. This subsystem is a cooling system; that one controls the flow of fuel to the heating system; that switch activates a conveyor to move parts to a milling machine.

Above that is the level of *abstract function*: this part of the plant is to provide energy; that part to transform or transport the energy; this part to assemble components; that part to deliver them to storage.

Finally, we have the most abstract level of all, the level that defines the *global purpose* of the entire system – to generate electricity, to manufacture refrigerators.

Maintenance personnel typically think about the lower levels of physical form and physical function. Managers are directly concerned with the higher levels of abstraction. Operators work at intermediate levels. The AH can be applied to all systems, including commercial, social, or economic systems (Rasmussen *et al.* 1995). To solve different kinds of problems, or to communicate with colleagues with different responsibilities, one must shift between conceptual levels, for what can be thought or expressed in the language of one level cannot be thought or expressed in another. Consider the difference between the meaning of "urgent" applied to product delivery dates by a manager and that of an

Table 11.2 Rasmussen's Abstraction Hierarchy

Typical Operations	Means–Ends Relations	Characteristic Modes of Though	Process Control Operations	Discrete Manufacturing
Produce and sell electricity to make a profit for the business	GOALS AND CONSTRAINTS	Necessary and sufficient properties to link the performance of the system to its design goals. Language in terms of demands of environment	Produce 20,000 liters of pasteurized juice per day	Make 168 items in 12 hours to fill an order
Run the plant at full power to follow real-time demands	ABSTRACT FUNCTION	Necessary and sufficient properties to prioritize according to design specifications and set-points for mass–energy balances. Language in terms of abstract general properties, not specific to a particular plant.	Heat, pasteurize, and cool juice; collect spoiled juice; avoid emptying system or running pumps dry; maintain mass–energy balance	Fulfill scheduling plans
Control local properties such as temperature, energy generation, coolant flows, etc.	GENERAL FUNCTION	Necessary and sufficient properties to identify functions which must be controlled without regard to the particular instantiations of those functions in this particular plant.	Heat steam; pump feedstock; pump steam; raise temperature of feedstock in heat exchanger; maintain inventory of juice in vat; sense temperature of juice	Schedule action sequences on current jobs; ensure supply of parts for each job; satisfy quality criteria

Table 11.2 *Continued*

Typical Operations	Means–Ends Relations	Characteristic Modes of Though	Process Control Operations	Discrete Manufacturing
		Language in terms of well–known input–output relations and transfer functions		
Use particular subsystems to control flows, pressures, core reactivity, etc. Start a pump. Change rod positions	PHYSICAL PROCESSES AND ACTIVITIES	Necessary and sufficient properties to control particular work activities, choose and use equipment, predict the results of intervention, diagnose and maintain subsystems. Language related to physical systems and processes	Control rate of each pump; control temperature of steam; control energy supply to boiler; switch flow according to temperature; enable energy exchange in heat exchangers	Control movements of individual AGVs, perform machining, inspection, assembly, pallet loading and unloading, lubricate robots
Open a valve, replace a switch	PHYSICAL FORM AND RELATIONS IN THE CONTROL ROOM	Necessary and sufficient properties to categorize, identify, and operate a particular component, to physically explore the topology of the system, and to repair components. Language related to designer's and architect's specification of the system	Vats, pumps, pipes, heaters, switches, thermometers, heat exchangers, displays, controls, etc.	AGV, pallets, numerically controlled machines, inspection cell, robots, parts for assembly, etc.

operator controlling a chemical reaction; or the fact that during fault diagnosis operators shift between topographic search (in which they search for the part of the plant which is faulty at the level of physical form), and symptomatic search (in which they try to interpret functional changes in the behavior of variables) (Rasmussen 1986).

Means–Ends Hierarchy

Each level of the AH represents the goal or end which the level below subserves as a means, so that the AH is also a means–ends hierarchy. Problem-solving often requires switching conceptual frameworks – look for a means, at a lower level, to serve the end (goal) perceived to exist at a higher. When moving down the hierarchy we move from social, economic, and psychological goals to physical goals. High up the hierarchy, goals are concerned with purpose. Lower down they are concerned with physical causality (Rasmussen 1986).

Part–Whole Decomposition

Orthogonal to the abstraction hierarchy is part–whole decomposition (PWD). At each AH level one can think about the system at different levels of detail. At the highest level of the AH, for example, there are plans for production by the whole plant, by different sub-divisions, by different assembly lines or individual machines or individual worker; at the level of physical form one might look for a leak in the overall appearance of a room containing a reaction vessel, or at the finest level examine a particular welded seam to see if its integrity is intact. (For further details, see Rasmussen 1986, p. 119.)

AH and PWD represent the context of operators' cognitive and physical behavior when interacting with human–machine systems, but they are not descriptions of behavior or mental activity. They provide conceptual frameworks to support cognitive and physical task analyses, and to define the informational and control needs of automatic controllers and human operators. They determine the load on memory and the information content of decisions. The means–ends hierarchy, on the other hand, includes both psychological ...d physical teleologies.

...Ladder

...man–machine interaction is summarized in the decision ladder
...sion of which is shown in Figure 11.2. The word "operator"
...s used generically to refer to a traditional control room
...crete manufacturing process while walking about
...ce technician, a supervisor, a manager – in fact, to
...s in industrial or commercial contexts. The DL shows
...g with the receipt of information from displays, through
...ng, to the selection of plans and action taken to affect the
more detail below.

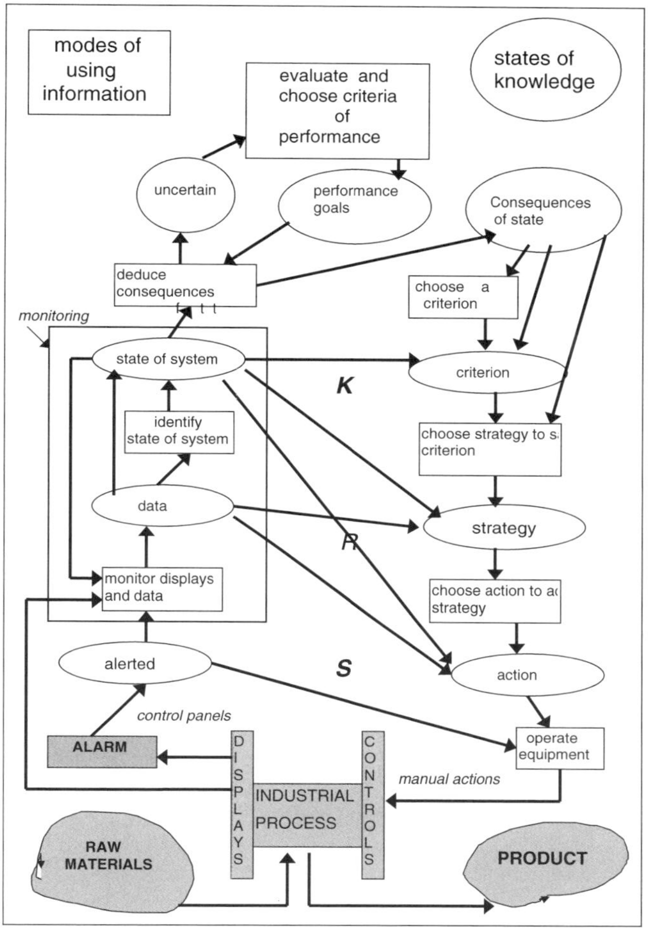

Figure 11.2 Rasmussen's decision ladder

Classification of Behavior: SBB, RBB, and KBB

Rasmussen assigns behavior to one of three categories: skill-based, rule-based, or knowledge-based behavior (SBB, RBB and KBB). This taxonomy has found very widespread acceptance as a heuristic among engineers and engineering psychologists. It summarizes many psychological ideas in a way that is useful for systems design and analysis.

SBB appears after prolonged practice or where there is a high degree of stimulus–response compatibility, and is typical of perceptual-motor skills. It can probably be identified with the automatic processing described by Shiffrin and Schneider (1977). SBB is typically effortless, highly efficient, fast, and prone only to errors that Reason (1990) calls "slips." It involves little or no deliberate thought. It is typical of expert operators in high bandwidth manual control, such as in driving or piloting skills, or in over-learned, rapid discrete responses to alarms. Since industrial operators may have thousands of hours' practice, SBB can appear even when there is not consistent mapping between information and response (see also Durso *et al.* 1987).

RBB involves using procedures, whether written or memorized. It seems to be the most common kind of behavior in real-world tasks. It is typically modeled in so-called expert systems: "If Condition A, then do X. If Condition B, then do Y." (Such rule-based systems are sometimes called "production systems" in cognitive science. It is important to note that this is a different meaning from industrial production in the sense of manufacturing.) Conditions may be recognized perceptually or may require inference. They may be as simple as a temperature, or may be complex, such as there being a certain percentage of jobs completed and one numerically controlled lathe out of three faulty with only four hours left to complete an order. Field studies suggest that people typically choose to work with RBB and avoid deep reasoning if possible. The time/reliability curves of fault diagnosis are probably due to repeated RBB (Wohl 1982; Moray 1986). RBB errors may arise from errors of state recognition, or from errors of selection of action, and are prone to "lapses" of working memory and to both of Reason's "mistake" mechanisms – pattern matching and frequency gambling (Reason 1990).

KBB occurs when neither SBB nor RBB is possible. Operators find themselves in a situation that seems completely novel. The state of the system cannot be identified, or there is no well-specified rule to follow. They must reason deeply to understand the state of the system and to decide what to do. Academic cognitive psychology has typically been concerned with KBB (Wason & Johnson-Laird 1972; Johnson-Laird 1983), because it requires logical reasoning. Such logical reasoning is rare in real work in real-time industrial systems. It is sometimes seen in fault management, although even then, as emphasized by studies of naturalistic decision-making (Klein *et al.* 1993), deep reasoning is avoided by experts. KBB errors are typically "mistakes" (Reason 1990); they are rare but have significant consequences (Woods & Roth 1988). It is likely that exceptionally long fault diagnosis times are due to a switch from RBB to KBB (Wohl 1982).

Signals, Signs, and Symbols

Rasmussen suggests that SBB, RBB, and KBB imply different semiotics, respectively signals, signs, and symbols. The value of a variable may have several meanings, and Rasmussen (1986) gives the example of a meter with an associated control. During normal operation the position of the pointer is read with respect to the set-point, the commanded value. If the observed value is too low or high, the operator responds with SBB using the deviation from the set-point as an error *signal* in closed–loop control, and turns the control knob to exclude the disturbance and return the pointer to the set-point. If the plant is in an unusual state, such as start-up, the pointer may have a different expected value. The temperature of a subsystem may rise only late in the start-up process. If operators know that the plant is in the expected low-temperature state, they should not use the control to try to drive the instrument reading to the normal set-point. A reading far from normal may require one action during start-up, and a different response in normal operating mode. Hence RBB is required: "If the plant is cold, do not use the control to force the pointer to the normal set-point. If the plant is in full power operating mode, null any error to drive the pointer to the normal set-point." In this case Rasmussen describes the displayed information as a *sign*. Signs indicate contexts within which different RBBs are appropriate. Finally, operators may find that the indicator reading is quite abnormal, a value which they have never seen, which was not included in training, and which makes no sense – there are no well-defined rules to follow. The first response might be to press the "calibrate" button to make sure that the meter is properly set up. If the abnormal reading persists, the displayed information is symbolic of something that requires KBB, reasoning, experiments, perhaps further information. In this case the value of the variable is a *symbol* of the system state, rather than an indicator of what to do (as in SBB or RBB).

SBB, RBB, and KBB describe behavior: signals, signs, and symbols describe the logical status and cognitive value of displayed information that supports choices of adaptive behavior, and the cognitive strategy to be adopted. Novices typically begin by using KBB or RBB, depending on their training and the design of the human–machine interface, and progress at least to a stable pattern of performance at RBB. If the bandwidth of the system is high, if stimulus response compatibility is high, and if behavior can be practiced sufficiently, operators will often achieve SBB (see, e.g., Crossman & Cooke 1974; Moray *et al.* 1986). For a related model of skill acquisition, see McRuer and Krendel (1957, 1959, reprinted 2005).

Sociotechnical Aspects of Cognition in Work

Sociotechnical factors affect cognition and behavior. If training and operating procedures emphasize an absolute primacy of rules, with no freedom for operators to diverge from the formal regulations imposed by management, action will be extremely constrained. A managerial regime that punishes infringement of tightly written operating procedures may prevent operators taking any action at all if an unforeseen situation does not match any rules. Operators can justify inaction because it is not their responsibility to cope with unforeseen events using KBB, only to follow instructions (RBB). A liberal regime where creativity is encouraged will permit the maximum use of human intelligence in the face of unforeseen events. But flexibility has a price: it can lead operators to force the system into unforeseen states. This balance between creativity and prescription is central to the design problem of sociotechnical systems (Zuboff 1988; Reason 1990; Hollnagel 1993, 1998; Rasmussen *et al.* 1995). Hollnagel and Woods (2005) have recently described an approach to system design which they call *cognitive systems engineering,* which emphasizes the importance of thinking of the human and machine as a *joint cognitive system* (*JCS*) rather than as separate entities. They suggest that it is the properties of the JCS that must be understood, rather than human cognition per se.

Workers rarely work alone, and this implies a social dimension to cognition. For example, Moray *et al.* (1992) describe a case where telephone communication was as important as an elaborate computer-based information system in the response to a nuclear power incident, and where cognition was distributed over a team of more than ten people during emergency management. De Keyser (1981) noted that steel mill workers relied extensively on telephone messages to confirm control room displays even when given a modern computer-based control room. Several early papers make the same point (Crossman 1974; Edwards & Lees 1974a; Englestadt 1974; Lees 1974), and in recent years there has been increasing interest in distributed decision-making, where decisions are the product of groups or teams (Hutchins 1995; Cooke *et al.* 2000; Langan-Fox *et al.* 2000) study of cognition in naval pilotage is a classic account of such phenomena, and the work of Rochlin and LaPorte (see Laporte & Consolini 1991) shows how even in a sociotechnical system that one might expect to be prone to failure, good sociotechnical organization can produce a remarkably high level of safe performance. There are major cultural differences among workers in different countries (Moray 2004; see Cooke *et al.*, Chapter 10, this volume).

COGNITIVE FUNCTIONS IN INDUSTRIAL SYSTEMS

To apply a theory of cognition to a real work situation requires a *task analysis* to define environmental constraints and the cognitive behavior required (Kirwan & Ainsworth 1992; Hoffman & Woods 2000). Vicente (1999) argues instead for a *cognitive work analysis*, and Hollnagel and Woods (2005) for a radically different approach. Here we will note cognitive activities typical of many industrial tasks.

Planning and Scheduling

Planning supports behavior under time constraints. In DMS, scheduling is the central planning operation, requiring a rich mental model of the process and interaction with sophisticated computer programs, since scheduling algorithms are often computationally extremely demanding. In CPCS and hybrid systems planning is also critical. (See Bainbridge (1974) for a verbal protocol from a CPCS with a flow chart of decision cycles that use time estimation to control the process.) European work emphasizes the crucial role of time as a cognitive variable (De Keyser 1981; De Keyser *et al.* 1987; De Cortis 1988; Hoc 1995, 1996; Cellier *et al.* 1996). For earlier studies, see Edwards and Lees (1974a), and a renewed emphasis in Hollnagel and Woods (2005).

Monitoring

In supervisory control (Sheridan 1992, 1997, 2002), the operators' primary task is to monitor the system to ensure that the system state is close to the desired state while automation exercises control. Monitoring involves attention, pattern recognition, dynamic attention allocation, decision-making, and perceptual-motor control. Attention and pattern recognition are used to decide whether to intervene manually if the system diverges from its desired state, or if windows of opportunity to increase efficiency can be found. In systems such as steel mills, some state variables such as noise, vibrations, and the color and appearance of hot metal can be monitored directly, providing what De Keyser (1981) calls "informal information." In NPP control rooms there are 1000–2000 displays and controls spread across a wall 20 meters or more long, or several hundred pages of information presented on computer screens. In DMS, some information may be displayed on a central computer console, with local displays on equipment scattered around the plant requiring operators to visit them to acquire information: or operators may need to watch directly AGVs, conveyors, etc. to see what is happening. The key cognitive processes in monitoring are attention and pattern recognition. A more generalized model for monitoring, incorporating sociotechnical factors, has recently been proposed by Vicente *et al.* (2004).

Constraint Recognition

System state space is the industrial equivalent of the "problem space" of artificial intelligence. The system's degrees of freedom define a multidimensional space of temperature, pressure, flow rates, mass inventory, queue length, machining time, etc. Within this space lie constraint boundaries that define regions of acceptable operation and conditions requiring intervention. Recent developments in displays put emphasis on displaying constraint boundaries to support creative responses by operators (Woods 1988; Woods & Roth 1988; Vicente 1992, 1998; Rasmussen *et al.* 1995; Vicente *et al.* 1996; Reising & Sanderson 2002). Fault diagnosis and management require an operator to understand the system's causal structure and to know where the plant state locus lies in relation to constraint boundaries, since by definition the plant should not be allowed to violate a constraint boundary, which may be hazardous or may lead to economic loss.

Function Allocation

This topic, one of the most important in industrial human factors, is treated comprehensively by Parasuraman & Lorenz (Chapter 16, this volume). Function allocation determines which tasks will be performed by humans and which by automation, and when control will pass from one to the other. This sort of decision requires one to know:

- the characteristics of the mechanical and automated system;
- the intentions of the designer: Why does the equipment behave in this way? What is the purpose of this pump in that location, and if it is malfunctioning, in what other way can the same result be achieved?
- the relative abilities of the human operator and the mechanized or automated systems.

Methods of function allocation such as "Fitts' List" (Fitts, 1951, reprinted 2005), based on a comparison of what humans and machines do better than each other, are unsatisfactory (Hancock & Scallen 1996; Hollnagel & Woods 2005). Engineering, psychological, and sociotechnical considerations are all needed (Sheridan 1992, 1997; Inagaki 1993, 1995; Grote *et al.* 1995; Parasuraman & Riley 1997; Parasuraman *et al.* 2000; Weiringa 1997; Wei *et al.* 1998; Siemieniuch *et al.* 1999). Technical advances now allow almost any human ability to be simulated by machines (at a price). With increasing machine intelligence adaptive function allocation includes a social relation involving mutual trust and an understanding of mutual authority between human and machine (Rouse 1988; Woods 1988; Woods & Roth 1988; Inagaki 1993, 1995; Moray *et al.* 1994, 1995; Scerbo 1996; Parasuraman & Riley 1997; Sheridan 1997; Moray *et al.* 2000). Some quantitative models exist, mostly based on queuing theory, but the dimensions of trust and complacency in the relations between humans and machines have been increasingly emphasized, and attention has also been given to organizational factors (Lee & Moray 1992, 1994; Parasuraman *et al.* 1993; Muir 1994; Riley 1994, 1996; Muir & Moray 1996; Tan & Lewandowsky 1996; Moray & Inagaki 2001; Moray *et al.* 1995; Lee & See 2004).

Social and Motivational Factors

Effective cognition involves social dynamics and motivation. The strategic goals of management and executives may have time constants of weeks or even years: the tactical goals of operators have time constants of the order of minutes or hours; the action goals of operators or maintenance technicians during an emergency may lie in the range of seconds. Coordination and communication among personnel are of the utmost importance. A workforce that understands the long-term goals of its management, and which trusts that management is likely to work well, make good decisions, pay close attention to its task, and develop good patterns of communication which support coordination and mutual understanding. A management which is sensitive to the needs of the workforce and trusts the operators is more likely to invest in good equipment and training and to allow creative experiment than one which is not (Zuboff 1988; Rasmussen *et al.* 1995). Reason (1990, 1997) notes that many violations of work rules are not malicious, but represent accumulated "work wisdom" arising from practice and embodying expertise. During major emergencies radical departures from normal practice may be needed. If management is willing to accept violations as experiments in good faith, and if "whistleblowing" to identify problems is encouraged, then the dynamics of social interaction in the workplace will support efficient performance of cognitive tasks.

In this regard LaPorte and Consolini (1991) on effective systems are particularly interesting, and describe systems characteristics that promote error detection and exceptionally safe operation, arising from self-organizing properties of human-machine systems rather than the application of rigid rules. (There may, however, be important cultural differences that have not yet been studied. Hofstede (1984, 1994) reports that workers from different cultures show great differences in socio–technical characteristics.)

Mental Models

Operators develop *mental models* of their systems. The existence of such mental models has long been taken for granted by engineers and psychologists in human–machine systems research (Edwards & Lees 1974a. For reviews of mental models in industrial contexts, see Wilson and Rutherford 1989; Bainbridge 1991; Rutherford *et al.* 1992; Moray 1997a, 1998); for comparable classical laboratory work, see Gentner and Stevens 1983; Johnson-Laird 1983). The concept is rich, and care is needed to avoid its becoming just another way of saying that operators understand the system. However it has been shown that a successful controller *must* be a model of the controlled process (Conant & Ashby 1970).

Rasmussen's classification of behavior is helpful in classifying mental models. In SBB, mental models can be identified with human operator transfer functions (McRuer and Krendel 1959, reprinted 2005, 1976; Young 1969, 1973; Sheridan and Ferrell 1974). In RBB, mental models are probably mental look-up tables entered by pattern recognition fed by direct perception of displays, or by calculations on an array of multivariate state space variables (Dutton and Starbuck 1971, reprinted 2005; Beishon 1974). In other cases they are the remembered contents of rule sets constructed in the mind. KBB models are probably mental representations of systems in the form of verbal (declarative) knowledge, and also sets of mental images.

In this last sense, models for KBB, operators' mental models most resemble those discussed in basic research (Gentner & Stevens 1983; Johnson-Laird 1983). There are, however, important differences. In academic experiments subjects can form exact and complete mental models, isomorphic to the problem. The universe to be embodied in a model is complete in the data provided by the experimenter. By contrast, mental models constructed by workers in complex systems are not isomorphs but homomorphs of the real world, many-to-one mappings in which information is lost in the interests of simplification and mental economy. While most accounts of mental models in laboratory research seem to imply that mental models reside in working memory, many engineering psychologists think of them as long-term representations of operating experience. Mental models reside in long-term memory, whence they may be recalled in whole or in part for use in working memory.

Mental models of real systems are always incomplete and imperfect, since workers never experience all possible states of even a simple system. Operators may form multiple models of a given system, representing final cause, material cause, etc. Indeed, Rasmussen's abstraction hierarchy can be thought of as a set of progressively more compact mental models, since one can form mental models of mental models (Moray 1989, 1997a, 1998). Workers frequently modify their mental models on the basis of experience so that the relations among their different ways of thinking about a system change. There is empirical evidence that models that support normal operation may not generalize to abnormal operation, even in quite simple systems.

It is often said that interface design, procedures, and training should support operators' mental models (e.g., Wickens 1991). However, this should be done only if the models are correct, and it is one of the tasks of cognitive engineering to ensure that mental models are as accurate as possible. Clearly this involves training, although training centered on model creation has not been much explored. A major part of acquiring expertise is the construction of good mental models, and in industrial settings these often must be shared among team members (Langan-Fox *et al.* 2000).

Fault Detection and Management

One of the most important roles for human operators is the detection, diagnosis, and management of faults (Rasmussen & Rouse 1981). This requires problem-solving in dynamic environments, where the problem may change rapidly and where the outcomes often involve high hazards and payoffs. Generally, faults propagate so that a single localized failure produces a cascade of further problems, requiring operators to change frames of reference and problem spaces dynamically. This is particularly difficult because people seem able to think about only one problem at a time, and are unable or unwilling to switch between concurrent problems (Moray & Rotenberg 1989; Woods 1994; Weiringa 1997; Wei 1998). Industrial systems have alarms, but these are often insufficient to support fault management, especially in large systems. Sensors can fail, or minor faults become accepted as chronic plant states and so hide important changes (Kasperson 1992), what one might call "crying sheep" rather than "crying wolf." As Reason (1990) and many others have noted, the "defense in depth" design of hazardous industrial systems can make it harder to manage faults. Such systems are designed with much redundancy, so that not even several concurrent failures are sufficient to challenge plant safety. A progressive degradation of safety systems may be hidden until the moment of final catastrophic failure. There is one well-documented case where no fewer than seven safety systems failed simultaneously, although a probabilistic risk assessment of such an event would suggest that its probability is less than 10^{-14}, which one would normally regard as zero. Such events constitute "fundamental surprises" (Lanir 1986; Sarter *et al.* 1997) arising from "resident pathogens" (Reason 1990, 1997). In large systems alarms and sensors are often faulty and frequently "cry wolf," so that when the real fault occurs it may go unnoticed (Kemeny 1979).

Cognition in DMS: Scheduling

The great majority of research has been concerned with CPCS, but there are some features of discrete systems that are particularly interesting. In particular, and central to DMS, is scheduling. The phrase "mental model" has many meanings (Moray 1997a, 1998), but studies in DMS settings, particularly when scheduling is involved and because RBB is preferred to KBB, suggest that in such systems mental models are look-up tables. In their classic paper "Finding Charlie's Run-Time Estimator," Dutton and Starbuck (1971) provide a particularly clear account of practical cognition and an operator's mental. "Charlie" was responsible for scheduling in a factory making cloth, controlling a machine on which cloth was woven, then cut longitudinally ("ripped") and transversely ("cut"). His task was to estimate the time it would take to fill orders. Dutton and Starbuck worked with him for a year, measuring his behavior objectively, conducting interviews, and taking verbal protocols.

The number of possible schedules was of the order of several thousand combinations, (the product of the number of variables and their range of values); but Charlie mentally could accurately estimate the timing of orders, apparently using the following variables:

- the kind of cloth being produced;
- the raw material of which the cloth was to be made;
- the set-up of the ripper (which makes the longitudinal cuts);
- the number of changes of width required;
- the speed of the machine in yards per hour;
- the average length of rips;
- the sum of rip length;
- the value of this sum divided by the speed;
- "several other factors."

Charlie considered them in an almost invariable sequence, indicating a methodical approach to his mental calculations. Dutton and Starbuck constructed two models of how Charlie estimated scheduling time. One was a quantitative engineering model, based on their observations, while the second was based on Charlie's own account of what he was doing.

The quantitative equation was:

$$T = aR + (b + g\ W)L$$

Where:

T = the sum of the times for the segments scheduled
R = the number of "ripper set-ups" used
W = the weight per square yard of the cloth
L = the length in yards of the material to be produced
a = time required for "set-up"
b + g W = time per yard produced.

The model based on what Charlie told them of how he worked was equivalent to:

$$T = L/S \tag{1}$$

Where:

$$S = f(A, \text{type of cloth, texture, properties of material}) \tag{2}$$

And:

S = speed measured in yards/hour
A = mean length of a "rip"
(Note that $S = 1/(a/A + b + gW)$ even if Charlie was unaware of the fact.)

Dutton and Starbuck comment, "Charlie thus uses two non-linear relations, of which one is quite complex, in order to construct a simple linear relation." This latter is then used to schedule the task. The authors remark that relation (1) seems to be a description of a mental model rather than a true equation, and (2) is effectively a very large, multidimensional look-up table, with between 2000 and 5000 entries. Mental look-up tables probably cause less mental workload than calculations, although it would require prolonged experience to develop one. (See Crossman 1959, reprinted 2005; Towill 1974) for the time needed to develop industrial skills.) Charlie seems to be using a combination of RBB (the look-up table) and KBB (reasoning), based on a mental model or models built up by long experience, which enable him to avoid direct calculation. Beishon (1974) also concluded that in a scheduling task, operators use large mental look-up tables rather than mathematical reasoning.

Charlie's task appears to have been one in which scheduling was completed prior to the beginning of the run. Sanderson examined some of the subtleties of dynamic intervention in the acquisition of scheduling skills (Buss 1988; Sanderson 1989; Singalewitch 1992; Seiler 1994). She developed optimal algorithms for a simulated DMS, and investigated how operators acquire supervisory control skills in scheduling. After some hours of practice, the combination of human and optimal automation showed an increase in output of around 15 per cent over automation alone, despite the fact that the automation algorithm was optimal in the strong mathematical sense over the time horizon of the production run. The tendency for hybrid human–machine systems to be better than either alone is well attested (Sanderson 1989).

The operators seemed to operate rationally but opportunistically on a short time horizon. They might halt an empty AGV on its way to a distant destination because they could see that a task at an intermediate location was about to be completed. By pausing until this latter was finished, the AGV could transport it to an intermediate destination on the way to the AGV's final destination (as algorithmically programmed with a time horizon of the complete task, due to last nearly an hour). The time lost in the delay was more than recovered by avoiding an extra circuit of the track to deal subsequently with the second job. Humans used short time horizon opportunistic intervention to improve the overall performance of the human–machine combination over either automation or manual control alone. Sanderson's group added opportunistic rule-based strategies to the long time horizon algorithm, and found that automated control approached, but never completely matched, the symbiotic behavior. (Note that industrial scheduling is increasingly automated, and the opportunities for short-term intervention by operators is decreasing.)

A detailed analysis of the human role in DMS based on field studies can be found in Wiers (1997), Crawford & Wiers (2001), and McKay & Wiers (2003). Wiers' analysis broadly supports the results quoted above from laboratory and earlier field studies. For a model of the role of the human in scheduling see Sanderson (1989, 1991) and Sanderson & Moray (1990). Jackson *et al.* (2004) have recently proposed a global qualitative model for the role of humans in scheduling. For an overview of the relation between scheduling models and cognitive psychology models, see Dessouky *et al.* (1995). For a general review of the human factors of manufacturing see Karwowski *et al.* (1997).

COGNITION IN THE DL CYCLE

We can relate cognition in industrial tasks to laboratory research by examining the activities associated with the elements of Rasmussen's DL (see Figure 11.2), starting at the bottom left element of Figure 11.2 and considering each of the information-processing activities in turn.

Alarms

A typical event initiating the DL cycle is an alarm that alerts the operator to monitor information. This may cause a rapid SBB response, such as to hit an emergency shutdown switch. The automatic, "thoughtless," skill-based path from signal detection to action is indicated by the arrow marked S. Such SBB is error-prone if the relation between perception and action violates either stimulus–response compatibility, or stimulus–response population stereotypes. (NPP regulations commonly require operators to monitor the automatic safety systems for 20–30 minutes before intervening, because of the high probability of error with very rapid responses, essentially the speed–accuracy tradeoff.)

Another response to an alarm is to scan displays and acquire data from sources such as indicators, computer screens, the physical appearance of material such as molten steel, the position or movement of an object on a conveyor belt, or the number of items in a queue. Such observations support decision-making when there is no SBB available. Signal Detection Theory (Swets 1996) can be used to model information acquisition at this stage.

Coupling causes difficulty. It is extremely rare for a single alarm to appear. At least in CPCS an abnormal state is almost certain to propagate disturbances throughout the plant. Several hundred alarms occurred during the first minute of the accident at Three Mile Island, and by the end of two or three minutes almost every alarm was illuminated (Kemeny 1979). Such a state carries no diagnostic information save that "something is terribly wrong." The problem of cascading alarms is discussed by Woods (1994), and several reviews of alarms and warnings have appeared (Stanton 1994; Laughery *et al.* 1995). De Keyser (1981; De Keyser *et al.* 1987) reports that workers in a steel mill sometimes took action to correct a situation before the alarm sounded and used the alarm as a form of feedback to measure the success of their intervention.

Monitor Displays and Data

To *monitor* a system is to distribute attention over sources of information to keep track of plant state. To *sample* is to observe a single source of data. A monitoring cycle typically takes several seconds, since operators must scan a computer screen or a large control panel using head and eye movements, page through computer displays, walk around the control room, speak to colleagues directly or by telephone, or glance through a window to see what is happening on the plant floor. These behaviors, not details of central nervous system physiology, are the mechanisms of attention relevant to industrial work. Attention in real work situations differs greatly from attention in laboratory studies. There may be hundreds or thousands of displays and controls distributed over many square meters of wall space or several hundred pages of computer displays. The values of variables may be strongly correlated one with another due to physical coupling. There are no well-defined trials. The duration of "stimuli" is indefinite and often at the choice of the observer, or may change too rapidly to track during faults: at Three Mile Island the hard copy printout was running nearly an hour behind the events (Kemeny 1979). The actions of operators change what will happen next. Values change continuously when they are not being observed.

There is no fixed value of attention-switching time and no limit to how long it may take to switch attention. If someone has to walk across a room, turn their eyes, head, or body, or use a mouse or keyboard to call up a page of data, the time taken to switch attention may be several seconds or longer. From both theory (Moray 1986; Senders 1964, 1983; Sheridan & Ferrell 1974) and empirical data, it is known that the greater the precision required in reading a display, the lower the signal-to-noise ratio of the display, and the more complex the display, the longer it takes to process the visual input. The fixation duration of eye movements, once a source is selected, has a lower limit of perhaps 200 milliseconds, but the upper limit is again indeterminate, and may be several seconds or more (e.g., if the observer fixates a changing display and tries to estimate its mean value).

The main factors controlling sampling are the rate of growth of uncertainty (due either to forgetting or the bandwidth of system events) and the expected value of significant events. If an observation shows a variable to be close to a constraint boundary, the next attentional sample will be taken earlier (Senders 1983; Leermakers 1995). The interval before the next sample will be reduced if a positive payoff is associated with the observation, and lengthened if observations are costly (Kvalseth 1977). Several models of sampling are reviewed in Moray (1986). Sampling is also used to update mental models.

Attention may be under conscious control (RBB or KBB) or may become skill-based and unconscious after prolonged experience of a system with stable statistical properties. Mental models may drive attention, and a particularly interesting case arises in what has been called "cognitive lockup" or "cognitive tunnel vision" (Moray 1981, 1986), which is seen in both laboratory and field studies (Edwards & Lees 1974a; Kemeny 1979;

Rasmussen & Rouse 1981). Real decisions are often quite different from the normative decision-making described in laboratory research. When a fault is detected, the first plausible hypothesis as to its cause tends to be adopted, attention becomes locked on to the suspect subsystem, and observers try to confirm the hypothesis, rather than test it (Reason 1990; Klein *et al.* 1993; Zsambok & Klein 1997). Other parts of the system are neglected so that later faults tend to remain untreated (Moray & Rotenberg 1989). Although usually thought of as an error, cognitive tunnel vision may better be regarded as a rational strategy based on an operator's realization that a fault first propagates within a tightly coupled subsystem. Iosif (1968, 1969a, 1969b, reprinted 2005) found that in a fossil fuel power plant mental models partitioned the plant into such subsystems. Operators' attention was distributed very unevenly over subsystems, and within each subsystem only one or two variables were sampled frequently, suggesting that those components were conveying enough information due to correlation among variables to reduce the sampling of others.

Identify State of System

Rasmussen's framework emphasizes pattern recognition, above all in RBB. Because of the weaknesses of human reasoning (Kahneman *et al.* 1982; Johnson-Laird 1983) which become worse under stress and time pressure, it is often better that displays should support direct pattern recognition rather than reasoning, because "solving a problem simply means representing it so as to make the solution transparent" (Simon 1981, p. 153), and because of people's known preference for RBB. In addition to recognizing the current state, workers must also be able to estimate the past dynamic history of the plant, predict its future trajectory through state space, and recognize where the plant is in relation to physical and sociotechnical constraint boundaries.

State identification is equivalent to complex pattern recognition. Models of sequential decision-making and the theory of signal detection (TSD) can be used to model event detection and state identification (Moray 1986). Something other is needed than TSD as used in laboratory studies, since the detection of drifts or the onset of instability in a CPCS involves the analysis of continuous signals (Taylor *et al.* 1967; Sheridan & Ferrell 1974). For industrial applications of TSD see Swets and Pickett (1982); Drury and Sinclair (1983); Swets (1996). Jerison (1967) argued that values of beta as high as 10 or 20 are unrealistic in laboratory experiments and invalidate TSD as a model for monitoring (vigilance), but calculating beta with costs and payoffs in real industrial tasks can lead to values of an order of magnitude greater. To trip (shut down) a power plant can cost a utility hundreds of thousands of dollars a day, while not tripping the plant can result, in the limit, in catastrophic failure with costs running into millions of dollars and severe social consequences including death to employees and others. Very high values of beta are realistic, and Moray (1982) found them in fault detection in a NPP.

Displays and Cognition

What displays best support the operator in complex systems? Some suggest that different display formats suit different users, and that users should be able to reconfigure interfaces to their preferred layout, symbology, and mode of presentation. Such systems could provoke accidents. Since teams, not individuals, often control complex processes, flexible adaptability could cause confusion. Many graphs and displays look superficially similar, and an operator might glance at displayed data without realizing that a colleague had reconfigured the displays. Moray and Gaines (Moray 1992) evaluated a flexible adaptable control panel for ships' engine rooms, and found that an experienced operator lost track of display–control relationships after he reconfigured them. We do not at present know how to choose an appropriate level of adaptability and flexibility in computerized control rooms. (See Kragt 1992 for examples of control room design.)

Designing Displays

Bennett and Flach (1992) provide an interesting introduction to the design of displays using the simple hydraulic system shown in Figure 11.3. Two inputs are controlled by valves V1 and V2, with flow rates shown by meters I1 and I2. At the output is a valve V3 and its flow meter O. The meter T shows the temperature of the fluid in the reservoir, whose fluid inventory is shown by the meter R. The system goal G1 is to hold the value of R at a particular set point and goal G2 is to achieve a specified flow rate through the system. (Multiple simultaneous goals are a common feature of industrial processes.)

The relation between the valve settings and the flow rates are given by:

$$I1 = K1.V1 \quad (1)$$

$$I2 = k2.V2 \quad (2)$$

$$O = k3.V3 \quad (3)$$

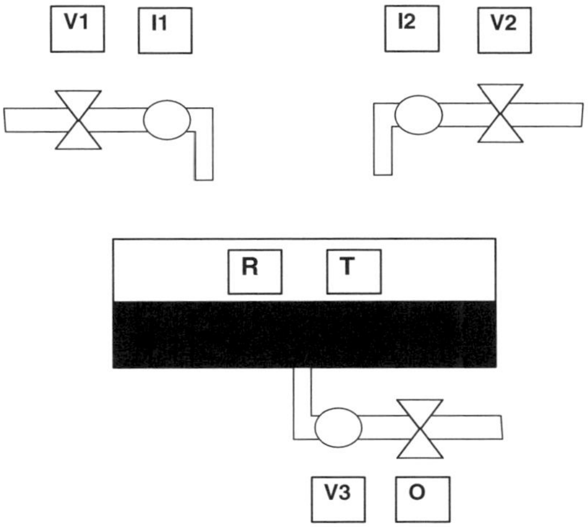

Figure 11.3 Bennett and Flach's hydraulic system

which can be rearranged to give:

$$k1 = I1/V1 \quad (1a)$$

$$k2 = I2/V2 \quad (2a)$$

$$k3 = O/V3 \quad (3a)$$

to show the relevant invariants.

Changes in the content of the reservoir are governed by the equation,

$$dR/dt = (V1 + V2) - V3 \quad (4)$$

which can be also expressed in terms of *k*s and Is.

Together, the values of the variables and the state equations (1)–(4) completely describe the system. What is the best display? In Figure 11.4, Bennett and Flach offer six possible designs. In A, B, and E the circles represent meters. C represents a mimic diagram, in which the circles are again meters or digital indicators. In F the circles represent lamps that may be lit or dark. D represents an "ecological interface display" (EID), to be discussed in more detail later. The columns in each display labeled P and D show respectively values which are directly perceptible from the display without any thought (P), and the values which must be derived from the displayed values by calculation (D).

It is unusual to display values such as *k1–k3*, but such information is useful diagnostically. These *k*s should be constant, since they are system invariants, part of the hardware definition. If *k3* is abnormally high, it implies that the flow is lower than expected for the given valve setting, which in turn indicates either that something is blocking the outflow pipe or that there is a fault in the sensor measuring the reservoir level, and that therefore the pressure head is lower than indicated. If *k* values are not displayed, the operator must calculate the ratio of I to V in order to check for constant *k*, that is, use KBB. Entries in the D column rely on human reasoning and increase mental workload.

Bennett and Flach do not discuss temporal information. Process operators like trend displays, which represent the (recent) past history of the process, and which allow them to extrapolate trends into the future (Kelly 1964, 2005; Edwards & Lees 1974a, 1974b). In the past trend graphs were produced as pen recordings, more recently as computer graphics (Woods 1986; Hansen 1995). Extrapolation into the future can be supported by predictor displays. These were originally proposed by Zeiboltz (Kelly 1964, 2005), and are becoming increasingly common (Wickens 1991; Sheridan 1992, 1997; Hansen 1995).

If it is best for operators to work at the SBB or RBB level, and avoid KBB, it is desirable to maximize the entries in the (P) column. Cognitive engineering should not always support thought and reasoning; it may be sometimes better to avoid it in favor of rules and recognition-based skills. Two kinds of displays deserve special emphasis, those based on emergent features, and so-called "ecological" displays.

"Emergent Feature" Displays

Detailed discussions of emergent features can be found in Carswell and Wickens (1987); Sanderson *et al.* (1989); Buttigieg and Sanderson (1991). Perhaps the best-known industrial

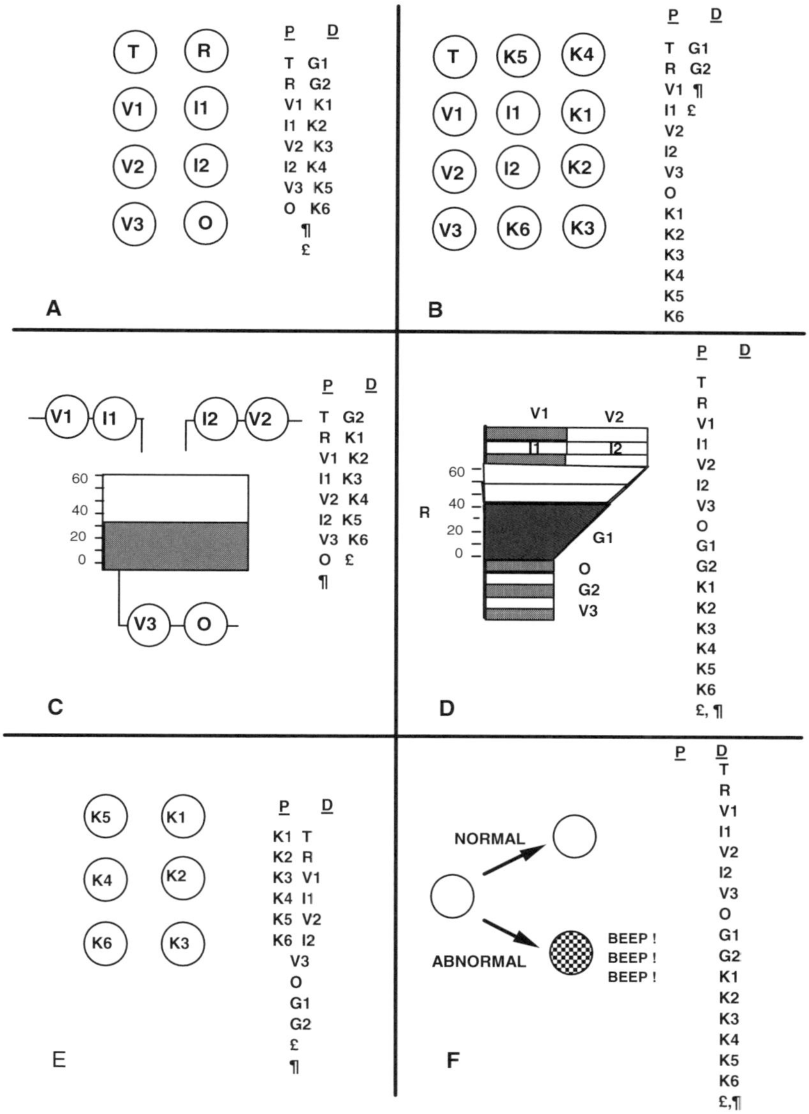

Figure 11.4 Bennett and Flach's examples of displays

example of an integrated display with emergent features is the "star" diagram, in which several variables are simultaneously displayed along the radii of a star, each variable having its zero value at the center of the circle, and normalized so that when each variable is at its expected value one can draw a polygon of constant radius, the emergent feature, by joining up the values (Coekin 1969; see Sheridan 1997 for an advanced form of this display). Any abnormality distorts the polygon.

Although attractive in principle, the use of star displays is problematic. There is no simple way to decide which variables to include in a star. Some configurations may be easier than others to read. Scaling to make radii equal when the plant state is normal may mean that changes in some variables are less perceptible than others. Some events may be easier to recognize when certain variables are on adjacent radii, but for others it may be better to have a different sequence. Nothing is known about how to optimize such displays. Little evaluation has been done. Woods *et al.* (1981) showed that detection of abnormalities was good with star displays (although they did not seem to aid diagnosis); but one group of users actively disliked a star display because it was difficult to recognize abnormal conditions. In a real system there is always enough drift or disturbance present to ensure that the variables do not fall on the "normal" circle even when the plant is operating normally.

"Ecological" Displays

The most important recent development in display design is the ecological interface display (EID). Consider Example D in Figure 11.4. The display shows directly the values of all the system state variables, inputs and outputs and the relations among them. The geometry of the display reveals the system state as the *shape* of the display. Again we may quote Simon (1981), "solving a problem simply means representing it so as to make the solution transparent."

Notice how the display supports directly. By suitable scaling, the length of the bars O, V3 and G2 can be made equal when the goal G2 is satisfied. Then the verticality of the straight line bounding the end of O, V3, and G2 is a directly perceptible indicator that the output flow goal is satisfied regardless of the quantitative values.

We can scale all variables and relations to produce a display in which all information is P, and none D. When running normally, the system is then represented by a vertical rectangle, and any departure from normality by a geometrical deformation of the rectangle. Furthermore, by choosing the geometry appropriately, any distortions indicate their cause. In example D of Figure 11.4 the reservoir is filling (the inflow to the reservoir is greater than the outflow), and the slope of the line on the right-hand end of the trapezoid resembles something that is filling. (Were it emptying, it would slope the other way.) This kind of display allows the system state to be assessed without quantitative calculations, using perception rather than cognition. Vicente summarizes thus the philosophy of EIDs as applied to large-scale systems:

> The approach . . . is based on an ecological perspective which demands that system design begin with, and be driven by, an explicit analysis of the constraints that the work environment imposes on behavior. Only by adopting such a perspective can designers ensure that the content and structure of the interface is compatible with the constraints that actually govern the work domain . . . The desired objective of this approach is to ensure that workers will acquire a veridical mental model of the work domain, so that their understanding corresponds, as closely as possible, to the actual behavior of the system with which they are interacting (e.g. the nuclear power plant). This is not to say that cognitive considerations are not important . . . Psychological factors come into play, but only after ecological constraints have been satisfied. After all, if ecological compatibility has not been established, then the design is doomed

> from the start . . . The argument for the ecological perspective . . . generalizes meaningfully to any application domain where there is an external reality – outside of the person and the computer – that imposes dynamic, goal-relevant constraints on meaningful behavior. For these correspondence-driven work domains, workers' mental models should correspond with this external reality. The only way to accomplish this objective efficiently is to adopt an ecological perspective by starting and driving the system design process by conducting an analysis of work constraints. (Vicente 1999)

The aim in EIDs is not to provide quantitative information about the values of variables ("data"), but to show the users where they are in constraint space ("information"). Appropriately designed EIDs should support all kinds of behavior (SBB, RBB, and KBB) and modes of thought at all levels of the abstraction hierarchy (physical form, physical function, general form, general function, high-level goals). This will allow the maximum freedom for workers to navigate in state space.

The importance of EIDs from a cognitive perspective is its insistence on perception rather than reasoning as the basis of adaptive behavior. There is some confusion about the relation between EIDs and Gibson's original description of the ecological psychology and adaptive behavior in the natural world (Gibson 1986; Flach *et al.* 1995; Hancock *et al.* 1995; Vicente 1999). Gibson's original concern was perceptual-motor skills in natural environments, and he proposed a "strong" ecological psychology that is best regarded as dealing with only such situations. As the human operator becomes increasingly remote from manual control of high bandwidth systems, strong ecological psychology becomes less and less relevant, and a careful reading of Gibson suggests that he explicitly excluded environments typical of industrial systems. Efforts by Shaw *et al.* (1995) to justify ecological psychology on the basis of dimensional analysis and the discovery of force related invariance are irrelevant, since through an appropriate human–machine interface any force, however small, can cause any acceleration, however great, by implementing appropriate interface transfer functions. The sense in which Rasmussen, Vicente, Sanderson and others use the term "ecological" should be distinguished from Gibson's original use. An interface is ecological when it displays perceptually the relevant system invariances and constraints.

In many systems there may be a "natural" or "canonical" representation which provides a natural geometry for the display (Beltracchi 1987; Rasmussen *et al.* 1995; Vicente *et al.* 1996) place great emphasis on looking for such displays. But research on cross-cultural display stereotypes suggests that there are very large cultural differences, and that *gestalten* that seem completely "natural" are often learned, and may have different meanings in different cultures (Moray 2004). EIDs are not instantly understandable, nor do they instantly provide affordances to all viewers, as Gibson claims for the ecology of the natural world. EIDs provide affordance for experts with domain knowledge, and even domain experts must have the symbology of the displays explained to them. Although intended for recognition-based behavior, paradoxically the design of EIDs is a challenge for *cognitive* psychology. The design of such interfaces is still as much an art as a science, although progress is being made (Harrison & Wells 2004; Burns & Hajdukiewicz 2004). There is evidence that EIDS are sometimes difficult to use, although good for fault management (Reising & Sanderson 2002), and for a conceptual criticism see Hollnagel and Woods (2005).

Deduce Consequences of State: Evaluate and Choose Criteria of Performance

Tracking the state of the system in an industrial process is equivalent to "situation awareness" in other domains (Endsley 1995; Endsley & Kiris 1995). However, the complexity and size of industrial systems and inadequate instrumentation or displays abnormal situations and faults may prevent operators from identifying system state. They must then proceed to higher levels of the DL and use KBB to develop strategies. The displayed data and information are used as inputs for reasoning using mental models, as operators try to drive the plant to a state that is understood, or is at least relatively safe and stable, and will provide time to develop strategies and tactics which lead to appropriate action.

SUMMARY

Both field studies and experiments on cognitive behavior are possible in real or realistic settings. Experimental work can be performed in the field, in simulators, or in the laboratory using "microworlds," realistic tasks that are sufficiently complex to call up realistic behavior from operators (Buss 1988; Sanderson 1989; Singalewitch 1992; Lee & Moray 1992, 1994; Muir 1994; Seiler 1994). Rasmussen *et al.* (1995, pp. 219–224) provide a particularly insightful discussion of the conditions under which laboratory studies are likely to produce ecologically valid results.

Parallels can be found between many concepts investigated in the cognitive psychology laboratory and behavior in field settings, including signal detection, pattern perception, attention, working memory, mental models and skill acquisition.

On the other hand, little laboratory research can be currently applied to human–machine systems design because of the oversimplified and "context-free" research settings used in the laboratory, which frequently prevent realistic behavior from appearing.

Applied cognitive research is a rich and fascinating field, with enormous importance to productivity, safety, and the job satisfaction of workers in an increasingly technological world. It provides deeply challenging intellectual problems for researchers, and a vivid setting for testing the predictive power of cognitive models, computational or otherwise. It further provides an outstanding opportunity to synthesize different fields of psychology, experimental, social and organizational, and in so doing give a richer meaning to "cognition".

The real world is the ultimate challenge for any psychological theory.

REFERENCES

Ashby, W. R. (1956). *An Introduction to Cybernetics*. London: Chapman and Hall.

Bainbridge, L. (1974). Analysis of protocols from a process control task. In E. Edwards & F. Lees (eds.), *The Human Operator in Process Control* (pp. 146–158). London: Taylor and Francis.

Bainbridge, L. (1978). Forgotten alternatives in skill and workload. *Ergonomics*, *21*(3), 169–185.

Bainbridge, L. (1983). The ironies of automation. *Automatica*, *19*, 755–779. Reprinted in N. Moray (ed.) (2005). *Ergonomics Major Writings* (Vol. 4, pp. 395–407). London: Taylor and Francis.

Bainbridge, L. (1991). Mental models in cognitive skills: the example of industrial process control. In A. Rutherford & Y. Rogers (eds.), *Models in the Mind*. New York: Academic Press.

Beishon, R. J. (1974). An analysis and simulation of an operator's behaviour in controlling continuous baking ovens. In E. Edwards & F. Lees (eds.), *The Human Operator in Process Control* (pp. 79–90). London: Taylor and Francis.
Beltracchi, L. (1987). A direct manipulation interface for water-based Rankine cycle heat engines. *IEEE Transactions of Systems, Man and Cybernetics*. SMC-17, 478–487.
Bennett, K. B. & Flach, J. M. (1992). Graphical displays: implications for divided attention, focused attention and problem solving. *Human Factors, 34*(5), 513–533.
Burns, C. & Hajdukiewicz, J. R. (2004) *Ecological Interface Design*. Boca Raton, FA: CRC Press.
Buss, T. (1988). Operator fault management in a small computer integrated manufacturing system. MSc Thesis, Engineering Psychology Research Laboratory, Department of Mechanical and Industrial Engineering, University of Illinois at Urbana-Champaign.
Buttigieg, M. & Sanderson, P. M. (1991). Emergent features in visual display design for two types of failure detection tasks. *Human Factors, 33*(6), 631–651.
Carswell, C. M. & Wickens, C. D. (1987). Information integration and the object display: an interaction of task demands and display superiority. *Ergonomics, 30*, 511–527.
Cellier, J-M., De Keyser, V. & Valot, C. (1996). *La Gestion du temps dans les environnements dynamiques*. Paris: Presses Universitaires de France.
Coekin, J. A. (1969). A versatile presentation of parameters for rapid recognition of total state. *International Symposium on Man–Machine Systems*. (58-MMS 4). New York: IEEE Conference Record 69.
Conant, R. C. & Ashby, W. R. (1970). Every good regulator of a system must be a model of that system. *International Journal of System Science, 1*, 89–97.
Cooke, N. J., Salas, E., Cannon-Bowers, J. A. & Stout, R. J. (2000). Measuring team knowledge. *Human Factors, 42*(1), 151–173.
Crawford, S. & Wiers, V. C. S. (2001). From anecdotes to theory: reviewing the knowledge of the human factors in planning and scheduling. In B. L. MacCarthy & J. R. Wilson (eds.), *Human Performance in Planning and Scheduling* (pp. 15–44). London: Taylor and Francis.
Crossman, E. R. (1974). Automation and skill. In E. Edwards & F. Lees (eds.), *The Human Operator in Process Control* (pp. 1–24). London: Taylor and Francis.
Crossman, E. R. & Cooke, F. W. (1974). Manual control of slow response systems. In E. Edwards & F. Lees (eds.), *The Human Operator in Process Control* (pp. 51–66). London: Taylor and Francis.
Crossman, E. R. F. W. (1959). A theory of the acquisition of speed skill. *Ergonomics, 2*, 153–166. Reprinted in N. Moray (ed.) (2005). *Ergonomics Major Writings* (Vol. 2, pp. 67–83). London: Taylor and Francis.
De Cortis, F. (1988). Dimension temporelle de l'activité cognitive lors des démarrages de systèmes complexes. *Le Travail Human, 51*, 1215–1238.
De Keyser, V. (1981). La fiabilité humaine dans les processus continus, les centrales thermo-electriques et nucléaires. *Technical Report 720-ECI-2651-C-(0) GCE-DGXII*, CERI, Bruxelles.
De Keyser, V., De Cortis, F., Housiaux, A. & Van Daele, A. (1987) Les communications homes–machines dans les systèmes complexes. Appendice, *Technical Report Contrat No. 8, Actions Nationales de Recherche En Soutien A Fast*. Université de Liège, Belgium.
Dessouky, M. I., Moray, N. & Kijowski, B. (1995). Taxonomy of scheduling systems as a basis for the study of strategic behavior. *Human Factors, 37*(3), 443–472.
Drury, C. G. & Sinclair, M. A. (1983). Human and machine performance in an inspection task. *Human Factors, 25*, 391–399.
Durso, F. T., Cooke, N. M., Breen, T. J. & Schvaneveldt, R. W. (1987). Is consistent mapping necessary for high-speed search? *Journal of Experimental Psychology: Learning, Memory and Cognition, 13*(2), 223–229.
Dutton, J. M. & Starbuck, W. (1971). Finding Charlie's run-time estimator. In J. M. Dutton & W. Starbuck (eds.), *Computer Simulation of Human Behavior*. New York: John Wiley & Sons. Reprinted in N. Moray (ed.) (2005), *Ergonomics Major Writings* (Vol. 4, pp. 367–383). London: Taylor and Francis.
Edwards, E. & Lees, F. (1974a). *The Human Operator in Process Control*. London: Taylor and Francis.

Edwards, E. & Lees, F. (1974b). *Process Control.* London: Institute of Chemical Engineers.
Endsley, M. R. (1995). Towards a theory of situation awareness in dynamic systems. *Human Factors, 37*(1), 32–64.
Endsley, M. R. & Kiris, E. O. (1995). The out-of-the-loop performance problem and level of control in automation. *Human Factors, 37*(2), 381–394.
Englestadt, P. H. (1974). Socio-technical approach to problems of process control. In E. Edwards & F. Lees (eds.), *The Human Operator in Process Control.* London: Taylor and Francis.
Fitts, P. M. (1951). *Some Basic Questions in Designing an Air-navigation and Air-traffic Control System* (pp. 5–11). Washington, DC: National Research Council. Reprinted in N. Moray (ed.) (2005) *Ergonomics Major Writings* (Vol. 4, pp. 367–383). London: Taylor and Francis.
Flach, J., Hancock, P., Caird, J. & Vicente, K. (1995). *Local Applications of the Ecological Approach to Human–Machine Systems* (Vol. 2). Hillsdale, NJ: Lawrence Erlbaum Associates.
Gentner, D. & Stevens, A. L. (1983). *Mental Models.* Hillsdale, NJ: Lawrence Erlbaum Associates.
Gibson, J. J. (1986). *The Ecological Approach to Visual Perception.* Hillsdale, NJ: Lawrence Erlbaum Associates.
Grote, G. S., Weik, T., Wafler, T. & Zolch, M. (1995). Criteria for the complementary allocation of functions in automated work systems and their use in simultaneous engineering projects. *International Journal of Industrial Ergonomics, 16*, 367–382.
Hancock, P., Flach, J., Caird, J. & Vicente, K. (1995). *Global Applications of the Ecological Approach to Human–Machine Systems* (Vol. 1). Hillsdale, NJ: Lawrence Erlbaum Associates.
Hancock, P. A. & Scallen, S. F. (1996). The future of function allocation. *Ergonomics in Design* (October), 24–29.
Hansen, J.-P. (1995). Representation of system invariants by optical invariants in configural displays for process control. In P. Hancock, J. Flach, J. Caird & K. Vicente (eds.), *Local Applications of the Ecological Approach to Human-Machine Systems* (pp. 208–233). Hillsdale, NJ: Lawrence Erlbaum Associates.
Harrison, J. & Wells, M. (2004). Advanced direct perception displays – addressing the problems that other decision support can't reach. *Journal of Defence Science, 9*(1), 30–40.
Hoc, J.-M. (1995). Planning in diagnosing a slow process. *Zeitschrift für psychologie, 203*, 111–115.
Hoc, J.-M. (1996). *Supervision et contrôle de processus: la cognition en situation dynamique.* Grenoble: Presses Universitaires de Grenoble.
Hoffman, R. R. & Woods, D. D. (eds.) (2000). Cognitive task analysis. Human Factors Special Section. *Human Factors, 42*, 1–101.
Hofstede, G. (1984). *Culture's Consequences.* Newbury Park, CA: Sage.
Hofstede, G. (1994). *Cultures and Organizations.* London: HarperCollins.
Hollnagel, E. (1993). *Human Reliability Analysis: Context and Control.* London: Academic Press.
Hollnagel, E. (1998). *Cognitive Reliability and Error Analysis Method.* Amsterdam: Elsevier.
Hollnagel, E. & Woods, D. D. (2005). *Joint Cognitive Systems: Foundations of Cognitive Systems Engineering.* London: Taylor and Francis.
Hutchins, E. (1995). *Cognition in the Wild.* Cambridge, MA: MIT Press.
Inagaki, T. (1993). Situation-adaptive degree of automation for system safety. *Proceedings of IEEE International Workshop on Robot and Human Communication* (pp. 231–236).
Inagaki, T. (1995). Situation-adaptive responsibility allocation for human-centered automation. *Transactions of the Society of Instrument and Control Engineers, 31*(3), 292–298.
Iosif, G. (1968). La stratégie dans la surveillance des tableaux de commande. I. Quelques facteurs determinants de caractère objectif. *Revue Roumanien de Science Social–Psychologique, 12*, 147–161. Reprinted in N. Moray (ed.) (2005). *Ergonomics Major Writings* (Vol. 4, pp. 249–268). London: Taylor and Francis.
Iosif, G. (1969a). La stratégie dans la surveillance des tableaux de commande. I. Quelques facteurs determinants de caractère subjectif. *Revue Roumanien de Science Social–Psychologique, 13*, 29–41.

Iosif, G. (1969b). Influence de la correlation fonctionelle sur parametres technologiques. *Revue Roumanien de Science Social-Psychologique*, *13*, 105–110. Reprinted in N. Moray (ed.) (2005). *Ergonomics Major Writings* (Vol. 4, pp. 269–281). London: Taylor and Francis.

Jackson, S., Wilson, J. R. & MacCarthy, B. L. (2004). A new model of scheduling in manufacturing: tasks, roles, and monitoring. *Human Factors*, *46*(3), 533–550.

Jerison, H. (1967). Signal detection theory in the analysis of human vigilance. *Human Factors*, *9*, 285–288.

Johnson-Laird, P. N. (1983). *Mental Models*. Cambridge, MA: Harvard University Press.

Kahneman, D., Slovic, P. & Tversky, A. (eds.) (1982). *Judgement under Uncertainty: Heuristics and Biases*. Cambridge: Cambridge University Press.

Karwowski, W., Warnecke, H. J., Hueser, M. & Salvendy, G. (1997). Human factors in manufacturing. In G. Salvendy (ed.), *Handbook of Human Factors* (2nd edn, pp. 1876–1925). New York: John Wiley & Sons.

Kasperson, R. E. (1992). The social amplification of risk. In S. Krinsky & D. Golding (eds.), *Social Theories of Risk* (pp. 153–178). Westport, CT: Praeger.

Kelly, C. (1964). *Manual and Automatic Control*. New York: John Wiley & Sons.

Kelly, C. (2005). Historical and predictor displays. In N. Moray (ed.). *Ergonomics Major Writings* (Vol. 3, pp. 251–262). London: Taylor and Francis.

Kemeny, J. G. (ed.) (1979). *The President's Commission on the Accident at Three Mile Island*. Washington, DC: US Government Printing Office.

Kirwan, B. & Ainsworth, L. K. (1992). *A Guide to Task Analysis*. London: Taylor and Francis.

Klein, G. A., Orasanu, J., Calderwood, R. & Zsambok, C. E. (1993). *Decision-making in Action: Models and Methods*. Norwood, NJ: Ablex.

Kragt, H. (1992). *Enhancing Industrial Performance: Experiences of Integrating the Human Factor*. London: Taylor and Francis.

Kuo, W. & Hsu, J. P. (1990). Update: simultaneous engineering design in Japan. *Industrial Engineering, 22*, 23–28.

Kvalseth, T. (1977). Human information processing in visual sampling. *Ergonomics*, *21*, 439–454.

LaPorte, T. R. & Consolini, P. M. (1991). Working in practice but not in theory: theoretical challenges of high-reliability organizations. *Journal of Public Administration Research and Theory*, *1*, 19–47.

Lanir, Z. (1986). *Fundamental Surprise*. Eugene, OR: Decision Research.

Langan-Fox, J., Code, S. & Langfield–Smith, K. (2000). Team mental models: techniques, methods, and analytic approaches. *Human Factors*, *42*(2), 242–271.

Laughery, K. R., Wogalter, M. S. & Young, S. L. (1995). *Human Factors Perspectives on Warnings*. Santa Monica, CA: Human Factors and Ergonomics Society.

Lee, J. D. & Moray, N. (1989). Making mental models manifest. *Proceedings of the 1989 IEEE International Conference on Systems, Man and Cybernetics*, Boston, MA, 56–60.

Lee, J. D. & Moray, N. (1992). Trust, control strategies and allocation of function in human–machine systems. *Ergonomics*, *35*, 1243–1270.

Lee, J. D. & Moray, N. (1994) Trust, self-confidence and operators' adaptation to automation. *International Journal of Human–Computer Studies*, *40*, 153–184.

Lee, J. D. & See, K. A. (2004). Trust in automation: designing for appropriate reliance. *Human Factors*, *46*(1), 50–80.

Leermakers, T. (1995). *Monitoring Behaviour*. Eindhoven: Eindhoven University of Technology.

Lees, F. (1974). Research on the process operator. In E. Edwards & F. Lees (eds.), *The Human Operator in Process Control* (pp. 386–425). London: Taylor and Francis.

McKay, K. N. & Wiers, V. C. S. (2003). Planners, schedulers and dispatchers: a description of cognitive tasks in production control. *Cognition, Technology and Work*, *25*(2), 82–93.

McRuer, D. T. & Krendel, E. (1957). *Dynamic Response of the Human Operator*. (WADC TR-56-254). Dayton, OH: Wright-Patterson AFB.

McRuer, D. T. & Krendel, E. (1976). *Mathematical Models of Human Pilot Behavior*. NATO AGARDograph No. 188. Brussels.

McRuer, D. T. & Krendel, E. S. (1959). The human operator as a servo system element. *Journal of the Franklin Institute, 267*(5/6), 1–49. Reprinted in N. Moray (ed.) (2005). *Ergonomics Major Writings* (Vol. 4, pp. 69–122). London: Taylor and Francis.

Moray, N. (1981). The role of attention in the detection of errors and the diagnosis of failures in man-machine systems. In J. Rasmussen & W. B. Rouse (eds.), *Human Detection and Diagnosis of System Failures*. New York: Plenum.
Moray, N. (1982). Subjective criteria used by nuclear power plant operators in making decisions about the normality of their equipment. *15th Proceedings of Human Factors Association of Canada*, Toronto.
Moray, N. (1986). Monitoring behavior and supervisory control. In K. R. Boff, L. Kaufman & J. P. Thomas (eds.), *Handbook of Perception and Human Performance* (Chapter 45). New York: John Wiley & Sons.
Moray, N. (1989). A lattice theory approach to the structure of mental models. *Philosophical Transactions of the Royal Society of London, series B*, *327*, 447–593.
Moray, N. (1992). Flexible interfaces can promote operator error. In H. Kragt (ed.), *Enhancing Industrial Performance* (pp. 49–64). London: Taylor and Francis.
Moray, N. (1997a). Models of models of . . . mental models. In T. B. Sheridan & T. Van Lunteren (eds.), *Perspectives on the Human Controller* (pp. 271–285). Mahwah, NJ: Lawrence Erlbaum Associates.
Moray, N. (1997b). Human factors in process control. In G. Salvendy (ed.), *Handbook of Human Factors* (2nd edn, pp. 1944–1971). New York: John Wiley & Sons.
Moray, N. (1998). Mental models in theory and practice. *Attention and Performance XVII* (pp. 223–258). Cambridge, MA: MIT Press.
Moray, N, (2004). Culture, context and performance. In M. Kaplan (ed.), *Cultural Factors in Ergonomics* (pp. 31–60). Amsterdam: Elsevier.
Moray, N. & Inagaki, T. (2001). Attention and complacency. *Theoretical Issues in Ergonomic Science*, *1*(4), 354–365.
Moray, N., Inagaki, T. & Itoh, M. (2000). Situation adaptive automation, trust and self-confidence in fault management of time-critical tasks. *Journal of Experimental Psychology: Applied*, *6*(1), 44–58.
Moray, N., Lee, J. D. & Hiskes, D. (1994). Why do people intervene in the control of automated systems? *Proceedings of the 1st Conference on the Human Factors of Automated Systems*. Washington, DC, February.
Moray, N., Lee, J. D. & Muir, B. M. (1995). Trust and human intervention in automated systems. In J.-M. Hoc, C. Cacciabue & E. Hollnagel (eds.), *Expertise and Technology: Cognition and Human–Computer Interaction*. Mahwah: Lawrence Erlbaum Associates.
Moray, N., Lootsteen, P. & Pajak, J. (1986). Acquisition of process control skills. *IEEE Transactions on Systems, Man and Cybernetics*, SMC-16, 497–504.
Moray, N. & Rotenberg, I. (1989). Fault management in process control: eye movements and action. *Ergonomics*, *32*, 1319–1342.
Moray, N., Sanderson, P. M. & Vicente, K. J. (1992). Cognitive task analysis of a complex work domain: a case study. *Reliability Engineering and Systems Safety*, *36*, 207–216.
Muir, B. M. (1994). Trust in automation: Part I – Theoretical issues in the study of trust and human intervention in automated systems. *Ergonomics*, *37*(11), 1905–1923.
Muir, B. M. & Moray, N. (1996). Trust in automation. Part II. Experimental studies of trust and human intervention in a process control simulation. *Ergonomics*, *39*(3), 429–461.
Norman, D. (1990). *The Design of Everyday Things*. New York: Doubleday.
Parasuraman, R., Molloy, R. & Singh, I. L. (1993). Performance consequences of automation-induced "complacency." *International Journal of Aviation Psychology*, *3*, 1–23.
Parasuraman, R. & Riley, V. (1997). Humans and automation: use, misuse, disuse, abuse. *Human Factors*, *39*(2), 230–253.
Parasuraman, R., Sheridan, T. B. & Wickens, C. D. (2000). A model for types and levels of human interaction with automation. *IEEE Transactions on Systems, Man, and Cybernetics*, SMC-30, 286–297.
Perrow, C. (1984). *Normal Accidents*. New York: Basic Books.
Rasmussen, J. (1986). *Information Processing and Human–Machine Interaction: An Approach to Cognitive Engineering*. Amsterdam: North-Holland.
Rasmussen, J., Pejtersen, A.-M. & Goodstein, L. (1995). *Cognitive Engineering: Concepts and Applications*. New York: John Wiley & Sons.

Rasmussen, J. & Rouse, W. B. (eds.) (1981). *Human Detection and Diagnosis of System Failures.* New York: Plenum.

Reason, J. (1990). *Human Error.* Cambridge: Cambridge University Press.

Reason, J. (1997). *Managing Risks of Organizational Accidents.* Aldershot: Ashgate.

Reising, D. V. C. & Sanderson, P. M. (2002). Ecological interface design for Pasteurizer II: a process description of semantic mapping. *Human Factors, 44*, 222–247.

Riley, V. (1994). A theory of operator reliance on automation. In M. Mouloua & R. Parasuraman (eds.), *Human Performance in Automated Systems: Recent Research and Trends* (pp. 8–14). Hillsdale, NJ: Lawrence Erlbaum Associates.

Riley, V. (1996). Operator reliance on automation. In M. Mouloua & R. Parasuraman (eds.), *Human Performance in Automated Systems: Theory and Applications* (pp. 19–35). Hillsdale, NJ: Lawrence Erlbaum Associates.

Rouse, W. B. (1988). Adaptive aiding for human-computer control. *Human Factors, 30*, 431–438.

Rutherford, A., Rogers, Y. & Bibby, P. A. (eds.) (1992). *Models in the Mind.* London: Academic Press.

Sanderson, P. M. (1989). The human planning and scheduling role in advanced manufacturing systems: an emerging human factors role. *Human Factors, 31*(6), 635–666.

Sanderson, P. M. (1991). Towards the model human scheduler. *International Journal of Human Factors in Manufacturing, 1*, 195–215.

Sanderson, P. M. & Moray, N. (1990). The human factors of scheduling behavior. In W. Karwowski & M. Rahini (eds.), *Ergonomics of Hybrid Automated Systems, II.* Amsterdam: Elsevier.

Sanderson, P. M., Flach, J. M., Buttigieg, M. A. & Casey, E. J. (1989). Object displays do not always support better integrated task performance. *Human Factors, 31*(2), 183–198.

Sarter, N. B., Woods, D. D. & Billings, C. E. (1997) Automation surprises. In G. Salvendy (ed.), *Handbook of Human Factors* (pp. 1026–1043). New York: John Wiley & Sons.

Scerbo, M. S. (1996). Theoretical perspectives on adaptive automation. In R. Parasuraman & M. Moulova (eds.), *Automation and Human Performance: Theory and Application.* Hillsdale, NJ: Lawrence Erlbaum Associates.

Seiler, M. (1994). The effects of heterarchical vs. hierarchical scheduling algorithms on human operator behavior in discrete manufacturing systems. MSc Thesis, Engineering Psychology Research Laboratory, Department of Mechanical and Industrial Engineering, University of Illinois at Urbana-Champaign.

Senders, J. W. (1964). The human operator as a monitor and controller of multi-degree of freedom systems. *IEEE Transactions on Human Factors in Electronics,* HFE-5, 2–5. Reprinted in N. Moray (ed.) (2005). *Ergonomics Major Writings* (Vol. 1, pp. 47–55). London: Taylor and Francis.

Senders, J. W. (1983). *Visual Sampling Processes.* Katholieke Hogeschool Tilburg, Netherlands and Hillsdale, NJ: Lawrence Erlbaum Associates.

Shaw, R. E., Flascher, O. M. & Kadar, E. E. (1995). Dimensionless invariants for intentional systems: measuring the fit of vehicular activities to environmental layout. In J. Flach, P. Hancock, J. Caird & K. Vicente (eds.), *Global Perspectives on the Ecology of Human–Machine Systems* (Vol. 1, pp. 293–358). Hillsdale, NJ: Lawrence Erlbaum Associates.

Sheridan, T. B. (1992). *Telerobotics, Automation, and Human Supervisory Control.* Cambridge, MA: MIT Press.

Sheridan, T. B. (1997). Supervisory control. In G. Salvendy (ed.), *Handbook of Human Factors* (2nd edn, pp. 1295–1327). New York: John Wiley & Sons.

Sheridan, T. B. (2002). *Humans and Automation: System Design and Research Issues.* New York: John Wiley and Sons.

Sheridan, T. B. & Ferrell, W. R. (1974). *Man-Machine Systems.* Cambridge, MA: MIT Press.

Shiffrin, R. M. & Schneider, W. (1977). Controlled and automatic human information processing II: perceptual learning, automatic attending, and a general theory. *Psychological Review, 84*, 127–190.

Siemieniuch C. E., Sinclair M. A. & Vaughan G. M. C. (1999). A method for decision support for the allocation of functions and the design of jobs in manufacturing, based on knowledge requirements. *International Journal of Computer-Integrated Manufacturing, 12*(4), 311–324.

Simon, H. (1981). *The Sciences of the Artificial.* Cambridge, MA: MIT Press.
Singalewitch, H. (1992). Learning strategies in a computer integrated manufacturing simulation. M.Sc. thesis, Engineering Psychology Research Laboratory, Department of Mechanical and Industrial Engineering, University of Illinois at Urbana-Champaign.
Singleton, W. T. (ed.) (1978). *The Study of Real Skills.* London: Academic Press.
Stanton, N. (ed.) (1994). *Human Factors in Alarm Design.* London: Taylor and Francis.
Swets, J. (1996). *Signal Detection Theory and ROC Analysis in Psychology and Diagnostics.* Mahwah, NJ: Lawrence Erlbaum Associates.
Swets, J. & Pickett, R. (1982). *Evaluation of Diagnostic Systems.* New York: Academic Press.
Tan, G. & Lewandowsky, S. (1996). A comparison of operator trust in humans versus machines. *INTERNET: CybErg International Electronic Conference.* Available: http://www.curtin.edu.auf conference/.
Taylor, M., Lindsay, P. H. & Forbes, S. M. (1967). Quantification of shared capacity processing in auditory and visual discrimination. *Acta Psychologica, 27,* 223–231.
Towill, D. R. (1974). A model for describing process operator performance. In E. Edwards & F. Lees (eds.) *The Human Operator in Process Control* (pp. 179–185). London: Taylor and Francis.
Vicente, K. J. (1992). Ecological interface design: theoretical foundations. *IEEE Transactions on Systems, Man, and Cybernetics*, SMC-22(4), 589–606.
Vicente, K. J. (1998). Improving dynamic decision-making in complex systems through ecological interface design: a research overview. *Systems Dynamics Review, 12,* 251–279.
Vicente, K. J. (1999). *Cognitive Work Analysis: Towards Safe, Productive and Healthy Computer-Based Work.* Mahwah, NJ: Lawrence Erlbaum Associates.
Vicente, K. J., Moray, N., Lee, J. D. *et al.* (1996). Evaluation of a Rankine cycle display for nuclear power plant monitoring and diagnosis. *Human Factors, 38*(3), 506–522.
Vicente, K. J., Murmaw, R. J. & Roth, E. M. (2004). Operator monitoring in a complex dynamic work environment: a qualitative cognitive model based on field observation. *Theoretical Issues in Ergonomics Science, 5*(5), 359–384.
Vierling, A. E. (1990). Machines can only produce as efficiently as the people who operate them. *Industrial Engineering, 22,* 24–26.
Volta, G. (1986). Time and decision. In E. Hollnagel, G. Mancini & D. D. Woods (eds.), *Intelligent Decision Support in Process Environments.* Berlin: Springer.
Wason, P. C. & Johnson-Laird, P. N. (1972) *Psychology of Reasoning: Structure and Content.* Cambridge, MA: Harvard University Press.
Wei, Z.-G. (1998). *Mental Load and Performance at Different Automation Levels.* Delft: University of Delft.
Wei, Z.-G., Macwan, A. P. & Weiringa, P. A. (1998). A quantitative measure for the degree of automation and its relation to system performance and mental load. *Human Factors, 40,* 277–295.
Weiringa, P. A. (1997). Operator support and supervisory control. In T. B. Sheridan & T. Van Lunteren (eds.), *Perspectives on the Human Controller* (pp. 251–260). Mahwah, NJ: Lawrence Erlbaum Associates.
Wickens, C. D. (1991). *Engineering Psychology and Human Performance.* New York: HarperCollins.
Wiener, E. L. & Curry, R. E. (1980). Flight-deck automation: promises and problems. *Ergonomics, 23*(10), 995–1011.
Wiers, V. C. S. (1997). *Human-Computer Interaction in Production Scheduling.* Eindhoven: Institute for Business Engineering and Technology Application.
Wilson, J. R. & Rutherford, A. (1989). Mental models: theory and application in human factors. *Human Factors, 31,* 617–634.
Wohl, J. G. (1982). Maintainability prediction revisited: diagnostic behavior, system complexity, and repair time. *IEEE Transactions on Systems, Man and Cybernetics*, SMC-12, 241–250.
Woods, D. D. (1986). Human factors challenges in process control: the case of nuclear power plants. In G. Salvendy (ed.), *Handbook of Human Factors.* New York: John Wiley & Sons.
Woods, D. D. (1988). Coping with complexity: the psychology of human behavior in complex systems. In L. P. Goodstein, H. B. Andersen & S. E. Olsen (eds.), *Tasks, Errors and Mental Models.* New York: Taylor and Francis.

Woods, D. D. (1994). Cognitive demands and activities in dynamic fault management: abductive reasoning and disturbance management. In N. Stanton (ed.), *Human Factors in Alarm Design* (pp. 63–92). London: Taylor and Francis.

Woods, D. D. & Roth, E. M. (1988). Cognitive systems engineering. In M. Helander (ed.), *Handbook of Human–Computer Interaction*. Amsterdam: North-Holland Elsevier.

Woods, D. D., Wise, J. A. & Hanes, L. F. (1981). An evaluation of nuclear power plant safety parameter display systems. *Proceedings of the Human Factors Society, 25th Annual Meeting.*

Young, L. R. (1969). On adaptive manual control. *IEEE Transactions on Man–Machine Systems,* MMS-10, 292–331.

Young, L. R. (1973). Human control capabilities. In J. F. Parker Jr. & V. R. West (eds.), *Bioastronautics Data Book*. Washington, DC: National Aeronautics and Space Administration.

Zsambok, C. E. & Klein, G. (1997). *Naturalistic Decision-making*. Marwah, NJ: Lawrence Erlbaum Associates.

Zuboff, S. (1988). *In the Age of the Smart Machine*. New York: Basic Books.

CHAPTER 12

Patient Safety in Health Care

Vimla L. Patel
Columbia University, USA
and
Jiajie Zhang
University of Texas at Houston, USA

Cognitive science has exerted a significant influence on academic medicine over the past three decades. However, the role of human cognition in achieving high quality care has not been fully appreciated by the health care community. There is a consensus that health care is not as safe and reliable as it could be, and that the research efforts of cognitive scientists and human factors researchers are on their way to correcting this situation. However, these efforts have not been as coordinated and integrated as they seem to be in non-medical industries. This chapter reviews some of the literature on cognition and human error for patient safety, including current trends in developing a culture of safety. We use a working definition of patient safety as the prevention of health care errors and the elimination or mitigation of patient injury caused by health care errors, as defined by the National Patient Safety Foundation. Health care error is further defined as an unintended health care outcome caused by a defect in the delivery of care to a patient. These errors are often precipitated by failures in cognitive functioning (perception, memory, attention, knowledge, action, inferences, and strategies), and constrained by social, cultural, and organizational factors. We focus on the cognitive aspects of human errors in health care that compromise patient safety.

A HISTORY OF PATIENT SAFETY

Human Errors in High-Risk Industries

The mind is associated with slips in actions, lapses in memory, and mistakes in thinking, reasoning, and decision-making. A slip of the tongue is usually inconsequential in daily life but in high-risk industries, such as aviation or nuclear power generation, such an error may trigger a catastrophic event. Various data show that human error is among the major causes of accidents in high-risk industries. For example, accidents caused by human error

Handbook of Applied Cognition: Second Edition. Edited by Francis T. Durso.

are: air traffic control – 90 per cent; automobiles – 85 per cent; nuclear power plants – 70 per cent; jet cargo transport – 65 per cent; petrochemical plants – 31 per cent (Van Cott 1994). Several high-profile accidents such as those at the Three Mile Island power plant, the *Challenger* disaster, and the Chernobyl nuclear reactor meltdown have exposed the catastrophic consequences of human error (Perrow 1984). The emergence of cognitive psychology in the 1960s and its progress over the past three decades provided theories of human error that allow the causes of accidents to be better understood. Psychological theories provide descriptions, explanations, and even predictions of error. Human errors are no longer considered to be random, unfortunate events that we can only passively observe; they can be reduced or even eliminated through intervention. Eliminating or mitigating the harmful consequences of errors is also important and easier to achieve.

Human Error in Health Care

Since the beginning of the twentieth century, one avenue has proved especially fertile for research on human error. Gestalt psychologists believed that errors are part of data reorganization, which is important for the solution to a problem (Dunker 1945). They also believed that the system with generic solutions memorized by the subjects is flagged by the memory of associated errors and failures. This logic inspired Dorner (1983) to carry out experiments with micro-worlds, simulating complex situations related to real life. This trend in psychology considered human error to have a beneficial and organizational role in cognition (Dorner 1983).

Just as technical safety is improved through the reduction of technical breakdowns, it seems reasonable to use a symmetrical rationale to improve human safety through the reduction of human error. This error-reduction concept was extensively explored for about 20 years. Studies focused on human reliability in engineering sciences, by considering the human component as an additional element in the system, similar to other technical components. It is often believed that adapting the success of industries such as civil aviation and nuclear power generation will make medicine just as safe, yet it has been argued that the situation is not as straightforward or as simple as it seems (Amalberti *et al.* 2005). These authors point out that an important difference lies in an industry's willingness to move away from historical and cultural precedents and beliefs that are linked to performance and autonomy. Patient safety is not yet a well-developed discipline. Definitions and concepts are evolving as experts debate error models and solutions to system problems. A working definition of patient safety has been "the prevention of health care errors, and the elimination or mitigation of patient injury caused by health care errors" (The National Patient Safety Foundation). Health care error is defined as an unintended health care outcome caused by a defect in the delivery of care to a patient. They can be classified as errors of commission (doing the wrong thing), omission (not doing the right thing), or execution (doing the right thing incorrectly). Errors may be generated by any member of the health care team in any health care setting. However, individuals who trigger errors may not be the root cause of errors.

In 1996, the Institute of Medicine (IOM) launched a concerted, ongoing effort focused on assessing and improving the nation's quality of care. The first phase of this *Quality Initiative* documented the serious and pervasive nature of the nation's overall quality problem, concluding that "the burden of harm conveyed by the collective impact of all of our health care quality problems is staggering" (Chassin & Galvin 1998). Their definition of quality is the degree to which health services for individuals and populations increase the likelihood of desired health outcomes and are consistent with current professional knowledge.

During the second phase, spanning the decade from 1999 to 2001, the Committee on Quality of Health Care in America set out a vision for how the health care system and related policies must be radically transformed in order to close the gap between what we know to be good quality care and what actually exists. Two reports were released during this phase: *To Err is Human: Building a Safer Health System* (Kohn *et al.* 1999) and *Crossing the Quality Chasm: A New Health System for the 21st Century* (Institute of Medicine [US] Committee on Quality of Health Care in America 2001). The former turned the spotlight on how tens of thousands of Americans die each year from medical errors and effectively put the issue of patient safety and quality on the radar screen of public and private policymakers. This report has greatly increased public awareness of the frequency, magnitude, complexity, and seriousness of medical errors. As the eighth leading cause of death in the US, ahead of motor vehicle accidents, breast cancer, and AIDS, medical errors were no longer ignored, and gained the immediate attention of academic, health care, and government organizations. The latter report describes broader quality issues and defines six aims for patient care: safety, effectiveness, patient-centered care, timeliness, efficiency, and equitability.

The third phase of the *Quality Initiative* has focused on operationalizing the vision of a future health system. These efforts focus on reform at three different, yet overlapping levels of the system to improve patient care: the environmental level; the health care organization level; and the interface between clinicians and patients. As a follow-up, a further report, *Keeping Patients Safe: Transforming the Work Environment of Nurses* (Child 2004), identifies solutions to problems in hospitals, nursing homes, and other health care environments that threaten patient safety through their effect on nursing care. The report's findings and recommendations address the related issues of management practices, workforce capability, work design, and organizational safety culture. Health care teams encounter many problems in trying to make medical care safe. The problem with trying to improve health care is that the focus is often on individual injuries rather than on the medical error itself (McNutt *et al.* 2002). A major practical limitation of the definition of an error is its focus on the outcome, rather than the root cause at the level of medical care (Perrow 1984).

The research on medical errors over the past few years has been programmatic, comprehensive, and diverse, as reflected in a large collection of research findings published in a two-volume handbook by the Agency for Health Research and Quality (Henriksen *et al.* 2005).

COGNITIVE FOUNDATIONS OF PATIENT SAFETY

It has been argued that patient safety efforts should focus on understanding and reducing medical errors (McNutt *et al.* 2002). The term "error," for psychologists, means the description of behavior that can be studied for its own sake in a nonjudgmental way, whereas others view it as the negative outcome for which someone should be blamed.

Medical error has been largely viewed by the health care industry in the latter perspective.

Medical error, or health care error, is an issue to study for cognitive science and engineering, not medicine, although knowledge of the practice of medicine is essential for the research and management of medical error. Cognitive factors are fundamental in medical errors, as can be seen from the very definition of medical errors and the view of the health care system hierarchy.

Medical errors are human errors in health care. By definition (Reason 1992; Kohn *et al.* 1999), human error is error in human actions, that is, human error is the failure of a planned sequence of mental or physical actions to achieve the intended outcome when this failure cannot be attributed to chance. Human actions are primarily cognitive; therefore, it is not surprising to see that errors are linked to cognitive processes of human action (Norman 1981; Reason 1992; Bogner 1994; Woods *et al.* 1994). To prevent human error, the systems in which people work must be adapted to their cognitive strengths and weaknesses and must be designed to mitigate the effects of human errors that do occur. To design such a system, it is critical to understand the underlying cognitive mechanisms of medical errors.

Let us consider the cognitive factors at the various levels of the health care system hierarchy at which medical errors might occur (Moray 1994; also see Zhang *et al.* 2003 for a modified version).

1. At the core level of the hierarchy, it is *individuals* who trigger errors, although individuals may not be the root cause of such errors. Cognitive factors of individuals, such as memory loss, attention-switching, deviations in skilled performance and actions, cognitive load, reasoning errors, decision biases, and faulty heuristics play the most critical role in understanding error (Reason 1992; Bogner 1994). This is traditionally the domain of research for cognitive psychology, cognitive science, and human factors.
2. *Individual–technology interaction*: Errors can occur in the interactions between an individual and technology. This is an issue of human–computer interaction and human factors (Norman 1988; Woods 1988; Flach 1990; Zhang & Norman, 1994; Helander *et al.* 1997; Zhang 1997; Vicente 1999; Hollnagel 2003; Nemeth 2003).
3. *Distributed systems*: Errors can be attributed to the social dynamics of interactions among groups of people and between people and technology. This is the issue of distributed cognition, computer-supported cooperative work, and the socio-technical approach to human-centered design (Woods 1988; Patel *et al.* 1989; Baecker 1993; Hutchins 1995a, 1995b; Xiao & Mackenzie 1998; Patel 1998; Berg 1999; Vicente 1999; Patel *et al.* 2000; Hollnagel 2003). A key issue at this level is to understand medical errors that are due to socio-technical factors, such as information flow, team dynamics, division of cognitive labor, communication, the practice of cognitive work, process reengineering, and cultural and environmental properties.
4. *Organizational structure*: Errors can be attributed to factors inherent in organizational structures such as coordination, cooperation, and collaboration among various units; communications, organizational change, organizational memory, group decision-making, and the standardization of work processes; and skills input and output (Nunamaker *et al.* 1991; Ackerman 1998; Ackerman & Halverson 1998; Te'eni 2001).
5. *Institutional functions*: Errors can be indirectly traced back to institutional policies and guidelines (McNutt *et al.* 2002).

6. *National regulations*: Errors can be reduced or prevented if systematic and comprehensive requirements such as usability and human factors testing for medical devices are mandated for vendors as a component in the approval process of medical devices (Sawyer *et al.* 1996).

Although the properties at the six levels of the system hierarchy can be studied independently, a cognitive foundation is essential for a comprehensive and in-depth understanding of medical errors across the full system hierarchy.

Understanding the cognitive basis of medical errors – patient injury resulting from poor medical management rather than the patient's disease – is an important step in reducing adverse events. However, it is only one part of the framework toward understanding medical errors. First, non-cognitive factors also contribute to medical errors. For example, fatigue and stress, which are not cognitive factors in the strict sense, can lead to breakdown of human information-processing (Krueger 1994). Second, not all adverse events are caused by medical errors. For example, a device malfunction, such as an infusion pump that delivers an incorrect dose due to a mechanical failure, may lead to an adverse event, but is not a medical error. Adverse events may also arise from system-level problems even when all the individuals working in the system do not make an error. For instance, McNutt *et al.* (2002) described a case resulting in cardiac arrest due to delays in care caused by organizational policies. Compliance with unproductive and inappropriate policy can also lead to adverse events (Bogner 1994). Another category of adverse events are those that are non-preventable. For example, a patient who gets their usual drug dose may unexpectedly suffer an unpredictable reaction.

TAXONOMIES OF MEDICAL ERRORS

To categorize, describe, explain, and predict medical errors, a fundamental first step is to develop a taxonomy of medical errors. Not surprisingly, various taxonomies of medical errors have been developed, with each emphasizing a different aspect of medical errors. We describe a few representative taxonomies based on cognitive factors, task factors, and event factors.

Cognitive Taxonomies

As discussed above, cognitive factors are a fundamental aspect of medical errors. Thus, one critical step toward understanding the cognitive mechanisms of various errors in medicine is to categorize them along cognitively meaningful dimensions. One of the pioneers of human error research was Freud (1914), who studied errors by collecting and analyzing many cases from everyday life. One important milestone in the study of human error is Norman's influential *Psychological Review* article (1981). To study human errors not just for the purpose of prevention, but also for the purpose of using errors as probes to understand human memory, action, and thinking, Norman used the psychological theories of schemata and actions to categorize slips, which are human errors due to the inaccurate performance of an otherwise correctly specified action.

Reason's book *Human Error* (1992) provided the first comprehensive review and systematic treatment of human error from a cognitive psychology perspective. The definition of human error Reason gave is widely accepted not just by psychologists but also by medical error researchers from other disciplines. Reason defines human error as a failure to achieve the intended outcome in a planned sequence of mental or physical activities. He divides human errors into two major categories: (1) slips that result from the incorrect execution of a correct action sequence; and (2) mistakes that result from the correct execution of an incorrect action sequence. From this top-level dichotomy more detailed categories were specified, such as skilled-based, rule-based, and knowledge-based errors.

In order to address the need of a cognitive framework specifically developed for medical errors, Zhang *et al.* (2004) developed a cognitive taxonomy of medical errors based on Reason's definition and Norman's "Action Theory" (Norman 1986, 1988). The aim was to make the framework comprehensive, descriptive, predictive, and generalizable. According to Norman (1986), any human action goes through seven stages: (1) establishing the goal; (2) forming the intention; (3) specifying the action specification; (4) executing the action; (5) perceiving the system state; (6) interpreting the state; and (7) evaluating the system state with respect to the goals and intentions. Figure 12.1 shows the cognitive taxonomy, where errors are divided into slips and mistakes, similar to Reason's two main categories. The slips and mistakes are divided into two more levels. An example of an execution slip is when a nurse intends to decrease a value using the decrement function, but pushes the down arrow key (which moves to the next field) instead of the minus key. An example of an evaluation slip is when a user presses the start button on an infusion pump after which the pump indicates that it has started infusing, so the user assumes the patient was receiving the drug; however, the user had forgotten to open the clamp on the hose, so no drug was being delivered.

This cognitive taxonomy can cover major types of medical error because a medical error is a human error in an action and any action goes through the seven stages of the

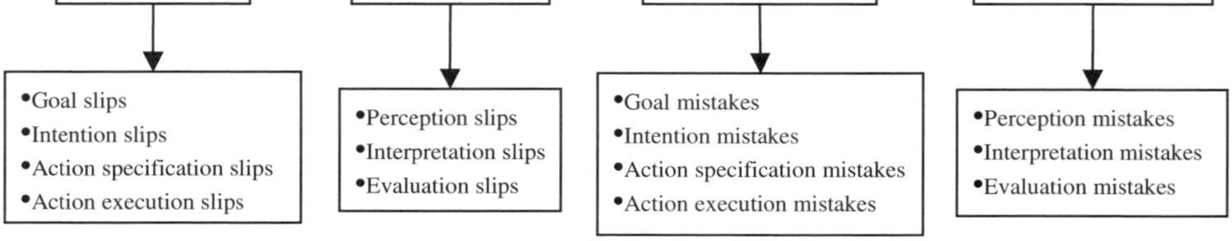

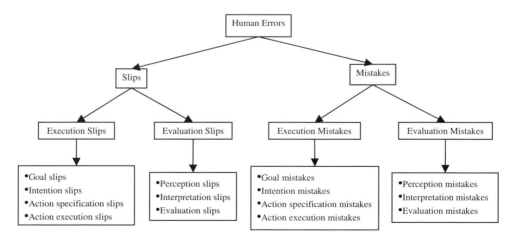

Figure 12.1 Cognitive taxonomy of medical errors. (From Zhang *et al.* 2004)

action cycle. Most reasoning and decision-making errors in medicine are under the category of mistakes in the taxonomy. They are due to incorrect or incomplete knowledge, or due to other factors. This taxonomy also provides preliminary analyses of underlying cognitive mechanisms for each category of errors and recommendations of intervention strategies. More recently, Malhotra and colleagues (2006) have extended this model to include communication between more than one health care provider.

Other Taxonomies

The National Coordinating Council for Medication Errors Reporting and Prevention (NCC MERP) has released a medication error taxonomy (1998). This provides a standard language and structure of medication error-related data for use in developing databases to analyze medication errors. It is organized into eight major categories: (1) patient information; (2) medication error event; (3) patient outcome; (4) product information; (5) personnel involved; (6) type of medication error; (7) causes; and (8) contributing factors. Each category has numerous attributes to be selected. For example, in Category 6, the type of medication error is categorized by dose omission, improper dose, wrong route of administration, wrong rate, monitoring, and other factors. This taxonomy, though quite elaborate, does not offer many useful explanations of mechanisms and recommendations for interventions. For example, Brixey *et al.* (2002) showed that the NCC MERP taxonomy is not equipped to handle complex medical error cases such as errors involving infusion pumps, which could be both device use errors and medication errors involving the use of devices. The NCC MERP taxonomy is basically for error reporting only.

Many taxonomies of medical errors are similar to the NCC MERP taxonomy, and are primarily for error reporting purposes. They are targeted at specific areas, such as primary care (Elder & Dovey 2002), nursing (Benner *et al.* 2002), family practice (Dovey *et al.* 2002), hospital accreditation and malpractice contexts (Victoroff 1997), medical education (Battles & Shea 2001), and other settings (Runciman *et al.* 1998).

Cognitive taxonomy is fundamental for the categorization, description, explanation, and prediction of medical errors. Other non-cognitive taxonomies are also essential for capturing the full spectrum of factors in health care settings. However, there is currently no single standardized nomenclature or universal classification system that is broad enough yet sufficiently detailed to encode medical error data from all health care delivery settings and application areas. To systematically categorize errors, assign mechanisms, collect frequency and other pertinent data, and map interventions, we need a single meta-taxonomy that is composed of multiple taxonomies, each of which categorizes medical errors along a specific set of dimensions. This is currently an active area of research.

COGNITIVE MECHANISMS OF MEDICAL ERRORS

Human errors occur due to non-cognitive and cognitive factors (Norman 1981; Reason 1992; Woods *et al.* 1994). Although non-cognitive factors such as organizational structure, automation, and policy are important for understanding medical errors, we believe that the fundamental mechanisms of medical errors are cognitive, although cognitive factors are not necessarily the root cause of the errors. Errors can be viewed as inevitable, yet cognitively useful phenomena that cannot be totally eliminated. In this view, human errors are products of cognitive activities in people's adaptation to their complex physical, social, and cultural environments. This cognitive approach stresses actions in conceptual understanding and thought processes during clinical problem-solving. The actions reflect the level of expertise and the demands of tasks in clinical performance. In order to manage errors during clinical decision-making, it is critical to understand how decisions are made and what underlying cognitive mechanisms are used to process information during interactions with patients, colleagues, and technology in the health care environment.

Three major categories of diagnostic error in medicine have been reported in the literature (Graber *et al.* 2002).

The first category is "no-fault errors," which occur when the disease is silent, atypical, and cannot be accounted for by the current state of medical knowledge. A rare misdiagnosis because it mimics a more common form of the disorder is also viewed as a no-fault error. These errors will inevitably decline as medical science advances and new syndromes are identified. However, such errors can never be eradicated because new diseases emerge, diagnostic tests are never perfect, patients are sometimes noncompliant, and physicians, at times, choose the most likely diagnosis over the correct one, illustrating the concept of necessary fallibility and the probabilistic nature of making a diagnosis (Graber *et al.* 2002).

The second category, "system errors," occurs when diagnosis is delayed or missed because of latent imperfections in the health care system, as described later in this chapter. This type of error can be reduced by system improvements, but can never be eliminated because these improvements lag behind and degrade over time, and each new fix creates the opportunity for novel errors. Tradeoffs also guarantee that system errors will persist, when resources are shifted.

The third category of diagnostic error is "cognitive errors." These reflect misconceptions, flawed reasoning, or incomplete knowledge. The limitations of human processing and the inherent biases in using heuristics guarantee that these errors will persist. Opportunities exist, however, for improving the cognitive aspect of diagnosis by adopting system-level changes (e.g., second opinions, decision-support systems, enhanced access to specialists) and by training designed to improve cognition or cognitive awareness. Diagnostic error can be substantially reduced, but never eradicated.

There are several strands of research which suggest possible general sources and types of errors that can occur in any workplace. Several potential categories of mistakes empirically identified are discussed below.

Conceptual Understanding

Misconceptions

Misconceptions refer to types of understanding that are at variance with scientific knowledge or empirically well-supported practice. They reflect stable beliefs that are rooted in productive knowledge and even partially correct knowledge. This understanding is flawed in some essential way and it is often difficult to refine this understanding into a correct conception.

Accurate knowledge of medical concepts is clearly important in medical decision-making, given that the decision strategies used are dependent on such knowledge. Lack of or faulty understanding can lead to conceptual errors, which can result in poor performance. Errors of this type can be especially difficult to identify because they are not easily captured by standard outcome-based measures. This phenomenon has been documented in studies of critical care physicians, where the problem was misunderstood, resulting in wrong recommendations being made for management of a patient in an intensive care unit. Studies also show that there are often dissociations between performance and knowledge in various critical care situations when one has to act quickly. For example, investigators studied the decision-making processes used by nurses in emergency (911) telephone triage, where the task was to assess the urgency of the caller's situation and provide the appropriate level of care (Leprohon & Patel 1995). By examining patient records and using follow-up phone calls to patients, they found that nurses correctly assessed all high-urgency cases (i.e., those where an ambulance was needed immediately), showed false positives (assessed the situation as more urgent than it actually was) in 38 per cent of cases, and showed false negatives (assessed the situation as less urgent that it actually was, thus potentially compromising patient health due to insufficient response) only 8 per cent of the time. On the whole, the nurses' judgments were accurate, or at least erred on the side of safety. However, analysis of the reasons underlying their decisions revealed that whereas their decisions may have been accurate, the reasoning behind their decisions was often not medically correct. This dissociation between performance and reasoning highlights the importance of examining not only resulting behaviors, but also the underlying processes of cognitive activity in order to identify errors.

This type of continuum of responses, from immediate response behavior involving minimal deliberation to the use of top-level pre-compiled plans, was also shown in studies of anesthesiologists in the surgical setting and the response of team members to unanticipated problems that can lead to adverse patient outcomes (Gaba 1992). Decision-making during highly ambiguous situations is most difficult, leading to more errors than in situations where there is less ambiguity.

Situational Factors and Type of Error

In addition to errors stemming from task complexity, misinterpretation or misuse of evidence, and underlying knowledge errors, the task or environmental characteristics can affect the nature of problem-solving and thus the nature of errors (see Durso *et al.*, Chapter 7, this volume). Patel and Arocha (2001) examined differences between health care teams in a surgical intensive care unit (SICU) and a medical intensive care unit (MICU) by following team members and attending morning rounds. They found that the different goals, subsequent differences in tasks, team member communication, and hierarchical distinctions influenced the probability and location of different types of errors. In the SICU, where patients are admitted straight from surgery and the ailments are usually known, the main goal is to monitor the patient for complications. On the other hand, the main goals of the MICU, where most of the patients are transfers from the emergency room (and thus less is known about them), are in identification of the patient's problem and stabilizing the patient. These different goals, in turn, resulted in vastly different communication styles.

Because of the differences in reasoning strategies employed in the MICU and SICU, the origin of errors also differs. Because problem-solving in the SICU is based more on automatic recognition of common patterns of data, errors may occur due to lack of vigilance or poor data interpretation. On the other hand, with the more deliberate processing seen in the MICU, errors could stem from data interpretation, inaccurate medical knowledge, or faulty reasoning processes (see the next section). Understanding the context surrounding decisions is thus critical to understanding the source and location of medical errors.

Sharp and Blunt Ends

The prevailing paradigm acknowledges that error in medical care has two distinct roots. At the "sharp end" is the individual provider who interacts with the patient and makes the mistake. At the "blunt end" are the latent flaws in the health care system which provide the setting, framework, and predisposition for the error to occur (Cook & Woods 1990; Graber *et al.* 2002). Blunt-end factors include the system's organizational structure, culture, policies, resources, the ground rules for interaction, and workload.

Medical devices are now seen as a common part of most health care systems, and the literature is littered with cases where poorly chosen medical devices compromise patient safety. Studies (e.g., Laxmisan *et al.* 2005) have shown how people with different types of expertise evaluate patient safety and device-related medical errors in the decision process of medical device purchasing. The authors found that clinicians (nurses and doctors, the sharp-end practitioners) focused on clinical and human aspects of errors, biomedical engineers (the blunt-end practitioners) focused on device-related errors, and administrators focused on documentation and training. The results show that the interpretations of the different individuals mirror their area of expertise, arguing for a broader representation within the health care system for safer choice of devices for health care practices.

Reasoning Processes

In addition to examining errors with respect to medical knowledge, task complexity, task urgency, and misinterpretation of evidence, there are also errors in the reasoning process itself. That is, while medical knowledge and interpretation of data may be accurate, deficits in how that information is used can generate errors. Two common deficits in reasoning are summarized below.

Biases in Reasoning

Reasoning bias is a deviation from normative and rational rules. Chapman and Elstein (2000) provide an overview of a number of biases in physicians' decision-making processes. These biases are grouped into three categories: (1) biases related to judging the likelihood of events; (2) biases related to preferences and values; and (3) biases related to the timing of decisions. Hindsight bias is an example of a bias related to judging the likelihood of events, after the event. It refers to the situation in which the individual revises their judgment as to the likelihood of an event occurring when they know the outcome. The phenomenon has been shown in decision-making by physicians (Arkes *et al.* 1995) as well as by nurses (Reece Jones 1995). In another interesting study, Brooks and colleagues (2000) demonstrated that while both experts and novices had difficulty making an accurate diagnosis when presented with a photograph of the key feature of a patient's problem, they showed a 20 per cent improvement when the features were described. Conversely, both experts and students reported seeing more of the features after the correct diagnosis were suggested to them. This pattern is similar to arriving at a hypothesis and then looking for evidence to support it (Patel *et al.* 2005).

Human beings use innovative and economical strategies to aid in problem-solving and decision-making; this is known as heuristics. These strategies are even more critical when the dense patient population and high degree of uncertainty exhibited in medical contexts taxes the processing capacities of physicians. The utility of heuristics lies in limiting the extent of purposeful search through data sets, and instead basing reasoning largely on past experience. By reducing redundancy, they have substantial practical value. A significant part of an emergency physicians' cognitive effort is based on heuristic thinking. Heuristics are rules of thumb, which develop with familiarity in the domain of application. The decisions based on heuristics have a high level of confidence associated with them and there is no way of checking the validity of the rules against the evidence. Heuristics are unlike the rules used to search for an explanation for a problem in that explanation involves evaluating pieces of evidence to provide a coherent account of the problem. The rules of thumb can result in errors in a number of ways, including the use of the availability heuristic, or judgment on the basis of how easily previous examples spring to mind; the anchoring heuristic, in which people stick to their initial impression of the case; framing effects, based on how the information is presented; blind obedience and premature disclosure (Tversky & Kahneman 1974). A combination of these types of results has been shown to produce serious misdiagnoses (Redelmeier 2005).

The use of heuristics introduces considerable bias in medical reasoning, resulting in a number of conceptual and procedural errors. These include misconceptions about laws governing probability, inaccurate instantiation of general rules to a specific patient at the problem, prior probabilities, perceptual illusion, and delusion of validity. These factors are described in studies reported by Croskerry and colleagues (2003, 2004).

Patel and colleagues have conducted a number of studies examining the use of heuristics by physicians (Patel & Groen 1986) and medical students (Arocha & Patel 1995). Most of these studies are summarized in Patel *et al.* (1994). A frequently used heuristic is the reliance on disease schemata during clinical diagnosis. Disease schemata are knowledge structures that have been formed from previous experience with diagnosing diseases, and contain information about relevant and irrelevant signs and symptoms. When physicians and medical students diagnose patients, they tend to rely on their schemata and base their reasoning on the apparent similarity of patient information with these schemata, instead of a more objective analysis of patient data. The schemata that are used in diagnosis often guide future reasoning about the patient, affecting what diagnostic tests are requested and how data are interpreted. This strategy is consistent with the fast and frugal heuristic where decision-makers use a 'take the best' algorithm, that is, look for recognizable patterns and cues in order to narrow the space for making decisions (Gigerenzer & Goldstein 1996).

This is similar to the "satisficing" principle (Simon 1957). Hashem and colleagues (2003) showed that there is a downside to experts' behaviors. Specialists tend to diagnose cases from outside their domain as though they fall within their areas of expertise, often assigning higher probabilities to diagnoses that are familiar to them than do clinicians who are expert in other areas. Studies of medical trainees show that they maintain their initial hypotheses, even if the subsequent data are contradictory. If the initial hypothesis is wrong, errors are likely to occur in diagnosis and treatment (Arocha & Patel 1995).

Croskerry and colleagues (2004) outlined cognitive dispositions to respond (CDRs) and affective dispositions to respond (ADRs) which influence diagnostic reasoning in medicine. In some instances, they lead to a correct diagnosis, but in others, they may compromise adequate diagnostic reasoning. CDRs are conceptualized as heuristics or shortcuts that are influenced by various contextual factors as well as past experience. ADRs constitute an important aspect of the diagnostic process, since affect can be influenced by a host of emotional and other personal factors. Interpersonal conflict as well as stress and fatigue are common factors influencing affect and may undermine the diagnostic process. These authors suggest that understanding cognitive and affective influences on the diagnostic process are crucial to identifying human error in the decision process. Croskerry (2003) also catalogued major cognitive biases in medicine and described a number of strategies for reducing them, which he calls "cognitive debiasing," a major one being metacognition, a reflective to the problem-solving approach that involves stepping back from the immediate problem to examine and reflect on the thinking process (see Sieck & Klein, Chapter 8, this volume).

Faulty Reasoning

Errors in diagnosis and prediction have been reported extensively in clinical case studies (Kassirer & Kopelman 1991). The authors draw heavily on the work of cognitive scientists, applying cognitive theory within a rich context of case material and describing a number of the more common cognitive biases employed in the clinical domain. This was a pivotal work in the development of a "clinical cognition" approach and in our understanding of the cognitive behavior of physicians.

A number of studies have identified cognitive errors that involve faulty reasoning by medical students (Patel *et al.* 1991) and clinicians (Patel & Ramoni 1997). This research was conducted under laboratory conditions and the authors found deficits in the reasoning of senior medical students, stemming from dependency effects and cyclical inferences. Such problems can also occur in clinical environments, where residents are unable to separate knowledge and inferences in high information density settings. In a pilot study of two medical emergency departments (Patel & Arocha 2001), it was found that the problem of cyclical inferences arose as a result of failure to maintain a separation between the flow of predictive and diagnostic reasoning, when predictive and diagnostic reasoning supported each other in a circular manner. When the medical knowledge of a resident trainee was adequate, diagnostic reasoning was used. However, when the knowledge was not sufficient, a mixture of predictive and diagnostic reasoning was most often used. In the emergency cases, there was a compounding of problems of dependency effects and cyclical inferences, where the major decision-making strategy was that of induction. In these circumstances, any use of induction (diagnosis) without an adequate basis for deduction (prediction), such as the ones afforded by well-developed classification schemata, would lead to inefficient, incomplete, and error-prone performance. Thus, induction as a strategy in the hands of novices can be dangerous.

METHODS FOR STUDYING MEDICAL ERRORS

Ethnographic Methods

The patient safety movement has evolved from a "phenotypical" study of the surface descriptors of medical error (the who, what, where, and when of adverse events) to a "genotypical" approach that seeks to identify how people, teams, and organizations coordinate activities, information, and problem-solving in order to cope with the complexities of situations that can arise in daily life (Woods *et al.* 1994). The link between cognitive error and decision-making, and the importance of characterizing the context, in which they are interconnected, necessitated the search for and development of methods for naturalistic study of error in the medical environment. Ethnography is one such approach, which is widely used in investigations in naturalistic environments.

Ethnography is considered much more than a set of methods; these methods are grounded in theory and philosophical principles. The strength of ethnography lies in its ability to uncover detailed insights into what people do. It allows in-depth study of real world environments that cannot be studied in laboratory settings. Typical ethnographic research on medical error involves studies of clinical workflow and collection of detailed observational data. These provide rich description of the workplace environment. Researchers usually take field notes and make event logs of human–computer interactions using participation/observation methods. They also conduct informal and formal interviews, and collect videotaped interactions, relevant documents, and photos to develop an understanding of the work environment.

A study carried out in an emergency department using ethnographic techniques of data collection (Laxmisan *et al.* 2005) identified critical failures in the workflow that compromised patient safety. One aspect of the failure was in the process of collaboration among clinical team members, especially during times of clinical shift change when information was not adequately transferred to the personnel in the next shift (e.g., the morning clinical team taking over from the night team). These "handovers" during shift changes are recognized as a vulnerable practice from patient safety standpoint (Kohn *et al.* 2000) even though they are essential in current health care work (Patterson *et al.* 2004a). Another facet – multitasking – identified as an important skill has also been recognized as an inefficient process and a major contributor to cognitive overload (Kirsh 2000; Rubinstein *et al.* 2001). Both handovers and multitasking are inherent to work practices in the emergency department. Research evidence from studies in human memory and cognition indicates that when two tasks are performed at the same time, the limited central processing channel creates a bottleneck effect for competing attentional demands which causes much of the observed slowing and lower precision of cognitive performance. If the effort that can be exerted at any time is limited, then any two tasks whose joint demands exceed that limit must be mutually interfering (Kahneman 1973). Frequent switching of attention from one task to another invariably increases error rates and completion times (Baddeley *et al.* 2001; Barrouillet *et al.* 2004). This bottleneck may reflect a structural limitation inherent in human cognitive architecture (Ruthruff *et al.* 2001). Extraneous cognitive load interferes with the primary goal of the task at hand (e.g., problem-solving) by making heavy demands on resources that become unavailable for the primary task.

Traditional ethnography (as used in anthropology and sociology) provides a rich set of data, but also generates a massive amount of data which may not be very useful for some of the focused cognitive analysis. Cognitive ethnography is becoming a useful tool for generating more focused data. It emerged from the adaptation and modification of three of the ten principles of prototypical ethnography outlined by Ball and Ormerod (2000). These include (1) replacing the principle of "intensity" with "specificity" of data collection; (2) replacing the principle of "independence," which states that the researcher must not have any existing theories, goals, or beliefs prior to observation, with "purposive" involving specific goals of the research; and (3) replacing "personalization" (which requires the researchers to make note of their own thoughts and feeling on their observations) with "verifiability" (validation of the results across various settings and observers). This adaptation of ethnography is useful in constraining the amount of data to be analyzed, and collecting data with a more specific goal in mind.

Case Analysis

Like case studies in medicine, psychology, and other fields, human error cases are important resources for understanding, describing, explaining, and even predicting human errors. In other safety-critical industries, case studies of catastrophic events were very valuable in identifying sources of error and providing directions for intervention. Most of the case studies are based on extensive accident reports. High-profile accidents such as Three Mile Island, *Challenger*, Chernobyl, and Bhopal are all cases that have been well documented and studied. Perrow's *Normal Accidents* (1984) presented case studies of many well-known disasters caused by human errors. NTSB (National Transportation Safety Board) publishes accident reports of airplane crashes, many of which were caused by human errors. These reports are an excellent resource for those conducting case studies.

Medicine is very different from these industries. Medical errors typically occur one at a time. Sometimes they go unnoticed, and sometimes even if they are noticed they are not reported for various reasons. The medical community has a very different culture and historically has been highly punitive for medical errors. Many medical error cases ended up in malpractice lawsuits. Despite these problems, case studies of medical errors are still feasible and valuable for understanding, categorization, explanation, and intervention. A well-documented case study of medical errors is the investigation of the Therac-25 accidents (Leveson & Turner 1993).

Distributed Cognition Methods

There is ample research evidence that the use of CPOE significantly reduces the rate of medical error and improves the quality of patient care (Bates *et al.* 1998; Kuperman *et al.* 2001; Chan 2002). The benefits have been widely recognized, but few institutions have successfully installed such systems. Despite the increasing consensus about the desirability of physician order entry systems, only about one in ten American hospitals presently have them (Ash *et al.* 2004).

The concept of distributed cognition is used in the health care domain to understand medical error in the context of high stress, high volume and incomplete information, such as critical care environment. This concept deals not only with the study of internal and external representations (Zhang & Norman, 1994), but also with the distribution and propagation of knowledge between individuals, artifacts, as well as the transformations sustained by structures when used by individuals and artifacts (Hutchins 1995b). This new approach allows the study of cognitive phenomena that are not observable at the individual level, such as cooperative work and socially distributed tasks such as those involved in health care, the nature of which are generally fluid and dynamic. An important part of the "world" is the interaction between individuals. In health care, cognition is distributed across different teams to function in a collaborative manner in order to deliver health care efficiently and effectively. This type of collaboration requires interaction, which has led to an increased focus on communication and teamwork. The composition of the team may represent different groups with their own agendas. For example, in an emergency room, we may have a medical team, a surgical team, medical nurses, and trauma nurses working with the same patient at the same time. The inherent benefits and problems of such a situation are the same as with any example of divided labor, the most important benefit of which is an increased efficiency in terms of time and quality. The composition of the team itself is dynamic, depending upon various factors like the time of the day and the nature of the task. Information and cognition flows across these individuals, groups, devices and the external world (see Cooke *et al.*, Chapter 10, this volume).

The intelligence required to solve a particular problem is often distributed across multiple individuals. When the cognitive load behind a task that requires collaboration for its execution is relatively low, and the decision to be made is easy, all members of the team have more or less equal standing. However, when the cognitive load is high, the cognition involved is usually distributed in a hierarchical manner.

The methodological approach outlined here incorporates methods such as generation of think-aloud protocols, cognitive task analysis, and cognitive walkthrough. They are used in conjunction with the Distributed Cognitive Resources analysis method to enrich and complement the interpretation of empirical data (Horsky *et al.* 2003).

Analytical methods derived from cognitive studies permit more direct observation and assessment of system usability. They allow analyses of psychological processes underlying performance in a variety of tasks, with an emphasis on providing a detailed characterization of the perceptual and cognitive processes that lead to observable behavior (Kluwe 1995). The methodological approach used in these studies follow two trajectories. One set of analyses is related to usability inspection in which all data are collected from tasks performed by the analysts. The visual contents of their computer monitors are recorded, along with their verbalizations, on videotape and transcribed. The results allow the formulation of system-specific and technology-general characterizations of user interaction afforded by the analyzed complex system. The analysis of subjects' behavior, from transcripts of their verbalized thoughts and from visual images, facilitates the identification and description of their interaction strategies. It also provides evidence about the ways in which external and internal resources facilitate performance and even contribute to the production of errors (e.g., Horsky *et al.* 2003). This combination of analytic techniques comparing analyst performance with empirical observations of practitioners has proven to be an effective strategy for the study of complex systems (Roth *et al.* 2002).

Modeling Methods

Medical error data are hard to collect prospectively because it is a low-probability event. In real-world settings we do not want to watch medical errors occurring due to negative outcome and ethical concerns. It would be useful to characterize cognitive mechanisms of human errors precisely with a mathematical or computational model so that medical errors can be generated, studied, and modeled. With the recent advances in cognitive modeling such as Act-R (Anderson *et al.* 2005), GOMS (Kieras 1997), SOAR (Newell 1991), and EPIC (Meyer & Kieras 1997a, 1997b) several computational models of errors in the context of human performance have been developed, such as by Byrne and Kirlik (2005). Altmann and Trafton (2002) and Trafton *et al.* (2003) have an initial computational model of interruptions in a human–computer interaction task context as it relates to human errors. In the Act-R model of pilot errors developed by Byrne and Kirlik (2005), pilots' strategies for taxiing an aircraft were modeled. The modeling results show that the details and dynamics of both the human cognitive system and the structure of the environment in which that system operates must be considered jointly and not in isolation.

One benefit of computational models is that they specify precise processes that can be simulated to test, evaluate, and predict various types of error-related behaviors. Computational modeling of medical errors has not yet started. While this is a challenging endeavor due the complexity of medical domains, it may nevertheless lead to fruitful results.

Usability Methods

Heuristic evaluation (Nielsen & Molich 1990; Nielsen 1992, 1994; Nielsen & Mack 1994) is a usability evaluation method for identifying violations of a set of well-established usability heuristics for good user interface design. This technique typically requires three or more expert usability evaluators to independently apply a set of usability heuristics to a product, identify violations of the heuristics, and assess the severity of each violation. Note that the term "heuristics" here is different from the term heuristics in the discussion of reasoning shortcuts or rules of thumbs. A heuristic for usability evaluation is a principle for good user interface design.

Zhang and colleagues (2003; Graham *et al.* 2004) modified the heuristic method and used it to study medical errors involved in infusion pump use. Infusion pumps are associated with many medication errors reported to FDA and published in the literature (Sawyer *et al.* 1996; Food and Drug Administration 1997). First, they used heuristic evaluation to discover usability problems that are likely to cause medical errors. Second, they used it to compare patient safety features of alternative medical devices, which is often useful in the purchasing process of medical devices. Third, they tried to demonstrate that heuristic evaluation is a good tool for medical device manufacturers to improve the patient safety features of their products during the design and redesign processes.

In one heuristic evaluation study, Zhang and colleagues (2003) applied 14 heuristics to evaluate the usability problems of two one-channel volumetric infusion pumps from two vendors. They focused on identifying usability problems that might be potential triggers for medical errors. They also compared the two infusion pumps in their usability and patient safety features. The evaluation showed that heuristics were violated a total of 192 times and 121 times for Pump 1 and Pump 2, respectively. Consistency and Visibility heuristics were the two most frequently violated heuristics for Pump 1, whereas Visibility was the most frequently violated heuristic for Pump 2. An example of a violation of the visibility heuristic would be: "When the 'enter' button is not pressed, after entering part or all of the value for 'Rate' and 'VTBI' (Volume To Be Infused), a message appears that reads 'complete entry'. It is not clear what it means. A better phrasing would be 'Press 'enter' to confirm value." In this case, users are apt to become confused by no clear delineation as to what action will come next. In terms of the number of heuristic violations, the results indicate that Pump 1 has more usability problems and thus may have a higher chance of generating medical errors. The findings from the heuristic evaluation of the two pumps are consistent with the frequencies of reported errors in FDA databases for the two pumps.

As a discount usability technique, heuristic evaluation is easy to use and master, efficient, effective, and useful. It can be used to identify a great proportion of major usability problems in a product in a timely manner with reasonable cost. Human errors in medical device use are largely due to interface design problems which can be potentially addressed through user-centered design. Because the quantity and severity of usability problems are usually correlated with the frequency of medical errors, heuristic evaluation is a method for indirectly assessing patient safety features in medical devices.

Task Analysis Methods

Task analysis is a critical component in cognitive systems engineering and usability engineering. It is the process of identifying the procedures and actions to be carried out and the information to be processed to achieve task goals. Hierarchical task analysis (HTA) is one of the most widely used forms of task analysis. It involves describing a task as a hierarchy of tasks and subtasks in several steps (Kirwan & Ainsworth 1992). Major tasks are identified first, followed by subtasks. This process of subdivision is continued until meaningful subtasks are exhausted and a hierarchy is established. Each task and subtask in the hierarchy is assigned a code indicating task level and sequence. By doing an HTA, the structures of the tasks and the interrelations of tasks and subtasks can be explicitly described. This process is useful for the understanding and design of user interfaces.

Chung, Zhang and colleagues (Chung *et al.* 2003; Jiajie Zhang *et al.* 2005) extended the traditional HTA to a method that can be used to evaluate and potentially predict medical errors. They called this method Extended Hierarchical Task Analysis (EHTA). The traditional HTA is limited and does not provide enough details about the cognitive processes and information-processing that is typically crucial for user interface design. EHTA added a few more steps that are especially useful for the prediction of medical errors. These extra steps include identification of system states, analysis of internal and external representations, and identification and estimation of error affordances.

In one study, Chung *et al.* (2003) analyzed single and triple channel pumps from Manufacturer A and Manufacturer B. Pumps from Manufacturer A are widely used, well recognized, and touted for their human-centered design. The pumps are claimed to have several human factors improvements over the previous technology. Nonetheless, a quick search through FDA device error reports makes it clear that they fall short of being problem-free. Pumps from Manufacturer B are a competing product. EHTA was used to analyze the two single- and two triple-channel pumps from Manufacturers A and B on two different tasks to show their intrinsic differences. The average number of steps needed to perform Task 1 and Task 2, the number of error affordances for Pump A and Pump B (both single and triple channels), and the actual use error data from FDA's MAUDE (Manufacturer and User Facility Device Experience) database (2001, 2002) were collected and compared. The results demonstrated that Pump A required more steps than Pump B, and Pump A has more error affordances than Pump B. In addition, this pattern is consistent with the FDA data on the actual error cases for Pump A and Pump B. Although more research is needed to improve EHTA, its initial success at predicting infusion pump use errors is encouraging.

CASE STUDY: OVERDOSE OF POTASSIUM CHLORIDE

This case study illustrates the errors that arise in complex systems of health care when the collaborative workflow of multiple players, working in a team and interacting with technology for delivery of safe patient care, breaks down (Horsky *et al.* 2005).

Recent advances in pharmacology research have brought to the market a number of new drugs that manage therapy more effectively or relieve previously untreated disease symptoms. As an effect of increased drug utilization, there is also a greater incidence of adverse effects of medications on hospitalized patients, frequently due to preventable prescribing errors (e.g., Patterson *et al.* 2004b). Incorrect dosing or the administration of an inappropriate drug can cause adverse drug events (ADE), ranging from mild discomfort to serious injury. Preventable ADEs are also associated with higher hospital costs to cover increased length of stay and additional treatment, and almost twice as great a risk of death. The ordering phase of patient drug therapy is the most common source of serious medication error. Computer-based provider order entry systems (CPOE) can dramatically reduce the number of these errors by assuring legibility and also by integrating decision-support and safety-related functions. CPOE systems often check in real time for drug interactions, alert to known patient allergies, and calculate dose adjustments according to patient's weight or renal function, decreasing significantly the likelihood of erroneous or unsafe doses. However, this positive effect of CPOE on prescribing safety can be compromised by the possibility of new kinds of errors specific to the inherent cognitive complexity of human computer interaction (Koppel *et al.* 2005).

The details of a dosing error event that occurred at one hospital were obtained from quality assurance reports, case and review reports provided by the organization's Significant Events Committee, recollections by involved parties obtained from interviews, and our own reconstruction from entries in ordering system usage logs (Horsky *et al.* 2005). This adverse event was related to the ordering of a potassium chloride (KCl) IV injection using an order entry system for an 85-year-old patient, admitted to the MICU with septic shock and respiratory failure. A high dose of potassium chloride was delivered due to errors and misperceptions by several care providers, compounded over several days by the propagation of an initial dosing error through the system. A summary of the problems identified is given below:

1. *Misconceptions about the relation between IV volume and time duration*: KCl can be delivered as an additive to maintenance IV fluid and dosed by limiting the *total volume* of fluid. However, IV fluids without additives are generally dosed by *volume per hour* for a specific period. The conceptual difference between *volume-limited* and *time-limited* dosing is crucial for correct dosing of IV with additives mixtures and may not be apparent from the way the entry form is presented to the user.
2. *Misconception of latest and dated laboratory results*: Misperception of the *latest* available serum potassium laboratory results as *current* played a role in erroneous assessment of the patient's status as hypokalemic. The most recent lab value did not reflect events and medication intake that took place between the time of measurement and the time the results were read by the provider and were therefore dated, that is they did not show the true current state of the patient.
3. *Inadequate clinical user training of safe and efficient ordering practices*: Procedural knowledge gained mostly from experience is often not sufficiently adaptable for successful backtracking or adequate error-recovery in non-routine situations likely to be encountered in practice. Inconsistent entry behavior in the repeated entry attempts suggested that the users were engaging in trial-and-error rather than using a skilled strategy and lacked sufficient conceptual understanding of the system.

CONCLUSIONS AND FUTURE DIRECTIONS

Human errors are viewed as products of cognitive activities in people's adaptation to their complex physical, social, and cultural environments. A cognitive approach stresses actions in conceptual understanding and thought processes during clinical problem-solving. The actions reflect the level of expertise and the demands of tasks in clinical performance. In order to manage errors in the clinical environment, it is critical to understand how decisions are made and what underlying cognitive mechanisms are used to process information during interactions with patients, colleagues, and support technology. Unlike the popular goal of achieving flawless performance (through development of error-free systems), we believe that the future trends will move toward collecting the empirical data on human performance that could be used to enhance and modify the current, more static, error taxonomy, which will guide development of adaptive systems that anticipate errors, respond to them, or substitute less serious errors that allow subsequent intervention before the errors result in an adverse event.

Mistakes are cognitively useful and cannot be totally eliminated. Psychology has acknowledged for a long time that errors act as flags on the learning curve (Seifert & Hutchins 1992). Errors are more frequent with beginners, and decrease with experience. Learning also leads to automation of behavior, resulting in an in-depth change in the nature of errors (Norman & Shallice 1986). In performance assessments, detection and recovery of failures is more important than the actual generation of failures.

Studies on patient safety from a cognitive point of view are increasingly moving toward investigations of "real-world" phenomena. The constraints of laboratory-based work prevent capturing the dynamics of real-world problems. This problem is particularly salient in critical care environments. In the best-case scenarios, this is creating the potential for great synergy between laboratory-based research and cognitive studies in the "wild." The concern with understanding and reducing medical errors provides a greater opportunity for cognitive scientists to apply cognitive theories and methodologies to a pressing practical problem in this domain.

Hollnagel *et al.* (2006) recently proposed a radically different view on medical error research in what they called *Resilience Engineering*. They point out that efforts to improve the safety of systems have often, if not always, been dominated by hindsight. In contrast, resilience engineering takes a radical step, not by adding one more concept to the existing vocabulary, but by proposing a completely new vocabulary, and therefore also a completely new way of thinking about safety. They argue that when research escapes from hindsight and from trying merely to explain what has happened, the sources of resilience usually allow people to produce success when failure threatens.

With the rapid advance of cognitive research on medical errors, cognitive interventions for reducing medical errors have surfaced. One major type of cognitive intervention is targeted training, based on research findings about clinicians' mistakes in thinking, reasoning, and decision-making. Another major type of cognitive intervention is through design of user interfaces in human–computer interactions. User interfaces can play an important role in the reduction of medical errors, although they are typically not considered as mandatory in the review and approval process of medical devices. In fact, health information systems are not even considered as medical devices requiring FDA approval. This trend, however, is changing, as the FDA has started to make recommendations of human factors considerations for medical device manufacturers (Sawyer *et al.* 1996; Food and Drug Administration 1997, 1998).

ACKNOWLEDGMENT

The preparation of this chapter was supported in part by Grant R01 LM007894-01A1 from the National Library of Medicine.

REFERENCES

Ackerman, M. S. (1998). Augmenting organizational memory: a field study of answer garden. *ACM Transactions on Information Systems*, *16*(3), 203–224.

Ackerman, M. S. & Halverson, C. (1998). Considering an organization's memory. Paper presented at the Proceedings of Computer-Supported Cooperative Work.

Altmann, E. M. & Trafton, J. G. (2002). Memory for goals: an activation-based model. *Cogntive Science*, *26*, 39–83.

Amalberti, R., Auroy, Y., Berwick, D. & Barach, P. (2005). Five system barriers to achieving ultrasafe health care. *Annals of Internal Medicine*, *142*, 756–764.

Anderson, J. R., Bothell, D., Byrne, M. D. & Lebiere, D. S. (2005). An integrated theory of the mind. *Psychological Review*, *111*(4), 1036–1060.

Arkes, H., Dawson, N., Speroff, T. *et al.* (1995). The covariance decomposition of the probability score and its use in evaluating prognostic estimates. *SUPPORT Investigators. Medical Decision Making*, *15*(2), 120–131.

Arocha, J. F. & Patel, V. L. (1995). Novice diagnostic reasoning in medicine: accounting for clinical evidence. *Journal of the Learning Sciences*, *4*, 355–384.
Ash, J. S., Gorman, P. N., Seshadri, V. & Hersh, W. R. (2004). Computerized physician order entry in US hospitals: results of a 2002 survey. *Journal of the American Medical Informatics Association*, *11*(2), 95–99.
Baddeley, A. D., Chincotta, D. & Adlam, A. (2001). Working memory and the control of action: evidence from task switching. *Journal of Experimental Psychology. General*, *130*(4), 641–657.
Baecker, R. M. (ed.) (1993). *Readings in Groupware and Computer-Supported Cooperative Work: Assisting Human–Human Collaboration.* San Francisco: Morgan Kaufmann.
Ball, L. J. & Ormerod, T. C. (2000). Putting ethnography to work: the case for a cognitive ethnography of design. *International Journal of Human–Computer Studies*, *53*, 147–168.
Barrouillet, P., Bernardin, S. & Camos, V. (2004). Time constraints and resource sharing in adults' working memory spans. *Journal of Experimental Psychology. General*, *133*(1), 83–100.
Bates, D. W., Leape, L. L., Cullen, D. J. *et al.* (1998). Effect of computerized physician order entry and a team intervention on prevention of serious medication errors. *JAMA: The Journal of the American Medical Association*, *280*(15), 1311–1316.
Battles, J. B. & Shea, C. E. (2001). A system of analyzing medical errors to improve GME curricula and programs. *Academic Medicine*, *76*(2), 125–133.
Benner, P., Sheets, V., Uris, P. *et al.* (2002). Individual, practice, and system causes of errors in nursing: a taxonomy. *The Journal of Nursing Administration*, *32*(10), 509–523.
Berg, M. (1999). Patient care information systems and health care work: a sociotechnical approach. *International Journal of Medical Informatics*, *55*, 87–101.
Bogner, M. S. (ed.) (1994). *Human Error in Medicine.* Hillsdale, NJ: Lawrence Erlbaum Associates.
Brixey, J., Johnson, T. R. & Zhang, J. (2002). Evaluation of a medical error taxonomy. In I. S. Kohane (ed.), *Proceedings of Amia 2002 Symposium* (pp. 71–75). Philadelphia: Hanley & Belfus.
Brooks, L., LeBlanc, V. & Norman, G. (2000). On the difficulty of noticing obvious features in patient appearance. *Psychological Science*, *11*(2), 112–117.
Byrne, M. D. & Kirlik, A. (2005). Using computational cognitive modeling to diagnose possible sources of aviation error. *International Journal of Aviation Psychology*, *15*(2), 135–155.
Chan, W. (2002). Increasing the success of physician order entry through human factors engineering. *Journal of Healthcare Information Management*, *16*(1), 71–79.
Chapman, G. B. & Elstein, A. S. (2000). Cognitive processes and biases in medical decision making. In G. B. Chapman & F. A. Sonnenberg (eds.), *Decision Making in Health Care: Theory, Psychology, and Applications* (pp. 183–210). New York: Cambridge University Press.
Chassin, M. R. & Galvin, R. W. (1998). The urgent need to improve health care quality. Institute of medicine national roundtable on health care quality. *JAMA: The Journal of the American Medical*, *280*, 1000–1005.
Child, A. P. (2004). *Keeping Patients Safe: Transforming the Work Environment of Nurses.* Washington, DC: National Academies Press.
Chung, P. H., Zhang, J., Johnson, T. R. & Patel, V. L. (2003). An extended hierarchical task analysis for error prediction in medical devices. *AMIA Annual Symposium Proceedings*, 165–169.
Cooke, N. J., Gorman, J. C. & Winner, J. J. (2007). Team cognition. Chapter 10, this volume.
Cook, R. I. & Woods, D. D. (1990). Operating at the sharp end: the complexity of human error. In M. Venturino (ed.), *Selected Readings in Human Factors* (pp. 255–310). Santa Monica, CA: Human Factors Society.
Croskerry, P. (2003). The importance of cognitive errors in diagnosis and strategies to minimize them. *Academic Medicine*, *78*(8), 781.
Croskerry, P., Shapiro, M., Campbell, S. *et al.* (2004). Profiles in patient safety: medication errors in the emergency department. *Academic Emergency Medicine*, *11*(3), 289–299.
Dorner, D. (1983). Heuristics and cognition in complex systems. In R. Gorner, M. Gorner & W. F. Bischof (eds.), *Methods of Heuristics.* Hillsdale, NJ: Lawrence Erlbaum Associates.
Dovey, S. M., Meyers, D. S., Phillips, R. L. Jr. *et al.* (2002). A preliminary taxonomy of medical errors in family practice. *Quality and Safety in Health Care*, *11*(3), 233–238.

Dunker, K. (1945). On problem solving. *Psychological Monographs*, *58*, 270.

Durso, F. T., Rawson, K. A. & Girotto, S. (2007). Comprehension and situation awareness. Chapter 7, this volume.

Elder, N. C. & Dovey, S. M. (2002). Classification of medical errors and preventable adverse events in primary care: a synthesis of the literature. *The Journal of Family Practice*, *51*(11), 927–932.

Flach, J. M. (1990). The ecology of human–machine systems. I: introduction. *Ecological Psychology*, *2*(3), 191–205.

Food and Drug Administration (1997). Improving patient care by reporting problems with medical devices: A medwatch continuing education article. Available at: http://www.fda.gov/medwatch/articles/mdr/mdr.pdf.

Food and Drug Administration (1998). Human factors implications of the new GMP rule. Overall requirements of the new quality system regulations. Available at: http://www.fda.gov/cdrh/humfac/hufacimp.html [June 27, 2000].

Freud, S. (1914). *Psychopathology of Everyday Life* (E. A. J. Strachey, Trans.). London: Ernest Benn.

Gaba, D. M. (1992). Dynamic decision-making in anesthesiology: cognitive models and training approaches. In D. A. Evans & V. L. Patel (eds.), *Advanced Models of Cognition for Medical Training and Practice* (pp. 123–147). New York: Springer-Verlag.

Gigerenzer, G. & Goldstein, D. (1996). Reasoning the fast and frugal way: models of bounded rationality. *Psychological Review*, *4*(103), 650–669.

Graber, M., Gordon, R. & Franklin, N. (2002). Reducing diagnostic errors in medicine: what's the goal? *Academic Medicine*, *77*, 981–992.

Graham, M. J., Kubose, T. K., Jordan, D. *et al.* (2004). Heuristic evaluation of infusion pumps: implications for patient safety in intensive care units. *International Journal of Medical Informatics*, *73*, 771–779.

Helander, M. G., Landauer, T. K. & Prabhu, P. V. (eds.) (1997). *Handbook of Human–Computer Interaction* (2nd edn). New York: North-Holland.

Henriksen, K., Battles, J. B., Marks, E. & Lewin, D. I. (2005). *Advances in Patient Safety: From Research to Implementation*. Rockville, MD: Agency for Healthcare Research and Quality.

Hollnagel, E. (ed.) (2003). *Hankbook of Cognitive Task Design*. Mahwah, NJ: Lawrence Erlbaum Associates.

Hollnagel, E., Woods, D. D. and Leveson, N. (eds.) (2006). *Resilience Engineering: Concepts and Precepts*. Aldershot: Ashgate.

Horsky, J., Kaufman, D. R., Oppenheim, M. I. & Patel, V. L. (2003). A framework for analyzing the cognitive complexity of computer-assisted clinical ordering. *Journal of Biomedical Informatics*, *36*(1–2), 4–22.

Horsky, J., Kuperman, G. J. & Patel, V. L. (2005). Comprehensive analysis of a medication dosing error related to CPOE. *Journal of the American Medical Informatics Association*, *12*(4), 377–382.

Hutchins, E. (1995a). *Cognition in the Wild*. Cambridge, MA: MIT Press.

Hutchins, E. (1995b). How a cockpit remembers its speed. *Cognitive Science*, *19*, 265–288.

Institute of Medicine (US) Committee on Quality of Health Care in America (2001). *Crossing the Quality Chasm: A New Health System for the 21st Century*. Washington, DC: National Academies Press.

Kahneman, D. (1973). *Attention and Effort*. Englewood Cliffs, NJ: Prentice-Hall.

Kassirer, P. K. & Kopelman, R. I. (1991). *Learning Clinical Reasoning*. Baltimore, MD: Williams & Wilkins.

Kieras, D. E. (1997). Goms model. In M. Helander, T. K. Launauer & P. Prabhu (eds.), *Handbook of Human Computer Interaction* (2nd edn). Amsterdam: North-Holland.

Kirsh, D. (2000). A few thoughts on cognitive overload. *Intellectia*, *30*, 19–51.

Kirwan, B. & Ainsworth, L. K. (1992). *A guide to Task Analysis*. London: Taylor and Francis.

Kluwe, R. H. (1995). Single case studies and models of complex problem solving. In P. A. Frensch & J. Funke (eds.), *Complex Problem Solving: The European Perspective* (pp. 269–291). Hillsdale, NJ: Lawrence Erlbaum Associates.

Kohn, L. T., Corrigan, J. M. & Donaldson, M. S. (eds.) (1999). *To Err is Human: Building a Safer Health System.* Washington, DC: National Academy Press.
Kohn, L. T., Corrigan, J. M., Donaldson, M. S. & Institute of Medicine (US). Committee on Quality of Health Care in America (2000). *To Err is Human: Building a Safer Health System.* Washington, DC: National Academy Press.
Koppel, R., Metlay, J. P., Cohen, A. *et al.* (2005). Role of computerized physician order entry systems in facilitating medication errors. *Journal of American Medical Association, 293*, 1197–1293.
Krueger, G. (1994). Fatigue, performance, and medical errors. In M. S. Bogner (ed.), *Human Errors in Medicine.* Hillsdale, NJ: Lawrence Erlbaum Associates.
Kuperman, G. J., Teich, J. M., Gandhi, T. K. & Bates, D. W. (2001). Patient safety and computerized medication ordering at brigham and women's hospital. *The Joint Commission Journal on Quality Improvement, 27*(10), 509–521.
Laxmisan, A., Malhotra, S., Keselman, A. *et al.* (2005). Decisions about critical events in device-related scenarios as a function of expertise. *Journal of Biomedical Informatics, 38*(3), 200–212.
Leprohon, J. & Patel, V. L. (1995). Decision-making strategies for telephone triage in emergency medical services. *Medical Decision Making, 15*(3), 240–253.
Leveson, N. G. & Turner, C. S. (1993). An investigation of theraz-25 accidents. *IEEE Computer, 18*, 41.
McNutt, R. A., Abrams, R. & Aron, D. C. (2002). Patient safety efforts should focus on medical errors. *JAMA: The Journal of the American Medical Association, 287*(15), 1997–2001.
Malhotra, S., Jordan, D., Shortliffe, E. H. & Patel, V. L. (2006). Workflow in critical care: piecing together your own puzzle. *Journal of Biomedical Informatics* (00).
Meyer, D. E. & Kieras, D. E. (1997a). A computational theory of executive cognitive processes and multiple-task performance: I. basic mechanisms. *Psychological Reivew, 104*(1), 3–65.
Meyer, D. E. & Kieras, D. E. (1997b). An overview of the epic architecture for cognition and performance with application to human-computer interaction. *Human–Computer Interaction, 12*(4), 391–438.
Moray, N. (1994). Error reduction as a systems problem. In M. S. Bogner (ed.), *Human Errors in Medicine.* Hillsdale, NJ: Lawrence Erlbaum Associates.
National Coordinating Council on Medication Error Reporting and Prevention (1998). Taxonomy of medication errors. Retrieved April 1, 2001. Available at: http://www.nccmerp.org/taxo0514.pdf.
Nemeth, C. (2003). *Human Factors Methods for Design: Making Systems Human-Centered.* London: Taylor and Francis.
Newell, A. (1991). *Unified Theories of Cognition.* Cambridge, MA: Harvard University Press.
Nielsen, J. (1992). Finding usability problems through heuristic evaluation. Paper presented at the Proceedings of ACM CHI'92.
Nielsen, J. (1994). *Usability Engineering.* Boston, MA: AP Professional.
Nielsen, J. & Mack, R. (eds.) (1994). *Usability Inspection Methods.* New York: John Wiley & Sons.
Nielsen, J. & Molich, R. (1990). Heuristic evaluation of user interfaces. Paper presented at the Proceedings of ACM CHI'90.
Norman, D. A. (1981). Categorization of action slips. *Psychological Review, 88*, 1–15.
Norman, D. A. (1986). Cognitive engineering. In D. A. Norman & S. W. Draper (eds.), *User Centered System Design.* Hillsdale, NJ: Lawrence Erlbaum Associates.
Norman, D. A. (1988). *The Psychology of Everyday Things.* New York: Basic Books.
Norman, D. A. & Shallice, T. (1986). Attention to action: willed and automatic control of behavior. In R. J. Davidson, G. E. Schwartz & D. Shapiro (eds.), *Consciousness and Self-regulation: Advances in Research* (Vol. 4). New York: Plenum.
Nunamaker, J. F., Dennis, A. R., Valacich, J. S. *et al.* (1991). Electronic meeting systems to support group work. *Communications of the ACM, 34*(7), 40–61.
Patel, V. L. (1998). Distributed and collaborative cognition in health care: implications for systems development. *Special Issue of Artificial Intelligence in Medicine, 12*(2), 93–195.

Patel, V. L. & Arocha, J. F. (2001). The nature of constraints on collaborative decision making in health care settings. In E. Salas & G. Klein (eds.), *Linking Expertise and Naturalistic Decision Making* (pp. 385–407). Mahwah, NJ: Lawrence Erlbaum Associates.

Patel, V. L. & Groen, G. J. (1986). Knowledge-based solution strategies in medical reasoning. *Cognitive Science*, *10*, 91–116.

Patel, V. L. & Ramoni, M. F. (1997). Cognitive models of directional inference in expert medical reasoning. In P. J. Feltovich & K. M. Ford (eds.), *Expertise in Context: Human and Machine* (pp. 67–99). Cambridge, MA: MIT Press.

Patel, V. L., Arocha, J. F. & Kaufman, D. R. (1994). Diagnostic reasoning and medical expertise. In D. L. Medin (ed.), *The Psychology of Learning and Motivation: Advances in Research and Theory* (Vol. 31, pp. 187–252). San Diego, CA: Academic Press.

Patel, V. L., Arocha, J. F. & Zhang, J. (2005). Thinking and reasoning in medicine. In K. J. Holyoak & R. G. Morrison (eds.), *Handbook of Thinking and Reasoning* (pp. 2298–2538). Cambridge: Cambridge University Press.

Patel, V. L., Cytryn, K. N., Shortliffe, E. H. & Safran, C. (2000). The collaborative health care team: the role of individual and group expertise. *Teaching and Learning in Medicine*, *12*(3), 117–132.

Patel, V. L., Evans, D. A. & Kaufman, D. R. (1989). Cognitive framework for doctor–patient interaction. In D. A. Evans & V. L. Patel (eds.), *Cognitive Science in Medicine: Biomedical Modeling* (pp. 253–308). Cambridge, MA: The MIT Press.

Patel, V. L., Groen G. J. & Norman, G. R. (1991). Effects of conventional and problem-based medical curricula on problem solving. *Academic Medicine*, *66*(7): 380–389.

Patterson, E. S., Roth, E. M., Woods, D. D. *et al.* (2004a). Handoff strategies in settings with high consequences for failure: lessons for health care operations. *International Journal for Quality in Health Care*, *16*(2), 125–132.

Patterson, E. S., Cook, R. I., Woods, D. D. & Render, M. L. (2004b). Examining the complexity behind a medication error: generic patterns in communication. *IEEE Transactions on Systems, Man and Cybernetics – Part A: Systems and Humans, 34*, 749–756.

Perrow, C. (1984). *Normal Accidents.* New York: Basic Books.

Reason, J. (1992). *Human Error.* Cambridge: Cambridge University Press.

Redelmeier, D. (2005). The cognitive psychology of missed diagnoses. *Annals of Internal Medicine*, *142*, 115–120.

Reece Jones, P. (1995). Hindsight bias in reflective practice: an empirical investigation. *Journal of Advanced Nursing*, *21*(4), 783.

Roth, E. M., Patterson, E. S. & Mumaw, R. J. (2002). Cognitive engineering: issues in user-centered system design. In J. J. Marciniak (ed.), *Encyclopedia of Software Engineering* (2nd edn). New York: John Wiley & Sons.

Rubinstein, J. S., Meyer, D. E. & Evans, J. E. (2001). Executive control of cognitive processes in task switching. *Journal of Experimental Psychology: Human Perception and Performance, 27*(4), 763–797.

Runciman, W. B., Helps, S. C., Sexton, E. J. & Malpass, A. (1998). A classification for incidents and accidents in the health-care system. *Journal of Quality in Clinical Practice*, *18*(3), 199–211.

Ruthruff, E., Pashler, H. E. & Klaassen, A. (2001). Processing bottlenecks in dual-task performance: structural limitation or strategic postponement? *Psychonomic Bulletin & Review*, *8*(1), 73–80.

Sawyer, D., Aziz, K. J., Backinger, C. L. *et al.* (1996). Do it by design: an introduction to human factors in medical devices. Available at: http://www.fda.gov/cdrh/humfac/doit.html.

Sieck, W. R. & Klein, G. (2007). Decision-making. Chapter 8, this volume.

Seifert, C. M. & Hutchins, E. (1992). Error as opportunity: learning in a cooperative task. *Human–Computer Interaction*, *7*(4), 409–435.

Simon, H. A. (1957). *Models of Man: Social and Rational; Mathematical Essays on Rational Human Behavior in Society Setting.* New York: John Wiley & Sons.

Te'eni, D. (2001). Review: a cognitive-affective model of organizational communication for designing it. *MIS Quarterly*, *25*(2), 251–312.

Trafton, J. G., Altmann, E. M., Brock, D. P. & Minitz, F. E. (2003). Preparing to resume an interrupted task: effects of prospective goal encoding and retrospective rehearsal. *International Journal of Human-Computer Studies*, *58*, 583–603.

Tversky, A. & Kahneman, D. (1974). Judgment under uncertainty: heuristics and biases. *Science*, *185*(4157), 1124–1131.

Van Cott, H. (1994). Human errors: their causes and reduction. In M. S. Bogner (ed.), *Human Errors in Medicine*. Hillsdale: NJ: Lawrence Erlbaum Associates.

Vicente, K. J. (1999). *Cognitive Work Analysis*. Mahwah, NJ: Lawrence Erlbaum Associates.

Victoroff, M. S. (1997). The right intentions: errors and accountability. *The Journal of Family Practice*, *45*(1), 38–39.

Woods, D. D. (1988). Cognitive systems engineering. In M. Helander (ed.), *Handbook of Human-Computer Interaction*. New York: North-Holland.

Woods, D. D., Johannesen, L., Cook, R. I. & Sarter, N. (1994). *Behind Human Error: Cognitive Systems, Computers and Hindsight*. Dayton, OH: Crew Systems Ergonomic Information and Analysis Center, WPAFB.

Xiao, Y. & Mackenzie, C. F. (1998). Team coordination and breakdowns in a real-life stressful environment. Paper presented at the Proceedings of the Human Factors and Ergonomics 42nd Annual Meeting.

Zhang, J. (1997). The nature of external representations in problem solving. *Cognitive Science*, *21*, 179–217.

Zhang, J., Johnson, T. R., Patel, V. L. *et al.* (2003). Using usability heuristics to evaluate patient safety of medical devices. *Journal of Biomedical Informatics*, *36*(1–2), 23–30.

Zhang, J. & Norman, D. A. (1994). Representations in distributed cognitive tasks. *Cognitive Science*, *18*(1), 87–122.

Zhang, J., Patel, V. L., Johnson, T. R. *et al.* (2005). Evaluating and predicting patient safety in medical device. In K. Henriksen, J. B. Battles, E. Marks & D. I. Lewin (eds.), *Advances in Patient Safety: From Research to Implementation*. Rockville, MD: Agency for Health Care Research and Quality.

Zhang, J., Patel, V. L., Johnson, T. R. & Shortliffe, E. H. (2004). A cognitive taxonomy of medical errors. *Journal of Biomedical Informatics*, *37*, 193–204.

CHAPTER 13

Skill in Sport

Bruce Abernethy
Institute of Human Performance, The University of Hong Kong, China & School of Human Movement Studies, The University of Queensland, Australia

Jonathan P. Maxwell, Robin C. Jackson, and Richard S. W. Masters
Institute of Human Performance, The University of Hong Kong, China

The domain of sport offers an incredibly rich and diverse "living laboratory" in which to study cognition and its links to human performance. Sports constantly test and extend the limits of human capability and present levels of time constraints and complexity far beyond those of more mundane activities. As the limiting factors to performance in many sports are more often than not cognitive than strictly motor, the sports domain consequently presents a unique natural environment in which to examine fundamental cognitive phenomena such as attention, memory, knowledge acquisition, visual search, and automaticity. The abundant supply of highly practiced athletes also presents the researcher with an interest in cognition with unique opportunities to examine skill learning and expert performance and provides an ideal situation in which to test, in a natural environment, the efficacy of many laboratory-derived concepts concerning human thinking and acting. Further, given the constant search in sports for new means of improving peak performance and consistency, of optimizing training and its efficacy, and of prolonging athletic careers, sport additionally provides a domain in which new ideas are encouraged and successful application of theory to practice is both highly sought and valued. Sport and the applied study of cognition therefore have significant complementary interests and goals and, consequently, much potentially to gain from mutual engagement.

Our purpose in this chapter is to provide a broad overview of research in cognition applied specifically to sport. We do so both to illustrate the contribution sports-based studies have made, and can make, to the understanding of cognition and to exemplify some of the many potential applications that studies of cognition can have to the enhancement of sports performance and participation. Given the breadth of the topic, our treatment is necessarily selective and illustrative rather than exhaustive and comprehensive. The chapter is organized into three main sections. The first provides a brief introduction to the history and contemporary scope of cognitive sports psychology; the second, an overview of current research and understanding on the effects of key cognitive factors on sports performance; and the third, an overview of some of the reciprocal, and frequently

Handbook of Applied Cognition: Second Edition. Edited by Francis T. Durso.

overlooked, effects of participation in sports and physical activity upon aspects of cognition. The second section in particular has strong cross-links to the earlier chapters in this handbook describing many of the fundamental elements of human cognition.

THE HISTORY AND SCOPE OF COGNITIVE SPORT PSYCHOLOGY

A Brief History of Cognitive Sport Psychology

Whereas scholarly interest in the relationship between sports participation and aspects of mental health can be traced back to the ancient Greeks, the first experimental works examining cognitive aspects of sports performance were probably undertaken in the late nineteenth century. Triplett (1898) compared the performances of track cyclists racing against each other or against the clock to demonstrate the social facilitatory effects of competition and the presence of others on performance. Anderson (1899) examined, as many have since, the effectiveness of mental training in improving skill and enhancing strength. By 1920, if not earlier, a number of laboratories were established in Europe for the systematic study of psychological aspects of sport – the most renowned among these being those of Carl Diem in Berlin and A. C. Puni in Leningrad (Wiggins 1984). Coleman Griffith from the University of Illinois established the first program of research on sports psychology in North America in the early 1920s, focusing attention on such issues as the reaction time and kinesthetic sensitivity of trained athletes (Kroll & Lewis 1970). Griffith's laboratory closed for financial reasons in 1932, after which relatively little theoretical and experimental work on sports psychology, aside from that influenced by the personality debates of the 1950s and 1960s, occurred until the mid-1960s and 1970s.

By the 1970s renewed programs of scholarly interest in the psychology of sport had emerged, marked, among other things, by the formation of professional societies (such as the International Society of Sport Psychology in 1965 and the North American Society for the Psychology of Sport and Physical Activity in 1967) and the initial publication of some specialist journals and texts (e.g., Cratty 1964; Singer 1968; Whiting 1969). Much of the work at this time was heavily reliant upon theories and paradigms imported directly from mainstream psychology, and consequently had a strong cognitive orientation. For example, research on motivation in sport was heavily influenced by the cognitive theories of attribution (Weiner 1972) and self-efficacy (Bandura 1977) and research on perception, knowledge, and expertise in sport was heavily influenced by the paradigms developed by de Groot (1966), Chase and Simon (1973), Anderson (1982), and others to help explain skill learning and performance in non-motor domains. An identifiable field of study – cognitive sport psychology (Straub & Williams 1984) – was apparent in the 1970s which applied the theories and methods of cognitive psychology to sport in an attempt to understand the cognitions and actions of both individual athletes and teams.

With increasing professionalization of both sports and sports psychology in the 1980s and the decades that followed, considerable interest and indeed emphasis developed on applied work. In particular, finding practical means of using knowledge from cognitive psychology to enhance athlete performance became a significant imperative for much of the research work. Studies on the cognitive skills of successful athletes (e.g., Mahoney & Avener 1977) and the development of means to assess and enhance the attentional skills of athletes (e.g., Nideffer 1976) were particularly influential, although arguably to the detriment of theory development and testing (Landers 1983). The study of movement control and coordination progressed significantly during this same period, influenced heavily by information-processing theories (e.g., Stelmach 1982). However, the distinct experimental bias within this work was toward laboratory-based studies of simple, untrained movements and this limited the extent to which the motor control and learning studies of the 1960s and 1970s generated knowledge that could be applied with ease to sports situations (e.g., Christina 1989). More detailed accounts of the historical development of research on sports psychology and on motor learning and control can be found in Massengale and Swanson (1997) and Schmidt and Lee (2005).

The Scope of Contemporary Cognitive Sports Psychology

A quick scan of the contents pages of contemporary texts on both sports psychology (e.g., Weinberg & Gould 2003; Morris & Summers 2004) and expert motor performance (e.g., Starkes & Ericsson 2003; Williams & Hodges 2004) reveals enormous scope and diversity within current research on cognition and skill in sports. Issues of interest range from traditional areas of focus such as personality, stress and anxiety, attention, motivation, self-confidence, perception, imagery, modeling, decision-making, mood states, team cohesion, social facilitation, and aggression through to more applied and emerging areas such as the identification and nurturing of talent, injury prevention and rehabilitation, and career management and transitions. All of these areas have a significant cognitive dimension and all have been influenced in some way by theory and data from cognitive psychology.

A major trend in recent decades has been the move away from a narrow focus primarily on sports psychology to a much broader focus on exercise, physical activity, and health behaviors in general. Associated with this widened focus and reflecting the heightened awareness globally of the profound public health significance of regular physical activity (World Health Organization 2004) has been a broadening of interest from a singular focus on sports performance to one that also addresses issues of sports (and physical activity) participation. Such a trend is especially significant as it reflects a recognition that the importance of cognitive factors may not be limited to the extent to which cognition can influence sports performance. The reciprocal influence that involvement in sport (or more broadly, physical activity) may have on facets of cognition and cognitive function may be equally, if not more, important. In the sections that follow we look at examples of research that has examined the influence of cognitive factors on sports performance and the influence of sports participation on cognition. We present brief overviews of research on *some* of the key topics that have been examined as examples of applied research on cognition in sports (and physical activity).

EFFECTS OF COGNITIVE FACTORS ON SPORTS PERFORMANCE

It has long been recognized that simple, repetitive training of the muscular system is, in and of itself, insufficient to ensure successful sports performance. Sports performance has a high cognitive component, with skilled movement being heavily reliant upon the effective functioning of key cognitive elements such as pattern recognition, decision-making, knowledge formation, memory, and attention. Consequently, there has been considerable research interest in understanding cognitive processes as they operate in sports skills – both as a means of understanding more about cognition per se and as a window into discovering new and superior means of enhancing the learning and performance of sports skills. In this section we briefly review some of the research evidence from sports (and the motor domain, more generally) in relation to the interdependent cognitive processes of pattern recognition, anticipation, decision-making, knowledge development, attention, and skills learning. We examine why these cognitive processes are important in sport, how they are typically examined experimentally, and how some of the general findings and extant knowledge are of applied significance in suggesting new directions for performance enhancement.

The evidence on the role of selected cognitive processes in skilled performance and on the potential for these processes to be enhanced comes primarily from two different types of studies. Many studies make use of comparisons of experts and lesser skilled (frequently, novice) athletes as a means of determining whether particular cognitive functions are directly related to performance level, and hence potentially act as a limiting factor to skilled performance. Much is now known about the distinguishing attributes of expert performance in sport (e.g., Abernethy *et al.* 1998; Williams, Davids & Williams *et al.* 1999 for reviews), although much remains to be discovered about the differences in information pick-up and utilization that underpin these differences and about the practice (e.g., Ericsson *et al.* 1993; Helsen *et al.* 1998) and other contextual factors (e.g., relative age: Musch & Grondin 2001; diversity of experience: Baker *et al.* 2003) that contribute to the development of expert performance. Other knowledge about the role of cognitive processes in skilled performance has derived not from the studies of experts but from studies using more traditional learning paradigms. In these studies untrained or lesser skilled athletes, typically, are subjected to alternate forms of practice and both their sports performance and associated cognitive skills are measured either using a pre-/post-training design or by drawing comparisons to control groups who receive usual or no training. The advantage of the expertise approach is that it provides access to participants who have experienced literally millions of trials of practice – orders of magnitude more practice than is typically experienced in the laboratory. The advantage of the learning paradigm approach is that it permits tight (prospective) control of the specific amount and type of practice undertaken in a way that is typically not possible within the expertise paradigm.

Pattern Recognition, Anticipation, and Decision-Making

Many sports place significant demands on the performer to respond not only accurately, but also extremely quickly. For example, in baseball, a fast ball pitch may travel at a speed exceeding 40 m/s and take only marginally more than 400 ms from its release by the pitcher to when it reaches the batter (Tresilian 2004). In this time, the batter must accurately recognize the type of pitch that has been thrown, determine when and where it will arrive, and, assuming it is in the strike zone, organize and execute an appropriate swing of the bat to make good contact with the ball. Even allowing for a relatively short bat swing movement time of 150–200 ms (Hubbard & Seng 1954) and a response latency of 200 ms, it is evident that the decision as to whether or not to swing at the pitch must be based, at least in part, upon information gleaned prior to the pitcher actually releasing the ball. Calculations of the time constraints associated with other sports tasks such as returning a serve in tennis, batting in cricket, goal-tending in ice-hockey, and goal-keeping against soccer penalty kicks similarly suggest that key decisions must often be made prior to ball flight information becoming available (Glencross & Cibich 1977) and must therefore, presumably, be based on information available from the opponent's movement pattern. This has led to considerable interest in the perceptual processes underlying rapid decision-making and anticipatory processes in sports and to research attempting to determine how successful players (experts) are able to perform with high accuracy in time-constrained situations while still appearing unhurried and as if having "all the time in the world."

A number of different lines of evidence are now available to demonstrate that expert performers in fast ball sports can indeed pick up useful information in advance of ball flight from the movement patterns of their opponents and can do so in a superior manner to less skilled performers. Chronometric analyses of the behavioral responses of performers in reactive situations support the presence of systematic skill-related differences in the timing of anticipatory movements. For example, Hennemann and Keller (1983) conducted a frame-by-frame analysis of a server and receiver in tennis and found that the better receiver prepared sooner in the serving sequence of their opponent. Similarly, Howarth *et al.* (1984) compared high-skilled and less-skilled squash players' responses and also found that the more skilled players initiated responses earlier than their less-skilled counterparts. Moreover, when taking into account response latency, initiation of anticipatory movement by high-skilled players appeared to be based on information gleaned prior to the opponent hitting the ball whereas less-skilled players responded after their opponent had struck the ball, presumably on the basis of early ball-flight information.

Experimental evidence on the time course of information pick-up by players of different skill levels has been derived largely through the use of the temporal visual occlusion paradigm. In this paradigm, participants typically view video images of the movement patterns of opponents (such as the opponent's service action in tennis) with the images designed to simulate, as accurately as possible, the display normally available to the player in the natural setting. The amount of visual information available to participants is then systematically varied by occluding the display at a number of different times before and after key events (such as ball–racquet contact in the tennis example). The task of the participants, who are typically players of different skill level, is to predict the type, direction, or landing position of the ball on the basis of the information available to them.

In the first published study to examine the use of "advance cues," Jones and Miles (1978) compared the ability of 32 professional tennis coaches and 60 novices to predict the landing location of tennis serves occluded at different time periods. The coaches, who were all former experienced players, outperformed the novices when viewing clips occluded either shortly after the ball had been struck (+126 ms) and shortly *before* contact (−42 ms), and performed significantly better than chance levels on both conditions. The coaches, unlike the novices, were able to make use of advance information to predict serve direction. Subsequent studies have largely replicated these findings. The consistent observation that experts are better able to use early visual information to anticipate (and "read ahead") than their less-skilled counterparts has been shown to hold true not only in tennis (e.g., see Buckolz *et al.* 1988; Goulet *et al.* 1989) but also in the other fast ball sports of cricket (Abernethy & Russell 1984), badminton (Abernethy & Russell 1987a), volleyball (Wright *et al.* 1990), squash (Abernethy 1990), soccer (Williams & Davids 1998); as well as in the martial art, karate (Mori *et al.* 2002). In the majority of studies, expert players perform above chance level, even at very early points of occlusion, and show an earlier ability to benefit from the increased information contained within consecutive occlusion points. Moreover, the expert advantage is retained even when simple point-light displays (Johansson 1973) are presented containing the pure biological motion of the opponent but eliminating all other visual details. This suggests that experts are better attuned to the essential kinematic features of their opponents' movement patterns (Abernethy *et al.* 2001).

The relationship between skill level and the ability to extract essential information from patterns is not simply restricted to individual fast ball sports but also holds true more generally in relation to the pick-up of essential information in team ball sports, such as basketball, football, and hockey, which are replete with offensive and defensive play patterns. Classical recall and recognition paradigms from cognitive psychology (e.g., Chase & Simon 1973; Charness 1979) have been used to demonstrate the expert superiority for recalling player positions in briefly presented slides of game situations from sports (e.g., Allard *et al.* 1980; Starkes 1987) and for recognizing such patterns when they are presented amongst other patterns not previously encountered (e.g., Abernethy *et al.* 1994; Williams & Davids 1995). The expert advantage, however, only holds for displays depicting structured game situations and either reduces or completely disappears if the displays contain the usual elements (e.g., offensive and defensive players) but without their usual relations (e.g., the players moving around randomly before or after the game is completed). This demonstrates that the experts' advantage is not due to some generic superiority in the encoding, processing, and recall of all types of visual information but is specific to their domain of expertise and the knowledge and skills they have developed through extensive practice in the domain.

In the case of both individual tasks (like baseball batting) and team tasks (like responding to a football offense) a major challenge to understanding the mechanisms underpinning skilled pattern perception, and to developing means of accelerating the usual rate of acquisition of pattern reading skills, is being able to identify the specific cues that players of different skill levels use to encode and interpret particular patterns. A number of different approaches have been developed to attempt to trace and identify this information. Verbal reports have been used by some researchers (e.g., Tenenbaum *et al.* 1996; Williams & Davids 1998), but such approaches may be problematic as the determination of what visual information is picked up and used may be largely automatic and implicit, and performers may not necessarily have verbal access to their own processing strategies. Given this concern, more direct approaches that either manipulate the visual information available through different forms of spatial occlusion or measure the visual search patterns of performers of different skill levels are generally favored.

In the spatial occlusion paradigm, different regions of the display that contain cues that may be useful for pattern perception are selectively occluded and the impact on anticipatory performance is measured. The underlying rationale is that whereas masking or removing features of the display that are critical for anticipation will disrupt performance relative to the normal, unoccluded display condition, occlusion of non-critical information will not disrupt performance (see Figure 13.1). In a study of anticipation in badminton players, Abernethy and Russell (1987a) masked visibility to the opposing player's arm and racquet, the racquet only, the player's head, the player's lower body, or an irrelevant background feature, and required players of different skill levels to anticipate the direction and

Figure 13.1 An example of the use of the spatial occlusion method. The panel on the left contains all the advance movement pattern information available to help predict the direction of the tennis player's serve whereas in the other panels information arising from the motion of the arm and racquet (middle panel) and from the lower body (right panel) has been selectively removed. The relative prediction performance between these different conditions can help determine the importance to anticipation of the particular cue or combination of cues that has been masked

force of strokes on the basis of the advance information presented to them. Expert prediction performance was found to be disrupted by the occlusion of both the arm and the racquet whereas the prediction performance of the novices was only disrupted when the racquet was masked. Loss of vision of the player's head or lower body had no impact on either skill group. The inference that can be drawn from this is that expert players are not only able to pick up advance information from the motion of the racquet as do the novices but can also pick up information from the earlier occurring, more proximal motion of the arm holding the racquet – information to which the less skilled performers are not attuned. With the acquisition of expertise comes the capacity to use additional, earlier sources of information to guide pattern perception and the early initiation of appropriate movement responses.

An alternative means of attempting to determine skill-related differences in information usage for pattern perception and anticipation is to measure the visual search patterns of players, using standard eye-movement recording procedures. Although there are no reliable, systematic differences between experts and novices in terms of their basic visual functions, such as static and dynamic visual acuity, depth perception, contrast sensitivity, and central peripheral awareness (Williams *et al.* 1999), differences in the location, duration, and order of fixations made on particular patterns might be expected. In one of the first studies using eye-movement recording in sport, Bard and Fleury (1976) compared the visual search patterns of experienced and novice varsity basketball players as they viewed static slide displays depicting 28 schematic representations of typical offensive situations. They found that the better players made significantly fewer fixations and were also more likely to fixate upon the "empty space" between players than were novice players.

Subsequent studies measuring sport-related visual search patterns in the laboratory (e.g., Williams *et al.* 1994) and in the natural playing environment (e.g., Martell & Vickers 2004), have proved somewhat inconsistent in their findings. In some studies, expert–novice differences in the distribution of fixations have been evident (e.g., Goulet *et al.* 1989; Williams & Davids 1998), whereas in others (e.g., Abernethy & Russell 1987b) the search patterns of the different skill groups have been indistinguishable even though there have been pronounced concurrent differences in information pick-up and anticipation. The visual search patterns of even experts show considerable inter- and intra-group variability. For example, in on-court testing of the return-of-serve in five highly ranked university tennis players, Singer *et al.* (1998) found that three players followed the ball toss (two with 100 per cent pursuit tracking, one with 100 per cent saccades), one fixated entirely on the racquet, and the other player had 40 per cent pursuit tracking and 60 per cent of fixations on the expected ball toss area.

In hitting skills such as are required in batting in baseball (Bahill & LaRitz 1984) and cricket (Land & McLeod 2000), experienced performers frequently make predictive saccades to key events, such as the predicted release point for the pitch or the predicted point of ball-bounce in cricket but are unable to track the ball continuously up to the point of contact with the bat as the angular velocity of the ball in its final stages exceeds the tracking capacity of the ocular system. Interestingly, players nevertheless report having watched the ball all the way to the bat and having seen the actual bat–ball contact. There are clearly some instances in which features of visual search show expertise-related differences although, equally, it is apparent that eye-movement behaviors present only a poor proxy for actual visual information-processing. Eye movements and visual attention can be disassociated (e.g., Shulman *et al.* 1979) and, for expert perception and performance in sports, the way in which visual information is processed ("seeing") is clearly more critical than simply where one "looks."

Expert anticipation and decision-making are undoubtedly influenced not only by what information can be picked up on any occasion from the specific movement pattern of the opposing player or team, but also by more general knowledge about situational probabilities and context acquired through years of domain-specific experience. In baseball batting, for instance, predictions and decisions by experts are likely based not only on information derived from the pitcher's current movement pattern (or biomechanics) but also from more global knowledge about the pitcher's favored pitches and pitch sequences and how these may be influenced by contextual factors such as the score, the count, and past records against other players and teams (Newell 1974). Whereas considerable research effort has been expended on examining skill-related differences in the pick-up of information from the unfolding of current events, there has been relatively little systematic examination of experts' ability to make use of these situational probabilities. This is surprising at one level, given the long-standing laboratory evidence that advance knowledge of stimulus probabilities and sequential dependencies can profoundly reduce reaction time (Hyman 1953) but most likely reflects the difficulty in finding suitable, naturalistic paradigms through which to realistically manipulate situational probabilities. Some notable work has been undertaken in this area nevertheless. For example, Alain and Proteau (1980), in studies of racquet ball players, showed that the initiation point of anticipatory movement is directly affected by the situational probabilities assigned by players to the likelihood of particular events. Paull and Glencross (1997) found that both high-level and lower-level baseball players were able to use strategic game information (e.g., the count, the game score, and the number of hits recorded against the pitcher) to decrease decision time and error scores when facing a variety of pitches displayed on a life-size screen and Gray (2002) demonstrated that prior expectations held by the batter regarding the pitch sequence and count not only influenced the timing of the baseball swing but also produced effects on swing timing that were predictable from a two-state Markov model.

In an applied sense, knowledge about the nature of expertise in pattern recognition, anticipation, and decision-making in sports is of most use if this knowledge can be used to enhance skill learning and performance beyond existing means. This inevitably means that training studies must be conducted, yet to date only relatively few studies have addressed this specific question of whether training techniques can be designed that enhance perceptual skills beyond what can be achieved simply through sport-specific experience and existing practice methods. The search for means of training pattern recognition skills for sports has quite a lengthy history, although the majority of experimental work is quite recent.

Haskins (1965) developed a training film in which tennis players responded to shots occluded either 167 ms or 21 ms after racquet–ball contact. Following two training sessions, it was reported that players improved their on-court response times by an average of 69 ms when facing serves from the player depicted in the training film. Abernethy *et al.* (1999) conducted a perceptual training intervention with novice tennis players in which the players received formal instruction about the biomechanical properties of the forehand and backhand drive shots and formal instruction about the most important cues for anticipating shot depth and direction, interspersed with sessions in which they practiced using this knowledge to make verbal or physical responses to serves. The results of this and similar studies (e.g., Farrow *et al.* 1998; Scott *et al.* 1998) have been encouraging in terms of showing improvements in anticipatory skill, as measured by performance on laboratory temporal occlusion tasks. There has also been encouraging recent evidence that perceptual training benefits seen in the laboratory can transfer to improved performance in the natural performance setting, as indicated by faster decision times and/or improved accuracy (Williams *et al.* 2002, 2003). Williams *et al.* (2003), for example, reported that a single, 45-minute training session was successful in significantly decreasing a novice field-hockey goalkeeper's decision time for penalty flicks in both laboratory and field scenarios.

Thus far the perceptual training interventions that have been reported in the sports domain have varied enormously in frequency and duration (from a single 45-minute session to 16 20-minute sessions), in mode of presentation (normal speed vs. slow motion), and in the degree of explicit information provided (from "tips" to formal biomechanical-based instruction). Consequently, it is unclear whether the same underlying processes mediate improvements across the different training regimes and to what extent the improved performances reported are a result of low-level perceptual adaptation or cognitive mediation. Improved understanding of these issues would seem critical for the development of optimally effective training programs. To this end a number of researchers (e.g., Rowe & McKenna 2001) have now begun to examine the attentional demands of anticipatory processes and the properties of less directive perceptual training interventions.

Training techniques that attempt to create implicit learning conditions (e.g., Farrow & Abernethy 2002; Raab 2003) or invoke (guided) discovery learning (Williams *et al.* 2002; Smeeton *et al.* 2005) may be considered less directive. Implicit learning, as described in greater detail in the next section, refers to situations in which information the learner acquires information without necessarily intending to do so, and, as a consequence, such information is generally very difficult to verbalize (Berry & Dienes 1993). Research on implicit perceptual training has been stimulated by studies suggesting that making performers aware of the regulatory features of the environment sometimes disrupts performance (Green & Flowers 1991; Magill 1998), and by work suggesting that motor skills that are learned implicitly may be more robust under stress (Masters 1992; Hardy *et al.* 1996). Thus far, evidence for benefits associated with implicit perceptual training interventions relative to explicit methods is equivocal (Jackson 2003; Poulter *et al.* 2005) and is dogged by a number of difficult conceptual and methodological challenges (e.g., Dienes & Berry 1997; Stadler 1997; Jackson & Farrow 2005). Equivalent improvements have been apparent, to date, between explicit and guided discovery learning conditions, the latter being conditions in which performers are directed to focus upon information-rich regions of the display but are not informed about the location of the specific critical cues or about the link between such cues and event outcome (Williams *et al.* 2002). Clearly, considerable further experimental examination of different forms of perceptual training interventions is needed to help apply existing knowledge on expertise to training and to develop procedures that can consistently and optimally accelerate the acquisition of those perceptual skills known to be critical for expert performance in many sports.

Knowledge, Attention, and Motor Skill Learning

The idea that expert motor performance in sport is characterized by a high degree of automaticity is widely accepted (e.g., Logan 1985; Schmidt & Lee 2005). Functional benefits associated with automatic motor performance include fluent movement (Salmoni 1989), apparent effortlessness, resistance to disruption, reduced physiological cost, and less reliance on attentional resources, particularly working memory (Schmidt & Wrisberg 2004). The movement patterns of less skilled performers, on the other hand, tend to be jerky, effortful, easily disrupted, and attention-demanding. The novice athlete faces a considerable challenge if their ultimate goal is the achievement of expert performance. The learner has to deal with multiple information sources and integrate them with the numerous functional degrees of freedom that characterize the human musculoskeletal system. This process is slow and unpredictable, the learner often experiences demotivating performance plateaus, eventual success is far from guaranteed, and progress may be dogged by injury. In addition, it has been estimated that a minimum of ten years or 10,000 hours of dedicated, deliberate practice is required to acquire expertise (Ericsson *et al.* 1993). Consequently, it is no surprise that athletes, coaches, movement scientists, physical educators, and sports psychologists have sought to understand the learning process and develop ways to enhance it.

Theoretical approaches to skills acquisition in sport can be divided roughly into two camps: cognitive approaches, characterized by sundry adaptations of traditional stage theories developed by Fitts and Posner (1967) and Anderson (1983, 1993), and the ecological approaches emerging from the influences of Bernstein (1967) and Gibson (1979). (See Abernethy *et al.* 1994 for an overview of these contrasting approaches as they apply to motor expertise.) The cognitive approaches are generally based on the distinction between procedural and declarative knowledge, but vary in terms of how they conceptualize the development, progression, administration, and interaction between these two types of knowledge in motor skill acquisition. Declarative knowledge, within the sports context, refers to verbalizable rules, techniques, or methods that are applied to achieve optimal performance. Procedural knowledge drives action and is typified by the idea of motor programs or schemas (Henry & Rogers 1960; Keele 1968; Schmidt 1988) which are generalized instructional sets that oversee the execution of a class of movements, such as those required in throwing, catching, and locomotion.

The most popular models of skills acquisition in sport describe a learning progression from declarative to procedural knowledge. Anderson's (1983, 1993) ACT* and ACT-R model of cognitive architecture and Fitts' (1964) stage theory of skills acquisition typify the notion that skills are first acquired as a set of declarative rules that are applied by conscious processes (presumably working memory) to guide learning. Declarative rules are gradually transformed through practice into procedural knowledge that guides performance without recourse to working memory resources (Fitts & Posner 1967). Whilst originally addressing the acquisition of cognitive skills, Anderson has claimed that motor skills are an example of procedural skills and should follow similar learning principles.

The stage theory of skills learning has permeated approaches to sports coaching and remains the predominant theoretical approach to athlete tuition (Beilock & Carr 2004). In a typical coaching situation, athletes are given verbal instructions (often coupled with demonstrations highlighting the validity of such instructions) that are designed to impart an exact model of how to perform the skill. The learner is expected to integrate all of this information and somehow reproduce an approximate copy. Further instruction and practice fine-tune the movement until perfection (or thereabout) is achieved. The early declarative phase is characterized by conscious processing, with the learner adopting a problem-solving approach (Glencross 1992). As learning progresses the skill begins to appear fluent, is performed more automatically, with less and less variation (Salmoni 1989), and specific performances are often difficult retrospectively to describe in detail (Beilock & Carr 2001). Automatic performance places fewer demands on attention and is resistant to change or disruption (Fitts 1964; Neves & Anderson 1981) – characteristics of control that are clearly highly desirable and advantageous for performance in many, if not all, competitive sports.

Support for the applicability of stage theory in sport has been provided by comparisons of the attentional demands the performance of specific skills place upon expert and novice performers. Leavitt (1979), for example, demonstrated that skating speed is considerably reduced when novice ice hockey players are required to complete concurrent secondary tasks, such as dribbling a puck, but are not reduced in experts. This observation was interpreted as support for the gradual proceduralization of the skating skill with its associated automaticity. Allard and Burnett (1985) also provided evidence that motor skills in basketball are gradually proceduralized and that sport experts build up specialized declarative and procedural knowledge in much the same way that experts in more cognitive skills develop domain-specific specialized knowledge.

Recent years have seen growth in the volume of research examining the supposed automaticity of expert performance. Beilock and her colleagues (2002, 2004; Gray 2004) have repeatedly demonstrated that expert performers are unhindered by the imposition of a variety of secondary tasks. For example, Gray (2004) had expert and novice baseball batters respond to a stimulus (high- or low-pitched tones) whilst attempting to hit slow- or fast-pitched virtual balls. Participants were required to state the frequency of the tone (high or low), an externally focused dual task, or whether the bat was traveling down or up on "impact" with the ball, an internally or movement-focused dual task. Gray discovered that the batting accuracy of experts was robust under secondary task loading that focused attention externally, but relatively poor when the secondary task focused attention on movement execution. Novices, however, demonstrated the opposite pattern of results, exhibiting better performance when focusing on skill execution. Beilock *et al.* (2002) reported similar results for expert and novice golfers performing a putting task, and for expert/novice soccer players performing a dribbling task. These findings suggest that expert performance is indeed characterized by a high degree of automaticity, whereas the performance of novices tends to benefit from a high degree of cognitive control, commensurate with stage models of learning. Beilock and Carr (2001) also demonstrated that experts are less able than are novices to describe the details of specific performances. This is again consistent with the idea that expert performance is automatic rather than consciously controlled, whereas the reverse is true for novices.

In recent years the idea that knowledge is first acquired declaratively and then proceduralized has been called into question (e.g., Seger 1994; Maxwell *et al.* 2003; Masters & Maxwell 2004; Sun *et al.* 2005). This challenge to conventional dogma has developed because of a growing body of anecdotal and experimental evidence that procedural skills can be acquired in the absence of an accumulation of task-relevant declarative knowledge. Very young children, for instance, can acquire fundamental movement skills, such as crawling, walking, and pointing, but are unable to engage in detailed discussions of the mechanical idiosyncrasies of the acts (using declarative knowledge), suggesting the independent development of procedural knowledge for at least some skills.

Perhaps the best-known experimental demonstration of perceptual–motor skill proceduralization, without the corresponding accrual of declarative knowledge, has come from studies using the serial reaction time (SRT) task. The SRT task requires learners to attend and react to a repeating sequence of four possible stimuli. Typically, the learner's performance improves (measured by reaction time and in some cases accuracy), but they are unable to report the details of the sequence (Nissen & Bullemer 1987; Cohen *et al.* 1990; Curran & Keele 1993). Evidence of independent procedural learning has also been provided from the study of neurologically impaired patients. Amnesic patients have great difficulty acquiring new cognitive skills, but are frequently unimpaired with regard to motor (procedural) skill acquisition and retention (e.g., Corkin 1968). Similar findings have since been reported for other neurologically impaired populations (e.g., Knopman & Nissen 1991; Masters *et al.* 2004).

Unsurprisingly, the direct application to sports of findings from studies using SRT tasks (with their relatively small motor component) and neurologically impaired patients is not without its problems. Fortunately, a growing body of research is now available, demonstrating that principles derived from the cognitive literature are applicable to more complex sports skills. One of the first studies to provide evidence of motor learning in the absence of declarative learning had participants performing the pursuit tracking equivalent of the SRT task (Pew 1974). Participants utilized a joystick to follow a waveform presented on an oscilloscope. The waveform consisted of three sections of which the middle section was invariant (i.e. repeating) whilst the first and last sections were randomly generated on each trial. Pew found that participants improved their performance on the repeated section with practice; however, when questioned, participants were unaware that they had learnt a repeating sequence. Similar findings have been reported by several researchers using the same task (e.g., Magill & Hall 1989; Wulf & Schmidt 1997) and a dynamic balancing variant (Shea *et al.* 2001). In all cases, performance increased on the repeating section in the absence of explicit awareness (although for a critique, see Perruchet *et al.* 2003).

Using a more complex, sports-specific task – golf putting – Masters (1992) also demonstrated procedural learning without a concomitant increase in declarative knowledge. Masters had participants perform a secondary task whilst putting. The secondary task of random-letter generation (Baddeley 1966) was hypothesized to prevent the acquisition of declarative knowledge by preventing the rehearsal of task-relevant information in working memory. After 400 learning trials participants failed to report substantial amounts of declarative knowledge of the putting skill. Additionally, their putting performance improved over trials, demonstrating that procedural learning had occurred. By demonstrating procedural learning in the absence of task-relevant declarative knowledge, Masters concluded that participants had acquired the motor skill implicitly. Masters (1992) also demonstrated that the performance of implicit learners improved under evaluation-induced psychological stress whilst the performance of explicit learners (who were able to report a large pool of declarative knowledge) degraded. The accrual of declarative knowledge appeared to be detrimental to skilled performance under pressure. The basic finding of procedural without declarative learning has since been replicated several times in golf putting (e.g., Hardy *et al.* 1996; Maxwell *et al.* 2000, 2001, 2003), table tennis (Liao & Masters 2001), and, as noted in the previous section, in some aspects of perceptual learning (Farrow & Abernethy 2002; see also Jackson 2003).

These and other findings have led several authors to propose new theories of skills acquisition that postulate alternative interactions between declarative and procedural knowledge. Willingham and Goedert-Eschmann (1999) have proposed that declarative and procedural knowledge are accrued in parallel. Initially, behavior is controlled by explicit, declarative knowledge. Once the procedural or implicit representation has developed to such an extent that it can support behavior, explicit knowledge is no longer used. Gentile (1998) proposed a similar model of functional skills acquisition, but labeled the processes explicit and implicit rather than declarative and procedural. The explicit process describes the functional relationship between the performer and their environment, whereas the implicit process determines the functional dynamics of the movement in relation to force production and efficiency. Gentile suggested that these processes act in parallel and that the explicit process is rapid, whereas the implicit process is slow and requires substantial practice. When performing a golf-putting task both explicit and implicit processes might be used in parallel. The performer uses information from the environment and the outcome of their actions to explicitly establish the relationship between their actions and the desired outcome. That is, they explicitly modify their technique, by testing hypotheses, to conform to the task demands. Implicit knowledge is developed through continued repetition of the task and may require relatively stable environmental conditions for optimal learning.

Sun and colleagues (e.g., Sun 1997; Sun *et al.* 2001, 2005) proposed a model whereby skill acquisition progresses from declarative to procedural in some situations (e.g., in intellectual skills), but progresses in the opposite direction for "lower-level" skills (particularly those with high movement content). Both types of knowledge may develop independent of the other, but can interact to bring about optimal performance. This theory is mirrored in the motor domain by Masters and Maxwell's (2004) conceptualization of implicit and explicit motor learning. On the basis of their experimental findings (e.g., Masters 1992; Maxwell *et al.* 2000), these authors argued that procedural knowledge can be acquired and applied independent of working memory resources (Maxwell *et al.* 2003) whereas the accrual and application of declarative knowledge requires the availability of working memory. Whilst not dismissing the idea that declarative information can be used to partially control motor output (Beek 2000), Masters and Maxwell have claimed that attempts to control movement via conscious processing of declarative knowledge often hinder the accurate expression of procedural knowledge. Corroborating evidence is available from the "choking," reinvestment, and self-consciousness literature (e.g., Baumeister 1984; Masters *et al.* 1993; Bawden *et al.* 2001).

There are obviously many characteristics, in addition to a high degree of automaticity, that set the expert sports performer apart from the novice. Expert performance is characterized by a high degree of flexibility that is functionally important in unstable environments (e.g., a baseball batter receiving slow, fast, or curve pitches to variable locations). For some, this presents a paradox for the idea that experts rely almost exclusively on automatic processes (e.g., Beek 2000; Rossano 2003). Beek (2000) stated that automatic processes are difficult to alter once they are initiated; therefore, responses cannot be altered in the face of changing demands. Clearly, experts are capable of changing responses to even rapidly changing stimuli. This observation suggests a high degree of online cognitive control over action. One solution to this problem is to suppose that there is a complex interaction between controlled and automatic processes with the former able to inhibit the latter at any point (see Libet 1985 for a similar argument on the function of consciousness; see also Rossano 2003 for an intriguing argument on the role of evolution in consciousness and expertise). Unfortunately, interactions between controlled and automatic processing are difficult to interpret because they depend on the particular theoretical framework within which they are evaluated and the degree of primary and secondary task integration or chunking cannot be easily predicted (Heuer & Wing 1984).

Another solution to the automaticity vs. flexibility paradox may reside within the ecological and dynamic systems approaches to human movement. In contrast to traditional cognitive models of skills learning, these complementary approaches to motor learning downplay the contribution of cognition and focus rather on the development of direct relationships (affordances) between the environment and the performer along with the extent to which movement control can be supported by intrinsic effects arising from the natural dynamics of the neuromusculoskeletal system (e.g., Kelso 1995; Beek *et al.* 2003). As the learner becomes more acquainted with environmental properties, the generation of new movement solutions becomes easier. From this perspective, movement generation can retain both a degree of automaticity and flexibility.

Although direct perception–action coupling and the underlying non-linear dynamics of the human motor system may account for many low-level movements (e.g., intercepting a moving object and producing rhythmic movements) some researchers (e.g., Summers 1998) have argued that such approaches have intrinsic constraints and difficulty in explaining the more complex, goal-directed skills that are typical of sport (but see also Davids *et al.* 1994; Handford *et al.* 1997 for a counter-view). Consequently, cognitive approaches to skills acquisition remain popular despite the growing interest in ecological views. The marrying of cognitive and ecological perspectives is perhaps inevitable (Abernethy & Sparrow 1992; Summers 2004) and increasingly attempts are being made to recognize the contribution that attention, decision-making, intentions, and personal goals play in determining, or at least modifying, the dynamics of motor skills coordination and control (e.g., Temprado *et al.* 1999; Davids & Button 2000).

Understanding the processes that lead to expertise in sport is interesting from a theoretical point of view, but is unlikely to occupy the attention of athletes who are focused on achieving excellence. The practical application of theory pertaining to the optimization of learning and performance has proved to be a productive avenue of enquiry for sports scientists who are interested in the applied aspects of their trade. Early attempts to establish optimal learning conditions examined the effect of presenting augmented feedback, in the form of knowledge of results (KR), on learning. Originally, KR was seen as one of the most important augmented information sources, without which learning could not proceed (Bilodeau *et al.* 1959; Schmidt & Lee 2005). However, it soon became clear that presenting KR after every trial often enhanced immediate performance, but degraded learning as measured by delayed no-KR retention and transfer tests (Lavery 1962; Schmidt *et al.* 1989). Providing average KR, conversely, depressed performance but enhanced learning. This led a number of authors (e.g., Holding 1965; Annett 1969) to suggest that KR functions as guidance for the learner, directing change or stability. Salmoni *et al.* (1984) postulated that the learner comes to rely on KR when it is provided after every trial; thus, performance deteriorates when KR is removed. Providing KR averaged over a number of trials alleviates the dependency effect. Knowledge of performance (qualitative information about the nature of movement pattern) has been found to affect learning in similar ways to KR (Swinnen 1996; Wulf & Shea 2004).

Feedback schedules have been manipulated in various ways to achieve optimal performance. Lai and Shea (1999), for example, provided bandwidth feedback to learners of a sequential tapping task that required the acquisition of precise inter-tap timing. Bandwidth feedback typically involves a qualitative statement (e.g., "correct") when performance falls within a specified limit of accuracy and quantitative feedback for performances outside the limits. Lai and Shea found that bandwidth feedback improved learning relative to quantitative KR presented on every trial and argued that the provision of bandwidth KR enhanced response stability (i.e., reduced trial-to-trial variability), a factor that is associated with the enhancement of the generalized motor program (Schmidt & Bjork 1992). A recent extension of the KR work, involving learners' preferences, provided evidence that presenting KR for preferred trials was beneficial for learning (Janelle *et al.* 1995; Janelle *et al.* 1997). Learners favor receiving KR when they believe they have performed well (Chiviacowsky & Wulf 2005), presumably to reinforce their intrinsic perception of good performance.

The effect on learning of manipulating several other factors external to the learner has also been assessed. Experimental evidence exists to demonstrate that variable (random) practice enhances learning relative to blocked practice (e.g., Shea & Morgan 1979; Goode & Magill 1986), modeling can enhance learning through observation (e.g., Landers & Landers 1973; McCullagh 1986; Griffin & Meaney 2000), and breaking complex skills into parts then chaining them may help the acquisition of complex skills (e.g., Wightman & Lintern 1985; Park *et al.* 2004). Manipulating the learning environment such that few errors are made during learning seems to have a number of benefits on subsequent performance, including superior accuracy and greater automatization, even after relatively few trials of practice (Maxwell *et al.* 2001; Poolton *et al.* 2005).

The search for enhancement strategies has not been restricted to manipulations of the external environment – attempts have also been made to enhance skills learning via the learner's internal mental processes. Given that it is logically important that athletes attend to the correct information source when either learning a new skill or performing an old skill, Wulf and colleagues (for a review see Wulf & Prinz 2001) proposed that directing attention internally to the dynamics of movement (e.g., the movement of the arm, wrist, and fingers when pitching in baseball) may be detrimental to learning whereas attending externally to the effects of movement (e.g., the ball's flight) may enhance learning. Wulf *et al.* (1998) reported the first experimental test of this proposal using a slalom-ski task. They demonstrated that, compared to focusing on the movement of the feet, attending to the effects of movement on the apparatus (a platform that moved across two bowed bars in a side-to-side slalom-like movement) resulted in better performance on a delayed retention test. The benefits of an external focus of attention have since been replicated several times in a variety of sports, including golf chipping (Wulf *et al.* 1999), tennis (Wulf *et al.* 2000), volleyball and soccer (Wulf *et al.* 2002), and have been shown to hold for both novice and expert performers (Wulf *et al.* 1999; 2002).

Relatedly, Singer *et al.* (1993) proposed a Five-Step Strategy that involves "learning to prepare for the act, to image, to focus on a meaningful cue, to execute with a quiet mind and to evaluate" (p. 21). The key features of this strategy are that when performing the action attention is directed at an external cue (step 3) and the mind is clear of conscious thought (step 4). The efficacy of the Five-Step approach has been demonstrated in a number of studies (e.g., Singer & Suwanthada 1986; Singer *et al.* 1989; 1993), and appears to be particularly effective in tasks with a high motor component and low cognitive demand (Kim *et al.* 1996).

An alternative learning strategy was recently proposed by Liao and Masters (2001), which may enhance performance in demanding situations. This technique, termed *analogy learning*, is designed to minimize the amount of information being consciously processed by reducing a number of task-relevant "rules" into a simple, all-encompassing biomechanical metaphor (Masters 2000). For example, the metaphor of imagining oneself moving the bat up the hypotenuse of a right-angled triangle in hitting top-spin forehand strokes in table tennis encapsulates all the biomechanical requirements of actually executing such a stroke. Liao and Masters found that the performance of learners given an analogy was unaffected by the imposition of a secondary cognitive load, whereas the performance of a group who received copious verbal instruction was impaired by the secondary load. A recent study has also demonstrated that, compared with instructed learners, analogy learners are better able to make tactical decisions whilst playing table tennis (Poolton *et al.* 2006). Further development of enhanced approaches to the learning of movement skills is of great practical significance to those involved in the coaching and performance of sports and will logically progress in concert with, rather than independent of, improved understanding of the fundamental role of different cognitive factors in the control and acquisition of goal-directed movements.

EFFECTS OF SPORTS PARTICIPATION ON COGNITION

For many people participation in sports, in either a competitive or a recreational mode, represents the major means through which they gain regular physical activity. With the increasing recognition that regular physical activity has profound health benefits that extend beyond protection against the early onset of chronic diseases (such as cardiovascular disease, diabetes, osteoporosis, and some forms of cancer) to other factors such as mental health, sleep quality, and positive self-concept, that also have a direct bearing on quality of life, there has been growing interest in understanding whether, and how, regular participation in sport and physical activity may influence different mental processes.

In this section we very briefly overview the evidence on the relationship between participation in physical activity and some selected aspects of cognitive functioning and stress coping as examples of this emerging research activity. Reminiscent of the situation in the previous section, the evidence of the links between participation and cognition comes generally from two different types of studies: (1) largely descriptive studies that compare different cognitive functions and attributes between self-selected groups of regular exercisers and non-exercisers; and (2) more controlled interventions in which the level of physical activity is directly manipulated and cognitive functions are measured at multiple time periods before, during, and after the exercise bout(s). Almost without exception the studies examine physical activity involvement rather than sport participation per se, so the link to sport is generally inferential. A key variable mediating and moderating many of the findings to date on exercise effects on mental processes is the type of exercise and the period over which it is experienced. A particularly critical distinction in this respect is that drawn between the *acute* (short-term) effects of physical activity and the adaptive effects arising from *chronic* (longer-term) engagement in activity.

Sport, Physical Activity, and Cognitive Function

A number of reviews have been conducted over the past two decades on the impact of exercise/physical activity on different aspects of cognitive function (e.g., Tomporowski & Ellis 1986; Etnier *et al.* 1997; Biddle *et al.* 2000; McMorris & Graydon 2000) and many comment on the inconsistent and inconclusive nature of much of the evidence, especially the early evidence in which appropriate methodological controls were frequently lacking. Nevertheless, more recent studies and reviews (e.g., Tomporowski 2003) point to clearer evidence that physical activity may systematically influence at least some aspects of cognitive function and performance.

Recent electroencephalographic studies (e.g., Polich & Lardon 1997; Nakamura *et al.* 1999) indicate that frequent exercisers (i.e., people engaged in chronic levels of physical activity) are more likely to show heightened cortical activation than less active individuals. This evidence is consistent with animal work indicating that exercise promotes neurogenesis, that exercised animals are superior on maze learning tasks to sedentary controls (van Praag *et al.* 1999), and that activity elicits different gene expression patterns, frequently in genes known to be associated with brain function (Tong *et al.* 2001).

The effects of acute bouts of exercise appear to be quite selective to different facets of information-processing and the direction and period of sustenance of the effects (beneficial or detrimental) appears to be contingent upon the exercise intensity and severity (Tomporowski 2003). Participation in acute exercise appears to have little or no effect on perceptual and sensory aspects of information-processing (e.g., Allard *et al.* 1989) but can have a significant facilitatory effect on both the speed and accuracy of decision-making as measured by both simple and choice reaction time tasks (e.g., Paas and Adam 1991; McMorris *et al.* 1999) and on the speed of response preparation (e.g., Fleury & Bard 1987). Acute exercise appears to have a particular effect on memory, bringing about improvements in the blocking of irrelevant and the selection of relevant information (e.g., Lichtman & Poser 1983) although in the absence of any apparent effect on the capability to retrieve information from working memory (Tomporowski *et al.* 1987). There is evidence to indicate that these facilitatory effects of exercise on selected cognitive functions can be reversed to detrimental ones if the exercise bout is of sufficient duration or intensity to induce significant dehydration (Cian *et al.* 2000; Tomporowski 2003). Clearly, much more needs to be done to explain the mechanism of these various effects of exercise participation on cognition and to harness them for individual and public health benefit.

Sport, Physical Activity, and Coping with Stress

Whereas the study of the relationship between exercise and cognitive function is in its relative infancy, there is a quite sizeable body of literature available examining the relationship between participation in regular physical activity and psychological health. This is especially true in relation to the availability of studies examining the role of exercise in the prevention and treatment of depression and anxiety – psychological disorders with significant cognitive components. There are many recent reviews of this evidence (e.g., Brown 1990; McAuley 1994; US Department of Health & Human Services, 1996; Morgan 1997) and their conclusions are relatively consistent.

A variety of evidence from both cross-sectional (e.g., Stephens 1988) and cohort (e.g., Farmer *et al.* 1988; Weyerer 1992) studies of the general population points to a strong inverse association between level of physical activity participation and the prevalence of anxiety and depression. This evidence is complemented by controlled intervention studies demonstrating that regular exercise is equally, if not more, effective than other forms of psychotherapy for the treatment and management of both anxiety (e.g., Martinsen & Stephens 1994) and depression (e.g., Greist *et al.* 1979). Other evidence is available indicating quite enduring reductions in anxiety and stress-coping from even single bouts of acute aerobic activity or weight-training (e.g., O'Connor *et al.* 1993; Landers & Petruzzello 1994).

How participation in physical activity, such as that provided through participation in sports and other forms of exercise, influences psychological health is not entirely clear, although a number of different mechanisms have been proposed (see McAuley & Rudolph 1995 for a review). Biological explanations have been suggested based on the release of endorphins during exercise and around the moderated release of the stress-related hormones, such as cortisol and the catecholamines. Psychological mechanisms have been advanced based on improvements in self-efficacy that are known to accompany regular activity. Like many fields in the study of human behavior and cognition, understanding more about the interface and linkage between psychological states and biological events is necessary to develop a fuller understanding of the relationship between participation in exercise and individual differences in stress-coping and propensity toward anxiety and depression. Although participation in sports and physical activity may also have a number of potentially negative psychological consequences (e.g., see Sallis & Owen 1999, pp. 48–50) for a brief review), it is clear from the evidence to date that the cognitive skills developed through participation in physical activity may have both widespread and enduring implications for cognitions underpinning psychological health and thus have important applied significance for the enhancement of general well-being. Relatedly, there is growing evidence that cognitive skills and strategies learned in the domain of sport may transfer to other performance domains, such as the work environment, and this has become increasingly an area of interest for researchers interested in the facilitation of the career paths and prospects of athletes post-retirement (e.g., Mayocchi & Hanrahan 2000).

SUMMARY, CONCLUSIONS, AND FUTURE DIRECTIONS

There are strong reciprocal interactions between cognition and sport – the full significance and potential of which is only beginning to be understood. The efficacy with which fundamental cognitive processes, such as attention, function has a profound bearing on human perceptual-motor skill and, through this, a direct bearing on sports performance. Continued attempts to understand more about how cognition influences motor processes will provide benefit to enhancing basic knowledge about key cognitive processes, their generalizability, and their response to moderating factors such as extensive practice and intensive competitive pressure and to providing new pathways for performance enhancement in sport and related domains. Conversely, it is also increasingly apparent that involvement in sports, and other forms of physical activity, can have both short- and long-acting influences on cognitive function, and cognitively-mediated mental states, such as anxiety, self-efficacy, and general feelings of well-being. Understanding more about how exercise influences cognition again offers enormous potential benefits for both an enhanced fundamental understanding of brain function (and biological-psychological interrelations) and development of new and improved means for promoting positive health and well-being in its broadest sense. Transdisciplinary investigative approaches at the interface between cognitive science, neuroscience and kinesiology offer exciting future opportunities for advancing fundamental and applied knowledge about the important, and many and varied, relationships between cognition and sport.

REFERENCES

Abernethy, B. (1990). Expertise, visual search and information pick-up in squash. *Perception, 19*, 63–77.

Abernethy, B., Burgess-Limerick, R. J. & Parks, S. (1994). Contrasting approaches to the study of motor expertise. *Quest, 46*, 186–198.

Abernethy, B., Gill, D., Parks, S. L. & Packer, S. T. (2001). Expertise and the perception of kinematic and situational probability information. *Perception, 30*, 233–252.

Abernethy, B., Neal, R. J. & Koning, P. (1994). Visual-perceptual and cognitive differences between expert, intermediate and novice snooker players. *Applied Cognitive Psychology, 8*, 185–211.

Abernethy, B. & Russell, D. G. (1984). Advance cue utilization by skilled cricket batsmen. *The Australian Journal of Science and Medicine in Sport, 16*, 2–10.

Abernethy, B. & Russell, D. G. (1987a). Expert-novice differences in an applied selective attention task. *Journal of Sport Psychology, 9*, 326–345.

Abernethy, B. & Russell, D. G. (1987b). The relationship between expertise and visual search strategy in a racquet sport. *Human Movement Science, 6*, 283–319.

Abernethy, B. & Sparrow, W. A. (1992). The rise and fall of dominant paradigms in motor behaviour research. In J. J. Summers (ed.), *Approaches to the Study of Motor Control and Learning* (pp. 3–45). Amsterdam: Elsevier Science.

Abernethy, B., Wann, J. P. & Parks, S. (1998). Training perceptual-motor skills for sport. In B. C. Elliott (ed.), *Training in Sport: Applying Sport Science* (pp. 1–68). Chichester: John Wiley & Sons.

Abernethy, B., Wood, J. M. & Parks, S. (1999). Can the anticipatory skills of experts be learned by novices? *Research Quarterly for Exercise and Sport, 70*, 313–318.

Alain, C. & Proteau, L. (1980). Decision making in sport. In C. H. Nadeau, W. Halliwell, K. M. Newell & G. C. Roberts (eds.), *Psychology of Motor Behavior and Sport – 1979* (pp. 465–477). Champaign, IL: Human Kinetics.

Allard, F., Brawley, L., Deakin, J. & Elliot, F. (1989). The effect of exercise on visual attention performance. *Human Performance*, 2, 131–145.

Allard, F. & Burnett, N. (1985). Skill in sport. *Canadian Journal of Psychology, 39*, 294–312.

Allard, F., Graham, S. & Paarsalu, M. L. (1980). Perception in sport: basketball. *Journal of Sport Psychology, 2*, 14–21.

Anderson, J. R. (1982). Acquisition of cognitive skill. *Psychological Review, 89*, 369–406.

Anderson, J. R. (1983). *The Architecture of Cognition*. Cambridge, MA: Harvard University Press.

Anderson, J. R. (1993). *Rules of the Mind*. Hillsdale, NJ: Lawrence Erlbaum Associates.

Anderson, W. G. (1899). Studies in the effects of physical training. *American Physical Education Review, 4*, 265–278.

Annett, J. (1969). *Feedback and Human Behaviour*. Harmondsworth: Penguin Books.

Baddeley, A. D. (1966). The capacity for generating information by randomisation. *Quarterly Journal of Experimental Psychology, 18*, 119–129.

Bahill, A. T. & LaRitz, T. (1984). Why can't batters keep their eyes on the ball? *American Scientist, 72*, 249–253.

Baker, J., Côté, J. & Abernethy, B. (2003). Sport-specific practice and the development of expert decision-making in team ball sports. *Journal of Applied Sport Psychology, 15*, 12–25.

Bandura, A. (1977). Self-efficacy: toward a unifying theory of personality change. *Psychological Review, 84*, 191–215.

Bard, C. & Fleury, M. (1976). Analysis of visual search activity during sport problem situations. *Journal of Human Movement Studies, 3*, 214–222.

Baumeister, R. F. (1984). Choking under pressure: self-consciousness and paradoxical effects of incentives on skilful performance. *Journal of Personality and Social Psychology, 46*, 610–620.

Bawden, M. A. K., Maynard, I. W. & Westbury, T. (2001). The effects of conscious control of movement and dispositional self-consciousness on golf putting performance. *Journal of Sports Sciences, 19*, 68–69.

Beek, P. J. (2000). Toward a theory of implicit learning in the perceptual-motor domain. *International Journal of Sport Psychology, 31*, 547–554.

Beek, P. J., Jacobs, D. M., Daffertshofer, A. & Huys, R. (2003). Expert performance in sports: views from the joint perspectives of ecological psychology and dynamical systems theory. In J. L. Starkes & K. A. Ericsson (eds.), *Expert Performance in Sports: Advances in Research on Sport Expertise* (pp. 321–342). Champaign, IL: Human Kinetics.

Beilock, S. L., Bertenthal, B. I., McCoy, A. M. & Carr, T. H. (2004). Haste does not always make waste: expertise, direction of attention, and speed versus accuracy in performing sensorimotor skills. *Psychonomic Bulletin and Review, 11*, 373–379.

Beilock, S. L. & Carr, T. H. (2001). On the fragility of skilled performance: what governs choking under pressure? *Journal of Experimental Psychology: General, 130*, 701–725.

Beilock, S. L. & Carr, T. H. (2004). From novice to expert performance: memory, attention, and the control of complex sensori-motor skills. In A. M. Williams & N. J. Hodges (eds.), *Skill Acquisition in Sport: Research, Theory and Practice* (pp. 309–327). London: Routledge.

Beilock, S. L., Carr, T. H., MacMahon, C. & Starkes, J. L. (2002). When paying attention becomes counterproductive: impact of divided versus skill-focused attention on novice and experienced performance of sensorimotor skills. *Journal of Experimental Psychology: Applied, 8*, 6–16.

Bernstein, N. (1967). *The Coordination and Regulation of Movement*. Oxford: Pergamon Press.

Berry, D. C. & Dienes, Z. (1993). *Implicit Learning: Theoretical and Empirical Issues*. Hove: Lawrence Erlbaum Associates.

Biddle, S. J. H., Fox, K. R. & Boutcher, S. H. (2000). *Physical Activity and Psychological Well-Being*. London: Routledge.

Bilodeau, E. A., Bilodeau, I. M. & Schumsky, D. A. (1959). Some effects of introducing and withdrawing knowledge of results early and late in practice. *Journal of Experimental Psychology, 58*, 142–144.

Brown, D. R. (1990). Exercise, fitness, and mental health. In C. Bouchard, R. J. Shephard, T. Stephens, J. R. Sutton & B. D. McPherson (eds.), *Exercise, Fitness, and Health: A Consensus of Current Knowledge* (pp. 607–626). Champaign, IL: Human Kinetics.

Buckolz, E., Prapavesis, H. & Fairs, J. (1988). Advance cues and their use in predicting tennis passing shots. *Canadian Journal of Sport Sciences*, *13*, 20–30.

Charness, N. (1979). Components of skill in bridge. *Canadian Journal of Psychology*, *33*, 1–16.

Chase, W. G. & Simon, H. A. (1973). The mind's eye in chess. In W. G. Chase (ed.), *Visual Information Processing* (pp. 215–282). New York: Academic Press.

Chiviacowsky, S. & Wulf, G. (2005). Self-controlled feedback is effective if it is based on the learner's performance. *Research Quarterly for Exercise and Sport*, *76*, 42–48.

Christina, R. W. (1989). Whatever happened to applied research in motor learning? In J. S. Skinner, C. B. Corbin, D. M. Landers, P. E. Martin & C. L. Wells (eds.), *Future Directions in Exercise and Sport Science Research* (pp. 411–422). Champaign, IL: Human Kinetics.

Cian, C., Koulmann, N., Barraud, P. A. *et al.* (2000). Influences of variations in body hydration on cognitive function: Effects of hyperhydration, heat stress, and exercise-induced dehydration. *Journal of Psychophysiology*, 14, 29–36.

Cohen, A., Ivry, R. & Keele, S. (1990). Attention and structure in sequence learning. *Journal of Experimental Psychology: Learning, Memory and Cognition*, *16*, 17–30.

Corkin, S. (1968). Acquisition of motor skill after bilateral medial temporal lobe excision. *Neurosychologia*, *6*, 225–265.

Cratty, B. J. (1964). *Movement Behavior and Motor Learning.* Philadelphia: Lea & Febiger.

Curran, T. & Keele, S. W. (1993). Attentional and non-attentional forms of sequence learning. *Journal of Experimental Psychology: Learning, Memory and Cognition*, *19*, 189–202.

Davids, K. & Button, C. (2000). The cognition-dynamics interface and performance in sport. *International Journal of Sport Psychology*, *31*, 515–521.

Davids, K., Handford, C. & Williams, M. (1994). The natural physical alternative to cognitive theories of motor behaviour: an invitation for interdisciplinary research efforts in sports science? *Journal of Sports Sciences*, *12*, 495–528.

de Groot, A. D. (1966). Perception and memory versus thought. In B. Kleinmuntz (ed.), *Problem Solving Research, Methods and Theory* (pp. 19–50). New York: John Wiley & Sons.

Dienes, Z. & Berry, D. C. (1997). Implicit learning: below the subjective threshold. *Psychonomic Bulletin and Review*, *4*, 3–23.

Ericsson, K. A., Krampe, R. T. & Tesch-Römer, C. (1993). The role of deliberate practice in the acquisition of expert performance. *Psychological Review*, *100*, 363–406.

Etnier, J. L., Salazar, W., Landers, D. M. *et al.* (1997). The influence of physical fitness and exercise upon cognitive functioning: a meta-analysis. *Journal of Sport and Exercise Psychology*, *19*, 249–277.

Farmer, M. E., Locke, B. Z., Moscicki, E. K. *et al.* (1988). Physical activity and depressive symptoms: the NHANES I Epidemiologic Follow-up Study. *American Journal of Epidemiology*, *128*, 1340–1351.

Farrow, D. & Abernethy, B. (2002). Can anticipatory skills be learned through implicit video-based perceptual training? *Journal of Sports Sciences*, *20*, 471–485.

Farrow, D., Chivers, P., Hardingham, C. & Sasche, S. (1998). The effect of video-based perceptual training on the tennis return of serve. *International Journal of Sport Psychology*, *29*, 231–242.

Fitts, P. M. (1964). Perceptual-motor skill learning. In A. W. Melton (ed.), *Categories of Human Learning.* New York: Academic Press.

Fitts, P. M. & Posner, M. I. (1967). *Human Performance.* Belmont, CA: Brooks/Cole.

Fleury, M. & Bard, C. (1987). Effects of different types of physical activity on the performance of perceptual tasks in peripheral and central vision and coincident timing. *Ergonomics*, *30*, 945–958.

Gentile, A. M. (1998). Implicit and explicit processes during acquisition of functional skills. *Scandinavian Journal of Occupational Therapy*, *5*, 7–16.

Gibson, J. J. (1979). *The Ecological Approach to Visual Perception.* Boston, MA: Houghton Mifflin.

Glencross, D. J. (1992). Human skill and motor learning: a critical review. *Sport Science Review*, *1*, 65–78.

Glencross, D. J. & Cibich, B. J. (1977). A decision analysis of games skills. *Australian Journal of Sports Medicine*, *9*, 72–75.

Goode, S. L. & Magill, R. A. (1986). The contextual interference effect in learning three badminton serves. *Research Quarterly for Exercise and Sport, 57,* 308–314.

Goulet, C., Bard, C. & Fleury, M. (1989). Expertise differences in preparing to return a tennis serve: a visual information processing approach. *Journal of Sport and Exercise Psychology, 11,* 382–398.

Gray, R. (2002). "Markov at the bat": a model of cognitive processing in baseball batters. *Psychological Science, 13,* 542–547.

Gray, R. (2004). Attending to the execution of a complex sensorimotor skill: expertise differences, choking, and slumps. *Journal of Experimental Psychology: Applied, 10,* 42–54.

Green, T. D. & Flowers, J. H. (1991). Implicit versus explicit learning processes in a probabilistic, continuous fine-motor catching task. *Journal of Motor Behavior, 23,* 293–300.

Greist, J. H., Klein, M. H., Eischens, R. R. *et al.* (1979). Running as treatment for depression. *Comprehensive Psychiatry, 20,* 41–54.

Griffin, K. & Meaney, K. S. (2000). Modeling and motor performance: an examination of model similarity and model type on children's motor performance. *Research Quarterly for Exercise and Sport, 71,* A-56, 67.

Handford, C., Davids, K., Bennett, S. & Button, C. (1997). Skill acquisition in sport: some implications of an evolving practice ecology. *Journal of Sports Sciences, 15,* 621–640.

Hardy, L., Mullen, R. & Jones, G. (1996). Knowledge and conscious control of motor actions under stress. *British Journal of Psychology, 87,* 621–636.

Haskins, M. J. (1965). Development of a response recognition training film in tennis. *Perceptual and Motor Skills, 21,* 207–211.

Helsen, W. F., Starkes, J. L. & Hodges, N. J. (1998). Team sports and the theory of deliberate practice. *Journal of Sport and Exercise Psychology, 20,* 12–34.

Hennemann, M. & Keller, D. (1983). Preparatory behaviour in the execution of a sport-related movement: The return of service in tennis. *International Journal of Sport Psychology, 14,* 149–161.

Henry, F. M. & Rogers, D. E. (1960). Increased response latency for complicated movements and a "memory drum" theory of neuromotor reaction. *Research Quarterly, 31,* 448–458.

Heuer, H. & Wing, A. M. (1984). Doing two things at once: Process limitations and interactions. In M. M. Smyth & A. M. Wing (eds.), *The Psychology of Human Movement* (pp. 183–213). London: Academic Press.

Holding, D. H. (1965). *The Principals of Training.* Oxford: Pergamon Press.

Howarth, C., Walsh, W. D., Abernethy, B. & Snyder, C. W. (1984). A field examination of anticipation in squash: Some preliminary data. *Australian Journal of Science and Medicine in Sport, 16,* 6–10.

Hubbard, A. W. & Seng, C. N. (1954). Visual movements of batters. *Research Quarterly, 25,* 42–57.

Hyman, R. (1953). Stimulus information as a determinant of reaction time. *Journal of Experimental Psychology, 45,* 188–196.

Jackson, R. C. (2003). Evaluating the evidence for implicit perceptual learning: a re-analysis of Farrow and Abernethy (2002). *Journal of Sports Sciences, 21,* 503–509.

Jackson, R. C. & Farrow, D. (2005). Implicit perceptual training: How, when, and why? *Human Movement Science, 24,* 308–325.

Janelle, C. M., Barba, D. A., Frehlich, S. G. *et al.* (1997). Maximizing performance effectiveness through videotape replay and a self-controlled learning environment. *Research Quarterly for Exercise and Sport, 68,* 269–279.

Janelle, C. M., Kim, J. & Singer, R. N. (1995). Subject-controlled performance feedback and learning of a closed motor skill. *Perceptual and Motor Skills, 81,* 627–634.

Johansson, G. (1973). Visual perception of biological motion and a model for its analysis. *Perception and Psychophysics, 14,* 201–211.

Jones, C. M. & Miles, T. R. (1978). Use of advance cues in predicting the flight of a lawn tennis ball. *Journal of Human Movement Studies, 4,* 231–235.

Keele, S. W. (1968). Movement control in skilled motor performance. *Psychological Bulletin, 70,* 387–403.

Kelso, J. A. S. (1995). *Dynamic Patterns.* Cambridge, MA: MIT Press.

Kim, J., Singer, R. N. & Radlo, S. J. (1996). Degree of cognitive demands in psychomotor tasks and the effects of the five-step strategy on achievement. *Human Performance*, *9*, 155–169.
Knopman, D. & Nissen, M. J. (1991). Procedural learning is impaired in Huntington's disease: evidence from the serial reaction time task. *Neuropsychologia*, *29*, 245–254.
Kroll, W. & Lewis, G. (1970). America's first sport psychologist. *Quest*, *13*, 1–4.
Lai, Q. & Shea, C. H. (1999). Bandwidth knowledge of results enhances generalized motor program learning. *Research Quarterly for Exercise and Sport*, *70*, 79–83.
Land, M. F. & McLeod, P. (2000). From eye movements to actions: How batsmen hit the ball. *Nature Neuroscience*, *3*, 1340–1345.
Landers, D. M. (1983). Whatever happened to theory testing in sport psychology? *Journal of Sport Psychology*, *5*, 135–158.
Landers, D. M. & Landers, D. M. (1973). Teacher versus peer models: effect of model's presence and performance level on motor behaviour. *Journal of Motor Behaviour*, *5*, 129–139.
Landers, D. M. & Petruzzello, S. J. (1994). Physical activity, fitness, and anxiety. In C. Bouchard, R. J. Shephard & T. Stephens (eds.), *Physical Activity, Fitness, and Health: International Proceedings and Consensus Statement* (pp. 868–882). Champaign, IL: Human Kinetics.
Lavery, J. J. (1962). Retention of simple motor skills as a function of type of knowledge of results. *Canadian Journal of Psychology*, *16*, 300–311.
Leavitt, J. L. (1979). Cognitive demands of skating and stick-handling in ice hockey. *Canadian Journal of Applied Sport Sciences*, *4*, 46–55.
Liao, C. M. & Masters, R. S. W. (2001). Analogy learning: a means to implicit motor learning. *Journal of Sport Sciences*, *19*, 307–319.
Libet, B. (1985). Unconscious cerebral initiative and the role of conscious will in voluntary action. *Behavioural and Brain Sciences*, *8*, 529–566.
Lichtman, S. & Poser, E. G. (1983). The effects of exercise on mood and cognitive functioning. *Journal of Psychosomatic Research*, *27*, 43–52.
Logan, G. D. (1985). Skill and automaticity: relations, implications, and future directions. *Canadian Journal of Psychology*, *39*, 367–386.
McAuley, E. (1994). Physical activity and psychosocial outcomes. In C. Bouchard, R. J. Shephard & T. Stephens (eds.), *Physical Activity, Fitness and Health: International Proceedings and Consensus Statement* (pp. 551–568). Champaign, IL: Human Kinetics.
McAuley, E. & Rudolph, D. (1995). Physical activity, aging, and psychological well-being. *Journal of Aging and Physical Activity*, *3*, 67–96.
McCullagh, P. (1986). Model status as a determinant of observational learning and performance. *Journal of Sport Psychology*, *8*, 319–331.
McMorris, T. & Graydon, J. (2000). The effect of incremental exercise on cognitive performance. *International Journal of Sport Psychology*, *31*, 66–81.
McMorris, T., Meyers, S., Macgillivary, W. W. *et al.* (1999). Exercise, plasma catecholamine concentrations and performance of soccer players on a soccer-specific test of decision making. *Journal of Sports Sciences*, *17*, 667–676.
Magill, R. A. (1998). Knowledge is more than we can talk about: implicit learning in motor skill acquisition. *Research Quarterly for Exercise and Sport*, *69*, 104–110.
Magill, R. A. & Hall, K. G. (1989). *Implicit and explicit learning in a complex tracking task*. Paper presented at the annual meeting of the Psychonomic Society, Atlanta, GA.
Mahoney, M. J. & Avener, M. S. (1977). Psychology of the elite athlete: An exploratory study. *Cognitive Therapy and Research*, *1*, 135–141.
Massengale, J. D. & Swanson, R. A. (eds.) (1997). *History of Exercise and Sport Sciences*. Champaign, IL: Human Kinetics.
Martell, S. G. & Vickers, J. N. (2004). Gaze characteristics of elite and near-elite athletes in ice hockey defensive tactics. *Human Movement Science*, *22*, 689–712.
Martinsen, E. W. & Stephens, T. (1994). Exercise and mental health in clinical and free-living populations. In R. K. Dishman (ed.), *Advances in Exercise Adherence* (pp. 55–72). Champaign, IL: Human Kinetics.
Masters, R. S. W. (1992). Knowledge, knerves and know-how: the role of explicit versus implicit knowledge in the breakdown of a complex motor skill under pressure. *British Journal of Psychology*, *83*, 343–358.

Masters, R. S. W. (2000). Theoretical aspects of implicit learning in sport. *International Journal of Sport Psychology*, *31*, 530–541.

Masters, R. S. W., MacMahon, K. M. A. & Pall, H. S. (2004). Implicit motor learning in Parkinson's disease. *Rehabilitation Psychology*, *49*, 79–82.

Masters, R. S. W. & Maxwell, J. P. (2004). Implicit motor learning, reinvestment and movement disruption: what you don't know won't hurt you? In A. M. Williams & N. J. Hodges (eds.), *Skill Acquisition in Sport: Research, Theory and Practice* (pp. 207–228). London: Routledge.

Masters, R. S. W., Polman, R. C. J. & Hammond, N. V. (1993). "Reinvestment": A dimension of personality implicated in skill breakdown under pressure. *Personality and Individual Differences*, *14*, 655–666.

Maxwell, J. P., Masters, R. S. W. & Eves, F. F. (2000). From novice to no know-how: A longitudinal study of implicit motor learning. *Journal of Sport Sciences*, *18*, 111–120.

Maxwell, J. P., Masters, R. S. W. & Eves, F. F. (2003). The role of working memory in motor learning and performance. *Consciousness and Cognition*, *12*, 376–402.

Maxwell, J. P., Masters, R. S. W., Kerr, E. & Weedon, E. (2001). The implicit benefit of learning without errors. *Quarterly Journal of Experimental Psychology*, *54*, 1049–1068.

Mayocchi, L. & Hanrahan, S. (2000). Transferable skills for career change. In D. Lavallee & P. Wylleman (eds.), *Career Transitions in Sport: International Perspectives* (pp. 95–110). Morgantown, WV: Fitness Information Technology.

Morgan, W. P. (1997). *Physical Activity and Mental Health*. Champaign, IL: Human Kinetics.

Mori, S., Ohtani, Y. & Imanaka, K. (2002). Reaction times and anticipatory skills of karate athletes. *Human Movement Science*, *21*, 213–230.

Morris, T. & Summers, J. (2004). *Sport Psychology: Theory, Applications and Issues* (2nd edn). Brisbane: John Wiley & Sons.

Musch, S. & Grondin, J. (2001). Unequal competition as an impediment to personal development: a review of the relative age effect in sport. *Developmental Review*, *21*, 147–167.

Nakamura, Y., Nishimoto, K., Akamatu, M. *et al.* (1999). The effect of jogging on the P300 event related potentials. *Electromyography and Clinical Neurophysiology*, *39*, 71–74.

Neves, D. M. & Anderson, J. R. (1981). Knowledge compilation: mechanisms for the automatisation of cognitive skills. In J. R. Anderson (ed.), *Cognitive Skills and Their Acquisition*. Hillsdale, NJ: Lawrence Erlbaum Associates.

Newell, K. M. (1974). Decision processes in baseball batters. *Human Factors*, *16*, 520–527.

Nideffer, R. M. (1976). The test of attentional and interpersonal style. *Journal of Personality and Social Psychology*, *34*, 394–404.

Nissen, M. J. & Bullemer, P. (1987). Attentional requirements of learning: evidence from performance measures. *Cognitive Psychology*, *19*, 1–32.

O'Connor, P. J., Bryant, C. X., Veltri, J. P. & Gebhardt, S. M. (1993). State anxiety and ambulatory blood pressure following resistance exercise in females. *Medicine and Science in Sports and Exercise*, *25*, 516–521.

Paas, F. G. W. C. & Adam, J. J. (1991). Human information processing during physical exercise. *Ergonomics*, *34*, 1385–1397.

Park, J-H., Wilde, H. & Shea, C. H. (2004). Part–whole practice of movement sequences. *Journal of Motor Behaviour*, *36*, 51–61.

Paull, G. & Glencross, D. (1997). Expert perception and decision making in baseball. *International Journal of Sport Psychology*, *28*, 35–56.

Perruchet, P., Chambaron, S. & Ferrel-Chapus, C. (2003). Learning from implicit learning literature: comment on Shea, Wulf, Whitacre, and Park (2001). *Quarterly Journal of Experimental Psychology*, *56A*, 769–778.

Pew, R. W. (1974). Levels of analysis in motor control. *Brain Research*, *71*, 393–400.

Polich, J. & Lardon, M. T. (1997). P300 and long-term physical exercise. *Electroencephalography and Clinical Neurophysiology*, *103*, 493–498.

Poolton, J. M., Masters, R. S. W. & Maxwell, J. P. (2005). The relationship between initial errorless learning conditions and subsequent performance. *Human Movement Science*, *24*, 362–378.

Poolton, J. M., Masters, R. S. W. & Maxwell, J. P. & Raab, M. (2006). Learning by analogy improves decision making in table tennis. Unpublished paper.

Poulter, D. R., Jackson, R. C., Wann, J. P. & Berry, D. C. (2005). The effect of learning condition on perceptual anticipation, awareness, and visual search. *Human Movement Science*, *24*, 345–361.

van Praag, H., Christie, B. R., Sejnowski, T. J. & Gage, F. H. (1999). Running enhances neurogenesis, learning, and long-term potentiation in mice. *Proceedings of the National Academy of Sciences of the United States of America*, *96*, 13427–13431.

Raab, M. (2003). Implicit and explicit learning of decision making in sports is affected by complexity of situation. *International Journal of Sport Psychology*, *34*, 273–288.

Rossano, M. J. (2003). Expertise and the evolution of consciousness. *Cognition*, *89*, 207–236.

Rowe, R. M. & McKenna, F. P. (2001). Skilled anticipation in real-world tasks: Measurement of attentional demands in the domain of tennis. *Journal of Experimental Psychology: Applied*, *7*, 60–67.

Sallis, J. F. & Owen, N. (1999). *Physical Activity and Behavioral Medicine*. Thousand Oaks, CA: Sage.

Salmoni, A. W. (1989). Motor skill learning. In D. H. Holding (ed.), *Human Skills* (2nd edn, pp. 261–332). London: John Wiley & Sons.

Salmoni, A., Schmidt, R. A. & Walter, C. B. (1984). Knowledge of results and motor learning: A review and critical reappraisal. *Psychological Bulletin*, *95*, 355–386.

Schmidt, R. A. (1988). Motor and action perspectives on motor behaviour. In O. G. Meijer & K. Roth (eds.), *Complex Motor Behaviour: "The" Motor-Action Controversy* (pp. 3–44). Amsterdam: Elsevier.

Schmidt, R. A. & Bjork, R. A. (1992). New conceptualisations of practice: common principals in three paradigms suggest new concepts for training. *Psychological Science*, *3*, 207–217.

Schmidt, R. A. & Lee, T. D. (2005). *Motor Control and Learning: A Behavioral Emphasis* (4th edn). Champaign, IL: Human Kinetics.

Schmidt, R. A. & Wrisberg, C. A. (2004). *Motor Learning and Performance* (3rd edn). Champaign, IL: Human Kinetics.

Schmidt, R. A., Young, D. E., Swinnen, S. & Shapiro, D. C. (1989). Summary knowledge of results for skill acquisition: support for the guidance hypothesis. *Journal of Experimental Psychology: Learning, Memory, and Cognition*, *15*, 352–359.

Scott, D., Scott, L. M. & Howe, B. L. (1998). Training anticipation for intermediate tennis players. *Behaviour Modification*, *22*, 243–261.

Seger, C. A. (1994). Implicit learning. *Psychological Bulletin*, *115*, 163–196.

Shea, C. H., Wulf, G., Whitacre, C. A. & Park, J. H. (2001). Surfing the implicit wave. *Quarterly Journal of Experimental Psychology*, *54*, 841–862.

Shea, J. B. & Morgan, R. L. (1979). Contextual interference effects on the acquisition, retention, and transfer of a motor skill. *Journal of Experimental Psychology: Human Performance and Perception*, *5*, 179–187.

Shulman, G. L., Remington, R. W. & McLean, J. P. (1979). Moving attention through visual space. *Journal of Experimental Psychology: Human Perception and Performance*, *5*, 522–526.

Singer, R. N. (1968). *Motor Learning and Human Performance*. New York: Macmillan.

Singer, R. N., DeFranscesco, C. & Randall, L. E. (1989). Effectiveness of a global learning strategy practiced in different contexts on primary and transfer self-paced motor tasks. *Journal of Sport and Exercise Psychology*, *11*, 290–303.

Singer, R. N., Lidor, R. & Cauraugh, J. H. (1993). To be aware or not aware? What to think about while learning and performing a motor skill. *The Sport Psychologist*, *7*, 19–30.

Singer, R. N. & Suwanthada, S. (1986). The generalisability effectiveness of a learning strategy on achievement on related closed motor skills. *Research Quarterly for Exercise and Sport*, *57*, 205–214.

Singer, R. N., Williams, A. M., Frehlich, S. G. *et al.* (1998). New frontiers in visual search: an exploratory study in live tennis situations. *Research Quarterly for Exercise and Sport*, *69*(3), 290–296.

Smeeton, N. J., Williams, A. M., Hodges, N. J. & Ward, P. (2005). The relative effectiveness of various instructional approaches in developing anticipation skill. *Journal of Experimental Psychology: Applied*, *11*, 98–110.

Stadler, M. A. (1997). Distinguishing implicit and explicit learning. *Psychonomic Bulletin & Review*, *4*, 56–62.
Starkes, J. L. (1987). Skill in field hockey: the nature of the cognitive advantage. *Journal of Sport Psychology*, *9*, 146–160.
Starkes, J. L. & Ericsson, K. A. (eds.) (2003). *Expert Performance in Sports: Advances in Research on Sport Expertise*. Champaign, IL: Human Kinetics.
Stelmach, G. E. (1982). Information-processing framework for understanding human motor behavior. In J. A. S. Kelso (ed.), *Human Motor Behavior: An Introduction* (pp. 63–91). Hillsdale, NJ: Lawrence Erlbaum Associates.
Stephens, T. (1988). Physical activity and mental health in the United States and Canada: evidence from four population surveys. *Preventive Medicine*, *17*, 35–47.
Straub, W. F. & Williams, J. M. (eds.) (1984). *Cognitive Sport Psychology.* Lansing, NY: Sport Science Associates.
Summers, J. J. (1998). Has Ecological Psychology delivered what it promised? In J. P. Piek (ed.), *Motor Behavior and Human Skill: A Multidisciplinary Approach* (pp. 385–402). Champaign, IL: Human Kinetics.
Summers, J. J. (2004). A historical perspective on skill acquisition. In A. M. Williams & N. J. Hodges (eds.), *Skill Acquisition in Sport: Research, Theory and Practice* (pp. 1–26). London: Routledge.
Sun, R. (1997). Learning, action, and consciousness: a hybrid approach towards modeling consciousness. *Neural Networks*, *10*, 1317–1331.
Sun, R., Merrill, E. & Peterson, T. (2001). From implicit skills to explicit knowledge: a bottom-up model of skill learning. *Cognitive Science*, *25*, 203–244.
Sun, R., Slusarz, P. & Terry, C. (2005). The interaction of the explicit and the implicit in skill learning: a dual-process approach. *Psychological Review*, *112*, 159–192.
Swinnen, S. P. (1996). Information feedback for motor skill learning: a review. In H. N. Zelaznik (ed.), *Advances in Motor Learning and Control* (pp. 37–66). Champaign, IL: Human Kinetics.
Temprado, J. J., Zanone, P. G., Monno, A. & Laurent, M. (1999). Attentional load associated with performing and stabilizing preferred bimanual patterns. *Journal of Experimental Psychology: Human Perception and Performance*, *25*, 1575–1594.
Tenenbaum, G., Levy-Kolker, N., Sade, S. *et al.* (1996). Anticipation and confidence of decisions related to skilled performance. *International Journal of Sport Psychology*, *27*, 293–307.
Tomporowski, P. D. (2003). Effects of acute bouts of exercise on cognition. *Acta Psychologica*, *112*, 297–324.
Tomporowski, P. D. & Ellis, N. R. (1986). The effects of exercise on cognitive processes: a review. *Psychological Bulletin*, *99*, 338–346.
Tomporowski, P. D., Ellis, N. R. & Stephens, R. (1987). The immediate effects of strenuous exercise on free recall memory. *Ergonomics*, *30*, 121–129.
Tong, L., Shen, H., Perreau, V. M. *et al.* (2001). Effects of exercise on gene-expression profile in the rat hippocampus. *Neurobiology of Disease*, *8*, 1046–1056.
Tresilian, J. R. (2004). The accuracy of interceptive action in time and space. *Exercise and Sport Sciences Reviews*, *32*, 167–173.
Triplett, N. (1898). The dynamogenic factors in pacemaking and competition. *American Journal of Psychology*, *9*, 507–553.
US Department of Health and Human Services (1996). *Physical Activity and Health: A Report of the Surgeon General.* Atlanta, GA: US Department of Health and Human Services, Centers for Disease Control and Prevention, National Center for Chronic Disease Prevention and Health Promotion.
Weinberg, R. S. & Gould, D. (2003). *Foundations of Sport And exercise Psychology* (3rd edn). Champaign, IL: Human Kinetics.
Weiner, B. (1972). *Theories of Motivation: From Mechanism to Cognition.* Chicago, IL: Markham.
Weyerer, S. (1992). Physical inactivity and depression in the community: evidence from the Upper Bavarian Field Study. *International Journal of Sports Medicine*, *13*, 492–496.
Whiting, H. T. A. (1969). *Acquiring Ball Skills: A Psychological Interpretation.* London: Bell.

Wiggins, D. K. (1984). The history of sport psychology in North America. In J. M. Silva & R. S. Weinberg (eds.), *Psychological Foundations of Sport* (pp. 274–286). Champaign, IL: Human Kinetics.

Wightman, D. C. & Lintern, G. (1985). Part-task training strategies for tracking and manual control. *Human Factors, 27*, 267–283.

Williams, A. M. & Davids, K. (1995). Declarative knowledge in sport: a by-product or experience or a characteristic of expertise? *Journal of Sport and Exercise Psychology, 17*, 259–275.

Williams, A. M. & Davids, K. (1998). Visual search strategy, selective attention, and expertise in soccer. *Research Quarterly for Exercise and Sport, 69*, 111–128.

Williams, A. M., Davids, K., Burwitz, L. & Williams, J. G. (1994). Visual search strategies of experienced and inexperienced soccer players. *Research Quarterly for Exercise and Sport, 65*, 127–135.

Williams, A. M., Davids, K. & Williams, J. G. (1999). *Visual Perception and Action in Sport.* London: E. & F. N. Spon.

Williams, A. M. & Hodges, N. J. (eds.) (2004). *Skill Acquisition in Sport: Research, Theory and Practice.* London: Routledge.

Williams, A. M., Ward, P. & Chapman, C. (2003). Training perceptual skill in field hockey: is there transfer from the laboratory to the field? *Research Quarterly for Exercise and Sport, 74*, 98–103.

Williams, A. M., Ward, P., Knowles, J. M. & Smeeton, N. (2002). Anticipation skill in a real-world task: measurement, training, and transfer in tennis. *Journal of Experimental Psychology: Applied, 8*, 259–270.

Willingham, D. B. & Goedert-Eschmann, K. (1999). The relation between implicit and explicit learning: evidence for parallel development. *Psychological Science, 10*, 531–534.

World Health Organization (2004). Global Strategy on Diet, Physical Activity and Health. World Health Assembly Resolution WHA 57: 17, May.

Wulf, G., Höß, M.,& Prinz, W. (1998). Instructions for motor learning: differential effects of internal versus external focus of attention. *Journal of Motor Behavior, 30*, 169–179.

Wulf, G., Lauterbach, B. & Toole, T. (1999). The learning advantages of an external focus of attention in golf. *Research Quarterly for Exercise and Sport, 70*, 120–126.

Wulf, G., McConnel, N., Gärtner, M. & Schwarz, A. (2002). Enhancing the learning of sport skills through external-focus feedback. *Journal of Motor Behavior, 34*, 171–182.

Wulf, G., McNevin, N. H., Fuchs, T. *et al.* (2000). Attentional focus in complex motor skill learning. *Research Quarterly for Exercise and Sport, 71*, 229–239.

Wulf, G. & Prinz, W. (2001). Directing attention to movement effects enhances learning: a review. *Psychonomic Bulletin and Review, 8*, 648–660.

Wulf, G. & Schmidt, R. A. (1997). Variability of practice and implicit motor learning. *Journal of Experimental Psychology: Learning, Memory & Cognition, 23*, 987–1006.

Wulf, G. & Shea, C. H. (2004). Understanding the role of augmented feedback: the good, the bad, and the ugly. In A. M. Williams & N. J. Hodges (eds.), *Skill Acquisition in Sport: Research, Theory, and Practice* (pp. 121–144). London: Routledge.

Wright, D. L., Pleasants, F. & Gomez-Meza, M. (1990). Use of advanced visual cue sources in volleyball. *Journal of Sport & Exercise Psychology, 12*, 406–414.

CHAPTER 14

Aviation

Christopher Wickens
University of Illinois at Urbana-Champaign

Flying an aircraft is one of the greatest challenges to the cognitive capabilities of humans, involving as it does the knowledge of how to control a vehicle that defies the natural forces of gravity. From the standpoint of cognitive psychology, the task of flying will be considered from three different, but intersecting perspectives: the cognitive analysis of the different tasks a pilot must carry out (Seamster *et al.* 1997); a description of the physical characteristics of the aircraft system that is the focus of those tasks; and a representation of the pilot's information-processing structures that are most critical, in different combinations, to achieving those tasks. In this chapter, we first describe the physical characteristics of airplane flight that impose so heavily upon the pilot's cognitive capabilities. Then, after representing the pilot as an information-processing system, we proceed to describe the cognitive demands imposed by the following aviation task categories: aviating, navigating, communicating, and systems management. Within each category, we discuss ways in which the design of aircraft and of the airspace is evolving to remediate (but sometimes exacerbate) those demands. Then we address two general issues, falling within the purview of cognitive psychology, that transcend the different task categories: actions and tasks and the cognitive issues of automation.

THE AIRCRAFT AS A DYNAMIC SYSTEM

Effective control of any complex dynamic system depends upon the operator possessing an accurate *mental model* of the system from which to establish expectancies of system response to environmental and control inputs (Bellenkes *et al.* 1997; Moray 1997). The foundations of the mental model of the aircraft are based in its dynamics, represented schematically in Figure 14.1a, which presents a graphic presentation of the aircraft. Figure 14.1b presents a more schematic and abstract version of its dynamic elements. As shown in both figures, the aircraft can be characterized first by control of its *attitude* (orientation or rotation) in three-dimensional space, a vector defined by *pitch*, *bank* (or roll), and *yaw*. As shown in the middle row of Figure 14.1b, as the aircraft moves forward, its attitude parameters then produce rates of change, vertical velocity generally being influenced by

Handbook of Applied Cognition: Second Edition. Edited by Francis T. Durso.

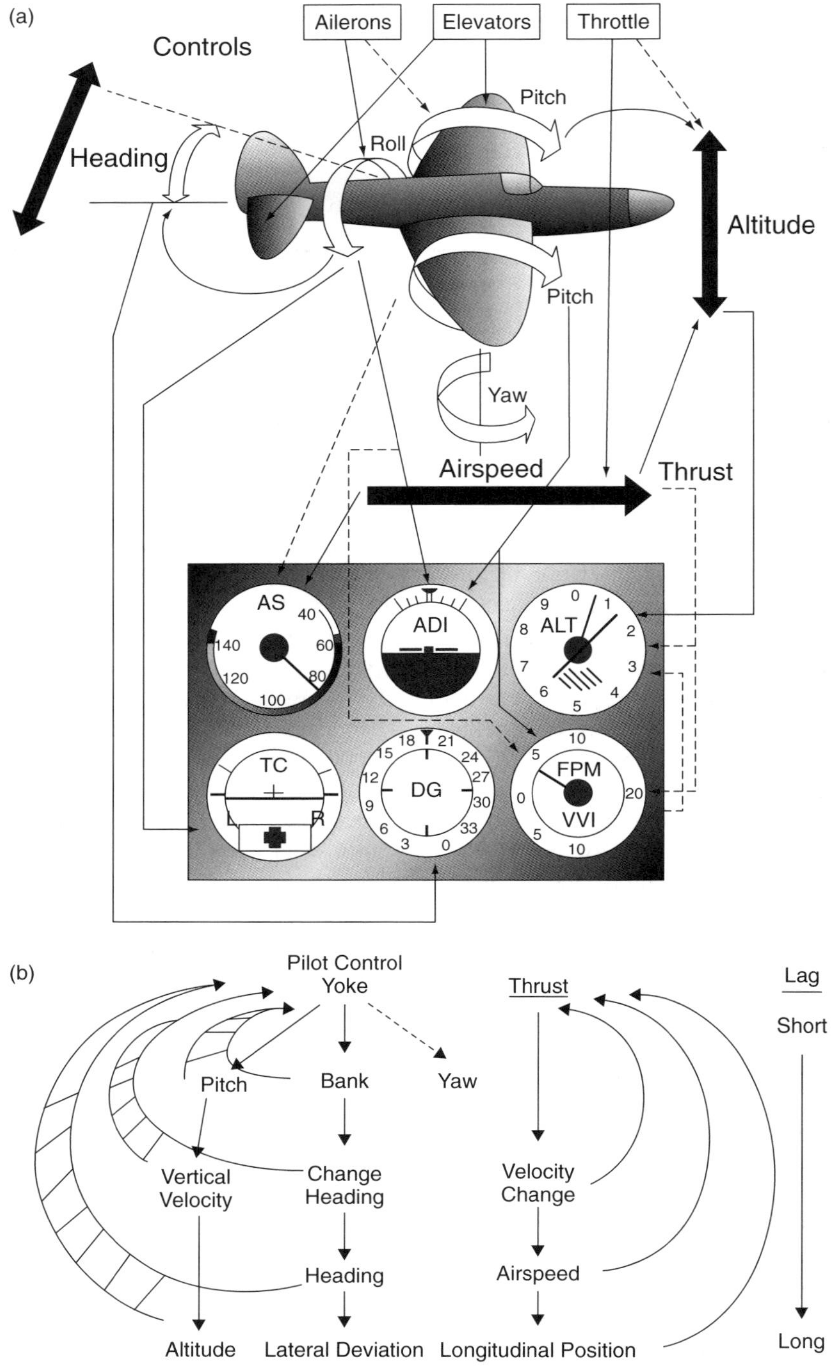

Figure 14.1 A representation of flight dynamics: (a) shows the relation between three flight control inputs (top boxes), the movement (heavy black arrows) and rotation (heavy white arrows) of the aircraft, and how these movements are displayed to the pilot in six critical flight instruments (bottom). Within the instrument panel, across the top row are displays of airspeed, attitude (pitch and bank) and altitude. Across the bottom row are displays of turning style, heading (compass) and vertical velocity. The thin dashed lines represent sources of "cross-coupling" between axes of flight. (b) Represents the flight axes in more schematic form. The pilot directly controls inner loop variables at the top, to affect control of middle and outer loop variables toward the bottom

pitch, and heading change being influenced primarily by roll. Changes in forward movement (acceleration) are primarily influenced by the thrust from the aircraft engines. As shown in the next row of Figure 14.1b, the changes along the vertical, heading, and forward motion (longitudinal) dimensions, produce new *positions* in altitude, heading, and airspeed. Finally, as shown in the bottom row, heading and airspeed produce lateral deviations (from a desired flight path), and longitudinal position along the flight path, respectively. This causal sequence of aircraft dynamic behavior is represented by the three embedded control loops in Figure 14.1b. These may be referred to as inner loop, middle loop and outer loop control.

As shown in Figure 14.1a, in most aircraft the pilot has, or can assume, direct control over pitch, bank, and thrust. Using these parameters the pilot must perform two fundamental tasks which we shall discuss in more detail below: maintaining stable flight control and lift or *aviating* (avoid stalling the aircraft such that it falls out of the air), and *navigating* to reach certain desired points in three-dimensional space and avoid other hazardous regions (bad weather, terrain, other aircraft). Because the aviate task is accomplished by maintaining an adequate velocity of airflow relative to the wings' orientation, it depends critically upon control of attitude (pitch and bank) and airspeed. The navigate task is based upon control of the variables, altitude (above ground or above sea level), lateral deviation, and longitudinal position, at the bottom level of Figure 14.1b, since these are the variables that define positions in three-dimensional airspace.

Three characteristics of the aviate and navigate tasks impose very complex cognitive demands on the pilot: first, as noted, control of the attitude parameters of pitch and roll must serve two, not always compatible tasks: preventing stall (aviate), and using these to influence rate of change, which will in turn influence position, in order to satisfy navigational goals. Second, control of the outer loop navigational variables is *sluggish*. This is shown by the causal sequence of arrows in Figure 14.1b. The pilot must control inner loop parameters to influence middle loop parameters, and use these in turn to influence outer loop parameters. As a result, the latter variables of lateral and vertical position change slowly; they have a greater *lag*, as shown to the right of the figure. This lag will be amplified on larger aircraft. The control of sluggish systems is a cognitive challenge, because it requires a great degree of *mental prediction and extrapolation* (Wickens 1986; Wickens & Hollands 2000). Third, as reflected in the dashed arrows in Figure 14.1a, the causal effects of control variables is not as simple as the representation in Figure 14.1b suggests. This is because the three axes of flight show considerable *crosstalk*, such that, for example, changes in bank affect pitch (the aircraft will pitch down if its wings are not level), and changes in pitch affect airspeed (pitch down increases airspeed), while changes in speed can affect altitude (slowing the aircraft will cause it to lose altitude).

A representation of the pilot as an information-processing system is shown in Figure 14.2, which integrates the collective findings of years of studies from basic and applied cognitive psychology (see Wickens & Hollands 2000; Wickens & Carswell 2007). Within the figure, the pilot is represented monitoring the airspace world, both inside and outside the cockpit, by selectively deploying his/her senses, in order to notice and process relevant events. This is the role of *selective attention*. What is passed on from this selective process is then *perceived*, whether these events are discrete, like the appearance of a cockpit alert, or continuous, like the flow of the ground beneath a landing airplane. This perceptual interpretation of the world is said to be guided by both *bottom-up* processes, analyzing the flow of information from the senses, and *top-down processes*, characterizing the heavy

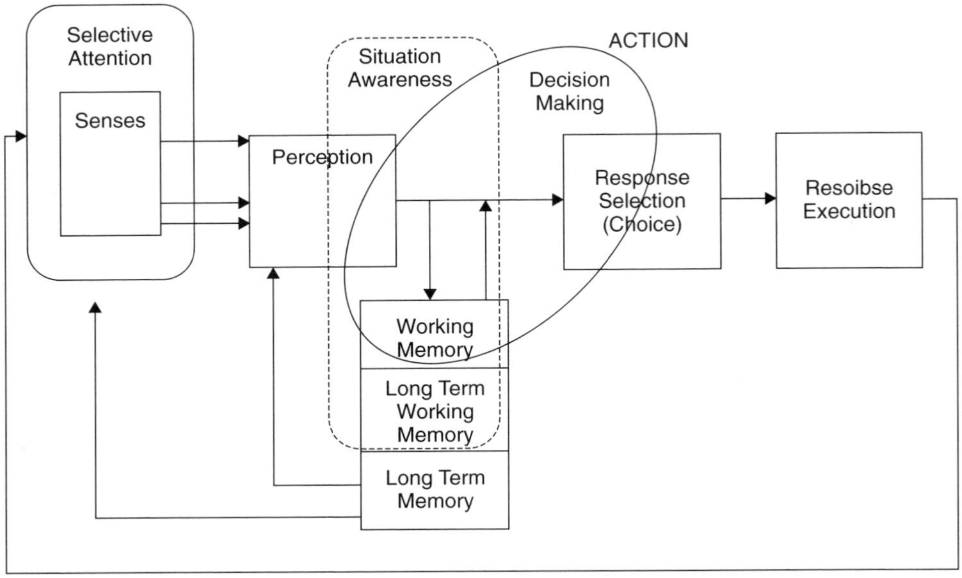

Figure 14.2 Representation of the pilot as an information-processing system

role of expectancy stored in long-term memory. These expectancies lead us to perceive what we expect to perceive, even if the sensory message is unclear, or, in fact, is different from what is expected.

Sometimes the pilot's perception may immediately trigger a selected and then executed action, as when a perceived deviation from the desired altitude leads to a corrective movement of the yoke control. Such an action often has consequences to the environment, and so leads to feedback to the senses (Jagacinski & Flach 2003). But often, the contents of perception lead to an evolving updating of *situation awareness* of the dynamic situation both within and outside the cockpit, as represented in the dashed box, and discussed fully in Chapter 7 above (see also Endsley 1995; Wickens 2002). Two properties of situation awareness are particularly critical. First, good situation awareness really involves the blending of the cognitive processes of perception and *working memory*. Working memory is that rehearsable but very vulnerable temporary store of information the pilot might use to retain, for example, an air traffic control instruction until it is executed. Those very limited properties of working memory are well documented in extensive research (Baddeley 1986). Situation awareness also includes what is called "long-term working memory" (Kintch & Ericsson 1995), information that, while not actively rehearsed, can be rapidly retrieved if necessary. Second, situation awareness, understanding the temporary state of affairs and its future implications, provides the basis of effective *aeronautical decision-making*: the appropriate choice of action, such as whether to continue a flight, or divert in the face of deteriorating weather. The process of decision-making, shown in the oval in Figure 14.2, will not be discussed in this chapter, and the interested reader should consult O'Hare (2003). Finally, we note that many of these processes are *resource-limited* (Norman & Bobrow 1975), which means that carrying out concurrent operation is sometimes difficult (e.g., studying a map while talking), and sometimes nearly impossible (e.g., listening to the copilot while speaking to air traffic control).

The pilot must, at a minimum, bring these processes to bear on the tasks of aviating and navigating. But these core tasks often spawn others. Because the airspace must usually be shared with other users, it is necessary to *communicate* with other aircraft or with air traffic control, to avoid collision. Because the aircraft itself depends on the functioning of many other mechanical, hydraulic, digital, and electrical *systems*, it is often necessary for the pilot to understand what those systems are doing (systems management). In addition, any aircraft has a *mission requirement* (e.g., transport passengers or cargo, engage in rescue, surveillance or combat). Finally, carrying out the aviation, navigation, communications, and systems subtasks generally requires judgment and knowledge of very specific *procedures and actions*. The pilot must accomplish tasks within these various categories, as well as *prioritize* among them (Schutte & Trujillo 1996), a prioritization scheme that generally dictates a hierarchy of aviate, navigate, communicate, systems management (sometimes known as ANCS), but often may need to temporarily deviate from it. We discuss each of these major task categories in the following sections, before discussing cognitive issues brought about by their automation.

AVIATE: MAINTAINING STABILITY

As shown in Figure 14.1a, the requirement to maintain adequate airflow over the wings, to avoid stalling and to direct the aircraft in a way that satisfies the outer loop navigational goals, is a complex process. A pilot may rely on one of two generic sources of visual information to accomplish this. When flying in good weather, *visual contact* information is provided by the view of the earth outside the aircraft, using the flow of information across the visual field (Gibson 1979; Warren & Wertheim 1990) to update the pilot's attitude awareness. For example, the angle and vertical location on the windscreen of the horizon line provide an accurate representation of bank and pitch, respectively. When flying toward or along a textured surface as in an approach to landing, the pilot may use the texture gradient to judge altitude changes, and may use texture flow to judge ground speed, and the orientation of the flight path related to the ground plane (Haber 2003; Palmisano & Gillam 2005).

While such holistic or ecological visual cues are intuitive and can be rapidly perceived, many of them are imprecise, subject to visual illusion (Previc & Ercoline 2004), and, of course, may be unavailable at night or in poor weather. Furthermore, since they are all based on ground features, none of them offers reliable information regarding velocity through the air (airspeed vector) which, as pointed out above, is a critical variable for preventing stall. As a consequence of these shortcomings, all conventional aircraft have been equipped with a minimum standard set of (generally six) instruments, shown at the bottom of Figure 14.1a.

Visual Scanning

Examination of cockpit visual scanning (Fitts *et al.* 1950; Carbonnell *et al.* 1968; Harris & Christhilf 1980; Bellenkes *et al.* 1997) has revealed important differences between the six flight instruments, in terms of the frequency and dwell duration with which they are scanned (selective attention), and how these differences in turn are affected by pilot skill levels. These skill-related differences implicate changes in the pilot's mental model of the flight dynamics. For example, a repeated finding from cockpit scanning research is that the attitude directional indicator, or "artificial horizon," shown in the upper center of the instrument panel, is the most important instrument. It is visited most frequently, and the gaze dwells there longest when it is visited (Harris & Christhilf 1980; Bellenkes *et al.* 1997). Two reasons can be offered for its importance. First, it is the only instrument which offers two channels of information integrated into one – the horizon line both pitches and banks, hence conveying the two most critical aspect of attitude; second, as noted in Figure 14.1b, pitch and bank represent the most rapidly changing inner loop information source (highest bandwidth) which simultaneously serves two task goals: maintaining stability (aviate), and influencing (and thereby *predicting*) the middle and outer loop parameters to affect navigational goals (bank → heading → lateral position; pitch → altitude = vertical position). Collectively, these features establish the ADI as both the most important and the most informative instrument, hence, explaining its scanning parameters.

Visual scanning analysis has revealed important differences between experts and novices and good and poor performing pilots (Bellenkes *et al.* 1997; Wickens *et al.* 2006). For example, experts more than novices tend to look more at predictive instruments (and therefore better compensate for lags), as well as show a scan pattern more sensitive to cross-coupling, both facets reflecting a more accurate mental model. Many other aspects of expert/novice differences in aviation are discussed in Seamster *et al.* (1997), and more general discussion of expert/novice differences in cognition can be found in Chapter 4.

Solutions to Visual Demand Problems

The scanning costs here are substantial enough that aircraft designers have pursued three avenues to alleviate these attention demands. First, capitalizing on electronic display technology, efforts are being made to improve the symbology by providing more integrated and cognitively compatible information. Figure 14.3 provides an example, in which predictive information is explicitly and intuitively displayed (rather than needing to be cognitively derived), via the three-dimensional "pathway in the sky" extending into the future (Theunissen 1997; Prinzel *et al.* 2004; Alexander *et al.* 2005). The naturalistic ego-referenced viewpoint, and three-dimensional pathway are compatible with the way we naturally move through the environment, and so such displays provide easy-to-fly, intuitive, and precise control. Also, vertically-oriented instruments representing airspeed and altitude have often replaced "round dial" instruments, hence presenting a more cognitively compatible representation of these linear "higher-lower" quantities (Roscoe 1968; Wickens & Hollands 2000).

Second, many aircraft can present this critical flight information in a "head-up" location, superimposed on the outside world, hence in theory reducing the visual attention demands away from the visual view outside the cockpit (Figure 14.4; Weintraub & Ensing 1992; Wickens *et al.* 2004).

Figure 14.3 Example of a three-dimensional "highway in the sky" flight instrument, superimposed on a three-dimensional synthetic display of terrain. The small white inverted "T" is a prediction symbol that shows where the plane will be in five seconds

While HUDs do improve the ability of the pilot to divide attention between the instruments and the outside world, relative to a head-down configuration (Fadden *et al.* 1998, 2001; Wickens *et al.* 2004), because of the reduction in scanning that results from the overlay, they do not guarantee parallel processing. Such parallel processing or divided attention between inside and outside may be hindered because of the clutter caused by overlapping imagery (Wickens & Long 1995; Fadden *et al.* 2001). In particular, the perception of unexpected and non-salient events that are viewed in or through a HUD image appears to suffer (Wickens & Long 1995; Fadden *et al.* 1998, 2001). However, when HUDs can be designed such that their instruments overlay or "conform" to features of the world beyond, like the horizon line or runway outline shown in Figure 14.4 upper left, then pilots may effectively "fuse" HUD information with the environmental information, creating a single visual "object." Research in visual attention has shown the success with which attention can be more readily divided across the features of one object (Kramer & Jacobson 1991; Jarmasz *et al.* 2005) than of several. Hence, not surprisingly, HUDs with conformal imagery appear to do a better job of supporting the division of attention between instruments and the far domain (Wickens & Long 1995; Fadden *et al.* 1998, 2001).

Third, designers have pursued the option of using *autopilots* to control the short lag, high bandwidth inner loop variables of pitch and bank, as well as the mid-loop variables of heading change (turn) and altitude change, an issue we discuss in the context of the *flight management system*. Such automation does not relieve the pilot from needing to be aware of these inner-loop variables, but does unburden the need for the continuous monitoring of these high BW instruments necessary for continuous active manual control.

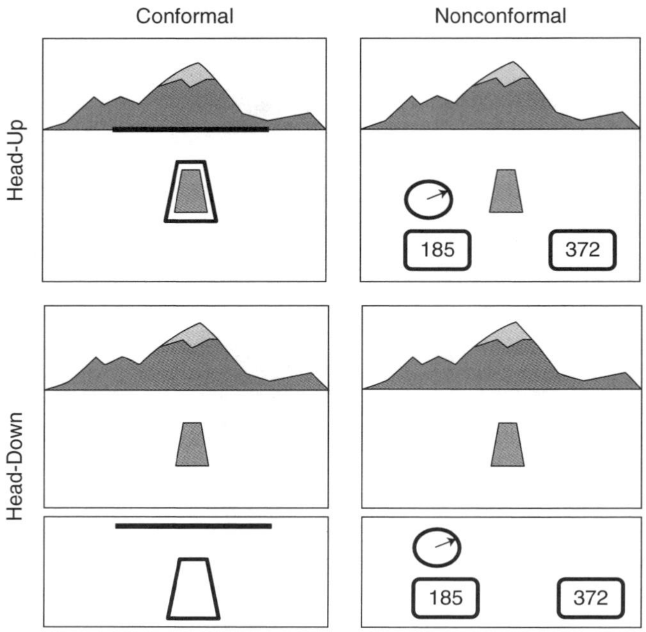

Figure 14.4 Example of a head-up display (top two panels). The instrument panel containing both conformal (the horizon line and runway outline) and nonconformal information (the round dial gauges) is superimposed on the view of the "far" domain. The bottom two panels show this lane info head down

NAVIGATION

The pilot's navigational task is critical. Several examples of *controlled flight into terrain* or CFIT (Wiener 1977) have exemplified the dangers when pilots flying a perfectly stable airplane, lose awareness of their three-dimensional position with respect to the terrain, and crash. Less severe in their consequences, but still of major concern, are instances in which pilots, initially flying in good visibility, find themselves flying into bad weather or clouds, for which they do not have qualifications (Wiegmann *et al.* 2002). In the previous section we explained how pilots could control their orientation and trajectory in three-dimensional space via the control of inner- and middle-loop variables. In this section we consider the cognitive factors involved in *understanding* or *maintaining spatial awareness* of their actual position and of the locational goals – paths, trajectories, and destinations – to pursue, and of hazards to avoid (weather, air traffic, and terrain) (Wickens 1999, 2003; Wickens *et al.* 2005). Such aviation navigational issues can be addressed in two contexts: in *visual contact flight*, the pilot has the terrain in sight, and navigates by virtue of a map, while searching the airspace for possible traffic and bad weather. In *instrument flight* (which must be assumed in poor visibility, but may also be characteristic of much flight in good visibility), the pilot navigates by reference to navigational instruments and air traffic control, assuming the latter has kept the path ahead clear of other traffic.

Visual Flight: The Role of Navigational Checking

In visual flight, the pilot's navigational task is supported by a map, often a two-dimensional paper display, or increasingly, the GPS electronic map. As a flight proceeds, the pilot continuously updates awareness of location, by confirming a correspondence between the image of the terrain perceived in the forward field of view, and an inferred position represented on the map (Aretz 1991; Williams *et al.* 1996; Schreiber *et al.* 1998; Hickox & Wickens 1999; Figure 14.5). If correspondence is confirmed, positional awareness is maintained. If it is not confirmed, the pilot may be considered lost.

As with image comparison in basic cognitive psychology (Shepard & Cooper 1982), so in map comparison the pilot must perform various types of cognitive image transformations to assure that the map (where I should be) corresponds with the view in the real world (where I am).

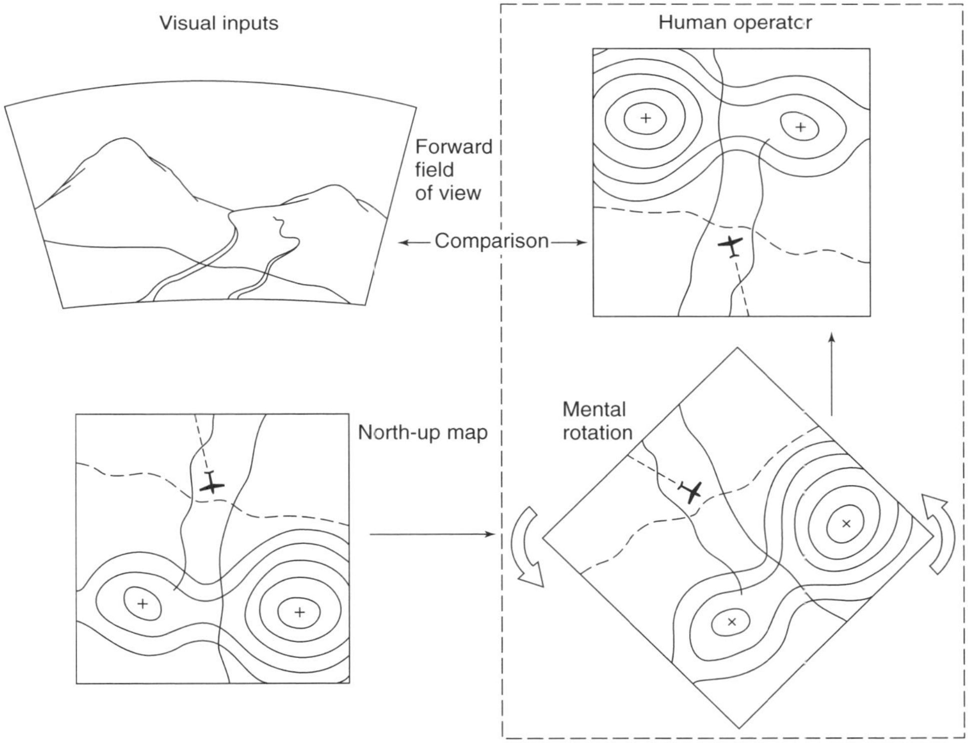

Figure 14.5 Representation of the navigational checking task and its transformations. A forward field of view (upper left) must be compared with a north-up map view (lower left) to assure their congruence or correspondence. To make this comparison pilots will mentally rotate this map to a track-up position (right column), and then envision the two-dimensional rotated image (upper right) as it would appear in three dimensions. The mental rotation component can be eliminated by directly displaying the map in track-up mode (upper right), and the envisioning component can be eliminated by displaying the map in three dimensions

In particular, as shown in Figure 14.5, these include: (1) *lateral mental rotation*, if the map is held in a north-up orientation in order to read its text, while the pilot is heading in a direction other than north; and (2) three-dimensional *envisioning*, in order to imagine the three-dimensional appearance of the terrain, represented on the two-dimensional map. The latter two operations are represented in Figure 14.5.

The findings of transformation costs in navigational checking have a direct bearing on the development of electronic maps to support visual navigation (Hickox & Wickens 1999); to minimize these costs, currently most electronic maps rotate laterally so that up is in the direction of travel, and the aviation community is beginning to design three-diemsnional maps that present the world in a three-dimensional perspective (Olmos *et al.* 1997; Prinzel *et al.* 2004). We discuss more features of electronic map design below.

Instrument Flight

Traditional navigational displays to assist the pilot when the terrain cannot be viewed have not served the pilot's cognitive processes very well for several reasons (Wickens 2003). A digital display of distance along a track to or from a fixed navigational beacon presents information, sometimes indicating the distance *to* a beacon being approached, and sometimes indicating the distance *from* a beacon that has been passed, thus leading to an *inconsistent* representation. The pilot's awareness of lateral deviation from the ground track must be perceived from an analog indicator that violates principles of motion compatibility (Roscoe 1968; Wickens & Hollands 2000), by depicting a moving flight path symbol and a stationary aircraft symbol, when in actuality it is the airplane that moves. Finally, the indication of altitude, obtained from the traditional analog round dial altimeter, is obtained from a third separated location in the cockpit, and registers altitude above sea level, rather than above the ground, the hazard that is the cause of controlled flight into terrain accidents. Thus, to obtain a true three-dimensional sense of position the pilot must integrate three sources of separately located, differently, and inconsistently represented information. Such a task imposes heavily on working memory and cognitive information integration capabilities, a violation of the *proximity compatibility principle* which states that items needing to be integrated for a task should be integrated or displayed close together in a display (Wickens & Carswell 1995; Wickens 2003).

Fortunately, good human factors assistance, coupled with advanced display technology, has been applied to improve navigational awareness in the design of dynamic electronic maps. For example, the cockpits of most advanced and transport category aircraft are equipped with integrated representations of position in the lateral and longitudinal axes, the so-called *horizontal situation display* (Fadden *et al.* 1991; Wickens 2003). Furthermore, such maps are designed to rotate to a track-up orientation in order to maintain congruence between the visual representation of position, and the manual control of that position (e.g., a leftward position on the map is pursued by a leftward movement of the control); and this map rotation is as beneficial in instrument flight as it is in visual flight (Wickens *et al.* 1996). Current technology allows the aircraft position to be established on the basis of satellite-based communications (the Global Positioning System) rather than ground-based navigational beacons.

We now discuss two particular challenges imposed by this advanced display technology: designing three-dimensional displays; and addressing clutter.

Three-Dimensional Displays

Three-dimensional displays, such as that shown in Figure 14.3, are beginning to be considered for navigation. Not only does the prediction and preview of such displays support smooth, stable, and easy flying (aviate), but the pathway or highway provides an accurate, spatially compatible (and flexible) command trajectory to support navigation (Prinzel *et al.* 2004; Alexander *et al.* 2005). Furthermore, the three-dimensional display can also "host" the display of hazards to be avoided in the forward path, particularly terrain, as shown in Figure 14.3. This supports visual, contact-like flight in low visibility. However the three-dimensional hazard display in the relatively egocentric frame shown in Figure 14.3 has the important limitation that it cannot render hazards located above, below, and to the side of the aircraft (e.g., traffic on a 90 degree collision course), nor the representation of hazards at greater distances. In the absence of such representation on the very compelling primary flight display shown in Figure 14.3, there is a danger that the pilot might "cognitively tunnel" attention to the forward path and lose global spatial awareness of other hazards not located there (Wickens & Prevett 1995; Wickens 2005).

Under these circumstances, the electronic map can be made to host these wider-ranging hazard representations, in directions beyond the forward path. But should this also be a three-dimensional display? Research suggests that it is very important that such displays do contain an analog representation of vertical information, which the two-dimensional map does not support (Hughes 2004; Alexander *et al.* 2005), but when the vertical information is presented on a three-dimensional perspective display of hazards, this invites problems of the *ambiguity* of precisely locating hazards in three-dimensional space on the two-dimensional surface of a three-dimensional display (McGreevy & Ellis 1986; Wickens & Prevett 1995; Wickens 2003). At present the perceptual and cognitive issues of presenting hazard and navigational information on a three-dimensional display involve tradeoffs of sufficient complexity that they cannot be addressed here (see Wickens 1999, 2000, 2003; Wickens *et al.* 2005 for a further discussion).

Clutter

A second cognitive challenge in developing navigational/hazard displays is that of clutter. Two forces create clutter in electronic maps. First, the large scope necessary for long-range navigational planning often forces a vast amount of material to be depicted in a restricted spatial region on the cockpit panel. Second there is a legitimate desire for integrating information about traffic, terrain, and weather all on a single panel, a design decision that makes good sense when it is realized that a pilot may need to mentally integrate such information when choosing a safe path of travel (Kroft & Wickens 2003). However from a cognitive perspective, clutter has two serious drawbacks. First, it slows visual search for target information, as the number of "things" that have to be examined increases (Remington *et al.* 2000; Yeh & Wickens 2001), replicating the classic serial self-terminating search model (Neisser 1963). On a cluttered cockpit map, this slowing of search may be as long as 4–5 seconds. Second, clutter hinders the reading of information once it is located, replicating the failures of focused attention from closely arranged items in space (Eriksen & Eriksen 1974; Broadbent 1982).

Some designers have chosen to address issues of clutter by developing computer-based *decluttering* tools, in which a switch can turn off classes of information deemed temporarily irrelevant (Mykityshyn *et al.* 1994; Kroft & Wickens 2003). However, such devices invite the danger of "out of sight out of mind" (Wickens *et al.* 2003). That is, the pilot may erase information that, at the time, may appear irrelevant (in order to aid focused attention on the relevant), only to forget the existence of that erased information at a time when it suddenly becomes directly relevant to a navigational decision, perhaps because it has changed while hidden. Rensink (2002) refers to this as blindness for a "completed" change. For example, a pilot might declutter weather information, and hence fail to realize the approach of hazardous weather. Thus more effective solutions to clutter may involve low lighting or "layering" information at different intensities, rather than erasing it entirely (Kroft & Wickens 2003).

COMMUNICATIONS

Cockpit communications can be categorized into three sorts. First, the pilot and air traffic controller are both involved in an intricate network of ground-to-air voice communications which is particularly, although not exclusively, focused on the navigational subtask. Second, personnel within the flight deck (i.e., pilot and copilot) must often communicate among themselves. Third, pilots may communicate with an on-board "mission" crew, such as flight attendants on a commercial flight (Chute & Wiener 1995). Flight deck communications, whether within the aircraft, or with the ground, is highly vulnerable to human error. Such breakdowns may occasionally result in tragedy, as when a communications error led the pilot of a 747 aircraft to mistakenly believe that he had been granted clearance for takeoff (Hawkins 1993). The takeoff proceeded while another 747 was still on the runway, and the resulting collision caused more than 500 deaths.

While the absolute frequency of incorrect air-to-ground communications is relatively small (estimated to be approximately 10 per cent; Morrow *et al.* 1993), this number is still large enough to warrant serious concern for its causes, many of which are based on cognitive factors. We focus our discussion here most directly on air-to-ground communications, rather than intra-cockpit communications, because the former have generally been better analyzed, studied, and proceduralized. Furthermore, the latter are more heavily influenced by characteristics of social and personality psychology, and hence beyond the scope of this chapter (Foushee 1984; Wiener *et al.* 1993).

Task analysis of the communications process reveals that a "unit" of communications generally includes (1) a *transmission* typically from controller to pilot relaying an instruction (e.g., "United 486, climb to flight level 210 and turn to heading 180; anticipate climb to 240"); (2) a subsequent *readback* or acknowledgment which contains the source, and repeats all the key features of the transmission ("Roger; United 486 flight level 210, heading 180 anticipate 240"); and (3) a *covert monitoring* of the readback by the message transmitter (in this example the air traffic controller), to ensure that the message sent was accurately read back by the recipient. Such an accurate readback is implicitly assumed by the controller to indicate that the pilot will comply with the instruction. One class of errors in the process are *procedural* errors in which, for example, a readback is incomplete or missing altogether, or in which a controller fails to deliver instructions in standard terminology. A second class of errors are *transmission* errors, in which a communication is heard incorrectly. In some cases this error may be detected (by the transmitter) in the readback; in other cases it may not be, particularly if the procedural error of a readback failure occurs. The vulnerabilities in the communications process can readily be linked to four well-known characteristics of human information-processing: procedural knowledge, cognitive workload, expectancies and working memory limitations, and we describe the interlocking influences of these factors as follows.

Under some circumstances, often resulting from lack of experience, standard communications procedures are violated, perhaps via an incomplete readback (Morrow *et al.* 1993) or an improper sequence as described above. Also controllers may sometimes deliver a single message that is considerably longer than that which is procedurally recommended (Morrow *et al.* 1993), because long messages impose on the pilots' limits of working memory.

The likelihood of both controller and pilot procedural errors may be amplified by the effects of high cognitive workload and time pressure. For example, higher cockpit workload may lead the pilot to truncate, and possibly eliminate, the appropriate readback, whereas high controller workload (coupled with the time cost required to initiate and complete each communications exchange) may lead the controller to deliver a long string of instructions in a single message, rather than dividing this message across two or more shorter communications. This choice is made for the sake of efficiency because the single message will shorten the total amount of time the controller must deal with each individual aircraft. For the pilot, and particularly, the controller, high workload can eliminate careful readback monitoring (Redding 1992).

The cognitive bias of expectancy-driven top-down processing, which causes us to hear what we expect to hear, can itself amplify the influence of the factors described above. Whenever the bottom-up signal quality of communications is made more difficult (e.g., by low acoustic quality, or by a rapidly spoken long message) the pilot's bias will be to hear the expected message. Thus, if an unexpected or unusual item is delivered in the communications, an error in understanding is invited. Furthermore, the controller expects the pilot to read back the transmission as it was delivered (as is typically the case, a typicality that is the very basis for the expectancy). Hence, in the covert monitoring component of the transmission sequence, the controller may *fail* to detect a pilot's incorrect readback; what Monan (1986) has described as the "hearback" problem (ATC: "reduce speed to 220." Pilot response: "Roger: speed 200").

Finally, the limited capacity of working memory is clearly evident in the communications transmission errors that are observed (Loftus *et al.* 1979; Morrow *et al.* 1993). The contents of any sequence of instructions must be maintained in working memory until it is fully read back, and beyond that, until it is written down, entered into a computer, or actually executed on the flight controls. The more chunks that a transmission contains, or the more rapidly it is delivered (hence, leading to less opportunity for rehearsal or deeper encoding of each chunk), the greater is the chance of forgetting. Such forgetting may often result from confusion, such as a pilot transposing digits (115 vs. 151), or even confusing the three critical message components – heading, airspeed, and flight level – all of which are generally expressed as three-digit numbers as in the example above.

Solutions to such communications problems can readily be found in the form of *data link* (Kerns 1999; Navarro & Sikorski 1999; Helleberg & Wickens 2003), a digitized communications system, beginning to be introduced in the next generation of aircraft, whereby instructions flow between ground and air over digital channels, rather than voice-based radio. Such a system has at least three cognitive advantages over the conventional radio channels. First, because communications data would be available (and therefore preservable) electronically in the cockpit, it can be visually displayed and maintained, hence offloading the limited capacity working memory system (Helleberg & Wickens 2003). Second, because of its availability in digital form, it may be displayed in a multimedia fashion, hence capitalizing on both human's facility with redundant information (Garner & Morton 1969) and certain principles of cognitive display compatibility (e.g., a spatial trajectory instruction can be represented spatially on an electronic navigation display, rather than, or in addition to, being presented in verbal form (Hahn and Hansman 1992). Third, visual display may be less interruptible of ongoing tasks, an issue we address below.

SYSTEMS MONITORING AND MANAGEMENT

The fourth major task domain within the cockpit is that associated with monitoring (and occasional control over) aircraft systems. As with many other process monitoring tasks (Moray 1986, 1997; Parasuraman 1987), the task of aircraft systems monitoring takes on tremendous importance on the rare occasions when systems do malfunction. In such cases the speed of detection becomes a critical factor, as does the speed and accuracy with which diagnosis and selection of remedial action are accomplished (Rasmussen & Rouse 1981).

In this domain, designers of automation have provided a valuable service by providing pictorially based, easy to interpret graphics of many aspects of systems monitoring tasks, the so-called Electronics Instrument Caution and Advisory System or EICAS. Furthermore, to attenuate the clutter associated with the massive number of systems to monitor on the modern transport aircraft, as well as to allow integrated depiction of textual and status information, designers have gone to menu-based *multifunction displays*, in which multiple pages of information can be examined (albeit sequentially) through a single viewport. While this centralized computer-based graphics image capability has many advantages, it also raises some important cognitive issues regarding the structure of the computer database (Seidler & Wickens 1992; Wickens & Seidler 1997), and the extent to which this organizational structure matches the pilot's cognitive model of systems relatedness (Roske-Hofstrand & Paap 1986). Where the design mismatches the pilot's mental model, added time costs in navigating through the data base are invited.

PILOT'S PROCEDURES AND ACTIONS

Much of task selection in aviation is *procedural*. Tasks are carried out at certain pre-designated times or sequences during a flight. For example, the landing gear must be lowered prior to landing and raised after takeoff; particular communications must be initiated when the aircraft transitions between ATC sectors in the airspace. With repeated practice, the pilot builds up what are called "schemata" of the appropriate procedures and actions to be performed at the appropriate times. The airlines put great emphasis on training pilots in what they call "standard operating procedures" (Degani & Wiener 1993; Hawkins 1993; Orlady & Orlady 2000), capturing many of these sequences of tasks or actions. Correspondingly, there is great emphasis on "proceduralizing" most aspects of air traffic control, through standard communications protocols, standardized aircraft departure and arrival routes and so forth (Wickens *et al.* 1997). Most of these procedures depend upon a vast array of declarative knowledge, nearly all of which is backed up by published federal air regulations (FARs), operating manuals, and checklists (Orlady & Orlady 2000). The various procedures, such as configuring the airplane for takeoff, dealing with a malfunctioning instrument, filing a flight plan, or checking the status of the aircraft prior to engine start, have two general attributes: *how* they should be carried out, and *when* they should be done.

While extensive training, practice, and rehearsal may be necessary to assure that procedures are carried out fluently, such training is never entirely sufficient to assure safe flight because the appropriate sequence of procedures will not have been learned well by the student pilot and may occasionally be forgotten or missed even by the skilled pilot. Hence procedures-following is always supported by the checklist.

Checklists

Because of human frailties in both declarative knowledge (*how*), and prospective memory (*when*; Harris & Wilkins 1982), an absolutely critical memory support for the pilot is the *checklist* (Degani & Wiener 1993). The pilot will have several checklists for both routine and emergency procedures, each listing the nature of the procedure (characterizing the "how"), in the sequential order in which it should be accomplished (characterizing the "when"), thus providing what Norman (1988) has characterized as "knowledge in the world."

Yet even such a valuable support as the checklist is vulnerable to certain cognitive frailties. Two in particular are related to *expectancy-driven processing* and *selective attention*. As an example of the former, it is possible that a checklist might ask the pilot to "check that switch X is on." If the normal state of switch X is in the "on" position, the pilot may "see" the switch in that state, based on expectancy alone, rather than making a careful evaluation based upon bottom-up visual inspection of the switch itself (Mosier *et al.* 1992). In this example the tendency for the top-down processing is reinforced by the greater ease with which people judge "true positive" responses in a word picture comparison task (Clark & Chase 1972), which characterizes the information-processing demands of the checklist item.

Selective attention also plays a role in checklist following, as the pilot's eyes must move down the list from item to item. Here the orderly sequence may be disrupted. While disruptions may sometimes only be minor, as when the eyes must move away to assure that the item is in the appropriate "checked" state, there is always a danger that such a diversion can disrupt the orderly sequential flow of attention down the list. When diversions of attention are large or long, they can be more likely to lead to a disruption of the flow, as occurred tragically in 1987 when pilots of a commercial airliner taxiing prior to takeoff at Detroit Metropolitan Airport had their attention disrupted from the checklist by a required take-off runway change directed from air traffic control (Wiener 1988). When the pilots' attention returned to the list, it apparently did so one item *beyond* the last item prior to the interruption. The missing item turned out to be the critical one of setting the flaps and slats for takeoff. This omission compromised the amount of lift generated by the plane, and left it with too little altitude to clear obstructions after it left the runway. Over 100 lives were lost in the resulting crash.

High levels of time pressure may amplify expectancy-driven top-down processing as above, and may also influence selective attention by causing a pilot to rush through and finish a checklist prematurely and turn attention toward another activity, hence leaving the final items uncompleted (Degani & Wiener 1993). Such instances may occur, for example, if ATC suddenly requests an expedited procedure (preparation for takeoff, or final approach to landing), in order to maximize traffic flow.

As with so many of the vulnerabilities that we have described above, good human factors, along with automation, are suggested as a remedy for some of the problems with checklists (Palmer & Degani 1991; Degani & Wiener 1993). For example, to avoid time-pressure problems, "killer items" (those with catastrophic consequences if undone) should never be placed toward the end of a checklist. Electronic checklists can require that each item be actively "checked" by the pilot providing a machine readable input (e. g., a touch screen overlaying the list), and hence offering a monitoring device that could prevent the error of omission described above (Palmer & Degani 1991; Bresley 1995). Checked items turn green, while unchecked items remain red, offering a salient, attention-capturing sign that a checklist has not been completed. While such an approach would not address the problems associated with expectancy-driven processing (Mosier *et al.* 1992), these could be addressed, in some circumstances, by sensors in the aircraft that could sense and self-report their state (e.g., the switch in the previous example could report that it is in the "off" position, and alert or suggest that the pilot should turn it "on" Bresley (1995).

Cockpit Task Management

While it might be ideal if all of a pilot's tasks could be proceduralized and therefore supported by checklists, in practice, this is not possible. There are simply too many unexpected events that can occur in the airspace, and in some emergencies checklists cannot predict (and therefore dictate) all the appropriate actions to be taken. Furthermore, numerous situations exist when two (or more) tasks compete for the pilot's attention, and he or she must then choose which to perform and which to defer, if they cannot be accomplished in parallel. The issues of *cockpit task management* (CTM; Funk 1991; Chou *et al.* 1996; Dismukes 2001), or *strategic workload management* (Hart & Wickens 1990), or interruption management (McFarlane & Latorella 2002) describe the characteristics of such strategies that are employed by the pilot choosing which tasks to perform, which to delay or "shed" and which tasks may interrupt or "preempt" other ongoing tasks (see also Adams *et al.* 1995). We identify below, three general characteristics that appear to underlie breakdowns in task management.

Preemption and the ANCS Hierarchy

In aviation, the ANCS hierarchy can often be used to define an "optimal" prioritization or importance ordering of tasks, and there is little doubt that air safety is compromised by poor cockpit task management when more important tasks are allowed to be preempted or superseded by those of lesser importance. Such a conclusion comes from several sources. For example, the crash of Eastern Airlines Flight 401 into the Florida Everglades in 1972 resulted because pilots became fixated on a landing gear problem (systems management), failing to heed a loss of altitude (aviate), which resulted from an accidentally disengaged autopilot (Wiener 1977). Indeed, Chou *et al.* (1996) have documented that 23 per cent of 324 NTSB reported accidents during the period 1960–89 had poor CTM as one underlying cause. Raby and Wickens (1994) found that, although pilots were generally fairly optimal in task management, they tended not to exhibit highly sophisticated rescheduling routines when workload was unexpectedly increased. Furthermore, the better performing pilots in a high workload simulation tended to switch attention between tasks more frequently than those pilots who performed less well. Raby and Wickens (1994) and Laudeman and Palmer (1995) both found that better performing pilots were more optimal in *when* they performed the higher priority activities, tending to accomplish these earlier.

Other investigators have studied interruptions, in which the performance of certain ongoing tasks is terminated by the arrival of a new task (Damos 1997; Dornheim 2000; Dismukes 2001; McFarlane & Latorella 2002). Analyzing a series of videotaped scenarios, in which professional pilot crews handled unexpected circumstances, Damos (1997) found that in ATC communications (the third task on the ANCS hierarchy) would often interrupt or preempt a pilot's involvement with navigational planning tasks, which may be considered a second level task, a characteristic that can be described as non-optimal task management. In contrast, however, pilots were fairly effective at protecting the hand flying of the aircraft (Aviate: first priority) from being interrupted. Latorella (1996) and Dismukes (2001) have also noted the preemptive nature of ATC communications into a pilot's ongoing task, an issue that will be addressed below. A general finding too is the extreme vulnerability of visual monitoring (necessary for maintaining stage 1 situation awareness) to interruptions.

Auditory Preemption

Noteworthy in the discussion above is the finding that the disruptive communications task (no. 3 on the hierarchy) often interferes with no. 2 navigation, which is primarily a visual task. This pattern seems to reflect a more general tendency for auditory preemption. At least two reasons for such preemption can be offered. First, auditory onsets are inherently (and biologically) attention-grabbing, perhaps because they are omni-directional (Spence and Driver 1997; Banbury *et al.* 2001). This would explain their near-universal preference for use in high-priority alarms (Stanton 1994). Second, because of working memory limitations, people want to keep attention directed to an auditory task until it is completed, so that material is not forgotten from working memory (Latorella 1996). Hence they will deal with an auditory communications immediately when it arrives.

If auditory events tend to preempt visual ones, then visual events by contrast do so to a much lesser extent. This has a positive facet of flexibility in that, when material is presented visually the pilot can divert attention from the task supported by that visual material, and return to it later knowing that it will still be perceptually available (unlike the decaying representation of auditory material in working memory). Thus the visually presented data link, described in section 5, enables that flexibility to operate with communications tasks (Helleberg & Wickens 2003). But the negative facet is that our visual modality is relatively insensitive to noticing changes (Carpenter 2001; Rensink 2002), in elements like cockpit-displayed traffic and weather (Muthard & Wickens in press; Iani & Wickens in press).

Cognitive Tunneling

A final problem in task management results when a pilot "tunnels," or focuses attention on a particular activity for a longer period than is optimal, and therefore fails to switch attention visually (via scanning) or cognitively (via thought) to tasks deserving of attention (Wickens 2005). Dismukes (2001) has noted the extent to which the task of failure management tends to induce such tunneling. Wickens (2005) has reviewed a number of studies that suggest that highly realistic immersed three-dimensional displays, as discussed above (see Figure 14.3), also induce attentional tunneling, and a resulting neglect of scanning to the outside world beyond the cockpit displays, thereby rendering the pilot vulnerable to events and hazards that may not be registered on those displays.

COGNITIVE FACTORS IN AEROSPACE AUTOMATION

The previous sections have identified several ways in which automation may be considered to remedy the cognitive challenges of aviation. Indeed automation, both in the cockpit and in the ATC control room, has both increased the efficiency of air transport, and saved lives. For example, each successive generation of more highly automated aircraft has a higher safety record (Sparaco 1998), and automated alerts and warning systems (discussed below) have prevented potential collisions with other aircraft and with the terrain.

Automation is sometimes represented in the framework of the stages of pilot information-processing activities that it replaces (or augments – see Figure 14.2; Parsuraman *et al.* 2000). For example automation may (1) direct selective attention via techniques such as cuing or filtering; (2) draw inferences or assessment about the current and future state of the airspace (e.g., conflict warnings), or aircraft (e.g., smart failure diagnostics, Hicks and DiBrito 1998); (3) select or recommend; or (4) execute actions. Across all these stages (see Wickens 2002), automation has a number of well-documented strengths, but weaknesses as well.

Problems with Automation

Much has been written about human factors problems with automation (e.g., Parasuraman & Riley 1997; Parasuraman and Lorenz, Chapter 16, this volume), even when the automa-

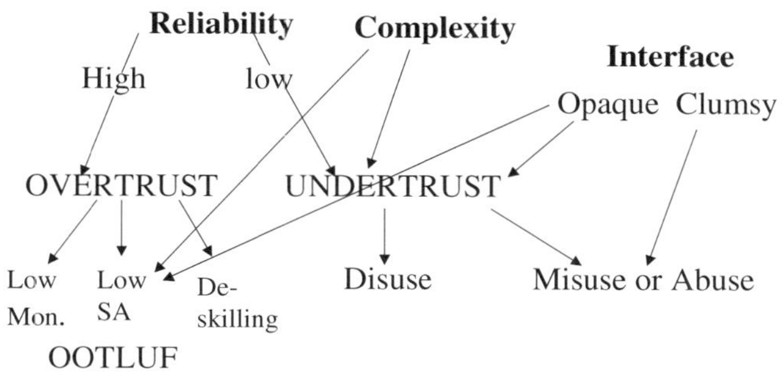

Figure 14.6 Some human cognitive factors underlying automation

tion functions better than the human capabilities that it replaced (or is relieving a great amount of mental workload). As applied particularly to automation of aerospace systems, we represent these problems in Figure 14.6. The figure identifies three important attributes of automation in **bold face** across the top (reliability, complexity and interface properties), two critical cognitive states in CAPITALS, related to human trust in and dependence upon the automation, and a set of behavioral consequences that flow from these properties, mediated by human the human's cognitive state. Starting at the left, if automation is extremely reliable, it breeds the danger of over-trust, sometimes described as "complacency" (Parasuraman *et al.* 1993). Three behavioral consequences of this are that the operator will:

1. no longer monitor (low mon) the processes controlled or supervised by the automation (trusting it to "do right");
2. lose situation awareness of the current state of what automation is doing, a joint consequence of not watching it, and of the fact that people are less proficient at remembering the consequence of an action when they have witnessed another agent doing it, than when they have done it themselves: this is the "generation effect" (Slamecka & Graf 1978; Hopkin 1995);
3. lose skill at performing the task manually if they need to do this once the automation has failed, since this task had been repeatedly done by automation in the past.

These three cognitive/behavioral changes present no problem *unless* automation fails, and the human must suddenly step "into the loop." Under such circumstances the human will be slower to detect the failure, slower to understand the current state and future implications and therefore choose the appropriate actions, and less skilled in executing those actions. These three symptoms of over-trust are often joined to define what is called the "out of the loop unfamiliarity" (OOTLUF) syndrome.

In contrast, automation whose reliability is low – for example, the alert system that gives too many false warnings – is one of three causes that breed *under-trust* in automation. This influence of low reliability is joined by the influence of a high degree of "opacity" of the automation – the inability of the user to see or learn what is going on within the "black box" (Sarter and Woods 1997); and of a high degree of complexity of the automation (its algorithms and functionality; Degani 2003), further hampering the user's ability to understand what the automation is doing. In isolation, or in combination, all three of these influences breeding under-trust may cause the user to stop using the automation (disuse, as when we no longer heed an alarm), or possibly even "misuse" or "abuse" the automation (Parasuraman & Riley 1997). In this representation it is worth noting the common influence of unreliability and opacity/complexity. While a complex/opaque automation system such as the flight management system we discuss below, may actually carry out its function reliably, it may do things that are surprising to the user, leading the user to assume that automation is actually unreliable, with the consequent distrust (Sarter & Woods 1997, 2000).

In discussing problems with automation, as depicted in Figure 14.6, it is important to include the clumsy nature that is often inherent in the interface with which the pilot must program (or reprogram) what the automation is doing. For example, while it is generally found that the flight management system (see below) reduces workload, in order to change a runway assignment while on an approach, 28 programming steps are required. Such clumsy features of the automation interface invite misuse.

While the number of automated systems on the flight deck and in Air Traffic Control is large, including such systems as datalink, and the automated checklist as we have discussed above, we single out two in particular for more extensive discussion: alerting systems, because of their ubiquity in the air and on the ground (ATC); and the flight management system (FMS), because it has often served as the prototype for both what is right and what is wrong with automation.

Imperfect Alerting Automation

Within the taxonomy of automation stages described above (information selection, integration, action choice, and execution), an important generic class are those automated systems that warn or alert operators to dangerous conditions (Pritchett 2001). In essence these functions may combine stage 1 and stage 2 automation. Simple alerts that replace human monitors (like the engine temperature alert) are stage 1 attention guiders that call the pilots' attention to the critical signal. More complex inference-makers, like those diagnostic systems that infer a particular root cause failure from a collection of symptoms (Hicks & DiBrito 1998), or an impending mid-air collision by integrating trajectory information are stage 2 automation examples. By diagnosing "what is" or predicting "what will be," they implicitly direct visual attention to the relevant displays of system state, as well as direct cognitive attention to the relevant hypotheses.

Both stages of automation have in common two key aspects. (1) Both can be represented within the framework of signal detection theory, with its two classes of errors – misses (a dangerous condition exists that automation fails to detect) and false alerts (an alert is raised when all is well). (2) Such automation is often asked to perform tasks where automation will be imperfect and hence these automation errors actually occur with some frequency (reliability is less than 1.0), often because of the probabilistic nature of the world that automation is trying to overcome (consider automated weather forecasts). This is particularly true when automation is designed to support the prediction of future states across long prediction intervals: the crystal ball becomes hazier the further into the future we look.

Referring to Figure 14.6, we find that the effectiveness of such diagnostic alerting systems is based on trust or dependence. Trust is a psychological state. Dependence describes the actual behavioral consequences of trust, the degree of use or disuse of the automation (Parasuraman & Riley 1997). With regard to the diagnostic automation typical of alerting systems, Meyer (2004) has distinguished between the dependence states of *reliance* and *compliance*. Reliance is fostered by miss-free automation; that is, an automation system that never (or rarely) fails to detect a critical condition when one occurs. The reliant pilot or controller will have plenty of spare capacity to carry out other concurrent tasks besides monitoring the process that automation is also monitoring. But, the (now very rare) automation miss that *does* occur might well be missed by the complacent, over-dependent, over-reliant human operator. In contrast, the skeptical operator, with lower reliance, will then allocate more attention to monitoring the "raw data" which the automation is also monitoring, but as a consequence will have fewer resources available for concurrent tasks.

Compliance describes the operator's tendency to respond in a timely fashion whenever the system diagnoses a dangerous or important situation (e.g., the alarm or alert sounds). High compliance is bred by a false alarm-free system. Conversely, a false alarm-prone system will degrade compliance, leading to the so-called "cry wolf" syndrome where all alerts may be dealt with on a non-urgent basis, or ignored altogether, including those that should be attended because they are true (Breznitz 1983; Sorkin 1989).

Naturally, the lower reliability confronting more challenging automation diagnosis (e.g., a prediction of traffic collision with longer look-ahead time; Thomas & Rantanen 2006), may decrease both reliance and compliance, as miss and false alert rates rise respectively. However, the designer of the alert system has a choice of where to place the "threshold" of the alert, corresponding to setting the response criterion (β) of signal detection theory, in order to achieve the optimal balance between the two types of errors. Dixon and Wickens (2006), studying system failure alerts in unmanned air vehicles, found that a designer-adjusted threshold with higher misses indeed reduced reliance; concurrent tasks suffered but operators were quite proficient in detecting the events when the automation missed the system failure. However a false alert-prone system not only degraded compliance (delayed pilot response to all alerts), but also appeared to disrupt the symptoms of reliance as well, suggesting that false alerts may be overall more damaging to human performance with automation. This finding was reflected in the reports of pilots concerning alerting systems in real aircraft (Bliss 2003), where the false alert problem was viewed as more severe than the miss problem.

Whether the problem is misses or false alerts, if alerting systems are asked to carry out diagnostic tasks in which they may be forced to be imperfect (e.g., because of long look-ahead times), at least two solutions may be imposed. First, it is logical to provide the operator with some view of the "raw data" upon which the automation is making its diagnosis or prediction, so that the veracity of the alert can be checked if needed. Second, it is important to provide the operator with training and understanding of the inevitability that alerting system errors will occur in such circumstances; so that appropriate oversight of the raw data is maintained, and false alerts are not viewed as an indictment of the system leading to disuse.

The Flight Management System

The flight management system (FMS) is an example of a system that implements stages 3 and 4 automation, and is a fixture on all commercial air carriers. It decides how (where and how fast) to fly the plane to implement pilot goals, and then executes those responses.

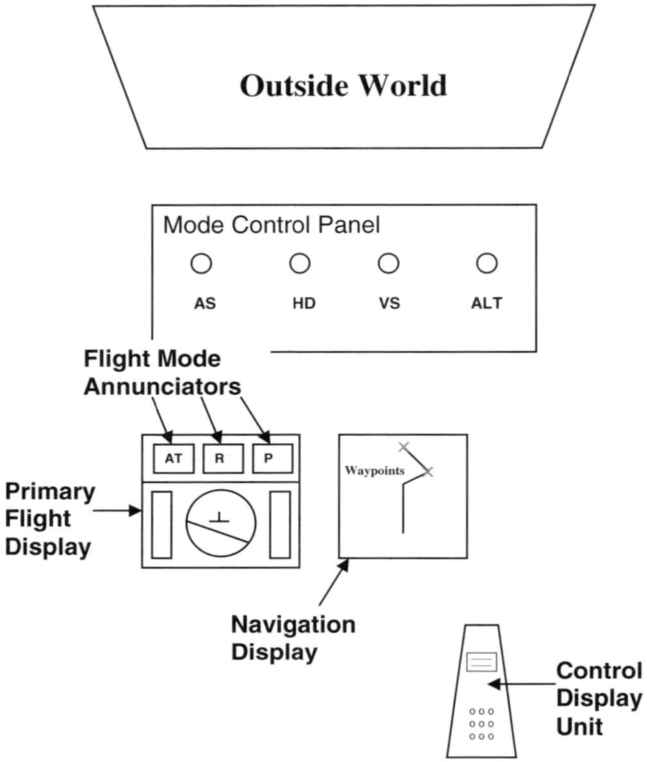

Figure 14.7 Components of the Flight Management System, as described in the text. The flight mode annunciator abbreviations are AT (auto throttle), R (roll: lateral control), and P (pitch: vertical control)

More specifically, the FMS is a collection of autopilots, combined with an intelligent logic, that can accomplish the goal of navigating the aircraft to varying points and along varying trajectories in three-dimensional space (Sarter & Woods 1994, 1995, 1997; Sherry & Polson 1999). The FMS actually consists of a number of components, distributed throughout the flight deck, as shown in Figure 14.7. The pilot can program the FMS through a flight management computer, housed in a control display unit (CDU) which is typically positioned between the seats. This programming may be accomplished before a route is flown (i.e., on the ground). Then the FMS will fly the aircraft along various three-dimensional trajectories by setting various *modes* of operation: for example, climbing at a particular rate (feet per minute) or angle with the ground, reaching particular waypoints over the ground at particular times, and adjusting particular speeds. Because the three-dimensional trajectories must be accomplished and coordinated in time, this is sometimes referred to as "four-dimensional navigation," with time as the fourth dimension.

The pilot may intervene with this automation at any time, either by reprogramming through the CDU, or by setting in particular target values to a device called a *mode control panel* mounted at the top of the instrument panel just below the windshield. The pilot may also view what the automation is doing, or is about to do, as this is represented spatially on a two-dimensional electronic map, the navigation display, and symbolically, through a set of three small windows, known as the *flight mode annunciators*, positioned at the top of the primary flight displays.

While the FMS can be programmed to fly extremely efficient routes, both selecting (stage 3 automation) and executing (stage 4), control of heading, location, and altitude, past experience has identified a number of human factors problems for the pilot (e.g., Sarter & Woods 1994, 1997, 2000), problems that have led to accidents (Dornheim 1995) as well as incidents where highly qualified pilots will ask what the FMS is doing and why, in response to its sometimes surprising actions (Funk & Lyall 1999).

Many of these problems can be well represented within the context of Figure 14.7. Thus while the reliability of the FMS is high, it is nevertheless sometimes subject to under-trust because of its overwhelming complexity and features of its interface. Regarding complexity, the FMS has many *modes* particularly in accomplishing vertical flight (five different ways of changing altitude, for example), and these modes can be combined in many different ways (Degani 2003). Furthermore, the logic within the FMS allows the plane to transition from one mode to another (a stage 3 decision) without any direct action from the pilot at the time of the transition. This transition may involve both activating certain modes (e.g., a speed control mode, once a certain target altitude is reached), or in some cases deactivating a mode. Thus, because of the generation effect described above, the pilot will lose situation awareness of the changing modes (and resulting state of the aircraft), compared to a situation in which she were directly controlling the aircraft with the yoke and throttle.

These problems of under-trust are exacerbated by three properties of the interface:

1. It is somewhat opaque, contributing to the loss of situation awareness. Many of the mode changes that go on within the FMS, particularly in the complex vertical flight, are represented to the pilot only by non-spatial changes in symbolic abbreviations posted on the flight mode annunciators. Not only are these not intuitive or easy to understand, but their actual occurrence often goes unnoticed by the pilot busy scanning the full cockpit (Wickens *et al.* 2003), a failure of bottom-up attention capture (Nikolic *et al.* 2004).
2. There is no spatial analog representation of the complex vertical navigation that would correspond to the spatial map (navigation display) for lateral navigation. Instead, symbolic representation of vertical behavior is found in text on the pages of the flight management computer, visible in the CDU, and in alphanumeric mode abbreviations visible within the FMA windows. Thus, there is a violation of display compatibility in representing symbolically, the inherently spatial information regarding vertical flight (Wickens & Hollands 2000).
3. The information concerning overall status of the FMS is, as shown in Figure 14.7, spatially distributed about the cockpit. Yet this information needs to be integrated in the mind (a violation of the proximity compatibility principle; Wickens and Carswell 1995; Wickens 2003).

It is at least evident that designers are aware of these issues, and some effort is being made to support better situation awareness, particularly by considering graphic analog vertical situation displays (Hughes 2004), and developing fewer and more intuitive symbolic labels for FMS-related flight modes (Sherry & Feary 2005).

CONCLUSIONS

This chapter has really only scratched the surface of the multitude of cognitive challenges confronting the pilot. Indeed because of space, we have neglected entirely discussing the important cognitive issues related to pilot judgment and problem-solving, as well as those related to pilot training and instruction (see Garland *et al.* 1999; Orlady and Orlady 2000; and Tsang and Vidulich 2003 for further information on these topics). Another area that we believe will represent an important future in aviation psychology is computational models (Foyle & Hooey 2007). Such models have the advantage of generating predictive data as to how pilots and controllers will respond to new technology and new procedures, without requiring time-consuming and expensive human-in-the-loop simulations. Thus they should become vital tools in ensuring the continued safety of the airspace and its human users.

REFERENCES

Adams, M. J., Tenney, Y. J. & Pew, R. W. (1995). Situation awareness and the cognitive management of complex systems. *Human Factors*, *37*(1), 85–104.

Alexander, A. L., Wickens, C. D. & Hardy, T. J. (2005). Synthetic vision systems: the effects of guidance symbology, display size, and field of view. *Human Factors*, *47*(4), 693–707.

Aretz, A. J. (1991). The design of electronic map displays. *Human Factors*, *33*(1), 85–101.

Baddeley, A. D. (1986). *Working Memory*. Oxford: Clarendon Press.

Banbury, S. P., Macken, W. J., Tremblay, S. & Jones, D. M. (2001). Auditory distraction and short-term memory: phenomena and practical implications. *Human Factors*, *43*, 12–29.

Bellenkes, A. H., Wickens, C. D. & Kramer, A. F. (1997). Visual scanning and pilot expertise: the role of attentional flexibility and mental model development. *Aviation, Space, and Environmental Medicine*, *68*(7), 569–579.

Bliss, J. (2003). An investigation of alarm related accidents and incidents in aviation. *International Journal of Aviation Psychology*, *13*(3), 249–268.

Bresley, B. (1995, April–June). 777 flight deck design. *Airliner*, 1–9.

Breznitz, S. (1983). *Cry-Wolf: The Psychology of False Alarms*. Hillsdale, NJ: Lawrence Erlbaum Associates.

Broadbent, D. E. (1982). Task combination and selective intake of information. *Acta Psychologica*, *50*, 253–290.

Carbonnell, J. R., Ward, J. L. & Senders, J. W. (1968). A queuing model of visual sampling: experimental validation. *IEEE Trans. on Man–Machine Systems, MMS-9*, 82–87.

Carpenter, S. (2001). Sights unseen. *APA Monitor*, *32*, 54–57.

Chou, C., Madhavan, D. & Funk, K. (1996). Studies of cockpit task management errors. *International Journal of Aviation Psychology*, *6*, 307–320.

Chute, R. D. & Wiener, E. L. (1995). Cockpit–cabin communication: I. a tale of two cultures. *The International Journal of Aviation Psychology*, *5*(3), 257–276.

Clark, H. H. & Chase, W. G. (1972). On the process of comparing sentences against pictures. *Cognitive Psychology*, *3*, 472–517.

Damos, D. L. (1997). Using interruptions to identify task prioritization in Part 121 air carrier operations. *Proceedings of the 9th International Symposium on Aviation Psychology*. Columbus, OH: Ohio State University.

Degani, A. (2003). *Taming HAL*. New York: Palgrave Macmillan.

Degani, A. & Wiener, E. L. (1993). Cockpit checklists: concepts, design and use. *Human Factors*, *35*(4), 345–360.

Dismukes, K. (2001). The challenge of managing interruptions, distractions, and deferred tasks. *Proceedings of the 11th International Symposium on Aviation Psychology*. Columbus, OH: Ohio State University.

Dixon, S. R. & Wickens, C. D. (2006). Automation reliability in unmanned aerial vehicle flight control: evaluating a reliance-compliance model of automation dependence in high workload. *Human Factors*, *48*(3).

Dornheim, M. A. (1995, January 30). Dramatic incidents highlight mode problems in cockpit. *Aviation Week and Space Technology*, 57–59.

Dornheim, M. A. (2000, July 17). Crew distractions emerge as new safety focus. *Aviation Week and Space Technology*, 58–65.

Endsley, M. R. (1995). Toward a theory of situation awareness in dynamic systems. *Human Factors*, *37*(1), 85–104.

Eriksen, B. A. & Eriksen, C. W. (1974). Effects of noise letters upon the identification of a target letter in a non-search task. *Perception & Psychophysics*, *16*, 143–149.

Fadden, D. M., Braune, R. & Wiedemann, J. (1991). Spatial displays as a means to increase pilot situational awareness. In S. R. Ellis, M. K. Kaiser & A. J. Grunwald (eds.), *Pictorial Communication in Virtual and Real Environments* (pp. 173–181). London: Taylor and Francis.

Fadden, S., Ververs, P. M. & Wickens, C. D. (1998). Costs and benefits of head-up display use: a meta-analytic approach. *Proceedings of the 42nd Annual Meeting of the Human Factors & Ergonomics Society* (pp. 16–20). Santa Monica, CA: Human Factors Society.

Fadden, S., Ververs, P. M. & Wickens, C. D. (2001). Pathway HUDS: are they viable? *Human Factors*, *43*(2), 173–193.

Fitts, P., Jones, R. E. & Milton, E. (1950). Eye movements of aircraft pilots during instrument landing approaches. *Aeronautical Engineering Review*, *9*, 24–29.

Foushee, H. C. (1984). Dyads and triads at 35,000 feet: factors affecting group process and aircrew performance. *American Psychology*, *39*, 885–893.

Foyle, D. & Hooey, B. (2007). *Human performance modeling in aviation*. Mahwah, NJ: Lawrence Erlbaum Associates.

Funk, K. (1991). Cockpit task management: preliminary definitions, normative theory, error taxonomy, and design recommendations. *The International Journal of Aviation Psychology*, *1*(4), 271–286.

Funk, K. & Lyall, B. (1999). Special issue on aircraft automation. *International Journal Aviation Psychology*, *9*(2), 107–108.

Garland, D. J., Wise, J. A. & Hopkin, V. D. (eds.) (1999). *Handbook of Aviation Human Factors*. Mahwah, NJ: Lawrence Erlbaum Associates.

Garner, W. R. & Morton, J. (1969). Perceptual independence: definitions, models, and experimental paradigms. *Psychological Bulletin*, *72*, 233–259.

Gibson, J. J. (1979). *The Ecological Approach to Visual Perception*. Boston, MA: Houghton Mifflin.

Haber, R. (2003). Perception and attention during low altitude high speed flight. In P. Tsang & M. Vidulich (eds.), *Principles and Practice of Aviation Psychology*. Mahwah, NJ: Lawrence Erlbaum Associates.

Hahn, E. C. & Hansman, R .J. (1992). Experimental studies on the effect of the effect of automation and pilot situational awareness in the data ink ATC environment. *SAE AEROTECH Conference and Exposition*. Warrendale, PA: Society of Automotive Engineers, Inc.

Harris, R. L. Sr. & Christhilf, D. M. (1980). What do pilots see in displays? *Proceedings of the 24th Annual Meeting of the Human Factors Society* (pp. 22–26). Santa Monica, CA: Human Factors Society.

Harris, J. R. & Wilkins, A. J. (1982). Remembering to do things: a theoretical framework and an illustrative experiment. *Human Learning*, *1*, 123–136.

Hart, S. G. & Wickens, C. D. (1990). Workload assessment and prediction. In H. R. Booher (ed.), *MANPRINT: An Approach to Systems Integration* (pp. 257–296). New York: Van Nostrand Reinhold.

Hawkins, F. H. (1993). *Human Factors in Flight*. Brookfield, VT: Ashgate.

Helleberg, J. & Wickens, C. D. (2003). Effects of data-link modality and display redundancy on pilot performance: an attentional perspective. *The International Journal of Aviation Psychology, 13*(3), 189–210.

Hickox, J. C. & Wickens, C. D. (1999). Effects of elevation angle disparity, complexity, and feature type on relating out-of-cockpit field of view to an electronic cartographic map. *Journal of Experimental Psychology: Applied, 5*(3), 284–301.

Hicks, M. & DiBrito G. (1998). Civil aircraft warning systems: whose calling the shots? In G. Boy, C. Graeber & J. M. Robert (eds.), *International Conference on Human–Computer Interaction in Aeronautics* (HCI-Aero 98, pp. 205–212). Montreal, Canada: École Polytechique de Montréal.

Hopkin, D. (1995). *Human Factors in Air Traffic Control*. London: Taylor and Francis.

Hughes, D. (2004, November 29) Boeing, airbus go vertical, vertical innovation. *Aviation Week & Space Technology*, 59–61.

Iani, C. & Wickens, C. D. (in press). Factors affecting task management in aviation. *Human Factors*.

Jagacinski, R. J. & Flach, J. M. (2003). *Control Theory for Humans*. Mahwah, NJ: Lawrence Erlbaum Associates.

Jarmasz, J., Herdman, C. M. & Johannsdottir, K. (2005). Object-based attention and cognitive tunneling. *Journal of Experimental Psychology: Applied, 11*, 3–18.

Kerns, K. (1999). Human factors in air traffic control/flight deck integration: implications of data-link simulation research. In D. J. Garland, J. A. Wise & V. D. Hopkin (eds.), *Handbook of Aviation Human Factors* (pp. 519–546). Mahwah, NJ: Lawrence Erlbaum Associates.

Kintch, W. & Ericsson, K. A. (1995). Long-term working memory. *Psychological Review, 102*, 211–245.

Kramer, A. F. & Jacobson, A. (1991). Perceptual organization and focused attention: the role of objects and proximity in visual processing. *Perception and Psychophysics, 50*, 267–284.

Kroft, P. D. & Wickens, C. D. (2003). Displaying multi-domain graphical database information: an evaluation of scanning, clutter, display size, and user interactivity. *Information Design Journal, 11*(1), 44–52.

Latorella, K. A. (1996). Investigating interruptions: an example from the flightdeck. *Proceedings of the 40th Annual Meeting of the Human Factors and Ergonomics Society* (pp. 249–253). Santa Monica, CA: Human Factors and Ergonomics Society.

Laudeman, I. V. & Palmer, E. A. (1995). Quantitative measurement of observed workload in the analysis of aircrew performance. *The International Journal of Aviation Psychology, 5*(2), 187–198.

Loftus, G., Dark, V. & Williams, D. (1979). Short-term memory factors in ground controller/pilot communication. *Human Factors, 21*, 169–181.

McFarlane, D. C. & Latorella, K. A. (2002). The score and importance of human interruption in human-computer interface design. *Human Computer Interaction, 17*(1), 1–61.

McGreevy, M. W. & Ellis, S. R. (1986). The effect of perspective geometry on judged direction in spatial information instruments. *Human Factors, 28*, 439–456.

Meyer, J. (2004). Conceptual issues in the study of dynamic hazard warnings. *Human Factors, 46*, 196–204.

Monan, W. P. (1986). *Human Factors in Aviation Operations: The Hearback Problem* (NASA Contractor Report 177398). Moffett Field, CA: NASA Ames Res. Ctr.

Moray, N. (1986). Monitoring behavior and supervisory control. In K. R. Boff, L. Kaufman & J. P. Thomas (eds.), *Handbook of Perception and Performance* (Vol. 2, pp. 40–1/40–51). New York: John Wiley and Sons.

Moray, N. (1997). Human factors in process control. In G. Salvendy (ed.), *The Handbook of Human Factors and Ergonomics* (2nd edn). New York: John Wiley & Sons.

Morrow, D., Lee, A. & Rodvold, M. (1993). Analysis of problems in routine controller–pilot communication. *The International Journal of Aviation Psychology, 3*(4), 285–302.

Mosier, K. L., Palmer, E. A. & Degani, A. (1992). Electronic checklists: implications for decision making. *Proceedings of the 36th Annual Meeting of the Human Factors Society* (pp. 7–11). Santa Monica, CA: Human Factors Society.

Muthard, E. K. & Wickens, C. D. (in press). The influence of prior beliefs and imperfect automation on safety critical event detection and plan fixation. *International Journal of Aviation Psychology*.

Mykityshyn, M. G., Kuchar, J. K. & Hansman, R. J. (1994). Experimental study of electronically based instrument approach plates. *The International Journal of Aviation Psychology*, *4*(2), 141–166.

Navarro, C. & Sikorski, S. (1999). Datalink communication in flight deck operations: a synthesis of recent studies. *The International Journal of Aviation Psychology*, *9*(4), 361–376.

Neisser, U. (1963). Decision time without reaction time. *American Journal of Psychology*, *76*, 376–385.

Nikolic, M. I., Orr, J. M. & Sarter, N. B. (2004). Why pilots miss the green box: how display context undermines attention capture. *The International Journal of Aviation Psychology*, *14*(1), 39–52.

Norman, D. (1988). *The Psychology of Every Day Things*. New York: Harper and Row.

Norman, D. A. & Bobrow, D. G. (1975). On data-limited and resource-limited processes. *Cognitive Psychology*, *7*, 44–64.

O'Hare, D. (2003). Aeronautical decision making: metaphors models and methods. In P. Tsang & M. Vidulich (eds.), *Principles and Practices of Aviation Psychology*. Mahwah, NJ: Lawrence Erlbaum Associates.

Olmos, O., Liang, C.-C. & Wickens, C. D. (1997). Electronic map evaluation in simulated visual meteorological conditions. *International Journal of Aviation Psychology*, *7*(1), 37–66.

Orlady, H. W. & Orlady, L. M. (2000). *Human Factors in Multi-Crew Flight Operations*. Brookfield, VT: Ashgate.

Palmer, E. & Degani, A. (1991). Electronic checklists: evaluation of two levels of automation. *Proceedings of the 6th International Symposium on Aviation Psychology*. Columbus, OH: The Ohio State University, Department of Aviation.

Palmisano, S. & Gillam, B. (2005). Visual perception of touchdown point during simulated landing. *Journal of Experimental Psychology: Applied*, *11*, 19–30.

Parasuraman, R. (1987). Human–computer monitoring. *Human Factors*, *29*, 695–706.

Parasuraman, R. & Lorenz, B. (2007). Automated and interactive real-time systems, Chapter 16, this volume.

Parasuraman, R. Molloy, R. & Singh, I. L. (1993). Performance consequences of automation-induced complacency. *International Journal of Aviation Psychology*, *3*(1), 1–23.

Parasuraman, R. & Riley, V. (1997). Humans and automation: use, misuse, disuse, abuse. *Human Factors*, *39*, 230–253.

Parasuraman, R., Sheridan, T. B. & Wickens, C. D. (2000, May). A model for types and levels of human interaction with automation. *IEEE Transactions on Systems, Man & Cybernetics*, *30*(3), 286–297.

Previc, F. & Ercoline, W. R. (2004). *Spatial Disorientation in Aviation*. Reston, VA.: American Institute of Aeronautics and Astronautics Inc.

Prinzel, L. J. III Comstock, O. R., Glaab, L. J., Kromer, L. J., Arthur, J. L. & Berry, S. S. (2004). The efficacy of head-down and head-up synthetic vision display concepts for retro- and forward-fit of commercial aircraft. *The International Journal of Aviation Psychology*, *14*(1), 53–77.

Pritchett, A. (2001). Reviewing the role of cockpit alerting systems. *Human Factors & Aerospace Safety*, *1*, 5–38.

Raby, M. & Wickens, C. D. (1994). Strategic workload management and decision biases in aviation. *International Journal of Aviation Psychology*, *4*(3), 211–240.

Rasmussen, J. & Rouse, W. (eds.) (1981). *Human Detection and Diagnosis of System Failures*. New York: Plenum.

Redding, R. E. (1992). Analysis of operational errors and workload in air traffic control. *Proceedings of the 36th Annual Meeting of the Human Factors Society* (pp. 1321–1325). Santa Monica, CA: Human Factors Society.

Remington, R. W., Johnston, J. C., Ruthruff, E., Gold, M. & Romera, M. (2000). Visual search in complex displays: factors affecting conflict detection by air traffic controllers. *Human Factors*, *42*(3), 349–366.

Rensink, R. A. (2002). Change detection. *Annual Review of Psychology*, *53*, 245–277.

Roscoe, S. N. (1968). Airborne displays for flight and navigation. *Human Factors*, *10*, 321–332.
Roske-Hofstrand, R. J. & Paap, K. R. (1986). Cognitive networks as a guide to menu organization: an application in the automated cockpit. *Ergonomics*, *29*, 1301–1311.
Sarter, N. B. & Woods, D. D. (1994). Pilot interaction with cockpit automation II: an experimental study of pilots' model and awareness of the flight management system. *The International Journal of Aviation Psychology*, *4*(1), 1–28.
Sarter, N. B. & Woods, D. D. (1995). How in the world did we ever get into that mode? Mode error and awareness in supervisory control. *Human Factors*, *37*(1), 5–19.
Sarter, N. B. & Woods, D. D. (1997). Team play with a powerful and independent agent: operational experiences and automation surprises on the Airbus A-320. *Human Factors*, *39*(4), 553–569.
Sarter, N. & Woods, D. D. (2000). Team play with a powerful and independent agent: a full-mission simulation study. *Human Factors*, *42*(3), 390–402.
Schreiber, B. T., Wickens, C. D., Renner, G. J. *et al.* (1998). Navigational checking using 3D maps: the influence of elevation angle, azimuth, and foreshortening. *Human Factors*, *40*(2), 209–223.
Schutte, P. C. & Trujillo, A. C. (1996). Flight crew task management in non-normal situations. *Proceedings of the 40th Annual Meeting of the Human Factors and Ergonomics Society* (pp. 244–248). Santa Monica, CA: Human Factors and Ergonomics Society.
Seamster, T. L., Redding, R. E. & Kaempf, G. L. (1997). *Applied Cognitive Task Analysis in Aviation*. Brookfield, VT: Ashgate.
Seidler, K. & Wickens, C. D. (1992). Distance and organization in multifunction displays. *Human Factors*, *34*, 555–569.
Shepard, R. N. & Cooper, L. A. (1982). *Mental Images and Their Transformations*. Cambridge, MA: MIT Press/Bradford Books.
Sherry, L. & Feary, M. (2005). Invalid entry, try again: analysis of human–computer interaction in response to error messages of the flight management system. In R. Jensen (Ed) *Proceedings of the International Symposium of Aviation Psychology.*
Sherry, L. & Polson, P. G. (1999). Shared models of flight management system vertical guidance. *The International Journal of Aviation Psychology*, *9*(2), 139–154.
Slamecka, N. J. & Graf, P. (1978). The generation effect: delineation of a phenomenon. *Journal of Experimental Psychology: Human Learning and Memory*, *4*, 592–604.
Sorkin, R. (1989). Why are people turning off our alarms? *Human Factors Bulletin*, *32*, 3–4.
Sparaco, (1998, January 5). Airbus: automated transports safer than older aircraft. *Aviation Week and Space Technology*, 40–41.
Spence, C. & Driver, J. (1997). Audiovisual links in attention: implications for interface design. In D. Harris (ed.), *Engineering psychology and Cognitive Ergonomics* (Vol. 2, pp. 185–192). Brookfield, VT: Ashgate.
Stanton, N. (ed.) (1994). *Human Factors in Alarm Design*. Bristol, PA: Taylor and Francis.
Theunissen, E. (1997). Integrated Design of a Man-Machine Interface for 4-D Navigation. Doctoral dissertation, Faculty of Electrical Engineering, Delft University of Technology, The Netherlands.
Thomas, L. C. & Rantanen, E. M. (2006). Human factors issues in implementation of advanced aviation technologies: a case of false alerts and cockpit displays of traffic information. *Theoretical Issues of Ergonomics Science* [in press].
Tsang, P. & Vidulich, M. (2003). *Principles and Practices of Aviation Psychology*. Mahwah, NJ: Lawrence Erlbaum Associates.
Warren, R. & Wertheim, A. H. (eds.) (1990). *Perception and Control of Self-motion*. Hillsdale, NJ: Lawrence Erlbaum Associates.
Weintraub, D. J. & Ensing, M. J. (1992). *Human Factors Issues in Head-Up Display Design: The Book of HUD* (SOAR CSERIAC State of the Art Report 92–2). Dayton, OH: Crew System Ergonomics Information Analysis Center, Wright-Patterson Air Force Base.
Wickens, C. D. (1986). The effects of control dynamics on performance. In K. R. Boff, L. Kaufman & J. P. Thomas (eds.), *Handbook of Perception and Performance* (Vol. 2, pp. 39-1–39-60). New York: John Wiley & Sons.
Wickens, C. D. (1999). Frames of reference for navigation. In D. Gopher & A. Koriat (eds.), *Attention and Performance* (Vol. 16, pp. 113–144). Orlando, FL: Academic Press.

Wickens, C. D. (2000). Human factors in vector map design: the importance of task-display dependence. *Journal of Navigation*, *53*(1), 54–67.

Wickens, C. D. (2002). Situation awareness and workload in aviation. *Current Directions in Psychological Science*, *11*(4), 128–133.

Wickens, C. D. (2003). Aviation displays. In P. Tsang & M. Vidulich (eds.), *Principles and Practices of Aviation Psychology* (pp. 147–199). Mahwah, NJ: Lawrence Erlbaum Associates.

Wickens, C. D. (2005). Attentional tunneling and task management. *Proceedings of the 13th International Symposium on Aviation Psychology*. Dayton, OH.

Wickens, C. D. & Carswell, C. M. (1995). The proximity compatibility principle: its psychological foundation and relevance to display design. *Human Factors*, *37*(3), 473–494.

Wickens, C. D. & Carswell, C. M. (2007). Human information processing. In G. Salvendy (ed.), *The Handbook of Human Factors and Ergonomics* (3rd edn). New York: John Wiley & Sons.

Wickens, C. D. & Hollands, J. (2000). *Engineering Psychology and Human Performance* (3rd edn). Englewood Cliffs, NJ: Prentice-Hall.

Wickens, C. D., Liang, C-C., Prevett, T. & Olmos, O. (1996). Electronic maps for terminal area navigation: effects of frame of reference and dimensionality. *International Journal of Aviation Psychology*, *6*(3), 241–271.

Wickens, C. D. & Long, J. (1995). Object- vs. space-based models of visual attention: implications for the design of head-up displays. *Journal of Experimental Psychology: Applied*, *1*(3), 179–194.

Wickens, C. D., Mavor, A. S. & McGee, J. P. (eds.) (1997). *Flight to the Future: Human Factors in Air Traffic Control*. Washington, DC: National Academy Press.

Wickens, C. D., Mumaw, R. & Sarter, N. B. (2003). Pilots' monitoring and task management strategies and performance on glass cockpit aircraft: beyond anecdotal evidence. *Proceedings of the 2003 International Symposium for Aviation Psychology*. Dayton, OH.

Wickens, C. D., Muthard, E. K., Alexander, A. L. *et al.* (2003). The influences of display highlighting and size and event eccentricity for aviation surveillance. *Proceedings of the 47th Annual Meeting of the Human Factors and Ergonomics Society*. Santa Monica, CA: Human Factors and Ergonomics Society.

Wickens, C. D. & Prevett, T. (1995). Exploring the dimensions of egocentricity in aircraft navigation displays. *Journal of Experimental Psychology: Applied*, *1*(2), 110–135.

Wickens, C. D. & Seidler, K. S. (1997). Information access in a dual-task context: testing a model of optimal strategy selection. *Journal of Experimental Psychology: Applied*, *3*(3), 196–215.

Wickens, C. D., Ververs, P. & Fadden, S. (2004). Head-up display design. In D. Harris (ed.), *Human Factors for Civil Flight Deck Design* (pp. 103–140). Brookfield, VT: Ashgate.

Wickens, C., Vincow, M. & Yeh, M. (2005). Applications of visual spatial thinking. In A Mikayi & P. Shah (eds.), *Cambridge Handbook of Visual Spatial Thinking*. Cambridge: Cambridge University Press.

Wickens, C. D., McCarley, J. S., Alexander, A. L. *et al.* (2006). Attention-situation awareness (A-SA) model of pilot error. In D. Foyle & B. Hooey (eds.), *Human Performance Modeling in Aviation*. Mahwah, NJ: Lawrence Erlbaum Associates.

Wiegmann, D. A., Goh, J. & O'Hare, D. (2002). The role of situation assessment and flight experience in pilots' decisions to continue visual flight rules flight into adverse weather. *Human Factors*, *44*(2), 189–197.

Wiener, E. L. (1977). Controlled flight into terrain accidents: system-induced errors. *Human Factors*, *19*, 171–181.

Wiener, E. L. (1988). Cockpit automation. In E. L. Wiener & D. C. Nagel (eds.), *Human Factors in Aviation* (pp. 433–461). San Diego, CA: Academic Press.

Wiener, E. L., Kanki, B. C. & Helmreich, R. L. (eds.) (1993). *Cockpit Resource Management*. San Diego, CA: Academic Press.

Williams, H., Hutchinson, S. & Wickens, C. D. (1996). A comparison of methods for promoting geographic knowledge in simulated aircraft navigation. *Human Factors*, *38*(1), 50–64.

Yeh, M. & Wickens, C. D. (2001). Attentional filtering in the design of electronic map displays: a comparison of color-coding, intensity coding, and decluttering techniques. *Human Factors*, *43*(4), 543–562.

CHAPTER 15

Driving

Geoffrey Underwood, David Crundall, and Peter Chapman
University of Nottingham, UK

Driving is a skill that most of us acquire, even though it seems daunting to the novice sitting behind the steering wheel for the first time. The combinations of actions required for the vehicle to maintain progress, plus the need to collect information from the perceptual world for vehicle guidance and for interactions with other traffic, requires the novice to master a series of perceptual-motor subskills. Complete novices sometime declare changing gear to be totally impossible, and if cognitive psychologists were to design such a task from scratch they might be inclined to agree. The need to co-ordinate movements of gear stick, clutch, and accelerator at a precise moment called by the engine speed, and while continuing to stay in lane and avoid any close encounters with other road users might seem to overload the driver's resources. After a few months of practice the novices' views will have changed, and as well as performing previously "impossible" coordinated actions they will be able to debate which CD should be put on the in-car entertainment system, or argue about incidents in last night's football match. The change from overloaded novice to skilled driver is one of the main themes of this chapter, in which we will first analyze the perceptual tasks involved in vehicle control in part to help understand the paradox of why novices show little sensitivity to changing driving conditions. One explanation is that they do not scan complex roads for potentially dangerous events because they are perceptually limited, and so they need to look directly at the road in front in order to steer their vehicle. After discussing the perceptual task facing the driver, we will consider alternative explanations based on the availability of the drivers' cognitive resources, and the drivers' situation awareness, before we discuss the relationship between what the driver does and what the driver remembers doing.

PERCEPTUAL PROCESSES IN DRIVING

When newly qualified drivers encounter difficult driving conditions, their search of the road becomes stereotypical and inflexible. As conditions require more negotiation between drivers, at junctions and with slip roads introducing merging traffic, for example, novices seem particularly vulnerable. Their inspection of the environment for potential hazards

Handbook of Applied Cognition: Second Edition. Edited by Francis T. Durso.

becomes inadequate at exactly the time when difficulties are more likely to occur. When their cognitive load is increased by the appearance of multiple hazards, novice drivers tend to look inflexibly at the road directly ahead. This was the result of a study reported by Crundall and Underwood (1998) in which eye movements were recorded. Drivers of differing experience drove an instrumented vehicle along low-traffic rural roads, a suburban housing estate, and a multi-lane highway with traffic that merged from both left and right. Novice drivers searched along the horizontal meridian no differently on the dual carriageway than they did on the relatively quiet rural road, suggesting perhaps that they were insensitive to changes in the complexity of the environment, or that they were insufficiently skilled to be able to respond to these changes. Falkmer and Gregersen (2001) reported a similar finding from a Swedish study, in that their learner drivers scanned the roadway less on a high-demand city route than on a less demanding rural road. This is a paradoxical result, with relatively unskilled drivers restricting their scanning for hazards on exactly those roadways where hazards were most likely to appear.

In order to be safe on the roads we need to stay in lane, maintain manageable speeds and headways, navigate corners and bends by turning the steering wheel through the optimum angle, and to be able to brake and avoid hazards as they occur. The primary input to these motor control tasks is however visual. To understand successful driving, we must therefore first consider the different sources of visual information that drivers attend to, and their reasons for doing so. This section will review research that has attempted to unpack the role of vision in driving, assessing the state of understanding concerning where drivers look (and why) during driving.

Where Do Drivers Look?

It is accepted that visual input is by far the most important source of driving information, accounting for nearly 90 per cent of all relevant information (Sivak 1996). It is also axiomatic that attention is limited and that drivers cannot attend to every stimulus in the driving scene. On a rural road with no traffic, this does not pose a problem, as the majority of the visual information that is available is irrelevant. In fact, under these circumstances the driver will have spare attentional capacity that could be easily devoted to interesting, but irrelevant, stimuli. In undemanding conditions, experienced drivers can devote up to 50 per cent of their time to inspection of the scenery (e.g., Hughes & Cole 1986; Land & Lee 1994; Green 2002). The demands placed on a driver can increase, however, to a point where there are not enough resources to monitor every relevant stimulus in view. This may occur due to an increase in the number of task-relevant stimuli (such as an increase in traffic density, or an increase in visual clutter that may mask potential hazards, such as driving through a congested urban street). Alternatively, increased speed, decreased visibility, lack of experience, alcohol, drugs, and fatigue can all result in tasks requiring more attention if progress is to be maintained. Whatever the cause of the increase in demands on attention, the driver must make important decisions about what to attend to, often without previewing them prior to selection for further processing. This is the *scheduling problem* that questions how drivers can make these decisions without access to all the information required to correctly prioritize them (see also Shinoda *et al.* 2001). A number of strategies and tactics are available to these drivers, however, to ensure that

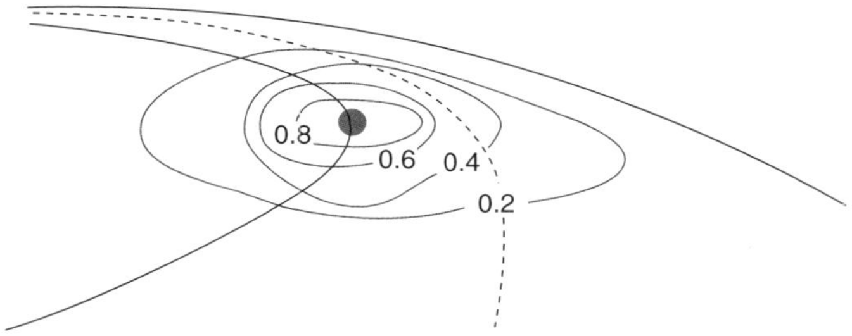

Figure 15.1 A contour plot showing the proportions of fixations to fall on a left-hand bend, with the epicenter being the tangent point (from Land & Lee 1994)

visual sampling is directed toward task-relevant information, while being inhibited from the unnecessary inspection of task-irrelevant stimuli.

The most important strategy is remarkably obvious: look straight ahead. The focus of expansion is generally synonymous with the direction of the vehicle, at least on straight roads, and is unsurprisingly the fixation location most favored by experienced drivers (Mourant & Rockwell 1972; Underwood *et al.* 2003a). There are varying estimates of the amount time spent fixating the road at a far preview distance, though studies have shown that 80–94 per cent of fixations can fall on the road ahead under varying circumstances (Mourant *et al.* 1969; Lansdown *et al.* 1999; Brackstone & Waterson 2004).

Despite this predisposition to look straight ahead, drivers will still avert their gaze from this location for considerable periods of time, with some studies finding mean fixations within the car of over one second (e.g., Rockwell 1988), while average fixations on mirrors tend to be in the region of 0.5–1 seconds (Mourant & Rockwell 1972; Brackstone & Waterson 2004). When drivers are not gazing straight ahead however, the majority of fixations tend to fall to the left and right of the focus of expansion, inspecting pedestrians, parked cars, and other potential sources of hazards. This creates an elongated inspection window, with the majority of fixations falling along the horizontal plane with relatively few fixations in the vertical plane (Chapman & Underwood 1998a, 1998b). The elongated pattern of fixations is also depicted in Figure 15.1, which shows the proportion of fixations made upon different parts of the roadway while steering around a bend. This pattern of fixation distribution reflects the locations of task-relevant stimuli, though it is not simply reactive to these locations. Inexperienced drivers tend not to have such a wide spread of fixations in the horizontal plane, and have been noted to make more fixations in the vertical plane (Mourant & Rockwell 1972; Evans 1991; Crundall & Underwood 1998). This suggests that the horizontal bias is developed or learnt with experience. Experienced drivers must therefore prioritize certain areas of the visual field, based on the learned probabilities of task-relevant stimuli being present in these locations. Such learned probabilities can, however, be much more specific. For instance, Shinoda *et al.* (2001) found that drivers in a simulator were more likely to detect the masked onset of a stop sign if it appeared at a junction rather than on a straight road. They argued that stop signs were searched for only at the junctions because drivers had developed a strong association between junctions and traffic signs.

The horizontal prioritization of visual search has also been noted in scan path analyses. Liu (1998) compared fixation transitions from one area of the visual scene to another, and found that some of these transitions were statistically more likely to occur than others. These strings of fixations (recorded while participants drove a circuit in a simulator) formed reliable scan paths that would reoccur. The most robust pattern was characterized by a shift in the position of the eyes from the focus of expansion to either the left or right edge of the road. Underwood *et al.* (2003a) also found that the focus of expansion, or even middle distances in the road, provided important cornerstones for two and three fixation scan paths.

Distraction and Attention: Phone Use while Driving

One current issue in driving psychology that has given rise to much debate is the role of cellular telephone use in accident liability. This section briefly discusses the evidence for this, and possible underlying causes. Violanti and Marshall (1996) suggested that less than an hour of cellular telephone use per month can increase accident liability five-fold. Other studies have noted degradations in gap judgment (Brown *et al.* 1969), insensitivity to road conditions (Haigney *et al.* 2000), a decline in headway and lane maintenance (Brookhuis *et al.* 1991; Briem & Hedman 1995; Reed & Green 1999; Haigney *et al.* 2000), and a decrease in the ability to respond to discrete driving events such as brake lights (McKnight & McKnight 1993; Lamble *et al.* 1999; Irwin *et al.* 2000; Strayer & Johnston 2001; Hancock *et al.* 2003; Strayer *et al.* 2003; Patten *et al.* 2004). One obvious reason for such interference with the driving task is that hand-held cell phones require visual and motor interaction which may compete with the demands of driving. Inappropriate prioritization of phone and driving subtasks can easily result in drivers paying insufficient attention to the road during the occurrence of a sudden hazard. This problem with hand-held units is well documented (Brookhuis *et al.* 1991; Briem & Hedman 1995; Wikman *et al.* 1998; Goodman *et al.* 1999), and has led to a ban on their use when driving on British roads.

In one particular study, Garcia-Larrea *et al.* (2001) used event-related brain potentials to identify a decline in the readiness of participants to make a motor response due to the use of a hand-held phone. However, an additional level of interference was also noted, for both hand-held and hand-free units, suggesting a general decrease in attention to sensory inputs. Many other studies have replicated the degrading effects of hand-free cell phones upon driving tasks (e.g., Lamble *et al.* 1999; Strayer & Johnston 2001; Patten *et al.* 2004).

Considering the influence of hand-free communications upon driving performance, one might expect that conversing with passengers in the same vehicle might have a similar effect. The evidence does not support this, however (Kames 1978; Fairclough *et al.* 1991; Parkes 1991; though see Sagberg 2001). There are several reasons why this might not be the case. The nature of the conversation between a driver and a remote speaker may be qualitatively different from a conversation with a passenger in its intensity and focus. Furthermore, the driver may engage in some form of visualization of the remote speaker or the context that the remote speaker is communicating from. This internal visual process may then compete with resources devoted to external stimuli. A third possibility is that an in-car conversation may be paced according to the demands of the drive. The shared visual experience may allow a passenger to predict when the driver needs to concentrate on the road. The passenger may then limit the demands of the conversation at these points. Similarly, the driver may feel more comfortable stopping a conversation mid-sentence with a passenger, whereas they might feel socially obliged to maintain a conversation with a remote speaker who would not be aware of why the driver might suddenly stop talking.

Gugerty *et al.* (2004) investigated this conversation-suppression hypothesis using pairs of naïve participants in a laboratory setting. The driver performed a number of driving-related tasks while engaged in a word game with a partner. The in-car condition allowed the partner to see the same task information on the screen as the driver while the remote condition removed all shared visual experience. They predicted that the partner would slow the conversation when they shared the visual experience as they would be more aware of the demands placed on the driver. The results of the first experiment, however, actually found that the conversation was slower in the remote condition, and driving performance was also degraded. A second experiment increased the difficulty of the verbal task and removed differences in verbal response times between the remote and in-car conditions. While they could make conclusions about the overall speed of the word game across the remote and in-car conditions, they did not vary task demands during a conversation to see if the driver or partner modulated the conversation according to the demands.

A recent study by Crundall *et al.* (2005a) addressed the conversation-suppression hypothesis under real driving conditions. The rate of naturalistic conversation was measured during driving across a number of roads of varying demand. Conversations were held remotely via cell phones, or with in-car passengers (half of whom were blindfolded so that they did not share the same visual experience as the driver). The results suggested that remote speakers are less likely to modulate their conversation than in-car passengers (even the blindfolded passengers; see Figure 15.2).

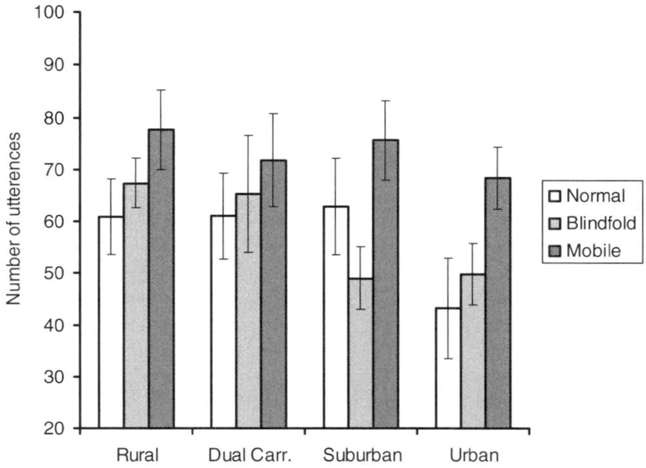

Figure 15.2 The number of utterances produced by a conversational partner as a passenger (NORMAL), as a blindfolded passenger (BLINDFOLD), or as a remote speaker (MOBILE). Only MOBILE speakers fail to reduce their conversation on difficult urban roads (Crundall *et al.* 2005a)

Table 15.1 A classification of different types of information that the driver may process

	Monitoring	Planning
Selection	*Ambient* e.g., Lane maintenance	*Tactical* e.g., Changing lanes
Search	*Anticipatory* e.g., Hazard perception	*Strategic* e.g., Route navigation via road signs

The current conclusions from cell phone research agree that the real danger of remote conversations cannot be eliminated by restricting the use of hand-held units, though the underlying reasons why hands-free remote conversations are still dangerous is still under investigation.

What Information Do Drivers Seek?

The information that drivers seek when they move their eyes around the visual scene while driving can be split into four different categories along the two dimensions shown in Table 15.1. Table 15.1 does not include the factors of attraction and distraction of attention by various road-related stimuli, but instead is concerned with the reasons that drivers need, monitor, and seek out particular sources of information, and how these are important to the safety of the driving task.

Ambient information refers to sources of information that are continuously present, but generally do not need to be fixated in order to benefit from them. An example is the use of lane markings to maintain lane position. Land and Horwood (1995) found that though a far preview of the road ahead was vital to successful steering, more immediate feedback of lane position was given by the lane markers just in front (to the left and right) of a simulated vehicle. Participants rarely looked directly at this source of information, but when the lane markers near the vehicle were obscured, steering performance deteriorated. Land and Horwood concluded that lane marker information was taken in through peripheral vision and provided immediate feedback of the lateral displacement of the simulated vehicle allowing participants to immediately correct any deviations. Though we refer to this information as ambient, under certain conditions foveal demand may increase to such an extent that peripheral attention to such ambient sources is reduced (Crundall *et al.* 1999, 2002). This may force drivers to fixate on the lane markings in order to extract lane position information, especially in novices who are considered to be constantly under conditions of higher demand than more experienced drivers (e.g., Mourant & Rockwell 1972; Crundall *et al.* 2005b).

We use the term *tactical* to describe information that is present in the scene for much of the time (as with ambient information), but the driver chooses when to seek out this information, and will execute a specific pattern of eye movements immediately prior to a planned movement. This type of information differs from ambient information in that the extraction of information from tactical sources is more difficult and will almost always require the driver to foveate these sources. Steering can also provide us with an example from this category. Though lane maintenance requires ambient information from lane markers close to the car, successful steering through a bend also requires information about the curvature of the bend from a preview of the road ahead. Eye-tracking studies indicate that the tangent point of the curve appears to be extremely important in the calculation of steering angle (e.g., Land & Lee 1994, see Figure 15.1; Land & Tatler 2001), though other characteristics of the roadway might be expected to influence gaze as well. When drivers have a clear view of the road beyond the bend, the tangent point is less important to them (Underwood *et al.* 1999), suggesting perhaps that certain types of road may invite inspection of the tangent point more than others. The road used in the Land and Lee study was on a steep hillside, with little opportunity to see beyond each bend, and so their three drivers may have simply been looking as far ahead as they could, taking their eyes to the tangent point. Researchers have estimated that there is an internal buffer of 0.8–1 seconds, which allows the extracted information from the tangent point to be converted into movements of the steering wheel (Donges 1978; Land 1998).

Another example of tactical shifts of overt attention comes from research undertaken by Salvucci and Liu (2002) looking at the time course of a lane change in a simulator. They recorded lane position and steering wheel angle, and attempted to relate these measures to the amount of time participants fixated the start lane and the destination lane. The measures were split into five temporal categories. The central category is timed from the average point at which a driver announced an intention to change, up to the point at which driver reported that the maneuver was completed (LC). The two categories either side represent five-second windows before (BLC) and after (ALC) the lane change, while the outermost categories reflect baseline measures of lane keeping before and after the change (LK). The amount of overt attention devoted to the start lane begins to drop while attention to the destination lane starts to increase several seconds before the participant reports the intention to change lanes. This effect (and the small increase in mirror usage) is a very clear indication of how drivers modify their visual search to seek out tactical information that will help them execute specific maneuvers.

The third category defined in Table 15.1 requires drivers to actively monitor specific sources of information when they occur in the driving scene in the *anticipation* that certain responses may be required if the stimuli demand it. This can include the monitoring of speed limit signs to ensure one is driving within the limit, or more active monitoring of potentially dangerous areas of the visual field that may require an emergency response. These types of monitoring are generally subsumed under the term *hazard perception*, which has been described as situation awareness for dangerous situations during driving (Horswill & McKenna 2004). For instance, oncoming traffic should not interfere with the forward motion of the driver provided she has no intention of crossing the path of the contraflow lane. Most drivers will, however, devote some attention to oncoming traffic, even under demanding conditions (Crundall *et al.* 2005b). Though our driver may have no intention of crossing the contraflow lane, the only way she can gain insight into the intentions and capabilities of the oncoming driver is to infer it from looking at their behavior. Indication signals, lane position, and speed are just a few of the variables that need to be processed quickly for the driver to decide whether a response is required. If the oncoming driver is indicating to cross our driver's path and actually begins to edge out, then an evasive maneuver may be required. Likewise, if the oncoming driver is weaving erratically, or perhaps approaching a parked vehicle which must be overtaken, there is the possibility that our driver may have to make an emergency response. The oncoming car is therefore a highly relevant stimulus which may need to be fixated and monitored in case a hazardous situation develops, though in the vast majority of such cases no hazard occurs and our driver proceeds as intended.

Hazard perception is now recognized by several countries such as the UK and Australia as a vital and complex skill that learner drivers need to demonstrate before they are given a full license. Several studies have demonstrated that experienced drivers respond faster to the appearance of a hazard on film clips taken from the driver's point of view (McKenna & Crick 1994; Renge 1998) and it seems that much of this benefit may accrue from experienced drivers' improved deployment of both overt and covert attention (Chapman & Underwood 1998a; Crundall *et al.* 1999, 2002, 2003; Underwood *et al.* 2002a; Crundall 2005). It appears that new drivers need to learn the likely sources of hazards through guided practice and experience, so that they can search out these areas of the visual scene when driving and monitor them.

An example was reported by Fisher *et al.* (2003) who had drivers of varying experience drive through a series of scenarios in a driving simulator. The more experienced drivers were more likely to fixate specific sources of potential hazards in this study. One example scenario required the participant to drive through a junction that had a pedestrian crossing marked on the road. On the approach to the junction the participants could see a large hedge that obscured the pavement next to the crossing. This hedge could easily also obscure a pedestrian who might suddenly emerge and step into the road. The experienced drivers were more likely to fixate this hedge and monitor it until this potential source of a hazard was passed. They suggest that continued exposure to driving leads to the development of schemas for eye movements in potentially dangerous situations, allowing the driver to quickly locate and then monitor these sources of information.

We have also found evidence to suggest that highly experienced drivers are more likely to seek out and monitor potential hazard locations (Crundall *et al.* 2003, 2005b). This study compared the eye movements of police drivers (trained to pursuit standard) with matched control drivers and novices while performing a hazard perception task. Three different types of driving film clip were used: police pursuits, emergency responses, and control drives (with the first two filmed from police cars involved in real incidents). During pursuits all participants tended to look at the fleeing vehicle for a high proportion of the time, though the police drivers made better use of those moments when they were not fixating the lead car, monitoring other potential hazard locations such as parked cars, pedestrians, and side roads. We believe that this represents a schema developed by pursuit drivers that assigns priorities to secondary sources of hazard.

The final category in Table 15.1 refers to the *strategic* use of information that must be sought out and incorporated into a relatively long-term plan. Temporal distinctions between tactical and strategic plans are, however, hard to quantify. Instead, it might be prudent to distinguish between tactical and strategic information acquisition on the basis of which cognitive processes are involved. The decision to cross a lane of oncoming traffic requires the driver to fixate oncoming traffic in order to judge whether the maneuver can be completed without a collision. This time-to-collision (TTC) calculation is a qualitatively different process from fixating the tangent point when navigating a curve. Strategic use of information is conscious, whereas, in our definition, the tactical use of information is often part of a compiled behavior that the driver may not be fully aware of.

The most obvious example of strategic information acquisition is navigation using road signs. Though road signs may be missed if they are unexpected (Shinoda *et al.* 2001), or ignored if there are more pressing demands (Crundall *et al.* 2005b), they provide a predictable source of information that allow a hierarchy of plans to be constantly updated. Zwahlen *et al.* (2003) have analyzed the eye movements of drivers acquiring information from road signs and found that a diagrammatic guide sign tended to receive two or three fixations. The first fixation was said to reflect the initial acquisition of information and was consistently longer than the last fixation that was said to reflect a confirmation of sign content. Unfortunately, research has rarely gone further than assessing the acquisition and response to information stored in single, or at best repeated, road signs. A comprehensive look at the integration of road sign information within long term plans is necessary.

The calculation of time-to-collision (TTC) is another example of the strategic use of information. For instance, when waiting to turn across the path of oncoming traffic, the driver must make a decision concerning the distance and speed of the oncoming vehicle. Though this process can be temporally similar to many tactical uses of information, a TTC decision requires cognitive processes in-between the input and output, and is available to subsequent introspection. The precise nature of the relevant visual information for this task is still debated (Schrater *et al.* 2001), though again this is a task that can be improved with experience, as drivers learn to relate visual information to their own actions (e.g., Recarte & Nunes 1998).

A LIFETIME OF DRIVING: FROM NEWLY QUALIFIED NOVICE TO AGING DRIVER

As we have seen, novice drivers scan hazardous roads in a curiously maladaptive way, tending to look straight ahead, and not showing any sensitivity to changes in driving conditions. Why should novice drivers fail to scan for hazards such as other vehicles merging with intersecting trajectories on the roads most likely to present them with dangers? The explanations to be considered here suggest that (1) novices need to look at road markers in order to steer the vehicle, because unlike experienced drivers they cannot use peripheral vision to collect information about the relationship of the vehicle to the immediate environment; (2) novices are unable to allocate sufficient cognitive resources to visual search on these roads because they have not yet automatized the subskills required for the co-ordination of the vehicle controls; and (3) novices may *choose* not to look around them because they have an inadequate mental model of the dangers present on these roads – they have incomplete situation awareness (see Durso *et al.*, Chapter 7, this volume; Gugerty 1997; Horswill & McKenna 2004). These three hypotheses are not mutually exclusive, of course. It is possible that the novice has difficulties in maintaining lane position, in thinking about much else than controlling the vehicle so keep it moving at the same speed as the other traffic, and in forming an understanding of what the other road users are doing and what they are likely to do in the near future. As we become more skilled in handling the vehicle, with the automatization of sub-skills, cognitive resources are released and can be allocated to other tasks such as hazard surveillance, and general observation of the traffic for the enrichment of situation awareness. With increasing practice the novice no longer has to concentrate on the position of the gear lever and the coordinated sequence of clutch pedal depression and release when changing gear. More and more they are able to think about the traffic around them while performing this operation apparently without thinking about it. Increased skill is associated with an increase in the capacity for acquiring information about the situation around them. At the same time as they are developing their vehicle handling skills through practice, they gain experience of traffic events that include accidents, near-accidents, and hazardous conjunctions of traffic that further develop their situation awareness by providing knowledge of possible events. When they next encounter similar situations they will have an increased awareness of the potential danger, and will scan the scene more extensively than previously.

The three hypotheses emphasize (1) steering control limitations; (2) vehicle control limitations; and (3) the driver's situation awareness or mental model. The first two hypotheses are closely related, with steering control being a special case of the demands of vehicle control. Mourant and Rockwell (1972) and Summala *et al.* (1996) have demonstrated that novices tend to look at a part of the road closer to the vehicle than do experienced drivers, suggesting that they have not yet learned the use of peripheral vision for steering. If they must look at road markers close to the vehicle, then they will have limited scope for looking at other objects in the roadway. The relationship between steering and gaze has been discussed in some detail above, and here we will consider the alternative hypotheses.

Our second hypothesis sees central cognitive resources being occupied in many aspects of vehicle control, including the maintenance of the vehicle's position relative to other traffic, so that the novice driver does not have the mental resources available for scanning the road scene and acquiring new information about potential hazards. We know that varying the demand of the driving task will cause variations in their acquisition of information, for experienced drivers at least. (It is difficult to envisage conducting a study in which a novice's resources are reduced by a secondary task, while they negotiate difficult traffic.) Recarte and Nunes (2000) and Robinson *et al.* (1972) found that mirror-checking was reduced as the mental load of driving increased. Mirror-checking is a useful measure in determining the cognitive load of driving, because it is not an essential part of vehicle control except when lane-changing, unlike speed and vehicle positioning control. Underwood *et al.* (2002b) have reported that mirror-checking also varied with driving experience, with greater selectivity of the mirror used in experienced drivers during lane-changing maneuvers. Schweigert and Bubb (2001) also reported fewer fixations on mirrors and other non-essential objects as driving demands increase. As the demands of a secondary task increased, drivers compensated by reducing the frequency of glances to their mirror and also by increasing the distance to the car ahead (see also Recarte & Nunes 2000). This evidence is consistent with the view that when driving demands increase, experienced drivers can reallocate their cognitive resources and modify their inspection of the available scene.

Perhaps novices stereotypically look straight ahead when driving because they have inadequate situation awareness. The third hypothesis explains differences in the search patterns of novice and experienced drivers as a product of the knowledge base developed through their previous traffic encounters. As drivers interact with other vehicles and observe the behavior of road users, they accumulate a mental catalogue of events that happen on different kinds of roads, and of their probability of occurring. These situation-specific expectancies in driving or "scripts" can help guide drivers through environments that are new in themselves, but that are sufficiently similar to previously encountered circumstances for them to generalize their behavior. A novice necessarily has an impoverished catalogue by comparison with an experienced driver, built mainly as a walker, cyclist, or passenger. It is possible, therefore, that when novices scan the dual carriageway to a lesser extent than the experienced drivers, they are doing so this because they are unaware of the dangers associated with this particular type of road. They perhaps have insufficient exposure to this kind of road from which to build a mental model of the probable behavior of other vehicles, are unable to predict where other vehicles will be a few seconds later, and do not recognize the demands of inter-weaving lanes of traffic.

Underwood *et al.* (2002a) sought evidence to discriminate between these hypotheses. Novice and experienced drivers have previously inspected different types of roads in different ways, but this may be due to the resources required for vehicle control, or due to differences in their mental models of driving encounters. We tested between the hypotheses by eliminating the need to control a vehicle, and the task was essentially one of observation and prediction. Drivers sat in the laboratory and watched film clips recorded from a car as it traveled along five different roads, including the roads used by Crundall and Underwood (1998), again observing scanning differences between experienced and inexperienced drivers. Their task was to make a key-press response if they saw an event that would cause a driver to take evasive action, and while they watched the films their eye movements were recorded. If novices have restricted search patterns because their resources are allocated to vehicle control, then eliminating this component of the driving task should have resulted in visual search patterns in the laboratory equivalent to those of experienced drivers. However, if their search patterns result from a mental model that does not inform them of the particular hazards associated with dual carriageways, then they should continue to restrict the extent of their searches while watching recordings of these situations in a non-interactive, view-only task. The results indicated that the two groups of drivers were thinking about the scene differently, even though their resources were not occupied by the demands of vehicle control.

Our use of a laboratory task in which drivers watch film-clips is some distance from an actual driving task, and its validity can be questioned as a measure of driving ability. The purpose, however, was not to assess driving performance but to observe how novice drivers scan a road scene when they do not have to control the vehicle. The task indicated differences between novice and experienced drivers that support the hypothesis that their inspection of the roadway is limited not because they have limited mental resources residual from the task of vehicle control, but have an impoverished mental model of what is likely to happen. Their mental model will develop as they encounter these kinds of roads and gain experience of vehicles changing lanes in their proximity, but it also possible that they could be made more aware of the problems associated with these roads through training targeted at the need to search for potential hazards. Chapman *et al.* (2002) have demonstrated the effective use of hazard-awareness training with novices. As drivers acquire experience they inspect the roadway differently, and at the same time their accident liability decreases. Some very experienced drivers are not at reduced risk, of course – elderly drivers may have many years' and many miles' experience, and in a recent study we observed their scanning behavior while they watched the same kinds of film clips as we have just described (Underwood *et al.* 2005).

The Aging Driver

Driving experience results in extensive changes in the intake of information from the roadway and in vehicle control. These changes are reflected in reduced accident liability.

What happens as we get older and acquire extensive driving experience is that we also suffer increased liability to cognitive and visual impairment. Older drivers are aware of the impact of these problems and compensate by changing their driving habits – not driving at night or in heavy traffic, for instance. Do elderly drivers also change their intake of information with changed scanning behavior? A difficulty in investigating the relationship between age and scanning patterns is that the contributions of possible impairments must be determined and excluded. For example, studies of visual impairment in older adults have established that age is often associated with the prevalence of reduced acuity and light sensitivity, as well as increased incidence of deficits such as cataracts and macular degeneration (e.g., Weale 1992; Klein *et al.* 1995, 1996; Klaver *et al.* 1998; van der Pols *et al.* 2000). Visual impairment has a consequence for driving ability, with accident risk increased by the prevalence of cataracts, visual attentional disorder (Owsley *et al.* 1991; Owsley *et al.* 2001), and weak relationships have sometimes been reported between road traffic accident risk and poor acuity (Hofstetter 1976; Slade *et al.* 2002). Older drivers have an increasing accident liability as a direct consequence of this increasing liability to visual impairment (Wood & Troutbeck 1994; Wood 1999). In addition, increasing age is associated with an increasing risk of neurological damage and cognitive impairments that can have consequences for driving ability (e.g., Nouri & Lincoln 1993; McKenna *et al.* 2004). Many studies have compared impaired patients with age-matched controls, with declining driving skills in evidence. For example, in a longitudinal study of on-road driving skills, Duchek *et al.* (2003) found decrements in older adults in general and especially for early-stage Alzheimer's patients. Decrements were observed over a two-year period. A driving instructor made assessments during a 45-minute road test in traffic along a predetermined route, scoring the drivers for their ability to maintain a set speed, correctly signal, change lanes, react to other drivers, etc., with all drivers showing declining ability over time. In a comparison of younger, unimpaired older, and impaired older drivers, Wood (1999) found differences between all three groups, with visual impairments being associated with poor sign detection and slower on-road driving on a closed test track. Older drivers have more visual and cognitive problems than younger experienced drivers, and these problems are associated with increased crash risk.

Research has given more emphasis to investigations of the abilities of elderly drivers with known impairments than to those who are old but who do not have clinical deficits. Laboratory studies have also indicated an age-related decrement in driving skills in unimpaired individuals. Andersen *et al.* (2000), for example, found an age-related decrement in the judgment of screen-displayed collisions, especially at higher speeds. The comparison in that study was between younger and older drivers who had comparable acuity. In contrast, Ball and Owsley (2003) argued that in the absence of disease or functional impairment there is no evidence of adverse effects of aging upon driving ability. Using a different approach comparing older and younger drivers, Hakamies-Blomqvist *et al.* (2002) also concluded that when distance driven was matched, there was no difference between the old and the young in their accident rates per mile driven.

A reduction in the "useful field of view" of older drivers might be expected to result in changes in the ways that drivers scan the roadway. Ball and Owsley and their colleagues have argued that the Useful Field of View (UFOV) test is an effective way of predicting "unsafe" drivers (e.g., Ball & Owsley 1991; Owsley *et al.* 1991, 2001; Ball *et al.* 1988). The UFOV test requires the detection of target objects that are shown above threshold but very briefly. Three subtests assess processing speed, divided attention, and selective attention, with a composite score indicating the reduction in the functional field of view. The useful field of view is defined in these studies as the area of the visual field over which we can use briefly presented information, and the UFOV test is claimed to provide a measure of pre-attentive processes in the detection of peripheral targets. This differs from the field of view determined by visual perimetry in that it also relies on the cognitive abilities necessary for the deployment of attention and for rapid information-processing. The UFOV test makes good predictions about the relationship between the size of the visual field and accident liability. For example, there is a strong relationship between UFOV scores and recent road accident history, in the absence of a similar predictive association for visual processing variables such as visual acuity, contrast sensitivity, and disability glare (Owsley *et al.* 1998), and with a 40 per cent reduction of the useful field of view these drivers were more than twice as likely to have experienced a road accident. Independent support for the predictive value of the useful field of view has come from a study with a driving simulator reported by Rog *et al.* (2004). The detection of peripheral signals deteriorated over time on a monotonous driving task, and older drivers were impaired relative to young drivers. Changes in the size of the useful field of view are also prompted by the occurrence of hazards. Crundall *et al.* (1999, 2002) found that the detection of peripheral targets by drivers watching film clips varied according to changes in the current demand, with reduced detection when the driver's attention was focused on the hazard. Changes to the size and shape of the useful field of view could be expected to prompt changes in scanning behavior while driving or watching films depicting driving situations such as the hazard clips, and this prediction prompted the Underwood *et al.* (2005) study.

Scanning and Hazard Detection by Older Drivers

Underwood *et al.* (2005) recorded the eye fixations of younger and older drivers with no impairment, while they watched sequences of events filmed from a moving vehicle traveling along a range of roadways. The film clips occasionally showed driving hazards such as pedestrians walking into the pathway of the recording vehicle, or the appearance of a slow-moving road user such as a cyclist who would require evasive steering on the part of the driver of the recording vehicle. The investigation employed the hazard detection task used in our previous studies, and that gives an indication of a vitally important driving skill that is now part of the driver licensing test in the UK and elsewhere. Of particular interest were fixation patterns made during the hazardous events – events that would cause the driver of a vehicle to brake or change direction in order to avoid a collision.

All drivers are sensitive to hazardous situations and respond by rapidly redirecting their gaze in the direction of the hazardous road user. Older drivers were no different in the Underwood *et al.* (2005) study, and when hazards appeared, then whatever they had been looking at, they moved their eyes to the hazardous object – the pedestrian stepping into the roadway or the cyclist who was causing the vehicle to brake. Their scan paths resembled those of the experienced drivers who were 30 years younger, but an interesting difference did emerge in the reporting of hazards. When an event occurred that would require evasive action the laboratory participants pressed a response key, and there were no differences in response time or in the numbers of hazards correctly detected. The similarity of scan paths, the efficacy of a hazard in capturing attention, and the reaction to hazard onset were similar for our younger and older drivers, suggesting that there is no age-related decrement in drivers with no visual or cognitive impairment. However, the older drivers made a large number of false positives, pressing the response key when no evasive action was demanded. There are a number of possible explanations of this difference between younger and older drivers. Perhaps we get more cautious as we get older and see danger where none exists, or perhaps older drivers have richer mental models with more experiences of hazardous situations encoded within them from actual driving events. If older drivers have memories of a large number of dangerous situations encountered during their driving careers, then situations that would look innocuous to a less experienced driver may remind them of a an event in their past that did develop perilously and perhaps even resulted in an accident. The relationship between our driving experiences and our memories of driving events will now be discussed in more detail.

MEMORY PROCESSES IN DRIVING

There are two ways to think about memory processes in driving. One is to focus on the role of short-term memory in allowing drivers to attend to and combine multiple sources of transient information. Such an approach focuses on using theories such as Baddeley's (1986, 2003) model of working memory, or Wickens' multiple-resource theory (e.g., 1980) to predict the optimal modalities and timing for the presentation of information to the driver. Groeger (2000) provides a good review of such an approach, including speculation as the approximate brain regions involved in different aspects of working memory as applied to driving. The other aspect of memory processes in driving, and one that is more intuitive for the non-psychologist, is to explore longer-term memory for driving events: what does the driver actually remember of the driving experience? Clearly, much of the low-level details of car control is unlikely to be remembered, perhaps because these components of driving only receive controlled attentional resources in the very earliest stages of learning to drive. Indeed, such aspects are often thought of as textbook examples of automatic activities (e.g., Shiffrin & Schneider 1977; Schneider *et al.* 1984; though see Duncan *et al.* 1992; Groeger & Clegg 1998). One of common distinctions between automatic and controlled activities is given by Shiffrin (1997) as memory effects and although it is not possible to precisely equate explicit memory with controlled processes (Shiffrin 1997; Jacoby *et al.* 1997), most people would expect to have some explicit memory for most of their more complex actions and experiences during driving.

There are many reasons to think that it is important to remember events that we experience while driving. From a research perspective, road safety researchers very commonly rely on drivers' self-reports of their own behaviors, the kinds of events they experience while driving, and their own accident and near-accident records (Chapman & Underwood 2000; but see also Wright 1997). In measures of situation awareness during driving participants are often required to recall the locations of cars within simulated scenarios (e.g., Gugerty 1997), and failures of recall are interpreted as failures of situation awareness rather than failures of memory. More practically, many everyday driving decisions depend on memory for recently experienced information (e.g., the last speed limit sign passed, direction, distance, and warning signs), and on information that has been gained from previous drives (e.g., locations of congestion, road works, etc.). Such memory becomes particularly important in safety-critical situations where the driver may have the opportunity to remember potential sources of danger. These memories may be specific to individual locations, such as hidden side roads or deceptive bends, or may be more generic, for example, memory for the kinds of situations or behaviors that have resulted in previous accidents or near-accidents. Another situation where memory for events is particularly important is in the courtroom. It has frequently been noted that eyewitness testimony is one of the most powerful sources of evidence in the trials (e.g., Ainsworth 1998), and the confidence of an eyewitness in their memory is one of the most critical factors in determining the weight that jurors will give to evidence (Cutler & Penrod 1995). Those involved in road traffic accidents are often required to give insurance statements or even testimony in court about the events leading up to an accident. The assumption is frequently made that such memory should be complete and accurate, and any inaccuracies or omissions in descriptions may be treated as deliberate attempts at deception. It is thus of great importance to understand what drivers' memories are actually like for typical driving situations, and the factors which may enhance or impair drivers' memories. This is particularly important given that much of the available evidence suggests that drivers may have extremely poor memory for what they have experienced.

Driving without Memory

One of the most compelling reasons to suspect that drivers' memories may be fallible is the "time-gap" experience (e.g., Chapman *et al.* 1999a, *1999*b). Reed (1972) gives the following description of such experiences:

> After a long drive the motorist will quite commonly report that at some point in the journey he "woke up" to realise that he had no awareness of some preceding period of time. People often describe this, with some justification, as a "gap in time", "a lost half-hour" or "a piece out of my life". The strangeness of the experience springs partly from "waking up" when one is already awake. But mainly it is due to the knowledge of a blank in one's temporal awareness. (Reed 1972, p. 18)

Phrases such as "highway hypnosis" (Brown 1991) and "driving without attention mode" (Kerr 1991) have been used to describe the phenomenon; however, the actual experience is one of a memory failure and does not necessarily imply any failure of attention. Clearly, there will be cases where such reports are directly related to driver sleepiness (e.g., Horne & Reyner 1995); however, the missing experience is often of sufficient duration and complexity to suggest that this is unlikely to be a sufficient explanation for the majority of reports. Chapman *et al.* (1999a) reported that around 90 per cent or respondents in questionnaire studies admit to experiencing such memory failures, in a microcassette recorder diary study they go on to explore the frequency and nature of such experiences in a sample of 33 regular drivers. During the course of the study, participants reported 172 separate instances of time-gaps while driving, ranging from as little as five seconds up to as much as an estimated 25 minutes. Such experiences were generally terminated by the requirement for relatively complex driving (e.g., the arrival at a particular junction) though on 5 per cent of occasions the time-gap was only terminated by the driver arriving at the wrong location. From a practical perspective such experiences may be important as predictors of accident involvement – Chapman *et al.* found a significant correlation between the frequency of report for time-gaps and for near-accidents even after confounding variables had been excluded. From a theoretical perspective they give us strong reason to believe that our memory for much of our everyday driving may be extremely poor. Unfortunately, the unpredictable nature of time-gaps makes direct memory tests from such periods difficult to achieve; however, one area where direct memory testing after everyday driving has been attempted is in exploring drivers' memory for road signs.

A pioneering series of studies was carried out in Sweden by Johansson and colleagues (Johansson & Rumar 1966; Johansson & Backlund 1970) using a paradigm in which a police roadblock was set up and drivers were questioned about the last road sign they had passed. There has been relatively good agreement among these studies and others using similar paradigms (e.g., Hakkinen 1965; Shinar & Drory 1983) on the relatively low incidence of accurate memory. A typical result from the roadblock paradigm is that approximately half the drivers can accurately recall the last sign passed. Recall performance in these studies has been found to vary systematically with the type of sign used, being best for speed limits and worst for relatively rare warning signs. In some cases as few as 2 per cent of drivers have been found to be able to recall the last road sign they had passed (e.g., the bumpy road sign tested by Milosevic and Gajic 1986). While this paradigm is frequently criticized because of the delay between passing the sign and testing, and because of the possible interfering effects of being stopped by the police, studies using a variety of other techniques have found similarly low levels of recall for many signs (Luoma 1986, 1988, 1991; Macdonald & Hoffmann 1991; Fisher 1992). One important thing to note about such studies is that levels of appropriate response to such signs are often much higher than levels of correct recall (Summala and Hietamaki 1984; see also Crundall & Underwood 2001), for potential priming effects of road signs, and comparison of implicit and explicit measures of situation awareness (Gugerty 1997). This supports the idea given by the time-gap literature that even relatively complex driving situations and appropriate driving actions may frequently be wholly forgotten by the driver soon after the event. If the underlying reason for such failures is simply that nothing of note has occurred during these periods of driving, then this may be of little consequence, but if it is possible that more serious events such as hazardous situations or actual accidents could be forgotten, then the implications are of great concern.

Heightened Awareness and Memory in Dangerous Situations

One simple prediction would be that memory for dangerous situations would generally be much better than that for more mundane everyday driving. Chapman and Groeger (2004) set out to explore this prediction by having drivers view and rate a series of films of everyday driving situations differing in the level of risk present. After viewing the films, the drivers were given a surprise recognition memory test in which they were required to identify the previously viewed sections from among a series of similar films. Contrary to the prediction, no simple relationship between risk and recognition performance was observed. Instead, subjective risk appeared to improve memory in generally dangerous situations, but impair memory for generally safer situations. A detailed exploration of these results caused Chapman and Groeger (2004) to conclude that memory was not improved overall in risky situations, but did appear to focus on different aspects of the scene. A particular suggestion is that in dangerous situations drivers may have enhanced memory for central information at the expense of memory for peripheral information. This idea is consistent with the changes in UFOV discussed earlier, and with the idea of "weapon focus" in eyewitness testimony (e.g., Loftus 1979), in which the victim of a violent crime might report extremely good memory for the weapon being wielded, but no memory for the assailant's face. The simplest explanation for weapon focus effect in memory is that it reflects the pattern of attention at the time of the event. If a victim never looked at their assailant's face it is perhaps unsurprising that they will have poor memory for this later. In the case of driving, we have already reviewed evidence relating to UFOV and describing the typical patterns of eye movements in safer and more dangerous situations. Chapman and Underwood (1998a) found relatively little evidence for any simple focus on centrally spatial information in dangerous situations, but did find that such situations reduced the spread of search, increased individual fixation durations, and reduced saccade distances. Moreover, they found that such focusing effects were particularly pronounced for novice drivers.

The direct relationship between eye movements and memory in driving situations was explored in a study by Underwood *et al.* (2003b). In that study novices or experienced drivers viewed film clips of driving scenes as described by Chapman and Underwood (1998a, 1998b) and also used in studies described above, but the film was frequently stopped and the drivers were required to answer questions about items that had been on the screen either centrally or peripherally. Each test item was scored as to whether it had been fixated prior the question being asked. Around 75 per cent of spatially central items and 50 per cent of peripheral items were fixated and these proportions were roughly the same whatever the experience level of the drivers. In turn, approximately 80 per cent of questions relating to central items were answered correctly, compared with 60 per cent of questions about peripheral items, though in this case there was a group difference, with experienced drivers answering significantly more questions about peripheral items correctly than novice drivers did.

Some participants in the study fixated virtually all the central items, and generally went on to remember them correctly. However, when these high-performing participants were removed from the analysis it was possible to conduct a systematic analysis of how memory for items depended on having fixated them. In these cases correct recall for fixated objects was at 51 per cent, while correct recall for unfixated objects was dramatically poorer at 21 per cent. These effects interacted with whether items appeared centrally or peripherally such that for fixated objects performance was better for central than peripheral items (65 per cent vs. 37 per cent) while for unfixated objects performance was extremely poor for both central and peripheral items (18 per cent and 23 per cent respectively). Thus there was a clear advantage for central information over peripheral information in both fixation data and in recall data. In both cases this advantage was more marked in films showing hazardous driving situations than those showing normal ones. For non-fixated information, memory was generally extremely poor, but was actually better in normal situations than hazardous ones. When information had been fixated, memory was actually better in hazardous situations, but only when it was central. The greater probability of fixation and enhanced memory for central information in hazardous situations is consistent with the recognition results from Chapman and Groeger (2004), while the lower probability of remembering unfixated items in dangerous situations is consistent with the idea of attention narrowing in such situations.

Longer-Term Memory for Driving Events

When drivers are asked to remember and date the accidents that they have been involved in, a surprising pattern emerges. If a large number of such reports are aggregated by the date drivers provide for the accidents, the largest number of accidents occurs in the previous year. The number of accidents reported from previous years reduces steadily the longer ago the time period being considered is. This result remains even when the amount of driving being done by the sample in each of the years is taken into account. Of course, we know from actual accident statistics that younger, less experienced drivers are more likely to be involved in accidents. If accident reports and dates were accurate, we would thus expect the number of self-reported accidents to be higher rather than lower in more distant time periods. The simplest explanation for such findings is that drivers routinely forget their own road accidents at a rate that can be estimated to be approximately one third per year (Maycock *et al.* 1996). Even limiting the analysis to injury accidents leaves a forgetting rate that has been estimated as 18 per cent per annum. This is a surprising suggestion, but it is one that is consistent with reports from the more general memory literature showing that 14 per cent of people involved in an injury-provoking road accident did not remember it a year later, and over 25 per cent of people discharged from a hospital failed to report the event a year later (Loftus 1993).

When less serious events such as near-accidents are considered, the rate of forgetting may be much faster. Chapman and Underwood (2000) asked 80 regular drivers to keep a micro-cassette recorder in their car and report a selection of driving events including accidents and near-accidents after each journey. When these reports were compared to a separate laboratory-based delayed memory interview with the same drivers a dramatic difference was observed. Estimates of mileages and numbers of journeys were roughly consistent whether they came from the in-car reporting condition or the delayed recall condition; however, estimates for the number of near-accidents were dramatically different. A total of 382 events were described as near-accidents from the in-car condition, while only 69 were described from a matched time period when delayed recall was required. Thus over 80 per cent of drivers' near-accidents appear to be routinely forgotten over a delay which in this case was always less than two weeks. Analysis of the pattern of near-accident types in the two conditions allowed Chapman and Underwood to conclude that the most likely events to be forgotten were those where there was little actual danger of an accident, and for which the driver did not feel to blame. More serious near-accidents and those where the driver admitted that they were completely to blame for the event were notably less likely to be forgotten, but still produced implied forgetting rates of over 50 per cent. The fact that drivers were less likely to forget accidents for which they felt to blame may be a comforting example of an adaptive rather than self-serving memory bias. It might have been predicted that drivers would over-report cases where they felt another driver was in the wrong, either to bolster self-esteem, or as a function of a misperception of blame at the time of the incident. Indeed, drivers in the immediate report condition did describe around 180 incidents for which they were definitely not to blame, and less than 80 for which they admitted full blame. However, the same drivers were later more likely to remember their full blame near-accidents than their blame-free ones, suggesting that they may actually have the adaptive ability to selectively learn from their mistakes.

The findings from a variety of types of study of drivers' memory seem to be remarkably consistent. Long-term memory for driving events is strikingly poor. In some cases this absence of memory is so dramatic as to be actually noted by the driver as a specific time-gap experience, in other cases it emerges only incidentally as a memory correction factor that is required when looking at self-reported accident rates (e.g., Maycock *et al.* 1996). Memory performance is slightly better when we know that the driver did actually look at the item for which their memory is being tested, but there is still clear evidence for memory failures in these cases, and suggestions from work on traffic signs that even signs which elicited the correct behavioral response from the driver in terms of speed modification have been routinely forgotten moments later. It is tempting to conclude that the poor memory for such events is because of their mundane and repetitious nature. However, memory for more dangerous events, near-accidents, and actual driving accidents is also generally poor. Simple increases in risk do not appear to improve people's memory for driving situations, though dangerous events may elicit slightly better memory performance, coupled with a focus in memory on central information and a corresponding impairment in memory for peripheral information. Further increases in danger do render events less likely to be forgotten, but not to the point where memory is perfect. Even actual road accidents involving injury to one of the participants appear to be routinely forgotten at surprisingly high rates.

CONCLUSIONS

The transition from novice, through experienced driver to aging driver is accompanied by a number of changes in behavior. The intake of information from the environment is initially stereotyped and focused more on control of the vehicle's position than with more experienced drivers. Skill acquisition is associated with the development of richer situation awareness, and even when not in control of a vehicle, novice drivers fail to inspect a displayed roadway as extensively as they will when they are more experienced. Elderly drivers continue to inspect the roadway and detect hazards effectively, even though they are more cautious in declaring what is a hazardous situation. This again may be a product of an extensive driving history resulting in a richer catalogue of memories of hazardous experiences.

REFERENCES

Ainsworth, P. B. (1998). *Psychology, Law and Eyewitness Testimony*. Chichester: John Wiley & Sons.

Andersen, G. J., Cisneros, J., Saidpour, A. & Atchley, P. (2000). Age-related differences in collision detection during deceleration. *Psychology and Aging*, *15*, 241–252.

Baddeley, A. D. (1986). *Working Memory*. Oxford: Oxford University Press.

Baddeley, A. D. (2003). Working memory: looking back and looking forward. *Nature Reviews Neuroscience*, *4*, 829–839.

Ball, K. K., Beard, B., Roenker, D. L. *et al.* (1988). Age and visual search: expanding the useful field of view. *Journal of the Optical Society of America A*, *5*, 2210–2219.

Ball, K. K. & Owsley, C. (1991). Identifying correlates of accident involvement for the older driver. *Human Factors*, *33*, 583–595.

Ball, K. K. & Owsley, C. (2003). Driving competence: it's not a matter of age. *Journal of the American Geriatrics Society*, *51*, 1499–1501.

Ball, K. K., Owsley, C., Stalvey, B. T. *et al.* (1998). Driving avoidance and functional impairment in older drivers. *Accident Analysis and Prevention*, *30*, 313–322.

Brackstone, M. & Waterson, B. (2004). Are we looking where we are going? An exploratory examination of eye movement in high speed driving. In *Proceedings of the 83rd Transportation Research Board Annual Meeting* (Paper 04-2602, CD-ROM). Washington, DC: Transport Research Board.

Briem, V. & Hedman, L. R. (1995). Behavioural effects of mobile telephone use during simulated driving. *Ergonomics*, *38*, 2536–2562.

Brookhuis, K., De Vries, G. & De Waard, D. (1991). The effects of mobile telephoning on driving performance. *Accident Analysis and Prevention*, *23*, 309–316.

Brown, I. D. (1991). Highway hypnosis: implications for road safety researchers and practitioners. In A. G. Gale *et al.* (eds.), *Vision in Vehicles III*. Amsterdam: Elsevier.

Brown, I. D., Tickner, A. H. & Simmonds, D. C. V. (1969). Interference between concurrent tasks of driving and telephoning. *Journal of Applied Psychology*, *53*, 419–424.

Chapman, P. & Groeger, J. A. (2004). Risk and the recognition of driving situations. *Applied Cognitive Psychology*, *18*, 1231–1249.

Chapman, P., Ismail, R., Avellano, T. & Underwood, G. (1999a). Time gaps while driving. In G. B. Grayson (ed.), *Behavioural Research in Road Safety IX*. Crowthorne: Transport Research Laboratory.

Chapman, P., Ismail, R. & Underwood, G. (1999b). Waking up at the wheel: accidents, attention and the time-gap experience. In A. G. Gale *et al.* (eds.), *Vision in Vehicles VII*. Amsterdam: Elsevier.

Chapman, P. & Underwood, G. (1998a). Visual search of driving situations: danger and experience. *Perception*, *27*, 951–964.

Chapman, P. & Underwood, G. (1998b). Visual search of dynamic scenes: event types and the role of experience in viewing driving situations. In G. Underwood (ed.), *Eye Guidance in Reading and Scene Perception* (pp. 371–396). Oxford: Elsevier.

Chapman, P. & Underwood, G. (2000). Forgetting near-accidents: the roles of severity, culpability and experience in the poor recall of dangerous driving situations. *Applied Cognitive Psychology*, *14*, 31–44.

Chapman, P., Underwood, G. & Roberts, K. (2002). Visual search patterns in trained and untrained novice drivers. *Transportation Research F: Psychology and Behaviour*, *5*, 157–167.

Crundall, D. (2005). The integration of top-down and bottom-up factors in visual search during driving. In G. Underwood (ed.), *Cognitive Processes in Eye Guidance*. Oxford: Oxford University Press.

Crundall, D., Bains, M., Chapman, P. & Underwood, G. (2005a). Regulating conversation during driving: a problem for mobile telephones? *Transportation Research Part F*, *8*, 197–211.

Crundall, D., Chapman, P., France, E., Underwood, G. & Phelps, N. (2005b). What attracts attention during police pursuit driving? *Applied Cognitive Psychology*, *19*, 409–420.

Crundall, D., Chapman, P., Phelps, N. & Underwood, G. (2003). Eye movements and hazard perception in police pursuit and emergency response driving. *Journal of Experimental Psychology: Applied*, *9*, 163–174.

Crundall, D. & Underwood, G. (1998).The effects of experience and processing demands on visual information acquisition in drivers. *Ergonomics*, *41*, 448–458.

Crundall, D. & Underwood, G. (2001). The priming function of road signs. *Transportation Research Part F*, *4*, 187–200.

Crundall, D., Underwood, G. & Chapman, P. (1999). Driving experience and the functional field of view. *Perception*, *28*, 1075–1087.

Crundall, D., Underwood, G. & Chapman, P. (2002). Attending to the peripheral world while driving. *Applied Cognitive Psychology*, *16*, 459–475.

Cutler, B. L. & Penrod, S. D. (1995). *Mistaken Identification: The Eyewitness, Psychology, and the Law.* Cambridge: Cambridge University Press.

Donges, E. (1978). A two-level model of driver steering behavior. *Human Factors, 20*, 691–707.

Duchek, J. M., Carr, D. B., Hunt, L. *et al.* (2003). Longitudinal driving performance in early-stage dementia of the Alzheimer type. *Journal of the American Geriatrics Society, 51*, 1342–1347.

Duncan, J. D., Williams, P., Nimmo-Smith, I. & Brown, I. D. (1992). The control of skilled behavior: learning, intelligence and distraction. In D. E. Meyer & S. Kornblum (eds.), *Attention and Performance XIV.* Cambridge, MA: MIT Press.

Evans, L. (1991). *Traffic Safety and the Driver.* New York: Van Nostrand Reinhold.

Fairclough, S. H., Ashby, M. C., Ross, T. & Parkes, A. M. (1991). Effects of hands free telephone use on driving behaviour. In: *Proceedings of the ISATA Conference.* Florence, Italy.

Falkmer, T. & Gregersen, N. P. (2001). Fixation patterns of learner drivers with and without cerebral palsy (CP) when driving in real traffic environments. *Transportation Research F, 4*, 171–185.

Fisher, D. L., Pradhan, A. K., Hammel, K. R. *et al.* (2003). Are younger drivers less able than older drivers to recognize risks on the road? *Injury Insights,* February/March, *1*, 2–7.

Fisher, J. (1992). Testing the effect of road traffic signs' informational value on driver behavior. *Human Factors, 34*, 231–237.

Garcia-Larrea, L., Perchet, C., Perrin, F. & Amenedo, E. (2001). Interference of cellular phone conversations with visuomotor tasks: an ERP study. *Journal of Psychophysiology, 15*, 14–21.

Goodman, M. J., Bents, F., Tijerina, L. & Wierwille, W. W. (1999). Using cellular telephones in vehicles: safe or unsafe? *Transportation and Human Factors, 1*, 3–42.

Green, P. (2002). Where do drivers look while driving (and for how long)? In R. E. Dewar & P. L. Olson (eds.), *Human Factors in Traffic Safety* (pp. 77–110). Tucson, AZ: Lawyers and Judges Publishing.

Groeger, J. A. (2000). *Understanding Driving: Applying Cognitive Psychology to a Complex Everyday Task.* Hove: Psychology Press.

Groeger, J. A. & Clegg, B. A. (1998). Automaticity and driving: time to change gear conceptually In J. A. Rothengatter & E. Carbonell Vaya (eds.), *Traffic and Transport Psychology: Theory and Application* (pp.137–146). Amsterdam: Elsevier.

Gugerty, L. (1997). Situation awareness during driving: explicit and implicit knowledge in dynamic spatial memory. *Journal of Experimental Psychology: Applied, 3*, 42–66.

Gugerty, L., Rakauskas, M. & Brooks, J. (2004). Effects of remote and in-person verbal interactions on verbalization rates and attention to dynamic spatial scenes. *Accident Analysis and Prevention, 36*, 1029–1043.

Haigney, D., Taylor, R. G. & Westerman, S. J. (2000). Concurrent mobile (cellular) phone use and driving performance: task demand characteristics and compensatory processes. *Transportation Research Part F, 3*, 113–121.

Hakamies-Blomqvist, L., Raitanen, T. & O'Neill, D. (2002). Driver aging does not cause higher accident rates per km. *Transportation Research Part F: Traffic Psychology and Behaviour, 5*, 271–274.

Hakkinen, S. (1965). *Perception of Highway Traffic Signs.* Reports from Talja, the Central Organization for Traffic Safety in Finland, 1.

Hancock, P. A., Lesch, M. & Simmons, L. (2003). The distraction effects of phone use during a crucial driving manoeuvre. *Accident Analysis and Prevention, 35*, 501–514.

Hofstetter, H. W. (1976). Visual acuity and highway accidents. *Journal of the American Optometric Association, 47*, 887–893.

Horne, J. A. & Reyner, L. A. (1995). *Falling Asleep at the Wheel* (TRL Report 168). Crowthorne: Transport Research Laboratory.

Horswill, M. S. & McKenna, F. P. (2004). Drivers' hazard perception ability: situation awareness on the road. In S. Banbury & S. Tremblay (eds.), *A Cognitive Approach to Situation Awareness.* Aldershot: Ashgate.

Hughes, P. K. & Cole, B. L. (1986). What attracts attention when driving? *Ergonomics, 29*, 377–391.

Irwin, M., Fitzgerald, C. & Berg, W. (2000). Effect of the intensity of wireless telephone conversation on reaction time in a braking response. *Perceptual and Motor Skills*, *90*, 1130–1134.

Jacoby, L. L., Yonelinas, A. P. & Jennings, J. M. (1997). The relation between conscious and unconscious (automatic) influences: a declaration of independence. In J. D. Cohen & J. W. Schooler (eds.), *Scientific Approaches to Consciousness*. Mahwah, NJ: Lawrence Erlbaum Associates.

Johansson, G. & Backlund, F. (1970). Drivers and road signs. *Ergonomics*, *13*, 749–759.

Johansson, G. & Rumar, K. (1966). Drivers and road signs: a preliminary investigation of the capacity of car drivers to get information from road signs. *Ergonomics*, *9*, 57–62.

Kames, A. J. (1978). A study of the effects of mobile telephone use and control using design on driving performance. *IEEE Transactions on Vehicular Technology, VT-27*, 282–287.

Kerr, J. S. (1991). Driving without attention mode (DWAM): a formalisation of inattentive states while driving. In A. G. Gale *et al.* (eds.), *Vision in Vehicles III*. Amsterdam: Elsevier.

Klaver, C. C. W., Wolfs, R. C. W., Vingerling, J. R. *et al.* (1998). Age-specific prevalence and causes of blindness and visual impairment in an older population: the Rotterdam Study. *Archives of Ophthalmology*, *116*, 653–658.

Klein, R., Klein, B. E. & Lee, K. P. (1996). Changes in visual acuity in a population: the Beaver Dam Eye Study. *Ophthalmology*, *103*, 1169–1178.

Klein, R., Wang, Q., Klein, B. E. *et al.* (1995). The relationship of age-related maculopathy, cataract, and glaucoma to visual acuity. *Investigative Ophthalmology and Visual Science*, *36*, 182–191.

Lamble, D., Kauranen, T., Laakso, M. & Summala, H. (1999). Cognitive load and detection thresholds in car following situations: safety implications for using mobile (cellular) telephones while driving. *Accident Analysis and Prevention*, *31*, 617–623.

Land, M. F. (1998). The visual control of steering. In L. R. Harris & M. Jenkin (eds.), *Vision and Action* (pp. 163–180). Cambridge: Cambridge University Press.

Land, M. F. & Horwood, J. (1995). Which parts of the road guide steering? *Nature*, *377*, 339–340.

Land, M. F. & Lee, D. N. (1994). Which parts of the road guide steering? *Nature*, *369*, 742–744.

Land, M. F. & Tatler, B. W. (2001). Steering with the head: the visual strategy of a racing driver. *Current Biology*, *11*, 1215–1220.

Lansdown, T. C., Parkes, A. M., Fowkes, M. & Comte, S. (1999). Visual allocation of expert and novice drivers. In A. Gale *et al.* (eds.), *Vision in Vehicles VII* (pp. 393–402), Amsterdam: Elsevier.

Liu, A. (1998). What the driver's eye tells the car's brain. In G. Underwood (ed.), *Eye Guidance in Reading and Scene Perception*. Oxford: Elsevier.

Loftus, E. F. (1979). *Eyewitness Testimony*. Cambridge, MA: Harvard University Press.

Loftus, E. F. (1993). The reality of repressed memory. *American Psychologist*, *48*, 518–537.

Luoma, J. (1986). *The Acquisition of Visual Information by the Driver: Interaction of Relevant and Irrelevant Information* (Reports from Liikenneturva 32/1986). Helsinki: Liikenneturva – Central Organization for Traffic Safety.

Luoma, J. (1988). Drivers' eye fixations and perceptions. In A. G. Gale *et al.* (eds.), *Vision in Vehicles II*. Amsterdam: Elsevier.

Luoma, J. (1991). Perception of highway traffic signs: interaction of eye fixations, recalls and reactions. In A. G. Gale *et al.* (eds.), *Vision in Vehicles III*. Amsterdam: Elsevier.

Macdonald, W. A. & Hoffmann, E. R. (1991). Drivers' awareness of traffic sign information. *Ergonomics*, *34*, 585–612.

McKenna, F. P. & Crick, J. L. (1994). *Hazard Perception in Drivers: A Methodology for Testing and Training* (Transport Research Laboratory Report, 313). Crowthorne: Transport Research Laboratory.

McKenna, P., Jefferies, L., Dobson, A. & Frude, N. (2004). The use of a cognitive battery to predict who will fail an on-road driving test. *British Journal of Clinical Psychology*, *43*, 325–336.

McKnight, A. J. & McKnight, A. S. (1993). The effect of cellular phone use upon driver attention. *Accident Analysis and Prevention*, *25*, 259–265.

Maycock, G., Lester, J. & Lockwood, C. R. (1996). *The Accident Liability of Car Drivers: The Reliability of Self Report Data* (TRL Report 219). Crowthorne: Transport Research Laboratory.

Milosevic, S. & Gajic, R. (1986). Presentation factors and driver characteristics affecting road-sign registration. *Ergonomics*, *29*, 807–815.
Mourant, R. R. & Rockwell, T. H. (1972). Strategies of visual search by novice and experienced drivers. *Human Factors*, *14*, 325–335.
Mourant, R. R., Rockwell, T. H. & Rackoff, N. J. (1969). Drivers' eye movements and visual workload. *Highway Research Record*, *292*, 1–10.
Nouri, F. M. & Lincoln, N. B. (1993). Predicting driving performance after stroke. *British Medical Journal*, *307*, 482–483.
Owsley, C., Ball, K., McGwin, G. *et al.*(1998). Visual processing impairment and risk of motor vehicle crash among older adults. *Journal of the American Medical Association*, *279*, 1083–1088.
Owsley, C., Ball, K., Sloane, M. E. *et al.* (1991). Visual/cognitive correlates of vehicle accidents in older drivers. *Psychology and Aging*, *6*, 403–415.
Owsley, C., Stalvey, B. T., Wells, J. *et al.* (2001). Visual risk factors for crash involvement in older drivers with cataract. *Archives of Ophthalmology*, *119*, 881–887.
Parkes, A. M. (1991). Drivers' business decision making ability whilst using carphones. In E. Lovessey (ed.), *Contemporary Ergonomics: Proceedings of the Ergonomic Society Annual Conference* (pp. 427–432). London: Taylor and Francis.
Patten, C. J. D., Kircher, A., Östlund, J. & Nilsson, L. (2004). Using mobile telephones: cognitive workload and attention resource allocation. *Accident Analysis and Prevention*, *36*, 341–350.
van der Pols, J. C., Bates, C. J., McGraw, P. V. *et al.* (2000). Visual acuity measurements in a national sample of British elderly people. *British Journal of Ophthalmology*, *84*, 165–170.
Recarte, M. A. & Nunes, L. M. (1998). Effects of distance and speed on time to arrival estimation in an automobile: two classes of time? In A. Gale *et al.* (eds.), *Vision in Vehicles VI*. Amsterdam: Elsevier.
Recarte, M. A. & Nunes, L. M. (2000). Effects of verbal and spatial-imagery tasks on eye fixations while driving. *Journal of Experimental Psychology: Applied*, *6*, 31–43.
Reed, G. (1972). *The Psychology of Anomalous Experience*. London: Hutchinson University Library.
Reed, M. P. & Green, P. (1999). Comparison of driving performance on-road and in a low-cost simulator using a concurrent telephone dialling task. *Ergonomics*, *42*, 1015–1037.
Renge, K. (1998). Drivers' hazard and risk perception, confidence in safe driving, and choice of speed. *Journal of the International Association of Traffic and Safety Sciences*, *22*, 103–110.
Robinson, G. H., Erickson, D. J., Thurston, G. L. & Clark, R. L. (1972). Visual search by automobile drivers. *Human Factors*, *14*, 315–323.
Rockwell, T. H. (1988). Spare visual capacity in driving – revisited. In A. Gale *et al.* (eds.), *Vision in Vehicles II* (pp. 317–324). Amsterdam: Elsevier.
Rogé, J., Pébayle, T., Lambilliotte, E. *et al.* (2004). Influence of age, speed and duration of monotonous driving task in traffic on the driver's useful visual field. *Vision Research*, *44*, 2737–2744.
Sagberg, F. (2001). Accident risk of car drivers during telephone use. *International Journal of Vehicle Design*, *26*, 57–59.
Salvucci, D. D. & Liu, A. (2002). The time course of a lane change: driver control and eye-movement behaviour. *Transportation Research Part F*, *5*, 123–132.
Schneider, W., Dumais, S. T. & Shiffrin, R. M. (1984). Automatic and controlled processing and attention. In R. Parasuraman & D. R. Davies (eds.), *Varieties of Attention*. Orlando, FL: Academic Press.
Schrater, P. R., Knill, D. C. & Simoncelli, E. P. (2001). Perceiving visual expansion without optic flow. *Nature*, *410*, 816–819.
Schweigert, M. & Bubb, H. (2001). Eye movements, performance and interference when driving a car and performing secondary tasks. Paper presented at the *Vision in Vehicles 9* conference, Brisbane, August.
Shiffrin, R. M. (1997). Attention, automatism, and consciousness. In J. D. Cohen & J. W. Schooler (eds.), *Scientific Approaches to Consciousness*. Mahwah, NJ: Lawrence Erlbaum Associates.

Shiffrin, R. M. & Schneider, W. (1977). Controlled and automatic human information processing: perceptual learning, automatic attending, and a general theory. *Psychological Review, 84*, 127–190.

Shinar, D. & Drory, A. (1983). Sign registration in daytime and nighttime driving. *Human Factors, 25*, 117–122.

Shinoda, H, Hayhoe, M. M. & Shrivastava, A. (2001). What controls attention in natural environments? *Vision Research, 41*, 3535–3545.

Sivak, M. (1996). The information that drivers use: is it indeed 90 per cent visual? *Perception, 25*, 1081–1089.

Slade, S. V., Dunne, M. C. M. & Miles, J. N. V. (2002). The influence of high contrast acuity and normalised low contrast acuity upon self-reported situation avoidance and driving crashes. *Ophthalmic and Physiological Optics, 22*, 1–9.

Strayer, D. L., Drews, F. A. & Johnston, W. A. (2003). Cell phone-induced failures of visual attention during simulated driving. *Journal of Experimental Psychology: Applied, 9*, 23–32.

Strayer, D. L. & Johnston, W. A. (2001). Driven to distraction: dual task studies of simulated driving and conversing on a cellular telephone. *Psychological Science, 12*, 462–466.

Summala, H. & Hietamaki, J. (1984). Drivers' immediate responses to traffic signs. *Ergonomics, 27*, 205–216.

Summala, H., Nieminen, T. & Punto, M. (1996). Maintaining lane position with peripheral vision during in-vehicle tasks. *Human Factors, 38*, 442–451.

Underwood, G., Chapman, P., Brocklehurst, N. *et al.* (2003a). Visual attention while driving: sequences of eye fixations made by experienced and novice drivers. *Ergonomics, 46*, 629–646.

Underwood, G., Chapman, P. Berger, Z. & Crundall, D. (2003b). Driving experience, attentional focusing, and the recall of recently inspected events. *Transportation Research F: Psychology and Behaviour, 6*, 289–304.

Underwood, G., Chapman, P., Bowden, K. & Crundall, D. (2002a). Visual search while driving: skill and awareness during inspection of the scene. *Transportation Research F, 5*, 87–97.

Underwood, G., Crundall, D. & Chapman, P. (2002b). Selective searching while driving: the role of experience in hazard detection and general surveillance. *Ergonomics, 45*, 1–12.

Underwood, G., Chapman, P., Crundall, D. *et al.* (1999). The visual control of steering and driving: where do we look when negotiating curves? In A. G. Gale, I. D. Brown, C. M. Haslegrave & S. P. Taylor (eds.), *Vision in Vehicles VII.* Amsterdam: Elsevier.

Underwood, G., Phelps, N., Wright, C. *et al.* (2005). Eye fixation scan paths of younger and older drivers in a hazard perception task. *Ophthalmic and Physiological Optics, 25*, 346–356.

Violanti, J. M. & Marshall, J. R. (1996). Cellular phones and traffic accidents: an epidemiological approach. *Accident Analysis and Prevention, 28*, 265–270.

Weale, R. A. (1992). *The Senescence of Human Vision.* Oxford: Oxford University Press.

Wickens, C. D. (1980). The structure of attentional resources. In R. Nickerson & R. Pew (eds.), *Attention and Performance VIII.* Hillsdale, NJ: Lawrence Erlbaum Associates.

Wikman, A., Nieminen, T. & Summala, H. (1998). Driving experience and time-sharing during in-car tasks on roads of different width. *Ergonomics, 41*, 358–372.

Wood, J. M. (1999). How do visual status and age impact on driving performance as measured on a closed circuit driving track? *Ophthalmic and Physiological Optics, 19*, 34–40.

Wood, J. M. & Troutbeck, R. (1994). Effect of visual impairment on driving. *Human Factors, 36*, 476–487.

Wright, D. (1997). Answering survey questions. In G. B. Grayson (ed.), *Behavioural Research in Road Safety VII.* Crowthorne: Transport Research Laboratory.

Zwahlen, H. T., Russ, A. & Schnell, T. (2003). Driver eye scanning behavior while viewing ground-mounted diagrammatic guide signs before entrance ramps at night. Paper presented at the 82nd Annual Meeting of the Transportation Research Board, January 12–16, Washington, DC.

CHAPTER 16

Automated and Interactive Real-Time Systems

Bernd Lorenz
German Aerospace Center, Braunschweig, Germany
and
Raja Parasuraman
George Mason University, Fairfax, USA

INTRODUCTION

People employed in safety-critical occupations – pilots, air-traffic controllers, power plant operators, intensive care personnel, military commanders, maintenance staff, and others – work in complex systems embedded within a larger socio-technical system. Four important features characterize such workplaces. First, *human safety* requires that the combined human–machine system be operated correctly. At stake are the lives of both the operators and the general public: consider, for example, the consequences of a failure in the control systems of a nuclear power plant. Second, the task demands imposed on the human operator are primarily *cognitive*: information must be continuously absorbed, integrated into meaningful assessment, and transformed into efficient planning and decision-making for timely actions. Other tasks simultaneously compete for the operator's limited attention resources, making this cognitive activity error-prone, with the potential of catastrophic consequences. Third, the *social aspect* refers to the need for efficient communication and collaboration between team members to accomplish system goals. Finally, complex safety-critical systems are embedded within a natural, event-driven, dynamic, and therefore not fully predictable, *real-time* environment.

Advances in the technical component of these systems have been stimulated by the decrease in size and cost and increase in power, speed, and "intelligence" of microcomputers. This has led to increased automation, not just in the workplace, but also in transportation, the home, and in entertainment. The economic benefits that automation can provide (or is perceived to offer) are the primary driver for the introduction of more automation. The trend of introducing increasing levels of automation in safety-critical workplaces is particularly challenging because of the four features described above. The

Handbook of Applied Cognition: Second Edition. Edited by Francis T. Durso.

expectation is that automation will enhance system performance by freeing up the limited mental resources of the human operator, reduce the likelihood of human error, or prevent errors from becoming a safety hazard. Because human error is thought to be a leading cause in 60–70 per cent of accidents (O'Hare *et al.* 1994; Boeing 2004), research efforts focus on this issue. Some regard automation as a safeguard against unreliable humans. Others see it as a complete misconception of the accident statistics and emphasize the human role in creating safety. Whereas the first position strives to limit the role of the human, the second focuses on empowering the role of the human operator.

Over the past two decades, a substantial body of knowledge has shown that the intended benefits of automation are not always achieved or are not cost-free (Wiener 1988; Billings 1997; Sheridan 2002). Serious problems, in most cases unanticipated by the designer, emerge when human control is simply replaced by automation and the resulting new role of the human is either ignored or not specifically designed for (Wiener & Curry 1980; Bainbridge 1983; Sarter & Woods 1992; Woods 1994a; Abbott *et al.* 1996; Parasuraman & Mouloua 1996; Billings 1997; Parasuraman & Riley 1997; Wickens & Hollands 2000; Sheridan 2002; Sheridan & Parasuraman 2006).

In contrast to older technology, advanced automation provides more "degrees of freedom" to system designers in defining the solution space of the design concept. Consequently, function allocation decisions, that is, decisions at the level of human and automation involvement, become paramount. Any changes in the distribution of work between humans and automation imply changes in the role of the human operator. Given the capability of today's technology, many more human activities can, in principle, be automated. As Wiener and Curry (1980) put it cogently, "The question is no longer whether one or another function can be automated but, rather, whether it should be" (p. 995). The increased flexibility in the decision as to what to automate implies a proportionate increase of opportunities for the designer to make suboptimal design tradeoffs.

Chapter Overview

In this chapter we focus on human performance issues involving operators interacting with complex, real-time, automated systems. We define the human role in automated systems in terms of three generic concepts of human-centered automation: the human as a *supervisor*; an *individual operator*; and a *team member*. First, the *supervisory control* paradigm and related research are discussed. The *levels of automation* paradigm is then presented as an approach to reason about the individual operator role and their associated human factors cost and benefit considerations. Finally, *collaborative frameworks* are discussed with reference to the team member role. The chapter concludes with a summary and some thoughts about the human role in automated systems that go beyond the boundaries of human performance issues.

On a final precursory note, this review predominantly refers to aviation to exemplify the central issues and principles arising in human–automation interaction. One reason is that the human-centered approach to automation received a significant input from experience in this domain. A second reason is that we base our review on *empirical* research rather than on conjecture or theoretical speculation. Most research of human–automation interaction has been carried out in aviation and other transportation systems such as driving and shipping. It would be appropriate to discuss automation in the home, in commercial activities like banking, in the marketplace, in leisure activities, and so forth, but there is simply little or no scientific research on human–automation interaction in these domains, although there are several "thought" pieces in each of these areas. Furthermore, aircraft operations occur in a formal working context where tasks are prescribed in detail by written operating procedures and the job-holders represent a comparatively homogeneous population of highly skilled operators. Judgments as to what actions are appropriate or inappropriate in a given operational situation are less controversial compared to other complex working environments. These features contributed to the fact that the flight deck of commercial transport jets became the most targeted field for the study of skilled complex human performance. Nevertheless, we also present empirical research derived from simplified research vehicles such as laboratory tasks or "microworlds," as well as research examples from other domains, including process control, military operations, the medical domain, and robotics.

HUMAN-CENTERED DESIGN PHILOSOPHY

A human-centered design philosophy requires an explicit description of the human role. There is consensus in the aviation community that the two key front-end operators in air transportation – pilots and air traffic controllers – will be ultimately responsible for the safety of the flight and for safe separation of aircraft, respectively (Billings 1991, 1997; Palmer *et al.* 1995; Tarnowski 1999; Kelly 2004). Equivalent variations of this role statement would apply to operators of other safety-critical domains such as process control, intensive medical care, military systems, and others. We can regard this statement as a mandatory function allocation decision addressing the role of the human operator at the highest level of abstraction, which should become the primary driver for function allocation decisions at lower levels of abstraction.

The human-centered approach (Billings 1997) stipulates that the *human operator must be in command and have the final authority over automation.* In turn this means that *the human operator must be involved* in the operation of an automated system. Of course, operators cannot be involved in *every* function needed to accomplish the overall mission. Thus a generic high-level guiding principle for the allocation of functions across human and automated resources is needed. New automation should not be introduced merely because it is feasible. Rather, automation must result in significant safety and operational benefits. Despite the general consensus on these generic principles of human-centered automation there is a less consensus as to how they can be translated into automation design practice, or as Sarter *et al.* (1997) put it, "the road to technology-centered solutions is paved with user-centered intentions (p. 1926).

Ultimate responsibility for safety cannot be allocated to a machine. Thus, any design must support the human who acts in this role. Which functions are critical and which less critical to this role? There is a large gap between this abstract role statement and the level of functions for which a function allocation decision is sought. But the gap can be bridged by the articulation of human roles at an intermediary level of abstraction above the task level. This suggests three important roles (see also Palmer *et al.* 1995): the human as *an individual operator*; *a team member*; and a *supervisor.* These roles are interdependent rather than mutually exclusive. At the core is the role of a supervisor. This is nested into that of a team player, which in turn is nested into that of an individual operator (see

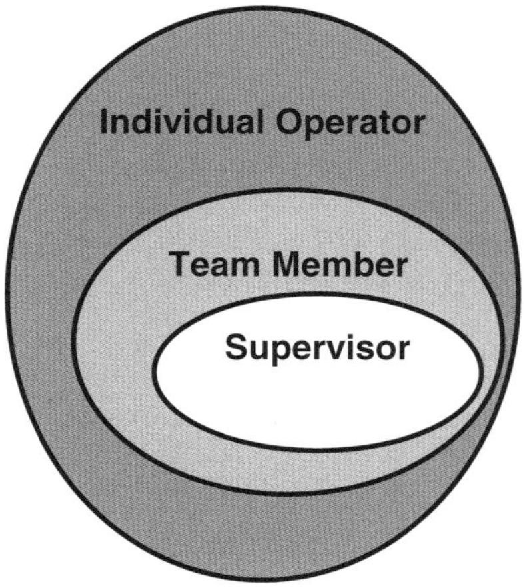

Figure 16.1 Nested concept of human roles to organize guidance for the design of automation support

Figure 16.1). Thus, the conception is that both the team member and the supervisor roles emerge because the human does not work alone. Some new work activities such as coordination and communication are created when automation is introduced, similar to when a colleague joins a working team. This new activity is part of the team member role and there are special forms of this coordination activity that belong to the supervisory role. Coordination can be achieved only by additional efforts that combine the individual working contributions of other actors, human and machine, to the work as a whole. This is often underestimated when designers assume that automation simply substitutes an action that is previously done by the human, what Billings (1997) refers to as the substitution myth.

The role concept also indicates that there should be *congruence* in the distribution of functions between the human and automation, i.e., their concurrent work should complement each other (Jordan 1963; Billings 1997; Hollnagel 1999). Reasoning about congruence contrasts to the traditional approach of function allocation originally proposed by Fitts (1951) of using a list of isolated, single, low-level functions and to allocate those functions to the machine when the machine outperforms the human, and vice versa. Such an approach does not consider functions in their operational context; nor does it take their complex interaction into account (Dearden *et al.* 2000). As we will see, the supervisor role is matched by a subordinate delegate role. One of the central views we develop in this chapter is that such reasoning about congruence in terms of role-matching lends itself more easily to search for congruence at lower levels of abstraction, e.g., at a task level in terms of a flexible pattern of task-based roles shared between human and automated agents (Miller & Parasuraman in press), or even lower at the level of functions (Hollnagel 1999). In the following, the three human roles will guide the identification of useful frameworks supporting a review of relevant empirical human factors research on human-automation interaction problems.

THE SUPERVISORY CONTROL PARADIGM

A representational framework for the human role as a supervisor can be taken from the supervisory control paradigm introduced by Sheridan (1992). In this view, the human should be predominantly involved in activities that support his or her role of a supervisor. The congruent role of automation is one of a subordinate to whom the supervisor delegates a set of tasks. Sheridan (1992) decomposes supervisory control into five generic elements (see Figure 16.2). These are:

Planning what task to do and how to do it: This includes the attainment of a comprehensive understanding of the mission, setting goals, and formulating a strategy to do the task. This activity primarily takes place in advance of the actual operation or mission.

Teaching the automation: This includes the translation of goals into detailed instructions to the computer.

Monitoring the automation's execution of the plan: This includes the observation of the mission progress to make sure that everything is going as planned and to identify either the completion of an automated sub-task or an event indicating a major exception.

Intervening to abort or assuming control: When an exceptional situation (e.g., a failure) is identified the human must step in to solve the problem. This may involve degrading or entirely revoking authority delegated to automation, updating the instructions while at the same time managing the disturbance.

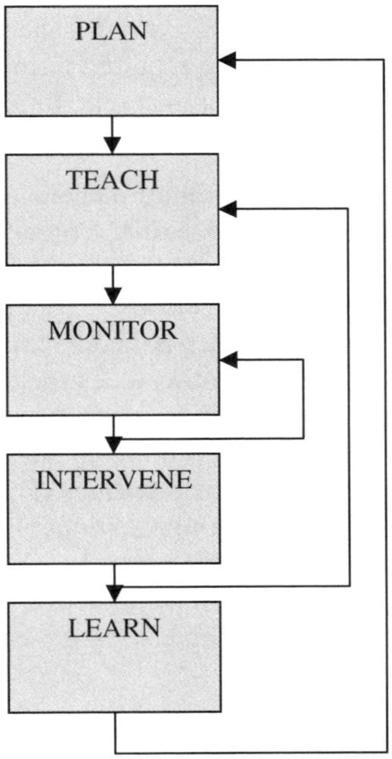

Figure 16.2 Nested loops concept of supervisory control tasks (from Sheridan 1992)

Learning from experience: This means ensuring that the experience made during the mission improves the understanding of its problems to ensure that in the future all four preceding tasks can gain the largest possible benefit.

Sheridan (1992) conceives these five categories as nested loops (see Figure 16.2). *Planning* and *learning* denote strategic subtasks of the supervisory role that primarily take place off-line or out of the loop in relation to the inner-loop that closes from monitoring to itself and intervening that closes back to teaching. The human–automation interaction issues are not as striking as with *teaching*, *monitoring*, and *intervention*, all of which characterize real-time activities embedded in the working situation. The real-time activity of the human that is challenging the top-level role of being responsible the most is *intervention*. All five categories emphasize the transition from a normal to an exceptional off-routine situation as the primary area of concern in the fulfillment of the supervisory role. *Planning* will be poor when it does not properly prepare for contingencies. Likewise, the largest potential of *learning from experience* is gained from exceptional situations with which a crew has successfully coped.

In the following, we turn our focus on the interplay between the inner and middle loops, which operate at a tactical time scale that is highly sensitive to deficiencies in the coupling of human and automation resources.

Human Monitoring and Intervention

The Out-of-the Loop Phenomenon

There is a potential performance cost when human operators are placed in a passive monitoring role while simultaneously being required to intervene should the automation fail. In her seminal work on "ironies of automation," Bainbridge (1983) discussed three main concerns arising from this practice:

1. Operators lack sufficient practice to maintain manual and cognitive skills over long periods of operation controlled by automation. Consequently, they cannot intervene efficiently. The decay of mental arithmetic skills from disuse due to electronic calculators is an everyday example. The *generation effect* (Slameca & Graf 1978; McNamara & Healy 1995), or learned material that is better remembered when self-produced rather than when it is simply copied or observed, provides another example.
2. Monitoring itself as the dominant job left for the operator is much more difficult for a human to accomplish than it may appear. Studies on monitoring efficiency using targets of low probability in monotonous vigilance settings (Davies & Parasuraman 1982) as well as in more enriched automated working settings (Parasuraman 1987) give ample evidence that humans are poor passive monitors.
3. The switch from being a passive monitor to an active troubleshooter often occurs in complex, high-workload, high-tempo, and stressful conditions. This increases the potential of human error.

These three concerns characterize the key attributes of a performance dilemma often referred to as the *out-of-the-loop performance problem* (Endsley & Kiris 1995; Endsley & Kaber 1999; Endsley *et al.* 2003) or *out-of-the-loop unfamiliarity* syndrome (Wickens & Hollands 2000). In aviation, for example, introduction of the autopilot raised the concern that pilots might not be able to detect failures in the operation of automatic controllers in a timely manner when not actively controlling the aircraft (Ephrath & Young 1981). Wickens & Kessel (1981) examined this problem by means of a laboratory tracking task and compared the performances of two groups who were required to detect subtle changes in the control dynamics of the tracking loop. The first group, who performed the task manually, detected these events faster than the second group, who observed the automatic control of the task. Wickens and Kessel explained this effect with the absence of a haptic cue in the latter group. The finding is in agreement with a similar laboratory experiment reported by Ephrath and Young (1981) and with Young (1969). However, Curry and Ephrath (1977) and Ephrath and Young (1981) in a second experiment involving a high-fidelity flight simulation found the opposite.

Evidence that active involvement in the control of a task can be detrimental to supervisory control was reported by Jentsch *et al.* (1999) in a study of human–human role allocation. They analyzed over 300 civilian incidence reports and found a link between loss of situation awareness and aircrew role assignment. It turned out that: (1) loss of situation awareness occurred more frequently when the captain was at the controls than when the first officer was; and (2) the pilot flying was more likely to lose situation awareness than the pilot not flying. They attribute this finding to the twofold burden of captains when engaging in active flight control while simultaneously maintaining the "big picture" needed to fulfill their role in setting global goals and elaborating problem-solving strategies. This explanation points to conflicting demands between the supervisory and the individual operator role as a controller of the system. On the one hand, the monitoring role engenders a loosening of the coupling between the operator and the system with the consequence of reducing the amount of available information about the system behavior. On the other hand, the relief from controlling a process frees capacity that could be devoted to fault detection and recovery (Moray 1986). We will encounter a tradeoff of this kind below when we present research on decision-making functions using the levels of automation approach to discuss the individual operator role in more detail.

Over-reliance

Operators tend to become over-reliant on automation perceived to be highly reliable. As a result, the automated function is less frequently monitored and automation failures are missed or not detected in time for effective intervention. This phenomenon, often referred to as *automation complacency*, has received considerable attention (Billings *et al.* 1976; Wiener 1981; Parasuraman *et al.* 1993; Parasuraman and Riley 1997; Metzger & Parasuraman 2001). Studies have shown that complacent behavior (as measured by automation failure detection rate) varies with task load. For example, complacency is greater when multiple tasks have to be performed than in single task conditions (Thackray & Touchstone 1989; Parasuraman *et al.* 1993; Singh *et al.* 1997), suggesting that complacency should better be conceived as suboptimal attention resource management (Parasuraman *et al.* 1993). However, attention must be allocated to many sources in most real-time interactive systems, which implies that even with an optimal sampling not all critical failure signals can be detected (Moray & Inagaki 2001; Moray 2003). Therefore, complacent behavior should not be inferred solely on the basis of detection failures but should be substantiated in addition by information sampling indicators, e.g., parameters of eye movement analyses

(Metzger & Parasuraman 2001) or by recordings of display activation patterns (Bahner *et al.* 2006).

A driver of complacent behavior may be an implicit decision heuristic on behalf of the human to reduce cognitive effort. Such a tendency is generally observed in a variety of problem solving tasks (Wickens & Hollands 2000). An effort-reducing task strategy is also a characteristic element of a phenomenon quite similar to complacency referred to as *automation bias*, which Mosier and Skitka (1996) define as a "tendency to use automation cues as a heuristic replacement for vigilant information seeking and processing" (p. 205).

Trust in Automation

Another important variable of the working situation for the understanding of automation complacency is the reliability of an automated system. If a system is completely unreliable, then presumably complacency would be unlikely. Similarly, a supervisor who observes unreliable behavior in her subordinate would either dismiss this person, limit the range of authorized decisions, or would more frequently and closely check his output. The latter strategy would occur at the expense of resources that could be devoted to other supervisory tasks. Not checking the subordinate's output frequently may result in a failure to stop a process that is not well handled by the subordinate from escalating into trouble. *Trust* is, therefore, as relevant a construct to understand human–automation interaction as it is for human–human interaction. A dominant view is that trust should be *calibrated*, that is be neither too high nor too low (Lee & See 2004). Both forms of mis-calibration (i.e., over-trust and hence complacency, as well as under-trust leading to unjustified disuse) should be avoided (Parasuraman & Riley 1997). Typically, a high level of reliability engenders human trust in automation (Lee & Moray 1992, 1994). However, the relationship between reliability and trust is not that simple. Lee and Moray (1992) conducted experiments using complex process control simulations in which they carefully observed under what conditions their participants decided to use automation support or to opt for manual control. They collected ratings of the subjectively perceived automation reliability and found that this was highly correlated with automation use, which is not that surprising. They also collected ratings on their confidence in their own ability to control the process. Their results indicate a complex moderating effect of both self-confidence and trust on automation use. If the level of self-confidence is greater than the level of trust, participants opted for manual control. If the reverse was true, i.e., the level of trust was higher than the level of self-confidence, participants would opt for automation. Thus, the absolute level of reliability is less important than the level of trust it engenders in relation to self-confidence. A recent thorough theoretical examination of the concept of trust in automation can be found in Lee and See (2004).

Teaching Automation

Assuming manual control in case of an exceptional situation is equivalent to a complete revocation of authority previously delegated to the automation device. We may characterize this pattern as escaping from the supervisory role to the individual operator role in full manual control. As Figure 16.2 suggests, there is the alternative option for the operator to keep the automated device engaged but teach it to accommodate to the off-routine situational demand. There are some important human performance issues concerning the efficiency of teaching automation in such a situation.

Clumsy Automation

Recall that teaching automation means translating the goals and intentions of the supervisor into instructions to be given to the automated device, typically a computer. In the aviation context, a new clearance from air traffic control represents an unexpected situation that forces the cockpit crew to reprogram the flight management computer. Re-programming the flight management computer, which is the job of the non-flying pilot, absorbs important attention resources also needed for monitoring the outside scene and the activities of the flying pilot. Sumwalt *et al.* (1999) searched the Aviation Safety Report System (ASRS) database for incidents of pilot errors in flight monitoring and report that 30 per cent of errors occurred during re-programming of the flight management system. To some extent this is due to the poor interface design of the Control and Display Unit (CDU), which requires the pilot to browse through several pages involving many keystrokes (Sarter *et al.* 1997). This sudden transition from a period of low to unexpectedly high workload as task demands escalate has been termed *clumsy automation* (Wiener 1988). Clumsy automation is an indication of a mismatch, or lack of congruence, between the human supervisory role and the role of automation as an assistant. Flight crews often solve the clumsy automation problem by resorting to full manual control.

Automation Opacity

The more competent an automated device is, the more complex can be the instruction given to it by the supervisor, and hence the more powerful the automated agent will become (Sarter & Woods 2000). Once the instruction has been activated the automation is enabled to act autonomously in the absence of further immediate operator input. If after a long period of autonomously controlled operation an anomaly occurred it may become very difficult for the operator to identify the root causes if the contribution (e.g., error-compensating influences of the automation) to the overall pattern of system responses cannot easily be inferred and is, therefore, not fully understood (Woods 1994b). *Automation opacity* (Billings 1997) refers to an automated agent that does not give the appropriate feedback on its own action (Norman 1990) to establish situation awareness needed by the supervisor to diagnose the situation and anticipate how the situation will evolve in response to her input.

THE LEVELS OF AUTOMATION APPROACH

In the preceding section we have discussed some important human performance concerns related to the human–automation relationship which assigns the human too passive a role. The performance deficiencies resulting from this passive role can be summarized as a state of poor situation awareness in the short term and a loss of skills in the long term. We have also pointed out that the supervisor role has its merits in reducing workload. In conclusion, there is a tradeoff between the goals of maintaining situation awareness while at the same time moderating the workload. It seems clear that the supervisor role must be enriched with more active elements in the overall task design. The active elements pertain to the individual operator role. But what type of tasks should be reclaimed by the human? To what extent should the range of tasks allocable to automation be limited?

These questions take us closer to the key guiding principle of human-centered automation stated above, namely that the *human must be involved*. At the outset we can state that the nature of tasks in which the operator must be involved is primarily *cognitive*. By this we mean that we cannot only describe the observable motor or vocal actions of the operator, but must consider the information-processing underlying action. We can identify four broad generic task dimensions, each defined by a stage within an information-processing sequence or cycle: information acquisition, information analysis, decision-making on action selection, and action implementation (Parasuraman *et al.* 2000). The first two stages include the three components of Endsley's conception of situation awareness which is formally defined as "the perception of the elements in the environment within a volume of time and space, the comprehension of their meaning and the projection of their status in the near future" (Endsley 1988, in Endsley 1995a, p. 36). Stage 1 corresponds to perception and stage 2 to comprehension and anticipation. With an information-processing view we also can derive a definition of automation that better addresses human performance aspects of the individual operator role. Thus, we can define automation as "any sensing, detection, information-processing, decision-making, or control action that could be performed by humans but is actually performed by a machine" (Moray *et al.* 2000, p. 44). Central to Parasuraman *et al.* (2000) is the assumption that automation is not an all-or-nothing phenomenon, but can vary along different degrees or levels of automation (LOA). Finding an adequate function allocation, i.e. finding functions where the operator must be involved, becomes a matter of reasoning about desirable rather than feasible LOA. Second, desirable LOA may differ by the four generic processing stages. Most of them will be forms of partial rather than total automation. There are alternative taxonomies of automation to distinguish various forms of partial automation (Sheridan & Verplank 1978; Ntuen & Park 1988; Shoval *et al.* 1993; Billings 1997; Semple 1998; Endsley & Kaber 1999; Dearden 2001; Kaber & Endsley 2004). Here, we use the four-stage structure of the Parasuraman *et al.* (2000) model to review relevant human factors studies that throw some light on the question as to where and to what extent the human needs to be involved to ensure best performance in the supervisory as well as in the individual operator role. For that purpose we first address human performance studies where automation is primarily applied to the acquisition and analysis of automation. This is followed by studies that examined the effects of automating decision-making and action implementation.

Automation of Information Acquisition and Analysis

Humans use their senses to take in information. Most important for the operator are the visual, auditory, and haptic senses. Technology offers sensors for the same purpose. Even if we disregard sensors of a purely technical nature that sense aspects of the environment unavailable to the human (e.g., ambient pressure, speed, acceleration, heading, etc.), there are still many sensors with "seeing" capabilities that acquire information that can also be acquired by human senses, albeit with different capabilities. These include television and infra-red cameras and various forms of forward-looking radar sensors. The number increases if we add those sensors that need a connecting infrastructure in the environment. In aviation, ground-based radio systems and radio navigation aids enable the surveillance and guidance of aircraft as they travel through airspace. The present-day trend of using powerful, small mobile computers with wireless access to a worldwide information network can be regarded as imbedding automation of information acquisition into the everyday life.

Moreover, digital technology enables the processing of sensor data. Thus, the operator could be presented not with the raw data but with a subset that in addition can be organized in a way to support the task at hand. The key function of the second class of information analysis in the Parasuraman *et al.* (2000) model is the process by which data from different sources are combined to become meaningful information. The boundary between automation that supports acquisition and automation that supports analysis is not easy to draw. The distinction between bottom-up and top-down processing may help to clarify this issue. Top-down attention processes are guided by goals, intentions, and expectancies as opposed to bottom-up processes that are guided by sensory properties responsible for stimulus salience. The modes complement each other. Top-down processing draws upon limited working memory resources and helps to further structure the compound of information into relevant and irrelevant parts. The bottom-up mode is necessary to override top-down processing so as to facilitate the intake of information contradictory to the expectation or of information calling for a change in the priority setting linked to concurrent goals. Thus, we could relate the acquisition stage to the bottom-up and the analysis stage to the top-down component. Automated cueing, highlighting, and filtering all change the salience of the stimulus environment and can so be classified as stage 1 automation subcategories. However, strictly speaking, most of these functions require at least some of top-down analysis, too. Thus, even a simple automated cueing algorithm must have access to the goal state (threshold) enabling the comparison with the sensed state and hence the subsequent cueing of the deviation to the operator. Automated cueing considered this way replaces information analysis and should then be classified as stage 2 automation. As we cannot solve this problem other than by lumping both classes into one we proceed in a pragmatic way and present auto-enhancing, auto-detection, and auto-notification systems as stage 1 automation as these forms of automation primarily support attention guidance in favor of the perception component of situation awareness. Auto-integration and auto-diagnosis will then be discussed as forms of stage 2 automation as the implied human performance issues are linked to a far more complex output of intelligent information automation that supports the discovery of higher-order properties inherent in the multiplicity of information sources. These forms of automation address the comprehension and anticipation component of situation awareness.

Auto-Enhancing Information Salience

Display enhancement to guide the attention of an operator is similar to a laboratory task situation where the participants receive perceptual cues that help to direct their attention to important features or targets embedded within a noisy stimulus background. As this type of automation supports visual search, any simple features that create a "pop-out" effect (Treisman 1982) can be used for such target cueing, e.g., highlighting certain display elements (Wickens *et al.* 2003). A filter algorithm that samples sensor data and presents only a subset of relevant data (to avoid information overload) represents an even higher LOA.

In reality, however, many situations are ambiguous with regard to what information is relevant or irrelevant. This raises the question as to the potential performance cost that results from a deficiency of cueing or filtering the highest priority target information. In other words, what is the impact on operator performance if the cued information is actually less relevant than another uncued source? Posner's (1980) cueing paradigm has inspired a series of studies examining this question. Yeh *et al.* (1999) evaluated the potential benefits for using helmet-mounted displays (HMD) by soldiers and measured their performance on a target detection task for this purpose. Participants "walled" in an immersive display environment searched for simulated tanks, landmines, nuclear devices, and soldiers. Cueing presented on a simulated HMD was fully reliable on some targets, and absent on others, including some of higher priority. It was found, as expected, that cued targets were detected significantly faster than uncued targets. However, when a target was cued, and a second target, which was uncued but considered a higher priority target, was present at the same time, the higher priority target was likely to be ignored in favor of reporting the lower priority target that was cued. Merlo *et al.* (1999) and Yeh and Wickens (2001) confirmed this finding using a similar experimental task. Note that participants were made aware that the cueing algorithm was not completely reliable. Target cueing supports focused attention, which is beneficial only when the piece of information with the highest priority value is cued. The performance cost of cueing low-priority information results from the reduced ability of the operator to draw off the allocation of attention from the cued source in favor of the more important pieces of information.

The performance cost noted in these cueing studies is referred to as cognitive fixation, or attention tunneling (Wickens & Long 1995; Martin-Emerson & Wickens 1997; Yeh *et al.* 1999; Fadden *et al.* 2001; Yeh & Wickens 2001). Wickens (2005) defines attention tunneling "as the allocation of attention to a particular channel of information, diagnostic hypothesis or task goal, for a duration that is longer than optimal, given the expected cost of neglecting events on other channels, failing to consider other hypotheses, or failing to perform other tasks" (p. 620). Thus, attention tunneling can be regarded as a stage 1 processing deficiency which may limit the processing efficiency in the subsequent stage of information analysis in that not all information that needs to be integrated for an appropriate situation assessment is made available in a timely way. Information cueing research suggests that target cueing should not be used when it is not highly reliable. Rather, Endsley *et al.* (2003) recommended a lower LOA by supporting operators in their manual search processes, for example, by providing means to declutter displays from unwanted information in a user-initiated fashion.

Auto-Detection Devices

An LOA in which the visual search function is shared between the human and automation characterizes systems that Allen and Kessel (2002) refer to as conventional auto-detection devices that became prevalent in military surveillance operations. In a conventional auto-detection setting, both the computer and the human operator scan the same signals, e.g., synthetic aperture radar (SAR), sonar, or aerial photos, and both agents analyze these signals for a target or threat. If the computer raises an alarm on the operator's display, it is the role of the operator to inspect and subsequently dismiss or confirm the alarm. According to Allen and Kessel (2002) this type of computer support is perceived as an additional load and source of annoyance rather than assistance to the operator as in most cases there is no performance gain above the level of performance achieved by the operator working without the automation. The consequence is that most operators are inclined to switch off auto-detection (see also Parasuraman & Riley 1997). The reason is that the detection algorithms make errors that misguide the operator. As these shortcomings were anticipated by the designers it appears quite reasonable that they subordinate the automated solutions to the human expert. Allen and Kessel (2002) argue that this *total* subordination, and thus the removal of any responsibility from the auto-detection device, is the core problem of its inefficiency and hence disuse. Therefore, they postulate two elements of an efficient but still imperfect auto-detection device. First, a deficiency in the human operator that the device is able to address needs to be identified. In other words, an aspect of performance requirement, e.g., a specific demand on knowledge, memory, or speed, has to be recognized, if only temporarily or occasionally, where the device outperforms the human. Second, the identified capability of the automated device needs to be balanced with its assigned responsibility so as to avoid both too much as well as too little responsibility. According to Allen and Kessel (2002), the criterion for such a balancing should be minimization of mission cost and mission risk. These costs and risks, in turn, directly result from consequences of the uncertain operation that may incur either missed genuine targets or non-targets mistaken for targets (false alarms). This balance principle "requires that the costs and risks borne by the detector be commensurate with the detector's ability, being neither so great as to jeopardize those who rely on the detector, nor so little as to make the detector inconsequential" (Allen & Kessel 2002, p. 5). This again points to the importance of trust discussed above.

Auto-notification Devices

An automated notification system is involved when monitoring is totally allocated to automation at a higher LOA of information acquisition. This type of automation became prevalent with the use of Internet-based communication systems such as email or instant messaging which provide a visual or auditory alert or a combination of both when a new message has been received. Acquisition of information with automated notification systems is entirely computer-initiated. Such automated service that works continuously in the background frees the user from intermittent manual inspection, thereby allowing the operator to accomplish other tasks. If the notification message is a reminder (e.g., of a meeting appointment or an approaching deadline), it supports also human prospective memory, i.e., remembering to execute an intention formed a certain amount of time prior to the time when this action becomes due (Brandimonte *et al.* 1996). In any case, these notifications are interruptions with potential disruptive performance consequences (McFarlane & Latorella 2002). They must be integrated with the user's ongoing activity. System alerts are one form of interruptions on the flight deck. The crew is required to manage the interruption to maintain a coherent task flow by coordinating the interrupted with the interrupting task made imminent by the alert. We may want a notification system that is intelligent enough to take important parameters of the current task context of the user into account. A comprehensive review of human factors issues associated with human interruption in complex systems is given in McFarlane and Latorella (2002).

Auto-integration Devices

As noted earlier, the key element of information analysis is the process by which data become information. Information is the result of the relation between data, the context to which the data refer, and the user's intentions, expectations, or interests (Woods 1995). This data-to-information relationship can be rather complex, for example, in systems of high dimensionality such as process control where operators often have difficulties discovering causal relationships among multiple variables and their interactions from their state values (Moray 1997). Making constraints of the dynamic working domain visible in the interface is a major goal of effective interface design. The computer medium provides the designer with a large amount of flexibility to determine which of the many constraints of the working domain should be represented in the interface. A guiding principle is to create semantic mapping (Bennett & Flach 1992). This is achieved when the intrinsic constraints of the work domain are directly mapped onto the structure and the dynamic behavior of the display elements. An example of such constraints is the relationship between pressure, the valve state (open vs. closed), and the flow rates in the pipe system of a processing plant. System failures are indicated by violations in the constraints that characterize the health of the system (e.g., a leak in a valve that causes the downstream flow rate to be less than normal). However, the designer has to recognize that the constraints exist at multiple levels, reflecting the hierarchical structure of the work domain. Therefore, it is important to develop a multilevel representation format that describes the various layers of constraint in a work domain. This is what Vicente and Rasmussen (1992) refer to as the abstraction hierarchy, which is the key element in their ecological interface design (EID) philosophy. Higher levels represent functional information about system purposes, whereas lower levels represent physical information about how the system purposes are implemented in system components. Vicente (1996) describes a detailed example showing how the semantic mapping principle in the EID framework can inform the design of an interface supporting fault diagnosis in a simplified thermal-hydraulic process control microworld. Vicente (1996) reports a series of experiments using this research vehicle, suggesting that the representation of higher-order functional constraint information in the display led to faster fault detection and more accurate fault diagnoses. Furukawa *et al.* (2003) developed a new display for Vicente's (1996) microworld. This made the automation's intentions (i.e., goals and means) visible in the display. They found that such an intention-represented EID display improved the operators' ability to prevent conflicts with the automated controllers as compared to the standard EID display. Effken *et al.* (1997) used an interactive computer environment of a hemodynamic system to test various ecological multilevel interfaces that made anatomical and causal constraints of the hemodynamic system visible. With these integrated displays, nursing students and experienced critical care nurses Effken *et al.* (1997) found improved speed and accuracy in the diagnosis and improved selection of drug treatment decisions in response to simulated clinical problem states. Furukawa *et al.* (2003) found empirical evidence derived from a simplified flight simulation task suggesting a benefit of an integrated display in the mitigation of the complacency phenomenon discussed previously. Lorenz *et al.* (2004), using a microworld that simulated complex fault management (FM) in a simplified atmosphere control system of a spacecraft, also found faster and more accurate fault diagnoses when the pattern of constraint violations was visualized by an additional integrated display as compared to the sole display of raw data. However, the integrated display simultaneously deteriorated the performance of one of the embedded secondary tasks which required the participants to selectively read out raw data from a single state indicator. This pattern of effects points to a performance tradeoff between focused attention and information integration (Bennett & Flach 1992) and is consistent with the theoretical underpinnings of the proximity-compatibility principle proposed by Wickens and Carswell (1995) to provide guidance in display design for a balanced solution of this tradeoff problem.

Automated Diagnosis

Automated target detection and notification devices generally prompt operators to assess the situation and to infer the need for action. Such an assessment may be rather difficult in complex highly coupled process control systems, for example, where a failure of a component tends to impact other parts of the system causing a cascade of subsequent alerts (Moray 1997). Treating the "downstream" failure does not solve the problem: rather the operator must diagnose the root cause. Model-based expert systems are developed to provide the operator with automated assistance in root-cause determination of a fault. If such an expert system should operate online, the challenge for the designer is to make such a system aware of the context and also congruent with the mental model of the operator. The problem is that even the brightest and most knowledgeable design teams cannot anticipate the variety of circumstances that can affect the operation of the system over its entire lifecycle. Encountering problems for which the automated system was not designed can cause it to falsely assess the situation and hence misguide the operator toward a decision on an incorrect course of action. This is referred to as *automation brittleness* (Billings 1997) and characterizes the limitations of an embedded automated expert agent that works perfectly within its modeled operating range but degrades abruptly when events outside this envelope occur. There is some empirical evidence that placing automation in the critiquing role can help to mitigate the degrading impact of brittleness in automated medical diagnoses (Guerlain *et al.* 1995; Guerlain *et al.* 1999). A critiquing system provides guidance to the operators after rather than before they have made their decisions, similar to a coach who "looks over the shoulder" of the system operator.

As automated inference and diagnosis capabilities typify decision support systems that in most cases give advisories on the proper course of action, we will discuss further related human performance issues in the next section.

Automation of Decision-Making and Action Implementation

The stage of decision-making is a very important one in human–automation design. With the development of expert systems and other high-level decision aiding systems, it is clearly increasingly feasible to apply a very high LOA to this stage. Stage 2 and stage 3 automation, when combined, are commonly referred to as a decision support system (DSS). Crocoll and Coury (1990) studied to what extent stage 2 and stage 3 automation may differentially affect potential performance costs when the DSS is not fully reliable. They used a simulated air defense scenario and provided their participants either with automatic target identification or with a recommendation as to what action they should take against the targets. Both types of support were either perfectly reliable or failed on some occasions. A third manual condition served as a baseline reference. Performance improvements in terms of faster correct actions of equal size for both types of automation were found when the aid was perfectly reliable. Thus there was no incremental benefit derived from stage 3 automation. An unreliable DSS, however, led to higher performance disruptions in the group who received stage 3 automation. Sarter and Schroeder (2001) reported a similar result following the experimental comparison of two implementations of a DSS: a status and a command display, supporting pilots in the treatment of in-flight icing. Pilots in the status conditions received information about the location of the ice accretion, whereas pilots in the command conditions were given recommendations regarding an appropriate action to resolve the problem (power setting, flap setting, and pitch attitude). Consistent with Crocoll and Coury (1990), they found that accurate information from either type of automation resulted in improved handling of the ice accretion relative to baseline with no support. Again, there was no incremental performance gain for the command display. Performance with both displays dropped below a manual baseline when the information was inaccurate and this performance loss was greater in the group supported with the command display. In a further extension of this line of research Rovira, McGarry, and Parasuraman (in press) obtained similar results using a military command-and-control simulation.

The decision-making and action selection stage was also the focus of earlier suggestions for the definition of LOA. Endsley and Kiris (1995) used a five-category LOA scheme and presented their participants with a series of driver navigational problems for which they offered different forms of automated advisory according to the LOA scheme. They found that when the automated support was withdrawn unexpectedly, return-to-manual performance was degraded with increasing lack of involvement in problem-solving and decision-making which had taken place in normal trials prior to the failure. Moreover, situation awareness, which was probed from time to time during normal trials, was improved for those participants who were kept more actively involved in problem-solving. Endsley and Kaber (1999) applied a ten-level LOA taxonomy to examine the hypothesis that intermediate LOA improved performance by moderating mental workload while simultaneously maintaining situation awareness. This study could not confirm the straightforward inverse relationship between situation awareness indices probed during normal operation and the amount of out-of-the-loop performance problems during automation breakdown, as has been observed by Endsley and Kiris (1995). Improved rather than deteriorated SA was observed at higher as compared to lower LOA. Yet, the study points to the benefits of automated support in action implementation. This finding is in agreement with Kaber *et al.* (2000) who used a high-fidelity simulation of a tele-robotic task and also found that those LOA that provided computer assistance in action implementation promoted better maintenance of operator situation awareness and hence better manual performance during system failures, as compared with higher LOA in decision support.

Lorenz *et al.* (2002) studied LOA effects in normal and return-to-manual operation using an atmosphere management microworld. A simulated model-based reasoning agent offered decision support and provided fault management advisories at three LOA. During normal trials, participants who were supported with the two higher LOA that provided an automated fault diagnosis plus a list of recommended stabilization actions clearly outperformed the participants who received only a computerized fault-finding guide. In agreement with Kaber *et al.* (2000), the group supported with the LOA that provided assistance in action implementation performed best in return-to-manual trials. Lorenz *et al.* (2004) compared the two higher LOA that provided the same assistance in decision support but differed with regard to action implementation. Instead of using a return-to-manual paradigm, participants were confronted with more difficult failure modes which involved double-faults. In these trials the agent exhibited brittleness in terms of giving false or incomplete diagnoses or of failing to detect an anomaly at all, for example, when symptoms of the two faults involved masked each other. Again, it was found that agent support in action implementation during trials with reliable fault-management led to superior performance in the exceptional "brittle" trials. In both the Lorenz *et al.* (2002) study and the Lorenz *et al.* (2004) study, poor recovery from automation failure or brittleness, respectively, was associated with the tendency of participants to under-sample fault-relevant information during trials with reliable automation support.

In summary, the notion that automation of decision-making and action implementation functions can lead to out-of-the-loop unfamiliarity is less clear-cut than often thought. There is supporting evidence for this view from simple task paradigms (Wickens & Kessel 1981; Endsley & Kiris 1995). But the picture becomes complicated in more complex paradigms (Endsley & Kaber 1999; Kaber *et al.* 2000; Lorenz *et al.* 2002, 2004) or in the field as noted earlier (Jentsch *et al.* 1999) where the overall multiplicity of tasks and their nested character of inner and outer control loops indicate that there may be substantial workload and situation awareness benefits of the outer-loop supervisor role. This seems particularly important in situations when automation becomes brittle. Overall, there is converging evidence to support Billings' (1991) view that automation can benefit operators "first by relieving them from the burden of inner-loop control, second by providing them integrated information, and third by allowing them to manage at a higher level" (p. 17).

COLLABORATIVE FRAMEWORKS

Many authors suggest that human–system interaction should be designed for optimal mutual cooperation or "team play" (Malin & Schreckenghost 1992; Hoc & Lemoine 1998; Sarter & Woods 2000; Hoc 2001; Christoffersen & Woods 2002). Effective team play requires that team members operate from a *common ground* or *common frame of reference* of the actual situation. A common frame of reference refers to mutually held knowledge of the situation and is the result of merging the crew members' perceptions and their situation assessment, thus leading to effective decision-making and coordinated action (Endsley 1995b). While spoken communication prevails in human–human collaboration, the Human–Machine Interface (HMI) must similarly provide for effective human-automation collaboration.

The Common Work Space Concept

Principally, all four fundamental information-processing functions discussed previously must be represented in a virtual common frame of reference to support the coordination

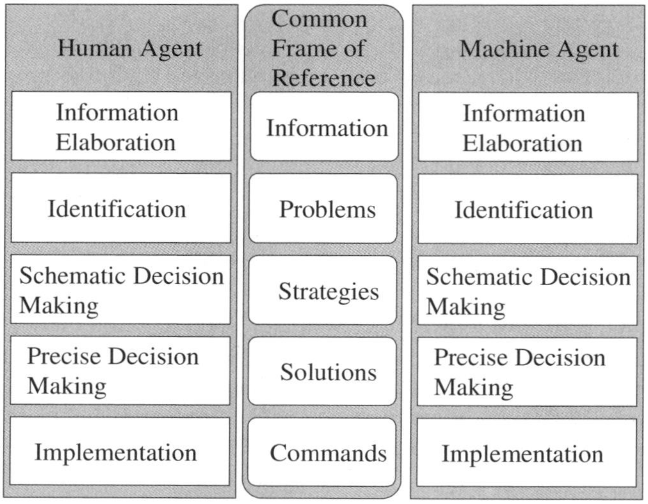

Figure 16.3 Contents of a common frame of reference for the implementation of cooperative activities (Debernard *et al.* 2002)

of joint agent activities. Figure 16.3 shows such a framework involving five generic information-processing classes proposed by Debernard *et al.* (2002; see also Riera and Debernard 2003). Their framework splits the decision stage into two classes of schematic and precise decision-making. For the technical implementation of this framework, Debernard *et al.* (2002) used the Common Work Spaces (CWS) approach developed in the domain of computer-supported cooperative work (CSCW) (Jones & Jasek 1997; Bannon 2001). To cooperate, agents pass on the products of the respective activities to form the content of the CWS, which are, in generic terms, *information*, *problems*, *strategies/solutions*, and *commands* enabling a sharing of their own frames of reference. Debernard *et al.* (2002; Pacaux-Lemoine and Debernard 2002) describe three forms of how inconsistency between agents' common frame of references and the content of the CWS can be solved through interaction with the CWS: *negotiation*, *acceptance*, and *imposition*. Negotiation aims at either modifying CWS content or the frame of reference of an agent on the basis of further explanations. Acceptance and imposition are reciprocal in that either an agent updates its frame of reference from the CWS, or alternatively, imposes its frame of reference to the CWS.

Riera and Debernard (2003) report two application projects, one of which applied this concept to study collaboration issues in the design of adaptive automation in air traffic control. In this project called AMANDA (Automation and MAN-machine Delegation of Action), the contents of the CWS (see Figure 16.4) were defined to enable collaborative interaction between a three-agent team of the two air traffic controllers (radar executive and planning controller) and an assistance tool (STAR) designed to support this team in the detection and resolution of conflicts in en route air traffic. Shared problem identification merges onto what is referred to as clusters. Clusters are a set of conflicts between two or more aircraft, including potential conflicts that may result from their resolution.

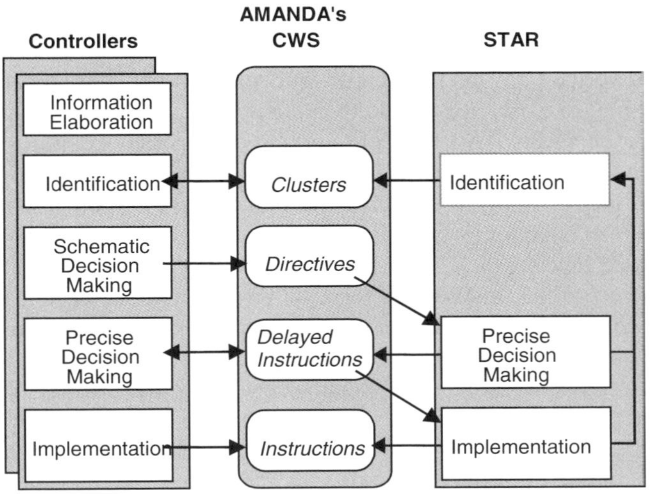

Figure 16.4 Common Work Space (CWS) for cooperative interaction of an air traffic controller team with a decision support tool (STAR) (from Hoc & Debernard, 2002)

Schematic decision-making at stage 3 takes the form of directives which are higher-level commands, e.g., "turn aircraft A behind aircraft B," as compared to lower-level delayed instructions resulting from precise decision-making, e.g., "turn aircraft A 30 degree to the left at 22:35." Finally, actions are implemented instructions following the resolution trajectories. Riera and Debernard (2003) describe three principles of collaboration between agents (see also Schmidt 1991). Arrows to and from the content elements of CWS in Figure 16.4 depict these principles. Clusters are generated in a so-called *debative* form of co-operation, i.e., all agents share this task and provide input to the CWS content. As Figure 16.4 shows, STAR does not engage in schematic decision-making, and hence does not generate strategies to solve conflicts. The know-how for schematic decision-making resides in the team of both controllers who develop the directives that define constraints for the tool to be taken into account in the production of resolution trajectories. This form of cooperation is termed *integrative*, because agents integrate different and complementary know-how to accomplish a task. Finally, cooperation can be characterized as *augmentative* when agents have similar know-how and divide the whole task among each other, because it may be too demanding to be performed by only one agent.

The Delegation Interface

Delegation interfaces (Miller & Parasuraman in press) are proposed as a real-time solution for flexible invocation and revocation of automation responsibility (autonomy) in a sense similar to that which occurs in successful human teams. An example of such a delegation interface is the Playbook design concept (Miller *et al.* 2000; Miller *et al.* 2004). This approach was guided by the metaphor of a sports team's manual of approved plays and the selection from among those plays by the team leader, e.g., the quarterback in

American football, and their execution by the team members, i.e., the other players. The Playbook interface provides a shared workspace that bears much in common with the CWS concept described above. The shared workspace allows the human supervisor to *compose a mission*, to *define plans*, and to *communicate goals* and *intentions* with subordinate automation agents. This form of interface permits the operator to delegate tasks to automation at a wide variety of functional levels of abstraction by provision of goals, or full or partial plans. Finally, the Playbook design concept supports the process of delegation by the human operator by providing a compiled set of plans, or "plays," with short, easily commanded labels which can be further modified as needed. This is the critical aspect of the concept that allows this form of flexible automation not to increase the workload associated with delegation, much as a sports team has an approved set of plays that facilitate task delegation by the team leader.

There are currently two sources of evidence concerning the efficacy of the delegation interface approach. First, a Playbook prototype for a mission planning and real-time control of unmanned air and ground vehicles has been developed (Parasuraman & Miller 2005). Second, initial experimental studies of the effects of delegation interfaces on human performance have been carried out (Parasuraman *et al.* 2005). These studies examined the use of a simple delegation interface on system performance during simulated human-robot teaming using the RoboFlag simulation environment. RoboFlag provided the operator with the ability to command simulated robots, individually or in groups, at several levels of complexity: by providing designated endpoints for robot travel, by commanding higher-level behaviors (or modes or plays) or by even higher "super-plays." The results showed that the multi-level tasking provided by the delegation interface allowed effective user supervision of robots, as evidenced by the number of missions successfully completed and the time for mission execution. However, further studies are needed in which more complex versions of delegation interfaces are evaluated.

SUMMARY AND CONCLUSIONS

The chapter has outlined frameworks to answer Wiener and Curry's question "Should we automate?" for interactive real-time systems that involve serious safety risks. There is broad agreement that automation should be used if there is a gain in efficiency and safety in the resulting human–automation system. Such an overall benefit can only be assured if the role of the human in the system is properly understood. The central view we have developed is that the search for congruence between human and automation should begin at the abstract and high level of roles. At the highest level, assignment to the human is mandatory because of the ultimate responsibility of the human operator for safety. We identified three supporting roles – supervisor, individual operator, and team member – and discussed their human performance requirements by reviewing relevant empirical human factors research. Insufficient active involvement was identified as a major impediment to the human being able to manage exceptional situations, as required by the supervisory role. We presented an information-processing view on levels of automation to support the search for answers to the question of where and to what extent the human needs to claim involvement. With respect to information acquisition and analysis, automated cueing, target detection, and notification systems, as well as information integration, were identified which have clear benefits if the resulting operator attention demands are carefully considered. At the same time, however, too active involvement in action implementation at lower system levels can be detrimental to system performance with the potential of compromising the human in the role of a supervisor. The collaborative role is also important, but additional empirical research is needed to understand its characteristics. Principles of collaboration can be implemented by allowing cooperation activities to be built around delegation-type interfaces such as the Common Work Space or the Playbook. These implementations allow for multiple and adaptable levels of automation which seems particularly crucial in unanticipated situations when human intelligence must intervene but is nevertheless in need of automation output at a reduced and easy-to-direct level of service to enable optimal access to all functionality for coping with this situation. As workload is typically high in such a situation, information access cost should be minimal by employing a similar, easy-to-direct level of service in the visualization of constraints at the required level of abstraction.

One of the challenges in the exploitation of these concepts and principles for the design of future systems, however, is that in many systems decisions are usually determined and fixed at an early design stage. Coordination and collaboration demands are often detected later. If proposed designs are to be analyzed with respect to both technical and human factors implications the requirement specification must support a clear, shared understanding between the main professionals in the process of system development, i.e. the domain expert, the human factors specialist, and the systems engineer. At an early design stage such a shared understanding will be essential for a preliminary assessment of relevant human–system integration concerns such as workload, operator situation awareness, technical feasibility, potential cost, and likely system performance. Promising approaches are diverse and include matured quantitative formal models of human performance (Corker 2000; Schweickert *et al.* 2003), expanded formal verification methods for the examination of human–automation interaction (Degani & Heymann 2002), linking cognitive levels of automation frameworks to engineering system representations such as use-case models (Harrison *et al.* 2003), and the use of intermediate design artifacts guided by cognitive task analyses (Potter *et al.* 2002). All these approaches strive at a better coupling between the top-down analysis of requirements of human involvement in system operation and the actual bottom-up building of the system.

The term *role* is central in this chapter. Role has many connotations, particularly in the psychosocial or sociological sense. We have confined our reasoning on the human role to the interaction with automated systems within safety-critical working environments. Here, roles are envisaged as an aggregate of tasks at a mission level for which we could make an account on responsibility and required human authority. It should not be neglected, however, that some broader reasoning about the human role is necessary when we look at the job level and, moreover, the organizational level. As technology changes, so do jobs. This suggests the need to widen the scope of investigation to aspects such as motivation and job satisfaction. Changes in the mix of tasks and in the amount of responsibility assigned to the human may lead to fundamental role transitions that have an impact on the congruency between self-concept, perceived job demand, and the expectations of the organization and the society to the job-holder (Neale & Griffin 2006). At present, pilots, for example, still undergo a sophisticated selection and training process to become an airline pilot both contributing to a high level of self-esteem, appreciation by society, and joy in the fulfillment of their job. Automation may make them feel that they have become less important. As Billings (1997) notes, "every self-respecting pilot would agree that a cognitively difficult, complex flight followed by a skilful manually flown approach and a safe, gentle landing provides an intellectual satisfaction second to few others. What a waste to hand over to the machine" (p. 64). Surveys on pilots' attitudes toward automation, however, did not reveal profound indications of automation-induced job dissatisfaction (Curry 1985; Wiener 1985, 1989). On the contrary, pilots mostly expressed pride in flying a modern high-technology aircraft. Nevertheless, concerns about negative role transitions need to be taken seriously. At present many air traffic controllers worry about their role in a future air traffic management. Answers to the question "Should we automate?" in face of these considerations need much broader conceptual frameworks to guide deliberate system development decisions.

REFERENCES

Abbott, K., Slotte, S., Stimson, D. *et al.* (1996). *The Interfaces between Flightcrews and Modern Flight Deck Systems* (Report of the FAA Human Factors Team). Washington, DC: Federal Aviation Administration.

Allen, N. J. M. & Kessel, R. T. (2002). The roles of human operator and machine in decision aid strategies for target detection. Paper presented at the RTO HFM Symposium on "The role of humans in intelligent and automated systems," Warsaw, Poland, October 7–9, 2002. RTO-MP-088, 3-1-14. Neuilly-sur-Seine: NATO/RTO.

Bahner, J. E., Hueper, A.-D. & Manzey, D. (2006). Complacency in automated fault management: how to keep operators alert towards possible failures of automated aids? Paper presented at the International Ergonomics Association (IEA) Conference, July 10–14 2006, Maastricht, The Netherlands.

Bainbridge, L. (1983). Ironies of automation. *Automatica*, *19*, 775–779.

Bannon, L. J. (2001). Toward a social and societal ergonomics: a perspective from computer-supported cooperative work. In M. McNeese, E. Salas & M. Endsley (eds.), *New Trends in Cooperative Activities: Understanding System Dynamics in Complex Environments* (pp. 9–21). Santa Monica, CA: Human Factors and Ergonomic Society.

Bennett, K. B. & Flach, J. M. (1992). Graphical displays: implications for divided attention, focused attention, and problem solving. *Human Factors*, *34*, 513–533.

Billings, C. E. (1991). *Human Centered Aircraft Automation: A Concept and Guidelines* (NASA Tech. Memorandum 102885). Moffet Field, CA: NASA Ames Research Center.

Billings, C. E. (1997). *Aviation Automation: The Search for a Human-Centered Approach.* Hillsdale, NJ: Lawrence Erlbaum Associates.

Billings, C. E., Lauber, J. K., Funkhouser, H. *et al.* (1976). *NASA Aviation Safety Reporting System* (Tech. Memo. No. TM-X-3445). Moffet Field, CA: NASA Ames Research Center.

Boeing (2004). *Statistical Summary of Commercial Jet Airplane Accidents. Worldwide Operations 1959–2003.* Seattle/Washington: Author. Available at http://www.boeing.com/news/techissues/pdf/statsum.pdf [June 17, 2004].

Brandimonte, M., Einstein, G. O. & McDaniel, M. A. (1996). *Prospective Memory: Theory and Applications.* Mahwah, NJ: Lawrence Erlbaum Associates.

Christoffersen, K. & Woods, D. D. (2002). How to make automated systems team players. In E. Salas (ed.), *Advances in Human Performance and Cognitive Engineering Research, Vol. 2.* Amsterdam: Elsevier.

Corker, K. M. (2000). Cognitive models and control: human and system dynamics in advanced airspace operation. In N. B. Sarter & R. Amalberti (eds.), *Cognitive Engineering in the Aviation Domain* (pp. 13–42). Mahwah, NJ: Lawrence Erlbaum Associates.

Crocoll, W. M. & Coury, B. G. (1990). Status or recommendation: selecting the type of information for decision-aiding. *Proceedings of the Human Factors and Ergonomics Society 34th Annual Meeting* (pp. 1524–1528). Santa Monica, CA: HFES.

Curry, R. E. (1985). *The Introduction of New Cockpit Technology: A Human Factors Study.* NASA TM 86659. Moffett Field, CA: NASA Ames Research Center.

Curry, R. E. & Ephrath, A. R. (1977). Monitoring and control of unreliable systems. In T. B. Sheridan & G. Johannsen (eds.), *Monitoring Behavior and Supervisory Control.* New York: Plenum.

Davies, D. R. & Parasuraman, R. (1982). *The Psychology of Vigilance.* London: Academic Press.

Dearden, A. (2001). IDA-S: a conceptual framework for partial automation. In A. Blandford, J. Vanderdonckt & P. Gray (eds.), *People and Computers XV – Interaction without Frontiers.* Proceedings of IHM-HCI 2001. Berlin: Springer.

Dearden, A., Harrison, M. & Wright, P. (2000). Allocation of function: scenarios, context and the economics of effort. *International Journal of Human–Computer Studies, 52,* 289–318.

Debernard, S., Cathelain, S., Crévits, I. & Poulain, T. (2002). AMANDA project: delegation of tasks in the air-traffic control domain. In M. Blay-Fournarino, A.-M. Pinna-Dery, K. Schmidt & P. Zaraté (eds.), *Cooperative Systems Design* (pp. 173–190). Amsterdam: IOS.

Degani, A. & Heymann, M. (2002). Formal verification of human–automation interaction. *Human Factors, 44,* 28–43.

Effken, J. A., Kim, N.-G. & Shaw, R. E. (1997). Making the constraints visible: testing the ecological approach to interface design. *Ergonomics, 40,* 1–27.

Endsley, M. (1988). Design and evaluation for situation awareness enhancement. In *Proceedings of the Human Factors Society 32nd Annual Meeting* (pp. 97–101). Santa Monica, CA: Human Factors Society.

Endsley, M. R. (1995a). Measurement of situation awareness in dynamic systems. *Human Factors, 37,* 65–84.

Endsley, M. R. (1995b). Toward a theory of situation awareness in dynamic systems. *Human Factors, 37,* 32–64.

Endsley, M. R., Bolté, B. & Jones, D. G. (2003). *Designing for Situation Awareness: An Approach to User-Centered Design.* New York: Taylor and Francis.

Endsley, M. R. & Kaber, D. B. (1999). Level of automation effects on performance, situation awareness and workload in a dynamic control task. *Ergonomics, 42,* 462–492.

Endsley, M. R. & Kiris, E. O. (1995). The out-of-the-loop performance problem and level of control in automation. *Human Factors, 37,* 281–394.

Ephrath, A. R. & Young, L. R. (1981). Monitoring vs. man-in-the-loop detection of aircraft control failures. In J. Rasmussen & W. B. Rouse (eds.), *Human Detection and Diagnosis of System Failures* (pp. 143–154). New York: Plenum Press.

Fadden, S., Ververs, P. M. & Wickens, C. D. (2001). Pathway HUDs: are they viable? *Human Factors, 43,* 173–193.

Fitts, P. M. (1951). Engineering psychology and equipment design. In S. S. Stevens (ed.), *Handbook of Experimental Psychology* (pp. 1301–1306). New York: John Wiley & Sons.

Furukawa, H., Parasuraman, R. & Inagaki, T. (2003). Supporting system-centered view of operators through ecological interface design: two experiments on human-centered automation. In *Proceedings of the Human Factors and Ergonomics Society* (pp. 567–571). Santa Monica, CA: Human Factors and Ergonomics Society.

Guerlain, S., Smith, P. J., Obradovich, J. *et al.* (1999). Interactive critiquing as a form of decision support: an empirical evaluation. *Hunan Factors, 41,* 72–89.

Guerlain, S., Smith, P. J., Obradovich, J. *et al.* (1995). The Antibody Identification Assistant (AIDA), an example of a cooperative computer support system. In *Proceedings of the 1995 IEEE International Conference on Systems, Man and Cybernetics* (pp. 1909–1914). New York: International Institute of Electrical and Electronics Engineers.

Harrison, M. D., Johnson, P. D. & Wright, P. C. (2003). Relating the automation of functions in multiagent control systems to a system engineering representation. In E. Hollnagel (ed.), *Handbook of Cognitive Task Design* (pp. 503–524). Mahwah, NJ: Lawrence Erlbaum Associates.

Hoc, J-M. (2001). Towards a cognitive approach to human-machine cooperation in dynamic situations. *International Journal of Human–Computer Studies, 54,* 509–540.

Hoc, J-M. & Debernard, S. (2002). Respective demands of task and function allocation on human–machine cooperation design: a psychological approach. *Connection Science, 14,* 283–295.

Hoc, J. M. & Lemoine, M. P. (1998). Cognitive evaluation of human-human and human–machine cooperation modes in air traffic control. *International Journal of Aviation Psychology, 8*, 1–32.

Hollnagel, E. (1999). From function allocation to function congruence. In S. Dekker & E. Hollnagel (eds.), *Coping with Computers in the Cockpit* (pp. 29–53). Aldershot: Ashgate.

Jentsch, F., Barnett, J., Bowers, C. A. & Salas, E. (1999). Who is flying this plane anyway? What mishaps tell us about crew member role assignment and air crew situation awareness. *Human Factors, 41*, 1–14.

Jones, P. & Jasek, C. (1997). Intelligent support for activity management (ISAM): an architecture to support distributed supervisory control. *IEEE Transactions on Systems, Man, and Cybernetics – Part A: Systems and Humans, 27*, 274–288.

Jordan, N. (1963). Allocation of functions between man and machines in automated systems. *Journal of Applied Psychology, 47*, 161–165.

Kaber, D. B. & Endsley, M. (2004). The effects of level of automation and adaptive automation on human performance, situation awareness and workload in a dynamic control task. *Theoretical Issues in Ergonomics Science, 5*, 113–153.

Kaber, D. B., Onal, E. & Endsley, M. R. (2000). Design of automation for telerobots and the effect on performance, operator situation awareness and subjective workload. *Human Factors and Ergonomics in Manufacturing, 10*, 409–430.

Kelly, B. D. (2004). Flight deck design and integration of commercial air transports. In D. Harris (ed.). *Human Factors for Civil Flight Deck Design* (pp. 3–31). Aldershot: Ashgate.

Lee, J. D. & Moray, N. (1992). Trust, control strategies and allocation of function in human–machine systems. *Ergonomics, 35*, 243–1270.

Lee, J. D. & Moray, N. (1994). Trust, self confidence, and operators' adaptation to automation. *International Journal of Human–Computer Studies, 40*, 153–184.

Lee, J. D. & See, K. A. (2004). Trust in automation: designing for appropriate reliance, *Human Factors, 46*, 50–80.

Lorenz, B., Di Nocera, N. & Parasuraman, R. (2004). Examination of the proximity-compatibility principle in the design of displays in support of fault management. In D. de Waard, K. A. Brookhuis & C. M. Weikert (eds.), *Human Factors in Design* (pp. 213–229). Maastricht: Shaker.

Lorenz, B., Di Nocera, F., Röttger, S. & Parasuraman, R. (2002). Automated fault-management in a simulated space flight micro-world. *Aviation, Space, and Environmental Medicine, 73*, 886–897.

Mc Farlane, D. C. & Latorella, K. A. (2002). The scope and importance of human interruption in human-computer interaction design. *Human–Computer Interaction, 17*, 1–61.

Mc Namara, D. S. & Healy, A. F. (1995). A generation advantage for multiplication skill training and nonword vocabulary acquisition. In A. F. Healy & L. E. Bourne Jr (eds.), *Learning and Memory of Knowledge and Skills*. Thousand Oaks, CA: Sage.

Malin, J. & Schreckenghost, D. L. (1992). *Making Intelligent Systems Team Players: Overview for Designers (NASA Techn. Mem. 104751)*. Houston, TX: Johnston Space Center.

Martin-Emerson, R. & Wickens, C. D. (1997). Superimposition, symbology, visual attention, and the head-up display. *Human Factors, 39*, 581–601.

Merlo, J. L., Wickens, C. D. & Yeh, M. (1999). *Effect of Reliability on Cue Effectiveness and Display Signaling, Technical Report, ARL-99-04/FED-LAB-99-3*. Urbana, IL: University of Illinois, Institute of Aviation, Aviation Human Factors Division.

Metzger, U. & Parasuraman, R. (2001). Automation-related "complacency": Theory, empirical data, and design implications. In *Proceedings of the Human Factors and Ergonomics Society 45th Annual Meeting* (pp. 463–467). Santa Monica, CA: Human Factors and Ergonomics Society.

Miller, C. A., Goldman, R., Funk, F. *et al.* (2004). A playbook approach to variable autonomy control: application for control of multiple, heterogeneous unmanned air vehicles. *Proceedings of FORUM 60, the Annual Meeting of the American Helicopter Society*. Baltimore, MD, June 7–10.

Miller, C. A. & Parasuraman, R. (in press). Designing for flexible interaction between humans and automation: delegation interfaces for supervisory control. *Human Factors*.

Miller, C. A., Pelican, M. & Goldman, R. (2000). "Tasking" interfaces to keep the operator in control: In M. E. Benedict (Ed.), *Proceedings of the 5th International Conference on Human Interaction with Complex Systems* (pp. 87–91). Urbana, IL: University of Illinois at Urbana Champaign.

Moray, N. (1986). Monitoring behavior and supervisory control. In K. Boff, L. Kaufman & J. Thomas (eds.), *Handbook of Perception and Human Performance* (Vol. 2, pp. 40–1, 40–51). New York: John Wiley & Sons.

Moray, N. (1997). Human factors in process control. In G. Salvendy (ed.), *Handbook of Human Factors and Ergonomics* (2nd edn, pp. 1944–1971). New York: John Wiley & Sons.

Moray, N. (2003). Monitoring, complacency, scepticism and eutactic behaviour. *International Journal of Industrial Ergonomics, 31*, 175–178.

Moray, N. & Inagaki, T. (2001). Attention and complacency. *Theoretical Issues in Ergonomics Science, 1*, 354–365.

Moray, N., Inagaki, T. & Itoh, M. (2000). Adaptive automation, trust, and self-confidence in fault management of time-critical tasks. *Journal of Experimental Psychology: Applied, 6*, 44–58.

Mosier, K. L. & Skitka, L. J. (1996). Human decision makers and automated decision aids: made for each other? In R. Parasuraman & M. Mouloua (eds.), *Automation and Human Performance: Theory and Applications* (pp. 201–220). Mahwah, NJ: Lawrence Erlbaum Associates.

Neale, M. & Griffin, M. A. (2006). A model of self-held work roles and role transitions. *Human Performance, 19*, 23–41.

Norman, D. A. (1990). The problem with automation: inappropriate feedback and interaction, not "over-automation." *Philosophical Transactions of the Royal Society of London, B 327*, 585–593.

Ntuen, C. A. & Park, E. H. (1988). Human factors issues in teleoperated systems. In W. Karwowski, H. R. Parsaei & M. R. Wilhelm (eds.), *Ergonomics of Hybrid Automated Systems I*. Amsterdam: Elsevier.

O'Hare, D., Wiggins, M., Batt, R. & Morrison, D. (1994). Cognitive failure analysis for aircraft accident investigation. *Ergonomics, 37*, 1855–1869.

Pacaux-Lemoine, M-P. & Debernard, S. (2002). Common work space for human–machine cooperation in air traffic control. *Control Engineering Practice, 10*, 571–576.

Palmer, M. T., Rodgers, W. H., Press, H. N. *et al.* (1995). *A Crew-Centered Flight-Deck Philosophy for High-Speed Civil Transport (HSCT) Aircraft.* NASA Technical Memorandum 109171. Hampton, VA: NASA Langley Research Center.

Parasuraman, R. (1987). Human–computer monitoring. *Human Factors, 29*, 695–706.

Parasuraman, R., Galster, S., Squire, P. *et al.* (2005). A flexible delegation interface enhances system performance in human supervision of multiple autonomous robots: empirical studies with RoboFlag. *IEEE Transactions on Systems, Man & Cybernetics – Part A: Systems and Humans, 35*, 481–493.

Parasuraman, R. & Miller, C. (2005). Delegation interfaces for human supervision of multiple unmanned vehicles: theory, experiments, and practical applications. In H. Pedersen & N. Cooke (eds.), *Human Factors of Remotely Operated Vehicles.* New York: Plenum.

Parasuraman, R., Molloy, R. & Singh, I. L. (1993). Performance consequences of automation-induced "complacency." *The International Journal of Aviation Psychology, 3*, 1–23.

Parasuraman, R. & Mouloua, M. (1996). *Automation and Human Performance.* Mahwah, NJ: Lawrence Erlbaum Associates

Parasuraman, R. & Riley, V. A. (1997). Humans and automation: use, misuse, disuse, abuse. *Human Factors, 39*, 230–253.

Parasuraman, R., Sheridan, T. B. & Wickens, C. D. (2000). A model of types and levels of human interaction with automation. *IEEE Transactions on Systems, Man, and Cybernetics – Part A: Systems and Humans, 30*, 286–297.

Posner, M. I. (1980). Orienting of attention. *Quarterly Journal of Experimental Psychology, 32*, 3–25.

Potter, S. S., Elm, W. C., Roth, E. M. *et al.* (2002). Using intermediate design artifacts to bridge the gap between cognitive analysis and cognitive engineering. In M. McNeese & M. Vidulich (eds.), *Cognitive Systems Engineering in Military Aviation Environments: Avoiding Cogminutia Fragmentosa* (Chapter 5, pp. 137–166). Wright-Patterson AFB, OH: Human Systems Information Analysis Center.

Riera, B. & Debernard, S. (2003). Basic cognitive principles applied to the design of advanced supervisory systems for process control. In E. Hollnagel (ed.), *Handbook of Cognitive Task Design* (pp. 255–281). Mahwah, NJ: Lawrence Erlbaum Associates.

Rovira, E., McGarry, K. & Parasuraman, R. (in press). Effects of imperfect automation on decision-making in a simulated command and control task. *Human Factors.*

Sarter, N. B. & Schroeder, B. K. (2001). Supporting decision-making and action selection under time pressure and uncertainty: the case of in-flight icing. *Human Factors, 43*, 573–583.

Sarter, N. B. & Woods, D. D. (1992). Pilot interaction with cockpit automation: operational experiences with the Flight Management System. *The International Journal of Aviation Psychology, 2*, 303–321.

Sarter, N. B. & Woods, D. D. (2000). Team play with a powerful and independent agent: a full-mission simulation study. *Human Factors, 42*, 390–402.

Sarter, N., Woods, D. & Billings, C. E. (1997). Automation surprises. In G. Salvendy (ed.), *Handbook of Human Factors and Ergonomics* (2nd edn, pp. 1926–1943). New York: John Wiley & Sons.

Schmidt, K. (1991). Cooperative work: a conceptual framework. In J. Rasmussen, B. Brehmer & J. Leplat (eds.), *Distributed Decision-Making: Cognitive Models for Cooperative Work* (pp. 75–110). Chichester: John Wiley & Sons.

Schweickert, R., Fisher, D. L. & Proctor, R. W. (2003). Steps toward building mathematical and computer models from cognitive task analyses. *Human Factors, 45*, 77–103.

Semple, W. G. (1998). Information, decision or Action? – The role of IT in fast jet mission systems. In *Proceedings of the 1998 AGARD Conference MP3.* Neuilly-sur-Seine: NATO Advisory Group on Aerospace Research & Development.

Sheridan, T. B. (1992). *Telerobotics, Automation, and Human Supervisory Control.* Cambridge, MA: MIT Press.

Sheridan, T. B. (2002). *Humans and Automation: System Designs and Research Issues.* Santa Monica, CA and New York: Human Factors and Ergonomics Society and John Wiley & Sons.

Sheridan, T. B. & Parasuraman, R. (2006). Humans and automation: a review of recent research. In R. Nickerson (ed.), *Reviews of Human Factors and Ergonomics* (Vol. 1, pp. 89–129). Santa Monica, CA: Human Factors & Ergonomics Society.

Sheridan, T. B. & Verplank, W. L. (1978). *Human and Computer Control of Undersea Teleoperators.* Massachusetts Institute of Technology, Cambridge, MA: Man–Machine Systems Laboratory, Department of Mechanical Engineering (Tech. Rep.).

Shoval, S., Koren, Y. & Borenstein, J. (1993). Optimal task allocation in task agent control state space. In *Proceedings of the IEEE Conference on Systems, Man and Cybernetics* (pp. 27–32). Piscataway, NJ: IEEE Press.

Singh, I. L., Molloy, R. & Parasuraman, R. (1997). Automation induced monitoring inefficiency: role of display location. *International Journal of Human–Computer Studies, 46*, 17–30.

Slameca, N. J. & Graf, P. (1978). The generation effect: delineation of a phenomenon. *Journal of Experimental Psychology: Human Learning and Memory, 4*, 592–604.

Sumwalt, R. L., Morrison, R., Watson, A. & Taube, E. (1999). What ASRS data tell about inadequate flight monitoring. In R. S. Jensen & L. A. Rakovan (eds.), *Proceedings of the 10th International Symposium on Aviation Psychology* (pp. 977–982). Columbus, OH: Ohio State University.

Tarnowski, E. (1999). *Airbus Cockpit Philosophy.* (Ref.: AI/ST-D/SR–148–05/99). Blagnac, France: Airbus Industries.

Thackray, R. I. & Touchstone, R. M. (1989). Detection efficiency on an air traffic task with and without computer aiding. *Aviation, Space, and Environmental Medicine, 60*, 744–748.

Treisman, A. M. (1982). Perceptual grouping and attention in visual search for features and for objects. *Journal of Experimental Psychology: Human Perception and Performance, 8*, 194–214.

Vicente, K. J. (1996). Improving dynamic decision-making in complex systems through ecological interface design: a research review. *System Dynamics Review, 12*, 251–279.

Vicente, K. J. & Rasmussen, J. (1992). Ecological interface design: theoretical foundations. *IEEE Transactions on Systems, Man, and Cybernetics, 22*, 589–606.

Wickens, C. D. (2005). Attentional tunneling and task management. *Proceedings of the 13th International Symposium on Aviation Psychology* (pp. 620–625). Oklahoma City, OK, April 18–21.

Wickens, C. D. & Carswell, C. M. (1995). The proximity-compatibility principle: its psychological foundation and relevance to display design. *Human Factors*, *37*, 473–494.

Wickens, C. D. & Hollands, J. G. (2000). *Engineering Psychology and Human Performance*. Upper Saddle River, NJ: Prentice Hall.

Wickens, C. D. & Kessel, C. (1981). Failure detection in dynamic systems. In J. Rasmussen & W. B. Rouse (eds.), *Human Detection and Diagnosis of System Failures* (pp. 155–169). New York: Plenum.

Wickens, C. D. & Long, J. (1995). Object vs. space-based models of visual attention: implications for the design of head-up displays. *Journal of Experimental Psychology: Applied*, *1*, 179–193.

Wickens, C. D., Muthard, E. K., Alexander, A. L. *et al.* (2003). The influence of display highlighting and size and event eccentricity for aviation surveillance. *Proceedings of the 47th Annual Meeting of the Human Factors and Ergonomics Society* (pp. 149–153). Santa Monica, CA: Human Factors and Ergonomics Society.

Wiener, E. L. (1981). Complacency: is the term useful for air safety? In *Proceedings of the 26th Corporate Aviation Safety Seminar* (pp. 116–125). Denver, CO: Flight Safety Foundation, Inc.

Wiener, E. L. (1985). *Human Factors of Cockpit Automation: A Field Study of Flight Crew Transition*. NASA CR 177333. Moffett Field, CA: NASA Ames Research Center.

Wiener, E. L. (1988). Cockpit automation. In E. L. Wiener & D. C. Nagel (eds.), *Human Factors in Aviation* (pp. 433–461). San Diego, CA: Academic Press.

Wiener, E. L. (1989). *Human Factors of Advanced Technology ("Glass Cockpit") Transport Aircraft*. NASA CR 177528. Moffett Field, CA: NASA Ames Research Center.

Wiener, E. L. & Curry, R. E. (1980). Flight-deck automation: promises and problems. *Ergonomics*, *23*, 995–1011.

Woods, D. D. (1994a). Automation: apparent simplicity, real complexity. In M. Mouloua & R. Parasuraman (eds.), *Human Performance in Automated Systems: Current Research and Trends* (pp. 1–7). Hillsdale, NJ: Lawrence Erlbaum Associates.

Woods, D. D. (1994b). Cognitive demands and activities in dynamic fault management: abductive reasoning and disturbance management. In N. Stanton (ed.), *The Human Factors of Alarm Design*. London: Taylor and Francis.

Woods, D. D. (1995). Toward a theoretical base for representation design in the computer medium: ecological perception and aiding human cognition. In J. M. Flach, P. A. Hancock, J. Caird & K. J. Vicente (eds.), *Global Perspectives on the Ecology of Human-Machine Systems* (pp. 157–188). Hillsdale, NJ: Lawrence Erlbaum Associates.

Yeh, M. & Wickens, C. D. (2001). Display signaling in augmented reality: the effects of cue reliability and image realism on attention allocation and trust calibration. *Human Factors*, *43*, 355–365.

Yeh, M., Wickens, C. D. & Seagull, F. J. (1999). Target cueing in visual search: the effects of conformality and display location on the allocation of visual attention. *Human Factors*, *41*, 524–542.

Young, L. (1969). On adaptive manual control. *IEEE Transactions on Man–Machine Systems*, *10*, 292–331.

CHAPTER 17

Cognitive Models of Human–Information Interaction

Peter Pirolli
Palo Alto Research Center, USA

INTRODUCTION

Human–information interaction (HII) is an emerging branch of human–computer interaction (HCI) which is concerned with how people interact with and process outwardly accessible information such as the World Wide Web.[1] However, HII adopts an information-centric approach rather than the computer-centric approach to the field of human–computer interaction (Lucas 2000). Like HCI, HII is an application field that provides a complex test bed for theories of *cognitive architecture*. In turn, such theories provide the basis for *cognitive engineering models* that can yield predictions about technology and information design. This chapter provides an overview of cognitive architectures and cognitive engineering models in the context of human–information interaction.

The evolution of HCI toward the information-centric field of HII has occurred because of the increasing *pervasiveness* of information services, the increasing *transparency* of user interfaces, the *convergence* of information delivery technologies, and the trend toward *ubiquitous computing* (Lucas 2000). Access to the Internet is pervasive through land lines, satellite, cable, mobile devices, and wireless services. The field of HCI over the past two decades and more has led to the development of computers and computer applications that are increasingly transparent to users performing their tasks. In parallel, the business world around consumer media technologies shows excitement over the convergence of television, cell phones, PCs (personal computers), PDAs (Personal Digital Assistants), cars, set-tops, digital music players, and other consumer electronic devices, as well as the convergence among the means for transporting information, such as the Internet, radio, satellite, cable, and so on. Research on ubiquitous computing looks forward to a world in which computational devices are basically everywhere in our homes, mobile devices, cars, and so on, and these devices can be marshaled to perform arbitrary tasks for users. The net effect of these trends is to make computers invisible, just as electricity

Handbook of Applied Cognition: Second Edition. Edited by Francis T. Durso.

and electric motors are invisible in homes today (Norman 1998). As computers become invisible and information becomes copious and pervasive, we expect to see a continuing shift in studies from human–computer interaction to human–information interaction. Digital content is becoming independent of the particular physical storage devices and interaction devices. Rather than focus on the structure of devices and application programs, the focus of HII research centers on interaction with content and interactive media.

Although information is part of the focus of the field of HII, it is not the sole focus. HII continues to share with HCI a focus on the psychology of users. Information per se, whether in the classical sense (patterns of organization) or common sense (documents, email, summaries, document clusters, search results, etc.), is of limited interest. Information content has the potential to be used in ways that improve the achievement of human purposes. Information itself is best understood in relation to human use of that information, so human intentionality, psychology, and activity are crucial to providing coherence to the study of human–information interaction.

This chapter takes a particular approach to the psychology of HII, with a focus on the cognitive architectures and cognitive engineering models that are being extended to deal with HII questions. Cognitive engineering in the domains of HCI and HII is founded on the assumption that psychology ought to be able to predict the consequences of different technology designs. For instance, cognitive engineering models have been developed to address questions such as:

- How much time would it take to perform elementary tasks, like inserting, deleting, or moving text?
- How long will it take to learn the skills required for basic text editing?
- Will knowledge of other applications, such as a spreadsheet, transfer to the text editor?
- Will a user be able to figure out how to perform tasks (e.g., by exploration of the interface) without explicit instruction?
- How long will it take an experienced user to find an answer to a question using their PDA?
- What arrangement of information on a display yields more effective visual search?
- How difficult will it be for a user to find information on a website?

For modern information systems, iterative empirical testing and design revision are usually too expensive and too slow. One solution to this practical problem has been the development of *discount usability methods* (e.g., Nielsen & Mack 1974; Spool *et al.* 1999; Nielsen 2000) that employ low-cost techniques such as think-aloud usability tests and heuristic evaluations with small numbers of subjects (often experts in the target domain of interest), often using low-fidelity interface prototypes than can be easily redesigned. This method is aimed at rapidly uncovering bugs in the design at low cost. At the early stages of design, user interfaces often have so many bugs that this approach is productive. Cognitive engineering models form a complementary approach founded on the twin notions that prediction is a sign of understanding and control over the phenomena of interest, and a designer with an engineering model in hand can explore and explain the quantitative and qualitative effects of different design decisions before the heavy investment of resources for implementation and testing. This exploration of design space is more efficient because the choices among different design alternatives are better informed:

Rather than operating solely by intuition, the designer is in a position to know which avenues are better to explore and which are better to ignore. Nearly 40 years ago, when the first textbook on cognitive psychology was written (Neisser 1967), it would have been impossible to answer the questions listed above based on psychological theory alone. Only the first of these could have been answered in a restricted way nearly 25 years ago, when the first classic monograph on the psychology of HCI was written (Card *et al.* 1983). The second, third, and fourth questions could be answered at the time of publication of first edition of the *Handbook of Applied Cognition* (Pirolli 1999). Recent progress allows us to begin to address the last three questions. The continual accumulation of knowledge and progress in predictive power is a measure of the fruitfulness of the marriage of psychology and human–information interaction.

HUMAN–INFORMATION INTERACTION

During the 1990s, there was an explosion in the amount of information that became available to the average computer user, and the development of new technologies for accessing and interacting with all of that information. The late 1980s witnessed several strands of HCI research devoted to ameliorating problems of exploring and finding electronically stored information. It had become apparent that users could no longer remember the names of all their electronic files, and it was even more difficult for them to guess the names of files stored by others (Furnas *et al.* 1987). In the mid- to late 1980s HCI literature there were several proposals to enhance users' ability to search and explore external memory. Jones (1986) proposed the Memory Extender (ME), which used a model of human associative memory (Anderson 1983) to automatically retrieve files represented by sets of keywords that were similar to the sets of keywords representing the users' working context. Latent Semantic Analysis (LSA; Dumais *et al.* 1988) was developed to mimic human ability to detect deeper semantic associations among words, like "dog" and "cat," to similarly enhance information retrieval.

Hypermedia also became a hot topic during the late 1980s, with Apple's introduction of HyperCard in 1987, the first ACM Conference on Hypertext in 1987, and a paper session at the CHI '88 conference.[2] The very idea of hypertext can be traced back to Vannevar Bush's *Atlantic Monthly* article "As We May Think" (Bush 1945). Worried about scholars becoming overwhelmed by the amount of information being published, Bush proposed a mechanized private file system, the Memex, which would augment the memory of the individual user. It was explicitly intended to mimic human associative memory. Bush's article influenced the development of Douglas Engelbart's NLS (oNLine System), which was introduced to the world in a tour-de-force demonstration at the 1968 Fall Joint Computer Conference. The demonstration of NLS – a system explicitly designed to "augment human intellect" (Engelbart 1962) – also introduced the world to the power of networking, the mouse, and point-and-click interaction. Hypertext and hypermedia research arose during the late 1980s because PC power, networking, and user interfaces had evolved to the point where the visions of Bush and Engelbart could finally be realized for the average computer user.

The confluence of increased computing power, storage, and networking and information access and hypermedia research in the late 1980s set the stage for the widespread deployment of hypermedia in the form of the World Wide Web. In 1989, Tim Berners-Lee proposed a solution (Berners-Lee 1989) to the problems that were being faced by the CERN[3] community in dealing with distributed collections of documents, which were stored on many types of platforms, in many types of formats. This proposal led directly to the release of the World Wide Web in 1990. Berners-Lee's vision was not only to provide users with more effective access to information, but also to initiate an evolving web of information that reflected and enhanced the community and its activities. The emergence of the Web in the 1990s provided new challenges and opportunities for HCI. The increased wealth of accessible content, and the use of the Web as a place to do business, exacerbated the need to improve the user experience on the Web. The phenomenal growth of the Web, and the increasing pervasiveness of interaction with electronic content provided novel questions for cognitive architectures and engineering models, and initiated the development of information foraging theory, all of which are discussed in the next sections.

COGNITIVE ARCHITECTURES

Scientific understanding and prediction in the field of HII requires integrative psychological theories. Theories need to provide predictions at multiple time-scales of phenomena and provide explanations in multiple ways. Theories also have to integrate across the typical subdivisions of psychological theory. Cognitive architectures provide such integration and are consequently a good source of applied theory for HII.

The early growth of cognitive psychology during the 1950s and 1960s was characterized by research in largely independent experimental paradigms. Each such paradigm might involve variations on one or a few experimental tasks which were designed to address a few interesting questions about the nature of cognition. In a classic challenge to the field, Allen Newell (1973) argued that cognitive psychology could not make significant progress by this divide-and-conquer approach to research. Newell believed that understanding cognition, in even simple tasks, required an integrated theory of many cognitive processes and structures. Findings from one paradigm were surely relevant to the analysis of other paradigms. Progress, Newell (1973) argued, would require the development of theories that provide a unified way of accounting for all the diverse phenomena and tasks found in the individual paradigms.

One of the significant recent developments in theories of cognitive architecture has been the integration of perceptual-motor theories with cognitive theory. Interestingly, the inspiration for this effort came from an HCI cognitive engineering model developed by Card *et al.* (1983). This section will begin with a review of the Model Human Processor developed by Card *et al.* (1983) because of the importance of this model in both HCI and as a harbinger of recent developments in cognitive architectures

The Model Human Processor

The Model Human Processor (Figure 17.1) developed by Card *et al.* (1983) is a synthesis of findings from a diverse set of cognitive psychology paradigms. The purpose for its development was to provide a way for engineers to make zero-parameter predictions about performance with HCI systems.[4] The Model Human Processor is specified as (a) a set of

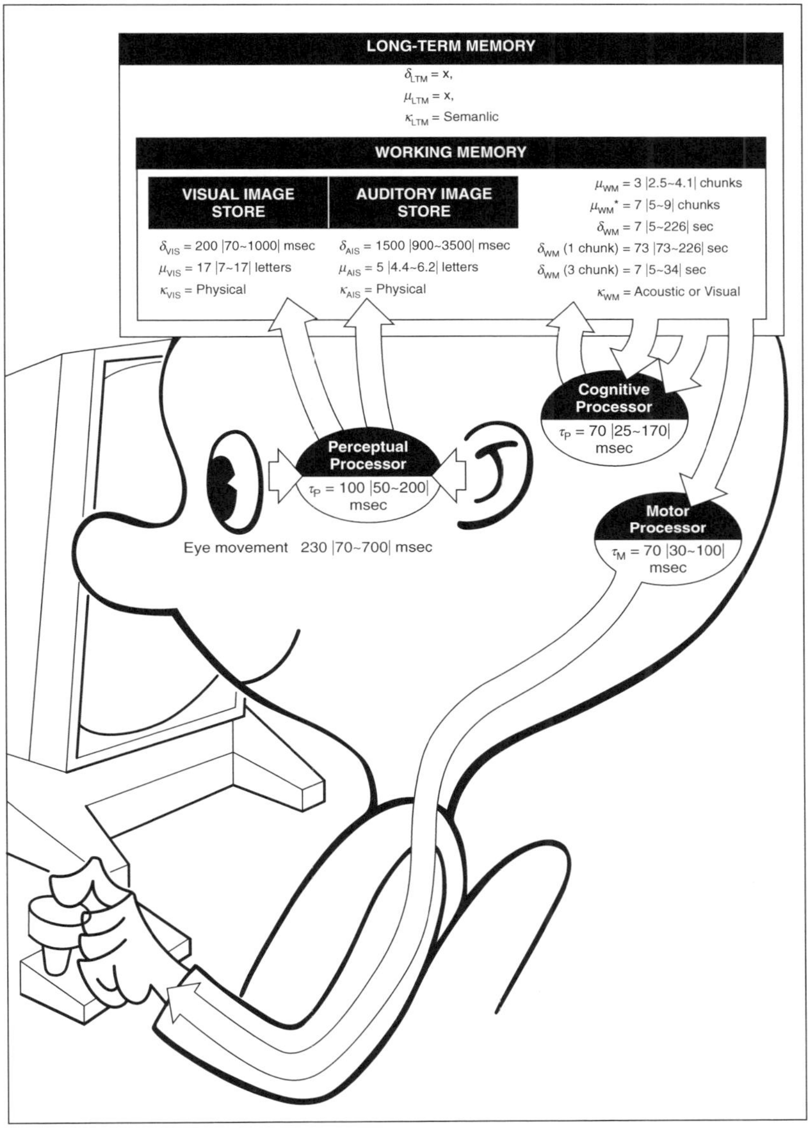

Figure 17.1 The Model Human Processor. Note that some estimates have changed since the original formulation. See text for details. From S. K. Card, T. P. Moran & A. Newell (1990), *The Psychology of Human–Computer Interaction* (p. 26). Hillsdale, NJ: Lawrence Erlbaum Associates. © 1983 by Lawrence Erlbaum Associates. Reprinted with permission

memories and processors and (b) a set of principles of operation. The processors and memories are summarized schematically in Figure 17.1. There are three subsystems for perceptual input, motor action, and cognition. The processors and memories in Figure 17.1 are characterized by a set of parameters:

- the storage capacity in terms of maximum number of items stored;
- the decay rate of an item (the time an item will reside in memory);
- the main type of code (representation type) of information, which may be physical, visual, acoustic, or semantic; and
- the cycle time (the time at which inputs to memory are updated).

The parameters are typical values extracted from the psychological literature. The general idea is that information is input from the world through the *perceptual processors*, into the visual and auditory stores. Some of this information makes its way into a *working memory*, which is operated on by the *cognitive processor*. The cognitive processor uses associations between information in working memory and *long-term memory* to make decisions and formulate actions. Actions in working memory trigger the *motor processor* to effect behavior in the world.

Card *et al.* (1983) define a set of principles of operation for the Model Human Processor (see also Pirolli 1999). The cognitive processor works through a *recognize–act cycle* on the contents of working memory. Working memory is assumed to be the information that a person is currently heeding – their focus of attention. These working memory structures are called *chunks* (Miller 1956; Simon 1974). In the recognize phase, information in working memory retrieves associated actions in long-term memory. The act phase of the cycle executes those retrieved actions and changes the contents of working memory. These associations between working memory information and effective actions in long-term memory are built from prior experience. The associations may be organized in the form of plans, such as plans of organized action for operating an interface. In the original Model Human Processor of Card *et al.* (1983), each recognize–act cycle takes 70 ms on average (Figure 17.1). Research since that original formulation has revised the recognize–act cycle time down to 50 ms (John & Kieras 1996a).

Working memory is assumed to be of limited capacity and rapid decay rate. For instance, without rehearsal, only about 3–7 chunks of information can be held in working memory for about seven seconds (Miller 1956). On the other hand, long-term memory is of very large capacity (Landauer 1986) and a very slow decay rate (Figure 17.1). It is the repository of the collective experience and learning of a person. It contains both factual knowledge as well as knowledge of how to perform procedures. Although long-term memory has effectively infinite capacity and permanent retention, there are factors that make retrieval less than perfect. These factors have to do with the ability of cues in working memory to retrieve associated information in long-term memory.

For the perceptual processor, it is assumed that auditory and visual stimuli trigger the appearance of representations in the auditory and visual memory stores. The representations in these memories encode mostly physical (non-symbolic) characteristics such as the intensity of a sound or the curvature of a line. These memories are also of limited capacity and very rapid decay (items have a half-life of 200 ms in the visual store and about 1500 ms in the auditory store). The perceptual processor has a cycle time of about 100 ms, which varies with stimulus intensity. The motor processor is assumed to operate with an approximately 70 ms cycle time. Many interactions with computers require movements of the hand or a hand-held mouse to some target location. The time to move the hand, or a mouse pointer, to a target may be calculated by Fitts' law (MacKenzie 2003), which depends on the distance to be traveled by the movement and the size of the target.

EPIC

Like the Model Human Processor, EPIC (Executive Process-Interactive Control) architecture (Kieras & Meyer 1997; Meyer & Kieras 1997a, 1997b) was developed with consideration of perceptual-motor aspects of behavior. One significant advance in EPIC is that it incorporates more recent and detailed results concerning human performance. A second significant advance is that it is actually a computer simulation system. EPIC models are constructed by specifying procedures as *production rules*. When such models are presented with the external stimuli for a task (the computer displays, keyboards, etc.) they follow the procedures for the tasks and simulate the time course of events on both the system side and human side of the HCI system.

In large part, EPIC has been developed to yield better models of attention and performance in multiple-task situations. These situations might occur in HCI, for instance, with certain computer operator jobs. Often, computer operators must coordinate and interleave their conversational tasks with a customer with database tasks with a computer. In cognitive psychology, the supervisory processes required to control and supervise other processes have traditionally been called *executive processes* – a carryover from the terminology of computer operating systems where an executive process oversees the other programs running on a computer. In EPIC, executive processes are considered to be the same as any other well-learned cognitive skill, and like other skills they are represented by production rules.

EPIC has been designed with the realization that perceptual and motor processors are complicated in their own right, and they have important interactions and constraints with cognition and executive control processes. How well people can handle multiple-task situations will depend on the structural constraints on perceptual processors, motor processors, limitations on working memory, etc. In contrast to traditional multi-tasking models, EPIC does not assume a single-channel attentional processor which must be switched from task to task, nor does it assume some limited central resource capacity on cognition. EPIC simply assumes that executive control processes must work around the structural limitations of the perceptual-cognitive-motor system. This assumption has led to successful models of attention and performance covering a large body of multi-task laboratory experiments (Kieras & Meyer 1997; Meyer & Kieras 1997a, 1997b). One of the areas of EPIC application in HII has been in understanding and making predictions about visual search over information. An application of EPIC is discussed below.

Figure 17.2 is a schematic for the EPIC architecture. It is a cognitive processor surrounded by perceptual and motor processors. The cognitive processor is controlled by production rules, and information flows through the perceptual processors, to the cognitive processor, and to the motor processors, which have feedback. To develop a specific model of a task situation requires the specification of production rules and the setting of perceptual-motor parameters. When combined with a simulator of the external environment, EPIC will simulate the serial and parallel actions required to perform the task.

The cognitive processor interacts with a working memory. Roughly, this working memory is equivalent to the short-term memory of the Model Human Processor. This working memory can also be thought of as a database that contains information representing goals and knowledge about the current state of affairs.

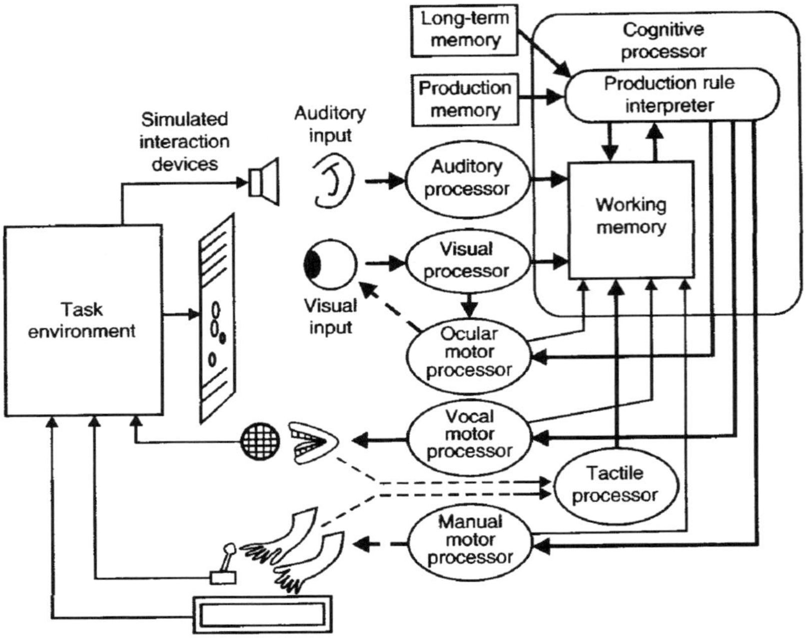

Figure 17.2 A schematic overview of the EPIC architecture. From An overview of the EPIC architecture for cognition and performance with application to human–computer interaction, *Human–Computer Interaction, 12,* 399. © 1998 by Lawrence Erlbaum Associates. Reprinted with permission

Production rules specify the flow of control of cognitive processing. Productions match to the working memory database and specify changes to the database or other actions to perform. Each production rule is of the form:

IF <condition> THEN <actions>

The condition of a rule specifies a pattern. When the contents of working memory match the pattern, the rule may be selected for application. The actions of the rule specify additions and deletions of content in working memory, as well as motor commands. These actions are executed if the rule is selected to apply.

The cognitive processor works on a 50 ms cycle. At the beginning of the cycle, working memory is updated by inputs from the perceptual processors, and by modifications that result from the application of production rules on the previous cycle. Production rules that match the contents from working memory are applied, and at the end of the cycle any motor commands that were issued are sent to the motor processor. All the production rules that match working memory are applied. The simultaneous application of production rules is a form of parallelism. Many other production systems (such as ACT-R discussed below) have limits of one production application per cycle. The perceptual and motor processors of EPIC are not necessarily synchronized with the 50 ms cognitive processor cycle. This means that perceptual inputs may have to "wait" on cognitive processing should they arrive before the beginning of the next cognitive cycle.

Working memory is partitioned into stores of different kinds of content. There are partitions of working memory for visual, auditory, and tactile information. These are slaved to the perceptual processors. That is, the outputs of those processors appear as representations in working memory. In addition, there are amodal partitions of working memory. One amodal partition is a control store that contains information about task goals and procedural steps. Another amodal partition is a general working memory that contains miscellaneous information that arises during the execution of a task.

As shown in Figure 17.2, EPIC has several perceptual processors. The time parameters associated the processing of the perceptual processors may be (a) *standard*, which come from surveys of the psychological literature and are felt to be relatively fixed across tasks, or (b) *typical*, which may vary from task to task.

There is a visual processor, which takes in stimuli from the visual scene and produces outputs in visual working memory. The visual processor has separate processors for the fovea, parafovea, and periphery. Each of these areas will produce different information from the same scene. For instance, the periphery may detect the sudden appearance of objects in the environment, the parafovea may detect the area occupied by a blob of text on a screen, and the fovea may detect the actual characters of the text. Each of these areas may have different time parameters on their processes. Event detection takes about 50 ms (periphery), while shape detection occurs about 100 ms later (parafovea), and pattern recognition about 250 ms later (fovea).

The auditory processor takes in sound stimuli and produces representations in auditory working memory. Again, different kinds of information-processing will take different amounts of time to output. The time to process a tone onset is about 50 ms, and a fully discriminated frequency appears about 250 ms later. After these outputs reach auditory working memory, they decay after about 4 s.

There are motor processors controlling the hands, eyes, and vocal tract (Figure 17.2). These can operate simultaneously. The cognitive processor sends commands to a motor processor by specifying the type and parameters of the movement to perform. The motor processor then translates these into a simulated movement. Movements are specified in terms of features. The time to execute a movement depends on movement features and the mechanical properties of the movements (e.g., the trajectory of movement of the hands).

The motor processors work in two phases: *preparation* and *execution*. In the preparation phase, a command is received from the cognitive processor and recoded into a set of movement features. For instance, to specify the tap of a finger on a key may require five features: the tap style, hand, finger, direction of movement, and extent of movement. The generation of each feature takes 50 ms, but features may be reused from previous movements, or generated in advance. For instance, tapping two different keys will share some features and allow the re-use of features. Tapping the same key twice will re-use all the features. If a movement can be anticipated, then the features can be prepared in advance. The execution phase has a delay of 50 ms to initiate the movement specified in the preparation phase. The physical movement depends on mechanical properties. For instance, the tap motion of a finger on the keyboard depends on a version of Fitts' law. The manual processor is capable of different movement styles such as punching keys, tapping, two-fingered patterns, pointing with a mouse, or pointing with a joystick. The occulomotor system has both voluntary motions (saccades) and involuntary (reflexive) motions. The vocal processor is capable of simple fixed utterances.

ACT

The ACT family of production system theories has the longest history of production system cognitive architectures. The seminal version of the ACT theory was presented in Anderson (1976), and it has undergone several major revisions since then (Anderson 1983, 1990, 1993; Anderson & Lebiere 1998; Anderson *et al.* 2004). Until recently, it has been primarily a theory of higher cognition and learning, without the kind of emphasis on perceptual-motor processing found in EPIC (Kieras & Meyer 1997) or the Model Human Processor (Card *et al.* 1983). The success of ACT as a cognitive theory has been historically in the study of memory (Anderson & Pirolli 1984; Anderson & Milson 1989), language (Anderson 1976) problem-solving (Anderson 1993) and categorization (Anderson 1991). As a learning theory, ACT has been successful (Anderson 1993) in modeling the acquisition of complex cognitive skills for tasks such as computer programming, geometry, and algebra, and in understanding transfer of learning across tasks (Singley & Anderson 1989). ACT has been strongly tested by application in the development of computer tutors (Anderson *et al.* 1990).

ACT-R, like previous versions of the ACT theory, contains assumptions about (1) knowledge representation, (2) knowledge deployment (performance), and (3) knowledge acquisition (learning). The current publicly released version of the architecture is ACT-R 5.0, which is illustrated in Figure 17.3. The architecture is arranged as a set of modules, each devoted to processing a particular kind of information, which are integrated and coordinated through a centralized production system module. Each module is assumed to

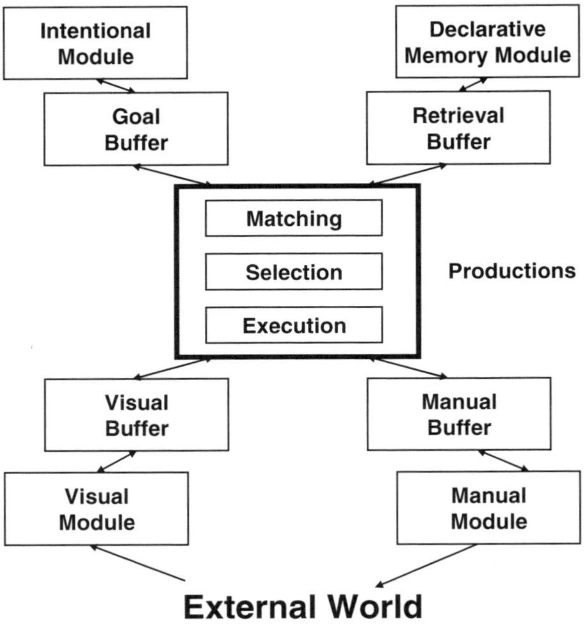

Figure 17.3 The ACT-R 5.0 architecture

deposit information into buffers associated with the module, and the central production system can only respond to the contents of the buffers, not the internal workings of the modules. This is consistent, for instance, with the observation that people do not have awareness of all of the retinal information in the visual field. The ACT-R 5.0 theory makes no claim about the complete set of modules that may eventually be identified. Each module, including the production module, has been hypothesized to occur in particular brain locations:

- Visual module (occipital cortex, and others) and visual buffers (parietal cortex) are based on EPIC's modules and keep track of objects and locations in the visual field.
- Manual module (motor cortex; cerebellum) and manual buffer (motor cortex) are based on EPIC's modules and is associated with control of the hands.
- Declarative module (temporal lobe; hippocampus) and retrieval buffer (ventrolateral prefrontal cortex) are associated with the retrieval and awareness of information from long-term declarative memory.
- Goal buffer (dorsolateral prefrontal cortex) keeps track of the goals and internal state of the system in problem-solving.
- Production system (basal ganglia) is associated with matching the contents of module buffers and coordinating their activity. The production includes components for pattern matching (striatum), conflict resolution (pallidum), and execution (thalamus). A production rule can be thought of as a formal specification of the flow of information from buffered information in the cortex to the basal ganglia and back again.

Historically, ACT-R provided limited, ad hoc modeling of perceptual-motor behavior. The production, declarative, and goal modules in ACT-R 5.0 are vestigial remnants of those earlier versions of ACT-R, and still remain the core of the current architecture. The declarative memory module and production system module store and retrieve information that corresponds to *declarative knowledge* and *procedural knowledge* (Ryle 1949). Declarative knowledge is the kind of knowledge that a person can attend to, reflect upon, and usually articulate in some way (e.g., by declaring it verbally or by gesture). Declarative knowledge includes the kinds of factual knowledge that users' can verbalize, like "The 'open' item on the 'file' menu will open a file." Procedural knowledge is the know-how we display in our behavior, without conscious awareness. For instance, knowledge of how to ride a bike and how to point a mouse to a menu item are examples of procedural knowledge. Procedural knowledge specifies how declarative knowledge is transformed into active behavior. Declarative knowledge in ACT-R is represented formally in terms of chunks (Miller 1956; Simon 1974). Whereas the information in the declarative memory module corresponds to personal episodic and semantic knowledge that promotes long-term coherence in behavior, the goal module stores and retrieves information that represents the internal intention and problem-solving state of the system and provides local coherence to behavior.

Chunks are retrieved from long-term declarative memory by an activation process. Activation may be interpreted metaphorically as a kind of mental energy that drives cognitive processing. Activation spreads from the current focus of attention, including goals, through *associations* among chunks in declarative memory. These associations are built up from experience, and they reflect how ideas co-occur in cognitive processing. Generally, activation-based theories of memory predict that more activated knowledge structures will receive more favorable processing. The spread of activation from one cognitive structure to another is determined by weighting values on the associations among chunks. These weights determine the rate of activation flow among chunks.

While sharing many commonalities with the EPIC perceptual-motor modules, ACT-R 5.0 does differ in several respects. The visual system in ACT-R 5.0 is separated into two components: (1) a *where* system that processes locations in the visual field, and a (2) *what* system that processes objects. Productions may request information from the "where" system by specifying a set of constraints based on visual properties (e.g., "an object that is colored red") or spatial location (e.g., "an object at the top of the screen") and the "where" system will return a chunk that matches those constraints. This supports the modeling of pre-attentive pop-out effects (Treisman & Gelade 1980) that occur, for example, when a display includes one red object amongst a set of green objects. In such a case, a production rule that requests "objects that are colored red" will cause the "where" system to return a chunk specifying the single red object displayed, and visual search time will be constant regardless of the number of green objects on the display. On the other hand, a production rule request for "an object that is colored green" will cause the "where" system to return a chunk that represents any one of the green objects, and the time to search for a particular green object will require repeated calls to the "where" system (a serial self-terminating search) that will exhibit time costs that depend on the number of other green objects in the display.

The "what" system of the visual module keeps track of visual objects. Production rules may request the "what" system to identify objects at a location, which causes the "what" system to shift visual attention to that location and return a declarative chunk that represent the object. ACT-R 5.0 supports a coarse model of visual attention in which visual search occurs at a rate of 185 ms per visual item, and a fine-grained model called EMMA (Salvucci 2001) in which the time for eye movements have time costs related to the eccentricity between the current focus of attention and the target location requested by a production.

Production rules are used to represent procedural knowledge in ACT-R. That is, they specify how to apply cognitive skill (know-how) in the current context, and how to retrieve and modify information in the buffers to other modules. Like EPIC, production rules in ACT-R have the basic IF<condition> THEN <actions> format. In ACT-R, each production rule has conditions that specify structures that are matched in buffers corresponding to information from the external world or other internal modules. Each production rule has actions that specify changes to be made to the buffers. As in EPIC, it is assumed that the cycle of production matching and execution takes about 50 ms to complete.

ACT-R 5.0 is a mix of parallel and serial processing. Modules may process information in parallel with one another. So, for instance, the visual modules and the motor modules may both operate at the same time. However, there are two serial bottlenecks in process. First, only one production may execute during a cycle (which is different than EPIC). Second, each module is limited to placing a single chunk in a buffer.

ACT-Scent

Seeking and gathering information for some purpose typically requires that users perform some mix of navigation through on-line information structures and the use of search engines. To model these activities requires a theory of how people perceive those information structures and then decide on the best course of action to take. An elaboration of the ACT-R architecture has been developed to model such activities. This architecture, called ACT-Scent[5] (Pirolli in press), was developed within a more general theoretical framework called Information Foraging Theory. This theory was developed to understand and predict information seeking and gathering behavior with complex technologies. Among other applications, Information Foraging Theory (Pirolli & Card 1999) has been used to develop cognitive models of Web navigation (SNIF-ACT 1.0 and 2.0 described below) that form the basis for a system that predicts Web usability. The theory is concerned with human behavior and technology involved in gathering information for some purpose, such as making a medical decision, finding a restaurant, or solving a programming problem.

Information Foraging Theory

Information Foraging Theory has adopted the *rational analysis* program initiated by Anderson (1989, 1990, 1991). The rational analysis approach involves a kind of reverse engineering in which the theorist asks (a) *what* environmental problem is solved, (b) *why* is a given behavioral strategy a good solution to the problem, and (c) *how* is that solution realized by cognitive mechanism. The products of this approach include (a) characterizations of the relevant goals and environment, (b) mathematical rational choice models (e. g., optimization models) of idealized behavioral strategies for achieving those goals in that environment, and (c) computational cognitive models. This methodology is founded on the heuristic assumption that evolving, behaving systems are well-designed (rational) for fulfilling certain functions in certain environments. Rational analysis is a variant form of an approach called *methodological adaptationism* that has also shaped research programs in behavioral ecology (e.g., Tinbergen 1963; Mayr 1983; Stephens & Krebs 1986), anthropology (e.g., Winterhalder & Smith 1992), and neuroscience (e.g., Glimcher 2003).

Rational Analysis

Anderson has used rational analysis to study the human cognitive architecture by assuming that natural information-processing mechanisms involved in such functions as memory (Anderson & Milson 1989; Anderson & Schooler 1991) and categorization (Anderson 1991) were well-designed by evolutionary forces to meet the problems posed by the environment. The key assumption behind rational analysis could be stated as

> *Principle of rationality*: The cognitive system optimizes the adaptation of the behavior of the organism.

As developed by Anderson (1990) rational analysis requires a focus on understanding the structure and dynamics of the environment. This understanding provides a rationale for the design of information-processing mechanisms. Anderson proposed the following recipe for rational analysis:

1. Precisely specify the goals of the agent.
2. Develop a formal model of he environment to which the agents is adapted.

3. Make minimal assumptions about the computational costs.
4. Derive the optimal behavior of the agent considering (1)–(3).
5. Test the optimality predictions against data.
6. Iterate.

Note, generally, the emphasized focus on optimal behavior under given goals and environmental constraints and the minimal assumptions about the computational structure that might produce such behavior.

Interaction with the information environment differs in a fundamental way from well-defined task environments that have been the dominant paradigms in HCI, such as expert text editing (Card *et al.* 1983) or telephone assistance (Gray *et al.* 1993). In contrast to such tasks in all but the most trivial cases, the information forager must deal with a *probabilistically textured* information environment (Brunswik 1952). In contrast to application programs such as text editors and spreadsheets, in which actions have fairly determinate outcomes,[6] foraging through a large volume of information involves uncertainties, for a variety of reasons, about the location, quality, relevance, veracity, and so on, of the information sought and the effects of foraging actions. The ecological rationality of information foraging behavior must be analyzed through the theoretical lens and tools appropriate to *decision making under uncertainty.* The determinate formalisms and determinate cognitive mechanisms that are characteristic of the HCI paradigm are inadequate for the job of theorizing about information foraging in probabilistically textured environments. Models developed in Information Foraging Theory draw upon probabilistic models, and especially Bayesian approaches, and they bear similarity to economic models of decision-making (rational choice) under uncertainty and engineering models.

ACT-Scent Architecture

Figure 17.4 presents the basic ACT-Scent architecture used in information foraging models (Pirolli 1997, 2005; Pirolli & Card 1999). It couples a simpler version of the ACT-R architecture to a module that computes *information scent.* Below, this chapter will present specific models of Web foraging (SNIF-ACT 1.0 and SNIF-ACT 2.0) developed within this architecture. The architecture includes a declarative memory containing chunks, a procedural memory containing production rules, and a goal memory containing the hierarchy of intentions driving behavior. The information scent module is a new addition to ACT that is used to compute the utility of actions based on an analysis of the relationship of content cues from the user interface to the user's goals.

A Spreading Activation Model of Information Scent

Information foraging behavior will often depend on assessments of the utility and costs of pursuing information items. In browsing for information on the Web, people must base navigation decisions on assessments of information scent cues associated with links from one Webpage to another. These information scent cues are the small snippets of text and graphics that are associated with Web links. Those cues are intended to represent tersely the content that will be encountered by choosing a particular link on one page and

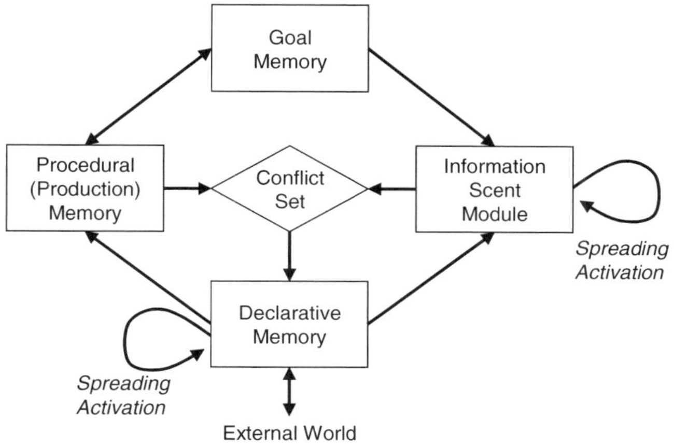

Figure 17.4 The ACT-Scent cognitive architecture

navigating to the linked page. When browsing the Web by following links, users must use these cues presented proximally on the web-pages they are currently viewing in order to make navigation decisions. The measure of information scent provides a means to predict how users will evaluate different links on a web-page, and as a consequence, the likelihood that a particular link will be followed.

The rational analysis of the use of information scent assumes that the goal of the information forager is to use proximal external information scent cues (e.g., a web-link) to predict the utility of distal sources of content (i.e., the web-page associated with a web-link), and to choose to navigate the links having the maximum expected utility. Pirolli (2005) decomposed this problem into three parts: (1) a Bayesian analysis of the expected relevance of a distal source of content conditional on the available information scent cues; (2) a mapping of this Bayesian model of information scent onto a mathematical formulation of spreading activation; and (3) a model of rational choice that uses spreading activation (Anderson & Pirolli 1984) to evaluate the utility of alternative choices of web-links. This rational analysis yielded a spreading activation theory of utility and choice.

The spreading activation theory of information scent assumes that the user's cognitive system represents information scent cues and information goals in cognitive structures called *chunks*. Figure 17.5 presents a schematic example of the information scent assessment subtask facing a Web user. Figure 17.5 assumes that a user has the goal of finding information about "medical treatments for cancer," and encounters a web-link labeled with the text that includes "cell," "patient," "dose," and "beam." The user's cognitive task is to predict the likelihood that a distal source of content contains desired information based on the proximal information scent cues available in the Web link labels. Each node in Figure 17.5 represents a cognitive chunk. Chunks representing information scent cues are presented on the right side of Figure 17.5, chunks representing the user's information need are presented on the left side. Also represented by lines in Figure 17.5 are *associations* among the chunks. The associations among chunks come from past experience. The strength of associations reflects the degree to which proximal information scent cues

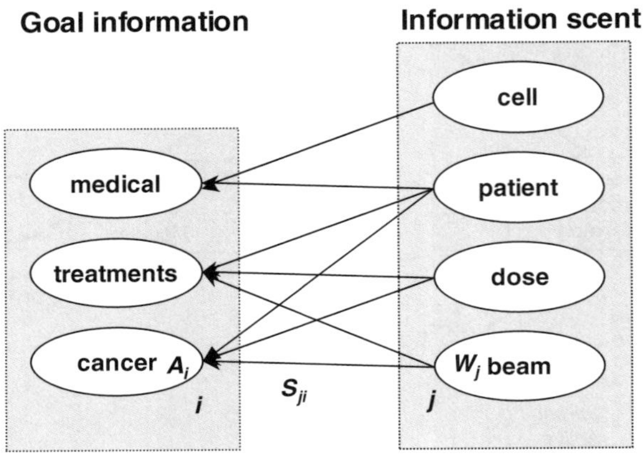

Figure 17.5 A cognitive structure in which cognitive chunks representing an information goal are associated with chunks representing information scent cues from a web-link

predict the occurrence of unobserved features. The strength of association between a chunk i and chunk j is computed as,

$$S_{ji} = \log\left(\frac{\Pr(i|j)}{\Pr(i)}\right) \tag{17.1}$$

Where $\Pr(i|j)$ is the probability (based on past experience) that chunk i has occurred when chunk j has occurred in the environment, and $\Pr(i)$ is the base rate probability of chunk i occurring in the environment. Equation 17.1 is also known as *Pointwise Mutual Information* (Manning & Schuetze 1999) or PMI.

It is assumed that when a user focuses attention on a web-link their attention to information scent cues activates corresponding cognitive chunks. Activation spreads from those attended chunks along associations to related chunks. For instance, activation would flow from the chunks on the right of Figure 17.5 through associations to chunks on the left of Figure 17.5. The amount of activation accumulating on the representation of a user's information goal provides an indicator of the likelihood that a distal source of information has desirable features based on the information scent cues immediately available to the user. For each chunk i involved in the user's goal, the accumulated activation received from all associated information scents chunks j is,

$$A_i = \sum_j W_j S_{ji} \tag{17.2}$$

where W_j represents the amount of attention devoted to chunk j. The total amount of activation received by all goal chunks i is just,

$$V = \sum_i A_i \tag{17.3}$$

The theory assumes that the utility of choosing a particular link is just the sum of activation it receives (Eqn 17.3) plus some random noise. From this assumption (see, Pirolli

2005) one can derive that the probability that a user will choose link L, having a summed activation V_L, from a set of links C on a Webpage, given an information goal, G, is

$$\Pr(L|G,C) = \frac{e^{\mu V_L}}{\sum_{k \in C} e^{\mu V_k}} \tag{17.4}$$

The information scent mechanisms are integral to modeling user judgments of which navigation action to take, including when to give up.

APPLICATIONS

This section illustrates the application of computational cognitive models to HII. This set of examples was selected to illustrate each of the three theories discussed above in three HII application domains. The examples include an EPIC model of visual search over information displays, ACT-R models of hand-held devices, and ACT-Scent models of seeking information on the Web.

EPIC Application: Visual Search of Hierarchical Information Displays

Many tasks involving interaction with information require visual navigation through displays of data that are hierarchically organized. Simple examples of such displays include menus (Hornof & Kieras 1997; Byrne *et al.* 1999) and web-pages. For instance, web-pages often arrange sets of links into groups (i.e., links within a group are proximal to one another and groups are spaced apart from one another), and provide distinctive labels for the visual groups. For instance, the home page for an on-line newspaper may contain visually grouped links labeled "Headlines," "Local," "Business," "Sports," "Entertainment," and so on. The benefits of such hierarchical arrangements are common wisdom in the design world (Spool *et al.* 1999).

Hornof and Halverson (2003) developed an EPIC model to make quantitative predictions regarding visual navigation of such hierarchically arranged information displays and to make predictions about the visual scan paths of users. Hornof and Halverson presented labeled and unlabeled layouts of one, two, four, or six groups of five text labels (pseudo-words). Figure 17.6 shows examples of a six-group labeled layout used in the experiment. Participants were visually presented a pseudo-word that would be their target for visual search, then they were presented with a display to search. In conditions in which labeled groups were presented, the users were presented with the group label from the group in which the target would be found, as well as the pseudo-word to find within the group. The location of the target in the display was random across trials.

Hornof and Halverson (2003) encoded a representation of the task and display into EPIC, along with the visual-perceptual features of the screen objects. Production rules were written to represent the cognitive strategies of study participants. Two strategies were found to fit the data:

- *Noisy-systematic search strategy* was used to predict data for the unlabeled layouts. This strategy assumes that people make a maximally efficient foveal sweep of the

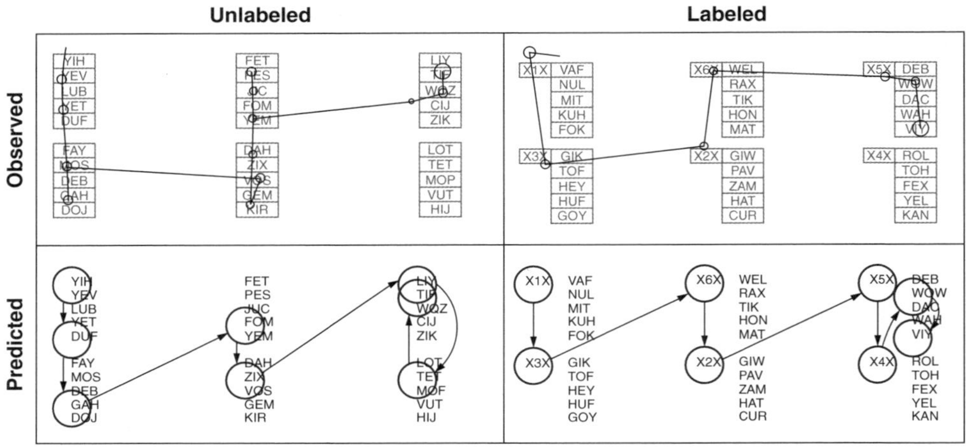

Figure 17.6 Observed fixation patterns (top) vs. those predicted by EPIC (bottom) for a six-group unlabeled display trial (left; modeled using a noisy-systematic strategy) and a six-group labeled display trial (right; modeled using a mostly systematic two-tiered search strategy). Circle diameters represent fixation duration in the observed data and represent foveal region in the predicted data

display which minimizes the number of fixations required to fixate the contents of the display in the high-resolution fovea (Hornof & Kieras 1997). The strategy is noisy because it sometimes overestimates how far to move the eyes.

- *Mostly systematic two-tiered search strategy* was used to predict eye movements on displays containing labeled groups. This strategy assumes that people first search labels until a target group is found, then search within that group. It is mostly systematic because it searches in an ordered fashion 75 per cent of the time, and random order 25 per cent of the time.

Figure 17.6 shows observed eye fixations patterns above eye movement patterns predicted by EPIC. One can observe good qualitative match of the model's search strategy to those of a participant. Figure 17.7 shows the fit of the model's prediction to observed visual search times. The model predicts the unlabeled visual search with an average absolute error of 8 per cent and the labeled visual search with an average absolute error of 6 per cent.

ACT-R Application: Information Seeking on a PDA

A cognitive engineering tool called CogTool (John *et al.* 2004; Luo & John 2005) has been developed to support the rapid development of a class of simple ACT-R models, called ACT-Simple, that correspond to the KLM (keystroke-level model) of Card *et al.* (Card *et al.* 1983). The scope of KLMs is limited to capturing the error-free performance of highly skilled users executing a single specific method on a given interface. Task execution is modeled in terms of time parameters associated with (a) the physical operators for

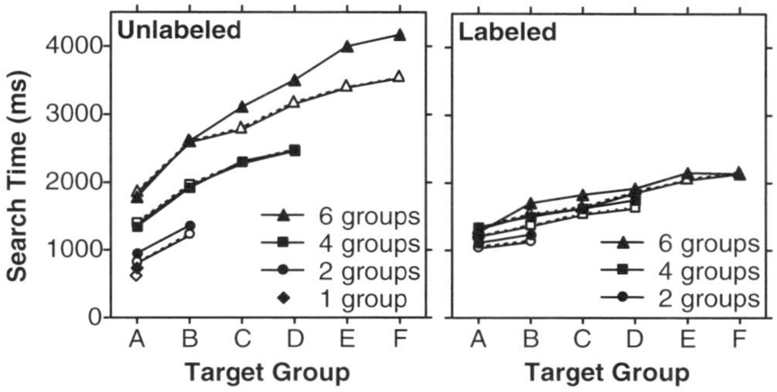

Figure 17.7 Observed search times (solid lines) and predicted (dashed lines) by the EPIC models using the noisy-systematic strategy (for unlabelled displays; left) and mostly systematic two-tiered search strategy (for labeled displays; right)

keystrokes, homing (moving the hands to a home location), drawing, (b) a generic mental operation (to capture time needed to think), and (c) system response time.

The development of CogTools has been guided by a set of principles aimed at accelerating the spread of cognitive engineering among user interface designers (John *et al.* 2004): (1) exploit tools already in widespread use among the design and cognitive modeling communities; (2) tightly couple design mockup tools to cognitive modeling tools so that changes to an user interface design are immediately reflected in changes to predictions of the cognitive model; and (3) avoid the need for programming by using such techniques as programming by demonstration.

CogTool allows a user interface designer to model an existing UI mocked up as existing web-pages. Alternatively, the designer may mock up a UI as web-pages using a web design application plus a palette of standard interface widgets such as buttons, check-boxes, text fields, pull-down menus, cascading menus, roll-over images, simulated speech-I/O, links, etc. The user interface mock-up defines the UI layout, as well as the effects of user actions (such as clicking on a button). The designer then may demonstrate a method of using the UI while recording the interaction with a tool called the Behavior Recorder. If there are alternative methods for performing some goal with the UI, then each method must be demonstrated. The resulting trace of behavior is assumed to represent an expert error-free execution of a given method for achieving some goal with the UI.

Each demonstration of a method with the UI is sent to a compiler that maps the behavior into a set of production rules that would generate the same behavior. These production rules implement a *press-key* ACT-Simple command that takes ~200–350 ms, a *move-mouse* ACT-Simple command that takes ~650–750 ms to move 500 pixels, a *move-hand* command that takes ~650–800 ms to execute, a *look-at* command that takes 150 ms, and a *think* command that takes 1200 ms. Most ACT-Simple commands compile to one production, and the *look-at* command compiles to two productions (one for shifting visual attention and one for ensuring encoding of a visual object).

Luo and John (2005) used CogTool to make predictions about use of the Palm Vx handheld PDA with an application that provides a city guide for New York City. The goal was to model performance times for alternative methods for using the city guide to find the open hours for the Metropolitan Museum of Art (MET). A Web-based storyboard mockup of the interface states and transitions that would result from a user performing these methods was created. An analyst demonstrated each method on the mockup using the Behavior Recorder. The demonstrated behavior trace was automatically compiled into ACT-Simple commands, which in turn were compiled into ACT-R production rules. The resulting ACT-R models were then run to provide the equivalent of a KLM performance prediction.

The methods analyzed were chosen to cover a range of interaction techniques possible with the Palm PDA. Four methods were studied: (1) map navigation, which involved clicking on increasingly more detailed maps to zoom in on the location of the MET; (2) soft keyboard, which involved tapping on a layout of alphanumeric characters to type in queries; (3) graffiti, which involved using a stylus to enter characters using the graffiti shorthand technique; and (4) scroll bar, which involved scrolling through a list of museums until the MET appeared. Users ($N = 10$) were asked to perform each of he methods ten times on Palm PDAs, following a practice phase. The average task times for the methods ranged from 9.00 s to 13.60 s, with map navigation being the fastest method and Graffiti being the slowest. The average CogTool prediction error for the four methods was 3.7 per cent (ranging from 1.38 to 7.43 per cent).

ACT-Scent Application: Seeking Information on the Web

The rational analysis of information scent presented above can be used to develop models of how users choose links on the Web. A similar rational analysis developed in Pirolli (2005) can be used to predict when users will leave a website. SNIF-ACT is a computation model developed in the ACT-Scent architecture based on these rational analyses. This section presents an overview of the SNIF-ACT model (Pirolli & Fu 2003; Pirolli 2005), as well as an automated Web usability system called Bloodhound (Chi *et al.* 2003) that was inspired by SNIF-ACT. For comparison, this chapter discusses a very similar Web usability analysis method called Cognitive Walkthrough for the Web (Blackmon *et al.* 2005; Kitajima *et al.* 2005) that is also based on the concept of information scent.

SNIF-ACT

SNIF-ACT assumes that users have the procedural knowledge necessary to use the browser, such as clicking on a link, or clicking on the "back" button to go back to the previous web-page. This procedural knowledge is represented as a set of production rules. SNIF-ACT also assumes that users have knowledge of the addresses of most popular Web search engines. This knowledge is represented as chunks in declarative memory.

In a SNIF-ACT simulation, information scent cues on a computer display activate chunks and activation spreads through the declarative network of chunks. The amount of activation accumulating on the chunks matched by a production is used to compute a utility score, which is used to evaluate and select productions. For instance, the utility of productions implementing the selection and clicking of links is based on the activation that spreads from the link that the productions match against.

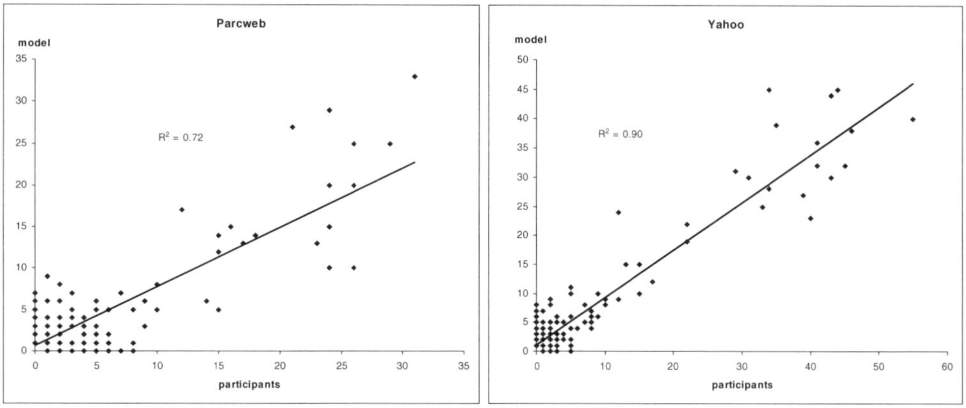

Figure 17.8 The scatter plots for the number of times links were selected by the model and by user at the Parcweb and Yahoo sites (eight tasks per site)

SNIF-ACT 1.0 (Pirolli & Fu 2003) was used to simulate four users working on two tasks each. Users were free to navigate anywhere on the Web to accomplish these tasks (for details, see Card *et al.* 2001). SNIF-ACT 2.0 (Pirolli 2005) was matched to data from 244 users. Users could work on eight tasks on two websites. Users were constrained to never leave the given website when performing their given task. Monte Carlo simulations with the model were used to generate data for the 16 tasks. For each task, the number of times SNIF-ACT was run was equivalent to the number of users observed on the task. Each point in Figure 17.8 plots data for a single link on a website, and each data point represents the number of users who selected that link, and the number of times SNIF-ACT selected the same link. Figure 17.8 shows that SNIF-ACT 2.0 provides good match to the data.

SNIF-ACT is a computational model derived from the rational analyses of Web navigation. The major assumption of the model is that Web navigations can be characterized by mechanisms that maximize expected information gain. Expected information gain is estimated by a spreading activation mechanism that calculates the relatedness of information goal and link text. The good fits to human data provide strong support for the use of information scent to characterize information-seeking decisions on the Web.

Bloodhound

The Bloodhound service (Chi *et al.* 2003) employs a Web user flow model to predict website usage patterns and identify Website navigation problems. The service employs a variation on a graph flow algorithm which abstracts away from the details of the SNIF-ACT model. This assumes that users come to a website with some information goal and forage for information by choosing links based on proximal information scent cues.

Figure 17.9 presents an overview of the process used by the Bloodhound service. A person (the *website analyst*) interested in performing a usability analysis of a website must indicate the website to be analyzed, and provide a text description representing a task that

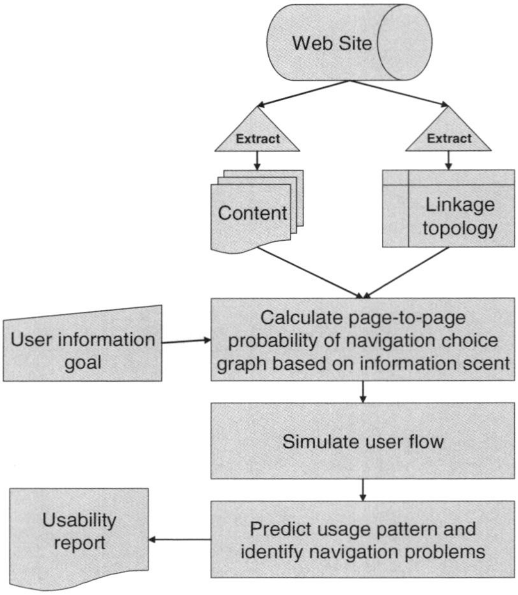

Figure 17.9 The conceptual flow chart for the processing done by the Bloodhound Web usability service

users are expected to be performing at the site. Bloodhound then must trawl the website to develop a representation of the linkage topology (the page-to-page links) and download the web-pages (content). From these data, Bloodhound analyzes the web-pages to determine the proximal information scent cues associated with every link on every page. At this point Bloodhound essentially has a representation of every page-to-page link, and the proximal cues associated with that link. From this, Bloodhound develops a graph representation in which the nodes are the website pages, the vertices are the page-to-page links at the site, and weights on the vertices represent the probability of a user choosing a particular vertex given the user's information goal and the proximal information scent cues associated with the link (e.g., Eqn 17.4). This graph is represented as a page-by-page matrix in which the rows represent individual unique pages at the site, the columns also represent website pages, and the matrix cells contain the navigation choice probabilities that predict the probability that a user with the given information goal, at a given page, will choose to go to a linked page. Using matrix computations (similar to those used in modeling a Markov process), this matrix is used to simulate user flow at the website by assuming that the user starts at some given webpage and iteratively chooses to go to new pages based on the predicted navigation choice probabilities. The user flow simulation yields predictions concerning the pattern of visits to web-pages, and the proportion of users that will arrive at target web-pages contain the information relevant to their tasks.

The Bloodhound service is provided over the Web. An input screen is provided to website analysts that allows them to enter specifications of user tasks, the website URL, and the target pages that contain the information relevant to those tasks. An analysis is then performed by Bloodhound and a report is then automatically generated that indicates such things as the predicted number of users who will be able to find target information relevant to the specified task, and intermediate navigation pages that are predicted to be highly visited that may be a cause of bottlenecks.

Chi *et al.* (2003) performed an evaluation of the capability of Bloodhound to predict actual user navigation patterns. Users were solicited to perform Web tasks at home, office, or place of their choosing and their performance was logged using a remote usability testing system. Four different types of website were studied with eight tasks of varying difficulty for each site. The comparison of interest was the match between observed and predicted usage patterns for each task and website. For each task + website, the observed data were the distribution of the frequency of page visits over every webpage. For instance, for a particular task + website, the home page might be visited 75 times, another page 25 times, and so on. The comparison was the distribution of page visits for that task and website as predicted by Bloodhound. Of the $4 \times 8 = 32$ combinations of websites and tasks, there were strong correlations (Pearson $r > 0.8$) of observed and predicted visitation frequencies for 12 cases, moderate correlations ($0.5 \leq r \leq 0.8$) for 17 cases, and weak correlations ($r < 0.5$) for 3 cases. Given that this was the first evaluation of Bloodhound the results seemed like a validation of the promise of the approach.

Cognitive Walkthrough for the Web

Cognitive Walkthrough for the Web (CWW) is a semi-automated method for finding and repairing Web usability problems that is similar in many ways to Bloodhound. CWW derives from a cognitive model called CoLiDes (Comprehension-based Linked model of Deliberate Search; Kitajima *et al.* 2000). Although CoLiDes differs in detail from SNIF-ACT, it shares the basic assumptions that the Web user has an information goal and information scent drives information-seeking behavior. CoLiDes uses a technique called Latent Semantic Analysis (LSA) to compute information scent. LSA (Landauer & Dumais 1997) assumes that the meaning of a word is associated with the meanings of all contexts that it has occurred in, while simultaneously the meaning of a message is associated with all the words it contains. In practice, the meaning of words is computed from a corpus of documents assumed to represent the linguistic environment of some population (e.g., college students). A word-by-document matrix, in which cell entries indicate the occurrence of some particular word in a particular document in the corpus is then extracted (typically, the log frequency of a word in a document), and submitted to a singular value decomposition (SVD) that is similar to factor analysis. This procedure computes a set of dimensions (substantially less than the number of documents) that may be interpreted to represent latent semantic factors. Each word can then be represented by its position in a space defined by these semantic factors. That is, each word will be represented as a vector of scores that indicate a position on each latent semantic factor. The psychological similarity of two words is just a distance measure between them in the semantic space defined by these latent factors. Dumais (2003) provides a survey of LSA applications in psychology and other fields. Turney (2001) has shown that PMI and LSA give very similar results on synonym tests. CoLiDes assumes that users' goals are represented as a collection of words, and links and web-page headings are represented by the text from the web-page, plus elaborations that consist of words that have high similarity to that text.

CWW identifies four kinds of problems, proposes repairs to those problems, and predicts the severity of those problems before and after repairs. The procedure (Blackmon *et al.* 2005) consists of:

1. Selecting a semantic space (generated from an appropriate document corpus) to represent a given user group.
2. Constructing a representative set of user goals for the website.
3. Simulate how users will parse a web-page into regions and sub-regions.
4. Simulate the elaboration of link text and heading text.
5. Apply LSA to obtain similarity scores from goals to Web headings and links. Mark the correct heading and link that should be chosen for each given goal.
6. Apply a set of problem identification rules.
7. Apply suggested repairs.
8. Apply problem severity formulae to predict severity for repaired and unrepaired problems.

The problem identification rules identify:

- *Weak link scent*, in which no correct links have strong similarity scores with the goal.
- *Unfamiliar links or headings*, which are indicated by LSA measures from the representative semantic space.
- *Competing headings*, which occur when a heading or associated sub-region on the web-page shows high similarity to the user's goal, but does not contain a correct link.
- *Competing links* in which there are links, other than the correct ones, that have high similarity to the user's goal.

Repairs to these problems typically involve substituting words to reduce the problem (e.g., by substituting words with high similarity to the goal in correct links with weak scent). Problem severity is predicted by a regression formula fit to data from a wide variety of tasks. The problem severity formula predicts the number of clicks required to get to a desired page on the analyzed web-page based on the familiarity of the correct link, the strength of scent of the correct link, and the number of competing links under competing headings.

GENERAL DISCUSSION

Computational cognitive models have been applied to an ever-broadening range of problems in human–computer interaction (Pirolli 1999). Recent applications in human–information interaction suggest that this record of success will continue. Cognitive architectures, such as EPIC, ACT-R, and ACT-Scent provide an integrated approach to modeling perception, motor action, and higher-order cognition. Their utility has been demonstrated in generating cognitive engineering models for such applications as visual search, mobile computing, and Web use.

Although working with such cognitive models directly requires some amount of training, the CogTool project (John *et al.* 2004; Luo & John 2005) suggests that standard rapid-prototyping tools for user interface design can be enhanced with built-in cognitive engineering evaluations. Similarly, the Bloodhound system (Chi *et al.* 2003) was targeted for use by Web designers with no training in cognitive engineering. The concept of information scent has been used to develop Web usability guidelines (Spool *et al.* 2004) and evaluation methods (Blackmon *et al.* 2002, 2005) for use by practitioners.

One of the significant challenges that lie ahead for cognitive models of HII is the problem of modeling the interpretation of content into actionable knowledge. For text, this involves using statistical language techniques such as PMI or LSA to build associative networks that support the mapping of external text onto user goals and procedural knowledge (e.g., the selection of production rules). For multimedia, this is much more difficult. Can we model how people make sense of the multimedia content with which they interact? This requires the integration of additional components for robust language comprehension, graphics understanding, rich knowledge representation, reasoning, knowledge acquisition, and meta-cognition, among other things. Many of these components have a long history of research in artificial intelligence and computational linguistics, but have yet to be incorporated into an integrated cognitive architecture such as the ones described in this chapter.

ACKNOWLEDGMENTS

The writing of this chapter has been supported in part by MDA 904-03-C-0404 to Stuart K. Card and Peter Pirolli.

NOTES

1 The term "human–information interaction" first appeared in the public literature in a birds-of-a-feather meeting title in 1995: Gershon, N. (1995, December). Human Information Interaction. In the *Proceedings of the Fourth International World Wide Web Conference* (http://www.w3.org/Conferences/WWW4/bofs/hii-bof.html).
2 The ACM is the Association for Computing Machinery, which is the main computer science organization, and CHI is the conference for the Computer Human Interaction special interest group of the ACM.
3 CERN is the European Organization for Nuclear Research, a multinational science community operating the world's largest particle physics laboratory.
4 Many models in psychology have free parameters that are estimated from the data to which the model is fit. A zero-parameter model is one in which no parameters need to be estimated from the data (all are set a priori).
5 Pronounced "accent."
6 Barring bugs, of course.

REFERENCES

Anderson, J. R. (1976). *Language, Memory, and Thought.* Hillsdale, NJ: Lawrence Erlbaum Associates.

Anderson, J. R. (1983). *The Architecture of Cognition.* Cambridge, MA: Harvard University Press.

Anderson, J. R. (1990). *The Adaptive Character of Thought.* Hillsdale, NJ: Lawrence Erlbaum Associates.

Anderson, J. R. (1991). The adaptive nature of human categorization. *Psychological Review, 98,* 409–429.

Anderson, J. R. (1993). *Rules of the Mind*. Hillsdale, NJ: Lawrence Erlbaum Associates.

Anderson, J. R., Bothell, D., Byrne, M. D. *et al.* (2004). An integrated theory of mind. *Psychological Review, 11*(4), 1036–1060.

Anderson, J. R., Boyle, C. F., Corbett, A. & Lewis, M. W. (1990). Cognitive modelling and intelligent tutoring. *Artificial Intelligence, 42*, 7–49.

Anderson, J. R. & Lebiere, C. (1998). *The Atomic Components of Thought*. Mahwah, NJ: Lawrence Erlbaum Associates.

Anderson, J. R. & Milson, R. (1989). Human memory: an adaptive perspective. *Psychological Review, 96*, 703–719.

Anderson, J. R. & Pirolli, P. (1984). Spread of activation. *Journal of Experimental Psychology: Learning, Memory, and Cognition, 10*, 791–798.

Anderson, J. R. & Schooler, L. J. (1991). Reflections of the environment in memory. *Psychological Science, 2*, 396–408.

Berners-Lee, T. (1989). *Information Management: A Proposal*. Geneva: CERN.

Blackmon, M. H., Kitajima, M. & Polson, P. G. (2005). Web interactions: tool for accurately predicting website navigation problems, non-problems, problem severity, and effectiveness of repairs. *CHI 2005, ACM Conference on Human Factors in Computing Systems, CHI Letters, 7*(1), 31–40.

Blackmon, M. H., Polson, P. G., Kitajima, M. & Lewis, C. (2002). Cognitive walkthrough for the web. *CHI 2002, ACM Conference on Human Factors in Computing Systems, CHI Letters, 4*(1), 463–470.

Brunswik, E. (1952). *The Conceptual Framework of Psychology*. Chicago: University of Chicago Press.

Bush, V. (1945). As we may think. *Atlantic Monthly, 176*, 101–108.

Byrne, M. D., Anderson, J. R., Douglass, S. & Matessa, M. (1999). Eye tracking the visual search of click-down menus. *CHI 1999, ACM Conference on Human Factors in Computing Systems, CHI Letters, 1*(1), 402–409.

Card, S. K., Moran, T. P. & Newell, A. (1983). *The Psychology of Human–Computer Interaction*. Hillsdale, NJ: Lawrence Erlbaum Associates.

Card, S. K., Pirolli, P., Van Der Wege, M. *et al.* (2001). Information scent as a driver of web behavior graphs: results of a protocol analysis method for web usability. *CHI 2001, ACM Conference on Human Factors in Computing Systems, CHI Letters, 3*(1), 498–505.

Chi, E. H., Rosien, A., Suppattanasiri, G. *et al.* (2003). The Bloodhound project: automating discovery of web usability issues using the infoscent simulator. *CHI 2003, ACM Conference on Human Factors in Computing Systems, CHI Letters, 5*(1), 505–512.

Dumais, S. T. (2003). Data-driven approaches to information access. *Cognitive Science, 27*, 491–524.

Dumais, S. T., Furnas, G. W., Landauer, T. K. *et al.* (1988). Using latent semantic analysis to improve access to textual information. Paper presented at the Conference on Human Factors in Computing Systems, CHI '88, Washington, DC.

Engelbart, D. C. (1962). *Augmenting Human Intellect: A Conceptual Framework* (No. AFOSR-3223). Menlo Park, CA: Stanford Research Institute.

Furnas, G. W., Landauer, T. K., Gomez, L. W. & Dumais, S. T. (1987). The vocabulary problem in human–system communication. *Communications of the ACM, 30*, 964–971.

Glimcher, P. W. (2003). *Decisions, Uncertainty, and the Brain: The Science of Neuroeconomics*. Cambridge, MA: MIT Press.

Gray, W. D., John, B. E. & Atwood, M. E. (1993). Project Ernestine: a validation of GOMs for prediction and explanation of real-world task performance. *Human–Computer Interaction, 8*, 237–309.

Hornof, A. J. & Halverson, T. (2003). Cognitive strategies and eye movements for searching hierarchical computer displays. *CHI 2003, ACM Conference on Human Factors in Computing Systems, CHI Letters, 5*(1), 249–256.

Hornof, A. J. & Kieras, D. E. (1997). Cognitive modeling reveals menu search is both random and systematic. Paper presented at the Conference on Human Factors in Computing Systems, CHI '97, New York.

John, B. E., & Kieras, D. E. (1996). The GOMS family of user interface analysis techniques: comparison and contrast. *ACM Transactions on Computer–Human Interaction*, *3*, 320–351.

John, B. E., Prevas, K., Salvucci, D. D. & Koedinger, K. (2004). Predictive human performance modeling made easy. *CHI 2003, ACM Conference on Human Factors in Computing Systems, CHI Letters*, *6*(1), 455–462.

Jones, W. P. (1986). The memory extender personal filing system. Paper presented at the Conference Human Factors in Computing System, CHI '86, Boston, MA.

Kieras, D. E. & Meyer, D. E. (1997). An overview of the epic architecture for cognition and performance with application to human-computer interaction. *Human–Computer Interaction*, *12*, 391–438.

Kitajima, M., Blackmon, M. H. & Polson, P. G. (2000). A comprehension-based model of web navigation and its application to web usability analysis. In S. McDonald, Y. Waern & G. Cockton (eds.), *People and Computers XIV, Usability or Else! Proceedings of HCI 2000* (pp. 357–373). Sunderland: Springer-Verlag.

Kitajima, M., Blackmon, M. H. & Polson, P. G. (2005). Cognitive architecture for website design and usability evaluation: Comprehension and information scent in performing by exploration. Paper presented at the Human Computer Interaction International, Las Vegas, NV.

Landauer, T. K. (1986). How much do people remember? Some estimates of the quantity of learned information in long-term memory. *Cognitive Science*, *10*, 477–493.

Landauer, T. K. & Dumais, S. T. (1997). A solution to Plato's problem: the latent semantic analysis theory of acquisition, induction, and representation of knowledge. *Psychological Review*, *104*, 211–240.

Lucas, P. (2000). Pervasive information access and the rise of human-information interaction. Paper presented at the Human Factors in Computing Systems, CHI 2000, The Hague.

Luo, L. & John, B. E. (2005). Predicting task execution time on handheld devices using the keystroke-level model. Paper presented at the CHI 2003, ACM Conference on Human Factors in Computing Systems, Late Breaking Results, Portland, OR.

MacKenzie, I. S. (2003). Motor behavior models for human-computer interaction. In J. M. Caroll (ed.), *HCI Models, Theories, and Frameworks* (pp. 27–54). San Francisco, CA: Morgan Kaufman.

Manning, C. D. & Schuetze, H. (1999). *Foundations of Statistical Natural Language Processing*. Cambridge, MA: MIT Press.

Mayr, E. (1983). How to carry out the adaptationist program? *American Naturalist*, *121*, 324–334.

Meyer, D. E. & Kieras, D. E. (1997a). A computational theory of executive cognitive processes and multiple-task performance: I. Basic mechanisms. *Psychological Review*, *104*(1), 3.

Meyer, D. E. & Kieras, D. E. (1997b). A computational theory of executive cognitive processes and multiple-task performance: Part 2. Accounts of psychological refractory-period phenomena. *Psychological Review*, *104*(4), 749.

Miller, G. A. (1956). The magical number seven plus or minus two: some limits on our capacity for processing information. *Psychological Review*, *63*, 81–97.

Neisser, U. (1967). *Cognitive Psychology*. New York: Appleton-Crofts.

Newell, A. (1973). You can't play 20 questions with nature and win: projective comments on the paper of this symposium. In W. G. Chase (ed.), *Visual Information Processing*. New York: Academic Press.

Newell, A. (1990). *Unified Theories of Cognition*. Cambridge, MA: Harvard University Press.

Nielsen, J. (2000). *Designing Web Usability*. Indianapolis, IN: New Riders.

Nielsen, J. & Mack, R. L. (eds.) (1974). *Usability Inspection Methods*. New York: John Wiley & Sons.

Norman, D. A. (1998). *The Invisible Computer*. Cambridge, MA: MIT Press.

Pirolli, P. (1997, March). Computational models of information scent-following in a very large browsable text collection. Paper presented at the ACM Conference on Human Factors in Computing Systems, CHI '97, Atlanta, GA.

Pirolli, P. (1999). Cognitive engineering models and cognitive architectures in human-computer interaction. In F. T. Durso, R. S. Nickerson, R. W. Schvaneveldt, S. T. Dumais, D. S. Lindsay

& M. T. H. Chi (eds.), *Handbook of Applied Cognition* (pp. 441–477). Chichester: John Wiley & Sons.

Pirolli, P. (2005). Rational analyses of information foraging on the web. *Cognitive Science*, *29*(3), 343–373.

Pirolli, P. (in press). *Information Foraging: A Theory of Adaptive Interaction with Information*. Oxford: Oxford University Press.

Pirolli, P. & Card, S. K. (1999). Information foraging. *Psychological Review*, *106*, 643–675.

Pirolli, P. & Fu, W. (2003). SNIF-act: a model of information foraging on the world wide web. In P. Brusilovsky, A. Corbett & F. de Rosis (eds.), *User Modeling 2003, 9th International Conference, UM 2003* (Vol. 2702, pp. 45–54). Johnstown, PA: Springer-Verlag.

Ryle, G. (1949). *The concept of mind*. London: Hutchinson.

Salvucci, D. D. (2001). An integrated model of eye movements and visual encoding. *Cognitive Systems Research*, *1*, 201–220.

Simon, H. A. (1974). How big is a chunk? *Science*, *183*, 482–488.

Singley, M. K. & Anderson, J. R. (1989). *Transfer of Cognitive Skill*. Cambridge, MA: Harvard University Press.

Spool, J. M., Perfetti, C. & Brittan, D. (2004). *Designing for the Scent of Information*. Middleton, MA: User Interface Engineering.

Spool, J. M., Scanlon, T., Schroeder, W. *et al.* (1999). *Website Usability*. San Francisco, CA: Morgan Kaufman.

Stephens, D. W. & Krebs, J. R. (1986). *Foraging Theory*. Princeton, NJ: Princeton University Press.

Tinbergen, N. (1963). On the aims and methods of ethology. *Zeitschrift für Tierpsychologie*, *20*, 410–463.

Treisman, A. M. & Gelade, G. (1980). A feature-integration theory of attention. *Cognitive Psychology*, *12*, 97–136.

Turney, P. D. (2001, September). Mining the web for synonyms: PMI-IR versus LSA on TOEFL. Paper presented at the Twelfth European Conference on Machine Learning, ECML 2001, Freiburg, Germany.

Winterhalder, B. & Smith, E. A. (1992). Evolutionary ecology and the social sciences. In E. A. Smith & B. Winterhalder (eds.), *Evolutionary Ecology and Human Behavior* (pp. 3–23). New York: de Gruyter.

CHAPTER 18

Personal Information Management

William Jones
University of Washington, USA
and
Brian H. Ross
University of Illinois, USA

INTRODUCTION

The efforts people make to understand and change their environment have long been characterized as acts of information-processing (e.g., Broadbent 1958). Increasingly, our modern environment is itself informational, consisting of and changed by documents, email messages, web-pages, blogs, wikis, etc. *Personal Information Management* (PIM) refers to both the practice and the study of the activities a person performs in order to acquire or create, organize, maintain, retrieve, use, and distribute the information needed to complete tasks (work-related and not) and to fulfill various roles and responsibilities (as parent, employee, friend, member of community, etc.). PIM places special emphasis on the manipulation of information as packaged into information items such as paper documents, electronic documents, email messages, Web references, handwritten notes, appointments entered in a calendar, and so on. How are information items organized into a person's life for effective use and re-use?

People want to have the right information in the right place, at the right time, in the right form to meet the current need. But this ideal is far from the reality for most people. People do not always find the right information in time to meet their current needs. The necessary information is never found or it is found too late to be useful. Or the information is encountered too soon and is then misplaced or forgotten entirely before opportunities for its application arrive.

Moreover, there is considerable overhead associated with even routine uses of information. In his highly influential article "Man–computer symbiosis," Licklider described his observations of his own working day: "About 85 per cent of my 'thinking' time was spent getting into a position to think, to make a decision, to learn something I needed to know."

Handbook of Applied Cognition: Second Edition. Edited by Francis T. Durso.

He concluded, "My choices of what to attempt and what not to attempt were determined to an embarrassingly great extent by considerations of clerical feasibility, not intellectual capability" (Licklider 1960, p. 4).

Many of us might reach similar conclusions concerning our own interactions with information. A seemingly simple email request, for example, can often cascade into a time-consuming, error-prone chore as we seek to bring together, in coherent, consistent form, information that lies scattered, often in multiple versions, in various collections of paper documents, electronic documents, email messages, Web references, etc. Can you give a presentation at a meeting next month? That depends . . . What did you say in previous email messages? When is your child's soccer match? Better check the paper flyer with scheduled games. Does the meeting conflict with a conference? Better check the conference website to get dates and program information. What have you already scheduled in your calendar? And so on. In their observations of people processing email, Bellotti *et al.* (2005) describe instances in which a single email message initiates a task involving several different software applications and lasting an hour or more.

A wide range of tools and technologies are now available for the management of personal information. But this diversity has become part of the problem, leading to *information fragmentation.* A person may maintain several separate, roughly comparable but inevitably inconsistent, organizational schemes. The number of organizational schemes increases if a person has several email accounts, uses separate computers for home and work, has a PDA or a smart phone, or uses any of a bewildering number of special-purpose PIM tools. Interest in the study of PIM has increased in recent years with the growing realization that new applications and new gadgets, for all the targeted help they provide, often do so at the expense of increasing the overall complexity of PIM.

The study of PIM shifts emphasis away from a person's interactions with a specific device or application and toward a broader look at a person's integrative use of information across tools and over time. But clearly, the point is not the information itself but what it represents and enables (and sometimes hinders). Information itself is usually not a very precious resource – people have too much of it. Even a document that a person has spent days or weeks writing is typically available in multiple locations (and, sometimes confusingly, in multiple versions). People manage information because information is the most visible, "tangible" way to manage other resources that *are* precious such as their time, money, energy, attention and, even, their sense of well-being.

Chapter Objectives, Scope, and Structure

PIM shares considerable, potentially synergistic overlap with disciplines such as cognitive science, human–computer interaction, information science, artificial intelligence, database management, and information retrieval. This chapter reviews PIM in the context of cognitive science and the study of human cognition. Even in this narrower context, the extent of common ground can easily overwhelm. For example, the way people process and manage information varies greatly depending upon the current task and their familiarity with or training in its completion. A person's practice of PIM can change dramatically over time and is heavily influenced by an external environment that includes other people, available technology, and organizational setting. Consequently, the study of situated cognition, distributed cognition, and social cognition (e.g., Suchman 1987; Fiske & Taylor 1991; Hutchins 1994) all have relevance to the study of PIM. Also highly relevant is the study of affordances provided by the environment and by the "everyday" (and often overlooked) objects of a person's environment (Gibson 1977, 1979; Norman 1988, 1990, 1993). People vary greatly in their approach to PIM-relevant behaviors such as planning and with respect to personality traits such as risk-aversion – making the study of individual differences and personality also relevant.

In short, the potential interactions between cognitive science and PIM are considerable, largely unexplored and well beyond the scope of a single chapter to review. The current chapter makes a modest start by attempting to relate current findings from PIM-related work to what might be called the classic findings of cognitive psychology (e.g., Neisser 1967). It was Neisser himself who expressed a concern that cognitive psychology was in danger of becoming "a narrow and uninteresting specialized field" unless the field took a more realistic turn that included "a greater effort to understand cognition as it occurs in the ordinary environment and in the context of natural purposeful behavior" (p. 7).

The study of PIM provides an excellent opportunity to take such a turn toward the realistic. Our understanding of PIM should be informed by basic findings of cognitive psychology. But the exchange is two-way. PIM can provide a wealth of everyday situations for the study of human cognition. PIM situations take the cognitive psychologist out of the laboratory and may even inspire revisions to some of the most cherished paradigms of cognitive psychology.

This chapter's objectives are to describe PIM, as both a practice we all engage in and as an area of study; and to give special attention to PIM as an area of productive interplay between applied research and basic research in cognitive psychology and, more generally, cognitive science.

The rest of the chapter is divided into the following sections:

1. A brief review of *influences on PIM*, historical and current.
2. An analysis of PIM that includes working definitions of *key concepts and a framework* in which these concepts are related.
3. A review of *research* relating to PIM – both applied and basic research from cognitive psychology.
4. A discussion of the need for *methodologies of PIM* and the special challenges associated with the study of PIM.
5. The *conclusion*, which gives special attention to the opportunity for a productive interplay between applied work in PIM and basic research in human cognition.

INFLUENCES ON PIM

The modern dialog on PIM is generally thought to have begun with Vannevar Bush's highly inspirational article "As we may think" (1945). Bush described his vision of a *memex* device which would greatly increase a person's ability to record, retrieve, and interrelate information. Licklider (1960, 1965), Engelbart (1963) and Nelson (1982) each advanced the notion that the computer could be used to extend the ability to process information and even to enhance the human intellect. The phrase "personal information management" was apparently first used in the 1980s (Lansdale 1988) in the midst of general excitement over the potential of the personal computer to greatly enhance the human ability to process information (Goldstein 1980; Jones 1986; Johnson *et al.* 1989). The 1980s also saw the advent of so-called "PIM tools," which provided limited support for the management of appointments and scheduling, "to do" lists, phone numbers, and addresses.

The past few years have seen a revival of interest in PIM as a serious area of inquiry focusing work from a diverse set of disciplines including cognitive science, human–computer interaction, database management, information retrieval, and library and information science. Renewed interest in PIM is double-edged. On one side, the pace of improvements in various PIM-relevant technologies gives us reason to believe that earlier visions of PIM may actually be realized in the near future. Digital storage can hold not only conventional kinds of information, but also pictures, photographs, music – even films and full-motion video. Digital storage is cheap and plentiful. Why not keep a record of everything we have encountered? Better search support may make it easy to pinpoint the information we need. The ubiquity of computing and the miniaturization of computing devices make it possible for us to take our information with us wherever we go and still stay connected to a larger world of information. However, on the "other side," renewed interest in PIM is spurred on by the awareness that new tools – for all the targeted help they provide – can still end up further complicating a person's overall information management challenge.

Much of the applied research reviewed in this chapter originates from practitioners in the field of *human–computer interaction* (HCI). However, much research in HCI remains focused on specific forms of information (e.g., email messages, web-pages, digital photographs), specific devices to aid the interaction and, increasingly, on group and organizational issues of HCI. In the study of PIM, the focus remains primarily on the individual but also broadens to include key interactions with information over time and across tools. PIM considers our personal use of information in all of its various forms, including paper. Although it is difficult to imagine a practice of PIM these days that does not involve computers, information is central, not computers.

There has been discussion in recent years of *human–information interaction* (HII) in contrast to HCI (Gershon 1995; Lucas 2000; Fidel & Pejtersen 2004; Pirolli 2006). Interest in HII in the HCI community is partly due to a realization that our interactions with information are much more central to our lives than are our interactions with computers. This realization is reinforced by the trends toward ubiquitous computing. Success in computing and, perhaps paradoxically, in HCI, may mean that the computer "disappears" (Streitz & Nixon 2005) into the backdrop of our lives much like electricity. If we get the "transparent interfaces" we want, we are then left with our information. However, recognition of the importence of the human–information interaction may be neither new nor recent. Fidel and Pejtersen (2004) assert that the terms human–information interaction and *human information behavior* represent essentially the same concept and can be used interchangeably. As such, HII-relevant discussions have been a long-time mainstay of the library and information science (LIS) field (see, for example, Belkin 1993). The study of PIM may provide a meeting ground for the productive exchange of information between HCI and LIS communities.

AN ANALYSIS OF PIM

An analysis of PIM begins with a discussion of working definitions for key concepts. These support the framework that organizes the chapter's review of PIM and some of its key points of intersection with cognitive science.

The Information Item and Related Concepts

PIM gives special attention to the *information item* as a packaging of information that can be acquired or created, stored, copied, moved, retrieved, sent, deleted, and otherwise manipulated either as a physical or virtual object. Information items come in many different forms, as reflected by the tools and materials used in their creation and manipulation. Examples include paper documents, electronic documents (e-documents) and other files, email messages, appointments in an on-line calendar, web-pages, or references (e.g., shortcuts, aliases) to any of the above. Paper documents, for example, are manipulated using such form-specific tools such as a physical desktop, paper clips, staplers, filing cabinets, etc. In our interactions with digital forms of information we depend upon the support of computer-based tools and applications such as email applications, file managers, and Web browsers.

It is striking to consider how much of our interaction with the world around us is now mediated by various information items. We consult the newspaper or a web-page to read the headlines of the day and to find out what the weather will be like (perhaps before we even bother to look outside). We learn of meetings via email messages. We receive the documents we are supposed to read for these meetings via email as well. On the output side, we fill out Web-based forms. We send email messages. We create and send out reports in paper and digital form. Technology enables new forms of information (email messages, web-pages, blogs) through which we project ourselves and our desires across time and space in ways that would never have occurred to our forebears.

The information item establishes a manageable level of abstraction for this chapter's review of PIM. Certainly, a person's interactions with an information item vary greatly depending upon its form. Interactions with incoming email messages, for example, are often driven by the expectation of a timely response and perhaps also by the awareness that, when an email message scrolls out of view without some processing, it is apt to be quickly forgotten. A person may make a paper printout of the same email message, to be folded, carried in a briefcase, marked up and ultimately discarded when its information has been consumed.

The limited space of this chapter focuses on essential *similarities* in the way people interact with information items, regardless of their form. Whether people are looking at a new email message in their inbox, a newly discovered website or the business card they have just been handed at a conference, many of the same basic decisions must be made: "Is this relevant (to me)? To what does it relate? Do I need to act now or can I wait? If I wait, can I get back to this item later? Where should I put it? Will I remember to look?"

At the same time, the information item does not blur to include all things informational. A hallway conversation between two people, for example, conveys information but is not itself a packaging of information. A conversation is not an information item. A cassette recording of this same conversation is an information item. The recording can be stored, sent, copied, and so on. A person's memory of an impending doctor's appointment is not an information item. The scrap of paper containing a written reminder of this appointment is an information item.

Another point concerning information items, in contrast, for example, to what we hear or see in our physical world, is that we can often defer processing until later. We can, and do, accumulate large numbers of information items for a "rainy day." This is quite unlike, for example, scenarios of situation awareness where acceptable delays in processing information are measured in seconds (Durso & Gronlund 1999).

A *personal space of information* (PSI) includes information that is "personal" for any of several reasons. Focus in this chapter is on the set of information items that are, at least nominally, under that person's control (but not necessarily exclusively so). A PSI contains a person's books and paper documents, email messages, e-documents, files and references to web-pages. A PSI also includes applications, tools (such as a desktop search facility) and constructs (e.g., associated properties, folders, "piles" in various forms) that support the acquisition, storage, retrieval, and use of the information items in a PSI.

A Conceptual Framework: PIM Activities to Map between Information and Need

The rest of this chapter is guided by a framework that derives from a basic assumption concerning PIM activities:

> PIM activities help to establish, use, and maintain a mapping between information and need.

This simple statement can be expanded with reference to Figure 18.1. Needs, as depicted in the leftmost column, can be expressed in several different ways. The need may come from within a person as she recalls, for example, that she needs to make plane reservations

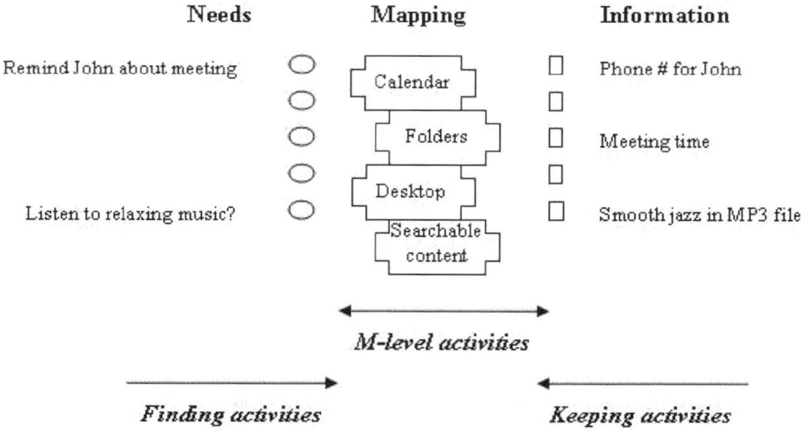

Figure 18.1 PIM activities viewed as an effort to establish, use and maintain a mapping between needs and information

for a trip. Or it may come via the question of a colleague in the hallway or a manager's request. Needs may also be evoked by an information item such as an email message or a Web-based form.

Information, as depicted in the rightmost column, is also expressed in various ways – as oral comments from a friend or as a billboard seen on the way to work or via any number of information items including documents, email messages, web-pages, and even handwritten notes.

Connecting between need and information is a mapping. Only small portions of the mapping have an observable external representation. Much of the mapping has only a hypothesized existence in the memory of an individual. Large portions of the mapping are potential and not realized in any form, external or internal. A sort function or a search facility, for example, has the potential to guide from a need to desired information.

But parts of the mapping can be observed and manipulated. The folders of a filing system (whether for paper documents, electronic documents, email messages or Web references), the layout of a desktop (physical or virtual), and the choice of names, keywords, and other properties for information items all forms parts of an observable fabric helping to knit need to information.

PIM activities and PIM-related research can be organized into this framework according to whether the initial focus is on a need, information or the mapping between need and information:[1]

- *Finding/re-finding activities* move from need to information. These activities affect the output of information from a PSI.
- *Keeping activities* move from information to need. These activities affect the input of information into a PSI.
- *Meta-level activities* focus on the mapping itself and on the overall management of the PSI. Efforts to maintain and organize regions of storage within a PSI – efforts to "get organized" in a physical office, for example, are one kind of meta-level activity.

RESEARCH RELATING TO PIM

Using the framework above, this section discusses PIM-related research, both applied and basic.

Finding: From Need to Information

People have needs. People find information to meet those needs. Needs can be large and nonspecific – the need for information to complete a review of a research area, for example – or small and simple – the need for a phone number. Many needs correspond to tasks (e.g., "get schedules and make airplane reservations"). But other needs may not fit tasks except by the broadest definition (e.g., "see that photograph of our vacation again").

In their efforts to meet needs, people seek. People search, sort, and browse. People scan through results lists or folder contents in an effort to recognize information items that relate to a need. These activities are all referred to in this chapter as *finding* activities.

Finding is broadly defined to include both acts of new finding where there is no previous memory of the needed information and acts of re-finding, where people are consciously trying to return to information items they have previously encountered. The information found can come from inside or outside a PSI. This chapter focuses on finding events where people are attempting to return to information they believe is in their PSI. But other variations in finding are also acts of PIM. And information inside the PSI can be used to support a more targeted, personalized search of the Web (e.g., Teevan *et al.* 2005).

Lansdale (1988) described a two-step process for information retrieval involving interplay between recall and recognition. Recall may mean typing in a search string or even an exact address for the desired information. In other cases, recall is less precise. A person may recall in which pile a paper document lies, but not its exact location within the pile. Or a person may have a rough idea when an email message was sent or an electronic document last modified. In a second step, then, information items or a representation of these, as delimited by the recall step, are scanned and, with success, the desired item is recognized and retrieved. The steps of recall and recognition can iterate to progressively narrow the search for the desired information – as happens, for example, when we move through a folder hierarchy to a desired file or email message or when we navigate through a website to a desired page. The recall/recognize two step can be seen as a dialog between people and their information environments.

But a successful outcome in a finding effort depends upon completion of another step preceding recall: a person must remember to look. A person may know exactly where an item is and still forget to look for the item in the first place. It is also useful to consider a final "repeat?" step, though this is essentially a variation of remembering to look. Meeting an information need often means assembling or reassembling a collection of information items relating to the task at hand. The finding activity must then repeat until the complete set of items is collected.

Failure to collect a complete set of information can sometimes mean failure for the entire finding episode. For example, a person may collect three of four items needed in order to decide whether to accept a dinner invitation next week. She consults a paper flyer, an events website and her on-line calendar and then, seeing no conflicts, accepts. Unfortunately, she did not think to look at a fourth item – a previously sent email in which she agreed to host a meeting of her book club that same evening.

Finding, then, can be viewed as a four-step with a possibility to fail at each step:

1. Remember to look.
2. Recall information about the information item that can help to narrow the subsequent scan.
3. Recognize the desired item(s).
4. Repeat, as needed, in order to "re-collect" the set of items needed for the current need.

Each step is now considered in more detail.

Remember to Look

Many opportunities to re-find and re-use information are missed for the simple reason that people forget to look. This failure occurs across information forms. In a study by

Whittaker and Sidner (1996), for example, participants reported that they forgot to look in "to do" folders containing actionable email messages. Because of mistrust in their ability to remember to look, people then elected to leave actionable email messages in an already overloaded inbox. Inboxes were often further loaded with copies of outgoing email messages that might otherwise be forgotten in a sent mail folder.

Web information is also forgotten. In one study of Web use, participants often complained that they encountered Web bookmarks, in the course of a "spring-cleaning," for example, that would have been very useful for a project whose time had now passed (Jones *et al.* 2002). In a study where participants were cued to return to a web-page for which they "had" a Web bookmark, this bookmark was used in less than 50 per cent of the trials (Bruce *et al.* 2004). Marshall and Bly (2005) report a similar failure to look for paper information (newspaper clippings). Many of us have had the experience of writing a document and then later discovering a similar document that we had previously authored.

If the old adage "out of sight, out of mind" is frequently true, then one way to remember is to keep items in view. Reminding is an important function, for example, of paper piles in an office (Malone 1983). Email messages in an inbox fulfill a similar function, at least until the messages scroll out of view (Whittaker & Sidner 1996). Barreau and Nardi (1995) observed that users often placed a file on the computer desktop in order to be reminded of its existence and of associated tasks to be completed.

Visibility helps. But a person must still be prepared to look. Piles on a physical desktop can, over time, recede into a background that receives scant attention. Likewise, as on-line advertisers surely know, people can learn to ignore sections of a computer's display. Also, the ability to manage items and keep track of items in view – whether on a computer screen or on the surfaces of a physical office – degrades, sometimes precipitously, as the number of items increases (Jones & Dumais 1986).

Attempts to compensate for the limitations of visible reminders can introduce other problems. People who adopt a strategy of repeatedly checking their email inboxes in order to respond to messages before these scroll out of view (and out of mind) may end up "living" in their email application with little time or attention left to accomplish work requiring sustained levels of concentration. People who immediately click through to interesting web-pages, for fear of forgetting to look at these later (even if they book-mark them) may have their session of Web use degenerate into an incoherent sequence of page views scattered across a wide range of topics with little to show for the experience.

There are many new ways in which a computer-based device might remind people of potentially useful information (Herrmann *et al.* 1999) including, for example, the spontaneous execution of searches that factor in words and other elements of the current context (Cutrell *et al.* 2006). However, these reminding devices must walk a fine line to avoid being either extremely annoying or ignored. These devices, like visible space, compete for a very precious and fixed resource: a person's attention.

Why is reminding so important? Why do people forget? Part of the answer goes back to a key problem of PIM: information fragmentation. Information items are scattered in different forms across different organizations. Support for grouping and interrelating items is still basic. The folder, for example, has changed little in its basic function since its introduction over 20 years ago as part of the desktop metaphor. Support for grouping, interrelating, and, more generally, support for the creation of external representations (e.g., of tasks or projects) that might support our internal representations is a topic of further discussion in both the keeping and meta-level sections.

Recall and Recognize

Recall and recognition are considered together as two sides of a dialog between a person and his information world. A person types a search word (recall) and then scans through a list of results (recognition). He clicks on a folder (recall) and then scans through a listing representing the items (e.g., email messages, files, Web references) within the folder.

Even as desktop search utilities improve, a preference persists for returning to information through what is alternately referred to as location-based finding, orienteering or, simply, browsing (O'Day & Jeffries, 1993; Barreau & Nardi 1995; Marchionini 1995; Teevan 2003). Habits change slowly and desktop search support continues to improve. Search is increasingly integrative and ever closer to an ideal where anything that can be remembered about an information item or the circumstances surrounding encounters with it (e.g., time of last use or nearby "landmark" events) can be used to help find this item (Lansdale 1988, 1991; Lansdale & Edmonds 1992; Cutrell *et al.* 2006). It is possible, then, that people may gradually shift toward a greater reliance on search.

But reasons to prefer browsing may be more basic. In response to a cue (such as an expression of information need) people are usually, but not always (Tulving & Thomson 1973), better at the recognition of an item from a set of alternatives than at its recall. Browsing reduces and distributes the amount that must be recalled and relies more on recognition (Lansdale 1988). Teevan *et al.* (2004) discuss additional considerations favoring what they term "orienteering," including *cognitive ease* (smaller steps, less burden on working memory), *sense of location* (and a greater sense of control), and a *richer context* in which to recognize and understand results. Basic research underlines the importance of context in recognition (Tulving & Thomson 1973; Tulving 1983).

Assuming people remember to look, how difficult is the return to an information item such as an e-document, email message or web-page previously seen? In a delayed cued recall study reported by Bruce *et al.* (2004), participants were asked to return to web-pages they had last visited up to six months prior by whatever means they chose. Participants did so quickly (retrieval times under a minute on average) and with success rates approaching 100 per cent. The small number of failures and time-out delays (>5 minutes) that did occur seemed primarily due to information fragmentation. For example, one participant was observed to look for a Web reference first in her Favorites, then in selected email folders, then in folders under "My Documents," before finally locating the Web reference inside a presentation she had saved to a network drive.

Repeat?

In many instances, the need is not for a single information item but for a set of items whose members may be scattered in different forms within different organizations. In the dinner scheduling example four different items needed to be retrieved in order to decide whether to accept a dinner invitation in the coming week. If the likelihood of successful retrieval of each item is strictly independent of the others, then the chances of successful retrieval of all relevant items goes down as their number increases. So even if the likelihood of success for each item is, say, 95 per cent, retrieval of all four items goes down to 81 per cent.

But the chance of success can be worse than would be expected for the independent retrieval of each of the items in the set. In situations of *output interference,* items retrieved first may interfere with the retrieval of later items in a set – perhaps because the act of retrieval itself strengthens the items first recalled at the expense of unrecalled items (Rundus 1971). Some of us may experience this effect when we try to think of everyone in a group of eight or nine friends. No matter whom we list first – and this can vary from time to time – the last one or two are often the hardest to remember.

The chances of successfully retrieving all members of a set can also be much better than predicted by a strict independence of individual retrievals. Obviously, retrieval is better if all items are in the same larger unit – a folder or a pile, for example. But then, it may make more sense to think of the folder or pile as the unit of retrieval. Retrieval may also be better than predicted by strict independence if items of a set have an internal organization or are interrelated to one another so that the retrieval of one item actually facilitates the retrieval of other items (e.g., Bower *et al.* 1969). One everyday example of what we might call *output facilitation* seems to occur, for example, when remembering the characters of a well-told story or a good movie.

Summary: Finding is Multi-step

Finding is a multi-step process with a possibility of stumbling at each step. First, people must *remember* to look. An item is retrieved through variations of searching or, more commonly for items in the PSI, browsing. Browsing and searching each involves an iterative interplay between basic actions of *recall* and *recognition*. Finally, in many situations of information need, people must *repeat* the finding activity several times in order to "re-collect" a complete set of information items.

Keeping: From Information to Need

Many events of daily life are roughly the converse of finding events: people encounter information and try to determine what, if anything, they should do with this information; i.e., people must match encountered information to anticipated need. Decisions and actions relating to encountered information are collectively referred to in this chapter as *keeping* activities. People may encounter an announcement for an upcoming event in the morning newspaper; or an "FYI" email may arrive with a pointer to a website. A successful effort to find new information frequently prompts keeping activity. A search of the Web, for example, often produces much more information than can be consumed in the current session. Both the decision to keep this information for later use and the steps to do so are keeping activities.

Keeping, more broadly considered, applies not only to information but also to channels of information. Subscribing to a magazine or setting the car radio to a particular station is a keeping decision. Keeping activities are also triggered when people are interrupted in the midst of a current task and look for ways of preserving current state so that work can be quickly resumed later (Czerwinski *et al.* 2004). People keep appointments by entering reminders into a calendar. People keep good ideas, or "things to pick up at the grocery store," by writing down a few cryptic lines on a sheet of paper.

Research relating to keeping points to the following conclusions:

- Keeping is difficult and error-prone.
- Keeping "right" has become harder as the diversity of information forms and supporting tools has increased.
- Some costs of keeping "wrong" have gone away, but challenges remain.

Keeping is Difficult and Error-prone

Keeping actions, such as bookmarking a website or setting a reminder flag on an email, are sometimes difficult both in the mechanics of execution and because these actions interrupt the current task (e.g., browsing the Web, reading email). Even more difficult is the decision that guides these actions.

The keeping decision is multifaceted. Is the information useful? If so, do special steps need to be taken to keep it for later use? How should the information be kept? Where? On what device? In what form should it be kept? Jones (2004) characterizes each keeping decision as a signal detection task[2] subject to a rational analysis of alternatives (Anderson 1990; see also Pirolli, Chapter 17, this volume).

There is a "gray area" of encountered information where determination of costs, reciprocal benefits, and outcome likelihoods is not straightforward. In the logic of signal detection, this middle area presents us with a "damned if you do and damned if you don't" choice. If we keep the information, we may never use it; if we don't keep it, we may later need it. Moreover, if we keep information in the wrong way – in the wrong folder, for example – we may pay twice: We don't find the information when we need it. Worse, when we later need other information in the folder, the incorrectly filed information gets in the way.

Filing information items – whether paper documents, e-documents or email messages – correctly in the right folders is a cognitively difficult and error-prone activity (Malone 1983; Lansdale 1988, 1991; Kidd 1994; Whittaker & Sidner 1996; Balter 2000). Difficulty arises in part because the definition or purpose of a folder is often unclear from the label (e.g., "stuff") and may change in significant ways over time (Kidd 1994; Whittaker & Sidner 1996; Whittaker & Hirschberg 2001). Determining a folder's definition may be at least as problematic as determining a category's definition (e.g., Wittgenstein 1953; Zadeh 1965; Rosch *et al.* 1976; Rosch 1978). Worse, people may not even recall the folders they have created and so create new ones to meet the same or a similar purpose (Whittaker & Sidner 1996).

If a person's use of folders is inconsistent, so too is a person's experience with incoming information. A person's experience of the same information item can change considerably as a function of the surrounding context (Martin 1968; Tulving & Thomson 1973). Context includes not only the external circumstances of an item's encounter, but also the anticipated circumstances of its later uses (Kwasnik 1989). The same person, on alternate days, may follow different schemes of classification within the same folder hierarchy. Sellen and Harper (2002) describe a study suggesting that 3 per cent of the paper documents in a typical office are misfiled and that 8 per cent are eventually lost. Perhaps the only surprise is that these figures are not higher.

There is little reason to believe that problems described above for folder use go away if we replace "folders" with "keywords" or "piles." Although items placed or left in piles retain greater visibility, they equally retain greater power to distract, confuse, or obscure if in the wrong pile. Moreover, as noted above, a person's ability to keep track of unlabeled piles is quite limited.

Keeping "Right" has Gotten Harder

An act of keeping might be likened to throwing a ball into the air toward a point where we expect to be at some future point in time and space. Keeping in accordance with future need has never been easy.

In her investigation into how people organize paper documents, Kwasnik (1989, 1991) identified a large number of, sometimes competing, considerations that might affect a document's classification. Considerations related, for example, to document attributes (e.g., author, topic, form), disposition (e.g., discard, keep, postpone), order/scheme, time, value (e.g., importance, interest, and confidentiality), and cognitive state (e.g., "don't know" and "want to remember").

Today, paper documents and books are still an important part of the average person's PSI (Whittaker & Hirschberg 2001; Sellen & Harper 2002). In addition, people must contend with the organization of e-documents, email messages, web-pages (or references to these) and possibly also a number of additional forms of digital information (each with their own special-purpose tool support) including phone messages, digitized photographs, music and videos. The number of keeping considerations further increases if a person has different email accounts, uses separate computers for home and work, uses a PDA, smart phone or special-purpose PIM tools.

People can and do freely convert from one form of information to another (Jones *et al.* 2002). People make paper printouts of e-documents, web-pages and email messages and scan paper documents for inclusion in e-documents. People send e-documents and Web references via email. People save email messages and web-pages into the same filing system that holds their electronic documents.

People can keep information in several different ways to be sure of having it later (Jones *et al.* 2002). A person may, for example, enter a client's phone number into a calendar (as a reminder to call) and into a contact database. But doing so can increase the later challenges of updating and synchronization (e.g., when the phone number changes). And still not all needs are met. Neither the calendar nor contact entry will help, for example, if the person needs to contact the client on his cell phone while stuck in traffic. We can hope that one day our information is more integrated. Perhaps we will carry gigabytes of information on a smart phone that we plug into computing environments with higher bandwidth as opportunity permits. For most of us, this day has not yet arrived.

Some Costs of Keeping "Wrong" Have Gone Away, but Challenges Remain

Recent developments in technology have dramatically reduced or even nullified some costs associated with keeping mistakes. These reductions invite a consideration of two "decision-free" extremes in keeping strategy: keep everything or keep nothing at all (Jones 2004). Unless people are doing video editing, for example, the storage cost of a false positive – of keeping digital information that's never used – is often negligible. Why not keep it all? Facilities to sort, search, and filter may even help to clear away the clutter so that people can focus on the more useful information. Many people appear to be following a modified "keep everything" approach, for example, in the management of incoming email by leaving it in the inbox, perhaps with occasional efforts to "spring clean" (Whittaker & Sidner 1996).

Some costs associated with a "miss" – not keeping information that turns out to be useful – are also decreasing dramatically. With ever-increasing amounts of information available in readily searchable form on the Web (or intranet counterparts), people often rely on re-finding methods that require no explicit keeping activity (Bruce *et al.* 2004). These "do nothing" methods include searching again or navigating from another website.

System support can also automate keeping in ways that combine local storage and reliance on the Web. The history and the "auto-complete" facilities in most Web browsers, for example, keep references locally to information that remains on the Web.

Approaches that automate keeping, or that free people from a need to decide what is kept, point to a dilemma identified by Lansdale (1988). People may not take the trouble to keep information for later use, either because doing so is too much trouble or because they are too confident of their ability to get back to the information later (Koriat 1993). Automated keeping can save people time and, more important, the distraction of leaving the current task in order to decide whether and how an item in view should be kept for future uses. But if people do not take actions to keep encountered information, they may be less likely to remember to look for this information later in the right situations.

Of relevance to Lansdale's dilemma are depth of processing effects (Craik & Lockhart 1972) and the *generation effect* (Slamecka & Graf 1978). The generation effect has been observed in the assignment of names for text editing commands (Jones & Landauer 1985) and in the assignment of tags to documents (Lansdale 1991). Research in *prospective memory* – the memory to perform an action in the future – also supports a prediction that activities taken when information is encountered may reduce the likelihood of memory failure later on (Terry 1988; O'Connail & Frohlich, 1995; Sellen *et al.* 1996; Ellis & Kvavilashvili 2000).

An alternative to "keep everything," "keep nothing," and "keep automatically" approaches are approaches that help people to "keep smarter," i.e., to make better decisions concerning future uses of encountered information. If people have prepared a clear plan, they are often more effective at keeping relevant information (including a recognition of its relevance) even when the plan and its goal are not the current focus of attention (Seifert & Patalano 2001).

Summary: Keeping is Multifaceted

Certainly keeping, like finding, can involve several steps. Keeping may even trigger an act of finding – as in finding the right folder or pile in which to place an information item. But the essential challenge of keeping stems from the multifaceted nature of the decisions about information needs. Is the information useful? Do special actions need to be taken to keep it for later use? Where? When? In what form? On what device? With no crystal ball to see into the future, answering these questions is difficult and error-prone. But the attempt to do so helps us to remember the information item later in appropriate circumstances. Some caution is advised against an over-reliance on well-intended attempts to automate these decisions. Complementary tool support for planning may be one way to ensure that key connections are made between encountered information and anticipated need. And a well-formulated plan has other benefits as well.

The Meta-level: Mapping between Need and Information

Meta-level activities, the third set of PIM activities, operate broadly upon collections of information within the PSI and on the mapping that connects need to information for these collections. At the level of keeping and finding, "managing" often equates with "getting by" (as in "I finally managed to find the information"). The meta-level puts a more proactive capital "M" spin on "Management". How can people take charge of their PIM practice? How should the information be structured? According to what schema? Following which strategies? How can tools help, either to structure or to obviate structuring? How is effectiveness of current practice measured? Policy decisions of privacy and security are also addressed at the meta-level (Karat *et al.* 2006). Who has access to what information under what circumstances? How to distribute information (medical information, airplane seating preferences, a résumé, etc.) for best effect?

This section considers two meta-level activities which are (and should be even more) related to one another: (1) maintenance and organization; and (2) making sense of information and planning its use.

Maintaining (too) Many Organizations (Maybe Tomorrow)

Differences between people are especially apparent in their approaches to the maintenance and organization of information. Malone (1983) distinguished between "neat" and "messy" organizations of paper documents. "Messy" people had more piles in their offices and appeared to invest less effort than "neat" people in filing information. Comparable differences have been observed in the ways people approach email (Mackay 1988; Whittaker & Sidner 1996; Balter 1997; Gwizdka 2002), e-documents (Boardman & Sasse 2004; Bruce *et al.* 2004) and Web bookmarks (Abrams *et al.* 1998; Boardman & Sasse 2004).

Across information forms, differences in approaches to organization correlate with differences in keeping strategy. For example, people who have a more elaborate folder organization – whether for paper documents, e-documents, email messages or Web bookmarks – tend to file sooner and more often. However, people are often selective in their maintenance of different organizations. Boardman and Sasse (2004), for example, classified 14 of 31 participants in their study as "pro-organizing" with respect to email and e-documents, but not with respect to bookmarks; seven of 31 participants only took the trouble to organize their e-documents. (The study did not include a look at organizations of paper documents.)

The fragmentation of information by forms poses special challenges for maintenance and organization. Folders with similar names and purposes may be created in different information organizations, especially for email messages and e-documents (Boardman &

Sasse 2004). Maintaining consistency is difficult and organizations can easily get out of synch; for example, people may have a "trips" email folder and a "travel" e-document folder. The fragmentation of information across forms also poses problems in the study of PIM (see the section on methods and methodologies of PIM below). It is difficult and time-consuming to study and compare a participant's organizational schemes across several different forms of information and tempting to focus primarily on a single form of information such as email messages or web-pages.

However, several studies have now looked at how the same person manages across different forms of information (Boardman & Sasse 2004; Ravasio *et al.* 2004; Jones *et al.* 2005). The following composite emerges:

- People do not generally take time out of a busy day to assess their organizations or their PIM practice in general.
- People complain about the need to maintain so many separate organizations of information and about the fragmentation of information that results.
- Even within the same folder organization, competing organizational schemes may suffer an uneasy co-existence with each other. People may apply one scheme on one day and another scheme the day after.
- Several participants in one study (Jones *et al.* 2002) reported making a special effort to consolidate organizations, for example, by saving Web references and email messages into a file folder organization or by sending e-documents and Web references in email messages.

"Meta-" is commonly used as in "beyond" (everyday PIM activities) or "about" (the mapping or a PIM practice overall).[3] But the studies referenced above also invoke a more original sense of "meta-" as in "after."[4] For many people, meta-level activities such as maintenance and organization occur only after other, more pressing, PIM activities of keeping and finding are done. This frequently means not at all. Activities of keeping and finding are triggered by many events in a typical day. Information is encountered and keeping decisions are made (if only the decision to do nothing). The information needed for a variety of routine activities (calling someone, planning the day's schedule, preparing for a meeting, etc.) triggers various finding activities.

Events triggering maintenance and organization of information are fewer and less frequent. For some people, these activities may be triggered by a corporate "clean desk" policy or a system administrator's message that an inbox is too full or possibly a New Year's resolution to get organized. Studies of PIM are themselves often a trigger. Boardman and Sasse reported, for example, that 12 participants in their study performed "ad hoc tidying" during the interview itself. In the Jones *et al.* (2005) study, all 14 participants made comments at the outset such as "I really should clean this up." Four participants actually insisted on interrupting the interview while they moved or deleted "old stuff that really shouldn't be there anymore."

As digital storage continues to increase in capacity and decrease in cost, maintenance, and organization activities are seldom prompted by "disk full" events. Even so, people often express an unease with their current maintenance of information as expressed by apologetic comments like "this is a mess" or in references to themselves as "a packrat" (Marshall & Bly 2005). Or, as one participant in Boardman and Sasse's study (2004, p. 585) said, "Stuff goes in but doesn't come back out – it just builds up."

Making Sense of Information and the Value of External Representations

Much of the experimental work reviewed so far may make us question the value of organizing information in our PSI. We have too many folder organizations to maintain and we frequently postpone and ignore issues of maintenance the way we might avoid straightening up a messy closet. Keeping (filing) information into a folder structure is difficult and mistakes are common. Storage is cheap. Search continues to improve. Is it still worthwhile to organize information? Or can we leave our information "flat" and depend upon search (and possibly sorting) as a primary means of access?

We now review research demonstrating that people organize information not only to insure its retrieval but for several other reasons as well. In the Jones *et al.* study (2005) participants listed a number of reasons for using folders even if they had access to a "perfect" desktop search facility:

- "I want to be sure all the files I need are in one place."
- "Folders help me see the relationship between things."
- "Folders remind me what needs to be done."
- "Folders help me to see what I have and don't have."
- "I use empty folders for information I still need to get."
- "Putting things into folders helps me to understand the information better."

In this study, a folder hierarchy developed for a project such as "wedding" often resembled a project plan or partial problem decomposition in which sub-folders stood for project-related goals and also for the tasks and sub-projects associated with the achievement of these goals. A "wedding dress" sub-folder, for example, organized information and tasks associated with the goal of selecting and fitting a wedding dress (including, for example, a "wedding dress trials" sub-subfolder).

Barsalou (1983, 1985, 1991) has long argued that many people's internal categories also arise to accomplish goals. His research demonstrates an ability to group together seemingly dissimilar items according to their applicability to a common goal. For example, weight watchers might form a category "foods to eat on a diet." Rice cakes, carrot sticks, and sugar-free drinks are all members of the category, even though they differ considerably in other ways. The best member is not necessarily like other category members. Instead, the best exemplar is the item that best accomplishes the goal, the ideal. Research by Markman and Ross (2003) suggests that an internal, goal-based organization for a set of items emerges as a by-product of the use of these items to accomplish goals. A person need not think explicitly about the goal-relatedness of items in order to internalize this organization.

This is not to suggest a direct mapping exists between goal-directed folders as an external form of information organization and goal-directed categories as an internal organization of concepts. However, it is reasonable to suppose that folders (and piles, property/value combinations, views, etc.) can form an important part of *external representations* (ERs) which, in turn, can complement and combine with *internal representations* (IRs) to form an integrated cognitive system (Hutchins 1994; Kirsh 2000).

Finding the right ER helps in *sense-making* (Dervin 1992), i.e., in efforts to make sense of the information. For example, the right diagram can allow one to make inferences more quickly (Larkin & Simon 1987). The way information is externally represented can produce huge differences in a person's ability to use this information in short-duration, problem-solving exercises (Kotovsky *et al.* 1985). Different kinds of representations, like matrices and hierarchies, are useful in different types of problems (Novick 1990; Novick *et al.* 1999; Cheng 2002). Russell *et al.* (1993) provide an analysis in which ERs are acquired and discarded according to an assessment of relative costs and benefits.

What are the long-term costs and benefits associated with the use of ERs for PIM – the ER that results from use of a particular filing scheme, for example? And, can tools change the cost/benefit equation to impact a person's willingness to invest in the expression and use of ERs? These are important, mostly unanswered questions, with implications both for the applied study of PIM and the more basic study of human cognition.

Efforts in tool support can benefit from basic research into how people plan. For example, support for a progressive refinement (top-down or bottom-up) must also allow for the dynamic, flexible changes people make to accommodate new information or to exploit new opportunities. This opportunistic aspect of planning has been noted in experiments ranging from ill-structured domains, such as errand planning (Hayes-Roth & Hayes-Roth 1979), to the highly structured Tower of Hanoi problem (Davies 2003).

Summary: Meta-level Activities are Important but Easily Overlooked

Meta-level activities are important to a successful PIM practice, but rarely urgent. There are few events in a typical day that direct our attention to meta-level activities such as maintenance and organization, making (overall) sense of an information collection, managing privacy and security or measuring and assessing the effectiveness of strategies and supporting tools. As a result, meta-level activities can easily become afterthoughts. Research into meta-level activities and their support also appears to get less attention than, for example, research into finding (which can draw upon support from established communities in information seeking and information retrieval). But it is at the meta-level that we may realize some of the most productive synergies between applied research in PIM and basic research in cognitive science.

METHODOLOGIES OF PIM

The development of methodologies especially suited to PIM is still in its infancy. There is a need for methodologies both to guide *descriptive* studies aimed at better understanding how people currently practice PIM and to guide *prescriptive* evaluations to assess proposed PIM solutions (which usually involve a tool but sometimes focus, instead, on a technique or strategy). PIM poses special challenges with respect to both its descriptive study and the prescriptive evaluation of proposed solutions:

1. *A person's practice of PIM is unique.* There is tremendous variation between people, even between people who have a great deal in common with each other with respect to profession, education and computing platform.
2. *PIM happens broadly across many tools, applications and information forms.* Moreover, people freely convert information from one to another form to suit their needs: emailing a document, for example, or printing out a web-page. Studies and evaluations that focus on a specific form of information and supporting applications – email, for example – run the risk of optimizing for that form of information at the expense of a person's ability to manage other forms of information.

3. *PIM happens over time.* Personal information has a lifecycle – for example, moving from an initial pile to a project folder and, later, to archival storage. Activities of keeping and finding directed to the same information item may be separated from each other by days, weeks or months. Basic PIM events of interest – like filing, creating a new folder, or the protracted search for a lost item of information – occur unpredictably and cannot be "scheduled." In addition, people can make significant changes in their practice of PIM over time.

One approach, then, is to create ethnographies of PIM in which a person and his/her practice of PIM is the subject of an exploratory, longitudinal case study. Design methodologies that place an emphasis on context and situation have obvious relevance including *contextual inquiry* (Beyer & Holtzblatt 1998), *situated activity* (Suchman 1983), and *situated design* (Greenbaum & Kyng 1991).

However, longitudinal case studies are time-consuming and it is not easy to find a representative sampling of participants able to commit to a multi-session study. Results may be very enlightening but do not, by themselves, form a proper basis for generalization. Results can often be used, however, to guide targeted single-session studies and surveys.

The effectiveness of PIM research can be improved through:

- *Development of reference tasks* (Whittaker *et al.* 2000). For example, there is a need for validated keeping and finding tasks that can be administered to participants as they work with their information.
- *Units of analysis.* Certainly a basic task or "to do" list item is one useful unit in the study of PIM (Bellotti *et al.* 2004) and promotes an approach in which PIM and personal task management are seen to be "two sides of the same coin" (but see Marshall & Bly 2005). The personal project (e.g., "re-model the house," "plan a summer vacation," "complete my part of the company's quarterly report") is a somewhat larger unit of analysis that also shows promise (Jones *et al.* 2005). A personal project has an internal structure and often involves considerable planning. Projects last from a few days to several months but are generally bounded in time. A project's planning and completion often involve a range of information forms (including paper) and a range of tools (computer-based and not). The study of a personal project may, therefore, provide a tractable way to study PIM without "falling into" existing tool-based partitions (e.g., by studying only email use or only Web use).

CONCLUSION: THE INTERPLAY BETWEEN PIM AND THE STUDY OF HUMAN COGNITION

PIM activities are usefully grouped according to their role in a person's ongoing effort to establish, use and maintain a mapping between information and need.

- *Finding* activities move people from a need to information that meets this need. Finding, and especially re-finding, is multi-step and problems can arise with each step. People must remember to look; people must combine actions of recall and recognition to actually locate an item; and often, these steps must be repeated to retrieve the set of items needed to complete a task.

- *Keeping* activities move people from encountered information to anticipated needs for which this information might be useful. The multifaceted nature of the keeping decision reflects the multifaceted nature of anticipated needs. We must make choices concerning location, organizing folder, form, and associated devices/applications.
- *Meta-level* activities focus on the mapping that connects information to need. Included are activities to *maintain* and *organize* collections of personal information and to *make sense of* the information in a collection. Management of privacy and security and the assessment of effectiveness for PIM tools and strategies are also meta-level activities. Although meta-level activities are important they are frequently overlooked since they are rarely prompted by the events of a typical day.

The study of PIM can benefit from, but can also enrich, the study of human cognition. For example, planning is a crucial aspect of performance in complex, dynamic, demanding tasks (Mumford *et al.* 2001). Increases in our basic understanding of planning carry practical implications for the design of PIM support. In return, the study of PIM presents real-world situations for the study of planning.

Situations of PIM may often suggest modifications in paradigms of inquiry. For example, the filing classification challenge that people often routinely complete is quite different from the task of a traditional experimenter-supervised, forced-choice classification paradigm: First, feedback, if it comes at all, may come only weeks or even months later and then is often only inferred not direct. Second, people are not limited to a fixed set of alternatives – they can create a new folder or they can decide not to file.

To take another example, PIM situations of keeping differ from the task of a standard prospective memory paradigm in at least two important respects. First, an information item may be encountered and kept days, months or even years before it is applied to a need. In contrast, the interval between intention and action in a prospective memory experiment is on the order of minutes to hours. Second, although prospective memory experiments have specific cues and intentions, an information item may be kept with no clear need in mind (Marshall & Bly 2005).

As these examples illustrate, the interplay between applied research in PIM and basic research in human cognition promises to be rich and mutually beneficial. To return to Neisser's quote at the beginning of this chapter, we might say that PIM provides a broad reality for the study of cognitive psychology. Cognitive psychology, in turn, can bring a deeper reality to our understanding of PIM.

ACKNOWLEDGMENTS

The authors gratefully acknowledge the helpful comments of Raymond Nickerson and two anonymous reviewers. The first author's work on this chapter is partially supported by the National Science Foundation #0097855.

NOTES

1 Certainly, some events of finding, keeping, and even at the meta-level involve no observable manipulation of information items and, therefore, fall outside the focus of PIM. A manager may see a recently hired employee, for example, and experience the need to retrieve the new

employee's name. She may remember that the employee's name is "Ted" without reference to external information items. (But she might also find out the employee's name by referring to a paper print-out that lists names of new employees.) Similarly, a sales person with a facility for remembering phone numbers might choose to commit the phone number for a new client to memory. But if, instead, he writes the number down, he has created an information item to be managed as part of his PSI.

2 The theory of signal detectability (TSD) (Peterson *et al.* 1954; Van Meter & Middleton 1954) has been applied elsewhere to a basic question of information retrieval: what does and does not get returned in response to a user's query (see, e.g., Swets 1963, 1969).

3 See the entry for "meta-" in the on-line Wikipedia: http://en.wikipedia.org/wiki/Meta-.

4 See, for example, the entry for "meta-" in the Merriam-Webster Online Dictionary (http://www.m-w.com/dictionary/Meta-).

REFERENCES

Abrams, D., Baecker, R. & Chignell, M. (1998). Information archiving with bookmarks: personal web space construction and organization. Paper presented at the ACM SIGCHI Conference on Human Factors in Computing Systems (CHI 1998), Los Angeles, CA.

Anderson, J. R. (1990). *The Adaptive Character of Thought*. Hillsdale, NJ: Lawrence Erlbaum Associates.

Balter, O. (1997). Strategies for organising email messages. In H. Thimbleby, B. O'Conaill & P. J. Thomas (eds.), *Proceedings of the Twelfth Conference of the British Computer Society Human Computer Interaction Specialist Group – People and Computers XII* (Vol. 12, pp. 21–38). Bristol: Springer.

Balter, O. (2000). Keystroke level analysis of email message organization. Paper presented at the ACM SIGCHI Conference on Human Factors in Computing Systems (CHI 2000), The Hague.

Barreau, D. K. & Nardi, B. A. (1995). Finding and reminding: file organization from the desktop. *SIGCHI Bulletin*, *27*(3), 7.

Barsalou, L. (1991). Deriving categories to achieve goals. In G. H. Bower (ed.), *The Psychology of Learning and Motivation* (Vol. 27, pp. 1–64). San Diego, CA: Academic Press.

Barsalou, L. W. (1983). Ad hoc categories. *Memory & Cognition*, *11*(3), 211–227.

Barsalou, L. W. (1985). Ideals, central tendency, and frequency of instantiation as determinants of graded structure in categories. *Journal of Experimental Psychology: Learning, Memory & Cognition*, *11*(1–4), 629–654.

Belkin, N. J. (1993). Interaction with texts: information retrieval as information-seeking behavior. In G. Knorz, J. Krause & C. Womser-Hacker (Eds.), *Information retrieval '93. Von der Modellierung zur Anwendung* (pp. 55–66). Konstanz: Universitaetsverlag Konstanz.

Bellotti, V., Dalal, B., Good, N. *et al.* (2004). What a to-do: Studies of task management towards the design of a personal task list manager. Paper presented at the Conference on Human Factors in Computing Systems (CHI 2004), Vienna.

Bellotti, V., Ducheneaut, N., Howard, M. *et al.* (2005). Quality vs. quantity: email-centric task-management and its relationship with overload. *Human–Computer Interaction*, *20*(1–2), 89–138.

Beyer, H. & Holtzblatt, K. (1998). *Contextual Design: Defining Customer-Centered Systems*. San Francisco, CA: Morgan Kaufmann.

Boardman, R. & Sasse, M. A. (2004). "Stuff goes into the computer and doesn't come out": a cross-tool study of personal information management. Paper presented at the ACM SIGCHI Conference on Human Factors in Computing Systems (CHI 2004), Vienna.

Bower, G. H., Clark, M. C., Lesgold, A. M. & Winzenz, D. (1969). Hierarchical retrieval schemes in recall of categorized word lists. *Journal of Verbal Learning and Verbal Behavior*, *8*, 323–343.

Broadbent, D. E. (1958). Perception and communication. London: Pergamon Press.

Bruce, H., Jones, W. & Dumais, S. (2004). Information behavior that keeps found things found. *Information Research*. http://informationr.net/ir/10-1/paper207.html

Bush, V. (1945). As we may think. *The Atlantic Monthly, 176*, 1 (July 1945), 641–649.

Cheng, P. C.-H. (2002). Electrifying diagrams for learning: principles for complex representational systems. *Cognitive Science*, *26*(6), 685–736.

Craik, F. I. M. & Lockhart, R. S. (1972). Levels of processing: a framework for memory research. *Journal of Verbal Learning and Verbal Behavior, 11*, 671–684.

Cutrell, E., Dumais, S. & Teevan, J. (2006). Searching to eliminate personal information management. *Communications of the ACM*, *49*(1), 58–64.

Czerwinski, M., Horvitz, E. & Wilhite, S. (2004). A diary study of task switching and interruptions. Paper presented at the ACM SIGCHI Conference on Human factors in Computing Systems (CHI 2004), Vienna.

Davies, S. P. (2003). Initial and concurrent planning in solutions to well-structured problems. *The Quarterly Journal of Experimental Psychology*, *56A*(7), 1147–1164.

Dervin, B. (1992). From the mind's eye of the user: the sense-making qualitative-quantitative methodology. In J. Glazier & R. Powell (eds.), *Qualitative Research in Information Management* (pp. 61–84). Englewood, CO: Libraries Unlimited.

Durso, F. T. & Gronlund, S. (1999). Situation awareness. In F. T. Durso, R. Nickerson, R. W. Schvaneveldt *et al.* (eds.), *The Handbook of Applied Cognition* (pp. 284–314). Chichester: John Wiley & Sons.

Ellis, J. & Kvavilashvili, L. (2000). Prospective memory in 2000: past, present and future directions. *Applied Cognitive Psychology*, *14*, 1–9.

Engelbart, D. C. (1963). A conceptual framework for the augmentation of man's intellect. In *Vistas in Information Handling*. London: VI Spartan Books.

Fidel, R. & Pejtersen, A. M. (2004). From information behaviour research to the design of information systems: the Cognitive Work Analysis framework. *Information Research*. http://informationr.net/ir/10-1/paper210.html

Fiske, S. T. & Taylor, S. E. (1991). *Social Cognition* (2nd edn). New York: McGraw-Hill.

Gershon, N. (1995). Human information interaction. Paper presented at the Fourth International World Wide Web Conference, Boston, MA.

Gibson, J. J. (1977). The theory of affordances. In R. E. Shaw & J. Bransford (eds.), *Perceiving, Acting, and Knowing: Toward an Ecological Psychology*. Hillsdale, NJ: Lawrence Erlbaum Associates.

Gibson, J. J. (1979). *The Ecological Approach to Visual Perception*. Boston, MA: Houghton Mifflin.

Goldstein, I. (1980). Pie: a network-based personal information environment. Paper presented at the Workshop on Research in Office Semantics, Chatham, Cape Cod, MA.

Greenbaum, J. M. & Kyng, M. (1991). *Design at Work: Cooperative Design of Computer Systems*. Hillsdale, NJ: Lawrence Erlbaum Associates.

Gwizdka, J. (2002). Reinventing the inbox: supporting the management of pending tasks in email. Paper presented at the ACM SIGCHI Conference on Human Factors in Computing Systems, Doctoral Consortium (CHI 2002), Minneapolis, MN.

Hayes-Roth, B. & Hayes-Roth, F. (1979). A cognitive modeling of planning. *Cognitive Science*, *3*, 275–310.

Herrmann, D., Brubaker, B., Yoder, C. *et al.* (1999). Devices that remind. In F. T. Durso, R. Nickerson, R. W. Schvaneveldt *et al.* (eds.), *Handbook of Applied Cognition* (pp. 377–407). Chichester: John Wiley & Sons.

Hutchins, E. (1994). *Cognition in the Wild*. Cambridge, MA: MIT Press.

Johnson, J., Roberts, T. L., Verplank, W. *et al.* (1989). The Xerox star: a retrospective. *Computer, 22*(9), 11–26, 28–29.

Jones, W. (1986). On the applied use of human memory models: the Memory Extender personal filing system. *International Journal of Man Machine Studies*, *25*, 191–228.

Jones, W. (2004). Finders, keepers? The present and future perfect in support of personal information management. *First Monday*. Available at: http://www.firstmonday.dk/issues/issue9_3/jones/index.html.

Jones, W. & Dumais, S. (1986). The spatial metaphor for user interfaces – experimental tests of reference by location versus name. *ACM Transactions on Office Information Systems*, *4*(1), 42–63.

Jones, W., Dumais, S. & Bruce, H. (2002). Once found, what then? A study of "keeping" behaviors in the personal use of web information. In *65th Annual Meeting of the American Society for Information Science and Technology (ASIST 2002)* (Vol. 39, pp. 391–402). Philadelphia, PA: American Society for Information Science & Technology.

Jones, W. & Landauer, T. K. (1985). Context and self-selection effects in name learning. *Behaviour & Information Technology*, *4*(1), 3–17.

Jones, W., Munat, C. & Bruce, H. (2005). The Universal Labeler: plan the project and let your information follow. Paper presented at the 68th Annual Meeting of the American Society for Information Science and Technology (ASIST 2005), Charlotte, NC.

Jones, W., Phuwanartnurak, A. J., Gill, R. & Bruce, H. (2005). Don't take my folders away! Organizing personal information to get things done. Paper presented at the ACM SIGCHI Conference on Human Factors in Computing Systems (CHI 2005), Portland, OR.

Karat, C. M., Brodie, C. & Karat, J. (2006). Usable privacy and security for personal information management. *Communications of the ACM*, *49*(1), 56–57.

Kidd, A. (1994). The marks are on the knowledge worker. Paper presented at the ACM SIGCHI Conference on Human factors in Computing Systems (CHI '94), Boston, MA.

Kirsh, D. (2000). A few thoughts in cognitive overload. *Intellectia*, *1*(30), 19–51.

Koriat, A. (1993). How do we know that we know? The accessibility model of the feeling of knowing. *Psychological Review*, *100*, 609–639.

Kotovsky, K., Hayes, J. R. & Simon, H. A. (1985). Why are some problems hard? Evidence from Tower of Hanoi. *Cognitive Psychology*, *17*(2), 248–294.

Kwasnik, B. H. (1989). How a personal document's intended use or purpose affects its classification in an office. Paper presented at the 12th Annual ACM SIGIR Conference on Research and Development in Information Retrieval (SIGIR 1989), Cambridge, MA.

Kwasnik, B. H. (1991). The importance of factors that are not document attributes in the organization of personal documents. *Journal of Documentation*, *47*(4), 389–398.

Lansdale, M. (1988). The psychology of personal information management. *Applied Ergonomics, 19*(1), 55–66.

Lansdale, M. (1991). Remembering about documents: memory for appearance, format, and location. *Ergonomics*, *34*(8), 1161–1178.

Lansdale, M. & Edmonds, E. (1992). Using memory for events in the design of personal filing systems. *International Journal of Man-Machine Studies*, *36*, 97–126.

Larkin, J. H. & Simon, H. A. (1987). Why a diagram is (sometimes) worth ten thousand words. *Cognitive Science*, *11*, 65–99.

Licklider, J. C. R. (1960). Man-computer symbiosis. *IRE Transactions on Human Factors in Electronics, HFE-1*, 4–11.

Licklider, J. C. R. (1965). *Libraries of the Future*. Cambridge, MA: The MIT Press.

Lucas, P. (2000). Pervasive information access and the rise of human-information interaction. Paper presented at the ACM SIGCHI Conference on Human Factors in Computing Systems, Extended Abstracts (CHI 2000), The Hague.

Mackay, W. E. (1988). More than just a communication system: diversity in the use of electronic mail. Paper presented at the Conference on Computer-Supported Cooperative Work (CCSW '88), Portland, OR.

Malone, T. W. (1983). How do people organize their desks: implications for the design of office information-systems. *ACM Transactions on Office Information Systems*, *1*(1), 99–112.

Marchionini, G. (1995). *Information Seeking in Electronic Environments*. Cambridge: Cambridge University Press.

Markman, A. B. & Ross, B. H. (2003). Category use and category learning. *Psychological Bulletin*, *129*(4), 592–613.

Marshall, C. C. & Bly, S. (2005). Saving and using encountered information: implications for electronic periodicals. In *Proceedings of the ACM SIGCHI Conference on Human Factors in Computing Systems (CHI 2005)* (pp. 111–120). Portland, OR: ACM Press.

Martin, E. (1968). Stimulus meaningfulness and paired-associate transfer: an encoding variability hypothesis. *Psychological Review, 75*, 421–441.
Mumford, M. D., Schultz, R. A. & Van Doorn, J. R. (2001). Performance in planning: processes, requirements and errors. *Review of General Psychology, 5*(3), 213–240.
Neisser, U. (1967). *Cognitive Psychology*. New York: Appleton-Century-Crofts.
Neisser, U. (1976). *Cognition and Reality: Principles and Implications of Cognitive Psychology.* San Francisco, CA: W. H. Freeman.
Nelson, T. H. (1982). *Literary Machines*. Sausalito, CA: Mindful Press.
Norman, D. A. (1988). *The Psychology of Everyday Things*. New York: Basic Books.
Norman, D. A. (1990). *The Design of Everyday Things*. New York: Doubleday.
Norman, D. A. (1993). *Things that Make Us Smart: Defending Human Attributes in the Age of the Machine*. Reading, MA: Addison-Wesley.
Novick, L. R. (1990). Representational transfer in problem solving. *Psychological Science, 1*(2), 128–132.
Novick, L. R., Hurley, S. M. & Francis, M. (1999). Evidence for abstract, schematic knowledge of three spatial diagram representations. *Memory & Cognition, 27*(2), 288–308.
O'Connail, B. & Frohlich, D. (1995). Timespace in the workplace: dealing with interruptions. Paper presented at the ACM SIGCHI Conference on Human Factors in Computing Systems, Extended Abstracts (CHI 1995), Denver, CO.
O'Day, V. & Jeffries, R. (1993). Orienteering in an information landscape: how information seekers get from here to there. Paper presented at the ACM SIGCHI Conference on Human Factors in Computing Systems (CHI 1993), Amsterdam.
Peterson, W. W., Birdsall, T. G. & Fox, W. C. (1954). The theory of signal detectability. *Institute of Radio Engineers Transactions, PGIT-4*, 171–212.
Pirolli, P. (2006). Cognitive models of human-information interaction. In F. T. Durso, R. S. Nickerson, R. W. Schvaneveldt *et al.* (eds.), *Handbook of Applied Cognition* (2nd edn). Chichester: John Wiley & Sons.
Ravasio, P., Schär, S. G. & Krueger, H. (2004). In pursuit of desktop evolution: user problems and practices with modern desktop systems. *ACM Transactions on Computer–Human Interaction, 11*(2), 156–180.
Rosch, E. (1978). Principles of categorization. In E. Rosch & B. B. Lloyd (eds.), *Cognition and Categorization* (pp. 27–48). Hillsdale, NJ: Lawrence Erlbaum Associates.
Rosch, E., Mervis, C. B., Gray, W. *et al.* (1976). Basic objects in natural categories. *Cognitive Psychology, 8*, 382–349.
Rundus, D. (1971). Analysis of rehearsal processes in free recall. *Journal of Experimental Psychology, 89*, 63–77.
Russell, D. M., Stefik, M. J., Pirolli, P. & Card, S. K. (1993). The cost structure of sensemaking. In *CHI 1993: Proceedings of the ACM SIGCHI Conference on Human Factors in Computing Systems* (pp. 269–276). Amsterdam: ACM Press.
Seifert, C. M. & Patalano, A. L. (2001). Opportunism in memory: preparing for chance encounters. *Current Directions in Psychological Science, 10*(6), 198–201.
Sellen, A. J. & Harper, R. H. R. (2002). *The Myth of the Paperless Office*. Cambridge, MA: MIT Press.
Sellen, A. J., Louie, G., Harris, J. E. & Wilkins, A. J. (1996). What brings intentions to mind? An in situ study of prospective memory. *Memory & Cognition, 5*(4), 483–507.
Slamecka, N. J. & Graf, P. (1978). The generation effect: delineation of a phenomenon. *Journal of Experimental Psychology: Human Learning and Memory, 4*, 592–604.
Streitz, N. & Nixon, P. (2005). Special issue: the disappearing computer. *Communications of the ACM, 43*(3), 32–35.
Suchman, L. (1983). Office procedure as practical action: models of work and system design. *ACM Transactions on Office Information Systems, 1*(14), 320–328.
Suchman, L. (1987). *Plans and Situated Actions: The Problem of Human–Machine Communication*. Cambridge: Cambridge University Press.
Swets, J. A. (1963). Information retrieval systems. *Science, 141*, 245–250.
Swets, J. A. (1969). Effectiveness of information retrieval methods. *American Documentation, 20*(1), 72–89.

Teevan, J. (2003). "Where'd it go?" Re-finding information in the changing web. Paper presented at the Student Oxygen Workshop, Gloucester, MA.
Teevan, J., Alvarado, C., Ackerman, M. S. & Karger, D. R. (2004). The perfect search engine is not enough: a study of orienteering behavior in directed search. Paper presented at the ACM SIGCHI Conference on Human Factors in Computing Systems (CHI 2004), Vienna.
Teevan, J., Dumais, S. T. & Horvitz, E. (2005). Personalizing search via automated analysis of interests and activities. Paper presented at the SIGIR 2005, Salvador, Brazil.
Terry, W. S. (1988). Everyday forgetting: data from a diary study. *Psychological Reports*, *62*, 299–303.
Tulving, E. (1983). *Elements of Episodic Memory*. Oxford: Oxford University Press.
Tulving, E. & Thomson, D. M. (1973). Encoding specificity and retrieval processes in episodic memory. *Psychological Review*, *80*(5), 359–380.
Van Meter, D. & Middleton, D. (1954). Modern statistical approaches to reception in communication theory. *Institute of Radio Engineers Transactions, PGIT-4*, 119–145.
Whittaker, S. & Hirschberg, J. (2001). The character, value and management of personal paper archives. *ACM Transactions on Computer–Human Interaction*, *8*(2), 150–170.
Whittaker, S. & Sidner, C. (1996). Email overload: exploring personal information management of email. In *CHI 1996: ACM SIGCHI Conference on Human Factors in Computing Systems* (pp. 276–283). Vancouver, BC: ACM Press.
Whittaker, S., Terveen, L. & Nardi, B. A. (2000). Let's stop pushing the envelope and start addressing it: a reference task agenda for HCI. *Human Computer Interaction*, *15*, 75–106.
Wittgenstein, L. (1953). *Philosophical Investigations*. New York: Macmillan.
Zadeh, L. A. (1965). Fuzzy sets. *Information and Control*, *8*, 338–353.

CHAPTER 19

Computer-Supported Cooperative Work

Gary M. Olson and Judith S. Olson
University of Michigan, USA

INTRODUCTION

We are social animals. We began by living in clusters and cooperating in our hunting and gathering. We still reside in communities and cooperate in work; we just do it differently. Over the millennia, we have invented tools and processes to help us cooperate, such as standardized time zones, telegraph and telephone, paper filing and accounting systems, and a host of other useful tools. We cooperate and coordinate by meeting. We converse face-to-face, by telephone and paper mail. We use blackboards, flipcharts, slides, acetate overheads, and duplicated paper handouts.

Our desire to communicate, relate, and work together has led us to develop supporting technologies while we move further and further away from each other physically. People converse long distance via instant messaging or voice over IP (digitized voice sent over the Internet), audio or video conferences, sometimes showing slides or projected work objects at all locations. People use fax, email with attachments, voicemail, and recently, blogs (web-logs, updateable websites that can be used to create shared asynchronous conversations) and wikis (a website that can be edited by anyone, and can be used to create shared documents or other useful material) to manage our asynchronous coordinated work. Today, people can successfully plan a global conference without ever meeting face-to-face; large corporations form world-wide teams of experts; people telecommute; and some organizations function entirely with mobile technology without the need for any physical offices. Wireless technology even removes the necessity for being "plugged in."

These same technologies also affect our collocated work. When we meet face-to-face, we present PowerPoint slides and take notes on our wireless laptops. While a speaker presents material, members of the audience look up related information on Google or even order books mentioned in the talk. We find our way to a meeting in an unfamiliar building by looking it up on GoogleMaps, complete with driving/walking directions and nearby coffee shops. Electronic calendars allow us to find a time to meet. We store our meeting decisions on a shared file system for use later.

Handbook of Applied Cognition: Second Edition. Edited by Francis T. Durso.

Computer Supported Cooperative Work (CSCW) is the study of how people work together using computer and communication technologies. This name emerged in the mid-1980s, first referring to a series of bi-annual meetings that constitute the principal forum for researchers in this area and now referring to the whole area of research. CSCW is a broadly interdisciplinary field, drawing on computer science, management information systems, information science, psychology, sociology, and anthropology. Within psychology there are roles for cognitive, social, and organizational theories and findings.

The field of CSCW is huge and growing. We cannot cover it all in this chapter. We have chosen a range of examples to illustrate the issues in CSCW research from a psychological perspective. We will do this through the following topics:

- An initial framework that helps define the overall issues in the area, including a brief survey of the kinds of technologies that have been developed for CSCW applications.
- A review of how CSCW relates to cognitive psychology along with the various critiques of psychological theories and methods and their implications.
- A survey of representative empirical findings to date on what happens when people use CSCW technologies.

It is easy to think of CSCW as a purely applied field. However, good applied work does not have to be at the expense of contributions to basic science. Stokes (1997) argued that the search for basic knowledge and attempts to solve practical problems are two separate dimensions of a 2×2 table rather than opposite ends of a continuum. He cited Pasteur as an instance of researcher who sought both basic understanding and practical applications. While some CSCW research can be quite applied in its focus, we feel that much of it falls into Pasteur's quadrant.

AN INITIAL FRAMEWORK

Just as it is impossible to answer the single overarching question, "How do computers affect people?" it is equally impossible to answer the question, "How do computers affect groups, organizations, and society?" The only possible answer is, "It depends." Before we present the empirical findings, it is imperative to adopt a vocabulary for the particular. If "it depends," what does it depend on?

Figure 19.1 shows a simple conceptual framework of the things that need to be described before we can sort out the various results. Figure 19.1 shows the three major determinants of the process the group members engage in and the eventual outcome. We have simplified the complexity of the real world for tutorial purposes. The world is not this neat and certainly not this linear; there are interesting interactions and feedback loops to explore. We present the framework briefly here; it is detailed elsewhere (Olson & Olson 1997).

The Group and Organization

The same technology can have a remarkably varied effect on groups that have different compositions, relationships, organizations, and contexts of time and location. A group that has members with similar and appropriate task skills will function differently than one that is *heterogeneous*. How these skills are used will differ in the presence of various

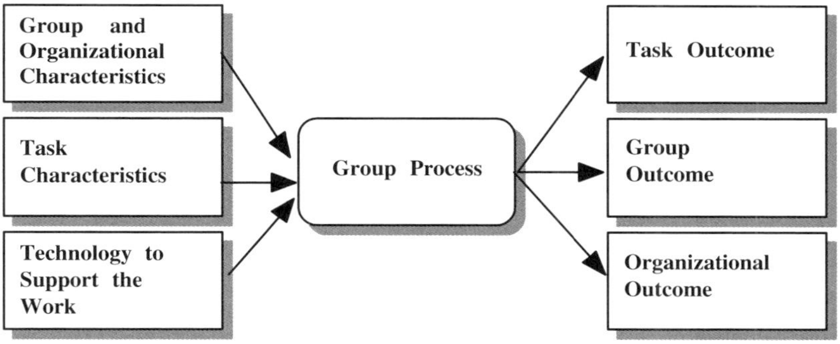

Figure 19.1 A simplified representation of the relationship between technology and behavioral consequences in group work (after Kraemer & Pinsonneault 1990; Olson & Olson 1997)

technologies. We know, for example, that strangers whose language skills are not fluent benefit from video conferencing, whereas established groups who are fluent and share a cultural background do just as well over audio conferencing (Gabarro 1990; Williams 1997; Veinott *et al.* 1999). Similarly, those groups that have established *trust* in each other can function cooperatively via email, where those that have not established trust quickly dissipate into non-cooperative behavior (Rocco 1998; Bos *et al.* 2002; Zheng *et al.* 2002). Technologies also fit or misfit with the group's *communication structure* (whether it takes place through hierarchical paths only or by free dissemination), and may be adopted or not depending on the organization's *reward* structure, work norms, or routines (Orlikowski 1992).

The Task

Tasks are described in everyday vernacular with such words as brainstorming, design, teaching, or decision-making, etc. But, if we are to understand how technologies support various kinds of tasks, this level of description is too coarse-grained. For example, some technologies support the generation of ideas and critiques well, but not the clarification of ideas or the organization of the ideas into a scheme or frame, all of which are part of design tasks. Most macro-tasks are made up of a mixture of smaller task units, and it is at that level that we believe tasks need to be described.

Tasks differ in the nature of the *material*, whether it consists of abstract ideas or concrete objects. The core *activities* themselves and their flow are differentially supported by technology. The work involves various amounts of exchange of information, planning, gathering or generating information, discussing to come to agreement, and planning and producing a product. Each of these subtasks may be supported by a different technology. There are also different *dependencies* among group members in performing the joint activity. Technologies that support group members' awareness of the moment-by-moment work of each other may help in highly dependent work, called tightly coupled work, but may indeed impede loosely coupled work because it is distracting. And tasks differ on something akin to *difficulty*, having to do with both the number of constraints that have to be satisfied and with their familiarity to the group members themselves. Technologies that make esoteric problems simple via representations, or those that compute constraint satisfaction, can differentially support tasks that differ on this key feature. Group interactions also have more *social* goals, such as finding out about the others, learning to trust them, establishing empathy, etc. As we will relate later, many of the newsgroups and on-line chat sessions are not intended to get work done, but rather to have a social exchange.

The Technologies

There are a number of different taxonomies of tasks (Hackman 1968; Steiner 1972; McGrath 1984).

Technologies for group work fall into clusters on two major dimensions:

- the setting in which the interaction takes place: the location and timing of the interaction; and
- what the technology supports: the object or the conversation.

First, technologies are intended for support of work that is either in the same or different *time* and the same or different *location* (Bullen & Bennett 1996).

On the left side of Figure 19.2 asynchronous work is represented, where people work independently on the project, conversing via email and shipping files to each other electronically for approval or editing. The arc at the top represents the transition to real-time work. Electronic calendars search for time when people can meet. Electronic Rolodexes keep track of people's contact information and background information to help determine whom to invite to a meeting.

The second dimension refers to what the technology is supporting. Technologies variously support the *object* of work (such as a proposal that is being developed by the group or the patient undergoing surgery) and/or the *conversation* on these objects. When people are face-to-face, it is usually easy for them to refer to the objects of the conversation and to maintain context. In supporting asynchronous work with today's technology, one can send files to one another (the objects) and converse by email, but it is difficult to specify in the conversation exactly what is being referred to. And, sometimes email itself serves a dual function, both sending an object (e.g., a list of courses offered in the next semester's curriculum) and engaging in conversation about it (e.g., asking for comments on proposed ideas).

The past decade has seen an explosion of commercial interest in technologies to support group work. A number of standard applications now include features to support collaboration (e.g., version control, annotations), and support for both synchronous and asynchronous conferencing via the Internet is widespread. Electronic mail has ever richer features, and electronic calendars are increasingly common. Project management and workflow tools are widely used to coordinate complex work.

As one might guess, technologies to support group work differ on a number of specifics, each of which has the potential of making significant differences in behavior. Unfortunately, many systems have been built but never formally evaluated; some have been evaluated only by the builders; and some have been evaluated in case studies, without any comparative evaluation. But it would be hard to enumerate all the possibilities of various designs and their consequences. It will be a long time before we understand the full set of interactions. Some researchers are beginning to do evaluations, and from them we can see trends, which we review below. Some trends confirm what we know about social psychology and communication; some are surprises warranting further investigation; and others, especially the emergent processes and far-reaching social impact, are new and bear examination by researchers in the more basic behavioral sciences.

The Process

The nature of the group, the kind of task they are engaged in, and the features of the technology affect how people behave. This is the focus of the center box in Figure 19.1. This process in turn affects the quality of the product, what they have learned, and how they feel about each other. Some researchers look for effects of groupware on the details of the process. To date, researchers have focused most on the *content* of the conversations in interactions, the *gestures* that accompany them, and various *timing* and *participation* measures. For example, some look in the content at the depth and breadth of the discussion and the time spent in various activities, distinguishing those related to the task itself, from those related to the organization of the activity and those in socializing or digression. Some catalog the turn-taking activity, including the number and kinds of interruptions people generate. And, some code the *affect* of each utterance, and how wide the participation is in the activity and the organizational roles of those that participate (e.g., whether he or she is someone with authority and power or not).

Task Outcomes

The literature on the effectiveness of groupware assesses impact in a number of different ways. These are illustrated on the right-hand side of Figure 19.1. Many studies measure the *task outcome*, counting the number of ideas or the quality of the product. These are measures that are often taken in comparative laboratory studies. It is difficult to measure task outcome in field settings because "success" depends on many things outside the group's control. Success is not often attributable solely to the adoption of a particular technology. Some people measure the participants' attitudes to the quality of the work, but it is well known that attitudes and performance are not always correlated (Eagly & Chaiken 1998; Petty & Wegener 1998). This well-established phenomenon has been shown in CSCW settings as well (e.g., Kottemann *et al.* 1994).

Group Outcomes

Other studies focus on *group outcomes*, assessing how technology affects people's

- understanding of what they decide;
- commitment to these decisions;
- satisfaction with the process or product; or
- follow-on attitudes.

Groups need to maintain themselves, to build trust and commitment, to help each other to fulfill their goals, and to learn. Some technologies (e.g., video) may affect the willingness of people to work together in the future. Others, like email or chats, may make people feel more connected or more isolated. We know, too, that trust is built when people meet face-to-face (Handy 1998) and lost through impoverished technologies. Interestingly, however, trust can be built through simple chat as long as the topic is not work-related but focused on the things the team members have in common (Zheng *et al.* 2002).

Organizational Outcomes

Few studies focus on *organizational outcomes*, longer-term effects of the adoption, and use of various technologies. Technologies may change a person's status in the organization, loyalty to that organization, learning (knowledge and skills), and work norms. Some have looked at how heterogeneity of the organization helps innovation, but hinders the ability of the individuals to get the innovation into a product-line (Burt 2004).

A few studies have looked at how technologies change an entire section of *society*, addressing issues about people's sense of community. Such studies are important not only for their implications for basic theory, but also more practically for policy formation and informing decisions about whether to fund large projects (Tenner 1996; Rochlin 1997).

PSYCHOLOGY AND CSCW

As mentioned in the Introduction, CSCW is a multidisciplinary field, and psychology is only one of a number of behavioral fields that have influenced research and theory. In fact, psychology has not necessarily provided the dominant conceptual and methodological ideas in CSCW, a state of affairs that some have suggested has impeded progress in CSCW (Finholt & Teasley 1998).

The various social sciences that contribute to CSCW have not always been happy partners. CSCW researchers from other social science traditions have singled out cognitive psychology for criticism, both theoretically and methodologically. Interestingly, many who were trained as cognitive psychologists and who are now among the most active CSCW researchers have become much more methodologically and theoretically eclectic.

Psychology has come in for criticisms from two quarters. The first is theoretical. Psychology has been criticized for seeking principles at too abstract a level of generality, at only the individual level, and thus failing to pay sufficient attention to the details of social and physical context (e.g., Suchman 1987; Lave 1988). An extensive debate has appeared in the published literature (e.g., Vera & Simon 1993, and an entire issue of *Cognitive Science* devoted to comments on their article). One result has been to widen the scope of cognitive theories and of the phenomena that are studied. Emerging theoretical perspectives such as distributed cognition represent attempts to incorporate a more explicit treatment of social and physical contexts into a psychological account of the kind of behavior seen with CSCW systems. A related move is to examine the cognitive behavior of aggregates of individuals, such as groups or organizations. We will look at these in more detail below.

A related criticism is methodological. Many areas of psychology depend on laboratory experiments for empirical evaluation of ideas. Critics charge that the situations and subjects used in many psychological experiments are not representative of typical group work. In contrast, much of the empirical work in CSCW is based on field observations, including ethnographic methods. Indeed, the methods of sociology and anthropology have played a major role in defining the empirical strategies of many CSCW researchers. Finholt and Teasley (1998) note how little of the research published in the meetings on CSCW have used experimental methods. They stress the value for CSCW research of using "reliable and proven measures of human behavior" drawn from psychological research in order to accumulate knowledge more quickly across studies. We have argued in more detail elsewhere (Olson *et al.* 1993; Olson & Olson 1997) that the external validity of experimental methods can be improved considerably. Improvement comes from the careful selection of tasks and subjects, and by coordinated field and laboratory investigations that explicitly analyze the similarities and differences between the two kinds of situations. Another research strategy is to conduct quasi-experiments in the field, using the kinds of design and analysis strategies discussed in Cook and Campbell (1979).

In the rest of this section we present several approaches that are representative of the new ways of conceptualizing group activity.

Distributed Cognition

A theoretical perspective known as distributed cognition (e.g., Wertsch 1985, 1991; Hutchins 1990, 1991, 1995a, 1995b; Rogers & Ellis 1994; Perry 2003) provides a framework for examining cognitive activity in its social and physical contexts. Cognitive processes and representations are characterized not only in terms of activity inside the heads of individuals, but also in the patterns of activity across individuals and in the material artifacts that mediate this activity. Hutchins has provided detailed accounts of cognitive activity in team settings to illustrate how this might work (e.g., shipboard navigation in Hutchins 1990, 1995a; flying a modern commercial jet in Hutchins 1995b).

All of the traditional phenomena of cognitive psychology are manifested in the interactions of individuals with their social and material world. In this view, the social setting and the artifacts serve to help us with:

- *Attention* (e.g., designing a large newspaper graphic to alert everyone to the fact that daylight saving time is imminent and our clocks have to change; cheerleaders using gestures to orchestrate a cheer).
- *Short-term memory* (e.g., moving a rule down a recipe to remind us of the steps already accomplished and to help us find what to do next).
- *Calculation* (e.g., using paper and pencil to do multiplication; constructing special tables to calculate in advance commonly encountered problems).
- *Long-term memory* (e.g., remembering where to find a book or who else knows something rather than committing to memory the contents of the book; giving each other hints until a word or past event or name can be recalled).
- *Cognitive representation* (e.g., plotting data on a graph so we can visually inspect it and gain insight through perceptual processing).

The most important implication of the theory of distributed cognition is that we can *design* the artifacts and the social processes to embody cognition. The field of CSCW is exactly about this act of design. How do we design the artifacts that support our needs in distributed cognition? How do we understand what is missing when we use certain kinds of technology that affect distributed cognition? The goal is to design new technology-based artifacts, or to design the processes that help distributed cognition thrive in new ways. But the idea of distributed cognition is also a new way of thinking that has significant implications for mainstream psychological theory.

Groups as Information Processors

The idea that cognition happens outside the head of an individual is expanded by Hinsz *et al.* (1997), who consider groups as collective information processors. According to this view, groups perform a variety of cognitive tasks, such as problem-solving, judgment, inference, and decision-making. The group attends, uses processing workspace, encodes, stores, and retrieves information in order to solve problems and make decisions. Hinsz *et al.*'s review of the small-group behavior literature follows these constructs, as illustrated in the following:

- *Goals*: Whether the group thinks that its goal is relationship-building or task-processing determines the ways in which people try to persuade each other.
- *Attention*: It appears that information must be held by at least two people before it will be brought to the attention of the group as a whole. Further, various kinds of information will be attended to depending on the time allowed to do a task.
- *Encoding*: Often heterogeneous people will not share the criteria that are to be brought to bear in making a decision, making the process difficult and consensus less likely.
- *Storage*: Presumably groups have the potential to store greater amounts of information than individuals because there are more heads involved. There is overhead in remembering the information shared by others as well as the individual items.
- *Retrieval*: Because more than one person stores a piece of information, members can correct each other's errors. But group members also stimulate recall and inhibit it by group actions (e.g., distracting from recall by changing the topic or helping recall by generating cues) (Gallupe *et al.* 1991; Hymes & Olson 1992).
- *Processing*: Individuals faced with a risky decision will take the risk of either no loss or a huge loss in favor of a sure moderate loss. Groups exaggerate this tendency.
- *Response*: If the group thinks there is one correct response, they share more of the individually held information during discussion than if they believe there is no correct response.
- *Feedback*: The literature shows that failure is typically attributed to someone else in the group or to the situation, but positive feedback is attributed to the whole group.
- *Overall*: Although some basic level of shared knowledge is necessary for groups to function, there is no perfect correlation between amount of shared knowledge and group effectiveness.

The authors synthesize from the findings two overarching questions about small-group behavior:

1. How do groups identify and apply the resources that group members bring to the task?
2. What are the processes by which these resources are combined to produce the outcome?

These lead to testable hypotheses about how people process pieces of information that can be examined in CSCW contexts.

Organizational Cognition

In a long tradition, going back at least to March and Simon (1958), organizations have been described as information-processing systems. Thus, it is not surprising that the vocabulary of cognition has been applied to the organization:

- knowledge (Nonaka & Takeuchi 1995);
- collective intelligence (Weick 1993; Weick & Roberts 1993);
- routines (Cyert & March 1963; Cohen & Bacdayan 1994);
- learning (Senge 1990; Argyris 1992; Argote 1999); and
- memory (Walsh & Ungson 1991; Walsh 1995).

These terms are particularly relevant to CSCW, since information technology's role in organizations is typically to alter the way in which information-processing is done (e.g., Ackerman 1998; Ackerman & Halverson 1998, 2000).

One important characteristic of cognitive activity that is as true of organizations as of individual minds is that some of the knowledge is explicit and easily accessible, while other knowledge is more tacit and procedural (Anderson 1982). Organizational routines are "multi-actor, interlocking, reciprocally-triggered sequences of actions" that are "a major source of the reliability and speed of organizational performance" (Cohen & Bacdayan 1994, p. 554). Routines at the organizational level are naturally built from cognitive procedures at the individual level, and share the characteristics of tacitness and automaticity. Based on these cognitive foundations we would expect routines to exhibit gradual acquisition, resistance to change, automatic invocation in response to social and physical cues, and limited access to verbal descriptions by the participants. Not surprisingly, they are a key element in the organizational response to new technologies.

Common Ground

The theory of common ground is relevant to the processes with which groups get their work done. The concept comes from researchers of the psychology of language, and focuses on the importance of conversational conventions and the constraints various communication channels put on our ability to come to a mutual understanding (e.g., Clark & Brennan 1991; Clark 1996; O'Conaill & Whittaker 1997; Monk 2003). For example, if we are conversing to come to an agreement on an issue, there are a number of steps we must go through, including offering, counter-offering, accepting, and agreeing that we are done. These conversational conventions are easy to keep track of when we are face-to-face, where immediate prior actions and the goal of the interaction are still in memory. But when we engage in a protracted conversation or when we conduct many of them interleaved, as we do in email, memory is put to the test. Our conventions must change if we are to manage it all.

Clark and Brennan (1991) have also enumerated a set of features that communication media have or do not have, which affect our ability to achieve common ground:

- *Co-presence*: we share the same environment and I can see and hear what you can see and hear.
- *Visibility*: we are visible to each other; our gestures and facial expressions can convey meaning.
- *Audibility*: we can hear each other; the tone of voice and timing can convey meaning.
- *Contemporality*: the message is received by one almost immediately after it is delivered.
- *Simultaneity*: messages can be sent and received simultaneously.
- *Sequentiality*: turns do not get out of order.
- *Reviewability*: messages can be re-read and revisited.
- *Revisability*: messages can be revised before being sent.

When we converse via videoconferencing, we have visibility, audibility, contemporality, simultaneity, and sequentiality. We do not see everything of the other location (copresence) and the messages can neither be reviewed nor revised. In instant messaging there is contemporality, but messages often get out of sequence. They are, however, revisable and reviewable. By enumerating these features of conversational media, one can predict the kinds of difficulty people will have in conversations, and how they will come to a common understanding to get their work done.

Findings from Social Psychology

CSCW exchanges theory and findings with social and organizational psychologists. Of particular interest is the work on how people categorize other individuals and the context in which they interact. This categorization drives people's ability to predict others' actions and behave appropriately (McCauley *et al.* 1980). People judge each other's intelligence by age and dress (e.g., we speak more slowly and simply to young children, and dress to be accepted in the cultures we visit); they gauge their expectations by the context in which they encounter other people (e.g., in the US, people expect to be served in order of arrival when they queue for service); they infer power and intent by a person's loudness and physical stature. All of these are characteristics that are disrupted in today's long-distance technologies. For example, people encounter those from other cultures in videoconferences and misinterpret their behaviors. They wrongly assess their intelligence because they dress differently and appear far away and are hard to hear.

Social psychology also has shown how, when people cannot communicate well, they become more self-serving even when cooperation would bring additional benefits. (Macy, 1991). This has been borne out in CSCW studies of long-distance teams who, because they could only communicate by email, communicated less, and so failed in their missions (Cummings 2001).

Social psychology has also studied variations in a group's motivation to contribute, coining the phrase "social loafing." Typically, people work less hard when they are part of a group. However, if people in the group are told that their input is unique (no one else can do what they can), if their output is visible, or if they believe that others will perform poorly, they will make more effort. This speaks to the motivational schemes that various online communities have instituted to keep contributions high (e.g., MovieLens; Ludford *et al.* 2004).

Activity Theory

Activity theory is less a theory than a set of concepts that help describe fully what is going on in a particular group situation (Nardi 1996). Unlike the information-processing orientation, activity theory views groups as having a history and culture through which they developed their ways of getting things done and invented or adapted tools to help them. Activity theory was developed in the early 1900s to contrast with psychoanalysis and behaviorism. More recently it has been adopted by researchers in CSCW to understand the use of tools and the organizational routines that people engage in to accomplish various goals. Any new tool introduced will disrupt the work through changing roles, routines, social interaction, etc.

Key features to describe and analyze in any work situation are:

- the goal (the object);
- the individuals (subjects);
- the community;
- the division of labor (roles);
- the rules (practice or praxis);
- the instruments.

Whereas previously listed theories concentrate on the activity itself, Activity Theory focuses more on the dynamics between individuals and where historically or in their culture various practices were developed.

Summary of Theories Related to CSCW

Referring to Figure 19.1, the theories listed there focus on different aspects of group characteristics and activities. *Distributed Cognition*, *Groups as Information Processors,* and *Organizational Cognition* borrow concepts from individual human information-processing to show how groups conduct their work – how attention, memory, calculation, decision-making, etc. are handled by various activities and artifacts in a group. They focus on the "Group Process" aspect and some of the "Technology to Support the Work." *Common Ground* and *Aspects of Social Psychology* similarly focus on the "Process" aspect, with some of the determinants of the "Team Members" to say how attitudes are formed, how people communicate, and their motivation to participate. The Clark and Brennan characteristics delineate "Technology to Support the Work." Interestingly, *Activity Theory* covers the "Group and Organizational Characteristics" with an expansion into history, culture, and rules. It focuses additionally on the instruments as "Technology to Support the Work," and highlights the importance of the group's goal. Most of these theories focus on how the work is done, with little regard for specifics about the task, group, or organizational outcomes.

FINDINGS ABOUT BEHAVIOR CHANGES WITH THESE TECHNOLOGIES

In the following section, we review some of the key findings that have implications for both the applied world and basic psychological research. We point to various reviews of the literature, where they exist, for a more complete discussion of the topic. We present the results using simple technology/situation categorizations, highlighting the features in Figure 19.1 within each category. That is, when appropriate, we describe specifically what *group* characteristics were present in the study, the *task* they undertook, and the details of the *technology*. We then describe the aspects of the *process* measured and the *outcomes*. We follow the categories of technology support in Figure 19.2, synchronous/asynchronous, collocated/remote, and support for the conversation/object.

Support for Face-to-Face Conversations

Technology has supported face-to-face meetings in a variety of ways. Some embed support for cognitive processes involved in problem-solving and decision-making. These structure the process of discussion (e.g., embodying nominal group technique or brainstorming), guide the way criteria are developed for decision-making (e.g., embodying stakeholder analysis), and determine how voting is accomplished (e.g., anonymously, with various voting and ranking algorithms). Others are more free-form. They allow people to create, view, and edit the object under discussion. These support the conversational grounding, the context and referents of the work.

Group Decision Support Systems (GDSS) are a common face-to-face system, which structure the group's problem-solving and decision processes. GDSSs build on decision support systems designed to aid individual decision-makers by adding a series of group tools to coordinate the decision-making. These systems are designed to support large, heterogeneous *groups* engaged in decision-making tasks, where their *task* consists of brainstorming alternatives and deciding among them. Most GDSSs require the services of a facilitator and someone to retrieve, run, and store results from one subtask to the other (e.g., Nunamaker *et al.* 1991). The attention of the group members is focused, as it should be, on the decisions they are making, and not on the complex task of orchestrating the technology and the group.

There has been a number of experimental evaluations of such systems, and there are several literature reviews that attempt to draw general conclusions from this work (Kraemer & Pinsonneault 1990; McLeod 1992; Hollingshead *et al.* 1993). These reviews conclude that the structured meeting support systems typically affect various *processes*, which in turn affect *outcomes*. Because many of these systems allow anonymous input, they typically produce meetings with more equal participation. Decision quality increases with the GDSS, but meetings require more time and produce decisions that are less satisfying to the participants than traditionally-supported meetings.

An interesting perspective on face-to-face meetings comes from recent work on radical collocation. Teasley *et al.* (2002) studied software teams who carried out their work while collocated in a war room for the duration of their project. Using a variety of software metrics, they found that these collocated teams had much better productivity than the company's baseline. Although at the outset members of these teams were wary about being collocated in this fashion, by the end of their projects they were much more satisfied. The war room setting provided them with immediate access to each other and to a large variety of artifacts (e.g., flipcharts and whiteboards, including electronic whiteboards). The richness of shared knowledge in this war room setting is currently difficult to emulate for remote groups.

Support for Remote Real-Time Conversation

There are many studies that compare face-to-face (FTF) with various forms of computer-mediation communication (CMC) (*technology*). There are some clear generalizations from such work, the main one being that CMC is more difficult to do than FTF, and requires more preparation and care (Siegel *et al.* 1986; McLeod 1992; Hollingshead *et al.* 1993; Straus & McGrath 1994; Olson *et al.* 1995; Straus 1996, 1997). A variety of things that come automatically with FTF are either difficult to support or absent in CMC (Whittaker & O'Conaill 1997; Olson & Olson 2000; Kiesler & Cummings 2002). Backchannel communication (*process*), which is important for modulating conversation, is either weak or nonexistent in CMC. Paralinguistic cues that can soften communication are often missing. Participants in CMC tend to have an informational focus, which means there is usually less socializing, less small talk. Over time this can lead to poorer social integration and organizational effectiveness (*organizational outcome*) (Nohria & Eccles 1992).

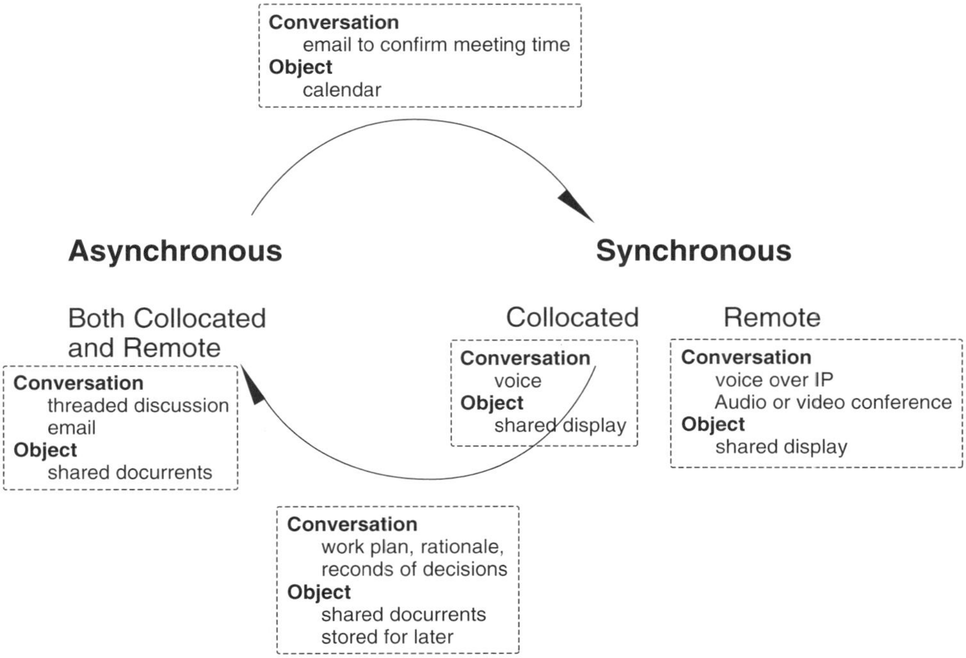

Figure 19.2 Representation of real-time and asynchronous work, transitions between them, and support of conversation and objects

CMC often introduces delay. This is well known to be very disruptive to communication (Krauss & Bricker 1966; Egido 1988; O'Conaill *et al.* 1993; Tang & Isaacs 1993; Ruhleder & Jordan 2001). Participants will communicate less information, be more frustrated with the communication, and actually terminate communication sessions sooner (*process*). Delay can be managed, but it takes special care among the participants, and turn-taking widgets must be present in the interface of the tools being used. For instance, if there is delay, then full-duplex open communication will not work, since participants will wait and then begin talking just when others begin, creating an awkward negotiation for who will take the next turn. The group must employ either a social protocol (e.g., like that used in radio communications with spacecraft) or a microphone-passing procedure with interface indications of who wants to talk next.

Text-Based Conversation

Text chat systems have existed for decades, and a number of research prototypes have been explored. However, recently, instant messaging (IM) has emerged as a popular communication medium, largely supported by commercial IM systems. While initially it was mostly used for socializing among friends and relatives, it has now emerged as a serious communication medium in organizations (Handel & Herbsleb 2002; Herbsleb *et al.* 2002). Muller *et al.* (2003) found in a survey study of three organizations that the introduction of IM led to significantly less use of such communication channels as email, voicemail, telephone, teleconference, pager, and face-to-face. They also found that IM was used for "substantive business purposes." Furthermore, in one of the organizations where they surveyed users after 24 months' usage they found that the substantive reasons for using IM increased. In a study of IM logs in an organization, Isaacs *et al.* (2002) found that a large proportion of IM conversations involved "complex work discussions." They found that IM users seldom switched to another communication channel once they were engaged in IM. Nardi *et al.* (2000) observed in a field study that workers used IM for a variety of purposes, not just for information exchange. Such matters as quick questions, scheduling, organizing social interactions, and keeping in touch with others were common uses of IM.

Other studies (Garcia & Jacobs 1999; O'Neill & Martin 2003) have shown that conversations in text chat or IM develop a fluency that bespeaks the limitations of the modality (*process and technology*). Users are able to carry on extended conversations, developing strategies for repairing misunderstandings. Even when multi-person text chats lead to multiple threads in the discussion, little thread confusion occurs (McDaniel *et al.* 1996). Thus, though it is easy to think of text chat or IM as a particularly impoverished communication channel, study after study of its use in real settings show that it is functional and is used for more than just awareness and coordination.

A number of creative ideas have been proposed for how to represent the other participants in an IM or chat session. We review these in detail in the section on Awareness, but we briefly mention some here because they are relevant to the modality question. Donath (2004) reviewed a series of ideas for how to show participation graphically, with some indication of the frequency and recency of their participation. The BABBLE system developed at IBM (Erickson *et al.* 1999) shows similar information, but in addition grouped it by "rooms" where different conversational threads are taking place.

While IM is a relatively new phenomenon in the workplace, it is clearly established as a useful and widely used tool. This will undoubtedly assist in the development of more sophisticated versions of the tool, as well as its integration into on-line conferencing systems. There is clearly much promise here. We have noticed, for example, that during audio or video conferences, IM or chat serves as a backchannel for side-conversations or debugging, an extremely useful adjunct to the core audio or video communication taking place in such conferences.

Audio and Video Conferencing

While it might seem desirable to always have the maximum communication and tool support possible, it is not always possible or even necessary to do so. Research shows that effective real-time collaboration can take place under a number of different arrangements, depending on the *task*, the characteristics of the *participants*, the specific geographical dispersion of the participants, and the processes employed to manage the interactions. There are also *organizational effects*, especially when the real-time collaborations are embedded in ongoing activities, as they almost always are.

For instance, early work (Williams 1977) showed that in referential communication tasks full-duplex audio is just as effective as FTF. Subsequent research comparing audio and video conferencing (see summaries in Finn *et al.* 1997; Cadiz *et al.* 2000) showed that for many tasks audio is sufficient, and that video adds nothing to task *effectiveness* though participants usually report they are more satisfied with video. There are important exceptions, however. Negotiation *tasks* are more effective with video (Short *et al.* 1976). This is probably because the more subtle visual cues to the participants' intentions are important in this kind of task. Further, Veinott *et al.* (1999) found that when *participants* have less common ground video helps. In their case, participants were non-native English speakers who were performing the task in English. For native speakers, audio was no better than video. Again, visual cues to comprehension and meaning likely played an important role. High quality video resulted in greater conversational fluency over high quality audio alone, especially as *group size* increased (Daly-Jones *et al.* 1998). There was also a higher rated sense of presence in the video conditions.

An important lesson to draw from this literature is that there are two broad classes by which we might assess whether video is important in real-time collaboration. On the one hand, except for *tasks* like negotiation, groups are able to get their *work done effectively* with high-quality audio. However, for things like *satisfaction*, conversational fluency, and a sense of presence, video adds value. These factors might be very important for long-term *organizational consequences* such as employee satisfaction. So far, no long-term studies have been done to examine this conjecture.

Audio quality is critical. Ever since Egido's (1988) early literature review, it has been reported over and over again that if the audio is poor quality, participants will develop a workaround. For instance, if the audio in a video conferencing system or the audio in an Internet conferencing system is poor, participants will turn to a phone conference.

But phone conferencing technology itself is not ideal. It is often difficult to remember who is in the conference, especially if it is very large. Turn-taking can be awkward. It can be difficult to tell speakers apart, since the phone system only transmits part of the audible frequencies of a voice. Experiments with three-dimensional audio have shown that these problems are easier to manage when a person's voice can be associated with a location in space, even if it is a virtual location (Gardner 1998; Lumbreras & Sanchez 1999; Leung & Chen 2003). But the current phone system does not support this, and no commercial VoiP systems do either.

Video can be presented in all kinds of ways, from large-screen displays in a conference room to small, poor quality windows on the desktop. The quality of video matters. Degraded video can convey bad affordances, such as lying or lack of interest (Horn *et al.* 2002).

However, even poor quality video can provide a sense of "presence," which can be important for sustaining *social relations*. Further, poor quality video can provide information about who is in the session, especially if there are locations where there are multiple participants. Not knowing who is actually there can be a big problem in CMC.

The social ergonomics of audio and video are also a key to their success. Many of the failures of audio conferencing, especially over the Internet, result from poor quality microphones, poor microphone placement, poor speakers, and interfering noises (e.g., air conditioning). Getting these details right is essential. Similarly, for video, camera placement can matter a lot. Huang *et al.* (2002) found that a camera angle that makes a person seem tall (as opposed to actually being tall) affects how influential he or she is in a negotiation *task*. Apparent height matters a lot. Other aspects of camera placement or arrangement of video displays might make a big difference as well.

Eye contact is a key linguistic and social mediator of the effectiveness of communication (Kendon 1967; Argyle & Cook 1976). It is very difficult to achieve eye contact in CMC systems. Many attempts have been made (Okada *et al.* 1994; Vertegaal 1999; Gale & Monk 2000; Vertegaal *et al.* 2001; Monk & Gale 2002; Grayson & Monk 2003), and at least the subjective reports are that these can be effective. But these all require special equipment or set-ups. And they don't scale very well to multi-party sessions.

Support for Face-to-Face and Remote Real-Time Sharing of Objects

Numerous studies demonstrate the centrality of shared work objects in collaboration (e.g., Whittaker *et al.* 1993; Suchman 1996; Teasley *et al.* 2002; Kraut *et al.* 2003). A number of early studies showed that when these objects are digital and can be jointly edited, further benefits accrued (Stefik *et al.* 1987; Olson *et al.* 1993). Being able to share such objects in face-to-face or distributed situations is now widely supported in a variety of commercial products.

Studies of the use of these technologies by small established *groups* doing design *tasks* show that the *quality* of the work is higher with these technologies than that with traditional support – with whiteboard or paper and pencil – but groups were slightly less *satisfied* (Olson *et al.* 1993). A detailed *process* analysis showed that the computer-supported groups, surprisingly, explored fewer options than the whiteboard groups while achieving higher quality. The tool was thought to help keep the groups more focused on the core issues, to have them waste less time on less important topics, and to capture what was said as they worked. This work was extended to evaluate the same technology in groups that were not collocated. In a second study, similar groups doing the same design task sat in different offices connected with a shared editor and either video and audio or audio-only connections. The quality of the work was nearly the same as that of groups meeting face-to-face using the shared editor (Olson *et al.* 1995).

The LiveBoard (a large, pen-based computer display much like an electronic whiteboard or flipchart; Elrod *et al.* 1992) has been evaluated in an extended case study of a *group* whose *task* it was to manage intellectual property issues. The team used the LiveBoard in conjunction with laptop note-taking and audio records for a period of two years. Their persistent use of the technology suggested that it was useful support for their work ("voting with their feet" by continuing to use it). Comments and suggestions they had along the way were incorporated into valued feature changes (Moran *et al.* 1996). They suggested that the system recognize various constructions that the team member recognized, such as lists, regions of the board, and outlines. By having the tool support the marks in the way the team members understood them, e.g., by having items in a list dragged around to rearrange them and having the rest of the list adjust position automatically around the moved item, the support for distributed cognition was smoother.

Nardi and colleagues (1995) observed a highly functional *surgical team* coordinate their work by having access to the surgeon's view of the surgery itself displayed on a monitor viewable by all. By seeing the progress of the surgery and both expected and unexpected actions, Nardi observed that the staff could smoothly prepare for the next step without the need for conversation. Using video in this way was seen as vastly superior to their previous coordination from only vague signals from their co-workers' words and gestures, many of which were confusing or absent under stress.

Several studies of groups working in real organizations have shown how powerful shared artifacts are in collaborative work (Olson & Teasley 1996; Teasley *et al.* 2002). Such artifacts are a critical element for coordinating the interactions among the participants and providing critical common ground to facilitate effective communication. Indeed, such artifacts function as an external memory for the group.

Asynchronous Support of Conversation

It is generally agreed that electronic mail is one groupware application that has seen considerable success (Sproull & Kiesler 1991; Satzinger & Olfman 1992; O'Hara-Devereaux & Johansen 1994; Anderson *et al.* 1995). The widespread dissemination of networks and personal computers has led to extensive use of email in organizations and from home. Now that email is common, it has many of the characteristics of other communication technologies such as the telephone. Demographic data on network connections, email use, and general connectivity all show the popular adoption of electronic communication as a form of human contact (Garton & Wellman 1995). Indeed, the problem now for many users is email overload (Whittaker & Sidner 1996).

Email has a number of well-known effects on human behavior. Because of its power to reach many subscribers quickly, it has changed the culture of the organizations in which it resides: it changes who talks to whom (Sproull & Kiesler 1991), what kind of person is heard from (Finholt *et al.* 1990), and the tone of what is said (Sproull & Kiesler 1991). With email, people who were previously thought to be under-performers find a voice. They are no longer impeded by shyness or difficulty with social interaction; they can speak without seeing other people. On the hand, forgetting that there is a human reading the message at the other end, and in the absence of feedback from the recipient, people tend to "flame," to write asocial, emotive messages that are either shocking, upsetting, or offensive. Hollingshead *et al.* (1993) and Arrow *et al.* (1996) suggest, however, that these effects dissipate in time.

Several studies have found that email is not only useful for direct communication, but people also find it especially useful for managing time, tasks, and information flow (Mackay 1989; Carley & Wendt 1991). Because email systems were not designed to support these secondary tasks, they support them poorly. Users spend enormous amounts of time managing their inboxes (Whittaker & Sidner 1996). Clearly something more is required. Since email is now used for so many functions beyond just communication, considerable work is going on about how to support this wider array of functions more effectively (e.g., Bellotti *et al.* 2003; Muller *et al.* 2004). The entire issue of *Human Computer Interaction* (2005) is entitled "Revisiting and reinventing email."

A very important new line of research addresses the consequence of the use of remote technologies to the development and loss of trust (*group outcome*). Recently, Rocco (1998) watched groups of six play a game that is a variant of the prisoner's dilemma. In this game individuals repeatedly decide what to invest in a common pool, and receive benefits either by cooperating (where everyone gets some positive benefit) or by "defecting," making a move that is personally beneficial but at the cost of making others lose. Rocco found that groups who were able to occasionally talk to each other face-to-face about the optimal strategy ended up achieving benefit through cooperation while those who discussed things by email defected more often. Importantly, however, those groups that met prior to the game and conducted a team-building activity eventually cooperated even when they were restricted to email. Bos *et al.* (2002) and Zheng *et al.* (2002) replicated and extended Rocco's findings, showing that having richer media for interacting during the task or using any of a variety of media to socialize ahead of time also led to increased trust.

Asynchronous Support of Sharing of Objects

A variety of objects are shared in the conduct of work. Documents such as work plans, proposals, requirements, etc. are often authored by many over time. People store finished documents for others to access. Even informal notes and meeting minutes can sometimes be valuable. A somewhat formal approach to this in the context of an organization is knowledge management, a set of methods and tools for creating an organizational memory. Obviously, the effectiveness of such repositories of information hinges on being able to find things. But remarkable advances in information retrieval and search methods make these tasks a lot easier. Since both knowledge management and information retrieval are huge topics in their own right, we will touch only briefly on these. Similarly, recent work on information retrieval and search has focused on how to make large, often heterogeneous collections of information useful.

Knowledge Management

An early instance of a tool that was intended to facilitate the keeping of organizational memory is Lotus Notes. For instance, a group can keep an open issue list in a form accessible to all interested parties, and construct workflow systems that automatically route information to the right people for additions and approvals. Some organizations have used Notes as repositories of corporate knowledge, capturing people's experience on previous projects, their heuristics for decision-making (e.g., pricing policies and exception handling), boilerplates for various kinds of proposals, etc.

However, three important case studies have shown the organizational consequences of introducing these kinds of technologies. In the first (Orlikowski 1992), consultants were asked to share their knowledge about various clients and engagements in a large Notes database so that others could benefit from their experience and insights. Two key issues prevented successful adoption. First, although consultants had to bill all their working hours to various clients, there was no account for them to use to bill the time devoted to data entry and learning of Notes. Second, consultants were promoted on the basis of their skill advantage over their co-workers, discouraging them from sharing their knowledge. So in this case the accounting/billing of time and the assessment of credit was misaligned with the capability the technology afforded, the objective of its introduction and the goals of its use. In a successful case in our experience, sales people shared their client contacts with each other. This sharing prevented the embarrassing occasions when two different sales people were telling a single client different stories. This use fitted the incentive scheme in which sales people received commissions on total sales as well as their individual sales.

In a third case study, software designers used Notes to keep their open issue list and to share information about future features or potential solutions to bugs (Olson & Teasley 1996). Their use of the system initially rose and then declined over 12 months. Interviews of the group members revealed that the team members were less and less inclined to use the application because they thought the manager was not participating. They saw no activity on his part and assumed he did not value their use of the system. In truth, the manager was participating regularly; he read the material but did not write. Unfortunately, Notes did not make reading activity visible in the interface.

More recent knowledge management explorations have looked at issues like finding expertise within an organization (McDonald & Ackerman 2000), making it easy to share the answers to repeated questions (Ackerman & McDonald 1996), and sharing recommendations in a variety of areas (Terveen *et al.* 1997). Brown and Duguid (2002) describe more generally the "social life of information" in a wide variety of venues.

Support for the Transition between Asynchronous and Real-Time Work: Awareness Support and Calendars

Group work is a mixture of synchronous and asynchronous activities. People meet to plan the work and assign individuals to do various subtasks. These people coordinate and clarify as they go, and periodically meet to align goals and plan the next steps. They move frequently between individual subtasks and coordination or clarification in real time. The following technologies would support these transitions.

First, project management software captures decisions made in meetings about who is doing what, and what the linkages or dependencies are between subtasks. These technologies help calculate the consequences of changes to the plan (by calculating the critical path) and indicate to team members who are waiting for work. Open issues lists and project management software are the tools to support the transition from real-time meetings to parallel, more independent work. These technologies suffer only from the time and effort involved in keeping them up-to-date; like writing and distributing meeting minutes, it requires someone to do it.

More difficult is the transition from asynchronous work to synchronous, both accessing an individual, so that one can converse or negotiate in real time, and calling meetings. Recognizing how difficult this is, some organizations expect workers to be at their desks at all times (and thus always reachable). Others schedule standing meetings, expecting full attendance whether one's expertise is needed or not. In lieu of these extreme solutions, some have adopted technologies to help people locate others or to assess when they can reach them so they can make contact.

One of the most comprehensive of these systems is Montage (Tang *et al.* 1994). Like Cruiser (Fish *et al.* 1993), Montage allows video "glances" into team members' offices so one can assess whether they are available for a phone or video conversation. If the glance instead reveals that the intended person is not there or not available, the seeker has several options. The seeker can leave an email message; can view the person's calendar to see when he or she might return or where they might be reached; or leave a "sticky note" on the screen of the person being sought, attracting the team member's attention immediately upon their return. In an evaluation of Montage which was deployed in a distributed workgroup, the results showed that people glanced at each other nearly three times a day, and in three-quarters of cases these were unacknowledged (i.e., people were there but did not respond to connect in a real-time video link). Any connections were brief (a little over one minute). And, although the additional access to calendars, email, and sticky notes were used infrequently, people reported valuing them highly.

Other uses of video to allow awareness of team members' activity have been tried. The VideoWindow at Bellcore was intended to encourage both ordinary meeting and casual interactions from remote sites over coffee (Fish *et al.* 1990). RAVE, a suite of systems at Rank Xerox EuroPARC (Gaver *et al.* 1992), was intended to support awareness of global activity, glances into individuals' offices, and point-to-point contact for close, intense work. Long-term use of video connectivity was analyzed in the Portland Experiment (Olson & Bly 1991). All of these systems have been studied within research lab settings, where modest amounts of sustained use were found. It would be extremely useful to have studies of these systems carried out in other kinds of organizational settings.

All of the implementations of awareness through video raise issues of privacy. Various solutions have been proposed, including introducing reciprocity (you are only on camera when you can see the person viewing you), warning (the sound of a "squeaky door opening" or approaching footsteps serves as a signal of an impending glance), viewee control over camera position, and showing recent snapshots as opposed to live immediate action (see Hudson & Smith 1996 for a discussion). One awareness system, Thunderwire (Hindus *et al.* 1996), used open audio instead of video. People realized the need for designing new norms in announcing oneself (because the hearers are blind), and negotiating inattention and withdrawal.

On-line calendars afford awareness as well as ease in scheduling meetings. PROFs calendar and Meeting Maker are two popular implementations. Both allow designation of who can write and who can read the calendar, as well as control over private portions of the calendar, where viewers can see that the person is busy, but not what they are doing. Although Grudin (1988) has designated this application as the quintessential misalignment of costs and benefits (the individual has to keep the calendar up to date if it is going to be of benefit to others), many organizations have adopted it successfully (Grudin & Palen 1997; Mosier & Tammaro 1997). A culture of sharing and accessibility supports the successful adoption of on-line calendars (Ehrlich 1987; Lange 1992).

Efforts to Support Communities

A number of recent projects investigated the needs of large-scale communities, both through user-centered design and by merely deploying a flexible technology and watching its use. Three main thrusts are relevant here: The study of home/community use of the World Wide Web, online "virtual communities," and the development of Collaboratories.

Home/Community Use of the World Wide Web

There are efforts to deploy various technologies in neighborhoods and communities. The intent is to learn what people value and what they might need in the future. One such effort is the HomeNet in the Pittsburgh area (Kraut *et al.* 1996). Families in the Pittsburgh area were given networked computers, and then the researchers followed their use of the technology over a number of years. Some interesting trends emerged. They found that teenage males are by far the heaviest users, although there is evidence that access to email for maintaining personal conversations and contacts is valued by all. There may even be long-term psychosocial effects of computer use, although the picture is complicated (Kraut *et al.* 1998; Kraut *et al.* 2002).

A second project is the Blacksburg Electronic Village (BEV) in Virginia (Carroll & Rosson 1996), another long-term project that has yielded rich results. Recently, Carroll *et al.* (2005) used the BEV project to develop a concept of "collective efficacy," derived from Bandura's (1997) concept of "self-efficacy." Those groups that feel they can overcome obstacles are more likely to succeed in sustaining their collective effort. Clearly, these kinds of long-term projects offer rich arenas for the exploration and development of psychological constructs.

On-Line Communities

Howard Rheingold (1993) established the word "virtual community" for the Internet sites that supported information exchange among a large number of people, many of whom do not know each other. There are such sites that are goal-oriented (e.g., wikipedia.org), support people who want to learn something (e.g., Moosecrossing), provide emotional support or advice for medical conditions (e.g., breastcancer.org), or that provide collected information to a professional community (e.g., Slashdot.org). A number of people are investigating what makes these successful, in that they are used, people participate, and satisfaction is high (Preece 2000; Ludford *et al.* 2004). Common findings are that the site has to be easily searchable, the tone and culture have to be set and maintained (especially in support groups), and that people will continue to contribute if they have a response. Some sites have set up elaborate and successful mechanisms for having content monitored for appropriateness. Slashdot in particular allows those who have posted good things to then rate other postings, and then rate the raters, all under the guise of gathering "kharma points." A site as big as Slashdot could not function without the masses helping with the monitoring (Lampe & Resnick 2004).

Collaboratories

A Collaboratory is the "combination of technology, tools and infrastructure that allow scientists to work with remote facilities and each other as if they were co-located" (Lederberg & Uncapher 1989, p. 6). A similar effort is underway in Europe under the name of "eScience."

One such Collaboratory effort is the Upper Atmospheric Research Collaboratory (UARC; later the Space Physics and Aeronomy Research Collaboratory, or SPARC), a set of technologies that allowed space scientists studying the upper atmosphere to view real-time data from various instruments (like incoherent scatter radar) around the world. They could align these views with models of what should be going on, and converse through a chat facility with the other scientists or graduate students. Finholt and Olson (1997) found that UARC theorists and data analysts are working together where they did not before. Also graduate students have access to remote mentors and can experience real-time data collection, where previously they might get the opportunity to go to a site once in their graduate training (Olson *et al.* 1998, 2001). The issue, really, is whether science is progressing faster or not, and since there is no real control group for this effort, we do not know.

There has been an explosive growth in collaboratories in virtually all areas of science. The Science of Collaboratories project at Michigan has identified more than 200 examples, and the list is growing (Olson 2004). It is clear that practicing scientists believe in the power of the kind of geographically distributed work that the Internet makes possible.

CONCLUSIONS

A great deal has been learned in CSCW about the nature of individuals and groups and organizations by borrowing from cognitive, social, and organizational psychology. At the same time CSCW has provided a rich venue in which to learn of new phenomena. For example, how trust is built and maintained in distant relationships sheds light on what trust is based on. When one is motivated to contribute to the common good in large-scale recommender systems sheds new light on theories of motivation and social capital. The listing of the theories in CSCW begs some researcher to integrate the factors and develop a more comprehensive theory. And, of course, with new technologies on the horizon (e.g., mobile connectivity to both people and massive filtered information), there are new test-beds with which to test our understanding of the social animals we are.

POINTERS TO THE PAST AND FUTURE RESEARCH IN THIS AREA

A number of sources exist that review subsets of the technologies and associated group behavior in greater depth. They are well worth pursuing for more detail and deeper analysis of cognition in CSCW. Six large volumes are anthologies of studies in this area:

- *Computer Supported Cooperative Work: A Book of Readings* (1988) edited by Greif. A set of classic papers from the early days.
- *Intellectual Teamwork: Social and Technological Foundations of Cooperative Work* (1990) edited by Galegher, Kraut, and Egido. Another collection of early classic papers.
- *Readings in Groupware and Computer Supported Cooperative* Work (1993) edited by Baecker. A useful collection of early work.
- *Video Mediated Communication* (1997) edited by Finn *et al.* Still the best source on video as a communication medium.
- *Coordination Theory and Collaboration Technology* (2001) edited by Olson, Malone & Smith. An influential set papers reporting work from the 1990s.
- *Distributed Work* (2002) edited by Hinds & Kiesler. A recent set of papers on geographically distributed work.

These excellent volumes, plus the *Proceedings on Computer Supported Cooperative Work* (CSCW) and the *European Computer Supported Cooperative Work* (ECSCW), the conferences that alternate meeting bi-annually, provide both the basics and the continuing progress in this exciting field. Other ACM conferences with substantial amounts of CSCW work are *GROUP* and *CHI*. Several journals also publish CSCW work: *Computer Supported Cooperative Work, Human Computer Interaction, ACM Transaction on Information Systems, Communication of the ACM, ACM Transactions on Computer–Human Interaction*, and *Journal of Computer-Mediated Communication.*

REFERENCES

Ackerman, M. (1998). Augmenting organizational memory: a field study of Answer Garden. *ACM Transactions on Information Systems, 17*, 203–224.

Ackerman, M. & Halverson, C. (1998). Considering an organization's memory. In *Proceedings of CSCW*. New York: ACM.

Ackerman, M. & Halverson, C. (2000). Reexamining organizational memory. *Communications of the ACM, 43*(1), 58–64.

Ackerman, M. & McDonald, D. (1996). Answer Garden 2: merging organizational memory with collaborative help. In *Proceedings of CSCW 1996*. New York: ACM.

Anderson, J. R. (1982). Acquisition of cognitive skill. *Psychological Review, 89*, 369–406.

Anderson, R. H., Bikson, T. K., Law, S. A. & Mitchell, B. M. (1995). *Universal Access to E-mail: Feasibility and Societal Implications*. Santa Monica, CA: RAND.

Argote, L. (1999). *Organizational Learning: Creating, Retaining and Transferring Knowledge*. Dordrecht: Kluwer.

Argyris, C. (1992). *On Organizational Learning*. Cambridge, MA: Blackwell.

Argyle, M. & Cook, M. (1976). *Gaze and Mutual Gaze*. New York: Cambridge University Press.

Arrow, H., Berdahl, J. L., Bouas, K. S. *et al.* (1996). Time, technology, and groups: an integration. *Computer Supported Cooperative Work, 4*, 253–261.

Baecker, R. M. (1993). *Readings in Groupware and Computer-Supported Cooperative Work*. San Mateo, CA: Morgan Kaufman.

Bandura, A. (1997). *Self-efficacy: The Exercise of Control*. New York: W. H. Freeman.

Bellotti, V., Ducheneaut, N., Howard, M. & Smith, I. (2003). Taking email to task: the design and evaluation of a task management centered email tool. In *Proceedings of CHI 2003*. New York: ACM.

Bos, N., Olson, J., Gergle, D. *et al.* (2002). Effects of four computer-mediated communication channels on trust development. *Proceedings of the Conference on Human Factors in Computing Systems, CHI02*, 135–140.

Brown, J. S. & Duguid, P. (2002). *The Social Life of Information*. Boston, MA: Harvard Business School Press.

Bullen, C. V. & Bennett, J. L. (1996). Groupware in practice: an interpretation of work experiences. In R. Kling (ed.), *Computerization and Controversy* (2nd edn, pp. 348–382). New York: Academic Press.

Burt, R. S. (2004). Structural holes and good ideas. *American Journal of Sociology, 110*, 349–399.

Cadiz, J., Balachandran, A., Sanocki, E. *et al.* (2000). Distance learning through distributed collaborative video viewing. In *Proceedings of CSCW 2000*. New York: ACM.

Carley, K. & Wendt, K. (1991). Electronic mail and scientific communication: a study of the Soar extended research group. *Knowledge: Creation, Diffusion, Utilization, 12*, 406–440.

Carroll, J. M. & Rosson, M. B. (1996). Developing the Blacksburg Electronic Village. *Communications of the ACM, 39*(12), 69–74.

Carroll, J. M., Rosson, M. B. & Zhou, J. (2005). Collective efficacy as a measure of community. In *Proceedings of CHI 2005* (pp. 1–10). New York: ACM.

Clark, H. H. (1996). *Using Language*. Cambridge: Cambridge University Press.

Clark, H. H. & Brennan, S. E. (1991). Grounding in communication. In L. Resnick, J. M. Levine & S. D. Teasley (eds.), *Perspectives on Socially Shared Cognition* (pp. 127–149). Washington, DC: APA.

Cohen, M. D. & Bacdayan, P. (1994). Organizational routines are stored as procedural memory: evidence from a laboratory study. *Organizational Science, 5*, 554–568.

Cook, T. D. & Campbell, D. T. (1979). *Quasi-Experimentation: Design and Analysis Issues for Field Settings*. Boston, MA: Houghton Mifflin.

Cummings, J. (2001) Work groups and knowledge sharing in a global organization. Unpublished doctoral dissertation. Carnegie Mellon University. Pittsburgh, PA.

Cyert, R. M. & March, J. G. (1963). *A Behavioral Theory of the Firm*. Englewood Cliffs, NJ: Prentice-Hall.

Daly-Jones, O., Monk, A. & Watts, L. (1998). Some advantages of video conferencing over high-quality audio conferencing: fluency and awareness of attentional focus. *International Journal of Human-Computer Studies, 49*(1), 21–58.

Donath, J. (2004). A semantic approach to visualizing online conversations. *Communications of the ACM, 45*(4), 45–49.

Eagly, A. H. & Chaiken, S. (1998). Attitude structure and function. In D. T. Gilbert, S. T. Fiske & G. Lindzey (eds.), *The Handbook of Social Psychology* (pp. 269–322). Boston, MA: McGraw-Hill.

Egido, C. (1988). Videoconferencing as a technology to support group work: a review of its failures. *Proceedings of the Conference on Computer Supported Cooperative Work*, 13–24.

Ehrlich, S. F. (1987). Strategies for encouraging successful adoption of office communication systems. *ACM Transactions on Office Information Systems, 5*, 340–357.

Elrod, S., Bruce, R., Gold, R. *et al.* (1992). LiveBoard: a large interactive display supporting group meetings, presentations, and remote collaboration. *Proceedings of Human Factors in Computing Systems, CHI'92*, 599–607.

Erickson, T., Smith, D. N., Kellogg, W. A. *et al.* (1999). Socially translucent systems: social proxies, persistent conversation, and the design of "BABBLE." In *Proceedings of CHI' 99*. New York: ACM.

Finholt, T. A. & Olson, G. M. (1997). From laboratories to collaboratories: a new organizational form for scientific collaboration. *Psychological Science*, 28–36.

Finholt, T., Sproull, L. & Kiesler, S. (1990). Communication and performance in ad hoc task groups. In J. Galegher, R. Kraut & C. Egido (eds.), *Intellectual Teamwork: Social and Technological Foundations of Cooperative Work*. Hillsdale, NJ: Lawrence Erlbaum Associates.

Finholt, T. A. & Teasley, S. D. (1998). The need for psychology in research on Computer Supported Cooperative Work. *Social Science Computing Review, 16*(1), 40–52.

Finn, K., Sellen, A. & Wilbur, S. (eds.) (1997). *Video-Mediated Communication*. Hillsdale NJ: Lawrence Erlbaum Associates.

Fish, R. S., Kraut, R. E. & Chalfonte, B. L. (1990). The VideoWindow system in informal communications. *Proceedings of the Conference on Computer Supported Cooperative Work*, 1–11.

Fish, R. S., Kraut, R. E., Root, R. & Rice, R. E. (1993). Video as a technology for informal communication. *Communications of the ACM*, *36*, 8–61.
Gabarro, J. (1990). The development of working relationships. In J. Galegher, R. E. Kraut & C. Egido (eds.), *Intellectual Teamwork*. Hillsdale, NJ: Lawrence Erlbaum Associates.
Gale, C. & Monk, A. (2000). Where am I looking? The accuracy of video-mediated gaze awareness. *Perception & Psychophysics*, *62*, 586–595.
Gallupe, R. B., Bastianutti, L. M. & Cooper, W. H. (1991). Unblocking brainstorms. *Journal of Applied Psychology*, *79*(1), 77–86.
Garcia, A. & Jacobs, J. (1999). The eyes of the beholder: understanding the turn-taking system in quasi-synchronous computer mediated communication. *Research on Language and Social Interaction*, *32*, 337–367.
Gardner, W. G. (1998). *3-D Audio Using Loudspeakers*. Norwell, MA: Kluwer.
Garton, L. & Wellman, B. (1995). Social impacts of electronic mail in organizations: a review of the research literature. In B. R. Burleson (ed.), *Communication Yearbook* (18). Thousand Oaks, CA: Sage.
Gaver, W. W., Moran, T., MacLean, A. *et al.* (1992). Realizing a video environment: EuroPARC's RAVE system. *Proceeding of the ACM Conference on Human Factors in Computing Systems (CHI'92)*.
Grayson, D. M. & Monk, A. (2003). Are you looking at me? Eye contact and desktop video conferencing. *ACM Transactions on Computer–Human Interaction*, *10*, 221–243.
Grudin, J. (1988). Why CSCW applications fail: problems in the design and evaluation of organizational interfaces. *Proceedings of the ACM Conference on Computer Supported Cooperative Work* (CSCW'88), 85–93.
Grudin, J. & Palen, L. (1997). Emerging groupware successes in major corporations. *Lecture Notes in Computer Science*, *1274*, 142–153.
Hackman, J. R. (1968). Effects of task characteristics on group products. *Journal of Experimental Social Psychology*, *4*, 162–187.
Handel, M. & Herbsleb, J. D. (2002). What is chat doing in the workplace? *Proceeding of the ACM Conference on Computer Supported Cooperative Work (CSCW 2002)*.
Handy, C. (1998). *The Hungry Spirit beyond Capitalism: A Quest for Purpose in the Modern World*. New York: Broadway Books.
Herbsleb, J. D., Atkins, D. L., Boyer, D. G. *et al.* (2002). Introducing instant messaging and chat in the workplace. *Proceeding of the ACM Conference on Human Factors in Computing Systems (CHI'02)*, 171–178.
Hindus, D., Ackerman, M. S., Mainwaring, S. & Starr, B. (1996). Thunderwire: a field study of an audio-only media space. *Proceeding of the ACM Conference on Computer Supported Cooperative Work* (CSCW'96), 238–247.
Hinsz, V. B., Tindale, R. S. & Vollrath, D. A. (1997). The emerging conceptualization of groups as information processors. *Psychological Bulletin*, *121*(1), 43–64.
Hollingshead, A. B., McGrath, J. E. & O'Connor, K. M. (1993). Group performance and communication technology: a longitudinal study of computer-mediated versus face-to-face work. *Small Group Research*, *24*(3), 307–333.
Horn, D. B., Olson, J. S. & Karasik, L. (2002). The Effects of Spatial and Temporal Video Distortion on Lie Detection Performance. Short paper presented at CHI 2002, Minneapolis, MN April 20–25.
Huang, W., Olson, J. S. & Olson, G. M. (2002). Camera angle affects dominance in video-mediated communication. In *Proceedings of CHI 2002*. New York: ACM.
Hudson, S. E. & Smith, I. (1996). Techniques for addressing fundamental privacy and disruption tradeoffs in awareness support systems. *Proceeding of the ACM Conference on Computer Supported Cooperative Work* (CSCW'96), 248–257.
Hutchins, E. (1990). The technology of team navigation. In J. Galegher, R. E. Kraut & C. Egido (eds.), *Intellectual Teamwork: Social and Technological Foundations of Cooperative Work* (pp. 191–220). Hillsdale, NJ: Lawrence Erlbaum Associates.
Hutchins, E. (1991). The social organization of distributed cognition. In L. B. Resnick, J. M. Levine & S. D. Teasley (eds.), *Perspectives on Socially Shared Cognition* (pp. 283–307). Washington: American Psychological Association.

Hutchins, E. (1995a) *Cognition in the Wild*. Cambridge, MA: MIT Press.

Hutchins, E. (1995b) How a cockpit remembers its speeds. *Cognitive Science*, *19*, 265–288.

Hymes, C. M. & Olson, G. M. (1992). Unblocking brainstorming through use of a simple group editor. *Proceedings of the ACM Conference on Computer Supported Cooperative Work (CSCW'92)*, 99–106.

Isaacs, E., Walendowski, A., Whittaker, S. *et al.* (2002). The character, functions, and styles of instant messaging in the workplace. In *Proceedings of CSCW 2002*. New York: ACM.

Kendon, A. (1967). Some functions of gaze direction in social interaction. *Acta Psychologia*, *26*, 22–63.

Kiesler, S. & Cummings, J. N. (2002). What do we know about proximity and distance in work groups? A legacy of research. In P. J. Hinds & S. Kiesler (eds.), *Distributed Work* (pp. 57–80). Cambridge, MA: MIT Press.

Kottemann, J. E., Davis, F. D & Remus, W. R. (1994). Computer assisted decision making: performance, beliefs, and the illusion of control. *Organizational Behavior and Human Decision Processes*, *57*, 26–37.

Kraemer, K. L. & Pinsonneault, A. (1990). Technology and groups: assessments of empirical research. In J. Galegher, R. Kraut & C. Egido (eds.), *Intellectual Teamwork.: Social and Technological Foundations of Cooperative Work*. Hillsdale, NJ: Lawrence Erlbaum Associates.

Krauss, R. M. & Bricker, P. D. (1966). Effects of transmission delay and access delay on the efficiency of verbal communication. *Journal of the Acoustical Society*, *41*, 286–292.

Kraut, R. E., Fussell, S. R. & Siegel, J. (2003). Visual information as a conversational resource in collaborative physical tasks. *Human-Computer Interaction*, *18*(1–2), 13–39.

Kraut, R., Kiesler, S., Boneva, B. *et al.* (2002). Internet paradox revisited. *Journal of Social Issues*, *58*(1), 49–74.

Kraut, R., Patterson, M., Lundmark, V. *et al.* (1998). Internet paradox: a social technology that reduces social involvement and psychological well-being? *American Psychologist*, *53*(9), 1017–1031.

Kraut, R., Scherlis, W., Mukhopadhyay, T. *et al.* (1996). HomeNet: a field trial of residential internet services. *Proceeding of the ACM Conference on Human Factors in Computing Systems (CHI'96)*, 284–291.

Lampe, C. & Resnick, P. (2004). Slash(dot) and burn: distributed moderation in a large online conversation space. *Proceeding of the ACM Conference on Human Factors in Computing Systems (CHI'04)*, 1–8.

Lange, B. M. (1992). Electronic group calendaring: experiences and expectations. In D. Coleman (ed.) *Groupware* (pp. 428–432). San Mateo, CA: Morgan Kaufman.

Lave, J. (1988). *Cognition in Practice*. Cambridge: Cambridge University Press.

Lederberg, J. & Uncapher, K. (1989). *Towards a National Collaboratory: Report of an Invitational Workshop at the Rockefeller University*. Washington, DC: National Science Foundation, Directorate for Computer and Information Science.

Leung, W. H. & Chen, T. (2003). A multi-user 3-D virtual environment with interactive collaboration and shared whiteboard technologies. *Journal of Multimedia Tools and Applications*, *20*(1), 7–23.

Ludford, P. J., Cosley, D., Frankowski, D. & Terveen, L. (2004). Think different: increasing online community participation using uniqueness and group dissimilarity. In *Proceedings of CHI 2004* (pp. 631–638). Vienna, Austria.

Lumbreras, M. & Sanchez, J. (1999). Interactive 3D sound hyperstories for blind children. In *Proceedings of CHI 99*. New York: ACM.

McCauley, C. C., Stitt, L. & Segal, M. (1980). Stereotyping: from prejudice to prediction. *Psychological Bulletin*, *87*, 195–208.

McDaniel, S. E., Olson, G. M. & Magee, J. S. (1996). Identifying and analyzing multiple threads in computer-mediated and face-to-face conversations. *Proceeding of the ACM Conference on Computer Supported Cooperative Work* (CSCW'96), 39–47.

McDonald, D. W. & Ackerman, M. S. (2000). Expertise recommender: a flexible recommendation system and architecture. In *Proceedings of CSCW 2000*. New York: ACM.

McGrath, J. E. (1984). *Groups: Interaction and Performance*. Englewood Cliffs, NJ: Prentice-Hall.

Mackay, W. E. (1989). Diversity in the use of electronic mail: a preliminary inquiry. *ACM Transactions on Office Information Systems, 6*(4), 380–397.

McLeod, P. L. (1992). An assessment of the experimental literature on electronic group support: results of a meta-analysis. *Human–Computer Interaction, 7*, 257–280.

Macy, M. W. (1991) Learning to cooperate: Stochastic and tacit collusion in social exchange. *American Journal of Sociology, 97*, 808–843.

March, J. G. & Simon, H. A. (1958). *Organizations*. New York: John Wiley & Sons.

Monk, A. (2003). Common ground in electronically mediated communication: Clark's theory of language use. In J. M. Carroll (ed.), *HCI Models, Theories, and Frameworks: Toward a Multidisciplinary Science* (pp. 265–289). San Francisco, CA: Morgan Kaufmann.

Monk, A. & Gale, C. (2002). A look is worth a thousand words: full gaze awareness in video-mediated communication. *Discourse Processes, 33*, 257–278.

Moran, T. P., Chiu, P., Harrison, S. *et al.* (1996). Evolutionary engagement in an ongoing collaborative work process: a case study. *Proceedings of the ACM Conference on Computer Supported Cooperative Work* (CSCW'96), 150–159.

Mosier, J. N. & Tammaro, S. G. (1997). When are group scheduling tools useful? *Computer Supported Cooperative Work, 6*, 53–70.

Muller, M. J., Geyer, W., Brownholtz, B. *et al.* (2004). One hundred days in an activity-centric collaboration environment based on shared objects (pp. 375–382). In *Proceedings of CHI 2004*. New York: ACM.

Muller, M. J., Raven, M. E., Kogan, S. *et al.* (2003). Introducing chat into business organizations: toward an Instant Messaging Maturity Model. *Proceedings of the 2003 International ACM SIGGROUP*.

Nardi, B. A. (ed.) (1996). *Context and Consciousness: Activity Theory and Human Computer Interaction*. Cambridge, MA: MIT Press.

Nardi, B. A., Kuchinsky, A., Whittaker, S. *et al.* (1995). Video-as-data: technical and social aspects of a collaborative multimedia application. *Computer Supported Cooperative Work, 4*, 73–100.

Nardi, B. A., Whittaker, S. & Bradner, E. (2000). Interaction and outeraction: instant messaging in action. In *Proceedings of CSCW 2000*. New York: ACM.

Nohria, N. & Eccles, R. G. (eds.) (1992). Networks and organizations: structure, form, and action. Boston, MA: Harvard Business School Press.

Nonaka, I. & Takeuchi, H. (1995). *The Knowledge-Creating Company: How Japanese Companies Create the Dynamics of Innovation*. New York: Oxford University Press.

Nunamaker, J. F., Dennis, A. R., Valacich, J. S. *et al.* (1991). Electronic meeting systems to support group work. *Communications of the ACM, 34*(7), 40–61.

O'Conaill, B. & Whittaker, S. (1997). Characterizing, predicting and measuring video-mediated communication: a conversational approach. In K. Finn, A. Sellen & S. B. Wilbur (eds.), *Video Mediated Communication* (pp. 107–131). Mahwah, NJ: Lawrence Erlbaum Associates.

O'Conaill, B., Whittaker, S. & Wilbur, S. (1993). Conversations over videoconferences: an evaluation of the spoken aspects of video mediated communication. *Human–Computer Interaction, 8*, 389–428.

O'Hara-Devereaux, M. & Johansen, R. (1994). *Global Work: Bridging Distance, Culture & Time*. San Francisco: Jossey-Bass.

Okada, K., Maeda, F., Ichicawaa, Y. & Matsushita, Y. (1994). Multiparty videoconferencing at virtual social distance: MAJIC design. In *Proceedings of CSCW 94*. New York: ACM.

Olson, G. M. (2004). Collaboratories. In W. S. Bainbridge (ed.), *Encyclopedia of Human–Computer Interaction*. Great Barrington, MA: Berkshire Publishing.

Olson, G. M., Atkins, D. E., Clauer, R. *et al.* (1998). The upper atmospheric research collaboratory. *Interactions, 5*(3), 48–55.

Olson, G. M., Atkins, D., Clauer, R., Weymouth, T., Prakash, A., Finholt, T., Jahanian, F., & Rasmussen, C. (2001) Technology to support distributed team science: The first phase of the Upper Atmospheric Research Collaboratory (UARC) (pp. 761–783) In G. M. Olson, T. Malone & J. Smith (Eds.), *Coordination theory and collaboration technology*. Hillsdale, NJ: Lawrence Erlbaum Associates.

Olson, G. M. & Olson, J. S. (1997). Research on computer supported cooperative work. In M. G. Helander, T. K. Landauer & P. V. Prabhu (eds.), *Handbook of Human-Computer Interaction* (pp. 1433–1456). Amsterdam: North-Holland.

Olson, G. M. & Olson, J. S. (2000). Distance matters. *Human–Computer Interaction, 15*, 139–179.

Olson, J. S., Olson, G. M. & Meader, D. K. (1995). What mix of video and audio is useful for remote real-time work? *Proceedings of ACM Conference on Human Factors in Computing Systems. CHI'95*, 362–368.

Olson, J. S., Olson, G. M., Storrøsten, M. & Carter, M. (1993). Groupwork close up: a comparison of the group design process with and without a simple group editor. *ACM Transactions on Information Systems, 11*, 321–348.

Olson, J. S. & Teasley, S. (1996). Groupware in the wild: lessons learned from a year of virtual collocation. *Proceeding of the ACM Conference on Computer Supported Cooperative Work* (CSCW'96), 419–427.

Olson, M. H. & Bly, S. A. (1991). The Portland experience: a report on a distributed research group. *International Journal of Man–Machine Studies, 34*, 211–228.

O'Neill, J. & Martin, D. (2003). Text chat in action. In *Proceedings of GROUP '03*. New York: ACM.

Orlikowski, W. J. (1992). Learning from Notes: organizational issues in groupware implementation. In *Proceedings of the Conference on Computer Supported Cooperative Work* (pp. 362–369). November, Toronto: ACM/SIGCHI & SIGOIS, NY.

Perry, M. (2003). Distributed cognition. In J. M. Carroll (ed.), *HCI Models, Theories, and Frameworks: Toward a Multidisciplinary Science* (pp. 192–222). San Francisco, CA: Morgan Kaufmann.

Petty, R. E. & Wegener, D. T. (1998). Attitude change: multiple roles for persuasion variables. In D. T. Gilbert, S. T. Fiske & G. Lindzey (eds.), *The Handbook of Social Psychology*. (pp. 322–390). Boston, MA: McGraw-Hill.

Preece, J. (2000). *Online Communities: Designing Usability and Supporting Sociability*. New York: John Wiley & Sons.

Rheingold, H. (1993). *The Virtual Community: Homesteading on the Electronic Frontier*. New York: HarperPerennial.

Rocco, E. (1998). Trust disappears over email but it can be repaired with initial face-to-face contact. *Proceeding of the ACM Conference on Human Factors in Computing Systems* (CHI'98), 496–502.

Rochlin, G. I. (1997). *Trapped in the Net: The Unanticipated Consequences of Computerization*. Princeton, NJ: Princeton University Press.

Rogers, Y. & Ellis, J. (1994). Distributed cognition: an alternative framework for analysing and explaining collaborative working. *Journal of Information Technology, 9*(2), 119–128.

Ruhleder, K. & Jordan, B. (2001). Co-constructing non-mutual realities: Delay-generated trouble in distributed interactions. *Computer Supported Cooperative Work, 10*, 113–138.

Satzinger, J. & Olfman, L. (1992). A research program to assess user perceptions of group work support *Proceeding of the ACM Conference on Human Factors in Computing Systems* CHI'92, 99–106.

Senge, P. M. (1990). *The Fifth Discipline: The art and Practice of the Learning Organization*. New York: Doubleday Currency.

Short, J., Williams, E. & Christie, B. (1976). *The Social Psychology of Telecommunications*. New York: John Wiley & Sons.

Siegel, J., Dubrovsky, V., Kiesler, S. & McGuire, T. W. (1986). Group processes in computer-mediated communication. *Organizational Behavior and Human Decision Processes, 37*, 157–187.

Sproull, L. & Kiesler, S. (1991). *Connections: New Ways of Working in the Networked Organization*. Cambridge, MA: MIT Press.

Steiner, I. D. (1972). *Group Process and Productivity*. New York: Academic Press.

Stefik, M., Foster, G., Bobrow, D. *et al.* (1987). Beyond the chalkboard: computer support for collaboration and problem solving in meetings. *Communications of the ACM, 30*, 32–47.

Stokes, D. E. (1997). *Pasteur's Quadrant: Basic Science and Technological Innovation*. Washington, DC: Brookings Institution.
Straus, S. G. (1996). Getting a clue: the effects of communication media and information distribution on participation and performance in computer-mediated and face-to-face groups. *Small Group Research*, *1*, 115–142.
Straus, S. G. (1997). Technology, group process, and group outcomes: testing the connections in computer-mediated and face-to-face groups. *Human–Computer Interaction*, *12*, 227–266.
Straus, S. G. & McGrath, J. E. (1994). Does the medium matter: the interaction of task and technology on group performance and member reactions. *Journal of Applied Psychology*, *79*, 87–97.
Suchman, L. (1987). *Plans and Situated Action: The Problem of Human–Machine Communication*. Cambridge; Cambridge University Press.
Suchman, L. (1996). Constituting shared workspaces. In Y. Engeström & D. Middleton (eds.), *Cognition and Communication at Work* (pp. 35–60). New York: Cambridge University Press.
Tang, J. C. & Isaacs, E. (1993). Why do users like video? *Computer Supported Cooperative Work*, *1*, 163–196.
Tang, J. C., Isaacs, E. A. & Rua, M. (1994). Supporting distributed groups with a Montage of lightweight interactions. *Proceeding of the ACM Conference on Computer Supported Cooperative Work* (CSCW'94), 23–34.
Teasley, S. D., Covi, L. A., Krishnan, M. S. & Olson, J. S. (2002). Rapid software development through team collocation. *IEEE Transactions on Software Engineering*, *28*, 671–683.
Tenner, E. (1996). *Why Things Bite Back: Technology and the Revenge of Unintended Consequences*. New York: Alfred A. Knopf.
Terveen, L., Hill, W., Amento, B. *et al.* (1997). PHOAKS: a system for sharing recommendations. *Communications of the ACM*, *40*(3), 59–62.
Veinott, B., Olson, J. S., Olson, G. M. & Fu, X. (1999). Video helps remote work: speakers who need to negotiate common ground benefit from seeing each other. In *Proceedings of CHI 99* (pp. 302–309). New York: ACM.
Vera, A. H. & Simon, H. A. (1993). Situated Action: a symbolic interpretation. *Cognitive Science*, *17*(1), 7–48.
Vertegaal, R. (1999). The GAZE groupware system: mediating joint attention in multiparty communication and collaboration. In *Proceedings of CHI'99*. New York: ACM.
Vertegaal, R., Slagter, R., van der Veer, G. & Nijholt, A. (2001). Eye gaze patterns in conversations: there is more to conversational agents than meets the eye. In *Proceedings of CHI 2001*. New York: ACM.
Walsh, J. P. (1995). Managerial and organizational cognition: notes from a trip down memory lane. *Organizational Science*, *6*, 280–321.
Walsh, J. P. & Ungson, G. R. (1991). Organizational memory. *Academy of Management Review*, *16*, 57–91.
Weick, K. E. (1993). The collapse of sensemaking in organizations: the Mann Gulch disaster. *Administrative Science Quarterly*, *38*, 628–652.
Weick, K. E. & Roberts, K. H. (1993). Collective mind in organizations: heedful interrelating on flight decks. *Administrative Science Quarterly*, *38*, 357–381.
Wertsch, J. V. (1985). *Vygotsky and the Social Formation of Mind*. Cambridge, MA: Harvard University Press.
Wertsch, J. V. (1991). *Voices of the Mind: A Sociocultural Approach to Mediated Action*. Cambridge, MA: Harvard University Press.
Whittaker, S., Geelhoed, E. & Robinson, E. (1993). Shared workspaces: how do they work and when are they useful? *International Journal of Man–Machine Studies*, *39*(5), 813–842.
Whittaker, S. & O'Conaill, B. (1997). The role of vision in face-to-face and mediated communication. In K. Finn, A. Sellen & S. B. Wilbur (eds.), *Video Mediated Communication*. (pp. 23–49). Mahwah, NJ: Lawrence Erlbaum Associates.
Whittaker, S. & Sidner, C. (1996). Email overload: exploring personal information management of email. *Proceeding of the ACM Conference on Human Factors in Computing Systems* (CHI'96), 276–283.
Williams, E. (1977). Experimental comparisons of face-to-face and mediated communication: a review. *Psychological Bulletin*, *84*, 963–976.

Williams, G. (1997). Task conflict and language differences: opportunities for videoconferencing. *Proceedings of the European Computer Supported Cooperative Work* (ECSCW'97).

Zheng, J., Veinott, E., Bos, N. *et al.* (2002). Trust without touch: jumpstarting long-distance trust with initial social activities. *Proceedings of the Conference on Human Factors in Computing Systems, CHI02*, 141–146.

CHAPTER 20

Online Courses

Ruth H. Maki and William S. Maki
Texas Tech University, USA

INTRODUCTION

College instructors are being encouraged to develop online courses, and more entire degree programs are becoming available online. For example, in a recent survey of chairs of psychology departments, Piotrowski and Vodanovich (2004) found that 50 per cent of the psychology chairs in the United States surveyed reported that their departments use the Internet in teaching to a moderate degree. About 75 per cent of the department chairs expressed favorable attitudes toward Internet-based instruction. The chairs predicted that computer-based instruction is likely to be part of the standard curriculum in psychology in the future. However, in spite of generally positive attitudes about and fairly frequent usage of Web-based instruction, the evidence on learning from online courses relative to traditional face-to-face courses is mixed.

In this chapter, we review this literature and draw some conclusions about the circumstances under which learning is enhanced by online presentations and about the circumstances under which learning may be hampered. In the literature on distance education and online learning, different terms are often used to describe the two kinds of courses. Online courses employing the Internet and the World Wide Web are a subset of possible modes of distance education, which includes delivery by CD-ROM, video tape, and remote classrooms. We include only studies using online instruction in this chapter. The terms Web-based and online are used interchangeably. We focus on online courses which were compared to traditional courses. Traditional courses are taught on site, in the "face-to-face" mode, often employing lectures and supplemented with discussion, demonstrations, and video presentations. The terms traditional and face-to-face are used interchangeably. Almost all the traditional courses used lecture as the primary classroom activity.

The literature on online instruction is large. Searching for online (Web-based) instruction in PsychInfo produced 3946 articles. Adding other databases, such as Educational Resources Information Center (ERIC), increases this number. In order to make this review manageable, we limited our review to those studies that included a comparison between a traditional course and an online course or that compared baseline performance with performance following online learning. We eliminated studies that used Web-based exer-

Handbook of Applied Cognition: Second Edition. Edited by Francis T. Durso.

cises as supplements to a traditional course (e.g., Dufresne *et al.* 2002). We did not include studies that compared different modes of distance instruction, such as interactive television vs. delivery over the Internet (Lilja 2001). Although it would be useful to know what components of a Web-based course are effective, there are very few studies that included such a comparison and that also included measures of learning. Some studies compare technical aspects of online materials, such as amount of white space on the pages (e.g., Bradshaw & Johari 2002), but we did not review these because we were interested in more global aspects of learning from online courses.

The review and commentary are organized around the four questions related to learning and behavior in online classes as compared to more traditional face-to-face classes:

- How much is learned?
- What influences study behaviors?
- Are students more or less satisfied?
- Which individual differences modulate learning and satisfaction?

For each of these questions, conclusions from meta-analyses are presented, followed by a review of representative studies. For each section of the review, we first present our published work which resulted from comparisons between traditional and online versions of general psychology courses at Texas Tech University. Our studies are highlighted because they were designed using principles from cognitive psychology that are known to improve learning. In addition, they are among the very few that have evaluated online courses using experimental or quasi-experimental designs. In spite of the availability of appropriate designs (Stalcup & Maki 2002; Maki 2005) it was observed that very few of the published studies concerned with online learning have employed such designs. In addition, we selected a subset of studies from the literature that compared online learning to traditional face-to-face learning. We categorized these based on their characteristics and their outcomes in order to determine what factors influence learning and satisfaction in online vs. traditional courses. These studies are described in Table 20.1. To preview our findings, our review of the literature will show that many variables affect learning and satisfaction in online courses, but almost every one of these variables affects learning and satisfaction in a similar way in traditional face-to-face courses. Therefore, having the traditional comparison group is critical. Following a review of research on each of the four questions, we will draw some lessons from the literature and from our own research about the design and evaluation of online courses.

HOW MUCH IS LEARNED?

Previous Reviews on Amount of Learning

Most of the recent reviews of online instruction have focused on learning, so these reviews are most relevant to the first question involving amount of learning. Dillon and Gabbard (1998) reviewed empirical studies in which hypermedia was used to present course material. They defined hypermedia as "hypertext, multimedia, and related applications involving the chunking of information into nodes that could be selected dynamically" (Dillon & Gabbard 1998, p. 323). Based on eight studies, they concluded that the amount learned from a hypermedia environment or from standard text on paper shows little difference in

Table 20.1 Methodology, contingencies, and effects reported in articles comparing online and face-to-face courses

Reference	Methodology	Type of Course	Required Weekly Assignments	Learning Effect	Satisfaction Effect
Bernardo *et al.* (2004)	Pre-experiment	Experimental Surgery (undergraduate)	Yes	Improvement from pretest to posttest	No comparison group
Cahill and Cantanzaro (1997)	Pre-experiment	Spanish	Yes	Online better	–
Casanova (2001)	Pre-experiment	College Chemistry	Yes	Online better	–
Chou and Liu (2005)	Quasi-experiment	Computers – Junior High	Yes	Online better	Online higher
Dutton *et al.* (2001)	Pre-experiment	Computer Programming	Yes	Online better	–
Johnson (2001)	Pre-experiment	Political Science	Yes	Face-to-face better (n.s.)	–
Johnson (2002)	Quasi-experiment	Biology	Yes	No difference	No difference
Logan and Conerly (2002)	Pre-experiment	Library Science	Yes	No difference	Qualitative
Maki *et al.* (2000)	Quasi-experiment	Psychology	Yes	Online better	Face-to-face higher
Poirier and Feldman (2004)	Experiment	Psychology	Yes	Online better	Online higher
Schutte (1997)	Experiment	Statistics	Yes	Online better	Online higher
Summers *et al.* (2005)	Quasi-experiment	Statistics	Yes	No difference	Face-to-face higher
Hiltz (1993)	Pre-experiment	Sociology, Computer Science, Statistics, Management	No	No difference	No comparison
Jeannette and Meyer (2002)	Quasi-experiment	Horticulture Continuing Education	No	No difference	–
LaRose *et al.* (1998)	Experiment	Telecommunications	No	No difference	No difference
Wang and Newlin (2000)	Pre-experiment	Statistics	No	Face-to-face better	No difference
Brown and Liedholm (2002)	Pre-experiment	Economics	??	Face-to-face better	–
Buchanan *et al.* (2001)	Pre-experiment	Library and Information Science	??	No difference	Qualitative

Table 20.1 *Continued*

Reference	Methodology	Type of Course	Required Weekly Assignments	Learning Effect	Satisfaction Effect
Campbell *et al.* (2002)	Pre-experiment	Accounting	??	Online better	Mixed
Collins (2000)	Pre-experiment	Biology	??	No difference	No comparison
Cooper (2001)	Pre-experiment	Computer Applications	??	Online better (no statistics)	Face-to-face better (no statistics)
Fallah and Ubell (2000)	Pre-experiment	Telecommunications	??	No difference	–
Neuhauser (2002)	Pre-experiment	Management	??	No difference	No difference
Parker and Gemino (2001)	Quasi-experiment	Business Administration Systems Analysis	??	Conceptual-Online better Procedural-Face-to-face better	–
Piccoli *et al.* (2001)	Quasi-experiment	Management Information Systems	??	No difference	Face-to-face higher
Ryan (2000)	Quasi-experiment	Construction Equipment	??	No difference	Mixed
Sankaran *et al.* (2000)	Quasi-experiment	Business Computers	??	No difference	–
Schulman and Sims (1999)	Pre-experiment	Various Business, Education, and Environmental Studies	??	No difference	–
Schoenfeld-Tacher *et al.* (2001)	Quasi-experiment	Histology	??	Online better	–
Thirunarayanan and Perez-Prado (2001–2002)	Pre-experiment	Teaching English as a Foreign Language	??	No difference	–
Waschull (2001)	Pre-experiment	Psychology	??	No difference	No difference
Wegner *et al.* (1999)	Pre-experiment	Education	??	No difference	Online higher (no statistics)

Note: All courses were college courses unless noted otherwise. The methodology judgment was based on categorization used by Cook and Campbell (1979). Pre-experimental designs included posttest only, and pretest and posttest single group designs. Quasi-experimental designs included designs with multiple pre-treatment measures and multiple post-treatment measures, and the non-equivalent control group design. True experimental designs used random assignment to courses. Only significant effects are reported, except in a few cases in which statistics were not conducted or the statistical conclusions were inappropriate.

measures of comprehension (e.g., Van der Berg & Watt 1991). However, tasks that required rapid searching through a large amount of information (such as searching for references containing topical information) do show some advantage with hypermedia as opposed to paper text (Lehto *et al.* 1995). Dillon and Gabbard's (1998) general conclusion from the early studies that they reviewed is that the value of hypermedia in education is severely limited.

Three fairly large meta-analyses have been published recently, each focusing on somewhat different aspects of online learning. Bayraktar (2001–2002) reviewed studies on computer-assisted instruction in science education. Each of the 42 studies in Bayraktar's analysis compared a high school or college science class (physics, chemistry, biology, general science, or physical science) in which computer-assisted instruction was used with a class using traditional instruction. In some cases, the computerized material replaced other classroom activities and, in others, the computer-assisted material supplemented other course materials. Bayraktar included only experimental or quasi-experimental studies. Overall, students learned more in the classes that included computer-assisted instruction. Of the 108 effect sizes used in the analysis, 70 showed a positive effect of computer-assisted instruction and 38 showed that traditional instruction was better than computer-assisted instruction. The average student in a computer-assisted class would exceed the performance of 62 per cent of the students in a traditional class. Bayraktar coded several other aspects of the studies that also produced effects. Using the computer purely for drill and practice produced less learning in computer-assisted courses than in traditional courses, but using the computer for simulations and tutorials produced better learning in computer-assisted courses. Interestingly, one of the largest effects related to the year of the publication, with publications in the 1970s producing the largest effects and publications in the 1990s producing the smallest. Bayraktar attributed this to a Hawthorne effect, that is, computer-assisted instruction was more novel in the earlier years and students may have responded positively to the novelty. Length of treatment also produced a difference in effect size, with larger effects occurring for classes in which the computer-assisted instruction lasted for four weeks or less and smaller effects occurring for longer treatments. This may also be due to a Hawthorne effect related to the novelty of the treatment. Effects were larger when computers were used to supplement instruction and smaller when computers replaced regular instruction. Most of the studies discussed here involved more extensive use of computers to replace traditional instruction, so smaller effects may be seen than those reported by Bayraktar (2001–2002).

Shachar and Neumann (2003) conducted a meta-analysis to compare the performance of students enrolled in distance education and in traditional classrooms. Not all of the studies they used involved course delivery over the Web, but most did. Shachar and Neumann included only studies that had no severe methodological flaws; and discarded studies that did not have appropriate comparison groups and that did not report sample sizes, means, and standard deviations. Of the 259 eligible studies published between 1990 and 2002, 86 met their criteria. They found that the distance education groups outperformed the traditional groups in 66 per cent of the studies, placing the mean performance in the distance education groups at the 65th percentile of the traditional groups. Thus, distance education produced learning that was superior to that of traditional classroom settings.

A meta-analysis by Bernard *et al.* (2004) reached a different conclusion. Their meta-analysis differed from Shachar and Neumann's (2003) in that it included all studies of distance learning for which the sample size, mean, and standard deviation could be determined. Rather than eliminating studies with poor methodology, Bernard *et al.* coded each study in terms of the quality of its methodology. Although many of the studies included in their meta-analysis had been used by Schachar and Neumann, Bernard *et al.* included many more studies – a total of 232. Bernard *et al.* coded the medium used for distance education (e.g., video, CD-ROM, World Wide Web), and distinguished between synchronous and asynchronous comparisons. The comparison was synchronous if the traditional group met at the same time as the distance education group was completing their course. Thus, the synchronous distance education group included videoconferencing, interactive television, and/or simultaneous web-casts. Students participated in the course at the same time. In asynchronous comparisons, the classroom and distance conditions were not linked in time. Students in the asynchronous online courses communicated via email, and did their coursework at any time. Bernard *et al.* also coded nine pedagogical features of each course, including systematic instructional design features, advance course information given to students, and a number of measures related to the amount of student–instructor and student–student contact.

In Bernard *et al.*'s meta-analysis, the difference in performance in the distance and face-to-face courses produced an effect size that was essentially zero. However, the synchronous comparisons produced a significant negative effect, indicating that the traditional methods produced more learning than the distance methods. For asynchronous comparisons, however, the distance groups significantly outperformed the traditional groups, although the effect was small.

Bernard *et al.* (2004) conducted a multiple regression to relate effect size to quality of the methodology, pedagogical requirements, and medium (e.g., Web-based, interactive television, CD). The medium accounted for significant variance only when it was entered into the regression first. The quality of the study was the best predictor of effect size. Studies with better controls produced larger differences in favor of the distance courses. The pedagogy used in the distance course was also important, with better performance in distance groups when there was more face-to-face contact with other students, advance information about the course given to students, and more opportunity for mediated communication with the instructor.

Generally, these meta-analyses indicate that learning in distance courses is often greater than learning in face-to-face courses. However, factors other than the course medium are important in determining superior learning in distance courses. These include strong methodology, asynchrony in the distance course, and opportunities for online students to interact with the instructor and other students. In discussing the studies comparing online and face-to-face courses that we reviewed in Table 20.1, we will emphasize methodology and pedagogy.

General Psychology Online at Texas Tech University

Performance and student satisfaction were measured in online and face-to-face courses in general psychology at Texas Tech University across four semesters, using a nonequivalent-groups pretest–posttest design (Cook & Campbell 1979). Students were not randomly assigned to online vs. face-to-face sections. They signed up for a specific section at a specific time. Initial differences in knowledge were controlled by covariance techniques.

Online and face-to-face sections were taught by the same instructor, and students read the same textbook, covered the same material, and took the same examinations. Students in the face-to-face class were expected to attend 50-minute classes, three days a week, but attendance was not mandatory. Classes consisted of lectures, videos, and demonstrations, but students in the face-to-face class did not have access to online materials.

The online course design incorporated principles from cognitive psychology, distributed learning, active engagement with course material, and immediate feedback from practice quizzes. Evidence for the importance of distributed learning on very long-term retention comes from a study by Bahrick *et al.* (1993). They manipulated the distribution of learning by having participants relearn materials after intervals of up to one month, and they then measured memory over long periods of time, of up to five years. Bahrick *et al.* showed that material learned in a distributed way is remembered much longer than material learned in a massed way. Given that the goal of the Texas Tech study was to encourage long-term learning, online course requirements were imposed so that students would interact with the material several times in a distributed way. Students could not use massed learning by reading all of the material immediately before the examinations, as was possible in the face-to-face course.

Passive lectures were replaced with three weekly assignments which encouraged active engagement with course material. (1) Each week, students were advised to preview the topic by studying outlines or reading answers to frequently asked questions. Then, they took a quiz over this preview material. This preview was intended to serve as an advance organizer of the week's material. Similar activities have been shown to facilitate learning from text (Rothkopf & Bisbicos 1967; Mayer *et al.* 1984). (2) Students were required to pass two mastery quizzes consisting of questions from a large pool of items. They received immediate feedback on each question along with an explanation of why each answer was correct or incorrect. (3) Students in the online course did an interactive exercise often involving participation in a demonstration of a psychological phenomenon (such as a short-term memory task) and answering questions about the activity. In addition, there was a synchronous component in the online course: students met once a week to see their pooled data from the exercise or to do some other interactive exercise.

Performance on a difficult set of test questions was measured at the beginning and end of each type of course. These content questions were drawn from a practice test for the Psychology Graduate Record Examination (GRE; Educational Testing Service 1994). Performance for the online and face-to-face classes was also compared on the common unit and final examinations. Attitudes toward the course were measured at the beginning and end of the course. Questions about workload were asked in the two courses. Data on students' year in college and their major were collected. All students answered items related to the Big Five personality factors (McCrae & Costa 1987): conscientiousness, agreeableness, introversion, emotional stability, and intellectualism or openness to experience. Conscientiousness was expected to play a role in online course success because online learning needs to be self-directed. A subset of the students in the online and face-to-face courses came to the laboratory to be tested for comprehension ability as measured by the Multimedia Comprehension Battery (MMCB) developed by Gernsbacher and Varner (1988). The MMCB consists of six narratives: two presented as written text, two presented as spoken text, and two presented visually as a series of pictures. At the end of each text, students wrote short answers to 12 questions; their answers were scored using the procedures developed by Gernsbacher and Varner.

Over the four semesters, examination performance in the online versions of general psychology courses was higher than in the face-to-face versions. In addition, students in the online sections learned more than did students in face-to-face sections, as indicated by a greater increase in scores on the practice GRE questions from the beginning to the end of the semester. Maki *et al.* (2000) reported the learning differences across two semesters for about 100 students in each of the two types of courses. The groups did not differ on the GRE questions at the beginning of the semester. However, they differed significantly at the end of the course. Performance increased about 10 per cent from the beginning to the end of the course in the online group, but only about 5 per cent in the face-to-face group. The online group also scored significantly higher on the three unit and final examinations. None of these effects was modulated by instructor or semester.

Many course components were equated in the Texas Tech studies, including instructor, text material, and examinations. Students self-selected the courses, but individual differences in prior knowledge about psychology were controlled by using scores on a pretest as a covariate. Still, medium was confounded with specific course content because instructors taught the material in the face-to-face courses in their "usual" way, including lectures, demonstrations, discussion, and video tapes. Several characteristics of the online environment could mediate the differences in learning between the online and face-to-face courses. The online environment allowed for required interaction with the material. All activities carried points related to students' grades, so most students completed the weekly exercises. Similar required activities probably would have boosted the scores of students in the traditional courses also.

What Makes Online Courses Effective?

The results of Maki *et al.* (2000) led to the hypothesis that specific requirements for students in online courses but the absence of parallel requirements for traditional courses results in better learning in online courses. Using the bibliographies in previous reviews and electronic databases, we searched for studies that compared an online version of an entire course with the traditional version of the same course or studies that compared baseline performance with performance following online learning. We restricted this review to those studies ($N = 32$) that used the Internet for online delivery and that reported some measure of achievement (course grades, final examination score, or performance on some problem set). Thus studies of distance learning that employed other media (such as CD-ROMs or video broadcasts) were excluded. References that were included in this summary of learning outcomes are shown in Table 20.1. Of those 32 studies, 18 also reported some quantitative measure of satisfaction, usually in the form of standard course evaluations in which the course and/or instructor were rated, although comparisons of satisfaction in traditional and online courses were not always reported. The satisfaction results will be discussed later in the section comparing satisfaction in online and traditional courses.

Quality of the Experimental Design

Consistent with the reviews cited above, our review of the literature comparing online and face-to-face courses showed that the quality of the experimental design was related to the learning outcome. In general, academic performance was better in online courses in those studies that had high quality evaluation designs. Table 20.1 shows the studies that we reviewed comparing online and face-to-face courses. Only 13 of the studies employed true experimental or quasi-experimental designs. Of the remaining 19, 18 were posttest only, nonequivalent groups designs. This type of design suffers from selection effects, which are a severe threat to internal validity (Cook & Campbell 1979). In the other study, Bernardo *et al.* (2004) randomly selected students from a traditional course to participate in an online version of the course. However, they reported only changes in performance from a pretest to a posttest, and no comparisons with performance in the traditional course. This pretest–posttest design suffers from maturation effects, another severe threat to internal validity (Cook & Campbell 1979).

Weekly Requirements

In addition to coding each study in terms of its design, we attempted to code each study in terms of whether there were weekly requirements (such as required online quizzes) imposed in the online course. Table 20.1 is organized by the presence of explicit weekly course requirements. Such requirements were imposed in 12 of the studies. Of these, seven (58 per cent) showed better performance in the online course, three (25 per cent) showed no difference, and one (8 per cent) showed better performance in the face-to-face course. The other study showed an improvement from pretest to posttest in an online course. This contrasts with the situation in the four studies in which specific weekly requirements were not imposed. Of the four studies in that category, three (75 per cent) showed no online vs. face-to-face difference, and one (25 per cent) showed better performance in the face-to-face course. Of the remaining 16 cases in which we could not determine if weekly requirements were imposed, three studies (19 per cent) showed a significant difference favoring the online class, 11 (58 per cent) showed no difference, and only one (6 per cent) showed a significant difference in favor of the face-to-face course. An additional study showed mixed results, with online students performing better on conceptual material and face-to-face students performing better on procedural skills.

This analysis suggests that the imposition of weekly requirements is an important factor in determining whether online courses produce more learning than face-to-face courses. Strict weekly requirements, which can be more easily imposed and monitored in online than in face-to-face courses, lead to better performance in online than in face-to-face courses. We should, however, make one more qualifying observation. The large number of reports classified as "unknown" with respect to requirements for online students is indicative of an appalling lack of specifics in those reports. Frequently, the online course components and activities are listed, but there is no mention of exactly what the students were expected to do with them, and often there is no mention of course credit for those activities.

In spite of these caveats, we propose that a primary reason for discrepancies in the literature is the type of requirements placed on students, with stringent contingencies leading to superior performance in online courses. Better performance in Texas Tech's online psychology course than in the traditional course can be attributed to such contingencies. Another study that supports the contingency hypothesis is described below. However, contingencies do not fully explain the discrepancies among outcomes, so studies showing other potentially important factors are also described.

An example of an experimental study with structured requirements is Poirier and Feldman (2004). They randomly assigned students to participate in either a large lecture course or in an online course. Although the number of students who were randomly assigned in each group was small ($N = 11$ and $N = 12$), students taking the online course performed better on examinations than students taking the lecture course. In addition to reading a textbook, the online students had several requirements each week that involved course material: participating in two online discussions and completing several activities on the Web. With these specific requirements, students in the online course performed better on examinations than did students assigned to the face-to-face course.

In contrast, Wang and Newlin (2000) reported a study in which the online course was relatively unstructured. Students in the online course were required to attend two biweekly lectures in online chat rooms. In addition, they were encouraged to use an electronic forum board and email messages. Students did not post messages on the forum very often, averaging a total of 4.67 postings over the 15-week course (fewer than one a week). They read an average of 84 postings over the 15 weeks (fewer than six a week). In addition to low averages, there was wide variability in how often students interacted with the forum board. Students in both the online and traditional sections had homework, but apparently it was not done online. There did not appear to be any specific requirements to ensure that students in the online group interacted regularly with the material. Wang and Newlin found no differences on unit examinations for online and traditional versions of statistical methods courses, and they reported better performance on the final examination in the traditional course. Apparently, there were no explicit contingencies to ensure that online students interacted with course material, so it is not surprising that those students did not learn better than students in the traditional face-to-face course.

Collaboration in Online Courses

Students in Wang and Newlin's (2000) online course also differed from those in their traditional course in that they were encouraged to collaborate on unit examinations prior to the final examination, and they were allowed to use their books and notes on unit examinations. Students in the traditional course could not collaborate and they could not use books and notes on any examination. Students in both types of courses were not permitted to collaborate or use books and notes on the final examination. Collaboration on unit examinations, along with the use of books and notes, may have hampered preparation for the individual final examination for online students, whereas students in the traditional course may have been better prepared because all of their examinations were individual.

There is also evidence that increased collaboration may facilitate learning in online courses. Schutte (1997) reported a large difference (20 percentage points) in favor of students in an online statistics course over those in a face-to-face statistics course. He attributed this to an inability on the part of students in the online course to ask questions of the professor in a face-to-face way. To compensate, students formed study groups and collaborated in their learning. Schutte attributed the benefits of online learning to this. Jung *et al.* (2002) compared three versions of an online course: a standard course in which students interacted mainly with Web-based materials; a collaborative course in which groups of learners participated in discussions; and a social interaction course in which instructors interacted individually with online students. Learning was better in the social interaction version of the course than in the standard version, with the collaborative version of the course falling in between. Adding more student collaboration and personal contact with the instructor may facilitate learning in online courses.

Learning Concepts vs. Procedures

The type of material that is tested may also explain some of the discrepancies in the literature. Parker and Gemino (2001) tested both abstract and conceptual material, and students' abilities to use technical tools, such as software applications. Students in online courses performed better than students in face-to-face courses on the conceptual material, but students in face-to-face courses performed better in the use of technical tools. Parker and Gemino concluded that online learning is better suited to teaching concepts than teaching procedures. However, this conclusion needs to be qualified. The online course format involved much asynchronous discussion and the discussion format may be helpful for conceptual understandings. Other studies (e.g., Shute 1995) have shown that the acquisition of procedural skills was enhanced by computer-based training so a different course format might have improved learning of technical tools in the Parker and Gemino study.

Conclusions about Learning in Online Courses

Although a general review of the online vs. face-to-face learning literature shows mixed results, we believe that we can conclude that online learning produces positive results relative to traditional courses when college courses are structured with clear contingencies. This does not, however, support the conclusion that the medium by which a course is delivered is responsible for increased learning. The nature of the online environment allows for frequent requirements that can be easily monitored. That is, students learn more in online than in traditional courses because they are required to do more in online than in traditional courses. In the next section, specific student behavior in interacting with online course material is discussed.

WHAT INFLUENCES STUDY BEHAVIORS?

There are few studies in the literature that address the question of student study behaviors in online courses. The meta-analyses (Bayraktar, 2001–2002; Shachar & Neumann 2003; Bernard *et al.* 2004) did not code any factors related to study behavior. One of the advantages of online instruction is that it provides opportunities to record students' interactions with course materials. These data may provide insights into the effectiveness of various instructional manipulations that go beyond how students perform on tests and how satisfied they are with courses. Given the richness of the available data, it is surprising that only a few researchers have reported the frequency with which students visit various types of web-pages ("hits").

Taraban *et al.* (1999) used electronic logs to investigate study behaviors in an early version of the online course at Texas Tech University. As noted earlier, this online general psychology course was highly structured (Maki *et al.* 2000). Students were required to meet weekly deadlines in order to gain course points. Each week, they were required to complete two online activities for course points: pass two interactive quizzes with immediate feedback at 80 per cent or better, and complete a computerized demonstration and answer questions about it. In addition, online students received points for attending a class each week. In later versions of the online course (Maki & Maki 2000), points were awarded for preview activities – quizzes covering chapter outlines or lists of frequently asked questions. In earlier versions of the course (Taraban *et al.* 1999), students were merely advised to engage in those preview activities (i.e., without quizzes and without explicit course credit). In the face-to-face course, the students simply were assigned reading material and encouraged to come to class three times a week. For all students, unit examinations occurred every three weeks.

In the online course described by Taraban *et al.* (1999), voluminous records of student behaviors were collected. Records included logs of "hits" on the course website and electronic mail logs (the method of recording quiz results). In addition, 20 students were asked to report the time they spent on the course, day-by-day. The interest here is in the distribution of study behaviors over time. Were such behaviors controlled by the contingencies of the quiz system? If so, the frequencies of quiz-related behaviors would peak just prior to scheduled quizzes and exams. The course was organized into three-week units, with each unit terminated by a unit exam. During the 21 days before each exam, online quizzes were required at the end of each week. Taraban *et al.* (1999) reported that quiz submission frequencies were minimal during the first five days of each one-week quiz cycle and accelerated during the last two days of the cycle. Students' subjective reports of study times corresponded to the objective data. Students' behavior showed a scalloping effect with little activity early in the unit cycle and much activity at the end of the cycle.

Other activities for which the contingencies were not explicit showed different patterns. For example, in the online course described by Taraban *et al.* (1999), the chapter outlines were intended to serve as advance organizers, but there was no point value attached to studying the outlines. If the student behaviors conformed to the intent, then the hits on outline pages should have occurred early each week. Instead, outline page counters showed little activity during the first two weeks of each examination cycle but accelerated rapidly during the week before the examination. Apparently, the students used the outlines for *re*view rather than the intended *pre*view. Students in the online course studied these outlines just before mid-term examinations when study of the outlines had no course points attached.

Wang and Newlin (2000) correlated course grades with the frequency of usage of the course website. Total hits on the course homepage, number of postings written, and number of postings read all correlated positively with course grade (which did not include credit for these activities). Students in the online course who were more actively involved with course material performed better in the class than those who were less involved. Because there were no explicit contingencies to regulate student involvement, there was wide variability in how often students interacted with online course materials.

Elvers *et al.* (2003) studied procrastination in online courses vs. traditional courses. Students in both types of courses had access to the same materials on the World Wide

Web, but there were no contingencies related to accessing these materials. The difference between the two courses was that Web-based material supplemented lectures and the textbook in the face-to-face course, but Web-based material supplemented only the textbook in the online course; there were no lectures. Elvers *et al.* recorded the first date on which a student accessed the website relative to the test over material covered on the webpages. The difference between these two dates was a measure of procrastination, with smaller differences showing more procrastination. Procrastination scores were not significantly different for the online and traditional courses. However, correlations between procrastination scores and exam scores were significantly larger in the online than in the traditional courses. That is, students who delayed more tended to do worse on examinations, and this was especially true in the online course. More students in the online courses than in the traditional courses reported that it was easy to get behind on coursework. This suggests that procrastination is more of a problem in online courses where Web-based material is the only supplement to the textbook than in traditional courses where lectures, which are distributed uniformly over time, supplement the textbook.

Heffner and Cohen (2005) reported numbers of hits on various types of course webpages. They found the greatest number of hits on the pages that included material related to requirements (lecture topics, assignment due dates, links to Web-based reading assignments) and to pages designed for review for the final examination. Pages that were not required, such as instructor biographies and links to psychology-related websites, were accessed rarely. Bernardo *et al.* (2004) reported that pages containing required readings and informative pages (such as the syllabus, tutorials, and lists of technical support staff) were viewed most frequently, and the message board and frequently-asked-question pages were viewed least frequently.

Student self-reports showed a similar pattern of usage. In the online courses at Texas Tech (Maki *et al.* 2000), students were asked how often they used course components. Students reported that they used the course syllabus more than once a week, and that they used the announcement page, the chapter outlines, and the frequently asked questions about once a week. This is consistent with course requirements. Links to related sites, however, were rarely used overall, and they were never used by 46 per cent of the students. Use of these links had no consequences; they were included so that interested students could learn more.

Results from Maki *et al.* (2000); Bernardo *et al.* (2004) and Heffner and Cohen (2005) showed that students rarely use the links that have no point values attached. Wang and Newlin (2000) apparently had no contingencies attached to reading and writing postings to their electronic forum, and students varied widely in how often they did this. Components of online courses are used with a frequency that reflects the course requirements, supporting the conclusion that students' behaviors are guided by explicit course contingencies. The point values assigned to components of online courses are strong determiners of how those components will be used. Contingencies are known to be strong determinants of behavior (Ferster & Skinner 1957), so it is not surprising that they are effective in online courses. When no value is assigned to course components, the components will be used in sometimes unpredictable ways, if used at all. Essentially the same point was made by Hiltz (1997): "Simply making an [asynchronous learning network] available and telling students to use it . . . does not insure its use. If it is not a 'required' and graded, integral part of the course, the majority of the students will never use it at all" (p. 2). The same point has been made elsewhere (Maki & Maki 1997; 2000; Taraban *et al.* 1999).

ARE STUDENTS MORE OR LESS SATISFIED?

Although student satisfaction is not specifically cognitive in nature, it is important for an instructor's decision about whether to instruct an online course. Thus, knowledge about likely patterns of satisfaction with online learning is important from an instructional point of view.

Previous Reviews of Course Satisfaction

In their meta-analysis, Bernard *et al.* (2004) studied effect sizes for attitudes toward the course in addition to the amount learned. Overall they found that attitudes toward the distance courses were more negative than attitudes toward the traditional courses, especially in the synchronous cases. Course attrition was greater in the distance than in the traditional courses, especially when the distance course was asynchronous. Although each measure of satisfaction favored the traditional course over the distance course, Bernard *et al.* emphasized that there was very large variability in effect sizes across studies. They were able to capture some of that variance in satisfaction with methodology and pedagogical variables, but wide variability remained.

Satisfaction in General Psychology Online at Texas Tech University

Consistent with Bernard *et al.*'s meta-analysis, students in Maki *et al.*'s (2000) online course were less satisfied with the course than were students in the face-to-face course. Students in the face-to-face courses gave significantly higher ratings to questions pertaining to interest in psychology, the chances of recommending the course to a friend, and enrolling in the same section again. In particular, having a live instructor appears to have increased the satisfaction scores (see Williams & Ceci 1997). Interestingly, for the satisfaction measures, the interactions between course format and instructor and between course format and semester were significant. Unlike the learning measures, satisfaction seems driven by instructor personality and time of year, as well as by course format. Moreover, students in the online classes thought that the course involved more work than a traditional course, and this perception may have negatively influenced overall course satisfaction (Maki *et al.* 2000).

Students also rated course components in Maki *et al.*'s (2000) study. Generally, online course components were rated highly. The required weekly quizzes with feedback were rated the highest, as very useful. Chapter outlines, interactive computer exercises, and frequently asked questions were rated as moderately useful. The least popular aspect of the online course was the weekly class meetings, although these were rated between slightly and moderately useful. Thus, in spite of the fact that students in online courses gave lower overall ratings of satisfaction than students in face-to-face courses, the online students rated most course components quite positively.

Variables that Influence Course Satisfaction

Table 20.1 shows the satisfaction outcomes for studies included in our literature review that reported satisfaction measures. Many of the studies in Table 20.1 did not report satisfaction in either online or face-to-face courses, and several studies reported satisfaction measures for the online course but not for the face-to-face course. Thus, we were able to use fewer data than for the learning measure. Nevertheless, our review suggests that global satisfaction measures do not differentiate online from face-to-face methods of instruction. Of the 15 studies that included a quantitative comparison of satisfaction in online and face-to-face courses, four (27 per cent) reported higher satisfaction in the online courses, five (33 per cent) reported no differences, and four (27 per cent) reported greater satisfaction in the face-to-face than in online courses. Several other studies reported mixed results across different measures of satisfaction. Table 20.1 suggests that there is no clear relationship between weekly requirements and overall satisfaction with online courses.

Just as Maki *et al.*'s (2000) study can be cited as evidence for greater satisfaction in face-to-face courses than in online courses, other studies can be cited to show greater satisfaction with online than face-to-face courses. Schutte (1997), who found much better learning in online courses, also found higher satisfaction in the online course. Students reported a great deal of student-to-student collaboration in that study, which may explain the greater satisfaction in the online course. Jung *et al.* (2002) found that students' satisfaction with online courses was greater in their collaborative online course in which class discussions occurred than in less collaborative versions of their online courses. This suggests that increasing required collaboration among students in online courses might be one way to increase their satisfaction. There was little student-to-student collaboration in the Maki *et al.* (2000) courses, so this may help to explain the lower satisfaction in the online version of the course.

Somewhat surprisingly, several studies have reported that online students report more student-to-student contact (Hiltz 1993; Schutte 1997; Campbell *et al.* 2002; Poirier & Feldman 2004), more student–instructor interaction (Poirier & Feldman 2004), or more instructor availability (Campbell *et al.* 2002) relative to face-to-face courses. As with learning, the structure of the course (e.g., whether students interact; responsiveness of the instructor) probably determines the level of student satisfaction in online courses.

Other variables, such as perceived workload and specific instructor, may also contribute to the variability in satisfaction noted by Bernard *et al.* (2004) and observed in our review of the literature. The literature is mixed on whether perceived workload is greater in online than in traditional courses. Consistent with the findings of Hiltz (1993) and Schutte (1997), Maki *et al.* (2000) reported that students found the online course to involve more work than their face-to-face courses. However, Jeannette and Meyer (2002) and Poirier and Feldman (2004) reported no differences in perceived workload for face-to-face and online courses. Thus satisfaction differences do not appear to correlate with differences in perceived workload. Specific instructor, however, is an important determinant of satisfaction in face-to-face courses but not in online courses (Maki & Maki 2003).

In Maki *et al.*'s (2000) study, the most positive ratings for the online course were given to questions involving the flexibility of the course and the requirement of coming to class only once a week. Students were moderately positive about having to learn on their own. They did not think that more lectures were needed. However, students did not perceive the online course as being more efficient than traditional courses. Hiltz (1993) also reported that students did not perceive online courses as more efficient than traditional courses. Other studies have also reported that online courses are viewed as more flexible and convenient than face-to-face courses (e.g., Schutte 1997; Wegner *et al.* 1999; Cooper 2001; Jeannette & Meyer 2002). Students in the courses described by Wegner *et al.* (1999) and Cooper (2001) appreciated the opportunity to learn independently in the online courses. However, Wegner *et al.* also reported that students complained about the lack of direction in the course and the lack of content. Students made comments such as "I had to teach myself."

Neuhauser (2002) reported that students in online courses rated components such as chapter pretests, chapter reviews, assignments, and online lectures highly. In fact, students in the online courses rated chapter pretests and chapter reviews more highly than did students in face-to-face courses. The only course component that was favored more by students in the face-to-face course than in the online course (although not significantly) was class discussions. Summers *et al.* (2005) reported that online students gave significantly lower ratings to class discussions than face-to-face students.

Hiltz (1993) used multiple regression to predict satisfaction ratings for the online versions of courses, but she did not conduct a similar analysis for face-to-face courses. The 18 predictor variables, including ratings of course convenience, ratings of ease of access to the professor, and ratings of course involvement, explained 67 per cent of the variance in overall satisfaction. Thurmond *et al.* (2002) conducted a similar multiple regression analysis to determine predictors of overall satisfaction in online courses. Amount of time studying for the course, participation in discussions, and knowing the instructor did not predict significant variance in satisfaction. However, Thurmond *et al.* found that satisfaction was highest among students who perceived that the instructor's comments were timely, who acknowledged a variety of ways to assess learning, and who worked in teams or groups. Although these variables may be important for satisfaction in online courses, they are probably also important in traditional courses (Maki & Maki 2003).

WHAT INDIVIDUAL DIFFERENCES MODULATE LEARNING AND SATISFACTION?

Individual Differences in Amount Learned from Online Courses

Maki and Maki (2003) conducted analyses from four semesters with 659 students in online and face-to-face courses in order to understand what variables related to learning. Course format, semester and time of course, instructor, student's year in college, student's major, Big Five personality characteristics (conscientiousness, openness to experience, emotional stability, introversion, and agreeableness), and student's perceived workload were entered in a hierarchical multiple regression analysis to predict learning. Each of these variables was also entered into the regression as an interaction with course format in order to determine whether the variable affected learning in online courses more or less than in face-to-face courses.

After removing variability due to pre-course knowledge, course format accounted for significant variance in learning with online students performing better. Year in college accounted for significant variance with more advanced students performing better than less advanced students. Major also accounted for significant variance, with science and technology majors and humanities majors performing better than other groups. More introverted students and those who were more intellectual (both Big Five personality characteristics) performed better on tests. However, none of these variables interacted with course format, suggesting that certain types of students did better in both face-to-face and online courses.

Several other studies also show that certain types of students do better in online courses, but students with those characteristics also perform better in traditional courses. Navarro and Shoemaker (1999) compared online and face-to-face course formats on seven student characteristic variables, including gender, ethnicity, distance lived from campus, age, and grade-point average. Although several of these characteristics were related to course performance, they found that none of these variables interacted with course format. Sankaran and Bui (2001) compared performance of surface learners (who learn by rote repetition) and deep learners (who learn by relating and elaborating concepts) in online and face-to-face courses. Whereas deep learners performed better, this was true for both types of courses. Another study, using a different type of learning style, showed no effects. Neuhauser (2002) found that preferred mode of learning (visual, auditory, or kinesthetic) and temperament (sensation/judging, sensation/perceiving, intuition/feeling, intuition/thinking) did not predict performance in either online or face-to-face courses. Each of these studies showed similar effects of student characteristics in online and face-to-face comparison groups, indicating that it is important to include a comparison group before concluding that certain types of students are particularly well suited for online courses.

There are several other studies in which student characteristics were used to predict performance in online courses with no comparison to traditional course control groups. Hiltz (1993) used multiple regression to predict grades in online courses, but she did not perform a similar analysis for traditional courses. She found that both ability and attitude explained variance in course performance. Her measure of ability, scores on the Verbal Scholastic Assessment Test (SAT) scores, related positively to course performance. Verbal ability, along with perceived course convenience, were the only significant predictors of course performance from among 12 predictor variables, but the regression analysis explained only 14 per cent of the variance in grades. Kim and Schniederjans (2004) investigated the relationship between the Big Five personality factors and performance in an online course. They found that all five factors in the Big Five were related to examination performance. Wang and Newlin (2000) found that online course performance correlated significantly with locus of control, mastery motivation, and need for cognition. The researchers in these three studies did not use face-to-face courses as a comparison groups. The literature suggests that the variables they identified as effective for learning in online courses would correlate with performance in traditional courses also.

An interaction between student characteristics and course format is necessary to show that some specific characteristics make students particularly well suited for online courses as opposed to traditional face-to-face courses. Maki and Maki (2003) added questions in the second year of their course to try to identify variables that might interact with class format. The only variable that predicted performance in online courses but not in face-to-face courses was students' preference for class discussion. Students who indicated high liking for class discussion did more poorly in the online course than students who indicated less preference for class discussion, but preference for class discussion had no effect on examination performance in the face-to-face course. Other variables, such as computer anxiety, frequency of use of the World Wide Web, a desire to work independently, and expected examination performance at the beginning of the course affected examination performance, but not differentially between online and face-to-face courses. Thus, Maki and Maki (2003) found several variables that affected performance in online and face-to-face courses, but very few predicted performance differentially for the two course formats.

Online courses, as compared to face-to-face courses, might be especially beneficial for students of low or high comprehension ability. To test this, Maki and Maki (2002) measured comprehension ability of a subset of students taking the online and face-to-face sections of the general psychology course. The intent was to determine if the differential gains in content knowledge could be accounted for by an aptitude-treatment interaction (Snow & Yalow 1982). Comprehension ability was defined by the combined score of the written, auditory, and pictorial portions of the MMCB (Gernsbacher & Varner 1988). The MMCB score was used as a predictor of performance on course examinations and on the difficult psychology content questions. After variance from pre-course scores on the content questions was removed, Maki and Maki (2002) found an interaction between the MMCB and course format for both examination scores and posttest scores on the content questions. This interaction occurred because students with higher comprehension ability scores performed better in the online course than in the face-to-face course, but students who were lower in comprehension ability did not differ in their performance across course format. Thus, the online course benefited students who were high in comprehension ability rather than boosting performance of students who have less ability.

Similar interactions between ability and format of learning materials have been found by in two earlier studies, although these did not involve entire courses. Recker and Pirolli (1995) compared learning of a computer program using traditional text or hypertext. Students with more previous knowledge learned more from the hypertext version than from the standard text, but students with less prior knowledge learned less from hypertext than from traditional text. Shute and Gawlick-Grendell (1994) compared learning from a computer-based statistics tutor with learning from a paper-and-pencil workbook. Participants were divided into high and low cognitive abilities based on a series of cognitive ability tests. High-ability participants performed better in the computer-based tutorial, but participants with lower cognitive abilities performed about the same with the two tutorial formats.

The literature discussed so far shows that higher-ability students learn more in hypermedia presentations than in lecture presentations, but lower-ability students do not show this difference. However, in other studies, use of hypermedia has tended to equalize the performance of lower- and higher-ability students because the hypermedia environment provides more learning aids. Shute (1995) showed that lower-ability learners benefited more from an intelligent tutor than did higher-ability learners, but only in the learning of procedural skills and not in gaining conceptual knowledge. In a study using economics courses, Brown and Liedholm (2002) found that female students performed more poorly than male students in face-to-face economics courses, but the difference was smaller and not significant in online economics courses. They attributed the better performance of females to the use of non-timed, Web-based problems that were not available in the face-to-face courses. It appears to be possible to design hypermedia materials in a way that benefits lower-ability students.

Individual Differences in Satisfaction in Online Courses

The literature on satisfaction is similar to that on learning. Very few studies show interactions between satisfaction and course format. Maki and Maki (2003) used multiple regression analyses to predict student satisfaction. For this analysis, potential predictor variables were course format, semester, instructor, perceived workload, examination performance, year in college, major, and Big Five personality scores. Course format explained significant variance with greater satisfaction associated with the face-to-face course. After variance related to course format was removed, the only other significant predictors of variance were instructor, workload, and examination performance. Students who thought they worked less hard and who did better on examinations were more satisfied with the course. However, none of the variables interacted with course format, suggesting that the variables did not differentially predict performance in online and face-to-face courses. In the second phase of this study with more specific questions, Maki and Maki (2003) found that a preference for class discussion interacted with course format. Students liked the face-to-face course more if they preferred class discussion, but this variable was unrelated to course satisfaction in the online course.

Sankaran *et al.* (2000) compared predictors of learning and satisfaction in online and face-to-face courses. They reported that students with a positive attitude toward the Web format learned more in the Web-based course than in a face-to-face course, but students with a positive attitude toward the face-to-face format learned more in the face-to-face course than in the Web-based course. However, possible conclusions from their study are limited because they did not report statistical tests of the implied interaction.

In another a study that compared course formats, Benbunan-Fich and Hiltz (2003) conducted regression analyses to identify predictors of students' perceptions of learning (but not actual learning) in online, mixed, and face-to-face courses. They found that several variables predicted greater perceptions of learning including motivation to learn, amount of collaboration with other students, active involvement in the course, and convenience of the course. However, these variables showed similar relationships to perceived learning in online, face-to-face, and mixed course formats.

Conclusions about Individual Differences in Online Courses

Our review of studies to determine which characteristics of students interact with course format yielded very few examples of interactions. In many cases, characteristics of success in online courses were reported without any comparison with face-to-face courses. In other cases, there were main effects of student characteristics, but interactions between characteristics and course format were not found. This is true for both learning and satisfaction measures. Maki and Maki's (2002) study of ability differences in online and face-to-face courses is one of the few in the literature that shows an interaction between an ability measure and course format. Students with higher comprehension abilities performed better in the online course than in the face-to-face course, but this was not true for students with lower abilities. Generally, personality characteristics that lead to successful online course performance also lead to successful face-to-face course performance.

CONCLUSIONS

We began this chapter by asking four questions about online learning. Table 20.2 summarizes the answers to these questions based on our research and other recent studies.

How Much is Learned?

Clark (1994) was correct when he argued that it is the structure of a course that determines learning and not the medium in which the course is offered. When online courses are structured so that course credit is attached to regularly occurring online activities (such as quizzes and homework problems), learning from such courses can be better than face-to-face learning. Unstructured online courses with few requirements can also produce greater learning than face-to-face courses if extensive collaboration among students occurs.

What Influences Study Behaviors?

Placing value on the online activities in the form of course credit is critical to maintaining student interactions with the course. Perhaps an unfortunate side-effect of the cognitive revolution has been the tendency to believe that cognitive aids, delivered online, are in and of themselves sufficiently motivating to keep student interest in and use of those aids at high levels. This belief is simply wrong. Students behave in a way prescribed by the matching law (see Anderson 2000, p. 139). If the relative reinforcing value of an online activity is zero, the proportion of effort expended on that activity is also zero. Moreover, the temporal distribution of such value controls the distribution of student interactions with online activities; proper use of the contingencies may provide cognitive benefits in the form increased retention because of distributed study.

Are Students More or Less Satisfied?

Bernard *et al.*'s (2004) meta-analysis and other well-controlled studies have shown less satisfaction in online than in face-to-face courses. However, the meta-analysis also showed substantial variability in satisfaction results (Bernard *et al.* 2004). Satisfaction depends on such things as amount of collaboration among students, instructor enthusiasm, and perceptions of the workload and its distribution. Students generally rate components of online courses highly, even if they give lower overall ratings to online than to face-to-face courses.

Which Individual Differences Modulate Learning and Satisfaction?

Students with high comprehension ability benefit more from online relative to face-to-face courses than do students with lower comprehension ability. However, students with lesser abilities have been reported to benefit from intelligent tutoring on specific skills. Students

Table 20.2 Conclusions about learning and satisfaction in online versus face-to-face courses

Conclusion	References	Strength of Conclusion
Learning		
Course structure and not the medium of presentation determines learning.	Clark (1994); this review	Supported by most studies
Online courses with structured requirements produce more learning han face-to-face courses	Table 20.1, this review	Exceptions exist in the literature
Unstructured courses that require more collaboration among online learners than face-to-face learners produce more learning.	Jung *et al.* (2000); Schutte (1997)	Explanation is post hoc
Student Behavior		
Students' interaction with online materials is guided by contingencies.	Bernardo (2004); Heffner and Cohen (2005); Taraban *et al.* (1999)	Relevant to learning in general.
Materials placed online without contingencies will be used rarely or with large variability.	Heffner and Cohen (2005); Bernardo (2004); Maki *et al.* (2000); Wang and Newlin (2000)	Supported by several studies.
Satisfaction		
Satisfaction may be higher in online or face-to-face courses, independently of learning differences.	Bernard *et al.* (2000); Maki *et al.* (2000); Summers *et al.* (2005)	Mixed results
Collaboration among students may increase satisfaction.	Jung *et al.* (2002); Schutte (1997)	Shown in several studies
Students rate online course components highly even if they prefer traditional courses.	Maki *et al.* (2000); Neuhauser (2002)	Shown in several studies.
Individual Differences		
Students with higher verbal abilities do better in online than face-to-face courses, but students with lower verbal abilities show no difference.	Maki and Maki (2002); Recker and Pirolli (1995); Shute and Gawlick-Grendell (1994)	Shown in several studies, but exceptions exist.
Students who prefer class discussion do more poorly in and are less satisfied with online than face-to-face courses.	Maki and Maki (2003)	Shown only in one study.
Many personality and learning style variables influence learning in online courses, but they also influence learning in traditional courses.	Maki and Maki (2003); Navarro and Shoemaker (1999); Sankaran and Bui (2001)	Shown in al studies that used a traditional comparison group.

who prefer class discussion do more poorly and are less satisfied with online than with face-to-face courses than are students who show lower preferences for class discussion. When appropriate designs have been used, individual differences in personality characteristics and learning styles that predict learning and satisfaction in online courses also predict them in traditional courses.

The answer to the individual differences question raises a methodological issue that we repeatedly encountered in our literature review and prompts us to make two recommendations. First, many of the reports comparing online and traditional courses used designs that were so flawed that it is impossible to draw valid conclusions from them. Future studies of online instruction (including evaluations of specific technology-based cognitive aids) need to employ sound experimental or quasi-experimental designs that have been available to the educational community for decades (Campbell & Stanley 1963; Cook & Campbell 1979). There is no good reason to do otherwise. Second, the level of reporting in most comparative studies, even those containing proper controls, usually has lacked enough detail to enable replication. We encountered disturbing tendencies to list online activities without elaboration and to refer to face-to-face courses as if all such courses were procedurally identical. Future studies of online learning need to be reported in enough detail so that other educators can evaluate and implement specific aspects of both traditional and online courses.

We close this chapter with one other observation and a glimpse into the future of online learning research and development. Our review of the literature complements recent meta-analytical work in finding that online learning is no worse than, and often no better than, that achieved by traditional courses. Pedagogy accounted for more variance in effect size than did course medium (Bernard *et al.* 2004). The specific activities in which the students engage, then, appear more important than the media by which the activities are delivered, a view consistent with that of Clark (1994) who argued that media per se do not influence learning. We probably are never going to be able to answer the question about whether online learning is more effective than face-to-face learning because the answer depends upon how the learning in each course format is structured. Future research should be aimed at the application of specific principles from cognitive psychology in online courses. We know that factors such as level of processing of material, distribution of learning experiences, testing versus continued study of material, and exposure to multiple examples of concepts influence learning. The online environment provides an ideal opportunity to test the application of these cognitive processes in a real-world setting in that each of these variables can be manipulated in online materials. In addition, students' frequency of interaction with the materials can be measured. A program of research that includes comparisons of online courses containing specific cognitive components known to influence learning in the laboratory would allow both researchers and educators to understand which of these components are most effective in actual educational settings.

AUTHOR NOTE

The development of the online General Psychology course and the evaluation research summarized in this chapter was supported by Grant NSF DUE-9752349 from the National Science Foundation to R. H. Maki and W. S. Maki ("Using Technology to Transform

Instruction and Improve Learning in Introductory Psychology"). Address correspondence to Ruth.Maki@ttu.edu or Bill.Maki@ttu.edu.

REFERENCES

Anderson, J. R. (2000). *Learning and Memory: An Integrated Approach* (2nd edn). New York: John Wiley & Sons.

Bahrick, H. P., Bahrick, L. E., Bahrick, A. S. & Bahrick, P. E. (1993). Maintenance of foreign language vocabulary and the spacing effect. *Psychological Science, 4*, 316–322.

Bayraktar, S. (2001–2002). A meta-analysis of the effectiveness of computer-assisted instruction in science education. *Journal of Research on Technology in Education, 34*, 173–188.

Benbunan-Fich, R. & Hiltz, S. R. (2003). Mediators of the effectiveness of online courses. *IEEE Transactions on Professional Communication, 46*, 298–312.

Bernard, R. M., Abrami, P. C., Lou, Y. *et al.* (2004). How does distance education compare with classroom instruction? A meta-analysis of the empirical literature. *Review of Educational Research, 74*, 379–439.

Bernardo, V., Ramos, M. P., Plapler, H. *et al.* (2004). Web-based learning in undergraduate medical education: development and assessment of an online course on experimental surgery. *International Journal of Medical Informatics, 73*, 731–742.

Bradshaw, A. C. & Johari, A. (2002). Effects of white space in learning via the web. *Journal of Educational Computing Research, 26*, 191–201.

Brown, B. W. & Liedholm, C. E. (2002). Can Web courses replace the classroom in principles of microeconomics? *American Economic Review, 92*, 444–448.

Buchanan, E., Xie, H., Brown, M. & Wolfram, D. (2001). A systematic study of Web-based and traditional instruction in an MLIS program: success factors and implications for curriculum design. *Journal of Education for Library and Information Science, 42*, 274–288.

Cahill, D. & Catanzaro, D. (1997). Teaching first-year Spanish on-line. *Calico Journal, 14*, 97–114.

Campbell, M., Floyd, J. & Sheridan, J. B. (2002). Assessment of student performance and attitudes for courses taught online versus onsite. *Journal of Applied Business Research, 18*, 45–51.

Campbell, D. T. & Stanley, J. C. (1963). *Experimental and Quasi-Experimental Designs for Research*. Chicago, IL: Rand-McNally.

Casanova, R. S. (2001). Student performance in an online general college chemistry course. Retrieved May 18, 2005. Available at: http://www.chem.vt.edu/confchem/2001/c/04/capefear.html.

Chou, S-W. & Liu, C-H. (2005). Learning effectiveness in a Web-based virtual learning environment; a learner control perspective. *Journal of Computer-assisted Learning, 21*, 65–76.

Clark, R. E. (1994). Media will never influence learning. *Educational Technology Research &Development, 42*, 21–29.

Collins, M. (2000). Comparing Web correspondence and lecture versions of a second-year nonmajor biology course. *British Journal of Educational Technology, 31*, 21–27.

Cook, T. D. & Campbell, D. T. (1979). *Quasi-Experimentation: Design & Analysis Issues for Field Settings*. Boston, MA: Houghton Mifflin.

Cooper, L. W. (2001). A comparison of online and traditional computer applications classes. *T H E Journal, 28*, 52–56.

Dillon, A. & Gabbard, R. (1998). Hypermedia as an educational technology: a review of the quantitative research literature on learner comprehension, control, and style. *Review of Educational Research, 68*, 322–349.

Dufresne, R., Mestre, J., Hart, D. M. & Rath, K. A. (2002). The effect of Web-based homework on test performance in large enrollment introductory physics courses. *Journal of Computers in Mathematics and Science Teaching, 21*, 229–251.

Dutton, J., Dutton, M. & Perry, J. (2001). Do online students perform as well as lecture students? Retrieved May 26, 2005. Available at: http://www4.ncsu.edu/unity/users/d/dutton/public/research/online.pdf.

Educational Testing Service. (1994). *GRE: Practicing to Take the Psychology Test* (3rd edn). Princeton, NJ: Educational Testing Service.

Elvers, G. C., Polzella, D. J. & Graetz, K. (2003). Procrastination in online courses: performance and attitudinal differences. *Teaching of Psychology, 30*, 159–162.

Fallah, H. M. & Ubell, R. (2000). Blind scores in a graduate test: conventional compared with Web-based outcomes. Retrieved May 26, 2005. Available at: www.aln.org/publications/magazine/v4n2/fallah.asp.

Ferster, C. B. & Skinner, B. F. (1957). *Schedules of Reinforcement*. New York: Appleton-Century-Crofts.

Gernsbacher, M. A. & Varner, K. R. (1988). *The Multi-media Comprehension Battery* (Tech. Rep. No. 88–3). Eugene, OR: Institute of Cognitive and Decision Sciences.

Heffner, M. & *Cohen*, S. H. (2005). Evaluating student use of Web-based course material. *Journal of Instructional Psychology*, *32*, 74–81.

Hiltz, S. R. (1993). Correlates of learning in a virtual classroom. *International Journal of Man–Machine Studies*, *39*, 71–98.

Hiltz, S. R. (1997). Impacts of college-level courses via asynchronous learning networks: some preliminary results. Retrieved May 26, 2005. Available at: http://www.aln.org/publications/jaln/index.asp.

Jeannette, K. J. & Meyer, M. H. (2002). Online learning equals traditional classroom training for master gardeners. *Hort Technology*, *12*, 148–156.

Johnson, M. (2002). Introductory biology online: assessing outcomes of two student populations. *Journal of College Science Teaching*, *31*, 312–317.

Johnson, S. M. (2001). Teaching introductory international relations in an entirely Web-based environment: comparing student performance across and within groups. *Education at a Distance, 15*(1). Retrieved May 27, 2005. Available at: http://www.usdla.org/html/journal/JAN01_Issue/article01.html.

Jung, I., Choi, S., Lim, C. & Leem, J. (2002). Effects of different types of interaction on learning achievement, satisfaction, and participation in web-based instruction. *Innovations in Education and Teaching International*, *39*, 153–162.

Kim, E. B. & Schniederjans, M. J. (2004). The role of personality in web-based distance education courses. *Communications of the ACM*, *47*, 95–98.

LaRose, R., Gregg, J. & Eastin, M. (1998). Audiographic telecourses for the Web: an experiment. *Journal of Computer-Mediated Communication, 4*. Retrieved May 26, 2005. Available at: http://www.ascusc.org/jcmc/vol4/issue2/larose.html#ABSTRACT.

Lehto, M., Zhu, W. & Carpenter, B. (1995). The relative effectiveness of hypertext and text. *International Journal of Human-Computer Interaction*, *7*, 293–313.

Lilja, D. J. (2001). Comparing instructional delivery methods for teaching computer systems performance analysis. *IEEE Transactions on Education*, *44*, 35–40.

Logan, E. & Conerly, K. (2002). Students creating community: an investigation of student interactions in a Web-based distance learning environment. Retrieved May 27, 2005. Available at: http://www.icte.org/T01_Library/T01_253.pdf.

McCrae, R. R. & Costa, P. T. Jr (1987). Validation of the five-factor model of personality across instruments and observers. *Journal of Personality and Social Psychology*, *52*, 81–90.

Maki, R. H. & Maki, W. S. (2003). Prediction of learning and satisfaction in online and lecture courses. *Journal of Educational Computing Research*, *28*, 187–219.

Maki, R. H., Maki, W. S., Patterson, M. & Whittaker, P. D. (2000). Evaluation of an Online introductory psychology course: I. learning and satisfaction in online versus lecture courses. *Behavior Research Methods, Instruments & Computers*, *32*, 230–239.

Maki, W. S. (2005). Assessing outcomes. *Invention and Impact: Building Excellence in Undergraduate Science, Technology, Engineering, and Mathematics (STEM) Education*. Washington: National Science Foundation.

Maki, W. S. & Maki, R. H. (1997). Learning without lectures: a case study. *IEEE Computer, 30*, 107–108.

Maki, W. S. & Maki, R. H. (2000). Evaluation of a Web-based introductory psychology course: II. contingency management to increase use of online study aids. *Behavior Research Methods, Instruments & Computers*, *32*, 240–245.

Maki, W. S. & Maki, R. H. (2002). Multimedia comprehension skill predicts differential outcomes of Web-based and lecture courses. *Journal of Experimental Psychology: Applied*, *8*, 85–98.
Mayer, R. E., Dyck, J. L. & Cook, L. K. (1984). Techniques that help readers build mental models from scientific text: definitions pretraining and signaling. *Journal of Educational Psychology*, *76*, 1089–1105.
Navarro, P. & Shoemaker, J. (1999). The power of cyberlearning: an empirical test. *Journal of Computing in Higher Education*, *11*, 29–54.
Neuhauser, C. (2002). Learning style and effectiveness of online and face-to-face instruction. *American Journal of Distance Education*, *16*, 99–113.
Parker, D. & Gemino, A. (2001). Inside online learning: comparison conceptual and technique learning performance in place-based and ALN formats. *Journal of Asynchronous Learning*, *5*, 1–11. Retrieved May 19, 2005. Available at: http://www.aln.org/publications/jaln/v5n2/v5n2_parkergemino.asp.
Piccoli, G., Ahmad, R. & Ives, B. (2001). Web-based virtual learning environments: a research framework and a preliminary assessment of effectiveness in basic IT skills training. *MIS Quarterly*, *25*, 401–426.
Piotrowski, C. & Vodanovich, S. J. (2004). Is Web-based instruction popular in psychology? A national survey. *Computers in Human Behavior*, *20*, 727–732.
Poirier, C. R. & Feldman, R. S. (2004). Teaching in cyberspace: online versus traditional instruction using a waiting-list experimental design. *Teaching of Psychology*, *31*, 59–64.
Recker, M. & Pirolli, P. (1995). Modeling individual differences in students' learning strategies. *Journal of the Learning Sciences*, *4*, 1–38.
Rothkopf, E. Z. & Bisbicos, E. E. (1967). Selective facilitative effects of interspersed questions on learning from written materials. *Journal of Educational Psychology*, *87*, 455–467.
Ryan, R. C. (2000). Lecture and online construction equipment and methods classes. *THE Journal*, *27*, 78–82.
Sankaran, S. R. & Bui, T. (2001). Impact of learning strategies and motivation on performance: a study in Web-based instruction. *Journal of Instructional Psychology*, *28*, 191–198.
Sankaran, S. R., Sankaran, D. & Bui, T. X. (2000). Effect of student attitude to course format on learning performance: an empirical study in web vs. lecture instruction. *Journal of Instructional Technology*, *27*, 66–73.
Schoenfeld-Tacher, R., McConnell, S. & Graham, M. (2001). Do no harm – A comparison of the effects of on-line vs. traditional delivery media on a science course. *Journal of Science Education and Technology*, *10*, 257–265.
Shachar, M. & Neumann, Y. (2003, October). Differences between traditional and distance education academic performances: a meta-analytic approach. *International Review of Research in Open and Distance Learning*, 1–19. Retrieved May 27, 2005. Available at: http://www.irrodl.org/content/v4.2/shachar-neumann.html.
Schulman, A. H. & Sims, R. L. (1999). Learning in an online format versus an inclass format: an experimental study. *THE Journal Online*, *26*. Retrieved May 27, 2005. Available at: http://www.thejournal.com/magazine/vault/a2090.cfm.
Schutte, J. G. (1997). Virtual teaching in higher education: the new intellectual superhighway or just another traffic jam? Retrieved May 26, 2005. Available at: http://www.csun.edu/sociology/virexp.htm.
Shute, V. J. (1995). SMART: student modeling approach for responsive tutoring. *User Modeling and User-Adapted Interaction*, *5*, 1–44.
Shute, V. J. & Gawlick-Grendell, L. A. (1994). What does the computer contribute to learning? *Computers in Education*, *23*, 177–186.
Snow, R. E. & Yalow, E. (1982). Education and intelligence. In R. J. Sternberg (ed.), *Handbook of Human Intelligence* (pp. 493–585). Cambridge: Cambridge University Press.
Stalcup, K. A. & Maki, W. S. (2002). Learning about learning on the web (Review of the book *Learning and Teaching on the World Wide Web*). *Applied Cognitive Psychology*, *16*, 863–864.
Summers, J. J., Waigandt, A. & Whittaker, T. A. (2005). A comparison of student achievement and satisfaction in an online versus a traditional face-to-face statistics class. *Innovative Higher Education*, *29*, 233–250.

Taraban, R., Maki, W. S. & Rynearson, K. (1999). Measuring study time distributions: implications for designing computer-based courses. *Behavior Research Methods, Instruments & Computers*, *31*, 263–269.

Thurmond, V. A., Wambach, K. & Connors, H. R. (2002). Evaluation of student satisfaction: determining the impact of Web-based environment by controlling for student characteristics. *The American Journal of Distance Education*, *16*, 169–189.

Thirunarayanan, M. O. & Perez-Prado, A. (2001–2002). Comparing Web-based and classroom-based learning: a quantitative study. *Journal of Research on Technology in Education*, *34*, 131–137.

Van der Berg, S. & Watt, J. (1991). Effects of educational setting on student responses to structured hypertext. *Journal of Computer-Based Instruction*, *18*, 118–124.

Wang, A. Y. & Newlin, M. H. (2000). Characteristics of students who enroll and succeed in psychology online classes. *Journal of Educational Psychology*, *92*, 137–143.

Waschull, S. B. (2001). The online delivery of psychology courses: attrition, performance, and evaluation. *Teaching of Psychology*, *28*, 143–147.

Wegner, S. B., Holloway, K. C. & Garton, E. M. (1999). The effects of Internet based instruction on student learning. *Journal of Asynchronous Learning Networks, 3*. Retrieved May 27, 2005. Available at: http://www.aln.org/alnweb/journal/Vol3_issue2/Wegner.htm.

Williams, W. M. & Ceci, S. J. (1997, September/October). "How'm I doing?" Problems with student ratings of instructors and courses. *Change*, *29*, 13–23.

SECTION 3

Applied Cognition in Human–Social Systems

CHAPTER 21

Instruction

Lindsey E. Richland, Marcia C. Linn, and Robert A. Bjork
University of California, USA

COGNITION AND INSTRUCTION: BRIDGING LABORATORY AND CLASSROOM SETTINGS

Researchers who conduct laboratory studies of memory, reasoning, and forgetting, almost always with undergraduate students as participants, have much in common with researchers who conduct classroom studies of memory, reasoning, and cumulative understanding, usually with pre-college students as participants. Yet studies within these two settings have traditionally used distinct research methods and addressed different questions (Linn 1990; Brown 1992; Collins 1992; Shonkoff & Phillips 2000; Shavelson & Towne 2002; Bell *et al.* 2004). This chapter focuses on ways that research deriving from laboratory and classroom traditions can be mutually informative. In particular, this chapter focuses on studies that both address the cognitive mechanisms underlying learning *and* seek answers to questions of genuine educational importance. While this chapter has broad implications for practitioners, its primary goal is to encourage traditional laboratory researchers to broaden research programs to address complex, educationally relevant learning.

We begin with a consideration of conditions that have fostered the separation between laboratory and classroom research traditions. We then discuss two methodological approaches utilized in recent projects that broaden basic cognitive research on learning and increase its educational relevance. One approach consists of laboratory research designed to examine whether existing laboratory findings and principles extend to materials and retention intervals that are educationally realistic. The second approach consists of classroom studies that test whether principles of learning derived from laboratory research can upgrade instruction in actual classrooms. We conclude with recommendations for research methods that bridge the gap between the laboratory and classrooms and have the potential to address real-world educational problems often considered intractable. We specifically advocate partnerships among the varied stakeholders, including laboratory and classroom researchers, to address the pressing dilemmas facing educational policy makers today.

Handbook of Applied Cognition: Second Edition. Edited by Francis T. Durso.

Rationale: Getting Beyond the Basic vs. Applied Distinction

Traditional psychological research on learning has made an implicit distinction between basic and applied investigations. Basic research, aimed at understanding human cognitive processes, has been associated with laboratory-based studies using simple, clearly defined materials, controlled conditions, and delays on the order of minutes or hours. Applied research, aimed at improving classroom instruction and promoting lifelong learning, has been associated with classroom-based studies using complex curriculum materials and assessments of students' understanding, retention, and transfer across retention intervals extending to months or years.

The overall distinction between basic and applied research has been challenged in recent years (Stokes 1997). This distinction can lead researchers to assume that any work conducted in a use-based setting, such as a classroom, is by definition an application of some finding. In contrast, Stokes (1997) argues that research in complex contexts can yield generalizable insights in its own right. Stokes argues that many important basic scientific discoveries have emerged from attempts to solve applied problems (e.g., Pasteur's germ theory of disease).

We suggest that the basic vs. applied distinction is unhelpful in research on learning and instruction because the boundaries have become blurred. The implication that basic research is necessary to guide and inform applied research is not consistent with numerous classroom studies that yield powerful findings (e.g., diSessa 2000; Songer *et al.* 2003). Instead, work in areas such as design-based research illustrates how generalizable principles of learning and instruction can be derived from iterative attempts to design and improve classroom instruction (e.g., Brown 1992; Cobb *et al.* 2003; Shavelson *et al.* 2003; Linn *et al.* 2004). Recent psychological studies also support this view by showing that educational research conducted in classroom settings (Anderson *et al.* 2004; Klahr & Li 2005) yields unique, valuable basic research insights. These studies can raise new questions for investigation and reveal unexplored assumptions made within laboratory studies (e.g., Brown 1992; Richland *et al.* 2004). Classroom studies document important educational variables, such as the role of everyday experience with physics, which are neglected in laboratory work. Classroom work can also reveal whether cognitive mechanisms identified to impact learning for simple stimuli and following short delays also guide learning for more complex materials and longer delays. Finally, classroom studies often reveal unintended consequences of laboratory findings when implemented in settings that are part of a complex system (Schofield 1995).

We suggest that the historic distinction between basic and applied research has fueled the separation between laboratory and classroom-based research. This has led to largely separate bodies of literature and reduced the cross-fertilization of ideas and findings across these settings. Stokes' (1997) framework of *use-based research* has inspired both researchers and the National Science Foundation to emphasize the utility of research that begins with educational questions or currently intractable instructional debates as sources for investigating general mechanisms underlying learning (Klahr & Li 2005). We suggest that this framework can help forge connections between laboratory and classroom-based research traditions.

Desirable Difficulties: Implications for Classroom Learning

Many commonly accepted findings from laboratory studies of learning have quite provocative and potentially important implications for education. This chapter focuses on one such cluster of laboratory-based research findings that have demonstrated the beneficial effects of increasing the apparent difficulty of initial learning opportunities. These are findings that have been categorized as "desirable difficulties," a term Bjork (1994, 1999) used to describe principles for designing instruction that make learning *seem* more difficult during acquisition, slowing the *apparent* rate of acquisition, but lead to increased long-term retention and transfer. These principles are largely counterintuitive, and teachers and students alike are regularly misled to believe that the rate of acquisition is an effective predictor of learning. However, laboratory-based research has demonstrated that this is unreliable and instead, greater difficulty and slow acquisition can be markers of richer encoding and longer-term retention.

Such desirable difficulties include using tests rather than presentations as learning events (e.g., Gates 1917; Glover 1989; McDaniel & Fisher 1991; Roediger & Karpicke 2005); spacing rather than massing study sessions (for reviews see Dempster 1988, 1989, 1996; Lee & Genovese 1988; Glenberg 1992); interleaving rather than blocking to-be-learned materials and tasks (see, e.g., Shea & Morgan 1979; Carlson & Yaure 1990); and varying the conditions of practice rather than keeping conditions constant and predictable (e.g., Catalano & Kleiner 1984; Homa & Cultice 1984; Reder *et al.* 1986; Mannes & Kintsch 1987). Each of these desirable difficulties has been well replicated in controlled experiments, usually with simple verbal or motor tasks and short retention intervals, and in a few cases with more complex real-world tasks, especially in the cognitive-motor domain. Whether such manipulations can enhance learning in the classroom remains, however, largely an open issue.

Recent studies have begun to bridge from the traditional laboratory studies to more educationally relevant materials and settings, and this process has raised new questions and areas for study. This body of research provides an excellent window into the processes of forging connections between laboratory and classroom studies of learning. Investigations have taken two approaches: (1) determining how far theoretical principles derived from laboratory research extend to educationally relevant curricula materials and substantial delays; and (2) determining how to design classroom interventions to enable all students to meet the goals of everyday instruction. In the sections that follow, we discuss representative research programs that take each approach to investigate learning principles within the cluster of desirable difficulties. We consider advantages and challenges inherent within each approach.

APPROACH 1: INCREASING THE EDUCATIONAL RELEVANCE OF LABORATORY STUDIES

Many foundational studies of learning have been conducted with simple materials, such as word pairs, word lists, or simple motor tasks, which may engage quite different processing than do more familiar and complex types of educational materials. These studies also typically measured retention over short time-intervals, not over the kinds of long-term intervals that are fundamental to the educational process and classroom contexts. We review several research programs that have employed the methodological strategy of conducting laboratory studies that are more educationally relevant than the classic studies. These efforts are conducted in the laboratory and build directly on prior research on cognitive mechanisms, but they extend basic explanations to learning that is more relevant to classroom settings.

Extending the Effects of Testing and Generation

Test effects have been explored by both classroom researchers and laboratory researchers, albeit in quite different ways. In laboratory research, test effects have typically been studied with respect to their effect on information retrieval. In classroom research, test effects have been studied primarily in the context of embedding alternative types of assessments into instruction.

Building on the laboratory tradition, research on the retrieval of information as a function of test vs. study trials has recently been extended to more educationally realistic materials by Roediger and Karpicke (2005). The test effect, namely, that tests are learning events in the sense that they enhance subsequent recall of the tested materials, has been demonstrated with a wide variety of materials and tasks in studies dating back at least to Gates's (1917) research on recitation. Overall, the history of laboratory research on test effects has demonstrated that the retrieval processes engaged by tests have several important effects: They retard forgetting of the retrieved material (e.g., Gates 1917; Hogan & Kintsch 1971; Bjork 1975; Whitten & Bjork 1977; Thompson *et al.* 1978; McDaniel & Mason 1985; Wheeler & Roediger 1992; Wheeler *et al.* 2003); they potentiate subsequent study trials (e.g., Izawa 1970); and they can impair the subsequent recall of information that is in competition with the retrieved information (e.g., Anderson *et al.* 1994). These studies have used simple materials (typically word lists, paired associates, or picture sets) to demonstrate such effects.

In the educational research domain, recent writings on assessment stress the importance of tests as components of the curriculum and emphasize performance assessments that can engage students not only in assessing their own understanding, but in learning about specific topics as a part of the assessment (Pellegrino *et al.* 2001; Shavelson & Towne 2002). In classroom studies, researchers have shown the advantage of inserting questions in study materials (see, e.g., Hamaker 1986). When educators design study materials with embedded questions that require student responses, they find that conceptual comprehension of the instruction is increased (Palinscar & Brown 1984; Scardamalia & Bereiter 1991; Chi 2000; Davis & Linn 2000). Importantly, these projects emphasize the role of conceptual tests that tap complex cognition such as making predictions, critiquing evidence, integrating topics, or building on prior knowledge. At the same time, the growing emphasis on accountability in schooling has increased reliance on standardized tests that often ask students to retrieve unconnected pieces of information and do not serve as learning events. A growing body of research demonstrates the advantages of using assessments that require the same cognitive activities emphasized in instruction and suggest that when tests ask for recall only, classroom instruction often relies on recall as well (Black & Wiliam 1998).

Extending Test Effects to Educational Materials

Roediger and Karpicke (2005) demonstrate the relevance of laboratory findings about the test effect's impact on retention to educationally relevant reading comprehension tasks. Participants in two studies studied short prose passages selected from the Test of English as a Foreign Language (TOEFL; Rogers 2001). They then had the opportunity to study some of these materials again and were also given a free-recall comprehension test on the other passages (without feedback). Finally, retention of the material was tested at a five-minute, two-day, or a one-week delay in a between-subject design. The results exhibit a striking interaction: In the immediate (five-minute) condition, participants recalled more in the study–study condition than they did in the study–test condition. After a delay of either two or seven days, however, participants showed greater memory for passages that had been tested rather than re-studied.

In a second experiment, Roediger and Karpicke examined the effects of repeated test opportunities as compared to more intensive study. In a between-subjects design, participants either studied a prose passage four times consecutively (SSSS), studied it three times consecutively and then were tested (SSST), or studied it once and were tested three times (STTT). Recall was then tested after five minutes or after one week. As in the prior experiment, Roediger and Karpicke found that there was a short-term benefit for re-studying the passage multiple times. After a week's delay, however, participants who were tested during the learning phase performed much better than learners who only studied the passage, and there was an additional small benefit for testing multiple times over testing once. Interestingly, students reported that the SSSS condition was least interesting, but predicted they would learn the most.

This study demonstrates that for complex prose passages, testing is a more powerful learning event than direct study over the long term, although direct study can show greater benefits in the short term. By increasing the educational validity of the materials implemented in this study as well as the test format, these researchers provide an important bridge to educational settings. The interaction between condition with retention interval obtained by Roediger and Karpicke replicates earlier laboratory findings, particularly those obtained by Hogan and Kintsch (1971), and thus provides a good example of a laboratory finding that carries over to materials and retention intervals that are educationally realistic. Recent studies have demonstrated success in incorporating tests into undergraduate psychology courses (Leeming 2002; McDaniel, 2004) indicating that the extension of this research to instruction is useful. Leeming (2002) gave 192 students short tests at the beginning of every class period in four psychology courses, and found higher course grades, higher retention, greater satisfaction, and fewer course withdrawals from participating students than from prior courses with only four total exams.

When advocating for the use of tests as learning events, a second question emerges from this research. Specifically, what is the effect on recall of incorrect materials either generated or considered during a test event? For example, if a test is in multiple-choice format and the learner considers three incorrect alternatives for every problem, will the test effect improve their false memory for these items as correct responses?

These questions are under investigation by Roediger and Marsh (2005) and McDermott (2006). In Roediger and Marsh's study, undergraduate participants who studied text materials were tested on the materials they read, as well as materials they did not study but might have known from prior experience. They were then tested on multiple-choice problems with two, four, or six alternatives and asked to answer every question, even if they had to guess. After a short delay, participants were given a cued-recall test on both the studied and unstudied materials and for materials tested earlier and not tested earlier. Participants were asked not to guess on this final test.

Roediger and Marsh found that the test effect was replicated overall, that is, there were benefits on the final cued-recall test of having been tested earlier via multiple-choice items. A closer examination of their results reveals, however, that the effect decreased linearly with the number of alternatives. The test effect was most pronounced when questions were initially tested with only two alternatives, it was less strong with four alternatives, and even less effective with six alternatives. Second, the number of false lures given as answers in the second test increased linearly with the number of alternatives, such that the fewest were given when initially tested with two alternatives and the most were given when initially tested with six alternatives. Participants had been asked not to guess, which suggests that production of the false lures reflected false beliefs that these answers were correct. Analyses revealed that participants who remembered and continued to choose an answer they incorrectly selected during the first test drove these error data.

These studies suggest that the test effect leads to increased retention when students produce correct information, but also enables students to learn material that is inaccurate, if they generate the inaccurate information in response to test questions. This raises the issue of feedback and explicit error correction.

Extending Laboratory Studies of Feedback

Research on feedback has a long tradition within studies of learning, and these recent results suggest that the use of testing as a learning event requires consideration of feedback strategies. Pashler *et al.* (2003) found, for example, that adding feedback to tests can foster subsequent correct recall even under conditions such as delaying the test which increase the likelihood of an error being made. Feedback has been demonstrated to be powerful in both laboratory and classroom studies, though there is reason to believe that optimal feedback conditions for learning may be somewhat different across settings and materials.

We discuss two research areas in which laboratory-based studies of feedback can be informative to educational practice. One such body of research has focused on the role of differences in the *timing* of feedback, specifically the amount of delay between when a learner is tested and when they receive feedback. Insights into the optimal timing for feedback are useful in organizing classroom instruction and designing technological learning environments.

Kulik and Kulik (1988) conducted a meta-analysis of experimental research on feedback timing using simple and educational tests. Interestingly, some discrepancies about the optimal feedback emerged based upon the nature of the learned materials. The meta-analysis revealed that immediate feedback tended to be more effective than longer delayed feedback when learning materials were more complex educational tests and in educational settings. This finding resonates with studies showing that when teachers return student homework and tests quickly, students learn more (Sloane & Linn 1988). In contrast, delayed feedback was more effective for simple stimuli and abstract materials in laboratory settings. Differences in the posttest materials may provide some insight into this finding. In the majority of the applied studies, the posttest materials were different from the exact items tested during the feedback training. By contrast, the majority of the tests of abstract material examined posttest scores on the identical training materials. Because educators are often more concerned with learners' ability to develop knowledge that can transfer to tests that have somewhat different features from the initial learning context, so the laboratory-based studies may be more relevant. Thus, increased delays to feedback could lead to greater retention but less flexibility in knowledge representations.

Alternatively, subtle differences in the time-scales between studies may also impact the different patterns of feedback delays on learning. For instance, the delayed feedback in the educational settings was typically given after day or week delays. In contrast, delayed feedback in laboratory settings and with simple stimuli tended to be given after each item or at the end of the test, with delays of the order of minutes or hours. The Kulik and Kulik (1988) findings might indicate that a short delay to feedback, on the order of minutes or hours, would be most optimal in a classroom setting.

Another factor may have been that only a small selection of the laboratory studies, and none of the applied studies, tested the impact of feedback timing on a delayed test. In the motor literature and cognitive tests where items are learned during testing, immediate feedback is demonstrated to be more effective than delayed feedback on a test after a minimal delay, though delayed feedback is reliably more effective after a longer test delay (see, e.g., Kulhavy 1977; Schmidt *et al.* 1989; Winstein & Schmidt 1990; Schmidt 1991). Based on these types of findings, the desirable-difficulty framework would recommend delayed feedback in order to produce longer-term retention, although short-term gains might be obtained through immediate feedback (Bjork 1994, 1999). More research is necessary to determine whether this would hold in more complex settings, or whether, as indicated in Kulik and Kulik's (1988) analysis, there are multiple determinants for the impact of feedback on longer-term retention.

Laboratory research has also been able to focus on the relationship between specific characteristics of test items and feedback. For instance, recent studies have clarified the interplay between confidence in incorrect prior knowledge and feedback on educational materials. Butterfield and Metcalfe (2001) found that errors made with high confidence were "hyper-corrected" by feedback – that is, the errors were most likely to be replaced by correct answers on a delayed test. In this study, participants were tested on their prior knowledge for general information trivia items. People were asked to rate their confidence in the accuracy of their responses to free recall questions, and then were given immediate feedback. Feedback consisted of both a statement of their accuracy and the correct response if they had been in error.

Butterfield and Metcalfe were thus able to identify high confidence errors, that is, items on which a given participant had initially indicated high confidence in their accuracy, but that in fact were errors. After a delay, participants were given a final test on a subset of the same set of trivia items, half that were answered correctly, and half that were answered incorrectly. People were asked to produce the answer they believed to be most correct and to produce two other responses that came to mind. One might expect that the high confidence errors would be resistant to change, and thus these items would be less accurate at posttest. In contrast, findings revealed that participants were more likely to correct errors for content in which they had originally expressed high confidence in their accuracy.

People did remember their initial answers, and frequently listed them within the three potential responses, but they successfully identified that these were not correct.

These findings build on early studies in which learners who answered a question incorrectly were found to study feedback more carefully if they had previously assumed the answers were correct than if they had not expected to answer the question correctly (Kulhavy & Stock 1989). Interestingly, these authors also found that these results could be increased by adding a small delay of minutes between test and feedback. This dovetails nicely with the emerging principle that a short delay to feedback may be optimal for promoting longer-term retention of some complex content.

Overall, these data reveal that feedback can play a substantial role in making testing an effective learning opportunity. In particular, these laboratory-based studies provide insights into the optimal timing of feedback, the interaction of feedback and content complexity, and the interaction between feedback and confidence ratings. Determining ideal feedback strategies can have implications for classroom teachers and for the design of technology-based curricula. The role of feedback in correcting high-confidence errors is particularly important since these are likely to be persistent sources of misconceptions within classroom learning when uncorrected. Care needs to be taken, however, in attempting to remedy strongly held beliefs because these often have experience-based justifications that deserve attention (diSessa 2000; Linn & Hsi 2000). For example, when students argue that metals are colder than wood at room temperature because they feel colder, the remedy needs to respect the tactile evidence and help learners reinterpret their experiences.

Extending the Generation Effect

A second learning principle identified in the laboratory that is closely related to the test effect is the generation effect (Slamecka & Graf 1978). In the test-effect studies, students typically answer questions that address information studied earlier in the experiment. In generation-effect studies, a similar procedure is sometimes employed, making the two effects essentially the same, or participants are asked to generate answers based on their prior knowledge, not based on recently studied information (thus, to give a simple example, participants might be asked to generate the incomplete words in "A weather phenomenon: Th**d*r and L*gh*n**g"). Generation is then compared to conditions in which learners only read or listen to the material. As in the case of test effects, materials that are generated tend to be recalled better than words that are studied, and often recalled much better (see, e.g., Jacoby 1978). Because classroom learning relies upon both acquisition of new knowledge and retrieval of prior knowledge, both laboratory-based learning principles have relevance. Generation provides one specific framework for conceptualizing *active participation* in classroom instruction, by enabling learners to retrieve prior knowledge as part of their acquisition of new learning. Engaging students in active participation has been a major part of educational reform recommendations, though the precise meaning of this term has been interpreted in many ways.

In the decades since the initial generation-effect experiments, such as the study by Slamecka and Graf, which tended to employ simple materials, the generation effect has been found to be robust, with a wide set of more educationally relevant materials. deWinstanley (1995), for example, replicated the generation effect using trivia facts and

Pesta *et al.* (1999) demonstrated that the generation effect improves recall of multiplication facts.

Educationally, another important question is whether students can learn the benefit of generation as a learning strategy, and thus whether its use during instruction will lead students to improve their own learning. Learning to learn has long been a primary goal of educational settings (Brown 1992). deWinstanley and Bjork (2004) investigated whether students could learn to use the generation effect to improve their own reading comprehension and whether student participants would learn to monitor and use generation methods independently when they participated in an experiment in which they could experience the benefits of generation over study. In two experiments, participants studied two paragraphs of science text which were each presented one phrase at a time. In a within-subjects manipulation, participants were either required to generate a critical word in each phrase or were asked to read the critical word. People completed a first paragraph in which they were given both read and generated phrases and were tested on that paragraph, via a fill-in-the-blank test for the critical words, before moving on to the second paragraph. The order of the paragraphs was counterbalanced across subjects.

For the first of the studied paragraphs, deWinstanley and Bjork replicated the generation effect, showing that learners retrieved items they had generated more successfully than items they had read. Surprisingly, following the second paragraph, participants performed as well on items they had read as words they had generated and at about the level of the generated items in the first paragraph. This finding, replicated in a second and third experiment, lends support for the conclusion proposed by deWinstanley and Bjork that learners discovered a more effective processing strategy by their second study opportunity. Specifically, they argue that participants observed the benefit of generation in the first paragraph and then used this technique on their own for the second paragraph even for items that were designated as *read* phrases. They also demonstrate in two studies that when learners were not allowed to compare their own read and generated performance, they did not show the same change in performance. Rather, the generation condition had an advantage over read for all paragraphs. This is a potentially important finding because it provides insight into how the design of generation-effect experiences can be used to train children more generally in academic and study skills. The generation effect has not been replicated in all study designs, but these findings may provide some insight into students' understanding of the generation effect and how they can learn to apply this strategy to their own learning.

Recent experimental studies have used students' allocations of study time to demonstrate that metacognitive awareness of desirable-difficulty principles and test difficulty can impact students' decisions about how to control their own learning (Metcalfe & Kornell 2003; Son 2004; Kornell & Metcalfe in press). These studies revealed that if students have limited study time, they monitor and control the timing for study repetitions (Son 2004) and length of study (Metcalfe & Kornell 2003; Kornell & Metcalfe in press) based upon the apparent difficulty of the learning materials in reliable, productive ways. Thus with the deWinstanley and Bjork (2004) findings, these experiments suggest that students could learn to exert control over their available study time in optimal ways through educational experiences with desirable difficulty.

In summary, studies of the test effect and the generation effect jointly shed light on the importance of asking students to respond to questions in the course of learning. These studies also provide insight into the role of desirable difficulties within instruction as a means for improving student learning and study skills. Expert learners who have a good understanding of their own learning processes may institute self-testing activities that enable them to learn more effectively. These studies suggest, however, that most learners benefit from prompts or manipulations that increase the likelihood that they generate responses and, as a result, examine their own learning.

Extending the Effects of Spacing to Educationally Realistic Retention Intervals

Another major limitation of many cognitive psychological theories for informing educational practice is that memory for learning is tested only after minutes or hours, or at most a day or two. Recent projects have begun to address whether laboratory findings extend to educationally realistic retention intervals. An illustrative set of studies by Pashler and his colleagues (Cepeda *et al.* 2006) have examined whether the spacing effect, a robust effect in laboratory studies, extends to educationally meaningful retention intervals. The spacing effect refers to the memory benefit that occurs when there is an interval between repetitions of study materials as opposed to study sessions that are consecutive, or massed. A closely related effect is the lag effect, which refers to the retention benefits of increasing the length of spacing intervals when compared with shorter spacing intervals (e.g., Tzeng 1973; Thios & D'Agostino 1976). For reviews of spacing and lag effects, see Dempster (1989, 1996).

In a quantitative meta-analysis of existing research on spacing in verbal learning paradigms, Cepeda *et al.* (2006) examined the relationship between the length of intervals between successive practice opportunities and retention. In an analysis of 317 experiments from 184 articles, they compared 958 accuracy values, 839 assessments of distributed practice, and 169 effect sizes. Overall, they found a strong positive effect of spacing over massing on long-term retention, but they also found that increasing the spacing interval beyond a certain optimal point, which is longer than the final retention interval, results in a slight decrease in long-term retention. Thus, for a given retention interval, an increase in inter-study interval causes test performance to first increase and then decrease. This meta-analysis clarifies early findings that drew attention to the power of inter-study intervals during list learning (e.g., Glenberg 1976), and highlights the importance of the length of the retention interval in decisions about the optimal timing of study.

Cepeda *et al.* (2006) noted that their meta-analysis reveals some important limitations of current laboratory research on spacing, especially that very few studies examine recall performance after delays of weeks, months, and years, that is, across educationally realistic retention intervals. They also noted that to explore applications of the spacing effect to children's learning, given educationally realistic retention intervals, it becomes necessary to understand how developmental effects interact with the effects of spacing.

As an important step in examining the spacing effect across realistic intervals, Cepeda *et al.* (2006, unpublished paper) examined foreign language, factual, and visual object learning with a substantial range of inter-study intervals and retention intervals out to six months in some cases. Again, the results suggest that some spacing vs. massing is very beneficial, but that for any given retention interval there is an optimal spacing interval and that further spacing has deleterious, if slight, effects. Cepeda *et al.* also argued that the non-monotonic relationship between the inter-study interval and retention interval takes the form that as the retention interval increases, the optimal spacing interval is a decreasing fraction of the final retention interval. These studies build on prior research demonstrating the potential for very long-term retention of educational content following spaced practice (e.g., Bahrick & Phelps 1987).

In a study of the spacing effect using mathematical materials, Rohrer and Taylor (in press) taught undergraduates how to calculate the number of permutations of a letter string in which at least one letter was repeated. Learners were then given ten practice trials, either all at once or spaced over two sessions with a one-week delay. Participants were tested one or four weeks later. Spaced practice resulted in poorer performance at the one-week interval, but better performance after the four-week delay. Additional study practice during massing made no difference – spacing was still better. This study, along with others, suggests that the spacing effect is useful not only for rote, memorized, items, but also for materials that require some generalization and application to new content features.

Studies of the spacing effect have useful implications for classroom learning. Curriculum designers and teachers make many decisions about spacing of tests as well as spacing of topics. These laboratory studies of spaced testing indicate that spaced testing of previously learned material could be quite powerful. They also imply the benefit of cumulative tests in educational settings that prompt re-study for information across a school year, or even multiple years. Unfortunately, these are not extremely common within current classroom practice, where most tests are considered final assessments of a single curriculum topic and are not repeated over spaced intervals.

The implications for curriculum organization are more nuanced. The benefits of spacing suggest a rationale for practices such as the spiral curriculum, in which a large number of topics are studied each year and then are reintroduced at regular intervals over multiple school years. Education assessments do not seem, however, to provide good support for the effectiveness of spiral curricula; indeed, some have argued that the spiral curriculum is one of the reasons why American students perform less well than their international counterparts on international comparison tests in mathematics and science (Schmidt *et al.* 2001). The realities of schooling mean that a spiral curriculum increases the total number of topics covered in a given academic year. Dramatic differences in the number of topics covered have been reported between countries that do well on international comparison tests, such as Japan and the Czech Republic, and countries that do poorly, such as the United States. For example, in Japan in middle school science, eight topics are covered, while the average for American classrooms is over 60 (Linn *et al.* 2000).

Thus, the generalization of the spacing effect to educational contexts invites new questions for study. For example, most studies of the spacing effect rely on retention of individual ideas, rather than the development of conceptual understanding. Research is needed to clarify how the spacing effect works for accumulating conceptual knowledge of topics. Nevertheless, research to date on the spacing effect clearly reveals advantages for spaced study for the long-term retention that is a hallmark of successful classroom instruction.

Overlearning in the Laboratory and Implications for the Classroom

The use of assessments as learning events raises the open question: Can there be too much of a good thing? Recent educational reforms that tout the use of standardized assessment measures to hold teachers and schools accountable for students' performance, termed "high stakes accountability," has led to increased instruction using drill practice in which learners practice on test items even after demonstrating success. Overlearning, as a laboratory procedure, consists of continued study or practice after some criterion level of mastery or recall has been achieved. Laboratory studies, some tracing back many decades, suggest that overlearning can enhance long-term retention. From an educational practice standpoint, however, two questions are relevant: (1) Do such results also obtain with educationally realistic materials and retention intervals? (2) If so, does the benefit due to overlearning justify the additional expenditure of time? While the answers to these questions are not yet known, some progress has been made toward understanding the impact of overlearning with classroom materials.

Research by Rohrer *et al.* (2005) provides some insight. In one of their experiments, designed to examine whether the benefits of overlearning are maintained over time, they had participants learn word pairs that linked cities and countries. There was a standard learning condition that consisted of five learning trials for the to-be-learned pairs, and an overlearning condition that consisted of 20 such trials. Retention tests were administered at one, three, or nine weeks. At all retention intervals participants in the overlearning condition performed better than did participants in the standard condition, but the magnitude of the difference fell substantially across those intervals. In a second experiment, the overlearning group studied the materials twice as many times as did the comparison group. On a test administered four weeks later, there were no significant differences between groups.

Caution is always necessary when interpreting the absence of differences, but these findings may well have implications for classroom practices. Specifically, they question the value of popular drill activities in mathematics and reading. From these data, it appears that students would be better off spending time learning new material rather than overlearning old material, such as math facts, through repeated testing in preparation for high-stakes assessments.

The spacing of repeated learning opportunities may also have a direct impact on the efficacy of overlearning. In a study examining the effects of a spaced repetition of previously overlearned high school mathematics content, Bahrick and Hall (1991) examined life-span retention of high school algebra and geometry concepts. These authors used cross-sectional data to compare the retention of learners who had learned the material in one time period, during high school, to the retention of learners who had restudied the same overlearned material in a later college course. They found strong relationships such that when the initial learning was spaced over several years, retention for the content remained high up to 50 years later. In contrast, when initial learning was concentrated in a single year, or a shorter time period, forgetting proceeded rapidly. The researchers found near-chance performance levels for the relevant mathematical materials when tested after the life-span retention intervals.

Overall, these studies suggest that overlearned material has the potential to remain in memory indefinitely when acquisition is spaced over a considerable interval. Without spacing repeated learning opportunities, however, overlearning may not provide a substantial benefit for long-term retention. More research is necessary to determine the optimal relationship between spacing and overlearning, but together these projects urge rethinking of the popular use of repetitive-drill instruction that is concentrated into a single time frame.

Summary

As revealed in this selective review, a growing group of cognitive psychologists has begun to extend classical studies of learning to materials and retention intervals that are educationally realistic. The initial findings suggest, in some cases, that laboratory phenomena demonstrated with simple materials and short retention intervals often *do* generalize, but in other cases there are reasons to be cautious in basing educational practices on laboratory findings obtained with materials and intervals that are unrealistic.

Overall, these studies support the claim that taking certain measures to increase the initial difficulty of a learning event can result in greater learning and retention over time. The following specific recommendations emerge from these laboratory studies of desirable difficulty using educational materials or delays:

- Studying information by reading is less effective than studying by testing. So, tests can and should be used as tools for learning and engagement as well as assessment. However, careful thought should be given to the role of false alternatives (e.g., multiple-choice questions) since these can result in increased memory for this incorrect information if not corrected. Feedback might reduce the learning for this incorrect information viewed during testing.
- Feedback is an essential part of students' learning, but the timing for when it is given is critical. In classroom settings, immediate feedback seems to be more effective than feedback after a long delay, but this may depend upon instructional goals and the length of measured delay. Specifically, a short delay (e.g., hours or a day) may be more effective than either immediate feedback after seconds or a long delay of multiple days or longer. Shorter delays (seconds up to one day) may also improve generalized knowledge acquisition, while relatively longer delays (minutes to weeks) improve memorization of precise facts. Further, feedback may have more of an impact on certain materials than for others – for instance, high confidence items that are incorrect.
- Memorization of classroom content can be improved by spacing repetitions of study rather than training on the content all at once. But it is important to ensure that the period between intervals is not so great that the prior knowledge is forgotten. Thus, for example, a spiral curriculum model of allowing an entire year or more to pass between revisits to a topic may be too long. Feedback may be important in ensuring that items are not forgotten, as well as the length of delay.
- Repeated drills on content may result in short-term memory benefits but this type of overlearning practice is not likely to improve longer-term retention. So, if memorization for content over a period of months or years was the goal, increasing intervals to days, weeks, or months between drills would be a better strategy to improve students' long-term memory.
- Learning experiences in which students see the benefits of desirable difficulties can be useful in enhancing their metacognitive sophistication and likelihood of using them to organize their own study. This has been shown in particular for the benefits of generation over more passive reading.

These are important principles with direct implications for classroom learning. Even so, the act of applying these general strategies to classroom instruction often raises new questions. It is critical, therefore, to research desirable-difficulty learning principles in the classroom as well as in the laboratory. In the next section we provide recent examples of research that raise the main issues inherent in truly bringing laboratory findings to the classroom.

APPROACH 2: TESTING LEARNING PRINCIPLES IN CLASSROOM SETTINGS

Classrooms and laboratories prompt learners to activate quite different motivational and attentional states, which can make it challenging to define cognitive principles that will generalize across settings. For this reason, laboratory researchers interested in educational learning are beginning to test cognitive principles in their context of interest: classrooms. These projects have varying research goals, including determining whether principles learned from the laboratory generalize to classroom learning, assessing whether principles derived from laboratory studies can improve classroom learning, and developing principles for the design of future curricula. Some research groups work directly with classroom teachers to develop curricula based on cognitive principles (e.g., Brown & Campione 1994; Gelman & Brenneman 2004). Other groups take advantage of technological tools to deliver instruction in regular classes (e.g., Anderson *et al.* 1995; Linn *et al.* 2004; Metcalfe *et al.* 2006, unpublished paper). Research projects in these latter two veins are reviewed to demonstrate available strategies for taking laboratory findings into classroom contexts.

Interventions Integrated into Curriculum Materials

Researchers committed to curricular reforms based on laboratory findings face a tradeoff between educational realism and research control, and often a parallel tradeoff between practitioner and professional support for the work. We describe recent examples of initiatives along this continuum, and consider both the benefits and challenges inherent in the alternative research designs.

Controlled Interventions into Classrooms

One methodology for determining whether laboratory-based learning principles generalize to more dynamic, complex classroom settings and materials is to constrain classroom instruction to create a lab-like setting. This approach can be achieved using designs in which students are pulled out for small-group testing, or where tasks are administered using a controlled technology platform that students complete individually. An example of the latter type is a study recently conducted by Metcalfe *et al.* (2006, unpublished paper) in which a computer game interface was used to embed science and English vocabulary instruction into an after-school program.

Metcalfe *et al.* designed instruction that integrated multiple learning principles consistent with the desirable-difficulty framework. They sought to demonstrate that these principles could be used together to improve long-term retention of standards-based science and English vocabulary. The study was conducted with at-risk sixth-grade students at an urban inner-city school. For five weeks, the students interacted with a game-like format in which multiple-learning principles were integrated. Among others, these included testing, generation, spaced practice, and feedback. There was also a no-study control. As predicted by the laboratory research, the game-like incorporation of learning principles did enhance students' learning and retention, after a week's delay, of the task vocabulary. The researchers also replicated these effects with English-language learners who used the technology to learn English vocabulary.

These findings provide support for the argument that the desirable-difficulties framework may have direct implications for classroom instruction. The main advantage of this study design is greater educational realism while maintaining experimental rigor and control over the execution of the instruction. This enables easily interpretable comparisons between instructional manipulations. The highly engaging task environment also has the advantage that students are likely to benefit from the difficulty manipulations, because they are only effective if a learner overcomes the challenges. The main disadvantage is that the computer program provides such support that there is still little evidence gained about the likelihood that an educator could successfully implement these principles within the myriad demands of an everyday classroom. For example, students' motivation levels in a group setting could lead to differences in how these principles operate when implemented by a teacher.

Interventions into Classroom Curricula

A second strategy for extending laboratory-based learning principles into the classroom is the introduction of interventions into classroom curricula. Such interventions require partnerships of researchers, teachers, administrators, and curriculum designers. Given these complex partnerships, creating control conditions for these studies is more difficult than it is for laboratory studies.

In a recent program of research that has made direct impact on multiple early childhood educational settings, Gelman and Brenneman (2004) describe a long-term collaboration with science teachers to develop Preschool Pathways to Science. The initiative draws on cognitive developmental theories of domain specificity, which is the theoretical argument that children's development of knowledge structures differs between content areas (see Gelman 1998). Most traditional theories of cognition and development describe domain-general processes, but a class of domain-specific learning theories (domain-specific, core knowledge and rational-constructivist) emerged in response to accumulating evidence for young children's fairly sophisticated conceptual capacities in several areas, including quantitative, physical, and biological reasoning. These domain-specific learning theories have implications for the design of learning environments. In particular, they imply the benefits of domain-relevant inputs to build on existing knowledge structures.

The Preschool Pathways to Science curriculum is a science and math program for young children in which tasks are designed in to build on domain-specific knowledge structures through selected domain-relevant inputs. Inputs included scientific vocabulary and skills with the scientific method such as observing data, predicting, and assessing predictions. The curriculum program also incorporated key advances in educational design such as constructivist learning environments and connected concepts. These led to tasks jointly developed by teachers and researchers such as making predictions, observing, and assessing predictions for "what is inside an apple."

This study is very different in form from the laboratory-based manipulations of desirable difficulty described above. As such, it raises several important issues for projects operating in classrooms settings. First, in pre-school through grade 12 educational settings, the researcher must grapple with developmental questions as well as pure information-processing considerations. Second, the content being taught is central to the learning study, as opposed to being a secondary consideration as it is during explorations of domain-general learning processes in the laboratory. Third, collaborative partnerships are extremely effective strategies for applying research findings to meet real classroom needs. Though, they also make findings difficult to separate from the specific setting (e.g., teacher skill set, administrator support, children's characteristics, etc). In addition, due to the highly collaborative, intensive nature of these partnerships, randomized experimental designs comparing interventions are often impractical or impossible.

Even so, research-based interventions through collaborations with classroom teachers are an important strategy for bridging laboratory and classroom learning. These interventions can produce generalizable principles for wide spread implementation, though researcher support may be necessary to ensure productive implementation of these principles.

Curriculum Interventions Using Technological-Enhanced Learning Environments

Collaborative interventions into classroom curriculum can also be conducted using technology-enhanced learning environments. This strategy allows for systematic tests of more general learning principles that coordinate with everyday classroom instruction. These environments deliver consistent instruction, allowing for some control over the inputs going to students, while also freeing the teacher to work individually with students in ways he or she might do ordinarily. Two examples of technology-enhanced learning environments that support this kind of research are the cognitive tutors, built by Anderson (Anderson *et al.* 1995), and the Web-Based Inquiry Science Environment (WISE, http://wise.berkeley.edu).

Anderson and his colleagues have used an architecture developed to model cognition, called Adaptive Control of Thought (ACT) theory, to design tutors that enhance student learning for procedural knowledge in the domains of algebra, geometry, and LISP programming. Procedural knowledge is emphasized over declarative knowledge, since it is assumed that inert knowledge can be learned more easily, while teaching successful knowledge manipulation and strategy use is more of an instructional challenge. These technological tools guide students to perform geometry proofs and algebra symbol manipulations successfully, as well as to consult other resources such as text and visualizations to understand these complex topics (Anderson *et al.* 1995; Koedinger & Anderson 1998; Corbett *et al.* 2001).

Tutors are now being designed in collaborations with curriculum experts to fit with state curriculum standards and as such have been much more fully integrated into high school classroom math and computer science instruction. These newer models also employ a knowledge-tracing technique, first implemented in the LISP tutor, in which mastery of a skill is broken into components, and students' acquisition of each component is assessed separately and required before advancement to a next instructional section.

The tutors are based on principles derived from the updated ACT-R theory, and build on the notion that instruction should be developed with reference to the cognitive competence being taught. Specifically, these tutors provide learners with some instruction, and then facilitate practice with problem solving by guiding students toward an expert solution model. The tutors invoke a "model-tracing approach," which means that a model is constructed for how an expert would solve the problem, and then learners are guided via immediate, corrective feedback to that model. The learner's response entries are evaluated for whether they are "on-path" or "off-path" actions, so generally there is a constraint that the program must be able to recognize the type of approach being used by the learner. Constraints on students' solution attempts are somewhat more minimal than in other such model-tracing tutors, but even so this approach allows for rapid diagnosing of errors and misconceptions.

Evaluation of the cognitive tutors has demonstrated their effectiveness in helping students learn algebra and geometry. In addition, researchers have examined the impact of the social context on student learning, in an attempt to understand how the cognitive tutors contribute to student success. These studies reveal several important aspects of the cognitive tutors that lead to their impact. First and foremost, students using the cognitive tutors are motivated to continue to attempt to solve algebra and geometry problems. In addition, students using the tutors benefit from creative representations of geometry proofs using means–ends analysis and algebra problems. Furthermore, as Schofield (1995) demonstrates, the cognitive tutors enable teachers to complete the text curriculum efficiently and to ensure that students who have gaps in their knowledge are able to practice the important skills necessary for them to persist in the course.

Using the cognitive-tutor technology, Anderson and his colleagues have been able to carry out well-controlled studies comparing various approaches to instruction. The cognitive tutor gathers information each second or more frequently, compared to many research studies that only gather information at the end of a day, week, or unit. Thus, researchers have an opportunity to look closely at the struggles that students face and to provide a greater understanding of educational innovations that might contribute to learning. Anderson *et al.* (2004), for example, describe eye-tracking studies that allow analysis of students' attentional process when looking at educational materials. These studies suggest that many of the ideas that govern the design of textbooks may be quite inadequate. Textbook designers often create materials designed to appeal to textbook selection committees rather than designed to improve student learning. The Anderson *et al.* (2004) eye-tracking study suggests that students' eye movements and attention are easily drawn to pictures of people and animals, and away from, for example, graphs and charts. Thus, when textbook publishers create attractive and busy pages, they may inadvertently be distracting students from the crucial information necessary for learning.

Work by researchers using the Web-based Inquiry Science Environment (WISE, http://wise.berkeley.edu) affords similar kinds of semi-controlled instruction that seamlessly integrates into classroom curriculum. WISE is an Internet-based platform that delivers science curriculum modules using inquiry-based activities. Many modules have been created through partnerships between teachers and researchers to teach standards-based science curriculum to students from approximately grades 6 through 12. Teachers can selectively identify modules that are relevant to their science instruction, and can incorporate them into their yearly curriculum. WISE provides a library of freely available modules on science content, such as astronomy, light propagation, thermal equilibrium,

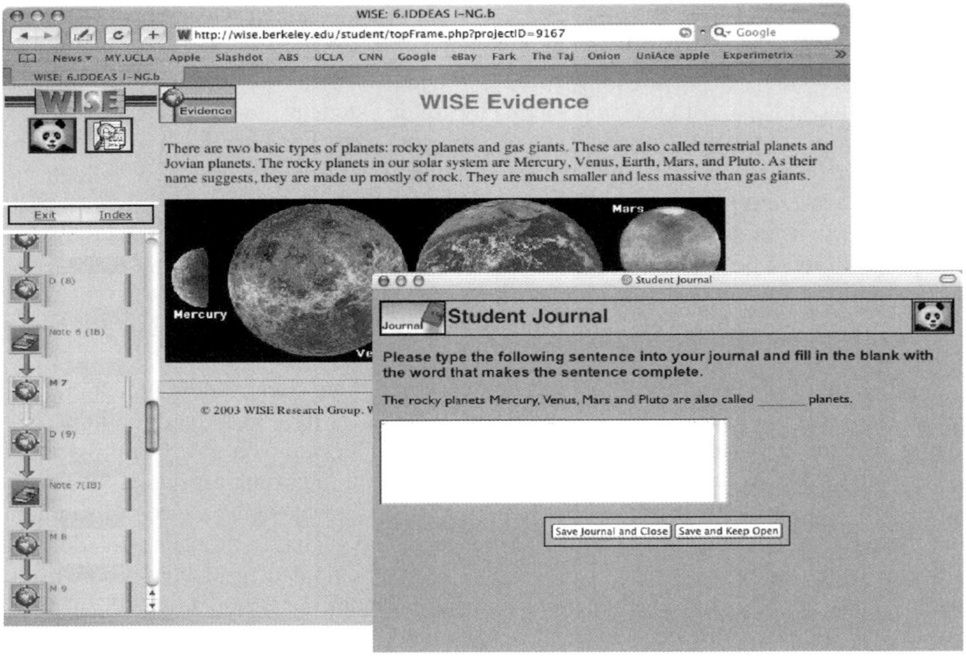

Figure 21.1 Sample screens of WISE software. Information presentation and embedded prompts

and chemical reactions. These modules are also customizable, so a teacher could alter any module to best fit their teaching needs. The customizability also makes them feasible for comparative research, and embedded assessments allow for many sources of data about students' learning process.

Classroom observations of students using WISE projects reveal similarly effective benefits to those found with the cognitive tutors. Students working on science projects guided by the WISE technology tend to spend more time writing notes and conducting experiments than they did with traditional instructional materials (Linn & Hsi 2000). In addition, studies comparing different forms of animations, alternative forms of prompts, and varied discussion tools help clarify the factors that contribute to effective learning (Linn *et al.* 2004).

WISE allows designers, for example, to embed specific generation questions within the activities (see Figure 21.1). Research by Davis (1998) shows that the type of questions selected for generation can impact student learning. In Davis's work, generation questions varied along the dimension of specificity. One set of generic questions asks students to reflect on what they have learned and identify gaps in their understanding. Another set of more specific questions asks students about specific links that they might have made among materials that they had studied. Davis found that the generic questions, which ask students to self-diagnose the gaps in their understanding, were more successful than the specific questions, which students often found somewhat confusing to interpret or found too easy, and therefore said, "Well, I already know that." The Davis results resonate with the deWinstanely and Bjork study (2004), suggesting that allowing learners to assess their own learning through experience can be an effective strategy to improve their metacognitive awareness and learning skills.

Technological learning environments allow researchers to investigate the cognition underlying learning within classroom curricula and provide some measure of control over the instructional inputs. Even so, there are often limits on the generalizability of these findings to other instruction. The results of these studies often serve to improve the technological intervention itself, rather than seek to provide generalizable knowledge for use in designing alternative learning environments.

Design-Based Research

A field of design-based research has emerged to meet the goal of developing generalizable knowledge about the processes of designing effective classroom curriculum interventions. Researchers have begun to study the design process and construct databases of principles that guide and impact designers (e.g., Barab & Squire 2004; Kali *et al.* 2005). Cognition is conceptualized as being closely tied to the learning context. This research, therefore, moves away from the assumption that lies at the heart of laboratory research traditions, namely that learning principles derived in one setting can be necessarily applied to a new setting.

This body of work derives from the notion of "design experiments," as initially framed by Collins (1992) and Brown (1992). They described a process of doing experimental research that was situated within classrooms as a means for developing a generalizable body of knowledge about how cognition could be best enhanced in classroom settings. Design experiments (e.g., Brown 1992) are educational interventions that seek to investigate the basic processes of learning and instruction by manipulating classroom contexts in systematic ways. These interventions reveal the complex interplay between classroom curricula, roles of students and teachers, and assessment, all of which Brown argued must be understood and manipulated to fully characterize learning in educational settings. The nature of the interrelationships between these factors made clear experimental manipulations impossible, and involved a tradeoff between experimenter control and realism in data.

This framework has developed into a field of design-based research, in which researchers identify ways to conduct classroom research that leads to optimized learning as well as strategies to guide future designers (e.g., Cobb *et al.* 2003; Shavelson *et al.* 2003; Shavelson *et al.* 2003; Linn *et al.* 2004) characterize design studies as having several common features, though the studies themselves vary widely. They argue that design studies are typically *interventionist* and *theory-driven* in that they test theory by modifying everyday instructional activities, *iterative*, such that they contain successive modified replications of the interventions, and *utility-oriented*, in that they are concerned with producing benefits for classroom instruction. They are also *process-focused*, such that they are concerned with tracing the evolution of student and/or institutional beliefs in general as well as in response to the intervention, *multi-leveled* in developing links between classroom instruction and broader school or district structures, and *collaborative* between researchers and these various educational partners. These studies also differ from more traditional experimental studies in that multiple types of data are collected. Generally, researchers collect a detailed record of the entire study, which may include ethnographic and interview data, design process data, and evidence of student engagement and learning throughout. These data often result in a more complex picture of learning than traditional posttest performance data reveal.

Overall, this research approach is provocative and provides an alternative strategy for conceptualizing educational research. Interestingly, few of the design principles highlighted in this work have focused on learning principles deriving from laboratory research on cognition. Rather, research in this field has tended to focus on principles developed from classroom-situated learning (Kali 2006). While important and revealing, this reliance may also reflect missed opportunities to apply the rich body of laboratory-based research on learning principles, including the benefits of desirable difficulties.

Parallel Studies in Classroom and Laboratory Contexts

In our own collaborative research, we have sought to assess the relevance and applicability of certain laboratory-based learning principles to classroom curriculum through combined laboratory and classroom studies. Our partnership of cognitive psychologists, educational researchers, classroom teachers, policymakers, technology experts, and discipline experts has led to the design of studies in laboratory and classroom contexts that extend findings from laboratory studies using more educationally relevant materials. This research has been conducted with the aim of developing design principles for generalization to other instructional interventions.

Conducting parallel studies in the laboratory and the classroom allows us to test both whether factors identified as important in the laboratory impact classroom learning, and to identify factors explaining performance in the classroom. Our goal is to examine whether the principles within the desirable-difficulties framework (Bjork 1994, 1999), such as generation rather than reading, spacing rather than massing, and interleaving rather than blocking, have the potential to improve instruction. From a research methodology perspective, we have integrated laboratory and classroom studies to investigate further the value of desirable difficulties in educationally realistic learning contexts. Findings from this project so far indicate that these benefits extend to educationally realistic materials and retention intervals.

More specifically, our approach was to examine whether incorporating desirable difficulties into the design of WISE science learning modules could increase their effectiveness. Our initial goal was to examine, under controlled conditions and using introductory psychology students as participants, whether certain difficulties remained desirable when introduced into the learning of educationally realistic materials. In carefully controlled laboratory studies at UCLA, we have focused on three desirable difficulties: interleaving rather than blocking materials to be learned; having learners generate rather than re-read material presented earlier on in the study phase, and spacing rather than massing practice. Experiments have explored the relevance of these principles to science educational content. We have also used parallel materials to test these same desirable difficulties in classroom learning settings. Through the use of the WISE platform, we were able to conduct very comparable studies in both the laboratory and middle school science classrooms. This strategy allowed us to map closely between laboratory findings, which could be carefully controlled, and classroom findings, which provide insight into the generalizability of these principles from the laboratory to real educational instruction.

In one such experiment we adapted an existing WISE module on astronomy, one that covers the characteristics of planets that are important for the existence of life and is relevant to middle and high school science curriculum standards. The module covered two main characteristics: the mass of a planet, and a planet's distance from its sun. The effects of generation and interleaving, two desirable difficulties, and their interaction, were tested via a 2×2 design, which resulted in four conditions: Interleaving plus Generation, Interleaving plus Reading, Blocking plus Generation, and Blocking plus Reading. Interleaving was manipulated by varying whether the instruction described all of the information about the role of the Mass of a planet and then all of the information about the Distance of a planet (Blocked), or whether the instruction alternated randomly between these two sets of information (Interleaved). Generation was manipulated by varying the study opportunities that learners were given. After learning new information, they were either given a review sentence to copy into their notes (read condition) or they were asked to generate a word to fill a blank within the review sentence (generate).

The results we obtained (from a total of 96 participants) largely replicated the effects of generation and interleaving which have been obtained in laboratory studies using simpler materials. Learners who generated during study opportunities recalled significantly more of the material than learners who had simply re-read and copied the reviewed information. Interleaving materials led to greater ability to integrate information (a main goal of science education) than blocking materials, although there was little impact of interleaving on recall for facts taught during the instruction. These findings supported the hypothesis that these principles could impact complex science curriculum content learning, though the benefits of interleaving were not as large or consistent as the benefits of generation. Even so, the generation manipulation was not as challenging or active as what is advocated by science education curriculum designers.

In a second study using the interleaved version of the WISE astronomy module, the generation effect was explored using more educationally important, complex generation questions. In a between-subjects design, participants were given generation prompts that required either free response answers that integrated multiple pieces of information from either Mass OR Distance content (Single-Topic), or free response answers that integrated information from Mass AND Distance content (Topic-Integration). The latter is a more complex knowledge-integration type of reasoning, and mirrors science education pedagogical goals for students' thinking. Performance was tested on study questions, retrieval prompts, during instruction and on new questions after a two-day delay. Data from 55 undergraduates revealed that the Topic-Integration generation was more difficult and resulted in lower performance during learning but led to higher performance on new questions on a posttest following a two-day delay (Richland *et al.* 2005). This suggests that complex generation led to learning above and beyond only retention of the information generated successfully.

While these findings supported the extension of generation and interleaving principles to classroom-relevant technology environments and materials, a further step was necessary to determine whether they would impact learning in a classroom context. As argued by design-based researchers, the close relationship between cognition and context could make these principles unlikely to impact science curriculum learning within a classroom setting. Thus, a slightly modified version of the same WISE module was tested in eighth-grade classrooms in a California Bay Area public middle school. The experiment involved 140 students. As in the laboratory experiments, Interleaving and Generation were manipulated between-subjects in a 2 × 2 design. Generation was manipulated between simple generation (single fact, as in the first WISE experiment described above) and complex Intra-category generation (as in the second WISE Experiment described above). Importantly, findings revealed main effects of both generation and interleaving, indicating that these desirable difficulties have benefits that extend into the dynamic, less controlled, classroom context (Cheng 2004). When tested on new questions on a posttest, students who performed complex, inter-category generation scored higher than students who performed single fact generation. Similarly, students who were taught through interleaved material scored higher on posttest problems than students who were taught through blocked materials.

Interpreting Laboratory and Classroom Findings

Conducting parallel studies in laboratory and classroom settings has revealed dilemmas that signal underlying questions about the nature of learning. They have also led to promising research designs. If the goal of classroom learning is to have students hold up new ideas to existing views, sort out promising perspectives, link new information to related information, and organize ideas, then experimental studies of the recall of a single isolated idea may obscure the complexities of the process. The desirable difficulties that we set out to investigate, while distinct in prior laboratory settings, are more difficult to distinguish in classroom instruction. For example, the test effect and the generation effect have many similarities in complex learning of science. Testing of individuals on complex topics requires asking them to generate ideas that frequently incorporate their personal prior scientific knowledge. Yet generation is a more complex task than distinguishing whether or not a term is the correct match to a stimulus. As a result, the test effect and the generation effect become conflated when valid assessments are included in instruction.

More importantly, spacing and interleaving are conflated in complex learning because successful understanding of the topic requires making sense of related ideas, not just overcoming interference or forgetting. When teachers space instruction of specific topics, they introduce other course-related activities in between. Most often, this will include learning about alternative content within the same domain that has connections to the spaced topic (e.g., a second science topic may be taught during spaced intervals of a science lesson). When students organize their own study they may connect the spaced topic to material they encounter between repetitions. In the process of making sense of the spaced topic, students inevitably consider connections with topics and experiences that they encounter within the same classroom context. By contrast in laboratory studies, spacing and interleaving are differentiated by the degree of interference that the interleaved activity introduces. Interleaved topics are intended to slightly interfere with the learning of each individual topic. Spacing manipulations ideally do not involve active interference so much as opportunities for forgetting.

The complex interconnectedness of the cognitive processes underlying classroom instruction has traditionally made it difficult to extrapolate learning principles developed from the laboratory directly to the design of classroom instruction. Research conducted in the laboratory tradition typically focuses on single, isolated manipulations such as spacing (Bahrick & Phelps 1987), generation (Slamecka & Graf 1978), or testing (Gates 1917). In contrast, classroom interventions tend to require attention to multiple, connected manipulations. For this reason, design-based researchers have critiqued findings from laboratory studies as unclear as far as their applicability to the widely interconnected classroom setting, whereas laboratory researchers have critiqued design-based research findings as non-diagnostic as to what factor, or combination of factors, may be responsible for observed effects.

The types of studies reviewed in this chapter are increasingly filling this bi-directional gap. Laboratory researchers are extending their studies to more complex, realistic tasks and materials. Design-based researchers are using more carefully controlled classroom curriculum interventions and technology-based environments to determine how laboratory results can inform classroom practice. This body of research is growing and has the potential to provide insights into future strategies to build upon and extend laboratory research.

Overall, as this discussion suggests, desirable difficulties may have important implications for classroom learning. Understanding how they work together and how they contribute to the development of an integrated and cohesive view of a particular domain of knowledge requires investigations and research studies that go beyond examining desirable difficulties in isolation and in laboratory settings. Because implementing desirable difficulties is often counterintuitive, they are frequently neglected in classroom instruction. Teachers and students alike are regularly misled by the impression that ease of acquisition indicates successful learning. Laboratory data demonstrates that student views of their own learning often directly contradict their level of retention (Bjork 1994, 1999; Simon & Bjork 2001). Thus, this is an area in which laboratory principles of learning can have real benefits for classroom instructional design.

CONCLUSIONS

As efforts to bridge laboratory and classroom contexts in order to understand learning suggest, these activities are both important and complex. On the one hand, laboratory studies provide clear indications of specific learning principles that work reliably in laboratory studies. As research reported here suggest, however, these clear learning principles must be examined in more complex settings and with more educationally relevant materials before they can be easily applied to a classroom learning environment. The difficulties stem not just from the challenges of the materials, but also because the mechanisms that determine the clarity of these principles rely on the lack of interference or connections among the materials that are typically used in these studies.

When researchers attempt to generalize these learning principles, verified in the laboratory, to classroom contexts, they must combine them with understanding of how people learn more interconnected ideas, such as those of mathematics and science domains. These interconnections are central to extending laboratory findings to classroom settings and crucial in ensuring that individuals who are trained in our schools can engage in lifelong learning (Linn 1995; Linn & Hsi 2000; Linn *et al.* 2004). The process of lifelong learning depends on regularly revisiting ideas and making sense of their connections. Lifelong learning involves more than recalling isolated information and really rests on the importance of making analogies and inferences about when to use information, when to combine information, and when to distrust information. Learners in classroom settings need to build a more and more integrated understanding of their ideas if they are to become productive contributors to society and to lead fruitful lives.

Furthermore, studies of learning in complex settings offer an opportunity to connect learning and design. Learning principles emerging from laboratory studies can lead to new ideas that apply to the design of instructional materials. Criteria for the design of new instruction are increasingly being captured as *design principles* (e.g., Linn *et al.* 2004; Quintana *et al.* 2004; Kali 2006). These studies raise the challenge of linking learning principles and design principles to inform educational interventions. Today, researchers are beginning to connect research in complex settings, features of instruction, and design principles (Quintana *et al.* 2004; Kali 2006). Design principles capture the results of effective designs in guidelines that can be used by future designers and combined in *design patterns* (Linn & Eylon in press). Design patterns describe sequences of activities that have the potential of promoting effective understanding. These sequences, such as *predict, observe, explain*, might be a way to combine the learning principles emanating from laboratory studies with research findings when these principles are tested in classroom settings.

Efforts to merge research conducted in laboratories and research conducted in classrooms meets the goals of use-based research, identified by Stokes (1997). Several features of successful collaborations bridging laboratory and classroom contexts have emerged. First, these collaborations typically involve a partnership of researchers with expertise in laboratory and classroom learning. This leads to productive cross-fertilization of ideas, theoretical traditions, and research strategies.

Second, these ventures typically conduct classroom studies that compare educationally viable alternatives to applying the findings from the laboratory study conducted with more complex materials. Classroom studies must meet stringent criteria, such as not entailing a risk that an intervention will impede student learning. As a result, some comparisons that might be fruitful in the laboratory, such as ones designed to demonstrate the ineffectiveness of a given manipulation, are inappropriate in the classroom. An important virtue of partnerships between laboratory researchers and educational scientists is that manipulations that are at risk of being ineffective, as well as effective, can be tested in the laboratory before being considered for the classroom. In short, bridging laboratory and classroom contexts to create a science of learning offers both daunting challenges and exciting opportunities – for improving student learning, teacher learning, and school effectiveness. We are just beginning on this important trajectory.

In summary, this chapter constitutes an argument that there are compelling theoretical and practical reasons for carrying out research that bridges multiple contexts. To remedy long-standing disconnections between laboratory and classroom research, we argue for partnerships between cognitive scientists and educational researchers and we advocate an interplay of studies that incorporate educationally relevant materials and delays into laboratory studies and test findings from laboratory studies in classroom settings.

Research on cognition and instruction is *both* timely and important. It tackles problems and opportunities that characterize our educational system, and addresses the need for lifelong learning in a world that is ever more complex and rapidly changing. It builds on a foundation of informative laboratory and classroom research. And, most importantly, it responds to an eagerness among cognitive and educational scientists to bridge the laboratory and classroom settings.

AUTHOR NOTES

Preparation of this chapter was supported by Grants 011237 and 030141 from the Institute of Educational Sciences and by Collaborative Activity Grant 014448 from the James S. McDonnell Foundation. This material is also based upon work supported by the National Science Foundation under grants Nos. 9873180, 9805420, 0087832, and 0334199. Any opinions, findings, and conclusions or recommendations expressed in this material are those of the authors and do not necessarily reflect the views of the National Science Foundation, Institute of Education Sciences, or James S. McDonnell Foundation. The authors gratefully acknowledge helpful discussions of these ideas with members of the Web-based Inquiry Science Environment group and the Technology Enhanced Learning in Science center. The authors appreciate help in production of this paper from David Crowell and Jonathan Breitbart, and we thank Jason Finley for his contributions to the experimental work we report.

REFERENCES

Anderson, M. C., Bjork, R. A. & Bjork, E. L. (1994). Remembering can cause forgetting: retrieval dynamics in long-term memory. *Journal of Experimental Psychology: Learning, Memory, and Cognition*, *20*, 1063–1087.

Anderson, J. R., Corbett, A. T., Koedinger, K. & Pelletier, R. (1995). Cognitive tutors: lessons learned. *The Journal of Learning Sciences*, *4*, 167–207.

Anderson, J. R., Douglass, S. & Qin, Y. (2004). How should a theory of learning and cognition inform instruction? In A. Healy (ed.), *Experimental Cognitive Psychology and Its Applications*. Washington, DC: American Psychological Association.

Bahrick, H. P. & Hall, L. K. (1991). Lifetime maintenance of high school mathematics content. *Journal of Experiment Psychology: General*, *120*, 20–33.

Bahrick, H. P. & Phelps, E. (1987). Retention of Spanish vocabulary over 8 years. *Journal of Experimental Psychology: Learning, Memory & Cognition*, *13*, 344–349.

Barab, S. A. & Squire, K. D. (2004). Design-based research: putting a stake in the ground. *Journal of the Learning Sciences*, *13*, 1–14.

Bell, P., Hoadley, C. M. & Linn, M. C. (2004). Design-based research in education. M. C. Linn, E. A. Davis & P. Bell (eds.), *Internet Environments for Science Education* (pp. 73–88). Mahwah, NJ: Lawrence Erlbaum Associates.

Bjork, R. A. (1975). Retrieval as a memory modifier: an interpretation of negative recency and related phenomena. In R. L. Solso (ed.), *Information Processing and Cognition* (pp. 123–144). New York: John Wiley & Sons.

Bjork, R. A. (1994). Memory and metamemory considerations in the training of human beings. In J. Metcalfe and A. Shimamura (eds.), *Metacognition: Knowing about Knowing*. (pp. 185–205). Cambridge, MA: MIT Press.

Bjork, R. A. (1999). Assessing our own competence: heuristics and illusions. In D. Gopher and A. Koriat (eds.), *Attention and Performance XVII. Cognitive Regulation of Performance: Interaction of Theory and Application* (pp. 435–459). Cambridge, MA: MIT Press.

Black, P. & Wiliam, D. (1998). Assessment and classroom learning. *Assessment in Education: Principles, Policy, and Practice*, *5*(1), 7–74.

Brown, A. L. (1992). Design experiments: theoretical and methodological challenges in creating complex interventions in classroom settings. *The Journal of the Learning Sciences, 2*(2), 141–178.

Brown, A. L. & Campione, J. C. (1994). Guided discovery in a community of learners. In K. McGilly (ed.), *Classroom Lessons: Integrating Cognitive Theory and Classroom Practice* (pp. 229–270). Cambridge, MA: MIT Press.

Butterfield, B. & Metcalfe, J. (2001). Errors made with high confidence are hypercorrected. *Journal of Experimental Psychology: Learning, Memory, and Cognition, 27,* 1491–1494.

Carlson, R. A. & Yaure, R. G. (1990). Practice schedules and the use of component skills in problem solving. *Journal of Experimental Psychology: Learning, Memory & Cognition, 16,* 484–496.

Catalano, J. F. & Kleiner, B. M. (1984). Distant transfer in coincident timing as a function of variability of practice. *Perceptual & Motor Skills, 58,* 851–856.

Cepeda, N. J., Pashler, H., Vul, E., Wixted, J., & Rohrer, D. (2006). Distributed practice in verbal recall tasks: a review and quantitative synthesis. *Psychological Bulletin, 132,* 354–380.

Cheng, B. (2004). IDDEAS: classroom studies of desirable difficulties implemented in astronomy curricula. Paper presented at the American Education Research Association Conference. San Diego, CA.

Chi, M. T. H. (2000). Self-explaining expository tests: the dual process of generating inferences and repairing mental models. In R. Glaser (ed.), *Advances in Instructional Psychology* (Vol. 5, pp. 161–238). Mahwah, NJ: Lawrence Erlbaum Associates.

Cobb, P., diSessa, A., Lehrer, R. & Schauble, L. (2003). Design experiments in educational research. *Educational Researcher, 32,* 9–13.

Collins, A. (1992). Toward a design science of education. In E. Scanlon & T. O. Shea (eds.), *New Directions in Educational Technology* (pp. 15–22). New York: Springer-Verlag.

Corbett, A. T., Koedinger, K. R. & Hadley, W. H. (2001). Cognitive tutors: from the research classroom to all classrooms. In P. S. Goodman (ed.), *Technology Enhanced Learning: Opportunities for Change* (pp. 235–263). Mahwah, NJ: Lawrence Erlbaum Associates.

Davis, E. A. (1998). Scaffolding students' reflection for science learning. Unpublished doctoral dissertation, University of California at Berkeley, CA.

Davis, E. A. & Linn, M. C. (2000). Scaffolding students' knowledge integration: prompts for reflection in KIE. *International Journal of Science Education, 22,* 819–837.

Dempster, F. N. (1988). The spacing effect: a case study in the failure to apply the results of psychological research. *American Psychologist, 43,* 627–634.

Dempster, F. N. (1989). Spacing effects and their implications for theory and practice. *Educational Psychology Review, 1,* 309–330.

Dempster, F. N. (1996). Distributing and managing the conditions of encoding and practice. In E. L. Bjork & R. A. Bjork (eds.), *Memory* (Vol. 10, E. C. Carterette & M. P. Friedman, eds.), *Handbook of Perception and Cognition.* New York: Academic Press.

deWinstanley, P. A. (1995). A generation effect can be found during naturalistic learning. *Psychonomic Bulletin & Review, 2,* 538–541.

deWinstanley, P. A. & Bjork, E. L. (2004). Processing strategies and the generation effect: implications for making a better reader. *Memory and Cognition, 32,* 945–955.

diSessa, A. A. (2000). *Changing Minds: Computers, Learning, and Literacy.* Cambridge, MA: MIT Press.

Gates, A. I. (1917). Recitation as a factor in memorizing. *Archives of Psychology, 6*(40), 104.

Gelman, R. (1998). Domain specificity in cognitive development: universals and nonuniversals. In M. Sabourin, F. Craik & M. Robert (eds.), *Advances in Psychological Science, Vol. 2, Biological and Cognitive Aspects.* Hove: Psychology Press.

Gelman, R. & Brenneman, K. (2004). Science learning pathways for young children. *Early Childhood Research Quarterly, 19,* 150–158.

Glenberg, A. M. (1976). Monotonic and nonmonotonic lag effects in paired-associate and recognition memory paradigms. *Journal of Verbal Learning and Verbal Behavior, 15,* 1–16.

Glenberg, A. M. (1992). Distributed practice effects. In L. R. Squire (ed.), *Encyclopedia of Learning and Memory* (pp. 138–142). New York: Macmillan.

Glover, J. A. (1989). The "testing" phenomenon: not gone but nearly forgotten. *Journal of Educational Psychology, 81*, 392–399.

Hamaker, C. (1986). The effects of adjunct questions on prose learning. *Review of Educational Research, 56*, 212–242.

Hogan, R. M. & Kintsch, W. (1971). Differential effects of study and test trials on long-term recognition and recall. *Journal of Verbal Learning and Verbal Behavior, 10*, 562–567.

Homa, D. & Cultice, J. (1984). Role of feedback, category size, and stimulus distortion on the acquisition and untilization of ill-defined categories. *Journal of Experimental Psychology: Learning, Memory, and Cognition, 10*, 83–94.

Izawa, C. (1970). Optimal potentiating effects and forgetting-prevention effects in paired-associate learning. *Journal of Experimental Psychology, 83*, 340–344.

Jacoby, L. L. (1978). On interpreting the effects of repetition: solving a problem versus remembering a solution. *Journal of Verbal Learning and Verbal Behavior, 17*, 649–667.

Kali, Y. (2006). Collaborative knowledge-building using the Design Principles Database. *International Journal of Computer Support for Collaborative Learning, 1*(2), 187–201.

Kali, Y., Spitulnik, M. & Linn, M. (2005). Design principles for educational software. Retrieved January 10, 2005, Available at: http://www.design-principles.org/dp/index.php

Klahr, D. & Li, J. (2005). Cognitive research and elementary science instruction: from the laboratory, to the classroom, and back. *Journal of Science Education and Technology, 14*, 217–238.

Koedinger, K. R. & Anderson, J. R. (1998). Illustrating principled design: the early evolution of a cognitive tutor for algebra symbolization. *Interactive Learning Environments, 5*, 161–180.

Kornell, N. & Metcalfe, J. (2006). Study efficacy and the region of proximal learning framework. *Journal of Experimental Psychology: Learning, Memory, & Cognition, 32*, 609–622.

Kulhavy, R. W. (1977). Feedback in written instruction. *Review of Educational Research, 58*(1), 79–97.

Kulhavy, R. W. & Stock, W. A. (1989). Feedback in written instruction: the place of response certitude. *Educational Psychology Review, 1*(4), 279–308.

Kulik, J. A. & Kulik, C. C. (1988). Timing of feedback and verbal learning. *Review of Educational Research, 58*, 79–97.

Lee, T. D. & Genovese, E. D. (1988). Distribution of practice in motor skill acquisition: learning and performance effects reconsidered. *Research Quarterly for Exercise and Sport, 59*, 277–287.

Leeming, F. C. (2002). The exam-a-day procedure improves performance in psychology classes. *Teaching of Psychology, 29*, 210–212.

Linn, M. C. (1990). Establishing a science and engineering base for science education. In M. Gardner, J. G. Greeno, F. Reif, A. H. Schoenfeld, A. diSessa & E. Stage (eds.), *Toward a Scientific Practice of Science Education* (pp. 323–341). Hillsdale, NJ: Lawrence Erlbaum Associates.

Linn, M. C. (1995). Designing computer learning environments for engineering and computer science: the Scaffolded Knowledge Integration framework. *Journal of Science Education and Technology, 4*, 103–126.

Linn, M. C., Davis, E. A. & Bell, P. (2004). Inquiry and technology. In M. C. Linn, E. A. Davis & P. Bell (eds.), *Internet Environments for Science Education* (pp. 3–28). Mahwah, NJ: Lawrence Erlbaum Associates.

Linn, M. C. & Eylon, B.-S. (in press). Science education: integrating views of learning and instruction. In P. A. Alexander & P. H. Winne (eds.), *Handbook of Educational Psychology* (2nd edn). Mahwah, NJ: Lawrence Erlbaum Associates.

Linn, M. C. & Hsi, S. (2000). *Computers, Teachers, and Peers: Science Learning Partners.* Mahwah, NJ: Lawrence Erlbaum Associates.

Linn, M. C., Lewis, C., Tsuchida, I. & Songer, N. B. (2000). Science lessons and beyond: why do U.S. and Japanese students diverge? *Educational Researcher, 29*(3), 4–14.

McDaniel, M. A. & Fisher, R. P. (1991). Tests and test feedback as learning sources. *Contemporary Educational Psychology, 16*, 192–201.

McDaniel, T. R. (1994). College classrooms of the future: megatrends to paradigm shifts. *College Teaching, 42*(1), 27–31.

McDaniel, M. A. & Mason, M. E. J. (1985). Altering memory representations through retrieval. *Journal of Experimental Psychology: Learning, Memory, and Cognition*, *11*, 371–385.
McDermott, K. B. (2006). Paradoxical effects of testing: repeated retrieval attempts enhance the likelihood of later accurate and false recall. *Memory & Cognition*, *34*, 261–267.
Mannes, S. M. & Kintsch, W. (1987). Knowledge organization and text organization. *Cognition and Instruction*, *4*, 91–115.
Metcalfe, J. & Kornell, N. (2003). The dynamics of learning and allocation of study time to a region of proximal learning. *Journal of Experimental Psychology: General*, *132*, 530–542.
Metcalfe, J., Kornell, N. & Son, L. K. (2006). A cognitive-science based program to enhance study efficacy in a high and low-risk setting. Submitted for publication.
Palinscar, A. S. & Brown, A. L. (1984). Reciprocal teaching of comprehension-fostering and comprehension-monitoring activities. *Cognition and Instruction*, *1*, 117–175.
Pashler, H., Zarow, G. & Triplett, B. (2003). Is temporal spacing of tests helpful even when it inflates error rates? *Journal of Experimental Psychology: Learning, Memory & Cognition*, *29*, 1051–1057.
Pellegrino, J. W., Chudowsky, N. & Glaser, R. (2001). *Knowing What Students Know: The Science and Design of Educational Assessment*. Washington, DC: National Academy Press.
Pesta, B. J., Sanders, R. E. & Murphy, M. D. (1999). A beautiful day in the neighborhood: what factors determine the generation effect for simple multiplication problems? *Memory and Cognition*, *27*, 106–115.
Quintana, C., Reiser, B. J., Davis, E. A. *et al.* (2004). A scaffolding design framework for software to support science inquiry. *Journal of the Learning Sciences*, *13*(3), 337–386.
Reder, L. M., Charney, D. H. & Morgan, K. I. (1986). The role of elaborations in learning a skill from an instructional text. *Memory and Cognition*, *14*, 64–78.
Richland, L. E., Bjork, R. A., Finley, J. R. & Linn, M. C. (2005). Linking cognitive science to education: generation and interleaving effects. In B. G. Bara, L. Barsalou & M. Bucciarelli (eds.), *Proceedings of the Twenty-Seventh Annual Conference of the Cognitive Science Society*. Mahwah, NJ: Lawrence Erlbaum Associates.
Richland, L. E., Holyoak, K. J. & Stigler, J. W. (2004). Analogy use in eight-grade mathematics classrooms. *Cognition and Instruction*, *22*, 37–60.
Roediger, H. L. & Karpicke, J. D. (2006). Test-enhanced learning: taking memory tests improves long-term retention, *Psychological Science*, *17*(3), 249–255.
Roediger, H. L. & Marsh, E. J. (2005). The positive and negative consequences of multiple-choice testing. *Journal of Experimental Psychology: Learning, Memory and Cognition*, *31*, 1155–1159.
Rogers, B. (2001). *TOEFL CBT Success*. Lawrenceville, NJ: Peterson's.
Rohrer, D. & Taylor, K. (in press). The effects of overlearning and distributed practice on the retention of mathematics knowledge. *Applied Cognitive Psychology*.
Rohrer, D., Taylor, K., Pashler, H. *et al.* (2005). The effect of overlearning on long-term retention. *Applied Cognitive Psychology*, *19*, 361–374.
Scardamalia, M. & Bereiter, C. (1991). Higher levels of agency for children in knowledge-building: a challenge for the design of new knowledge media. *Journal of the Learning Sciences*, *1*, 37–68.
Schmidt, R. A. (1991). Frequent augmented feedback can degrade learning: evidence and interpretations. In G. E. Stelmach & J. Requin (eds.), *Tutorials in Motor Neuroscience* (pp. 59–75). Dordrecht: Kluwer.
Schmidt, R. A., Young, D. E., Swinnen, S. & Shapiro, D. C. (1989). Summary knowledge of results for skill acquisition: support for the guidance hypothesis. *Journal of Experimental Psychology: Learning, Memory, and Cognition*, *15*, 352–359.
Schmidt, W. H., McKnight, C. C., Houang, R. T. *et al.* (2001). *Why Schools Matter: A Cross-National Comparison of Curriculum and Learning*. San Francisco, CA: Jossey-Bass.
Schofield, J. W. (1995). *Computers and Classroom Culture*. New York: Cambridge University Press.
Shavelson, R. J., Phillips, D. C., Towne, L. & Feuer, M. J. (2003). On the science of education design studies. *Educational Researcher*, *32*(1), 25–28.

Shavelson, R. J. & Towne, L. (2002). *Scientific Research in Education*. Washington, DC: National Academy Press.

Shea, J. B. & Morgan, R. L. (1979). Contextual interference effects on the acquisition, retention, and transfer of a motor skill. *Journal of Experimental Psychology: Human Learning and Memory*, *5*, 179–187.

Shonkoff, J. P. & Phillips, D. A. (eds.) (2000). *From Neurons to Neighborhoods: The Science of Early Childhood Development*. Washington, DC: National Academy Press.

Simon, D. A. & Bjork, R. A. (2001). Metacognition in motor learning. *Journal of Experimental Psychology, Learning, Memory, and Cognition*, *4*, 907–912.

Slamecka, N. J. & Graf, P. (1978). The generation effect: delineation of a phenomenon. *Journal of Experimental Psychology: Human Learning and Memory*, *4*, 592–604.

Sloane, K. & Linn, M. C. (1988). Instructional conditions in Pascal programming classes. In R. E. Mayer (ed.), *Teaching and Learning Computer Programming: Multiple Research Perspectives*. Hillsdale, NJ: Lawrence Erlbaum Associates.

Son, L. K. (2004). Spacing one's study: evidence for a metacognitive control strategy. *Journal of Experimental Psychology: Learning, Memory, and Cognition*, *30*, 601–604.

Songer, N. B., Lee, H.-S. & McDonald, S. (2003). Research towards an expanded understanding of inquiry science beyond one idealized standard. *Science Education*, *87*(4), 490–516.

Stokes, D. E. (1997). *Pasteur's Quadrant: Basic Science and Technological Innovation*. Washington, DC: Brookings Institute.

Thios, S. J. & D'Agostino, P. R. (1976). Effects of repetition as a function of study-phase retrieval. *Journal of Verbal Learning and Verbal Behavior*, *15*, 529–536.

Thompson, C. P., Wegner, S. K. & Bartling, C. A. (1978). How recall facilitates subsequent recall: a reappraisal. *Journal of Experimental Psychology: Human Learning and Memory*, *4*, 210–221.

Tzeng, O. J. L. (1973). Stimulus meaningfulness, encoding variability, and the spacing effect. *Journal of Experimental Psychology*, *99*, 162–166.

Wheeler, M. A., Ewers, M. & Buonanno, J. (2003). Different rates of forgetting following study versus test trials. *Memory*, *11*, 571–580.

Wheeler, M. A. & Roediger, H. L. (1992). Disparate effects of repeated testing: Reconciling Ballard's (1913) and Bartlett's (1932) results. *Psychological Science*, *3*, 240–245.

Whitten, W. B. & Bjork, R. A. (1977). Learning from tests: the effects of spacing. *Journal of Verbal Learning and Verbal Behavior*, *16*, 465–478.

Winstein, C. J. & Schmidt, R. A. (1990). Reduced frequency of knowledge of results enhances motor skill learning. *Journal of Experimental Psychology: Learning, Memory, and Cognition*, *16*, 677–691.

CHAPTER 22

Cognitive Rehabilitation

Barbara A. Wilson
MRC Cognition and Brain Sciences Unit, UK
The Oliver Zangwill Centre for Neuropsychological Rehabilitation, UK

OVERVIEW

This chapter is concerned with the rehabilitation of cognitive deficits in people who have survived an injury or other insult to the brain. The topics addressed are those which currently engage the interest of clinicians actively working in the field. In rehabilitation centers for survivors of brain injury the typical patient will be a young man who has sustained a traumatic brain injury in a road traffic accident. He will probably not have severe motor problems. He is likely to have memory and attention deficits; his planning, reasoning, judgment, and problem-solving skills will have been affected. He may be anxious and have mood swings. His social skills may be impaired. His friends may drift away. He has probably lost his job and there may be frequent arguments at home. Of course, not everyone will have all of these difficulties but the picture painted above will be familiar to anyone working in the area of cognitive rehabilitation.

Following a brief history of rehabilitation, definitions of the term "cognitive rehabilitation" are considered. The definition preferred is based on McLellan (1991), namely that cognitive rehabilitation is a process whereby people disabled by injury or disease work with professional staff and others to alleviate or ameliorate cognitive deficits resulting from an insult to the brain. The chapter continues with a section about theoretical influences on cognitive rehabilitation. Given the complexity of the problems faced by people with brain injury, no one theory, model, or framework is sufficient to address all the difficulties faced by patients and their families so it is essential to have a wide theoretical base if one is to achieve best clinical practice. The chapter continues with an account of some of the main changes in rehabilitation over the past 25 years. These include (1) partnership with patients and families; (2) use of goal-setting to plan and evaluate rehabilitation; (3) recognition that the treatment of emotional problems should be an integral part of cognitive rehabilitation; (4) the increasing use of technology, particularly in helping people to compensate for their cognitive deficits; (5) starting rehabilitation in intensive care; and (6) not being constrained by one theoretical approach. Current approaches to rehabilitation are then considered. These include the exercise approach, approaches derived

Handbook of Applied Cognition: Second Edition. Edited by Francis T. Durso.

from cognitive neuropsychological theories, the combined approach, and the holistic approach. Consideration is given to the practice of rehabilitation, including information collected from a survey of psychologists engaged in brain injury rehabilitation. A case study is then presented to illustrate the process of cognitive rehabilitation before the summary and conclusions.

HISTORICAL BACKGROUND

Although the first program to describe itself as providing "cognitive rehabilitation" appears to be that initiated by Leonard Diller in New York in 1976 (Diller 1976), his program was not the first to offer treatment for cognitive disorders. In Germany in the First World War, for example, Goldstein, Poppelreuter, and others were providing help to brain-damaged soldiers (Boake 1996). The first book written on rehabilitation appears to be Poppelreuter's (1917), who describes a program for helping soldiers to return to work; and it is interesting to note that many of his ideas are incorporated into contemporary vocational rehabilitation programs. Poppelreuter argued for an interdisciplinary approach between psychology, neurology, and psychiatry, and in a paper published in 1918 he emphasized the importance of the patient's own insight into the effects of disabilities and treatment. Goldstein (1942), also writing about the consequences of injury in the First World War, stressed the importance of cognitive and personality deficits following brain injury, and referred to techniques that we would now call "cognitive rehabilitation strategies" (Prigatano 1986). In 1918, Goldstein, according to Poser *et al.* (1996), was concerned with decisions as to whether to try to restore lost functioning or to compensate for lost or impaired functions. This debate is still being argued today. Goldstein's interest in work (vocational) therapy, like that of his fellow countryman Poppelreuter, is reflected in modern rehabilitation. Poser *et al.* (1996) remind us that "Many of the rehabilitation procedures developed in special military hospitals during World War One are still in use today in modern rehabilitation – at least to some extent" (p. 259).

In the Second World War, both Luria, working in what was then the Soviet Union, and Zangwill, in the United Kingdom, were active in treating cognitive problems seen in the survivors of gunshot wounds to the head. Christensen and Caetano (1996), in a paper describing Luria's contributions to neuropsychological rehabilitation, suggested that the Second World War was the most significant factor in Luria's development of neuropsychological rehabilitation methods. Zangwill also reported to a friend, Richard Gregory, that this was the most creative period of his life (Gregory, personal communication). One important principle, stressed by both Luria and Zangwill, was that of "functional adaptation," whereby an intact skill is used to compensate for a damaged one; and we have already seen that Goldstein was committed to a similar concept. Luria's own publications, and his book with Naydin, Tsvetkova, and Vinarskaya (Luria 1963, 1970; Luria *et al.* 1969) are well worth reading today for the insights they offer. So too is Zangwill's (1947) paper, in which he discusses, among other things, the principles of re-education, and refers to three main approaches to rehabilitation: "compensation," "substitution," and "direct retraining." This appears to be the first time anyone had categorized rehabilitation in this way. In Zangwill's words, "We wish to know in particular how far the brain injured patient may be expected to compensate for his disabilities and the extent to which the injured human brain is capable of re-education." This question is as pertinent in the twenty-first century as it was during the Second World War.

Programs from Israel, such as those described by Najenson *et al.* (1974) and Ben-Yishay (1978), have also been very influential. Ben-Yishay (1996) describes in some detail the origins of his approach, the evolution of the therapeutic milieu concept, and the philosophy behind his thinking. In 1966, after the Yom Kippur war, he was living in New York and was asked by the Israeli government to set up a program for the soldiers who had survived brain injury. He started his "Milieu Therapy" (Ben-Yishay 1996), which was the precursor of the holistic programs that will be discussed later in this chapter. The Milieu approach recognized the importance of the social and emotional consequences of brain injury and suggested that if these are not treated, rehabilitation of cognitive deficits will fail. The reason it is so important to address the psychological as well as the cognitive issues is because it is futile to separate the cognitive sequelae of brain injury from the emotional, social, and functional sequelae. After all, how we think, remember, communicate, and solve problems affects how we feel emotionally and how we behave, and vice versa. Survivors of brain injury are at risk of a range of emotional, behavioral, and psychiatric disorders (Williams & Evans 2003). It is often hard to separate out these different disorders and all should be treated. For a more detailed discussion of the psychosocial disorders associated with brain injury the reader is referred to Williams and Evans (2003), a collection of 17 papers on this topic.

WHAT DO WE UNDERSTAND BY THE TERM "COGNITIVE REHABILITATION"?

There are several definitions of the general term "rehabilitation" and of the more specific "cognitive rehabilitation." Perhaps one of the most inclusive and coherent, and one that I shall adhere to for the purpose of this discussion, is McLellan's (1991): "[rehabilitation] is a process by which people disabled by injury or disease work together with professional staff, relatives, and members of the wider community to achieve their optimal physical, psychological, social, and vocational wellbeing" (p. 785). One of McLellan's main points is that rehabilitation is a two-way, interactive process in which the person with disability is one of the central players. This is unlike other branches of medicine such as surgery or pharmacological therapy where the patient remains a passive recipient of the treatment.

How, then, should we define "*cognitive* rehabilitation"? There have been several attempts since Diller's term gained popular usage in the 1980s. One of its earliest advocates was Gianutsos (1980), who described it as "a service designed to remediate disorders of perception, memory, and language" (p. 37). This is now seen as rather limiting as it omits the cognitive disorders of attention, planning, organization, and spatial awareness. Wood (1990) stated that, "Cognitive rehabilitation uses an assortment of procedures to improve or restore a diverse collection of abilities and skills" (p. 3). This definition is perhaps too imprecise and can be compared with the more detailed definition offered by Sohlberg and Mateer (1989), who argue that "Cognitive rehabilitation . . . refers to the therapeutic process of increasing or improving an individual's capacity to process and use incoming information so as to allow increased functioning in everyday life. This includes both methods to restore cognitive function and compensatory techniques" (pp. 3–4). Sohlberg and Mateer elaborate by stating: "Cognitive rehabilitation applies to therapy methods that actually retrain or alleviate problems caused by deficits in attention, visual processing, language, memory, reasoning/problem solving, and executive functions" (p. 4).

Ben-Yishay and Prigatano (1990) offer a variation of this when they suggest that cognitive rehabilitation is "the amelioration of deficits in problem solving abilities in order to improve functional competence in everyday situations" (p. 395). Is poor problem-solving ability the basic underlying deficit in all people with cognitive deficits following brain injury? What about patients with a pure amnesic syndrome who, despite severe memory deficits, do not appear to have difficulties with problem-solving tasks? Ben-Yishay and Prigatano might argue that such patients are unable to solve problems *which allow them to compensate* and thus surviving in their own environments.

To return to McLellan's definition, we can modify this to define cognitive rehabilitation as a process whereby people disabled by injury or disease work with professional staff and others to alleviate or ameliorate cognitive deficits resulting from an insult to the brain. This process involves attempts to help survivors of brain injury and their families understand, bypass, come to terms with, and reduce such cognitive deficits. However, even this definition is insufficient in terms of current thinking, which recognizes that survivors of brain injury are likely to face emotional, behavioral, and social difficulties in addition to their cognitive problems. It follows that because these various consequences of brain injury are interlinked and hard to disentangle, it is probably more accurate to include them in the broader term "neuropsychological rehabilitation" as this has sufficient breadth to encompass behavioral, psychological, and social consequences of brain injury.

THEORETICAL INFLUENCES ON COGNITIVE REHABILITATION

Gianutsos (1991) suggests that cognitive rehabilitation is born of mixed parentage, including neuropsychology, occupational therapy, speech and language therapy, and special education. Others refer to different fields: McMillan and Greenwood (1993), for example, believe that rehabilitation draws on clinical neuropsychology, behavioral analysis, cognitive retraining, and group and individual psychotherapy. Still others believe only one "parent" is necessary, and these tend to be supporters of the use of theories from cognitive neuropsychology to inform treatment. Coltheart (1984), in the first issue of the prestigious journal *Cognitive Neuropsychology*, argues that rehabilitation programs should be based on a theoretical analysis of the nature of the disorder to be treated. Mitchum and Berndt (1995) suggest that the goal of cognitive rehabilitation is "the development of rational therapies that are based upon a theoretical analysis of the nature of the disorder that is targeted for treatment" (p. 13).

Most people working in cognitive rehabilitation agree that theoretical models are necessary for appropriate treatment although many of them might also argue that they are not necessarily sufficient on their own. The situation is made more complex because there is disagreement as to what constitutes a theoretical model. Gianutsos (1991), for example, claims that cognitive rehabilitation is the application of theories of cognitive sciences to traumatic brain injury (TBI) rehabilitation. Apart from the fact that it is not only people with TBI who receive cognitive rehabilitation, Gianutsos's approach does not appear to be influenced by theories from cognitive science as she favors the repeated practice approach whereby patients or clients engage, for the most part, in computerized cognitive exercises (Gianutsos 1981, 1991). There is little, if any, presence in these papers of theories of cognitive neuroscience.

The most influential theories are without doubt those from cognitive neuropsychology, particularly from the fields of language and reading (see, e.g., Seron & Deloche 1989; Coltheart *et al.* 1991; Mitchum & Berndt 1995). Although it is true that theoretical models from cognitive neuropsychology have been highly influential in helping us to understand and explain related phenomena (Wilson & Patterson 1990) and in helping us to develop assessment procedures, the trap waiting for them is rehabilitation irrelevance (Robertson 1991). Wilson (1997) also argues that because models from cognitive neuropsychology tell us *what* to treat and not *how* to treat, they are insufficient on their own to guide us through the many intricate processes involved in the rehabilitation process.

Theories and models from learning theory and behavioral psychology have also been used in rehabilitation since the 1970s (Ince 1976; Lincoln 1978), and in cognitive rehabilitation (Wilson 1991). For example, behavioral assessments are employed in many cognitive programs to (1) identify and measure variables that control behavior, (2) select treatment, and (3) evaluate treatment. Numerous approaches from behavior therapy and behavior modification can and have been adopted to help people with memory, perceptual, reading, and language disorders (Wilson 1999). A behavioral analysis approach is usually incorporated into cognitive rehabilitation because it provides a structure, a way of analyzing cognitive problems, a means of assessing everyday manifestations of cognitive problems, and a means of evaluating the efficacy of treatment programs. It also, of course, supplies us with many existing treatment strategies such as shaping, chaining, modeling, desensitizing, flooding, extinction, positive reinforcement, response cost, and so forth, all of which can be modified or adapted to suit particular rehabilitation purposes.

Pioneered by Diller (1976); Ben-Yishay (1978), and Prigatano (1986), the holistic approach is now seen as one of the most effective ways of providing cognitive rehabilitation to survivors of brain injury and is now much in evidence. Most holistic programs are concerned with increasing a client's awareness, alleviating cognitive deficits, developing compensatory skills, and providing vocational counseling. All such programs provide a mixture of individual and group therapy. They differ from the combined approach primarily in their recognition of the importance of treating emotional problems at the same time as treating the cognitive and social difficulties.

Inherent in the holistic approach are theories and models of emotion, which are becoming increasingly important in cognitive rehabilitation, as evidenced, for example, by a recent special issue of the journal *Neuropsychological Rehabilitation* focusing entirely on biopsychosocial approaches in neuropsychological rehabilitation (Williams & Evans 2003).

Prigatano (1995, 1999) believes that dealing with the emotional effects of brain injury is essential to rehabilitation success. Social isolation, anxiety, and depression are common in survivors of brain injury (Wilson 2002a). Gainotti (1993) distinguishes three main factors causing emotional and psychosocial problems after brain injury: those due to neurological factors, those due to psychological or psychodynamic factors, and those due to psychosocial factors. An example of the first might be someone with frontal lobe damage leading to loss of control and anger outbursts. An example of the second would be someone with reduced cognitive abilities and consequent loss of self-esteem, together with depression, because of an inability to engage in his or her previous profession. An example of the third might be someone who loses all friends and colleagues following a brain injury and is thus very socially isolated. It is possible that these different types of emotional problems may overlap. Other models and theories that need to be taken into account are those pertaining to pre-morbid personality, neurological, physical, and biochemical models as well as models of emotional behavior such as those from cognitive behavior therapy (CBT).

Ever since Beck's (1976) highly influential *Cognitive Therapy and Emotional Disorders* appeared, CBT has become one of the most important and best validated psychotherapeutic procedures (Salkovskis 1996). An update of Beck's model appeared in 1996. Williams *et al.* (2003) discuss CBT with survivors of TBI. Analytic psychotherapy is also used in rehabilitation practice, and Prigatano (1999) is one of the best-known advocates of this approach with survivors of brain injury.

Because survivors of brain injury are likely to have a mixture of cognitive and non-cognitive problems, no one theory, model, or framework is sufficient to deal with the range, or indeed complexity, of problems faced by those requiring cognitive rehabilitation. In Diller's (1987) words, "While current accounts of remediation have been criticised as lacking a theoretical base, it might be more accurate to state that remediation must take into account several theoretical bases" (p. 9). We need to have some understanding of theories of assessment, recovery, learning, personality, and plasticity, to name but a few. In an attempt to illustrate the complexity of rehabilitation and to persuade those that believe one theoretical approach is sufficient, Wilson (2002a) published a provisional model of cognitive rehabilitation (reproduced in Figure 22.1). This model illustrates the fact that rehabilitation is a complex process, and many factors need to be taken into account, including the family, the nature and severity of brain injury, and evaluation of the efficacy of treatment, as well as cognitive and emotional difficulties.

CHANGES IN REHABILITATION OVER THE PAST 25 YEARS

There have been a number of changes in the practice of neuropsychological rehabilitation over the past 25 years, including the following six that have been particularly influential. First, as inferred earlier, rehabilitation is now seen as a partnership between patients, families, and health care staff. In the 1970s and 1980s staff at rehabilitation centers would tell the person with the disability what to expect in and from rehabilitation, they would determine what areas to work on, what goals to set, what was achievable, and what was not. Doctors, psychologists, and therapists would decide that Mrs. Brown would learn an alternative communication system to compensate for her language deficits or that Mr. Smith would undergo scanning training to reduce his unilateral neglect. In the late 1980s the philosophy began to change – at least in some centers – so that in many rehabilitation programs today, clients and families are asked about their expectations. Rehabilitation goals are discussed and negotiated between all concerned; now, in many if not most rehabilitation centers, families, clients, and staff work together to determine the aims and purposes of the rehabilitation program.

The focus of treatment is on improving aspects of everyday life and, as Ylvisaker and Feeney (2000) say, rehabilitation involves personally meaningful themes, activities, settings, and interactions. Evans (2003) illustrates this approach in his case description of David, a man with attention and planning problems following a stroke. Tate *et al.* (2003) also intimate the importance of partnership in the descriptions of their service for people

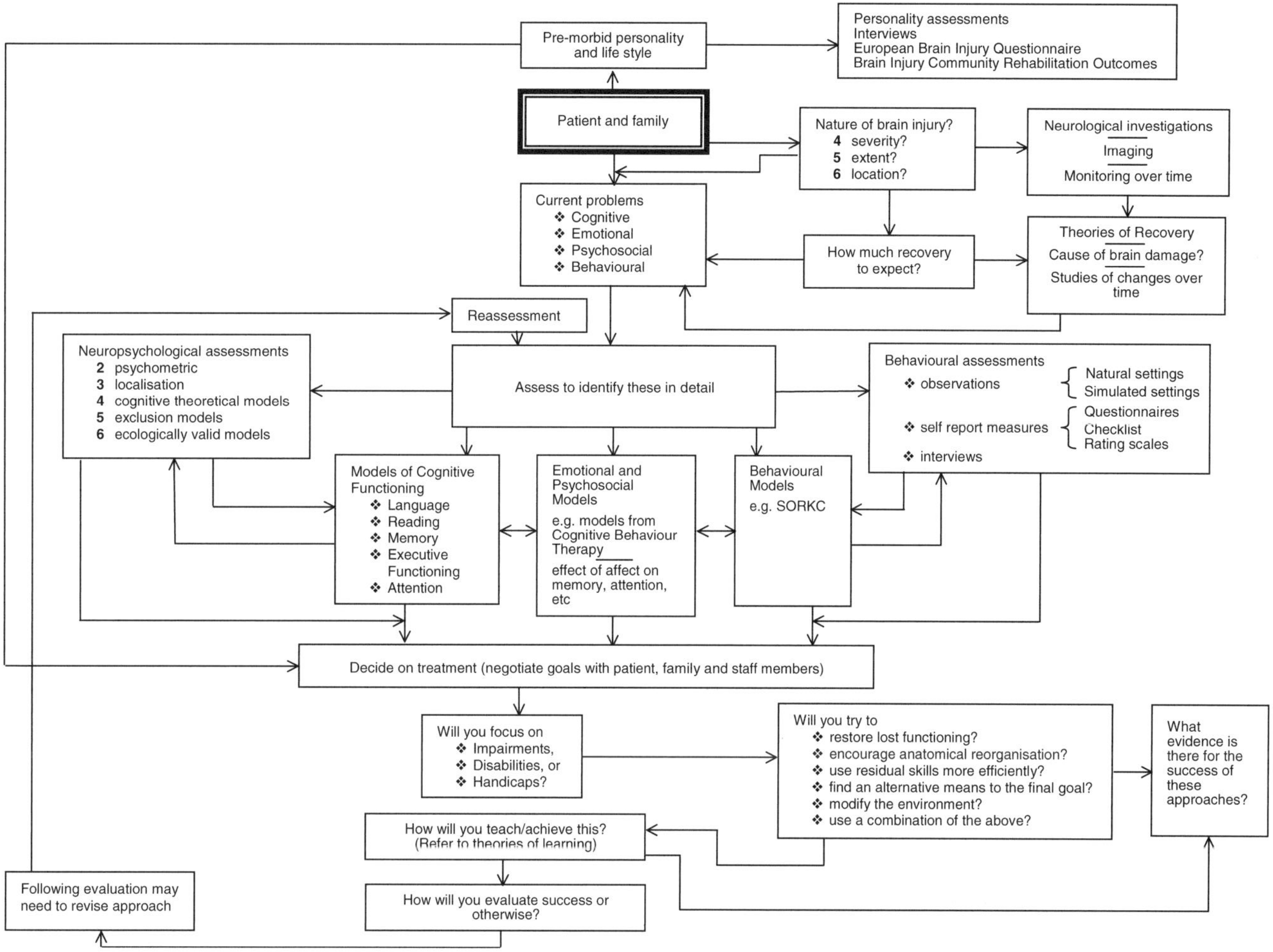

Figure 22.1 A provisional model of cognitive rehabilitation. This figure illustrates many of the factors that need to be taken into account when assessing, planning and evaluating rehabilitation programs. Not all components will be used for every patient but practitioners should be aware of the complexity and the need to draw on a number of theories, models and frameworks

with brain injury, and Clare (2003) describes how people with dementia select their own targets for treatments.

A second major change is in the use of goal planning to design and evaluate the efficacy of rehabilitation. Goal planning allows treatment to be tailored to the individual needs of people with brain injuries and their families. Although this approach is not new and has been used in rehabilitation settings for a number of years with different diagnostic groups, including people with brain injury, the last two decades have seen more centers adopt this method when planning rehabilitation. Goal planning makes sense to staff, clients, and families. Wilson *et al.* (2002) provide a fairly detailed description of goal planning used in the successful treatment of a man who sustained both a head injury and a stroke. Manly (2003) discusses the targeting of functional goals in treatment; and Williams (2003) says goal-setting procedures are one of the main components of programs dealing with cognitive and emotional disorders. Goal planning is now a well-established procedure; it is one of the major ways of ensuring a client-centered approach and thus achieving a genuine partnership.

The third main change, again inferred earlier, involves the increasing recognition that cognition, emotion, social functioning, and behavior are interlinked and should all be addressed in the rehabilitation process. This is the underlying principle of holistic programs. Wilson *et al.* (2000) have developed a British holistic program based on the principles of Ben-Yishay (1978) and Prigatano (1986), which is conducted at the Oliver Zangwill Centre for Neuropsychological Rehabilitation in Ely, Cambridgeshire. Williams (2003), in a discussion of the rehabilitation of emotional disorders following brain injury, says that survivors are at particular risk of developing mood disorders. He goes on to say that this is one of the key areas for development in neurological services.

The fourth major change is in the increased use of technology to help people compensate for their difficulties. Sophisticated technology such as positron emission tomography and functional magnetic resonance imaging are enhancing our understanding of brain damage (e.g., Menon *et al.* 1998). To what extent these methods can improve our rehabilitation programs remains to be seen. At present they are limited in helping us plan the actual process of rehabilitation.

What is clear, however, is the value of technology for reducing everyday problems of people with neurological damage. One of the major themes in rehabilitation is the adaptation of technology for the benefit of people with cognitive impairments. Computers can, for example, be used as cognitive prosthetics, as compensatory devices, as assessment tools or as a means for training. Given the current expansion in information technology, this is likely to be an area of growth and increasing importance in the next decade. One of the earliest papers describing the use of an electronic aid with a person with brain damage was by Kurlychek (1983), who showed that a real-life problem, in this case involving the checking of a timetable, could be overcome. In 1986, Glisky and Schacter taught memory-impaired people computer terminology, and one of their participants was able to find employment as a computer operator. Kirsch and his colleagues (1987) designed an interactive task guidance system to assist brain-injured people perform everyday tasks. Boake (2003) includes discussion of some of the early computer-based programs. Since then, there have been numerous papers reporting successful use of technology with brain-injured people. Wilson *et al.* (2001) used a randomized control crossover design to demonstrate that it is possible to reduce the everyday problems of neurologically impaired people with memory and/or planning problems. Another area where technology is likely to play an increasing role in the future is virtual reality (VR). VR can be used to simulate real-life situations and thus be beneficial for both assessment and treatment (Brooks *et al.* 1999). Kapur *et al.* (2004) present an up-to-date review of external memory aids and computer resources in the management of organic memory deficit.

The fifth main change is the recognition that rehabilitation should begin in the first days after brain injury when people may still be in coma or the vegetative state. Perhaps one of the most significant developments in rehabilitation over the past few years has been in the assessment and management of people with disorders of consciousness or states of reduced awareness (Jennett 2002). Jennett and Teasdale (1977), the authors and developers of The Glasgow Coma Scale (GCS–1977), define coma as "giving no verbal response, not obeying commands and not opening the eyes spontaneously or to stimulation" (p. 878). The Royal College of Physicians Working Group (1996) describes the characteristics of people in the vegetative state, and Giacino and Whyte (2005) give an up-to-date description of coma, vegetative state, and the minimally conscious state.

Several assessment tools have been developed to measure the behavior of people in reduced states of awareness, one of them being the Wessex Head Injury Matrix (WHIM; Shiel *et al.* 2000). The WHIM can also be used to set goals for treatment. The goal planning approach is followed here in much the same way as described earlier, with the exception that the client will not be able to participate in goal selection. The goals, of course, will be different from those set for people in the later stages of recovery. Whereas a rehabilitation goal for someone in a rehabilitation center a year or two post-injury might be connected with work or driving or using a compensatory system, the goal for someone just emerging from coma might be to increase eye contact or to establish a method of communication. Shiel (2003) discusses rehabilitation of people in states of reduced awareness and presents four case studies to illustrate some of the principles involved.

The sixth major change is one we have already discussed: the acknowledgment that rehabilitation requires a broad theoretical base because no one theory, model, or framework is sufficient to address all the problems faced by people with neuropsychological deficits. Boake (2003) describes the different methodologies that influenced some of the historical figures in the field. Manly (2003) refers to numerous theories of attention that have guided treatment approaches in this difficult area. The neurobehavioral model of Wood (1987, 1990) has influenced Alderman (2003) in his treatment of brain-injured people with severe behavior problems. Clare (2003), in her discussion of rehabilitation for people with dementia, draws upon theories of memory, psychotherapy, emotion, and other work. From these and other studies it can be seen that ethical and effective neuropsychological rehabilitation requires a synthesis and integration of several frameworks, theories, and methodologies to achieve its aims and ensure effective clinical practice.

CURRENT APPROACHES TO REHABILITATION

We will first look at the recent history of rehabilitation to see where current approaches to rehabilitation come from. An important paper on rehabilitation of people with brain injury, written by Zangwill, appeared in 1947 in which he discussed, among other things, the principles of re-education. He referred to three main approaches: compensation, substitution, and direct retraining. As far as we know, he was the first to categorize approaches to cognitive rehabilitation in this way, although others have since developed, modified, and extended this classification system (e.g., Buffery & Burton 1982; Miller 1984). Primarily working with people with aphasia, Zangwill also addressed problems of attention, memory, and initiative. The questions he raised are still pertinent at the beginning of the twenty-first century. His concern with the extent to which the injured human brain is capable of re-education and when the circumstances are such that we should teach compensatory skills still grips practitioners, and the issue remains unresolved. Age at insult, diagnosis, the number of insults sustained by an individual, the pre-morbid status of the individual's brain, and available resources such as psychosocial support are just a few of the probable influencing factors. Age, often thought to be an important variable, is perhaps less clear-cut than many believe (Kennard 1940; Kolb 2004). Robertson (1999, 2002) and Kolb (2004) discuss further the issues of recovery.

Zangwill (1947) defined compensation as a "reorganization of psychological function so as to minimize or circumvent a particular disability" (p. 63). He believed that compensation for the most part took place spontaneously, without explicit intention by the patient, although in some cases it could occur by the patient's own efforts or as a result of instruction and guidance from the psychologist/therapist. The examples of compensation offered by Zangwill include giving a person with aphasia a slate to write on, or teaching someone with a right hemiplegia to write with the left hand.

By substitution Zangwill meant "the building up of a new method of response to replace one damaged irreparably by a cerebral lesion" (p. 64). He recognized that this was a form of compensation but taken much further, where the end result was obtained by other than normal means through re-education. Lip-reading for people who are deaf and Braille for people who are blind would be examples of substitution. We used the tactile sense as a substitute in the rehabilitation of a patient with aphasia who could no longer read through the visual route. The man was taught initially to trace the letters, then pretend to write them on his knee with his fingertip, and eventually to manage without the tactile sense except when faced with difficult words. Two cases in which this method was used successfully are reported in Wilson (1999).

The third of Zangwill's methods was "direct retraining." He considered this to be training at the highest level. Whereas compensation and substitution were the methods of choice for functions that "do not genuinely recover" (1947, p. 65), he thought that some damaged functions could be restored through training. He admitted that some improvement might be due to overcoming the effects of shock (or "diaschisis" to use von Monakov's (1914) term), but that in other cases it was possible for true re-education to occur. The examples provided are relearning of multiplication tables by people with dysphasia and the relearning of motor skills through physiotherapy. Zangwill was rather tentative about direct retraining and did not conceal the fact that he could not provide real evidence. He concluded that "direct, as opposed to substitutive training has a real though limited part to play in re-education" (1947, p. 66). Robertson and Murre (1999) introduced somewhat similar (although less tentative) views when they said that compensatory strategies should be the treatment of choice for people who are *not* expected to recover; whereas for those who are expected to recover (e.g., those without severe lesions), assisted recovery (akin to direct retraining) can be effective. This may be true for some cognitive functions such as language and attention, but it would not appear to be true for other functions such as memory, where there is little evidence for restoration of function once the initial recovery period has passed (Kapur *et al.* 2002). Whether this is due to the neural networks involved (e.g., are there fewer alternative pathways in memory than in attention?) or to the fact that those surveyed in the literature have more severe deficits is not clear.

Currently, there appear to be four main ways of providing cognitive rehabilitation (Wilson 1997), with Zangwill's ideas incorporated into most of these approaches: (1) cognitive retraining through exercise; (2) theoretical models from cognitive neuropsychology; (3) a combined approach deriving treatment strategies from a number of different fields, and (4) holistic.

Advocates of the cognitive retraining through exercise approach provide a set of exercises for patients to work through. These are often computerized, but paper-and-pencil exercises are also used. The rationale behind this approach is that exercising damaged cognitive skills will remediate the underlying deficit or alternatively such exercises will teach people how to deal with the damaged skills. The early programs, including that Diller's (1976), also employed this approach and some, such as Gianutsos (1991), still believe this is the way cognitive rehabilitation should be carried out. While it is clearly recognized that people need to practice skills and the learning of information if they are to retain new knowledge, it sometimes appears that advocates of cognitive retraining are claiming more for the methodology, seemingly believing that *practicing* a deficient skill can *remediate* that skill. This is akin to the idea of cognition being like a "mental muscle" so that if we practice a weak cognitive ability, then we strengthen it. This is a somewhat controversial viewpoint. A famous experiment (Ericsson *et al.* 1980) taught undergraduates to improve their performance on a forward digit span task. One young man was particularly successful. From a normal span of seven he improved with repeated practice until he could repeat back 80 digits in the correct order after hearing them once only. A prodigious feat and one might think his memory had improved. However, when tested on a letter span task his span was still at the normal 7 ± 2. In other words, he had improved on the specific task he practiced, but this did not generalize to other tasks so his memory overall was no better than before. This is one of the problems with the practice approach to rehabilitation: people tend to improve on the task or tasks they are working on, but the underlying deficit is unchanged. In addition to the lack of generalization, this approach does not address real-life problems such as inability to use the telephone or drive a car, which I have argued on many previous occasions (Wilson 1999, 2002b), should be the main focus of rehabilitation; neither does it address the emotional, social, or behavioral consequences of brain injury. Furthermore, there is little evidence in support of its effectiveness (Robertson 1990; Sloan & Ponsford 1995; Wilson 1999).

The second approach based on theoretical models from cognitive neuropsychology uses a cognitive model to specify, often very precisely, the deficit of an individual patient. As stated above, models of language and reading have been particularly influential (Seron & Deloche 1989; Coltheart 1991; Mitchum & Berndt 1995). The rationale is that in order to treat a deficit we have to understand its nature, and we need to understand how the function we are interested in is normally achieved in people without brain damage. The belief that detailed assessment informed by theoretical cognitive models can identify what needs to be rehabilitated highlights, perhaps, the major difference between academic and clinical neuropsychologists. For those working in clinical practice, the focus of rehabilitation is not on an impairment identified by a theoretically informed model but on real-life problems experienced by patients and families. Simply focusing on impairments identified by models will not inform us as to how to treat a patient for these everyday problems. The models themselves do not address the emotional, behavioral, and social sequelae of brain injury; they do not usually address issues of generalization. They are, therefore, best suited to patients with very specific deficits rather than to those with a range of cognitive problems such as we encounter in the more typical rehabilitation patient.

The above argument is not detracting from the fact that models of cognitive functioning are important. We need to know the cognitive strengths and weaknesses of each individual patient in order to ensure we are not asking the cognitively impossible in our treatment programs; and we must identify an individual's strengths so these can be harnessed to overcome the weaknesses. We need to be able to explain why certain apparent anomalies occur (e.g., why someone can read nouns but not verbs); we need to make predictions about future behaviors; and we need models to help us develop assessment procedures. To emphasize these points it is worth noting that before the dual-route model of reading was published (Coltheart 1985), most psychologists assessed reading skills with word lists and comprehension passages; but since the introduction of this and other models of reading the assessment of these disorders has been revolutionized. We now consider regular and irregular words, parts of speech, word-length effect, age of acquisition, concrete and abstract words, and "easy to image" vs. "hard to image" words. My point here is not that these theoretical models are unimportant, but rather that they are insufficient on their own to deal with the complex issues faced in rehabilitation.

The third approach combines theories and models from a number of different fields to try to deal with the wide variety of problems encountered by people with brain injury. The rationale is that we need to take elements from a number of fields in order to reduce the everyday problems seen in rehabilitation practice. Perhaps the three most commonly used models and theories relied upon by followers of the combined approach come from: neuropsychology, which helps us to understand the organization of the brain; cognitive psychology, which provides us with models to explain phenomena and make predictions; and behavioral psychology, which provides us with a range of treatment strategies that can be used or modified in teaching new skills or reducing inappropriate behaviors. One of the advantages of behavioral psychology is that generalization is typically built in to the treatment program. These are not the only fields contributing to rehabilitation, however, and theories of plasticity, emotion, linguistics, phenomenology, and so forth can all be used to enhance our clinical practice.

The combined approach has been used in cognitive rehabilitation for decades, with Goodkin (1969), Ince (1976), Lincoln (1978), and Wood (1990) among the early proponents. Its use today is obvious in the work of Alderman (1996) and Wilson *et al.* (2003). One criticism that has been made of this approach, and in particular about the use of techniques from behavioral psychology, is that it does not address people's feelings and emotions. While this is perhaps not entirely true, it can nevertheless be argued that before holistic approaches came into prominence it was likely that there was little formal recognition of the need to address emotional issues. Another problem that could result from both the cognitive theoretical approach and the behavioral approach is that practitioners might tend to concentrate on one problem area, such as language or memory, to the exclusion of the whole spectrum of difficulties faced by patients and their families.

As stated earlier, the holistic approach is now much in evidence. Ben-Yishay and Prigatano (1990) provide a hierarchical model of stages in the holistic approach that patients must work through in rehabilitation. These are, in chronological order, (1) engagement (interventions which are meant to optimize alertness, basic attention, and concentration), (2) awareness (interventions to make the patient aware and willing to undergo intensive rehabilitation), (3) mastery and (4) control (these are two stages in which the focus of rehabilitation is on the amelioration of cognitive and personality deficits and to helping patients use compensatory strategies, (5) acceptance (is arrived at when the patient has met the challenges and accepts the changes), and (6) identity ("the culmination of the successful resolution of all the preceding stages when the patient becomes reintegrated in the community" (pp. 400–401)). Holistic programs appear to follow these stages explicitly or implicitly, and they make clinical sense. The main criticism of this approach is its initial high cost. While holistic programs are probably cost-effective in the long term (Mehlbye & Larsen 1994; Prigatano & Pliskin 2002; Wilson & Evans 2002), they are nevertheless expensive in the short term. Another possible criticism is that we do not know whether or not all the components offered in a holistic program are essential. Do we, for example, have to provide both group and individual therapy or will one of these be sufficient? Do we have to work through the hierarchical stages and help people understand and accept what has happened or not? In order to determine the essential components we would need a huge, multi-center study and this is probably impractical. However good these programs are, it is probably true to say that they could be improved by incorporating the best aspects of the other approaches.

In summary, I would argue that in order to ensure ethical and effective cognitive rehabilitation it would be advisable to take on board the most positive components of each approach. For this we would need to: (1) rehearse and practice new skills and information to prevent loss of information; (2) be guided by cognitive models to understand the cognitive strengths and weaknesses of our patients; (3) have a broad theoretical base so as to be able to address the multitude and complexity of problems faced by survivors of brain injury; and (4) employ the holistic model in clinical practice because cognition, emotion, and behavior are interlinked and should all be addressed.

THE PRACTICE OF REHABILITATION

The provisional model of rehabilitation provided by Wilson (2002a) synthesizes a number of different models that have influenced the field. The two basic assumptions are that neuropsychological rehabilitation is concerned with the amelioration of cognitive, social, and emotional deficits caused by an insult to the brain, and the main aims of such rehabilitation are to enable people with disabilities to (1) achieve their optimum level of well-being; (2) reduce the impact of their problems on everyday life; and (3) help them return to their own, most appropriate environments. From this it follows that no one model, theory, or framework can deal with all the difficulties facing people with brain impairments. These often include multiple cognitive impairments as well as accompanying social, emotional, and behavioral problems.

In order to understand which parts of Wilson's (2002a) synthesized model were most used by practicing psychologists engaged in neuropsychological rehabilitation, a questionnaire was designed and sent to 60 British and Australian psychologists. These were selected on the basis of having full practitioner membership of the Division of Neuropsychology and working in brain injury rehabilitation (for the British members) or Australian members working in brain injury rehabilitation who attended a satellite meeting in rehabilitation in Ayers Rock in 2004. One or more questions were generated for each component of the model. Thus, in order to know whether or not clinicians assessed pre-morbid personality, the question was asked: "Do you assess pre-morbid personality – Yes or No? If yes, is this through informal interview/formal interview/formal assessment procedure (please state which one/other)." Respondents were asked to check all that applied to them and their situation, and allowed to add any other comments about pre-morbid personality. In order to find out about treatment influences we included the following question: "Which of the following treatment approaches do you use? (please check all that apply): (a) those derived from cognitive neuropsychological theory, (b) those derived from behavioral psychology, (c) those derived from theories of emotion (including CBT), (d) those derived from psychoanalytic theory, (e) other (please specify)." They were also allowed to provide any other comments about treatment approaches.

Forty-five people (75 per cent) responded and some of the main results are summarized below.

All responders said they tried to find out about patients' likes and interests, and all said they employed a goal-setting approach. All but two said they assessed pre-morbid personality and all but three said they assessed present personality. The most frequently used treatment approaches derived from models of cognitive behavior therapy, (67 per cent) cognitive neuropsychological theory (37 per cent) and behavioral models (24 per cent). Psychodynamic models were used by only 3 per cent of respondents. Most practitioners tried to reduce disabilities (the everyday problems) and handicaps (environmental and societal hindrances to the successful achievement of goals) rather than impairments (the physical and mental difficulties directly caused by the insult, for example restoring damage to cells destroyed by a stroke). Several strategies are employed to do this, the most frequent being compensatory techniques; making use of residual skills; and restructuring the environment (between 90 and 100 per cent using these). Restorative approaches and attempts at anatomical reorganization were rarely used.

It would seem, judging from this small survey, that practicing psychologists in rehabilitation use a range of theoretical models and approaches in their clinical work, thus confirming the view that we need a broad theoretical base when dealing with the complex problems experienced by people with brain injury.

A CASE STUDY TO ILLUSTRATE THE PROCESS OF COGNITIVE REHABILITATION

Vince was involved in a road traffic accident at the age of 19, when the car he was driving span out of control. He sustained a severe head injury and was in a coma for five days. He made a gradual return to full consciousness and received early inpatient rehabilitation plus several weeks of outpatient rehabilitation, which included physiotherapy and occupational therapy. Six months post-injury Vince tried to return to work as a trainee chef. He was asked to leave after a few months because of late time-keeping, distractibility, and generally poor performance. He tried to get other jobs but was unsuccessful and became increasingly moody and withdrawn. He tried a number of voluntary unpaid jobs but none lasted. He was referred to the psychiatric service because of depression and was seen as an outpatient for three years.

At this point, his psychiatrist referred Vince to our center. He lived with his parents and usually stayed in bed until early afternoon each day. Vince was offered a one-day preliminary assessment and attended with his parents. Neuropsychological tests were administered and Vince was interviewed by two members of the interdisciplinary team. His parents were also interviewed and completed some questionnaires about Vince's behavior and mood. Vince's main complaints were (a) memory (he did not know what he was supposed to do each day); (b) speech (he felt himself rushing and forgetting what he wanted to say); (c) writing and spelling (he avoided tasks involving writing); (d) mood (his mood was low and he often became frustrated and angry); (e) he felt he lacked a purpose to his life; and (f) he became tired very easily. His main goals were to find a job, have some purpose to his life, and gain self-confidence.

Vince and his parents discussed the possibility of coming to the unit for a period of rehabilitation. Funding was sought and obtained from his local health authority and he returned for a two-week detailed assessment. His main problems, as identified by the staff, involved verbal memory, attention, low mood, poor anger control, some difficulties with comprehension of speech, and overly fast, dysfluent speech. He engaged well with the program, contributed to group discussions, and was able to identify (potentially) realistic goals. At the end of this period all parties agreed that Vince should come on the full six-month program of which the first three months would be full-time and during the second three-month period he would attend the rehabilitation centre for two days a week. The remaining 2–3 days a week would be spent trying to reintegrate into work or further education. Again, funding was sought and obtained from his local health authority.

Once Vince came for the full program eight goals were set to be achieved by the time of discharge.

Vince will:

1. Be in work (either paid or unpaid) for three days a week by the time of discharge.
2. Demonstrate the consistent use of an external memory aid (e.g., a filofax or diary) for organizing his activities a week in advance.
3. Learn and demonstrate the techniques for tolerating frustration and managing his anger.
4. Demonstrate reduced speed of speech, as rated by his parents and the speech and language therapist.
5. Identify situations in which he needs extra support to help him cope with stressful situations.
6. Be in charge of his own medication.
7. Engage in a leisure activity twice weekly.
8. Attend a driving assessment to determine whether he can resume driving.

Short-term goals and action plans were set to help Vince achieve these goals. For example, for goal 2 (using an external memory aid) the first short-term goal was that Vince should accompany his occupational therapist to look at possible aids at the memory clinic and select one for Vince. The second was that Vince should learn to enter and store a message in the aid. The next short-term goal was that Vince should enter and retrieve three messages. He then went on to use the aid to remind him to take his medication (with a therapist supervising and prompting if necessary). He gradually built up the ability to use the aid and to use it to remember to do other everyday tasks such as telephone for an appointment to join the leisure centre.

For his frustration, mood, and anger management problems Vince had both individual and group psychological support using CBT and anger management techniques as described by Williams and Evans (2003).

As the most important long-term goal for Vince was finding (and keeping) a job, his work trial is described in some detail. At the beginning of the program he was helped to identify potential areas of work, together with problem areas that had prevented him keeping a job in the past. He wanted to work somewhere where he could help people and had been interested in hospitals and medical situations, so his first work trial (one day a week for four weeks) was set up with the portering service of the local hospital. This began five weeks into the program. The main purpose of this initial trial was to assess Vince's potential for work as a porter. The short-term goals set to help Vince reach the long-term goal were to:

1. Identify the skills necessary to work as a porter.
2. Identify any factors that might preclude him working as a porter.
3. Use the strategies learned at the center in a work environment (e.g., his diary, requesting clarification of instructions, etc.).

Vince achieved these objectives in the first four weeks of the second trial. In the second four weeks Vince's shifts were increased in length and he was given the opportunity to work in different areas of the hospital.

Regular verbal and written feedback was obtained from the portering manager, and staff from the rehabilitation centre were also able to shadow Vince at work for part of the time.

Although the four-week trial was successful and this kind of work seemed appropriate, Vince found the local hospital was too quiet. So, a further work trial was arranged in a busy teaching hospital, which was also nearer Vince's home. This trial began a month after the end of the first and about three months after Vince started the program. He worked for three days a week for four weeks and this was then extended.

Feedback from the manager was positive. Vince enjoyed the work and when he completed the rehabilitation program he stayed at the hospital as a volunteer until a paid post became available. Staff helped Vince prepare an application form and he was given the job. He remains in the same post at the time of writing. He also left his parents' home and now lives in his own flat.

SUMMARY AND CONCLUSIONS

Cognitive rehabilitation is a process whereby people disabled by injury or disease work with health service staff and others to alleviate or remediate cognitive deficits arising from a neurological insult. It is now recognized that cognitive, emotional, social, and behavioral difficulties are often hard to separate (how we feel affects how we think and how we behave) and all should be addressed in rehabilitation programs (Prigatano 1999). Following traumatic brain injury, cognitive, and emotional problems are more handicapping than physical problems (Ponsford 1995).

Cognitive problems, including those of attention, processing of visual and verbal information, memory, language, problem-solving, and reasoning are common after brain injury. These need to be recognized, assessed, and treated by specialist cognitive rehabilitation teams. Each team should include a clinical neuropsychologist working with occupational therapists and speech and language therapists. Emotional, social, and behavioral consequences of brain injury should be addressed within cognitive rehabilitation. Rehabilitation should be structured through goal-setting to ensure it focuses on practical problems, is tailored to individual needs, and avoids the artificial distinction between many outcome measures and real-life functioning. Patients and families should be involved in choosing and setting the goals of rehabilitation.

As demonstrated in this chapter, there is considerable evidence that cognitive rehabilitation can improve cognitive functioning of individuals by teaching them to compensate for their problems, by helping them to learn more efficiently, or through achieving partial or full restoration of function.

REFERENCES

Alderman, N. (1996). Central executive deficit and response to operant conditioning methods. *Neuropsychological Rehabilitation, 6*, 161–186.

Alderman, N. (2003). Rehabilitation of behaviour disorders. In B. A. Wilson (ed.), *Neuropsychological Rehabilitation: Theory and Practice* (pp. 171–196). Lisse, The Netherlands: Swets & Zeitlinger.

Beck, A. T. (1976). *Cognitive Therapy and Emotional Disorders.* New York: International Universities Press.

Ben-Yishay, Y. (ed.) (1978). *Working Approaches to Remediation of Cognitive Deficits in Brain Damaged Persons (Rehabilitation Monograph).* New York: New York University Medical Center.

Ben-Yishay, Y. (1996). Reflections on the evolution of the therapeutic milieu concept. *Neuropsychological Rehabilitation, 6*, 327–343.

Ben-Yishay, Y. & Prigatano, G. P. (1990). Cognitive remediation. In M. Rosenthal, E. R. Griffith, M. R. Bond & J. D. Miller (eds.), *Rehabilitation of the Adult and Child with Traumatic Brain Injury* (2nd edn, pp. 393–409). Philadelphia: F.A. Davis.

Boake, C. (1996). Editorial: historical aspects of neuropsychological rehabilitation. *Neuropsychological Rehabilitation, 6*, 241–243.

Boake, C. (2003). Cross-cultural issues in historical perspective: culture-fair tests, norms, and interpretations. *Clinical Neuropsychologist, 17*, 98–99.

Brooks, B. M., McNeil, J. E., Rose, D. F. *et al.* (1999). Route learning in a case of amnesia: a preliminary investigation into the efficacy of training in a virtual environment. *Neuropsychological Rehabilitation, 9*, 63–76.

Buffery, A. W. H. & Burton, A. (1982). Information processing and redevelopment: towards a science of neuropsychological rehabilitation. In A. Burton (ed.), *The Pathology and Psychology of Cognition.* London: Methuen.

Christensen, A.-L. & Caetano, C. (1996). Romanovich Luria (1902–1977): contributions to neuropsychological rehabilitation. *Neuropsychological Rehabilitation, 6*, 279–303.

Clare, L. (2003). Rehabilitation for people with dementia. In B. A. Wilson (ed.), *Neuropsychological Rehabilitation: Theory and Practice* (pp. 197–215). Lisse, The Netherlands: Swets & Zeitlinger.

Coltheart, M. (1984). Editorial. *Cognitive Neuropsychology, 1*, 1–8.

Coltheart, M. (1985). Cognitive neuropsychology and reading. In M. Posner & O. S. M. Marin (eds.), *Attention and Performance XI* (pp. 3–37). Hillsdale, NJ: Lawrence Erlbaum Associates.

Coltheart, M. (1991). Cognitive psychology applied to the treatment of acquired language disorders. In P. Martin (ed.), *Handbook of Behavior Therapy and Psychological Science: An Integrative Approach* (pp. 216–226). New York: Pergamon Press.

Coltheart, M., Bates, A. & Castles, A. (1991). Cognitive neuropsychology and rehabilitation. In M. P. D. Partz & M. Leclercq (eds.), *La Réeducation neuropsychologique de l'adulte.* Paris: Publications de la Société de Neuropsychologie de Langue Française.

Diller, L. (1976). A model for cognitive retraining in rehabilitation. *The Clinical Psychologist, 29*, 13–15.
Diller, L. (1987). Neuropsychological rehabilitation. In M. J. Meier, A. L. Benton & L. Diller (eds.), *Neuropsychological Rehabilitation* (pp. 3–17). Edinburgh: Churchill Livingstone.
Ericsson, K. A., Chase, W. G. & Falcon, S. (1980). Acquisition of a memory skill. *Science, 208*, 1181–1182.
Evans, J. J. (2003). Rehabilitation of executive deficits. In B. A. Wilson (ed.), *Neuropsychological Rehabilitation: Theory and Practice* (pp. 53–70). Lisse, The Netherlands: Swets & Zeitlinger.
Gainotti, G. (1993). Emotional and psychosocial problems after brain injury. *Neuropsychological Rehabilitation, 3*, 259–277.
Giacino, J. & Whyte, J. (2005). The vegetative and minimally conscious states: current knowledge and remaining questions. *Journal of Head Trauma Rehabilitation, 20*, 30–50.
Gianutsos, R. (1980). What is cognitive rehabilitation? *Journal of Rehabilitation, 1*, 37–40.
Gianutsos, R. (1981). Training the short- and long-term verbal recall of a post-encephalitis amnesic. *Journal of Clinical Neuropsychology, 3*, 143–153.
Gianutsos, R. (1991). Cognitive rehabilitation: a neuropsychological specialty comes of age. *Brain Injury, 5*, 363–368.
Glisky, E. L. & Schacter, D. L. (1986). Long-term retention of computer learning by patients with memory disorders. *Neuropsychologia, 26*, 173–178.
Goldstein, K. (1942). *Aftereffects of Brain Injury in War.* New York: Grune and Stratton.
Goodkin, R. (1969). Changes in word production, sentence production and relevance in an aphasic through verbal conditioning. *Behaviour Research and Therapy, 7*, 93–99.
Ince, L. P. (1976). *Behavior Modification in Rehabilitation Medicine.* Baltimore, MD: Williams & Wilkins.
Jennett, B. (2002). *The Vegetative State: Medical Facts, Ethical and Legal Dilemmas.* Cambridge: Cambridge University Press.
Jennett, B. & Teasdale, G. (1977). Aspects of coma after severe head injury. *Lancet, 1*, 878–881.
Kapur, N., Glisky, E. L. & Wilson, B. A. (2002). External memory aids and computers in memory rehabilitation. In A. D. Baddeley, M. D. Kopelman & B. A. Wilson (eds.), *Handbook of Memory Disorders* (2nd edn, pp. 757–783). Chichester: John Wiley & Sons.
Kapur, N., Glisky, E. L. & Wilson, B. A. (2004). External memory aids and computers in memory rehabilitation. In A. D. Baddeley, M. D. Kopelman & B. A. Wilson (eds.), *The Essential Handbook of Memory Disorders for Clinicians* (pp. 301–327). Chichester: John Wiley & Sons.
Kennard, M. A. (1940). Relation of age to motor impairment in man and subhuman primates. *Archives of Neurology and Psychiatry, 44*, 377–397.
Kirsch, N. L., Levine, S. P., Fallon-Krueger, M. & Jaros, L. A. (1987). The microcomputer as an "orthotic" device for patients with cognitive deficits. *Journal of Head Trauma Rehabilitation, 2*, 77–86.
Kolb, B. (2004) Mechanisms of cortical plasticity after neuronal injury. In J. Ponsford (ed.), *Rehabilitation and Recovery of Function.* New York: Guilford.
Kurlychek, R. T. (1983). Use of a digital alarm chronograph as a memory aid in early dementia. *Clinical Gerontologist, 1*, 93–94.
Lincoln, N. B. (1978). Behavioural modification in physiotherapy. *Physiotherapy, 64*, 265–267.
Luria, A. R. (1963). *Restoration of Function after Brain Injury.* New York: Pergamon Press.
Luria, A. R. (1970). *Traumatic Aphasia.* The Hague: Mouton.
Luria, A. R., Naydin, V. L., Tsvetkova, L. S. & Vinarskaya, E. N. (1969). Restoration of higher cortical functions following local brain damage. In P. J. Vinken & G. W. Bruyn (eds.), *Handbook of Clinical Neurology* (Vol. 3, pp. 368–433). New York: Elsevier.
McLellan, D. L. (1991). Functional recovery and the principles of disability medicine. In M. Swash & J. Oxbury (eds.), *Clinical Neurology* (pp. 768–790). Edinburgh: Churchill Livingstone.
McMillan, T. M. & Greenwood, R. J. (1993). Models of rehabilitation programmes for the brain-injured adult – II: model services and suggestions for change in the UK. *Clinical Rehabilitation, 7*, 346–355.
Manly, T. (2003). Rehabilitation for disorders of attention. In B.A. Wilson (ed.), *Neuropsychological Rehabilitation: Theory and Practice* (pp. 23–52). Lisse, The Netherlands: Swets & Zeitlinger.

Mehlbye, J. & Larsen, A. (1994). Social and economic consequences of brain damage in Denmark. In A.-L. Christensen & B. P. Uzzell (eds.), *Brain Injury and Neuropsychological Rehabilitation: International Perspectives* (pp. 257–267). Hillsdale, NJ: Lawrence Erlbaum Associates.

Menon, D. K., Owen, A. M., Williams, E. J. *et al.* (1998). Cortical processing in the persistent vegetative state revealed by functional imaging. *Lancet*, *352*, 200.

Miller, E. (1984). *Recovery and Management of Neuropsychological Impairments*. Chichester: John Wiley & Sons.

Mitchum, C. C. & Berndt, R. S. (1995). The cognitive neuropsychological approach to treatment of language disorders. *Neuropsychological Rehabilitation*, *5*, 1–16.

von Monakow, C. (1914). *Localization in the Cerebrum and the Degeneration of Functions through Cortical Sources*. Wiesbaden: J. F. Bergmann.

Najenson, T., Mendelson, I., Schechter, I. *et al.* (1974). Rehabilitation after severe head injury. *Scandinavian Journal of Rehabilitation Medicine*, *6*, 5–14.

Poppelreuter, W. (1917). *Disturbances of Lower and Higher Visual Capacities Caused by Occiptal Damage* (J. Zihl & L. Weiskrantz, Trans.). Oxford: Clarendon Press.

Ponsford, J. L. (1995). Assessment and management of behavior problems. In J. Ponsford, S. Sloan & P. Snow (eds.), *Traumatic Brain Injury: Rehabilitation for Everyday Adaptive Living* (pp. 165–194). London: Lawrence Erlbaum Associates.

Poser, U., Kohler, J. A. & Schönle, P. W. (1996). Historical review of neuropsychological rehabilitation in Germany. *Neuropsychological Rehabilitation*, *6*, 257–278.

Prigatano, G. P. (1986). Personality and psychosocial consequences of brain injury. In G. P. Prigatano, D. J. Fordyce, H. K. Zeiner *et al.* (eds.), *Neuropsychological Rehabilitation after Brain Injury* (pp. 29–50). Baltimore, MD and London: Johns Hopkins University Press.

Prigatano, G. P. (1995). Personality and social aspects of memory rehabilitation. In A. D. Baddeley, B. A. Wilson & F. N. Watts (eds.), *Handbook of Memory Disorders* (pp. 603–614). Chichester: John Wiley & Sons.

Prigatano, G. P. (1999). *Principles of Neuropsychological Rehabilitation*. New York: Oxford University Press.

Prigatano, G. P. & Pliskin, N. H. (eds.) (2002). *Clinical Neuropsychology and Cost Outcome Research: A Beginning*. Hove: Psychology Press.

Robertson, I. H. (1990). Does computerised cognitive rehabilitation work? A Review. *Aphasiology*, *4*, 381–405.

Robertson, I. H. (1991). Book review. *Neuropsychological Rehabilitation*, *1*, 87–90.

Robertson, I. H. (1999). Theory-driven neuropsychological rehabilitation: the role of attention and competition in recovery of function after brain damage. In D. Gopher & A. Koriat (eds.), *Attention and Performance XVII. Cognitive Regulation of Performance: Interaction of Theory and Application* (pp. 677–696). Cambridge, MA: MIT Press.

Robertson, I. H. (2002). Cognitive neuroscience and brain rehabilitation: a promise kept (Editorial). *Journal of Neurology, Neurosurgery and Psychiatry*, *73*, 357.

Robertson, I. H. & Murre, J. M. J. (1999). Rehabilitation of brain damage: brain plasticity and principles of guided recovery. *Psychological Bulletin*, *125*, 544–575.

Royal College of Physicians Working Group (1996). The permanent vegetative state. *Journal of the Royal College of Physicians*, *30*, 119–121.

Salkovskis, P. M. (ed.) (1996). *Frontiers of Cognitive Therapy*. New York: Guilford Press.

Seron, X. & Deloche, G. (eds.) (1989). *Cognitive Approaches in Neuropsychological Rehabilitation*. Hillsdale, NJ: Lawrence Erlbaum Associates.

Shiel, A. (2003). Rehabilitation of people in states of reduced awareness. In B. A. Wilson (ed.), *Neuropsychological Rehabilitation: Theory and Practice* (pp. 253–269). Lisse, The Netherlands: Swets & Zeitlinger.

Shiel, A., Horn, S. A., Wilson, B. A. *et al.* (2000). The Wessex Head Injury Matrix (WHIM) main scale: a preliminary report on a scale to assess and monitor patient recovery after severe head injury. *Clinical Rehabilitation*, *14*, 408–416.

Sloan, S. & Ponsford, J. (1995). Managing cognitive problems. In J. Ponsford, S. Sloan & P. Snow (eds.), *Traumatic Brain Injury: Rehabilitation for Everyday Adaptive Living*. Hove: Lawrence Erlbaum Associates.

Sohlberg, M. & Mateer, C. (1989). *Introduction to Cognitive Rehabilitation: Theory and Practice*. New York: Guilford Press.

Tate, R. L., Strettles, B. & Osoteo, T. (2003). Enhancing outcomes after traumatic brain injury: a social rehabilitation approach. In B. A. Wilson (ed.), *Neuropsychological Rehabilitation: Theory and Practice* (pp. 137–169). Lisse, The Netherlands: Swets & Zeitlinger.

Williams, W. H. (2003). Neuro-rehabilitation and cognitive behaviour therapy for emotional disorders in acquired brain injury. In B. A. Wilson (ed.), *Neuropsychological Rehabilitation: Theory and Practice* (pp. 115–136). Lisse, The Netherlands: Swets & Zeitlinger.

Williams, W. H. & Evans, J. (2003). *Neuropsychological Rehabilitation: Special Issue on Biopsychosocial Approaches in Neurorehabilitation*. Hove: Psychology Press.

Williams, W. H., Evans, J. J. & Wilson, B. A. (2003). Neurorehabilitation for two cases of post-traumatic stress disorder following traumatic brain injury. *Cognitive Neuropsychiatry*, *8*, 1–18.

Wilson, B. A. (1991). Behaviour therapy in the treatment of neurologically impaired adults. In P. R. Martin (ed.), *Handbook of Behavior Therapy and Psychological Science: An Integrative Approach* (pp. 227–252). New York: Pergamon Press.

Wilson, B. A. (1997). Cognitive rehabilitation: how it is and how it might be. *Journal of the International Neuropsychological Society*, *3*, 487–496.

Wilson, B. A. (1999). *Case Studies in Neuropsychological Rehabilitation*. New York: Oxford University Press.

Wilson, B. A. (2002a). Towards a comprehensive model of cognitive rehabilitation. *Neuropsychological Rehabilitation*, *12*, 97–110.

Wilson, B. A. (2002b). Management and remediation of memory problems in brain-injured adults. In A. D. Baddeley, M. D. Kopelman & B. A. Wilson (eds.), *Handbook of Memory Disorders* (2nd edn, pp. 655–682). Chichester: John Wiley & Sons.

Wilson, B. A., Emslie, H. C., Quirk, K. & Evans, J. J. (2001). Reducing everyday memory and planning problems by means of a paging system: a randomised control crossover study. *Journal of Neurology, Neurosurgery and Psychiatry*, *70*, 477–482.

Wilson, B. A. & Evans, J. J. (2002). Does cognitive rehabilitation work? Clinical and economic considerations and outcomes. In G. Prigatano (ed.), *Clinical Neuropsychology and Cost-Outcome Research: An Introduction* (pp. 329–349). Hove: Psychology Press.

Wilson, B. A., Evans, J., Brentnall, S. *et al.* (2000). The Oliver Zangwill Centre for Neuropsychological Rehabilitation: a partnership between health care and rehabilitation research. In A.-L. Christensen & B. P. Uzzell (eds.), *International Handbook of Neuropsychological Rehabilitation* (pp. 231–246). New York: Kluwer Academic/Plenum.

Wilson, B. A., Evans, J. J. & Keohane, C. (2002). Cognitive rehabilitation: a goal-planning approach. *Journal of Head Trauma Rehabilitation*, *17*, 542–555.

Wilson, B. A., Herbert, C. M. & Shiel, A. (2003). *Behavioural Approaches in Neuropsychological Rehabilitation: Optimising Rehabilitation Procedures*. Hove: Psychology Press.

Wilson, B. A. & Patterson, K. E. (1990). Rehabilitation and cognitive neuropsychology: does cognitive psychology apply? *Journal of Applied Cognitive Psychology*, *4*, 247–260.

Wood, R. Ll. (1987). *Brain Injury Rehabilitation: A Neurobehavioural Approach*. London: Croom Helm.

Wood, R. Ll. (1990). Towards a model of cognitive rehabilitation. In R. L. Wood & I. Fussey (eds.), *Cognitive Rehabilitation in Perspective* (pp. 3–25). London: Taylor and Francis.

Ylvisaker, M. & Feeney, T. (2000). Reconstruction of identity after brain injury. *Brain Impairment*, *1*, 12–28.

Zangwill, O. L. (1947). Psychological aspects of rehabilitation in cases of brain injury. *British Journal of Psychology*, *37*, 60–69.

CHAPTER 23

Personnel Selection and Testing

Margaret E. Beier
Rice University, USA
and
Phillip L. Ackerman
Georgia Institute of Technology, USA

COGNITIVE ABILITIES IN PERSONNEL SELECTION AND TESTING

Suppose you need to select new employees to work in your organization. Should you take a random sample of applicants for the job, or select applicants on the basis of some information? Would you like to know which applicants would most likely succeed in an extensive training program, or which applicants would be most likely to be competent or top performers? The answers to such questions can be found in the use of cognitive and other assessments in selection. Such assessments provide a quick and objective source of information that often far exceeds the ability of a manager to make predictions about the success of job applicants based on subjective judgments or intuition. Basic and applied research on cognitive abilities represents one of the most successful applications of psychology over the past 100 years. From educational to occupational selection, tests and other assessment procedures have been used to make selection both efficient and fair.

Organizations spend billions of dollars recruiting and selecting employees (Cascio 1998). As such, having effective selection systems – those that help identify potentially high-performing employees for specific jobs is important. Selection involves a series of steps, of which the actual choosing of a new employee is only one. The series of steps is longer or shorter, depending on how elaborate the selection procedure is and the specific attributes of the job in question. However, in the development of valid selection procedures, each of these steps must be, at a minimum, thoughtfully considered. These include: (1) determining the relevant traits and requirements for each job (What skills does a successful employee in this job have? What type of ability and personality traits does he/she possess?); (2) assessing these traits in job candidates; (3) predicting performance of candidates; and (4) selecting a candidate to hire.

Cognitive abilities historically have been, and continue to be, the most effective and efficient predictors of job performance. Meta-analyses conducted to estimate the relationship between general cognitive ability and job performance report that, although the mean

Handbook of Applied Cognition: Second Edition. Edited by Francis T. Durso.

correlation differs by job type (e.g., 0.53 for manager and 0.27 for sales clerk; Hunter and Hunter 1984), general ability is significantly predictive of performance for essentially all jobs. Even though non-ability traits such as personality are predictive of performance in some jobs (Barrick & Mount 1991), abilities are generally a more effective and consistent determinant of performance at work. It is perhaps also important to note that there are instances when general cognitive abilities are less important for selection purposes. When the cost of training is low, and when there is a reasonable expectation that most employees will gain the requisite skills for the job, and when the applicant pool includes individuals who already possess the requisite job knowledge and skill, the emphasis on cognitive abilities is minimized.

The goal of this chapter is to examine the linkages between applied cognitive psychology and personnel selection and to provide an overview of personnel selection. However, personnel selection is a broad field and includes the treatment of non-ability traits such as personality, motivational states, vocational interests, applicant reactions to selection systems, and so on. Because we aim to focus on ability and selection, an in-depth treatment of these aspects of personnel selection is outside of the scope of this chapter. The interested reader is referred to Schmitt and Chan (1998) and Guion (1998). who provide comprehensive overviews of the field of personnel selection.

Overview

This chapter is presented in five sections. First, we define important concepts in the study of skills, abilities, and individual differences. Second, we briefly review the history of ability testing in industrial psychology. Third, we review methods of selection and assessment, and discuss issues of fundamental importance to testing – i.e., reliability and validity. Fourth, we consider the role of cognitive ability and more narrow abilities in personnel selection. Finally, we discuss some additional considerations for using ability testing in selection, such as typical and maximal performance, group differences in test performance, and predicting team performance.

SKILLS, ABILITIES, AND INDIVIDUAL DIFFERENCES

It is important to make a distinction between *abilities* and *skills* in the context of personnel selection. Skills can be thought of as representing a malleable aspect of individual performance, such as would result from practice on a task or job training. In contrast, abilities are considered to be more general traits that are relatively stable, at least where adults are considered. (Abilities in young children can change substantially over brief periods; Fleishman 1972.) Skills and abilities are interrelated in that specific abilities are related to skill acquisition for certain tasks required for certain jobs (e.g., psychomotor ability facilitates learning how to type; general cognitive ability predicts skill acquisition related to job performance across most jobs) and skills are sometimes described in terms of the abilities to which they are most closely related (e.g., an individual's skill at writing clearly might be described by some as verbal ability).

The study of individual differences is broadly focused on providing tools for the "objective quantification of the characteristics of individuals within a given population"

(Ackerman & Humphreys 1991, p. 224). In the employment context, two types of individual differences have traditionally been studied. The study of *intra-individual differences* is concerned with the changes of an attribute within a person over time (such as individual skill development during training). Typically, those who seek to develop more effective training programs, or those interested in understanding how employees develop expertise on the job, examine intra-individual differences. For example, trainers are interested in the development or improvement of job skills for each individual in a training program.

To the degree that organizations can successfully develop competencies in all job applicants, then consideration of ability differences between individuals is not much of an issue. However, when training programs are expensive or when they cannot develop all individuals to be competent for a job, consideration of *inter-individual differences* (such as in the domain of cognitive abilities) becomes important for achieving competence in new workers. The study of *inter-individual differences* is concerned with the differences *between* individuals, and it is the basis of personnel selection. In a selection context for example, a group of job applicants might be compared in terms of cognitive ability and other job-related skills or knowledge. Those with the most favorable assessments in terms of the job in question are those that are selected. The traits that are generally relevant in a selection context are knowledge, skills, cognitive abilities, and other non-ability characteristics such as personality and motivational traits. The assessment of inter-individual differences in job candidates allows a rank-ordering of candidates so organizations can select the best candidates for a given job, which depends, of course, on the requirements for each job.

Researchers also consider inter-individual differences and intra-individual differences together – specifically to examine *inter-individual differences in intra-individual change*. For example, it is likely that the relative level of cognitive ability of job applicants (i.e., inter-individual differences in ability) would predict which individuals would acquire more skills in a training program (i.e., intra-individual differences in skill acquisition). Relatively recent methodological advancements have simplified the investigation of inter-individual differences in intra-individual change. These methods facilitate the examination of between-person differences in within-person change and are known by various names such as individual growth models, multilevel models, mixed models, and hierarchical linear models (see Singer & Willett 2003 for a thorough presentation of this methodology). While researchers have long examined the relations among inter-individual differences and intra-individual change, the recent methodological developments allow for a more precise analysis of the inter-individual differences that account for variance in within person change (intra-individual differences) at different stages of skill acquisition, while avoiding some of the pitfalls of measuring change over time (see, e.g., Cronbach & Furby 1970). Yeo and Neal (2004) recently used this methodology to examine the relations among cognitive ability, effort intensity, and additional personality and motivational variables and skill acquisition over 30 trials of an air traffic control task. Their results show interesting patterns of interactions between ability, effort, non-ability traits, and task performance throughout practice, and provide an excellent example of examining inter-individual differences in intra-individual change.

In summary, individuals differ in both their ability to learn during training and on the job, and in their ability to perform well on the job after training. These inter-individual and intra-individual differences imply payoffs or costs to organizations. The assessment of an applicant's ability and non-ability traits allows for selection of the most qualified applicants for each job.

HISTORY OF ABILITY TESTING IN INDUSTRIAL PSYCHOLOGY

Early Work

There are two fundamentally different approaches to the use of ability (or aptitude) tests in employment settings, though they represent different ends of a continuum. The first method is to focus on the abilities that are critical to a particular job or job task, and to devise a selection measure that is based on the abilities that are identified. The second method is to focus on broad abilities or general intelligence, as a means of selecting those applicants who are the most highly intelligent. The first approach is exemplified by Münsterberg's (1913) creation of a test for motormen. The second approach is exemplified by the work of Yerkes and his colleagues (Yoakum & Yerkes 1920) in the creation and application of the Army Alpha Test. There is a third approach that is not exactly an assessment of ability; rather, it focuses on domain knowledge and skills. However, such measures are relevant to the discussion of abilities in that they often share substantial communality, and there are some instances where it is difficult to determine whether one is assessing ability or skill. We discuss the early developments of these approaches below.

Münsterberg (1913)

Probably the first instance of ability testing for industrial selection in modern psychology was performed by Münsterberg (1913). Münsterberg set out to determine whether a test could be devised for assessing the critical cognitive abilities of individuals selected for the job of electric train (what is now typically called street-car or light rail) motormen. He first performed a rudimentary analysis of job requirements and the sources of train accidents (e.g., pedestrian intrusion on the rail tracks). From this point, he departed from the more traditional approach of building a high-fidelity simulator to assess individuals on the task. Instead, he abstracted the underlying ability to perform the task (e.g., identifying accident threats and reacting to them), and then created a test that included a series of cards with abstract objects of red or black, with an indication of how fast they could move, and whether they can only move in parallel to an illustrated track or can move perpendicular to the track. The examinee's task was to turn a hand crank that advanced the view of the track, and to take note of any objects that represented track intrusion threats. Performance was measured by the amount of time taken to traverse the track and by the number of omissions (or missed threats). For validation purposes, Münsterberg examined three groups of concurrent employees (those designated by management as highly skilled, those who were average performers, and those who just missed being dismissed for poor performance), along with some Harvard students. After determining that the test differentiated among the differently performing groups, Münsterberg provided a set of cut-score recommendations for whether individuals should be selected for the job of motorman.

Where Münsterberg's use of an ability test was specifically focused on selection, later developments in the 1910s included another important use of ability testing that is typically found only in military or other large-scale assessments, that of classification. That is, in the selection situation, one only need determine whether an applicant is suitable for the job, which is established with a cut-off score. Of course, another strategy in selection testing is to rank-order individuals on the basis of ability, in order to select the best of the applicants. This course of action is most useful when there are more applicants that exceed the cut-off score than there are jobs slots to fill. Classification in its purest sense occurs when the organization must accept all job candidates, but the organization may attempt to maximize overall effectiveness by placing the candidates in the jobs for which they will be best suited. The development of the Army Alpha and Army Beta tests involved both selection and classification purposes, since the Army was dealing with a large number of draftees who needed to be evaluated for both overall suitability and, if suitable, where the best assignment to jobs should be made.

The First World War

Prior to the First World War, there were only a couple of omnibus intelligence tests in existence that were suitable for adult assessment (e.g., the Yerkes *et al.* 1915 point scale), and none had been used in an employment context. However, through the efforts of a small group of psychologists led by Robert Yerkes (see Yoakum & Yerkes 1920), the US Army agreed to provide for the development and implementation of large-scale intelligence testing of conscripts. According to Yoakum and Yerkes (1920, p. xi):

> The purposes of psychological testing are (a) to aid in segregating the mentally incompetent, (b) to classify men according to their mental capacity, (c) to assist in selecting competent men for responsible positions.

Yerkes and his team started with the work of Binet (who had created individual intelligence tests for children), and of Otis (who was in the process of developing a group-administered test of intelligence). Ultimately, they created two versions of an omnibus intelligence test that could be administered simultaneously to large groups of adult examinees.

Army Alpha and Army Beta

The Alpha test was the major test of intelligence used by the Army in the First World War. Like the Binet tests, it included several scales that were aggregated to yield a single, overall score for each individual. The tests included scales of math word problem-solving, general information, synonyms-antonyms, rearranged sentences, number series, word analogies, and so on. Because the test used written verbal material, or required that the examinee follow verbal instructions given in English, the test clearly required that the examinee be literate in written and spoken English. This created a serious difficulty for conscripts who were either illiterate or not competent English speakers, since the test would be clearly inappropriate for the ability assessment of such individuals. Thus, a second test was created that was entirely non-verbal, both in instruction and in test content.

This was the Army Beta test, and it consisted of mazes, counting, spatial series, digit-symbol, number comparison, figures with missing features, and paper-folding tests. In later analyses, it is important to note that there were many problems with the Beta test, in that many examinees did not understand what was required of them (given that instructions were presented in pantomime), and for other issues, such as the fact that verbal abilities were not evaluated in the context of an overall intelligence score.

Over 1.7 million tests were administered to conscripts during the First World War, though the use of the tests for selection and classification was haphazard at best, given that each camp commander determined whether or not to take the test results into account for specific assignments. The success of this testing program perhaps lay partly in the demonstration that it was possible to do large-scale group intelligence testing of adults, and partly in the efforts by the psychologists after the war to popularize the Army Alpha and its descendants for use in industrial selection situations.

Trade Tests

In addition to the development of omnibus intelligence tests, the Army had a great need for evaluating whether conscripts were skilled in the various trades (e.g., machinists, truck drivers). The goal of this testing program was to separate the men into one of four categories "(1) novices, (2) apprentices, (3) journeymen, and (4) experts" (see Hull 1928). Three different kinds of tests were constructed: verbal, picture, and performance tests. The verbal and picture tests were tests of declarative knowledge about the trade in question, whereas the performance tests were essentially job sample tests. As noted by Hull (1928), the purposes of trade tests and aptitude (or ability) tests are different, but there is in fact much greater similarity between the verbal and picture trade tests and tests of, for example, mechanical ability. The critical differences between these two kinds of tests have to do with test specificity and the demands for prior knowledge. When individual examinees have similar background exposure to the test content, regardless of test specificity and demands for prior knowledge, a trade test is essentially an ability test. When the examinees differ in prior experience, then the demands for prior knowledge may shift the test from an ability assessment to an achievement or skill/knowledge assessment. Although this is a consideration that should apply to all ability tests, in practical terms it is a critical issue when tests are not specifically designed to minimize the value of prior experience for test performance.

Test specificity, on the other hand, is a consideration most often when the criterion job task performance is similarly specific. Numerous tests were created in the 1920s and later which focused on abilities for particular jobs. For example, at a very specific level, tests of clerical abilities (e.g., Andrew & Paterson 1934) focused on predicting proofreading and filing proficiency, while more general tests, such as the Stenquist Mechanical Aptitude Test (Stenquist 1923), focused on a large variety of jobs that involve working with one's hands.

Post-First World War to the Second World War

By the early 1920s, modified Alpha tests were used for selection in education (i.e., college and university admissions; see Ackerman 1996 for a more extensive review), and selection in industrial settings. For example, Toops (1926) reported a survey of 110 colleges and university intelligence testing practices, in the period 1918–1924. He found that while only 7 per cent of the institutions were using some kind of intelligence test for selection in 1918, 60 per cent of the institutions were using intelligence tests for selection in 1924, and another 12 per cent were using them on an experimental basis. Many of the remaining schools were also using intelligence tests, but only for specific departments, and not across the entire institution. Industry also embraced the use of both omnibus intelligence tests in the same period. Although a parallel survey was not completed, an examination of the life insurance sales industry, indicated by the mid-1930s, over a quarter million copies of a single test based on the Army Alpha (the Life Office Management Association "LOMA" test) had been used by over 200 companies (Ferguson 1952). To get an idea of how ubiquitous ability tests became over the post-First World War period, consider that Hildreth's (1933) Bibliography of Mental Tests and Rating Scales listed some 3000 measures. In Bingham's (1937) review of aptitude tests, he noted six major categories of cognitive ability measures used in employment settings, as follows: (1) manual aptitudes, (2) mechanical aptitudes, (3) clerical aptitudes, (4) omnibus measures of intelligence, (5) scientific aptitude, and (6) art judgment. According to Bingham, however, this vast proliferation of ability tests was not uniformly a good thing, since many of these tests would not withstand scientific scrutiny in terms of reliability and validity considerations.

As noted by Tiffin (1952), one of the major reasons for the development of many industrial testing programs during the period 1930–1935 was that this was the height of the Depression era. In that context, the number of job applicants was many times greater than the number of job openings so that organizations were much more oriented to job selection than recruitment. In contrast, as the US entered the period of the Second World War, the use of ability tests shifted from selection to placement (or classification). As noted above, when there are more job openings than applicants, the organization's main goal is to maximize the effectiveness of the individuals by placing them in the jobs for which they are best suited.

The Second World War

The entry of the US into the Second World War provided for a major advance in the development and application of ability assessment measures. In contrast to the efforts of psychologists in the First World War, ability tests were used in almost every aspect of selection and classification. In the US Navy, the Basic Test Battery was administered to over two million recruits (Stuit 1947). The Basic Test Battery was composed of a General Classification Test (sentence completion, opposites, and analogies), a Reading Test, an Arithmetical Reasoning Test, a Mechanical Aptitude Test (including block counting, mechanical comprehension, and surface development scales), and a Mechanical Knowledge Test. The Basic Test Battery was used for classification of enlisted men for assignment to specific Navy training centers. Cut-scores were established as "acceptance requirements for 46 types of enlisted men's training programs" (Stuit 1947, p. 61).

Several special aptitude tests were also created for specific tasks (e.g., Combat Information Center, Pre-Radar Officer, Radio Technician, Radio Code, and Sonar Pitch Memory), though these tests were used with less success than the Basic Test Battery. The Navy also administered a series of tests for the purposes of selection into officer training. For example, the Officer Classifications Test was administered to over 100,000 officers. These tests were similar to standard omnibus intelligence tests (including, e.g., tests of verbal, mechanical, mathematical, and spatial abilities measures). These tests were also used in some cases for classification purposes, but to a limited and non-systematic degree.

The Army Air Forces had a program for selection and classification that was somewhat smaller than that of the Navy, in terms of number of recruits tested. The Army Air Forces (AAF) Aviation Psychology Research Program tested about 600,000 recruits during the Second World War. However, the scope of their program was much more extensive and intensive. The first problem was that there were relatively few individuals in the civilian sector with any kind of aviation experience prior to the war. In addition, because of the highly complex nature of some of the assignments (e.g., pilot, navigator), the specificity of the skills needed (e.g., radar operator, flexible gunner, aircraft maintenance), and the more substantial consequences of the failure of any one individual for an aircraft, the need for selection and classification precision was somewhat greater for the AAF than it was for many of the assignments made by the Navy. By the end of the war, the Aviation Psychology Program had 200 officers, 750 enlisted men, and 500 civilian staff (Flanagan 1948). The 17-volume set of reports published after the war describe not only the efforts in developing and validating new tests of abilities (e.g., Gibson 1947; Guilford & Lacey 1947; Melton 1947), but also new methods of test validation, classification, applied statistics, performance appraisal, and the like (e.g., Thorndike 1947; Flanagan 1948).

Although the AAF used a general intelligence measure for selection and classification purposes (the AAF Qualification Examination), most of the efforts of this group focused on developing ability tests for specific classifications, especially for pilots, navigators, bombardiers, radar operators, and gunners. Literally hundreds of ability tests were created by this group and subjected to evaluation of reliability and validity for selection and classification purposes. Based on this research, the AAF ultimately adopted a two-stage ability testing program. The AAF Qualification Examination was administered as a first screening, for selection purposes. If the recruits passed the initial screening test, they were then administered the AAF Aircrew Classification Test. Scores on this second test were used for assignment for further training into one of the specific jobs, from pilot to gunner. The ability tests and procedures were so successful in terms of reducing washout rates and overall success that they were subsequently adopted by the Royal Air Forces (England) and the French Air Forces (see, e.g., Flanagan 1948).

Post-Second World War

Since the Second World War, ability testing has continued to develop in terms of administering omnibus intelligence tests for employment selection purposes and tests that are specific to particular occupations or fields. For example, one of the most popular tests of general intelligence is the Wonderlic Personnel Test. This is an adaptation of the original Otis Self-Administering Test (Tiffin 1952), and has been in continuous use since 1937. According to the publisher (Wonderlic.Com 2005), "Since 1937, more than 120 million people at thousands of organizations worldwide have taken the [test]." Similarly, the proliferation of specialized ability tests for particular occupations is well documented by the Buros Mental Measurement Yearbook (Spies & Plake 2005), which is published every couple of years, and includes reviews of hundreds of different tests for general and specific job selection purposes.

ASSESSMENT IN PERSONNEL SELECTION

There are many different approaches to designing personnel selection systems to predict job or training performance, but the overall process is generally the same (Schmitt & Chan 1998). First, a job analysis is conducted to identify all requisite job tasks. From this analysis, hypotheses about what ability and non-ability traits (e.g., ability, knowledge, and skill specific to the job) will be necessary for performing each task are developed. Decisions are then made about how to assess each of the relevant traits with a pool of job candidates. Assessment can take many forms, including job interviews, assessment centers, work sample performance, and paper-and-pencil tests. Each assessment method has advantages and disadvantages depending on the skills and traits in question. Many organizations will use a combination of methods to ensure assessment of all relevant traits for a job. Job interviews represent a ubiquitous selection method and consist of a candidate interacting with a representative from the organization. Interviews are typically used to fill gaps of information in the applicant's resume or application, and to assess factors that can only be assessed in a face to face interaction (e.g., appearance, poise, interpersonal competence). Cognitive ability is only weakly related to interview scores (Cortina *et al.* 2000) and interviews are generally not used to assess cognitive ability in any formal way.

Assessment centers are techniques used for assessment of a small group of individuals using multiple methods or exercises. Assessment exercises are typically tailored for a specific job or organization – exercises are selected because they reflect a major aspect of job performance for the job in question. Assessment exercises are usually performance-type tests such as work simulations which vary in their fidelity to real work (Guion 1998). For example, a popular assessment center exercise is the Leaderless Group Discussion in which a group of applicants is given a problem to solve and parameters for solving it. In this exercise, applicants are generally scored based on their interactions and leadership initiative (many variations of the exercise exist – scoring depends on the attributes of interest and the job in question). Cognitive ability can also be assessed as part of an assessment center process, but generally this process is no different than typical ability assessments (i.e., paper-and-pencil tests). Meta-analytic research has shown that assessment centers are valid predictors of job performance (mean $r = 0.37$, Schmidt & Hunter 1998) but their reliability and validity vary greatly. They are also much more expensive to implement than other selection methods.

Work sample assessments are performance tests that use a sample of job performance taken under typical circumstances – the type of performance assessed is a "standardized abstraction of work actually done on the job" (Guion 1998, p. 510). These types of assessments are good predictors of job performance (mean $r = 0.54$ reported by Schmidt & Hunter 1998) but typically cannot be given to applicants who have no job experience.

Compared to work sample assessment, assessment centers, and interviews, paper-and-pencil assessments are generally less expensive to administer and usually have higher reliability and predictive validity. These measures also have added advantages in that they do not require experience with a job, are easily scored, are objective, and most can be easily administered in a group setting (Guion 1998). Recently, traditional paper-and-pencil trait assessments used in organizations (e.g., the Wonderlic, Wonderlic.com) have been transferred to computer administration, which has added advantages in terms of ease of administration and scoring. However, there are potential disadvantages to computerized testing in terms of control over the conditions of administration of the test, falsification of identities of test-takers, and security of the items included in the test. These disadvantages are most problematic when computerized tests are administered remotely without proctoring or supervision (e.g., via the Internet).

Normed and validated measures of general cognitive ability can be purchased for use. However, in the event that assessment of more narrow abilities or skills associated with a specific job is desired, organizations can develop their own measures. This is more easily said than done, however, and requires attention to all aspects of test development from defining the construct, developing items, piloting the measure, to administration of the test to ensure that the new test is reliable, valid for the job in question, and legally defensible (see the Standards for Educational and Psychological Testing, American Educational Research Association, American Psychological Association & National Council on Measurement in Education 1999 for a discussion of test development, and Guion 1998 for a discussion of test development in personnel selection). Even if measures are purchased off the shelf, an organization is responsible for making sure the measures are reliable and valid for their intended purpose. Reliability and validity will be discussed next.

RELIABILITY AND VALIDITY

Reliability

Reliability refers to the stability and consistency of a measure. A measure is considered reliable when it yields consistent results – for example, when the rank-ordering of a group of individuals is consistent across multiple administrations of a test. However, rank-ordering of individuals across multiple administrations of a test may be imperfectly stable for reasons that are not related to the construct the test is measuring. For example, an examinee taking a cognitive ability measure may feel more or less anxious or feel more or less alert on one testing occasion than another. As such, all individual test scores (and all average scores for a group) contain a certain level of measurement error and a certain amount of error free performance that can be assessed. In classical test theory the variance associated with error free performance is called true score variance. Classical test theory is simply, $\sigma_x^2 = \sigma_T^2 + \sigma_E^2$; where σ_x^2 is the variance of the observed score; σ_T^2 is the variance associated with the true score and σ_E^2 is random error variance. True score variance is the variance related to the construct of interest (e.g., general cognitive ability, job knowledge). Error variance is random variance. In a traditional classical test theory framework, reliability coefficients can be conceptualized as the ratio of true score variance to observed variance (Traub 1994).

Reliability coefficients associated with classical test theory fall into three main categories: test–retest, alternate forms (both considered indices of the stability of a measure), and internal consistency. An in-depth review of these reliability estimates is outside of the scope of this chapter – reviews can be found (Traub 1994). The different types of reliability estimates related to classical test theory are somewhat limited in that there is not a single approach that addresses both internal consistency and stability. Generalizability theory is an alternative method for evaluating reliability or the dependability of a measure that accounts for both the internal consistency and stability of a measure without the two occasions needed to assess test–retest and alternative forms reliability (Cronbach *et al.* 1972). This approach requires collecting data within an analysis of variance experimental design which allows the experimenter to simultaneously estimate and separate the variance associated with the individual, the test occasion, and the test items. Generalizability theory also allows for the identification of different sources of measurement error (e.g., random vs. systematic; see Guion 1998 for an application example of generalizability theory).

Classical test theory also has the limitation that the characteristics of the examinee cannot be disentangled from the characteristics of the test. For example, in classical test theory, the difficulty associated with each item (calculated as the proportion of examinees that get the correct response) is dependent on the sample from which the data are collected. As such, summary data on item and test difficulty, variability, and inter-item relations differ, depending on the levels of the trait (e.g., level of ability) that exist in the sample. Item response theory (IRT) addresses this issue. In the IRT framework, item characteristic curves (ICCs) map the probability of a correct response for each item given different levels of the trait (ability). These ability levels are stable across samples which means that the probably of a correct response for each item is based on the ability of the person responding, rather than the number of people at that ability level in the sample. In other words, in theory, the parameters of the ICC equation are invariant across samples.

Parameter invariance has many advantages. Because it separates item statistics from the samples from which they are obtained, difficulty can be more clearly determined for each item. In this way, IRT is oriented toward each individual item and allows for the design of tests with groups of items that have particular characteristics for certain populations of examinees. Computer adaptive testing (CAT) uses branching algorithms to display items based on examinee responses to initial items of moderate difficulty, requiring the examinee to respond to fewer items per test than traditional, linear tests (although a very large item bank must be developed and validated for use in the CAT format). Some CAT algorithms are based on IRT and are used in personnel selection (Borman *et al.* 2001), although there are still drawbacks to this approach, such as the large sample sizes required for IRT analyses, which are prohibitive for most research and applications.

Validity

Although reliability is essential for establishing validity, it is not sufficient (e.g., tests can reliably measure the wrong construct). Validity is the extent to which the inferences drawn from a test are accurate. For example, scores from the Graduate Record Examination are used as part of selection for graduate students at most universities. Tests of perceptual speed and cognitive ability might be used to select airline pilots for training. Based on the scores of these tests, inferences are made about performance in graduate school and performance on the job – that is, those scoring above a certain level on a test will be top performers. In a selection context, validity concerns the accuracy of these inferences.

The statistical framework for personnel selection is generally correlational, and people who do selection in organizations are mainly interested in how well assessment measures (predictors) are correlated with job performance (criterion). The examination of the relationship between predictor and criterion provides evidence of criterion validity. In a selection context, this correlation is also called the *validity coefficient* (Guion 1998). Linear regression models are typically used to predict performance on a criterion given a level of performance on a predictor. This model assumes the relationship between the predictor and criterion is linear (i.e., higher scores on the predictor always result in higher scores on the criterion). This is a fairly safe assumption – the linearity of predictor and criterion is a robust finding in selection research (see, e.g., Coward & Sackett 1990).

Validity coefficients are the basis for determining the utility of a test. The classical validation model, which is based on the validity coefficient, implies that the higher the validity coefficient, the more valuable the test. For example, an ability test that is correlated 0.30 with job performance will be more useful than another test that is correlated 0.20 with job performance. The validity coefficient is not the only consideration for examining the usefulness of a test, however. Taylor and Russell (1939) identified factors in addition to the validity coefficient that affect the usefulness of a test, including the selection ratio and the base rate. The *selection ratio* is the proportion of people in the applicant pool who are hired. The *base rate* is the proportion of present employees and employees in the applicant pool who would be considered successful if no selection procedure were introduced. The Taylor–Russell tables (Taylor & Russell 1939) incorporate the validity coefficient, the selection ratio, and the base rate to estimate the proportion of selected applicants who will subsequently be judged as successful (the success ratio; Cascio 1998).

The Taylor–Russell tables (Taylor & Russell 1939) highlight some general trends in selection and the utility of measures (Schmitt & Chan 1998). (1) When the validity coefficient is zero, the success ratio (the proportion of selected applicants subsequently judged as successful) will be equal to the base rate. (2) The larger the validity coefficient, the higher the success ratio will be. (3) Lower selection ratios will lead to greater success ratios. Lower selection ratios benefit organizations because they imply that the organization has many applicants to choose from to fill each position. When the selection ratio is large there are fewer applicants for each position.

When the base rate is already high (over 0.50), a selection system may not pay off for the organization. This is because the success ratio would be high in the absence of a selection system. The greatest increase in successful applicants selected occurs when the base rate is 0.50.

We can develop a few examples to illustrate the importance of the base rate and selection ratio using the Taylor-Russell tables (Taylor & Russell 1939). Supposes a new battery of tests has a validity coefficient of $r = 0.50$. When the selection ratio is 0.50 (half of the applicants can be selected), and the base rate is 0.30, then the success ratio would be 0.44 (i.e., 44 out of 100 employees would be successful). Next we will illustrate the benefit to the organization of a lower selection ratio. Now suppose that the selection ratio was lower, 0.05, and that the validity coefficient and base rate remain the same as above. The success ratio in this case would be 0.72 (28 per cent more than Example 1). In our third example, we will illustrate how changes to the base rate affect the success ratio. If the selection ratio was 0.50 (as in Example 1) and the base rate was also 0.50 (compared to 0.30 in Example 1), and the validity coefficient remains the same as Example 1, the success ratio would be 0.67 (23 per cent more than Example 1).

The validity coefficient is also quite important in estimating the utility of a selection system. Validity coefficients for assessments used in selection generally range from 0.20 to 0.50. When the base rate is 0.50, and the selection ratio is low (0.05), the success ratios for validity coefficients of 0.20 and 0.50 are 0.67 and 0.88 respectively. The Taylor–Russell tables (Taylor & Russell 1939) are useful in evaluating new selection procedures, but they have a few limitations such as requiring dichotomous evaluation of performance (e.g., employees are considered as either successful or unsuccessful in determining the success ratio), and they do not include the cost of the selection procedure in evaluating the payoff. More current utility analysis procedures address these issues (Cabrera & Raju 2004).

Although researchers and practitioners may focus on the validity coefficients associated with their assessment measures, research conducted to validate selection procedures is much broader than a focus on the correlation between predictors and criteria. Building theory and testing hypotheses about how predictors and criteria are related must include a consideration of the relations among the measures and the underlying constructs they represent (Binning & Barrett 1989). Psychological constructs are theoretical variables that are inferred from many different types of evidence. As such, arguments for their validity include multiple types of evidence such as relations to other variables (i.e., an examination of whether anticipated positive relations with similar constructs and/or near zero or negative relations with dissimilar constructs are found), evidence based on test content (i.e., observation of whether the test content is related to the construct it is intended to measure), evidence based on response processes (i.e., observation of whether the test taps the processes it is designed to measure – e.g., is a cognitive ability test designed to assess math reasoning simply assessing arithmetic ability?), and evidence based on the internal structure of the test (i.e., an examination of the degree to which the test items conform to the proposed structure of the test, AERA, APA & NCME 1999). Establishing the validity of a test to measure the underlying psychological construct of interest is a difficult task, requiring examining evidence for validity from multiple sources.

COGNITIVE ABILITIES AND JOB PERFORMANCE

Many different conceptualizations of the structure of cognitive abilities have been proposed, each of varying levels of complexity. Guilford (1956) proposed a complex model which included 120 factors. Spearman's (1927) model proposed only one general ability factor, *g*, in addition to variance specific to the test, or *s*. Hierarchical models were also proposed by Vernon (1950) and later by Horn and Cattell (1966). These hierarchical models generally incorporated the concept of general ability at the top of the hierarchy and different content-specific abilities on the second level of the hierarchy depending on the theory. Carroll (1993) factor analyzed hundreds of studies on abilities and based on his re-analysis, developed an ability hierarchy that is generally accepted as reflecting the structure of abilities. The result of Carroll's review and re-analysis is graphically displayed in Figure 23.1. The figure shows *g* at the top of the hierarchy and a second order of abilities which include Gf (the raw processing and reasoning ability; Horn & Cattell 1966) and Gc (knowledge acquired through experience and education; Horn & Cattell 1966) as well as visual perception, auditory perception, learning and memory, and speed.

We can examine the intra-individual differences in general ability (the change in ability within a person over time) to understand the differences in predictive validities for general

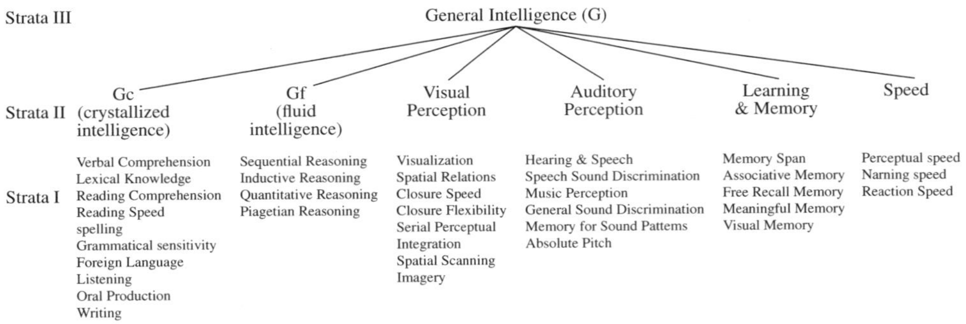

Figure 23.1 A structure of ability constructs derived from information in Carroll (1993). Strata III = third-order construct (general intelligence); Strata II = second-order constructs; Strata I = first-order constructs

cognitive ability and different types of jobs. Ackerman's (1988) theory of the ability determinants of performance during skill acquisition provides a framework for understanding how the consistency of tasks required on the job might moderate the relationship between general ability and job performance. Ackerman's theory states that for most tasks, cognitive ability will be an important predictor of performance when tasks are new. Tasks that lend themselves to proceduralization in this framework are those that are consistently mapped (Schneider *et al.* 1984). As expertise develops through practice on consistently mapped tasks, performance becomes more and more automatized. As performance becomes automatized, performance becomes less dependent on cognitive resources (e.g., attentional resources). In cases where the task is relatively simple and dependent on speed of perception and response coordination, performance becomes more associated with other abilities such as psychomotor and perceptual speed abilities (Ackerman & Cianciolo 2000). As opposed to consistently mapped tasks, variably mapped tasks are not automatized, and require continuous controlled processing, meaning that some focus and application of attention and ability will be required for task performance.

Murphy (1989) developed a framework for examining the stability of validity coefficients in job performance based on Ackerman's (1988) theory of skill acquisition. The different phases involved in job performance in Murphy's model mirror the stages in Ackerman's model of skill acquisition. The transition stage is when the employee must process and acquire new information (i.e., cannot rely on past experiences). In the employment context, this phase happens when an employee is new to a job or when the major duties or responsibilities of a job change. The maintenance stage is when most major job tasks are "well learned and can be performed with minimal mental effort" (Murphy 1989, p. 190). In this phase, Murphy hypothesized that ability may no longer have a direct effect on job performance. Rather, it is likely that ability influences the initial acquisition of job knowledge, which in turn influences job performance in situations where processing novel information is not necessary. The view that ability influences job performance through job knowledge is supported by research conducted by Hunter (1986) and a series of studies by Borman and colleagues (1991; 1993; 1995).

The framework provided by Ackerman (1988) and later modified by Murphy (1989) can be used to understand the change in the validity of general cognitive ability for predicting job performance over time. For example, evidence suggests that standardized tests are good at predicting initial performance in college or graduate school, but that the validity of these measures declines after the first year (Lin & Humphreys 1977). Hulin *et al.* (1990) examined the validity coefficients of general mental ability and more specific abilities for a variety of criteria. They found evidence for declining predictive validities over time for general mental ability as well as more specific abilities examined. They concluded that validity coefficients necessarily decline as a function of time. However, others have pointed out that declines in the predictive validity of cognitive ability over time are not ubiquitous for all jobs, but are a function of the types of predictors and criteria examined (Ackerman 1989; Barrett *et al.* 1992) and that if the right predictors are selected, they may show increased predictive validities over time. For example, jobs that continually require a high level of cognitive demand may not show declines in the validity of general ability for predicting job performance over time. For jobs involving more simple tasks where performance is predicated on coordination of responses, a psychomotor ability measure may increase in its predictive validity over time. What is important is selecting a predictor that is matched to the tasks required by the job.

Farrell and McDaniel (2001) have more recently examined Ackerman's (1988) theory of skill acquisition in an applied setting. Their findings generally supported the theory of the ability determinants of performance during skill acquisition. That is, for jobs including relatively more consistent tasks, general cognitive ability was the strongest predictor of job performance initially, but the predictive validity of cognitive ability declined with experience (psychomotor ability becoming more important over time). For jobs that included relatively more inconsistent tasks, general cognitive ability remained the strongest predictor of job performance throughout task performance.

Job Complexity

The relationship between cognitive ability and job performance is related to the complexity of the job in question (e.g., Hunter & Hunter 1984). Unfortunately, complexity classifications can be relatively uninformative (Murphy 1989). Hunter (1983) derived five levels of job complexity which, in order from most to least complex, are: (1) managerial/professional, (2) complex technical setup, (3) skilled crafts, technicians, supervisors, administrative, (4) semiskilled, and (5) unskilled. Hunter defines complexity in terms of the extent to which workers use data, things, or people on their jobs. This definition does not necessarily address complexity in terms of the cognitive resources required for job tasks, which limits its value in terms of understanding how cognitive abilities are related to job performance for specific job tasks. This is important because, while we know that general cognitive ability is related to job performance for most jobs, and we have general theories about why it is more or less related to performance depending on the job in question, there is not an understanding of the cognitive processes tapped for job performance in specific job tasks.

An alternative to Hunter's (1983) framework was proposed by Wood (1986). Wood provided an extensive definition of task complexity that included three dimensions: component complexity, coordinative complexity, and dynamic complexity. *Component complexity* is a function of the number of distinct acts needed to perform a task. *Coordinative complexity* is a function of the relations between inputs to the task and resulting products.

Dynamic complexity is a function of changes in the environment that affect the relations between task inputs and products – a measure of the stability of the relations between inputs and outputs over time. Wood's definition of task complexity has generally not been adopted in applied research, perhaps because it involves a deeper level of analysis of each of the component tasks involved in a job than is practical in applied research settings. That is, jobs are likely to have an overwhelming number of tasks to be analyzed in Wood's framework (e.g., job analysis results can result in a listing more than 150 tasks associated with one job; Guion 1998). It may be that a more general scheme that borrows from Wood's (1986) framework would suffice. That is, describing job complexity could be done in terms of the relative number of consistently mapped to variably mapped tasks involved in a job – analogous to Wood's dynamic complexity dimension.

Narrow Abilities and Job Performance

When little or no information is available about the job in question, general cognitive ability is good predictor of job performance because it is a very broad construct. In contrast, when very detailed job/task information is available, it may be possible to select employees based on a narrower set of ability constructs that are uniquely associated with performance on the specific job. There is an associated increase in risk in selecting narrower abilities, because a mismatch between predictor and criterion may result in much lower validity coefficients than using measures of general ability. However, there is an increase in potential benefit in terms of increased validity if there is a tighter match between predictor and criterion (see Wittmann & Süß 1999).

Although not explicitly examined in the applied literature, narrower abilities like Gf and Gc are potentially important for predicting job success, especially for older workers. That is, there is evidence that Gf abilities decline with advancing adult age, while Gc remains relatively stable or even increases through the lifespan (Cattell 1987). In this context Gc abilities can be thought of as a skill (e.g., a malleable aspect of performance which changes as a result of training or practice) as opposed to an ability. Ackerman and colleagues' research findings suggest that older adults will be disadvantaged when measures used in personnel selection emphasize Gf type abilities for predicting job performance (Ackerman & Rolfhus 1999; Ackerman 2000). Although Gf abilities might be important for many jobs, it is likely that Gc abilities (such as job knowledge) provide some compensation for declines in Gf for older workers. Indeed, job knowledge has been identified as the main mediator for the relation between cognitive ability and job performance (Hunter 1986; Borman *et al.* 1991, 1993).

Because Gc-type abilities remain stable or increase with advancing age and job knowledge is an important predictor of job performance, one might expect that the relation between age and job performance is positive. The results of research in this area however, are mixed. Meta-analytic research has found both a positive relationship between job performance and age (Waldman & Avolio 1986) and no significant relationship (McEvoy & Cascio 1989; Sturman 2003). However, these studies used rudimentary descriptions of job complexity as discussed previously (e.g., professional or non-professional) that do not necessarily elucidate the relation between age, job performance, and the types of cognitive abilities required for job tasks.

ADDITIONAL CONSIDERATIONS FOR THE USE OF ABILITY TESTS IN SELECTION

Below we review some additional issues that are relevant to personnel selection: the match between predictor and criterion in terms of typical and maximal performance, group differences in test performance and bias, and a trend toward teams in organizations.

Typical and Maximal Performance

Most cognitive ability tests are given under conditions of maximum performance. The instructions for these tests direct individuals to "do their best," soliciting maximum motivation for performance from test takers. Many cognitive ability tests used for selection purposes are considered high stakes tests in that the test-taker has a lot riding on successful performance (educational and employment opportunities). The question is, are these tests, which are administered under conditions that solicit maximum motivation for performance, matched with the criterion of interest, that is, what a person will do on a typical workday? In other words, are these measures of what an individual "can do" when they have maximum motivation the best predictors of what they "will do" on the job (Campbell 1990)?

Cronbach (1949) was the first to identify a classification scheme for measures of typical and maximal performance (see also Ackerman 1994 for a review; Fiske & Butler 1963). Cronbach identified most ability tests as measures of maximal performance and personality tests as measures of typical performance. In contrast to ability tests, for example, the instructions for personality tests direct respondents to think about what they would typically do in a situation. Research has shown that using maximal predictors (e.g., cognitive ability) to predict typical performance is problematic and that maximal performance measures are more consistent in their prediction of maximal performance than typical performance (Sackett *et al.* 1988; DuBois *et al.* 1993).

What might predict typical performance better than cognitive ability measures? While some researchers assert that tests of job knowledge are tests of maximal performance (Schmitt & Chan 1998; Schmitt *et al.* 2003), knowledge can also be conceptualized as representative of typical intellectual engagement. This is because knowledge acquired through the lifespan can be thought of as the cumulative result of a lifetime of learning (Ackerman 1994). Job knowledge does indeed account for incremental variance over measures of general cognitive ability for predicting job performance (e.g., Schmidt & Hunter 1998).

Measures of job knowledge, however, are not always appropriate in a selection context, mainly because an applicant may not possess any knowledge of the available job. It may be that more general knowledge can serve as an indicator of typical intellectual engagement. For example, recent research suggests existing general knowledge is predictive of knowledge acquired in typical learning situations (Beier & Ackerman 2005). These findings suggest that Gc or general knowledge is an index of how skilled people are at acquiring knowledge and can predict what people can learn. If used for personnel selection, general knowledge tests might be broadly work-relevant – assessing knowledge related to work in general (e.g., having productive meetings) vs. job knowledge specific to a job (e.g., knowledge of specific forms related to a procedure). Clearly, more research is needed to understand the role of more general knowledge and domain specific knowledge for predicting job performance.

Group Differences and Adverse Impact

As discussed, measures of cognitive ability are generally good predictors of job performance across essentially all jobs (Hunter & Hunter 1984; Schmidt & Hunter 1998). However, one problem with these tests is that there exist significant and pervasive racial group differences in mean performance (Ones *et al.* 2004). Mean performance for African-Americans is generally about one standard deviation lower than Caucasians. It is also interesting to note that there are pervasive gender differences favoring men in test performance as well, especially on tests of visual-spatial ability, and quantitative skill (Halpern 2000). Women do outperform men on average on many tests of verbal ability, but this finding is not universal. For example, men score better than women on average on both the verbal and quantitative portions of the SAT (although the difference between the genders is much greater for the quantitative section of the SAT; Halpern 2000, p. 127).

These group differences in test performance may result in adverse impact when measures of cognitive abilities are used for selection. *Adverse impact* exists when members of one group are less likely to be hired (i.e., have a lower selection ratio) than members of another group (Guion 1998). Adverse impact alone is not sufficient reason to determine that a selection system is unfair or biased. However, when adverse impact exists, organizations must be able to defend the selection procedure on the grounds that it is a valid predictor of performance (i.e., provide evidence for criterion validity) and job relevant (provide evidence for construct and content related validity; Guion 1998).

To assess the fairness of a test used for selection, it is important to consider whether group differences in mean performance represent bias in the measures, or represent true underlying differences in ability that are associated with job performance. This involves looking not only at the difference in means in test performance, but also at the distributions for each group (i.e., standard errors) and the validity coefficients for predicting performance for each group. Differential validity refers to whether the test in question has different validity coefficients for different groups. Differential validity of a test will result in different regression lines for predicting performance for different groups. Bias is said to exist if the predictor consistently under- or over-predicts on the *common* regression line for one group over another (Humphreys 1952; Cleary 1968). To date, there is little evidence of differential validity based on group membership for cognitive ability tests used to predict job performance (see Ones *et al.* 2004 for a review). In fact, when differential validity exists, the common regression line usually serves to over-predict performance for protected groups (Guion 1998).

Stereotype threat is a theory that endeavors to account for the group differences found in test performance (Steele & Aronson 1995). Stereotype threat is "being at risk of confirming, as self-characteristic, a negative stereotype about one's group" (Steele & Aronson 1995, p. 797). The notion is that stereotype threat inhibits performance in situations where the stereotype of a group to which a person belongs is activated. Steele and Aronson posit that taking a test that is aimed at measuring intellectual ability will induce stereotype threat for African-Americans because of the stereotype that African-Americans are less intellectually able than White Americans. Steele and Aronson activated stereotype threat in an experimental setting and found that performance for African-Americans was adversely affected under conditions of stereotype threat. These findings have been replicated in subsequent laboratory studies and for different groups (e.g., women and mathematical performance; Cadinu *et al.* 2005). Although there is evidence for stereotype threat in laboratory studies, stereotype threat did not fully account for group differences in ability testing in Steele and Aronson's study (Sackett *et al.* 2004).

There is also some argument about the size of the effects and the usefulness of Stereotype Threat for understanding group differences in test performance outside laboratory environments. Cullen *et al.* (2004) examined two datasets collected in applied settings for evidence of stereotype threat. One dataset included SAT scores and GPA and the other included ASVAB scores and job proficiency for military jobs as part of a large-scale project on selection and classification conducted for the military (i.e., Army Project A; see Campbell & Knapp 2001 for information about this research project). They found no evidence that scores on the SAT or ASVAB under-predicted performance for women or minority groups – that is, they found no evidence that stereotype threat introduced bias in selection in applied settings. More work is being done to examine the causes and possible remedies to group differences in tests used for selection. Needless to say, the adverse impact that results from using measures of cognitive ability is one of the most vexing issues facing selection researchers and practitioners.

Team Performance

Recently, much research in I/O psychology has focused on a perceived movement in organizations from individual jobs to team-based work environments. Team research incorporates team dynamics (which is one of the fundamental topics in the small-group literature) but also includes a focus on the task or tasks done by the group, and the technology associated with task completion (Kozlowski & Bell 2003). A thorough treatment of teams in organizations is outside of the scope of this chapter; a comprehensive overview is provided by Kozlowski and Bell (2003).

The necessity to hire people to fit into a team environment has implications for personnel selection. Depending on how each organization rewards behavior, ratings of job performance for each individual on a team will generally include an evaluation of team performance. Working together effectively on a team requires both adequate task performance and teamwork and implies an increased focus on interpersonal skills and personality traits for selection. Cognitive ability remains a key trait for selecting individuals to work on teams (Barrick *et al.* 1998), but there is some evidence that it is not sufficient for predicting performance in the team environment. Non-ability factors such as the leadership qualities and personality traits of the individuals on the team and the homogeneity/diversity of the *composition* of these traits within the team are also important predictors of team performance.

CONCLUSIONS

From the beginning of the history of personnel testing through today, the study of cognitive ability has been central to personnel selection. Even though cognitive ability accounts for a substantial portion of variance in job performance (i.e., about 25 per cent under the best circumstances), there is clearly quite a lot of variance in job performance left for which to account. Prediction may be maximized by a more precise analysis of the types of abilities required by job tasks and an assessment of these abilities in potential employees. Non-ability traits such as personality have also shown promise for accounting for incremental variance in job performance (Kanfer & Kantrowitz 2002) and these traits are likely even more important for team performance (Kozlowski & Bell 2003). The future will likely bring many innovations in the area of selection research. However, it is likely that cognitive ability will continue to play a major role in choosing the best applicants for jobs.

REFERENCES

Ackerman, P. L. (1988). Determinants of individual differences during skill acquisition: cognitive abilities and information processing. *Journal of Experimental Psychology: General, 117*, 288–318.

Ackerman, P. L. (1989). Within-task intercorrelations of skilled performance: implications for predicting individual differences? (A comment on Henry & Hulin 1987). *Journal of Applied Psychology, 74*, 360–364.

Ackerman, P. L. (1994). Intelligence, attention, and learning: maximal and typical performance. In D. K. Detterman (ed.), *Current Topics in Human Intelligence, Vol. 4: Theories of Intelligence* (pp. 2–27). Norwood, NJ: Ablex.

Ackerman, P. L. (1996). A theory of adult intellectual development: process, personality, interests, and knowledge. *Intelligence, 22*, 229–259.

Ackerman, P. L. (2000). Domain-specific knowledge as the "dark matter" of adult intelligence: Gf/Gc, personality and interest correlates. *Journal of Gerontology: Psychological Sciences, 55B*, P69–P84.

Ackerman, P. L. & Cianciolo, A. (2000). Cognitive, perceptual-speed, and psychomotor determinants of individual differences during skill acquisition. *Journal of Experimental Psychology: Applied, 6*, 259–290.

Ackerman, P. L. & Humphreys, L. G. (1991). Individual differences theory in industrial and organizational psychology. In M. D. Dunnette & L. M. Hough (eds.), *Handbook of Industrial and Organizational Psychology* (Vol. 1, pp. 223–282). Palo Alto, CA: Consulting Psychologists Press.

Ackerman, P. L. & Rolfhus, E. L. (1999). The locus of adult intelligence: knowledge, abilities, and nonability traits. *Psychology and Aging, 14*, 314–330.

American Educational Research Association, American Psychological Association & National Council on Measurement in Education (1999). *Standards for Educational and Psychological Testing.* Washington, DC: American Educational Research Association.

Andrew, D. M. & Paterson, D. G. (1934). *The Minnesota Vocational Test for Clerical Workers* (Rep. No.). Employee Stabilization Research Institute.

Barrett, G. V., Alexander, R. A. & Doverspike, D. (1992). The implications for personnel selection of apparent declines in predictive validities over time: a critique of Hulin, Henry, and Noon. *Personnel Psychology, 45*, 601–617.

Barrick, M. R. & Mount, M. K. (1991). The big five personality dimensions and job performance: a meta-analysis. *Personnel Psychology, 44*, 1–26.

Barrick, M. R., Stewart, G. L., Neubert, M. J. & Mount, M. K. (1998). Relating member ability and personality to work-team processes and team effectiveness. *Journal of Applied Psychology, 83*, 377–391.

Beier, M. E. & Ackerman, P. L. (2005). Age, ability, and the role of prior knowledge on the acquisition of new domain knowledge: promising results in a real-world learning environment. *Psychology and Aging, 20*, 341–355.

Bingham, W. V. D. (1937). *Aptitudes and Aptitude Testing.* New York: Harper & Brothers.

Binning, J. F. & Barrett, G. V. (1989). Validity of personnel decisions: a conceptual analysis of the inferential and evidential bases. *Journal of Applied Psychology, 74*, 478–494.

Borman, W. C., Buck, D. E., Hanson, M. A. *et al.* (2001). An examination of the comparative reliability, validity, and accuracy of performance ratings made using computerized adaptive rating scales. *Journal of Applied Psychology, 86*, 965–973.

Borman, W. C., Hanson, M. A., Oppler, S. H. *et al.* (1993). Role of early supervisory experience in supervisor performance. *Journal of Applied Psychology, 78*, 443–449.

Borman, W. C., White, L. A. & Dorsey, D. W. (1995). Effects of rate task performance and interpersonal factors on supervisor and peer performance ratings. *Journal of Applied Psychology, 80*, 168–177.

Borman, W. C., White, L. A., Pulakos, E. D. & Oppler, S. H. (1991). Models of supervisory job performance ratings. *Journal of Applied Psychology, 76*, 863–872.

Cabrera, E. F. & Raju, N. S. (2004). Utility analysis: current trends and future directions. *International Journal of Selection and Assessment, 9*, 92–102.

Cadinu, M., Maass, A., Rosabianca, A. & Kiesner, J. (2005). Why do women underperform under stereotype threat? Evidence for the role of negative thinking. *Psychological Science, 16*, 572–578.

Campbell, J. P. (1990). Modeling the performance prediction problem in industrial and organizational psychology. In M. D. Dunnette & L. M. Hough (eds.), *Handbook of Industrial and Organizational Psychology* (Vol. 1, pp. 687–732). Palo Alto, CA: Consulting Psychologists Press.

Campbell, J. P. & Knapp, D. J. (2001). *Exploring the Limits in Personnel Selection and Classification.* Mahwah, NJ: Lawrence Erlbaum Associates.

Carroll, J. B. (1993). *Human Cognitive Abilities: A Survey of Factor-analytic Studies.* New York: Cambridge University Press.

Cascio, W. F. (1998). *Applied Psychology in Human Resource Management* (5th edn). Upper Saddle River, NJ: Prentice-Hall.

Cattell, R. B. (1987). *Intelligence: Its Structure, Growth, and Action.* New York: Elsevier.

Cleary, T. A. (1968). Test bias: prediction of grades of Negro and white students in integrated colleges. *Journal of Educational Measurement, 5*, 115–124.

Cortina, J. M., Goldstein, N. B., Payne, S. C. *et al.* (2000). The incremental validity of interview scores over and above cognitive ability and conscientiousness scores. *Personnel Psychology, 53*, 325–351.

Coward, W. M. & Sackett, P. R. (1990). Linearity of ability-performance relationships: a reconfirmation. *Journal of Applied Psychology, 75*, 297–300.

Cronbach, L. J. (1949). *Essentials of Psychological Testing.* New York: Harper.

Cronbach, L. J. & Furby, L. (1970). How we should measure "change" – or should we? *Psychological Bulletin, 74*, 68–80.

Cronbach, L. J., Gleser, G. C., Nanda, H. & Rajaratnam, N. (1972). *The Dependability of Behavioral Measurements: Theory of Generalizability for Scores and Profiles.* New York: John Wiley & Sons.

Cullen, M. J., Hardison, C. M. & Sackett, P. R. (2004). Using SAT-grade and ability-job performance relationships to test predictions derived from stereotype threat theory. *Journal of Applied Psychology, 89*, 220–230.

DuBois, C. L. Z., Sackett, P. R., Zedeck, S. & Fogli, L. (1993). Further exploration of typical and maximum performance criteria: definitional issues, prediction, and white–black differences. *Journal of Applied Psychology, 78*, 205–211.

Farrell, J. N. & McDaniel, M. A. (2001). The stability of validity coefficients over time: Ackerman's (1988) model and the General Aptitude Test Battery. *Journal of Applied Psychology, 86*, 60–79.

Ferguson, L. W. (1952). A look across the Years 1920 to 1950. In L. L. Thurstone (ed.), *Applications of Psychology* (pp. 1–17). New York: Harper and Brothers.

Fiske, D. W. & Butler, J. M. (1963). The experimental conditions for measuring individual differences. *Educational and Psychological Measurement, 23*, 249–266.

Flanagan, J. C. (ed.) (1948). *The Aviation Psychology Program in the Army Air Forces* (Report No. 1). Army Air Forces aviation psychology program research reports #1. Washington, DC: US Government Printing Office.

Fleishman, E. A. (1972). On the relation between abilities, learning, and human performance. *American Psychologist, 27*, 1017–1032.

Gibson, J. J. (ed.) (1947). *Army Air Forces Aviation Psychology Program Research Reports: Motion Picture Testing and Research* (Report No. 7). Washington, DC: US Government Printing Office.

Guilford, J. P. (1956). The structure of intellect. *Psychological Bulletin, 53*, 267–293.

Guilford, J. P. & Lacey, J. I. (eds.) (1947). *Army Air Forces Aviation Psychology Program Research Reports: Printed Classification Tests* (Report No. 5). Washington, DC: US Government Printing Office.

Guion, R. M. (1998). *Assessment, Measurement, and Prediction for Personnel Decisions*. Mahwah, NJ: Lawrence Erlbaum Associates.

Halpern, D. F. (2000). *Sex Differences in Cognitive Abilities* (3rd edn). Mahwah, NJ: Lawrence Erlbaum Associates.

Hildreth, G. H. (1933). *Bibliography of Mental Tests and Rating Scales*. New York: Psychological Corporation.

Horn, J. L. & Cattell, R. B. (1966). Refinement and test of the theory of fluid and crystallized general intelligences. *Journal of Educational Psychology, 57*, 253–270.

Hulin, C. L., Henry, R. A. & Noon, S. L. (1990). Adding a dimension: time as a factor in the generalizability of predictive relationships. *Psychological Bulletin, 107*, 328–340.

Hull, C. L. (1928). *Aptitude Testing*. New York: World Book Company.

Humphreys, L. G. (1952). Individual differences. *Annual Review of Psychology, 3*, 131–150.

Hunter, J. E. (1983). *Test Validation for 12,000 Jobs: An Application of Job Classification and Validity Generalization Analysis for the General Aptitude Test Battery* (US Employment Service Test Research Report No. 45). Washington, DC: US Department of Labor.

Hunter, J. E. (1986). Cognitive ability, cognitive aptitudes, job knowledge, and job performance. *Journal of Vocational Behavior, 29*, 340–362.

Hunter, J. E. & Hunter, R. F. (1984). Validity and utility of alternative predictors of job performance. *Psychological Bulletin, 96*, 72–98.

Kanfer, R. & Kantrowitz, T. M. (2002). Ability and non-ability predictors of job performance. In S. Sonnentag (ed.), *Psychological Management of Individual Performance* (pp. 27–50). Hoboken, NJ: John Wiley & Sons.

Kozlowski, S. W. J. & Bell, B. S. (2003). Work groups and teams in organizations. In W. C. Borman, D. R. Ilgen, R. J. Klimoski & I. B. Weiner (eds.), *Handbook of Psychology: Vol. 12. Industrial and Organizational Psychology* (pp. 77–105). Hoboken, NJ: John Wiley & Sons.

Lin, P. & Humphreys, L. G. (1977). Predictions of academic performance in graduate and professional school. *Applied Psychological Measurement, 1*, 249–257.

McEvoy, G. M. & Cascio, W. F. (1989). Cumulative evidence of the relationship between employee age and job performance. *Journal of Applied Psychology, 74*, 11–17.

Melton, A. W. (ed.) (1947). *Army Air Forces Aviation Psychology Program Research Reports: Apparatus Tests* (Report No. 4). Washington, DC: US Government Printing Office.

Münsterberg, H. (1913). *Psychology and Industrial Efficiency*. Boston, MA: Houghton Mifflin.

Murphy, K. R. (1989). Is the relationship between cognitive ability and job performance stable over time? *Human Performance, 2*, 183–200.

Ones, D. S., Viswesvaran, C. & Dilchert, S. (2004). Cognitive ability in selection decisions. In O. Willhelm & R. W. Engle (eds.), *Handbook of Understanding and Measuring Intelligence* (pp. 431–468). Thousand Oaks, CA: Sage.

Sackett, P. R., Hardison, C. M. & Cullen, M. J. (2004). On interpreting stereotype threat as accounting for African American–White differences on cognitive tests. *American Psychologist, 59*, 7–13.

Sackett, P. R., Zedeck, S. & Fogli, L. (1988). Relations between measures of typical and maximum job performance. *Journal of Applied Psychology, 73*, 482–486.

Schmidt, F. L. & Hunter, J. E. (1998). The validity and utility of selection methods in personnel psychology: practical and theoretical implications of 85 years of research findings. *Psychological Bulletin, 124*, 262–274.

Schmitt, N. & Chan, D. (1998). *Personnel Selection: A Theoretical Approach*. Thousand Oaks, CA: Sage.

Schmitt, N., Cortina, J. M., Interick, M. J. & Weichmann, D. (2003). Personnel selection and employee performance. In W. C. Borman, D. R. Ilgen, R. J. Klimoski & I. B. Weiner (eds.), *Handbook of Psychology: Vol. 12. Industrial and Organizational Psychology* (pp. 77–105). Hoboken, NJ: John Wiley & Sons.

Schneider, W., Dumais, S. T. & Shiffrin, R. M. (1984). Automatic and control processing and attention. In R. Parasuraman & D. R. Davies (eds.), *Varieties of Attention* (pp. 29–61). New York: Academic Press.

Singer, J. D. & Willett, J. B. (2003). *Applied Longitudinal Data Analysis: Modeling Change and Event Occurrence.* Oxford and New York: Oxford University Press.

Spearman, C. (1927). *The Nature of "Intelligence" and the Principles of Cognition.* New York: Macmillan.

Spies, R. A. & Plake, B. S. (2005). *The Sixteenth Mental Measurements Yearbook.* Lincoln, NE: Buros Institute of Mental Measurement.

Steele, C. M. & Aronson, J. (1995). Stereotype threat and intellectual test performance of African Americans. *Journal of Personality and Social Psychology, 69,* 797–811.

Stenquist, J. L. (1923). Measurements of mechanical ability. In *Teachers College Contributions to Education* (No. 130). New York: Columbia University.

Stuit, D. B. (ed.) (1947). *Personnel research and test development in the Bureau of Naval Personnel.* Princeton, NJ: Princeton University Press.

Sturman, M. C. (2003). Searching for the inverted U-shaped relationship between time and performance: a meta-analysis of the experience/performance, tenure/performance, and age/performance relationships. *Journal of Management, 29,* 609–640.

Taylor, H. C. & Russell, J. T. (1939). The relationship of validity coefficients to the practical effectiveness of tests in selections: discussion and tables. *Journal of Applied Psychology, 23,* 565–578.

Thorndike, R. L. (1947). *Research Problems and Techniques* (Report No. 3). Army Air Forces aviation psychology program research reports #3. Washington, DC: US Government Printing Office.

Tiffin, J. (1952). *Industrial Psychology.* New York: Prentice-Hall.

Toops, H. A. (1926). The status of university intelligence tests in 1923–24. *Journal of Educational Psychology, 17,* 23–36, 110–124.

Traub, R. E. (1994). *Measurement Methods for the Social Sciences Series, Vol. 3: Reliability for the Social Sciences.* Thousand Oaks, CA: Sage.

Vernon, P. E. (1950). *The Structure of Human Abilities.* New York: John Wiley & Sons.

Waldman, D. A. & Avolio, B. J. (1986). A meta-analysis of the age differences in job performance. *Journal of Applied Psychology, 71,* 33–38.

Wittmann, W. W. & Süß, H. (1999). Investigating the paths between working memory, intelligence, knowledge, and complex problem-solving performances via Brunswik Symmetry. In P. L. Ackerman, P. C. Kyllonen & R. D. Roberts (eds.), *Learning and Individual Differences: Process, Trait, and Content Determinant.* Washington, DC: American Psychological Association.

Wonderlic.Com. Available at: http://www.wonderlic.com/products. Retrieved January 15, 2005.

Wood, R. E. (1986). Task complexity: definition of the construct. *Organizational Behavior and Human Decision Processes, 37,* 60–82.

Yeo, G. B. & Neal, A. (2004). A multilevel analysis of effort, practice, and performance: effects of ability, conscientiousness, and goal orientation. *Journal of Applied Psychology, 89,* 231–247.

Yerkes, R. M., Bridges, J. W. & Hardwick, R. S. (1915). *A point Scale for Measuring Mental Ability.* Baltimore, MD: Warwick & York.

Yoakum, C. S. & Yerkes, R. M. (1920). *Mental Tests in the American Army.* London: Sidgwick & Jackson, Ltd.

CHAPTER 24

Mental Illness and Mental Health

Megan E. Hughes
Temple University, USA
Catherine Panzarella
Child, Adolescent & Family Division
Mental Health Association of Southeastern Pennsylvania, USA
Lauren B. Alloy
Temple University, USA
and
Lyn Y. Abramson
University of Wisconsin-Madison, USA

A COGNITIVE PERSPECTIVE ON MENTAL ILLNESS AND MENTAL HEALTH

Cognitive psychologists examine the ways in which individuals perceive, interpret, and recall situations and how their perceptions relate to their behavior and emotions. The cognitive perspective on mental illness suggests that a negative misinterpretation of events and situations is central to the development of psychological disturbance. Although negative misinterpretations are present in different types of psychopathology, not all misinterpretations are necessarily detrimental. In fact, some misinterpretations may actually play a role in the maintenance of mental *health*. For example, non-depressed individuals are less accurate in some of their interpretations than depressed individuals (Alloy & Abramson 1988). Thus, mental health outcomes cannot be predicted simply by the presence of misperceptions and misinterpretations, but more specifically by their type and frequency (*cognitive content*) as well as the manner in which the information is processed (*cognitive processes*).

In this chapter, we review the theory and evidence that connect attention, memory, and interpretation biases to a range of psychological disorders. We begin with a discussion of a few basic constructs and methods used in cognitive psychology. We then review relevant

Handbook of Applied Cognition: Second Edition. Edited by Francis T. Durso.

cognitive research on several mental disorders. Panic disorder, specific phobia, and unipolar depression are included because they are highly prevalent disorders that have long been a central focus of cognitive theory and research. Bipolar disorder was added because its combination of high and low moods poses a particular challenge to cognitive theory. Anorexia nervosa and bulimia nervosa are highlighted because they provide good examples of the complicated interplay between cognitive and biological factors. Dissociative identity disorder is included because of its fascinating implications for memory research. Finally, the chapter concludes with a discussion of the cognitive factors in mental health and the emerging field of positive psychology. This chapter is an updated version of the one published in 1999 (Panzarella *et al.* 1999). Although there is some overlap with the earlier version, this chapter has incorporated the most relevant current research on each disorder and includes the new topics of bipolar depression and positive psychology.

BASIC CONCEPTS UTILIZED IN THE STUDY OF COGNITIVE MODELS OF MENTAL HEALTH

Although thoughts that are deliberative or conscious are important, it is fleeting thoughts, which are not in full awareness, often referred to as *automatic thoughts* (e.g., Beck *et al.* 1979), that are of particular interest to mental health researchers. Automatic thoughts are influenced by deeper organizational structures called *schemata*. Schemata contain generalized beliefs about the self and the world, called *core beliefs* (e.g., Beck *et al.* 1979), as well as functional processing mechanisms for handling the wide variety of information that is available to a person at any one time.

Schemata theoretically assist people in processing complex environmental information by: (1) selecting only a fraction of incoming stimuli for processing; (2) abstracting meaning from incoming information and favoring storage of the meaning rather than a veridical representation of the original stimulus; (3) using prior knowledge to assist in processing and interpreting information; and (4) integrating information to favor creation of internal consistency over external veracity (Alba & Hasher 1983). Schemata pertaining to the self are of greatest interest to mental health researchers. Markus (1977) defines self-schemata as "cognitive generalizations about the self, derived from past experience, that organize and guide the processing of self-related information contained in the individual's social experiences" (p. 64). Researchers have identified characteristics of self-schemata uniquely associated with different disorders. For example, depressed individuals show evidence of self-schemata characterized by a negative view of the self and information-processing biased toward pessimistic interpretations of events. Before describing the research on schemata and cognitive content associated with various mental disorders, we will briefly present some of the methods that have been developed for studying cognitive phenomena in mental disorders.

METHODS USED TO STUDY COGNITIVE CONTRIBUTIONS TO MENTAL HEALTH

Self-report is still one of the most widely used methodologies for studying cognition. However, self-reports can be inaccurate because individuals may be unaware of or unwilling to report certain thoughts. Some of the methodologies that attempt to circumvent the problems of direct self-report are briefly described in Table 24.1.

APPLYING THE COGNITIVE PERSPECTIVE TO PARTICULAR DISORDERS

Anxiety Disorders

Anxiety disorders involve excessive fears, worries, or time spent trying to control worrisome thoughts (American Psychiatric Association 2000). Substantial research by cognitive theorists implicates two cognitive biases in the development and maintenance of anxiety disorders: selective attention toward threatening stimuli and overestimation of the threat inherent in relatively benign stimuli. Here, we will present some of the research findings from panic disorder, where the feared stimulus is internal (e.g., fear of going mad) and specific phobia, where the feared stimulus is external (e.g., spiders).

Panic Disorder

A *panic attack* is characterized by the sudden onset of somatic symptoms such as heart palpitations, chest pain, dizziness, sweating, and trembling, as well as cognitive symptoms such as fear of dying or losing control (American Psychiatric Association 2000). Panic disorder is diagnosed when an individual has recurrent, unexpected panic attacks and, for at least a month, has concerns about future attacks, worries about implications of panic attacks, or changes his or her behavior related to the attacks (e.g., avoids locations where panic attacks occurred; American Psychiatric Association 2000). The latest US National Comorbidity Survey Replication (NCS-R) found a 12-month prevalence for panic disorder of 2.7 per cent in English-speaking Americans (Kessler *et al.* 2005b). The same study estimates the lifetime prevalence of panic disorder in English-speaking Americans to be 4.7 per cent (Kessler *et al.* 2005a). Panic disorder is often accompanied by *agoraphobia*, the fear of being in situations (e.g., being outside the home, being on a bridge, or traveling in a plane) where it may be difficult to escape or get help (American Psychiatric Association 2000).

D. M. Clark's (1986) cognitive model of panic disorder, based on Beck *et al.*'s (1985) cognitive model of anxiety disorders, suggests that individuals who have panic attacks tend to have a cognitive bias to interpret their somatic sensations catastrophically. That is, they misinterpret normal daily sensations such as breathlessness after climbing a flight of stairs or sweating in a stressful meeting as signaling a dangerous outcome such as a heart attack or loss of control (Clark *et al.* 1989). D. M. Clark (1986) claims that individuals who have panic attacks interpret either an internal (e.g., heart palpitation, anxious thought) or external (e.g., hot room, feared situation) stimulus as a sign of danger, leading them to experience anxious apprehension and *catastrophic cognitions*. In this state, the individual experiences many somatic sensations that, when interpreted in a catastrophic way, increase the individual's sense of threat and apprehension. This cycle continues to build and leads to a full-blown panic attack. Individuals with panic disorder also tend to be hyper-vigilant in scanning their bodies for the feared sensations and avoiding situations

Table 24.1 Common cognitive psychology methodologies

Type of Method	Description	
Reaction-Time	Technique	Participants react to stimuli (i.e., push a key on a computer to label an adjective as "me" or "not me").
	Dependent Variable	Amount of time it takes to respond to a stimulus.
	Relevance	Differences in reaction times are attributed to differences in underlying cognitive processes.
	Representative Example	Alloy *et al.* (1997) Depressed participants were faster at labeling adjectives that fit their self-view ("inferior") compared to words that did not fit self-schema ("adept").
Ambiguous Stimuli	Technique	Participants determine the meaning of an ambiguous stimulus.
	Dependent Variable	The interpretation chosen (i.e., slay vs. sleigh).
	Relevance	Interpretations are thought to be related to underlying schemata.
	Representative Example	Mathews *et al.* (1989) Participants write down their interpretation of words that were presented through a tape-recorder. Anxious participants were significantly more likely to make threat word interpretations (i.e. "slay" vs. "sleigh") than normal controls.
Competing Stimuli	Technique	Participants presented with two different stimuli simultaneously, forcing them to attend to only one.
	Dependent Variable	Measuring the type of stimuli to which the participants attend.
	Relevance	Individuals with certain disorders will attend to or be distracted by stimuli that are consistent with their cognitive biases.
	Representative Example	Treisman and Geffen (1967); Burgess *et al.* (1981) Participants wearing earphones heard different words in each ear. They were asked to attend to and repeat the message in one ear and to press a button when they heard certain words in either ear. Anxious participants detected significantly more fear-relevant phrases in the unattended passages than did controls.
Emotional Stroop	Technique	In the original task, individuals are shown a series of color words (i.e., green, red) printed in different colored ink. If asked to name the color of ink for each word, participants are distracted by the written color name and demonstrate slower reaction times (Stroop 1935). Instead of using color words, the *emotional* Stroop task asks participants to name the ink color for words that are likely to be of relevance to certain people (i.e. "failure" for a depressed participant).
	Dependent Variable	Time to read words.
	Relevance	Investigators make inferences about the attentional processing of individuals with particular psychological profiles.
	Representative Example	Gotlib and McCann (1984) Dysphoric students take longer to name the ink colors of negative words than neutral or positive words (non-dysphoric students do not).

Table 24.1 *Continued*

Type of Method	Description	
Priming	Technique	In priming tasks, participants are typically presented with a stimulus that activates hypothetical mental structures (e.g., depressive self-schemata) without the participant being fully aware of the activation (Segal & Ingram 1994). Priming could be done in a variety of ways, including having people compare lists of words that include threat words or read a story that induces a negative mood.
	Dependent Variable	A variety of dependent variables are used.
	Relevance	These studies rely on the assumption that cognitive and affective information is interconnected, so that activating one type of information makes the other more accessible (Bower 1981).
	Representative Example	Teasdale and Dent (1987) Recovered depressives and never-depressed controls completed an adjective recall measure while in a normal mood state and after a negative mood induction. The formerly depressed group recalled more negative adjectives than the never-depressed group after the negative mood induction (they performed the same when not primed).
Judgment of Covariation	Technique	Participants are asked to estimate the extent to which to events are connected.
	Dependent Variable	Degree of contingency estimate.
	Relevance	Errors in contingency estimations can provide information on an individual's cognitive biases (Nisbett & Ross 1980).
	Representative Example	Alloy and Abramson (1979, Experiments 1–4) Depressed and non-depressed participants were asked to estimate the degree of contingency between pressing a button and turning on a light. Although the experimenters varied the contingency, depressed participants were more accurate in their estimation whereas non-depressed participants overestimated the control they had.
Psycho-physiological	Technique	Various techniques. Electroenchepalograms (EEG) measure the electrical activity of the brain. Functional magnetic resonance imaging (fMRI) measures neural activity by assessing changes in brain blood flow. Eye-blink magnitude is measured as an implicit indicator of negative interpretations of ambiguous stimuli.
	Dependent Variable	Various measurements from each technique.
	Relevance	Psychophysiological measures provide information about potential biological correlates of cognitive changes.
	Representative Example	Lawson *et al.* (2002) Eye-blink magnitude was used to measure interpretations of ambiguous stimuli (i.e., _loom, could be interpreted as gloom or bloom). An eye-blink magnitude study demonstrated that depressed individuals have a bias to interpret ambiguous stimuli in a negative way.

that have led to panic in the past (Clark *et al.* 1989). Such avoidance reduces the individual's ability to disconfirm their catastrophic beliefs and may lead to agoraphobia.

Studies demonstrate that carbon dioxide inhalation, sodium lactate infusion, and hyperventilation can induce panic-like somatic symptoms in individuals, with panic disorder patients more likely to have full panic attack responses than normal controls or individuals with other anxiety disorders (for a review, see Rapee 1995). There is evidence to suggest that cognitions mediate the relationship between biological panic-inducing agents and panic attacks (for a review, see Khawaja & Oei 1998). In one study, one group of participants with panic disorder was given information about the sensations that they might experience during a carbon dioxide inhalation challenge and another group was given no information. Those in the no explanation condition had more catastrophic cognitions and panic symptoms than their informed counterparts (Rapee 1986). D. M. Clark *et al.* (1989) reported that panic patients interpret somatic sensations more negatively than controls or non-panic anxious patients on explicit self-report forms. They also were faster at completing sentences that utilized panic words (e.g., dying, choking, insanity) than those who used neutral words (whereas the reaction times of normal controls did not differ between sentence types). In another study, of current panic patients who read cards with somatic sensations followed by catastrophic interpretations, 83 per cent had panic attacks, whereas no remitted panic disordered patients or non-panic controls had panic attacks (Clark *et al.* 1989). Furthermore, cognitive behavioral treatment outcome studies suggest that catastrophic cognitions were reduced during successful treatment of panic disorder (Westling & Ost 1995) and that reductions in catastrophic cognitions during treatment predicted maintenance of these improvements (Clark *et al.* 1989).

Although the preceding studies support the role of catastrophic cognitions in panic attacks, Stoler and McNally (1991) reported that the catastrophic cognitions of remitted panic disorder patients continued to be more like those of panic disorder clients than like those of normal controls. Furthermore, data from retrospective self-report suggest that a significant minority of attacks is not preceded by conscious catastrophic interpretations at all (Rachman *et al.* 1988). The existence of nocturnal panic attacks, when an individual wakes in the middle of a panic attack, raises further questions about the necessity of catastrophic cognitions in the onset of panic attacks (Bouton *et al.* 2001). Craske *et al.* (2002) addressed this criticism in a laboratory sleep study. Individuals were told that an audio tone would signal physiological changes during sleep. One group of participants was told that physiological changes were normal during sleep and another group was told that they were unexpected. Regardless of any true physiological changes during sleep, the experimenters produced an audio tone to wake participants. Those who had been told not to expect physiological changes had more nocturnal panic symptoms than those who were expecting such changes. Although the experimenters concluded that catastrophic cognitions can lead to panic attacks outside of the realm of awareness, this idea rests on the assumption that there are no conscious cognitions during sleep. Furthermore, Roth *et al.* (2005) note that Craske *et al.*'s (2002) conclusion makes it nearly impossible to disprove that catastrophic cognitions have a causal role in panic attack onset. The catastrophic cognition debate points to one of the most frustrating features of this research, the fact that there is not yet a way to measure, with certainty, the role of specific cognitive content aside from problematic self-report. Given the current state of the literature, however, there is enough evidence to suggest that catastrophic cognitions do play a role in the cause or exacerbation of panic symptoms.

Cognitive research has also examined memory and attentional biases in panic disorder. Individuals with anxiety disorders, including panic disorder, demonstrate a bias to attend to and remember more threatening and negative information (see Mogg & Bradley 1998 for a review). In the explicit domain, people with panic disorder recalled more anxiety-related than non-anxiety-related words from a previous rating task, whereas normal controls showed the opposite pattern (McNally *et al.* 1989). Although some research has found that panic disorder patients have attentional biases toward threatening stimuli as evidenced by taking longer to read threat words on emotional Stroop tasks than normal controls (Ehlers *et al.* 1988; Lundh *et al.* 1999), other, more recent work has not found these differences (Kampman *et al.* 2002). Some evidence suggests that attentional biases in panic disorder appear to be specific to physical threat words compared with social threat words (Hope *et al.* 1990). However, other research has found that panic disorder participants have attentional bias for all threat words on an emotional Stroop task, compared to social anxiety sufferers who specifically focused on social concerns (Maidenberg *et al.* 1996). Adding to the confusion, some research suggests that panic disorder subjects do not differ on Stroop tasks from other anxiety disorder patients, including obsessive-compulsive disordered participants (McNally *et al.* 1992; McNally *et al.* 1994). In summary, although the literature suggests that attentional biases do exist in panic disorder, it is not clear if these biases are distinct from those found in other anxiety disorders. Psychophysiological studies comparing the attentional biases of different anxiety disorder patient groups offer one way to expand this conflicting literature beyond simple Stroop task designs.

Much of the cognitive theory of panic focuses on catastrophic cognitions, attentional bias toward threat, and other negative cognitions. However, researchers have suggested that panic disorder outcome is also mediated by positive cognitions, such as changes in self-efficacy and coping (i.e. Beck *et al.* 1985; Bandura 1988; Casey *et al.* 2004). Beck and Clark's (1997) information-processing model of anxiety suggests that there are three stages in processing new information. It is in the third stage, when individuals engage in a metacognitive assessment of their coping resources, that positive cognitions can be used to avoid escalation into a panic attack (Beck & Clark 1997). Specifically, if certain safety cues are present, or if individuals believe in their ability to cope with the threat, they can avoid a panic attack. Beck and Clark (1997) then suggest that treatments for this anxiety should, in part, focus on increasing metacognitive beliefs in coping skills. Casey *et al.* (2005) reported on a cognitive behavioral therapy treatment outcome study that supports a mediational role for changes in both negative *and* positive cognitions. In comparison to their waitlist control counterparts, panic disorder participants in the treatment condition had significantly greater reductions in catastrophic cognitions about their somatic sensations as well as larger increases in panic self-efficacy.

In addition to coping skills, *safety cues* may lead to positive cognitions in the face of potential panic symptoms. A safety cue can be an object, location, or person whose presence allows individuals with panic disorder to experience fewer symptoms of fear, anxiety, or avoidance (Carter *et al.* 1995). For example, some agoraphobics fear venturing away from their home (safety cue) without the presence of a close family member (safety cue). There is mixed evidence about the presence of safety cues as a mediator between biological challenge and panic outcome. Some research suggests that safety cues have no effect on outcome and other research supports the fact that the presence or absence of safety cues does, indeed, mediate the occurrence of a panic reaction (Rapee *et al.* 1991; Carter *et al.* 1995).

Although an understanding of their exact roles requires more clarification, research suggests that catastrophic cognitions, attentional biases, self-efficacy beliefs, and safety cues are important negative and positive cognitive factors that influence the likelihood and severity of panic symptoms. Despite our growing understanding of cognitive biases in panic and other disorders, advanced cognitive research must do more than just demonstrate the presence of such biases concurrent with a disorder. Rather, it will be necessary to examine the mechanisms of change in interventions and, for the cognitive perspective to hold, show that changes in cognitive biases mediate treatment outcome (Hollon *et al.* 1987; Kazdin 2001; Kazdin & Nock 2003; for a discussion of this issue in panic disorder, see Casey *et al.* 2004).

Specific Phobia

Specific phobia is a persistent, marked fear of some clearly identifiable object or situation such as animals or heights (American Psychiatric Association 2000). When phobics are exposed to their feared stimulus, they experience anxiety even though they understand the fear to be unreasonable. People with specific phobias attempt to avoid exposure to their feared stimuli, which may cause interference with functioning (American Psychiatric Association 2000). The 12-month prevalence estimate for specific phobia is 8.7 per cent and the lifetime prevalence is 12.5 per cent (Kessler *et al.* 2005a, 2005b).

Cognitive researchers have posited that phobics engage in memory and attention biases when faced with their feared stimulus. Indeed, Wessel and Merckelbach (1998) demonstrated that when presented with a bulletin board with pictures of spiders, babies, and pens, spider phobics had better free recall of threat-relevant information and worse recall of threat-irrelevant information than control subjects. In an attention study, individuals with fears of snakes or spiders were able to find pictures of their feared object faster than normal controls. Their times did not differ from normal controls when searching for pictures that did not depict their feared item (Ohman *et al.* 2001). Finally, in an emotional Stroop task, spider phobics named the ink colors of threatening words slower than neutral ones (Lavy *et al.* 1993). This finding suggests that their heightened attention to the threatening words interfered with their performance on the color-naming task (Lavy *et al.* 1993). Thus, an initial read of the literature would suggest that phobics are "better" at attending to and remembering their feared stimulus than participants not presented with a feared stimulus.

Becker and Rinck (2004) provide another possibility. They suggest that results indicating that phobics are better at attending to threat stimuli may actually be the result of signal detection differences. Their theory asserts that responses to ambiguous stimuli are made of two parts: discriminating the target stimulus from other stimuli; then implementing a *response criterion* (the likelihood of responding "yes" or "no" when presented with a stimulus that is difficult to discern). The authors hypothesized that anxious individuals are more likely to have a liberal response bias than non-anxious controls and thus respond "yes" more often. They would then show a pattern of getting more "hits" and "false alarms" than someone with a conservative response bias, who would show more "correct rejections" and "misses" (Becker & Rinck 2004). Given this pattern of results, the effect may not be that phobics are truly better at attending to threat stimuli but that they are more likely to interpret a stimulus as threatening, even if it is not. Becker and Rinck (2004) used a signal detection paradigm with high spider fear participants and found that they were, in fact, no better at detecting pictures of spiders than non-spider fear controls, but that they were more likely to rate non-spiders (beetles) as spiders. Thus, preliminary evidence suggests that at least some of the effects typically attributed to attentional biases in phobics are actually associated with signal detection biases.

Phobics also appear to have *covariation biases*, biases in which they inflate the likelihood of two events occurring together. Specifically, a series of studies suggests that individuals with specific phobias have a covariation bias toward connecting their feared stimulus with aversive outcomes (Tomarken *et al.* 1989). In these studies, phobics are presented with fear-relevant and fear-irrelevant pictures which are then randomly followed either by a shock, a tone, or nothing. Studies using women with high or low fear of snakes or spiders demonstrated that high fear women rated the association between fear-relevant stimuli and electric shock as higher than those with low fear (Tomarken *et al.* 1989, 1995). Research also finds that treated spider phobics no longer demonstrated the covariation bias and, in another sample, the presence of a covariation bias at end of treatment predicted higher likelihood of relapse (de Jong *et al.* 1992, 1995). However, two studies suggest that covariation biases may develop in all individuals who are presented with blood-injury stimuli or pictures of disgusted faces, not just those who have blood-injury or social phobias (Mineka *et al.* 1996, unpublished; Pury & Mineka 1997). The authors propose that some stimuli, those that generate negative affect in all participants (i.e., blood-injury stimuli), will lead to covariation biases in all participants (not just those with phobic-level fear).

In addition to covariation biases, individuals with specific phobias may also have a perceptual bias to see their feared stimuli as being especially menacing (Riskind *et al.* 1995). In one study, participants with high spider fear were more likely than low-fear participants to expect that a spider in a room would move toward them instead of toward other individuals in the room (Riskind *et al.* 1995). Research on this looming maladaptive style suggests that it may be an important cognitive vulnerability to phobic anxiety (Riskind *et al.* 2000).

Finally, Teachman *et al.* (2001) used an Implicit Association Test to demonstrate that phobics have negative automatic associations to their feared stimuli. Spider and snake phobics were shown pictures and asked to label them in their correct category: spider or snake. In each trial, the two category labels were paired with different positive and negative descriptors (e.g., spider–good and snake–bad; spider–danger and snake–safety). The researchers predicted that spider phobics would be faster to correctly label a spider picture when the word spider was paired with a negative descriptor than when it was paired with a positive descriptor. The reaction time results suggested that the two phobic groups did indeed demonstrate negative implicit associations (e.g., bad, afraid, danger, and disgusting) to their feared stimulus but not to their non-feared stimulus. Teachman and Woody (2003) went on to assess changes in implicit associations of spider phobics from pre- to post-exposure therapy. Although exposure therapy was effective in reducing the "afraid" and "disgusting" implicit associations, there were no changes in the "danger" and "bad" associations (Teachman & Woody 2003). Thus, treatment reduced some, but not all, of the implicit associations.

In summary, phobia research finds clear memory, attention, and perceptual biases in phobic individuals. Exposure to feared stimuli has been a successful treatment in disconfirming at least some of these biases and cognitions. Future work should address the inconsistencies found in the covariation literature and examine whether the amelioration of specific cognitive biases mediates phobia treatment outcome.

Mood Disorders

Mood disorders may involve either high (manic disorder) or low (major depressive disorder) moods, or a combination of the two (bipolar disorders). Mood disorders are diagnosed based on the length, severity, and patterning of depressive and manic episodes. A depressive episode is characterized by symptoms including depressed mood or loss of interest in nearly all activities, accompanied by changes in appetite, sleep, and psychomotor activity, and loss of energy, difficulty concentrating, feelings of worthlessness, and suicidal thoughts (American Psychiatric Association 2000). A manic episode is characterized by high mood, expansive mood, or irritability, in combination with reduced need for sleep and increases in self-esteem, talking, racing thoughts, distractibility, goal-directed activity, and impulsivity (American Psychiatric Association 2000). It is estimated that the 12-month prevalence of major depressive disorder in English-speaking Americans is 6.7 per cent and the lifetime prevalence is 16.6 per cent (Kessler *et al.* 2005a, 2005b). Although less common than unipolar depression, bipolar disorders do affect a significant portion of the population. The twelve-month prevalence in English-speaking Americans is 2.6 per cent and lifetime prevalence is 3.9 per cent (Kessler *et al.* 2005a, 2005b).

Major Depressive Disorder

Beck and colleagues have developed a theory and system of psychotherapy to identify and reduce the cognitive biases in psychiatric disorders including depression (e.g., Beck *et al.* 1979; Burns 1980; for a review of cognitive therapy theory and outcomes, see Beck 2005). Depressed individuals view the self, world, and future more negatively than non-depressed individuals (Beck *et al.* 1979; Engel & DeRubeis 1993). For example, depressed individuals tend to over-generalize negative events, take responsibility for negative events that are not in their control, and disqualify or ignore positive information. Like panickers, depressives are in a vicious cycle in which low moods are maintained by negative beliefs: generalized negative expectations about self, world, and future lead to a proclivity to process information in a negatively biased manner, which then confirms their negative expectations. Although empirical studies have consistently demonstrated that depressive thinking is more negative than cognition in non-depressed people, it is not clear whether depressives actually distort information in a negative direction, or whether their negative thinking is realistic. Many studies have found that although negative in content, depressives' perceptions and inferences about themselves are actually more accurate than those of non-depressed persons, who typically show optimistic biases and distortions in self-perception (for a review of "depressive realism" studies, see Alloy and Abramson 1988). In one task, participants were asked to judge the degree of contingency between pressing a button and turning on a light. Non-depressed participants showed an "illusion of control" bias to overestimate the control they had over the situation (Alloy & Abramson 1979, Experiments 1–4). In line with this theory, EEG data demonstrated that non-depressed controls had a bias for recognizing positive stimuli, but depressed individuals did not have a bias for negative stimuli (Deldin *et al.* 2001). Alternatively, it may be that people who are mildly depressed process information about themselves more accurately than either non-depressives who show optimistic biases or more severely depressed persons who display negative distortions (Ackerman & DeRubeis 1991). Researchers who support this position propose that the conditions of the "depressive realism" studies are not generalizable to the real world (Pacini *et al.* 1998). Pacini *et al.* found that depressed individuals do demonstrate unrealistically negative biases when experimental conditions are more life-like than those used in the depressive realism studies. Despite this disagreement about the extent to which the thoughts are realistic, it is quite clear that the thinking of depressed individuals is more negative than that of their non-depressed counterparts.

Information-processing biases also play a role in depressed affect. Although there is evidence that depression is associated with a general slowing in information-processing (Tsourtos *et al.* 2002), dysphoric participants process negative self-referent information more easily than non-dysphoric participants (Bargh & Tota 1988). Lawson *et al.* (2002) used an eye-blink measure to demonstrate that individuals in the highest third of scores on a self-report depression measure had a more negative interpretation, as measured by larger blink magnitudes, to ambiguous stimuli than those in the lowest third. These negative processing biases may predict increases in depression symptoms even after controlling for current depressive symptoms and lifetime history of depression (Rude *et al.* 2002). Rude *et al.* (2002) presented undergraduates with an ambiguous stimuli task in which they were asked to unscramble ambiguous verbal stimuli (e.g., "winner born I am loser a"). While under a cognitive load (having to remember a six-digit number), individuals who interpreted the sentence in a negative way (e.g., unscrambling the group of words to read "I am a born loser") had more symptoms of depression four to six weeks later than individuals who unscrambled it in a positive way (e.g., "I am a born winner"). Thus, in the laboratory, depressed individuals have a consistent pattern of automatically interpreting stimuli in a negative way. If these studies are generalizable to real-world experiences, one can easily imagine a depressed individual's dysphoric mood fueled by his or her negative interpretation of feedback from a professor, boss, or significant other.

The Stroop task is another method commonly used to assess depressive cognitions in the laboratory. Although several emotional Stroop task studies demonstrate that depressed individuals do have interference from negative words (e.g., Gotlib & McCann 1984), other studies do not support this finding (Hill & Knowles 1991; Mogg *et al.* 1993; Gilboa & Gotlib 1997). Given these inconclusive findings, it is important to assess depressive cognitions in another way. Alloy *et al.* (1997) performed a rigorous test of whether or not negative self-schemata exist independent of mood state. Non-depressed participants were labeled as being at high or low risk for depression based on their cognitive styles. Individuals from both groups were administered a self-schema task battery at the beginning of the study. They then completed measures of dysphoria every six weeks. Alloy and colleagues found that cognitively high-risk participants exhibited more negative self-referent information processing than cognitively low-risk participants at Time 1 (controlling for BDI scores) despite the fact that all participants were *not* clinically depressed at that time. In addition, participants' negative self-referent processing at Time 1 predicted onsets of major and minor depressive episodes during the two-year follow-up period. Further evidence suggests that negative self-referent information may be especially important in depression, specifically. Using a similar self-referent task, Gotlib *et al.* (2004) found that depressed individuals remembered more negative self-referent words than participants with social phobia or normal controls. Thus, research suggests that negative self-referent information processing may be involved with the development of depression, specifically, and occurs independently of current dysphoric mood.

Despite its independence from self-referent information-processing, negative affect *is* associated with social cognition deficits. Depressed and non-depressed individuals who were given a negative mood induction were less accurate in their social judgments, including assessments of teaching ability, relationship type, and understanding of nonverbal cues (Ambady & Gray 2002). Interestingly, this effect was nullified when participants had a distraction (cognitive counting) task to perform while making relationship-type judgments (Ambady & Gray 2002). These social cognition findings provide an interesting contrast to the depressive realism studies described above that suggest that depressed individuals may be more accurate in their negative self-referent judgments, including the degree of control they exert in a situation. However, although depressed individuals may range in the extent to which their judgments and interpretations are biased, they are consistently more negative than those who are not experiencing depressed mood.

Depressed individuals also evidence memory biases. They report fewer explicit positive memories than non-depressed controls (for a review, see Blaney 1986). They attend to and display better explicit recognition memory for pictures of sad faces than happy faces (Ridout *et al.* 2003; Gotlib *et al.* 2004). Depressed individuals have *over-general memories* (those that are characterized as being categorical and generalized, instead of specific; J. M. G. Williams 1996). Other research on memory has demonstrated an implicit bias for negative memories in certain tasks (for a review, see Watkins 2002). Implicit biases are found in conceptual procedures, such as a task in which the participant is asked to pay attention to the meaning of a word (Watkins 2002). However, implicit biases are not found in purely perceptual tasks, those in which a person has to attend to only a stimulus's perceptual feature (e.g., a word-stem completion task; Watkins 2002). Despite the lack of negative bias in implicit perceptual tasks, the overall depression memory literature paints a bleak picture. It appears that, in addition to a host of concurrent biases, depression even makes it less likely that one will remember positive, specific memories from the past.

Our discussion of depression thus far indicates that, in comparison to non-depressed individuals, depressed individuals have more negative thinking, information-processing biases, social cognition impairment, and several types of memory biases. The hopelessness theory of depression attempts to understand the causal role that these biases may have in the development of some depressive episodes. The theory posits that a style to make consistently negative interpretations in interaction with negative life-events plays a causal role in the development of some depressions (Abramson *et al.* 1989). The depressive inferential style involves attributing negative events (e.g., failed test) to global and stable causes (e.g., "I'm stupid") instead of explanations that are specific (e.g., "This particular test was especially hard") and short-lived (e.g., "I'll study harder next time"). The hopelessness theory also suggests that depressed individuals infer that negative consequences will follow from a negative event and that the occurrence of the negative event indicates flaws in oneself. Many studies have supported the hopelessness theory of depression (e.g., Metalsky *et al.* 1987, 1993; Nolen-Hoeksema *et al.* 1992; Alloy *et al.* 1997; Alloy & Clements 1998; Hankin *et al.* 2005). The Cognitive Vulnerability to Depression (CVD) Project was a prospective, high-risk design study that followed a large sample of undergraduates for five years (Alloy *et al.* 2005). Participants were selected for low- and high-risk groups at study onset, according to the extent to which they endorsed *dysfunctional attitudes* (e.g., perfectionism) and *negative inferential style* (i.e., negative inferences about causes, consequences, and self-worth implications of negative life-events; Alloy *et al.* 2005). Analyses from the project suggest that participants' cognitive style, inferences, and attributions remained consistent over time (Steinberg 1998; Raniere 2000). During the first 2½ years' follow-up, high cognitive vulnerability prospectively predicted first onsets and recurrences of major and minor depressive disorders and hopelessness depression (Alloy *et al.* 2006b; for a review of CVD Project findings, see Alloy *et al.* 2005). Looking at the data retrospectively, individuals in the high cognitive risk group had higher lifetime histories of major depression and hopelessness depression than did participants in the low-risk group (Alloy *et al.* 2000).

Other prospective and treatment outcome studies also support the role of negative thinking patterns in the development of depression. A negative cognitive style, including dysfunctional attitudes, mediated by a negative view of the future (but not of the self), predicted increases in depressed mood immediately after rejection from a college (Abela & D'Alessandro 2002). Similarly, in a large longitudinal study of pregnant women, those who had a negative self-schema were more likely to develop depression during the follow-up period (Evans *et al.* 2005). In a treatment study, individuals who received cognitive therapy for a year as part of their post-discharge randomized treatment had a smaller association between their negative cognitions and their depressive symptoms than those in groups who did not receive cognitive therapy (Beevers & Miller 2005). Thus, as their depression symptoms increased, individuals who received cognitive therapy did not display increases in negative cognitions as quickly as those who did not receive therapy. The authors suggest that cognitive therapy was able to disrupt the connection between negative thoughts and depression symptoms. Thus, research supports the cognitive theory of depression in two ways: the presence of depressive cognitions prospectively predicts depression symptoms and treatment targeting these cognitions is effective in reducing the depressogenic effect of negative cognitions.

Although the previous research is supportive of the cognitive theory, any successful cognitive theory of depression must meet an additional explanatory challenge. There is a large increase in the onset of depression during adolescence. A gender difference in depression rates also emerges in adolescence, so that by adulthood, women are twice as likely to be depressed as men (Nolen-Hoeksema & Girgus 1994). Several theories that include biological, social, cognitive, and other factors have attempted to explain the emergence of the gender difference in depression at adolescence (Cyranowski *et al.* 2000; for reviews, see Nolen-Hoeksema & Girgus 1994; Hankin & Abramson 2001). One cognitive theory is Nolen-Hoeksema's (1987) response style theory of depression (RST). Nolen-Hoeksema (1987) introduced the idea of rumination, the repetitive thinking about the causes and consequences of one's negative mood. Nolen-Hoeksema and colleagues have found that, when in a sad or anxious mood, women are more likely to ruminate than men (Nolen-Hoeksema *et al.* 1999; Nolen-Hoeksema & Jackson 2001). Ruminative thinking is associated with an inflexible cognitive style and perseverative thinking, and appears to be a stable characteristic that does not change over time (Nolen-Hoeksema *et al.* 1993, 1994; Davis & Nolen-Hoeksema 2000). Studies across different settings, including laboratory mood inductions in undergraduates and clinical samples, conclude that utilizing a ruminative response style maintains dysphoric mood (Morrow & Nolen-Hoeksema 1990; Nolen-Hoeksema & Morrow 1993; Butler & Nolen-Hoeksema 1994; Kuehner & Weber 1999; Ciesla & Roberts 2002; Vickers & Vogeltanz-Holm 2003). After engaging in a rumination task, dysphoric individuals rate themselves as less likely to engage in pleasant activities that might improve their mood (Lyubomirsky & Nolen-Hoeksema 1993). They also are more impaired in concentration, memory tasks, and problem-solving skills (Lyubomirsky & Nolen-Hoeksema 1995; Hertel 1998; Lyubomirsky *et al.* 2003). In addition to these other negative outcomes, research has demonstrated that rumination predicts prospective onsets of major depression episodes and increases anxious mood (Just & Alloy 1997; Nolen-Hoeksema 2000; Spasojevic & Alloy 2001; Vickers & Vogeltanz-Holm 2003). Given its theoretical and predictive utility, rumination has become an important new variable of interest to cognitive researchers.

Teasdale has also expanded the cognitive theory of depression, noting that it is not the presence of dysfunctional thoughts that lead to depression, but rather one's *reactivity* to these dysfunctional thoughts (Teasdale & Dent 1987). The researchers note that when people believe that their dysfunctional thoughts are valid, a previously mild dysphoric mood can spiral down into depression. They propose that this spiral can be avoided by increasing *metacognitive awareness* (Teasdale *et al.* 2002). That is, they propose interventions that train depressed individuals to see their negative thoughts as simply mental events that may not be valid (Teasdale *et al.* 2002). Research findings support the theory. Increasing participants' ability to see negative thoughts as mental events reduced their likelihood of relapse (Lau *et al.* 2004; Ma & Teasdale 2004). Interestingly, Segal *et al.* (1999) found that recovered patients in euthymic moods did not differ in dysfunctional thoughts depending on whether they had been treated with cognitive therapy or pharmacotherapy (Segal *et al.* 1999). However, when given a negative mood induction, the cognitive therapy groups had lower dysfunctional attitudes than did their pharmacotherapy counterparts. Thus, those with cognitive interventions had less reactivity to the dysfunctional thoughts, theoretically reducing their risk for relapse. Teasdale's work has highlighted the importance of metacognition in depression.

In summary, cognitive research on depression supports the idea that depressives have highly developed negative self-schemata that lead to memory and attentional biases for negative events and stimuli. The tendency to then believe in and ruminate on these negative thoughts and feelings furthers the downward spiral into depression.

Bipolar Depression

Although less common than unipolar depression, bipolar disorder causes severe functional impairment (for a review, see Zarate *et al.* 2000). Traditionally, researchers have focused on the important role that genetic, psychosocial, and biological variables play in the development of bipolar disorder (Healy & Williams 1989; Potash & DePaulo 2000; Jones *et al.* 2005). In more recent years there has been an exciting increase in research on the contribution of cognitive factors.

There are many cognitive deficits associated with bipolar disorder. Researchers find that manic episodes may be especially impairing (Rubinsztein *et al.* 2001). For example, although manic individuals demonstrate similar deficits in planning ability and pattern and spatial recognition memory as individuals who are depressed, neuropsychological tests show that manic episodes are associated with more memory, attention, and problem-solving deficits than bipolar depressive episodes (Murphy *et al.* 1999; Sweeney *et al.* 2000).

Researchers have asked if the cognitive deficits that are present during bipolar episodes remit after successful treatment. Some studies have demonstrated the return of functioning after bipolar symptom remission. For example, executive functioning is restored in remitted bipolar patients without alcohol dependence (van Gorp *et al.* 1998). However, other studies suggest that certain cognitive deficits remain even after mania has subsided. These include information processing and visuospatial recognition, sustained attention, and verbal and declarative memory deficits (i.e. inability to remember a list of words that has been presented several times; Fleming & Green 1995; van Gorp *et al.* 1998; van Gorp *et al.* 1999; Rubinsztein *et al.* 2000; Clark *et al.* 2002). These continued cognitive deficits may be evidence of a "scar" from bipolar disorder (van Gorp *et al.* 1998) and may play a role in future relapses (*Psychological Medicine* 2003). In support of a scar hypothesis, van Gorp *et al.* (1998) found significant correlations between the duration and number of episodes of mania and depression and poor performance on cognitive assessments. However, one important caveat from all of this research should be noted: medication side-effects may contribute to the continued deficits. Although at least one study noted that cognitive deficits were not different between patients treated with lithium and those either on a different medication or no medication, this study was limited by its small sample size (L. Clark *et al.* 2002). In summary, research suggests that although euthymic bipolar participants do regain functioning after episode remission, many cognitive deficits remain. Research is mixed on which functions are restored and is complicated by issues of comorbidity and psychotropic medication use.

Given the wide range of affect displayed in bipolar disorder, studies that incorporate affect and self-esteem in the cognitive tasks are of special interest. Several studies suggest that individuals in a manic phase have different affective responses than euthymic or depressed individuals. For example, in one study, manic, unipolar depressed, and control participants were asked to respond to either "happy" or "sad" words flashed on a screen (Murphy *et al.* 1999). On this affective shifting task, manic participants exhibited quicker reaction times to happy stimuli than sad stimuli. The depressed participants showed the opposite pattern. Murphy and colleagues (1999) also found that in this affective task, manic participants had more difficulty with inhibiting incorrect responses (not responding to distracter words) and focusing their attention, whereas members of the depressed group had more trouble shifting their attention (i.e., longer reaction times after the target was shifted from happy to sad words). Lyon *et al.* (1999) gave several measures of social cognition to participants in a manic phase, in a bipolar depressive phase, and controls. As one might expect, the individuals in a manic phase demonstrated general positive self-schemata on several explicit measures of self-esteem and schemata. However, they showed lower self-esteem on implicit tasks (Stroop, implicit memory for positive and negative descriptor words; Lyon *et al.* 1999). This pattern of results supports the intriguing hypothesis that manic individuals engage in a "manic defense," covering up their implicit negative self-esteem with an outward demonstration of positiveness. Thus, studies in manic individuals suggest that although their affect is positive, their internal self-schemata may be negative. This contradiction may be especially important in determining the course of the disorder.

The complex pattern of cognitive deficits and affective biases in bipolar disorder poses a challenge to cognitive theorists. Alloy and colleagues have addressed this challenge by extending the hopelessness theory of depression to bipolar disorder, hypothesizing that cognitive vulnerability in combination with stress can lead to bipolar episodes (Alloy *et al.* 1999). The researchers found that attributional style and dysfunctional attitudes remained consistent as untreated cyclothymic and dysthymic participants cycled through their moods (Alloy *et al.* 1999). College students with a lifetime history of a unipolar mood disorder, those with a lifetime history of a bipolar mood disorder, and controls with no mood disorder history were assessed at Time 1 and then one month later at Time 2 (Reilly-Harrington *et al.* 1999). In the bipolar group, negative attributional style for negative events (but not positive events), dysfunctional attitudes, and negative self-schemas at Time 1 interacted with life stressors between Time 1 and Time 2 to predict increases in manic symptoms at Time 2 (Reilly-Harrington *et al.* 1999). In another study, positive life-events were not related to manic symptoms in psychiatric patients with bipolar disorders, although goal-attainment life-events did predict manic symptoms over the two months following the event (Johnson *et al.* 2000). These studies suggest that negative cognitive style and negative life-events are importantly involved in bipolar symptomatology. However, data from other studies do not provide such a clear picture. One longitudinal prospective study of individuals with bipolar spectrum disorders suggests that it is *positive* life-events that interact with *positive* cognitive style to predict hypomanic symptoms (Francis-Raniere *et al.* 2005). In another study, Johnson and Fingerhut (2004) found that cognitive vulnerability measures did not predict changes in mania symptoms at all. Thus, the relationship of negative and positive cognitive styles and life-events with bipolar spectrum outcome is in need of further clarification (Alloy *et al.* 2006a). Although there is emerging evidence that cognitive factors (including affective and social cognitions) play a role in bipolar disorder impairment, future studies will need to more fully examine these cognitions at work.

Eating Disorders

Eating disorders are diagnosed when an individual's eating behaviors are severely disturbed and associated with a psychological condition (American Psychiatric Association 2000). Two common eating disorders are anorexia nervosa (AN), in which people restrict their eating patterns so that they are significantly underweight, and bulimia nervosa (BN), diagnosed when episodes of binge eating are followed by compensatory behaviors to prevent weight gain (American Psychiatric Association 2000). Hoek and van Hoeken (2003) reviewed data from epidemiological studies and found an average reported prevalence for AN in young females of 0.3 per cent. They reported a 1 per cent prevalence rate of BN in young women and 0.1 per cent in young men. Eating disorders tend to appear in adolescence and are much more common in females than in males (Pawluck & Gorey 1998). Importantly, individuals may fluctuate between AN and BN in their lifetimes. In one study, 24 per cent of current bulimics met criteria for a past diagnosis of anorexia (Agras *et al.* 2000).

AN is diagnosed when a person's weight is less than 85 per cent of what would be expected, the individual has a fear of gaining weight, either restricts food intake or purges food in some way, and the person's concern about shape influences self-evaluation (American Psychiatric Association 2000). BN is diagnosed when episodes of binge eating are followed by compensatory behaviors to prevent weight gain. Such behaviors include vomiting, exercise, fasting, and misuse of medications (American Psychiatric Association 2000).

Anorexia Nervosa and Bulimia Nervosa

Attention, memory, and interpretation biases have been implicated as cognitive variables that influence the occurrence and course of eating disorders (Williamson *et al.* 2001). The fact that individuals with eating disorders tend to think obsessively about food and their weight and shape has been especially noted in the literature (Gleaves *et al.* 2000). Schotte *et al.* (1990) used a dichotic listening task to show that bulimics selectively attend more than normal controls to words pertaining to bodyweight. Over-evaluation of shape and weight was one predictor of the persistent course of eating pathology in a five-year prospective study of bulimics (Fairburn *et al.* 2003). A meta-analysis of prospective and experimental studies of disordered eating found that cognitive variables, including the internalization of the thin ideal (related to the over-evaluation of weight and shape), were causal risk and maintenance factors for bulimic behavior (Stice 2002).

Waller *et al.* (2000) proposed that there is actually a layer of negative core beliefs underlying these shape, weight, and food-related negative schemata thought to characterize eating disordered individuals (Clark *et al.* 1989; Vitousek & Hollon 1990; Vitousek & Orimoto 1993; Cooper 1997). Waller *et al.* (2000) had women complete a questionnaire about their core beliefs and then complete eating behavior diaries for two weeks. They found that, indeed, certain underlying negative core beliefs predicted bulimic behaviors. Specifically, defectiveness/shame predicted severity of vomiting, whereas emotional inhibition predicted severity of bingeing. In another study, fearful cognitions relating to weight gain, rejection, and intimacy, among other factors, explained 27 per cent of the variance in a female college student sample's self-reported eating pathology (Teachman & Brownell 2000). These findings suggest that it may also be useful to address more general and deeper core beliefs in the treatment of eating disorders instead of just surface cognitions about shape, weight, and food (Waller *et al.* 2000).

Fairburn *et al.* (2003) proposed a "trans-diagnostic" theory of eating disorders that incorporates many factors to explain the maintenance of all eating pathology. The authors suggest that individuals with disordered eating are perfectionists and are cognitively biased to over-evaluate their eating, shape, and weight. This combination results in dieting and weight-control measures, which in bulimics leads to binge eating and compensatory behaviors and in anorexics leads to a "starvation syndrome" (Fairburn *et al.* 2003). Thus, the difference between the two disorders is found in the balance struck between over- and under-eating and individuals may fluctuate between BN and AN in their lifetimes (Fairburn *et al.* 2003). Stressful interpersonal life-events, intolerance to experiencing strong emotions, low self-esteem, and perfectionism are implicated as factors that maintain eating pathology (Fairburn *et al.* 2003).

Although Fairburn *et al.* (2003) suggest that AN and BN have similar underlying cognitive structures, Keel and Klump (2003) present quantitative and qualitative data suggesting that the disorders are unique, with possibly different genetic bases. Furthermore, cognitive biases that are present in eating disorders may be a result and not a cause of the pathology (Polivy & Herman 2002). For example, research on food restriction suggests that restricting anorexics have lower oxytocin levels, which may be a result of their starvation and a cause of some of the cognitive deficits they exhibit (Demitrack *et al.* 1990). Furthermore, non-eating disordered individuals who fasted for 24 hours displayed slower reaction times to a Stroop task using food-related words (Channon & Hayward 1990). Thus, teasing apart the cognitive factors in eating disorders is especially difficult given the physical side-effects of restricted eating. Although research reliably demonstrates cognitive differences in individuals with eating disorders compared to healthy controls, some of these differences may be attributable, at least in part, to unhealthy eating behaviors and other biological and social factors. Given the conflict between the cognitive and genetic data and the biological variables inherent in a disorder that revolves around food, it will be important for prospective studies to further explore the role of genetic, biological, and cognitive factors in the etiology of eating disorders.

Dissociative Disorders

Dissociative disorders are diagnosed when there is a breakdown in the integration of the cognitive functions of consciousness, memory, identity, or perception (American Psychiatric Association 2000). Dissociation is a common experience. For example, when driving, many of us have arrived at a location without being conscious of having experienced the entire trip. However, if a car had suddenly come to a halt in front of us during the drive, our attention would have been quickly reallocated to the task of stopping our car. Dissociation is also a common response of healthy adults during extremely stressful experiences (Morgan *et al.* 2001). Morgan and colleagues (2001) assessed Army survival training course participants before and after the intensely stressful 19-day program. The researchers found that 96 per cent of participants in two studies endorsed having experienced dissociative symptoms as a result of the stressful program (Morgan *et al.* 2001). Although dissociation occurs in healthy adults, it becomes problematic when the dissociation is of critical functions like memory of past events rather than incidental aspects of the environment. This section will focus on dissociative identity disorder (DID), formerly known as multiple personality disorder.

Dissociative Identity Disorder

In DID, an individual's identity is fragmented into more than one distinct part that exerts control over their behavior (American Psychiatric Association 2000). Individuals with DID display amnesia for personal information to a level that surpasses normal forgetfulness (American Psychiatric Association 2000). Each identity state or personality may have a different name, self-image, and personal history and have differing ability to remember the experiences of the other identities (American Psychiatric Association 2000). DID is rare, although the rates have increased in recent years (American Psychiatric Association 2000).

Importantly, cognitive studies of memory in DID are often limited by their small sample size and lack of experimental design. This body of literature is not as advanced as that of depression or anxiety and should be evaluated within this limited context.

There is significant controversy about DID. Some researchers believe that it is overdiagnosed (Lindsay & Read 1994; Piper 1994). The *sociocognitive model of DID* argues that therapists and the media have a role in creating the disorder in individuals by teaching people how to display multiple personalities and encouraging this behavior (Spanos 1994). The sociocognitive model does not, however, claim that individuals with DID are *con-*

sciously creating a disorder that does not exist (Lilienfeld *et al.* 1999). Other researchers support the *post-traumatic theory*, suggesting that DID is a true reaction to childhood trauma (Bremner *et al.* 1996; Gleaves 1996). The *cognitive perspective* on DID suggests that the disorder involves disrupted memory and focuses on assessing implicit and explicit memory between and within identified alter-egos, without necessarily commenting on whether or not an individual has truly separate personalities.

Case and experimental studies are mixed on whether or not explicit and implicit memories transfer across personalities (Kihlstrom 2001). In an experimental study of 12 DID participants, although explicit memory for neutral and emotional words was impaired between identity states, implicit memory generally remained intact (Elzinga *et al.* 2003). In another study, DID participants, controls pretending to have DID, and normal controls were assessed for recall and recognition of neutral stimulus words (the DID and simulated DID groups were asked to remember different lists for each identity; Huntjens *et al.* 2003). Although 21 of 31 DID participants reported having no explicit memory for lists learned by alternate identities, there were no differences in recall and recognition scores between DID participants and controls, suggesting that explicit learning did occur. These mixed findings suggest that more work is necessary before researchers can fully understand the memory dysfunction in DID.

Psychophysiological measures provide another way to approach the DID debate. Although case studies show that different identities have different EEG and fMRI profiles, this apparent support for the post-traumatic theory may be related solely to the different emotions experienced as different alter-egos are presented (Merckelbach *et al.* 2002). In support of this skeptical view, Merckelbach and colleagues (2002) described a study in which undergraduates feigning DID demonstrated different psychophysiological responses for words they were asked to remember and forget, but were able to demonstrate the same memory for words as individuals not asked to feign DID. Merckelbach *et al.* (2002) concluded that researchers should view DID identities as metaphors and not truly distinct personalities. Again, although promising, current psychophysiological data do not provide the key to settling this debate.

Some researchers have looked to other areas of memory research to inform the DID debate. The dispute over recovered memories of childhood abuse is another controversial topic related to the capabilities of memory (for a study in support of recovered memories, see Williams 1994; for a study suggesting the falsehood of these memories, see Clancy *et al.* 2000). In fact, although most people can be deceived into endorsing memories for events that did not occur, there are also some people who no longer endorse remembering independently corroborated past abuse. Although a thorough description of the false memory debate is beyond the scope of this chapter, it is important to note that evidence from both sides of the debate highlight the fact that memory is fallible and displays individual differences (for a review, see Mazzoni & Scoboria, Chapter 30, this volume).

Although there is enough evidence on each side to keep the contentious debate alive, existing implicit memory and psychophysiological data cannot fully support either of the two main theories of DID. What is clear is that individuals who experience these memory and dissociation problems do experience a great deal of subjective distress related to these difficulties. Although it is challenging to reach definitive conclusions about the exact nature of the memory disturbance in DID, this disorder reminds researchers of the importance of examining individual differences in memory capabilities.

APPLYING THE COGNITIVE PERSPECTIVE TO MENTAL HEALTH

One theme that was interwoven in this chapter is the fact that cognitive biases can undermine healthy functioning. However, mental health is not defined simply as the presence of entirely reality-based cognitions. In fact, individuals who have positively biased views of themselves, the world, and their ability to exert control over events seem to be more resilient to anxiety and depression than people who are realistic or have negatively biased perceptions (e.g., Alloy *et al.* 1981; Alloy & Abramson 1988; Taylor & Brown 1988). Three positive biases seem to be particularly important for positive mental health: (1) unrealistically positive self-evaluation; (2) an exaggerated belief in personal control and mastery; and (3) unrealistic optimism (Taylor & Brown 1988, 1994).

The propensity for people to make internal, stable, and global attributions for positive events in their lives and not for negative events is known as the self-serving attributional bias. A meta-analytic review of this literature found that this is a strong and consistent effect in normal populations and is attenuated in individuals with depression, anxiety, and ADHD (Mezulis *et al.* 2004).

It has been proposed that self-enhancement is actually a psychologically unhealthy defense mechanism, repressing underlying negative self-beliefs (e.g., Eysenck 1994). However, Updegraff and Taylor (2000) reviewed the literature and, overall in the presence of stressful life events, self-enhancement is associated with better mental health outcomes. Furthermore, self-enhancers were found to have healthier baseline biological markers (perhaps implying a long-term biological protective role for self-enhancement) and healthier responses to a stress task than low self-enhancers (Taylor *et al.* 2003). Positive illusions may serve as moderators of psychosocial stress by increasing individuals' ability to cope with stressful life events including illnesses such as AIDS and breast cancer (Taylor *et al.* 1992; Taylor & Armor 1996; Taylor & Aspinwall 1996). In fact, HIV-positive individuals with positive illusions about their disease had a longer latency before developing symptoms and longer survival time than those who did not (Taylor *et al.* 2000).

Non-depressed individuals display an inflated sense of control over positive outcomes. Alloy and Clements (1992) gave undergraduates a computerized judgment of covariation test and then a laboratory stressor in the form of an unsolvable block design. Participants who had illusions of control at Time 1 were less likely to display negative mood reactions immediately after the unsolvable block design puzzle and less likely to become discouraged or depressed after the occurrence of negative life events at a one-month follow-up. The authors concluded that illusions of control helped people to cope with adversity in part by reducing discouragement in the face of negative life events.

Positive psychology is a subfield that endeavors to promote mental health, an area of psychology that most researchers ignore (Seligman *et al.* 2005). Seligman and colleagues research "positive emotion, positive character, and positive institutions" in the aim of "making people lastingly happier" (p. 410). Seligman and colleagues have used cognitive research on positive cognitions to create interventions that focus on creating an optimistic explanatory style and preventing depression (for a review, see Gillham *et al.* 2001). Simple Internet-based interventions, such as having individuals record the cause of three things that went well each day, demonstrated lasting reductions in depressive symptoms at a six-month follow-up (Seligman *et al.* 2005). Despite these encouraging findings, it is important to note that individuals with severe disorders require in-person and multi-modal treatments.

Although cognitive research tends to focus more on mental illness outcomes than on mental health, important work is being done to understand the role of cognitions in feeling good and positive adjustment. It appears that some level of positive cognitive distortion is present in healthy individuals and may lead to improved functioning, health, and happiness.

CONCLUSION

It is important to note that although this chapter has focused on cognitive contributions to mental illness, most psychologists agree that a host of other factors, including biology, genetics, and the environment also play a role in mental health outcomes (Kendall & Dobson 1993). Although teasing apart the specific role of cognition is difficult, some important conclusions can be drawn from the literature. First, cognitive biases occur in both mental illness and mental health. For example, individuals with anxiety disorders perceive and process threat-related information, whereas those with depression perceive and process negative information. Eating disorders are characterized by an over-evaluation of shape and weight. DID is related to cognitive disruption in memory. Even mental health is associated with *positive* biases about the self. Second, successful cognitive treatments may work to change some of an individual's underlying negative cognitive structures. If this is indeed the case, cognitive flexibility is of utmost importance to successful treatments for many of the mental illnesses discussed in this chapter.

The findings suggest several exciting new directions for both basic and applied research. First, for cognitive theories to hold, we must move beyond an understanding of cognitive biases by studying metacognition (for anxiety, see Beck & Clark 1997; for depression, see Teasdale *et al.* 2002; for Generalized Anxiety Disorder, see Wells 1995), cognitive process and mediation (Clark 2001; Kazdin 2001), and how cognitive factors interact with important emotion, neurobiology, and sociocultural variables (Dalgleish 2004). Second, we must apply what we have learned from cognitive research to prevention efforts and mental health outreach. Already, cognitive therapies have demonstrated relapse prevention capabilities superior to those of pharmacological treatments alone (Hollon *et al.* 2005). Given this success, researchers must also assess the common factors across different forms of psychotherapy, such as the quality of the therapeutic relationship, in order to improve our understanding of the process of therapy (Casey *et al.* 2005).

In summary, the cognitive study of mental illness is at a crossroads. Traditional theory, basic research, and applied treatments have substantially expanded our ability to understand and treat mental illness. In all three of these arenas, future research should aim to increase our understanding of the role of cognition in the *process* of creating mental illness and mental health.

REFERENCES

Abela, J. R. Z. & D'Alessandro, D. U. (2002). Beck's cognitive theory of depression: a test of the diathesis-stress and causal mediation components. *British Journal of Clinical Psychology*, *41*, 111–128.

Abramson, L. Y., Metalsky, G. I. & Alloy, L. B. (1989). Hopelessness depression: a theory-based subtype of depression. *Psychological Review, 96*, 358–372.

Ackerman, R. & DeRubeis, R. J. (1991). Is depressive realism real? *Clinical Psychology Review, 11*, 565–584.

Agras, W. S., Walsh, B. T., Fairburn, C. G. *et al.* (2000). A multicenter comparison of cognitive-behavioral therapy and interpersonal psychotherapy for bulimia nervosa. *Archives of General Psychiatry, 57*, 459–466.

Alba, J. W. & Hasher, L. (1983). Is memory schematic? *Psychological Bulletin, 93*, 203–231.

Alloy, L. B. & Abramson, L. Y. (1979). Judgment of contingency in depressed and nondepressed students: sadder but wiser? *Journal of Experimental Psychology: General, 108*, 441–485.

Alloy, L. B. & Abramson, L. Y. (1988). Depressive realism: four theoretical perspectives. In L. B. Alloy (ed.), *Cognitive Processes in Depression* (pp. 223–265). New York: Guilford Press.

Alloy, L. B., Abramson, L. Y., Murray, L. A. *et al.* (1997). Self-referent information processing in individuals at high and low cognitive risk for depression. *Cognition and Emotion, 11*, 539–568.

Alloy, L. B., Abramson, L. Y., Safford, S. M. & Gibb, B. E. (2005). The Cognitive Vulnerability to Depression (CVD) project: current findings and future directions. In L. B. Alloy & J. H. Riskind (eds.), *Cognitive Vulnerability to Emotional Disorders* (pp. 33–61). Hillsdale, NJ: Lawrence Erlbaum Associates.

Alloy, L. B., Abramson, L. Y. & Viscusi, D. (1981). Induced mood and the illusion of control. *Journal of Personality and Social Psychology, 41*, 1129–1140.

Alloy, L. B., Abramson, L. Y., Walshaw, P. D. & Neeren, A. M. (2006a). Cognitive vulnerability to unipolar and bipolar mood disorders. *Journal of Social and Clinical Psychology, 25*, 727–755.

Alloy, L. B., Abramson, L. Y., Whitehouse, W. G. *et al.* (2006b). Prospective incidence of first onsets and recurrences of depression in individuals at high and low cognitive risk for depression. *Journal of Abnormal Psychology, 115*, 145–156.

Alloy, L. B. & Clements, C. M. (1992). Illusion of control: invulnerability to negative affect and depressive symptoms after laboratory and natural stressors. *Journal of Abnormal Psychology, 101*, 234–245.

Alloy, L. B. & Clements, C. M. (1998). Hopelessness theory of depression: tests of the symptom component. *Cognitive Therapy and Research, 22*, 303–335.

Alloy, L. B., Just, N. & Panzarella, C. (1997). Attributional style, daily life events, and hopelessness depression: subtype validation by prospective variability and specificity of symptoms. *Cognitive Therapy & Research, 21*, 321–344.

Alloy, L. B., Reilly-Harrington, N. A., Fresco, D. M. *et al.* (1999). Cognitive styles and life events in subsyndromal unipolar and bipolar mood disorders: stability and prospective prediction of depressive and hypomanic mood swings. *Journal of Cognitive Psychotherapy: An International Quarterly, 13*, 21–40.

Alloy, L. B., Whitehouse, W. G., Lapkin, J. B. *et al.* (2000). The Temple-Wisconsin Cognitive Vulnerability to Depression Project: lifetime history of axis I psychopathology in individuals at high and low cognitive risk for depression. *Journal of Abnormal Psychology, 109*, 403–418.

Ambady, N. & Gray, H. M. (2002). On being sad and mistaken: mood effects on the accuracy of thin-slice judgments. *Journal of Personality and Social Psychology, 83*, 947–961.

American Psychiatric Association (2000). *Diagnostic and Statistical Manual of Mental Disorders* (4th edn revd.). Washington DC: American Psychiatric Association.

Bandura, A. (1988). Self-efficacy conception of anxiety. *Anxiety Research, 1*, 77–98.

Bargh, J. A. & Tota, M. E. (1988). Context-dependent automatic processing in depression: accessibility of negative constructs with regard to self but not others. *Journal of Personality and Social Psychology, 54*, 925–939.

Beck, A. T. (2005). The current state of cognitive therapy: a 40-year retrospective. *Archives of General Psychiatry, 62*, 953–959.

Beck, A. T. & Clark, D. A. (1997). An information processing model of anxiety: automatic and strategic processes. *Behaviour Research and Therapy, 35*, 49–58.

Beck, A. T., Emery, G. & Greenberg, R. L. (1985). *Anxiety Disorders and Phobias: A Cognitive Perspective*. New York: Basic Books.

Beck, A. T., Rush, A. J., Shaw, B. F. & Emery, G. (1979). *Cognitive Therapy of Depression*. New York: Guilford Press.

Becker, E. S. & Rinck, M. (2004). Sensitivity and response bias in fear of spiders. *Cognition and Emotion, 18*, 961–976.

Beevers, C. G. & Miller, I. W. (2005) Unlinking negative cognition and symptoms of depression: evidence of a specific treatment effect for cognitive therapy. *Journal of Consulting and Clinical Psychology, 73*, 68–77.

Blaney, P. H. (1986). Affect and memory: a review. *Psychological Bulletin, 99*, 229–246.

Bouton, M. E., Mineka, S. & Barlow, D. H. (2001). A modern learning theory perspective on the etiology of panic disorder. *Psychological Review, 108*, 4–32.

Bower, G. H. (1981). Mood and memory. *American Psychologist, 36*, 129–148.

Bremner, J. D., Krystal, J. H., Charney, D. S. & Southwick, S. M. (1996). Neural mechanisms in dissociative amnesia for childhood abuse: relevance to the current controversy surrounding the "False Memory Syndrome." *American Journal of Psychiatry, 153*, 71–82.

Burgess, I. S., Jones, L. M., Robertson, S. A. *et al.* (1981). The degree of control exerted by phobic and non-phobic verbal stimuli over the recognition behaviour of phobic and non-phobic subjects. *Behaviour Research and Therapy, 19*, 233–243.

Burns, D. D. (1980). *Feeling Good: The New Mood Therapy*. New York: Morrow.

Butler, L. D. & Nolen-Hoeksema, S. (1994). Gender differences in responses to depressed mood in a college sample. *Sex Roles, 30*, 331–346.

Carter, M. M., Hollon, S. D., Carson, R. & Shelton, R. G. (1995). Effects of a safe person on induced distress following a biological challenge in panic disorder with agoraphobia. *Journal of Abnormal Psychology, 104*, 156–163.

Casey, L. M., Newcombe, P. A. & Oei, T. P. S. (2005). Cognitive mediation of panic severity: the role of catastrophic misinterpretation of bodily sensations and panic self-efficacy. *Cognitive Therapy and Research, 29*, 187–200.

Casey, L. M., Oei, T. P. S. & Newcombe, P. A. (2004). An integrated cognitive model of panic disorder: the role of positive and negative cognitions. *Clinical Psychology Review, 24*, 529–555.

Casey, L. M., Oei, T. P. S. & Newcombe, P. A. (2005). Looking beyond the negatives: a time period analysis of positive cognitions, negative cognitions, and working alliance in cognitive-behavior therapy for panic disorder. *Psychotherapy Research, 15*, 55–68.

Channon, S. & Hayward, A. (1990). The effect of short-term fasting on processing of food cues in normal subjects. *International Journal of Eating Disorders, 9*, 447–452.

Ciesla, J. A. & Roberts, J. E. (2002). Self-directed thought and response to treatment for depression: a preliminary investigation. *Journal of Cognitive Psychotherapy: An International Quarterly, 16*, 435–453.

Clancy, S. A., Schacter, D. L., McNally, R. J. & Pitman, R. K. (2000). False recognition in women reporting recovered memories of sexual abuse. *Psychological Science, 11*, 26–31.

Clark, D. A. (2001). The persistent problem of negative cognition in anxiety and depression: new perspectives and old controversies. *Behavior Therapy, 32*, 3–12.

Clark, D. A., Feldman, J. & Channon, S. (1989). Dysfunctional thinking in anorexia and bulimia nervosa. *Cognitive Therapy and Research, 13*, 377–387.

Clark, D. M. (1986). A cognitive approach to panic. *Behaviour Research and Therapy, 24*, 461–470.

Clark, D. M., Salkovskis, P. M., Gelder, M., *et al.* (1989). Tests of a cognitive theory of panic. In I. Hand & H. V. Wittchen (eds.), *Panic and Phobias 2* (pp. 149–158). Berlin: Springer-Verlag.

Clark, D. M., Salkovskis, P. M., Ost, L. G. *et al.* (1997). Misinterpretation of body sensations in panic disorder. *Journal of Consulting & Clinical Psychology, 65*, 203–213.

Clark, L., Iversen, S. D. & Goodwin, G. M. (2002). Sustained attention deficit in bipolar disorder. *The British Journal of Psychiatry, 180*, 313–319.

Cooper, M. (1997). Cognitive theory in anorexia nervosa and bulimia nervosa: a review. *Behavioural & Cognitive Psychotherapy, 25*, 113–145.

Craske, M. G., Lang, A. J., Rowe, M. *et al.* (2002). Presleep attributions about arousal during sleep: nocturnal panic. *Journal of Abnormal Psychology, 111*, 53–62.

Cyranowski, J. M., Frank, E., Young, E. & Shear, M. K. (2000). Adolescent onset of the gender difference in lifetime rates of major depression: a theoretical model. *Archives of General Psychiatry, 57*, 21–27.

Dalgleish, T. (2004). Cognitive approaches to posttraumatic stress disorder: the evolution of multirepresentational theorizing. *Psychological Bulletin, 130*, 228–260.

Davis, R. N. & Nolen-Hoeksema, S. (2000). Cognitive inflexibility among ruminators and nonruminators. *Cognitive Therapy and Research, 24*, 699–711.

Deldin, P. J., Keller, J., Gergen, J. A. & Miller, G. A. (2001). Cognitive bias and emotion in neuropsychological models of depression. *Cognition and Emotion, 15*, 787–802.

Demitrack, M. A., Lesem, M. D., Listwak, S. J. *et al.* (1990). CSF oxytocin in anorexia nervosa and bulimia nervosa: clinical and pathophysiologic considerations. *American Journal of Psychiatry, 147*, 882–886.

Ehlers, A., Margraf, J., Davies, S. & Roth, W. T. (1988). Selective processing of threat cues in subjects with panic attacks. *Cognition and Emotion, 2*, 201–219.

Elzinga, B. M., Phaf, R. H., Ardon, A. M. & van Dyck, R. (2003). Directed forgetting between, but not within, dissociative personality states. *Journal of Abnormal Psychology, 112*, 237–243.

Engel, R. A. & DeRubeis, R. J. (1993). The role of cognition in depression. In K. S. Dobson and P. C. Kendall (eds.), *Psychopathology and Cognition* (pp. 83–119). San Diego, CA: Academic Press.

Evans, J., Heron, J., Lewis, G. *et al.* (2005). Negative self-schemas and the onset of depression in women: longitudinal study. *British Journal of Psychiatry, 186*, 302–307.

Eysenck, H. J. (1994). Neuroticism and the illusion of mental health. *American Psychologist, 49*, 971–972.

Fairburn, C. G., Cooper, Z. & Shafran, R. (2003). Cognitive behaviour therapy for eating disorders: a "transdiagnostic" theory and treatment. *Behaviour Research and Therapy, 41*, 509–528.

Fairburn, C. G., Stice, E., Cooper, Z. *et al.* (2003). Understanding persistence in bulimia nervosa: a 5-year naturalistic study. *Journal of Consulting & Clinical Psychology, 71*, 103–109.

Fleming, K. & Green, M. F. (1995). Backward masking performance during and after manic episodes. *Journal of Abnormal Psychology, 104*, 63–68.

Francis-Raniere, E. L., Alloy, L. B. & Abramson, L. Y. (2006). Depressive personality styles and bipolar spectrum disorders: prospective tests of the event congruency hypothesis. *Bipolar Disorders, 8*, 382–399.

Gilboa, E. & Gotlib, I. H. (1997). Cognitive biases and affect persistence in previously dysphoric and never-dysphoric individuals. *Cognition & Emotion, 11*, 517–538.

Gillham, J. E., Reivich, K. J. & Shatte, A. J. (2001). Building optimism and preventing depressive symptoms in children. In E. C. Chang (ed.), *Optimism & Pessimism: Implications for Theory, Research, and Practice* (pp. 301–320). Washington, DC: American Psychological Association.

Gleaves, D. H. (1996). The sociocognitive model of dissociative identity disorder: a reexamination of the evidence. *Psychological Bulletin, 120*, 42–59.

Gleaves, D. H., Lowe, M. R., Snow, A. C. *et al.* (2000). Continuity and discontinuity models of bulimia nervosa: a taxometric investigation. *Journal of Abnormal Psychology, 109*, 56–68.

van Gorp, W. G., Altshuler, L., Theberge, D. C. & Mintz, J. (1999). Declarative and procedural memory in bipolar disorder. *Biological Psychiatry, 46*, 525–531.

van Gorp, W. G., Altshuler, L., Theberge, D. C. *et al.* (1998). Cognitive impairment in euthymic bipolar patients with and without prior alcohol dependence: a preliminary study. *Archives of General Psychiatry, 55*, 41–46.

Gotlib, I. H., Kasch, K. L, Traill, S. *et al.* (2004). Coherence and specificity of information-processing biases in depression and social phobia. *Journal of Abnormal Psychology, 113*, 386–398.

Gotlib, I. H. & McCann, C. D. (1984). Construct accessibility and depression: an examination of cognitive and affective factors. *Journal of Personality and Social Psychology, 47*, 427–439.

Hankin, B. L. & Abramson, L. Y. (2001). Development of gender differences in depression: an elaborated cognitive vulnerability-transactional stress theory. *Psychological Bulletin, 127*, 773–796.

Hankin, B. L., Fraley, R. C. & Abela, J. R. Z. (2005). Daily depression and cognitions about stress: evidence for a traitlike depressogenic cognitive style and the prediction of depressive symptoms in a prospective daily diary study. *Journal of Personality and Social Psychology, 88*, 673–685.

Healy, D. & Williams, J. M. G. (1989). Moods, misattributions, and mania: an interaction of biological and psychological factors in the pathogenesis of mania: *Psychiatric Developments, 1*, 49–70.

Hertel, P. T. (1998). Relation between rumination and impaired memory in dysphoric moods. *Journal of Abnormal Psychology, 107*, 166–172.

Hill, A. B. & Knowles, T. H. (1991). Depression and the "emotional" Stroop effect. *Personality and Individual Differences, 12*, 481–485.

Hoek, H. W. & van Hoeken, D. (2003). Review of the prevalence and incidence of eating disorders. *International Journal of Eating Disorders, 34*, 383–396.

Hollon, S. D., DeRubeis, R. J. & Evans, M. D. (1987). Causal mediation of change in treatment for depression: discriminating between nonspecificity and noncausality. *Psychological Bulletin, 102*, 139–149.

Hollon, S. D., DeRubeis, R. J., Shelton, R. C. *et al.* (2005). Prevention of relapse following cognitive therapy vs. medications in moderate to severe depression. *Archives of General Psychiatry, 62*, 417–422.

Hope, D. A., Rapee, R. M., Heimberg, R. G. & Dombeck, M. J. (1990). Representations of the self in social phobia: vulnerability to social threat. *Cognitive Therapy and Research, 14*, 177–189.

Huntjens, R. J. C., Postma, A., Peters, M. L. *et al.* (2003). Interidentity amnesia for neutral, episodic information in dissociative identity disorder. *Journal of Abnormal Psychology, 112*, 290–297.

Johnson, S. L. & Fingerhut, R. (2004). Negative cognitions predict the course of bipolar depression, not mania. *Journal of Cognitive Psychotherapy, 18*, 149–162.

Johnson, S. L., Sandrow, D., Meyer, B. *et al.* (2000). Increases in manic symptoms after life events involving goal attainment. *Journal of Abnormal Psychology, 109*, 721–727.

Jones, S. H., Hare, D. J. & Evershed, K. (2005). Actigraphic assessment of circadian activity and sleep patterns in bipolar disorder. *Bipolar Disorders, 7*, 176–186.

de Jong, P. J., van den Hout, M. A. & Merckelbach, H. (1995). Covariation bias and the return of fear. *Behaviour Research and Therapy, 33*, 211–213.

de Jong, P. J., Merckelbach, H., Arntz, A. & Nijmam, H. (1992). Covariation detection in treated and untreated spider phobics. *Journal of Abnormal Psychology, 101*, 724–727.

Just, N. & Alloy, L. B. (1997). The response styles theory of depression: tests and an extension of the theory. *Journal of Abnormal Psychology, 106*, 221–229.

Kampman, M., Keijsers, G. P. J., Verbraak, M. J. P. M. *et al.* (2002). The emotional Stroop: a comparison of panic disorder patients, obsessive-compulsive patients, and normal controls, in two experiments. *Journal of Anxiety Disorders, 16*, 425–441.

Kazdin, A. E. (2001). Progression of therapy research and clinical application of treatments require better understanding of the change process. *Clinical Psychology: Science and Practice, 8*, 143–151.

Kazdin, A. E. & Nock, M. K. (2003). Delineating mechanisms of change in child and adolescent therapy: methodological issues and research recommendations. *Journal of Child Psychology and Psychiatry, 44*, 1116–1129.

Keel, P. K. & Klump, K. L. (2003). Are eating disorders culture-bound syndromes? Implications for conceptualizing their etiology. *Psychological Bulletin, 129*, 747–769.

Kendall, P. C. & Dobson, K. S. (1993). On the nature of cognition and its role in psychopathology. In K. S. Dobson and P. C. Kendall (eds.), *Psychopathology and Cognition* (pp. 3–17). San Diego, CA: Academic Press.

Kessler, R. C., Berglund, P., Demler, O. *et al.* (2005a). Lifetime prevalence and age-of-onset distributions of *DSM-IV* disorders in the National Comorbidity Survey Replication. *Archives of General Psychiatry, 62*, 593–602.

Kessler, R. C., Chiu, W. T., Demler, O. & Walters, E. E. (2005b). Prevalence, severity, and comorbidity of 12-month *DSM-IV* Disorders in the National Comorbidity Survey Replication. *Archives of General Psychiatry, 62*, 617–627.

Khawaja, N. G. & Oei, T. P. S. (1998). Catastrophic cognitions in panic disorder with and without agoraphobia. *Clinical Psychology Review, 18*, 341–365.

Kihlstrom, J. F. (2001). Dissociative disorders. In P. P. Sutker & H. E. Adams (eds.), *Comprehensive Handbook of Psychopathology* (3rd edn, pp. 259–276). New York: Kluwer Academic/Plenum.
Kuehner, C. & Weber, I. (1999). Responses to depression in unipolar depressed patients: an investigation of Nolen-Hoeksema's response styles theory. *Psychological Medicine*, *29*, 1323–1333.
Lau, M. A., Segal, Z. V. & Williams, J. M. G. (2004). Teasdale's differential activation hypothesis: implications for mechanisms of depressive relapse and suicidal behavior. *Behaviour Research and Therapy*, *42*, 1001–1017.
Lavy, E. H., van den Hout, M. A. & Arntz, A. (1993). Attentional bias and spider phobia: conceptual and clinical issues. *Behaviour Research and Therapy*, *31*, 17–24.
Lawson, C., MacLeod, C. & Hammond, G. (2002). Interpretation revealed in the blink of an eye: depressive bias in the resolution of ambiguity. *Journal of Abnormal Psychology*, *111*, 321–328.
Lilienfeld, S. O., Lynn, S. J., Kirsch, I. *et al.* (1999). Dissociative identity disorder and the socio-cognitive model: recalling lessons from the past. *Psychological Bulletin*, *125*, 507–523.
Lindsay, D. S. & Read, J. D. (1994). Psychotherapy and memories of childhood sexual abuse: a cognitive perspective. *Applied Cognitive Psychology*, *8*, 281–338.
Lundh, L. G., Wikstrom, J., Westerlund, J. & Ost, L. G. (1999). Preattentive bias for emotional information in panic disorder with agoraphobia. *Journal of Abnormal Psychology*, *108*, 222–232.
Lyon, H. M., Startup, M. & Bentall, R. P. (1999). Social cognition and the manic defense: attributions, selective attention, and self-schema in bipolar affective disorder. *Journal of Abnormal Psychology*, *108*, 273–282.
Lyubomirsky, S., Kasri, F. & Zehm, K. (2003). Dysphoric rumination impairs concentration on academic tasks. *Cognitive Therapy and Research*, *27*, 309–330.
Lyubomirsky, S. & Nolen-Hoeksema, S. (1993). Self-perpetuating properties of dysphoric rumination. *Journal of Personality and Social Psychology*, *65*, 339–349.
Lyubomirsky, S. & Nolen-Hoeksema, S. (1995). Effects of self-focused rumination on negative thinking and interpersonal problem solving. *Journal of Personality and Social Psychology*, *69*, 176–190.
Ma, S. H. & Teasdale, J. D. (2004). Mindfulness-based cognitive therapy for depression: replication and exploration of differential relapse prevention effects. *Journal of Consulting and Clinical Psychology*, *72*, 31–40.
McNally, R. J., Amir, N., Louro, C. E. *et al.* (1994). Cognitive processing of idiographic emotional information in panic disorder. *Behaviour Research and Therapy*, *32*, 119–122.
McNally, R. J., Foa, E. B. & Donnell, C. D. (1989). Memory bias for anxiety information in patients with panic disorder. *Cognition and Emotion*, *3*, 27–44.
McNally, R. J., Riemann, B. C., Louro, C. E. *et al.* (1992). Cognitive processing of emotional information in panic disorder. *Behaviour Research and Therapy*, *30*, 143–149.
Maidenberg, E., Chen, E., Craske, M. *et al.* (1996). Specificity of attentional bias in panic disorders and social phobia. *Journal of Anxiety Disorders*, *10*, 529–541.
Markus, H. (1977). Self-schemata and processing information about the self. *Journal of Personality and Social Psychology*, *35*, 63–78.
Mathews, A., Richards, A. & Eysenck, M. (1989). Interpretation of homophones related to threat in anxiety states. *Journal of Abnormal Psychology*, *98*, 31–34.
Merckelbach, H., Devilly, G. J. & Rassin, E. (2002). Alters in dissociative identity disorder: metaphors of genuine entities. *Clinical Psychology Review*, *22*, 481–497.
Metalsky, G. I., Halberstadt, L. J. & Abramson, L. Y. (1987). Vulnerability to depressive mood reactions: toward a more powerful test of the diathesis-stress and causal mediation components of a reformulated theory of depression. *Journal of Personality and Social Psychology*, *52*, 386–393.
Metalsky, G. I., Joiner, T. E., Hardin, T. S. & Abramson, L. Y. (1993). Depressive reactions to failure in a naturalistic setting: a test of the hopelessness and self-esteem theories of depression. *Journal of Abnormal Psychology*, *102*, 101–109.
Mezulis, A. H., Abramson, L. Y., Hyde, J. S. & Hankin, B. L. (2004). Is there a universal positive bias in attributions?: a meta-analytic review of individual, developmental, and cultural differences in the self-serving attributional bias. *Psychological Bulletin*, *130*, 711–747.

Mogg, K. & Bradley, B. P. (1998). A cognitive-motivational analysis of anxiety. *Behaviour Research and Therapy, 36*, 809–848.
Mogg, K., Bradley, B. P., Williams, R. & Mathews, A. (1993). Subliminal processing of emotional information in anxiety and depression. *Journal of Abnormal Psychology, 102*, 304–311.
Morgan, C. A., Hazlett, G., Wang, S. *et al.* (2001). Symptoms of dissociation in humans experiencing acute, uncontrollable stress: a prospective investigation. *American Journal of Psychiatry, 158*, 1239–1247.
Morrow, J. & Nolen-Hoeksema, S. (1990). Effects of responses to depression on the remediation of depressive affect. *Journal of Personality & Social Psychology, 58*, 519–527.
Murphy, F. C., Sahakian, B. J., Rubinsztein, J. S. *et al.* (1999). Emotional bias and inhibitory control processes in mania and depression. *Psychological Medicine, 29*, 1307–1321.
Nisbett, R. & Ross, L. (1980). *Human Inference: Strategies, and Shortcomings of Social Judgment.* Englewood Cliffs, NJ: Prentice-Hall.
Nolen-Hoeksema, S. (1987). Sex differences in unipolar depression: evidence and theory. *Psychological Bulletin, 101*, 259–282.
Nolen-Hoeksema, S. (2000). The role of rumination in depressive disorders and mixed anxiety/depressive symptoms. *Journal of Abnormal Psychology, 109*, 504–511.
Nolen-Hoeksema, S. & Girgus, J. S. (1994). The emergence of gender differences in depression during adolescence. *Psychological Bulletin, 115*, 424–443.
Nolen-Hoeksema, S., Girgus, J. S. & Seligman, M. E. P. (1992). Predictors and consequences of childhood depressive symptoms: a 5-year longitudinal study. *Journal of Abnormal Psychology, 101*, 405–422.
Nolen-Hoeksema, S. & Jackson, B. (2001). Mediators of the gender differences in rumination. *Psychology of Women Quarterly, 25*, 37–47.
Nolen-Hoeksema, S., Larson, J. & Grayson, C. (1999). Explaining the gender difference in depressive symptoms. *Journal of Personality and Social Psychology, 77*, 1061–1072.
Nolen-Hoeksema, S. & Morrow, J. (1993). Effects of rumination and distraction on naturally occurring depressed mood. *Cognition and Emotion, 7*, 561–570.
Nolen-Hoeksema, S., Morrow, J. & Fredrickson, B. L. (1993). Response styles and the duration of episodes of depressed mood. *Journal of Abnormal Psychology, 102*, 20–28.
Nolen-Hoeksema, S., Parker, L. E. & Larson, J. (1994). Ruminative coping with depressed mood following loss. *Journal of Personality and Social Psychology, 67*, 92–104.
Ohman, A., Flykt, A. & Esteves, F. (2001). Emotion drives attention: detecting the snake in the grass. *Journal of Experimental Psychology: General, 130*, 466–478.
Pacini, R., Muir, F. & Epstein, S. (1998). Depressive realism from the perspective of cognitive-experiential self-theory. *Journal of Personality and Social Psychology, 74*, 1056–1068.
Panzarella, C., Alloy, L. B., Abramson, L. Y. & Klein, K. (1999). Cognitive contributions to mental illness and mental health. In F. T. Durso, R. S. Nickerson, R. W. Schvaneveldt *et al.* (eds.), *Handbook of Applied Cognition*. New York: John Wiley & Sons.
Pawluck, D. E. & Gorey, K. M. (1998). Secular trends in the incidence of anorexia nervosa: integrative review of population-based studies. *International Journal of Eating Disorders, 23*, 347–352.
Piper, A. Jr (1994). Multiple personality disorder. *British Journal of Psychiatry, 164*, 600–612.
Polivy, J. & Herman, C. P. (2002). Causes of eating disorders. *Annual Review of Psychology, 53*, 187–213.
Potash, J. B. & DePaulo, J. R. Jr. (2000). Searching high and low: a review of the genetics of bipolar disorder. *Bipolar Disorders, 2*, 8–26.
Psychological Medicine. (2003). [Editorial]. Cognition in mania and depression. *Psychological Medicine, 33*, 959–967.
Pury, C. L. S. & Mineka, S. (1997). Covariation bias for blood-injury stimuli and aversive outcomes. *Behaviour Research and Therapy, 35*, 35–47.
Rachman, S., Lopatka, C. & Levitt, K. (1988). Experimental analyses of panic – II. Panic patients. *Behaviour Research and Therapy, 26*, 33–40.
Raniere, D. F. (2000). Long-term stability of inferences about major stressful life-events: Comparing retrospective report among individuals at high versus low cognitive risk for depression. Unpublished doctoral dissertation, Temple University, Philadelphia, PA.

Rapee, R. M. (1986). Differential response to hyperventilation in panic disorder and generalized anxiety disorder. *Journal of Abnormal Psychology*, *95*, 24–28.

Rapee, R. M. (1995). Psychological factors influencing the affective response to biological challenge procedures in panic disorder. *Journal of Anxiety Disorders*, *9*, 59–74.

Rapee, R. M., Telfer, L. A. & Barlow, D. H. (1991). The role of safety cues in mediating the response to inhalations of CO_2 in agoraphobics. *Behaviour Research and Therapy*, *29*, 353–355.

Reilly-Harrington, N. A., Alloy, L. B., Fresco, D. M. & Whitehouse, W. G. (1999). Cognitive styles and life events interact to predict bipolar and unipolar symptomatology. *Journal of Abnormal Psychology*, *108*, 567–578.

Ridout, N., Astell, A. J., Reid, I. C. *et al.* (2003). Memory bias for emotional facial expressions in major depression. *Cognition and Emotion, 17*, 101–122.

Riskind, J. H., Moore, R. & Bowley, L. (1995). The looming of spiders: the fearful perceptual distortion of movement and menace. *Behaviour Research and Therapy, 33*, 171–178.

Riskind, J. H., Williams, N. L., Gessner, T. L. *et al.* (2000). The looming maladaptive style: anxiety, danger, and schematic process. *Journal of Personality & Social Psychology, 79*, 837–852.

Roth, W. T., Wilhelm, F. H. & Pettit, D. (2005). Are current theories of panic falsifiable? *Psychological Bulletin, 131*, 171–192.

Rubinsztein, J. S., Fletcher, P. C., Rogers, R. D. *et al.* (2001). Decision-making in mania: a PET study. *Brain, 124*, 2550–2563.

Rubinsztein, J. S., Michael, A., Paykel, E. S. & Sahakian, B. J. (2000). Cognitive impairment in remission in bipolar affective disorder. *Psychological Medicine, 30*, 1025–1036.

Rude, S. S., Wenzlaff, R. M., Gibbs, B. *et al.* (2002). Negative processing biases predict subsequent depressive symptoms. *Cognition and Emotion, 16*, 423–440.

Schotte, D. E., McNally, R. J. & Turner, M. L. (1990). A dichotic listening analysis of body weight concerns in bulimia nervosa. *International Journal of Eating Disorders, 9*, 109–113.

Segal, Z. V. & Ingram, R. E. (1994). Mood priming and construct activation in tests of cognitive vulnerability to unipolar depression. *Clinical Psychology Review, 14*, 663–695.

Segal, Z. V., Gemar, M. & Williams, S. (1999). Differential cognitive response to a mood challenge following successful cognitive therapy or pharmacotherapy for unipolar depression. *Journal of Abnormal Psychology, 108*, 3–10.

Seligman, M. E. P., Steen, T. A., Park, N. & Peterson, C. (2005). Positive psychology progress: empirical validation of interventions. *American Psychologist, 60*, 410–421.

Spanos, N. P. (1994). Multiple identity enactments and multiple personality disorder: a sociocognitive perspective. *Psychological Bulletin, 116*, 143–165.

Spasojevic, J. & Alloy, L. B. (2001). Rumination as a common mechanism relating depressive risk factors to depression. *Emotion, 1*, 25–37.

Steinberg, D. (1998). Predictors of relapse and recurrence in depression: The scar hypothesis and impact of depressive episodes. Unpublished doctoral dissertation, Temple University.

Stice, E. (2002). Risk and maintenance factors for eating pathology: a meta-analytic review. *Psychological Bulletin, 128*, 825–848.

Stoler, L. S. & McNally, R. J. (1991). Cognitive bias in symptomatic and recovered agoraphobics. *Behaviour Research and Therapy, 29*, 539–545.

Stroop, J. R. (1935). Studies on interference in serial verbal reactions. *Journal of Experimental Psychology, 18*, 643–662.

Sweeney, J. A., Kmiec, J. A. & Kupfer, D. J. (2000). Neuropsychologic impairments in bipolar and unipolar mood disorders on the CANTAB neurocognitive battery. *Biological Psychiatry, 48*, 674–685.

Taylor, S. E. & Armor, D. A. (1996). Positive illusions and coping with adversity. *Journal of Personality, 64*, 873–898.

Taylor, S. E. & Aspinwall, L. G. (1996) Mediating and moderating processes in psychosocial stress: appraisal, coping, resistance, and vulnerability. In H. B. Kaplan (ed.), *Psychosocial Stress: Perspectives on Structure, Theory, Life-Course, and Methods* (pp. 71–110). San Diego, CA: Academic Press.

Taylor, S. E. & Brown, J. D. (1988). Illusion and well-being: a social psychological perspective on mental health. *Psychological Bulletin, 103*, 193–210.

Taylor, S. E. & Brown, J. D. (1994). Positive illusions and well-being revisited: separating fact from fiction. *Psychological Bulletin*, *116*, 21–27.

Taylor, S. E., Kemeny, M. E., Aspinwall, L. G. *et al.* (1992). Optimism, coping, psychological distress, and high-risk sexual behavior among men at risk for acquired immunodeficiency syndrome (AIDS). *Journal of Personality and Social Psychology*, *63*, 460–473.

Taylor, S. E., Kemeny, M. E., Reed, G. M. *et al.* (2000). Psychological resources, positive illusions, and health. *American Psychologist*, *55*, 99–109.

Taylor, S. E., Lerner, J. S., Sherman, D. K. *et al.* (2003). Are self-enhancing cognitions associated with healthy or unhealthy biological profiles? *Journal of Personality and Social Psychology*, *85*, 605–615.

Teachman, B. & Brownell, K. D. (2000). Fearful cognitions associated with eating pathology: psychometric properties of a new scale. *Eating Disorders*, *8*, 283–297.

Teachman, B. A., Gregg, A. P. & Woody, S. R. (2001). Implicit associations for fear-relevant stimuli among individuals with snake and spider fears. *Journal of Abnormal Psychology*, *110*, 226–235.

Teachman, B. A. & Woody, S. R. (2003). Automatic processing in spider phobia: implicit fear associations over the course of treatment. *Journal of Abnormal Psychology*, *112*, 100–109.

Teasdale, J. D. & Dent, J. (1987). Cognitive vulnerability to depression: an investigation of two hypotheses. *British Journal of Clinical Psychology*, *26*, 113–126.

Teasdale, J. D., Pope, M., Moore, R. G. *et al.* (2002). Metacognitive awareness and prevention of relapse in depression: empirical evidence. *Journal of Consulting and Clinical Psychology*, *70*, 275–287.

Tomarken, A. J., Mineka, S. & Cook, M. (1989). Fear-relevant selective associations and covariation bias. *Journal of Abnormal Psychology*, *98*, 381–394.

Tomarken, A. J., Sutton, S. K. & Mineka, S. (1995). Fear-relevant illusory correlations: what types of associations promote judgmental bias? *Journal of Abnormal Psychology*, *104*, 312–326.

Treisman, A. & Geffen, G. (1967). Selective attention: perception or response? *The Quarterly Journal of Experimental Psychology*, *19*, 1–17.

Tsourtos, G., Thompson, J. C. & Stough, C. (2002). Evidence of an early information processing speed deficit in unipolar major depression. *Psychological Medicine*, *32*, 259–265.

Updegraff, J. A. & Taylor, S. E. (2000). From vulnerability to growth: positive and negative effects of stressful life events. In J. H. Harvey & E. D. Miller (eds.), *Loss and Trauma: General and Close Relationship Perspectives* (pp. 3–28). New York: Brunner-Routledge.

Vickers, K. S., Vogeltanz-Holm, N. D. (2003). The effects of rumination and distraction tasks on psychophysiological responses and mood in dysphoric and nondysphoric individuals. *Cognitive Therapy and Research*, *27*, 331–348.

Vitousek, K. B. & Hollon, S. D. (1990). The investigation of schematic content and processing in eating disorders. *Cognitive Therapy and Research*, *14*, 191–214.

Vitousek, K. B. & Orimoto, L. (1993). Cognitive-behavioral models of anorexia nervosa, bulimia nervosa, and obesity. In K. S. Dobson & P. C. Kendall (eds.), *Psychopathology and Cognition* (pp. 191–243). San Diego, CA: Academic Press.

Waller, G., Ohanian, V., Meyer, C. & Osman, S. (2000). Cognitive content among bulimic women: the role of core beliefs. *International Journal of Eating Disorders*, *28*, 235–241.

Watkins, P. C. (2002). Implicit memory bias in depression. *Cognition and Emotion*, *16*, 381–402.

Wells, A. (1995). Meta-cognition and worry: a cognitive model of generalized anxiety disorder. *Behavioural and Cognitive Psychotherapy*, *23*, 301–320.

Wessel, I. & Merckelbach, H. (1998). Memory for threat-relevant and threat-irrelevant cues in spider phobics. *Cognition and Emotion*, *12*, 93–104

Westling, B. E. & Ost, L. G. (1995). Cognitive bias in panic disorder patients and changes after cognitive-behavioral treatments. *Behaviour Research and Therapy*, *33*, 585–588.

Williams, J. M. G. (1996). Depression and the specificity of autobiographical memory. In D. C. Rubin (ed.), *Remembering Our Past: Studies in Autobiographical Memory* (pp. 244–267). Cambridge: Cambridge University Press.

Williams, L. M. (1994). Recall of childhood trauma: a prospective study of women's memories of child sexual abuse. *Journal of Consulting & Clinical Psychology*, *62*, 1167–1176.

Williamson, D. A., Zucker, N. L., Martin, C. K. & Smeets, M. A. M. (2001). Etiology and management of eating disorders. In H. E. Adams & P. B. Sutker (eds.), *Comprehensive Handbook of Psychopathology* (3rd edn, pp. 641–670). New York: Kluwer Academic/Plenum.

Zarate, C. A., Tohen, M., Land, M. & Cavanagh, S. (2000). Functional impairment and cognition in bipolar disorder. *Psychiatric Quarterly*, *71*, 309–329.

CHAPTER 25

Media

Richard Jackson Harris, Elizabeth T. Cady, and Christopher P. Barlett
Kansas State University, USA

Here is a little quiz. Do each of the following as best you can:

1. Hum the theme music from the movie *Jaws*.
2. Sing *Thriller* by Michael Jackson.
3. Name the six characters on *Friends*.

Most people can accurately do each of these, because it is virtually impossible to escape the influence of mass media. It is not the scope of this chapter to attempt to define exactly what the mass media are, because the concept of *media* is evolving and means different things to different people. While mass media have traditionally been seen as encompassing print (newspapers and magazines) and electronic/broadcast (radio and television), recent technology has blurred the distinctions between media and entertainment and between mass and personal media. Such activities as using the Internet, watching a movie, or playing video games are often considered a part of media. People spend more time each week watching television than in any other activity, except sleeping and working (Harris 2004). In 2003, 13- and 14-year-olds spent almost 14 hours a week watching television and almost 17 hours on the Internet (Weaver 2003a). Seventy per cent of college students play video games at least "once in a while" (Weaver, 2003b). Moreover, there are around 1500 daily and 8000 weekly newspapers and over 11,000 different magazines published in the US (Wilson & Wilson 1998).

Mass media can benefit society by reporting daily news, playing the Top 40 music hits, or televising public service announcements. However, there are also some negative aspects to media. For example, violent television and video games have been blamed for everything from a casual attitude toward mayhem to the 1999 Columbine High School shootings. Whether positive or negative, the mass media clearly do affect people's lives. Although social psychologists have been studying these effects for decades, only more recently have cognitive psychologists seriously begun to look at mass media, exploring their effects on certain cognitive processes. This chapter discusses the general cognitive processes of attention, comprehension and memory, and decision-making, and discusses how the media influences each. Media are a major source of knowledge, and how

Handbook of Applied Cognition: Second Edition. Edited by Francis T. Durso.

individuals process that information is vitally important to understanding their effects on attitudes and behavior.

ATTENTION

Attention has long been an important area of study in cognitive psychology. Sternberg (2003) defines attention as a means of reducing the total amount of information that exists in the environment to a smaller amount that affords further processing, making attention clearly relevant to the mass media with its abundance of information. Specifically, cognitive psychologists studying media effects are concerned with allocation of attention and multi-tasking of media, both of which greatly affect media consumers and producers.

Allocation of Attention to Media

Since the media often contain large quantities of information, and people have limited processing ability, much media content is necessarily only incompletely processed. Although this issue applies to all media, research has predominantly focused on how people allocate attention to television. Although the average person watches 3–4 hours of television a day, having the television switched on does not necessarily mean that everyone in the room is fully attending to it. When the television is on, adults and children will attend to it 58–75 per cent of the time (Schmitt *et al.* 2003).

However, children do not attend to all television equally. They attend more to television when they fully comprehend the program (Anderson *et al.* 1981). For example, children pay more attention to child-based content than adult-based content (Luecke-Aleksa *et al.* 1995) and attend to children's television programs twice as much when no toys are present in the room competing for their attention as when toys are present (Lorch *et al.* 1979). Cognitive development is enhanced when actively attending to educational television programming (Anderson *et al.* 2000), and children attend better to television programs when there are short scenes, much movement, and purposeful character behavior (Schmitt *et al.* 1999).

Sometimes a media message may require considerable attentional resources, and other times much fewer. This distinction is captured by the Elaboration Likelihood Model (ELM), which posits two methods through which the consumer may be persuaded (Petty *et al.* 2002). The *central* route involves active processing of the content by a thinking person, while the *peripheral* route assumes a more direct effect of the superficial aspects of the media or message (e.g., attractiveness of source) on a relatively passive viewer. Persuasion through the peripheral route requires little attention allocation and occurs when the person has low motivation or inadequate background knowledge needed to process the message. Motivation to attend to a message for central processing would occur when the person believes that the information has relevance or wants to learn more and elaborate on that information. When such elements are missing, superficial aspects of the message, such as a sexy model or the presence of a celebrity spokesperson, may lead to persuasion through the peripheral route (Petty *et al.* 2002). The ELM also relates to comprehension and decision-making, which will be discussed later in the chapter.

Media and Multi-tasking

Seldom do people sit and actively attend to only the medium in front of them. Rather, they often multi-task, dividing their attention between the media source and an unrelated task. Simultaneously attending to two messages or activities that require controlled (conscious) processing is very difficult due to the limited capacity of attentional resources. Researchers have examined performance on certain cognitive tasks, such as reading comprehension or recalling information, in the presence of certain media such as music or television.

Ransdell and Gilroy (2001) found that when background music was playing, undergraduates showed disrupted writing fluency (words generated per minute) while writing essays, suggesting that background music consumes cognitive resources. Likewise, attending to music can hinder other tasks. For instance, attending to song lyrics while driving is distracting and negatively impacts driving performance (Anderson *et al.* 2003). Individuals tend to drive significantly faster when listening to fast tempo music compared to slow tempo or no music (Brodsky 2001). In a simulated driving vigilance task, listening to high-intensity music increased reaction time for stimuli in the periphery in a high-demand condition (Beh & Hirst 1999). These studies suggest that music may have a negative effect on driving under difficult conditions.

Like background music, background television can adversely affect performance on certain cognitive tasks. Armstrong and Chung (2000) found that students reading newspaper articles later scored lower on recall tasks if television had been on in the background. Pool *et al.* (2003) found that Dutch children's homework completion time and total number of correct answers was hindered by a Dutch-language soap opera in the background but not by an English-language music video or no television at all (which may be a function of the differing languages of the media modality). Armstrong and Sopory (1997) found that background television had a negative effect on performance on the Brooks Visual-Spatial Working Memory Task. Although much of this research has shown that people have great difficulty simultaneously performing two tasks requiring conscious attention, this is not always so. Wickens (2002) offered an explanation for this apparent inconsistency by arguing that there is less interference in multi-tasking if the two stimuli do not use the same sensory modalities or coding channels (e.g., auditory vs. visual). This helps explain why many people are better able to perform two very different tasks that require conscious attention, such as solving algebra problems and listening to music.

Sometimes there may be performance decrements even when people believe they can successfully multi-task two tasks simultaneously. For example, many people drive while using a cell phone, not only to talk but also to browse the Internet, watch a movie, answer email, instant message, or play games. Research using driving simulators has shown, however, that drivers talking on either hand-held or hand-free cell phones make more driving errors and have longer reaction times than those not using the phones. In some cases the distraction can impair a driver as much or more than being legally drunk or slow the reaction time of a 20-year-old to that of the average 70-year-old (Matthews *et al.* 2003; Strayer *et al.* 2003; Strayer *et al.* 2005).

Thus, although a considerable degree of multi-tasking with media sources is possible, it comes at a serious cost to performance on some other activity like driving or doing homework.

COMPREHENSION AND MEMORY

Comprehension of both linguistic and pictorial information in media involves many cognitive structures and processes, such as working memory to store and transform information, knowledge schemata to organize construction of memory representations, and cognitive heuristics to guide retrieval. In addition, individuals must possess sufficient background knowledge of the topic in order to fully comprehend the material (Ericsson & Kintsch 1995). Since the process of comprehension thus has direct ramifications for the quality and quantity of material later remembered, comprehension and memory will be considered together in this section.

Long-term Working Memory

Traditionally, working memory was conceived of as the momentary storage of information needed to complete an immediate cognitive task. This type of memory has limits on both the amount and duration of the information and does not have the flexibility to allow individuals to stop a cognitive activity, in contrast to reading, which requires memory to keep track of plot and characters, and then resume the activity without decreased performance or the need to review information already read (Ericsson & Kintsch 1995). To correct for this limitation of the working memory model, Ericsson & Kintsch (1995) introduced the concept of long-term working memory (LTWM), which allows for greater flexibility, although it requires domain-specific knowledge in the area of discourse. In terms of media, long-term working memory allows us to keep track of all the characters and plots in a complicated movie or novel over a longer time frame than what is available in traditional working memory (Butcher & Kintsch 2003). For example, an individual can watch a mystery movie and remember critical information and clues long enough to solve the mystery. Previously read information is stored in long-term memory as the new information is processed, and any connections between the two serve as the retrieval cues underlying LTWM (Ericsson & Kintsch 1995).

Skill involved in LTWM consists of using easily retrieved cues in short-term working memory to rapidly recover information from long-term memory. Since long-term memory has a theoretically unlimited capacity, experts on a topic can readily store huge amounts of information about that topic. When media consumers watch a television show or read a magazine, their LTWM performs two functions. The first involves the immediate activation of background knowledge of the situation, which remains in LTWM in case it is needed for making an inference to understand the new material. This prerequisite knowledge arises from a lifetime of social and sensory experience, as well as knowledge of consistent patterns in certain media genres (Butcher & Kintsch 2003). The second use of LTWM in comprehension involves the maintenance of the situation model constructed throughout the reading process. In other words, the reader or viewer understands the input by making inferences and building a model of the events. As the reader or viewer learns new information, LTWM keeps the model activated so it can be updated (Butcher & Kintsch 2003).

Schemata

Encoding information into long-term memory draws upon schemata, structures of knowledge in the long-term memory of the perceiver. These cognitive structures become the framework for accepting incoming episodic information, which then becomes integrated into a memory representation that reflects both the prior schematic information and the new stimulus input (Bartlett 1932; Brewer & Nakamura 1984).

While schemata provide a framework for encoding new information, integration between the two sources of information has been argued to occur at the situation model or mental model level of representation (Kintsch 1998). A situation model involves the activation and integration of both mental schemata and currently attended information in the environment, leading to the observer's real-time monitoring and understanding of the situation, environments, and other individuals (Zwaan & Radvansky 1998). Such integration at the level of the situation model ultimately leads to schema modification. If the new information is congruent with the activated schema, the information will be integrated into the existing schema. If the information is incongruent, accommodation occurs, which may result in the formation of a new schema.

Although we generally form and modify schemata through direct experience, certain schemata may be formed through vicarious experience, especially through the media (Harris 2004). For example, a teenager growing up in rural Nebraska might have a schema about life in New York City, although she has never visited there. Instead, she might build her knowledge base from information gained from both entertainment and news media. Thus, her schema relies heavily on the view of reality projected by the producers of that media. Similarly, another teenager living in Los Angeles might form a schema of rural life based on what he sees in the media, which would necessarily reflect the views of the media producers, who may have limited life experience with rural life. Media might also inform the contents of schemata about certain groups of individuals, such as ethnic minorities or people from other countries. The influence of the media on this knowledge base increases as the amount of life experience with those groups decreases.

In addition, stored schemata may affect comprehension of media events (Harris 2004). For example, a person watching a basketball game on television follows the events of the game by using schematic information about basketball to understand the actions of the players or referees. The same happens in media entertainment genres, especially if the viewer can identify in some way with the characters or situations in the show, which allows the viewer to retrieve particular schemata to comprehend the plot. For example, a teenager watching a teen drama will comprehend it differently than an adult viewer. In much the same way that schemata guide understanding of real world events, comprehension of the media proceeds using previously known information.

Activity schemata, called scripts, organize information about events and aid in comprehending events or the media. Low & Durkin (2000) found that even young children aged 5–11 years use a script to comprehend television shows. The children were shown one of two abridged versions of a crime drama. One version showed the story in the common form (i.e., scenes in the order of crime, investigation, chase, arrest, and court), while the other rearranged the same scenes. The youngest children recalled the story best when they saw the common form, although older children were able to understand the other version, indicating that while young children use well-defined scripts to understand television, older children display more flexibility (Low & Durkin 2000).

Framing

Framing by the media involves choices made by producers regarding what information to provide the public and how to communicate it. One important use of a frame is to inform the public what issues it should think of as important (Cohen 1963), what communications researchers call "agenda-setting" (McCombs & Reynolds 2002). The frame of a news report thus affects how viewers understand the issue under discussion. The media employ frames to emphasize certain aspects of the world while downplaying others. By doing so, they help ensure that the input is attended to and comprehended in certain ways (Entman 1993). For example, if the media are the only source from which people acquire information about a particular sport, fans will only learn what fits into the frame employed by the media.

On a more local scale, even a minor change in the wording of an advertisement may activate a frame, which then guides cognitive processing. For example, consider meat advertised as "75 per cent lean" vs. "only 25 per cent fat." Consumers evaluate the former more favorably than the semantically identical latter wording (Levin & Gaeth 1988). Similarly, most consumers prefer receiving a "discount" rather than a "surcharge," even if the final cost is the same. A positive frame leads to construction of a more positive image of the product.

Frames perform four specific functions. First, they identify the issues and problems that merit media coverage. Second, frames articulate the reasons and agents that have led to these problems. Third, they judge the causes in terms of certain moral tenets. In this way, the viewers learn who is to blame and how those people should be judged. Finally, frames give specific suggestions for dealing with these issues (Entman 1993). In this way, the frame chosen by the media producers can influence the thoughts, attitudes, and beliefs of the viewer.

Frames can occur in four stages within the mass communication process. First, the media producers utilize their own frames or schemata (Entman 1993) to determine what to communicate to the public. This agenda-setting technique begins by increasing the relevance of a topic until the media consumers focus their attention, thoughts, and actions on it (McCombs & Reynolds 2002). In this way, the media producers begin to shape the opinions of the public. For example, sports media use a frame that values the athletic accomplishments of males more than those of females, so sports reporters focus on men's sports far more than on women's. This contributes to the public valuing men's sports and athletes more than women's.

Second, the media message itself incorporates specific images, words, or sources of information that stem from the specific frames (Entman 1993). Taking the sports media example, the language used to describe male athletes usually focuses on their strength or abilities, while the language describing female athletes highlights their physical appearance (Halbert & Latimer 1994; Eastman & Billings 2000; Billings *et al.* 2002). Third, the prevalent social culture provides certain frames that are common across many people within a society. In other words, although the mass media choose to focus on men's sports at the expense of women's, these media frames in part reflect a culture that tends to value athleticism in males more than in females (Kane 1988). Finally, viewers bring their own frames to the media experience. For example, a woman who has participated in sports might be more likely to focus on the athletic accomplishments portrayed in the media than on the appearance of the athletes.

Framing can also affect coverage of political campaigns, which in turn can affect voters' knowledge and behavior about the candidates. For example, Jamieson and Waldman (2003) identified two predominant negative frames in press discussion of candidates George W. Bush and Al Gore in the US Presidential election in 2000. Bush was seen as dim-witted and highly prone to speech errors ("Dumbo" frame), while Gore was seen as stretching the truth and trying to pander to all constituencies ("Pinocchio" frame). With these frames guiding the media stories about the candidates, Bush's speech errors and ignorance of certain facts ("Who is the leader of Pakistan?") were widely reported, while Gore's stretching of the truth ("I invented the Internet") and inconsistent statements to different groups received more attention. Conversely, speech errors and lack of knowledge were not noted in Gore, while factual misstatements and "pandering" from Bush slipped by largely unnoticed. Interestingly enough, after the 9/11 terrorist attacks, the Dumbo frame to describe Bush essentially disappeared in favor of a "strong leader" frame. Many commented how Bush had changed as a leader as a result of responding to the attacks, but it may have more been the reporters covering the President who changed (Jamieson & Waldman 2003).

Comprehension of News

News offers a useful domain in which to test people's cognition in a real-world setting, which has both applied and theoretical importance (Price & Czilli 1996; McCombs & Reynolds 2002). News stories in all media are typically fairly short, self-contained pieces. Schneider & Laurion (1993) found that people's assessment of what they had remembered from radio news was quite accurate. With television, however, the simultaneous presence of the visual and auditory information provides the potential of these modalities either complementing or interfering with each other. In general, memory for pictorial material is better than memory for verbal material (Graber 1990), and memory overall is better if there is a close fit between the video and the audio components, such as when the video illustrates exactly what the reporter is describing. When the relationship is less clear or when the video and audio portions evoke different previous information from the viewer's memory, comprehension and memory for the new information suffer (Mundorf *et al.* 1990; Grimes 1991). Memory for persons in the news can also be affected by the viewers' social attitudes, such as Whites being more likely to identify an African-American than a Caucasian as a criminal suspect (Oliver & Fonash 2002; Gibbons *et al.* 2005). Assuming the video and audio portions are congruent, children remember news presented on television better than news presented only on radio or in print, even if the latter contains illustrations (Walma van der Molen & van der Voort 2000).

The Availability Heuristic and the Importance of Vivid Exemplars

Often in comprehension of media, compelling exemplars are critically important. A cognitive heuristic called *availability* posits that we draw conclusions about the frequency or typicality of an event or instance based on how readily we can retrieve relevant exemplars from memory (Tversky & Kahneman 1973, 1974). These easily retrieved examples are then seen as highly typical, when in fact that may not be the case. If the first examples of

Arabs that come to mind are villains from film entertainment and terrorists from news, we may come to believe a larger proportion of Arabs are terrorists than is in fact the case. The positive potential of this principle is also considerable; for example, if Will Truman of the popular sitcom *Will and Grace* becomes the prime example of a gay man, the social perception by heterosexuals of gay men might be improved considerably. Entertainment presents numerous vivid and memorable exemplars of diverse people and situations; when the distribution of these exemplars deviates strongly from the real-world distribution, the risk of viewers having a skewed view of the world markedly increases.

The Power of Vivid Exemplars

Sometimes an unusually attractive or respected person or character can greatly influence attitudes or behavior in positive ways. For example, after a sexy "hunk" actor played a deaf character in a popular Brazilian soap opera, interest in learning sign language soared. When NBC news anchor Katie Couric invited *Today* show viewers to watch her colon exam live in 2000, requests for colonoscopies to screen for colon cancer rose 20 per cent, almost surely saving numerous lives (Bjerklie 2003). Bonds-Raacke *et al.* (in press) found that heterosexuals who thought about a positive gay character on TV had more positive attitudes toward gay men than those heterosexuals who thought about a either negative gay character or an unmarried character.

One basic aspect of human cognition is that the rich sensory experience of our world must be organized into meaningful knowledge categories for interpretation and storage in memory. Specific and highly available exemplars or instances of particular categories or classes of events often come to represent the entire category, whether or not they are in fact truly representative. Which exemplars will prevail to mentally define the category depends on the two major factors of frequency and vividness. The more often an instance occurs, the more representative it will seem (Harris *et al.* in press). For example, if a large number of African-American men in movies are criminals or drug dealers, many viewers (especially those with limited life experience with African-American men) will come to see that image as typical of Black men.

A particularly vivid example is highly memorable and thus is very readily called to mind when thinking of that category. For example, after the 1975 blockbuster movie *Jaws* portrayed numerous shark attacks on swimmers at ocean beaches, coastal resorts reported a significant loss in business. The highly vivid fictional attacks from *Jaws*, though extremely rare in real life, were readily remembered and taken to be far more typical beach experiences than was in fact the case. Vivid cases that elicit high levels of arousal (such as a shark attack) are especially memorable, as are vivid cases that are frequently repeated (Harris *et al.* 2006).

Gibson & Zillmann (1994) found that readers of a magazine news story about carjacking evaluated the crime as both more serious and more frequent if the story had contained an extreme example (victim killed in the crime) than if it had been less extreme (victim injured little or not at all).

Comprehension of Risk

Media reporting of vivid exemplars of crimes play a large role in people's assessment of their personal risk. Even though violent crime rates in most places fell precipitously between 1990 and 2005, most of the public believed they had risen, perhaps because there has been a 400 per cent increase in American network news coverage of murders during this period. Most news stories are heavy on coverage of specific events and exemplars and much lighter on deeper inquiry and analysis of causes or historical background.

Language and framing of the exemplars also affect the audience's assessment of their personal risk from threats such as disease or violence. News reports routinely cover rare but dramatic deaths like homicides or national disasters more heavily than they do more frequent but less dramatic deaths such as those from heart disease or stroke. In addition, sensational risk factors for crimes and diseases, such as the use of illicit drugs, are covered more extensively than more prevalent risk factors such as obesity (Glassner 1999). One model of why people fear very unlikely events stems from exemplification theory, which provides a framework for memory of events (Zillmann 2002). As people watch a news report, they attend to and subsequently recall the information it contains according to three principles. First, if the event covered is concrete rather than abstract, it is more likely to be recalled. For example, given two stories on flesh-eating bacteria, one interviewing a victim who developed the disease after contracting strep and a second giving the actual rates of infection (which are very low) but without any specific examples of people who caught strep without developing the bacteria complication, viewers later recall the more vivid and concrete interview and overestimate the occurrence of flesh-eating bacteria (Glassner 1999).

Second, events judged to be important are attended to and recalled better than events judged to be irrelevant, especially if the events contain emotion-laden information. Because highly emotional events would have been more relevant to survival in the evolutionary past, humans have a well-developed limbic system that enables superior encoding of memories during times of strong emotion (Zillmann 2002). Highly emotional news photos, such as a shot of a bloody, disfigured body of an accident or war victim, evoke activation in the amygdala, and these pictures are better recalled (Levine & Pizarro 2004). However, the encoding of the immediately preceding text may be disrupted by the picture (Loftus & Burns 1982; Christianson & Loftus 1987; Newhagen & Reeves 1992). Furthermore, verbal material presented during or after the intense image is remembered shortly afterward as well as or, in the case of material presented immediately after the image, sometimes even better than material without an accompanying intense image. Apparently, the intense emotional image disrupts the rehearsal in working memory for the immediately preceding information, much as a head injury can produce retroactive amnesia for events just preceding the impact. However, the intense picture is itself highly memorable and may enhance memory for subsequent related information by serving as a mental model or organizational schema for the construction of a memory representation.

Third, the occurrence of widely publicized similar events inflates one's estimation of the frequency of that category of events. After several school shootings that took place in the US in the late 1990s, many people began to fear being shot at school and to believe that school violence was epidemic, despite the fact that the probability of violence in schools was declining and remained very low. The same occurred after the terrorist attacks of 9/11. Overall, heavy coverage of violent crime in the media leads to overestimates of the frequency of crime, although actual crime rates in the US declined from 1993 to 2005 (Bureau of Justice 2005).

Such mis-cognitions may have serious consequences. A gruesome story about the abduction and murder of a child evokes strong emotions in viewers, causing them to attend to the story and recall it readily as a highly available and typical exemplar of the class of events "child disappearances." As a result, people overestimate the probability of such events and misunderstand their typical character. The intense emotion induced by the story will then cause the viewer to fear child abduction by a stranger, even though the large majority of child disappearances are runaways and the perpetrator in 76 per cent of actual child abductions is a non-custodial parent or someone else known to the child (OJJDP 2000).

In addition to news, entertainment media contribute to viewers' overestimation of risk. Criminal behavior prevails in entertainment media, especially police dramas and action adventure shows. Although less than 1 per cent of the crimes committed in the US are murders, half of media crimes are murders (Oliver 1994; Bushman & Anderson 2001). In addition, mentally ill characters in the media are portrayed as violent 72 per cent of the time (Signorielli 1989), although the proportion of mentally ill individuals who are violent in reality is only 11 per cent (Teplin 1985).

Portrayals of Ethnic Groups

Vivid exemplars may also be taken as typical representatives of various social groups. Although the number of African-Americans on American television has greatly increased since the 1960s and now approximates the proportion in the general population, they still tend to disproportionately appear in situation comedies or police dramas (Greenberg *et al.* 2002). In contrast, Latinos, although even greater in numbers than African-Americans in the general population, comprise only 2 per cent of prime-time TV characters (Poniewozik 2001), mostly in comedic, criminal, or police roles. Native Americans in media are almost entirely Plains Indians from TV and movie westerns; thus, most Americans' prototypical "Indian" became a Plains Indian, not a Navajo, Kwakiutl, Cherokee, or Iroquois. With the decline of the genre of Westerns, Native Americans have all but disappeared from the media, although the vivid Plains buffalo-hunting image persists.

The small number of characters overall, combined with the stereotypical portrayal of minorities in the media, can thus lead to prejudiced views of these groups, especially in those majority group viewers with limited life experience with members of the group in question (Greenberg *et al.* 2002). Givens and Monahan (2005) used an indirect measure of prejudice consisting of determining if various adjectives accurately described a target individual, who was either an African American woman or a White woman. They found that participants who had previously seen a video clip showing a highly sexualized African American woman (the "Jezebel" image) were faster to respond to adjectives related to Jezebels than were participants in the control condition. This indicates that media portrayals can make prejudiced attitudes more accessible. Children, especially those who have limited real-life experience with people unlike themselves, use television and movies as practice on which to build thoughts, emotions, and opinions, or to learn behaviors to employ when faced with others of a different race. Thus, the potential of television in creating, strengthening, or reducing prejudice is great (Graves 1999).

Content analyses do not tell the whole story of how these portrayals affect the audience's perception. A strong character in an immensely popular TV show might "drench" the viewer with an image of the minority that remains strong despite other portrayals the viewer might see. In this way, certain actors and characters, such as Bill Cosby's Dr Cliff Huxtable from *The Cosby Show*, will exert far more influence on the perceptions of the group being portrayed than the many other less seen exemplars of the same group (Greenberg 1988). However, viewing examples of individuals who do not fit into a stereotype will not necessarily easily change stereotypes held by the viewer. Richards and Hewstone (2001) define subtyping as the process of grouping those who deviate from a stereotype into a new category separate from the stereotyped group. Rather than relaxing the standards for inclusion into the stereotyped group and thus changing the stereotype, subtyping allows for stereotype maintenance. This occurs more with less typical group members than with more typical ones. On the other hand, subgrouping refers to the process of sorting individuals into several groups based on specific similarities, although those individuals are still viewed as being part of the larger, stereotyped group. This allows for variation within the stereotyped group and can serve to lessen the stereotype (Richards & Hewstone 2001).

Exemplars and the Peripheral Route to Persuasion

Recall from the discussion of the Elaboration Likelihood Model (ELM) that the central route to persuasion makes less use of heuristics such as availability in cognitive processing, while the peripheral route relies strongly on them (Petty *et al.* 2002). Many of the negative effects of using heuristics to process information in the media can be overcome by actively processing that information. For example, motivating viewers to process information deeply can lessen cultivation effects, which occur when viewers perceive the external world as similar to the world portrayed in the media (Gerbner *et al.* 2002; Shrum 2002). Although media consumers tend to ignore base-rate information in favor of higher-impact exemplars, if someone believes that information given in base-rate terms will be helpful, he or she will attend to it (Zillmann 2002). Anything that makes base-rate information more salient thus contributes to overall media literacy.

Autobiographical Memory

Autobiographical memory consists of knowledge about events or experiences that have occurred in one's own life, including experiences that involve the media (Conway & Pleydell-Pearce 2000; Conway 2001). Autobiographical memory contains both sensory-perceptual and abstract semantic knowledge. The first leads to a relatively exact memory trace, leading to a mental replay for portions of the event, while the latter concerns a person's unique history, which affects one's interpretation of the event. Due to the presence of these types of knowledge, memories can be accurate in terms of both objective reality and one's self-concept (Anderson & Conway 1997). Rich memories for event-specific knowledge often are encoded with imagery, which helps elicit vivid memories. Although we do not tend to remember as many supporting details from events that did not occur as from those that did, we can also recall vivid but false memories of events that never happened (Garry *et al.* 1996; Garry & Polaschek 2000; Sharman *et al.* 2005). These attributions of reality can be influenced by the motivation, biases, and experiences, as well as metacognitive skills, of the person recalling the event (Mitchell & Johnson 2000), thus reflecting the malleability of memory.

Autobiographical memory can be studied by presenting some type of cue and asking for a memory related to that cue. In media research, these cues often relate to autobiographical memories of events, characters, or programs watched at some point in one's life. This method allows research into the effects on children of antisocial messages in media, such as sex or violence (Harrison & Cantor 1999; Hoekstra *et al.* 1999; Cantor *et al.* 2003). By asking adults about their memories of seeing an R-rated movie as a child, for example, one can indirectly study effects without exposing young participants for research purposes. Although there is an inherent problem of the inability to verify the memories of the experience of watching a media event, the major interest is the remembered experience, with objective accuracy of the memories of less concern than the participant's memory of them (Harris *et al.* 2005). In such a study, the participant might be instructed to think of the overall experience of watching a frightening or sexually themed movie in their childhood. Once the experience has been recalled, the participant rates various aspects of the event on several dimensions. For example, the experience of watching a frightening movie might be rated for negative effects (e.g., insomnia) or positive effects (e.g., enjoyment) experienced. Using the autobiographical memory technique in this way allows probing, albeit indirectly and retrospectively, of the effects of seeing characters or events under more ecologically valid viewing circumstances, rather than in a short segment viewed in more artificial situations.

Music also plays a large role in autobiographical memory, and participants make more accurate time estimates of when a song had been popular when they use associated autobiographical memories as cues (Bartlett & Snelus 1980). Both college students and adults aged 66–71 best remember and most prefer music that was popular during their adolescence, although the older adults did not remember those songs as well as the younger group overall, unless the song evoked a strong emotional memory (Schulkind *et al.* 1999).

DECISION-MAKING

Decision-making involves selecting from among choices or possible outcomes. The media influence decision-making in terms of what products to buy, which candidate to vote for, or whether a defendant is guilty or innocent. This section discusses how media affect judgments and decisions in response to advertising and news.

Influencing Purchase Decisions

The goal of most advertising is to persuade consumers to buy products or use services. Social psychology has long been interested in factors that determine how people are persuaded by messages. In order for an advertisement to significantly impact the viewer, three elements need to be involved: the communicator, the message, and the recipient (Hovland *et al.* 1953). Source (communicator characteristics) and content (message characteristics) are two factors that influence how people make decisions as a function of exposure to media.

Source

The source factor includes credibility and likeability, both components of who is delivering the message. Credibility involves the perceived expertise of the source. If the source of the information is credible (i.e., a prestigious journal vs. a popular magazine), participants will rate the prestigious source as more trustworthy (Hovland & Weiss 1951). Furthermore, participants rate people who appear knowledgeable, smart, or have impressive credentials to be experts (Hass 1981). An example of this includes an advertisement of a person in a lab coat with a stethoscope selling aspirin. This person may not be a doctor (and in some cases may actually admit this in the ad) but still has the appearance of a medical expert. Unless the message is of great importance, viewers will probably accept the message without much scrutiny and fail to use central processing techniques of the sort outlined in the ELM model (Petty *et al.* 2002) to question the apparent expertise of the spokesperson (Maddux & Rogers 1980).

Another source variable is likeability, which relates to how attractive, charming, athletic, or popular the source is (Hovland *et al.* 1953). Michael Jordan made commercials for Hanes underwear and Ballpark Franks years after his retirement, and supermodels are paid to sell underwear, jeans, and beer. Such advertisements can be very effective because of the attractive or knowledgeable source, even if that source has no more expertise than the viewer about the product (Harris 2004). One explanation for the perception of knowledge in the spokesperson may be affect infusion, in which an individual relies in part on affective information to reach a conclusion that requires judging incoming information (Forgas 1995). This model suggests that if Michael Jordan has a positive affective tag associated with him, and the judgment needs to be made efficiently (which is often the case with short commercial advertisements), then the affect-as-information heuristic (Schwartz 1990) is implemented. This leads to the source being perceived as credible, even if the actors have no prior experience with the product.

Content

The content factor involves the information in the ad and how this information is presented as important to consumers and advertisers (Hovland *et al.* 1953). For example, some Butterfingers candy bar ads state what the candy is made of and how good it tastes, while others show characters from *The Simpsons* eating the candy.

Several different types of advertising appeals have been shown to influence memory (Harris 2004). One popular appeal is humor, which has spawned considerable psychological research. Furnham and Mori (2003) found that people scored higher on a cued recall test of ad content if the ad was humorous, while Krishnan and Chakravarti (2003) found that memory for brand names was higher if the ad was humorous. Finally, people have a better memory for ad content if it contained a cartoon than if it did not (Gunter *et al.* 2002).

Another class of appeals is emotional ads, which appeal to one's feelings, such as a commercial with a grandfather hugging his grandchild. Studies have shown that products in emotional ads were better recalled than those in neutral ads (Hornik 1989; Friestad & Thorson 1993). One particularly potent kind of emotional appeal is the fear advertisement, which implies some sort of threat if the consumer does not heed the message. An example is the anti-drug spot with an egg in a frying in a pan and a voiceover message, "This is your brain. . . . This is your brain on drugs. . . . Any questions?" This commercial sends the message that taking drugs will "fry" your brain. Fear appeals can be very effective. Smokers were more likely to quit after viewing ads that involved a fear appeal (Smith & Stutts 2003), especially if the viewer was an adult smoker (Beaudoin 2002). The one caveat about fear appeals is that they may be counterproductive if the fear threat is so strong as to invoke defenses in the viewer (Witte 1994).

Individual Difference Variables

The final factor that significantly contributes to the advertisement's effectiveness is individual differences in the recipient. One such attitudinal variable is self-monitoring, where high self-monitors are individuals who attempt to adapt their personality to the environment and low self-monitors do not adapt to differing situations (Snyder 1974). High self-monitors are more likely to pay for a product that has numerous images advertised, whereas low self-monitors are more likely to pay for a product that has more quality-oriented (functional value of the product) ads (Snyder & DeBono 1985). These researchers suggest that high self-monitors will be more likely to respond to advertisements that are image-oriented because that may be another manifestation of the desire to strive to blend in across differing situations, while low self-monitors may be interested in content-based advertisements because that quality will be consistent across most environments (Snyder & DeBono 1985).

Another individual difference variable that affects decision-making is the need for cognition, which is the desire to understand and make sense of the surrounding world (Cohen *et al.* 1955). Research has shown that when an advertising argument is strong, both high and low need for cognition individuals will rate their attitudes toward and evaluate the message more positively. If a message is weak, however, low need for cognition individuals will rate and evaluate the message more positively than high need for cognition individuals (Cacioppo *et al.* 1986). In other words, if the message contains a strong argument, people will generally rate it as more positive. However, the salience of the message strength is more important to individuals high in need for cognition, and they will rate an advertisement as more positive if it is strong and as more negative if it is weak, compared to low need for cognition individuals (Cacioppo *et al.* 1986).

The Effect of News on Decision-Making

Decision-making is also important in areas of media other than advertising. One of the most important areas involves news coverage.

One issue concerns the effect of media publicity on juror decision-making. Jurors' exposure to specific pretrial publicity about a case does affect verdicts (Carroll *et al.* 1986; Shaw & Skolnick 2004). Lurid pretrial information about a rape or murder case increases the likelihood of a conviction and cannot be erased by a judge's direction to disregard the information. Another concern involves general pretrial publicity and jurors' exposure to information about other cases involving similar issues. Greene and Wade (1987) had students either not read any story or read a news magazine story about (a) the brutal rape of an elderly woman, or (b) the wrongful conviction of a man for a rape to which someone else subsequently confessed. Later, in what was presented as an unrelated experiment, all participants acted as jurors for a different court case. Compared to the control group, twice as many (20 per cent vs. 10 per cent) who had read of the brutal rape said that the defendant in the second case was "definitely guilty." Although 57 per cent of those reading about the prior miscarriage of justice called the new defendant "probably not guilty," only 25 per cent did so after reading about the brutal rape, probably due to having that very available instance in their memory (cf. Tversky & Kahneman 1973; Zillmann 2002). In the real world, jurors' prior exposure to such examples is all but impossible to control because such cases receive heavy media coverage. As we have seen, a powerful, vivid example can do much to drive future information-processing and behavior (Zillmann 2002).

In general, individuals maintain activation of information given in the media or in trials, even if that information has been specifically recanted. Johnson and Seifert (1998) had readers determine to which of two possible characters an anaphoric reference applied, and found that the readers tended to recall incorrect characters even when the information had been corrected in the same passage. This indicates that misinformation as well as true information affects readers' text comprehension. This holds true in mock juries as well, although introducing suspicion about the motives of those presenting false information reduces the effect of the misinformation. Fein *et al.* (1997) performed two different experiments in which participants read a transcript of a trial and then indicated guilt of the defendant. When the participants read news stories casting the defendant in a negative light prior to reading the transcript, they were more likely to give a guilty verdict despite reading the judge's instructions to consider only the information presented in the trial. However, participants who read the stories along with an interview with the defendant's lawyer who presented reasons to suspect the news media's motives were less likely to vote guilty than those who read the media stories only. Similarly, participants who read statements in the transcript that were followed by an objection and instructions to the jury to disregard that information were more likely to vote guilty than those who did not read the critical statements or those who also read a statement raising suspicion about why the prosecutor introduced the evidence.

Media news coverage frequently provides information that corrects or updates previously presented reports. In the case of the 2003 Iraq war, much information was presented as unconfirmed and then updated, and more was imparted as true and later retracted or corrected (Lewandowsky *et al.* 2005). They presented respondents in three countries with news statements related to the Iraq war and asked them about their memory of those events. If they recalled the event, they were later asked to state whether initial information had been retracted, indicating that the original statement was false. The American respondents believed that both true and false retracted events were true, while Germans and Australians believed the true events but not those that had been discounted. Lewandowsky *et al.* (2005) also found that the Americans believed in different justifications of the war than those in the other countries, specifically that they were more likely to agree with US policy. Those participants who harbored suspicions about the reasons for war were more likely to discount the misinformation than those who were not suspicious, regardless of nationality. Similar to Fein *et al.* (1997), this indicates that original reports are remembered even when they are later retracted, although those who suspect the reasons behind introducing false information are more likely to update their information and make decisions based on the corrected information than those having no suspicions (Lewandowsky *et al.* 2005).

Political Media

Considerable research has looked at the various ways the media can influence political campaigns and elections. Houston *et al.* (1999) asked participants to examine the campaigns of two different candidates. One campaign had a positive focus, while the other had a negative focus, and the participants were asked which candidate they liked. Results showed that the positive campaign elicited a more positive evaluation than the negative campaign. Benoit (1999) looked at US Presidential nomination addresses between 1960 and 1996, and found that nominees used more acclaiming strategies (emphasizing their own positions) than attacking strategies (attacking the opponent's positions). Overall, Democratic nominees used more acclaiming strategies and Republicans employed more attacking strategies. If a candidate used a negative focus campaign strategy that was seen as justified, people rated that candidate more favorably (Budesheim *et al.* 1996).

Political ads are another way of imparting political messages and ideas to voters. Some purposes of political advertising are name recognition, agenda-setting, image-building, issue exposition, and fundraising (Harris 2004). Like the campaigns, political advertisements also differ in emotional valence, with positive ads emphasizing the candidate's strengths and negative ads attacking the opponent. In terms of memory, negative ads are recalled better than positive ads, even though voters do not like them as well (Garramone *et al.* 1990; Faber 1992). Kaid (1997) found that using a negative ad did affect the voter's image of the candidate, thus potentially influencing voting behavior. This presents a challenge for campaign strategists. Positive ads lead to a more favorable impression of, but poorer memory for, the candidate. On the other hand, negative ads increase recall but decrease approval of the candidate.

Politicians in the media can also provide information in the form of reminders of our own mortality. This might come in the reference to gruesome crime stories, threats of terrorism, or news of epidemics. Terror management theory (Pyszczynski *et al.* 2003) posits that such reminders of mortality can lead to more punitive judgments, the derogation of others, and generally defensive behaviors. Many years of programmatic research (summarized in Pyszczynski *et al.* 2003) have supported the idea that the manipulation of mortality salience leads to such behaviors. Some have used terror management theory for an explanation of the success of US President George W. Bush in his 2004 re-election campaign; by continually speaking about the 9/11 attacks and the threat of future attacks, he kept the mortality salience elevated, thus contributing to voters accepting his hard line internationally and refusing to "change horses" in leadership. Landau *et al.* (2004) performed several studies that forced participants in the US to contemplate death before reading a statement that cast Bush and his actions in a highly positive light. Increasing mortality salience for participants led to more agreement with these statements as well as more intention to vote for Bush. Moreover, when participants thought about death their support for Presidential candidate John Kerry decreased, and these feelings of support were independent of the participants' political opinions. These results were replicated when participants were provided reminders about the World Trade Center and 9/11.

MEDIA LITERACY

In the early years of media effects research, investigators noticed the power of media in bringing about change in the attitudes or beliefs of the consumer. This direct effects model assumed large, immediate, and most often negative effects on the audience. Although this paradigm dominated early media research, more recently researchers have viewed media as having more modest effects, which depend greatly on the attention, comprehension, memory, and perception of the consumer (Perse 2001). A few people are heavily affected, a larger number modestly affected, while many others are not affected at all. While these effects can be moderated by the prior knowledge of the viewer (Petty *et al.* 2002), a very important moderator is the level of media literacy the viewer has (Johnson 2001).

Media literacy involves the skill of questioning, appraising, and processing media, whether video, audio, or print. The area of media literacy that most directly utilizes cognition is the stage of analyzing and asking questions about the message. According to Johnson (2001), once consumers interpret the meaning of a media message, the media-literate among them may use metacognitive skills to determine why the interpretation process led to that specific meaning, including such factors as understanding the use of stereotypes and the motivations of the producers. This may involve reflecting on the message while examining it from multiple perspectives, all of which are clearly central (as opposed to peripheral) processing in the sense of the Elaboration Likelihood model (Petty *et al.* 2002). For example, Sagarin *et al.* (2002) found that providing short training might enable participants to judge the persuasiveness of authority appeals based on whether the authority has a legitimate reason to provide information about the product. Participants receiving the training rated illegitimate spokes-models as less persuasive than did participants in the control group. This result was enhanced when participants were shown that they themselves could fall prey to these types of appeals.

Because the media use framing and other techniques to set their agenda, consumers must develop a certain degree of media literacy in order to discover that agenda and fully comprehend the information appearing in the media. This learning process must occur for each source the consumer uses, in order to allow for full comprehension of both the new information and the agendas behind it (Cohen 1963). For example, if a regular viewer of Fox News switches to CNN, she will experience a transition period before completely understanding which issues, and which viewpoints on those issues (i.e., its agenda), are given the most weight on the new channel. (See Potter 2001 for a thorough discussion of various aspects of media literacy.)

Case Study of Media Literacy: Misleading Advertising

One public policy media literacy issue clearly amenable to cognitive research is the question of deceptive, or misleading, advertising. If consumers construct a meaning of an ad that is at variance with the facts, they are deceived or misled (Harris *et al.* 1983; Burke *et al.* 1988; Richards 1990). Determining whether an ad is misleading is not the same as assessing its literal truth. The truth of a claim may be resolved by examining reality. Being misleading, however, is a function of the understanding of the consumer.

It is thus a cognitive question and must be inferred from an assessment of a person's understanding of an ad. Some blatantly false statements are unlikely to mislead anyone ("Our cookies are made by elves in a tree"; "At these prices the cars will fly out the door"). On the other hand, advertising that makes only true statements may mislead when the consumer is led to infer unsubstantiated claims about a product that were never explicitly stated.

Several different types of linguistic constructions may mislead without actually lying by inviting the consumer to infer beyond the information stated. One common class of true but potentially misleading claims are hedge words (e.g., *may, could help*), which weaken a claim without denying it, e.g., "Scrubble Shampoo *may help* get rid of dandruff *symptoms*," or "Rainbow Toothpaste *fights* plaque." Another common manner of implying false information is the elliptical comparative, e.g., "Fibermunchies have *more* vitamin C," or "Powderpower laundry detergent cleans *better*," without stating the standard to which the product is being compared.

A causal relationship may be implied when no more than a correlation in fact exists, as in the juxtaposition of two imperatives ("Help your child excel in school. Buy an Apricot home computer" or "Shed those extra pounds. Buy the Blubberbuster massage belt"). In neither case does the ad state that buying the product will have the desired effect, but the causal inference is easy to draw. Something unfavorable may be implied about a competitor's products or services, without stating so directly. For example, consumers may infer from statements like "If we do your taxes and you are audited by the IRS, we will accompany you to the audit" or "Our company gives refunds quickly if your traveler's checks are lost or stolen" that the competing companies do not provide the same service, whereas in fact they do.

Incomplete reporting of scientific evidence may also imply more than what is stated. For example, "Three out of four doctors recommended Zayer Aspirin" would not be false if only four people were questioned. Claiming that "2,000 dentists recommended brushing with Laser Fluoride" without reporting the sample size is also potentially misleading. Our minds fill in the missing information in ways favorable to the advertiser (Harris *et al.* 1983). Comparison advertising may employ very selective attribute comparisons to imply a much more global impression. For example, "The Egret Pistol has more front-seat leg room than a Dodge Intrepid, more rear-seat headroom than a Nissan Maxima, and a larger trunk than a Toyota Camry" may imply that the car has a more spacious interior on most or all dimensions than any of the competitors.

In experimental studies, people do in fact make the inferences described and remember the inferred information as having been stated in the ad (e.g., remembering that a toothpaste prevents cavities when the ad only said it fights cavities). This stable finding occurs with a variety of dependent measures and is increasingly strong with longer retention intervals between exposure to the ad and the memory test (Russo *et al.* 1981; Burke *et al.* 1988; Harris *et al.* 1989; Gardner & Leonard 1990; Harris *et al.* 1993). Training people not to make such inferences is difficult, because the tendency to infer beyond given information is very strong. However, training participants to individually analyze ads, identify potential unwarranted inferences, and rewrite ads to imply something more or less strongly, has some positive effect in teaching them to put a brake on this natural inference-drawing activity (Bruno & Harris 1980). Such research has direct implication for media literacy programs.

CONCLUSION

As this chapter has shown, cognitive processes affect and are affected by one's experience with the media. As the media become more technologically advanced and pervasive, researchers must continue to examine the possible effects of those media on consumers. Examining how consumers attend to, comprehend, remember, evaluate, and act upon the information presented in the media will provide greater understanding of the effects of all types of media. One area of research that holds promise in this area is media literacy. Although the potential exists for positive benefits from the media (e.g., learning about and understanding people with whom one has no contact), there is also the danger of negative effects (e.g., learning incorrect information). As former Federal Communications Commissioner Nicholas Johnson said many years ago in reference to television, "All television is educational. The only question is, 'What is it teaching?'" (Liebert & Schwartzberg 1977, p. 170).

AUTHOR NOTE

Thanks are expressed to Stephan Lewandowsky, Tuan Tran, Nicole Peck, Kristen Geri, and two anonymous reviewers for helpful comments on earlier drafts of this manuscript.
Correspondence may be addressed to rjharris@k-state.edu.

REFERENCES

Anderson, C. A., Carnagey, N. L. & Eubanks, J. (2003). Exposure to violent media: the effects of songs with violent lyrics on aggressive thoughts and feelings. *Journal of Personality and Social Psychology*, *84*, 960–971.

Anderson, D. R., Bryant, J., Wilder, A. *et al.* (2000). Researching *Blue's Clues*: viewing behavior and impact. *Media Psychology*, *2*, 179–194.

Anderson, D. R., Lorch, E. P., Field, D. E. & Sanders, J. (1981). The effects of TV program comprehensibility on preschool children's visual attention to television. *Child Development*, *52*, 151–157.

Anderson, S. J. & Conway, M. A. (1997). Representation of autobiographical memories. In M. A. Conway (ed.), *Cognitive Models of Memory*. Cambridge, MA: MIT Press.

Armstrong, G. B. & Chung, L. (2000). Background television and reading memory in context. *Communication Research*, *27*, 327–352.

Armstrong, G. B. & Sopory, P. (1997). Effects of background television on phonological and visuo-spatial working memory. *Communication Research*, *24*, 459–480.

Bartlett, F. C. (1932). *Remembering: A study in Experimental and Social Psychology* (5th reprinting). London: Cambridge University Press.

Bartlett, J. C. & Snelus, P. (1980). Lifespan memory for popular songs. *American Journal of Psychology*, 93, 551–560.

Beaudoin, C. E. (2002). Exploring antismoking ads: appeals, themes, and consequences. *Journal of Health Communication*, *7*, 123–137.

Beh, H. C. & Hirst, R. (1999). Performance on driving-related tasks during music. *Ergonomics*, *42*, 1087–1098.

Benoit, W. L. (1999). Acclaiming, attacking, and defending in presidential nominating acceptance addresses, 1960–1996. *Quarterly Journal of Speech*, *85*, 247–267.

Billings, A. C., Halone, K. K. & Denham, B. E. (2002). "Man, that was a pretty shot": an analysis of gendered broadcast commentary surrounding the 2000 men's and women's NCAA Final Four basketball championships. *Mass Communication & Society*, *5*, 295–315.

Bjerklie, D. (2003). *Time*, 73(July 28).

Bonds-Raacke, J. M., Cady, E. T., Harris, R. J. *et al.* (in press). Remembering gay/lesbian media characters: can Ellen and Will improve attitudes toward homosexuals? *Journal of Homosexuality*.

Brewer, W. F. & Nakamura, G. V. (1984). The nature and functions of schemas. In R. S. Wyer & T. K. Srull (eds.), *Handbook of Social Cognition*. Hillsdale, NJ: Lawrence Erlbaum Associates.

Brodsky, W. (2001). The effects of music tempo on simulated driving performance and vehicular control. *Transportation Research. Part F, Traffic Psychology and Behaviour*, *4*, 219–241.

Bruno, K. J. & Harris, R. J. (1980). The effect of repetition on the discrimination of asserted and implied claims in advertising. *Applied Psycholinguistics*, *1*, 307–321.

Budesheim, T. L., Houston, D. A. & DePaola, S. J. (1996). Persuasiveness of in-group and out-group political messages: the case of negative political campaigning. *Journal of Personality and Social Psychology*, *70*, 523–534.

Bureau of Justice (2005). Key crime and justice facts at a glance. Retrieved June 29, 2005, Available at: http://www.ojp.usdoj.gov/bjs/glance.htm#Crime.

Burke, R. R., DeSarbo, W. S., Oliver, R. L. & Robertson, T. S. (1988). Deception by implication: an experimental investigation. *Journal of Consumer Research*, *14*, 483–494.

Bushman, B. J. & Anderson, C. A. (2001). Media violence and the American public: scientific facts versus media misinformation. *American Psychologist*, *56*, 477–489.

Butcher, K. R. & Kintsch, W. (2003). Text comprehension and discourse processing. In A. F. Healy & R. W. Proctor (eds.), *Handbook of Psychology Volume 4: Experimental Psychology*. Hoboken, NJ: John Wiley & Sons.

Cacioppo, J. T., Petty, R. E., Kao, C. F. & Rodriguez, R. (1986). Central and peripheral routes to persuasion: an individual difference perspective. *Journal of Personality and Social Psychology*, *51*, 1032–1043.

Cantor, J., Mares, M. L. & Hyde, J. S. (2003). Autobiographical memories of exposure to sexual media content. *Media Psychology*, *5*, 1–31.

Carroll, J. S., Kerr, N. L., Alfini, J. J. *et al.* (1986). Free press and fair trial: the role of behavioral research. *Law and Human Behaviour*, *10*, 187–202.

Christianson, S. & Loftus, E. F. (1987). Memory for traumatic events. *Applied CognitivePsychology*, *1*, 225–239.

Cohen, A. R., Stotland, E. & Wolfe, D. M. (1955). An experimental investigation of need for cognition. *Journal of Abnormal and Social Psychology*, *51*, 291–294.

Cohen, B. C. (1963). *The Press and Foreign Policy*. Princeton, NJ: Princeton University Press.

Conway, M. A. (2001). Sensory-perceptual episodic memory and its context: autobiographical memory. In A. Baddeley, J. P. Aggleton & M. A. Conway (eds.), *Episodic Memory: New Directions in Research* (pp. 53–70). Oxford: Oxford University Press.

Conway, M. A. & Pleydell-Pearce, C. W. (2000). The construction of autobiographical memories in the self-memory system. *Psychological Review*, *107*, 261–288.

Eastman, S. T. & Billings, A. C. (2000). Sportscasting and sports reporting: the power of gender bias. *Journal of Sport and Social Issues*, *24*, 192–213.

Entman, R. M. (1993). Framing: toward clarification of a fractured paradigm. *Journal of Communication*, *43*, 51–58.

Ericsson, K. A. & Kintsch, W. (1995). Long-term working memory. *Psychological Review*, *102*, 211–245.

Faber, R. J. (1992). Advances in political advertising research: a progression from if to when. *Journal of Current Issues and Research in Advertising*, *14*, 1–18.

Fein, S., McCloskey, A. L. & Tomlinson, T. M. (1997). Can the jury disregard that information? The use of suspicion to reduce the prejudicial effects of pretrial publicity and inadmissible testimony. *Personality and Social Psychology Bulletin*, *23*, 1215–1226.

Forgas, J. P. (1995). Mood and judgment: the Affect Infusion Model (AIM). *Psychological Bulletin*, *117*, 39–66.

Friestad, M. & Thorson, E. (1993). Remembering ads: the effects of encoding strategies, retrieval cues, and emotional response. *Journal of Consumer Psychology*, *2*, 1–23.
Furnham, A. & Mori, T. (2003). The effect of programme context on memory for humorous television advertisements in Japan. *Psychologia: An International Journal of Psychology in the Orient*, *46*, 53–66.
Gardner, D. M. & Leonard, N. H. (1990). Research in deceptive and corrective advertising: progress to date and impact on public policy. *Current Issues and Research in Advertising*, *12*, 275–309.
Garramone, G. M., Atkin, C. K., Pinkleton, B. E. & Cole, R. T. (1990). Effects of negative political advertising on the political process. *Journal of Broadcasting and Electronic Media*, *34*, 299–311.
Garry, M., Manning, C. G., Loftus, E. F. & Sherman, S. J. (1996). Imagination inflation: imagining a childhood event inflates confidence that it occurred. *Psychonomic Bulletin & Review*, *3*, 208–214.
Garry, M. & Polaschek, D. L. L. (2000). Imagination and memory. *Current directions in psychological Science*, *9*, 6–10.
Gerbner, G., Gross, L., Morgan, M. *et al.* (2002). Growing up with television: cultivation processes. In J. Bryant & D. Zillmann (eds.), *Media Effects: Advances in Theory and Research* (2nd edn, pp. 43–67). Mahwah, NJ: Lawrence Erlbaum Associates.
Gibbons, J. A., Taylor, C. & Phillips, J. (2005). Minorities as marginalized heroes and prominent villains in the mass media: music, news, sports, television, and movies. In R. Walker & D. J. Herrmann (eds.), *Cognitive Technology: Essays on the Transformation of Thought and Society* (pp. 149–171). Jefferson, NC: McFarland.
Gibson, R. & Zillmann, D. (1994). Exaggerated versus representative exemplification in news reports: perception of issues and personal consequences. *Communication Research*, *21*, 603–624.
Givens, S. M. B. & Monahan, J. L. (2005). Priming mammies, jezebels, and other controlling images: an examination of the influence of mediated stereotypes on perceptions of an African American woman. *Media Psychology*, *7*, 87–106.
Glassner, B. (1999). *The Culture of Fear: Why Americans are Afraid of the Wrong Things*. New York: Basic Books.
Graber, D. A. (1990). Seeing is remembering: how visuals contribute to learning from television news. *Journal of Communication*, *40*, 134–155.
Graves, S. B. (1999). Television and prejudice reduction: when does television as a vicarious experience make a difference? *Journal of Social Issues*, *55*, 707–725.
Greenberg, B. S. (1988). Some uncommon television images and the Drench Hypothesis. In S. Oskamp (ed.), *Television as a Social Issue* (pp. 88–102). Newbury Park, CA: Sage.
Greenberg, B. S., Mastro, D. & Brand, J. E. (2002). Minorities and the mass media: television into the 21st century. In J. Bryant & D. Zillmann (eds.), *Media Effects: Advances in Theory and Research* (2nd edn, pp. 333–351). Mahwah, NJ: Lawrence Erlbaum Associates.
Greene, E. & Wade, R. (1987). Of private talk and public print: general pre-trial publicity and juror decision-making. *Applied Cognitive Psychology*, *1*, 1–13.
Grimes, T. (1991). Mild auditory-visual dissonance in television news may exceed viewer attentional capacity. *Human Communication Research*, *17*, 268–298.
Gunter, B., Baluch, B., Duffy, L. J. & Furnham, A. (2002). Children's memory for television events: effects of programme-advertisement congruency. *Applied Cognitive Psychology*, *16*, 171–190.
Halbert, C. & Latimer, M. (1994). "Battling" gendered language: an analysis of the language used by sports commentators in a televised coed tennis competition. *Sociology of Sport Journal*, *11*, 298–308.
Harris, R. J. (2004). *A Cognitive Psychology of Mass Communication* (4th edn). Mahwah, NJ: Lawrence Erlbaum Associates.
Harris, R. J., Bonds-Raacke, J. M. & Cady, E. T. (2005). What we remember from television and movies: using autobiographical memory to study mass media. In R. Walker & D. J. Herrmann (eds.), *Cognitive Technology: Essays on the Transformation of Thought and Society* (pp. 130–148). Jefferson, NC: McFarland.

Harris, R. J., Cady, E. T. & Tran, T. Q. (2006). Comprehension and memory. In J. Bryant & P. Vorderer (eds.), *Psychology of Entertainment* (pp. 71–84). Mahwah, NJ: Lawrence Erlbaum Associates.

Harris, R. J., Dubitsky, T. M. & Bruno, K. J. (1983). Psycholinguistic studies of misleading advertising. In R. J. Harris (ed.), *Information Processing Research in Advertising* (pp. 241–262). Hillsdale, NJ: Lawrence Erlbaum Associates.

Harris, R. J., Pounds, J. C., Maiorelle, M. J. & Mermis, M. M. (1993). The effect of type of claim, gender, and buying history on the drawing of pragmatic inferences from advertising claims. *Journal of Consumer Psychology, 2*, 83–95.

Harris, R. J., Trusty, M. L., Bechtold, J. I. & Wasinger, L. (1989). Memory for implied versus directly asserted advertising claims. *Psychology & Marketing, 6*, 87–96.

Harrison, K. & Cantor, J. (1999). Tales from the screen: enduring fright reactions to scary media. *Media Psychology, 1*, 97–116.

Hass, R. G. (1981). Effects of source characteristics on cognitive responses and persuasion. In R. E. Petty, T. M. Ostrom & T. C. Brock (eds.), *Cognitive Responses in Persuasion* (pp. 141–172). Hillsdale, NJ: Lawrence Erlbaum Associates.

Hoekstra, S. J., Harris, R. J. & Helmick, A. L. (1999). Autobiographical memories about the experience of seeing frightening movies in childhood. *Media Psychology, 1*, 117–140.

Hornik, J. (1989). Temporal instability as a moderating factor on advertising effectiveness. *Journal of Business Research, 18*, 89–106.

Houston, D. A., Doan, K. & Roskos-Ewoldsen, D. (1999). Negative political advertising and choice conflict. *Journal of Experimental Psychology: Applied, 5*, 3–16.

Hovland, C. I., Janis, I. L. & Kelley, H. H. (1953). *Communication and Persuasion*. New Haven, CT and London: Yale University Press.

Hovland, C. I. & Weiss, W. (1951). The influence of source credibility on communication effectiveness. *The Public and Opinion Quarterly, 15*, 635–650.

Jamieson, K. H. & Waldman, P. (2003). *The Press Effect: Politicians, Journalists, and the Stories that Shape the Political World*. New York: Oxford University Press.

Johnson, H. M. & Seifert, C. M. (1998). Updating accounts following a correction of misinformation. *Journal of Experimental Psychology: Learning, Memory and Cognition*, 24, 1483–1494.

Johnson, L. J. (2001). *Media, Education, and Change*. New York: Peter Lang.

Kaid, L. L. (1997). Effects of the television sports on images of Dole and Clinton. *American Behavioral Scientist, 40*, 1085–1094.

Kane, M. J. (1988). Media coverage of the female athlete before, during, and after Title IX: *Sports Illustrated* revisited. *Journal of Sport Management, 2*, 87–99.

Kintsch, W. (1998). *Comprehension: A Paradigm for Cognition*. Cambridge: Cambridge University Press.

Krishnan, S. & Chakravarti, D. (2003). A process analysis of the effects of humorous advertising executions on brand claims memory. *Journal of Consumer Psychology, 13*, 230–245.

Landau, M. J., Solomon, S., Greenberg, J. *et al.* (2004). Deliver us from evil: the effects of mortality salience and reminders of 9/11 on support for President George W. Bush. *Personality and Social Psychology Bulletin, 30*, 1136–1150.

Levin, I. P. & Gaeth, G. J. (1988). How consumers are affected by the framing of attribute information before and after consuming the product. *Journal of Consumer Research, 15*, 374–378.

Levine, L. J. & Pizarro, D. A. (2004). Emotion and memory: a grumpy overview. *Social Cognition, 22*, 530–554.

Lewandowsky, S., Stritzke, W. G. K., Oberauer, K. & Morales, M. (2005). Memory for fact, fiction, and misinformation: the Iraq War 2003. *Psychological Science, 16*, 190–195.

Liebert, R. & Schwartzberg, N. (1977). Effects of mass media. *Annual Review of Psychology, 28*, 141–174.

Loftus, E. F. & Burns, T. E. (1982). Mental shock can produce retrograde amnesia. *Memory & Cognition, 10*, 318–323.

Lorch, E. P., Anderson, D. R. & Levin, S. R. (1979). The relationship of visual attention children's comprehension of television. *Child Development, 50*, 722–727.

Low, J. & Durkin, K. (2000). Event knowledge and children's recall of television based narratives. *The British Journal of Developmental Psychology, 18*, 247–267.

Luecke-Aleksa, D., Anderson, D. R., Collins, P. A. & Schmitt, K. L. (1995). Gender consistency and television viewing. *Developmental Psychology*, *5*, 773–780.

McCombs, M. & Reynolds, A. (2002). News influence on our pictures of the world. In J. Bryant & D. Zillmann (eds.), *Media Effects: Advances in Theory and Research* (pp. 1–18). Mahwah, NJ: Lawrence Erlbaum Associates.

Maddux, J. E. & Rogers, R. W. (1980). Effects of source expertness, physical attractiveness, and supporting arguments on persuasion: a case of brains over beauty. *Journal of Personality and Social Psychology*, *39*, 235–244.

Matthews, R., Legg, S. & Charlton, S. (2003). The effect of cell phone type on drivers' subjective workload during concurrent driving and conversing. *Accident Analysis & Prevention*, *35*, 451–457.

Mitchell, K. J. & Johnson, M. K. (2000). Source monitoring: attributing mental experiences. In E. Tulving & F. I. M. Craik (eds.), *The Oxford Handbook of Memory* (pp. 179–195). New York: Oxford University Press.

Mundorf, N., Drew, D., Zillmann, D. & Weaver, J. (1990). Effects of disturbing news on recall of subsequently presented news. *Communication Research*, *17*, 601–615.

Newhagen, J. E. & Reeves, B. (1992). The evening's bad news: effects of compelling negative television news images on memory. *Journal of Communication*, *42*, 25–41.

Office of Juvenile Justice and Delinquency Prevention (2000). *Kidnapping of Juveniles: Patterns from NIBRS (NCJ 181161)* (Authors: D. Finkelhor & R. Ormrod).

Oliver, M. B. (1994). Portrayals of crime, race, and aggression in "reality-based" police shows: a content analysis. *Journal of Broadcasting and Electronic Media*, *38*, 179–192.

Oliver, M. B. & Fonash, D. (2002). Race and crime in the news: whites' identification and misidentification of violent and nonviolent criminal suspects. *Media Psychology*, *4*, 137–156.

Perse, E. M. (2001). *Media Effects and Society*. Mahwah, NJ: Lawrence Erlbaum Associates.

Petty, R. E., Priester, J. R. & Briñol, P. (2002). Mass media attitude change: implications of the elaboration likelihood model of persuasion. In J. Bryant & D. Zillmann (eds.), *Media Effects: Advances in Theory and Research*. Mahwah, NJ: Lawrence Erlbaum Associates.

Poniewozik, J. (2001). What's wrong with this picture? *Time*, 80–82 (May 28).

Pool, M. M., Koolstra, C. M. & van der Voort, T. H. A. (2003). The impact of background radio and television on high school students' homework performance. *Journal of Communication*, *53*, 74–87.

Potter, W. J. (2001). *Media Literacy* (2nd edn). Thousand Oaks CA: Sage.

Price, V. & Czilli, E. J. (1996). Modeling patterns of news recognition and recall. *Journal of Communication*, *46*, 55–78.

Pyszczynski, T. A., Solomon, S. & Greenberg, J. (2003). *In the Wake of 9/11: The Psychology of Terror*. Washington, DC: American Psychological Association.

Ransdell, S. & Gilroy, L. (2001). The effects of background music on word processing writing. *Computers and Human Behavior*, *17*, 141–148.

Richards, J. I. (1990). *Deceptive Advertising*. Hillsdale, NJ: Lawrence Erlbaum Associates.

Richards, Z. & Hewstone, M. (2001). Subtyping and subgrouping: processes for the prevention and promotion of stereotype change. *Personality and Social Psychology Review*, *5*, 52–73.

Russo, J. E., Metcalf, B. L. & Stevens, D. (1981). Identifying misleading advertising. *Journal of Consumer Research*, *8*, 119–131.

Sagarin, B. J., Cialdini, R. B., Rice, W. E. & Serna, S. B. (2002). Dispelling the illusion of invulnerability: the motivations and mechanisms of resistance to persuasion. *Journal of Personality and Social Psychology*, *83*, 526–541.

Schmitt, K. L., Anderson, D. R. & Collins, P. A. (1999). Form and content: looking at visual features of television. *Developmental Psychology*, *35*, 1156–1167.

Schmitt, K. L., Woolf, K. D. & Anderson, D. R. (2003). Viewing the viewers: viewing behaviors by children and adults during television programs and commercials. *Journal of Communication*, *53*, 265–281.

Schneider, S. L. & Laurion, S. K. (1993). Do we know what we've learned from listening to the news? *Memory & Cognition*, *21*, 198–209.

Schulkind, M. D., Hennis, L. K. & Rubin, D. C. (1999). Music, emotion, and autobiographical memory: they're playing your song. *Memory & Cognition*, *27*, 948–955.

Schwartz, N. (1990). Feelings as information: informational and motivational functions of affective states. In E. T. Higgins & R. Sorrentino (eds.), *Handbook of Motivation and Cognition: Foundations of Social Behavior* (Vol. 2, pp. 527–561). New York: Guilford Press.

Sharman, S. J., Manning, C. G. & Garry, M. (2005). Explain this: explaining childhood events inflates confidence for those events. *Applied Cognitive Psychology*, *19*, 67–74.

Shaw, J. I. & Skolnick, P. (2004). Effects of prejudicial pretrial publicity from physical and witness evidence on mock jurors' decision making. *Journal of Applied Social Psychology*, 34, 2132–2148.

Shrum, L. J. (2002). Media consumption and perceptions of social reality: effects and underlying processes. In J. Bryant & D. Zillmann (eds.), *Media Effects: Advances in Theory and Research*. Mahwah, NJ: Lawrence Erlbaum Associates.

Signorielli, N. (1989). The stigma on mental illness on television. *Journal of Broadcasting and Electronic Media*, *33*, 325–331.

Smith, K. H. & Stutts, M. (2003). Effects of short-term cosmetic versus long-term health fear appeals in anti-smoking advertisements on the smoking behavior of adolescents. *Journal of Consumer Behavior*, *3*, 157–177.

Snyder, M. (1974). The self-monitoring of expressive behavior. *Journal of Personality and Social Psychology*, *30*, 526–537.

Snyder, M. & DeBono, K. G. (1985). Appeals to image and claims about quality: understanding the psychology of advertising. *Journal of Personality and Social Psychology*, *49*, 586–597.

Sternberg, R. J. (2003). *Cognitive Psychology* (3rd edn). Belmont, CA: Wadsworth.

Strayer, D. L., Drews, F. A., Crouch, D. J. & Johnston, W. A. (2005). Why do cell phone conversations interfere with driving? In R. Walker & D. J. Herrmann (eds.), *Cognitive Technology: Essays on the Transformation of Thought and Society* (pp. 51–68). Jefferson, NC: McFarland.

Strayer, D. L., Drews, F. A. & Johnston, W. A. (2003). Cell phone induced failures of visual attention during simulated driving. *Journal of Experimental Psychology: Applied*, *9*, 23–52.

Teplin, L. A. (1985). The criminality of the mentally ill: a dangerous misconception. *American Journal of Psychiatry*, *142*, 593–599.

Tversky, A. & Kahneman, D. (1973). Availability: a heuristic for judging frequency and probability. *Cognitive Psychology*, *5*, 207–232.

Tversky, A. & Kahneman, D. (1974). Judgment under uncertainty: heuristics and biases. *Science*, *185*, 1124–1131.

Walma van der Molen, J. H. & van der Voort, T. H. A. (2000). The impact of television, print, and audio on children's recall of the news. *Human Communication Research*, *26*, 3–26.

Weaver, J. (2003a). Teens tune out TV, log on instead. Retrieved July 25, 2003, Available at: http://www.msnbc.msn.com/id/3078614/.

Weaver, J. (2003b). College students are avid gamers. Retrieved July 18, 2003. Available at: http://www.msnbc.msn.com/id/934589/.

Wickens, C. D. (2002). Multiple resources and performance prediction. Theoretical Issues in *Ergonomics Science*, *3*, 159–177.

Wilson, J. R. & Wilson, S. L. R. (1998). *Mass Media/Mass Culture* (4th edn). New York: McGraw-Hill.

Witte, K. (1994). Fear control and danger control: a test of the extended parallel process model (EEPM). *Communication Monographs*, *61*, 113–134.

Zillmann, D. (2002). Exemplification theory of media influence. In J. Bryant & D. Zillmann (eds.), *Media Effects: Advances in Theory and Research*. Mahwah, NJ: Lawrence Erlbaum Associates.

Zwaan, R. A. & Radvansky, G. A. (1998). Situation models in language comprehension and memory. *Psychological Bulletin*, *123*, 162–185.

CHAPTER 26

Consumer Psychology

Joseph W. Alba
University of Florida, USA

and

J. Wesley Hutchinson
University of Pennsylvania, USA

Cognitive psychology continues to exert a guiding influence on consumer research. We discuss this relationship in terms of two main problem areas: the cognitive antecedents of decision-making and decision-making processes. The antecedents of consumer decision-making constitute an eclectic set of topics that are seldom integrated into a common framework. These topics include consumer response to marketing actions (such as advertising and pricing), information search (in memory as well as the external environment), and consumer expertise. Research on these cognitive antecedents tends to be descriptive in nature and draws from the mnemonic, interpretive, perceptual, and learning effects traditionally examined by cognitive psychologists. In contrast, research on decision processes tends to be concerned with methods for discerning the nature of the decision process and deviations from normative behavior. Such research draws on psychometrics and economics in addition to cognitive psychology.

COGNITIVE ANTECEDENTS OF DECISION-MAKING

From the perspective of economics and management science, the inputs to decision-making are well specified by the definition of the decision problem. From a cognitive perspective, however, the inputs to real-world decision-making are poorly specified and may include information available in the immediate environment, knowledge retrieved from memory, and inferences based on a combination of internal and external inputs. We focus on two broad categories of cognitive antecedents to consumer decision-making: buyer responses to the marketing actions of sellers and the results of goal-oriented buyer behaviors.

Handbook of Applied Cognition: Second Edition. Edited by Francis T. Durso.

Consumer Responses to Marketing Actions

It is traditionally held that firms have four general tools for influencing consumers' decisions: advertising (and related promotional devices), pricing, physical distribution and display of the product, and the product itself. Most research that has investigated the cognitive antecedents of decision-making has focused on the first two. Distribution has received far less formal investigation, although managerial heuristics often make assumptions about consumer information-processing. Product has been studied in a variety of contexts and is an inherent component of the normative approaches to decision-making described later. In this section we discuss consumer response to products primarily under the rubric of brand equity.

Advertising

Whereas managers' concerns tend to revolve around the effectiveness of their advertising, behavioral scientists have mainly investigated the role advertising plays in persuasion. One area in which these interests converge is in the study of ad recall. The prevailing wisdom, supported by anecdotal and proprietary research, is that memory for advertising can be extremely low. In part, the problem is one of limited attention and a consequent failure to encode. Ads are typically viewed in distracting and uninvolving settings. Academic research has generally examined more favorable climates in which attention, per se, is not a limiting factor, but where competitive effects loom large. Consistent with basic memory research, memory for information contained in advertisements appears to be governed by attention and elaboration (e.g., Kardes & Kalyanaram 1992; Zhang & Markman 1998; Sengupta & Gorn 2002) and by competitive interference, which itself is moderated by such real-world considerations as the modality of the message, message variability, cognitive structure (expertise) of the receiver, processing style, cues present at the time of recall, and the structural, evaluative, and semantic similarity of competing messages (Alba & Chattopadhyay 1985, 1986; Burke & Srull 1988; Keller 1991; Unnava *et al.* 1994; Pieters & Bijmolt 1997; Law 2002; Krishnan & Chakravarti 2003).

More provocative than the pure mnemonics of advertising is the question of how advertising influences consumers. A broad construal of consumer learning argues that the market needs to convey information about three types of decision inputs: search attributes, experience attributes, and credence attributes (Darby & Karni 1973). Search attributes typically consist of visual and verbal cues that are open to inspection, often prior to purchase, and therefore fall within the scope of stimuli traditionally studied by cognitive and decision researchers. These attributes include product ingredients, technical specifications, and price – attributes that should be most compatible with traditional advertising formats. Experience attributes, such as flavor, cannot be assessed fully from description and therefore require consumption. Credence attributes represent information that cannot be obtained through search or experience within a reasonable period of time and therefore must be informed by another party. For example, the relative efficacy of competing brands of toothpaste is difficult to evaluate, and one may take an expert's advice in lieu of conducting an error-prone time-series experiment.

Those who endorse a caveat emptor philosophy of regulation speak of the ubiquity of search and experience attributes which, by their nature, afford the opportunity to make informed decisions. Caveat emptor is less consistent with the findings and intuitions of decision researchers. The issue is not whether consumers can make optimal decisions or should bear the responsibility for those decisions, but rather consumers' ability to learn from the environment (Hoch & Deighton 1989; Alba & Hutchinson 1991). Those who view consumers as imperfect learners argue that advertising may exert a variety of influences that enhance or distort the accurate accrual of product beliefs, regardless of attribute type. In the case of search attributes, advertising may "frame" the buying decision by persuading consumers to place greater or lesser weight on different product attributes, by defining the ideal point for a product category, or by inhibiting recall and consideration of particular decision criteria (Sanbonmatsu *et al.* 2003; cf. Bettman & Sujan 1987; Mandel & Johnson 2002). In the case of experience attributes, advertising may create expectations that guide evaluation when objective quality is difficult to discern, such as when objective information is voluminous (Deighton 1984), the choice set is efficient (Ha & Hoch 1989), and sensory information fails to indicate a clearly superior alternative (Hoch & Ha 1986). More worrying is the finding that expectations may guide evaluation of taste goods when the alternatives are not entirely ambiguous (Levin & Gaeth 1988; Hoegg & Alba 2006), and may even alter the perceived efficacy of products possessing experience attributes (Shiv *et al.* 2005).

Consumer researchers have also borrowed from traditional cognitive paradigms to highlight two additional distorting effects of advertising. First, repeated exposure to advertised claims increases the perceived validity of those claims, particularly among consumer segments that are most likely to face memory deficits (see, e.g., Law *et al.* 1998; Hawkins *et al.* 2001; Skurnik *et al.* 2005). Second, post-consumption advertising may alter memory for the consumption episode such that reconstructive processes lead to recollections that are more positive than the experience itself (Braun 1999), especially among consumers who have little product expertise (Cowley & Janus 2004).

Brand Equity

Brand names continue to exert considerable influence on consumer decision-making even in an era in which true product uniqueness is becoming increasingly difficult to maintain (Keller 2003). This paradox can be understood in the context of the assets of a name and the environment in which firms must compete. The assets include awareness, meaning, and loyalty; the environment is one in which noise abounds.

Awareness. Brand awareness is important not only because familiarity has well-documented affective implications (Zajonc & Markus 1982; Moore & Hutchinson 1985) but also, as discussed below, because competitive pressures raise the importance of being recognized in a stimulus-based decision environment and recalled in a memory-based decision environment (cf. Srinivasan *et al.* 2005). For present purposes it is sufficient to note that mere inclusion in the consumer's choice set is a powerful predictor of consumer choice (Nedungadi 1990; Shocker *et al.* 1991).

Meaning. Environmental noise and cognitive limitations similarly raise the value of the meaning component of brand equity. The original purpose of a brand was to signal unique quality. Brands continue to serve this function, and much more. When consumers lack the resources, motivation, or ability to assess relative quality across offerings, brands provide heuristic value and enhance consumer welfare (whenever the signals are accurate). Over time, competition, commoditization, and elementary strategic considerations have sharpened the signaling value of brands such that many brands signal not only general quality but also specific meaning (e.g., Ivory is gentle). In a multidimensional product space, brands represent different locations. When the dimensions are product benefits, brands facilitate choice by distinguishing one offering from another on meaningful decision criteria. Moreover, if a brand becomes synonymous with a benefit and consumers use brand names heuristically, the brand may dominate its competitors even when it lacks true competitive superiority as defined by objective product specifications. Thus, a brand name can provide a competitive advantage that is slow to erode.

Finally, brands possess not only present value but also potential value. When brands assume specific meanings, firms can leverage those meanings to extend into other product categories. Although inferences regarding the firm's underlying competence play a role in guiding perceptions of quality (Bottomly & Holden 2001), the true power of a brand is revealed by its ability to facilitate entry into a category in which the firm possesses no structural competence (Broniarczyk & Alba 1994a; see also Meyvis & Janiszewski 2004). For example, Brinks may be viewed as a competent provider of home security systems even though such products lack manufacturing synergy with Brinks' original service.

Loyalty. Brand loyalty is a cherished goal of most firms. Loyal consumers provide a consistent and predictable revenue stream, exhibit less price sensitivity than other consumers, and can serve as endorsers of the brand to non-users. A range of causes may underlie loyalty, anchored at one end by objective brand utility and at the other by emotional attachment (Jacoby 1971; Fournier 1998). Between these poles is a variety of rational, semi-rational, and irrational reasons why consumers exhibit brand loyalty or, more generally, a "status quo bias" (see Samuelson & Zeckhauser 1988).

On the utility-based side is loyalty driven by the costs of switching, such that consumers remain loyal not because the chosen brand possesses superior quality but because net utility for the chosen brand is higher when search and learning costs associated with switching to a competing brand are taken into account. Switching costs also come in the form of potential rewards, as in the case of frequency programs. Consumers remain loyal at least until they can redeem the points they have accumulated toward a reward. Although computing net utility is economically appropriate, recent research has shown that a medium used to represent progress toward the reward may take on illusory value and thereby distort the choice process (Hsee *et al.* 2003; van Osselaer *et al.* 2004).

Loyalty may obtain also from (over-)confidence that one's chosen brand is objectively superior to competing brands, which in turn may be driven by asymmetric knowledge about the chosen and non-chosen options. Greater knowledge about a satisfactory incumbent brand and mistaken assessments of its uniqueness have been shown to result in erroneous beliefs about its superiority over competing brands (Kardes & Kalyanaram 1992; Muthukrishnan 1995; Muthukrishnan & Kardes 2001).

Appropriately viewed as irrational is loyalty due to sunk costs. Consumers may make an investment and then forgo superior courses of action to justify the original decision or avoid the appearance of wastefulness that accompanies abandonment of the initial investment (cf. Arkes & Blumer 1985; Cripps & Meyer 1994; Boulding *et al.* 1997). It is interesting, however, that these sunk investments can be mentally depreciated such that their effect on a present decision diminishes as the interval between the time of the investment and the time of the decision widens (Gourville & Soman 1998).

Independent of the sunk-cost effect is the endowment effect, as exemplified by the higher prices demanded by individuals when selling a good than the purchase prices individuals would willing to pay to obtain the same good (Thaler 1980; Kahneman *et al.* 1990). The difference between the selling and purchase prices can be staggering and do not necessarily require actual possession (Sen & Johnson 1997). Evidence suggests that both buyers and sellers focus on what they will forgo as a consequence of the transaction. Buyers focus on their outlay, whereas sellers focus on the benefits of the good (Carmon & Ariely 2000).

Lastly, consumers may remain loyal to a brand due to the risks associated with switching. Similarly, consumers may be motivated to choose particular options to avoid regret that could accompany the selection of different options. As Simonson (1992) argues, conventional options represent the norm and may prompt greater regret if forgone in favor of an option that ultimately proves to be less attractive. In the consumer world, the conventional option may be the market leader or the brand generally purchased by an individual.

Pricing

Traditional economic models of consumer behavior assume rational response to market prices such that an individual compares the (positive) utility of consuming a product to the (negative) utility of its cost and then opts to purchase the product if the net utility is positive. Although it is certainly true that consumers consider costs and benefits when making a purchase decision, their reactions to prices may be influenced as much by psychological factors as by the economic tradeoffs.

Reference Prices. The attractiveness of a price is driven in part by comparison to a reference price (Winer 1986). Research and common experience suggest that consumers seek "good deals" rather than balanced exchanges of utility. However, consumers are not entirely self-serving in their view of a transaction and are willing to acknowledge the vendor's need to make a profit (Kahneman *et al.* 1986). The problems for the vendor are that consumers possess arbitrary and idiosyncratic beliefs about the size of the allowable profit and tend to overestimate the profit realized by the vendor (Bolton *et al.* 2003). Vendors may respond legitimately by educating consumers about product value and the costs required to deliver that value (Thaler 1985; Gourville 1998) or somewhat less forthrightly by manipulating reference points, such as through the use of artificially high comparison prices (cf. Urbany *et al.* 1988).

Of course, the ability to frame a price or price increase is dependent in part on the consumer's level of knowledge, which varies considerably across individuals. Whereas one segment of consumers (sometimes referred to as "price vigilantes") may engage in frequent price comparison, others appear to have vaguer notions of the going rate (see Vanhuele & Dreze 2002). Among the latter, price perception will be influenced by cues present at the point of purchase (cf. Lattin & Bucklin 1989; Mayhew & Winer 1992). Again, some vendors may attempt to educate consumers about the attractiveness of their prices whereas others may operate contrary to consumers' interest by falsely signaling a price reduction (Inman *et al.* 1990) or by providing misleading heuristic cues (see Alba 2002).

Mental Accounting. A final peculiarity of human behavior driven by monetary reference points is the tendency to treat money as less fungible than it is (Thaler 1985; Prelec & Lowenstein 1998). Individuals possess a total personal wealth but often divide that wealth into budgetary categories, each of which has its own reference point. Thus, an expenditure will be deemed acceptable or unacceptable depending on the category from which it is mentally deducted. For example, a $100 meal might be considered prohibitive if deducted from the weekly food budget but quite acceptable if purchased while on vacation and deducted from the vacation budget.

Goal-Oriented Consumer Behaviors

We consider two broad classes of activities undertaken by consumers in their attempt to acquire informational inputs for decision-making. The first consists of searching the external environment for relevant factual information; the second consists of searching memory. As a precursor we briefly review the literature on optimal search and learning, which serves as a normative reference point for many descriptive studies.

Optimal Information Search and Learning

Consumer research has been influenced by work in economics and statistics that attempts to describe how utility-maximizing consumers should behave in acquiring information. Two types of problems have been the main foci of this research: information search and learning. The optimal search problem is typically defined as one in which previously unknown information is revealed with certainty. The search process is modeled as drawing a sample of a given size from some population that varies in the values being optimized. The consumer then decides either to choose the best option in that sample or draw a new sample. The act of drawing a sample is assumed to have a cost (based on factors such as search effort and the opportunity cost of time).

Price search is a classic example. Consider a consumer who is shopping for apples. The consumer might draw a sample of prices by visiting a grocery store and examining the prices of the different types of apples available at the store. Having acquired this information, the consumer either buys apples at that store or visits another store. For most search problems of this type, the optimal policy is to determine the optimal sample size for each draw and then continue drawing samples until the best current option is better than the statistically expected value of continued search, which is often called a *reservation value* (e.g., McKenna 1987; see Hutchinson & Meyer 1994, for a brief overview of optimal dynamic decision-making). The actual computation of the sample size and the reservation value can be quite complex, but the rule itself is simple. A number of researchers have examined variations of this problem tailored to realistic consumer situations (Hauser & Wernerfelt 1990; Roberts & Lattin 1991; Feinberg & Huber 1996; Moorthy *et al.* 1997). Optimal search has also been examined experimentally. Similar to other empirical tests of optimal decision-making, humans are found to respond to manipulated variables in ways that are directionally correct but often not precisely optimal (e.g., Meyer & Assuncao 1990).

The issue of learning is typically defined in terms of uncertainty reduction, with optimal behavior defined in terms of Bayesian updating. A great deal of research in psychology has documented the ways in which humans deviate from Bayesian learning (e.g., Grether 1980; Tversky & Koehler 1994; Gigerenzer & Hoffrage 1995; Kruschke 1996; March 1996). Bayesian learning has frequently been assumed in the normative models developed in economics and marketing, but direct empirical tests in consumer contexts have been rare (Roberts & Urban 1988; Chatterjee & Eliashberg 1990; Lippman & McCardle 1991). Instead, most consumer research on both information search and learning has been primarily descriptive and has examined cognitive models without explicit reference to optimal behavior other than to identify the key tradeoff between the cost and benefits of information acquisition.

Information Search Behavior

A common finding is that consumers engage in less than exhaustive search (Urbany *et al.* 1989), sometimes appropriately and sometimes not.

External Search. Although lack of expertise should motivate information acquisition, novices may search sparingly because they lack the knowledge required to conduct an appropriate search (Brucks 1985). Search will also be inhibited by high levels of knowledge whenever experts reasonably restrict search to the most diagnostic information available or inappropriately dismiss novel information as uninformative (Johnson & Russo 1984; Wood & Lynch 2002). Urbany *et al.* (1989) identify a worst-case scenario involving a low-search segment of consumers (the "blissfully uninformed") who admit to knowing little about how to make optimal decisions within a product class, but simultaneously express great confidence in being able to identify the best brand.

Errors in reasoning may also play a role in suboptimal search behavior. For example, consistent with the assumption of a nonlinear value function (e.g., Kahneman & Tversky 1979; Thaler 1985), consumers may perform less price search when the potential cost saving is computed on a high base price than when the same saving is computed on a low base price (Grewal & Marmorstein 1994). Consumers also may forgo choice and investigate other options when alternatives are *added* to the choice set (Tversky & Shafir 1992; Dhar 1997). More generally, expansive choice sets may prompt procrastination, which can have staggering implications for consumer welfare, such as when retirement planning is forestalled (Iyengar & Lepper 2000). Finally, consumers may overgeneralize from very limited product experience (Hoch & Deighton 1989). If the experience is negative, further sampling may be quickly but prematurely terminated.

External information search represents perhaps the most mature domain of consumer research. However, the topic has been reawakened by the development of the Internet as a search tool (see Alba *et al.* 1997). The implications for both consumer and vendor welfare are far from clear; however, preliminary evidence suggests that electronic media may enable consumers to realize greater efficiency and closer matches to preference but that the benefits are contingent on the specifics of the search environment, consumer exploitation of the medium's potential, and the vendor's ability to influence the search process (see, e.g., Ariely 2000; Johnson *et al.* 2003; Ratchford *et al.* 2003; Johnson *et al.* 2004; Diehl & Zauberman 2005). Firmer conclusions await additional research.

Internal Search. It is natural to think about search in terms of the external environment. Indeed, when the decision task is completely "stimulus-based," as in some supermarket contexts, consumers can view a relatively complete set of brands and product specifications. In other instances, however, the environment may provide scant information, thereby requiring the consumer to rely on recalled options and attributes (Alba *et al.* 1991).

Several studies have examined the role of memory phenomena in the formation of consideration sets and have produced results consistent with the basic memory literature (see Shocker *et al.* 1991 for a review). For example, Nedungadi (1990) showed that priming of a non-salient subcategory can dramatically increase choice probabilities for brands in the same subcategory; Alba and Chattopadhyay (1985, 1986) showed that brand recall can be reduced via provision of a subset of available brands, not unlike memory inhibition achieved through part-list cuing. In the larger retail environment, perceptions of product variety appear to be unaffected by substantial reductions in the number of brands carried if total space devoted to the product category is held constant and only non-favorites are deleted (Broniarczyk *et al.* 1998), a finding that is also consistent with recall-inhibition or attention-deflection processes.

Mitra and Lynch (1995) showed how the effects of advertising on memory for product information can affect price sensitivity. Advertising enhances the retrieval of comparable alternatives at the time of choice, thereby prompting greater price sensitivity (cf. Lynch & Ariely 2000). However, the content of advertising also differentiates items, essentially providing consumers with retrievable information that could justify the selection of higher priced options.

Hutchinson *et al.* (1994) developed and empirically estimated a stochastic model of brand-name recall. Retrieval time was found to be inversely related to prior usage (which presumably reflects consideration and preference), the overall presence of the products in the marketplace (similar to frequency of instantiation; Barsalou 1985), and the marketing efforts of manufacturers (e.g., amount of money spent advertising the brand). Desai and Hoyer (2000) found that consideration sets constructed from memory are large and have greater variety in familiar than unfamiliar usage situations (holding product category constant). Cowley and Mitchell (2003) found that consumers who encode information about brands in the context of a given usage situation later recall mainly brands that are appropriate for that situation but have difficulty recalling brands for a new usage situation. However, consumers who have high levels of knowledge about the product category do not exhibit this limitation.

Once a consumer has constructed a set of brands for consideration, there remains the task of making a final choice. Not all attribute information is recalled equally well, and traditional memory determinants, such as perceptual salience, repetition, cuing, rehearsal, elaboration, and interference influence the inputs into a decision (Alba & Hutchinson 1987; Soman 2001). Similarly, the decision itself may influence the type of information that is subsequently recalled. For example, attributes of chosen alternatives are preferentially recalled over attributes of unchosen alternatives (Biehal & Chakravarti 1982), and reasons that support a decision are preferentially recalled over contradictory reasons (Dellarosa & Bourne 1984).

These results notwithstanding, an interesting development in the study of memory-based decision-making is the frequent failure to observe a strong relationship between attribute recall and persuasion. A widely accepted explanation is that most judgments are made upon receipt of information. Once formed, they may be retrieved directly without reliance on memory for the attributes on which they are based. On the presumably rare occasions when an initial judgment is not generated, significant correlations between judgment and attribute recall should obtain (see Hastie & Park 1986).

Although such "judgment-referral" has been implicated in many decision contexts, consumer research has shown it to be an incomplete account of decision-making. One simple reason is that memory for product judgments is subject to the same inhibitory processes as memory for other types of information; that is, when judgments differ across multiple options, interference may reduce memory for the judgment of any particular option (Baumgardner *et al.* 1983; Keller 1991).

More important than interference, however, is the nature of the task confronting the consumer. Unlike social judgment, purchase situations frequently require consumers to make a choice among competing options rather than an assessment of a single target. A key moderator of the use of prior judgments vis-à-vis product attributes is the "diagnosticity" of the recalled information (Feldman & Lynch 1988). In some choice contexts, global judgments will not be sufficient to discriminate among alternatives. Most competing brands are attractive in some sense, and therefore the formation of preferences may require more precise inputs. Evidence suggests that when comparative judgments or choices are made and the global evaluations are not sufficiently diagnostic, attribute recall predicts preference (Chattopadhyay & Alba 1988; Lynch *et al.* 1988).

Of course, much depends on the precision of memory. When specific attributes cannot be recalled but a decision is demanded nonetheless, consumers will retrieve and use whatever information is deemed next most diagnostic. Such information may include memorable but misleading peripheral cues and abstract summaries of specific attributes (Alba *et al.* 1992).

Inference-making. Inference-making may substitute for effortful external search or compensate for failed internal search, but with the attendant danger that inferences can be erroneous and resistant to correction (cf. Johar & Simmons 2000). Consumer research on the inference process has focused primarily on the bases for product inference. Results are largely consistent with the larger body of research on human inference but also illuminate the influence of cues that are specific to product contexts. Thus, consumers engage in reconstructive, schema-based processes when unable to recall the sponsor of an advertisement or event (Johar & Pham 1999) and engage in category-based inference when trying to determine the likely benefits of a new technology (Moreau *et al.* 2001; Gregan-Paxton *et al.* 2005).

Consumer research has been particularly concerned with the manner in which consumers deal with missing attribute information. Such research possesses a degree of novelty within the larger inference literature due to the fact that missing-attribute inferences can be based on a variety of legitimate product-related rationales. The objective of consumer research has been not only to document the use of these rationales but also to establish dominance relationships when rationales conflict. Results suggest that the inferred value of a missing attribute can be based on the overall assessment of the brand (an evaluative-consistency inference), data-based inter-attribute correlations, and the amount of variance in the attribute level across brands within a product category. Also unique to the consumer context is a meta-cognitive rationale based on the manner in which markets are structured. Thus, if two brands are viable in the marketplace, a consumer might infer that a brand that is inferior on one attribute is superior on a missing attribute, simply because a dominated alternative would be forced from the market (Chernev & Carpenter 2001). Across these various rationales, however, it appears that a dominating basis for inference is the theory that ties attributes together in the consumer's world view. For example, consumers make strong inferences about product durability from warranty cues and appear to do so even when the intuition runs counter to the empirical inter-attribute correlation and other legitimate bases for inference (Broniarczyk & Alba 1994b).

Finally, an enduring question concerns the extent to which consumers generate inferences spontaneously. The record is mixed, although there are clear demonstrations of spontaneity. However, consumers also may refrain from inference, relying instead on the attributes common to the choice alternatives while rationalizing their inattention to missing information. Thus, if the option that is superior on common attributes is also missing an attribute, the missing attribute may be viewed as inconsequential; on the other hand, if the inferior option is missing an attribute, the missing information may be treated as a reason to reject it from the choice set (Kivetz & Simonson 2000). Such a tendency would be consistent with a more general bias to interpret any ambiguous information in a way that favors the option for which the consumer has an initial predisposition (Russo *et al.* 1998).

Learning and the Development of Consumer Expertise

Product exposure does not ensure the development of expertise or improvement in decision quality. We briefly discuss consumer knowledge across the broad spectrum from familiarity to true expertise. More complete reviews within the consumer context can be found in Alba and Hutchinson (1987), Hutchinson and Eisenstein (2006) and more generally Chi *et al.* (1988); Palmeri *et al.* (2004), and Shanteau and Stewart (1992).

Familiarity. Researchers in both marketing and psychology have found evidence that "mere" familiarity has a positive effect on attitudes and choices. For example, the classic mere exposure effect has been demonstrated in consumer situations involving brand names and product packages (Janiszewski 1993; see also Kunst-Wilson & Zajonc 1980; Zajonc & Markus 1982; Gordon & Holyoak 1983; Obermiller 1985). Additionally, Moore and Hutchinson (1985) found evidence that familiarity mediates the delayed positive effect of affective reactions to advertising (regardless of whether the initially affective response was positive or negative). Finally, many researchers have found that typicality generally has a positive effect on brand preferences, although preferences for novelty and moderate levels of schema incongruity have also been reported (Gordon & Holyoak 1983; Barsalou 1985; Nedungadi & Hutchinson 1985; Martindale & Moore 1988; Loken & Ward 1990; Veryzer & Hutchinson 1998).

Learning and Prediction. There is scant evidence that consumers are well informed or are rapid learners. Surveys of consumers' factual knowledge can produce disappointing results (Alba & Hutchinson 1991), and rule learning does not appear to be a particular strength (Hutton *et al.* 1986). Available evidence suggests that, as with other topics discussed thus far, failure to learn appropriate rules stems from a combination of poor logic, low motivation, and information-processing constraints.

Meyer (1987) examined consumer learning of multi-attribute rules. He found that, despite multiple learning trials, consumers were more likely to learn the quality associated with particular exemplars than the underlying attribute rule that governed quality. Consumers were also quicker to learn positive than negative exemplars. Although the use of exemplars as an optimizing strategy can be criticized (see Hutchinson & Alba 1997), exemplar heuristics are not rare and a "positive-exemplar heuristic" can be viewed as reasonable if consumers adopt a "good-enough" criterion for product choice.

A similar explanation may be provided for consumers' tendency to draw erroneous conclusions from advocacy messages (see Hoch & Deighton 1989). A brand may stake a claim to superiority by promoting an attribute it shares with its competitors and may do so with the hope that consumers are unlikely to understand that the attribute does not apply uniquely (cf. Kruschke 1996). Nonetheless, if the attribute is causal, reliance on it may result in unwarranted loyalty to the brand but may not necessarily result in a loss of welfare.

Processing constraints also may contribute to the formation of erroneous rules. Cognitive psychologists have long distinguished between analytic and holistic categorization processes (e.g., Brooks 1978). The former refers to correct categorization based (typically) on a single diagnostic attribute; the latter refers to classification based on an object's overall similarity to other category instances. Hutchinson and Alba (1991) demonstrated, however, that when meaningful product information is used to construct stimuli and salience varies significantly across attributes, classification is neither analytic nor holistic. Rather, decisions are based on a small subset of salient attributes that typically includes both diagnostic and non-diagnostic information. They also found that intentional learning exhibits more analytic classification than does incidental learning. Eisenstein and Hutchinson (2006) obtained a related result when they examined differences between learning to predict specific prices and learning to predict threshold-based price categories that were defined by decision goals. Threshold learning exhibited strong effects of attention that depended on the placement of the threshold.

Consumer learning can also be inhibited by conceptually driven processes. As in other areas of human endeavor, consumers possess strong prior beliefs about the state of the world, including beliefs about brand superiority, country-of-origin effects, and the price–quality relationship. Consumers may cling to these beliefs even in the face of contradictory data, especially when the environment imposes processing constraints. For example, independent tests report low empirical correlations between price and quality (Lichtenstein *et al.* 1991), yet consumers appear to rely heavily on price as a signal of quality, particularly when perception and recall of price and quality information is made difficult (Pechmann & Ratneshwar 1992) or when the density and presentation format of the information provide consumers with latitude to engage in confirmatory processing (Broniarczyk & Alba 1994c).

Finally, learning can be suppressed by basic inhibitory processes that, unlike the aforementioned processes, are exacerbated by the motivation to learn. Consistent with a long-established, cross-species phenomenon, learning of the predictive relationship between one product attribute and a product criterion (e.g., quality) can be "blocked" by prior learning of predictive relationship between a different attribute and the same criterion (van Osselaer & Alba 2000). If the originally learned attribute is perfectly predictive of the criterion, subsequently encountered attributes may fail to gain associative strength, particularly when consumers deliberately attempt to identify predictive cues (van Osselaer & Janiszewski 2001).

Although consumer learning can be inefficient and errorful, simple interventions can improve performance significantly. For example, the mere provision of a "consumption vocabulary," operationalized as a set of attribute labels and descriptions, can improve cue learning and preference consistency (West *et al.* 1996). Similarly, consumers who are provided evaluative criteria exhibit an enhanced sensory memory for the product and greater resistance to later attempts to distort that memory (Shapiro & Spence 2002).

Between-Groups Differences in Expertise. Consumer researchers and marketing managers have had a long-standing interest in the cognitive effects of extensive experience with specific products. In particular, whenever innovative new products are introduced, the entire population must learn about the costs and benefits of that product. Moreover, consumers differ widely in knowledge about even well-established products and brands, depending on their personal experiences. For example, one might be very knowledgeable about motorcycles but not sewing machines or about one's favorite soft drink but not the favorite of one's spouse. These differences have important implications for issues ranging from information search to product safety (cf. Chi *et al.* 1988). Thus, there is a growing interest in the areas of consumer expertise and knowledge. Alba and Hutchinson (1987) reviewed a broad spectrum of consumer and cognitive research in an attempt to characterize consumer expertise and distinguish it from product familiarity. Although the constructs are clearly related, Alba and Hutchinson define familiarity as "the number of product-related experiences that have been accumulated by the consumer" and expertise as "the ability to perform product-related tasks successfully." From this perspective, most early research in this area used measures of familiarity or ownership, whereas more recent research has included measures of expertise (Brucks 1986). Ratchford (2001) provides a complementary view of consumer expertise that uses the theory of human capital developed in economics by Gary Becker (e.g., Becker 1993). This perspective emphasizes that consumption results in "learn-by-doing" knowledge that, when treated as human capital, has predictable effects on economic behavior. For example, consumers will invest the time and effort needed to gain expertise to the extent that it produces future benefits, such as heightened satisfaction from more effective product usage or reduced search costs for future purchases.

As discussed earlier, research on external information search suggests an inverted-U relationship with consumer expertise (i.e., the highest levels of search occur at moderate levels of expertise). Expert–novice comparisons among consumers have also found expert-superiority effects in the size and structure of memory for brand names and factual information (Hutchinson 1983; Mitchell & Dacin 1996; Cowley & Mitchell 2003), the ability to match products to usage situations correctly (Mitchell & Dacin 1996; Cowley & Mitchell 2003), the ability to take advantage of mass customization in product choice (Dellaert & Stremersch 2005), the ability to use brand-specific associations rather than general brand image in evaluating products (Dillon *et al.* 2001), and the ability to predict market prices (Spence & Brucks 1997; Eisenstein & Hutchinson 2006). Similarly, a number of studies have examined how various consumer-related abilities develop during childhood (Brucks *et al.* 1988; Macklin 1996; John 1997). One finding that is common to many of these studies is that experts are able to identify the most diagnostic information for decision-making, thereby reducing their effort and increasing their accuracy. As noted, however, these benefits can be offset by diminished search activity and overconfidence (e.g., Wood & Lynch 2002).

CONSUMER DECISION-MAKING

Consumer research has focused much of its attention on how individuals make purchase decisions. There are many other types of decisions that consumers make, including what information is needed, where and when to shop prior to purchase, how to use or consume previously purchased products, and when such products are no longer needed. However, the purchase decision is central to most business applications because that transaction marks the point at which money changes hands and an effect is exerted on the buyer, the seller, and the economy as a whole.

Models of Preference and Choice

Although there are many variations, the standard model of the purchase decision is a stage model in which the consumer first recognizes a need, collects information (either from memory or from external sources), combines that information in some way to form product preferences, chooses a specific product, and finally consumes the product (thus achieving the initial goal and obtaining feedback that can be used in future decision-making). Typically the chosen product is most preferred among those available; however, in some models, memory failures, cognitive biases, or information-processing errors can result in the choice of less preferred alternatives. Need recognition, information acquisition, and consumption are often assumed to encompass a wide variety of activities that may occur over an extended period (see earlier discussions). The act of purchase, however, is typically a singular event. Thus, a very common research paradigm is to control both motivation and input information experimentally and then measure preferences or observe choice behavior (usually without consumption feedback). In many ways, this conforms to the traditional stimulus–response paradigms used in cognitive psychology. There is a fundamental difference, however. In typical cognitive tasks, the experimenter knows or defines a "correct" response a priori. For most purchase tasks, "correctness" is unknown because different individuals have different needs and goals and, therefore, value choice alternatives differently. Although some paradigms contrive methods to control such heterogeneity (e.g., by asking subjects to make a purchase for a hypothetical individual with explicitly defined values), most consumer research must include measures of individual preferences. Often, and especially in academic research, these measures provide methodological controls for testing other hypotheses of interest (e.g., factors that change preferences, affect comprehension and recall, etc.). Equally often, and especially in commercial applications, measures of preference and choice are of direct interest because they guide managerial decisions about what products and services to develop and what prices to charge.

Measuring Consumer Preference

The measurement models used for assessing consumer preferences derive from two research domains in psychology: attitude formation and psychometric analysis. In particular, fundamental measurement (Krantz *et al.* 1971), information integration (Anderson 1981), expectancy-value (Fishbein & Ajzen, 1975), and multi-attribute utility theory (Keeney & Raiffa 1976) have been highly influential, and the methods of those paradigms are often directly applied in consumer research.

Three general approaches to measuring preferences are most common. First, the survey methods of attitude and public opinion research are commonly employed to assess consumer preferences for actual or hypothetical products and consumer perceptions (or beliefs) about the attributes products possess. Preference measures are then modeled as a function of attribute perceptions and other variables using some appropriate statistical methods (e.g., Bagozzi 1982; Lilien *et al.* 1992).

The second general approach to measuring preferences is conjoint analysis. Although influenced by the classic work of Krantz and Tversky (e.g., 1971) on axiomatic foundations and of Anderson (1981) and Lynch (1985) on model-testing, marketing research has developed an extensive academic literature on the design, analysis, and validation of data from conjoint experiments. These methods have been widely applied in commercial settings to guide product development and understand how identifiable groups of consumers (often called segments) differ in product preferences (e.g., Louviere 1988; Carroll & Green 1995).

The third approach uses psychometric methods such as factor analysis, multidimensional scaling, and joint-space analysis to represent preferences among existing products as distances from an ideal product in an underlying space (Cooper 1983). As with conjoint analysis, marketing researchers began applying these methods and developing specialized versions in parallel with their development in psychology in the 1970s (e.g., Shepard *et al.* 1972; Cooper 1983). As in psychology, the psychometric methods used to uncover cognitive structure have been complemented by more experimental research on natural categories and graded structure (Nedungadi & Hutchinson 1985; Ratneshwar & Shocker, 1991; Urban *et al.* 1993; Hutchinson *et al.* 1994).

Context Effects

As a result of the widespread use of these preference scaling methods, consumer researchers have also investigated many of the context effects that have been identified in the cognitive literature. Two of these have been particularly important, not only because of their implications for models of the judgment process but also because they highlight systematic sources of measurement error that have pragmatic implications. First, there are the effects of stimulus range and frequency that were first noted by Parducci (1965; see also Gescheider 1988). The focus in this research is on the separation of the effects of "response language" from those of psychological impressions. Presumably, the latter are a more valid indicator of true preferences. To the extent that the stimulus range affects psychological impressions (even transiently), consumers are at risk to be biased in their decisions by the specific set of alternatives available. In general, consumer research supports the existence of range effects at both levels (i.e., response language and psychological impressions; see Cooke *et al.* 2004); however, these effects appear to be reduced substantially by experience (Lynch *et al.* 1991). Thus, novice consumers are at greater risk than experts (see also Alba & Hutchinson 1987).

The second important context effect that has influenced consumer researchers is preference reversal (e.g., Schkade & Johnson 1989; Tversky *et al.* 1990). The basic finding is that willingness-to-pay measures of preference (in which subjects report specific prices that create indifference between two alternatives) are systematically reversed when subjects are presented with a discrete choice. For example, the average indifference price for a high quality product compared to a low quality product priced at $50 might be $100; however, the vast majority of subjects nevertheless choose the $50 low-quality product over a $95 high-quality product. This result is problematic for both the economic theory of rational consumer behavior and commercial applications of preference measurement. In marketing, there has been considerable research on the development of measurement methods in which subjective ratings and discrete choices produce consistent and reliable estimates of preference (Louviere *et al.* 2000). In general, such convergence is possible, but researchers must be vigilant about the differences between preference and choice tasks.

Predicting Consumer Choice

In recent years, there has been a widespread trend toward collecting and modeling discrete choice data in the laboratory and the field. The impetus for this trend is simply that consumers participate in markets by making choices. Few real-world behaviors resemble the types of judgments measured by ratings scales, and research on attitude–behavior consistency cautions against taking rating scale responses at face value (Petty *et al.* 1991).

As in the case of preference modeling, consumer choice modeling has been strongly influenced by work in psychology (especially Luce 1959; Tversky 1972) and in econometrics (especially McFadden 1986). Often called the Bradley-Terry-Luce model (after independent development by Bradley & Terry 1957; Luce 1959) in the psychological literature, the *attraction model* of aggregate and individual level choice is ubiquitous. In its simplest form, the probability of choosing item x from the set of choice alternatives A is $v(x) / \Sigma_{y \in A} v(y)$, where v is a positive-valued function that represents the attractiveness of each item. There is abundant evidence in both psychology (e.g., Tversky & Sattath 1979) and consumer research (e.g., Kahn *et al.* 1987) that this model fails to account for key aspects of both aggregate- and individual-level choice. In particular, the model exhibits the formal property of independence from irrelevant alternatives. (Often abbreviated IIA, this property requires that the addition of one or more choice alternatives decreases the choice probabilities for existing alternatives by a constant percentage.) However, it is frequently observed that a new choice alternative draws its share disproportionately from alternatives that are similar to it, as when a conservative Independent Party candidate hurts the Republican candidate more than the Democratic candidate in an election. This is called the *similarity effect* and was first described by Debreu (1960). A wide array of more sophisticated models has been developed in a number of disciplines to account for these and other known choice phenomena. It is beyond the scope of this chapter to review these models; however, excellent reviews of the consumer choice literature can be found in the

McFadden (1986), Meyer and Kahn (1991), Louviere *et al.* (2000), and Chakravarti *et al.* (2005).

Despite its failure as a complete model of choice, the attraction model is often a good and easily estimated approximation. As such, it has proved to be a widely used "work-horse" as part of more complex models in need of a decision-making component. The exponential, or multinomial logit, version of the attraction model has proved especially useful in this regard, as it has in cognitive models of memory and classification (see, e.g., Nosofsky 1984), mainly because of its mathematical and statistical properties. The most influential application of this model in consumer research is the analysis of scanner panel data by Guadagni and Little (1983). (Scanner panel data are collected from samples of consumers who, for a fee, allow all of their food store purchases to be tracked electronically.) These researchers examined purchases of regular ground coffee over a two-year period and showed that a multinomial logit model that incorporated price, promotion, and brand loyalty (as measured by past purchases) provided an excellent predictive model of future purchases, including conditions of changed price and promotion. The model is very rudimentary from a cognitive perspective and can be thought of as a simple response model for stimuli defined by price and promotion plus a simple learning component (similar to associative reinforcement models such as described by Rescorla and Wagner 1972 and Kruschke 1996). In fact, more recent and sophisticated statistical models that distinguish between structural state dependence, habit persistence, and unobserved heterogeneity are relatively simple from a cognitive perspective (e.g., Roy *et al.* 1996; see also Hutchinson 1986; Camerer & Ho 1999). However, they establish important benchmarks for testing cognitively based models with observations of real-choice behavior in complex environments.

Methodologically, the explicit incorporation of population heterogeneity into models of choice behavior has proven to be particularly important and is often ignored in cognitive research (although there are certainly exceptions). The basic insight from a wide variety of research is that observed market-level behavior and estimated choice model parameters can strongly suggest dynamic properties, such as those discussed earlier, that are spurious or distorted when heterogeneity in the population is ignored (e.g., Roy *et al.* 1996; Hutchinson *et al.* 2000).

Choice Context Effects

Virtually all quantitative models of choice satisfy a formal property called *regularity* (i.e., choice probabilities can only decrease or remain unchanged whenever an alternative is added to the choice set). However, consumer researchers have found several manipulations of the stimulus context that result in systematic violations of regularity. The first of these, *attraction* or *decoy effects*, arises when a two-item choice set is expanded by the addition of a third item that is dominated by one, but not the other, of the original two items (Huber *et al.* 1982). For example, the original set might contain items that differ in price and quality such that the higher quality item is also higher in price (i.e., neither item dominates the other). If a third item is added that is similar to the high-price item but slightly higher in price and slightly lower in quality, then a decoy effect arises. Few subjects choose the new item because it is dominated by the original high-price item. However, the original high-price item is chosen more frequently when the third item is present than when it is absent – a violation of regularity. The explanation of this effect is still a matter of intense debate, but there can be no doubt that it is a serious problem for traditional models of choice that are not context-sensitive (see Heath & Chatterjee 1995).

More recently, Simonson (1989; Simonson & Tversky 1992) has demonstrated violations of IIA and regularity without using dominated alternatives. As an example, assume that most people choose the lower priced item in the two-item set described earlier. If a third item is added that is higher in price and quality than the original high-price item by an amount that is approximately equal to that which separated the original two, the original high-price item benefits significantly and often in violation of regularity. This result has been dubbed the *compromise effect* because the original high-price item looks like a mid-price item in the new choice set. Again, the explanation is controversial; however, Tversky and Simonson (1993) have developed a model in which loss-aversion is the main explanatory principle.

Heuristics and Biases in Decision-making

The previous section describes how the models and methods of cognitive psychology have been applied and extended to understand consumer preferences and choices among options that are known with certainty. In this section, we briefly review aspects of the large, multidisciplinary literature on risky decision-making that have most influenced consumer research.

The Influence of Behavioral Decision Research

There are many excellent reviews of behavioral decision research (e.g., Payne *et al.* 1993; Camerer 1995; Mellers *et al.* 1998), and therefore we will not attempt to provide a comprehensive summary here. Rather, we will describe the ways in which this research has affected consumer research. That consumers are "boundedly rational" (i.e., limited in their ability to conform to the strategic behavior of economic theory) has been widely accepted in marketing for a long time as a result of both academic research (e.g., Simon 1955; Tversky & Kahneman 1974) and practitioner observations about market phenomena (e.g., Howard & Sheth 1969; Krugman 1965). Moreover, much of our earlier discussion of the cognitive antecedents of decision-making illustrate the many cognitive factors that contribute to these limitations. One articulation of this perspective is the adaptive decision-making framework of Payne *et al.* (1993). Drawing on work in cognitive psychology, organizational behavior, and consumer research, these authors propose that choices in the marketplace result from a process of strategy selection. Consumers are able to use a wide variety of strategies to make any given decision. These strategies range from conscious, explicit rules to unconscious, automatic processes that serve as decision heuristics. The strategies vary in the effort they require and the accuracy with which they achieve decision objectives. Consumers choose among strategies based on their assessment of the effort–accuracy tradeoff. This choice may not be strictly optimal, but it is assumed to generally be adaptive and intelligent (Payne *et al.* 1993). Luce *et al.* (2001) have extended this approach in an important way by showing that, in addition to cognitive effort, emotional factors contribute to decision strategy selection (see also Loewenstein *et al.* 2001).

In particular, they show that decisions involving tradeoffs among desirable benefits are emotionally difficult for consumers, who respond either by working harder (problem-focused coping) or avoiding the decision (emotion-focused coping). A key implication of this general approach is that as decision tasks become more complex or emotionally stressful, simplifying strategies are more likely to be adopted. Simpler strategies are generally less accurate and more susceptible to the biasing effects of task and context variables.

Within the adaptive decision-making framework, the most influential work has been that of Simon (1955; Newell & Simon 1972) and Tversky and Kahneman (1974). Many early (and still widely used) models of consumer behavior used Simon's problem-solving framework (e.g., Bettman, 1979; Howard & Sheth 1969). Similarly, many consumer-oriented tasks have been used to replicate and extend results on mental accounting (Thaler 1985, discussed earlier), agenda effects (Kahn *et al.* 1987), and loss-aversion (Hardie *et al.* 1993; see next section). In fact, these effects can be viewed as a more theoretical account of well-known marketing practices in advertising to "position" a product by influencing the relative salience of attribute information.

Prospect Theory

Arguably, the most influential contribution from decision research on current consumer research has been prospect theory (Kahneman & Tversky 1979; Tversky & Kahneman 1992). This model has two key components that differentiate it from expected utility models (and subjective expected utility models): a weighting function that transforms probabilities into decision weights (which overweights small probabilities, underweights large probabilities, and does not conform to the algebra of probability), and a value function for outcomes that is referent dependent (i.e., piecewise separated by a reference point into gains and losses) and loss-averse (i.e., losses valued more than objectively equivalent gains).

Evidence supporting the prospect theory weighting function has been found in consumer markets for insurance (Johnson *et al.* 1993) and the perceived risks of products and services (Slovic *et al.* 1982; Johnson 2004). Johnson *et al.* showed that the factors known to create overestimation in the perceived frequencies of risk often lead to associated increases in the purchase of insurance or in the prices consumers are willing to pay for insurance. A dramatic real-world example of these effects occurred in 1990 when media attention to a (dubious) prediction led to a threefold increase in the sales of earthquake insurance over the previous year, with most sales occurring in the two months prior to the predicted quake (which did not occur).

In contrast to the relatively small amount of consumer research focused on the weighting function, an enormous amount of research has been focused on the value function. For example, the most common explanation given for the compromise effect discussed earlier is loss-aversion (e.g., Tversky & Simonson 1993; Kivetz *et al.* 2004). Loss-aversion is also the most frequent explanation of the widely observed endowment effect discussed earlier (Kahneman *et al.* 1990; Tversky & Kahneman 1991; Novemsky & Kahneman 2005). The essence of the effect is that the value of a possession is perceived as much higher for sellers than for buyers because sellers see it as a loss and buyers see it as a gain. Buyer–seller discrepancies have been observed in the laboratory for a wide variety of goods and services. Moreover, a number of robust real-world phenomena have been similarly attributed to loss-aversion. In behavioral finance, the famous puzzle of the equity premium has been attributed to loss-aversion. The equity premium puzzle arises from the fact that for most of the twentieth century stock returns were about 8 per cent higher than bond returns. Qualitatively, such an outcome is expected, based on standard economic theory because stocks are riskier than bonds and most investors are risk-averse to some degree. The puzzle is that the degree of risk-aversion required to account for the 8 per cent difference is absurdly high. Asset pricing models that incorporate loss-aversion are able to explain the puzzle (although the explanation is complex; see Camerer 2000; Barberis & Thaler 2003, for reviews of prospect theory explanations of anomalies in financial markets).

Despite the widespread adoption of loss-aversion as an explanation for many types of consumer behavior in the lab and real markets, several major problems have been identified that challenge loss-aversion as a fundamental property of all purchase transactions. First, loss-aversion is not always observed. For example, the similarity between buyers' price bids and choice equivalents suggests that buyers do not experience loss-aversion for the money they are bidding for a good (otherwise, these prices would be significantly lower than their choice equivalents). This result led Tversky and Kahneman (1991) to hypothesize that there is no loss-aversion for items given up in "routine" transactions, including the riskless purchase of goods with money. This hypothesis and the empirical results for routine transactions have proven controversial, however (see Bateman *et al.* 2005). Recently, Novemsky and Kahneman (2005) reported a carefully constructed set of experiments containing both riskless and risky decisions that test the boundaries of loss-aversion. They conclude that there is no loss-aversion when goods are exchanged "as intended." Of course, this argument requires a yet-to-be-developed model of consumer intentions, but it is certainly meant to include routine purchases. A seeming contradiction to this conclusion is found in the results of Hardie *et al.* (1993), who modeled consumer scanner panel data for orange juice purchases and found that, given reasonable definitions for reference points, there were larger coefficients for increases in prices and decreases in quality than for changes in the opposite direction, an outcome that supports loss-aversion for routine transactions. However, Bell and Lattin (2000) analyzed the same data (and similar data for 11 other product categories) and showed than most of the estimated loss-aversion for prices was due to heterogeneity. Price-sensitive consumers tend to buy lower-priced products than less sensitive consumers; consequently, they have lower reference prices, and most prices they face are perceived as losses. Conversely, consumers with low price sensitivity have higher reference prices and therefore face prices that are mostly perceived as gains. Thus, when the model estimates separate components for losses and gains it confounds the value function with differences between consumers in price sensitivity. When Bell and Lattin explicitly modeled heterogeneity in price sensitivity, loss-aversion was dramatically reduced or eliminated; however, a significant effect remained for seven of 12 products.

Overall, it is difficult to reach a general conclusion about loss-aversion for money in routine purchases. Heterogeneity may have exaggerated these effects, but they still appear to be present for some products. Novemsky and Kahneman (2005) present compelling evidence for no loss-aversion in buying, but are forced to speculate about differences in subject pools (i.e., heterogeneity) to reconcile their results with those of Bateman *et al.* (2005). Finally, although not designed to test loss-aversion, per se, the previously noted findings of Hsee *et al.* (2003; see also van Osselaer *et al.* 2004) have shown that the medium of immediate payments (e.g., frequent-flyer miles or bonus points that are later converted to money, goods, or services) determines decisions more than final outcomes. Even more than money, the intermediate payment mechanisms in these experiments are devoid of intrinsic value. This result runs counter to the idea that people do not think of possessing and consuming money in the same way they think of other, more tangible items – one reason given for an absence aversion for buying. Because "routine purchases" represent such a large amount of actual consumer behavior, expanding our knowledge of the nuances and boundaries of loss-aversion is an important issue for both theoretical and applied research in decision-making.

Another challenge to prospect theory and loss-aversion can be found in recent research on the compromise effects discussed earlier. Kivetz *et al.* (2004) showed that a model based on contextual concavity is as good or better than a model based on loss-aversion. Contextual concavity postulates that all attribute values are viewed as gains relative to the lowest value present in the immediate choice context and that the value function is concave. Loss-aversion models typically put the reference point in the middle of the range of stimulus values and thus create a similar type of overall concavity. The differentiating aspects of loss (e.g., convex losses) seem to hurt rather than help in fitting the data.

CONCLUSIONS AND FUTURE DIRECTIONS

Our overly simple model of consumer behavior argues that consumers are exposed to information, react to information, and make decisions based on that information. Our objective has been to illustrate the cognitive influences on a category of human endeavor that is an integral part of everyday life. In addition, we have tried to describe the points of overlap between cognitive psychology and consumer research. In some cases, such as in the study of memory, consumer research has contextualized some basic effects first reported in the cognitive literature; in other cases, such as in the study of information search, the inspiration runs in the opposite direction; in yet others, such as in the study of loyalty and preference, the influence is, or should be, mutual.

Many emerging issues promise an exciting future for consumer research. A sampling includes the roles of metacognition (Alba & Hutchinson 2000; see also Schwarz 2004, and commentaries), consciousness (Bargh 2002; Dijksterhuis *et al.* 2005, and commentaries), and the interplay of deliberative and visceral forces (Loewenstein 2001). The influence of cognitive psychology on consumer behavior shows no sign of abating.

REFERENCES

Alba, J. W. (2002). Frequency effects in consumer decision-making. In P. Sedlmeier & T. Betsch (eds.), *Etc.: Frequency Processing and Cognition*. (pp. 259–270). New York: Oxford University Press.

Alba, J. W. & Chattopadhyay, A. (1985). Effects of context and part-category cues on recall of competing brands. *Journal of Marketing Research*, *22*, 340–349.

Alba, J. W. & Chattopadhyay, A. (1986). Salience effects in brand recall. *Journal of Marketing Research*, *23*, 363–369.

Alba, J. W. & Hutchinson, J. W. (1987). Dimensions of consumer expertise. *Journal of Consumer Research*, *13*, 411–454.

Alba, J. W. & Hutchinson, J. W. (1991). Public policy implications of consumer knowledge. In P. N. Bloom (ed.), *Advances in Marketing and Public Policy* (Vol. 2, pp. 1–39). Greenwich, CT: JAI Press.

Alba, J. W. & Hutchinson, J. W. (2000). Knowledge calibration: what consumers know and what they think they know. *Journal of Consumer Research*, *27*, 123–156.

Alba, J. W., Hutchinson, J. W. & Lynch, J. G. Jr. (1991). Memory and decision-making. In T. S. Robertson & H. H. Kassarjian (eds.), *Handbook of Consumer Behavior* (pp. 1–49). Englewood Cliffs NJ: Prentice-Hall.

Alba, J., Lynch, J., Weitz, B. *et al.* (1997). Interactive home shopping: consumer, retailer, and manufacturer incentives to participate in electronic marketplaces. *Journal of Marketing*, *61*, 38–53.

Alba, J. W., Marmorstein, H. & Chattopadhyay, A. (1992). Transitions in preference over time: the effects of memory on message persuasiveness. *Journal of Marketing Research*, *29*, 406–416.

Anderson, N. H. (1981). *Foundations of Information Integration Theory*. New York: Academic Press.

Ariely, D. (2000). Controlling the information flow: effects on consumers' decision-making and preference. *Journal of Consumer Research*, *27*, 233–248.

Arkes, H. R. & Blumer, C. (1985). The psychology of sunk cost. *Organizational Behavior and Human Decision Processes*, *35*, 124–140.

Bagozzi, R. P. (1982). A field investigation of causal relations among cognitions, affect, intentions, and behavior. *Journal of Marketing Research*, *19*, 562–584.

Barberis, N. & Thaler, R. (2003) A survey of behavioral finance. In G. M. Constanides, M. Harris & R. Stulz (eds.), *Handbook of the Economics of Finance* (pp. 1053–1123). Greenwich, CT: JAI Press.

Bargh, J. A. (2002). Losing consciousness: automatic influences on consumer judgment, behavior, and motivation. *Journal of Consumer Research*, *29*, 280–285.

Barsalou, L. W. (1985). Ideals, central tendency, and frequency of instantiation as determinants of graded structure. *Journal of Experimental Psychology: Learning, Memory, and Cognition*, *11*, 629–654.

Bateman, I., Kahneman, D., Munro, A. *et al.* (2005). Testing competing models of loss aversion: an adversarial collaboration. *Journal of Public Economics*, *89*, 1561–1580.

Baumgardner, M. H., Leippe, M. R., Ronis, D. L. & Greenwald, A. G. (1983). In search of reliable persuasion effects: II. Associative inference and persistence of persuasion in a message-dense environment. *Journal of Personality and Social Psychology*, *45*, 524–537.

Becker, G. (1993). *Human Capital*. Chicago: University of Chicago Press.

Bell, D. R. & Lattin, J. M. (2000). Looking for loss aversion in scanner panel data: the confounding effect of price response heterogeneity. *Marketing Science*, *19*, 185–200.

Bettman, J. R. (1979). *An Information Processing Theory of Consumer Choice*. Reading, MA: Addison-Wesley.

Bettman, J. R. & Sujan, M. (1987). Effects of framing on evaluation of comparable and noncomparable alternatives by expert and novice consumers. *Journal of Consumer Research*, *14*, 141–154.

Biehal, G. & Chakravarti, D. (1982). Information-presentation format and learning goals as determinants of consumers' memory retrieval and choice processes. *Journal of Consumer Research*, *8*, 431–441.

Bolton, L. E., Warlop, L. & Alba, J. W. (2003). Consumer perceptions of price (un)fairness. *Journal of Consumer Research*, *29*, 474–491.

Bottomly, P. A. & Holden, S. J. S. (2001). Do we really know how consumers evaluate brand extensions? Empirical generalizations based on secondary analysis of eight studies. *Journal of Marketing Research*, *38*, 494–500.

Boulding, W., Morgan, R. & Staelin, R. (1997). Pulling the plug to stop the new product drain. *Journal of Marketing Research*, *34*, 164–176.

Bradley, R. A. & Terry, M. E. (1957). Rand analysis of incomplete blocks designs, I: the method of paired comparisons. *Biometrika*, *39*, 324–345.

Braun, K. A. (1999). Postexperience advertising effects on consumer memory. *Journal of Consumer Research*, *25*, 319–334.
Broniarczyk, S. M. & Alba, J. W. (1994a). The importance of the brand in brand extension. *Journal of Marketing Research*, *31*, 214–228.
Broniarczyk, S. M. & Alba, J. W. (1994b). The role of consumers' intuitions in inference making. *Journal of Consumer Research*, *21*, 393–407.
Broniarczyk, S. M. & Alba, J. W. (1994c). Theory versus data in prediction and correlation tasks. *Organizational Behavior and Human decision Processes*, *57*, 117–139.
Broniarczyk, S. M., Hoyer, W. D. & McAlister, L. (1998). Consumers' perceptions of the assortment offered in a grocery category: the impact of item reduction. *Journal of Marketing Research*, *35*, 166–176.
Brooks, L. (1978). Nonanalytic concept formation and memory for instances. In E. Rosch & B. B. Lloyd (eds.), *Cognition and Categorization* (pp. 169–211). Mahwah, NJ: Lawrence Erlbaum Associates.
Brucks, M. (1985). The effects of product class knowledge on information search behavior. *Journal of Consumer Research*, *12*, 1–16.
Brucks, M. (1986). A typology of consumer knowledge content. In R. J. Lutz (ed.), *Advances in Consumer Research* (Vol. 13, pp. 58–63). Provo, UT: Association for Consumer Research.
Brucks, M., Armstrong, G. M. & Goldberg, M. E. (1988). Children's use of cognitive defenses against television advertising: a cognitive response approach. *Journal of Consumer Research*, *14*, 471–482.
Burke, R. R. & Srull, T. K. (1988). Competitive interference and consumer memory for advertising. *Journal of Consumer Research*, *15*, 55–68.
Camerer, C. F. (1995). Individual decision-making. In J. Kagel & A. E. Roth (eds.), *Handbook of Experimental Economics* (pp. 587–703). Princeton, NJ: Princeton University Press.
Camerer, C. F. (2000). Prospect theory in the wild: evidence from the field. In D. Kahneman & A. Tversky (eds.), *Choices, Values, and Frames* (pp. 288–300). New York: Cambridge University Press/Russell Sage Foundation.
Camerer, C. & Ho, T.-H. (1999). Experience-weighted attraction learning in games: a unifying approach, *Econometrica*, *67*, 827–874.
Carmon, Z. & Ariely, D. (2000). Focusing on the forgone: how value can appear so different to buyers and sellers. *Journal of Consumer Research*, *27*, 360–370.
Carroll, J. D. & Green, P. E. (1995). Psychometric methods in marketing research: Part I, conjoint analysis. *Journal of Marketing Research*, *32*, 385–391.
Chakravarti, D., Sinha, A. R. & Kim, J. (2005). Choice research: a wealth of perspectives. *Marketing Letters, 16*, 173–182.
Chatterjee, R. & Eliashberg, J. (1990). The innovation diffusion process in a heterogeneous population: a micromodeling approach. *Management Science*, *36*, 1057–1079.
Chattopadhyay, A. & Alba, J. W. (1988). The situational importance of recall and inference in consumer decision-making. *Journal of Consumer Research*, *15*, 1–12.
Chernev, A. & Carpenter, G. S. (2001). The role of market efficiency intuitions in consumer choice: a case of compensatory inferences. *Journal of Marketing Research*, *38*, 349–361.
Chi, M. T. H., Glaser, R. & Farr, M. J. (1988). *The Nature of Expertise*. Hillsdale, NJ: Lawrence Erlbaum Associates.
Cooke, A. D. J., Janiszewski, C., Cunha, M. *et al.* (2004). Stimulus context and the formation of consumer ideals. *Journal of Consumer Research*, *31*, 112–123.
Cooper, L. (1983). A review of multidimensional scaling in marketing research. *Applied Psychological Measurement*, *7*, 427–450.
Cowley, E. & Janus, E. (2004). Not necessarily better but certainly different: a limit to the advertising misinformation effect on memory. *Journal of Consumer Research*, *31*, 229–223.
Cowley, E. & Mitchell, A. A. (2003). The moderating effect of product knowledge on the learning and organization of product information. *Journal of Consumer Research*, *30*, 443–454.
Cripps, J. D. & Meyer, R. J. (1994). Heuristics and biases in timing the replacement of durable products. *Journal of Consumer Research*, *21*, 304–318.
Darby, M. R. & Karni, E. (1973). Free competition and the optimal amount of fraud. *Journal of Law and Economics*, *16*, 66–86.

Debreu, G. (1960). Review of R. D. Luce, individual choice behavior: a theoretical analysis. *American Economic Review*, *50*, 186–188.

Deighton, J. (1984). The interaction of advertising and evidence. *Journal of Consumer Research*, *11*, 763–770.

Dellaert, B. G. C. & Stremersch, S. (2005). Marketing mass-customized products: striking a balance between utility and complexity. *Journal of Marketing Research*, *42*, 219–227.

Dellarosa, D. & Bourne, L. E. Jr (1984). Decisions and memory: differential retrievability of consistent and contradictory evidence. *Journal of Verbal Learning and Verbal Behavior*, *23*, 669–682.

Desai, K. K. & Hoyer, W. D. (2000). Descriptive characteristics of memory-based consideration sets: influence of usage occasion frequency and usage location familiarity. *Journal of Consumer Research*, *27*, 309–323.

Dhar, R. (1997). Consumer preferences for a no-choice option. *Journal of Consumer Research*, *24*, 215–231.

Diehl, K. & Zauberman, G. (2005). Searching ordered sets: evaluations from sequences under search. *Journal of Consumer Research*, *31*, 824–832.

Dijksterhuis, A., Smith, P. K., van Baaren, R. B. & Wigboldus, D. H. J. (2005). The unconscious consumer: effects of environment on consumer behavior. *Journal of Consumer Psychology*, *15*, 193–202.

Dillon, W. R., Madden, T. J., Kirmani, A. & Mukherjee, S. (2001). Understanding what's in a brand rating: a model for assessing brand and attribute effects and their relationship to brand equity. *Journal of Marketing Research*, *38*, 415–429.

Eisenstein, E. & Hutchinson, J. W. (2006). Action-based learning: goals and attention in the acquisition of market knowledge. *Journal of Marketing Research*, *43*, 244–258.

Feinberg, F. M. & Huber, J. (1996). A theory of cutoff formation under imperfect information. *Management Science*, *42*, 65–84.

Feldman, J. M. & Lynch, J. G. Jr (1988). Self-generated validity and other effects of measurement on belief, attitude, intention, and behavior. *Journal of Applied Psychology*, *73*, 421–435.

Fishbein, M. & Ajzen, I. (1975). *Belief, Attitude, Intention, and Behavior: An Introduction to Theory and Research*. Reading, MA: Addison-Wesley.

Fournier, S. (1998). Consumers and their brands: developing relationship theory in consumer research. *Journal of Consumer Research*, *24*, 343–373.

Gescheider, G. A. (1988). Psychophysical scaling. *Annual Review of Psychology*, *39*, 169–200.

Gigerenzer, G. & Hoffrage, U. (1995). How to improve bayesian reasoning without instruction: frequency formats. *Psychological Review*, *102*, 684–704.

Gordon, P. C. & Holyoak, K. J. (1983). Implicit learning and generalization of the "mere exposure" effect. *Journal of Personality and Social Psychology*, *45*, 492–500.

Gourville, J. T. (1998). Pennies-a-day: the effect of temporal reframing on transaction evaluation. *Journal of Consumer Research*, *24*, 395–408.

Gourville, J. T. & Soman, D. (1998). Payment depreciation: the behavioral effects of temporally separating payments from consumption. *Journal of Consumer Research*, *25*, 160–174.

Gregan-Paxton, J., Hoeffler, S. & Zhao, M. (2005). When categorization is ambiguous: factors that facilitate the use of a multiple category inference strategy. *Journal of Consumer Psychology*, *15*, 127–140.

Grether, D. M. (1980). Bayes rule as a descriptive model: the representativeness heuristic. *Quarterly Journal of Economics*, *95*, 537–557.

Grewal, D. & Marmorstein, H. (1994). Market price variation, perceived price variation, and consumers' price search decisions for durable goods. *Journal of Consumer Research*, *21*, 453–460.

Guadagni, P. M. & Little, J. D. C. (1983). A logit model of brand choice calibrated on scanner data. *Marketing Science*, *2*, 203–238.

Ha, Y.-W. & Hoch, S. J. (1989). Ambiguity, processing strategy, and advertising-evidence interactions. *Journal of Consumer Research*, *16*, 354–360.

Hastie, R. & Park, B. (1986). The relationship between memory and judgment depends on whether the judgment task is memory-based or on-line. *Psychological Review*, *93*, 258–268.

Hardie, B. G. S., Johnson, E. J. & Fader, P. S. (1993). Modeling loss aversion and reference dependence effects on brand choice. *Marketing Science*, *12*, 378–394.

Hauser, J. R. & Wernerfelt, B. (1990). An evaluation cost model of consideration sets. *Journal of Consumer Research*, *16*, 393–408.

Hawkins, S. A., Hoch, S. J. & Meyers-Levy, J. (2001). Low-involvement learning: repetition and coherence in familiarity and belief. *Journal of Consumer Psychology*, *11*, 1–11.

Heath, T. B. & Chatterjee, S. (1995). Asymmetric decoy effects on lower quality versus higher quality brands: meta-analytic and experimental evidence. *Journal of Consumer Research*, *22*, 268–284.

Hoch, S. J. & Deighton, J. (1989). Managing what consumers learn from experience. *Journal of Marketing*, *53*, 1–20.

Hoch, S. J. & Ha, H.-Y. (1986). Consumer learning: advertising and the ambiguity of product experience. *Journal of Consumer Research*, *13*, 221–233.

Hoegg, J. & Alba, J. W. (2006). Linguistic framing of sensory experience: there is some accounting for taste. In T. M. Lowrey (ed.), *Psycholinguistic Phenomena in Marketing Communications*. Mahwah, NJ: Lawrence Erlbaum Associates.

Howard, J. A. & Sheth, J. N. (1969). *The Theory of Buyer Behavior*. New York: John Wiley & Sons.

Hsee, C. K., Yu, F., Zhang, J. & Zhang, Y. (2003). Medium maximization. *Journal of Consumer Research*, *30*, 1–14.

Huber, J., Payne, J. W. & Puto, C. (1982). Adding asymmetrically dominated alternatives: violations of regularity and the similarity hypothesis. *Journal of Consumer Research*, *9*, 90–98.

Hutchinson, J. W. (1983). Expertise and the structure of free recall. In R. P. Bagozzi and A. M. Tybout (eds.), *Advances in Consumer Research* (Vol. 10, pp. 585–589). Provo, UT: Association for Consumer Research.

Hutchinson, J. W. (1986). Discrete attribute models of brand switching. *Marketing Science*, *5*, 350–371.

Hutchinson, J. W. & Alba, J. W. (1991). Ignoring irrelevant information: situational determinants of consumer learning. *Journal of Consumer Research*, *18*, 325–345.

Hutchinson, J. W. & Alba, J. W. (1997). Heuristics and biases in the "eye-balling" of data: the effects of context on intuitive correlation assessment. *Journal of Experimental Psychology: Learning, Memory, and Cognition*, *23*, 591–621.

Hutchinson, J. W. & E. M. Eisenstein (2006). Consumer learning and expertise. In C. P. Haugtvedt, P. Herr & F. Kardes (eds.), *Handbook of Consumer Psychology*. Mahwah, NJ: Lawrence Erlbaum Associates.

Hutchinson, J. W., Kamakura, W. & Lynch, J. G. (2000). Unobserved heterogeneity as an alternative explanation for "reversal" effects in behavioral research. *Journal of Consumer Research*, *27*, 324–344.

Hutchinson, J. W. & Meyer, R. J. (1994). Dynamic decision-making: optimal policies and actual behavior in sequential choice problems. *Marketing Letters*, *5*, 369–382.

Hutchinson, J. W., Raman, K. & Mantrala, M. (1994). Finding choice alternatives in memory: probability models of brand name recall. *Journal of Marketing Research*, *31*, 441–461.

Hutton, R. B., Mauser, G. A., Filiatrault, P. & Ahtola, O. T. (1986). Effects of cost-related feedback on consumer knowledge and consumption behavior: a field experimental approach. *Journal of Consumer Research*, *13*, 327–336.

Inman, J. J., McAlister, L. & Hoyer, W. D. (1990). Promotion signal: proxy for a price cut? *Journal of Consumer Research*, *17*, 74–81.

Iyengar, S. S. & Lepper, M. R. (2000). When choice is demotivating: can one desire too much of a good thing? *Journal of Personality and Social Psychology*, *79*, 995–1006.

Jacoby, J. (1971). A model for multi-brand loyalty. *Journal of Advertising Research*, *11*, 25–30.

Janiszewski, C. (1993). Preattentive mere exposure effects. *Journal of Consumer Research*, *20*, 376–392.

Johar, G. V. & Pham, M. T. (1999). Relatedness, prominence, and constructive sponsor identification. *Journal of Marketing Research*, *36*, 299–312.

Johar, G. V. & Simmons, C. J. (2000). The use of concurrent disclosures to correct invalid inference. *Journal of Consumer Research*, *26*, 307–322.

John, D. R. (1997). Out of the mouth of babes: what children can tell us. In M. Brucks & D. MacInnis (eds.), *Advances in Consumer Research* (Vol. 24, pp. 1–5). Provo, UT: Association for Consumer Research.

Johnson, E. J. (2004). *Rediscovering risk. Journal of Public Policy & Marketing, 23*, 8743–9156.

Johnson, E. J., Bellman, S. & Lohse, G. L. (2003). Cognitive lock-in and the power law of practice. *Journal of Marketing*, *67*, 62–75.

Johnson, E. J., Hershey, J., Meszaros, J. & Kunruether, H. (1993). Framing, probability distortion and insurance decisions. *Journal of Risk & Uncertainty*, *7*, 35–51.

Johnson, E. J., Moe, W. W., Fader, P. S. *et al.* (2004). On the depth and dynamics of online search behavior. *Management Science*, *50*, 299–308.

Johnson, E. J. & Russo, E. (1984). Product familiarity and learning new information. *Journal of Consumer Research*, *11*, 542–550.

Kahn, B., Moore, W. M. & Glazer, R. (1987). Experiments in constrained choice. *Journal of Consumer Research*, *14*, 96–113.

Kahneman, D., Knetsch, J. L. & Thaler, R. (1986). Fairness as a constraint on profit seeking: entitlements in the market. *American Economic Review*, *76*, 728–741.

Kahneman, D., Knetsch, J. L. & Thaler, R. H. (1990). Experimental tests of the endowment effect and the coarse theorem. *Journal of Political Economy*, *98*, 1325–1348.

Kahneman, D. & Tversky, A. (1979). Prospect theory: an analysis of decision under risk. *Econometrica*, *47*, 263–291.

Kardes, F. R. & Kalyanaram, G. (1992). Order-of-entry effects on consumer memory and judgment: an information integration perspective. *Journal of Marketing Research*, *29*, 343–357.

Keeney, R. L. & Raiffa, H. (1976). *Decisions with Multiple Objectives: Preferences and Value Tradeoffs*. New York: John Wiley & Sons.

Keller, K. L. (1991). Memory and evaluation effects in competitive advertising environments. *Journal of Consumer Research*, *17*, 463–476.

Keller, K. L. (2003). Brand synthesis: the multidimensionality of brand knowledge. *Journal of Consumer Research*, *29*, 595–600.

Kivetz, R. & Simonson, I. (2000). The effects of incomplete information on consumer choice. *Journal of Marketing Research*, *37*, 427–448.

Kivetz, R., Netzer, O. & Srinivasan, V. (2004) Alternative models for capturing the compromise effect. *Journal of Marketing Research*, *41*, 237–257.

Krantz, D. H., Luce, R. D., Suppes, P. & Tversky, A. (1971). *Foundations of Measurement* (Vol. 1). New York: Academic Press.

Krantz, D. H. & Tversky, A. (1971). Conjoint measurement analysis of composition rules in psychology. *Psychological Review*, *78*, 151–169.

Krishnan, H. S. & Chakravarti, D. (2003). A process analysis of the effects of humorous advertising executions on brand claims memory. *Journal of Consumer Psychology*, *13*, 230–245.

Krugman, H. E. (1965). The impact of television advertising: learning without involvement. *Public Opinion Quarterly*, *39*, 349–356.

Kruschke, J. K. (1996). Base rates in category learning. *Journal of Experimental Psychology: Learning, Memory, and Cognition*, *22*, 2–26.

Kunst-Wilson, W. R. & Zajonc, R. B. (1980). Affective discrimination of stimuli that cannot be recognized. *Science*, *207*, 557–558.

Lattin, J. M. & Bucklin, R. E. (1989). Reference effects of price and promotion on brand choice behavior. *Journal of Marketing Research*, *26*, 299–310.

Law, S. (2002). Can repeating a claim lead to memory confusion? The effects of claim similarity and concurrent repetition. *Journal of Marketing Research*, *39*, 366–378.

Law, S., Hawkins, S. A. & Craik, I. M. (1998). Repetition-induced belief in the elderly: rehabilitating age-related memory deficits. *Journal of Consumer Research*, *25*, 91–107.

Levin, I. P. & Gaeth, G. J. (1988). How consumers are affected by the framing of attribute information before and after consuming the product. *Journal of Consumer Research*, *15*, 374–378.

Lichtenstein, D. R. & Burton, S. & Karson, J. (1991). The effect of semantic cues on consumer perceptions of reference price ads. *Journal of Consumer Research*, *18*, 380–391.

Lilien, G. L., Kotler, P. & Moorthy, K. S. (1992). *Marketing Models*. Englewood Cliffs, NJ: Prentice-Hall.

Lippman, S. A. & McCardle, K. (1991). Uncertain search: a model of search among technologies of uncertain values. *Management Science, 37,* 1474–1490.

Loewenstein, G. (2001). The creative destruction of decision research. *Journal of Consumer Research, 28,* 499–505.

Loewenstein, G., Hsee, C. K., Weber, E. U. & Welch, N. (2001). Risk as feelings. *Psychological Bulletin, 127,* 267–286.

Loken, B. & Ward, J. (1990). Alternative approaches to understanding the determinants of typicality. *Journal of Consumer Research, 17,* 111–126.

Louviere, J. L. (1988). *Analyzing Decision-making: Metric Conjoint Analysis.* New York: Sage.

Louviere, J. L., Hensher, D. A. & Swait, J. D. (2000). *Stated Choice Methods: Analysis and Application.* London: Cambridge University Press.

Luce, M. F., Bettman, J. R. & Payne, J. W. (2001). Emotional decisions: tradeoff difficulty and coping in consumer choice. *Monographs of the Journal of Consumer Research, 1,* 1–209.

Luce, R. D. (1959). *Individual Choice Behavior.* New York: John Wiley & Sons.

Lynch, J. G. Jr. (1985). Uniqueness issues in the decompositional modeling of multiattribute overall evaluations: an information integration perspective. *Journal of Marketing Research, 22,* 1–19.

Lynch, J. G. Jr & Ariely, D. (2000). Wine online: search costs and competition on price, quality, and distribution. *Marketing Science, 19,* 83–103.

Lynch, J. G. Jr, Chakravarti, D. & Mitra, A. (1991). Contrast effects in consumer judgments: changes in mental representations or in the anchoring of rating scales? *Journal of Consumer Research, 18,* 284–297.

Lynch, J. G. Jr, Marmorstein, H. & Weigold, M. F. (1988). Choices from sets including remembered brands: use of recalled attributes and prior overall evaluations. *Journal of Consumer Research, 15,* 169–184.

McFadden, D. (1986). The choice theory approach to marketing research. *Marketing Science, 5,* 275–297.

McKenna, C. J. (1987). Theories of individual search behaviour. In J. D. Hey & P. J. Lambert (eds.), *Surveys in the Economics of Uncertainty* (pp. 91–109). Oxford: Basil Blackwell.

Macklin, M. C. (1996). Preschoolers' learning of brand names from visual cues. *Journal of Consumer Research, 23,* 251–261.

Mandel, N. & Johnson, E. J. (2002). When web pages influence choice: effects of visual primes on experts and novices," *Journal of Consumer Research, 29,* 235–245.

March, J. G. (1996). Learning to be risk averse. *Psychological Review, 103,* 309–319.

Martindale, C. & Moore, K. (1988). Priming, prototypicality, and preference. *Journal of Experimental Psychology: Human Perception and Performance, 14,* 661–670.

Mayhew, G. E. & Winer, R. S. (1992). An empirical analysis of internal and external reference prices using scanner data. *Journal of Consumer Research, 19,* 62–70.

Mellers, B. A., Schwartz, A. & Cooke, A. D. J. (1998). Judgment and decision-making. *Annual Review of Psychology, 49,* 447–477.

Meyer, R. J. (1987). The learning of multiattribute judgment policies. *Journal of Consumer Research, 14,* 155–173.

Meyer, R. J. & Assuncao, J. (1990). The optimality of consumer stockpiling strategies. *Marketing Science, 9,* 18–41.

Meyer, R. J. & Kahn, B. E. (1991). Probabilistic models of consumer choice. In T. S. Robertson & H. H. Kassarjian (eds.), *Handbook of Consumer Behavior* (pp. 85–123). Englewood Cliffs NJ: Prentice-Hall.

Meyvis, T. & Janiszewski, C. (2004). When are broader brands stronger brands? An accessibility perspective on the success of brand extensions. *Journal of Consumer Research, 31,* 346–357.

Mitchell, A. A. & Dacin, P. A. (1996). The assessment of alternative measures of consumer expertise. *Journal of Consumer Research, 23,* 219–239.

Mitra, A. & Lynch, J. G. Jr. (1995). Toward a reconciliation of market power and information Theories of advertising effects on price elasticity. *Journal of Consumer Research, 21,* 644–660.

Moore, D. L. & Hutchinson, J. W. (1985). The influence of affective reactions to advertising: direct and indirect mechanisms of attitude change. In L. Alwitt & A. A. Mitchell (eds.), *Psychological*

Processes and Advertising Effects: Theory, Research, and Application (pp. 65–87). Hillsdale, NJ: Lawrence Erlbaum Associates.

Moorthy, S., Ratchford, B. T. & Talukdar, D. (1997). Consumer information search revisited: theory and empirical analysis. *Journal of Consumer Research, 23*, 263–278.

Moreau, C. P., Markman, A. B. & Lehmann, D. R. (2001). "What is it?" Categorization flexibility and consumers' responses to really new products. *Journal of Consumer Research, 27*, 489–490.

Muthukrishnan, A. V. (1995). Decision ambiguity and incumbent brand advantage. *Journal of Consumer Research, 22*, 98–109.

Muthukrishnan, A. V. & Kardes, F. R. (2001). Persistent preferences for product attributes: the effects of the initial choice context and uninformative experience. *Journal of Consumer Research, 28*, 89–104.

Nedungadi, P. (1990). Recall and consumer consideration sets: influencing choice without altering brand evaluations. *Journal of Consumer Research, 17*, 263–276.

Nedungadi, P. & Hutchinson, J. W. (1985). The prototypicality of brands: relationships with brand awareness, preference and usage. In E. C. Hirschman & M. B. Holbrook (eds.), *Advances in Consumer Research* (Vol. 12, pp. 498–503). Provo, UT: Association for Consumer Research.

Newell, A. & Simon, H. A. (1972). *Human Problem Solving*. Englewood Cliffs, NJ: Prentice-Hall.

Nosofsky, R. M. (1984). Choice, similarity, and the context theory of classification. *Journal of Experimental Psychology: Learning, Memory, and Cognition, 10*, 104–114.

Novemsky, N. & Kahneman, D. (2005). The boundaries of loss aversion. *Journal of Marketing Research, 42*, 119–128.

Obermiller, C. (1985). Varieties of mere exposure: the effects of processing style and repetition on affective responses. *Journal of Consumer Research, 12*, 17–30.

van Osselaer, S. M. J. & Alba, J. W. (2000). Consumer learning and brand equity. *Journal of Consumer Research, 27*, 1–16.

van Osselaer, S. M. J., Alba, J. W. & Manchanda, P. (2004). Irrelevant information and mediated intertemporal choice. *Journal of Consumer Psychology, 14*, 257–270.

van Osselaer, S. M. J. & Janiszewski, C. (2001). Two ways of learning brand associations. *Journal of Consumer Research, 28*, 202–223.

Palmeri, T. J., Wong, A. C. N. & Gauthier, I. (2004). Computational approaches to the development of perceptual experience. *TRENDS in Cognitive Science, 8*, 378–386.

Parducci, A. (1965). Category judgment: a range-frequency model. *Psychological Review, 72*, 407–418.

Payne, J. W., Bettman, J. R. & Johnson, E. J. (1993). *The Adaptive Decision Maker*. Cambridge: Cambridge University Press.

Pechmann, C. & Ratneshwar, S. (1992). Consumer covariation judgments: theory or data driven? *Journal of Consumer Research, 19*, 373–386.

Petty, R. E., Unnava, R. H. & Strathman, A. J. (1991). Theories of attitude change. In T. S. Robertson & H. H. Kassarjian (eds.), *Handbook of Consumer Behavior* (pp. 241–280). Englewood Cliffs NJ: Prentice-Hall.

Pieters, R. G. M. & Bijmolt, T. H. A. (1997). Consumer memory for television advertising: a field study of duration, serial position, and competition effects. *Journal of Consumer Research, 23*, 362–372.

Prelec, D. & Lowenstein, G. (1998). The red and the black: mental accounting of savings and debt. *Marketing Science, 17*, 4–28.

Ratchford, B. T. (2001). The economics of consumer knowledge. *Journal of Consumer Research, 27*, 397–411.

Ratchford, B. T., Lee, M.-S. & Talukdar, D. (2003). The impact of the internet on information search for automobiles. *Journal of Marketing Research, 40*, 193–209.

Ratneshwar, S. & Shocker, A. D. (1991). Substitution in use and the role of usage context in product category structures. *Journal of Marketing Research, 28*, 281–295.

Rescorla, R. A. & Wagner, A. R. (1972). A theory of Pavlovian conditioning: variations in the effectiveness of reinforcement and nonreinforcement. In A. H. Black & W. F. Prokasy (eds.), *Classical Conditioning II: Current Research and Theory* (pp. 64–99). New York: Appleton-Century-Crofts.

Roberts, J. H. & Lattin, J. M. (1991). Developing and testing of a model of consideration set composition. *Journal of Marketing Research, 28*, 281–295.

Roberts, J. H. & Urban, G. (1988). Modeling multiattribute utility, risk, and belief dynamics for new consumer durable brand choice. *Management Science, 34*, 167–185.

Roy, R., Chintagunta, P. K. & Haldar, S. (1996). A framework for investigating habits, "the hand of the past," and heterogeneity in dynamic brand choice. *Marketing Science, 15*, 280–299.

Russo, J. E., Meloy, M. G. & Medvec, V. H. (1998). Predecisional distortion of product information. *Journal of Marketing Research, 35*, 438–452.

Samuelson, W. & Zeckhauser, R. (1988). Status quo bias in decision-making. *Journal of Risk and Uncertainty, 1*, 7–59.

Sanbonmatsu, D. M., Kardes, F. R., Houghton, D. C. *et al.* (2003). Overestimating the importance of the given information in multiattribute consumer judgment. *Journal of Consumer Psychology, 13*, 289–300.

Schkade, D. A. & Johnson, E. J. (1989). Cognitive processes in preference reversals. *Organizational Behavior and Human Decision Processes, 44*, 203–231.

Schwarz, N. (2004). Metacognitive experiences in consumer judgment and decision-making. *Journal of Consumer Psychology, 14*, 332–348.

Sen, S. & Johnson, E. J. (1997). Mere-possession effects without possession in consumer choice. *Journal of Consumer Research, 24*, 105–117.

Sengupta, J. & Gorn, G. J. (2002). Absence makes the mind grow sharper: effects of element omission on subsequent recall. *Journal of Marketing Research, 39*, 186–201.

Shanteau, J. & Stewart, T. R. (1992). Why study expert decision-making? Some historical perspectives and comments, *Organizational Behavior and Human Decision Processes, 53*, 95–106.

Shapiro, S. & Spence, M. T. (2002). Factors affecting encoding, retrieval, and alignment of sensory attributes in a memory-based brand choice task. *Journal of Consumer Research, 28*, 603–617.

Shepard, R. N., Romney, A. K. & Nerlove, S. B. (1972). *Multidimensional Scaling; Theory and Applications in the Behavioral Sciences*. New York: Seminar Press.

Shiv, B., Carmon, Z. & Ariely, D. (2005). Placebo effects in marketing actions: consumers may get what they pay for. *Journal of Marketing Research, 42*, 383–393.

Shocker, A., Ben-Akiva, M., Boccara, B. & Nedungadi, P. (1991). Consideration set influences on consumer decision-making and choice: issues, models, and suggestions. *Marketing Letters, 2*, 181–198.

Simon, H. (1955). A behavioral model of rational choice. *Quarterly Journal of Economics, 69*, 99–118.

Simonson, I. (1989). Choice based on reasons: the case of attraction and compromise effects. *Journal of Consumer Research, 16*, 105–118.

Simonson, I. (1992). The influence of anticipating regret and responsibility on purchase decisions. *Journal of Consumer Research, 19*, 158–174.

Simonson, I. & Tversky, A. (1992). Choice in context: tradeoff contrast and extremeness aversion. *Journal of Marketing Research, 29*, 281–295.

Skurnik, I., Yoon, C., Park, D. C. & Schwarz, N. (2005). How warnings about false claims become recommendations. *Journal of Consumer Research, 31*, 713–724.

Slovic, P., Fischoff, B. & Lichtenstein, S. (1982). Facts versus fears: understanding perceived risks. In D. Kahneman, P. Slovic & A. Tversky (eds.), *Judgment Under Uncertainty: Heuristics and Biases* (pp. 463–489). New York: Cambridge University Press.

Soman, D. (2001). Effects of payment mechanism on spending behavior: the role of rehearsal and immediacy of payments. *Journal of Consumer Research, 27*, 460–474.

Spence, M. T. & Brucks, M. (1997). The moderating effects of problem characteristics on experts' and novices' judgments. *Journal of Marketing Research, 34*, 233–247.

Srinivasan, V., Park, C. S. & Chang, D. R. (2005). An approach to the measurement, analysis, and prediction of brand equity and its sources. *Management Science, 51*, 1433–1448.

Thaler, R. (1980). Toward a positive theory of consumer choice. *Journal of Economic Behavior and Organization, 1*, 39–60.

Thaler, R. (1985). Mental accounting and consumer choice. *Marketing Science, 4*, 199–214.

Tversky, A. (1972). Elimination by aspects: a theory of choice. *Psychological Review*, *79*, 281–299.
Tversky, A. & Kahneman, D. (1974). Judgment under uncertainty: heuristics and biases. *Science*, *185*, 1124–1131.
Tversky, A. & Kahneman, D. (1991). Loss aversion in riskless choice: a reference dependent model. *Quarterly Journal of Economics*, *106*, 1039–1061.
Tversky, A. & Kahneman, D. (1992). Advances in prospect theory: cumulative representation of uncertainty. *Journal of Risk and Uncertainty*, *5*, 297–323.
Tversky, A. & Koehler, D. (1994). Support theory: a nonextensional representation of subjective probability. *Psychological Review*, *101*, 547–567.
Tversky, A. & Sattath, S. (1979). Preference trees. *Psychological Review*, *86*, 542–573.
Tversky, A. & Shafir, E. (1992). Choice under conflict: the dynamics of deferred decision. *Psychological Science*, *3*, 358–361.
Tversky, A. & Simonson, I. (1993). Context dependent preferences. *Management Science*, *39*, 1179–1189.
Tversky, A., Slovic, P. & Kahneman, D. (1990). The determinants of preference reversal. *American Economic Review*, *80*, 204–217.
Unnava, H. R., Burnkrant, R. E. & Erevelles, S. (1994). Effects of presentation order and communication modality on recall and attitude. *Journal of Consumer Research*, *21*, 481–490.
Urban, G., Hulland, J. S. & Weinberg, B. D. (1993). Premarket forecasting of new consumer durable goods: modeling categorization, elimination, and consideration phenomena. *Journal of Marketing*, *57*, 47–64.
Urbany, J. E., Beardon, W. O. & Weilbaker, D. C. (1988). The effect of plausible and exaggerated reference prices on consumer perceptions and price search. *Journal of Consumer Research*, *15*, 95–110.
Urbany, J. E., Dickson, P. R. & Wilkie, W. L. (1989). Buyer uncertainty and information search. *Journal of Consumer Research*, *16*, 208–215.
Vanhuele, M. & Dreze, X. (2002). Measuring the price knowledge shoppers bring to the store. *Journal of Marketing*, *66*, 72–85.
Veryzer, R. W. & Hutchinson, J. W. (1998). The influence of unity and prototypicality on aesthetic responses to new product designs. *Journal of Consumer Research*, *24*, 374–394
West, P. W., Brown, C. L. & Hoch, S. J. (1996). Consumption vocabulary and preference formation. *Journal of Consumer Research*, *23*, 120–135.
Winer, R. S. (1986). A reference price model of brand choice for frequently purchased products. *Journal of Consumer Research*, *13*, 250–256.
Wood, S. L. & Lynch, J. G. Jr. (2002). Prior knowledge and complacency in new product learning. *Journal of Consumer Research*, *29*, 416–426.
Zajonc, R. B. & Markus, H. (1982). Affective and cognitive factors in preferences. *Journal of Consumer Research*, *9*, 123–131.
Zhang, S. & Markman, A. B. (1998). Overcoming the early entrant advantage: the role of alignable and nonalignable differences. *Journal of Marketing Research*, *35*, 413–426.

CHAPTER 27

Protection of the Environment

Raymond S. Nickerson
Tufts University, USA

This chapter is intended to complement the one on the same topic that appeared in the first edition of this handbook. I do not repeat what was said in the earlier version regarding the nature of the problem of detrimental environmental change or regarding human behavior as an agent of that change. Accounts of the problem are readily available, not only in the earlier chapter, but in many publications (e.g., Geller *et al.* 1982; Gardner & Stern 1996; Oskamp 2000; Stern 2000; Nickerson 2003; Winter & Koger 2004; see also the series on "The state of the planet," beginning in the November 14, 1993, issue of *Science*). This chapter focuses on the question of what cognitive psychology, broadly defined, has to offer to help address the problem.

Environmental psychology has been a subdiscipline within psychology for a long time. Until fairly recently, the main focus of interest in the field was on the effects of environments, and especially built environments, on human safety, comfort, and performance. Relatively little attention was given, by comparison, to questions of how human behavior affected the natural environment and how behavior that was detrimental to the environment might be changed so as to be less so. Interest among psychologists in the latter class of questions has been growing, perhaps as a consequence of the greater attention that has been paid to environmental issues since the 1960s, not only by scientific publications, but also by the various news media.

Some see a new field of psychological research and application emerging as a consequence of the increasing interest among psychologists in the natural environment and what can be done to make human behavior more supportive of protecting it and maintaining a sustainable relationship to it. Conservation psychology, as this emerging field is called, is defined by Saunders (2003) as "the scientific study of the reciprocal relationships between humans and the rest of nature, with a particular focus on how to encourage conservation of the natural world" (p. 138). Conservation psychology is to be distinguished from environmental psychology more generally by its sharper focus on the natural environment. Its focus differs also from that of the closely related fields of ecological psychology (Barker 1968; Rogers-Warren & Warren 1977; Bronfenbrenner 1979; Catalano 1979) and ecopsychology (Roszak 1992; Roszak *et al.* 1995). Ecological psychology focuses on how behavior is affected by the context (sporting event, classroom, restaurant) in which it takes place;

Handbook of Applied Cognition: Second Edition. Edited by Francis T. Durso.

ecopsychology (a more recently coined term) represents an emerging interest in the implications for mental health of the way human beings connect with their surroundings. Ecological psychology, ecopsychology, and conservation psychology have some common interests but some notable differences as well (Fisher 2002; Beringer 2003; Reser 2003).

An assumption underlying this chapter is that cognitive psychology has much to offer the goal of mitigating detrimental environmental change. This assumption may require some defending, inasmuch as interest in environmental issues has not been a major driving force behind much research on cognition to date. It is clear, however, that many of the questions that arise when environmental protection is the focus are cognitive in nature. How are conflicting claims about the nature of the problem to be evaluated? How are specific risks associated with environmental change best assessed and communicated? How are attitudes and values relating to the environment formed and how do they affect behavior? What tradeoffs involving environmental and economic variables do people consider acceptable? How can the costs and benefits of alternative actions relevant to environmental change be accurately quantified, and the understanding of them by the general public facilitated? How is the value of clean air, clean water, wildlife habitat, recreational wilderness, and climate stabilization best assessed and communicated?

I want to argue that cognitive psychology can have an impact on this problem area not only by research motivated by such questions, but through the application of what is known about cognition from basic research. What is known about the strengths and weaknesses of human reasoning, for example, is relevant to an understanding of how people deal, or fail to deal, with various types of threats to the environment. The well-documented tendency to interpret data in such a way as to be consistent with existing assumptions or beliefs can help explain how people, including experts, can so readily disagree regarding the seriousness of alleged threats (Nickerson 1998). So too can the related tendency to oversimplify – to seek simple solutions to complex situations that are misperceived as simple (Spiro *et al.* 1991). The inclination to discount future costs and benefits when making decisions can go some distance toward accounting for people's general unwillingness to sacrifice much in the way of present benefits in order to avoid future costs (MacLean 1990). Studies of the effects of emotion on judgment and decision-making should provide insights into reactions people have to particular environmental threats and pro and con positions they take regarding proposed means of addressing them (Damasio 1994; Finucane *et al.* 2000).

Findings from studies of problem-solving techniques can inform attempts to deal with specific environmental issues. Work on group decision-making is germane to the question of how to get consensus within communities regarding how to deal with community problems. Work on social dilemmas can inform efforts to evoke cooperation for the common good among groups with different, perhaps conflicting, agendas. Techniques for transforming competitive and zero-sum conflicts into win-win situations should find uses in negotiations of decisions pertaining to the environment. An understanding of what facilitates or hinders the ability to see things from perspectives other than one's own should also find applications. It would be good to know why people often show little ability or inclination to think counterfactually, to explore "what if" scenarios, to search actively for problem solutions that might be better than alternatives already identified, or to be sufficiently critical of their own ideas. How to design messages both for ease of comprehension and for motivational effectiveness is a question of obvious relevance to the task of finding ways to modify behavior in the direction of greater environmental friendliness.

ASSESSMENT ISSUES

That detrimental environmental change caused by human behavior poses a genuine threat to the habitability of the planet is a belief that is sufficiently strongly held by many people to have evoked countless expressions of concern and motivated much activism. Assessing the nature and severity of the problem is a non-trivial challenge that relates to cognitive psychology in several ways. In the following, I note a few of the issues.

Evaluating What the Experts Say

Among numerous concerns about environmental change there is none more controversial than the possibility of global warming. Although I believe the prevailing view among scientists is that this worry is justified, as evidenced by the signing by 1600 scientists of a statement of intense concern (Union of Concerned Scientists 1992), the idea that global warming poses a serious threat has not lacked knowledgeable critics. A sense of the controversy relating to this issue can be obtained from the Marshall Institute report (Seitz *et al.* 1989), the *Science* article in which that report was discussed (Roberts 1989), several letters to the editor in response to this article (Jastrow 1990; Lindzen 1990; Nierenberg 1990), and the review of the dispute by White (1990). That the controversy continues is seen in the publication by Lomborg (2001) of an extensive challenge to the prevailing view and in the strong reactions this triggered, examples of which include essays by Schneider (2002), Holdren (2002), Bongaarts (2002) and Lovejoy (2002) in the same issue of *Scientific American*. Lomborg's (2002) reply appears in a later issue of the same volume. Numerous subsequent articles and commentaries appearing in *Science* and at various websites attest to the ongoing controversy surrounding the book, and more generally the issue.

Other evidences of differences of opinion among scientists are not hard to find. Reconstructed monthly temperatures in Europe from a variety of sources back to 1500 compared with those recorded in Europe during the late twentieth and early twenty-first centuries have led some investigators to conclude that the temperature during the latter period was very likely warmer than any other time during the past 500years (Luterbacher *et al.* 2004). But Soon and colleagues (Soon *et al.* 2003, Soon & Baliunas 2003) have published results they interpret to be inconsistent with this view.

One point on which there appears to be general agreement is that the task of determining whether global warming is really occurring, and if so as a result of human activities, is very difficult. Much of the concern is focused on the possible effects of warming on the polar regions, and the modeling of polar climate has proved to be especially difficult and the prediction of trends to be highly uncertain (Shindell 2003). The evidence is compelling that sudden dramatic and long-lasting changes in climate that could not be attributed to human activities have occurred many times in the past and are likely to happen in the future. Sources of the evidence include ice in cores drilled from the Greenland ice sheet, tree ring measurements, and ancient pollen and shells preserved in lake and ocean mud. Alley (2004) contends that the fact that large climate changes have occurred long before human behavior could have had any effect should not lessen concern about global warming today. He argues that climate change should be more of a worry now than ever, because the effect of the global warming could be to push other climate drivers to a point at which they lurch into a new and different state, and exactly what that state would be – whether it would usher in a period of greater warmth or cold – is impossible to assess.

In view of the inherent difficulty of the problem of determining whether global warming really is occurring as a consequence of human activities, and the non-trivial amount of disagreement among experts as to how to interpret the relevant data, how is the citizen who is not an expert in climatology or other related disciplines to decide what to believe? And how should policy decisions be made?

If we assume, or it becomes clear, that global warming really is occurring, there remains the difficulty of predicting its future effects. Will the consequences of the amount of increase that is likely to occur over the foreseeable future be good or bad on balance? Again, there are differences of opinion as to what the answer is. Some have argued that a modest temperature increase could be generally beneficial. On the other hand are numerous predictions of dire consequences of a continuing warming trend.

One calamitous prediction that has received a lot of press is the melting of the polar ice caps and a consequential rise in sea levels worldwide. According to Bindschadler and Bentley (2002), the ice cover of the part of Antarctica that lies mainly in the Western Hemisphere is enough to raise global sea level 5 meters if it were all to melt. Evidence that this body of ice has been disintegrating has been a major cause for concern. Bindschadler and Bentley note that many researchers now believe the ice sheet is shrinking more slowly than originally thought, but they note too that the dynamics of the sheet are not well understood. Sturm *et al.* (2003) estimate that air temperatures in the Arctic have increased by 0.5 degree Celsius each decade over the past 30 years and the area covered by sea ice has been decreasing by about 3 per cent per decade over the same period. These authors also point out that the web of feedback interactions in the Arctic is sufficiently complex that the causes of these changes and their significance for the future are not yet clear; however, that the changes are worrisome is not in doubt, they contend. Hansen (2004), who sees sea-level rise as a major threat, proposes a scenario to limit climate forcing that focuses on halting, or reversing, increase in air pollutants (soot, atmospheric ozone, and methane), and stabilizing the average fossil fuel carbon dioxide emissions over the next 50 years at about their current levels.

Another dire prediction also involves water, but in this case the concern is for the possibility of a reduction in an already stressed resource. Mountain snow serves as a reservoir of water. According to recent analysis of decades' worth of snow pack measurements, warming since the 1950s has resulted in considerable drops in snow pack levels throughout the American West over that time. Service (2004) contends that if even the most moderate regional warming predictions for the next 50 years come true, the western snow packs could be reduced by up to 60 per cent in some regions, with a resulting reduction in summertime stream flows of 20–50 per cent. This is not good news for a region that is already experiencing severe water problems.

Other claims about detrimental environmental change have also been controversial, albeit perhaps less vigorously contentious than the controversy about the threat of global warming. The threat of species extinction – destruction of wildlife habitat and other activities that have implications for the survival of particular species – is a case in point. The paleontological record makes it clear that species have come and gone throughout the history of the earth. Skepticism has been voiced by several paleontologists and statisticians about some of the more pessimistic estimates of the effects of human activities on the rate of species extinction at the present time (Gibbs 2001).

Some writers have argued that in assessing dire predictions of pending environmental disaster we are inclined to be untroubled by, or even to notice, previous alarming predictions that proved to be wrong.

> Politically correct thinking has spawned some monumental and near universally accepted inaccuracies that had ostensibly intelligent and educated authorities sounding the alarm that doomsday was coming. If the intent was to raise awareness – newspeak for scaring the dickens out of people into altering their attitudes and behaviors – they succeeded, at least until the myth was discredited. (Cummings & O'Donohue 2005, p. 5)

As examples of dire predictions that proved to be wrong – and forgotten – Cummings and O'Donohue point to Paul Ehrlich's (1968) warning that the world would run out of food and other resources before the twenty-first century, and Rachel Carson's (1962) prediction of the total disappearance of birds within 20 years because of pesticide use. Cummings and O'Donohue contend that burial of past alarms that have proved to be inaccurate is remarkably successful, and punctuate the claim with a reminder that only 30 years ago "society was bombarded with predictions that the use of fossil fuels was rapidly bringing about another ice age" (p. 6) and a pointer to a *Newsweek* (1975) article where the prediction can be found.

We should not ignore the possibility that the alarms that are criticized by Cummings and O'Donohue motivated behavior that helped the predicted disasters to be averted (banning of DDT, reclamation of some habitat, targeted rescue and restoration of some endangered species, etc.). But even so, it is hard to argue against the claim that as a society, and as individuals, we tend not to make much of an effort to evaluate past predictions with a view to deriving a better understanding of how much credence we should give to current ones.

Many of the issues that relate to detrimental environmental change are very complex. And the problem of getting an accurate understanding of the situation is exacerbated by selective presentations of facts and politically motivated exaggerations or obfuscations – tactics that appear to be employed more or less universally across the political spectrum. In short, it is exceedingly difficult for concerned people – especially, but not only, those without training in the relevant disciplines – to know how seriously to take predictions regarding the future environmental consequences of present human activities. This is a problem of human judgment and reasoning. How, when confronted with conflicting pronouncements from presumably credible sources, is one to determine what to believe? How does one determine the credibility of sources?

The problem for the lay person of evaluating conflicting claims regarding threats to the environment is amplified also by the fact that even the reporting of presumably hard data can be slanted, perhaps unwittingly, by the assumptions, earlier conclusions, or values of those who collected and interpreted the data. Holloway (1996) shows how this can work in a comparison of the methods used by groups with different vested interests to evaluate the recovery of Prince William Sound from the oil spill by the *Exxon Valdez* and the various interpretations of the results obtained: each group sees more or less what it is looking for. This should not come as a surprise to students of cognition. The tendency to see what one expects, or wants, to see in data is well documented in many contexts (Nickerson 1998).

The point I wish to emphasize is that assessing the condition of the environment and predicting the probable course of future environmental change conditional on human activities are daunting cognitive tasks. What is known about cognition (reasoning, decision-making, problem-solving) should find applications here. The large literature on human judgment, and especially reasoning heuristics and biases (base-rate neglect, confirmation bias, hindsight bias, attribution bias, overconfidence) contains many findings that should have applicability to the problem of assessing the relative plausibility of the various conflicting claims that are made about environmental change. I am not aware of many applications of this sort, however, so I mention it as an area of opportunity and challenge.

Risk Assessment

Environmental change is a matter of concern because many of the trends and predicted developments pose threats to health and comfort, if not to life. This being so, work that has been done on the assessment, communication and perception of risk, and on human response to risk is relevant to the general topic. Risk *assessment* involves bringing incidence statistics or expert opinion to bear on determining what the risks of specified events actually are. Risk *communication* means conveying information about specific risks to target audiences, including the general public. Risk *perception* refers to what people consider, rightly or wrongly, specific risks to be. All three topics are discussed in the chapter on environmental change in the earlier edition of the handbook. Here I want to focus on the question of how people come to believe what they do about the relative importance of various threats to the environment. Much of the relevant work has dealt with risks other than those associated with environmental change, but many of the findings are germane in this context. Gardner and Stern (1996) review research on how people perceive risks of various types, and offer several theoretical accounts of why people systematically misjudge risks in specific instances.

Perception of the relative likelihood of various situations often does not correspond closely to the likelihood of those situations as reflected in incidence statistics (Lichtenstein *et al.* 1978; Slovic *et al.* 1979) or in the opinions of experts (Burton *et al.* 1978; Gould *et al.* 1988). Poor reading comprehension and the fact that risk information is expressed in a variety of ways have been suggested as possible bases for misperception of risks (Sharlin 1986; Jeffery 1989; Atman *et al.* 1994). Accurate perception is impeded in some instances by the intensity of the emotional reactions of people on all sides of an issue (e.g., nuclear power generation, Levi & Holder 1986; Van der Pligt *et al.* 1986) and by the amount of dread that the possibility of a catastrophic incident evokes (Fischhoff *et al.* 1978).

The relative amount of media coverage given to different risks is believed by some to be a major determinant of the relative importance that people attach to those risks or of people's estimates of their probability of realization (Slovic *et al.* 1976; Combs & Slovic 1979; Rothman & Lichter 1987). This hypothesis gets support from the considerable increase in the perceived risk of nuclear contamination following the Chernobyl incident

(Verplanken 1989; Midden & Verplanken 1990; Renn 1990; Van der Pligt & Midden 1990).

Estimated costs of risks that can be realized only in the relatively distant future are likely to be discounted relative to estimated costs of risks that could be realized soon (Frederick *et al.* 2002; Hendrickx & Nicolaij 2004). Despite the importance of this fact, environmental risk discounting has not been the focus of much research (Hendrickx & Nicolaij 2004). Hendrickx and Nicolaihj note that, as is true of other types of risks, the degree of discounting of environmental risks increases, on average, with expected delay, but they note too that for sizeable percentages of the participants in studies they cite, such an increase was not found. Discounting, they conclude, is apparently less pronounced for environmental effects than for effects of other types. Their inclination is to attribute this difference to the strong role that ethical considerations play in people's reactions to environmental risks. They see the results of their own experimentation as supportive of dual-process theories of risk judgment, such as those proposed by Böhm and Pfister (2000), Finucane *et al.* (2000), Loewenstein *et al.* (2001) and Slovic *et al.* (2004), which hold that people evaluate risks with cognitive or analytic strategies but also on the basis of feelings and moral concerns.

Just as risks that can be realized in the near future are typically reacted to more strongly than comparable risks that can be realized only in the far future, so too are risks likely to be judged the more threatening the closer they are in space. Risks associated with nuclear power plants, hazardous waste incinerators, or toxic chemical production facilities are understandably likely to be of greater concern to people who live near them than to people who do not. But here too, there are some counter-indications. Lima (2004), for example, found that living near a hazardous waste incinerator can yield an increased perception of risk but can also have a habituation effect whereby the estimation of risk decreases over time. Although participants in this study who lived closest to the incinerator showed the habituation effect in their risk assessments, there was an increase in their reported psychological symptoms relating to mental health. Lima interpreted the results as suggestive of "a special cognitive effort to minimize the perceived threat," and to be compatible with theories of cognitive dissonance and cognitive adaptation as put forth by Festinger (1957) and Taylor and Brown (1988), respectively.

Habituation to environmental problems has been observed in a variety of contexts. People accustomed to living in smog are less likely to complain of it than are those who are not accustomed to it (Evans *et al.* 1982); recent migrants from rural areas are likely to judge a city to be noisier than are recent migrants from other urban areas (Wohlwill & Kohn 1973). Short-term adaptation effects in keeping with Helson's (1964) theory of adaptation level have been observed in studies of people's assessment of environmental quality; how attractive a particular forest scene is judged to be, for example, is likely to depend on the relative attractiveness of other scenes that are judged in the same session (Brown & Daniel 1987).

The misperception of risks can have negative consequences of more than one type. Underestimation of the seriousness of a risk more or less ensures that inadequate steps will be taken to avoid it, or to mitigate its effects; overestimation can result in unnecessary expenditures of resources to deal with it. Overestimation can also produce unnecessary apprehension and symptoms of chronic stress (Thomas 1983; Baum & Fleming 1993).

Ranking of Perceived Risks

Let us assume that risks associated with environmental change can be identified, which is to say that a list of such risks can be produced that most experts will accept as reasonably factual. Taking action aimed at reducing the probability that specific risks will be realized, or containing the undesirable consequences if they are, is likely to incur costs. It is important therefore to be able to judge the relative seriousness of the risks so resources can be expended efficiently. Inasmuch as it is the citizenry whose welfare is at stake and whose purse is underwriting the cost of whatever actions are taken, the citizenry should participate in deciding what is, and what is not, worth doing.

One technique for ranking risks, developed by researchers at Carnegie Mellon University, involves five interdependent steps (Florig *et al.* 2001; Morgan *et al.* 2001). The first three steps – identification of the risks that are to be ranked, identification of the attributes of those risks that are to be considered, use of the results of the first two steps in the preparation of the work sheets that are to be used in the ranking process – are performed by professionals. The final step – interpretation of the results – is also performed by professionals. The fourth step – the actual ranking of the risks – is performed by participants selected for that task. The ranking is done both holistically and on an attribute-by-attribute basis. Participants get to see how well their holistic rankings correspond to those implied by their responses to the attribute-by-attribute task, and to revise their rankings if they wish. Participants also work in small groups to produce group rankings. The procedure is time-consuming, but is designed to yield rankings that are the result of a thoughtful process (Willis *et al.* 2004).

Florig *et al.* (2001) are careful to note the limited expectations for risk-ranking. They see a ranking as one input to decision-making and not as a final recommendation for management priorities. They argue that allocation of resources to the reduction of specific risks should take into account not only the ranking, but the relative costs of reducing those risks. Morgan *et al.* (2000) note too the imprecise nature of the first step in the process – the defining of the risk categories to be ranked – and caution that the results of risk-ranking exercises can be very sensitive to the outcome of that step. But to the extent that risk-ranking can provide an accurate representation of how the general public and policy-makers assess the relative importance of the various major risks with which society must deal, it can usefully inform debate and the allocation of resources to risk reduction goals.

SOCIAL COGNITION

Oskamp (1995) points out that ecological concerns have been receiving increasing attention among social psychologists, one evidence of which is a growing number of column inches devoted to environmental problems in the *Journal of Social Issues*. He points out that, although many people think environmental problems must be solved by scientists and engineers, the fact that the problems stem from, or are exacerbated by, human behavior makes them an appropriate focus of research by social scientists. Such research is needed to inform public policy decisions, to plan and conduct public education programs, to anticipate the effects of possible government actions, and so on. Here we consider a few of the many ways in which social cognition relates to the problem of environmental change.

Attitudes, Values, and Affect

There appears to be a consensus among researchers that attitudes, as reflected in instruments designed to measure them, tend to be only moderately predictive of behavior (Ajzen & Fishbein 1980; Ajzen 2000; Bamberg 2003; Staats 2003; Poortinga *et al.* 2004). There is need for a better understanding of this surprising finding. Why the correlation between attitudes and behavior, especially as they relate to the environment, is not higher is an important question for research; however, that there is some correlation is also important information that can be applied to efforts to make behavior more environmentally friendly.

Several instruments have been developed to measure the degree to which individuals feel, or consider themselves, "connected" to nature (Dunlap & Van Liere 1978; Dunlap *et al.* 2000; Schultz 2001; Schultz *et al.* 2004). Mayer and Frantz (2004) developed a measure called the "connectedness to nature scale" (CNS) and took data obtained with it as evidence that people who show higher connectedness tend to engage in more eco-friendly behavior and to report a greater sense of personal well-being. They caution that the data demonstrate significant positive relationships among these variables, but that the nature of the cause-and-effect connections remains to be determined. And, as is true of methods for assessing attitudes, values, and affect generally, there is a need to be alert to the possibility of results being influenced by self-selection effects and demand characteristics of the task.

How environmental values manifest themselves in people's acceptance of policies addressing environmental problems can vary with socio-demographic variables such as people's positions, affiliations, income, and household size (Nilsson *et al.* 2004; Poortinga *et al.* 2004). Nilsson *et al.* (2004) found differences in this respect between decision-makers in the public sector and those in the private sector. Other investigators have found concern for the environment to be positively correlated with the extent to which one's values are self-transcendent and negatively correlated with the extent to which they are self-enhancing (Schultz & Zelezny 1998, 1999; Nordlund & Garvill 2002). How people become attached to or identify with specific places, or types of places, and the implications of such attachments for environmentally relevant behavior have begun to receive attention from researchers (Bott *et al.* 2003; Giuliani 2003).

Theoretical treatments of the effects of social norms as determinants of individuals' behavior include the theory of reasoned activation of Fishbein and Ajzen (1975), the theory of norm-activation of Schwartz (1977, 1999) and the value-belief-norm theory of Stern *et al.* (1999). These theories emphasize the roles of values and norms in motivating behavior that can be seen as socially beneficial if not altruistic. Each has been applied to behavior as it relates to environmental protection (Monroe 2003; Nilsson *et al.* 2004).

Education and Social Marketing

On the assumption that much of the problem of detrimental environmental change is a direct consequence of human behavior, one obvious approach to dealing with the problem is to attempt to effect the kinds of changes in behavior that would make it more environmentally benign. Reviews of work addressed to behavior change include Kollmus and Agyeman (2002), Vining and Ebreo (2002) and Nickerson (2003). Efforts to effect changes in behavior via large-scale public information campaigns have had some, but only relatively modest, success (Ester & Winett 1982; Condelli *et al.* 1984; Stern & Aronson 1984; Dennis *et al.* 1990; Dwyer *et al.* 1993). This is about the level of success realized by mass media campaigns aimed at modifying behavior in other areas of public interest (Wallack 1981; Roberts & Maccoby 1985).

This is not to disparage attempts to educate the public about the environmental consequences of specific behaviors, but simply to acknowledge that the evidence to date suggests that what can be accomplished in this fashion is probably relatively limited unless more effective informational techniques are developed. Ensuring that people understand the environmental consequences of specific behaviors appears not to be equivalent to motivating individuals to modify their ways of doing things in the direction of greater environmental friendliness. But if being well informed does not ensure environmentally friendly behavior, not being well informed more or less guarantees that one cannot be an effective agent of environmental preservation even if one is motivated to do so.

One goal of efforts to inform the public about environmental matters should be to improve people's understanding of the relative effectiveness of various actions they could take; it is possible for well-intentioned people to expend considerable effort to do things that have relatively little effect while being oblivious to other actions that would have much greater impact (Stern & Gardner 1981). Many consumers lack an accurate understanding of the energy demands of different household appliances (Kempton & Montgomery 1982; Kempton *et al.* 1985; Costanzo *et al.* 1986), or of the relative effectiveness of specific energy-conservation behaviors, such as turning off unused lights vs. making less frequent use of the clothes dryer (Dennis *et al.* 1990).

Here I want to focus on one aspect of the design of messages intended to inform individuals of how they can engage in behavior that is beneficial to the environment and to motivate them to do it. Much of the more recent relevant work relates to the concept of *social marketing*, which conveys the idea of motivating behavior by persuasive messages pointing out the benefits of that behavior. Having proved effective in other contexts, social marketing techniques seem well worth exploring for application when the objective is to make behavior more environmentally friendly (McKenzie-Mohr 2000; Monroe *et al.* 2000; Monroe 2003).

There is much evidence that people's behavior, as it relates to environmental change, is influenced by what they believe the behavior of their peers to be and by what they consider to be generally acceptable – or admirable – within their social contexts (Stern *et al.* 1986; Archer *et al.* 1987; Kahle & Beatty 1987; Cialdini *et al.* 1990; Jones 1990; Vining & Ebreo 1990). This might be seen as an argument for publicizing typical electrical energy use, water use, recycling activity, and other environmentally-relevant behavior, in the hope of bringing atypical behavior more in line with the norm (Pallak *et al.* 1980). One might wonder if this approach risks the possibility of influencing people who are doing better than average to modify their behavior in the direction of typicality, thereby offsetting gains realized from modifying the behavior of "underachievers" for the better. This is an empirical question that could be answered by research. An alternative approach could be to publicize examples of behavior that is atypical in the preferred direction, thereby providing role models worthy of emulation from an environmental point of view. Whether this approach would have the desired effect also is a question for research.

An approach to motivating environmentally friendly behavior that has been widely used is that of directly appealing to the public with signs and messages of various types: pleas and admonitions to recycle, to reduce waste, to walk sometimes instead of drive, to use public transportation when possible, to lower thermostats in winter and use air conditioning more sparingly in summer, and so on. It is increasingly common to see, in hotel rooms, printed messages requesting that one shorten the time spent in the shower, to volunteer to use the same sheets for two nights, to be willing to reuse towels – all for the sake of conserving water. It is of considerable interest, for both theoretical and practical purposes, to know what determines the extent to which such appeals are effective.

Cialdini (2005) reports an experiment in which hotel room appeals to reuse towels so as to conserve water were more effective when accompanied by the information that "almost 75 per cent of guests who are asked to participate in our new resource savings program do help by using their towels more than once" than when the information on participation rate was not provided. The same study showed a similar beneficial effect of the hotel informing guests that it had already made "a financial contribution to a nonprofit environmental protection organization in behalf of the hotel and its guests" (as distinct from promising to make such a contribution in the future) and requested that guests help recover the cost of the contribution by reusing towels. These results were seen to be consistent with other work showing the persuasive force of social norms and the general tendency of people to feel an obligation to reciprocate for favors done (Gouldner 1960; Schultz 1999; Cialdini 2001).

These are thought-provoking results, not only because they show the effectiveness of certain types of information in motivating desired behavior, but because they also raise an important issue. Suppose it is demonstrated beyond doubt that people are more likely to do X when informed that the majority of people do it, and that it is generally recognized that it would be good if everyone did it. It does not follow that claiming that the majority of people do X, independently of whether the claim is true, would be a good way to increase the percentage of people who do. Should one be tempted to make the inference, the temptation should be resisted, for both ethical and pragmatic reasons. The ethical argument is obvious, but if one does not find that compelling, there is the pragmatic concern that, inasmuch as the persuasiveness of a message depends in part on the credibility of its source as perceived by the message's recipients (McGuire 1969; Hass 1981), tailoring messages strictly for effect, without careful concern for their factuality, would eventually produce the kind of distrust and cynicism about the content of appeals that is already arguably the prevailing response to much advertising.

Much of the effort to effect behavioral change has appealed to people's sense of altruism (Schwartz 1977). Messages intended to encourage environmentally friendly behavior have typically been framed to appeal to altruistic motives, being "replete with references to 'saving,' 'helping,' or 'protecting,' actions that are done for the benefit of another" (Schultz & Zelezny 2003, p. 131). In view of the strong emphasis in many contemporary societies on self-enhancement (in contrast to self-transcendence), the question arises as to whether messages framed to appeal to self-enhancement motivation might be more effective in evoking the desired behavior than those that appeal to altruistic interests. Schultz and Zelezny give several examples of messages framed by the Biodiversity Project (Elder 2003) so as to have this type of appeal. They caution, however, that little is yet known of their effectiveness.

There appears to be general agreement among researchers that intrinsic motivation is more likely than extrinsic motivation (monetary incentives, pleading) to move people to engage in environmentally beneficial behavior over the long run (Levenson 1974; Deci &

Ryan 1985). Parnell and Larsen (2005) discuss several possible sources of intrinsic satisfaction or gratification that have been identified and that might motivate people to engage in environmentally beneficial behavior (e.g., the feeling of competence in dealing with a serious problem, a sense of participating with others in a socially beneficial endeavor).

One type of information that has proved to be effective in modifying behavior, or in sustaining change, at least for short periods of time, is feedback regarding the effectiveness of programs in which people have been asked to participate. For example, regular feedback regarding the effectiveness of efforts to increase participation in recycling programs has been shown to sustain increased levels of participation, at least over periods during which the feedback is provided, although, unhappily, the participation is likely to drop off when the feedback is discontinued (Kim *et al.* 2005).

Research on how attitudes and behavior relate to environmental change and how they might be modified for the better has produced many thought-provoking and useful results. The conclusions that can be drawn from this work have been limited in certain respects, however, because of constraints inherent to methods used, populations studied, and experimental tasks employed. The methods used often are limited to revealing correlational relationships among specific variables, which are informative and useful but that generally do not answer questions regarding the nature of cause-and-effect relationships that are involved. Recent work showing a strong correlation between the likelihood of people expressing an intention to recycle and the degree of correspondence between their descriptions of prototypical recyclers and their descriptions of themselves (Mannetti *et al.* 2004) illustrates the point. In Mannetti, Pierro, and Livi's terms, the finding demonstrates that identity similarity is a strong predictor of expressed intention to recycle, but it is not clear whether people are likely to express an intention to recycle because they see themselves as similar to prototypical recyclers or they see themselves as similar to recyclers because they have the intention to recycle. Possibly, too, such correlations could be the result, in part, of task demand characteristics.

Persuasiveness is more than a matter of logic and weight of evidence. The persuasiveness of an argument may depend not only on its content and logical form, but on more cosmetic aspects of the language in which it is expressed (Burgoon & King 1974; Burgoon & Bettinghaus 1980). Not surprisingly, people tend to be more easily persuaded by people to whom they are attracted than by people they dislike (Hovland *et al.* 1953). Both attractiveness and persuasiveness appear to vary with the degree to which people perceive others to be similar to themselves (Brock 1965; Bryne 1971). Mackie and colleagues found that people are likely to be persuaded by strong arguments made by in-group members although not by weak arguments made by in-group members, but to be relatively unmoved by arguments made by people outside the group, independently of their strength (Mackie *et al.* 1990; 1992).

Dealing with Social Dilemmas

Social dilemmas are situations in which self-interest tends to clash with the common good, as exemplified by the well-known metaphor of the "tragedy of the commons" (Hardin 1968). The prototypical situation is one in which short-term benefits from public resources can be enjoyed by a few members of a group, whereas the long-term costs are borne by the group as a whole. It was suggested in the chapter on the environment in the first edition of the *Handbook* that the occurrence of conflicts of the social-dilemma type seem bound to increase as concern about environmental problems continues to grow and especially as consumption increases both as a consequence of a growing world population (for projections and details, see Cohen 2003) and the economic development of many third world countries. This points up the need for better techniques both for anticipating conflicts so they can be avoided, and for resolving those that do occur so they do not escalate to crisis proportions.

Especially needed are approaches that can restructure zero-sum and win–lose conflicts into non-zero-sum and win–win situations, and those that can work despite reluctance on the part of parties to compromise. How to deal effectively with social dilemmas has been the focus of considerable research (Platt 1973; Messick & Brewer 1983; Ostrom 1990; Gardner & Stern 1996; Van Vugt 1997). Methods of study include computer simulations as well as experiments both in the laboratory and real-world settings. Studies of social dilemmas are a subset of the very large literature on competition, cooperation, negotiation, and policy-making much of which is relevant to the problem of making behavior more environmentally friendly.

Several efforts to address social dilemmas have realized considerable success (Berkes *et al.* 1989; Leavitt & Saegert 1989; Malle 1996; Ostrom *et al.* 1999), which is not to say that they have been problem free (Feeney *et al.* 1990). Developing a better understanding of the variables that determine the success or failure of attempts to deal with social dilemmas is one of the continuing challenges to research (Swap 1991), as is the discovery of more effective ways to evoke voluntary cooperative behavior in situations in which the natural tendency is likely to be to benefit at society's expense.

Although perhaps not social dilemmas in the sense of the "tragedy of the commons," situations that arise from efforts to deal with environmental problems sometimes put the interests of subsets of society in conflict with those of society as a whole. The problem of finding sites for the disposal or treatment of waste, especially toxic or hazardous waste, is among the more salient of such situations. No one questions the need for such facilities, but few people are willing to have them located in their own neighborhoods (Morell & Magorian 1980; Portney 1991; Kraft & Clary 1993).

The designation of protected areas for conservation purposes is often resisted much as is the siting of waste disposal facilities, but for different reasons. Residents of a region in which an area is designated for protection are likely to resist, especially if the area contains natural resources they are exploiting and the designation is being promoted by non-local authorities (Bonaiuto *et al.* 2002). Opposition is likely to be less strong, or even to give way to support, when the designated area does not contain natural resources that are being exploited by residents of the region and when residents can see advantages to the region of having the area protected (Carrus *et al.* 2005).

How one feels about designation of protected areas is likely to depend also on one's attitude toward nature generally; people who see nature as unattractive or scary (Bixler & Floyd 1997) are unlikely to have the same reaction as people who believe that experiencing nature can have a restorative effect on people suffering mental fatigue or be beneficial to health in general (Kaplan & Kaplan 1989; Dustin 1994; Irvine & Warber 2002).

DECISIONS AND TRADEOFFS

How decisions are made (or should be made) when the outcomes of possible options are not known with certainty is among the more extensively investigated subjects in cognitive psychology. Because the outcomes of various alternative approaches to perceived environmental problems are seldom known with certainty, much of this work should be relevant to the problem of dealing with environmental issues. The consequences of decisions made with respect to complex situations characterized by many interacting variables typically involve tradeoffs that are difficult, if not impossible, to predict with accuracy, or perhaps even to anticipate at all. This complicates, but makes even more critical, the study of decision-making aimed at environmental protection.

Decision-making under Uncertainty

Some applications of decision-making research have been made to environmental problems, but relatively few. The need for explicitly teaching students how to apply to environmental problems structured decision-making techniques, such as those discussed by Plous (1993) and Hammond *et al.* (1999), has been stressed by Arvai *et al.* (2004).

Fundamental to all decision-making activities is the determination of preferences among possible decision outcomes. Presumably people make selections among alternative courses of action on the basis of preferences they have among the expected consequences of those actions. Determining what the preferences are in specific instances turns out to be a nontrivial task, in part because people often cannot say with confidence what their preferences are, especially if they had not thought about them explicitly until being asked. One way of determining how much people value specific goods is to ask how much they would be willing to pay for them if they could be purchased (Kahneman & Knetsch 1992; Kahneman *et al.* 1993).

A limitation of the willingness-to-pay method of determining preferences is that one cannot be sure that people would actually pay what they say they would when nothing is really at stake. Another is that it is subject to certain context effects. For example, when asked how much they would be willing to pay for a good, A, which is a natural part of a larger good, B, they are likely to give a much larger figure if they are asked about good A in isolation than if they are asked about good A after having been asked about the more inclusive good B (Kahneman & Knetsch 1992; Kemp & Maxwell 1993).

Many researchers have found that preferences among decision outcomes can be determined not only by what the outcomes are, but by the way in which they are represented. This is generally known as the "framing effect" and it has been obtained in a variety of decision contexts including medicine (McNeil *et al.* 1982; Teigen & Brun 1999), gambling (Levin *et al.* 1986, 1988), and public opinion polls (Payne 1982; Moore 1992). It is easy to see how options that exist for dealing with environmental problems might evoke different responses from policy-makers or the general public, depending on such factors as whether questions are couched in terms of potential losses or potential gains (e.g., species lost or species saved; Tversky & Kahneman 1981) and on whether respondents are required to reveal preferences among alternatives by choosing some or by rejecting some (Shafir 1993).

Closely related to the framing effect is the phenomenon of "preference reversal," in which people express a preference for A over B when attempting to acquire one or the other but then attach a greater value to B than to A when pricing for resale (Lichtenstein & Slovic 1971; Slovic & Lichtenstein 1983; Goldstein & Einhorn 1987). Preference reversals have been found in the valuation of public goods and the measurement of environmental variables (Irwin *et al.* 1993; Kahneman & Ritov 1994).

Many other examples of findings of research on decision-making under uncertainty that might have implications for addressing problems of environmental change could be noted. The problem area holds many opportunities for the application of research methods that have been applied in other domains of decision-making or that have been used to study decision-making in the abstract.

Solutions vs. Tradeoffs

Sowell (1995) makes a compelling case that, at least in the context of addressing socially significant problems of interest to the general public, there are no solutions, only tradeoffs. Thinking in terms of solutions runs the risk of overlooking that what appears to be a solution to a particular problem when viewed from a narrow perspective can, and often does, turn out to have one or more unanticipated and undesired consequences when viewed from a broader perspective. Schwartz (1971) makes a similar point in noting that solutions to problems can turn out to be "quasi-solutions," because they generate unanticipated residue problems that are worse than the problems "solved." This is especially likely to be the case when the problem for which a solution is sought is complexly related to many variables, as is likely to be true of problems of environmental change. In many cases, the tradeoffs involved may remain unrecognized as such because the unanticipated and unwanted effects are delayed for a sufficiently long time that they may be perceived as independent of the decisions that produced them.

When the subject of tradeoffs is mentioned in the context of environmental change, one is likely to think immediately of situations in which environmental and economic interests conflict. Stiff resistance to policies intended to be protective of the environment is often motivated by concern for the perceived negative implications of those policies for economic development; and, conversely, proposals of economic development are often opposed because of concerns for their anticipated environmental effects. The development of more effective ways to resolve such conflicts is a major challenge to research, and cognitive psychology should have much to offer to this objective. Here I want to focus on tradeoffs that can be hidden in what can appear to be environmentally sound "solutions" to specific problems.

There are countless examples of developments that were viewed initially as totally beneficial that had hidden costs that only gradually came to light, sometimes after many years. The benefits of asbestos were recognized and exploited long before the hazards involved in its handling and use were widely recognized. The making of fire-resistant cloth from asbestos fibers spun like wool dates at least from the first century AD. In the United States, asbestos began to be used in insulating materials early in the nineteenth century; many products incorporating asbestos were marketed throughout the better part of the twentieth century and it was only during the 1970s that the popularity of this substance began to decline as some of the health implications of its handling began to come to light (Alleman & Mossman 1997).

Improvements in the process of synthesizing ammonia during the middle of the twentieth century made large-scale production of nitrogen-rich fertilizer economically feasible. The use of nitrogen fertilizer, production of which increased by a factor of eight between 1950 and 1980, became a major factor in ensuring the ability of farmers to grow enough crops to meet the world's food demands. However, introduction into the ground of large amounts of reactive nitrogen proved to be harmful to the environment in ways that were not anticipated. In addition to problems that can stem from the acidification of soil and the leaching of nitrates into ground and surface water (e.g., polluting of wells, eutrophication of lakes and streams) the use of nitrogen fertilizer also increases the amount of nitrous oxide in the atmosphere, problematic in view of the fact that a molecule of this compound absorbs about 200 times as much outgoing radiation as does a molecule of carbon dioxide (Smil 1997).

When invented by Thomas Midgley in 1931, chlorofluorocarbons (CFCs) were celebrated as an ideal solution to the environmental and safety problems represented by the toxic, flammable, corrosive chemicals such as ammonia and sulfur dioxide that were being used as coolants in home refrigerators at the time. Not until several decades later did the accumulation of CFCs in the stratosphere begin to be seen as possibly at least partially responsible for some thinning of ozone there (Molina & Rowland 1974; Rowland & Molina 1975).

Currently, there is great interest in the tapping of hydrogen as a major source of energy for motor vehicles, among other applications (Burns *et al.* 2002). As a basic fuel, hydrogen has much to recommend it from an environmental point of view, a major attraction being the fact that the main by-product of burning it is water. But the use of hydrogen is not without its own problems. While hydrogen fuel cells are more efficient than internal combustion engines and emit no greenhouse gases, the production of hydrogen is itself an energy-intense process which, if performed with fossil fuels, can have the same detrimental environmental effects as does burning fossil fuels in cars (Wald 2004). So there is the possibility of simply changing the locations of the polluting emissions. Storage and distribution of hydrogen also pose problems from a safety point of view. Transportation of hydrogen as a gas is inefficient, as compared with the transportation of gasoline; transportation of hydrogen in liquid form is less inefficient, but liquefying hydrogen is itself an energy-consuming process.

Despite undoubted environmental benefits that would be derived from the use of hydrogen as an automotive fuel (e.g., elimination of emissions of CO_2 and other pollutants at the point of use), whether a push to develop hydrogen cars is the best strategy for reducing the impact of automotive transportation on the environment, all factors considered, is not clear. This is important, because how resources for research are allocated now depends in large measure on what is believed about how progress on the emissions problem can best be made.

> If we were certain that hydrogen fuel was the only long-run solution to eliminating CO_2 emissions from cars, then it might make sense to focus R&D now, even though widespread deployment is decades away. If, however, we accept that there is considerable uncertainty about the optimum long-run solution, then early commitment to hydrogen fuel is unwise because it risks technological lock-in. (Keith & Farrell 2003, p. 316)

If there is a bona fide science of decision-making under uncertainty, this is a problem that seems ideally suited to its application.

All energy resources, renewable as well as non-renewable, have an environmental impact, although they differ with respect to both environmental and economic costs per unit of energy produced. Rank-ordering alternatives in terms of a single cost-benefit ratio that takes into account the various types of costs is not easy (Chow *et al.* 2003). A major challenge to cognitive psychology that relates directly to this problem is that of determining how to foster the kind of thinking that effectively takes easily overlooked consequences into account in the setting of goals and evaluation of approaches that are considered for realizing them. Spiro *et al.* (1991) argue that, especially in ill-structured domains, knowledge acquisition is often impeded by a "reductive bias," that is, a tendency to oversimplify what has to be learned.

> The more complex and ill-structured the domain, the more there is to be understood for any instructional topic; and therefore, the more that is unfortunately hidden in any single pass, in any single context, for any restricted set of purposes, or from the perspective of any single conceptual model. (p. 29)

The many-faceted nature of the problem of environmental change and the difficult-to-anticipate ramifications of many possible remedial actions invite oversimplification of the sort that Spiro *et al.* describe.

It is unlikely that all the unpleasant surprises that I have mentioned, and others of a similar kind, could have been avoided if only people had thought more carefully about the possible negative effects of innovations. Some of them might not have been anticipated no matter how careful the thinking had been. But it does appear to be the case that we are naturally inclined to think in uni-dimensional terms – to focus on how to attain a specific goal and to evaluate possible approaches only in terms of the probability of attaining that goal, without giving adequate consideration to possible unintended consequences. To the extent that research in cognitive psychology can discover ways to foster multi-dimensional thinking – thinking that actively seeks to identify possible effects of actions that are easily overlooked – that would be a substantive contribution to progress on the problem of detrimental environmental change. There is a need also for the development of effective means of educating the public to the importance of taking a broad view in assessing any new technology with respect to its potential environmental impact.

The need to recognize tradeoffs is illustrated also by the unanticipated negative effects of some of the approaches to water utilization and conservation that were generally considered appropriate during the twentieth century, typically involving the construction of dams, centralized treatment plants, and other large infrastructure projects. Whereas such approaches accomplished much good, unanticipated costs often included long-term ecological and environmental damage. Gleick (2003) points out that preference appears to be shifting toward less centralized smaller-scale projects, at least as complements to, if not replacements of, the larger-scale approaches. What is desired are "soft-path" techniques that will help meet water needs without incurring large, unwanted negative side-effects. Realization of the soft-path goals requires a better understanding of the specific needs that water (of different qualities) meets for various types of users (individual consumers, industry, agriculture, natural ecological systems) and the development of planning, decision-making, and management tools that are effective at various levels of organization (local, regional, national).

The problem of tradeoffs can also be seen in considerations that pertain to the cleanup of environmentally contaminated sites. What could be clearer than the desirability of cleaning up such sites? However, aggressive cleanup measures can themselves do environmental damage (Whicker *et al.* 2004), and in some cases health risks to cleanup workers can be greater than the public health risks of no action (Church 2001). These facts challenge the assumption that cleanup is always the best approach to environmental contamination. Especially where contamination is relatively slight and natural attenuation is relatively rapid, alternative approaches, perhaps involving monitored natural attenuation and the use of buffer zones, could arguably be safer, more environmentally friendly, and more economical. The situation points up the need for decision-making procedures aimed at achieving long-term protection of public health and ecosystems and that take into account not only risks associated with contamination but those associated with cleanup processes as well.

There seems little doubt that the choices relating to the environment that people will face, as individuals and as a society, will be difficult and probably increasingly so. Simple solutions will seldom be among the realistic options, although the tendency to think in uni-dimensional terms may deceive us into believing in simple solutions that do not exist. Again the problem is basically a cognitive one and the challenge is to find approaches to decision-making and planning that minimize unpleasant surprises.

CONCLUDING COMMENT

Where does protection of the environment fit among the various problems that we face as individuals, as a nation, as a species? There are plenty of serious problems in the world if one has a mind to pay attention to them: devastating famines, runaway epidemics, ethnic strife, brutally repressive political regimes. When one considers the big picture, is the problem of environmental change really worth getting excited about?

I believe it is. Famines, epidemics, atrocities stemming from political and ethnic strife unquestionably represent serious challenges to civilization, but their existence does not diminish the importance of changes in the quality of the environment that could have unhappy consequences for a very long time. Many scientists have shown sufficient concern about detrimental environmental change to have urged that the problem be addressed in tangible ways. Concern among the general population, and across socio-demographic categories, appears to have been increasing over the recent past (Fransson & Garling 1999). Interest in how human behavior contributes to the problem and how that behavior might be modified in the direction of greater environmental friendliness may be increasing among psychologists. It seems only natural that this should be so. Research on cognition has produced a considerable body of knowledge about how the mind works – sometimes remarkably well, sometimes less so – that should be applicable to any problems the effective addressing of which requires reasoning, problem-solving, decision-making and the like. Detrimental environmental change clearly is that type of problem.

Finally, a caveat. Much research on human cognition is open to the criticism that the results have been obtained in experiments that use puzzle-type tasks with college students, and that it is not clear how well they generalize to meaningful problems faced in real-life contexts outside the psychological laboratory, especially where the problems are complex and the stakes are high. The laboratory studies have produced many thought-provoking findings, and are suggestive of a variety of ways in which reasoning, problem-solving, and decision-making might be improved, but in most cases it would be good to have confirmation that the findings will hold with meaningful tasks in real-world contexts. The need for research with a broader participant base is especially great when matters of public concern are the focus of interest.

AUTHOR NOTE

I am grateful to Francis Durso, Robert Hoffman, and an anonymous reviewer for helpful comments on a draft of this chapter.

REFERENCES

Ajzen, I. (2000). Nature and operation of attitudes. *Annual Review of Psychology, 52*, 27–58.

Ajzen, I. & Fishbein, M. (1980). *Understanding Attitudes and Predicting Social Behavior.* Englewood Cliffs, NJ: Prentice Hall.

Alleman, J. E. & Mossman, B. T. (1997). Asbestos revisited. *Scientific American, 277*(1), 70–75.

Alley, R. B. (2004). Abrupt climate change. *Scientific American, 291*(5), 62–69.

Archer, D., Pettigrew, T., Costanzo, M. *et al.* (1987). Energy conservation and public policy: the mediation of individual behavior. In W. Kempton & M. Neiman (eds.), *Energy Efficiency: Perspectives on Individual Behavior* (pp. 69–92). Washington, DC: American Council on Energy-Efficient Economy.

Arvai, J. L., Campbell, V. E. A., Baird, A. & Rivers, L. (2004). Teaching students to make better decisions about the environment: lessons from the decision sciences. *The Journal of Environmental Education, 36*, 33–42.

Atman, C. J., Bostrom, A., Fischhoff, B. & Morgan, M. G. (1994). Designing risk communications: completing and correcting mental models of hazardous processes, Part I. *Risk Analysis, 14*, 779–788.

Bamberg, S. (2003). How does environmental concern influence specific environmentally relatied behavior? A new answer to an old question. *Journal of Environmental Psychology, 23*, 21–32.

Barker, R. G. (1968). *Ecological Psychology: Concepts and Methods for Studying the Environment of Human Behavior.* Stanford, CA: Stanford University Press.

Baum, A. & Fleming, I. (1993). Implications of psychological research on stress and technological accidents. *American Psychologist, 48*, 665–672.

Beringer, A. (2003). A conservation psychology with heart. *Human Ecology Review, 10*, 150–153.

Berkes, F., Feeney, D., McCay, B. J. & Acheson, J. M. (1989). The benefits of the common. *Nature, 340*, 91–93.

Bindschadler, R. A. & Bentley, C. R. (2002). On thin ice? *Scientific American, 287*(6), 98–105.

Bixler, R. & Floyd, M. (1997). Nature is scary, disgusting, and uncomfortable. *Environment and Behavior, 5*, 202–247.

Böhm, G. & Pfister, H. R. (2000). Action tendencies and characteristics of environmental risks. *Acta Psychologica, 104*, 317–337.

Bonaiuto, M., Carrus, G., Martorella, H. & Bonnes, M. (2002). Local identity processes and environmental attitudes in land use changes: the case of natural protected areas. *Journal of Environmental Quality, 21*, 369–385.

Bongaarts, J. (2002) Population: ignoring its impact. *Scientific American, 286*(1), 67–70.

Bott, S., Cantrill, J. G. & Myers, O. E. Jr. (2003). Place and the promise of conservation psychology. *Human Ecology Review, 10*, 100–112.

Brock, T. C. (1965). Communicator-recipient similarity and decision change. *Journal of Personality and Social Psychology, 1*, 650–654.
Bronfenbrenner, U. (1979). *The Ecology of Human Development*. Cambridge, MA: Harvard University Press.
Brown, T. C. & Daniel, T. C. (1987). Context effects in perceived environmental quality assessment: scene selection and landscape quality ratings. *Journal of Environmental, 7*, 233–250
Bryne, D. (1971). *The Attraction Paradigm*. New York: Academic Press.
Burgoon, M. & Bettinghaus, E. P. (1980). Persuasive message strategies. In M. E. Roloff & G. R. Miller (eds.), *Persuasion: New Directions in Theory and Research* (Vol. 8, pp. 141–169). Beverly Hills, CA: Sage.
Burgoon, M. & King, L. B. (1974). The mediation of resistance to persuasion strategies by language variables and active-passive participation. *Human Communication Research, 1*, 30–41.
Burns, L. D., McCormick, J. & Borroni-Bird, C. E. (2002). Hydrogen fuel-cell cars could be the catalyst for a cleaner tomorrow. *Scientific American, 287*(4), 64–73.
Burton, I., Kates, R. W. & White, G. R. (1978). *The Environment as Hazard*. New York: Oxford University Press.
Carrus, G., Bonaiuto, M. & Bonnes, M. (2005). Environmental concern, regional identity, and support for protected areas in Italy. *Environment and Behavior, 37*, 237–257.
Carson, R. (1962). *Silent Spring*. Boston, MA: Houghton Mifflin.
Catalano, R. (1979). *Health, Behavior, and the Community: An Ecological Perspective*. Elmsford, NY: Pergamon Press.
Chow, J., Kopp, R. J. & Portney, P. R. (2003). Energy resources and global development. *Science, 302*, 1528–1531.
Church, B. W. (2001). Environmental remedial action: are we doing more harm than good? *Environmental Science Pollution Research* (Special Issue 1), 9–24.
Cialdini, R. B. (2001). *Influence: Science and Practice* (4th edn). Needham Heights, MA: Allyn and Bacon.
Cialdini, R. B. (2005). Don't throw in the towel: use social influence research. *APS Observer, 18*(4), 33–34.
Cialdini, R. B., Reno, R. R. & Kallgren, C. A. (1990). A focus theory of normative conduct: recycling the concept of norms to reduce littering in public places. *Journal of Personality and Social Psychology, 58*, 1015–1026.
Cohen, J. E. (2003). Human population: the next half century. *Science, 302*, 1172–1175.
Combs, B. & Slovic, P. (1979). Causes of death: biased newspaper coverage and biased judgments. *Journalism Quarterly, 56*, 837–843.
Condelli, L., Archer, D., Aronson, E. *et al.* (1984). Improving utility conservation programs: outcomes, interventions, and evaluations. *Energy, 9*, 485–494.
Costanzo, M., Archer, D., Aronson, E. & Pettigrew, T. (1986). Energy conservation behavior: the difficult path from information to action. *American Psychologist, 41*, 521–528.
Cummings, N. A. & O'Donohue, W. T. O. (2005). Psychology's surrender to political correctness. In R. H. Wright & N. A. Cummings (eds.), *Destructive Trends in Mental Health* (pp. 3–27). New York: Routledge.
Damasio, A. R. (1994). *Descartes' Error: Emotion, Reason, and the Human Brain*. New York: G. P. Putnam's Sons.
Deci, E. L. & Ryan, R. M. (1985). *Intrinsic Motivation and Self-determinism in Human Behavior*. New York: Plenum.
Dennis, M. L., Soderstrom, E. J., Koncinski, W. S. Jr. & Cavanaugh, B. (1990). Effective dissemination of energy-related information: applying social psychology and evaluation research. *American Psychologist, 45*, 1109–1117.
Dunlap, R. E. & Van Liere, K. D. (1978). The new environmental paradigm: a proposed measuring instrument and preliminary results. *Journal of Environmental Education, 9*, 10–19.
Dunlap, R. E., Van Liere, K. D., Mertig, A. G. & Jones, R. E. (2000). Measuring endorsements of the New Ecological Paradigm: a revised NEP scale. *Journal of Social Issues, 56*, 425–442.

Dustin, D. (1994). Managing public lands for the human spirit. *Parks and Recreation*, *29*, 92–96.
Dwyer, W. O., Leeming, F. C., Cobern, M. K. *et al.* (1993). Critical review of behavioral interventions to preserve the environment: research since 1980. *Environment and Behavior*, *25*, 275–321.
Ehrlich, P. R. (1968). *The Population Bomb.* New York: Ballantine Books.
Elder, J. (2003). Biodiversity as a topic that needs public awareness and action. *Human Ecology Review*, *10*, 127.
Ester, P. A. & Winett, R. A. (1982). Toward more effective antecedent strategies for environmental programs. *Journal of Environmental Systems*, *11*, 201–221.
Evans, G. W., Jacobs, S. V. & Frager, N. B. (1982). Adaptation to air pollution. *Journal of Environmental Psychology*, *2*, 99–108.
Feeney, D., Berkes, F., McCay, B. J. & Acheson, J. M. (1990). The tragedy of the commons: twenty-two years later. *Human Ecology*, *18*, 1–19.
Festinger, L. (1957). *A Theory of Cognitive Dissonance.* Evanston, IL: Row, Peterson.
Finucane, M. L., Alhakami, A., Slovic, P. & Johnson, S. M. (2000). The affect heuristic in judgments of risks and benefits. *Journal of Behvioral Decision Making*, *13*, 1–17.
Fischhoff, B., Slovic, P., Lichtenstein, S. *et al.* (1978). How safe is safe enough? A psychometric study of attitudes towards technological risks and benefits. *Policy Science*, *9*, 127–152.
Fishbein, M. & Ajzen, I. (1975). *Belief, Attitude, Intention, and Behavior: An Introduction to Theory and Research.* Reading, MA: Addison-Wesley.
Fisher, A. (2002). *Radical Eco-psychology: Psychology in the Service of Life.* Albany, NY: State University of New York Press.
Florig, H. K., Morgan, M. G., Morgan, K. M. *et al.* (2001). A deliberative method for ranking risks (I): overview and test bed development. *Risk Analysis*, *21*, 913–921.
Fransson, H. & Garling, T. (1999). Environmental concern: conceptual definitions, measurement methods, and research findings. *Journal of Environmental Psychology*, *14*, 149–157.
Frederick, S., Loewenstein, G. & O'Donoghue, T. (2002). Time discounting and time preference: a critical review. *Journal of Economic Literature*, *40*, 351–401.
Gardner, G. T. & Stern, P. C. (1996). *Environmental Problems and Human Behavior.* Boston, MA: Allyn and Bacon.
Geller, E. S., Winett, R. R. & Everett, P. B. (1982). *Preserving the Environment: New Strategies for Behavior Change.* Elmsford, NY: Pergamon Press.
Gibbs, W. W. (2001). On the termination of species. *Scientific American*, *285*(5), 40–49.
Giuliani, M. V. (2003). Theory of attachment and place attachment. In M. Bonnes, T. Lee & M. Bonaiuto (eds.), *Psychological Theories for Environmental Issues* (pp. 137–170). Aldershot: Ashgate.
Gleick, P. H. (2003). Global freshwater resources: soft-path solutions for the 21st century. *Science*, *302*, 1524–1528.
Goldstein, W. & Einhorn, H. (1987). Expression theory and the preference reversal phenomenon. *Psychological Review*, *94*, 236–254.
Gould, L. C., Gardner, G. T., DeLuca, D. R. *et al.* (1988). *Perceptions of Technological Risks and Benefits.* New York: Russell Sage Foundation.
Gouldner, A. W. (1960). The norm of reciprocity: a preliminary statement. *American Sociological Review*, *25*, 161–178.
Hammond, J., Keeney, R. L. & Raiffa, H. (1999). *Smart Choices: A Practical Guide to Making Better Decisions.* Cambridge, MA: Harvard Business School Press.
Hansen, J. (2004). Defusing the global warming time bomb. *Scientific American*, *290*(3), 68–77.
Hardin, G. (1968). The tragedy of the commons. *Science*, *162*, 1243–1248.
Hass, R. G. (1981). Effects of source characteristics on cognitive responses in persuasion. In R. E. Petty, T. M. Ostrom & T. C. Brock (eds.), *Cognitive Responses in Persuasion* (pp. 141–172). Hillsdale, NJ: Lawrence Erlbaum Associates.
Helson, H. (1964). *Adaptation Level Theory.* New York: Harper and Row.
Hendrickx, L. & Nicolaij, S. (2004). Temporal discounting and environmental risks: the role of ethical and loss-related concerns. *Journal of Environmental Psychology*, *24*, 409–422.

Holdren, J. P. (2002). Energy: asking the wrong question. *Scientific American, 286*(1), 63–68.
Holloway, M. (1996). Sounding out science. *Scientific American, 275*(4), 106–112.
Hovland, C. I., Janis, I. L. & Kelley, H. H. (1953). *Communication and Persuasion: Psychological Studies of Opinion Change*. New Haven, CT: Yale University Press.
Irvine, K. N. & Warber, S. L. (2002). Greening healthcare: practicing as if the natural environment really mattered. *Alternative Therapies, 8*, 76–83.
Irwin, J., Slovic, P., Lichtenstein, S. & McClelland, G. (1993). Preference reversals and the measurement of environmental values. *Journal of Risk and Uncertainty, 6*, 5–18.
Jastrow, R. (1990). Global warming report (Letter to the Editor). *Science, 247*, 14–15.
Jeffery, R. W. (1989). Risk behaviors and health: contrasting individual and population perspectives. *American Psychologist, 44*, 1194–1202.
Jones, R. E. (1990). Understanding paper recycling in an institutionally supportive setting: an application of the theory of reasoned action. *Journal of Environmental Systems, 19*, 307–321.
Kahle, L. R. & Beatty, S. E. (1987). Cognitive consequences of legislating postpurchase behavior: growing up with the bottle bill. *Journal of Applied Social Psychology, 17*, 828–843.
Kahneman, D. & Knetsch, J. L. (1992). Valuing public goods: the purchase of moral satisfaction. *Journal of Environmental Economics and Management, 22*, 57–70.
Kahneman, D. & Ritov, I. (1994). Determinants of stated willingness to pay for public goods: a study in the headline method. *Journal of Risk and Uncertainty, 9*, 5–38.
Kahneman, D., Ritov, I., Jacowitz, K. E. & Grant, P. (1993). Stated willingness to pay for public goods: A psychological perspective. *Psychological Sciences, 4*, 310–315.
Kaplan, R. & Kaplan, S. (1989). *The Experience of Nature: A Psychological Perspective*. New York: Cambridge University Press.
Keith, D. W. & Farrell, A. E. (2003). Rethinking hydrogen cars. *Science, 301*, 315–316.
Kemp, M. A. & Maxwell, C. (1993). Exploring a budget context for contingent valuation estimates. In J. A. Hausman (ed.), *Contingent Valuation: A Critical Assessment*. Amsterdam: North-Holland.
Kempton, W., Harris, C. K., Keith, J. G. & Weihl, J. S. (1985). Do consumers know what works in energy conservation? *Marriage and Family Review, 9*, 115–133.
Kempton, W. & Montgomery, L. (1982). Folk quantification of energy. *Energy, 7*, 817–827.
Kim, S., Oah, S. & Dickinson, A. M. (2005). The impact of public feedback on three recycling-related behaviors in South Korea. *Environment and Behavior, 37*, 258–274.
Kollmus, A. & Agyeman, J. (2002). Mind the gap: why do people act environmentally and what are the barriers to pro-environmental behavior? *Environmental Education Research, 8*, 239–260.
Kraft, M. E. & Clary, B. B. (1993). Citizen participation and the NIMBY syndrome: public responses to radioactive waste disposal. *Western Political Quarterly, 44*, 299–328.
Leavitt, J. & Saegert, S. (1989). *From Abandonment to Hope: Community Households in Harlem*. New York: Columbia University Press.
Levenson, H. (1974). Activism and powerful others: distinctions within the concept of internal-external control. *Journal of Personality Assessment, 38*, 377–383.
Levi, D. J. & Holder, E. E. (1986). Nuclear power: the dynamics of acceptability. *Environment and Behavior, 18*, 385–395.
Levin, I. P., Chapman, D. P. & Johnson, R. D. (1988). Confidence in judgments based on incomplete information: an investigation using both hypothetical and real gambles. *Journal of Behavioral Decision Making, 1*, 29–41.
Levin, I. P., Johnson, R. D., Deldin, P. J. *et al.* (1986). Framing effects in decisions with completely and incompletely described alternatives. *Organizational Behavior and Human Decision Processes, 38*, 48–64.
Lichtenstein, S. & Slovic, P. (1971). Reversals of preference between bids and choices in gambling decisions. *Journal of Experimental Psychology, 89*, 46–55.
Lichtenstein, S., Slovic, P., Fischhoff, B. *et al.* (1978). Judged frequency of lethal events. *Journal of Experimental Psychology: Human Learning and Memory, 4*, 551–578.
Lima, M. L. (2004). On the influence of risk perception on mental health: living near an incinerator. *Journal of Environmental Psychology, 24*, 71–84.
Lindzen, R. S. (1990). Global warming report (letter to the Editor). *Science, 247*, 14.

Loewenstein, G., Weber, E. U., Hsee, C. K. & Welch, N. (2001). Risk as feelings. *Psychological Bulletin, 127*, 267–286.
Lomborg, B. (2001). *The Skeptical Environmentalist: Measuring the Real State of the World.* Cambridge: Cambridge University Press.
Lomborg, B. (2002). The skeptical environmentalist replies. *Scientific American, 286*(5), 14–15.
Lovejoy, T. (2002). Biodiversity: dismissing scientific process. *Scientific American, 286*(1), 69–71.
Luterbacher, J., Dietrich, D., Xoplaki, E. *et al.* (2004). European seasonal and annual temperature variability, trends, and extremes since 1500. *Science, 303*, 1499–1503.
McGuire, W. J. (1969). The nature of attitudes and attitude change. In G. Lindzey & E. Aronson (eds.), *The Handbook of Social Psychology* (Vol. 3, 2nd edn). Reading, MA: Addison-Wesley.
McKenzie-Mohr, D. (2000). Fostering sustainable behavior through community-based social marketing. *American Psychologist, 55*, 531–537.
Mackie, D. M., Gastardo-Conaco, M. C. & Skelly, J. J. (1992). Knowledge of the advocated position and the processing of in-group and out-group persuasive messages. *Personality and Social Psychology Bulletin, 18*, 145–151.
Mackie, D. M., Worth, L. T. & Asuncion, A. G. (1990). Processing of persuasive in-group messages. *Journal of Personality and Social Psychology, 58*, 812–822.
MacLean, D. E. (1990) Comparing values in environmental policies: moral issues and moral arguments. In P. B. Hammond & R. Coppock (eds.), *Valuing Health Risks, Costs, and Benefits for Environmental Decision Making* (pp. 83–106). Washington, DC: National Academy Press.
McNeil, B., Pauker, S., Sox, H. Jr. & Tversky, A. (1982). Comment on the elicitation of preferences for alternative therapies. *New England Journal of Medicine, 306*, 1259–1262.
Malle, K-G. (1996). Cleaning up the River Rhine. *Scientific American, 274*(1), 70–75.
Mannetti, L., Pierro, A. & Livi, S. (2004). Recycling: planned and self-expressive behavior. *Journal of Environmental Psychology, 24*, 227–236.
Mayer, F. S. & Frantz, C. M. (2004). The connectedness to nature scale: a measure of individuals' feeling in community with nature. *Journal of Environmental Psychology, 24*, 503–515.
Messick, D. M. & Brewer, M. B. (1983). Solving social dilemmas. In L. Wheeler & P. Shaver (eds.), *Review of Personality and Social Psychology* (Vol. 4). Beverly Hills, CA: Sage.
Midden, C. J. & Verplanken, B. (1990). The stability of nuclear attitudes after Chernobyl. *Journal of Environmental Psychology, 10*, 111–119.
Molina, M. J. & Rowland, F. S. (1974). Stratospheric sink for chlorofluoromethanes: chlorine atom catalysed destruction of ozone. *Nature, 249*, 810–812.
Monroe, M. C. (2003). Two avenues for encouraging conservaton behaviors. *Human Ecology Review, 10*, 113–125.
Monroe, M. C., Day, B. A. & Grieser, M. (2000). GreenCOM weaves four strands. In B. A. Day & M. Monroe (eds.), *Environmental Education and Communication for a Sustainable World* (pp. 3–6). Washington, DC: Academy for Educational Development.
Moore, D. W. (1992). *The Super Pollsters.* New York: Four Walls Eight Windows.
Morell, D. & Magorian, C. (1980). *Siting Hazardous Waste Facilities: Local Opposition and the Myth of Preemption.* Cambridge, MA: Ballinger.
Morgan, K. M., DeKay, M. L., Fischbeck, P. S. *et al.* (2001). A deliberative method for ranking risks (II): evaluation of validity and agreement among risk managers. *Risk Analysis, 21*, 923–937.
Morgan, M. G., Florig, H. K., DeKay, M. L. & Fischbeck, P. (2000). Categorizing risks for risk ranking. *Risk Analysis, 20*, 49–58.
Newsweek (1975). The cooling earth (April 28, pp. 11–53). New York: Newsweek.
Nickerson, R. S. (1998). Confirmation bias: a ubiquitous phenomenon in many guises. *Review of General Psychology, 2*, 175–220.
Nickerson, R. S. (2003). *Psychology and Environmental Change.* Mahwah, NJ: Lawrence Erlbaum Associates.
Nierenberg, W. A. (1990). Global warming report (Letter to the Editor). *Science, 247*, 14.
Nilsson, A., von Bergstede, C. & Biel, A. (2004). Willingness to accept climate change strategies: the effect of values and norms. *Journal of Environmental Psychology, 24*, 267–277.

Nordlund, A. & Garvill, J. (2002). Value structures behind proenvironmental behavior. *Environment and Behavior, 34*, 740–756.

Oskamp, S. (1995). Applying social psychology to avoid ecological disaster. *Journal of Social Issues, 51*, 217.

Oskamp, S. (2000). A sustainable future for humanity: how can psychology help? *American Psychologist, 55*, 496–508.

Ostrom, E. (1990). *Governing the Commons: The Evolution of Institutions for Collective Action.* Cambridge: Cambridge University Press.

Ostrom, E., Burger, J., Field, C. B. *et al.* (1999). Revisiting the commons: local lessons, global challenges. *Science, 284*, 278–282.

Pallak, M. S., Cook, D. A. & Sullivan, J. J. (1980). Commitment and energy conservation. In L. Bickman (ed.), *Applied Social Psychology Annual* (Vol. 1, pp. 235–254). Beverly Hills, CA: Sage.

Parnell, R. & Larsen, O. P. (2005). Informing the development of domestic energy efficiency iniatives: an everyday householder-centered framework. *Environment and Behavior, 37*, 787–807.

Payne, J. W. (1982). Contingent decision behavior. *Psychological Bulletin, 92*, 382–402.

Platt, J. (1973). Social traps. *American Psychologist, 28*, 641–651.

Plous, S. (1993). *The Psychology of Judgment and Decision-making.* New York: McGraw-Hill.

Poortinga, W., Steg, L. & Vlek, C. (2004). Values, environmental concern, and environmental behavior. *Environment and Behavior, 36*, 70–93.

Portney, K. E. (1991). *Siting Hazardous Waste Treatment Facilities.* New York: Auburn House.

Renn, O. (1990). Public response to the Chernobyl accident. *Journal of Environmental Psychology, 10*, 151–167.

Reser, J. P. (2003). Thinking through "conservation psychology": prospects and challenges. *Human Ecology Review, 10*, 167–174.

Roberts, D. F. & Maccoby, N. (1985). Effects of mass communication. In G. Lindzey & E. Aronson (eds.), *Handbook of Social Psychology* (3rd edn). New York: Random House.

Roberts, L. (1989). Global warming: blaming the sun. *Science, 246*, 992.

Rogers-Warren, A. & Warren, S. F. (eds.) (1977). *Ecological Perspectives in Behavior Analysis.* Baltimore, MD: University Park Press.

Roszak, T. (1992). *The Voice of the Earth: An Exploration of Eco-psychology.* New York: Simon and Schuster.

Roszak, T., Gomes, M. & Kanner, A. (1995). *Ecopsychology.* San Francisco, CA: Sierra Club Books.

Rothman, S. & Lichter, S. R. (1987). Elite ideology and risk perception in nuclear energy policy. *American Political Science Review, 81*, 383–404.

Rowland, F. S. & Molina, M. J. (1975). Chlorofluoromethanes in the environment. *Reviews of Geophysics and Space Physics, 13*, 1–35.

Saunders, C. D. (2003). The emerging field of conservation psychology. *Human Ecology Review, 10*, 137–149.

Schneider, S. (2002). Global warming: neglecting the complexities. *Scientific American, 286*(1), 62–65.

Schultz, P. W. (1999). Changing behavior with normative feedback interventions: a field experiment on curbside recycling. *Basic and Applied Social Psychology, 21*, 25–38.

Schultz, P. W. (2001). Assessing the structure of environmental concern: concern for the self, other people, and the biosphere. *Journal of Environmental Psychology, 21*, 327–339.

Schultz, P. W., Schriver, C., Tabanico, J. & Khazian, A. (2004). Implicit connections with nature. *Journal of Environmental Psychology, 24*, 31–42.

Schultz, P. W. & Zelezny, L. (1998). Values and proenvironmental behavior: a five-country survey. *Journal of Cross-Cultrual Psychology, 29*, 540–558.

Schultz, P. W. & Zelezny, L. (1999). Values as predictors of environmental attitudes: evidence for consistency across cultures. *Journal of Environmental Psychology, 19*, 255–265.

Schultz, P. W. & Zelezny, L. (2003). Reframing environmental messages to be congruent with American values. *Human Ecology Review, 10*, 126–136.

Schwartz, E. (1971). *Overskill.* New York: Ballantine Books.

Schwartz, S. H. (1977). Normative influences on altruism. In L. Berkowitz (ed.), *Advances in Experimental Social Psychology* (Vol. 10, pp. 221–279). New York: Academic.
Schwartz, S. H. (1999). A theory of cultural values and some implications for work. *Applied Psychology: An International Review*, *48*, 23–47.
Seitz, F., Jastrow, R. & Nierenberg, W. A. (1989). *Scientific Perspectives on the Greenhouse Problem*. Washington, DC: George C. Marshall Institute.
Service, R. F. (2004). As the West goes dry. *Science*, *303*, 1124–1127.
Shafir, E. (1993). Choosing versus rejecting: why some options are both better and worse than others. *Memory and Cognition*, *21*, 546–556.
Sharlin, H. I. (1986). EDB: a case study in communicating risk. *Risk Analysis*, *6*, 61–68.
Shindell, D. (2003). Whither Arctic climate? *Science*, *299*, 215–216.
Slovic, P., Finucane, M. L., Peters, E. & MacGregor, D. (2004). Risk as analysis and risk as feelings: some thoughts about affect, reason, risk, and rationality. *Risk Analysis*, *24*, 311–322.
Slovic, P., Fischhoff, B. & Lichtenstein, S. (1976). Cognitive processes and societal risk taking. In J. S. Carroll & J. W. Payne (eds.), *Cognition and Social Behavior* (pp. 165–184). Hillsdale, NJ: Lawrence Erlbaum Associates.
Slovic, P., Fischhoff, B. & Lichtenstein, S. (1979). Rating the risks. *Environment*, *21*(3), 14–20, 36–39.
Slovic, P. & Lichtenstein, S. (1983). Preference reversals: a broader perspective. *American Economic Review*, *73*, 596–605.
Smil, V. (1997). Global population and the nitrogen cycle. *Scientific American*, *277*(1), 76–81.
Soon, W. & Baliunas, S. (2003) Proxy climatic and environmental changes of the past 1000 years. *Climate Research*, *23*, 89–110.
Soon, W., Baliunas, S., Idso, C. *et al.* (2003). Reconstructing climatic and environmental changes of the past 1000 years: a reappraisal. *Energy and Environment*, *14*, 233–296.
Sowell, T. (1995). *The Vision of the Anointed: Self Congratulation as a Basis for Social Policy*. New York: Basic Books.
Spiro, R. J., Feltovich, P. J., Jacobson, M. J. & Coulson, R. L. (1991). Cognitive flexibility, constructivism, and hypertext: random access instruction for advanced knowledge acquisition in ill-structured domains. *Educational Technology*, *31*, 24–33.
Staats, H. (2003). Understanding proenvironmental attitudes and behavior: an analysis and review of research based on the theory of planned behavior. In M. Bonnes, T. Lee & M. Bonaiuto (eds.), *Psychological Theories for Environmental Issues* (pp. 171–201). Aldershot: Ashgate.
Stern, P. C. (2000). Psychology and the science of human-environment interactions. *American Psychologist*, *55*, 523–530.
Stern, P. C. & Aronson, E. (eds.) (1984). *Energy Use: The Human Dimension*. New York: Freeman.
Stern, P. C., Dietz, T., Abel, T. *et al.* (1999). A value-belief-norm theory of support for social movements: the case of the environmentalism. *Research in Human Ecology*, *6*, 81–97.
Stern, P. C., Dietz, T. & Black, J. S. (1986). Support for environmental protection: the role of moral norms. *Population and Environment*, *8*, 104–222.
Stern, P. C. & Gardner, G. T. (1981). Psychological research and energy policy. *American Psychologist*, *36*, 329–342.
Sturm, M., Perovich, D. K. & Serreze, M. C. (2003). Meltdown in the north. *Scientific American*, *289*(4), 60–67.
Swap, W. C. (1991). Psychological factors in environmental decision making: social dilemmas. In R. A. Chechile & S. Carlisle (eds.), *Environmental Decision Making: A Multidisciplinary Perspective* (pp. 14–37). New York: Van Nostrand Reinhold.
Taylor, S. E. & Brown, J. D. (1988). Illusion and well-being: a social cognitive perspective on mental health. *Psychological Bulletin*, *106*, 231–248.
Teigen, K. H. & Brun, W. (1999). The directionality of verbal probability expressions: effects on decisions, predictions, and probabilistic reasoning. *Organizational Behavior and Human Decision Processes*, *80*, 155–190.
Thomas, L. (1983). An epidemic of apprehension. *Discover*, *4*, 78–80.
Tversky, A. & Kahneman, D. (1981). The framing of decisions and the psychology of choice. *Science*, *211*, 453–458.

Union of Concerned Scientists (1992). *World Scientists' Warning to Humanity.* Cambridge, MA: Union of Concerned Scientists.
Van der Pligt, J., Eiser, J. R. & Spears, R. (1986). Attitudes toward nuclear energy. *Environment and Behavior, 18*, 75–93.
Van der Pligt, J. & Midden, C. J. H. (1990). Chernobyl four years later: attitudes, risk management and communication. *Journal of Environmental Psychology, 10*, 91–99.
Van Vugt, M. (1997). Concerns about the privatization of public goods: a social dilemma analysis. *Social Psychology Quarterly, 60*, 355–367.
Verplanken, B. (1989). Involvement and need for cognition as moderators of beliefs-attitude-intention consistency. *British Journal of Social Psychology, 28*, 115–122.
Vining, J. & Ebreo, A. (1990). What makes a recycler? A comparison of recyclers and nonrecyclers. *Environment and Behavior, 22*, 55–73.
Vining, J. & Ebreo, A. (2002) Emerging theoretical and methodological perspectives on conservation behavior. In R. B. Bechtel & A. Churchman (eds.), *Handbook of Environmental Psychology* (pp. 541–558). New York: John Wiley & Sons.
Wald, M. L. (2004). Questions about a hydrogen economy. *Scientific American, 290*(5), 66–73.
Wallack, L. M. (1981). Mass media campaigns: the odds against finding behavior change. *Health Education Quarterly, 8*, 209–260.
Whicker, F. W., Hinton, T. G., MacDonell, M. M. *et al.* (2004). Avoiding remediation at DOE sites. *Science, 303*, 1615–1616.
White, R. M. (1990). The great climate debate. *Scientific American, 263*(1), 36–43.
Willis, H. H., DeKay, M. L., Morgan, M. G. *et al.* (2004). Ecological risk ranking: development and evaluation of a method for improving public participation in environmental decision making. *Risk Analysis, 24*, 363–378.
Winter, D. & Koger, S. M. (2004). *The Psychology of Environmental Problems* (2nd edn). Mahwah, NJ: Lawrence Erlbaum Associates.
Wohlwill, J. F. & Kohn, I. (1973). The environment as experienced by the migrant: an adaptation level approach. *Representative Research in Social Psychology, 4*, 135–164.

CHAPTER 28

Juror Decision-Making

Ryan J. Winter
Florida International University, USA

and

Edith Greene
University of Colorado-Colorado Springs, USA

COGNITION AND JUROR DECISION-MAKING

Imagine a day in the life of a typical juror, whether in England, Canada, New Zealand, Scotland, Ireland, Australia, or the United States. Upon arrival in court he or she is beset by a complex system of rules and procedures that are well rehearsed and well understood by the professionals who work in those settings, but complicated and obtuse to the newcomer. In some jurisdictions, the complexity is amplified by the jury selection process. In Canada, for example, two lay "triers" selected from the pool of potential jurors determine whether their fellow jurors can be impartial. In the US, the prosecutor and defense attorneys dismiss potentially biased jurors based either on readily apparent juror prejudices or on attorneys' intuitions about prospective jurors' inclinations. The stated purpose of jury selection in these jurisdictions is to assure the court that those jurors who remain are impartial. But for the prospective juror the questioning process involves a number of complicated cognitive tasks, including reconstruction of the past, forecasting of the future, and inferential reasoning.

In any jury trial, empanelled members must sift through conflicting arguments and evidence presentations and a series of exhaustive jury instructions that frequently involve concepts and language unfamiliar to most laypeople. In England, Australia, and Canada, jurors hear summations of the evidence by the judge that may differ in significant ways from attorneys' arguments. Then, during their deliberations, jurors are asked to recall vast amounts of trial evidence, expected to understand and apply their instructions, and ultimately, to decide on an "appropriate" verdict.

These procedures beg the question, how *do* jurors decide on an "appropriate" verdict? How willing, able, and motivated are they to process the large volume of trial evidence, some of it contradictory in nature? How do they assess and combine disparate sources of information? By what process do they evaluate and use the trial evidence in reaching their decisions? How do their prior experiences and preconceptions regarding the judicial

Handbook of Applied Cognition: Second Edition. Edited by Francis T. Durso.

system influence their decision-making abilities? Hastie (1993) suggests that one reason psychologists are interested in jurors' judgments is that the juror's task is an inherently complex one that involves almost all higher-order thought processes of interest to cognitive psychologists.

In this chapter, we attempt to address some of the cognitive aspects of juror decision-making. Although other recent reviews of juror and jury decision-making exist (e.g., Greene *et al.* 2002; Levett *et al.* 2005), to our knowledge none looks explicitly at the cognitive processes involved in individual jurors' decision-making. We focus on the individual as the unit of analysis, leaving for now the nascent field of research that focuses on deliberating juries. Though jury deliberation presents a fascinating arena for examining the complex social interplay of several deliberating thinkers, focusing on the *juror* gives us the opportunity to explore in more precise detail how cognitive factors alone influence legal decision-making. Importantly, many studies have documented the crucial role that individual jurors' preferences play in reaching a final jury verdict. Indeed, the pre-deliberation verdict preferences of individual jurors predict the final outcome in the vast majority of cases (MacCoun & Kerr 1988; Devine *et al.* 2001). So because most of the work involved in determining the resolution of a case happens in the thoughts of individual jurors, it makes sense to hone in on reasoning processes at the individual level. These processes are highly determinative of the jury's final verdict.

To begin, we outline various cognitive models of juror decision-making that have been advanced and tested in recent decades. In the sections that follow, where possible, we apply aspects of these models to applied problems in the legal realm. Although cognitive mechanisms influence judgments in all areas of law (as evidenced by chapters in the 1999 edition of the *Handbook of Applied Cognition* that explored the cognitive mechanisms underlying eyewitness testimony and pre-trial publicity), we focus our review on three specific psycho-legal domains: juror decisions related to the death penalty, sexual harassment, and damage awards. Although these topics are primarily germane to American law, they present psychologically important issues that extend beyond the particular legal contexts involved. In addition, they represent "hot topics" in psychology and law that have generated a great deal of recent empirical work. So focusing our gaze their way will allow assessment of how cognitive principles apply both to decisions in these particular domains of American law and to legal decision-making more generally.

To presage an important point though, juror research has been a relatively disjointed enterprise, at least from the perspective of a cognitive theorist; with some exceptions, researchers have tended to test *legal* assumptions about juror behavior rather than assumptions that flow from models of cognition. Stated otherwise, cognitive models and the postulates that come from those models have had only modest and fleeting impact on our understanding of jurors' thought processes. Why is this so? We suspect that many psycho-legal researchers were initially drawn to this field because it values and rewards real-world applicability somewhat more than detailed theory development and refinement (though, of course, most would agree that there is nothing so useful as a good theory). This desire for relevance and application in the real world has, at some level and with some exceptions, tended to trump concerns about advancing basic cognitive theory.

Although the development of theory has not been at the forefront of scholarly work on juror decision-making, neither has that work been atheoretical. In fact, the prevailing *zeitgeist* has been to borrow concepts and measures from cognitive or social-cognitive theories and use them to examine the aptness of legal assumptions about jurors' behavior.

For example, various researchers (e.g., Dewitt *et al.* 1997; Chen & Chaiken 1999; Simon 2004) have examined how different modes of information-processing influence jurors' decision-making. Applying aspects of the elaboration likelihood model (ELM) proposed by Petty and Cacioppo (1986), Dewitt *et al.* have shown that, as ELM would predict, mock jurors who are not motivated to process scientific evidence in a thoughtful and effortful way are also less likely to attend to issue-relevant arguments presented during a trial. Borrowing concepts of coherence-based reasoning, Simon (2004) has shown that jurors' decisions involve a complex and nuanced set of cognitive processes that transform difficult choices into easier ones by amplifying one alternative perspective on the evidence and deflating competing perspectives. In essence, the cognitive system imposes coherence on complicated decisional tasks. Other theories of reasoning, e.g., belief bias, though not yet applied to the realm of juror decision-making, also posit that beliefs and attitudes affect construction of mental models and can bias reasoning performance (Evans *et al.* 1993; Klauer *et al.* 2000). They hold promise for future application. Finally, as we detail later in this chapter, Chen and Chaiken (1999), relying on a theory distinguishing systematic and heuristic reasoning, have shown that jurors faced with complicated cognitive tasks and lacking the motivation or ability to fully evaluate the evidence tend to rely on heuristic rules-of-thumb to determine a defendant's culpability.

In addition to the application of basic cognitive and socio-cognitive models to promote understanding of legal decisions, some psychologists have developed *de novo* theories of juror behavior to account for the ways that jurors think, reason, judge, and decide. We describe the models and predictions that flow from those theories next.

MODELS OF JUROR DECISION-MAKING

The ideal juror is one who can dispassionately listen to the trial evidence and is savvy enough to render a verdict based on rational and prejudice-free thought processes. The real juror, on the other hand, is not the blank slate that the judicial system prefers and presumes to exist. Rather, various cognitive factors affect jurors' abilities to process complex and lengthy trial information and make judgments based on that evidence in light of the legal parameters available to them. Models that describe this process tend to fall into one of two categories: mathematical approaches and explanation-based approaches. The most comprehensive review of these models is provided by Reid Hastie in an edited book entitled *Inside the Juror* (1993).

Three different models exemplify the mathematical approach: (1) probability theory (Schum & Martin 1993); (2) algebraic theory (Anderson 1981); and (3) stochastic processes (Kerr 1993). In all three, jurors are thought to engage in a series of "mental" calculations in which they weigh the relevancy and strength of each independent piece of trial evidence and translate the resulting score into an assessment of the defendant's culpability (in the realm of criminal law). This score is then compared to the criterion needed to find the defendant guilty (or, in civil law matters, liable). If the weight of the trial evidence meets the legal threshold for finding the defendant responsible, the juror will render that verdict. In a similar vein, Bayesian models rely on jurors' preconceptions about the defendant's culpability, factoring into this analysis the subjective links between pieces of evidence (Marshall & Wise 1975; Pennington & Hastie 1981; Schum & Martin 1982). These mathematical approaches are complex, and are dependent on the underlying assumption that jurors can conceptualize and weight pieces of trial information as separate and distinct entities (Hastie 1993; Ellsworth & Mauro 1998), an assumption not supported by more recent analyses of the jury decision-making process (Greene *et al.* 2002). Indeed, mathematically-based theories have generated relatively little empirical work in recent years as it has become clear that jurors do not necessarily process items of evidence as discrete entities or necessarily update their prior beliefs in light of that new evidence. More generally, we know that jurors' behavior does not conform to principles of probability.

Explanation-based approaches that emphasize jurors' cognitive organization or representation of the evidence have been favored by jury researchers in recent years. We describe the most widely cited explanation-based approach to jurors' cognitive behavior, the story model, in some detail. We also describe a second explanation-based approach, the heuristic-systematic model, that has been applied to juror decisions to explain the ways that jurors process evidence and use it to structure their choices. These models both portray the juror as an active decision-maker who interprets, evaluates, and elaborates on the trial information, rather than as a passive recipient who merely weighs each piece of evidence as a discrete entity and combines these elements in some probabilistic fashion.

The story model, developed by Pennington and Hastie (1981, 1986, 1988, 1993), posits that jurors construct a narrative storyline out of the evidence presented during the trial. There are three stages in this model: (1) evaluating the evidence through story construction; (2) learning about the various verdict options available; and (3) reaching a decision by fitting the story to the most appropriate verdict category (Pennington & Hastie 1993).

During the story construction stage, jurors use three kinds of information to create a plausible story: the evidence presented throughout the trial (such as testimony from the witnesses); their real-world knowledge of similar cases or crimes in their community; and their own generic expectations and experiences relevant to the issues in the case. In the process of constructing a narrative framework, various interpretations of the evidence can result in different stories. The juror will ultimately adopt the story that, in his or her mind, best fits the evidence and is most coherent (Pennington & Hastie 1993). In the second stage, jurors learn about the verdict options from the judge's instructions (in a homicide trial, these might include legal definitions of first-degree murder, second-degree murder, and manslaughter). In the final stage, jurors attempt to match the story that they constructed in the first stage to one of the second stage verdict categories using the legal rules and prescriptions provided by the trial judge. If the storyline fits the requirements of the verdict category under consideration, the juror will choose that verdict category. If the threshold is not met, the juror will search for a more appropriate verdict category.

Although the interpretative nature of story construction is likely to include a combination of accurate representations gleaned from the evidence presented during the trial, it may also involve unintended misrepresentations and even purposeful distortions (Smith 1991). Carlson and Russo (2001) posit that jurors engage in pre-decisional distortion, in which they interpret new trial evidence in a manner consistent with whichever verdict is tentatively favored at the time the evidence is presented. Jurors who tentatively favor the plaintiff (or defendant) early in the trial may interpret new information in a manner that supports that initial leaning. Carlson and Russo found such distortions to be particularly problematic in a sample of prospective jurors awaiting jury duty, whereas pre-decisional distortions among student participants were more limited. Such distortions challenge the legal system's requirement that jurors carefully consider and evaluate all trial information in a bias-free manner.

Empirical data show that jurors have a strong inclination to construct stories out of the evidence. In an early interview study, Pennington and Hastie (1981) asked jurors to "talk aloud" and respond to questions about the evidence and the judge's instructions as they made a decision about a homicide case. Jurors tended to organize the evidence into a narrative. Many of their stories included trial evidence that was only inferred (not actually presented) during the trial, reflecting the constructive nature of the adopted narrative. In addition, despite hearing the same trial information, those participants who chose a guilty verdict created different stories than those who chose the not guilty option.

Pennington and Hastie (1988) conducted a follow-up study to examine further the relationship between story construction and memory for evidence. They provided participants with various pieces of evidence that supported either a guilty or not guilty verdict and tested recognition of the evidence after the trial. Mock jurors recognized more evidentiary information consistent with their verdict choice than evidence inconsistent with that choice, suggesting the existence of pre-decisional distortion. Participants also falsely recognized verdict-consistent story elements that were not included in the original trial.

In a third study, Pennington and Hastie (1988) varied the manner in which the evidence was presented: both the defense and the prosecution presented their evidence using either a story-based approach (evidence presented in a story format) or a witness-based approach (evidence presented by a collection of witnesses who testified in no particular order). They found that when the prosecution used a story-based strategy and the defense did not, jurors convicted the defendant 78 per cent of the time. When the strategies were reversed, convictions dropped to 31 per cent. These findings suggest that the easier it is for jurors to construct a narrative, the more likely they are to render a verdict consistent with that story. This is not to imply that psychologists can reliably predict what kind of stories jurors will construct, as most personality and demographic characteristics have only weak relationships to juror verdicts. But according to Schuller & Yarmey (2001), the story model does provide an empirical framework through which researchers can test how cognitive and environmental factors influence juror decision-making.

Why do some jurors construct a guilt-based narrative while others create a not-guilty story? In answer to this question, Pennington and Hastie (1993) proposed that the constructive nature of story-generating is based on jurors' prior experiences, knowledge of the world, and ability to deal with the legal constraints placed upon them. Each juror has varying degrees of experience with issues related to the facts of a case, and this experience affects how he or she interprets both the trial evidence and the judge's instructions.

Other studies have shown the powerful influence of prior experiences and expectations on jurors' cognitive construction of evidence. Smith (1991) found, for example, that although lay definitions of legal rules often include legally incorrect information, jurors rely on these incorrect definitions when determining their verdicts. Likewise, they use crime prototypes (schemas based on "typical" crime elements) as models for determining whether a particular verdict alternative is appropriate, even if these prototypes are inconsistent with the facts and instructions in the current case (Smith 1991). Prior experience and real-world knowledge are only part of the story-generating process, however. Jurors' beliefs, attitudes, and cognitive capabilities also play a pivotal role in the processing of trial-relevant information, particularly when it comes to creating a plausible and coherent story framework.

Other explanation-based models stem from social-cognitive theories that propose a dual-processing approach to human information-gathering, whereby perceivers process information through either a passive, heuristic-based approach or a more active, systematic approach. One dual-process model that has attained some prominence in recent years and that has relevance to jurors' tasks is the heuristic-systematic model proposed by Chen and Chaiken (1999).

The heuristic-systematic model proposes that people process information along a heuristic/systematic continuum. Heuristic processing entails a nearly effortless appraisal of the available information, often using simple decision rules or rules-of-thumb (e.g., experts should be given deference) to evaluate information. Systematic processing, on the other hand, involves a more careful scrutiny of the available information (Chen *et al.* 1996). Though often more accurate than heuristic processing, decisions made using the systematic approach require greater cognitive effort on the part of information processors, who must have both the motivation and ability to fully evaluate information placed before them (Chen & Chaiken 1999). When either is lacking or when such information involves complex trial testimony and evidence, jurors may rely on heuristic rules-of-thumb to determine the defendant's culpability. For example, they may focus on the complexity of the testimony delivered by an expert witness or authority figure (Cooper *et al.* 1996), the number of plaintiffs involved in a lawsuit (Horowitz & Bordens 2000), the attractiveness of a witness (Catano 1980), the amount of evidence they are asked to evaluate during the course of the trial (Weinstock & Flaton 2004), or their prior knowledge and lay prototypes regarding the "typical" crime (Smith 1991). In each of these examples, jurors' reliance on heuristic shortcuts may undermine their ability to comprehend and integrate discrete pieces of evidence and apply those facts to the legal criteria provided by the judge (Greene & Ellis 2006).

In the following sections, we describe three applications of cognitive psychology to juror behavior in American law. In particular, we focus on subjects that have captured a great deal of empirical attention by psycho-legal researchers, namely capital punishment (in the realm of criminal law) and sexual harassment and damage awards (in civil law), but that have not been thoroughly examined through the lens of the cognitive psychologist. Where appropriate, we describe tests of the story model and dual-process model in these applied areas.

JUROR DECISION-MAKING IN CAPITAL PUNISHMENT CASES

A decision task that is uniquely American (though informative on jurors' assessments in all jurisdictions) is the determination of whether to sentence a convicted felon to death. Although European nations have no capital punishment, a surge of violent crime in Australia has raised the possibility of reinstating the death penalty, abolished in the 1960s, in that country (Forsterlee *et al.* 1999). So although only American jurors currently grapple with the uniquely finite nature of capital punishment, jurors in other jurisdictions may one day have to make these decisions as well. In the meantime, jurors in all trials are required to weigh competing sources of evidence and apply their assessments to legal standards provided by the judge – the inherently psychological tasks that we ask of capital jurors. So understanding jurors' decision-making in capital cases is broadly useful.

Because of the distinctive nature of capital punishment, this area of American criminal law has received special recognition by the courts (*Furman v. Georgia* 1972; *Gregg v. Georgia* 1976), which have adopted a series of specialized and explicit procedures to guide jurors' decision-making. These guidelines rely, implicitly, on beliefs about jurors' cognitive processes and, indeed, psychologists have examined the effects of these guidelines on jurors' decision-making processes in capital punishment cases.

Among the guidelines is a requirement that jurors who serve in a capital murder trial be "death-qualified." That is, they must be willing to impose the death penalty should the facts of the case warrant that punishment. Death qualification occurs during the jury selection of a capital trial, serving to exclude jurors whose beliefs about the death penalty are such that they would be unable or unwilling to impose it (*Witherspoon v. Illinois* 1968; *Wainright v. Witt* 1985; Butler & Moran 2002). In fact, jurors are excluded from capital trials if they are unwilling to impose the death penalty under any condition or if they are willing to *always* render a death verdict regardless of the case facts. One study estimated that 19 per cent of Californians hold the former view and 2.6 per cent ascribe to the latter (Haney *et al.* 1994). Other studies find comparable numbers.

A question that has garnered significant research effort asks how death qualification influences the overall decision-making capabilities of the jury. Death-qualified jurors do differ from jurors who are not death qualified (so-called "excluded jurors") in terms of their willingness to impose the death penalty, but they also differ in terms of their willingness to convict criminal defendants. Filkins *et al.* (1998) conducted a meta-analysis on the effects of death qualification on capital trial verdicts and found that death-qualified jurors were more likely than excluded jurors to convict the defendant and reached this decision long before they had to choose whether to sentence the defendant to death. Cowan *et al.* (1984) found similar results in their study of 288 mock jurors, where 75 per cent of death-qualified jurors convicted the defendant of homicide as did only 53 per cent of excluded jurors. In fact, a long line of research now documents that people who are excluded during the death qualification process are less punitive and less prosecution-oriented than those who serve in capital cases.

Death-qualified individuals also tend to favor crime control models of criminal justice (as opposed to due process models that focus on fair procedures), favor the point of view of the prosecution, mistrust criminal defendants and defense counsel, and take a more punitive stance against offenders (Fitzgerald & Ellsworth 1984). These individual preferences can have a dramatic impact on jurors' story constructions and on the verdicts they ultimately choose.

The story model posits that the prior experiences and worldviews of jurors (including death-qualified jurors) lead them to perceive trial information in a way that accommodates their individual attitudes. For example, an authoritarian attitude may provide an initial framework through which information presented during the trial is filtered, and the story that results is likely to be consistent with this initial belief structure. The juror who survives jury selection in a capital case may be especially likely to have this perspective; after all, he or she has agreed with governmental authorities (i.e., the prosecutor and judge) that the death penalty is appropriate in at least some circumstances. In addition, because jurors in capital cases have pondered the defendant's punishment before hearing any evidence of his guilt, their story construction may begin from a pro-prosecution stance, thinking that the defendant must be guilty and evaluating new evidence in light of that bias (Haney 1984).

Another of the guidelines formulated by the US Supreme Court (in *Gregg v. Georgia* 1976) is the bifurcation of capital trials into two phases: a guilt phase in which the defendant's guilt is assessed, and a penalty phase in which the sentence is determined. Although it provides some consistency sought by the courts, bifurcation also raises questions about jurors' competence to independently weigh and evaluate evidence presented during the two phases of a capital trial.

Empirical research now documents some of the problems with the two-phase bifurcated trial structure of capital punishment cases. Post-trial interviews of capital jurors conducted by researchers from the Capital Jury Project (a large research consortium that has examined jury behavior in 20–30 capital trials in each of 15 states in the US) reveal that jurors reach important conclusions during the guilt phase of the trial that have nothing whatsoever to do with the defendant's guilt. Many jurors questioned in these studies said that they relied on evidence presented during the guilt phase to reach personal decisions about punishment. In particular, these jurors tended to take an early stand favoring death. Jurors who took an early pro-life stand, on the other hand, were likely to point to the jury's deliberation (rather than the evidence presentation) as the point at which they reached a decision about punishment (Bowers *et al.* 1998). These findings suggest a strong primacy effect; many jurors are apparently influenced by the heinous character of the crime and the horrific nature of certain evidence (information that tends to be presented early in the trial), and wait for neither the evidence and arguments related to punishment nor for sentencing instructions from the judge before making their punishment choices. Furthermore, most jurors who took a premature stand on punishment were "absolutely convinced" of the correctness of their choice; in fact, jurors who reached these conclusions during the guilt phase were more firm in their beliefs than those who did so after hearing arguments, evidence, and instructions about sentencing. These premature punishment stands may influence the attention that jurors pay to discrete pieces of evidence and the weight that they accord that evidence during both the guilt and punishment phases of the trial, making them largely unreceptive to any contrary evidence that is presented later in the case (Bowers *et al.* 1998).

Jurors' ability to evaluate evidence presented during the penalty phase may be problematic as well. Jurors are supposed to consider two sources of evidence during this phase of the trial. First, they determine whether any aggravating factors are present. These are statutorily defined factors that make the defendant more worthy of death (e.g., that the crime was carried out in an especially heinous manner). If jurors find and agree upon aggravating factors, they then consider mitigating factors – any factors that make the defendant less deserving of the death penalty. Mitigating factors may be statutorily derived (e.g., the defendant was under extreme mental duress) or they may involve any non-statutory factor the juror may find relevant (e.g., the defendant was young; he has good parents).

A question of grave concern is how jurors weigh aggravating factors against the mitigating factors in determining the appropriateness of a death sentence. Some data suggest that jurors' attitudinal predispositions influence how they evaluate aggravating and mitigating evidence. For example, Butler and Moran (2002) found that death-qualified jurors were more likely to attend to and use aggravating factors and excluded jurors were more likely to attend to and use mitigating factors in their decision calculus. These findings fit squarely with the story model's prediction that an individuals' predispositions and expectations will influence the evidence evaluation stage of decision-making. The differential emphasis placed on these trial elements and the different story constructions that result obviously have a dramatic impact on the resulting verdicts.

Another question with relevance to cognition is whether capital jurors' appraisal of aggravating and mitigating factors, and their application of capital jury instructions more generally, is limited by poor comprehension of these legal dictates. To be sure, the legal instructions that accompany capital trials are written in complex and exacting language, and few, if any, jurors have experience with these concepts or terminologies. Lacking knowledge of the concepts involved and being unsure about how to apply the law, jurors may rely more on their predispositional biases than the legal prescriptions provided by the court. Stated otherwise, they rely on heuristic processing rather than a more in-depth, careful, and systematic approach. In story-model terminology, jurors may have difficulty reaching a logical and legally defensible decision because they were not adequately informed about their verdict options.

Several studies have examined jurors' comprehension of death penalty instructions. In a series of studies, Richard Wiener and his colleagues borrowed elements of the story model in an attempt to determine how well jurors understand and apply capital jury instructions. For example, Wiener *et al.* (1995) reasoned that death penalty jurors engage in active story construction, using the life histories of the defendant and the victim, the trial evidence, and their own prior experiences with homicides to construct plausible stories. They also hypothesized that jurors' narrative constructions of the evidence would incorporate potentially erroneous knowledge about relevant legal concepts and rules of law. Through interviews, they learned that jurors hold inaccurate and narrow definitions of capital trial instructions and that a majority of jurors confuse elements of aggravation with elements of mitigation. For example, 77 per cent of respondents inaccurately defined aggravation (24 per cent offered definitions that were too narrow and 52 per cent thought aggravation implied that *less* severe punishment was necessary). Further, 52 per cent inaccurately defined mitigation (42 per cent defined it too narrowly and 9 per cent thought mitigation implied that *more* severe punishment was appropriate). Lacking the ability to understand the jury instructions may have hindered each juror's chances of systematically processing relevant trial information.

Data from the Capital Jury Project further underscore jurors' inability to understand and apply aggravating and mitigating evidence. The US Supreme Court has ruled that jurors must find at least one statutorily defined aggravating factor in order to sentence the defendant to death (*Zant v. Stephens* 1983), and in some jurisdictions jurors may consider only certain factors as the basis for a death sentence. Yet, most jurors do not realize that they can consider only these defined aggravating factors and none other (Bowers & Foglia 2003). In addition, despite the fact that most state statutes require that aggravating circumstances be proven beyond a reasonable doubt, 30 per cent of jurors questioned at the conclusion of capital murder trials were unaware of this stringent requirement (Bowers & Foglia 2003).

The US Supreme Court has also ruled that jurors may consider *any* mitigating factors, not just those provided by statute (*Lockett v. Ohio* 1978). However, close to half of jurors interviewed as part of the Capital Jury Project were unaware of this prerogative. Even after hearing instructions to this effect, two-thirds of capital jurors did not realize that unanimity was not required to find mitigation; in fact, they can consider any factor in mitigation that they personally believe (Bowers & Foglia 2003). Importantly, these mistaken notions about how to handle aggravating and mitigating evidence all favor the sentence of death, rather than life imprisonment.

Can these misunderstandings be corrected, perhaps via rewriting, simplifying, or clarifying the penalty phase jury instructions? This possibility was examined by Wiener *et al.* (2004), who attempted to devise capital jury instructions that would assist jurors to overcome deficiencies in their instruction-based scripts. At the conclusion of a mock capital trial, jurors in this study received one of eight different versions of the instructions: (1) instructions currently used in Missouri; (2) control or baseline instructions in which all legal jargon and definitions were removed; (3) simplified instructions that were rewritten for improved clarity; (4) so-called "debunking instructions" that explained some of the common errors jurors make when applying the instructions; (5) flowchart instructions that provided a step-by-step graphic about how to proceed; and (6), (7), and (8) three practice instructions that allowed jurors to participate in a different capital trial case before judging the case at hand. (These jurors thus had prior experience with capital murder instructions.) All jurors then completed a series of questionnaires designed to assess their understanding of the instructions and then deliberated to a verdict.

Wiener *et al.* found that jurors given the approved Missouri instructions showed little understanding of how to proceed; their scores did not differ from the baseline condition in which no legal definitions were provided. However, mock jurors given the simplified instructions, debunking instructions, flowchart instructions, and the practice instructions understood the trial procedures and requirements better than jurors given the Missouri and the baseline instructions, suggesting that jurors who received some form of enhanced instructions relied less on their own (often mistaken) schemas of legal definitions. Rather, they applied the concepts embedded in the instructions in a more appropriate and rational manner. As in prior research (Wiener *et al.* 1995; 1998), jurors who poorly understood the instructions were more likely to give the defendant a death sentence than a sentence of life in prison, suggesting that enhancing jurors' understanding of their instructions may offset their reliance on predispositional, pro-prosecution biases.

Poor comprehension of capital sentencing instructions may explain another pervasive finding in the literature on death penalty jurisprudence, namely racial disparities in sentencing. Baldus *et al.* (1983) analyzed over 2000 manslaughter convictions from 1973 to 1979 and found that defendants who killed Whites were 11 times more likely to receive the death penalty than defendants who killed Blacks.[1] Some empirical evidence suggests that jurors' misunderstanding of capital instructions may lead them to render verdicts dependent, in part, on the racial characteristics of defendants and victims.

To explore the role of race and instruction comprehension in capital trials, Lynch and Haney (2000) presented 402 jury-eligible participants with a videotaped summary of a homicide trial in which the race of the defendant and the victim was varied. They found that those jurors who poorly understood the instructions were more likely to sentence the defendant to death. This was particularly true when the defendant was Black and the victim was White. (In this condition, 68 per cent of sentences were for death and 32 per cent were for life without parole. By contrast, when the defendant was White and the victim was Black, only 36 per cent of sentences were for death and 64 percent were for life without parole.) Poor comprehension may force jurors to evaluate the evidence and apply the law without judicial guidance, leading them to rely on idiosyncratic and potentially irrelevant factors such as racial stereotypes when constructing their legal narratives.

Dual-processing models may also explain these results. As instruction comprehension decreases, heuristic processing may allow jurors to focus on extralegal factors such as race. Without careful scrutiny of the trial evidence, jurors' prejudices and biases are given freer reign to influence story construction. If jurors' prototypes about crimes and criminal defendants are racially biased at the outset, those prototypes may be invoked to find minority defendants, or those who kill White victims, more worthy of death sentences.

Yet we also know that the story prototypes that capital jurors hold are complex and multifaceted. To study the manner in which potential jurors create prototypical death penalty stories, Wiener *et al.* (2002) interviewed 76 jury-eligible, death-qualified citizens and had them create stories revolving around a homicide. They found that several prototypes emerged, rather than one unifying storyline. Nonetheless, jurors' stories tended to include some key components of a homicide schema, though there were several variations and subcategories associated with each prototype. (It is important to note that this study did not focus on capital murder trials, which may provide a more unifying story framework for participants, particularly as crimes eligible for the death penalty are limited by thresholds of aggravation, i.e., capital cases typically involve brutal and heinous actions that arguably make the defendant worthy of the death penalty.)

Summary

Although US courts have scrutinized trial procedures in capital cases and have attempted to eliminate arbitrary and capricious decisions on the part of jurors by requiring capital juries to be death-qualified and by bifurcating capital trials, several problems remain and threaten the fairness of the process. Jurors who are deemed death-qualified tend to hold opinions more in line with the prosecution than the defense, and tend to render more guilty verdicts than their non-death-qualified peers. The story model proposes that jurors will construct a story from the available trial evidence using their own prior experiences and knowledge as a template. The prior experiences and belief structures of death-qualified jurors may be skewed in a punitive direction, may guide their interpretation of evidence presented during the guilt phase, and may account for the pro-prosecution stances they often assume.

A problematic feature of bifurcation is the fact that many jurors apparently lack the ability to withhold judgment about an appropriate penalty until they have heard evidence and instructions related to punishment; rather, they make premature decisions about punishment in response to evidence concerning the facts of the crime. Some commentators have called for separate juries to decide the issues of guilt and punishment in these cases. This procedural modification would certainly reduce concerns about the conviction-proneness of death-qualified jurors (assuming that jurors who determine guilt would not need to be death-qualified) and instances of premature judgments, but would reduce the efficiency of the courts.

Jurors' inability to comprehend and apply the penalty phase instructions seems more easily remedied, given the empirical data on improvements in comprehension that come with revised, simplified, and clarified instructions. Clearly, unfamiliar terminology and obtuse legal concepts impede jurors' abilities to weigh the evidence in a systematic and evenhanded fashion and increase the likelihood that jurors will resort to shortcut heuristic reasoning strategies. Less careful decision-making will result.

JUROR DECISION-MAKING IN SEXUAL HARASSMENT CASES

Legislation in the US prohibits employers from discriminating with regard to compensation, terms, conditions, or privileges of employment because of race, color, religion, sex, or national origin. Although these laws have enabled American women to gain legal support for their employment rights, little headway regarding sexual harassment, an issue of concern to many female employees, has been made in the years following enactment of these laws.

Much of this legal abeyance regarding sexual harassment resulted from an inability both to define sexual harassment and to provide guidelines for dealing with these often ambiguous workplace behaviors. Consequently, the US Equal Employment Opportunity Commission (EEOC) set out to clarify what does and does not constitute sexual harassment (EEOC 1980, revised 1993) and in so doing, outlined two types of sexual harassment claims. One form of sexual harassment quid pro quo occurs when employers take negative employment actions against complainants who reject sexual advances or requests for sexual favors (Andrew & Andrew 1997). This tit-for-tat harassment has been generally agreed upon by all US courts to constitute sexual harassment (Henry & Meltzoff 1998).

The second form of sexual harassment, hostile workplace sexual harassment, has created significant confusion in terms of an operational definition (*Harris v. Forklift Systems, Inc.* 1993). Hostile workplace sexual harassment refers to conduct that subjects employees to an "intimidating, hostile, or offensive working environment" (EEOC 1980, revised 1993, p. 74667). Such behaviors include "unwelcome sexual advances, requests for sexual favors, and other verbal or physical conduct of a sexual nature" (EEOC 1980, revised 1993, p. 74667). A key component of hostile workplace environment sexual harassment is that the behavior must be unwelcome by the target. That is, the plaintiff must show that she was offended by the conduct and that she suffered an injury from it (Conte 1997). In addition, according to this definition, the behavior must also be pervasive and severe in order to be deemed harassment (Andrew & Andrew 1997).

The complexity of sexual harassment claims extends to American courtrooms in cases where jurors are confronted with such thorny issues as contradictory claims about past behaviors, the need to assess those behaviors from the perspective of the complainant, and the task of evaluating the severity of invisible, emotional injuries. The story model has been invoked to explain how people determine whether sexual harassment has occurred. It can explicate some of the ways that jurors view incidents of sexual harassment in a trial setting.

To examine how story construction occurs during sexual harassment trials, Huntley and Costanzo (2003) examined post-trial narratives written by 112 mock jurors who took part in a sexual harassment trial simulation. The authors employed content analysis to examine jurors' responses. Two divergent narrative constructions emerged, one supporting the plaintiff (e.g., "she was an employee of good character who was understandably afraid to speak out against the harassment") and the other supporting the defendant (e.g., "the plaintiff was oversensitive and encouraged the sexual comments and advances"). When Huntley and Costanzo used these themes as mediators in a model that predicted verdicts in other sexual harassment cases, they found that the themes accounted for a significant amount of the variance with regard to the verdict, jurors' commitments to the verdict, and their confidence in that verdict. When constructing a story about alleged sexual harassment, jurors apparently rely on prototypes within that domain. Stated otherwise, jurors tend to organize the evidence in a sexual harassment trial into narrative structures that forecast their verdicts, as predicted by the story model.

In constructing these stories, jurors sometimes rely on their prior knowledge and experiences to evaluate a complainant's potentially harassing environment. According to the story model, after the evidence is organized into a narrative format, jurors must then apply the legal rules and standards that are intended to guide their verdict choices. Two legal standards are used to evaluate whether sexually harassing behaviors occurred. One standard, the *reasonable person* standard, asks whether the conduct in question would interfere with a reasonable person's work performance (*Rabidue v. Osceola* 1986). If so, the conduct is deemed harassing. A second standard, the *reasonable woman* standard, defines a hostile workplace as one in which a reasonable woman would find the conduct in question sufficiently severe or pervasive to alter the conditions of employment and create an abusive working environment (*Ellison v. Brady* 1991). The reasonable woman standard is based on the assumption that work is a distinctively different experience for women than for men, as each gender perceives certain interpersonal behaviors differently.

Some psychologists have asked how the reasonable person and reasonable woman standards are differentially applied in sexual harassment cases and whether the gender of the perceiver influences his or her evaluations. For example, Wiener *et al.* (1995) presented two written vignettes which described the facts of cases involving alleged hostile workplace harassment to both female and male participants and asked them to assess whether the conduct in question constituted harassment. Half of the participants applied the reasonable person standard and half used the reasonable woman standard. Although the authors found no differences based on legal standard, they did find that women were more likely to deem the conduct in the vignettes to be unwelcome, severe, and pervasive. They also found that women were more likely to see the conduct as negatively affecting the claimant's work performance and psychological wellbeing and to view the vignettes as being representative of a hostile working environment.

Further examination of the effects of differing legal standards on judgments of sexual harassment has shown that employees who receive the reasonable woman standard in mock juror research were more likely than those with the reasonable person standard to deem the behavior in question as sexual harassment (Wiener & Hurt 2000). Taking a slightly different approach, Perry *et al.* (2004) analyzed the outcomes of US federal district court cases of hostile environment sexual harassment that involved the reasonable woman standard. They found that these cases were somewhat more likely to be decided in favor of the plaintiff than cases that did not use this standard. Taken together, these findings imply that the reasonable woman standard may lower the threshold that a juror uses to decide whether an incident constitutes sexual harassment.

Do prior experiences with hostile or submissive victims impact sexual harassment decisions? To answer this question, Wiener *et al.* (2004) had participants read two sexual harassment cases in which the behavior of the complainant in the first vignette was varied (i.e., she acted in either a neutral, hostile, submissive, or hostile *and* submissive manner) whereas the complainant in the second vignette always acted in a neutral manner. The complainant's behavior activated behavior-consistent attitudes about that complainant (e.g., the hostile complainant was perceived as antagonistic, leading decision-makers to find less evidence of sexual harassment; the submissive complainant was perceived as needing protection, spurring benevolent judgments and increasing the chance of perceivers finding sexual harassment). In addition, these attitudes spilled over onto the second vignette (e.g., a hostile first complainant primed participants to see the second complainant as hostile, as well). In essence, the story script involving the first complainant carried over to the second scenario.

The dual-process model can also help us understand how jurors determine whether sexual harassment took place. According to this model, perceivers use well-rehearsed and easily retrievable attitude structures regarding sexual harassment, relying in part on the severity of the conduct. If the conduct is so severe that most people would see the behavior as sexually harassing (or so benign that few people would see it as harassing), then perceivers use heuristic processes to decide whether harassment took place. Such automatic processing allows the decision-maker to determine if the conduct was harassing without investing substantial cognitive energy (Bargh 1994; Wegner & Bargh 1998). For example, work environments filled with sexually explicit stimuli (e.g., sexual jokes and explicit photographs) clearly suggest a climate conducive to sexual harassment so observers' decisions about the likelihood of harassment in those settings may require little cognitive effort. On the other hand, rigidly controlled work environments that are demonstrably intolerant of these explicit behaviors may be easily classified as non-harassing. But when the sexual conduct and tolerance for sexual behavior in the workplace are intermediate or ambiguous in nature, perceivers must engage in a second processing stage, making a more effortful, systematic evaluation of the harassment claim.

At this point, the decision-maker is expected to rely on legal rules to guide his or her determination about the existence of harassment. Though processing at this stage is more systematic than during the first stage, the perceiver's motivation and ability to understand the legal rules will have a large impact on the final decision. Thus, legal criteria can guide perceivers' decisions to the extent that they are understood and applied correctly. If perceivers do not understand the legal criteria, they may use their own experiences and beliefs as reference points, measuring the purported sexual harassment against their own internal, subjective standards of welcome, pervasiveness, and severity (Wiener *et al.* 2004). The varying experiences that men and women have with regard to sexual harassment may thus influence how they view incidents of sexual harassment, especially when they lack the capacity to understand the nuances of the legal rules.

Summary

Courts have struggled with and reached different conclusions about the definition of sexual harassment and the appropriate standards to apply in assessing potentially harassing behaviors. These varying definitions and standards are ripe for psychological evaluation and indeed, psycho-legal researchers have asked, empirically, how laypeople think about potentially harassing behaviors. In particular, ambiguity inherent in the context of hostile workplace environments (ambiguity stemming from the need to understand the target's perceptions of the offensive behavior) has spawned considerable psychological research.

Empirical work testing postulates of the story model has shown that jurors tend to organize the evidence in a sexual harassment case into narrative structures that influence their choice of verdict and that their prior experiences with this topic serve to frame these choices. When measuring the constructed story against the legal requirements for sexual harassment, jurors viewing the behavior from the standpoint of a reasonable woman are somewhat more likely to find harassment than jurors using the reasonable person standard.

This relationship is not a strong one, however. Dual-processing theories may also explain sexual harassment determinations, as systematic processing may be required to fully understand the legal prescriptions and offset prior biases.

JURY DECISION-MAKING AND DAMAGE AWARDS

American jurors in civil cases have two theoretically independent decisions to make: first, who is responsible for causing the injuries or harm claimed by the plaintiff, and second, whether the plaintiff is entitled to compensation. Although psychologists have examined jurors' thought processes on both questions, considerable recent work has focused on the second, describing how jurors assess whether a plaintiff should receive damages and in what amount.

The determination of damages is no simple task; rather, it requires careful attention to the evidence concerning injuries and losses, evaluation of the credibility of expert witnesses who typically present this evidence, memory for highly detailed information, predictions about future suffering, and calculation of the funds that might reasonably compensate a victim for these losses. In addition, some jurors use the damage award to express their sentiments about the defendant's conduct. Consider the case of nine-year old Caitlyn Chipps, who suffered from cerebral palsy. Her parents sued their insurance company for repeatedly denying payment for their daughter's treatments. In 2000, after a month of testimony, six jurors, including Diane Leininger, delivered their verdict: $79.6 million, the largest damage award ever issued in an individual case in that jurisdiction (Curriden 2001). Why was the award so large? According to juror Leininger,

> We were stunned by the testimony. The company sent bonus checks to claims reviewers who saved the company money by denying the most medical claims for patients. And the company made its claims process so egregious and difficult just to increase their chances that families would eventually give up seeking reimbursement for treatments rather than continuing to fight to get their money . . . We had to send a message that would get not only Humana's attention but the attention of every [insurance company] out there. (Curriden 2001)

Although few juries award damages of this magnitude (in fact, there is significant controversy about whether damage awards are excessively high and growing in size; Seabury *et al.* 2004), this case illustrates the vast freedom that jurors are accorded in their decisions about damages. Judges send jurors off to deliberate with only minimal guidance about how their damage assessments should proceed (Greene & Bornstein 2000) and, at least in the realm of damages for non-economic losses like pain and suffering, with the disclaimer that the law provides no fixed standards by which to measure damages. It is no wonder that psychologists have been interested in examining the way that jurors make decisions on this largely unstructured task.

The primary focus of this research has been on the influence of various factors on the size and variability of damage awards. The severity of the plaintiff's injury has been a consistent and reliable predictor of compensatory damage awards, both in archival analyses (e.g., Bordens & Horowitz 1998; Vidmar *et al.* 1998) and in jury simulation studies (Feigenson *et al.* 2001; Greene *et al.* 2001). In general, people with significant injuries and losses receive more compensation than those with injuries and losses that are more negligible, a phenomenon termed "vertical equity."

But especially in the realm of non-economic damages, there are also large differences in awards for seemingly similar injuries, a phenomenon termed "horizontal inequity." Psychologists and policy analysts have wondered whether these inequalities are the result of differences in jurors' perceptions of harm to the plaintiffs, their monetary valuations of similarly perceived harms, the use of improper considerations such as personal characteristics of the litigants, or some combination of these factors. In general, the data suggest that jurors' perceptions of harm are consistently influenced by certain variables, such as the extent of the plaintiff's disability and the amount and duration of mental suffering, and not by variables such as the physical pain and disfigurement experienced by the plaintiff (Wissler *et al.* 1997). But some commentators (e.g., Kahneman *et al.* 1998) have suggested that damage awards are unpredictable because jurors have great difficulty translating their beliefs about harm into a monetary value. According to this argument, although jurors may agree about how severe an injury is, their choice of a monetary award often amounts to a stab in the dark. This occurs primarily because jurors must map their awards onto an unbounded magnitude scale. As a result, damage awards show a great deal of variability, particularly in the realm of punitive damages that are intended to punish the defendant for immoral and egregious behavior and to deter others. Finally, there is some, albeit minimal, support for the possibility that characteristics of the plaintiff, including age, race, and gender, can account for horizontal inequities in jury awards (Greene & Bornstein 2003).

Another explanation of horizontal inequity is that jurors miscalculate damage awards for plaintiffs who are partially responsible for their claimed losses. This situation arises when jurors apply rules of comparative negligence that have been enacted in most states. In these cases, jurors assign separate percentages of fault to the plaintiff and the defendant, and the plaintiff's damages are reduced proportionally (so, for example, if the plaintiff is deemed to be 25 per cent responsible for the accident and the jury awards $100,000, the plaintiff would receive only $75,000). But both archival (Hammitt *et al.* 1985; Shanley 1985) and experimental studies (Feigenson *et al.* 1997; Zickafoose & Bornstein 1999) show that damages are "doubly discounted" in these cases: jurors first discount their awards to reflect the plaintiff's wrongdoing, and the judge then further reduces the award to reflect the jury's decision about proportionate fault of the two parties. In the end, plaintiffs who are found comparatively negligent receive smaller gross damage awards than comparably injured non-negligent plaintiffs. Other studies have shown that with variations in the instructions (Sommer *et al.* 2001) or the verdict form used (Zickafoose & Bornstein 1999), even blameworthy plaintiffs are able to recover fully, however.

Psycho-legal research has explored jurors' use of heuristics in decisions about damages. They have learned, for example, that jurors apparently find it difficult to ignore evidence of the plaintiff's liability once they have been exposed to it, a phenomenon termed "hindsight bias." In terms of awarding compensation, jurors should be expected to examine the severity and nature of the plaintiff's injuries (after all, it is for these injuries that the plaintiff is receiving compensation) and the plaintiff's conduct (because if the plaintiff's actions contributed to his or her injuries, compensation is reduced accordingly). But jurors apparently also consider the conduct of the *defendant* in their calculation of damages, something that is contrary to the law's intentions. In theory, jurors should not increase their damage awards to reflect any revulsion over the defendant's conduct; neither should they decrease the award if they believe the defendant acted reasonably.

These premises were examined by Greene and colleagues (2001) in a jury analogue study. Mock jurors heard the evidence in a reenacted automobile negligence case in which the conduct of the defendant was described as either very careless (e.g., a truck driver was traveling 10 miles per hour over the speed limit through a construction zone, changing lanes rapidly, after having consumed alcohol), mildly careless (e.g., traveling near the speed limit with just one lane change immediately prior to the accident), or was not described at all. Jurors were asked to award damages to a plaintiff who was injured when the defendant lost control of the truck and crossed into oncoming traffic.

Data from individual jurors showed that they awarded more compensation when they had evidence of the defendant's conduct than when they did not. Thus, mock jurors fused their evaluation of the defendant's conduct with their evaluation of the plaintiff's injuries. Further evidence of this effect comes from the finding that jurors who heard about the defendant's conduct perceived the plaintiff as having sustained greater harm than jurors who did not hear about the defendant's behavior. Evidence of the defendant's carelessness, even when it was not particularly egregious, served to make the injury seem worse. These findings fit nicely within the framework of the story model, showing that jurors process evidence by constructing an overall narrative of the case, and demonstrating that jurors' interpretations of the evidence may be distorted to fit with the narratives they have created. More recent data suggest that this fusion of evidence can be partially offset by restructuring the task for jurors, essentially by separating the decisional components (i.e., liability, where defendant conduct *is* to be considered, and damages, where it is not) into separate segments of a trial and providing the evidence relevant to each decision separately (Smith & Greene 2005).

Another cognitive heuristic of relevance to damages determinations, the "simulation heuristic," is sometimes invoked when jurors evaluate events that have already taken place (typically with some negative ramifications for the plaintiff) and construct alternative simulations (or scenarios) of these events (Kahneman & Tversky 1982). Because most of this work has concerned simulations that lead to alternative outcomes (so-called "counterfactuals"), the research has been characterized as an investigation of counterfactual thinking. Counterfactual thinking arises in situations where people ponder what *might* have happened differently so that an alternative – typically better – outcome would have occurred. Jurors' damage awards can be influenced by counterfactual thinking. Mock jurors who could mentally mutate the defendant's behavior to undo an injurious act tended to find that behavior unreasonable and awarded the victim more compensation (Wiener *et al.* 1994).

A third heuristic used by jurors in determining damages is termed "anchoring-and-adjustment." A standard practice in many cases is for plaintiffs' attorneys to supply jurors with a number stating the amount of damages sought by their client (the *ad damnum*), and, on occasion, for defense attorneys to counter that figure with a lower number of their own. Psychologists have reasoned that because the judgment about damages involves uncertainty and jurors lack confidence in their own ability to assign monetary values to various injuries (Jacowitz & Kahneman 1995), these numbers serve as powerful anchors on jurors' decisions. The thinking is that jurors rely on these salient numerical reference points when making quantitative judgments, and that even if new evidence leads them to make adjustments away from the anchor, the resulting figure will still have been influenced by the anchor. This is the so-called anchoring and adjustment heuristic (Tversky & Kahneman 1974).

A number of empirical studies show the influence of the *ad damnum* on jurors' judgments about damages. In a particularly impressive demonstration of this effect, Hinsz and Indahl (1995) showed a reenactment of a wrongful death trial to mock jurors. The case was brought by the parents of two children who were killed in an automobile accident. In one condition, the plaintiff's lawyer requested $2 million, and in a second condition he requested $20 million. Despite hearing instructions to fairly and reasonably compensate the plaintiffs for their losses, jurors' mean awards varied dramatically as a function of the anchor: the mean award in the $2 million *ad damnum* condition was approximately $1.05 million and the mean from the $20 million condition was $9 million. The *ad damnum* functioned as an anchor and jurors reasoned heuristically after hearing that request.

Even extreme requests can function as anchors on subsequent judgments. In a mock personal injury trial, Chapman and Bornstein (1996) varied the *ad damnum*. In one condition, the hypothetical plaintiff claimed that her birth control pills led to her ovarian cancer and requested the large sum of $1 billion in compensation. Although she was perceived as more selfish and less honorable than a hypothetical plaintiff who asked for a more modest $5 million, still jurors awarded more to her than to the more reasonable plaintiff. Hastie *et al.* (1999) have shown dramatic effects of the *ad damnum* on resulting awards for punitive damages, as well.

We examine one final influence on jurors' decision-making regarding damages, namely trial complexity. The assessment of damages sometimes involves evaluation of extensive evidence – much of it highly technical – regarding multiple plaintiffs and defendants. In mass tort cases, for example, the issues being litigated are complex and the claimed losses are often immense. The cognitive tasks posed for jurors in the face of these complexities are enormous.

Using mock jury methodology, Irwin Horowitz and his colleagues have conducted several empirical studies to examine the effects of various aspects of trial complexity on decision-making about damages. Horowitz and Bordens (1988) asked how jurors make decisions about damages in trials involving multiple plaintiffs with differing degrees of injury from an environmental pollutant released by the defendant. They found clear evidence of a framing effect: jurors assessed damages for any given individual in light of the information available regarding other plaintiffs. Thus, the most severely injured plaintiff received lower damages when his case was aggregated with others, rather than tried separately, suggesting that the less severely injured plaintiffs pulled down jurors' responses to that outlier.

Complex cases also tend to involve highly complicated terminology, another issue of interest to Horowitz and his colleagues. Empirical examination of jurors' compensatory award judgments showed that they were affected by the complexity of the language used during the trial (Horowitz *et al.* 1996). Less complex language allowed jurors to discriminate more accurately among plaintiffs with differing degrees of injury, although jurors were able to award damages commensurate with a plaintiff's injuries only when less complex language was combined with low information load.

Other aspects of complex trials, including conflicting interpretations of law, multiple claims and counterclaims, and highly technical or scientific evidence presented by expert witnesses, raise questions about the competence of jurors to decide these cases fairly and rationally. Clearly, cognitive psychological research is relevant to this concern and psycholegal researchers would do well to borrow cognitive theories and findings to address this problem.

Summary

Because they lack clear guidelines, jurors have difficulty assessing damages. As a result, their awards are sometimes highly variable, and similarly injured plaintiffs are treated differently. We have suggested several reasons for these discrepancies, including the unbounded monetary scale that jurors use to assess damages and that invites variability, as well as inconsistencies in how jurors discount damages when the plaintiff is partly to blame. We have also described several cognitive heuristics or shortcuts that jurors rely on when making decisions about damages. We suspect that such reliance increases as the complexity of the decision increases. We know that trial complexity casts a long shadow over jurors as they attempt to wade through complicated and technical evidence and to understand and apply legal terms unfamiliar to most laypeople.

CONCLUSION

Jurors draw upon a number of cognitive processes in their attempts to make sense of the evidence presented at trial and to reach sensible verdicts. Among the cognitive processes are heuristic reasoning, memory reconstruction, language comprehension, schema acquisition and modification, and the induction and use of stereotypes. The study of juror decision-making can be enhanced by application of theories and principles derived from cognitive psychology. In this chapter, we have attempted to show that jurors' thinking can be accounted for both by the story model and dual-process model, cognitive theories that break the decision process into component parts and that predict how jurors' knowledge, expectations, attitudes, and motivation will influence their evaluation of the evidence and determination of a verdict. Although these models use different constructs and assume different mechanisms by which jurors reason and resolve controversies, both theories have been successfully invoked to describe the ways that jurors process and make sense of inherently complicated, unfamiliar information. In that respect, the theories are complementary rather than contradictory; both offer valid accounts of jurors' decision-making process and, in fact, can explain the same data.

Empirical analysis of jurors' decisions has tended to be influenced by legal theory rather than by basic cognitive psychological theory. Indeed, with the exception of mathematical models, which have actually generated few specific predictions about juror behavior and the more successful story and dual-process models, cognitive psychologists have tended to steer clear of the applied realm of decision-making by jurors. Perhaps the task is perceived as inherently complex and difficult to model. Perhaps the real-world setting is a deterrent to theorists. But applied psycho-legal researchers have tended to keep their distance from cognitive theorists, as well. Their reluctance to embrace cognitive theorizing may be a byproduct of the historic schism between basic and applied psychological research. Perhaps they fear that over-reliance on cognitive theory will impair their ability to make important connections to lawyers, judges, and policy-makers who have little understanding of psychological science. Whatever the reasons, our hope is that this chapter might, in some small way, encourage both cognitive psychologists and applied psycho-legal researchers to look to the law *and* to cognitive psychology as a source of inspiration for their empirical studies and as explanation for their findings.

NOTE

1 However, an updated study focusing on capital trials in Nebraska from 1973 to 1999 (Baldus *et al.* 2002) found that although minority defendants advanced further through the death penalty process than non-minority defendants, race did not have a differential impact on final sentences. This may be due to the small number of death penalty cases in Nebraska that involve minority members, limiting statistical power. At the time the Baldus team collected data, judges, rather than jurors, decided whether to sentence the defendant to death in Nebraska, a fact that may also account for discrepancies between this study and the 1983 study. Theoretically, judges have a more thorough and accurate knowledge of the law, and a considerable degree of experience that helps them avoid falling prey to their biases. Yet in 2002, the US Supreme Court ruled that judges will no longer decide death penalty sentences, and that death penalty determinations are in the province of an empanelled jury (*Ring v. Arizona* 2002). Whether racial bias will return to Nebraska and other states affected by the Court's opinion (Arizona, Colorado, Idaho, and Montana) is a question that may be answered in the next few years.

REFERENCES

Anderson, N. H. (1981). *Foundations of Information Integration Theory*. New York: Academic Press.

Andrew, M. J. & Andrew, J. D. (1997). Sexual harassment: the law. *Journal of Rehabilitation Administration*, *21*, 23–42.

Baldus, D. C., Pulaski, C. & Woodworth, G. (1983). Comparative review of death sentences: an empirical study of the Georgia experience. *Journal of Criminal Law and Criminology*, *74*, 661–753.

Baldus, D. C., Woodworth, G., Grosso, C. & Christ, A. M. (2002). Arbitrariness and discrimination in the administration of the death penalty: a legal and empirical analysis of the Nebraska experience (1973–1999). *Nebraska Law Review*, *81*, 486–753.

Bargh, J. A. (1994). The four horsemen of automaticity: awareness, intention, efficiency, and control in social cognition. In R. S. Wyer Jr. & T. K. Srull (eds.), *Handbook of Social Cognition* (Vol. 1: *Basic Processes*; Vol. 2: *Applications*, 2nd edn, pp. 1–40). Hillsdale, NJ: Lawrence Erlbaum Associates.

Bordens, K. & Horowitz, I. (1998). The limits of sampling and consolidation in mass tort trials: justice improved or justice altered? *Law and Psychology Review*, *22*, 43–66.

Bowers, W. & Foglia, W. (2003). Still singularly agonizing: law's failure to purge arbitrariness from capital sentencing. *Criminal Law Bulletin*, *39*, 51–86.

Bowers, W., Sandys, M. & Steiner, B. (1998). Foreclosed impartiality in capital sentencing: jurors' predispositions, guilt-trial experience, and premature decision-making. *Cornell Law Review*, *83*, 1476–1556.

Butler, B. M. & Moran, G. (2002). The role of death qualification in venirepersons' evaluations of aggravating and mitigating circumstances in capital trials. *Law and Human Behavior*, *26*, 175–184.

Carlson, K. A. & Russo, J. (2001). Biased interpretation of evidence by mock jurors. *Journal of Experimental Psychology – Applied*, *7*, 91–103.

Catano, V. (1980). Impact on simulated jurors of testimony as a function of non-evidentiary characteristics of witness and defendant. *Psychological Reports*, *46*, 343–348.

Chapman, G. B. & Bornstein, B. H. (1996). The more you ask for, the more you get: anchoring in personal injury verdicts. *Applied Cognitive Psychology*, *10*, 519–540.

Chen, S. & Chaiken, S. (1999). The heuristic-systematic model in its broader context. In S. Chaiken & Y. Trope (eds.), *Dual Process Theories in Social Psychology* (pp. 73–96). New York: Guilford Press.

Chen, S., Shechter, D. & Chaiken, S. (1996). Getting at the truth or getting along: accuracy- versus impression-motivated heuristic and systematic processing. *Journal of Personality and Social Psychology*, *71*, 262–275.

Conte, A. (1997). Legal theories of sexual harassment. In W. O'Donohue (ed.), *Sexual Harassment: Theory, Research, and Treatment* (pp. 50–83). Boston, MA: Allyn & Bacon.

Cooper, J., Bennett, E. A. & Sukel, H. L. (1996). Complex scientific testimony: how do jurors make decisions? *Law and Human Behavior, 20*, 379–394.

Cowan, C. L., Thompson, W. C. & Ellsworth, P. C. (1984). The effects of death qualification on jurors' predisposition to convict and on the quality of deliberation. *Law and Human Behavior, 8*, 53–79.

Curriden, M. (2001) Power of 12. *American Bar Association Journal, 8*(1), 26–41.

Devine, D., Clayton, L., Dunford, B. *et al.* (2001). Jury decision-making: 45 years of empirical research on deliberating groups. *Psychology, Public Policy, and Law, 7*, 622–727.

Dewitt, J., Richardson, J. & Warner, L. (1997). Novel scientific evidence and controversial cases: a social psychological examination. *Law and Psychology Review, 21*, 1–21.

Ellison v. Brady, 924 F. 2d 872 (9th Cir. 1991).

Ellsworth, P. C. & Mauro, R. (1998). Psychology and law. In D. T. Gilbert & S. T. Fiske (eds.), *Handbook of Social Psychology* (Vol. 2, 4th edn, pp. 684–732). New York: McGraw-Hill.

Equal Employment Opportunity Commission (EEOC) (1980, revised 1993). Guidelines and discrimination because of sex (Sec 1604.ii). *Federal Register, 45*, 74676–74677.

Evans, J., Over, D. & Manktelow, K. (1993). Reasoning, decision-making and rationality. *Cognition, 49*, 165–187.

Feigenson, N., Park, J. & Salovey, P. (1997). Effects of blameworthiness and outcome severity on attributions of responsibility and damage awards in comparative negligence cases. *Law and Human Behavior, 21*, 597–617.

Feigenson, N., Park, J. & Salovey, P. (2001). The role of emotions in comparative negligence judgments. *Journal of Applied Social Psychology, 31*, 576–603.

Filkins, J. W., Smith, C. M. & Tindale, R. S. (1998). An evaluation of the biasing effects of death qualification: a meta-analytic/computer simulation approach. In R. S. Tindale & L. Heath (eds.), *Theory and Research on Small Groups* (pp. 153–175). New York: Plenum.

Fitzgerald, R. & Ellsworth, P. C. (1984). Due process vs. crime control: death qualification and jury attitudes. *Law and Human Behavior, 8*, 31–51.

Forsterlee, L., Horowitz, I., Forsterlee, R. *et al.* (1999). Death penalty attitudes and juror decisions in Australia. *Australian Psychologist, 34*, 64–69.

Furman v. Georgia, 408 U S. 238 (1972).

Greene, E. & Bornstein, B. (2000). Precious little guidance: jury instruction on damage awards. *Psychology, Public Policy, and Law, 6*, 743–768.

Greene, E. & Bornstein, B. (2003). *Determining Damages: The Psychology of Jury Awards.* Washington, DC: American Psychological Association.

Greene, E., Chopra, S. R., Kovera, M. B. *et al.* (2002). Jurors and juries: a review of the field. In J. R. P. Ogloff (ed.), *Taking Psychology and Law into the Twenty-First Century* (pp. 225–284). New York: Kluwer Academic/Plenum.

Greene, E. & Ellis, L. (2006). Decision-making in criminal justice. In D. Carson, B. Milne, F. Pakes *et al.* (eds.), *Applying Psychology to Criminal Justice.* Chichester: John Wiley & Sons.

Greene, E., Johns, M. & Smith, A. (2001). The effects of defendant conduct on jury damage awards. *Journal of Applied Psychology, 86*, 228–237.

Gregg v. Georgia, 428 U.S. 153 (1976).

Hammitt, J. K., Carroll, S. J. & Relles, D. A. (1985). Tort standards and jury decisions. *Journal of Legal Studies, 14*, 751–762.

Haney, C. (1984). On the selection of capital juries: the biasing effects of the death-qualification process. *Law and Human Behavior, 8*, 121–132.

Haney, C., Hurtado, A. & Vega, L. (1994). "Modern" death qualification: new data on its biasing effects. *Law and Human Behavior, 18*, 619–633.

Harris v. Forklift Systems, Inc., 114 S. Ct. 367. (1993)

Hastie, R. (1993). *Inside the Juror: The Psychology of Juror Decision-making.* New York: Cambridge University Press.

Hastie, R., Schkade, D. & Payne, J. (1999). Juror judgments in civil cases: effects of plaintiff's request and plaintiff's identity on punitive damage awards. *Law and Human Behavior, 23*, 445–470.

Henry, J. & Meltzoff, J. (1998). Perceptions of sexual harassment as a function of target's response type and observer's sex. *Sex Roles*, *39*, 253–271.
Hinsz, V. B. & Indahl, K. E. (1995). Assimilation to anchors for damage awards in a mock civil trial. *Journal of Applied Social Psychology*, *25*, 991–1026.
Horowitz, I. A. & Bordens, K. (1988). The effects of outlier presence, plaintiff population size, and aggregation of plaintiffs on simulated civil jury decisions. *Law and Human Behavior*, *14*, 269–285.
Horowitz, I. A. & Bordens, K. S. (2000). The consolidation of plaintiffs: the effects of number of plaintiffs on liability decisions, damage awards, and cognitive processing of evidence. *Journal of Applied Psychology*, *85*, 909–918.
Horowitz, I. A., Forsterlee, L. & Brolly, I. (1996). Effects of trial complexity on decision-making. *Journal of Applied Psychology*, *81*, 757–768.
Huntley, J. E. & Costanzo, M. (2003). Sexual harassment stories: testing a story-mediated model of juror decision-making in civil litigation. *Law and Human Behavior*, *27*, 29–51.
Jacowitz, K. E. & Kahneman, D. (1995). Measures of anchoring in estimation tasks. *Personality and Social Psychology Bulletin*, *21*, 1161–1166.
Kahneman, D., Schkade, D. & Sunstein, C. R. (1998). Shared outrage and erratic awards: the psychology of punitive damages. *Journal of Risk and Uncertainty*, *16*, 47–84.
Kahneman, D. & Tversky, A. (1982). Subjective probability: a judgment of representativeness. In D. Kahneman, P. Slovic & A. Tversky (eds.), *Judgments under Uncertainty: Heuristics and Biases*. Cambridge: Cambridge University Press.
Kerr, N. (1993). Stochastic models of juror decision-making. In R. Hastie (ed.), *Inside the Juror: The Psychology of Juror Decision-making* (pp. 116–135). New York: Cambridge University Press.
Klauer, K., Musch, J. & Naumer, B. (2000). On belief bias in syllogistic reasoning. *Psychological Review*, *107*, 852–884.
Levett, L., Danielsen, E., Kovera, M. & Cutler, B. (2005). The psychology of juror and jury decision-making. In N. Brewer & K. Williams (eds.), *Psychology and Law: An Empirical Perspective*. New York: Guilford Press.
Lockett v. Ohio, *438* U.S. 586 (1978).
Lynch, M. & Haney, C. (2000). Discrimination and instructional comprehension: guided discretion, racial bias, and the death penalty. *Law and Human Behavior*, *24*, 337–358.
MacCoun, R. & Kerr, N. (1988). Asymmetric influence in mock jury deliberation: jurors' bias for leniency. *Journal of Personality and Social Psychology*, *54*, 21–33.
Marshall, C. F. & Wise, J. A. (1975). Jury decisions and the determination of guilt in capital punishment cases: a Bayesian perspective. In D. Wendt & C. Vlek (eds.), *Utility, Probability, and Human Decision-Making* (pp. 257–269). Norwell, MA: Reidel.
Pennington, N. & Hastie, R. (1981). Juror decision-making models: the generalization gap. *Psychological Bulletin*, *89*, 246–287.
Pennington, N. & Hastie, R. (1986). Evidence evaluation in complex decision-making. *Journal of Personality & Social Psychology*, *51*, 242–258.
Pennington, N. & Hastie, R. (1988). Explanation-based decision-making: effects of memory structure on judgment. *Journal of Experimental Psychology: Learning, Memory & Cognition*, *14*, 521–533.
Pennington, N. & Hastie, R. (1993). The story model for juror decision-making. In R. Hastie (ed.), *Inside the Juror: The Psychology of Juror Decision-making.* (pp. 192–221). New York: Cambridge University Press.
Perry, E., Kulik, C. & Bourhis, A. (2004). The reasonable woman standard: effects on sexual harassment court decisions. *Law and Human Behavior*, *28*, 9–27.
Petty, R. & Cacioppo, J. (1986). The elaboration likelihood model of persuasion. In L. Berkowitz (ed.), *Advances in Experimental Social Psychology* (Vol. 19, pp. 126–223). San Diego: Academic Press.
Rabidue v. Osceola Refining Co., 805 F.2d 611 (6th Cir. 1986).
Ring v. Arizona, *122* S. Ct. 2428 (2002).
Seabury, S., Pace, N. & Reville, R. (2004). Forty years of civil jury verdicts. *Journal of Empirical Legal Studies*, *1*, 1–25.

Schuller, R. A. & Yarmey, M. (2001). The jury: deciding guilt and innocence. In R. A. *Schuller* & J. R. P. Ogloff (eds.), *Introduction to Psychology and Law: Canadian Perspectives* (pp. 157–187). Toronto: University of Toronto Press.

Schum, D. A. & Martin, A. W. (1982). Formal and empirical research on cascaded inference in jurisprudence. *Law and Society Review, 17,* 105–151.

Schum, D. A. & Martin, A. W. (1993). Formal and empirical research on cascaded inference in jurisprudence. In R. Hastie (ed.), *Inside the Juror: The Psychology of Juror Decision-making* (pp. 136–174). New York: Cambridge University Press.

Shanley, M. G. (1985). *Comparative Negligence and Jury Behavior.* Santa Monica, CA: Rand Corporation.

Simon, D. (2004). A third view of the black box: cognitive coherence in legal decision-making. *University of Chicago Law Review, 71,* 511–586.

Smith, A. & Greene, E. (2005). Conduct and its consequences: attempts at debiasing jury judgments. *Law and Human Behavior, 29,* 505–526.

Smith, V. L. (1991). Prototypes in the courtroom: lay representations of legal concepts. *Journal of Personality and Social Psychology, 61,* 857–872.

Sommer, K. L., Horowitz, I. A. & Bourgeois, M. J. (2001). When juries fail to comply with the law: biased evidence processing in individual and group decision-making. *Personality and Social Psychology Bulletin, 27,* 309–320.

Title VII, Civil Rights Act of 1964 as amended in 1991 (42 U.S.C. Sec. 2000c-2(a)(1) (1997)).

Tversky, A. & Kahneman, D. (1974). Judgment under uncertainty: heuristics and biases. *Science, 185,* 1124–1131.

Vidmar, N., Gross, F. & Rose, M. (1998). Jury awards for medical malpractice and post-verdict adjustments of those awards. *DePaul Law Review, 48,* 265–299.

Wainright v. Witt, 469 U.S. 412 (1985).

Wegner, D. M. & Bargh, J. A. (1998). Control and automaticity in social life. In D. T. Gilbert & S. T. Fiske (eds.), *Handbook of Social Psychology* (Vol. 1, 4th edn, pp. 446–496). New York: McGraw-Hill.

Weinstock, M. P. & Flaton, R. A. (2004). Evidence coverage and argument skills: cognitive factors in a juror's verdict choice. *Journal of Behavioral Decision-making, 17,* 191–212.

Wiener, R., Gaborit, M., Pritchard, C. *et al.* (1994). Counterfactual thinking in mock juror assessments of negligence: a preliminary investigation. *Behavioral Sciences and the Law, 12,* 89–102.

Wiener, R. L. & Hurt, L. (2000). An interdisciplinary approach to understanding sexual conduct at work. *Psychology, Public Policy, and Law, 85,* 75–85.

Wiener, R. L., Hurt, L. E., Thomas, S. L. *et al.* (1998). The role of declarative and procedural knowledge in capital murder sentencing. *Journal of Applied Social Psychology, 28,* 124–144.

Wiener, R. L., Pritchard, C. C. & Weston, M. (1995). Comprehensibility of approved jury instructions in capital murder cases. *Journal of Applied Psychology, 80,* 455–467.

Wiener, R. L., Rogers, M., Winter, R. *et al.* (2004). Guided jury discretion in capital murder cases: the role of declarative and procedural knowledge. *Psychology, Public Policy & Law, 10,* 516–576.

Wiener, R. L., Richmond, T. L., Seib, H. M. *et al.* (2002). The psychology of telling murder stories: do we think in scripts, exemplars, or prototypes? *Behavioral Sciences and the Law, 20,* 119–139.

Wiener, R. L., Watts, B. A., Goldkamp, K. H. & Gasper, C. (1995). Social analytic investigation of hostile work environments: a test of the reasonable woman standard. *Law and Human Behavior, 19,* 263–281.

Wiener, R. L., Winter, R. J., Rogers, M. & Arnot, L. (2004). The effects of prior workplace behavior on subsequent sexual harassment judgments. *Law and Human Behavior, 28,* 47–67.

Wissler, R. L., Evans, D. L., Hart, A. J. *et al.* (1997). Explaining "pain and suffering" awards: the role of injury characteristics and fault attributions. *Law and Human Behavior, 21,* 181–207.

Witherspoon v. Illinois, 391 U.S. 510 (1968).

Zant v. Stephens, 462 U.S. 862 (1983).

Zickafoose, D. J. & Bornstein, B. H. (1999). Double discounting: the effects of comparative negligence on mock juror decision-making. *Law and Human Behavior, 23,* 577–596.

CHAPTER 29

Eyewitness Testimony

Daniel B. Wright
University of Sussex, UK and Florida International University, USA
and
Graham M. Davies
University of Leicester, UK

INTRODUCTION

Timothy Hiltsley and Ryan Boyd left a Wisconsin bar early one January morning in 2002. They met some people in the parking lot and two of these people went back to Hiltsley's for some marijuana. There, one of the people pulled a gun on Hiltsley, demanded money, then fled. Another robbery also occurred in the neighborhood, and police apprehended a suspect, Tyrone Dubose. They put Dubose in the back of a police car. Hiltsley was told that they had possibly caught "one of the guys" (*State v. Dubose* 2005, ¶13). Hiltsley was put in another police car and driven up to the car where Dubose was seated alone with a light shining on him. Hiltsley said that he was 98 per cent certain that this was the person who had held the gun to his head. Later that year, a jury convicted Dubose of the armed robbery.

This case raises a number of important issues with respect to the reliability of eyewitness testimony and also provides a good example of how psychology can influence legal decisions. For example:

1. Hiltsley thought that Dubose was somebody who frequented the liquor store that he worked in, and memory for familiar faces is better than for unfamiliar faces (Bahrick 1984; see also Bruce *et al.* 2001).
2. Hiltsley was "buzzed" from alcohol, which can impair the processing of new information. Paradoxically, alcohol can enhance memory for some previously encountered information, like arriving at the bar, because later information is not encoded and therefore does not interfere with this previously learned information (Wixted 2004, 2005).
3. Part of the incident was highly stressful, and this can negatively affect reliability of person recognition (Deffenbacher *et al.* 2004).
4. The relationship between confidence and accuracy is complex (Weber & Brewer 2004; Brewer 2006).

Handbook of Applied Cognition: Second Edition. Edited by Francis T. Durso.

5. Dubose is Black, Hiltsley is White, and generally cross-race identifications are less reliable than own-race identifications (Meissner & Brigham 2001).

But the main grounds for Dubose's appeal was whether the show-up, where Hiltsley was presented with a single person and told that he was a suspect, was unnecessarily suggestive. The original appeal was unsuccessful, but the Wisconsin Supreme Court ruled by a 4–3 majority that the show-up identification was not admissible as evidence.

The courts in the US generally frown upon show-ups but in *Stovall v. Denno* (1967) they have ruled that show-ups can be admitted, providing that they are not too suggestive and that the "totality of the circumstances" means the show-up was necessary. "Totality of the circumstances" is a legal phrase, but in *Stovall* it meant that the only witness was in the hospital and might not live. The police felt they needed to see if the witness could identify the suspect as soon as possible, since they did not know if they had time to construct a lineup. Another argument is that by not staging the show-up, they would have denied an innocent suspect his only chance of not being identified. The court in *Stovall* ruled the totality of the circumstances meant the show-up result could be used. In *State v. Dubose* the court argued that the circumstances were such that a lineup could have been produced. They concluded that "evidence obtained from an out-of-court show-up is inherently suggestive and will not be admissible unless, based on the totality of the circumstances, the procedure was necessary" (*State v. Dubose* 2005, ¶33).

The Wisconsin Supreme Court ruled only 4–3 in Dubose's favor, and Wisconsin stands out among US jurisdictions for this ruling. The dissenting opinions in this case were interesting for what they said about the use of psychology in courts and how judgments could affect police procedures. Justice Prosser argued that the non-eyewitness evidence was strong enough that the appeal should not have been successful. On this basis, Prosser presumably expects a retrial without the show-up identification would lead to conviction. Justice Roggensack argued that the reliability of the identification should be considered in its totality. She argued that the identification was likely to be reliable because of the assumed familiarity of the culprit, the lack of disguise, the length of the interaction, and that the identification occurred after only a brief time. She also felt the majority's reliance on "a disputed social science theory" (*State v. Dubose* 2005, ¶89) was misplaced. The main paper she refers to was Steblay *et al.*'s (2003) meta-analysis of show-ups vs. lineups. We discuss this paper below.

The argument from Roggensack is that in this case, the identification was reliable enough. Two counterarguments exist. First, the situation was one in which a show-up was not necessary. After all, according to Justice Prosser, there was much other evidence, enough to justify detaining Dubose and holding a lineup later. Also, neither suspect nor witness appeared near death's door, as in *Stovall*. Accordingly, the majority decision could send a signal to the police that show-ups should not be done unless they are essential, otherwise they will not be admissible (e.g., the post-*Dubose* ruling in *State v. Hibl* 2005). The second counterargument is that human memory, by its nature, is fallible. In concurring, Justice Butler states:

> The dissent cannot seriously argue … that eyewitness identifications are inherently reliable. What we have here is a legal fiction that is simply not borne out by the facts. Unless, and until, we improve eyewitness identification procedures so that the likelihood of irreparable misidentification is significantly reduced, we can no longer proceed as though all is good in the Land of Oz. (*State v. Dubose* 2005, ¶49)

Penrod (2003) has argued that if eyewitness identification was a new form of evidence, it would not be reliable enough to pass the stringent rules of evidence to be admissible in court.

Reading through *State v. Dubose*, and many other recent trial proceedings involving eyewitness identification, it is reassuring to see psychology research being discussed and influencing decisions. Similarly, when the US Department of Justice put forward guidelines for interviewing and identifications (Technical Working Group for Eyewitness Evidence 1999, hereafter *The Guide*) it was important that psychology played a central role as both information provider and sculptor of these recommendations (Wells *et al.* 2000). However, it is worrying to see the scale of errors. The Innocence Project (www.innocenceproject.org; see Scheck *et al.* 2003; Gross *et al.* 2005) in the US describes nearly 200 cases where DNA evidence has helped to exonerate innocent people convicted of crimes and the number of these cases continues to climb. Most of these people were convicted on the basis of faulty eyewitness evidence, and some were on death row. Dozens of similar projects have been created in the UK (www.innocencenetwork.org.uk) and the US. In fact, an *amicus brief* submitted by members of the Wisconsin Innocence Project (www.law.wisc.edu/fjr/innocence/Dubose.pdf) appears to have been a crucial influence on the court in deciding Dubose's appeal.

In this chapter we review some of the most important topics that applied cognitive and social psychologists have researched with respect to eyewitness testimony to discover how our discipline has advanced to such a stage so that Attorney Generals and Supreme Court justices take note.

Wells' Estimator and System Variable Classification

Wells (1978) provided a valuable framework for investigating eyewitness research topics, and in fact his distinction between estimator and system variables can be applied to many areas of science. Estimator variables are those which are naturally associated with the outcome variables. With reference to eyewitness testimony these are characteristics of the crime situation and the eyewitness that predict identification accuracy, and include findings like the longer someone has to view the culprit the higher the likelihood that they will make an accurate identification. System variables are those which can be manipulated by the system. With reference to eyewitness testimony these are variables under the control of the justice system and therefore can be altered if research shows that changes improve the reliability of the identifications. In *Dubose*, the believed familiarity, amount of exposure, that alcohol was involved, that a gun was used, that it was a cross-race identification, etc., are all estimator variables. Using a show-up rather than a lineup is a system variable. Because system variables are in principle under the control of the justice system, if mistakes are made in the procedure, this can lead to appeal. Therefore, appeals are usually made on the basis of system variable research. Expert testimony is given about both estimator and system variable research.

The purpose of this chapter is to review research into estimator and system variables over the last decade or so, since the publication of the first edition of this handbook (Wright & Davies 1999; see also Wells & Olson 2003; useful web-pages include eyewitness.utep.edu/bibliographies.html and www.psychology.iastate.edu/faculty/gwells/homepage.htm). As eyewitness testimony is one of the most researched topics in applied cognition (as shown from issues of *Applied Cognitive Psychology, Journal of Experimental Psychology: Applied*, and SARMAC conferences), our choice of topics is selective, but covers those we feel will have the largest impact over the next decade. The estimator variables we cover are: emotion and memory, own-race bias (ORB), and the potential problems of witnesses talking with each other. The system variables discussed are: interview procedures, credibility assessment, and conducting a lineup (in British terminology, an "identification parade").

ESTIMATOR VARIABLES

Emotion and Memory

Timothy Hiltsley had a gun pointed at his head. During many crimes the eyewitness is in a stressful situation. There are two important questions. First, how does this affect the reliability of subsequent testimony? Second, and arguably more important for the courts, is emotion associated with eyewitness accuracy? Emotion and memory are also discussed by Mazzoni and Scoboria (Chapter 30) this volume, in relation to false memories. While there is some overlap, the emotional events considered by eyewitness researchers are usually brief in duration, while many of the recovered memories refer to extended life periods. Further, in most of the recovered memory cases the "assailant's" identity is not as issue, but whether the event in question actually occurred.

To answer the first question, which is about the causal aspects of emotion, researchers have conducted carefully controlled laboratory studies where participants are randomly allocated either to a control or to an emotive condition, and their memories are compared. One of the main findings is that there is a narrowing of attention on the object creating the stress, which Loftus *et al.* (1987) call the *weapon focus effect*. This finding coincides with many eyewitness accounts where an eyewitness can report details of the .44 Magnum, but not Dirty Harry's face (nor the number of bullets fired).[1] A meta-analysis of these effects showed a small but reliable decrease in identification accuracy when a weapon was present (Steblay 1992).

Subsequent research has examined whether it is the emotive element per se that creates this attention focus, or whether any unusual item could focus attention. Pickel (1999; see also Mitchell *et al.* 1998) showed that presenting an unusual or out-of-context item can produce some of the same effects, a narrowing of attention focused on the unusual item. This suggests that processing both the weapon and the unusual object requires immediate attention, what Deffenbacher *et al.* (2004) call an orienting response. Therefore, novelty may be part of the reason for the weapon focus effect, but is it the only part?

Deffenbacher *et al.* (2004) describe another response to stress: a defensive response. They describe how this results from increased heart rate, blood pressure, etc., caused by anxiety and related stressors. Based on a meta-analysis of studies in which they felt a defensive response was likely to have occurred, they argued that stress negatively affects eyewitness accuracy. Further, they found the size of this effect was related to how realistic the stress manipulation was: the more realistic the manipulation is the greater the impairment. Thus, the effect of emotion is complex. The gun pointed at Hiltsley may have created an orienting response which can facilitate memory of some objects, but the stress of the whole situation may have created a defensive response which can impair memory.

The paragraphs above address whether a weapon and stress causally affect eyewitness accuracy. But a judge may often ask whether, in general, people in stressful situations have better or worse memory than people in non-stressful situations. This is a different question than the causal one and the above studies do not address it (Wright 2006). At first glance this should be an easy question to answer. Is there a correlation between emotion and accuracy? However, the answer depends on the sample of memories. If a collection of everyday memories are chosen, then there is likely to be a positive correlation, because emotive events tend to be important enough to remember (Burt *et al.* 1995). If we consider just events that produce lineups and operationalize stress by a weapon being used, then one of the surveys of lineups can be examined. Valentine *et al.* (2003, tables 8 and 9) compared crimes where a weapon was used vs. those where no weapon was used. The only statistically significant effect they found was that if a weapon was present, the eyewitness was less likely to identify a filler. This suggests a weapon being present is associated with better memory, but the effect is small (16 per cent vs. 24 per cent) and other surveys have failed to find any weapon effects (e.g., Wright & McDaid 1996; Behrman & Davey 2001).

In summary, the effects of emotion on eyewitness memory are complex. While highly stressful situations do involve to a greater extent certain physiological responses, highly stressful situations also are ones which often involve much post-event discussion and rehearsal. The physiological responses may involve a narrowing of attention, but also appear to generally impair cognition. It is important that courts do not consider the physiological responses in isolation. The reason for the emotional reaction is often what makes the event important, which increases the likelihood that it will be talked about with others. While this rehearsal may help to consolidate accurate reports, the act of verbalizing may impair later memories (see Meissner & Memon 2002) and make people less likely to report any information that may be remembered (Clare & Lewandowsky 2004), and, as discussed below, talking about events can allow errant memories from one person to infect another person's memories (Gabbert *et al.* 2003).

Own-Race Bias

There has been discussion about people being poor at recognizing people from other races since near the beginning of experimental psychology (e.g., Feingold 1914), but systematic investigation of what has become known as the own-race bias (ORB, sometimes called the cross-race effect) started with Malpass and Kravitz (1969). Feingold's (1914, p. 50) original speculation was that the ORB was due "to our familiarity, to our contact" with our own race. This is called the *contact* hypothesis. Meissner and Brigham (2001) examined 39 laboratory studies of ORB and found evidence for contact accounting for only a small part of the ORB.

A closer examination of Meissner and Brigham's (2001) meta-analysis is in order. The studies all had a similar form: participants were shown a large of number of faces and later given a recognition test of these faces plus fillers. They found that people were more likely to correctly recognize previously shown faces of their own race than of another race, and also more likely to falsely recognize faces of another race that were not shown.

On the basis of these studies they concluded that ORB was a reliable phenomenon when examined in this way. The average effect size was people being 2.2 times more likely to accurately recognize own-race faces compared with faces of other races. They also found that inter-racial contact predicted a small but reliable amount of the ORB.

There are concerns that the effect size may be different in laboratory situations, where the participants know that their memory will be tested and therefore can concentrate on each stimulus face, compared with more natural encounters with people of different races. To examine this, Wright *et al.* (2001) had either a White or a Black confederate approach either a White or a Black member of the public in a shopping center and ask a couple of questions. A few minutes later a research assistant approached the person, explained who she was, and asked them to identify the confederate from a lineup. They found an ORB for both Black and White participants using this more ecologically valid design. The effect size, a mean odds ratio of approximately 4, is considerably larger than the effects observed in the meta-analysis. This suggests that the effect may be stronger in more naturalistic encounters because people tend to pay more attention to others of their own race. In Valentine *et al.*'s (2003) archival study, they found the odds of a suspect identification were 1.38 times higher for own-race identifications than for cross-race identifications. This is lower than the other estimates, but overall, the data from different sources converge, demonstrating an ORB.

With the phenomenon of ORB clearly demonstrated, there have been four main strands of work expanding this basic finding. First, researchers have shown that other own-group biases exist. One of the most researched of these is an own-age bias (Wright & Stroud 2002; Lindholm 2005; Perfect & Moon 2005). The finding is that people are better at recognizing others of their own age. This research and other own-group bias research are in their infancy, but it appears that the main explanation for the ORB (the contact hypothesis) may not be tenable for these (Perfect & Moon 2005).

The second extension attempts to illuminate our understanding of the neuroscience of ORB. Cunningham *et al.* (2004) used functional imagery to look at brain activity when White people viewed Black and White faces. They found significant differences; there was greater activity in the amygdala area when seeing Black faces. The amygdala is an area associated with processing of emotional material. From Deffenbacher *et al.*'s (2004) review, if emotion processing creates a defensive response, this could be one of the reasons why White people have poor recognition memory for Black faces. This hypothesis is given further support by the finding that ORB is lessened (or eliminated) when people are in a good mood (Johnson & Fredrickson 2005). The leap from functional imagery studies to explanations of behavioral phenomena is large, but as in other areas of psychology, functional imaging techniques provide a different and sometimes valuable way of understanding a phenomenon.

The third extension is to focus on what "contact with other races" is and how it is measured or varied in order to see whether the small relationship between contact and ORB may be due to a poor conceptualization of contact and relying on self-assessment to measure contact. One of the most interesting studies was Ruth Dixon's undergraduate project (cited in Valentine *et al.* 1995). She compared two groups of White participants on memory for White and Black faces, tested at two points in time about eight weeks apart. The control group improved slightly with both sets of faces, as might be expected from practice. The experimental group spent the time between tests at a voluntary teaching project in either Ghana or Tanzania. Their recognition accuracy actually went down (slightly) for White faces, but their accuracy for Black faces went up by a large amount, so much that they were no longer exhibiting an ORB. This prospective study shows that experience with people from other races can improve memory accuracy for the other race. More recent studies have also used naturally occurring exposure to other races and have shown experience with other races improves memory (e.g., Sangrigoli *et al.* 2005).

The final extension is examining characteristics of own-race and other race memories using cognitive techniques, and incorporating theories from social psychology (e.g., Sporer 2001; Walker & Hewstone 2006). Some of the concentration relates to theories of face recognition, and whether it is better to represent faces within some multidimensional space (Valentine 1991) or as a set of features, where race is one feature (Levin 2000). Levin (2000) found that much of the ORB can be attributed to how people encode cross-race faces. People use much of their encoding processing to register that the person is from another race, which they do not do for own-race faces. Another recent approach is by Meissner *et al.* (2005) who used the widely assumed view in cognitive psychology that memory involves two processes (recollection and familiarity; for review, see Gronlund *et al.*, Chapter 5, this volume) to explore ORB. They found that the ORB mostly involves recollective processes. This suggests the familiarity process does not produce a bias and therefore that under certain circumstances, such as superficial encoding, an ORB would not be expected. However, further research of this type is necessary before it is possible to give accurate predictions of the ORB. These recent studies are important for theories of face recognition and potentially may be of great importance in the courtroom. If we are able to understand why people are inaccurate in certain situations, then it is possible that we will be better able to differentiate accurate from inaccurate memories.

Own-race bias is sometimes described as a phenomenon without an explanation. Because the phenomenon is part of folk psychology (the "they all look alike" belief) and is usually observed in empirical research, the presence of the effect is readily accepted. While the contact hypothesis also is intuitive, it has received less support because the effect sizes are often small. However, this may be due to the reliability of both the memory measure (as far as we know none of the papers in Meissner & Brigham 2001 reports reliability for the memory measures) and the contact measure. As measurement improves, contact may become a clearer frontrunner for an explanation, but it is important that researchers continue to look at the broader sociological and political reasons for why many people do not have much inter-racial contact.

Problems of Remembering Together

If you ask anyone from legal experts to first year undergraduates what they know about eyewitness research, they will tell you about one person and an area of research that began in the 1970s with confusing people about a stop sign and a yield sign. At memory conferences for 30 years researchers have talked about the "Beth-effect" (see Garry & Hayne 2006). The "Beth-effect" is the finding that post-event information can become incorporated into a memory for an original event. This was a radical departure from the existing memory theories at the time, and has helped to construct contemporary theories where memories are viewed as malleable in systematic and predictable ways. Post-event information research has branched out into many areas (Loftus 2005). Here we concentrate on one branch that is of particular forensic importance.

Paterson and Kemp (2006) found that for about 80 per cent of people who witnessed a crime there were other witnesses present. Of their sample, 86 per cent talked with the co-witnesses about the crime. When people discuss an event, this is a form of post-event information, and, as Paterson and Kemp have shown, it often occurs. If two witnesses recall an event differently and talk about the event, what one person's says can become part of the other person's memory. Marsh and Tversky (2004) have found that people admit that most retellings include distortions and many are inaccurate. This suggests that much of the information encountered when discussing events with co-witnesses will be inaccurate. While the 86 per cent estimate was based on their particular sample (of Australian undergraduates), even if the percentage of witnesses in the general population who talk with others is half this, this is still a large amount of time when potentially contaminating information could be presented to witnesses.

While there were some early studies on collaborative memory by Stephenson, Clark and colleagues (e.g., Stephenson *et al.* 1986; Clark *et al.* 1990) during the past decade several research groups have explored the phenomenon in more detail. The recent focus has been on errant information being transmitted from one person to others. It goes by different labels – for example, social contagion of memory (Roediger *et al.* 2001; Meade & Roediger 2002), response conformity (Schneider & Watkins 1996), co-witness information (Shaw *et al.* 1997), memory conformity (Wright *et al.* 2000; Gabbert *et al.* 2003), and social memory (Wright *et al.* 2005) – but regardless of the label the research shows that one person's response can become another person's memory.

Consider as an example a recent study by Gabbert and colleagues (in press). Participants arrived at the laboratory in pairs and were given several tasks, which included looking at pictures of complex scenes. They were later told to discuss these, and then were individually given a memory test. There were two tricks. The first was that the pictures they were given had a couple of minor differences. Therefore, when they discussed the scenes one person's accurate recollection would be erroneous for the other person. The second trick was that they told one person in the pair that she or he had viewed the scenes for twice as long as the other person, and told the other person that she or he had viewed the scenes for half as long. In fact, the times were the same. They found that the people who were told they viewed the scenes for less time were more likely to incorporate the errant pieces of information suggested by their partner into their individual recall than were the people told that they had viewed the scenes for longer.

During the last decade there have been many important findings about memory conformity. For example, it has been shown to work with the children (Schwarz *et al.* 2004) and older adults (Gabbert *et al.* 2003). Characteristics of the dialogue are also important, like the person who brings up the disputed information in the dialogue almost always is the one to convince the other person about this information (Gabbert *et al.* 2006). Certain items are also easier to implant in someone's memory. Roediger *et al.* (2001) have found that it is easier to introduce schema-consistent items than schema-inconsistent items, and Wright *et al.* (2005) showed that it is easier for a co-witness to add information to somebody else's memory than it is for them to remove information from a memory report.

What makes matters worse is that juries and courts often believe reports from multiple eyewitnesses as independent pieces of information. There are many ways that the eyewitnesses are not independent even if they do not talk (i.e., they see the same suspect in the lineup), but if the eyewitnesses talk with each other it is clear that one person's belief may have contaminated the others'. The courts should decide whether it is appropriate to accept potentially contaminated testimony, and if it is to be allowed, whether a warning should be given to jurors.

SYSTEM VARIABLES

Interview Procedures

In the *Dubose* investigation, the Wisconsin police interviewed the alleged victims at length. Despite the advances in forensic science of recent years, statements from witnesses remain the single most important source of information to the police. In recent years, psychologists have made major contributions to effective forensic interviewing of both adults and children. The goal has been to increase the amount of reliable information without decreasing accuracy. Sadly, hypnosis once advocated as a solution (Reiser 1989) has been shown in both experimental and field studies to increase suggestibility and fabrication, with attendant risks of miscarriages of justice (see Wagstaff 1999 for a review).

A more promising approach is the Cognitive Interview (CI; Fisher & Geiselman 1992). This technique has undergone numerous refinements and additions since its inception, fueled in part by the experiences of officers trained in its use. At the core of the original CI is the idea of applying techniques of memory retrieval derived from the laboratory to the practical problems of witness recall.

We describe details of the CI in Wright and Davies (1999), and more detailed descriptions can be found in Fisher and Geiselman (1992) and Memon *et al.* (2003), so here we shall only summarize the main issues. An important meta-analysis was published in Koehnken *et al.* (1999). There are four main cognitive techniques at the core of the CI:

1. *Reinstate the context.* People can recall more if in the same context as they encoded the information, even when they are told just to imagine themselves in the same context.
2. *Recall everything.* While this may lower the threshold for reporting information, and thus may allow some errors to be introduced, it encourages the eyewitness to report information that may not appear to be of forensic value to the eyewitness, but in fact could be a vital clue for the police investigator.
3. *Recall the event in different orders*, for example, both chronologically forward and backwards. Some research suggests that this may be beneficial, but it is often difficult to implement. More information is usually acquired because it involves multiple retrievals, but it is unclear how well this specific instruction is suited for the field.
4. *Recall the event from different perspectives.* Eyewitnesses are encouraged to report the event as it would have been seen by another eyewitness. Like the previous technique, there have been difficulties implemented this and its value may be do to the repeated retrieval than the specific instruction.

Early research comparing the CI (Bekerian & Dennett 1993) showed that the CI was able to produce much more information than the standard police interview, though this may say more about the poverty of the standard police interview than the value of the CI (Davies 1993). The standard police approach had been to ask many closed ended questions and not establish a rapport with the eyewitness. When Fisher and Geiselman (1992) updated the CI they stressed how this social element was important for creating a successful interview.

While the CI is a valuable tool, it should not be viewed as a perfect solution without need of modification. In fact, while it tends to produce more correct recall of past events when compared with other interviewing methods, some research also finds increased error rates. Researchers have looked at the CI to identify precisely the potent elements of the CI package that are responsible for its effectiveness. Studies on the relative importance of the original four mnemonic components suggest that the "recall everything" instruction combined with context reinstatement may be the most critical elements, with change in perspective and change of order producing only weak or equivocal effects (Milne & Bull 2002). Interestingly, surveys among serving police officers also show a preference for the former two instructions, with change of perspective or order being rarely used in practice (Kebbell *et al.* 1999). While context and detail appear to be powerful in facilitating retrieval, there is an obvious danger in asking victim witnesses to recreate their own rape or violent assault as it may produce secondary trauma (Kelly *et al.* 2005). Fisher and Geiselman (1992) suggest that if such witnesses are to be interviewed, they should be encouraged to use a third person narrative to distance themselves from the events.

The CI has been advocated in the US (*The Guide* 1999) and in the UK (Kebbell *et al.* 1999), and is beginning to be used in developing countries (Stein & Memon 2006). Adapted forms have proven to be useful for interviewing accident victims (Brock *et al.* 1999) and those with complex medical histories (Fisher *et al.* 2000). Versions of the CI have also been developed for interviewing children (Saywitz *et al.* 1992; see also Akehurst *et al.* 2003) and people with mild learning difficulties (Milne *et al.* 1999). There are many special considerations when interviewing children (Davies & Wescott in press).

The police continue to use the CI, but opposition to its widespread use in routine police enquiries arises due to the time it takes to administer relative to the traditional interview (Kebbell *et al.* 1999). Davis *et al.* (2005) have developed a shortened version of the CI, which drops order and perspective change, and claim to elicit 84 per cent of the information available from the full CI, with a 23 per cent saving in time. Further assessment of this shortened version is necessary.

Credibility Assessment

How can we be sure that what witnesses tell us is an honest account of what they remember? Tyrone Dubose was interviewed by the police at the time of his arrest and claimed he had no knowledge of the crime. Are there reliable signs that the police and the public can draw on to decide whether a person is telling the truth or not? Possible cues to deception can usefully be divided into four categories: behavioral, paralinguistic, physiological, and the content of the statement (Vrij 2000).

Behavioral and paralinguistic cues have traditionally been thought of as a rich source of information for establishing whether a person is telling the truth or not. Expansive claims have been made for the value of "body language" for detecting deception (Inbau *et al.* 2001; Walters 2003). However, research suggests that the number of such cues which reliably differentiate between truthful and fabricated statements is surprisingly small. A typical experiment will involve careful analysis of the non-verbal behavior of volunteers telling the truth or lying about their likes and dislikes of persons or products. DePaulo *et al.* (2003) conducted a meta-analysis of over 150 possible behavioral and paralinguistic measures of deception and found just three that were consistently associated with lying: a higher voice pitch; greater vocal stress or tension; and a shorter length of utterance. Even these differences, though statistically significant across a range of studies, were relatively modest in terms of effect size. It is also highly likely that even these effects are modulated by such factors as the opportunity for rehearsal, the seriousness of the lie, and the stress imposed upon the liar. Further, lying under experimental conditions may be very different than deceiving a court of law (DePaulo & Morris 2004; Sporer & Schwandt 2006). Sadly, it is apparent that there is no Pinocchio test!

What of the ability of the general public to detect lies? Research evidence confirms that their ability to detect deception under experimental conditions rarely rises much above chance. Vrij (2000) reviews nearly 40 studies which yielded accuracy rates of between 38 per cent and 64 per cent, where 50 per cent represents chance. One consistent finding is that the general public tends to show a "truth bias": they label more deceptive statements as true than not true (DePaulo *et al.* 1985). Perhaps all of us underestimate the frequency with which we are lied to in our general lives (DePaulo & Kirkendol 1989).

Are police officers, whose job entails routinely establishing the truth from deception, better judges than members of the public? Early experimental research suggested that they were no more accurate than members of the public (Vrij & Winkel 1993) and that training appeared to increase confidence but had little reliable impact on accuracy (Bull 2004). However, such experiments can be criticized as involving relatively trivial lies (pretending you prefer Coke to Pepsi, when the reverse is the case), rather than the so-called "high-stake" lies told by suspects during police interrogations. Mann *et al.* (2004) obtained video recordings through police sources of actual interrogations of individuals arrested for serious crimes, including rape and murder, for whom subsequent investigation had established either that they told the truth or had been grossly deceptive. Police officers unfamiliar with the cases involved viewed extracts from these recordings before deciding whether the suspect was being deceptive or not. Under these conditions, police officers were significantly more accurate than in the laboratory analogue studies: they averaged 64 per cent accuracy for the truthful statements and 66 per cent for the deceptive. However, as Vrij (2003) emphasizes, officers made many incorrect decisions. The explanation may lie in the officers' perceptions of what are accurate cues to deception. Surveys suggest that most British police officers believe that fidgeting and gaze-aversion are reliable signs of lying, yet actual analysis of police interviews where the suspect is known to have lied suggests that these are not reliably associated with deception: on the contrary, suspects showed a decrease in bodily movement and blink rate when lying at interview (Mann *et al.* 2002).

If humans are not reliable lie detectors, could a machine do any better? "Voice stress analyzers" are supposedly able to detect whether a person is lying from low frequency stress changes in the voice. Such machines can be used on recorded interviews or attached to telephones. However, the US National Research Council Report (2003) concluded that such devices were ineffective. As noted above, deception is significantly associated with raised voice pitch, but voice pitch can also be raised for a variety of other reasons, not least by the stress induced by being told that you are lying (the "Othello" error, Ekman 1989).

While the idea of telling whether you are being lied to on the phone is an attractive one, a practical device remains a dream. A much more widespread device for establishing truth is the lie detector or polygraph. This instrument simultaneously measures a person's respiration, blood pressure, heart rate, and frequently galvanic skin response (palmar sweating). The device is widely used in the interrogation of suspects in the US, Canada, Israel, and Japan, though not in the UK and many other European countries. The effectiveness of the machine is dependent on how it is used. Two common questioning procedures are the comparison question technique and the concealed knowledge test (Honts 2004).

The comparison question technique (CQT) is the most widely used in the US and involves comparing the physiological reaction of the accused to questions about the offense to questions which are either neutral (personal details) or control questions designed to arouse some emotion in even innocent persons (e.g., "Have you ever traveled on public transport without a ticket?"). The rationale is that while the innocent will show raised reactions to the control questions, but no systematic differences on the offense-related and neutral questions, the guilty will show an increased response on the offense-related questions relative to the other two types. Laboratory tests employ a mock crime paradigm when, for instance, some subjects enter a room and "steal" cash from a drawer while others are merely told about it. In one experiment brained polygraph operators identified 91 per cent of the "guilty" persons, and wrongly classified only 11 per cent of the innocent people as guilty (Honts 2004).

There are limitations on the realism achievable with laboratory tests and student participants are hardly representative of offender populations (Lykken 1998). The alternative is to conduct field studies, where experienced polygraphists examine anonymous output from actual interviews with suspects. Some will be from interviews where, based on other evidence, the suspect is assumed to have told the truth, while the remainder will have subsequently confessed and thus it is assumed they had lied during the examination. A survey of these field studies conducted as part of the report on the polygraph for the British Psychological Society (2004) gives figures of between 83 and 89 per cent correct decisions on guilty suspects but only 53–78 per cent of innocent suspects were correctly classified. Such high and unacceptable rates of error on innocent suspects are a source of continuing controversy, not least the ground truth of the original classifications: Were the confessions of guilt true or coerced, and were the innocent suspects really innocent? As the BPS report observes: a guilty suspect exonerated by a polygraph test is unlikely to say, "Well, actually I am guilty!"

The traditional alternative to the CQT is the concealed knowledge test (CKT). This operates by measuring a suspect's reaction to items connected to the crime but not publicly known. If, say, a bloodied glove was found at the crime scene, the suspect will be asked about this item alongside other decoy items. If the suspect shows a specific physiological reaction to mention of the glove, this will be taken as a sign of guilt. The CKT is widely used in Israel and has the advantage of not displaying the strong lie bias associated with the CQT (Elaad 1990). However, such privileged information is not available in many crimes; Podlesney (1990) estimated that material suitable for the CKT was available in only 9 per cent of cases investigated by the FBI. Further, there is the danger that the suspect may have acquired the critical information through entirely innocent means, such as the media or from the detectives in the course of the investigation. Both approaches appear vulnerable to countermeasures by forensically aware suspects; they include raising arousal to control items or reducing attention to relevant questions (Honts & Amato 2002). In the meantime, the search continues for new and even more foolproof measures of lie detection, such as evoked potentials (Iacono 1995; Rosenfeld 1995), but it is far from clear that such methods will be immune to the criticisms of the existing technology (British Psychological Society 2004).

A final source of information is the verbal content of the statement. One content-based system is Statement Validity Analysis (SVA), which is widely used for establishing the validity or otherwise of children's allegations of sexual abuse. The central tenet of SVA is that there are systematic differences in content and quality that differentiate a true statement from one that is fabricated. These relate to both the cognitive and motivational aspects of the statement. From a cognitive standpoint, a child who has experienced an event is likely to describe it in more detail, contain more irrelevancies, locate the event in a specific time and place, use reported speech and make reference to their own subjective experiences. As regards motivation, it is argued that children who are lying would not, for instance, readily admit to doubts about their own testimony, make spontaneous corrections to their story, or admit to a lack of memory for aspects of the event. Criteria-Based Content Analysis (CBCA) involves analyzing the transcripts of children's statements for the presence of 19 such criteria and combining these with other information concerning the nature of the allegation and the child concerned, reaching a decision on credibility. This was first introduced in Germany in 1954 and is still the method of choice for the German courts and many other countries in continental Europe (Koehnken 2004).

The first attempts at empirically validating the effectiveness of the CBCA did not begin until 1989, and since then there have been at least 37 published studies (Vrij 2005). As with the polygraph research, these can usefully be divided into laboratory experiments and field studies. In laboratory research, children may be invited to observe a staged event such as a magic show, or to describe a vivid, stressful incident from their past, such as being bitten by a dog. Subsequently, the content of their recall is compared to controls who merely imagine the events, which they are asked to describe as though they took part in them. In general such studies show that on the basis of total CBCA scores, between 67 and 91 per cent of truthful statements and between 64 and 100 per cent of lies were accurately identified. However, some criteria appear to be more frequent and diagnostic than others: in particular the cognitive, as opposed to the motivational, criteria (Vrij 2005). In field studies, transcripts of interviews with children who have been subsequently judged to have been honest or deceptive are analyzed for differences in the presence of the different criteria. Again, results generally favor the effectiveness of total CBCA scores in differentiating between the two groups of transcripts, though the problems of establishing ground truth apply as much to these studies as to those on the polygraph. In assessing the transcripts, the reliability of scoring some of the scales appears low (Lamb *et al.* 1997), a weakness possibly attributable to inadequate training (Koehnken 2004). Other problems for CBCA identified by Vrij (2005) include the clear correlation between the developmental age of the child and the number of criteria present, leading to concerns that younger children will be inappropriately labeled as deceptive; the lack of a clearly identifiable threshold in terms of numbers and strength of criteria for distinguishing between reliable and unreliable accounts, and the potential vulnerability of the system to coaching (Vrij *et al.* 2002).

In the UK and US, the adversarial system of justice makes it difficult to introduce expert evidence on credibility into the criminal court. SVA, though a potentially promising development, currently falls well short of the criteria set down in *Daubert v. Merrell Dow Pharmaceutical, Inc.* (1993) for the admission of such evidence (Vrij 2005). For the foreseeable future, in matters of credibility, the jury will continue to decide.

The Lineup

One of the most dramatic moments of a police investigation is when the eyewitness identifies, or fails to identify, the suspect in a lineup (sometimes called an identification parade). A lineup is where the eyewitness views a large number of people, usually including the suspect and several fillers (people known to be innocent), and decides if one of these people is the person they saw committing the crime. Lineups can be live, or use photographs or computer files (Valentine & Heaton 1999). It is dramatic because if the suspect is identified, this becomes important prosecution evidence which can often sway a jury toward a guilty verdict. If the suspect is not identified, that person is often released and the police begin new lines of enquiry (or end the investigation). People (including police officers, judges, and jurors) assume that memories are accurate in most situations, and therefore if an identification is made, it is assumed to be correct. In this section we describe the extent of errors in lineups and look at different ways in which identifications can be made.

The critical question for police, judges, and jurors is whether an identification is a good predictor of the suspect's guilt (Wells & Olson 2002). Penrod (2003; see also Levi 1998a) combined data from several archival studies (mainly Behrman & Davey 2001), laboratory identification studies (Steblay *et al.*'s 2001 meta-analysis), and mock witness studies (e.g., Valentine & Heaton 1999), with several assumptions about the recognition process (that similar processes occur in laboratory and field studies, that recognition is an all-or-none process with guessing, etc.) to calculate estimates. Penrod needed to calculate the overall amount of time that the suspect is the culprit, how often witnesses were guessing, and several other estimates that are likely to vary across jurisdictions. Given the number of approximations and assumptions, these are rough estimates. But he estimates that about half of the time when no identification is made the suspect is the culprit and about half of the time when a filler is identified the non-identified suspect is the culprit. These are important errors because often the culprit is released and may go on to commit more crimes. Further, police time may be lost if other investigative avenues are explored (It is also possible that another person could be falsely convicted of the crime.) When the suspect is identified, Penrod estimates that about 10–15 per cent of the time they are not the culprit. This is a large percentage considering the weight jurors place on identification evidence (Loftus 1974; Wright in press). The consequences of these errors are shown by the vast majority of people being exonerated by DNA evidence being originally convicted on the basis of errant eyewitness identification (Scheck *et al.* 2003; Gross *et al.* 2005).

One method that is sometimes used, particularly in the US, for an identification is a show-up (Dysart & Lindsay in press). An example of this is when Dubose sat in the back of a police car and was identified. The eyewitness is presented with a single person and asked whether this is the culprit. In Kassin *et al.*'s (2001) survey of eyewitness experts, 74 per cent believed that show-ups produced more misidentifications, most saying that this belief was based on the scientific literature. The court in *Dubose* argued that the show-up is a suggestive procedure and their decision has already affected other cases (e.g., *State v. Hibl* 2005). In making this argument the court cited Steblay *et al.*'s (2003) meta-analysis. The meta-analysis summarized data from eight articles which compared show-ups, where one person is presented to an eyewitness, and traditional simultaneous lineups, where the eyewitness views a number (usually six in the US and nine in the UK) of people and can either make an identification or not. They report that all studies had "unbiased lineup instructions" (p. 528).

Steblay *et al.* (2003) found that when the culprit was in the show-up/lineup, the correct identification rates were about the same. When the culprit was not present, 85 per cent of the show-up participants correctly rejected the show-up. This compares to only 57 per cent rejecting culprit absent lineups. At first glance this makes it appear that show-ups have an advantage. However, if the 43 per cent of errant identification in the culprit-absent lineups is spread equally across six people, then each person, including the suspect, would be picked only 7 per cent of the time. So, the likelihood of an innocent suspect being chosen is about twice as great in a show-up as in a lineup. There are many real cases where lineups are biased and the suspect is chosen more often than others by mock witnesses (Valentine & Heaton 1999), but there are also cases where the show-up is unduly biased, as in the *Dubose* case where the show-up was conducted in a police car. It is also worth noting that the small number of studies, individually, gave different results. It was only with the publication of Steblay *et al.*'s meta-analysis (first presented at a large conference in 2002, and so after Kassin *et al.*'s respondents answered their questions) that most researchers could have based their opinions on the scientific literature. Further, with only eight studies, second-order sampling error means that we should use these results with caution (Hunter & Schmidt 2004).

Kassin *et al.*'s (2001) respondents were probably willing to agree with the Wisconsin Supreme Court that show-ups are too suggestive prior to the meta-analysis because this is a logical conclusion from one of the most prominent views about how eyewitnesses make choices in a lineup. For 20 years, Lindsay, Wells, and their colleagues have argued and reported convincing evidence that eyewitnesses often assume that the culprit is present in the lineup and try to choose the person that looks most like how they remember the culprit (Wells & Olson 2003). If an eyewitness is presented with a single suspect, and if an eyewitness chooses the suspect that looks most like their memory of the culprit, then the single suspect is in a bad situation. It is probably even worse in real show-ups compared with laboratory studies, where participants are aware that the experimenters are likely to include some culprit-absent show-ups. An eyewitness is likely to assume that the police are presenting a suspect only if they think they have the right person. The wording that a police officer uses when presenting the show-up could reinforce this belief. While Steblay *et al.* (2003) only used studies with "unbiased instructions" it is likely that the phrases used by many police officers in show-ups reinforce the belief of the eyewitness that the person in the show-up is guilty. This means that a show-up may be even more suggestive than Steblay *et al.*'s results suggest.

Lindsay and Wells (1985) developed and tested an alternative lineup, called the sequential lineup, which takes into account that eyewitnesses sometimes treat the identification task as an attempt to choose the person who looks most like the culprit. Rather than showing all people in the lineup simultaneously, eyewitnesses are shown each person individually and asked if that person is the culprit. If they say "no," they are shown the next person. Eyewitnesses are not allowed to go back to previously discounted people, and once a person (a suspect or a filler) has been positively identified the lineup is over. These two factors are important because they emphasize that eyewitnesses are supposed to make absolute rather than relative judgments of each person.

In another meta-analysis by Steblay and colleagues (2001) the traditional simultaneous lineup was compared with sequential lineups. When the culprit was present, 50 per cent of participants made a correct identification with a simultaneous lineup, but only 35 per cent did with the sequential lineup. When the culprit was not present, 49 per cent of the people using simultaneous lineups correctly rejected the lineup compared with 72 per cent of those in the sequential lineups. If we assume six-person lineups and each person in the lineup has an equal chance of being falsely identified, this suggests that when a suspect is not the target they will be chosen about 8.5 per cent in simultaneous lineups but only 4.7 per cent in sequential lineups. Thus, it appears that there may be a tradeoff between the culprit being identified more often with the traditional simultaneous lineups but also more false identifications. This has led several authors (e.g., Ebbesen and Flowe 2001; McQuiston-Surrett *et al.* 2006), to claim that the difference between the two procedures may simply be a difference in response criterion.[2] They argue that eyewitnesses in simultaneous lineups have a lower threshold for making an identification, but their identifications are approximately as accurate as those made from sequential lineups. However, Gronlund (2004) has shown that people do tend to use different strategies for the different types of lineup in accordance with Lindsay and Wells' predictions. This is a topic of much current debate (e.g., Meissner *et al.* 2005). While we agree with *The Guide* (1999) and the general belief within the research community that the sequential lineup is an improvement over the simultaneous lineup, this view has critics and all agree that there is room for improvement.

Two potential improvements have received much discussion. The first is Levi's (1998b) modified sequential lineup. He argues that the number of fillers should be increased to 20 or more and eyewitnesses should be allowed to make multiple identifications. His logic is that the larger number of fillers provides protection against an eyewitness guessing an innocent suspect. Allowing the eyewitness to see all the people in the lineup addresses a concern many legal experts have with the original sequential lineup. With the original sequential lineup a filler could be chosen before the suspect was viewed. Legal experts worry about this because they think jurors would want to know how the eyewitness reacts when faced with the suspect.

The second potential improvement was proposed by Pryke *et al.* (2004). Rather than just using a single sequential lineup, they ran separate lineups for the person's face, voice, body, and clothes. While it is possible that an eyewitness can guess an innocent suspect in one of these formats, somebody guessing the same innocent suspect in all of them is very unlikely. If six-person lineups are used, each person is equally likely to be chosen, and the result of one lineup is not related to the result of the others (i.e., they are independent), then the probability of guessing the suspect in all four lineups is $(1/6)^4 = 0.08$ per cent. This method is only possible if the eyewitness sees the face, body, and clothes, and hears the voice, but even if only two or three of these are available the probabilities are still just 3 per cent and 0.5 per cent, respectively. Thus, requiring a suspect identification in each of these formats to count as an identification should greatly lessen the number of innocent people identified, but it is a difficult task to correctly identify a culprit with each format. If there are three lineups and to count as an identification it is only necessary to identify the suspect in two, the chance of guessing this is: (1/6)(1/6)(5/6)3 = 7 per cent. To try to prevent this, Pryke *et al.* urge eyewitnesses not to guess. Their empirical tests of this are impressive. When a face is identified and only one other identification is made and it is of the same person, then in almost every case it was a correct identification. This appears to be a promising advance, but as said above, using multiple lineups will be possible only when the eyewitness has encoded these different attributes.

The final question we address is whether it is possible to ascertain whether an identification is accurate. We consider two aspects of an identification, the eyewitness's confidence and how quickly the identification was made. Lay people believe confident eyewitness reports, but research has shown that confidence does not imply accuracy. Brewer (2006) provides a detailed review of this research. Several decades ago Wells and Murray (1984) reviewed the literature on the confidence/accuracy relationship and found the average correlation was small ($r = 0.07$). Subsequent reviews have found larger correlations, but more importantly have identified situations when the correlation is likely to be larger and when it is likely to be small. Sporer *et al.* (1995) found the correlation to be larger when people made an identification, but smaller when people do not make an identification.

An important advance during the past decade regarding the confidence/accuracy relationship is the finding by Wells and Bradfield (1998) that telling eyewitnesses that they have identified the suspect increases their confidence while telling them that they have identified a filler decreases it. If somebody has errantly identified an innocent suspect the findings of Sporer *et al.* (1995) suggests that they might not be that confident in their identification. However, once they are told that they have identified the suspect their confidence increases and this increase in confidence may cause jurors to convict an innocent suspect. This is a potential lethal combination and explains why psychologists (e.g., Wells *et al.* 1998) state that an eyewitness's confidence should be measured after an identification but before the eyewitness receives any feedback.

The final topic is the speed of the identification. Within any given study, the general tendency is that people who naturally respond quickly tend to respond accurately. This finding should not be confused with the speed/accuracy tradeoff discussed in cognitive psychology where forcing participants to speed up on a task negatively affects accuracy. This illustrates the difference between an associative hypothesis (that fast responders tend also to be accurate) and a causal hypothesis (that increasing speed decreases accuracy, all other things being equal) (Wright 2006). The concern for identifications is with the associative hypothesis.

Dunning and Perretta (2002) analyzed data from several lineup studies. They came up with a "10–12-second" rule where identifications were generally accurate if they were within this time and more often incorrect if they were longer. Weber *et al.* (2004) examined the consistency of this rule and found that the precise time depends on several characteristics of the study. This questions the forensic utility of a critical latency period because different lineups (and their associated estimator and system variables) will have different characteristics and many of these will not be known. In the UK using response latency is even more difficult to use because, according to the rules, eyewitnesses have to view each person twice.

There have been two recent studies that have examined eyewitness confidence and identification speed using real lineups (Behrman & Richards 2005; Wright & Skagerberg in press). Behrman and Richards used the verbal descriptions often given by eyewitnesses and used these to calculate measures of confidence (phrases like "absolutely certain" as opposed to "not quite sure") and speed (phrases like "without hesitation" and "immediately"). They found eyewitnesses who identified fillers had lower confidence and slower responses than those who identified the suspect. Wright and Skagerberg asked eyewitness questions about confidence and speed after they had made an identification but before they knew whether they had chosen the suspect. They also found these measures differentiated between suspect and filler choosers. Further, they measured these variables after the eyewitnesses discovered if they had identified the suspect. As predicted from Wells and Bradfield (1998), confidence increased for people told they had chosen the suspect and decreased for those who had chosen a filler. These are important studies because they show that laboratory findings also occur in real eyewitness situations.

The lineup identification is a pivotal moment in a suspect's life. It can determine their freedom and in some jurisdictions their life. Because of the impact that identification evidence has on juror decision-making it is important to make sure that lineups produce as accurate results as possible. The wealth of psychology research on the topic helped the US Department of Justice to construct guidelines for conducting lineups (*The Guide* 1999). Not all the recommendations are routinely followed. Rulings like *Dubose* will encourage investigators to take more care in their investigations. However, the research literature is not static. Guidelines should not be as dynamic as the debates in the scientific literature, but they should be reviewed on a regular basis.

SUMMARY

Many eyewitness researchers have described the DNA cases from the Innocence Project, allowing the reader to empathize with the innocent people falsely imprisoned and speculate about how much more fortunate these people are than those falsely convicted in cases where DNA evidence could not be used to exonerate them. While these errors are critical, it is worth also considering the other type of error, where faulty eyewitness testimony allows the culprit to walk free. It is important that readers also empathize with the future victims of this person. It is up to society and experts in justice to decide the balance of these types of errors. This is not just determined by how jurors weight eyewitness evidence and use the reasonable doubt threshold, but also by how police and prosecutors weight eyewitness evidence. It is up to psychologists to indicate the diagnosticity of different types of evidence and to provide methods for examining these situations.

Eyewitness researchers can collectively be given a pat on the back. As Wells *et al.* (2000) discuss, after years of struggle to get courts to listen to us about psychology research (Loftus 1986), when the DNA showed that faulty eyewitness evidence caused many judicial errors and the justice system asked for help, psychologists already had a collection of recommendations to provide (Wells *et al.* 1998). While there are still difficulties implementing all the recommendations, this collection and *The Guide* are only a snapshot of the research that can inform police, judges, and jurors about eyewitness testimony. In this chapter we reviewed some of the areas where there has been active and important research during the past decade which can continue to have applied importance.

NOTES

1 For non-Clint Eastwood-aficionados the reference is: "I know what you're thinking: 'Did he fire six shots or only five?' Well, to tell you the truth, in all this excitement, I've kinda lost track myself. But being this is a .44 Magnum, the most powerful handgun in the world, and would blow your head clean off, you've got to ask yourself one question: 'Do I feel lucky?' Well, do ya, punk?" (*Dirty Harry* 1971).

2 A recent report (Mecklenburg 2006), which has received much discussion for its conclusions about using sequential vs. simultaneous lineups, compared data from double-blind sequential lineups with non-blind simultaneous lineups. This report found more suspect identifications and fewer filler identifications with the non-blind simultaneous lineups, which at first glance makes the simultaneous procedure appear better. However, given the differences between the conditions, it is difficult to ascertain which is responsible. Looking at the figures, there were remarkably low numbers of filler identification in the non-blind condition, suggesting that this might be the more important difference between conditions than the form of the lineup. Unfortunately, given that it is often not known whether the suspect is the culprit, and that both the form of the lineup and whether the administrator knew which person was the suspect varied across conditions, it is difficult to draw any conclusions from this study.

REFERENCES

Akehurst, L., Milne, R. & Koehnken, G. (2003). The effects of children's age and delay on recall in a cognitive or structured interview. *Psychology, Crime & Law, 9*, 97–107.

Bahrick, H. P. (1984). Semantic memory content in permastore: fifty years of memory for Spanish learned in school. *Journal of Experimental Psychology: General, 113*, 1–35.

Behrman, B. W. & Davey, S. L. (2001). Eyewitness identification in actual criminal cases: an archival analysis. *Law and Human Behavior, 25*, 475–491.

Behrman, B. W. & Richards, R. E. (2005). Suspect/foil identification in actual crimes and in the laboratory: a reality monitoring analysis. *Law and Human Behavior, 29*, 279–301.

Bekerian, D. A. & Dennett, J. L. (1993). The cognitive interview: reviving the issues. *Applied Cognitive Psychology, 7*, 275–298.

Brewer, N. (2006). Uses and abuses of eyewitness identification confidence. *Legal and Criminological Psychology, 11*, 3–23.

British Psychological Society (2004). *A Review of the Current Scientific Status and Fields of Application of Polygraphic Deception Detection*. Leicester: BPS.

Brock, P., Fisher, R. P. & Cutler, B. L. (1999). Examining the cognitive interview in a double-test paradigm. *Psychology, Crime & Law, 5*, 29–46.

Bruce, V., Henderson, Z., Newman, C. & Burton, A. M. (2001). Matching identities of familiar and unfamiliar faces caught on CCTV images. *Journal of Experimental Psychology: Applied, 7*, 207–218.

Bull, R. (2004). Training to detect deception from behavioural cues: attempts and problems. In P. A. Granhag & C. A. Stromwall (eds.), *Deception Detection in Forensic Contexts* (pp. 251–268). Cambridge: Cambridge University Press.

Burt, C. D. B., Mitchell, D. A., Raggatt, P. T. F. *et al.* (1995). A snapshot of autobiographical memory retrieval characteristics. *Applied Cognitive Psychology, 9*, 61–74.

Clare, J. & Lewandowsky, S. (2004). Verbalizing facial memory: criterion effects in verbal overshadowing. *Journal of Experimental Psychology: Learning, Memory, and Cognition, 30*, 739–755.

Clark, N. K., Stephenson, G. M. & Kniveton, B. H. (1990). Social remembering: quantitative aspects of individual and collaborative remembering by police officers and students. *British Journal of Psychology, 81*, 73–94.

Cunningham, W. A., Johnson, M. K., Raye, C. L. *et al.* (2004). Separable neural components in the processing of black and white faces. *Psychological Science, 15*, 806–813.

Daubert v. Merrell Dow Pharmaceutical, Inc. (1993). 113 S CT. 2786.

Davies, G. M. (1993). Witnessing events. In G. M. Davies & R. H. Logie (eds.), *Memory in Everyday Life* (pp. 367–401). Amsterdam: North-Holland.

Davies, G. M. & Westcott, H. L. (in press). Investigative interviewing with children: progress and pitfalls. In A. Heaton-Armstrong, E. Shepherd, G. Gudjonsson & D. Walchover (eds.), *Witness Testimony: Psychological, Investigative and Evidential Perspectives*. Oxford: Oxford University Press.

Davis, M. R., Mahon, M. & Greenwood, K. M. (2005). The efficacy of the mnemonic components of the cognitive interview: towards a shortened variant for time-critical investigations. *Applied Cognitive Psychology, 19*, 75–94.

Deffenbacher, K. A., Bornstein, B. H., Penrod, S. D. & McGorty, E. K. (2004). A meta-analytic review of the effects of high stress on eyewitness memory. *Law and Human Behavior, 28*, 687–706.

DePaulo, B. & Kirkendol, S. E. (1989). The motivational impairment effect in the communication of deception. In J. Yuille (ed.), *Credibility Assessment* (pp. 51–70). Dordrecht: Kluwer.

DePaulo, B. M., Lindsay, J. J., Malone, B. E. *et al.* (2003). Cues to deception. *Psychological Bulletin, 129*, 74–118.

DePaulo, B. M. & Morris, W. L. (2004). Discerning lies from truths: behavioral cues to deception and the indirect pathway of intuition. In P. A. Granhag & L. A. Stromwall (eds.), *The Detection of Deception in Forensic Contexts* (pp. 15–40). Cambridge: Cambridge University Press.

DePaulo, B. M., Stone, J. I. & Lassiter, G. D. (1985). Deceiving and detecting deceit. In B. R. Schlenker (ed.), *The Self in Social Life* (pp. 320–370). New York: McGraw-Hill.

Dunning, D. & Perretta, S. (2002). Automaticity and eyewitness accuracy: a 10- to 12-second rule for distinguishing accurate from inaccurate positive identifications. *Journal of Applied Psychology, 87*, 951–962.

Dysart, J. E. & Lindsay, R. C. L. (in press). The show-up identification procedure: what do we really know? In R. C. L. Lindsay, D. F. Ross, J. D. Read & M. Toglia (eds.), *The Handbook of Eyewitness Psychology, Memory for People*. Mahwah, NJ: Lawrence Erlbaum and Associates.

Ebbesen, E. B. & Flowe, H. D. (2001). Simultaneous v. sequential lineups: what do we really know? Unpublished manuscript available on http://www-psy.ucsd.edu/~eebbesen/SimSeq.htm.

Ekman, P. (1989). Why lies fail and what behaviours betray a lie. In J. C. Yuille (ed.), *Credibility Assessment* (pp. 71–82). Dordrecht: Kluwer.

Elaad, E. (1990). Detection of guilty knowledge in real-life criminal investigations. *Journal of Applied Psychology, 75*, 521–529.

Fisher, R. P., Falkner, K. L. & Trevisan, M. (2000). Adapting the cognitive interview to enhance long-term (35 years) recall of physical activities. *Journal of Applied Psychology, 85*, 180–189.

Fisher, R. P. & Geiselman, R. E. (1992). *Memory-enhancing Techniques for Investigative Interviewing: The Cognitive Interview*. Springfield, IL: C. C. Thomas.

Gabbert, F., Memon, A. & Allan, K. (2003). Memory conformity: can eyewitnesses influence each other's memories for an event? *Applied Cognitive Psychology, 17*, 533–543.

Gabbert, F., Memon, A. & Wright, D. B. (in press a). I saw it for longer than you: the relationship between perceived encoding duration and memory conformity. *Acta Psychologica*.

Gabbert, F., Memon, A. & Wright, D. B. (2006). Memory conformity: disentangling the steps towards influence during a discussion. *Psychonomic Bulletin & Review, 13*, 480–485.

Garry, M. & Hayne, H. (eds.) (2006). *Elizabeth Loftus: Contributions to Science, Law and Academic Freedom*. NJ: Lawrence Erlbaum Associates.

Gronlund, S. D. (2004). Sequential lineups: shift in criterion or decision strategy? *Journal of Applied Psychology, 89*, 362–368.

Gross, S. R., Jacoby, K., Matheson, D. J. *et al.* (2005). Exonerations in the United States, 1989 through 2003. *Journal of Criminal Law and Criminology, 95*, 523–560.

Honts, C. R. (2004). The psychophysiological detection of deception. In P. A. Granhag & C. A. Stromwall (eds.), *The Detection of Deception in Forensic Contexts* (pp. 103–126). Cambridge: Cambridge University Press.

Honts, C. R. & Amato, S. L. (2002). Countermeasures. In M. Kleiner (ed.), *Handbook of Polygraph Testing* (pp. 251–264). London: Academic Press.

Hunter, J. E. & Schmidt, F. L. (2004). *Methods of Meta-Analysis: Correcting Error and Bias in Research Findings* (2nd edn). Thousand Oaks, CA: Sage.

Iacono, W. G. (1995). Offender testimony: detection of deception and guilty knowledge. In N. Brewer & C. Wilson (eds.), *Psychology and Policing* (pp.155–171). Hillsdale, NJ: Lawrence Erlbaum Associates.

Inbau, F. E., Read, J. E., Buckley, J. P. & Jayne, B. C. (2001). *Criminal Investigations and Confessions* (4th edn). Gaithersburg, MD: Aspen.

Johnson, K. J. & Fredrickson, B. L. (2005). "We all look the same to me": positive emotions eliminate the own-race bias in face recognition. *Psychological Science, 16*, 875–881.

Kassin, S. M., Tubb, V. A., Hosch, H. M. & Memon, A. (2001). On the "general acceptance" of eyewitness testimony research. *American Psychologist, 56*, 405–416.

Kebbell, M. R., Milne, R. & Wagstaff, G. F. (1999). The cognitive interview: a survey of its effectiveness. *Psychology, Crime & Law, 5*, 81–100.

Kelly, L., Lovett, J. & Regan, L. (2005). *A Gap or a Chasm? Attrition in Reported Rape Cases.* London: Home Office RDS (HO Research Study 293).

Koehnken, G. (2004). Statement validity analysis and the "detection of truth". In P. A. Granhag & C. A. Stromwall (eds.), *The Detection of Deception in Forensic Contexts* (pp. 41–63). Cambridge: Cambridge University Press.

Koehnken, G., Milne, R., Memon, A. & Bull, R. (1999). A metaanalysis of the effects of the cognitive interview. *Psychology, Crime & Law, 5*, 101–116.

Lamb, M. E., Sternberg, K. J., Esplin, P. W. *et al.* (1997). Criterion-based content analysis: a field validation study. *Child Abuse and Neglect, 21*, 255–261.

Levi, A. M. (1998a). Are defendants guilty if they were chosen in a lineup? *Law and Human Behavior, 22*, 389–407.

Levi, A. M. (1998b). Protecting innocent defendants, nailing the guilty: a modified sequential lineup. *Applied Cognitive Psychology, 12*, 265–275.

Levin, D. T. (2000). Race as a visual feature: using visual search and perceptual discrimination tasks to understand face categories and cross-race recognition. *Journal of Experimental Psychology: General, 129*, 559–574.

Lindholm, T. (2005). Own-age biases in verbal person memory. *Memory, 13*, 21–30.

Lindsay, R. C. L. & Wells, G. L. (1985). Improving eyewitness identification from lineups: simultaneous versus sequential lineup presentations. *Journal of Applied Psychology, 70*, 556–564.

Loftus, E. F. (1974). Reconstructing memory: the incredible eyewitness. *Psychology Today, 8*, 116–119.

Loftus, E. F. (1986). Ten years in the life of an expert witness. *Law and Human Behavior, 10*, 241–263.

Loftus, E. F. (2005). Planting misinformation in the human mind: a 30-year investigation of the malleability of memory. *Learning & Memory, 12*, 361–366.

Loftus, E. F., Loftus, G. R. & Messo, J. (1987). Some facts about "weapon focus." *Law and Human Behavior, 11*, 55–62.

Lykken, D. T. (1998). *A Tremor in the Blood: Use and Abuses of Lie Detection.* New York: Plenum.

McQuiston-Surrett, D. E., Malpass, R. S. & Tredoux, C. G. (2006). Sequential vs. simultaneous lineups: a review of methods, data, and theory *Psychology, Public Policy and Law, 12*, 137–169.

Malpass, R. S. & Kravitz, J. (1969). Recognition of faces of own and other race. *Journal of Personality and Social Psychology, 13*, 330–334.

Mann, S., Vrij, A. & Bull, R. (2002). Suspects, lies, and videotape: an analysis of authentic high-stakes liars. *Law and Human Behavior, 26*, 365–376.

Mann, S., Vrij, A. & Bull, R. (2004). Detecting true lies: police officers' ability to detect deceit. *Journal of Applied Psychology, 89*, 137–149.

Marsh, E. J. & Tversky, B. (2004). Spinning the stories of our lives. *Applied Cognitive Psychology, 18*, 491–503.

Meade, M. L. & Roediger, H. L. III (2002). Explorations in the social contagion of memory. *Memory & Cognition, 30*, 995–1009.

Mecklenburg, S. H. (2006). *Report to the Legislature of the State of Illinois: The Illinois Pilot Program on Sequential Double-Blind Identification Procedures.* Illinois State Police.

Meissner, C. A. & Brigham, J. C. (2001). Thirty years of investigating the own-race bias in memory for faces: a meta-analytic review. *Psychology, Public Policy & Law, 7,* 3–35.

Meissner, C. A., Brigham, J. C. & Butz, D. A. (2005). Memory for own- and other-race faces: a dual-process approach. *Applied Cognitive Psychology, 19,* 545–567.

Meissner, C. A & Memon, A. (2002). Verbal overshadowing: a special issue exploring theoretical and applied issues. *Applied Cognitive Psychology, 16,* 869–872.

Meissner, C. A., Tredoux, C. G., Parker, J. F. & MacLin, O. H. (2005). Eyewitness decisions in simultaneous and sequential lineups: a dual-process signal detection theory analysis. *Memory & Cognition, 33,* 783–792.

Memon, A., Vrij, A. & Bull, R. (2003). *Psychology & Law: Truthfulness, Accuracy and Credibility of Victims, Witnesses and Suspects* (2nd edn). Chichester: John Wiley & Sons.

Milne, R. & Bull, R. (2002). Back to basics: a componential analysis of the original cognitive interview mnemonics with three age groups. *Applied Cognitive Psychology, 16,* 1–11.

Milne, R., Clare, I. C. H. & Bull, R. (1999). Using the cognitive interview with adults with mild learning disabilities. *Psychology, Crime & Law, 5,* 81–100.

Mitchell, K. J., Livosky, M. & Mather, M. (1998). The weapon focus effect revisited: the role of novelty. *Legal and Criminological Psychology, 3,* 287–303.

National Research Council (2003). *The Polygraph and Lie Detection. Committee to Review the Scientific Evidence on the Polygraph (2003).* Washington, DC: The National Academic Press.

Paterson, H. M. & Kemp, R. I. (2006). Co-witnesses talk: a survey of eyewitness discussion. *Psychology, Crime & Law, 12,* 181–191.

Penrod, S. (2003). Eyewitness identification evidence: how well are witnesses and police performing? *Criminal Justice Magazine, 54* (Spring), 36–47.

Perfect, T. J. & Moon, H. C. (2005). The own-age effect in face recognition. In J. Duncan, P. McLeod and L. Phillips (eds.), *Measuring the Mind.* Oxford: Oxford University Press.

Pickel, K. L. (1999). The influence of context on the "weapon focus" effect. *Law and Human Behavior, 23,* 299–311.

Podlesney, J. A. (1990). *A Lack of Operable Case Facts Restricts Applicability of the Guilty Knowledge Deception Detection Method in FBI Criminal Investigations.* Quantico, VA: FBI Technical Report.

Pryke, S., Lindsay, R. C. L., Dysart, J. E. & Dupuis, P. (2004). Multiple independent identification decisions: a method of calibrating eyewitness identifications. *Journal of Applied Psychology, 89,* 73–84.

Reiser, M. (1989). Investigative hypnosis. In D. Raskin (ed.), *Psychological Methods in Criminal Investigation and Evidence* (pp. 151–190). New York: Springer.

Roediger, H. L., Meade, M. L. & Bergman, E. T. (2001). Social contagion of memory. *Psychonomic Bulletin & Review, 8,* 65–371.

Rosenfeld, J. P. (1995). Alternative views of Bashore and Rapp's (1993) alternatives to traditional polygraphy: a critique. *Psychological Bulletin, 117,* 159–166.

Sangrigoli, S., Pallier, C., Argenti, A. M. *et al.* (2005). Reversibility of the other-race effect in face recognition during childhood. *Psychological Science, 16,* 440–444.

Saywitz, K., Geiselman, R. E. & Bornstein, G. K. (1992). Effects of the cognitive interview and practice on children's recall performance. *Journal of Applied Psychology, 77,* 744–756.

Scheck, B., Neufeld, P. & Dwyer, J. (2003). *Actual Innocence: When Justice Goes Wrong and How to Make it Right.* New York: New American Library.

Schneider, D. M. & Watkins, M. J. (1996). Response conformity in recognition testing. *Psychonomic Bulletin & Review, 3,* 481–485.

Schwarz, S., Roebers, C. M. & Schneider, W. (2004). Development of conformity and cognitive effects of social influence. *Zeitschrift für entwicklungpsychologie und padagogische psychologie, 36,* 173–181.

Shaw, J. S., Garven, S. & Wood, J. M. (1997). Co-witness information can have immediate effects on eyewitness memory reports. *Law and Human Behavior, 21,* 503–523.

Sporer, S. L. (2001). Recognizing faces of other ethnic groups: an integration of theories. *Psychology, Public Policy, and Law, 7,* 36–97.

Sporer, S. L., Penrod, S., Read, D. & Cutler, B. (1995). Choosing, confidence, and accuracy: a meta-analysis of the confidence-accuracy relation in eyewitness identification. *Psychological Bulletin, 118,* 315–327.

Sporer, S. L. & Schwandt, B. (2006). Paraverbal indicators of deception: a meta-analytic synthesis. *Applied Cognitive Psychology, 20*, 421–446.

State v. Dubose, 126 WI (2005).

State v. Hibl, No. 2004AP2936-CR (WI Ct. Appl., September 28, 2005).

Steblay, N., Dysart, J. E., Fulero, S. & Lindsay, R. C. L. (2001). Eyewitness accuracy rates in sequential and simultaneous lineup presentations: a meta-analytic comparison. *Law and Human Behavior, 25*, 459–473.

Steblay, N., Dysart, J. E., Fulero, S. & Lindsay, R. C. L. (2003). Eyewitness accuracy rates in police showup and lineup presentations: a meta-analytic comparison. *Law and Human Behavior, 27*, 523–540.

Steblay, N. M. (1992). A meta-analytic review of the weapon focus effect. *Law and Human Behavior, 16*, 413–424.

Stein, L. & Memon, A. (2006). Testing the efficacy of the Cognitive Interview in a developing country. *Applied Cognitive Psychology, 20*, 597–605.

Stephenson, G. M., Clark, N. K. & Wade, G. S. (1986). Meetings make evidence: an experimental-study of collaborative and individual recall of a simulated police interrogation. *Journal of Personality and Social Psychology, 50*, 1113–1122.

Stovall v. Denno, 388 US 293 (1967).

Technical Working Group for Eyewitness Evidence (1999). *Eyewitness Evidence: A Guide for Law Enforcement* (NCJ No. 178240). Washington, DC: U.S. Department of Justice, Office of Justice Programs.

Valentine, T. (1991). A unified account of the effects of distinctiveness, inversion and race in face recognition. *Quarterly Journal of Experimental Psychology, 43A*, 161–204.

Valentine, T., Chiroro, P. & Dixon, R. (1995). An account of the own-race bias and the contact hypothesis in terms of a face space model of face recognition. In T. Valentine (ed.), *Cognitive and Computational Aspects of Face Recognition: Explorations in Face Space*. London: Routledge.

Valentine, T. & Heaton, P. (1999). An evaluation of the fairness of Police lineups and video identifications. *Applied Cognitive Psychology, 13*, S59–S72.

Valentine, T., Pickering, A. & Darling, S. (2003). Characteristics of eyewitness identification that predict the outcome of real lineups. *Applied Cognitive Psychology, 17*, 969–993.

Vrij, A. (2000). *Detecting Lies and Deceit: The Psychology of Lying and Its Implications for Professional Practice*. Chichester: John Wiley & Sons.

Vrij, A. (2003). The assessment and detection of deceit. In D. Carson & R. Bull (eds.), *Handbook of Psychology in Legal Contexts* (2nd edn, pp. 67–88). Chichester: John Wiley & Sons.

Vrij, A. (2005). Criteria-Based Content Analysis: a qualitative review of the first 37 studies. *Psychology, Public Policy, and Law, 11*, 3–41.

Vrij, A., Akehurst, L., Soukara, S. & Bull, R. (2002). Will the truth come out? The effect of deception, age, status, coaching, and social skills on CBCA scores. *Law and Human Behavior, 26*, 261–283.

Vrij, A. & Winkel, F. W. (1993). Objective and subjective indicators of deception. *Issues in Criminological and Legal Psychology, 20*, pp. 51–57.

Wagstaff, G. F. (1999). Hypnotically induced testimony. In A. Heaton-Armstrong, E. Shepherd & D. Walchover (eds.), *Analysing Witness Testimony: A Guide for Legal Practitioners and Other Professionals* (pp. 162–177). London: Blackstone.

Walker, P. M. & Hewstone, M. (2006). Intergroup experience and the own-race face effect: a case study. *Applied Cognitive Psychology, 20*, 461–475.

Walters, S. B. (2003) *The Principles of Kinesic Interview and Interrogation* (2nd edn). Boca Raton, FL: CRC Press.

Weber, N. & Brewer, N. (2004). Confidence-accuracy calibration in absolute and relative face recognition judgments. *Journal of Experimental Psychology: Applied, 10*, 156–172.

Weber, N., Brewer, N., Wells, G. L., Semmler, C. & Keast, A. (2004). Eyewitness identification accuracy and response latency: the unruly 10–12-second rule. *Journal of Experimental Psychology: Applied, 10*, 139–147.

Wells, G. L. (1978). Applied eyewitness testimony research: system variables versus estimator variables. *Journal of Personality and Social Psychology, 36*, 1546–1557.

Wells, G. L. & Bradfield, A. L. (1998). "Good, you identified the suspect": feedback to eyewitnesses distorts their reports of the witnessing experience. *Journal of Applied Psychology, 83*, 360–376.
Wells, G. L., Malpass, R. S., Lindsay, R. C. L. *et al.* (2000). From the lab to the police station: a successful application of eyewitness research. *American Psychologist, 55*, 581–598.
Wells, G. L. & Murray, D. (1984). Eyewitness confidence. In G. L. Wells & E. F. Loftus (eds.), *Eyewitness Testimony: Psychological Perspectives* (pp. 155–170). New York: Cambridge University Press.
Wells, G. L. & Olson, E. (2002). Eyewitness identification: information gain from incriminating and exonerating behaviors. *Journal of Experimental Psychology: Applied, 8*, 155–167.
Wells, G. L. & Olson, E. (2003). Eyewitness identification. *Annual Review of Psychology, 54*, 277–295.
Wells, G. L., Small, M., Penrod, S., Malpass, Fulero, S.-M. and Brimacombe, C.A.E. (1998). Eyewitness identification procedures: recommendations for lineups and photospreads. *Law & Human Behavior, 22*, 603–647.
Wixted, J. T. (2004). The psychology and neuroscience of forgetting. *Annual Review of Psychology, 55*, 235–269.
Wixted, J. T. (2005). A theory about why we forget what we once knew. *Current Directions in Psychological Science, 14*, 6–9.
Wright, D. B. (in press). The impact of eyewitness identifications from simultaneous and sequential lineups. *Memory.*
Wright, D. B. (2006). Causal and associative hypotheses in psychology: examples from eyewitness testimony research. *Psychology, Public Policy, and Law, 12*, 190–213.
Wright, D. B., Boyd, C. E. & Tredoux, C. G. (2001). A field study of own-race bias in South Africa and England. *Psychology, Public Policy, and Law, 7*, 119–133.
Wright, D. B. & Davies, G. M. (1999). Eyewitness testimony. In F. T. Durso, R. S. Nickerson, R. W. Schvaneveldt *et al.* (eds.), *Handbook of Applied Cognition* (pp. 789–818). Chichester: John Wiley & Sons.
Wright, D. B. & McDaid, A. T. (1996). Comparing system and estimator variables using data from real lineups. *Applied Cognitive Psychology, 10*, 75–84.
Wright, D. B., Mathews, S. A. & Skagerberg, E. M. (2005). Social recognition memory: the effect of other people's responses for previously seen and unseen items. *Journal of Experimental Psychology: Applied, 17*, 200–209.
Wright, D. B., Self, G. & Justice, C. (2000). Memory conformity: exploring misinformation effects when presented by another person. *British Journal of Psychology, 91*, 189–202.
Wright, D. B. & Skagerberg, E. M. (in press). Post-identification feedback affects real eyewitnesses. *Psychological Science.*
Wright, D. B. & Stroud, J. N. (2002). Age differences in lineup identification accuracy: people are better with their own age. *Law and Human Behavior, 26*, 641–654.
Yuille, J. C. (1988). The systematic assessment of children's testimony. *Canadian Psychologist, 29*, 247–262.

CHAPTER 30

False Memories

Giuliana Mazzoni
University of Plymouth, UK
and
Alan Scoboria
University of Windsor, Canada

INTRODUCTION

> It was a small gray room, and there was a tall blond woman in glasses. I remember my sense of fear. The procedure lasted longer than I expected. There was a strong smell of disinfectant in the room.

This memory was reported by a Scottish student about a medical examination he underwent at the school health center when he was a child. About the same event, another Scottish student recalled:

> I was there with my mother. There were many people in the room. I was hungry. I felt the smell of gas used to put me asleep. A nurse held my hand but then all became a blur.

These two memories refer to the same specific medical procedure, having a school nurse slice off a small piece of skin from the little finger for a health test. Are these memories true or false? The content is relatively detailed, including the individuals present (the protagonist, mother, nurse), perceptual details (the nurse is described tall and blonde, the color of the room, smell of disinfectant or gas is described), emotional content (sense of fear), and actions (the nurse holding a hand). Had they not been located at the beginning of a chapter on false memories, these short narratives could easily be mistaken for true memories. In fact, they are false memories. No one born and raised in the region in which these descriptions were obtained ever received a medical test similar to that reported.

For the past three decades memory researchers have been fascinated by what has been called "memory's darker side" (Schacter 1999), the fact that people not only forget, they also distort the past to various degrees, sometimes to the extreme degree of remembering entire events that have not taken place (Loftus 2004). In some instances people even "remember" extremely implausible events like being the victims of rituals involving

Handbook of Applied Cognition: Second Edition. Edited by Francis T. Durso.

satanic abuse or being abducted by aliens. The term *false memory* has been applied to a wide array of phenomena in the psychological literature, ranging at extremes from erroneously recalling a word as having been on a previously presented list (e.g., Roediger & McDermott 1995) to elaborate autobiographical descriptions of personally experienced events (e.g., Loftus & Pickrell 1995). In the most general sense, false memory can be defined as any instance in which a memory is reported for an event or component of an event that has not been experienced.

False memories are quite easy to create and are considerably more frequent than the lay person might imagine. A large body of research has demonstrated that memory is (relatively) plastic, as evidenced by the hundreds of entries encountered during a literature search for "false memories" or "memory distortions." In this chapter we review some of these studies, analyze some of the mechanisms that are involved in the creation of false memories, and try to draw distinctions in the vast realm of false memory research. We focus in particular on false autobiographical memories, examining the mechanisms that make it possible for people to claim that they remember life events that did not in fact happen to them.

In the following sections, we will describe a number of false memory phenomena. We start by reporting research on situations in which only part of the memory is modified, sometimes with the aid of suggestive external intervention, sometimes by basic memory and inferential mechanisms alone (see Mazzoni 2002 for a detailed discussion of this distinction). Then we consider situations in which entirely new memories for complex autobiographical events are created.

MODIFYING MEMORIES FOR EXPERIENCED EVENTS

Prior to the 1980s, there were scattered studies of memory distortions in the literature (for detailed reviews, see Schacter 2001; Mazzoni 2002). Crucial to subsequent research were the pioneering work by Bartlett (1932) on memory representation, the related work on encoding and elaboration of complex verbal material developed during the 1970s (e.g., Bransford & Franks 1971), and the recently rediscovered work by Deese (1959) on the distortions produced by associative links among items on a list. More systematic bodies of research on memory distortions have since been developed, the most important being those on the misinformation effect, conjunction errors, and the Deese-Roediger-McDermott paradigm (DRM).

The Misinformation Effect

Research on the misinformation effect stems from the work of Elizabeth Loftus and collaborators. Loftus started her series of studies examining the effect of verbal material on memory for visual scenes. In a classical and frequently cited experiment (Loftus 1977), people watched slides depicting a car accident involving a green car. Half the participants were subsequently given misinformation embedded in the verbal description of the scene implying that the car was blue. After receiving the misinformation, a number of the participants reported on a subsequent recognition test that the car was blue, and some reported that the car was a color in between green and blue (some participants did not show any distortion).

This misinformation effect (for recent reviews see Loftus 2005a, 2005b) has been extensively studied because of its theoretical relevance and its important applications in the forensic arena. It is one of the factors that render eyewitness testimony less accurate, and it dovetails with the study of the effect of investigative interviews, which started with the pioneering work by Binet (1900) and Stern (1910). Their work, which has been confirmed by a substantial body of subsequent evidence (e.g., Gudjonsson 1984, 1988; Bull 1999; Lamb *et al.* 1999), indicates that post-event misinformation and type of interview modifies memory reports about an event. Research has clearly shown that the content of the questions asked and the type of feedback provided can severely impair the accuracy of an eyewitness report and modify the memory for the experienced event (Memon & Bull 1999). The empirical evidence has been so strong and unambiguous that in the UK the Home Office issued a series of guidelines prepared by panel of experts on how to proceed in interviewing children, and only interviews that follow those guidelines are accepted in court (Home Office 1992).

One of the theoretical issues raised during the 1980s concerned the locus and reasons for the change produced by the misinformation. The claim by Loftus and colleagues (1978) was that subsequent verbal misinformation modified and corrupted the memory trace of the visual information. This claim was later challenged by McCloskey and Zaragoza (1985; see also Zaragoza *et al.* 1987), who in a series of studies showed that part of the effect obtained by Loftus *et al.* could be explained by lack of memory for the original item. Others, however, have shown that under some circumstances the erroneous information can interfere and rewrite the original memory (e.g., Belli 1989; Tversky & Tuchin, 1989; Belli *et al.* 1992; Loftus 2005a; Okado & Stark 2005). Highly detrimental influences of verbal elaboration on visual memory have also been confirmed more recently in other domains. For example, verbal elaboration of visually presented faces seems to directly disrupt the appropriate processes that allow encoding and maintenance of visual information for faces (the verbal overshadowing effect; Schooler & Englster-Schooler 1990; Dodson *et al.* 1997).

Recent studies have also examined the effect of what can be called self-generated misinformation (Ackil & Zaragoza 1998; Zaragoza *et al.* 2001). Simulating what commonly occurs during interrogations, participants are asked to witness an event and are told to invent part of the scenes. In subsequent recognition and recall tests, the internally generated content is remembered with an elevated degree of confidence as being part of the witnessed scene (Mazzoni, Casciano & De Leo 2003), confirming that distortions of memories for an experienced event can be produced when the new, false contents are internally generated. The potentially deleterious effect of generation was shown also in a separate series of studies in which self-generated material (words taken from participants' dreams) were mistaken for words that had been presented on lists (Mazzoni & Loftus 1996; Mazzoni *et al.* 1999). Interestingly, dreamed words not only were erroneously recognized as experienced (i.e., seen on a list of words), they were also judged to be "remembered" when using a remember/know procedure. The remember/know judgment was used here as a measure of the subjectively perceived recollective quality of the memory. By assigning a "remember" judgment, participants were indicating that they not only remembered the dream words as having been presented on the list, they could also remember approximately in which position the words appeared in the list, how they were written, etc. We will see in a later section that the same recollective quality is assigned to false memories for words obtained with a different procedure.

Several explanations have been proposed for the classical misinformation effect. In addition to the idea that under some circumstances reporting the post-event misinformation is due to lack of memory for the original episode (McCloskey & Zaragoza 1985), the most commonly accepted explanation refers to problems in source monitoring, a diagnostic system that allows people to distinguish between various sources from which a mental representation might have originated. According to the source monitoring framework (Johnson *et al.* 1993; Lindsay & Johnson 2000), the source of a memory representation is identified by a series of monitoring processes that evaluate its characteristics. Internally generated representations are characterized by a series of cognitive processes that are absent from representations generated by external sources, which in turn are characterized by perceptual-like characteristics that are missing in internally generated sources.

The ability to identify the source of information has been proposed by Johnson (1988) as one of the key processes of the cognitive system and has been subsequently elaborated as a theoretical framework (Johnson *et al.* 1993). Source monitoring is predicated on the idea that the processes that created a memory representation are encoded as part of the memory representation itself. The information about these processes is then retrieved and the content of the memory is attributed to a specific source.

People are usually very good at discriminating between various sources of information, but under some circumstances this diagnostic system can fail. To the extent that memory characteristics are not clearly diagnostic about the source, memory errors can occur. In non-clinical populations, source monitoring errors are most often due to memory representations that contain an unusual amount of "wrong" characteristics (i.e., characteristics that belong to a different category). For example, the mental representation of an experienced stimulus that contains an unusual amount of cognitive characteristics could be easily confused with a thought or a dream. More common is the case of an internally generated representation (e.g., a mental image) that contains an unusual amount of perceptual characteristics, which can be mistaken for an experienced event and a real memory. In this case a false memory is created.

The source monitoring framework represents one of the two main theoretical accounts, not only of the misinformation effect, but of the more general phenomenon of false memories. theory, The other is fuzzy-trace theory (Reyna & Brainerd 1995; Brainerd & Reyna 2002, 2005; see also Reyna & Lloyd 1997; Lindsay & Johnson 2000 for the debate between proponents of fuzzy-trace theory and source monitoring theory). According to Brainerd and Reyna (2002, 2005), verbatim and gist memory traces coexist in episodic memory, where they are encoded and stored in parallel, although verbatim traces fade more quickly. Verbatim traces are memory "representations of the surface form of experienced items" (Brainerd & Reyna 2002, p. 165), whereas gist traces are "episodic interpretations of concepts . . . that have been retrieved as a result of encoding items' surface forms" (p. 165), and can be stored at various levels of specificity. Retrieving a memory involves activating both verbatim and gist traces. The likelihood of reactivating verbatim or gist traces depends on the nature of the retrieval cue (i.e., experienced cues reactivate verbatim traces; non-experienced cues reactivate gist traces), the strength of the traces, and the quicker fading of verbatim traces. Accessing gist traces, without corresponding verbatim traces, can create a false memory.

Memory Conjunction Errors

Another interesting false memory phenomenon is due to the "migration" of elements across episodes and is based on the idea that memory representations are not "holistic, indivisible entities" (Hannigan & Reinitz 2003, p. 434), but are made of separable parts that are combined, sometimes erroneously, when the memory is constructed. Evidence suggesting that stimuli and events are encoded as separable parts has been provided by an eclectic group of studies, including studies stemming from the source-monitoring framework. For example, very early studies on the tip-of-tongue phenomenon suggest that words can be encoded as sets of parts. People might recall only some aspects of the word (some letters, for example, or its position) without being able to recall the whole word (Brown & McNeill 1966; see also Koriat & Lieblich 1977), or they may recall the page that contained some information without being able to remember the content of the information itself (Zechmeister & McKillip 1972). The possibility that a memory consists of integrated parts that are represented separately has been proposed for the past three decades (e.g., Underwood *et al.* 1976), as has the possibility that memories for autobiographical events are created by the activation and integration of separable elements (Barsalou 1988; see also Conway & Pleydell-Pearce 2000 for an updated version of binding processes in autobiographical memory). Usually the binding process is successful in integrating parts that had occurred and were experienced together. However, under some circumstances, parts get integrated that belong to different stimuli or different episodes (Henkel *et al.* 1998).

When binding integrates elements that belong to different episodes, memory conjunction errors occur. These are similar to situations in which, for example, a witness misremembers an individual seen on the same day of a crime as having taken part in the crime (Ross *et al.* 1994). Memory conjunction errors have been obtained with compound words (Jones & Jacoby 2001; Jones *et al.* 2001; Reinitz & Hannigan 2004) and, more interestingly, with episodes (Reinitz *et al.* 1992; Hannigan & Reinitz 2003). In several studies, participants recognized novel stimuli that were constructed from parts of episodes that were experienced separately (Reinitz *et al.* 1992; Hannigan & Reinitz 2003). In another study, street signs and buildings that were presented in one virtual environment were attributed to a different virtual environment (Albert *et al.* 1999). Other studies have shown that conjunction errors are schema-dependent (Hannigan & Reinitz 2003), that is, participants falsely recognized more conjunction foils when the object was taken from the same schema than from a different schema.

Memory conjunction errors have also been studied in memories for diary events (Burt *et al.* 2004; Odegaard & Lampinen 2004) and the results have been interpreted as providing evidence for the role of binding processes in autobiographical memory. Burt *et al.* (2004) used entries in a diary written by participants several years before the test, and created various types of partially false autobiographical episodes that were then presented in a recognition test. These false episodes contained one element that was taken from other episodes (either location, or time, character, action or all elements together). The results of this study show that it is easier to accept as real an episode that is part of one's autobiography and contains only erroneous information about the location than to accept episodes that contain the other types of false information. Odegaard and Lampinen (2004) confirmed that people can accept as real episodes of their diary that contain false information.

Binding is not the only possible explanation of memory conjunction errors; familiarity is another option. Familiarity-based processes were invoked to explain the effect obtained by Jones *et al.* (2001), in which participants were presented with two sets of compound words (e.g., *stargaze* and *catfish*). One set was presented visually and the other aurally. On a subsequent recognition test participants tended to recognize not only compound words that had been presented, but also new compound words that were created by merging parts of two different original words (e.g., the new compound word *starfish*). The debate on whether merging of parts of items, or migration of elements across episodes, are due to binding or to familiarity remains unresolved (Reinitz & Hannigan 2001).

The DRM Paradigm

An extensively studied false memory phenomenon that seems to be guided by the way pre-existing knowledge is organized in memory was discovered in the late 1950s (Deese 1959) and rediscovered more recently (Roediger & McDermott 1995). When people are presented with lists of words that are taken from the strongest associates to a non-presented word, they often recall and recognize the non-presented word as having been presented (see also Read 1996), and the level of recall and recognition is similar to recall and recognition of words presented in the central part of the list (Stadler *et al.* 1999). For example, when the list includes words like "door, glass, pane, shade, ledge, sill, house, open, curtain, frame, view, breeze, sash, screen, shutter," people falsely recall and recognize the non-presented word "window." The lists usually comprise between 12 and 15 of the strongest associates to the critical lure (however see Robinson & Roediger 1997 for lists created with different criteria), and the words are usually presented in order of degree of association (taken from the associative norms of the language, in this case the Russell and Jenkins 1954 norms for English).

False memories for critical words in semantically-related lists are not due to artifactual demand characteristics (Lampinen *et al.* 1999), and they are reported with a high degree of confidence (Read 1996). Remember/know data indicate that false memories for critical lures have a strong recollective quality, which makes them difficult to eliminate. Participants claim that they "remember" the critical lure, whereas they "know" other intrusions or non-critical lures (Roediger & McDermott 1995). Furthermore, people not only "remember" the critical lure, they are willing to attribute the false memory to a specific source, for example to a specific voice (Payne *et al.* 1996; Mather *et al.* 1997).

Explicit warnings provided either before encoding (Gallo *et al.* 1997; McDermott & Roediger 1998; Libby & Neisser 2001; Neuschatz *et al.* 2001) or after study (McCabe & Smith 2002) decrease the probability of recognizing critical lures, but do not eliminate them. Similarly, repeated study test trials do not eliminate the effect completely (however see Dodhia and Metcalfe 1999; Goodwin *et al.* 2001; Watson *et al.* 2004 for conditions in which the effect is very low). Several studies have also observed reliable neural correlates of these false memories (e.g., Cabeza *et al.* 2001; Curran *et al.* 2001; Urbach *et al.* 2005).

In spite of their recollective quality, which makes them difficult to distinguish from true memories, some studies have suggested that true and false memories can be discriminated when the procedure triggers a more thorough analysis of the source of the information (Mather *et al.* 1997). This has been found to be true for both recall and recognition (e.g., Hicks & Marsh 1999; McCabe & Smith 2002).

The most popular theoretical explanation of the DRM phenomenon refers to both the activation of the associative network that links all words within a given list and an inability to monitor the source of the activation (Roediger & McDermott 1995). The role of source monitoring has been supported by studies showing that enhancing source monitoring processes usually diminishes the probability of reporting critical intrusions (e.g., McCabe & Smith 2002; however, see Hicks & Marsh 2001). Another compelling explanation of the DRM phenomenon has been provided by the fuzzy-trace theory, according to which the gist trace of the critical non-presented word is strongly activated during encoding. Verbatim traces of presented words fade rapidly, and the activation that remains is mostly at the gist level. Therefore, when people are asked to report their memory for the words in the list, all activated gist traces are reported as memories. It should be noted that spreading activation and fuzzy-trace theory are not necessarily incompatible.

FALSE MEMORIES FOR COMPLETELY NEW EVENTS

Up to this point we have reviewed work that shows some of the conditions under which false elements become part of the memory people report about stimuli and events that they have experienced. In all of these studies, a stimulus or event had in fact been experienced, and what is distorted is a particular element. Even in the DRM paradigm, the critical word is only one element of a complex event (i.e., seeing a list of related words). As Schooler (1998) notes, "when participants incorrectly recognize a related lure, they are not relying on new memory for something that never occurred. Rather, they are relying on an accurate gist memory in the absence of access to the verbatim component" (p. 133). In this section, we review studies examining the situations in which false memories are created for entire events that have not in fact occurred.

Evidence of the possibility of creating completely new false memories has been obtained mostly for autobiographical events. Indeed, the first studies in this area were triggered by the recovered memory controversy (see Read & Lindsay 1997), which started in the mid-1980s, when a large number of cases were reported in which adults, and in particular women, claimed to have recovered memories of child sexual abuse (see Lindsay & Read 1994). Whereas the tendency among a relatively sizeable proportion of therapists was to accept such claims as true, researchers were puzzled by the apparent ability to bring back to awareness the content of past traumatic events that had been forgotten for decades. These cases challenged the very concept of forgetting as a permanent loss of memory.

The attempt to understand what was happening in apparent recovered memory cases led to the development of the repressed memory controversy, which reached a level of acrimony that led some writers to talk about a "memory war" (e.g., Loftus 1997; for a comprehensive overview of the issues at stake, see Read & Lindsay 1997; for some more recent contributions, see McNally 2003; Dalenberg 2004; Tsai *et al.* 2004). On one side of this controversy, researchers tried to find ways to theoretically explain forgotten material as temporarily inaccessible memories, and concepts like psychogenic amnesia, implicit memory, and intentional suppression were proposed as possible explanations of memory repression and forgetting (Anderson & Green 2001; Smith *et al.* 2003; De Prince & Freyd

2004; Gleaves *et al.* 2004; Freyd *et al.* 2005). On the other side of the debate, researchers raised the question of whether recovered memories might be false, which led to the development of studies in which completely false memories were produced in participants. Memory researchers were joined by social psychologists, sociologists, and anthropologists in an attempt to assess the degree to which entirely false autobiographical memories can be implanted and to understand which cognitive and social/societal factors could influence the memory of a person to the point of creating a strong belief and a sometimes very detailed memory of personal events that had never happened. A middle ground has also been taken in this debate. For example, some corroborated cases of adult recovery of child sexual abuse have been found and analyzed (e.g., Schooler 1997, 2001). They show that people genuinely believe in the fact that they had "forgotten" traumatic events for many years, and had "recovered" them only during adulthood. In several of these cases, however, the sincere conviction turned out to be incorrect (these people had actually spoken about their abuse to others during those years, but they had forgotten these instances of recall), indicating the presence of a "forgot-it-all-along" bias in memory (Schooler 1997).

Before reviewing this literature we consider the distinction between autobiographical memory and autobiographical belief. This is a distinction which we believe to be critical to an accurate understanding of the data.

Autobiographical Beliefs and Autobiographical Memories

Many studies purporting to assess false autobiographical memories (e.g., Mazzoni & Loftus 1998; Paddock *et al.* 1998; Garry *et al.* 1999; Heaps & Nash 1999; Mazzoni *et al.* 1999) have done so using the Life Events Inventory (LEI). The LEI consists of a list of 20–40 events that range from relatively common (winning a toy at a fair) to very uncommon (shaking hands with the President). Participants are asked to rate how certain they are that each event had happened to them when they were a certain age (e.g., younger than four). Increases in LEI ratings produced by manipulations such as imagination have generally been interpreted as indicating the development of a false memory for the event. Strictly speaking, however, a statement that something has happened is an autobiographical belief and not necessarily a memory. Believing is not remembering. Instead, autobiographical belief (or knowledge) and autobiographical memory are distinct, partially independent constructs (Mazzoni & Kirsch 2002; Scoboria *et al.* 2004).

According to Tulving (2000), a mental event should be considered a memory only when it has episodic characteristics and feels like a memory (i.e., has recollective quality). Thus, one can hold a very strong belief or have certain knowledge that an event has occurred, without having any recollective experience of its occurrence. For example, we all know, and we are certain, that we were born, even though we do not remember our birth. The same is true for false events. Consider the question "Did you hear classical music in the hospital nursery during the first days of life?" Mazzoni and Vannucci (1999) elicited positive answers to this question after providing participants with misinformation about its likelihood (e.g., that most hospital nurseries in Italy broadcast classical music during a period of years including those in which the participants were born). The participants in this study did not develop memories of having heard the music, but they did acquire false autobiographical beliefs of having heard the music in the nursery. The distinction between autobiographical beliefs and memories has been sporadically made in the literature on false memories (Lindsay & Read 1994; Johnson & Raye 2000; Ost 2003; Smeets *et al.* 2005), but was first discussed in detail by Mazzoni and Kirsch (2002; also see Scoboria *et al.* 2004; Mazzoni in press), who presented a model describing the processes involved in the creation of an autobiographical belief.

Although false autobiographical beliefs are not necessarily false memories, they are nevertheless very important. Consider, for example, a person who falsely believes that she has been sexually abused by her father. The damage to her family and to herself may be the same whether or not she has a memory of its occurrence. A strong belief that something had happened can trigger emotions and activate behaviors that might have profound consequences, even if it is not accompanied by a recollective experience (Ost *et al.* 2002a). In addition, the development of false autobiographical beliefs may be part of the process by which false memories are subsequently created (Pezdek *et al.* 1997; Mazzoni *et al.* 2001; Mazzoni & Kirsch 2002). In the following sections, we examine data indicating procedures by which false autobiographical beliefs and memories can be generated, noting in each case whether memory, belief, or both were assessed.

Can You Trust Your Relatives?

In one of the first attempts to show that false memories for full-blown child autobiographical episodes could be created ex novo, Loftus and Pickrell (1995) had siblings of the participants act as confederates and describe a false event that had allegedly occurred to the participant during childhood. The false event was "getting lost in a shopping mall." Being told by a sibling that a certain unremembered (and false) event had occurred to them made subjects "remember" the event. Some subjects not only "remembered" what the sibling described, but were willing to add details and report a full-blown memory for the nonexistent event. Although it is clear that the influence of the sibling was crucial in creating the false memory, the specific variables responsible for the effect were not tested in this work.

The Loftus & Pickrell (1995) paradigm, since termed the "familial-informant false-narrative procedure" (Lindsay *et al.* 2004), has become prominent in studying the development of false autobiographical memories. Usually participants in these studies are told that a parent or another individual has informed the experimenter about a number of events which occurred to them during childhood. Some events are then presented in a narrative format for recognition, all but one of which are true events; experimenters add a false event, typically endorsed by parents as not having occurred. Participants are encouraged to try to recall unremembered events via procedures such as thinking about the event, imagining it in detail, and context reinstatement. This is typically done over two or more experimental sessions, and participants are encouraged to think about the event between sessions.

As reviewed by Lindsay *et al.* (2004), in eight published accounts reporting on nine experimental studies, rates of false memory formation have varied from 0 per cent to 56 per cent, with all but one study (in which an implausible event was used; Pezdek *et al.* 1997, Study 2) demonstrating creation of false memories in study participants. To evaluate the quality of memory reports provided by participants, Hyman and Pentland (1996) developed a coding procedure by which reports regarding false events are rated as *clear false memory*, *partial false memory*, *no memory but trying to recover*, or *no memory*.

Lindsay *et al.* (2004) note that of studies using these categories, 20 per cent of participants were classified as having complete false memories, and 17 per cent as having partial false memories. Using doctored photographs, Wade *et al.* (2002) found a 50 per cent false memory rate, and using actual class photographs Lindsay *et al.* demonstrated a 65 per cent false memory rate. In a recent investigation, Ost *et al.* (2005) used this paradigm to establish base rates of false memory formation about a childhood event that had not happened (i.e., going to the hospital at the age of four). Their data indicated that simply repeating interviews led to false memories in 23 per cent of the participants. Thus, false memories for autobiographical events are not rare occurrences.

False Memories in Therapy: Hypnosis, Age Regression, and Dream Interpretation

Many cases of recovered memories occur in therapy, and studies have assessed whether the likelihood of developing false memories for childhood events can be enhanced by suggestive therapeutic procedures. Suggestive techniques can have a strong influence on memory. For example, there is substantial evidence showing that hypnosis can modify autobiographical memories (for a recent review of hypnosis and memory in eyewitness testimony, see Mazzoni & Lynn in press). Hypnosis has long been used as a tool with the intent of recovering buried memories of traumatic events, with the aim of helping patients heal by bringing the memories into conscious awareness (a process also called abreaction in psychodynamic therapies). One of the first examples of such use of hypnosis can be found in a famous case treated by Janet (1889/1973), one of the founders of psychotherapy. Janet's patient, Maria, was age-regressed during hypnosis to her childhood to solve a number of hysteric pathological symptoms. Janet reported that in one instance she was able to remember a traumatic episode of her life (i.e., seeing a child with facial impetigo), and that by consciously reliving the memory of the trauma she was liberated from the symptoms. The belief that both therapist and patient shared was that the memory recovered in hypnosis was a true memory and was the cause of some of her symptoms. This belief has been relatively common among therapists, in particular in the US. For example, survey research (Poole *et al.* 1995) revealed that approximately one third of American psychologists sampled reported that they used hypnosis to help patients recall memories of sexual abuse (only 5 per cent of the British therapists did so). Subsequent discussions indicate that the issue of the use of hypnosis as a tool to recover repressed memories is still a topic of debate in both therapeutic (e.g., Lynn *et al.* 2003; Gleaves *et al.* 2004) and forensic (e.g., Scoboria *et al.* 2001; Coleman *et al.* 2001) arenas. Nevertheless, it seems clear that hypnosis and age regression can easily elicit false memories for autobiographical events, especially in highly suggestible individuals, although even low suggestible persons occasionally report pseudo-memories (Orne *et al.* 1996; Scoboria *et al.* 2001; for a review, see Lynn and Kirsch 2006; Mazzoni & Lynn in press).

One striking example of the dangerous effect of hypnosis on memory was reported by Laurence and Perry (1983). In their study, during hypnosis, highly suggestible participants were regressed to a night of the previous week and a suggestion was given that they heard a loud noise that awakened them. If they reported having heard the suggested noise, they were asked to describe it in detail. Sixty-three per cent of the participants accepted the suggestion and reported hearing the noise. Of these, 76 per cent subsequently developed false memories of the noise. Half of them remembered the noise clearly and were convinced that it had actually happened, whereas the others reported being somewhat confused about the source of the noise. The ease with which people in hypnosis can report believed-in false memories for autobiographical events has been confirmed by studies in which hypnotized participants reported recollections of childhood events that only rarely matched those of their parents (Nash *et al.* 1986), remembered playing with a doll that did not exist when they were children (Sivec & Lynn 1996), or reported memories of episodes that dated before the cutoff for infantile amnesia (Sivec *et al.* 1997; Marmelstein & Lynn 1999).

Although hypnotic suggestions can produce false memories, memories for traumatic childhood experiences have also been recovered in therapies in which hypnosis was not used, indicating that other, less suggestive therapeutic procedures might also create false memories. This question has been examined in a series of studies that assessed the effect of bogus dream interpretation on the creation of completely false childhood autobiographical memories (Loftus & Mazzoni 1998; Mazzoni & Loftus 1998; Mazzoni *et al.* 1999, 1999). Dream interpretation was selected because it is used in several types of therapy (primarily approaches influenced by classical psychoanalysis), and it has been proposed by some as a major road that leads to the discovery of buried memories for past events (Bass & Davis 1988; Blume 1990; Frederickson 1992; Terr 1994). For example, Frederickson (1992) stated that "buried memories of abuse intrude into your consciousness through dreams . . . Dreams are often the first sign of emerging memories" (p. 44); and, "Pool your perception to identify any memory fragments that seem to have intruded directly into the dream. . . . You also need to pinpoint any access symbols, which may provide entry into buried memories" (p. 134). Others even claim that dreams can be exact replicas of (traumatic) events (e.g., van der Kolk *et al.* 1984), and as such can help people remember the past. Dream interpretation can then become an integral part of the memory work used in the attempt to recover memories of suspected child abuse in therapy. The other reason for choosing this procedure is the symbolic nature of dream interpretation, which makes it possible to freely interpret any content, and to adapt the interpretation to any aim.

In the bogus dream interpretation studies, a clinical psychologist told participants that the content of the dream suggested that a certain event had happened to them in their childhood. Participants were asked to fill out a Life Events Inventory (LEI) that contained a number of events prior to and following an experimental manipulation. Participants were asked to rate how certain they were that the various events had happened to them before the age of three. This age was chosen because of convincing evidence showing that people cannot remember experiences that occurred before 2½–3 years of age (Howe & Courage 1997). Participants were selected on the basis of initially low ratings on the target events, the reason being that those who knew and had a memory for the event before the manipulation would have certainly not been influenced by the dream interpretation.

A few weeks later, in an allegedly different experiment, participants in the experimental group were asked to report either a recent or recurrent dream. Their dreams were interpreted by a clinical psychologist who followed a script. At first the clinical psychologist provided a symbolic interpretation of single elements of the dream; then he combined the elements and provided a full interpretation. The crucial element of the interpretation was to tell participants that the content of their dream (regardless of what it was) revealed the presence in their past of a mildly traumatic event that was buried in their memory. The nature of the mildly traumatic event differed in the various studies in terms of frequency, plausibility, and emotional intensity. Events included the experience of getting lost in a public space for more than one hour, being abandoned by one's parents for some time, choking on a small object, nearly drowning, etc. In all studies dream interpretation resulted in a sizeable percentage of participants increasing their conviction that the event had happened to them, and in some cases (up to 25 per cent) ratings moved from being very low to being relatively high, indicating that even a mildly suggestive procedure (bogus dream interpretation) that lasted no more than 30 minutes could have an effect on what people think had happened to them in their early childhood.

What could have made people increase their confidence in the occurrence of the target events? One possible explanation is misattribution of enhanced fluency or familiarity with the event created by the dream interpretation. Another explanation is source monitoring. Interestingly, individuals who were more prone to develop a false memory after dream interpretation were also better able to create very vivid mental images. During dream interpretation they might have created a vivid mental image of the event. The degree of vividness might have made them mistake the image for a memory, thus increasing the conviction that the event had occurred. Another explanation is that participants were persuaded that the event occurred, without actually remembering its occurrence. They had been informed by a credible expert that inaccessible childhood memories resided in their unconscious, and that dream symbolism could lead to accessing the information. Hence a rationale for not remembering was provided, as well as a credible method for accessing the unremembered information. Whether participants in these studies developed memories as well as beliefs that the events had occurred cannot be determined from the data.

One important element that might unintentionally lead to the creation of false memories in therapy is the presence of an initial bias in the therapist's interpretation of the symptoms. People are in general susceptible to biases that distort judgments and decisions, and this can also happen in therapy. As an example, Lindsay (1997) reports an interesting study by Oskamp (1965) demonstrating that the initial appraisal of a patient seems not to change over time. In that study, experienced clinicians as well as psychology students were asked the same questions about a patient's current attitudes, beliefs, etc., after being provided with four blocks of increasingly detailed and accurate background information about the patient. Although participants were invited to change their responses about beliefs and attitudes as they gathered more information about the patient, they rarely did so. Experienced clinicians were not more accurate than students, and all showed a high degree of confidence in their evaluations about the patient, no matter whether correct or incorrect.

In real-life cases, it is not infrequent to find false memories for child sexual abuse when the therapist from the very beginning works under the assumption that the symptoms are signs of sexual abuse. In such situations, therapists usually focus mainly on information that confirms the assumption and tend to overlook information that might falsify it. Confirmation bias is rather common and represents the human tendency to confirm, rather than disconfirm, one's beliefs. One heuristic that can contribute to confirmation bias is the tendency to confuse an implication for an equivalence. For example, finding that a patient has symptoms that could be a consequence of sexual abuse (e.g., post-traumatic stress symptoms), a therapist might conclude that sexual abuse has indeed occurred, without considering that the same symptoms can also be derived from other types of trauma. Another contributing heuristic is the phenomenon of illusory correlation, in which people erroneously perceive that two or more conceptually related phenomena are empirically correlated, when in fact they are not.

Imagination Inflation

"Imagination inflation" refers to a paradigm in which imagining an event increases the belief that it has happened or creates a memory of it having happened. In one of the first studies exploring the phenomenon of imagination inflation, Garry *et al.* (1996) had participants fill out an LEI pre- and post-manipulation. Between administrations, participants were asked to create a relatively simple mental image of a number of the events mentioned in the LEI (as "gave a friend a haircut" or "broke a window with your hand"). Results showed that imagining the events raised their rated likelihood of occurrence, compared to events that were not imagined. The effect was very small (less than one point on an eight-point rating scale), but very reliable, and it has been obtained in several subsequent studies (Heaps & Nash 1999; Sharman *et al.* 2004). Some studies (Paddock *et al.* 1998; Heaps & Nash 1999) have also revealed that the ability to create mental images was one of the individual differences (along with hypnotic suggestibility, dissociation, and external locus of control) that can predict imagination inflation. In some imagination inflation studies only participants who had very low initial certainty ratings for the target events were pre-selected, which gave rise to the criticism that the results could just be an artifact due to regression to the mean (Pezdek & Eddy 2001). This criticism, however, has been countered by Garry and collaborators (2001).

In another series of studies, repeated imagination led a sizeable percentage of participants to remember a non-experienced event, allegedly reported by parents of participants as having occurred before the age of six (Hyman *et al.* 1995; Hyman & Pentland 1996). Parents were contacted and asked to list episodes of their children's life up to age six. Unbeknown to participants, a new, false episode was added, which was the same for all participants. For example, in one case the episode was "spilling punch on the dress of the bride's mother" during a wedding at age six. Episodes for which participants had a memory were omitted, and only the unremembered ones were imagined on three subsequent trials. At the end of the third imagination, up to 25 per cent of the participants reported having a memory, sometimes vague but in other cases very detailed, of spilling the punch. Unlike studies relying on the LEI, these studies documented the creation of false memories, rather than false autobiographical beliefs.

Different opinions exist as to the role of demand characteristics, and whether they might encourage the creation and embellishment of unremembered events and eventual endorsement of false memories. Demand characteristics might play a substantial role in particular when the request to imagine is accompanied by statements from a number of authoritative sources (parents and experimenters) confirming that the event had happened (e.g., in the "familial-informant false-narrative procedure"; see Loftus and Pickrell 1995 for an example). The rationale is similar to what happens when a therapist suggests that a client attempt to recover a memory. Participants are informed that it is likely that they can recall the information, if only they try. Expectations for the general effectiveness of efforts to recover childhood memories, as well as the effectiveness of memory recovery procedures in aiding in the recovery process, are provided. Social pressure to keep trying is applied, and subjects are encouraged to expend cognitive resources over a number of days to trying to recall the event. This is clearly a complex set of procedures, capitalizing upon the combination of numerous cognitive and social psychological factors to produce a report of a false event. In contrast, "pure" imagination inflation studies (e.g., Garry *et al.* 1996) do not seem to capitalize on demand characteristics, as participants are simply told that the researchers are interested in how vividly they can imagine childhood events, and then asked what they remember about the events (see also Goff & Roediger 1998; Mazzoni & Memon 2003). In this case the creation of false memories is genuinely a product of imagination.

A commonly proposed explanation of imagination inflation is that imagined events share many characteristics with perceived events (e.g., the vividness of the mental image), and hence are mistakenly considered memories for experienced events (Johnson *et al.* 1993). Failures in source monitoring (i.e., in distinguishing between internally imagined and externally experienced events) have been demonstrated to be involved in imagination inflation (see Garry & Polaschek 2000; Libby 2003). Familiarity has also been hypothesized to be a factor in producing imagination inflation (Loftus & Bernstein 2005).

Are New Memories Necessarily False?

Despite the interest and the convergence of results of all the studies reported up to this point, critics have noted the possibility that those who increase their confidence that the event had happened or who report a memory for it might have uncovered an event that had in fact happened. This is possible even if the event is attributed to the period characterized by childhood amnesia, as they may have remembered a true event and erroneously attributed it to that period. How can one be certain that imagination can create false memories?

One way of addressing this problem was devised by Goff and Roediger (1998). Instead of referring to past events, the authors had participants perform or imagine a series of actions, or only hear about them. The next day, they had 1–5 imagination trials for various actions. Participants were asked to recognize actions several weeks later as having been heard, imagined, or performed. Imagination was found to lead participants to state that they had in fact performed actions which they had only imagined. A subsequent study (Thomas & Loftus 2002) confirmed that imagination can create source misattributions, even when the events are rather bizarre. However, these results do not indicate that imagination creates full-blown false memories; they simply confirm that imagination can influence source attribution and make people erroneously consider imagined (internally produced) events as having been experienced (externally produced).

A series of studies on non-existing mass media coverage represents another way to address the issue. Crombag *et al.* (1997) described another approach to the creation of false memories. In their study, participants in the Netherlands were asked if they recalled viewing video footage on television of the moment of impact when an airliner crashed into apartment blocks in Amsterdam. The crash was an historical fact, and there had been extensive media coverage of the aftermath of the crash; however, there was no video of the crash itself. They found that 66 per cent of study participants reported having seen the nonexistent video. In a subsequent study, Ost *et al.* (2002b) found that 44 per cent of individuals in their sample reported seeing a nonexistent video of the actual moment of the car crash that killed Diana, Princess of Wales. More recently, Jelicic *et al.* (2006) reported that 63 per cent of their study participants indicated remembering seeing nonexistent media footage of the assassination of a Dutch politician, and upon further questioning 23 per cent gave details of what they remembered from the film. This paradigm is compelling in that it demonstrates the relative ease with which people infer what they must have seen in the past based upon other sources of information, leading to rapid and relatively automatic false memory formation.

A clear way of demonstrating that imagination helps create false memories was devised by Mazzoni and Memon (2003), who chose an event that could not have happened to the sample of participants involved in the experiment (having a school nurse slicing off a small piece of skin from the little finger for a health test). Extensive investigation into the health policy of the Grampian region where the participants grew up showed that this procedure, allegedly performed after the Chernobyl explosion in order to test for nuclear contamination, never took place. In this study the role of demand characteristics was minimal. Participants were simply asked to imagine two events. No social pressure and no "familial-informant false-narrative procedure" were used. The study found that imagination not only increased the conviction that the event had happened, it also led approximately 25 per cent of the participants to "remember" the nonexistent event and describe their memories in some detail.

How are False Autobiographical Memories Created?

The two memory reports with which this chapter opened are examples of the false memories created via imagination for the impossible event for which memories were created in the (Mazzoni & Memon 2003) study. A closer look at these false memories provides insight into the processes that create false memories, at least false memories for autobiographical events. The first thing to consider is the presence of elements that are typical of the script for seeing a nurse (or doctor) for a medical intervention or examination: for example, a waiting room, the presence of a nurse, the smell of disinfectant, etc. This suggests that when creating a false memory for a non-experienced event, the schema or script for the event is activated, and subsequent processes fill in the gaps (see Lampinen *et al.* 2000). The second aspect to notice is the absence of a detailed description of the procedure in itself. This suggests that no gaps in the script can be filled about the specifics of the intervention, because no knowledge or information is available about it. The third aspect to notice is the presence of specific details (the room was small and gray, the nurse was tall, blonde, and wearing glasses, and so on). Where do these details come from? They could have been present in the mental images elaborated by the participants (we are currently assessing the extent to which full-blown false memories contain elements that were in the mental images). But they could also be separate (verbatim or gist) representations (or parts) of actually experienced events, which become activated by thinking about experiences of medical procedures. This suggests that when the memory of the nonexistent event is constructed, script activation, binding, and source monitoring problems converge in creating a mental event that is new (and does not have any correspondence in reality) but conveys the same recollective feeling as real memories.

This hypothesis is consistent with explanations of the creation of false memories that capitalize on the fact that retrieving a memory is a reconstructive process in which multiple parts are reactivated and linked together (Whittlesea 1997; Whittlesea & Leboe 2000; Whittlesea & Williams 2001). Some recent studies on the role of source monitoring in the creation of false memories via imagination are consistent with this explanation. People use object features to decide about the source of their memories (e.g., Geraci & Franklin 2004), and in some circumstances, elements from perceived events can be integrated into false memories for imagined events through binding (e.g., Lyle, *et al.* 2006; Lynn & Johnson, 2006). The presence of these perceived elements triggers the source monitoring decision that the (false) memory represents an event that had occurred and was actually perceived.

Event Plausibility

Pezdek and colleagues have suggested that false autobiographical memories can be implanted only for very plausible events (e.g., a mass for Catholic students and Sabbath service for Jewish students; Pezdek *et al.* 1997). Pezdek and Hodge (1999) first articulated the argument that the plausibility of events would differentially predict the degree to which memories for false events could be implanted. They observed that studies of false memory had succeeded in producing memories for highly plausible, benign events, which were not comparable with events such as childhood abuse which were discussed in the literature. In one study, they demonstrated the relative ease with which memory for a plausible event could be implanted (getting lost in a shopping mall), whereas no participants came to remember a relatively implausible event (receiving an enema).

Pezdek *et al.* (1997) hypothesized that the process by which false autobiographical memories are formed begins with the development of a false autobiographical belief, which in turn is dependent on the plausibility of the event. Subsequently, Mazzoni *et al.* (2001) proposed a three-step model, in which the evaluation of event plausibility is the first step in the development of false memories (see also Mazzoni & Kirsch 2002). In support of that hypothesis, Mazzoni (in press) reported evidence that prior to initiating a memory search to determine whether an event has happened to them, participants first make a quick plausibility assessment. A further memory search is undertaken only if the event is judged to be at least somewhat plausible, and the more plausible the event, the more intensive the memory search. Specifically, Mazzoni found that response times for answering the question "How certain are you that [event x] happened to you before the age of six?" depended on the perceived plausibility of the event, with highly implausible events being rejected almost immediately.

Although it is more difficult to instill a false memory for an implausible event than for a plausible one, the perceived plausibility of an event is malleable and can be changed by the provision of new information. Evidence for this was provided by Mazzoni *et al.* (2001), who showed that the perceived personal plausibility of a very implausible event (e.g., witnessing demonic possession or being kidnapped) can be increased by providing evidence that it is a more common event that one might suspect. The results of the study also showed that this increase in perceived plausibility enhances the likelihood of people believing that the event had happened to them.

FUTURE DIRECTIONS FOR FALSE MEMORY RESEARCH

In this chapter we have discussed the complexities of false memory, with a particular focus upon exploring factors involved in the fabrication of autobiographical events. Of particular importance is the distinction between autobiographical memory and autobiographical belief. Although having an autobiographical memory nearly always entails believing that the remembered event occurred, people often believe that events have occurred for which they have little or no memory. Relatively little is known about the formation of such autobiographical beliefs and their relationship to remembering, and considerable work is needed in the area.

An issue of theoretical concern that is in need of empirical resolution is whether all false memories are "created equally" (i.e., whether they are produced by the same underlying processes and mechanisms). There are reasons to think that they are (e.g., Roediger & McDermott 1999, 2000) and reasons to think that they are not (e.g., Pezdek & Lam in press). False autobiographical memories often represent complex narrative sequences, which reflect a perceptually rich memory representation conveying a sense of personal involvement, and involving affective reactions, emotions and cognitive reflections (e.g., Loftus & Pickrell 1995; Principe & Ceci 2002). They are created in an effortful way, require attentional and cognitive resources, and can be intentionally blocked. This is the case, for example, in false memories created via imagination, in which a mental image needs to be intentionally created and elaborated in order for the false memory phenomenon to appear. In contrast, false non-autobiographical memories do not refer to personally relevant experiences, do not possess narrative qualities, do not involve a sense of self-relevance, tend to be free of affective and emotional elements, seem to be effortlessly and automatically created during encoding, and remain rather impermeable to top-down processes (Seamon *et al.* 1998; Dodd & McLeod 2004).

Another reason for thinking that autobiographical and non-autobiographical false memories may not be created equally is the relative ease and difficulty with which they can be explained by various hypothesized mechanisms. Fuzzy-trace theory, for example, does a good job accounting for the DRM phenomenon and the misinformation effect, but falls short in explaining why individuals might report memories for complex bizarre events. The "core meaning" of events such as sexual abuse, alien abduction, and ritualistic satanic worship seems too extreme to argue that they are activations of previous gist traces. Clearly, individuals who develop such memories must uncritically accept suggested material and/or fabricate information in order to develop the memories.

Because of these differences, some writers have proposed limiting the term "false memories" to memories created for autobiographical events (Freyd *et al.* 2005; Pezdek & Lam, in press). However, basic research on non-autobiographical false memories has provided a major contribution toward understanding autobiographical false memories, and it seems almost certain that many cognitive mechanisms involved in false non-autobiographical memories are also involved in the production of autobiographical memories (Mazzoni 2002). As an example, it is thanks to basic research that such factors as source monitoring, knowledge activation, familiarity, and binding have been found to play a major role in the creation of false autobiographical memories. For this reason, we believe that all these phenomena can and should be called false memories. However, this should not result in overlooking differences between the two or disregarding the issue of ecological validity of an area of investigation that has such important applied and everyday implications (e.g., Cutshall & Yuille 1989). Whereas all false memories may share certain underlying mechanisms, autobiographical false memories may also involve processes (e.g., the role of "self") that are not an important factor in more basic false memory phenomena. Establishing the shared and unique processes involved in the creation of various types of false memories is an important task for future research.

Considerable work needs to be done dismantling the components of the complex autobiographical false memory paradigms, and asking questions such as: What is it about doctored photographs which so easily produces robust false childhood memories? To what degree are social influence, self-relevance, binding processes, schematic processes, source-monitoring, gist, familiarity, and a host of other potential influencing factors involved? How are these processes differentially involved in the formation of false beliefs and false memories? Finally, how important are false memories in the first place? At what point do people begin to behave in a significantly different manner due to having remembered something which never occurred?

The repeated finding that false memories are engendered in some people but not in others has stimulated a search for individual difference predictors of false memories. Several personality characteristics have been examined as potential correlates of the propensity to report both autobiographical and non-autobiographical false memories. These include dissociation (Eisen & Carlson 1998; Hyman & Billings 1998; Wilkinson & Hyman 1998; Winograd *et al.* 1998; Wright *et al.* 2005) hypnotic suggestibility (Barnier & McConkey 1992; Heaps & Nash 1999), self-monitoring (Hosch 1994), and absorption (Eisen & Carlson 1998; Platt *et al.* 1998). The results of these studies, however, are inconsistent, and only additional research can clarify the extent to which the tendency to create false memories can be predicted by individual differences.

CONCLUSION

Despite the vast array of false memory phenomena and the ease with which false memories are created under most circumstances, memory errors are frequently benign. As Schacter (1999) observes, there are numerous ways in which the human memory apparatus creates difficulties; however, for the large part memory is a functional, adaptive system. Even to the degree that past events are largely misrepresented or entirely fabricated on a day-to-day basis, there is often little consequence to individuals other than mild disagreement over the details. Indeed, there are many jokes related to husbands and wives recalling slightly different versions of events.

Memory errors become a serious problem when the accuracy of what occurred in the past becomes the focus of inquiry, which occurs frequently in the legal arena. Memory errors can also become a problem if they are created in therapy and are considered to represent true facts. This occurs mostly in certain misguided approaches to psychological therapy. It is not our intention to deny the existence of traumatic memories, but to warn about the ease with which false memories can be created, including false memories for traumatic events. Therapists can, and do, change for the better the way people think about themselves and their lives. However, it can be dangerous for a therapy becomes an investigation in the reality of patients' personal past. In this situation, there is a risk is of unintentionally implanting the idea of a trauma having taken place in a person's life as an explanation of the symptoms presented by the patient.

We end as we began, with a report of a potentially significant autobiographical experience, in which the person presents a complex scene with many details, accompanied by emotions and the personal certainty that it is a memory.

> I remember seeing a very bright light, becoming brighter and brighter until it was unbearable. I was terrorized. I woke up in a strange place, tied down and hooked up to some device, with tubes coming out of my nose and other parts of my body. There were strange creatures, grim, busying themselves around me. They cut my skin and probed the various apertures of my body. It was painful. (An alleged victim of alien abduction, US)

Is this memory true or false? Only two conclusions are possible. Either alien abduction is a reality, or richly detailed false memories for highly implausible events do indeed occur.

REFERENCES

Ackil, J. K. & Zaragoza, M. S. (1998). Developmental differences in eyewitness suggestibility and memory for source. *Journal of Experimental Child Psychology*. Special issue on Early Memory, *60*, 57–83.

Albert, W., Reinitz, M. T., Beusmans, J. & Gopal, S. (1999). Role of attention in spatial learning during simulated route navigation. *Environment & Planning*, *A31*, 1459–1472.

Anderson, M. C. & Green, C. (2001). Suppressing unwanted memories by executive control. *Nature*, *410*, 366–369.

Barnier, A. & McConkey, K. (1992). Reports of real and false memories: the relevance of hypnosis, hypnotizability, and context of memory test. *Journal of Abnormal Psychology*, *101*, 521–527.

Barsalou, L. W. (1988). The content and organization of autobiographical memories. In U. Neisser & E. Winograd (eds.), *Remembering Reconsidered: Ecological and Traditional Approaches to the Study of Memory* (pp. 193–243). New York: Cambridge University Press.

Bartlett, F. C. (1932). *Remembering: A Study in Experimental and Social Psychology*. Cambridge: Cambridge University Press.

Bass, E. & Davis, L. (1988). *The Courage to Heal*. New York: Harper & Row.

Belli, R. F. (1989). Influence of misleading postevent information: misinformation interference and acceptance. *Journal of Experimental Psychology: General*, *118*, 72–85.

Belli, R. F., Windschilt, P. D., McCarthy, T. T. & Winfrey, S. E. (1992). Detecting memory impairment with a modified test procedure: manipulating retention interval with centrally presented event item. *Journal of Experimental Psychology: Learning, Memory & Cognition*, *18*, 356–367.

Binet, A. (1900). *La Suggestibilité*. Paris: Schleicher frères.

Blume, E. S. (1990). *Secret Survivors: Uncovering Incest and its Aftereffects in Women*. New York: John Wiley and Sons.

Brainerd, C. J. & Reyna, V. F. (2002). Fuzzy-trace theory and false memory. *Current Directions in Psychological Science*, *11*, 164–169.

Brainerd, C. J. & Reyna, V. F. (2005). *The Science of False Memories*. New York: Oxford University Press.

Bransford, J. D. & Franks, J. J. (1971). The abstraction of linguistic ideas. *Cognitive Psychology*, *3*, 193–209.

Brown, R. & McNeill, D. (1966). The "tip-of-the-tongue" phenomenon. *Journal of Verbal Learning & Verbal Behavior*, *5*, 325–337.

Bull, R. (1999). Police investigative interviewing. In A. Memon & R. Bull (eds.), *Handbook of the Psychology of Interviewing*. Chichester: John Wiley & Sons.

Burt, C. D. B., Kemp, S. & Conway, M. (2004). Memory for true and false autobiographical event descriptions. *Memory*, *12*, 545–552.

Cabeza, R, Rao, S. M., Wagner, A. D. *et al.* (2001). Can medial temporal lobe regions distinguish between true and false? An event-related functional MRI study of veridical and illusory recognition errors. *Proceedings of the National Academy of Sciences*, *98*, 4805–4810.

Coleman, B. L., Stevens, M. J. & Reeder, G. D. (2001). What makes recovered-memory testimony compelling to jurors? *Law and Human Behavior*, *25*, 317–338.

Conway, M. & Pleydell-Pearce, C. W. (2000). The construction of autobiographical memories in the self-memory system. *Psychological Review*, *107*, 261–288.

Crombag, H. F. M., Wagenaar, W. A. & Van Koppen, P. J. (1997). Crashing memories and the problem of "source monitoring." *Applied Cognitive Psychology*, *10*, 95–104.

Curran, T. Schacter, D. L., Johnson, M. K. & Spinks, R. (2001). Brain potentials reflect behavioral differences in the true-false recognition. *Journal of Cognitive Neuroscience*, *13*, 201–216.

Cutshall, J. & Yuille, J. C. (1989). Field studies of eyewitness memory of actual crimes. In D. C. Raskin (ed.), *Psychological Methods in Criminal Investigations and Evidence* (pp. 97–124). New York: Springer.

Dalenberg, C. J. (2004). The war against recovered memories of trauma. *PsycCRITIQUES*, electronic collection.

Deese, J. (1959). On the prediction of occurrence of particular verbal intrusions in immediate recall. *Journal of Experimental Psychology*, *58*, 17–22.

De Prince, A. P. & Freyd, J. J. (2004). Forgetting trauma stimuli. *Psychological Science*, *15*, 488–492.

Dodd, M. D. & McLeod, C. M. (2004). False recognition without intentional learning. *Psychonomic Bulletin & Review*, *11*, 137–142.

Dodhia, R. M. & Metcalfe, J. (1999). False memories and sourse monitoring. *Cognitive Neuropsychology*, *16*(3–5), 489–508.

Dodson, C. S., Johnson, M. K. & Schooler, J. W. (1997). The verbal overshadowing effect: why descriptions impair face recognition. *Memory & Cognition*, *25*, 129–139.

Eisen, M. & Carlson, E. (1998). Individual differences in suggestibility: examining the influence of dissociation, absorption, and a history of childhood abuse. *Applied Cognitive Psychology*, *12*, S47–S61.

Frederickson, R. (1992). *Repressed Memories*. New York: Fireside/Parkside.

Freyd, J. J., Putnam, F. W., Lyon, T. D. *et al.* (2005). The science of child sexual abuse. *Science*, *308*, 501.

Gallo, D. A., Roberts, M. J. & Seamon, J. G. (1997). Remembering words not presented in lists: can we avoid creating false memories? *Psychonomic Bulletin & Review*, *4*(2), 271–276.

Garry, M. & Polaschek, D. L. L. (2000). Imagination and memory. *Current Directions in Psychological Science*, *9*, 6–10.

Garry, M., Frame, S. & Loftus, E. F. (1999). Lie down and let me tell you about your childhood. In S. D. Sala (ed.), *Mind Myths: Exploring Popular Assumptions about the Mind and Brain* (pp. 113–124). New York: John Wiley & Sons.

Garry, M., Manning, C., Loftus, E. F. & Sherman, S. J. (1996). Imagination inflation. *Psychonomic Bulletin and Review*, *3*, 208–214.

Garry, M., Sharman, S. J., Wade, K. A. *et al.* (2001). Imagination inflation is a fact not an artifact: a reply to Pezdek & Eddy. *Memory & Cognition*, *29*, 719–729.

Geraci, L. & Franklin, N. (2004). The influence of linguistic labels on source-monitoring decisions. *Memory*, *12*, 571–585.

Gleaves, D. H., Smith, S. M., Butler, L. D. & Spiegel, D. (2004). False and recovered memories in the laboratory and clinic: a review of experimental and clinical evidence, *Clinical Psychology: Science and Practice*, *11*, 3–28.

Goff, L. M. & Roediger, H. L. III (1998). Imagination inflation for action events: repeated imaginings lead to illusory recollection. *Memory & Cognition*, *26*, 20–33.

Goodwin, K. A., Meissner, C. A. & Ericsson, K. A. (2001). Toward a model of false recall: experimental manipulation of encoding context and the collection of verbal reports. *Memory & Cognition*, *29*, 806–819.

Gudjonsson, G. (1984). A new scale of interrogative suggestibility. *Personality and Individual Differences*, *7*, 195–199.

Gudjonsson, G. (1988). *The Gudjonsson Suggestibility Scales (GSS)*. Hove: Psychology Press.

Hannigan, S. L. & Reinitz, M. T. (2003). Migration of objects and inferences across episodes. *Memory & Cognition*, *31*, 434–444.
Heaps, C. & Nash, M. R. (1999). Individual differences in imagination inflation. *Psychonomic Bulletin & Review*, *6*, 313–318.
Henkel, L. A., Johnson, M. K. & De Leonardis, D. M. (1998). Aging and source monitoring: cognitive processes and neuropsychological correlates. *Journal of Experimental Psychology: General*, *127*, 251–268.
Hicks, J. L. & Marsh, R. L. (1999). Attempts to reduce the incidence of false recall with source monitoring. *Journal of Experimental Psychology: Learning, Memory & Cognition*, *25*, 1195–1209.
Hicks, J. L. & Marsh, R. L. (2001). False recognition occurs more frequently during source identification than during old-new recognition. *Journal of Experimental Psychology: Learning, Memory & Cognition*, *27*, 375–383.
Home Office (1992). *Memorandum of Good Practice: On Videorecorded Interviews with Child Witnesses for Criminal Proceedings*. London: Home Office.
Hosch, H. (1994). Individual differences in personality and eyewitness identification. In D. F. Ross, J. D. Read & M. P. Toglia (eds.), *Adult Eyewitness Testimony: Current Trends and Developments* (pp. 328–347). Cambridge: Cambridge University Press.
Howe, M. L. & Courage, M. L. (1997). The emergence and early development of autobiographical memory. *Psychological Review*, *104*, 499–523.
Hyman, I. & Billings, F. (1998). Individual differences and the creation of false childhood memories. *Memory*, *6*(1), 1–20.
Hyman, I. E., Husband, T. H. & Billings, F. J. (1995). False memories of childhood experiences. *Applied Cognitive Psychology*, *9*, 181–197.
Hyman, I. E. & Pentland, J. (1996). The role of mental imagery in the creation of false childhood memories. *Journal of Memory and Language*, *35*, 101–117.
Janet, P. (1889/1973). *L'Automatisme psychologique*. Paris: Alcan.
Jelicic, M., Smeets, T., Peters, M. J. V., Candel, I., Horselenberg, R. & Merkelbach, H. (2005). Assassination of a controversial politician: remembering details from another non-existent film. *Applied Cognitive Psychology,* Special Issue, *20*(5), 591–596.
Johnson, M. K. (1988). Discriminating the origin of information. In T. F. Oltmanns & B. A. Maher (eds.), *Delusional Beliefs* (pp. 34–65). New York: John Wiley & Sons.
Johnson, M. K. & Raye, C. L. (2000). Cognitive and brain mechanisms of false memories and beliefs. In D. L. Schacter (ed.), *Memory Brain and Beliefs* (pp. 85–36). Cambridge, MA: Harvard University Press.
Johnson, M. K., Hashtroudi, S. & Lindsay, D. S. (1993). Source monitoring. *Psychological Bulletin*, *114*, 3–28.
Jones, T. C. & Jacoby, L. L. (2001). Feature and conjunction errors in recognition memory: evidence for dual-process theory. *Journal of Memory & Language*, *44*, 82–102.
Jones, T. C., Jacoby, L. L. & Gellis, L. A. (2001). Cross-modal features and conjunction errors in recognition memory. *Journal of Memory & Language*, *44*, 131–152.
van der Kolk, B., Blitz, R., Burr, W., Sherry, S. & Hartmann, E. (1984). Nightmares and trauma: a comparison of nightmares after combat with lifelong nightmares in veterans. *American Journal of Psychiatry*, *141*, 187–190.
Koriat, A. & Lieblich, I. (1977). Memory pointers. *Acta Psychologica, 41*, 151–164.
Lamb, M. E., Sterberg, K. J., Orbach, Y. *et al.* (1999). Forensic interviews of children. In A. Memon & R. Bull (eds.), *Handbook of the Psychology of Interviewing*. Chichester: John Wiley & Sons.
Lampinen, J. M., Faries, J. M., Neuschatz, J. S. & Toglia, M. P. (2000). Recollection of things schematic: the influence of scripts on recollective experience. *Applied Cognitive Psychology*, *14*, 543–554.
Lampinen, J. M., Neuschatz, J. S. & Payne, D. G. (1999). Source attributions and false memories: a test of the demand characteristics account. *Psychonomic Bulletin & Review*, *6*, 130–135.
Laurence, J. R. & Perry, C. (1983). Hypnotically created memory among highly hypnotizable subjects. *Science*, *222*, 523–524.
Libby, L. K. (2003). Imagery perspective and source monitoring in imagination inflation. *Memory & Cognition*, *31*, 1072–1081.

Libby, L. K. & Neisser, U. (2001). Structure and strategy in the associative false memory paradigm. *Memory, 9*, 145–163.
Lindsay, S. D. (1997). Increasing sensitivity. In J. D. Read & S. D. Lindsay (eds.), *Recollections of Trauma: Scientific Evidence and Clinical Practice* (pp. 1–24). New York: Plenum.
Lindsay, D. S. & Johnson, M. K. (2000). False memories and the source monitoring framework: a reply to Reyna and Lloyd (1997). *Learning and Individual Differences, 12*, 145–161.
Lindsay, D. S., Hagen, L., Read, J. D. *et al.* (2004). True photographs and false memories. *Psychological Science, 5*, 149–154.
Lindsay, D. S. & Read, J. D. (1994). Psychotherapy and memories of childhood sexual abuse: a cognitive perspective. *Applied Cognitive Psychology*, 8, 281–338.
Loftus, E. F. (1977). Shifting human color memory. *Memory & Cognition, 5*, 696–699.
Loftus, E. F. (1997). Dispatch from the (un)civil memory war. In J. D. Read & S. D. Lindsay (eds.), *Recollections of Trauma: Scientific Evidence and Clinical Practice* (pp. 171–198). New York: Plenum.
Loftus, E. F. (2004). Memories of things unseen. *Current Directions in Psychological Science, 13*, 145–147.
Loftus, E. F. (2005a). Planting misinformation in the human mind: a 30-year investigation of the malleability of memory. *Learning and Memory, 12*, 361–366.
Loftus, E. F. (2005b). Searching for the neurobiology of the misinformation effect. *Learning & Memory, 12*, 1–2.
Loftus, E. F. & Bernstein, D. M. (2005). Rich false memories: the royal road to success. In A. F. Healy (ed.), *Experimental Cognitive Psychology and Its Applications* (pp. 101–113). Washington DC: APA Press.
Loftus, E. F. & Mazzoni, G. (1998) Changing beliefs and memories with imagination and personalized suggestions. Special Issue, Behavior therapy development and psychological science. *Behavior Therapy, 29*, 691–706
Loftus, E. F. & Pickrell, J. E. (1995). The formation of false memories. *Psychiatric Annals, 25*, 720–725.
Loftus, E. F., Miller, D. G. & Burns, H. J. (1978). Semantic integration of verbal information into a visual memory. *Journal of Experimental Psychology: Human Learning and Memory, 4*, 19–31.
Lyle, K. B., Bloise, S. M. & Johnson, M. K. (2006). Age-related binding deficits and the content of false memories. *Psychology and Aging, 21*(1), 86–95.
Lyle, K. B. & Johnson, M. K. (2006). Importing perceived features into false memories. Memory, *14*(2), 197–213.
Lynn, S. J. & Kirsch, I. (2006). *Essentials of Clinical Hypnosis: An Evidence-Based Approach.* Washington DC: APA Press.
Lynn, S. J., Lock, T., Loftus, E. F. *et al.* (2003). The remembrance of things past: problematic memory recovery techniques in psychotherapy. In S. O. Lilienfeld, S. J. Lynn & J. M. Lohr (eds.), *Science and Pseudoscience in Clinical Psychology* (pp. 205–239). New York: Guilford Press.
McCabe, D. P. & Smith, A. D. (2002). The effect of warnings on false memories in young and older adults. *Memory & Cognition, 30*, 1065–1077.
McCloskey M. & Zaragoza, M. (1985). Misleading postevent information and memory for events: arguments and evidence against memory impairment hypotheses. *Journal of Experimental Psychology: General, 114*, 1–16.
McDermott, K. B. & Roediger, H. L. III (1998). Attempting to avoid illusory memories. Robust false recognition of associats persists under conditions of explicit warnings and immediate testing. *Journal of Memory & Language, 39*, 508–520.
McNally, R. J. (2003). *Remembering trauma.* Cambridge, MA, Harvard University Press.
Marmelstein, L. & Lynn, S. J. (1999). Expectancies, group, and hypnotic influences on early autobiographical memory reports. *International Journal of Clinical and Experimental Hypnosis, 47*, 301–319.
Mather, M., Henkel, L. A. & Johnson, M. K. (1997). Evaluating characteristics of false memories: remember/know judgments and memory characteristics questionnaire compared. *Memory & Cognition, 25*, 826–837.

Mazzoni, G. (2002). Naturally-occurring and suggestion-dependent memory distortions. Target article. *European Psychologist*, *7*, 17–30.

Mazzoni, G. (in press). "Did you witness demonic possession?" A Response Time Analysis of the Relationship between Event Plausibility and Autobiographical Beliefs. *Psychonomic Bulletin & Review*.

Mazzoni, G., Casciano, M. & De Leo, G. (2003). *The Role of Confabulation and Type of Feedback in Distorting Memories for Events in Children*. European Congress of Developmental Psychology, Milan, August 27–31.

Mazzoni, G. & Kirsch, I. (2002). Autobiographical memories and beliefs: a preliminary metacognitive model. In T. Perfect & B. Schwartz (eds.), *Applied Metacognition* (pp. 121–145). Cambridge: Cambridge University Press.

Mazzoni, G. & Loftus, E. F. (1996). When dreams become reality. *Consciousness & Cognition*, *5*, 442–462.

Mazzoni, G. A. & Loftus, E. F. (1998). Dreaming, believing, remembering. In J. Rivera & T. R. Sarbin (eds.), *Believed-In Imaginings: The Narrative Construction of Reality*. APA Press.

Mazzoni, G. & Lynn, S. J. (in press). Using hypnosis in eyewitness memory: past and current issues. In R. C. L. Lindsay, M. Toglia, D. Ross & J. D. Read (eds.), *Handbook of Eyewitness Psychology: Memory for Events* (Vol. 1). Mahwah, NJ: Lawrence Erlbaum Associates.

Mazzoni, G. & Memon, A. (2003). Imagination can create false memories. *Psychological Science*, *14*(2), 186–188.

Mazzoni, G. & Vannucci, M. (1999). The provision of new information can change beliefs and memories about autobiographical events. Paper presented at the meeting of the Society of Applied Research in Memory and Cognition, Boulder, CO.

Mazzoni, G. A. L., Loftus, E. F. & Kirsch, I. (2001). Changing beliefs about implausible autobiographical events: a little plausibility goes a long way. *Journal of Experimental Psychology: Applied*, *7*, 51–59.

Mazzoni, G. A. L., Loftus, E. F., Seitz, A. & Lynn, S. J. (1999). Changing beliefs and memories through dream interpretation. *Applied Cognitive Psychology*, *13*, 125–144.

Mazzoni, G. A., Lombardo, P., Malvagia, S. & Loftus, E. F. (1999). Dream interpretation and false beliefs. *Professional Psychology: Research and Practice*, *30*, 45–50.

Mazzoni, G. A., Vannucci, M. & Loftus, E. F. (1999). Misremembering story material. *Journal of Criminological and Legal Psychology*, *4*, 93–110.

Memon, A. & Bull, R. (1999). *Handbook of the Psychology of Interviewing*. London: John Wiley & Sons.

Nash, M. J., Drake, M., Wiley, R. *et al.* (1986). The accuracy of recall of hypnotically age regressed subjects. *Journal of Abnormal Psychology*, *95*, 298–300.

Neuschatz, J. S., Payne, D. G., Lampinen, J. M. & Toglia, M. P. (2001). Assessing the effectiveness of warnings and the phenomenological characteristics of false memories. *Memory*, *9*, 53–71.

Odegaard, T. N. & Lampinen, J. M. (2004). Memory conjunction errors for autobiographical events: more than just familiarity. *Memory*, *12*(3), 288–300.

Okado, Y. & Stark, C. E. L. (2005). Neural activity during encoding predicts false memories created by misinformation. *Learning and Memory*, *12*, 3–11.

Orne, E. C., Whitehouse, W. G., Dinges, D. F. & Orne, M. T. (1996). Memory liabilities associated with hypnosis: does low hypnotizability confer immunity? *International Journal of Clinical and Experimental Hypnosis*, *44*, 354–369.

Ost, J. (2003). Essay review: seeking the middle ground in the "memory wars." *British Journal of Psychology*, *94*, 125–139.

Ost, J., Costall, A. & Bull, R. (2002a). A perfect symmetry? A study of retractors' experiences of making and then repudiating claims of early sexual abuse. *Psychology, Crime & Law*, *8*, 155–181.

Ost, J., Vrij, A., Costall, A & Bull, R. (2002b). Crashing memories and reality monitoring: distinguishing between perceptions, imaginations and "false memories." *Applied Cognitive Psychology*, *16*, 125–134.

Ost, J., Foster, S., Costall, A. & Bull, R. (2005). False reports of childhood events in appropriate interviews. *Memory*, *13*, 700–710.
Paddock, J. R., Joseph, A. L., Chan, F. M. *et al.* (1998). When guided visualization procedures may backfire: imagination inflation and predicting individual differences in suggestibility. *Applied Cognitive Psychology, 12*, S63–S76.
Payne, D. G., Elie, C. J., Blackwell, J. M. & Neuschatz, J. S. (1996). Memory illusions: recalling, recognizing and recollecting events that never occurred. *Journal of Memory and Language*, *35*, 261–285.
Pezdek, K. & Eddy, R. M. (2001). Imagination inflation: a statistical artifact of regression toward the mean. *Memory & Cognition*, *29*, 707–718.
Pezdek, K. & Hodge, D. (1999). Planting false childhood memories in children: the role of event plausibility. *Child Development*, *70*, 887–895.
Pezdek, K. & Lam, S. (in press). What research paradigms have cognitive psychologists used to study "false memory," and what are the implications of these choices? *Consciousness & Cognition*.
Platt, R., Lacey, S., Iobst, A. & Finkelman, D. (1998). Absorption, dissociation, fantasy-proneness as predictors of memory distortion in autobiographical and laboratory-generated memories. *Applied Cognitive Psychology*, *12,* S77–S89.
Pezdek, K., Finger, K. & Hodge, D. (1997). Planting false childhood memories: the role of event plausibility. *Psychological Science*, *8*, 437–441.
Poole, D. A., Lindsay, D. S., Memon, A. & Bull, R. (1995). Psychotherapists' opinions, practices, and experiences with recovery of memories of incestuous abuse. *Journal of Consulting and Clinical Psychology*, *68*, 426–437.
Principe, G. F. & Ceci, S. J. (2002). "I saw it with my own ears": the effect of peer conversation on preschoolers' reports of nonexperienced events. *Journal of Experimental child Psychology*, *83*, 1–25.
Read, J. D. (1996). From a passing thought to a false memory in 2 minutes: confusing real and illusory events. *Psychonomic Bulletin & Review*, *3*, 105–111.
Read, J. D. & Lindsay, D. S. (1997). *Recollection of Trauma: Scientific Evidence and Clinical Practice*. New York: Plenum.
Reinitz, M. T. & Hannigan, S. L. (2001). Effects of simultaneous stimulus presentation and attention switching on memory conjunction errors. *Journal of memory & Language*, *44*, 206–219.
Reinitz, M. T. & Hannigan, S. L. (2004). False memories for compound words: role of working memory. *Memory & Cognition*, *32*, 463–473.
Reinitz, M. T., Lammers, W. J. & Cochran, B. P. (1992). Memory conjunction errors: miscombination of stored stimulus features can produce illusions of memory. *Memory & Cognition*, *20*, 1–11.
Reyna, V. F. & Brainerd, C. J. (1995). Fuzzy-trace theory: an interim synthesis. *Learning and Individual Differences*, *7*, 1–75.
Reyna, V. F. & Lloyd, F. (1997). Theories of false memories in children and adults. *Learning and Individual Differences*, *9*, 95–123.
Robinson, K. & Roediger, H. L. (1997). Associative processes in false recall and false recognition. *Psychological Science*, *8*, 231–237.
Roediger, H. L. III & McDermott, K. B. (1995). Creating false memories. Remembering words not presented in lists. *Journal of experimental Psychology: Learning, Memory and Cognition*, *21*, 803–814.
Roediger, H. L. III & McDermott, K. B. (1999). False alarms and false memories. *Psychological Review*, *196*, 406–410.
Roediger, H. L. III & McDermott, K. B. (2000). Tricks of memory. *Current Directions in Psychological Science*, *9*, 123–127.
Ross, D. R., Ceci, S. J., Dunning, D. & Toglia, M. P. (1994). Unconscious transference and mistake identity: when a witness misidentifies a familiar with innocent person. *Journal of Applied Psychology*, *79*, 918–930.
Russell, W. A. & Jenkins, J. J. (1954). *The Complete Minnesota Norms for Responses to 100 Words from the Kent-Rosanoff Word Association Test* (Tech.Rep. No. 11 Contract N ONR 66126, Office of Naval Research).

Schacter, D. L. (1999). The seven sins of memory. Insights from psychology and cognitive neuroscience. *American Psychologist, 54*, 182–203.
Schacter, D. L. (2001). *The Seven Sins of Memory: How the Mind Forgets and Remembers*. Boston, MA: Houghton Mifflin.
Schooler, J. W. (1997). A cognitive corroborative case study approach for investigating discovered memories of sexual abuse. In J. D. Read & S. D. Lindsay (eds.), *Recollections of Trauma: Scientific Evidence and Clinical Practice* (pp. 379–387). New York: Plenum.
Schooler, J. W. (2001). Discovering memories for abuse in the light of meta-awareness. *Journal of Aggression, Maltreatment and Trauma, 4*, 105–136.
Schooler, J. W. (1998). The distinctions of false and fuzzy memories. *Journal of Experimental Child Psychology, 71*, 130–143.
Schooler, J. W. & Englster-Schooler, T. Y. (1990). Verbal overshadowing of visual memories: some things are better left unsaid. *Cognitive Psychology, 22*, 36–71.
Scoboria, A., Mazzoni, G., Kirsch, I. & Milling, L.S. (2001). Immediate and persisting effects of misleading questions and hypnosis on memory reports. *Journal of Experimental Psychology: Applied, 8*(1), 26–32.
Scoboria, A., Mazzoni, G., Kirsch, I. & Relyea, M. (2004). Plausibility and belief in autobiographical memory. *Applied Cognitive Psychology, 18*, 791–807.
Seamon, J. G., Luo, C. R. & Gallo, D. A. (1998). Creating false memories of words with and without recognition of list items: evidence for non-conscious processes. *Psychological Science, 9*, 20–26.
Sharman, S. J., Garry, M. & Beuke, C. J. (2004). Imagination or exposure causes imagination inflation. *American Journal of Psychology, 117*(2), 157–168.
Sivec, H. & Lynn, S. J. (1996). Early life events: hypnotic vs. nonhypnotic age regression. Unpublished manuscript, Ohio University. In S. J. Lynn *et al.* (eds.), *Hypnosis and Memory: Implications for the Courtroom and Psychotherapy*, in press.
Sivec, H. J., Lynn, S. J. & Malinoski, P. T. (1997). Early memory reports as a function of hypnotic and nonhypnotic age regression. Unpublished manuscript, State University of New York at Binghamton. In S. J. Lynn *et al.* (eds.), *Hypnosis and Memory: Implications for the Courtroom and Psychotherapy*, in press.
Smeets, T., Merkelbach, H., Horselenberg, R. & Jelicic, M. (2005). Trying to recollect past events: confidence, beliefs and memories. *Clinical Psychology Review, 25*(7), 917–934.
Smith, S. M., Gleaves, D. H., Pierce, B. H. *et al.* (2003). Eliciting and comparing false and recovered memories: an experimental approach. *Applied Cognitive Psychology, 17*, 251–279.
Stadler, M. A., Roediger, H. L. III & McDermott, K. B. (1999). Norms for word lists that create false memories. *Memory & Cognition, 27*, 494–500.
Stern, W. (1910). Abstract of lecture on the psychology of testimony and on the study of individuality. *American Journal of Psychology, 21*, 27–282.
Terr, L. (1994). *True Stories of Traumatic Memories, Lost and Found*. New York: Basic Books.
Thomas, A. K. & Loftus, E. F. (2002). Creating bizarre false memories through imagination. *Memory & Cognition, 30*, 423–431.
Tsai, A. C., Morsbach, S. K. & Loftus, E. F. (2004). In search of recovered memories. In W. T. O'Donohue & Levenski, E. R. (eds.), *Handbook of Forensic Psychology: Resource for Mental Health and Legal Professionals* (pp. 555–577). New York: Elsevier Science.
Tulving, E. (2000). *Memory, Consciousness and the Brain: The Tallin Conference*. New York: Psychology Press.
Tversky, B. & Tuchin, M. (1989). A reconciliation of the evidence on eyewitness testimony: comments on McCloskey & Zaragoza. *Journal of Experimental Psychology: General, 118*, 86–91.
Underwood, B. J., Kapelak, S. M. & Malmi, R. A. (1976). Integration of discrete verbal units in recognition memory. *Journal of Experimental Psychology: Human Learning & Memory, 2*, 293–300.
Urbach, T. P., Windmann, S. S., Payne, D. G. & Kutas, M. (2005). Mismaking memories. Neural precursors of memory illusions in electrical brain activity. *Psychological Science, 16*, 19–24.
Wade, K. A., Garry, M., Read, J. D. & Lindsay, D. S. (2002). A picture is worth a thousand lies: using false photographs to create false childhood memories. *Psychonomic Bulletin & Review, 9*, 597–603.

Watson, J. M., McDermott, L. B. & Balota, D. A. (2004). Attempting to avoid false memories in the Deese/Roediger–McDermott paradigm: assessing the combined influence of practice and warnings in young and old adults. *Memory & Cognition*, *32*, 135–141.

Wilkinson, C. & Hyman, I. (1998). Individual differences related to two types of memory errors: word lists may not generalize to autobiographical memory. *Applied Cognitive Psychology*, *12*, S29–S46.

Winograd, E., Peluso, J. & Glover, T. (1998). Individual differences in susceptibility to memory illusions. *Applied Cognitive Psychology*, *12*, S5–S27.

Whittlesea, B. W. A. (1997). Production, evaluation and perseveration of experiences: constructive processing in remembering and performance tasks. In D. Medin (ed.), *The Psychology of Learning and Motivation* (Vol. 37, pp. 221–264). New York: Academic Press.

Whittlesea, B. W. A. & Leboe, J. (2000). The heuristic basis of remembering and classification: fluency, generation and resemblance. *Journal of experimental Psychology: General*, *129*, 84–106.

Whittlesea, B. W. A. & Williams, L. D. (2001). The discrepancy-attribution hypothesis I: the heuristic bases of feeling of familiarity. *Journal of Experimental Psychology: Learning, Memory and Cognition*, *27*, 3–13.

Wright, D., Startup, H. & Mathews, S. (2005). Mood, dissociation and false memories using the Deese-Roediger–McDermott procedure. *British Journal of Psychology*, *96*, 283–293.

Zaragoza, M. S., Payment, K. E., Ackil, J. K., Drivdahl, S. B. & Beck, M. (2001). Interviewing witnesses: forced confabulation and confirmatory feedback increase false memories. *Psychological Science*, *12*, 473–477.

Zaragoza, M. S., McCloskey, M. & Jamis, M. (1987). Misleading postevent information and recall of the original event: further evidence against the memory impairment hypothesis. *Journal of Experimental Psychology: Learning, Memory & Cognition*, *13*, 36–44.

Zechmeister, E. B. & McKillip, J. (1972). Recall of place on the page. *Journal of Educational Psychology*, *63*, 446–453.

Author Index

Subject Index